POLICY FORMULATION AND ADMINISTRATION

Policy Formulation and Administration

A Casebook of
Top-Management Problems in Business

GEORGE ALBERT SMITH, JR., A.B., D.C.S.
Professor of Business Administration

C. ROLAND CHRISTENSEN, A.B., D.C.S.
George Fisher Baker, Jr., Professor of Business Administration

NORMAN A. BERG, S.B., D.B.A.
Assistant Professor of Business Administration

All of the
Graduate School of Business Administration
Harvard University

FIFTH EDITION · 1968
RICHARD D. IRWIN, INC.
HOMEWOOD, ILLINOIS

FIFTH EDITION

First Printing, January, 1968
Second Printing, September, 1968
Third Printing, June 1969

*Case material of the Harvard Graduate School of Business Administration
is made possible by the cooperation of business firms who may wish to
remain anonymous by having names, quantities, and other identifying
details disguised while basic relationships are maintained. Cases are
prepared as the basis for class discussion rather than to illustrate either
effective or ineffective handling of administrative situations.*

Library of Congress Catalog Card No. 67–30240

Acknowledgments

IT WOULD NOT be possible for the three of us, Professor Norman A. Berg having been added as a coauthor, to name all the people to whom we owe profound thanks for general help and encouragement in bringing out this new (fifth) edition. They include our colleagues at this Graduate School and our many friends at sister institutions. They also include the many leaders and their associates in the business firms and other institutions who have, in the interest of business education, given us permission to study their organizations and have allotted to us hours of time and virtually unlimited information. From both groups we have benefited by suggestions. Members of the second group often have helped us by supplying questions we had not known enough to ask. Then they have generously shared, in answer to the questions (theirs and ours), facts, and forthright and unashamed disclosures of their failures as well as of their successes.

The writing of some of the cases has been the work of one person; more often a case has been the work of more than one. Some we have written ourselves or have supervised the work of those who did write them. Without attempting to put names to cases, we will simply list the names of the writers. Our congratulations to them for work well done and our gratitude for their willing cooperation in aiding in this production are genuine and sincere. These people were at some time or still are (with a single exception) members of the faculty or staff of the Harvard Business School. Consequently we have had or still have frequent association with them. Many of their ideas and viewpoints to which we have had access, though less tangible than the cases, are nonetheless very real contributions to this book. The contributors are: C. A. Anderson; K. R. Andrews; J. F. Archer; N. H. Borden, Jr.; G. S. Gamble, Jr.; J. S. Garrison; W. D. Guth; E. R. Hanson; W. K. Harper; E. A. Helfert; C. W. Hofer; C. A. Hogg; R. M. Hower; T. C. Kienzle; J. M. Kinard; P. R. Lawrence; E. P. Learned; R. S. Meriam; T. C. Raymond; D. C. D. Rogers; A. Saitow; D. R. Schoen; D. H. Thain; S. Tilles; and A. R. Towl.

We thank the administrative officers of the Graduate School for providing us with time and encouragement, with financial support, and with secretarial, editorial, and proofreading help. Particularly do we appreciate the work of Miss Priscilla Winslow who has acted as most efficient manager in coordinating our efforts and the work of others in seeing this edition (and earlier ones) through the steps from conception to publication.

The cases in this book are with three exceptions copyrighted by the President and Fellows of Harvard College, and we are grateful for their permission to use them. Three of the cases are copyrighted by the Management Development Institute of Lausanne, Switzerland, and we thank the Director and Trustees of that Institute for allowing us to include them here.

December, 1967

GEORGE ALBERT SMITH, JR.
C. ROLAND CHRISTENSEN
NORMAN A. BERG

Table of Contents

Introduction ix

PART I
The Perspective of Top Management

Hammond Tire & Rubber Company, Inc. 3
United Industries 39
Wayland Company 54
HMH Publishing Company, Inc. 81
James Forsythe 106

PART II
Sizing up Situations, Formulating Policies, Discovering Opportun:ties, Assessing Risks, and Planning Programs of Action

Mathatronics, Inc. 133
Biddle Printing Company 160
Colony Trucking Company 186
Superb Biscuits, Inc. 209
Instruments, Incorporated 231
Heublein, Inc. (A) 251
Heublein, Inc. (B) 276

PART III
Organizing Administrative Personnel and Putting Plans into Action

Flawless Foundry and Equipment Company 297
Appleton Machine Company (A) 323
Appleton Machine Company (B) 344
The Rose Company 350
The Larger Company (A) 353
The Larger Company (B) 357
Consolidated Vultee Aircraft Corporation 359
Westinghouse Electric Corporation (A) 386
Westinghouse Electric Corporation (B_1) 393
Westinghouse Electric Corporation (B_2) 395

PART IV
Measuring, Controlling, and Motivating Administrative Personnel

Breitman & Company (A) 399
Breitman & Company (B) 448
A Note on the Manufacture and Distribution of Portland Cement in the
   United Kingdom 458
The Rugby Portland Cement Company Limited (A) 468
The Rugby Portland Cement Company Limited (B) 487
Precision Controls, Inc. 492
Business Machines Corporation 526
Linton Company, Inc. 554
Robbins, Inc. 587
Research, Inc. 590

PART V
Follow-up and Reappraisal

Aerosol Techniques, Inc. 607
Patterson & Swift, Inc. 634
Blakeston & Wilson 663
Superior Separator Company 687
Consolidated Drugs, Inc. 720

PART VI
Management of Foreign Operations

Devonian Electronic Components Ltd. (A) 749
Devonian Electronic Components Ltd. (B) 784
Godfrey L. Cabot, Inc. 800
Liebig's Extract of Meat Co. Ltd. 813

PART VII
The Business Leader and Public Responsibility

Auto-Start Manufacturing Company 843
Albert Manufacturing Company 854
Skyway Electronics, Inc. 863
Belcamp Hardware Company, Inc. 882

Introduction

THE PURPOSES of this fifth edition of *Policy Formulation and Administration* are essentially the same as were those of the previous editions. The new edition, however, has an additional author. At the request of Professors Smith and Christensen, Professor Norman Berg of the Harvard Business School Faculty is a coauthor. He has had successful research and teaching experience here and elsewhere, and he brings to this work a youthful outlook in this rapidly changing business world.

The book provides a selection of cases that can assist young men preparing for their first step up the ladder to top management. (Cases in the earlier editions also have been used with notable success in management programs for business executives at the Harvard Business School and other universities, as well as in in-company management development programs.) Study and discussion of these cases offer opportunities:

1. To learn what the functions of top management are.
2. To develop skill in envisaging goals; to delineate the functions that must be performed to achieve the goals; and to determine what activities are needed in workable combination to carry out the functions necessary to goal achievement.
3. To become familiar with "risk" and its place in top-management thinking.
4. To learn to identify and attract men to a business with the requisite technical and emotional abilities and to build them into a living, thinking, acting organization.
5. To develop ability to divide the work of a firm into logical and understandable assignments, with limitations on authority and at the same time with provisions for individual decision-making powers and opportunities for cooperation.
6. To learn to set standards for measuring performance.
7. To understand how to provide motivation for the members of the management group so they will apply their skills (which the organization needs) and in doing so find nutriment for their own needs.

8. To gain insight, self-confidence, imagination, and the ability to furnish leadership to the organization. Coupled with leadership is the willingness to take ultimate responsibility not only for the results of his own decisions but also for the results of the decisions and actions of all to whom he has delegated authority.

9. To understand and accept his responsibilities and those of the organization to the various sectors of society that are affected by the organization's actions—the investor, the worker, the supplier, the community, and the country; our private enterprise system is on trial in 1968 probably more than ever before.

The cases, it is clear, take their viewpoint primarily at the level of top management, including directors, where companywide objectives are set and departmental policies and activities are coordinated. This is the point of view of the Business Policy course at the Harvard Business School (the only required second-year course in the two-year program) and of the many similar courses, although the names may be different, at other universities, colleges, and business organizations here in the United States as well as throughout the world.

Each case in this book describes an actual situation (or situations) of an actual company as of the time the case was written. To preserve confidences, fictitious names have been used in some instances, and sometimes the geographical locations have been changed. In no instance has the industry been changed or the size of the company materially altered. Almost always the case contains information about the industry and its competitive conditions; some historical background about the company itself; financial and statistical data; information about products and production and marketing methods and facilities; the organization plan; and executive personnel. These cases are the raw materials that permit simulation in the classroom of the actual discussions carried on informally among managers and in board and committee rooms.

This edition contains 44 cases, 20 of which did not appear in the earlier editions. As has been the continuing policy, there are cases from many industries, from both large and small companies, and cases which ended many years ago, as well as ones of recent dates.

We are not unmindful that some users of our book would prefer all current cases. However, apart from the impossibility of producing such a book, we (and many others) believe there is value in including some classical cases that are not new. There are some basic reasons. For one, there is great pedagogical value in having some few cases that "happened quite a long time ago." If properly selected, they are not irrelevant to current problems and they add perspective as to what changes and what is timeless. Secondly, some of the older cases, in our view, present particular problems still applicable to our business society better than more recent cases could. Furthermore, we believe that the flood of mergers and acquisitions that has occurred in the past 15 years has absorbed a great and, perhaps, unhealthy amount of the time of top executives. Many business leaders have been acting as buyers and sellers of businesses rather than as administrators of productive business activities. We are not presuming to pass judgment on the ultimate value of this frenzy. We *do* think the attention of the public and of teachers and students of business may have been diverted unduly from the hard-core realities of managing the actual operations of the firm itself. Hence, in the older cases retained and in many of the new ones, we are sticking to a high percentage in which the discussion can readily focus on problems of operating management. Over time, our economy will be strong only if we have a growing number of responsible business leaders who understand and manage effectively the underlying and inescapable operations that result in the efficient distribution of useful goods and services.

The cases in this edition are from industries that manufacture, process, and/or supply: tires and other rubber products; patterns, models, and mock-ups; breathing apparatus; publications; entertainment; novelty items; banking and trustee activities; desk-type electronic computers; liquor and specialty food products; foundry products and foundry equipment; specialized industrial machinery; aircraft assemblies and completed aircraft; miscellaneous electric equipment for industrial and for consumer use; ladies' handbags and belts; cement; control devices for various uses; dictation equipment; wholesale grocery items; electronic equipment items; industrial research and development; gamma radiography equipment; electric power supply items; photographic products; fillings for aerosol products; electric relays; candy and confections; farm machinery; wholesale drugs; carbon black; specialty food items; automobile parts; and wholesale hardware.

It should be emphasized that our cases are not intended to be "examples" of right and wrong, good or bad. In no instance was a particular company selected because we believed it to be the "best" or the "worst" in its industry or because we thought it was "average" or "typical." Obviously, some of these firms had been well managed; others not so well. Some were in very good condition; others in critical condition. The important thing was that in the actual situations the persons responsible for the particular ventures were obliged to recognize and deal with the problems as they were. The problems might be desperate emergencies calling for drastic action. They might be basic policy decisions of long-range significance, even though not requiring emergency handling. Or they might be the somewhat less dramatic, but nonetheless important, problems of routine administration, keeping things going on an even keel from day to day.

It has been our experience and the experience of many other teachers that, by using cases such as these, a teacher and his students can together create "ways of thinking," "ways of feeling," and "ways of doing" that accelerate tremendously both intellectual growth and emotional development. An important by-product of case study and discussion is the accumulation of much information about business affairs. The main, though more elusive, products, however, are: insight, intellectual power, judgment, imagination, practical common sense, leadership ability, responsibility, and self-confidence.

THE QUESTIONS OR PROBLEMS IN THE CASES AND THEIR SOLUTIONS

At the top level, an executive does not have any "all-wise" adviser to inform him what problem or problems he should be watching or working on at a particular time. That he must decide himself. And he has no reference book to look into, no infallible aid to give him *the* solution. He must, nevertheless, find *some* solution, some workable solution. This he does by the use of experience and the exercise of his judgment, usually after discussion and consultation with others. And neither before a decision is made, nor after, can he be absolutely sure what action is *right* or *best.*

The administrator must be willing and able to work in a climate of uncertainty, which is often uncomfortable. He must accept the responsibility for reaching decisions under time pressures and on the basis of limited facts and in the face of many unknowns. He must work with people who, like himself, are imperfect. Almost always, some of his associates or other parties involved will disagree with him. He should take their disagreement and their views into account. Finally, however, he himself must analyze, decide, plan, and act. His is the usually lonesome situation of the possessor of ultimate responsibility. He inevitably will make some mistakes. If he is experienced and mature, he will expect this and will allow for it. He will hope to reach wise decisions most of the time. If he does, he is a successful business leader.

This clearly suggests that the cases do not include any "official" or "demonstrably correct" answers. We do not have either "official" questions or "approved" solutions. It is part of the student's task as it is part of an executive's task to discover questions and to distinguish the important from the unimportant. In some instances, we do not agree among ourselves as to exactly what the most fundamental problems or opportunities are; and in still more instances we do not agree on the best possible course of action. If we did, we would question the reality of our cases and perhaps also the quality and integrity of our own views. Complicated business situations such as are presented here are episodes taken out of business life. Since we are all different people, with our own special backgrounds and experiences, we will attach to these problems at least somewhat differing interpretations and envision somewhat differing or substantially differing solutions or courses of action.

We do have our own ideas about each of the cases we are offering; so do our colleagues who use them. In some instances, we hold our views with strong conviction. In others, we are much less sure of what we think. And we change our views from time to time. So we certainly do not feel that we *know* what should be done in each of the situations presented. The value of the cases in the classroom lies in their discussion, not in the giving or finding of an "authoritative" answer.

SIGNIFICANCE OF THE OUTLINE HEADINGS

As was true of its predecessors, this fifth edition has a fairly simple outline, planned for a schedule of approximately one case for each class day.

The outline, as before, has seven parts. Two are new and replace two we are omitting. One of the new ones is an expansion of *Control* into *Measuring, Controlling, and Motivating Administrative Personnel*. *Day to Day Administrative Problems* has disappeared as such and its subject matter is treated in other sections. *Management of Foreign Operations* has been added and its addition, we feel, is timely and a self-evident improvement.

The seven parts are:
1. The Perspective of Top Management
2. Sizing up Situations, Formulating Policies, Discovering Opportunities, Assessing Risks, and Planning Programs of Action
3. Organizing Administrative Personnel and Putting Plans into Action
4. Measuring, Controlling, and Motivating Administrative Personnel
5. Follow-up and Reappraisal
6. Management of Foreign Operations
7. The Business Leader and Public Responsibility

This organizational plan with its selected distribution of cases can give you as students a sense of the atmosphere in which top-level executives work and can make real to you the men in top management, with their range of human frailties and strengths. It also will make clear to you that the manager must work through and depend on other people; that he must engage in much routine work; that virtually all he can be sure of is "change" and the "unexpected." You will learn also that policy formulation is not always a formal process; that there often is a discrepancy between "stated" policy and policy as "practiced"; that much policy making is done (and should be) at fairly low levels in organizations; and that effective authority or leadership is not conferred from above but is earned and awarded from below.

As you progress in your study of the cases, many other important things will become clear. For example, you will be disabused of any idea that the executive discovers and solves one problem at a time. On the contrary, he deals with many problems concurrently, and at a different stage of development. Furthermore, the route of travel from size-up, through planning, organizing, putting plans into action, and control, to reapprisal is not a straight line. The route is much more like a circle. Even in dealing with one problem, the administrator goes around the circle many times. And, as we have said, he is busy with many circles. His job is never really finished.

PREPARING A CASE FOR CLASS

The question of how students should prepare a case for class has been put to us many times by our own students and also by people studying and teaching these cases elsewhere. Actually, the question is often phrased: "What is the *best* way to prepare a case?" That one we cannot answer, inasmuch as we do not think there is any *best* way. There are, no doubt, many good and useful ways. Each of us must develop the methods that serve him best. Moreover, we all must change our approach somewhat to deal with each new situation. And each case is a new situation. So there is no formula, no basic pattern, that we can pass on. We can, at most, make a few observations.

We recommend, with the qualifications just stated, the following to the student: We suggest you first read the case through to get a general impression of what it is about, how it seems to come out, and what kinds of information it contains. We think there is a real advantage in doing this first reading a day or two before the time when you must do your thorough and final preparation. There is value in having the general situation in mind in time to mull it over, both consciously and sub-consciously, for a while. That is true of any important problem one has to deal with—in school, in business, anywhere.

For the second reading, we suggest you take the time to proceed slowly and carefully, studying the tables and exhibits and making notes as you go. Perhaps some headings will occur to you under which you want to summarize what you believe are especially pertinent factors. The headings, of course, will vary from case to case. Moreover, what at first looks like a basic fact or issue may come to seem less important than something else as you work longer.

While going through these first two stages, you usually will find it worthwhile to ask yourself questions something like the following: "Does this company seem generally to be doing well, or not doing well?" "Is it making or losing money?" "Is its current financial situation strong or weak?" Next, perhaps: "On what basis must any one company compete with the others in this particular industry?" "At what kinds of things does a company have to be especially competent in order to succeed?" And then: "Does this company seem to be competent at those particular kinds of things?" If another company is getting along better, try to decide why. "How is the whole industry doing?" "Is it growing and expanding?" "Or is it static or declining?"

"Have the officers of this company selected appropriate and achievable objectives?" "Are the objectives good for society?" "Do the separate objectives fit together into one general program that makes sense and which, if carried out, would lead to success?" "Are the officers, in fact, carrying out the program?" "What, in the very nature of things, are the important functions in this situation?" "Does this company have sufficiently capable people in the key positions?" "Do they work together effectively?" "Does the nominal leader of the company really lead it?" "What do his record and his plans and his statements seem to indicate about his basic ability?"

Many other such questions may be asked, all of them helping you make your size-up of the company and its situation.

If you conclude that the company is doing well, that the management has sound plans and is made up of people with the kinds of ability needed for the present and the future, you presumably would advise the officers to continue in the present course, watching as they go along for any new developments.

If, however, you find signs of trouble and trace the trouble to funda-mental causes, you should end up with a reasonably compact statement of what basic issues or situations must be dealt with in order to get the company out of difficulty or to avert impending trouble.

Here you must set new goals, affirm some existing ones perhaps, and devise a program for advising management. You must explore and decide what you would like to see done. But you must be realistic and take into account all the limiting factors of the actual situation. You must, in effect, design a bridge (one that in reality could be built) to carry the company from where it is to where you think it should go.

The questions we have cited are only suggestions. You will think of others, and the sequence in which you put them to yourself is up to you. Perhaps, however, when you feel you are about at the end of your preparation, it will be well to ask: "Have I worked this thing through to the point where, if I really had a chance to talk to the persons responsible for this company, I could (1) talk intelligently with them about their company and their job in managing it; (2) show them why the main issues I have distilled out as a result of my analysis are really of first importance; and (3) give them a coordinated program of action that would be practical and would have a reasonable chance to succeed?"

We urge students to discuss the cases with one another while preparing them. Men in business discuss their problems with other key people. But be sure you do your own independent work and independent thinking. Do not be too stubborn to recognize a better idea than your own, but be sure you really understand and believe in it before you adopt it.

One more observation. Not infrequently, students express the wish for more information than is in a case; they feel they cannot make a decision without more facts. Do not hide behind that bogey. For one thing, business leaders never have all the facts they would like to have. And, as far as the cases are concerned, they all contain enough information to enable you to decide and recommend something sensible. Be sure you learn how to use, and do use, all the information you have.

OUTSIDE READING

Outside reading is not necessary in relation to specific cases. These cases make up the subject matter of a complete course. An instructor may wish to ask his students to read, during the course, a small number of books in various fields such as: directors and their functions; executive action; executive training. Such readings may add background for what can be developed in case discussions. But such reading is not necessary to full use of the cases.

The individual instructor will know better than we whether some particular outside readings will help his particular students. This is, we think, quite a personal matter, depending on the disposition and methods of the instructor and on the backgrounds and interests of the students themselves.

Taking a somewhat longer range view of background reading, we would point out that we urge our students, while they are in school and during the rest of their lives as well, to read widely and thoughtfully. This we suggest to all of you who study policy formulation and administration.

Read with discrimination as many books and magazine articles as you conveniently can in the areas of administration and leadership. There is a growing amount of good literature in these fields, and we believe it will increase in both quantity and quality as we all learn more about these subjects. Whatever you do read, do not regard it as necessarily authoritative or final, however. Read to stimulate your own thinking. Endeavor to keep aware of what is happening in our own society and in other societies. Be open-minded, but decide for yourself what ideas are good and profitable; have your own reasons for your conclusions. See how you can use what you read and what you conclude about it in your own situations. Let the sole objective be not that you aim to *know* more; let it rather be that you aim to be able to *achieve* more as an effective and useful leader. Having said that, let us add—and this is not a contradiction—that the acquisition of knowledge itself can help make of life a fuller and richer experience.

Read biographies and autobiographies of men and women who were or are themselves leaders in many fields. Read many kinds of history, with special attention to the people who were in the forefront of movements. Read a good daily paper and/or weekly news magazine in order to keep in touch with the world today. Furthermore, when reading such news, look at events through the eyes of the persons who head businesses, educational institutions, government agencies, churches, or other kinds of organizations, noting what kinds of decisions they make and what actions they have to take. This will make you appreciate, perhaps more than you do now, what the responsibilities of prominent leaders really are. You might also ask yourselves what you would do if you were in their positions.

We strongly suggest reading in many fields other than business, inasmuch as business is only one aspect—though a very important one—of our complicated civilization, all the parts of which influence and are influenced by one another. A business leader will be the more effective and more useful to society the better he understands human nature and the more fully he is acquainted with past and present movements in the arts, the sciences, and the humanities in our civilization and in other civilizations.

Clearly, such suggested readings as these are lifelong assignments and are not calculated to make easier the discussion of a particular case on a particular day in the classroom, although they may help sooner than one might suppose. Over a period of time, of course, such habits of reading can open up great sources of pleasure and also great sources of help, which, when combined with your own interpretations of your own experiences, can further your growth and development as human beings, your usefulness as citizens, and your capacity for service as administrators. If you do so grow and develop, you will be better able to deal wisely with the many "case problems" that will actually confront you in the several areas for which you have, or will have, responsibility—in business itself and elsewhere in life.

PART I

The Perspective of Top Management

Hammond Tire & Rubber Company, Inc.

IN AN INTERVIEW with the case writer in mid-September, 1965, Mr. Henry Hammond, Jr., Chairman of the Board of the Hammond Tire & Rubber Company of Plainville, Ohio, remarked:

There were over 300 manufacturers of tires in the United States when my grandfather founded this company in 1915; today there are only 12, and some of these may not last much longer in this intensively competitive industry. We have succeeded, I believe, because we have not tried to be a little Goodyear. To try to do everything the big boys do but on a small scale is a sure way to go broke in the tire business.

During most of the last 50 years, the company was run by a two-headed management "organization" consisting of my father in charge of sales and my uncle in charge of production. To some extent, neither side knew what the other was doing. In addition, I would say that neither of them was to any great extent *personally involved* in the company as a growing business operation. They ran it pretty much as a hobby, and although it was pretty successful as a hobby, it didn't show much growth as a business. Decisions were made on the basis of how these decisions would affect the personnel involved, rather than on a purely businesslike basis. As a result, our only significant periods of growth took place during World War II and the Korean conflict. We actually faced bankruptcy in 1936 and were saved by a $50,000 loan from the old Reconstruction Finance Corporation. The whole atmosphere was one of a relaxed, "don't-rock-the-boat" type of approach to business problems. There was absolutely no sense of urgency. By 1950, we'd been in business for 35 years, and I'm sure that everyone felt we could survive—just as we were—for another 35 years.

I joined the company in 1950, and this attitude of utter complacency disturbed me greatly. I felt we were just drifting. I also felt that my father's and uncle's relaxed approach to business showed most plainly in the quality of the other management personnel. We were very weak, anywhere you looked. Our criteria for selecting management personnel were almost nonexistent. I set about changing that; and since 1953, we have been extremely selective in *all* our hiring—factory, clerical, and management. Our organization has been transformed from a two-headed monster into a smoothly running team. Our production facilities have been modernized, and our sales organization has been completely reorganized. We have developed a sound technical capability, which has led to completely revamped product lines.

3

But above all else, Hammond is strong today because of the people we have attracted. Of course, Goodyear probably has more geniuses working for it than we have total employees. But the point is that we have a much higher percentage of top-notch people. If we don't make a lot of progress in the future, it will probably be because we got lazy or self-satisfied; it won't be because we weren't smart enough.

Now, as we start our second 50 years of operation, I believe it is important that we review our past and present development and evaluate our strategy for the future. Such a review is needed because of several changes that have recently taken place or are imminent in both major areas of business—truck tires and passenger tires.

In recent years, there has been a marked trend toward increased concentration in the trucking industry. Large, well-organized, and highly sophisticated firms are rapidly replacing outfits largely run by ex-truck drivers who were lucky enough to save some money and buy a few rigs. These large firms want to buy directly from the tire manufacturer. Hammond, however, has traditionally sold through independent tire dealers. Thus, if we agree to sell directly, we run the risk of damaging our dealer relationships; if we don't, we may lose a lot of business.

We also face the possibility of a major technological change in the production of truck tires. I am referring to the introduction of radial truck tires, which some people in the industry expect to account ultimately for 80 per cent of all truck tires produced. To produce radial tires we must develop new production skills and techniques, as well as invest large sums in capital expenditures.

In the passenger tire business two closely related changes have recently occurred, and two more will eventually have a major impact on our industry. The first change took place in 1957, when department stores discovered that they could make money selling tires. Since that time, the mass merchandisers have really moved in, and there has been a relative decline in the importance of the independent dealers. Since we presently sell about 80 per cent of our passenger tires to the independents, this trend is of great importance to us. As the sale of tires on a volume basis developed, a second trend became clear—the advertising and sale of passenger tires on a price basis. This has led to the introduction of undersized, understrength, third-line and fourth-line tires selling for as little as $9.95. Hammond, on the other hand, has traditionally produced only first-line and premium quality tires.[1]

Very much related to the cutthroat price competition and the introduction of low quality tires is the impending regulation of tire standards by the federal government. I have enthusiastically supported the idea of legally enforced standards, not only because I believe the consumer has a right to know what he is buying, but also because I believe these standards will materially improve our competitive ability.

Lastly, there is a real possibility—indeed, a probability—that one of these days we'll see the introduction of a 100-thousand-mile tire as original equipment on all new cars. When this happens, you can imagine the impact it will have on

---

[1] Although no uniform grading standards exist, first-line tires are generally the equivalent of original equipment tires.

firms like ours which sell exclusively in the replacement market. When cars begin going to the junkyard with their original tires still in place, our passenger tire sales will disappear almost overnight, and we must be prepared to survive this development. This is the reason why I have turned over all operating responsibilities to our president, William Porter, while I devote all my time to a search for companies we can acquire as part of a major diversification effort.

In September, 1965, Hammond was one of the smallest of 12 tire producers in the United States. In 1964 the company earned $317,000 after taxes on a sales volume of $10.3 million. Balance sheets and income statements for the 1957–64 period are presented in Exhibits 1 and 2, and a financial comparison between Hammond and four other small tire producers during the 1955–64 period is presented in Exhibit 3. Financial data on the major tire producers are presented in Exhibit 4.

In 1965 the company's sales were divided among its major product lines as follows:[2]

	Sales (in thousands)	Percentage	Units
Passenger car tires	$ 2,778	27	199,856
Heavy truck tires	4,631	45	77,950
Light truck tires	617	6	25,235
Tread rubber	1,441	14	.....
Tubes, tire repair materials, and nontire products	823	8	.....
Total	$10,290	100	303,041

Unlike most firms in the industry, Hammond sold all its tires under its own brands. Information on the company's four lines of passenger car tires and seven lines of truck tires is presented in Exhibit 5.

The company's 32-man sales force sold to about 900 active accounts in 21 states—all, with the exception of a large dealer in St. Louis, east of the Mississippi. Of these, about 700 were independent tire dealers, and the remainder were trucking firms to whom the company sold direct. In addition, some sales were made to dealers in 15 states where business was not actively solicited, and about 3% of the company's tires were sold through an agent in the export market. Although some Hammond dealers sold gasoline and oil products as a sideline, in all cases their major volume was in tires. No sales were made directly to automotive supply chains or through other channels of distribution, although some Hammond dealers resold the company's tires to service stations.

---

[2] These proportions had remained relatively constant during the previous five years.

Exhibit 1

HAMMOND TIRE & RUBBER COMPANY, INC. *Balance Sheets as of December 31, 1957–64* (Dollars in Thousands)

Assets	1964	1963	1962	1961	1960	1959	1958	1957
Cash (including U.S. treasury bills)	$ 410	$ 327	$ 384	$ 92	$ 190	$ 263	$ 342	$ 382
Accounts and acceptances receivable (net)	$1996	$2076	$1325	$1657	$1483	$1534	$1336	$1481
Inventory:								
Finished goods	$1050	$ 805	$ 813	$ 800	$1031	$ 772	$ 752	$ 705
Work in process	188	170	168	165	153	137	119	322
Raw materials	347	204	402	240	337	372	220	125
Total inventory	$1585	$1179	$1383	$1205	$1521	$1281	$1091	$1152
Prepaid expenses	$ 18	$ 14	$ 16	$ 81	$ 14	$ 14	$ 13	$ 6
Total current assets	$4009	$3596	$3108	$3035	$3208	$3092	$2782	$3021
Investments	$ 53	$ 161	$ 134	$ 68	$ ...	$ ...	$ ...	$ ...
Cash surrender value of life insurance	$ 47	$ 54	$ 46	$ 53	$ 32	$ 52	$ 46	$ 42
Property, plant & equipment:								
Land	$ 12	$ 12	$ 12	$ 12	$ 12	$ 12	$ 12	$ 12
Buildings	664	557	522	496	440	} $1669	} $1425	} $1014
Machinery and equipment	2200	1673	1439	1354	} 1484			
Molds and drums	547	473	435	408				
Total (at cost)	$3423	$2715	$2408	$2270	$1936	$1681	$1437	$1026
Less depreciation	2046	1822	1610	1407	1016	879	654	514
Net fixed assets	$1377	$ 893	$ 798	$ 863	$ 920	$ 802	$ 783	$ 512
Total assets	$5486	$4704	$4086	$4019	$4160	$3946	$3611	$3575

Liabilities	1964	1963	1962	1961	1960	1959	1958	1957
Current liabilities:								
Accounts payable	$ 617	$ 304	$ 527	$ 409	$ 379	$ 514	$ 429	$ 451
Accrued salaries, wages, commissions	153	160	102	107	} 457	} 439	} 490	} 374
Accrued taxes & other expenses	226	244	211	276				
Federal & state income taxes	190	259	6	18				
Current portion of long-term debt & notes payable	120	45	499	435	485	341	241	785
Total current liabilities	$1306	$1012	$1345	$1245	$1321	$1294	$1160	$1610
Long-term debt	1160	925	225	310	396	483	571	346
Net worth	3020	2767	2516	2464	2443	2169	1880	1619
Total liabilities	$5486	$4704	$4086	$4019	$4160	$3946	$3611	$3575

Source: Company records.

Exhibit 2

Hammond Tire & Rubber Company, Inc.

Income Statements Years Ending December 31, 1957–64

(Dollars in Thousands)

	1957	1958	1959	1960	1961	1962	1963	1964
Net sales	$7,720	$9,075	$10,686	$9,573	$7,620	$9,078	$9,563	$10,290
Cost of goods sold	6,190	7,045	8,232	7,085	6,012	7,212	7,103	7,459
Gross profit	$1,530	$2,030	$2,454	$2,488	$1,608	$1,866	$2,460	$2,831
Selling, shipping, administrative, and general expenses	1,206	1,369	1,646	1,878	1,533	1,772	1,897	2,179
	$ 324	$ 661	$ 808	$ 610	$ 75	$ 94	$ 563	$ 652
Other income (deductions)	21	(83)	(156)	157	(37)	(32)	(17)	(37)
Earnings before taxes	$ 345	$ 578	$ 652	$ 453	$ 38	$ 62	$ 546	$ 615
Provision for taxes	190	313	356	229	18	9	296	298
Net earnings	$ 155	$ 265	$ 296	$ 224	$ 20	$ 53	$ 250	$ 317

Source: Company records.

Exhibit 3

HAMMOND TIRE & RUBBER COMPANY, INC.

Financial Comparison—Hammond and Four Competitors, 1955–64

(Dollars in Thousands)

	Lee National Corporation	Mansfield Tire & Rubber Company	Mohawk Rubber Company	Seiberling Rubber Company	Hammond Tire & Rubber Company
NET SALES					
1955...................	$45,912	$74,556	$14,330	$45,987	$ 7,188
1956...................	46,582	61,558	15,127	46,634	7,238
1957...................	48,601	59,722	20,842	46,934	7,720
1958...................	46,559	63,634	25,513	48,134	9,075
1959...................	52,164	68,950	31,657	54,788	10,686
1960...................	44,299	61,958	32,326	48,026	9,573
1961...................	44,683	62,210	36,379	46,653	7,620
1962...................	45,592	70,335	37,575	45,232	9,078
1963...................	26,056	74,246	37,678	51,535	9,563
1964...................	n.a.	75,230	38,386	49,748	10,290
NET PROFIT					
1955...................	$ 1,750	$ 1,768	$ 321	$ 1,127	$ 220
1956...................	1,613	1,377	371	1,051	163
1957...................	1,763	1,523	563	943	155
1958...................	1,798	2,311	1,065	1,070	265
1959...................	1,522	2,282	1,219	1,191	296
1960...................	323	705	1,068	131	224
1961...................	212	870	1,751	(684)	20
1962...................	(840)	925	1,004	(826)	53
1963...................	(2,307)	972	1,281	102	250
1964...................	n.a.	532	1,304	(1,630)	317
CURRENT RATIO					
1955...................	4.26	2.07	2.89	2.48	1.94
1956...................	4.54	2.00	2.28	2.44	2.66
1957...................	6.18	2.09	1.83	2.27	2.34
1958...................	6.45	2.49	2.06	2.40	2.39
1959...................	5.83	2.74	1.99	3.53	2.37
1960...................	6.86	2.48	2.01	3.35	2.41
1961...................	6.07	2.41	2.14	3.19	2.37
1962...................	5.57	2.28	1.81	2.31	2.30
1963...................	9.85	2.30	3.49	1.86	3.55
1964...................	n.a.	3.66	3.35	1.45	3.07

Exhibit 3—Continued

	Lee National Corporation	Mansfield Tire & Rubber Company	Mohawk Rubber Company	Seiberling Rubber Company	Hammond Tire & Rubber Company
NET WORTH/TOTAL DEBT					
1955	3.88	1.29	3.19	1.53	1.12
1956	4.69	1.41	1.23	1.57	1.70
1957	6.78	1.57	1.02	1.50	1.16
1958	7.30	1.09	0.96	1.61	1.08
1959	6.66	1.08	0.87	1.28	1.22
1960	8.13	0.97	0.89	1.25	1.42
1961	7.25	0.98	0.83	1.21	1.58
1962	6.67	0.92	0.69	0.91	1.60
1963	12.70	1.00	0.83	0.72	1.43
1964	n.a.	0.95	0.80	0.53	1.23
INVENTORY TURNOVER*					
1955	3.21	4.71	4.93	3.98	6.74
1956	3.23	4.20	3.51	3.82	6.76
1957	3.69	4.08	4.65	3.89	5.37
1958	2.95	3.66	4.59	4.19	6.46
1959	3.26	3.72	4.29	3.91	6.43
1960	2.90	3.91	4.44	3.22	4.79
1961	3.40	3.24	4.13	3.87	4.99
1962	4.40	3.16	3.50	3.40	5.21
1963	7.30	3.34	4.54	3.44	6.03
1964	n.a.	2.85	4.90	3.40	4.70
SALES/WORKING CAPITAL					
1955	2.55	6.09	4.54	4.44	7.72
1956	2.48	5.57	4.16	4.43	6.29
1957	2.59	5.25	5.75	4.47	5.50
1958	2.39	4.16	4.65	4.31	5.61
1959	2.69	3.89	4.78	3.12	5.93
1960	2.37	3.88	4.58	2.98	5.08
1961	2.51	3.62	3.93	3.11	4.46
1962	2.73	3.82	4.10	2.68	5.20
1963	1.68	4.22	2.71	3.93	4.86
1964	n.a.	3.12	2.63	5.77	3.81
NET SALES/NEW PLANT					
1955	6.46	12.56	7.06	7.38	14.98
1956	6.75	8.53	4.46	7.38	16.83
1957	6.94	8.78	5.71	7.28	15.05
1958	6.05	7.52	6.80	7.79	11.52
1959	6.07	5.89	5.37	8.98	13.14
1960	5.15	4.05	4.89	6.86	10.44
1961	5.14	4.35	5.78	6.40	8.44
1962	5.07	5.29	4.88	5.79	11.38
1963	3.08	5.76	5.13	6.42	10.71
1964	n.a.	5.92	5.41	7.10	7.47

* Based on cost of goods sold.
Source: Company records.

Exhibit 4

HAMMOND TIRE & RUBBER COMPANY, INC.
Selected Financial Data of Major Tire Producers, 1955–64

	1964	1963	1962	1961	1960	1959	1958	1957	1956	1955
Net Sales (in millions of $)										
Goodyear	$2011	$1731	$1592	$1473	$1551	$1579	$1368	$1422	$1359	$1372
Firestone	1449	1382	1278	1183	1207	1188	1062	1159	1115	1115
U.S. Rubber	1087	980	1007	940	967	977	871	874	901	926
B. F. Goodrich	872	829	812	758	765	772	697	735	724	755
Net Income (in millions of $)										
Goodyear	$100.2	$81.2	$71.1	$76.2	$71.0	$76.0	$65.7	$64.8	$62.5	$59.7
Firestone	79.0	63.4	60.0	63.6	65.0	64.6	53.8	61.7	60.5	55.4
U.S. Rubber	30.1	22.1	25.7	27.1	30.7	35.6	22.7	29.7	31.9	33.6
B. F. Goodrich	34.0	27.1	26.3	31.0	30.0	37.6	35.5	39.4	43.8	46.7
Per Cent of Net Income to Net Sales										
Goodyear	5.0%	4.7%	4.5%	5.2%	4.6%	4.8%	4.8%	4.6%	4.6%	4.3%
Firestone	5.5	4.6	4.7	5.4	5.4	5.4	5.1	5.3	5.4	4.9
U.S. Rubber	2.8	2.3	2.6	2.9	3.2	3.6	2.6	3.4	3.5	3.6
B. F. Goodrich	3.9	3.3	3.2	4.1	3.9	4.9	5.1	5.4	6.0	6.2
Net Income per Share of Common Stock										
Goodyear	$ 2.81	$ 2.28	$ 2.00	$ 2.44	$ 1.99	$ 2.13	$ 1.85	$ 1.82	$ 1.75	$ 1.68
Firestone	2.75	2.21	2.09	2.22	2.27	2.26	1.89	2.18	2.17	1.99
U.S. Rubber	4.27	2.90	3.50	3.80	4.45	5.30	3.05	4.31	4.74	5.04
B. F. Goodrich	3.71	2.95	2.87	3.39	3.33	4.18	3.95	4.40	4.90	5.26

Source: Company annual reports.

In those states where sales were actively sought, the company's share of the passenger car replacement tire market ranged from .01% in Illinois and Rhode Island to 1.53% in Missouri, and in truck tires from .15% in Illinois to 4.39% in Ohio (see Exhibit 6).

Hammond Organization. Since March, 1963, when Henry Hammond, Sr., and his brother Paul Hammond retired as president and chairman, respectively, Henry Hammond, Jr., and William Porter had held the positions of chairman and president. Other members of the

Exhibit 5

HAMMOND TIRE & RUBBER COMPANY, INC.

Selected Data on Hammond Product Lines

Passenger Car Tires	Quality	Dealer Price*	"No Trade-in" Retail Price*
Eagle...................	Premium	$14.42	$38.60
Hawk...................	First-line	12.33	30.35
Falcon.................	Second-line	11.09	24.30
Winter Master..........	Premium	13.33	30.30

Truck Tires	Quality	Range of Sizes	Range of Retail Prices (Nylon)†
Super Highway..........	First-line	8.25–20—11.00–22	$ 95.30–$184.15
Super Distance..........	First-line	8.25–20—11.00–24	95.30– 191.25
Super Tread.............	Premium	8.25–20—10.00–22	100.50– 163.80
Duralug.................	Premium	7.00–15—12.00–24	41.15– 387.95
Roadmaster 100..........	Premium	6.70–15— 7.50–20	31.50– 75.45
Super Master...........	Premium	7.00–15— 9.00–20	46.55– 121.35
Super Winter Master......	Premium	6.70–15— 7.10–15	32.35– 35.80

* All prices shown are for 7.75–14 nylon cord, tubeless, blackwall tires, not including federal excise tax.
† Prices are for tube-type tires and do not include federal excise tax.
Source: Company records.

company's top management in 1965 were Philip Edwards, vice president of sales; Robert Gray, vice president of administration; George Roberts, vice president of manufacturing; and Peter Douglas, vice president of finance. All of these men had been hired since 1954 as part of an effort to strengthen the company's management. An organization chart is presented in Exhibit 7.

Company Ownership. Of the 60,000 shares of common stock outstanding, over 54,000 shares were owned by members of the Hammond family, with the remainder owned largely by (nonfamily) members of the management. No dividends had ever been paid on the common stock, and no future dividend payout was anticipated. The stock had

Exhibit 6

HAMMOND TIRE & RUBBER COMPANY, INC.

Market Penetration, in Percent—1964

	Passenger Tires and Inner Tubes	Truck and Bus Tires and Inner Tubes	Tread Rubber and Repair Material	Total Replacement Sales
Connecticut	0.33%	1.46%	1.23%	0.64%
Delaware	0.25	2.12	0.75	0.80
District of Columbia	0.22	0.06	1.68	0.26
Georgia	0.27	0.77	0.03	0.38
Illinois	0.01	0.15	0.17	0.06
Indiana	0.36	2.19	1.42	1.00
Kentucky	0.19	1.08	2.09	0.64
Maryland	0.10	1.07	0.53	0.40
Massachusetts	0.24	1.29	0.60	0.51
Michigan	0.06	0.68	1.28	0.30
Missouri	1.53	1.14	...	1.24
New Jersey	0.09	0.54	0.05	0.19
New York	0.19	1.24	2.04	0.55
North Carolina	1.11	3.58	2.09	2.01
Ohio	1.47	4.39	5.72	2.69
Pennsylvania	0.23	1.14	0.76	0.52
Rhode Island	0.01	1.24	0.34	0.33
South Carolina	0.59	2.30	1.52	1.16
Tennessee	0.23	0.46	0.26	0.30
Virginia	0.62	2.24	2.93	1.34
West Virginia	0.60	0.45	2.67	0.85
Wisconsin	0.07	1.08	0.19	0.33

Source: Company records.

never been traded, and a public offering in the foreseeable future was not expected. Of the 16,200 outstanding shares of $100 noncumulative 4% preferred stock, 13,560 were held by Plainville College and the Hammond Foundation, with the remainder owned by members of the Hammond family.

THE FIRST TWO GENERATIONS OF HAMMOND MANAGEMENT

For the first 15 years of its experience, the Hammond Tire & Rubber Company was operated as a sole proprietorship by its founder, Henry Hammond. During this period his two sons, Henry and Paul, graduated from college and entered the business. When their father died in 1930, each son inherited a 50% share of the company. At that time, Henry Hammond, Sr., assumed the title of president and the responsibility for the sales activities of the company. Paul Hammond became executive vice president in charge of all production activities. In describing the

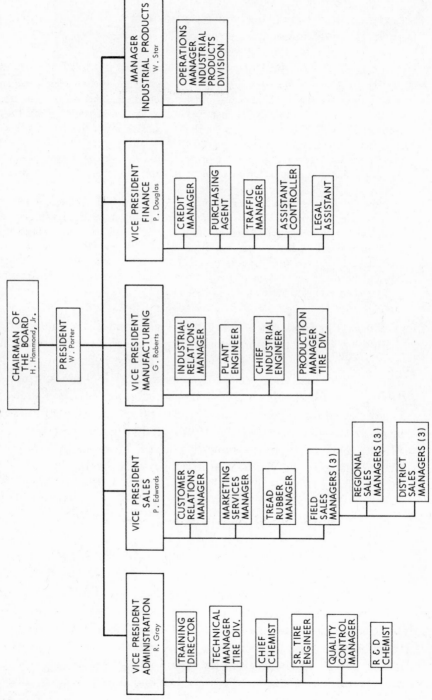

Exhibit 7

HAMMOND TIRE & RUBBER COMPANY, INC.

Organization—September 1965

CHAIRMAN OF THE BOARD
H. Hammond, Jr.

PRESIDENT
W. Porter

VICE PRESIDENT ADMINISTRATION
R. Gray

- TRAINING DIRECTOR
- TECHNICAL MANAGER TIRE DIV.
- CHIEF CHEMIST
- SR. TIRE ENGINEER
- QUALITY CONTROL MANAGER
- R & D CHEMIST

VICE PRESIDENT SALES
P. Edwards

- CUSTOMER RELATIONS MANAGER
- MARKETING SERVICES MANAGER
- TREAD RUBBER MANAGER
- FIELD SALES MANAGERS (3)
  - REGIONAL SALES MANAGERS (3)
  - DISTRICT SALES MANAGERS (3)

VICE PRESIDENT MANUFACTURING
G. Roberts

- INDUSTRIAL RELATIONS MANAGER
- PLANT ENGINEER
- CHIEF INDUSTRIAL ENGINEER
- PRODUCTION MANAGER TIRE DIV.

VICE PRESIDENT FINANCE
P. Douglas

- CREDIT MANAGER
- PURCHASING AGENT
- TRAFFIC MANAGER
- ASSISTANT CONTROLLER
- LEGAL ASSISTANT

MANAGER INDUSTRIAL PRODUCTS
W. Star

- OPERATIONS MANAGER INDUSTRIAL PRODUCTS DIVISION

Source: Company records.

operation of the company under the management of his father and uncle, Henry Hammond, Jr., remarked:

Evidently my grandfather never specified which son was to be the boss, with the result that our company grew up in the form of two totally separate organizations with no real coordination between them. The worst thing about working for such a company is that every now and then you're going to find yourself caught in the middle between the two bosses. After this has happened a few times, it will begin to dawn on you that you have three alternatives—quit, choose sides, or become a good tightrope walker. You can learn to stall on making a decision and can even train your bosses to make your decisions for you.

Now, do you see what kind of a management team you're liable to develop in a two-headed company? Do you think that really top-notch men will stay very long in a situation like that? Well, in our company's case, they didn't. In fact, it's amazing that good people were ever hired in the first place. It used to be a joke around town that the way to get hired by Hammond was "to be a good Lutheran boy and to have three or four relatives already working there." If you could pass these two criteria, you were in.

World War II Saves the Company. Hammond was severely hurt by the intense price competition initiated by the major tire producers during the Depression as they fought bitterly for the remains of a replacement tire market which decreased from sales of 43.9 million units in 1929 to 27 million units in 1936. Company records for 1934 showed a loss of $9,000 on a sales volume of $217,000, and although sales had increased to over $760,000 by 1940, profits in that year were only $1,490. This situation was radically altered, however, by a large increase in sales during World War II, as shown by the data below:

Year	Sales	Profit
1941	$1,097,145	$29,806
1942	1,539,368	23,806
1943	2,483,310	13,252
1944	3,086,385	20,280
1945	4,291,032	51,713

The Postwar Period—Continued Prosperity and Sudden Crisis. After the end of the war, the large pent-up civilian demand for replacement tires created a seller's market, and the company was forced to ration its tires among its dealers. At the same time, a profitable export market developed as a result of the severe damage suffered by European tire manufacturers during the war. Hammond rapidly expanded its export business to the point where it accounted for over 30% of total sales in 1947. In 1948, however, the availability of Marshall Plan dollars was sharply curtailed, and the company experienced the sudden loss of almost its entire export volume. In 1948 Hammond lost $5,000 on sales of $3 million, and the loss increased to over $58,000 in 1949, when sales fell to $2.2 million. The situation was considered to be so bad that the owners of the company gave serious consideration to selling out to one of its larger competitors.

The Korean War. Before a final decision to liquidate the company was made, however, the Korean War broke out in 1950, and the company benefited from a situation similar to the one experienced 10 years earlier during World War II. Once again it became necessary for Hammond to ration tires among its dealers while at the same time being able to expand production. Sales and profits during this period were:

Year	Sales	Profit
1950	$4,208,461	$146,468
1951	6,446,171	114,860
1952	5,625,997	117,155

THE THIRD GENERATION OF HAMMOND MANAGEMENT

In the summer of 1950, just after the start of the Korean War, Henry Hammond, Jr., joined the company after receiving a degree in business administration from the University of Illinois. He entered the production side of the company, and it was expected that he would eventually replace his uncle when the latter retired. In the interview with the case writer, Mr. Hammond described his first reactions in the firm:

When I joined the company I was appalled at the low caliber of our management people. Today, 15 years later, I am more convinced than ever that my first impression was correct. If I live to be a hundred, I'll never forget a remark made by Uncle Paul during my first week at Hammond. We were looking for an assistant to our lab technician, and the question of the proper salary for the job arose. Uncle Paul told me that it was company policy to pay a man one half of what he was worth for the first few years to see if he really wanted to work for the company. On the other hand, once a person was hired, he was never fired. We were sometimes called the "west-end branch of the Salvation Army."

Furthermore, our hiring procedures were about as crude as you can imagine. To hire people for work in the plant, for example, the production manager kept a large stack of completed applications on one corner of his desk. As new applications came in, his secretary added them to the top of the pile, and when the pile became too high, she would throw away the bottom three or four inches. Then, when a foreman announced that he needed one or two men to start work in his department "tomorrow," the production manager would start at the top of the pile and work his way down until he had found one or two men who could, literally, start the next day. Thus, we were hiring from a population of men who were currently unemployed or didn't have the courtesy to give their present employers any notice.

The situation hadn't hurt us too badly, however, since we did little hiring between World War II and 1950. And from the middle of 1950 until the end of 1952 we were completely occupied just trying to fill all the orders that were rolling in. Then the war boom started to collapse, and we found ourselves back in a competitive civilian economy. I realized then that major changes would have to be made in our operations if we were to escape another postwar crisis.

New Hiring Procedures. In 1953 Mr. Hammond convinced his father and uncle that the firm's method of hiring personnel, both plant and management, needed to be completely overhauled. To do this, the services of the Psychological Service of Cleveland (PSC) were engaged. PSC was a nonprofit organization specializing in the use of psychological tests for personnel selection. Starting in 1953, each potential employee of Hammond was required to take a battery of tests, and potential management personnel were intensively interviewed by a PSC psychologist, in addition to interviews by company executives. The first member of management hired using the new procedures was William Porter, Hammond's president in 1965. He entered the company as an industrial engineer, with the task of bringing the company's wage incentive system up to date.

PRODUCT DEVELOPMENT

Prior to 1958, Hammond relied almost exclusively on its major suppliers for the technical assistance needed for product development. A particularly close working relationship had been established with E. I. du Pont de Nemours & Company, suppliers of rayon and nylon tire cord, Neoprene synthetic rubber, and several rubber chemicals used in tire compounds. In exchange for Du Pont's technical assistance, Du Pont engineers used Hammond's production facilities and tires to test new Du Pont products. As a result of this outside help, Hammond's previous management had not felt it necessary to develop the company's own technical organization.

To strengthen the technical organization, Mr. Hammond hired Mr.

Robert Gray in November, 1958, to serve as chief chemist, and it was expected that Mr. Gray would eventually assume the position of technical director. Prior to joining Hammond, Mr. Gray had served for 8 years with the Seiberling Rubber Company as a rubber compounder, determining the proper mix of rubber, carbon black, and chemicals to be used in particular tires. When he talked with the case writer, Mr. Gray was 39 years old and held the position of vice president of administration. In this capacity he had formal responsibility for the company's product development, quality control, and training activities.

When I joined the company in 1958, I was amazed by the weakness of its technical organization. We were dependent upon our suppliers for technical advice; quality control activities were concerned almost exclusively with finished product inspection; no records were kept on product performance; and no knowledge existed about the actual applications in which our most important product, truck tires, were being used.

At that time, the company had a complacent attitude towards its products. People seemed to assume that Hammond tires were of the highest quality, and even though this assumption was false in several ways, the absence of knowledge about product performance made it difficult to challenge their position. Even our supposedly appealing advertising slogan, "Quality Since 1915," got us into trouble because it was interpreted by our employees as expressing a policy of producing the best tires possible, without any relationship to economic factors.

I believe the company was really trying to follow two conflicting product policies at the same time. On the one hand, we were trying to produce a quality product, able to compete with the best products of Goodyear and Firestone, while on the other hand we were trying to produce a tire which could be sold at a price 10% below the prices of competing lines. Furthermore, we assumed that because the name Hammond was not well-known, and because we did not have a sophisticated sales force, we had to make our tires larger and heavier in order to sell them.

It was my contention that a small company like Hammond could do something unique and get away with it. For instance, I suggested that we design a special tire to be sold as original equipment on a car such as the Chevy Corvette or the Ford Thunderbird. Bill Porter supported this idea for a while, but Henry Hammond, Sr., was violently opposed to it, and when a lot of internal friction developed, the idea was dropped.

The TX–35 Experience. In early 1960 the major tire producers initiated a 20% across-the-board decrease in the wholesale and retail prices of their tires. When Hammond's management determined that the company's premium tire, the Super Ride, could not be sold profitably at the new price levels, they ordered the development of a new premium product, the TX–35. This tire was both lighter and smaller than previous Hammond tires and thus represented a significant departure from the company's traditional products. In addition, it had a radically different tread design, with only three tread ribs, compared with the conventional five to seven rib construction. Unfortunately, the reduced number of ribs produced a high-pitched squeal during turns. The company's management believed that the competitive disadvantage which resulted from the tire's higher noise level was increased by the fact that the TX–35 was introduced at about the same time the major producers introduced their "Bucron" tires and promoted them largely on the basis of the quiet ride they delivered.

Hammond's dealers were extremely unhappy with the TX–35, and their failure to push the tire was believed to be a major factor behind a decrease in total sales from the 1959 high of $10.7 million to only $7.6 million in 1961.

When the full impact of the TX–35 failure became known, the company reintroduced the Super Ride tire, after making some modifications to lower its manufacturing cost. In addition, a new first-line tire, the Hammond Hawk, was added to the company's product lines. In order to introduce the Hawk as quickly as possible, it was originally manufactured using secondhand molds purchased from another tire company. Although the Hawk was considered to be old-fashioned in appearance, it was large and heavy, and dealers seemed to be pleased with it.

Recognizing that the steps described above were insufficient to place the company's passenger tires on a sound long-run competitive basis, Hammond started to develop a completely new Hawk tire, along with a new premium tire called the Eagle. These new lines were introduced in the spring of 1965 in conjunction with the company's 50th anniversary promotion.

Mr. Gray believed that the most important result of the company's product development program had been the parallel development of a sound technical capability. In September, 1965, Hammond employed six university-trained technical specialists and anticipated hiring more each year.

Product Development—Truck Tires. Mr. Gray also described problems of product development in the company's truck tire lines:

In 1958, Hammond was the only company in the industry still using Du Pont's Neoprene rubber in its truck tires—the result of the close relationship between the two companies. Although Neoprene originally had the advantage of good resistance to "channel cracking,"[3] by 1958 it was priced considerably higher than other synthetic rubbers on the market, in spite of the fact that it performed less satisfactorily at high operating temperatures. This latter characteristic was particularly important, because over the years there has been a steady increase in the length of truck trailers and, thus, in their weight. Their greater weight along with higher operating speeds has led to higher operating temperatures. As a result, the continued use of Neoprene rubber had a harmful effect on our ability to compete in the truck tire market. Unfortunately, however, our lack of knowledge of the field performance of our products prevented us from recognizing this problem as early as we should have. It was only when we began to lose a lot of truck tire business in 1960 that we stopped buying Neoprene and got off the Du Pont hook.

Additional difficulties have resulted from our failure to define the correct application or end-use of our truck tires and to insist that they be sold by our dealers only for this proper application. Last year, for instance, we had a problem with our "Duralug" tire—a tire with heavy "lugs" or cross ribs running perpendicular to the tread. We assumed that these tires were being used almost entirely in "on-the-road," or highway, applications, and we made several product changes to improve their high-speed performance. The result was a lighter tire that did not experience as much heat buildup in the tread. As soon as we started to distribute these modified tires, however, we began to receive many complaints of stone penetration—a type of damage that could only take place in "off-the-road" applications. We have therefore had to change our assumption, and we now believe that up to half of our Duralug tires are being operated off the road. Mistakes like this will be repeated unless we can develop a system which will give us much better feedback from the field.

PLANT MODERNIZATION PROGRAM

The only significant change which has taken place in the method of manufacturing tires during the last 10 years has been the introduction of the "Bag-O-Matic" curing press in 1952. Before this development, an airbag had to be manually inserted into each "green," or uncured, tire before the tire was placed in the curing press. The airbag, when inflated, served to hold the tire in the proper shape during the curing process. With Bag-O-Matic presses the uncured tires were placed in position without airbags, and the press, with its own airbag which automatically shaped the tire, was closed to complete the cure. As a result of eliminating the manual insertion of the airbag, the productivity of the curing department could be significantly increased.

Up until 1964, however, Hammond's management had not under-

---

[3] Channel cracks were splits that developed inside the grooves of a tire's tread. Combined with sufficient wear these cracks could lead to tire failure.

taken to modernize its production facilities, believing that machines did not have to be replaced as long as they were operating satisfactorily. During the late 1950's and early 1960's, therefore, Bag-O-Matic presses had been installed only at a rate of one press every two or three years, as the older presses wore out. By 1963, however, Hammond's management had become convinced that a major plant modernization program was necessary to lower production costs, and during 1964 ten Bag-O-Matic presses were installed at a cost of $50,000 per press.

At the end of 1965, there were 17 Bag-O-Matic presses in operation, and all but three of these incorporated equipment for the automatic loading and unloading of green and cured tires. The resulting increase in curing efficiency is shown by the fact that in 1964 only nine workers were required to cure 1,400 tires per day, while in 1954 there were 27 workers in the Curing Department when output was only 550 tires per day.

THE FINANCIAL CRISIS OF 1960

In 1959 the company's sales of tread rubber to tire recappers had grown to about 20% of total sales, and the machine which processed the tread-rubber compounds were being operated close to their capacity. Rather than expanding capacity at the Plainville plant, it was decided to build a tread-rubber plant in the southeastern U.S. Hammond's management believed that such a plant would enable the company to expand its tread-rubber sales in the Southeast by putting the company in a position to offer quicker delivery times to recappers in that area. In late 1959 a site in Palmerville, Georgia, was selected, and preliminary design work for the new plant was started in January, 1960. All plans for a new plant had to be abruptly terminated, however, as a result of a financial crisis which soon developed. Mr. Hammond described the crisis to the case writer:

> We didn't realize it at the time, but we were at that moment skating on thin financial ice. As a result of a failure to develop adequate financial controls, we had granted extended payment terms to too many dealers for too many dollars' worth of business in our "spring dating" program. Under this program, tires needed to build up dealer inventories for the spring selling season were sold and shipped during the first few months of the year although dealers were not billed for these tires until the late spring.
>
> By April of 1960, our cash position had deteriorated to the point where we simply could not pay all our bills. When we realized the seriousness of our

situation, we immediately quit granting extended terms to dealers, much to the dismay of our salesmen. They were competing with companies only too happy to sell tires and not get paid for them for 90 days. Unfortunately, we had exactly no alternatives, and our spring dating program disappeared overnight.

We managed to squeak through April, and in May the incoming cash flow was sufficient to enable us to pay all creditors. Obviously, any company which can't even pay its bills is not in shape to be starting a branch plant, and our Georgia adventure was indefinitely postponed. The experience showed us just how little we really knew about our financial situation and how poorly organized we were in our Financial Department. Actually, I'm being generous when I refer to a department because we really didn't have one then. Fortunately, we do now.

THE DEVELOPMENT OF A MARKETING ORGANIZATION

In September, 1965, Mr. Hammond believed that the major tasks in the development of a sound marketing organization had been accomplished. The last step in this process had been the appointment a month earlier of a field sales manager reporting to the vice president of sales, Mr. Edwards. It was hoped that without the responsibility to supervise the company's three regional sales managers, Mr. Edwards would have sufficient time for sales planning and the development of marketing policies.

Marketing Background. From 1930 until his retirement in March, 1963, Henry Hammond, Sr., was formally the director of the company's sales effort. Prior to World War II, however, he spent most of his time in the field as one of the company's two salesmen, and many important marketing decisions were made by Mr. M. P. (Flip) Jones, Hammond's sales office manager, when he talked with customers on the telephone.

In 1940 Mr. Hammond, Sr., hired three salesmen and returned to the home office. During the war and the immediate postwar period, sales problems were minimal, the result, first, of production for the armed forces and, later, for the tire-short domestic and overseas markets. Although the size of the sales force grew as additional salesmen were hired, the company continued to rely on a system of paying salesmen on a straight commission basis to provide an incentive for the sales effort, and no steps were taken to strengthen the sales organization in the home office.

In 1951 Henry Hammond, Sr., suffered a near-fatal heart attack. Realizing that a qualified replacement for his brother was necessary, and convinced that Mr. Jones was not the man for the job, Paul Hammond hired Mr. Frank Fairly as vice president of sales. Mr. Fairly made no significant changes in the marketing area, however, devoting almost his full attention to the company's advertising program.

In 1956 Henry Hammond, Jr., became alarmed about the situation. He described his feeling to the case writer:

Although I had no intention of getting into sales when I joined the company, the thought suddenly struck me in mid-1956 that I didn't know anything about sales at a time when we were exceedingly vulnerable in our Sales Department. No sales management people had been hired since Mr. Fairly became vice president of sales, and there were no qualified management candidates among our salesmen.

Therefore, with Bill Porter coming along well in production, I decided that if I were ever going to learn anything about sales, it had to be then. Acting on the theory that the best way to learn about sales is to get out and sell, I left Plainville, and for the next three years I worked as a salesman for the company in the field. By mid-1959 I thought I was ready to return to Plainville and take over our sales organization.

Upon my return I assumed the title of vice president of sales and started to run the sales end of the company. Fairly had already retired and Flip Jones resigned soon after I returned, so I immediately started to look for someone to work as my assistant and eventually become our sales manager. In the spring of 1960, I hired Philip Edwards for this job. At that time he was part owner and manager of the Pittsburgh branch of a retreading-equipment manufacturer, after previously starting his career in tire sales with the U. S. Rubber Company.

Our personnel problems in the marketing area were certainly not solved, however, when we hired Philip. By 1961 I realized that in addition to having a sales manager to supervise our field sales organization we needed a manager of marketing services, responsible for such things as advertising and promotion, sales planning, sales forecasting. Thus, in the fall of 1961, I hired Frank Williams for this position. Mr. Williams turned out to be neurotic and oversensitive, and he was simply unable to establish good working relationships within the company. Shortly after Bill Porter assumed total operating responsibility in the company, it was necessary to let Mr. Williams go, and he left in the fall of 1963. Bill can pick up the story from this point, and I suggest you talk to him.

Interview with William Porter. Following Mr. Hammond's suggestion, the case writer talked to Hammond's president, William Porter, about the recent development of the company's marketing organization:

My first attempt to replace Mr. Williams as director of marketing services failed. The man I hired in the fall of 1963, Mr. Peters, turned out to have a big "I" complex. Not content to run his own show, he attempted to exercise direct authority over our salesmen who reported to Philip Edwards. We could not tolerate this, so he left after just one year in the job.

Since we had failed twice to place someone in our marketing organization on a par with Philip Edwards, I decided that what we needed was a director of marketing in charge of all marketing activities with Philip reporting to him. For this job, I hired Paul Henderson in the fall of 1964. At first glance, Paul seemed to be a real world beater. He had been outstandingly successful as an account executive in our advertising agency and had made several brilliant presentations to us. Even though he had had no experience in the tire industry, I thought that his great sophistication in marketing was what we needed.

I was totally wrong. Soon after he joined the company, he started playing the "I've got a secret" game and refused to keep me informed about what he was doing. For example, one of the people in our Industrial Products Division convinced Paul that we needed to have an ultrasonic testing machine. I told him that we could not afford to purchase this expensive piece of equipment. Shortly thereafter, however, I began to hear people talking about ultrasonic experiments and was shocked to learn that, contrary to my orders, Paul had purchased the machine and had had it secretly installed in a garage he had rented downtown.

Paul also behaved in ways which I considered to be unethical—particularly when it came to recruiting people. For instance, one of his favorite tricks was to call the company of a man he wanted to hire and, pretending to be the representative of a credit agency, he would discover the man's address and telephone number. Then he would contact the man and try to get him to leave his present position.

This kind of behavior gradually began to undermine our entire organization. During the last few months before he left, I noticed that our weekly management meetings had deteriorated to the point where people were unwilling to discuss any of their problems with their associates. I wasn't aware of the reasons behind this, however, until I asked Paul to leave two months ago. As soon as he left everyone started to talk freely again. You can hardly imagine how this company bubbled over with joy when his dismissal was announced.

In describing my analysis of this development, I like to use the analogy of the behavior of airplane passengers when they pass through a severe thunderstorm. While the storm is around them, an almost complete silence descends upon the plane, but as soon as the storm is behind them and the plane emerges into blue skies, you can hear a great sigh of relief and everyone begins to speak.

Part of the difficulty we have had in getting a satisfactory marketing team probably stems from a failure to define the job to be done. In thinking about the case of Henderson, you must also remember that for several years Philip Edwards, Robert Gray, and I have formed a kind of inner group in our company. Therefore, to try to bring someone into a small organization and interject him between two members of such a group puts this person in a difficult position. I know that Paul thought that there was too much communication directly between Philip and me, and to some extent his criticism was probably valid.

Since Philip has only been in the sales vice president's position for a month, it is still too early to judge his effectiveness. He is probably the best tire salesman in the industry, but he has yet to prove himself as a manager.

Interview with Philip Edwards. To learn of the specific changes that had been made in Hammond's marketing operations, the case writer interviewed Mr. Edwards:

When I joined the company in May, 1960, I entered the most screwed-up sales organization I had ever seen. There were no quotas, no sales forecasts, no sales goals, no sales reports. No one in the home office even knew where the salesmen were. With no control over our sales activities, our salesmen were the real customers of the company, not the dealers who sold our tires. Obviously, it was impossible to plan with such a system.

Mr. Edward's first action was to require the salesmen to fill out route sheets and submit a weekly call report. Even these minor controls were resisted, however, and one salesman quit rather than "stand all that dirty paperwork." He then created the positions of three regional sales managers, each with a maximum of 12 salesmen under his supervision. And finally, Mr. Edwards instituted a salary-plus-commission compensation system to replace the straight commission system previously in force. Under the new system, which had been completely installed by January, 1963, each salesman was assigned a quota for his territory. When a salesman reached 90% of his quota, he began to earn a bonus of 1% of his salary for each percentage point increase in his sales, up to his assigned quota. Beyond this point, a salesman received a bonus of 2% of his salary for each percentage point gain in sales. Mr. Edwards said that he usually increased quotas 10% each year in those territories which were fully developed. In newly established territories, he said the annual quota increases were much larger, sometimes amounting to as much as 40%.

In late 1964, Mr. Edwards introduced a further modification in the company's sales compensation system whereby a salesman's bonus was raised or lowered on the basis of how the average gross margin of his sales compared with the average gross margin achieved by all salesmen. For each percentage point that a salesman's gross margin was higher than the company average, his bonus was increased by 10%; and for each decrease of 1% below the average gross margin, his bonus was decreased by 5%. This last change was designed to encourage the salesmen to push Hammond's high-margin products. For example, although the average gross margin on sales was 37.3% in 1965, tread-rubber sales to tire recappers, which represented 14% of total sales, earned a gross margin of only 22.7%. "Thus," Mr. Edwards remarked, "a salesman who sells a larger than average percentage of tread rubber will get clubbed when his bonus is computed."

Mr. Edwards had also devised a salary-plus-bonus compensation system for the three regional sales managers. When sales in a region reached 90% of quota, the regional managers received a bonus equal to

5% of their salary, and their salaries were increased an additional 2.5% for each 2% increase in the sales of their region. Eventually, Mr. Edwards planned on paying the regional managers a bonus based on the profits earned in their regions rather than on total regional sales. He believed, however, that it would be January of 1967 before this profit-center plan could be implemented.

With the appointment of a field sales manager to supervise the three regional sales managers, Mr. Edwards anticipated spending considerable time during 1966 on what he considered to be the two most important problem areas remaining in the company's marketing program—sales training and market research. The position of company training director had recently been created and a man hired to fill it. The new training director, reporting to Mr. Gray, was to be responsible for all training activities at Hammond. Mr. Edwards did not expect him to take a direct part in training salesmen, however, since he had had no previous experience in the tire industry. Mr. Edwards believed that such training should continue to be a responsibility of the regional sales managers.

In 1965 the company performed no market research on a continuing basis. Although Mr. Edwards believed that a market research program was needed, he was not yet sure how this function should be fitted into his sales organization.

PRODUCTION OPERATIONS, 1964–65

Mr. George Roberts, Hammond's vice president of manufacturing, discussed recent developments in the company's production operations. Before joining Hammond in May, 1964, Mr. Roberts had been vice president of operations of a large, plastic toy company for two years, after working 12 years as production manager and industrial relations manager at the Toledo, Ohio, plant of the Rockwell Manufacturing Company. While working for Rockwell, Mr. Roberts attended night school, receiving a bachelor's degree in industrial engineering from the University of Toledo in 1959.

During his first four months with Hammond, Mr. Roberts served as assistant to the president. In August, 1964, he was named production manager, and in the spring of 1965 he was promoted to the newly formed position of vice president of manufacturing. At the time of the interview, Mr. Roberts was 33 years old.

As vice president of manufacturing, I am responsible for coordinating the activities of our managers of production, industrial engineering, and industrial relations. Previously, these three men, plus our plant engineer, reported directly to the president, and my position was established to take this load off his shoulders.

When I became production manager, the most critical area needing improvement was labor relations. A few years previously, we had overhauled our incentive system and had eliminated many loose standards. But I think the pendulum had swung too far in the other direction. For example, in July, 1964, our curing room workers were being paid their hourly base pay of $2.11, even though under the previous incentive system these men had earned $3 per hour. Through an investment of $340,000 we had built a new curing room, and a dozen people had been taken off their jobs and assigned to other production operations. The result was a marked increase in efficiency accompanied by a lowering of morale.

To improve our labor relations, I adopted the use of union-management meetings, where I sit down with the executive board of the union four times a year to go over their problems and complaints. I think that their attitude has improved considerably in the past year because we now work together on common problems.

Our average incentive wages are now $2.50 per hour and some go as high as $3.55 per hour. I think, however, that we have lower labor costs than the major producers. We are the only company in the industry that does not negotiate with the Rubber Workers Union; we deal instead with the United Mine Workers Union. Although I don't have any specific data, I think that our lower wages are offset by our higher raw material and shipping costs. Normal raw material prices are f.o.b. Akron, and we have to pay the added costs of having our materials shipped to us here in Plainville.

The second most critical problem I faced when I took over this job was the need for better analyses of manufacturing requirements. In the past, the company had taken the attitude that they would follow the other fellow in the industry, doing what others did whether or not it was appropriate for Hammond. In addition, the production manager had taken upon himself the task of performing all economic analyses, making all decisions about plant layout, and handling the problems of industrial engineering. At present, however, the Industrial Engineering Department carefully analyzes the costs of any proposed changes in our production operations, and the plant engineer is responsible for making a careful economic evaluation of any new equipment purchases.

I believe that the major problems I encountered have now been eliminated, and we are making smaller refinements in our operations. My major goal is to develop a high-quality attitude among the workers. By making it right the first time we can reduce our scrap and rework costs. I recently hired a top-flight engineer to work on ways to reduce scrap costs, and I expect that this step will pay off very quickly. We also have a plant engineer second to none in the country.

One of my major concerns now is the need to increase our capacity. We are working three shifts a day, producing twice the output for which the plant was designed. We have real plant layout and material handling problems. For example, raw materials now enter the plant in six different places.

In the past three years we have made capital expenditures of over $1.8 million, but this is only the beginning. During the next five years we expect to spend $4 million on additional plant and equipment which will double our capacity. At the end of this program we shall have a much more rational flow of production.

We are presently experimenting with the development of a radial tire. If we introduce radials, it will require a complete change in worker training because of the precision required in radial construction. In some places where we now produce to tolerances of $\frac{1}{8}$ of an inch, radial production requires tolerances of $\frac{1}{100}$ of an inch.

I believe that a 100-thousand-mile tire will come along eventually, and that it will probably be made out of a plastic replacement for rubber. For instance, urethane tires were produced by the Germans in World War II, and many small industrial truck tires are now made from urethane. Because of urethane's high abrasion resistance, these tires last three to four times longer than conventional tires. There have also been some promising developments in the use of a mixture of rubber and styrene plastic.

RECENT FINANCIAL DEVELOPMENTS

In 1961 Mr. Peter Douglas joined Hammond as vice president of finance. Prior to that time, following a career as a CPA with a national accounting firm, Mr. Douglas had been the president of several smaller companies, each of which he had developed into profitable operations before selling to larger companies. At 57, Mr. Douglas was the oldest member of Hammond's management. Mr. Douglas described the financial development of Hammond:

When I joined the company, we had a controller but no financial man. We had a pretty good cost accounting system but very poor financial controls. Furthermore, the loans we had at that time were secured by warehouse receipts, a very expensive form of financing.

In 1962 we started a major plant modernization program, financed by a revolving loan from local banks. In 1964, however, we refinanced with loans of $600,000 from the Pittsburgh National Bank and $1.2 million from the Metropolitan Life Insurance Company.

I believe that anything that is sound can be financed and that one of the most important reasons why we have been able to secure adequate financing is the high caliber of the management group. With the exception of myself, this is a very young, dynamic organization. I've never been with a company that has the vim and vigor of Hammond, a company continually pushing ahead but, at the same time, keeping its feet on the ground.

The last three years have been spent in trying to educate our managers to use the accounting data we now give them. We make sales forecasts for each type of tire in our line, and these are translated into a manufacturing budget. Budget variances are analyzed monthly and the budget is revised every three months if necessary. I believe we have as many sales statistics as any of the larger companies in our industry, and we are very proud of what we are doing. Our main task now is to get more timely information to our management people.

Our earnings in the last few years have been somewhat understated because we have been taking as much depreciation as possible. Our plan now is to go for profits, and we are aiming at profits of $800,000 in 1966. You will also notice that we are highly leveraged, and I don't think you'll find another company of our size which has borrowed so much in relation to its net equity.

Credit Policies.   Hammond was the only company in the industry using trade acceptances in its sales to dealers, and at the end of 1965 over $1 million in acceptances had been drawn on the banks of the dealers. Mr. Douglas credited this form of financing sales with holding down the company's bad debt losses to a level of about $35,000 per year. "Our credit policy is one of aggressive collections," he said, "but with a selling orientation. I believe our collection manager knows our customers better than our salesmen, and there is close coordination between our sales and credit departments."

THE OUTLOOK FOR THE FUTURE

In the spring of 1965, in an effort to stimulate his associates to think about the long-term future of the company, Mr. Hammond asked each of them to complete a "secret ballot" listing how he believed the sales of the company would be divided among its major product classifications in 1980. The estimates of the Hammond management in millions of dollars were as follows:

	1980 Sales	Passenger Tire	Truck Tire	Industrial Products
H. Hammond	200	1	39	160
W. Porter	400	150	50	200
P. Edwards	640	160	160	320
R. Gray	575	130	145	300
G. Roberts	680	204	136	340
P. Douglas	200	15	35	150

The 100-Thousand-Mile Passenger Tire. There was no doubt in Mr. Hammond's mind that a 100-thousand-mile passenger car tire would be introduced as original equipment on all automobiles at some time in the 1965–80 period. As a result, he anticipated the virtual elimination of the company's passenger car tire business and had decided to devote his energies to a major diversification program. Mr. Porter agreed with Mr. Hammond that a 100-thousand-mile tire would eventually be developed, but he did not believe this would take place during the next 15 years. He told the case writer: "Because I see this event taking place further in the future, I do not see the urgency of our phasing out of the passenger tire business as fast as Henry does, and unlike Henry, I am quite willing to spend money in the tire business as long as we can have our investments pay back within the next five years." Mr. Edwards, on the other hand, believed there were several reasons why a 100-thousand-mile tire would not be introduced. He explained his position as follows:

Henry has tried to impress everyone in the company with the fact that products come and go in business. He talks about the 100-thousand-mile tire and even a form of hover craft which will not use tires at all. However, I believe we are fairly safe with our present products through 1980.

Although the 100-thousand-mile tire has already been researched, the cost of producing it now is so high that people would not be willing to pay for it. After all, most new car buyers intend to drive their cars for only about 25,000 miles before trading them in.

Another reason why the 100-thousand-mile tire will not come along in the foreseeable future is the fact that the automobile manufacturers don't want it; they like to have things begin to go wrong with their cars at about 25,000 miles. The first three things that start to go wrong are usually the tires, the battery, and the muffler, in that order. As soon as most car owners have to start putting money into their cars, they begin to think of trading them in on a new model. Automobile manufacturers are quite happy to have tires be the first things to go because they are able to disassociate themselves from the performance of a product made by other companies.

Changes in Channels of Distribution and Pricing Policy. In his opening remarks to the case writer, Mr. Hammond had mentioned the relative decline of the independent dealer as a distributor of tires and the growth of the mass merchandisers. He amplified his remarks as follows:

In spite of this relative decline, most industry experts see a continued growth in the tire sales of the independents on an absolute basis, and I believe we should continue to sell mainly in this market. The mass merchandisers in the big cities sell almost exclusively on a price basis and do not depend upon satisfied customers for repeat business. They also rely on the highly promoted reputation of the major producers. Because we are so small, however, we cannot engage in extensive consumer advertising, and we must rely on the personal relationship between the dealer and his customers to sell our tires. For this reason, our best market is and will continue to be in small-sized or medium-sized towns, where dealers know their customers personally. This also explains why we put almost all our advertising dollars in trade magazines aimed at the dealers and in cooperative newspaper advertising undertaken by our dealers.

I believe we should continue to give our dealers a tire which they can sell at a price a little below the price of the major brands but with a higher margin for themselves. We should make no pretense of being a full-line producer, but should take advantage of our small size by pointing out to our dealers that this permits us to produce a high-quality product at a lower cost. We should tell them, for instance, that we do not have multiple layers of branch management, have no expensive offices to maintain on the West Coast, do no expensive television advertising, and refuse to spend money flying blimps. Above all, we should continue to develop our ability to give our dealers fast action on their requests and quick answers to their questions, even though these answers may have to be "no." Right now, for example, we are setting up to handle all adjustment claims from our dealers in a maximum of 48 hours, compared with our old system which sometimes took as long as four to six weeks to process a claim.

Nor do I believe we should attempt to increase our geographical distribution west of the Mississippi. Even $20 million in sales is nothing in this industry, and it is much more efficient for us to try to increase our share of the market in our present area than to spread ourselves thin all over the country. Another reason for not expanding our area is that we can now dispose of our excess production at low prices outside our area if we get into a difficult situation without running into conflicts with our existing dealers.

Mr. Porter agreed with Mr. Hammond that the company should continue to attempt to expand its distribution through independent dealers in small towns and to limit its activities to its present geographic area. Mr. Edwards, however, was less sure about the wisest course of action for the company:

I am convinced that we cannot continue to do just more of what we have been doing. In the large cities it has become almost impossible to find an independent dealer for our products. Therefore, I have been investigating the possibility of selling to department stores or going into the private brand business. Many of the mass merchandisers have learned that it doesn't pay to sell inferior quality tires, and they may be ready to change to the higher quality levels we produce.

I am also concerned about our ability to continue to sell our truck tires through independent dealers. It is possible to divide truckers into two groups—those who operate about 20 rigs and those who operate more. The smaller outfits will continue to utilize outside services and will probably need to go through middlemen in buying their tires. Truckers operating more than 20 rigs, however, usually service their own equipment and want to purchase tires directly from the manufacturers. For the small trucker, the tire dealer or our own salesman can actually go around checking on such things as proper inflation, wheel alignment, and whether the tires are being removed at the right time for retreading. That is, they can act as maintenance departments for the truckers.

The large truckers, on the other hand, purchase tires mainly on a cost-per-mile basis, and they are particularly interested in the number of retreads they can get on a carcass. Selling on a cost-per-mile basis requires skilled salesmen who can analyze operating costs. I have thus told my salesmen to speak frankly with our dealers, telling them that if they cannot make the sales to the large trucking companies, we want to go in directly. Direct sales already make up 20% of our truck tire business, and the percentage is going up every year. I have already started to hire truck tire specialists for each region. These men will be responsible for all truck tire sales in their region, and in addition to working with the regular salesmen, I expect they will eventually spend a lot of time in direct selling.

One problem we face in truck tire sales is that of reciprocity. That is, the large truckers buy tires from those producers who use their trucks to transport their own materials. This practice has just about kept us out of the market composed of the ICC licensed operators.

While I agree that it would be unwise for us to attempt nationwide distribution all of a sudden, I believe some expansion is necessary. I thus plan on setting up sales territories in the states immediately west of the Mississippi in the coming year.

I believe we have some cost advantages over the major producers because of our lower wage rates and lower distribution costs. We don't have an expensive branch office type of operation. On the other hand, I have had to increase our distribution costs in the last year by establishing three branch warehouses. This step was necessary to give quicker delivery to our dealers.

We have traditionally followed a policy of pricing our tires at a level about 10% lower than the prices of the major producers. I believe that most of this saving has been passed along to the tire purchaser, even though we have no control over the final retail price. In recent months, however, price competition has grown so intense that we have had to abandon this policy, and I do not see us returning to it in the near future.

On the other hand, I do not intend to change our policy of not publishing a "Hammond price," or suggested retail price as most producers do. Last year one of the major producers was offering a suggested retail price only 14% higher than the dealer price. I don't see how their dealers could possibly operate profitably under those conditions. We just publish a "no trade-in price" and allow our dealers to mark our tires up to what the traffic will bear.

Introduction of a Second-Line Tire. At the end of 1965, plans were well under way to introduce a second-line tire for the first time in the company's history in the spring of 1966.[4] In commenting on this action, Mr. Porter said:

We claim that we have never made a second-line tire, but I'm not sure if we really believe this. For instance, the first Hawk tire was sold to our dealers for the same price they paid for the second-line tires of the major producers, and even though it was promoted as a 100-level tire, I'm sure many dealers sold it at a normal second-line price. In fact, the normal competitive situation in this industry is for the smaller producers to sell their tires at a price one level below

---

[4] Shortly after the preparation of this case, the company's second-line "Falcon" tire was introduced. The Falcon was sold at a dealer price of $11.09 and a "no trade-in" retail price of $24.30 (for the 7.75–14, nylon cord, tubeless, blackwall).

those of the major brands. Thus, the level of a tire is mainly one of price; as a measure of quality it is a relatively meaningless term. If our second-line tire turns out to be what I think it will, it will be a safe tire that represents a good customer value, and as far as I'm concerned, that's exactly our traditional product policy.

Mr. Gray was even less concerned about this proposed departure from tradition:

I believe our product policy can be expressed as producing tire products with a quality equal to or better than the average products of the major producers in the same price levels and for the same applications. Thus, as far as I'm concerned, we could go so far as to produce fifth-line tires and still be consistent with our policy.

Government Regulation of Tire Standards. By the fall of 1965, many industry observers expected that a federal law would be passed in 1966 establishing minimum standards of tire safety and perhaps including a uniform system of grade labeling. For several years, Mr. Hammond had been a leading spokesman among those pressing for such standards. In a statement submitted to the Federal Trade Commission in January, 1965, he said:

The average new car buyer can probably be pardoned for assuming that he can fill up his vehicle with people and baggage and then drive off—safely. If he had just bought a six-passenger wagon, he might be very surprised to learn that if he put six 170-pound men in it, each of whom had placed his 30-pound suitcase in the back of the vehicle, the tires might be overloaded by as much as 20%. If any one tire on this vehicle was underinflated by as little as four pounds, a three-hour turnpike trip at 65 m.p.h. would be a rather dangerous one.

At present, the average car driver is completely uninformed with regard to (1) the maximum rated load for his particular tire size, and (2) the empty weight of his car. These two rather important figures are not furnished to him by the vehicle manufacturers.

Our company feels that every new car should have in it a placard, easily visible from the driver's seat, showing the net number of pounds or people and/or baggage that can be put into the vehicle before the tires become loaded to the maximum allowed. Drivers would at least know then when they were skirting the danger area. As things stand now, the average driver simply doesn't give any thought to the matter—because no one has ever told him that he was placing himself, his passengers, and every oncoming driver in a potentially dangerous situation.

We think it's time somebody gave him some facts.

In his discussion with the case writer, Mr. Hammond explained the reasons behind his support of tire safety legislation:

When the third- and fourth-line tires were first introduced a few years ago, we were shocked that any reputable tire manufacturer would turn out such a product and allow it to fall into the hands of the poor unsuspecting consumer. For a while, we thought that this situation was a fad which would soon pass. Unfortunately, we were incorrect in that assumption.

Since our company only manufactures tires in the higher priced end of the spectrum, we quickly discovered that it was very difficult for us—being unknown to the consumer—to compete with the very low-priced tires. Our company policy on product quality would not allow us to "join them"—so we decided to beat them. Our approach was to start beating the drum for some kind of minimum tire quality standards. The industry bigwigs kept saying that it couldn't be done, but we had some very logical reasons as to why it could be done, and I am happy to say that our position will prevail. Our position has been that when the average American driver suddenly gets the idea that he needs some kind of protection when he goes to buy a tire, said American driver is going to get his legislators to pass some kind of a law which will provide the desired protection. There are only 12 tire producers, but there are millions of voter–drivers. Thus, it doesn't make any difference what the major rubber companies think.

The main social responsibility issue here is the need to protect the consumer from himself. In this industry, under present laws, a manufacturer can make tires out of chewing gum and old ties, and there is no way he can be prosecuted. It so happens that in this case a real need on the part of the public coincides with the competitive ax we have to grind in Hammond. Once the unsafe "cheapie" tires are off the market, we can breathe more freely here in Plainville.

Mr. Porter agreed that legally enforced tire standards would be established, but he was less sure about their impact on the company:

I am not sure that it is practicable to develop meaningful safety standards for tires, but since we are going to have these standards anyway, I believe we should take part in their formulation. In resisting tire standards against what appears to be an overwhelming public demand for them, I believe the industry has made a great mistake. All the industry has succeeded in accomplishing is a great deal of ill will.

I am afraid that the minimum standards will be set at a quality level somewhere around the present third-line tire. If so, there is a danger that the tire buyer will say, "If these tires are OK with the government, they are OK with me." This kind of reaction might well result in the reduction in sales of premium tires. The average car owner doesn't intend to keep his car until the second set of tires wears out. Therefore, if he can be assured of the safety of his replacement tires, he may purchase the cheapest "approved" tires he can find.

Messrs. Gray and Edwards were also concerned about the effect of the concern for tire safety on their company. Mr. Gray believed that the government standards would be set at a quality level between that of present second- and third-line tires, and that as these tires gained public acceptance, manufacturers such as Hammond would have less to sell. That is, the company could no longer promote its products on the basis of their greater safety. Mr. Edwards believed that people who were worried about tire safety were more likely to purchase a tire made by a major producer than to take a chance with the product of a company with a less well-known name and reputation.

Diversification.   Each member of Hammond's top management team believed that the company should make a major effort to diversify its activities. Mr. Hammond believed that the company's future development would take place in the field of industrial rubber products, and during the past year he had investigated over 40 companies which appeared to be potential acquisitions. He had reached his present position after analyzing the company's first attempt at diversification, which had been made in 1962 when it purchased the Willow Corporation, a manufacturer of fiberglass boats. He described this unsuccessful venture to the case writer:

Somewhere in about my second or third week with the company, the subject of diversification came up. We had just come through a bad year in 1949, and the subject of this particular meeting was the desirability of getting into other fields which would presumably remain profitable during the periodic slumps in the tire business. The meeting broke up on a theme of "everybody keep his eyes open for something new that we could get into, and when you see something interesting, bring it in and we'll look at it. If it looks good, we'll give it a try." Thus, getting us into new fields was everybody's business, and since everybody's business is nobody's business, it's no wonder that it took us 12 years before we made the first step.

In 1962 a consultant we were using mentioned a friend of his who was making fiberglass boats in his garage. This friend suggested that we get into the fiberglass boat business with himself as manager. We might actually have gotten started this way, if a representative of an investment banking firm hadn't casually mentioned that he knew of a fiberglass boat plant in Des Moines, Iowa, that was about to go broke. He was right, but we were hot for some kind of diversification, and the glamor of the boat business temporarily got the better of our business judgment. We bought the Willow Corporation for 15 cents on the dollar, and in looking back I can say that that was considerably more than it was worth.

Three years later, we came to the reluctant conclusion that we had gotten into the wrong business in the wrong place at exactly the wrong time. We were selling a big-ticket luxury item which had an extremely seasonal sales pattern, and we couldn't learn enough about selling boats fast enough to pull Willow out of the red. We finally sold off all the parts except the industrial fiberglass end of it and gave up the effort.

What did we learn from this experience? One thing was simply that if you are considering going into a field that requires a completely different marketing approach than you're used to, it might be a good idea to go out and call on some dealers who are presently in this particular business. You might learn pretty quickly just what some of the selling problems actually are. We also learned that if there isn't any fit between your present sales organization and the new field, you might ask yourself if you can afford to build up a completely new sales organization. A final lesson we learned was that taking a business which is losing money and then making it profitable is a skill that very few companies have. We may eventually develop such skills, but we don't have them yet.

By September, 1965, Mr. Hammond had developed a list of 13 criteria for the evaluation of potential acquisitions. These criteria were:

1. *Size of Company Being Acquired.* Prospects should have net sales between $500 thousand and $5 million.
2. *Management of Company Being Acquired.* The management must have similar basic philosophies to our own regarding product quality, desire for future growth, and honest dealing. Psychological Service of Cleveland evaluation of key management people must be satisfactory. Service companies (as opposed to product companies) should generally have a stronger management team. In general, one-man company situations should be avoided.
3. *Prospect's Field of Operations.* One-product companies should be avoided, unless the management team has enough demonstrated depth to come up with new (replacement) products as present product becomes obsolete. Prospect should offer either economies of manufacturing or economies of marketing when combined with our company. A qualified person in our own management must have some personal knowledge of and interest in the prospect's field—either through previous work experience or through some personal (hobby) interest in same. (This depends to some extent on the size and competence of the management team being acquired. The bigger and better, the less need for our "personal" involvement.)
4. *Prospect's Geographic Location.* Prospect should be in eastern half of U.S. and should be readily accessible, meaning that total air-ground travel time should not exceed three hours.
5. *Prospect's Financial Condition.* Prospect must be a profitable operation with at least a five-year history of same. Avoid businesses less than five years old.
6. *Prospect's Physical Facility.* Physical facility must present an appearance which indicates some effort being made toward keeping things shipshape. Sloppy housekeeping indicates sloppy management.
7. *Prospect's Reasons for Selling.* These must sound reasonable to us and must be subjected to as close a scrutiny as circumstances will allow. Those of our management who make this investigation must write, and circulate to our Board, a formal opinion as to the reasons why the prospect wishes to sell out. (Depends on the apparent "bargain" being offered.)
8. *Financial Feasibility of the Acquisition.* All deals are to be for cash only. We do not presently contemplate exchanging stock.
9. *Prospect's Union Relations.* These must be at least average or better. We are not interested in situations with a history of poor union relations.

Restrictive contracts which encroach on management prerogatives are grounds for our rejecting the deal.

10. *Moving Prospect's Physical Facilities.* We do not contemplate buying a company and then moving it to another location, except in very unusual circumstances. Too many valuable personnel are lost in the process. If we acquire a company for its marketing organization (field), we could consider moving the company without risking loss of field personnel.

11. *Long-Term Commitments.* Investigation of the prospect's long-term obligations must be made. Onerous leases, pension, retirement, profit sharing, or union contract items must be carefully evaluated in terms of our willingness to live with same.

12. *Complete Control.* We are probably not interested in anything less than 80% control of any prospective acquisition.

13. *Our Management Representatives.* No acquisition should be undertaken unless we have a qualified member of our management who can be assigned to the operation on a full-time basis for at least one year.

Using these criteria, Mr. Hammond had narrowed his list of potential acquisitions in the industrial rubber field from 40 down to four, and in early 1965 negotiations had been initiated with two of these companies. By the end of 1965, however, both negotiations had been terminated for various reasons, and no specific diversification steps were under way. The loan agreement with the Metropolitan Insurance Company provided that all acquisitions had to be approved by Metropolitan.

Mr. Porter also discussed the company's need to diversify:

Ever since 1956 I have felt very strongly about the need for our company to diversify, for it is basically unsound for a business to be so dependent upon one product—particularly a replacement product. I think it is still an open question, however, as to whether our diversification will be only in industrial rubber products. I hope it will not, for I do not see this kind of business as having as large a profit potential as some other things we could do.

For instance, I believe there are real opportunities for making money in the areas of education, recreation, and services. These are relatively undeveloped areas where someone can start something new. Growing in industrial rubber products, on the other hand, means taking business away from firms already well established. A steel mill, for example, which spends a few hundred dollars on rubber roller coverings will be very reluctant to change to an unknown supplier and take a chance on a shutdown that could cost thousands.

Recently I have been fooling around semiseriously with the idea of starting some kind of industrial education program. We had some experience in this kind of work when we conducted a training program here for Du Pont salesmen who were going to be selling to the rubber industry. Similar programs might be successful because with the exception of some work at one university there is no place where a man can learn about the rubber industry even though there is a great scarcity of such people as tire designers and tire developers.

In general, I believe our diversification should aim towards supplying a service rather than a product. For example, we might get into the management of a private hunting preserve, fishing preserve, or skiing area. In my opinion, skiing areas today are designed exclusively for the very good and very wealthy skier, and they are too fancy for the vast majority of people. If we could develop an area with gentle slopes which would appeal to a mass market and provide our service at a reasonable price, we might be able to do very well. I must admit, of course, that my interest in such activities is directly related to the fact that I am an outdoorsman. I can't think of any time when I would not prefer to be outdoors than indoors.

In addition to increasing sales of nontire products through acquisitions, Hammond was expanding its own production of nontire products, and an Industrial Products Division had been established in 1964.

At the end of 1965, this division was organized as a separate company, the Hammond Industrial Products Corporation. It was housed in a separate plant, financed by a $400,000 guaranteed mortgage from the Ohio Industrial Development Organization.

The Hammond Industrial Products Corporation produced rubber covered rolls, used primarily in the steel, paper, and glass industries. It also produced rubber and fiberglass linings for tanks and molded urethane products. Because of urethane's high abrasion resistance, it was finding increased applications in products ranging from protective shields for crane hooks to bearing seals.

Hammond's industrial product sales had amounted to about $100,000 in 1964, and they were expected to increase to about $200,000 in 1965. Although the company had not earned a profit on its nontire business, it was expected that profits would be generated in 1966.

MR. PORTER'S DILEMMA

Mr. Porter described what he considered to be a strategic dilemma facing his company:

I mentioned earlier that as a result of the coming government standards, I believe there may be a rush to the production of tires coming closer to the minimum standards. Thus, we may see a fading out of our Eagle and even our Hawk lines. After all, these tires have no really distinctive characteristics with which we can compete in the higher priced market. Thus, there is a real possibility that our second-line Falcon tire will become our major volume producer.

In the face of a diminishing market for our higher priced lines, we are caught on the horns of a dilemma. On the one hand, we could concentrate on the truck tire market, using a rifle versus a shotgun approach to sell people who recognize the cost-per-mile factors. We realize, however, that there is little possibility for significant growth in truck tire business, and thus, we would be pursuing a stagnant market.

On the other hand, we do not have consumer acceptance in the passenger tire market, and we would have to make a major investment to gain it. Our main hope here is the independent tire dealer. At present these dealers do not have the proper merchandising skills, and they are not being helped by the major producers. Perhaps we could put together some kind of package which would enable them to compete.

United Industries

UNITED INDUSTRIES was founded in 1945 by Mr. Peter Amato under the name of Middlesex Pattern Works. Mr. Amato, age 57, had been a craftsman in wood and metal for many years, having served a rigorous apprenticeship in his youth. For many years he had worked for General Electric at its Lynn, Massachusetts, plant.

From the date of its founding until 1956, the company's major product had been patterns. These were made primarily for the local foundry of General Electric but also for many of the other foundries in the Greater Boston area.

Patterns are solid pieces which are placed in a mold in order to impart the desired shape to a casting. A typical casting process would be to use a pattern to create, in sand, a depression of the size and shape of the desired casting. This is done by packing sand around the pattern. The pattern is then removed and the depression in the sand filled with molten metal.

United Industries made patterns of wood, metal, plastic, and clay. Since a single pattern can be used to produce many castings, patterns are often made in very small quantities; and an order for only one pattern of a particular kind is very common. Consequently pattern making is a highly skilled handcraft activity.

After 1956, the company's major product shifted from patterns to models and mockups. Net sales went from about $125,000 in 1957 to about $207,000 in 1961 (see Exhibit 1). Earned surplus went from $27,849 in 1957 to $81,191 in 1961 (see Exhibit 2). Financial ratios for this period are shown in Exhibit 3.

Models and mockups are three dimensional imitations of a device which differs from the real thing in several important ways. One important difference may be in actual size. A model may be either much smaller or much larger than the thing itself. Small-scale models are commonly used in architecture, factory layout, and chemical plant design. Large-scale models are used in product development.

A second important distinction between a model and the real thing may be in terms of the materials from which it is made. A full-scale model (often called a mockup) of wood or plastic may be desired as a

Exhibit 1

UNITED INDUSTRIES
Profit and Loss Statement
January 1 to December 31
(Thousands of Dollars)

	1957	1958	1959	1960	1961*
Gross sales	$127.1	$201.9	$257.2	$264.8	$211.4
Loss: Returns & allowances	1.2	1.1	6.8	4.1	4.0
Net sales	$125.9	$200.8	$250.3	$260.6	$207.4
Less: Labor	$ 58.2	$ 82.3	$107.3	$121.4	$102.7
Materials	19.5	32.4	40.9	40.6	23.9
Cost of goods sold	$ 77.7	$114.8	$148.2	$162.0	$126.6
Operating income	$ 48.1	$ 86.0	$102.1	$ 98.6	$ 80.7
Other income	1.8	..	..	5.5	5.4
Total income	$ 49.9	$ 86.0	$102.1	$104.1	$ 86.2
Operating expenses:					
Admin. salaries	$ 16.9	$ 20.0	$ 25.3	$ 20.5	$ 13.6
Office salaries	4.0	5.2	5.5	5.6	10.1
Rent	3.6	4.2	4.4	13.0	24.6
Repairs	2.0	2.8	2.3	4.4	10.1
Taxes	2.7	4.9	6.2	7.4	5.7
Contributions	..	0.2	0.3	0.2	..
Depreciation	2.9	4.6	6.0	5.5	4.3
Advertising	0.7	1.0	1.4	1.9	3.5
Travel expenses	1.3	1.6	1.7	1.5	0.4
Electricity, gas & fuel	1.7	1.9	2.2	3.2	3.7
Telephone	0.4	0.5	0.7	0.7	0.7
Office expenses	3.1	3.3	3.2	3.8	3.1
Freight	0.2	0.4	0.9	0.6	0.4
Insurance	1.0	1.3	1.6	2.6	2.0
Bad debts	..	..	0.4	..	..
Research & product development	..	..	4.1	..	..
Employee benefits:					
Insurance	0.6	0.9	1.6	3.2	2.3
Profit-sharing retirement plan	..	7.0	7.0	4.5	0.1
	$ 41.7	$ 60.6	$ 75.7	$ 78.5	$ 85.6
Profit before income tax	8.2	25.3	26.3	25.6	0.5
Federal income taxes	2.4	7.6	8.2	7.8	0.1
Net profit	$ 5.7	$ 17.6	$ 18.1	$ 17.7	$ 0.4

* Figures for 1961 reflect expenses incurred in the relocation of plant from 746 Broadway to 1901 Revere Beach Parkway.

less expensive way of reproducing a metal device for either display, instruction, or some other purpose where the durability of the actual material is not necessary. For example, United had made an aluminum and wood mockup of a jet engine for General Electric which was used to check the completed design, and subsequently for sales and exhibition purposes.

Exhibit 2

UNITED INDUSTRIES

Balance Sheet—December 31

(Thousands of Dollars)

Assets	1957	1958	1959	1960	1961*
Cash	$16.7	$27.1	$32.2	$ 47.4	$16.7
Receivables	9.8	21.3	27.7	30.1	28.1
Inventory	7.8	8.5	8.2	8.3	13.3
Total current assets	$34.3	$57.0	$68.1	$ 85.9	$58.1
Prepaid expenses	0.2	0.2	0.2	0.3	0.3
Deposits	0.6	0.6	0.6	0.6	0.1
Machinery & equipment	23.1	31.3	41.2	42.3	59.4
Less depreciation	13.6	18.3	19.5	25.1	26.0
Life insurance cash surrender value	1.0	1.8	2.5	3.4	4.3
Total assets	$45.8	$72.7	$93.2	$107.4	$96.2

Liabilities					
Accounts payable	$ 0.6	$ 3.6	$ 3.3	$ 1.9	$ 5.1
Accrued payroll	7.8	2.4	3.1	0.9	0.6
Accrued taxes	1.9	2.5	3.3	6.2	3.7
Accrued profit-sharing contribution	..	6.0	7.0	4.5	0.1
Federal income taxes	2.4	7.6	8.2	7.8	0.1
Total current liabilities	$12.9	$22.3	$24.9	$ 21.4	$ 9.9
Capital stock	5.1	5.1	5.1	5.1	5.1
Surplus	27.8	45.2	63.2	80.9	81.2
Total liabilities	$45.8	$72.7	$93.2	$107.4	$96.2

Reconciliation of Surplus					
Surplus at start	$22.5	$27.8	$45.2	$ 63.2	$80.9
Add: Tax income	8.2	25.3	26.3	25.6	0.6
Add: Increase in life insurance value	0.5	0.6	0.7	0.9	0.8
Total	$31.2	$53.8	$72.3	$ 89.7	$82.3
Less: Federal income tax	2.4	7.6	8.2	7.8	0.1
Less: Premium on life insurance	0.9	0.9	0.9	1.0	1.0
Total	$ 3.3	$ 8.6	$ 9.1	$ 8.8	$ 1.1
Surplus at end	$27.8	$45.2	$63.2	$ 80.9	$81.2

* Figures for 1961 reflect expenses incurred in the relocation of plant from 746 Broadway to 1901 Revere Beach Parkway.

Exhibit 3

UNITED INDUSTRIES

Selected Financial Ratios

Ratios	1957	1958	1959	1960	1961
Current assets/current liabilities	2.7	2.5	2.7	4.0	5.8
Operating income: % of net sales	38.0	43.0	41.0	38.0	39.0
Net profit after tax: % of net sales	4.5	8.8	7.3	6.8	0.2
Net profit after tax: % of net worth	17.3	35.1	26.6	20.8	0.4

The magnitude of the shift to models and mockups may be seen from the following table:

	Percentage of Total Sales
1956	15%
1957	30
1958–61	70

In explaining this shift in product mix, Mr. David E. Miller, marketing manager, said:

> The shift wasn't planned—it just happened that way. Models and mockups have much higher margins than patterns, so we pushed in that direction when the opportunity arose.
>
> The opportunity arose primarily because General Electric felt that Atkins & Merrill was high on price. Also, Atkins & Merrill was making models in fiberglass, and General Electric was interested in having them made of aluminum, which is much sturdier. We were in a position to do this because of our pattern-making experience and our casting facilities.
>
> Our big problem was convincing GE that we could do the job. Atkins & Merrill had that big, fancy plant, and we were just a cellar operation at the time.
>
> However, they were in the midst of developing the engine at the time, and they wanted quality models in a hurry. We were able to do the work. We were glad to have it because it came along just at the time when the pattern business was slack. It permitted us to keep the shop going.

In 1961, the name of the company was changed from Middlesex Pattern to United Industries. This took place at the same time that the company moved from the basement where it began operations to a two-story industrial building on Revere Parkway in Everett.

MANAGEMENT

The president, treasurer, and sole owner of United Industries was Mr. Amato. The other members of management in 1962 were Mr. R. H. Adams and Mr. David E. Miller. Mr. Adams, age 37, was production manager and had been with the company for over 15 years. Mr. Miller, age 26, was marketing manager. He had joined the company after having had previous marketing experience in other firms. Mr. Miller had an undergraduate training in engineering, and was a graduate of a leading eastern business school. He was also Mr. Amato's son-in-law.

MR. AMATO LOOKS AT HIS JOB

In an interview with the case writer, Mr. Amato made the following comment about his job:

I like this kind of work, and would do it even if I wasn't making any money. When you do something just for money, you don't always do the best job—you don't do it as well as something you do because you like it.

I couldn't stand a job where I did the same thing day after day. It's challenging to run this place, to solve the variety of problems we are faced with.

In fact, one reason I left the big company I used to work for as a pattern-maker was that I felt I couldn't grow any more. So I decided to leave.

If I had had more schooling, I might be working in a research group. I'd never get rich at it—but I'd be happy.

In the past, we have never refused a job because it was difficult—and we have never had a job that we couldn't do. I would say that the major strength of our organization is our ability to see the customer's problem and to have enough ingenuity to develop a solution for it.

I can see where, as a president, I have to project growth. After all, you either have to grow or fall by the wayside.

PERSONNEL

In 1962 United had 26 full-time employees. Twenty-one people worked on direct production activities, as follows:

Production Manager	1
Pattern Makers	7
Molder	1
Machinists	2
Apprentices	10
	21

In addition, there was one person assigned full time to maintenance. The remaining four employees were Mr. Amato, Mr. Miller, a clerk, and a typist.

Mr. Amato felt that one of his major problems was the lack of skilled craftsmen. Because most of the orders were either for a single item or a relatively small number of items, they had to be shaped and finished by relying almost entirely on simple tools and the worker's skill.

Craftsmen were very much in demand in the area and no pool of such men existed to meet the demand. On one occasion Mr. Amato inserted an ad for a patternmaker in a local newspaper. The only response was received from a 79-year-old man who was a retired patternmaker. One of the things that Mr. Amato was doing to remedy the situation was working with the vocational school in Everett in order to interest more young men in considering this kind of career. Mr. Amato was very much interested in training young men to be craftsmen. However, he had difficulty in doing this because of a shortage of qualified applicants.

The shortage of craftsmen was intensified by the unpredictability of orders being received. Also, there was a great deal of variation from month to month in the amount of work on hand (see Exhibit 4).

Employees were not unionized, but wage rates were approximately union scale for each craft. Time-and-one-half was paid after 40 hours, and double time for Sundays. The standard workweek was 48 hours, but because of the variations in orders received, it could be as low as 40 or as high as 60.

Exhibit 4

UNITED INDUSTRIES

Monthly Sales as a Percentage of Annual Sales, 1957–61

	1957	1958	1959	1960	1961
January	9.7	5.6	5.4	7.8	7.8
February	7.7	7.4	6.0	5.0	8.4
March	21.7	5.7	6.4	10.2	7.7
April	3.2	5.7	6.4	10.2	7.7
May	6.9	18.8	12.3	11.7	9.8
June	12.6	7.9	8.9	8.3	7.5
July	5.6	3.8	6.1	3.0	5.8
August	5.0	2.4	8.6	12.7	7.7
September	3.9	3.0	5.3	9.2	9.1
October	5.0	14.0	11.2	6.3	3.9
November	5.9	15.7	13.1	7.6	13.6
December	12.8	9.9	10.3	8.0	11.0
Total	100.0	100.0	100.0	100.0	100.0

All production employees participated in a profit-sharing fund into which 15% of profits before tax of each year were placed. Each employee's share was payable to him only upon termination of employment or retirement.

PRODUCTION

The building in which United was located was a two-story brick structure. There were 12,000 square feet on the first floor and 10,000 square feet on the second. The second floor was leased for a three-year period beginning in January, 1962, at an annual rental of $7,200. United occupied the entire first floor but currently used only 7,000 square feet of the total available space. The remainder was available to meet the needs of expansion. The building was owned by a trust set up by Mr. Amato; United paid an annual rental of $22,000 to the trust.

The work space was divided into four general areas: office, woodworking, metalworking, and foundry. Appropriate modern equipment was available in each of the areas.

The management felt that 1961 net sales of $207,000 could be doubled without requiring more than $15,000 in new equipment.

PRODUCT LINE

United had done work in a wide variety of fields and felt competent to provide a diversity of services, if orders could be obtained. Among the fields in which it had successfully provided service were developmental tooling, machine development, industrial design, and commercial exhibitions.

Developmental Tooling. Developmental tooling refers to tools made of materials that are less durable than those required for extensive production runs. They are less durable because they are made of materials which are easier to cut and form. This keeps the initial investment in tooling low until the final decisions concerning the production process are made. In addition, developmental tooling may be the only tools made for a job when the total expected production volume is low. Developmental tools are most commonly used in press operations, such as stamping and forming, since the cost of press dies is directly related to the durability of the die materials.

In explaining how the company got into developmental tooling, Mr. Miller said:

In 1960, we developed a way of making tools of kirksite, which is a good material for tooling on short-run jobs. We are the only ones in this area who do this kind of work. General Electric was especially interested in this service since they wanted to experiment with low-cost dies while they were getting their engines into production. However, now that GE is in full-scale quantity production, we have not only lost a lot of mockup business from them, we have also lost a lot of business for experimental tooling. In fact, we haven't had any mockups from them since April, 1961.

Prototypes. Prototypes are first-of-a-kind working models. They are, in a sense, the final phase of the design process—the tangible manifestation of the engineer's ideas. Many engineers felt, however, that a drawing of what they had in mind was as far as they had to go, and one of United's sales missions was to convince engineers of the desirability of a prototype model.

In its advertising, United presented the virtues of its prototype service as follows:

We at United feel that in creating prototypes—first-of-a-kind working models—we most fully demonstrate our unlimited imagination, flexibility, and skill.

Many designers and engineers have come to realize that our ingenuity and experience can play an integral part in their planning of new or revised products, components, processes, and equipment. Our expertly modeled prototypes offer that vital opportunity to actually prove the feasibility of a two-dimensional plan or calculated theory before extensive commitments are made. Prototypes enable the designer and engineer to study the physical relationships of component parts, one to another, and their cumulative relationship to the envelope design. They offer the opportunity for revisions, for additions, for improvements—without prohibitive expense.

.   .   .   .

In addition to their technical applications, prototypes aid the market research team. Prospective customers can actually try the new product, evaluate its usefulness, indicate its design appeal, and offer suggestions which might broaden the range of the product's sales potential.

United Industries had actively promoted its service of building prototypes, especially to manufacturers and designers that did not have their own manufacturing facilities. One of the groups toward whom this service was directed was small electronics firms. However, this business did not prove to be as great or as profitable as United had anticipated. The chief difficulty, Mr. Miller said, was "it costs a lot to do, and you have to bid more than most shops are willing to pay."

Product Development and Industrial Design. United had an arrangement with an industrial designer whereby they would build either models or prototypes of designs that he developed and would charge him a fixed rate. In return, he would provide them with industrial design services at a fixed rate.

In promoting this service to prospective customers, United's brochure described this service as follows:

The United Industries product development team produces ideas far enough advanced to stimulate the consumer and close enough to his purchasing habits for him to feel confident in buying it. Industrial applications are approached from a less aesthetic, more functional point of view.

We would welcome an opportunity to meet with you to discuss objectives and establish a general approach to your particular product design or redesign problem. Our well-rounded specialists adopt a practical approach to design. By designing within the limitations of your shop, our designers and engineers enable your company to hold production costs within reasonable limits.

Exhibits and Training Aids. United had prepared a number of displays for companies interested in exhibiting at trade shows.

Engineering Consulting. Recently, Mr. Miller had also taken on a job as engineering consultant to a company which had a machine that was not working properly. There was no manufacturing required on the job, which required several days of Mr. Miller's time.

Small Lot Production. United was also ready to supply plastic fabrications and castings in limited quantities.

MARKETING

Customers. In the years 1958–61, General Electric had been by far the company's major customer, with 65% to 70% of total sales being made to this one company. In the preceding years, this percentage was much lower since United had then been predominantly a pattern shop.

In addition to GE, most of United's sales were to a small number of firms. Ninety-four per cent of sales were to 20 customers in 1959, and 96% of sales were to 25 customers in 1960. No data were available for later years, but United estimates that from mid-1960 to mid-1961 it had from 75 to 100 active accounts who regularly submitted repeat orders, and from mid-1961 to mid-1962 from 100 to 125 active accounts. United had been actively striving to increase the number of active accounts it served in order to get some stability of work. Since an individual company did not have a continuous need for this kind of service, it felt it needed a greater number of customers.

Plastic fabrications were made by United to special order. They were usually completely handcrafted since only one or two might be ordered at a time. An example of such a fabrication was the air inlet duct used in the static testing of jet engines.

One adverse effect of increasing the number of accounts was that sales costs rose appreciably, reducing the profit margins. Another problem introduced by having a larger number of accounts was that a bunching of orders could have serious repercussions. Either work would have to be subcontracted, which was generally unprofitable, or the shop would have to go on a "crash" basis—with subsequent loss of quality, or else the bid on the job would have to have either a long delivery date or high margin—both of which were detrimental to United's relationship with its customers and to its general reputation.

Advertising. Early in 1962, 10,000 copies of a brochure describing United's products and facilities had been prepared at a cost of $5,000 for artwork and printing. United distributed these brochures in two ways: mailing and through McGraw-Hill's direct mail service. McGraw-Hill sent the brochures together with a covering letter to design engineers in Massachusetts. United's mailing was sent to firms all over New England selected from the *New England Directory of Manufacturers.* Speaking of this mailing in October, 1962, Mr. Miller said:

> Unlike the covering letter on the McGraw-Hill mailing, the one we sent out was typed on an autotyper, with the man's name inserted and his product

referred to specifically. We received ½% return in terms of inquiries on both mailings. Oddly enough, the personalization of the letters we sent did not seem to help.

We spent about $13,000 on the advertising, including my own time but not the overhead, and received about $11,000 in work.

In terms of actual business received, we got more out of McGraw-Hill's mailing than from our own. I think it's because we emphasized the engineering end more in that mailing.

Most of our quotes aren't coming from the advertising at all—they are coming from the yellow pages. We ask people how they happened to hear of us, and most of them say because of the yellow pages.

Exhibit 5 gives two examples of text from some of United Industries' recent advertising.

Manufacturers' Representatives. In the spring of 1962, five manufacturers' representatives were appointed: one for Washington, D.C., for federal government work; one for the state of Pennsylvania; one for the state of Maryland, and two for the states of New York and New Jersey with each covering a part of each state. These representatives would receive a commission of 10% of all sales originating in their

Exhibit 5

UNITED INDUSTRIES
Text from Recent Company Advertisements
Example 1

IMAGINATION

AND ABILITY TO FOLLOW THROUGH

United Industries enthusiastically looks for and accepts assignments which require exceptional ingenuity, inventiveness, resourcefulness and experience.

Since our beginning, nearly twenty years ago, it has been this imagination which has stimulated our growth. We at United are convinced that our greatest potential lies in our willingness and ability to exploit the knowledge and experience gained from past assignments. Such continual evaluation leads to new approaches, new materials and new methods with which to do those "impossible" jobs.

With several specialized departments working under one management, United offers a fully coordinated effort on all client problems. United's "first-of-a-kind" experience and service in the fields of product development, presentation and manufacture meet customer requirements for know-how, quality, delivery and cost.

Exhibit 5—Continued

Example 2

United's modern, well-equipped facilities plus the skills of our craftsmen enable us to assume complete responsibility for an entire project. For example: we can take an idea of any complexity, expressed in words or blueprints, and give it shape in the form of wood, metal, plastic or any other material. The coordinated efforts between our various shops cut costs, eliminate delivery delays and enable the customer to deal with a single responsible supplier.

In effect, we are saying that customer satisfaction is of primary importance at United Industries. We continually strive for this through the following four point program.

1. We believe "there is a better way to do it" . . . and we find it!
2. We deliver on time! Extra effort to meet customer expectations is assured.
3. We maintain a quality control system which insures customer acceptance.
4. Our quotations reflect our resourcefulness.

United's imagination—resourcefulness—skill can help your company improve its products and competitive position. We would welcome the opportunity to prove it!

CALL UNITED INDUSTRIES FOR ANY JOB WHICH REQUIRES AN UNUSUAL COMBINATION OF SKILLS, SUCH AS:

Engineering mockups · Prototypes · Scale models · Cutaways · Exhibits and displays—still and animated · Training devices · Low cost development tooling · Precision castings—aluminum and steel · Patterns · Reinforced plastic fabrications

territories whether or not they played any part in securing the sales. Their function was to seek out prospects and to make arrangements for United to submit bids on jobs. Job specifications would be sent to United and price proposals on all jobs would be made by United. Mr. Miller said of his representatives:

Most of our reps have not been productive. There is a lot of customer resistance to having this type of work done at plants located at some distance. The only rep to overcome this is the one working on the government account out of Washington, D.C. The government, being the government, will not generally use distance as a factor in disqualifying a vendor. As to the other reps, either our line is too broad or we haven't given them enough support.

Pricing. United Industries arrived at its proposed price for any job by estimating the number of hours of direct labor required, multiplying this number by $6.50, and adding to this figure the estimated cost of materials for the job. This formula was normally used, but $7 was substituted for $6.50 in proposing prices to customers who, it was believed, would accept the resultant higher price. The proposed price was also adjusted according to whether the plant was then working at or below capability with a 48-hour week. In the former case, a higher dollar rate would be used and in the latter a lower dollar rate. This adjustment was employed to a large degree as a means of regularizing production by discouraging new orders when at capacity and vice versa. Orders were not customarily turned down by admitting to the customer an inability to handle the job at the time but in effect by quoting a noncompetitive price to him. Due to the importance of General Electric as a customer, this policy was not followed on bids for this company; the price proposed on any job for this company was that secured by the formula with the $6.50 or lower rate inserted. The job, if awarded by General Electric to United, was, of course, accepted regardless of capacity considerations; if necessary, the plant was put onto a longer work-week or even onto a "crash" basis.

Due to the custom nature of the products, no two jobs were identical, and preparing price proposals involved considerable guesswork. Frequently a price proposal was made without benefit of exact specifications or detailed blueprints but instead on the basis of a sketch, a photograph, or a rough print. For each job undertaken, cost records were maintained to be compared upon completion of the job with the price agreed upon for the job.

Actual results on individual jobs varied from price equal to as much as twice the cost at one extreme to cost equal to twice the price at the other extreme. This wide range followed both from errors in estimating direct labor costs and from prices deliberately set either above or below the price indicated by the pricing formula (with the $6.50 per hour rate) as a means of either discouraging or encouraging the prospective customer to award the job to United. About one half of the jobs for which bids were submitted were awarded to United Industries.

Speaking of pricing in October, 1962, Mr. Miller said: "We've been running at breakeven, which is about $250,000 per year. Right now, we are quoting jobs to break even, without any profit in the estimates at all."

Competition. The firms listed in the yellow pages under "Model Makers" are shown in Exhibit 6.

Exhibit 6

UNITED INDUSTRIES

*Firms Listed in Yellow Pages of Boston Phone Book
under Classification "Model Makers"*

Firm	Employees	Location	Products and Services
Atkins & Merrill, Inc........	180	Sudbury	Industrial scale models (architectural, chemical, and engineering), product design, training and sales aids, mock-ups, prototypes, and production parts of reinforced fiberglass
Carlson Pattern Works.......	n.a.	Boston	Metal and wooden patterns
F. W. Dixon Co.............	25	Cambridge	Pattern and model shop
C. H. French Co.............	n.a.	Boston	Industrial models—aluminum molds for rubber and plastics
Harman F. Ward Associates..	n.a.	Halesite	Plant layout, architectural models, chemical components, product design
Morton Hollis Industrial Designers, Inc.............	n.a.	Boston	Product design and model making
J. P. Hussar...............	n.a.	Boston	n.a.
C. M. Jenkins Co...........	n.a.	Boston	n.a.
Mendall Pattern Works......	n.a.	Boston	n.a.
Madewell Co., Inc..........	60	Boston	Exhibits, point of sale displays, scale models
Master Model Co...........	n.a.	Boston	n.a.
Micro-Mechanics Co.........	n.a.	Wakefield	n.a.
Nelson Pattern Works.......	n.a.	Boston	n.a.
Norwood Pattern Works.....	n.a.	Norwood	n.a.
Pitman Studios.............	n.a.	Cambridge	n.a.
Scott Bros. Pattern Works....	n.a.	Somerville	n.a.
United Industries...........	26	Everett	(Large advertisement in center of page) mockups, prototypes, models, cutaways, training devices, development tooling, reinforced plastic products, aluminum precision products— Quality, satisfaction, prompt service
Van Buren, Inc.............	n.a.	Walpole	n.a.
Worcon Poli-Arts Co........	n.a.	Boston	Industrial and architectural scale models, product development, and model-making, prototypes, exhibit models, mockups

United considered its major competition to be Atkins & Merrill, Inc., the largest firm of this kind in the Greater Boston area.

Speaking of competitive conditions in October, 1962, Mr. David Miller said:

Since June we have had it very tough. The companies are all tightening up on costs. Things like exhibits are considered a luxury, and one of the first things to be chopped in a budget squeeze. Also, many engineers don't want to ask for a model, in order to keep their outside expenses down. The pinch is being felt by everyone. Even the little guy in the garage is cutting prices. And not only the little fellow—we recently lost a job to Atkins & Merrill—by 5%. They have traditionally been much higher than us on competitive bids because of their greater overhead. This means that they have been aroused and are really fighting for orders.

GOVERNMENT BIDS

One of the things that United was doing in October, 1962, in order to raise its volume was bidding on government jobs which required models or mockups. This work, however, was intensely competitive since firms from all over the United States submitted bids. One such job was an order for a number of full-scale mockups of space capsules to be made of fiberglass. Speaking of this job, Mr. Miller said:

I went down to Washington to look at it, and there were 31 companies down there participating in the bid. One of these is Lockheed, which has a couple of plants idle on the West Coast.

One of our problems now is how to bid on this job for NASA. If we get the job, we'll have to hire more people—and that's a problem. But we really need the work.

THE QUEST FOR A PROPRIETARY PRODUCT

In the summer of 1962, United had been apprehensive about its operating level, which was below its break-even point. In order to raise the operating level and in order to introduce a greater measure of stability into its operations, it began to think about having a product of its own.

At about this time, they sent out a mailing to architects who frequently use scale models. One architect gave the brochure to his son who is an agent for inventors. This man brought United a product, in prototype form, which appeared to have some commercial possibility.

Speaking of the product in October, 1962, Mr. Miller said:

We hope to develop and manufacture it. We have redesigned the original prototype, and quoted on making 100 units. We think the total market could be as much as one million units over the next five years. While we are primarily interested in manufacturing it, we would also be willing to take on the marketing, if the backer wants us to. The backer is simply a source of capital. He has the money, and has teamed up with the original inventor.

We have trimmed our estimate on this job as far as we could. We have cut the cost so much that it probably would not pay for them to try to go elsewhere to have it made. If we get the job, it will probably pay for all our overhead.

LOOKING AHEAD

Speaking of the company's future over the next few years, Mr. Miller said:

Three years from now, I see the model and mockup business as a small part of our annual volume—which by then should be about $2 million a year. Most of that will come from manufacturing small lots, although we have recently quoted on an order to produce 10,000 units of one small teaching machine.

If I take the most optimistic assumptions, next year's business might be as much as $1 million. But as it stands now, we don't have the equipment, or the people, or the money to do it. On the most pessimistic ones it could be as little as $300,000.

Mr. Amato saw the future of the company as follows:

Recent events indicate that our policy should be to encourage production business. If we could do that, we could increase our sales, and fill in the dips in our production volume. Also, the shortage of skilled personnel limits our expansion in our traditional product lines.

If we could get enough production business, there would be no limit to how large we could get. And we might even develop something of our own. We often spend a lot of time and effort on developing something far above what we get paid for, because we like to see it work. I see no reason why we couldn't do it for ourselves.

Wayland Company

"I GUESS I'm a fugitive from big business. After 20 years working for large companies, I was fed up with the frustrations, tension, and uncertainties caused by the internal politics in the vice-presidential class and decided to go in business for myself," Mr. Edward H. Cole, president of the Wayland Company, Wayland, Massachusetts, said in November, 1955.

I thought it might be nicer to build something for myself rather than to keep on trying to push things through committees. You know, there is an awful lot of featherbedding at the top of a large company. Still, it must take a really determined man to be the president of a large company; he must have stepped on many companies or people along the line. Originally, I never wanted to have a business of my own, but now I find it great fun to run a small company. You can get a great kick out of beating some of the big people and staying profitable. The real problem seems to be to keep a small company small. If you begin getting too many fingers in the pie, it slows down action, and the advantage of a small business is the ability to act quickly and be flexible. If you take that ability away, you have lost a good bit of the immediate advantage of smallness. In our three years of operation we have managed to stay small while growing, but we have not been profitable. We need at least another $20,000 invested in the business before we will break even. My cousin, the treasurer, and I thought we had enough money to get this business started profitably, but now we are in trouble.

Balance sheets and income statements for 1953 to 1955 are shown in Exhibits 1 and 2. Exhibit 2-A is prepared from Exhibits 1 and 2.

The Wayland Company was incorporated in Massachusetts in October, 1952, by Mr. Cole and a cousin in order to acquire the assets of the proprietorship of Mr. Ronald N. Furman, the inventor of a Self-contained breathing apparatus. Mr. Furman had developed the unit in 1951 while a consultant to the Burgin Machine Works; upon leaving this position, it was agreed that he and Burgin each would have one-half of any patent rights which might be granted on the unit. In 1952 Burgin had made a verbal agreement to produce the units and Mr. Furman to sell them. Wayland paid $4,000 for Mr. Furman's interest in the pending patents and the assets of his proprietorship. Both Mr.

Exhibit 1

WAYLAND COMPANY

Comparative Balance Sheet for Fiscal Years Ending October 31, 1953–55*

	1953 $	%	1954 $	%	1955 $	%
Assets						
Current Assets:						
Cash	$ 4,256	11.82	$ 1,103	3.57	$ 3,445	9.02
Accounts Receivable	5,150	14.31	6,231	20.17	9,332	24.42
Merchandise Inventory	12,145	33.74	10,760	34.84	13,637	35.69
Supplies	834	2.32	1,108	3.59	1,108	2.90
Total Current Assets	$22,385	62.19	$19,202	62.17	$27,522	72.03
Fixed Assets:						
Tools and Equipment	$ 1,844	5.12	$ 2,117	6.85	$ 1,918	5.02
Automobile	2,697	7.49	2,457	7.96	1,701	4.45
Office Equipment	1,547	4.30	1,469	4.76	1,543	4.04
Improvements	290	0.81	310	1.00	272	0.71
Total Fixed Assets	$ 6,378	17.72	$ 6,353	20.57	$ 5,434	14.22
Other Assets:						
Patents and Licenses	$ 3,764	10.45	$ 3,529	11.43	$ 3,294	8.62
Incorporation Expense	1,000	2.78	1,000	3.24	1,000	2.62
Prepaid Rent	500	1.39	500	1.62	500	1.31
Utility Deposits	75	0.21	75	0.24	75	0.19
Prepaid Insurance and Interest	1,097	3.05	225	0.73	386	1.01
Prepaid Royalties and Commissions	794	2.21	....	....	....	....
Total Other Assets	$ 7,230	20.09	$ 5,329	17.26	$ 5,255	13.75
Total Assets	$35,993	100.00	$30,884	100.00	$38,211	100.00
Liabilities						
Current Liabilities:						
Notes Payable—Bank	....	....	$ 5,000	16.19	$ 9,250	24.21
Notes Payable—Finance Co.	....	....	1,098	3.56	275	0.72
Notes Payable—Burgin Machine Works	$ 2,271	6.31	....	....	....	....
Accounts Payable—Trade	5,252	14.60	6,379	20.65	15,426	40.37
Employees' Stock Reserve Acct.	540	1.50	....	....	....	....
Employees' Withheld Taxes	363	1.01	161	0.52	117	0.31
Accrued Liabilities:						
Expenses	....	....	....	....	753	1.97
Royalties	....	....	381	1.23	1,107	2.90
Interest	....	....	....	....	345	0.90
Payroll Taxes	103	0.29	24	0.08	37	0.10
Municipal and State Taxes	4	0.00	203	0.66	9	0.02
Total Current Liabilities	$ 8,533	23.71	$13,246	42.89	$27,319	71.50
Other Liabilities:						
Notes Payable—Bank	$ 1,120	3.11	....	....	....	....
Notes Payable—Finance Co.	....	....	$ 275	0.89	....	....
Notes Payable—Officers	5,000	13.89	12,339	39.95	$ 5,819†	15.22
Total Liabilities	$14,653	40.71	$25,860	83.73	$33,138	86.72
Capital Stock	$41,500	115.30	$43,640	141.30	$51,840	135.67
Earned Surplus (Deficit)	(20,160)	(56.01)	(38,616)	(125.03)	(46,767)	(122.39)
Total Net Worth	$21,340	59.29	$ 5,024	16.27	$ 5,073	13.28
Total Liabilities and Net Worth	$35,993	100.00	$30,884	100.00	$38,211	100.00

* Balance sheet for start of business, November 1, 1952, not available.
† Maturing December 1, 1956.

Source: Auditor's report; percentages prepared by Harvard Business School staff.

Furman and the Burgin Machine Works were to receive a 3% royalty on the manufacturer's selling price of the Self-contained units; however, Mr. Furman sold his royalty rights to an individual employed by the Wayland Company early in 1954.

Under a written agreement with the Burgin Machine Works, Wayland had exclusive sales rights on the unit, while Burgin retained exclusive manufacturing rights. For the first six months Wayland was to pay Burgin on the tenth of the month following collection of the accounts receivable. In May, 1953, Wayland bought out Burgin's interest by paying $16,000 for the parts inventory, fixtures, and tools. "They could not produce as was required, and we were not satisfied with the quality of the products," Mr. Cole explained. Management later felt that $16,000 was an inflated cost. Wayland moved into rented quarters of 1,600 square feet and began to assemble the units itself, although it continued to buy all the parts.

In 1955 the organization consisted of six people: Mr. Cole, president; Miss Helen D. Cole, secretary and treasurer; Mr. Richard M. Tucker, design engineer; Mr. Paul A. Fuller, assistant to Mr. Cole; Mr. Herbert L. Carson, production manager; and Mrs. Audrey Bradley, secretary and senior employee.

PRODUCT LINE

The Wayland Company manufactured breathing equipment. The two principal products were the Pocketaire Self-contained breathing apparatus and the Pocketaire Portable oxygen unit. Both products are illustrated in the company advertisements shown in Exhibit 3. Self-contained units, which were used principally by firemen in rescue work, consisted of two cylinders containing oxygen, a regulator delivering a constant flow of oxygen, an air bag, a mask assembly, and a harness for attaching the apparatus to the body. Of the two cylinders, one supplied oxygen for the period of a rescue; when that tank was exhausted, the operator switched to the other cylinder that supplied five minutes of oxygen for escape. The interchangeable work cylinders came in three sizes: 5 minutes, 15 minutes, and 25 minutes, making the respective weights of the total unit 4½ pounds, 6½ pounds, and 9 pounds, and the prices $98.50, $118, and $126, respectively. The company also sold an industrial unit designed for use under safety suits. This unit had only one 15-minute cylinder; it weighed 4¾ pounds and cost $98.50. The $5.25 carrying case and the $4.50 goggles were optional equipment and not included in any of the

Exhibit 2

WAYLAND COMPANY

Comparative Statements of Profit or Loss for Fiscal Years Ending October 31, 1953–55

	1953 $	%	1954 $	%	1955 $	%	1956 $	%	1957 $	%
Net sales	$22,188	100.00	$38,170	100.00	$59,036	100.00				
Cost of goods sold:										
Beginning inventory	.....		12,145	31.82	10,760	18.22				
Purchases	23,613	106.42	11,935	31.27	26,896	45.56				
Outside contracting	448	2.02	2,249	5.89	2,194	3.72				
Less: Ending inventory	(12,145)	(54.74)	(10,760)	(28.19)	(13,637)	(23.10)				
Total	$11,916	53.70	$15,569	40.79	$26,213	44.40				
Gross profit before factory overhead	$10,272	46.30	$22,601	59.21	$32,823	55.60				
Factory overhead:										
Salaries	$ 2,066	9.31	$ 4,931	12.92	$ 5,694	9.65				
Insurance	.....	.....	.....	.....	363	0.61				
Rent, light, heat, telephone	1,740	7.85	1,475	3.87	846	1.43				
Depreciation—machinery, tools, and patents	1,269	5.72	299	0.78	541	0.92				
General (including repairs)	147	0.66	62	0.16	.....	.....				
Taxes on equipment and payroll	.....	.....	309	0.81	315	0.53				
Total	$ 5,222	23.54	$ 7,076	18.54	$ 7,759	13.14				
Gross profit on sales	$ 5,050	22.76	$15,525	40.67	$25,064	42.46				

Selling expenses:						
Salaries	$ 4,200	18.93	$12,028	31.51	$ 7,150	12.11
Royalties and commissions	2,230	10.05	3,203	8.39	2,246	3.81
Discounts allowed	.....	.....	664	1.74	1,095	1.86
Advertising	4,648	20.95	2,211	5.79	6,136	10.39
Auto and depreciation	1,695	7.64	1,531	4.01	.....	.....
Promotion and traveling	4,973	22.41	4,419	11.58	7,913	13.40
Taxes	.....	.....	375	0.98	241	0.41
Utilities	.....	.....	1,450	3.80	946	1.60
Insurance	.....	.....	1,103	2.89	211	0.36
Total	$17,746	79.98	$26,984	70.69	$25,938	43.94
General and administrative expenses:						
Salaries	$ 4,320	19.47	$ 2,215	5.80	$ 1,262	2.14
Payroll and property taxes	479	2.16	172	0.45	132	0.23
Office expenses	430	1.94	947	2.48	1,465	2.48
Legal and accounting	1,764	7.95	1,197	3.14	1,075	1.82
Insurance	821	3.70	1,130	2.96	255	0.43
Depreciation	172	0.78	176	0.46	216	0.37
Interest	.....	.....	247	0.65	839	1.42
Donations	12	0.05	.....	.....	.....	.....
Utilities	.....	.....	737	1.93	2,033	3.44
Total	$ 7,998	36.05	$ 6,821	17.87	$ 7,277	12.33
Net loss	($20,694)	(93.26)	($18,279)	(47.89)	($ 8,151)	(13.81)
Add: Discounts received	34	0.15	8	0.02	.....	.....
Services rendered	500	2.25	.....	.....	.....	.....
Less: Loss on sale of automobile			185	0.48	.....	.....
Net loss for year	($20,160)	(90.86)	($18,456)	(48.35)	($ 8,151)	(13.81)

Source: Auditor's report; percentages prepared by Harvard Business School staff.

Exhibit 2-A

WAYLAND COMPANY

Selected Balance Sheet and Operating Ratios

		October 31, 1953	October 31, 1954	October 31, 1955
(R)	Current ratio	2.62	1.45	1.01
($)	Net working capital	$13,852	$5,956	$203
(R)	Acid test ratio	1.20	0.64	0.51
(%)	Current assets to total assets	62.19	62.17	72.03
(%)	Total fixed assets to total assets	17.72	20.57	14.22
(R)	Net worth to debt	1.46	0.19	0.15
(%)	Net worth to total assets	59.29	16.27	13.28
(Days)	Receivables turnover*	83.56	58.77	56.91
(Days)	Inventory turnover†	....	264.80	167.53
(%)	Total assets to net sales	162.22	80.91	64.72
(%)	Fixed assets to net sales	28.75	16.64	9.20
(%)	Operation profit to net worth	(96.97)	(363.83)	(160.67)
(%)	Net profit to net worth	(94.47)	(367.36)	(160.67)

* Accounts receivable × 360/net sales.
† Average inventory × 360/cost of goods sold.
Source: Prepared from Exhibits 1 and 2 by Harvard Business School staff.

above manufacturer's suggested retail prices, to which management believed distributors adhered. Since all oxygen sold in the United States was medically pure, users could refill Pocketaire oxygen cylinders from any large-size standard cylinder in which the pressure was at least 1,800 pounds by using a recharging adapter sold by Wayland for $17.

The Portable oxygen unit was developed in 1953 in co-operation with Linde Air Products Company, a division of the Union Carbide and Carbon Corporation, and other manufacturers of oxygen gas. The 17-pound unit was packed either in a leatherette case designed to resemble a suitcase or in a hard-wearing fiber utility case and consisted of two small, standard medical oxygen cylinders with standard medical valves, a regulator, and disposable plastic face masks. The outfit, which supplied an hour of oxygen, cost $89.50 complete; the regulator alone sold for $34.50, and an adapter, which permitted using the regulator on large standard cylinders, cost $7. Principal purchasers were doctors and people with breathing difficulties who should have supplementary oxygen on hand in case of emergency.

Management believed the principal features of both lines of equipment were lightness, compactness, convenience, and low cost. Exhibit 4 shows pictures and gives descriptions of competing products. Management believed equipment competing with the Self-contained unit was either too heavy, too complicated, or took too long to put on before getting into the fire. A city fire department chief and the head of the city fire school, where the Self-contained unit was tested in 1952, wrote:

"We like Pocketaire because it goes on the firemen instead of on the trucks." A testimonial from the technical adviser of a city civil defense unit read as follows:

It has been interesting to note that in smoky fires, when unprotected men have been knocked out or reduced to copious tears, men wearing Pocketaire, without goggles, have experienced little or no lachrymation and no aftereffects.

Exhibit 3

WAYLAND COMPANY
Copies of Advertisements Showing Wayland Products

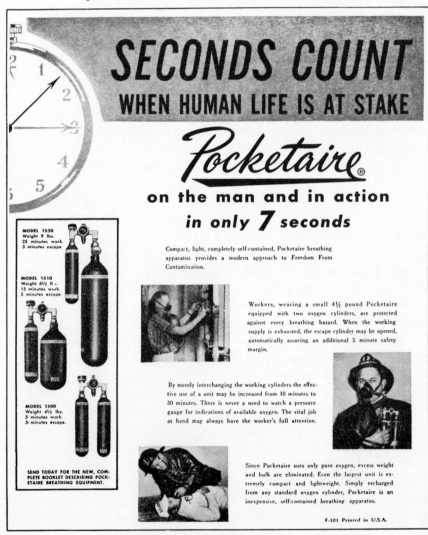

Your masks made possible seven rescues and a number of reconnaissance and ventilation tasks in heavy smoke and sulphur dioxide. The average citizen, to judge from his actions at Christmas and New Year, places small value on human

Exhibit 3—Continued

WAYLAND COMPANY
Copies of Advertisements Showing Wayland Products

Pocketaire
Breathing Equipment

Model 1510-S   **Weight 4¾ Lbs.**   **Life 15 Minutes**

The Model 1510-S Pocketaire is ideally suited for use in Safety Suits, as a smoke mask on aircraft, or wherever a small, light, self-contained breathing apparatus is necessary for work that can be completed in fifteen minutes or less.

Because the usual Pocketaire escape cylinder is without access in safety suits, and is unnecessary for fire fighting in confined areas such as in aircraft, it is not incorporated in the Model 1510-S in favor of lighter weight, smaller bulk, and lower cost.

Used with the modern, lightweight fire suit illustrated above, Pocketaire fits conveniently under the hood, with the cylinder slipped into a simple loop of fibreglass cloth. No suit alterations are necessary.

The wearer can clear the breathing bag at any time by flattening with external pressure through the hood, which discharges all rebreathed air out of the mask exhalation valve. The bag may then be immediately re-inflated with fresh, cool oxygen by pressing the recharging button on the end of the regulator. This button is easily operated through the hood with the gloved hand as illustrated. The recharging button is therefore protection against accidental deflation of the breathing bag due to unintentional external pressure.

Product of the Wayland Company, Wayland, Massachusetts

Exhibit 3—Continued

WAYLAND COMPANY

Copies of Advertisements Showing Wayland Products

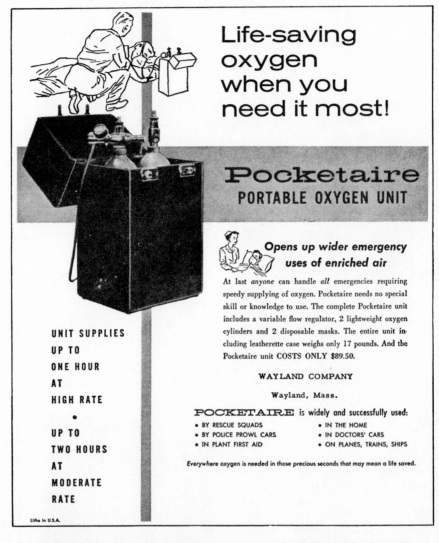

life. Lawyers, judges, and juries seem to value life at $7,500. Seven lives at $7,500, a total of $52,500, is a handsome return for the price of two masks. . . . Civil Defense bought three masks in 1953 and six in 1954. It intends to purchase six more within the next few weeks.

Mr. Tucker, design engineer, said the major criticisms of the Self-contained unit made by the potential customers were that: (1) it did

Exhibit 3—Continued

WAYLAND COMPANY

Copies of Advertisements Showing Wayland Products

not have the approval of the Bureau of Mines, which is the only government body approving mine safety equipment; (2) there was a build-up of carbon dioxide (CO_2) in the rebreathing bag under excessive work loads; and (3) the mask did not cover all the face.

The Bureau of Mines, in Schedule 13-C, set up minimum time limits for breathing equipment of one-half hour for escape purposes and one hour for all other uses. Commented Mr. Cole:

> In other words, our units may be used for escape from a mine but not to enter for rescue. In designing Pocketaire, it was our belief we could not produce the correct unit for which there was a vital need in the fire service for first-in men—a unit which would be light, compact, and easily carried as routine equipment for first entry of all fires—if we took into consideration the requirements of Schedule 13-C.

He pointed out that Pocketaire advertisements were accepted by the National Fire Protection Association's *Fireman Magazine;* Oklahoma A. & M.'s publication, *Protective Breathing Equipment;* and *Best's Safety Directory.* Both Mr. Fuller and Mr. Tucker agreed, however, that "The Bureau of Mines is still our big bugaboo, because their approval of products has been so well exploited by other suppliers."

Mr. Tucker said the problem of CO_2 build-up was really complicated. Some CO_2 stimulates breathing, but with hard exertion one breathes more deeply and some CO_2 accumulates in the rebreathing bag; however, the wearer can clear the bag by flattening it and then immediately reinflate it with oxygen by pressing a button on the front of the regulator. It would be possible, Mr. Tucker thought, to add a canister of chemicals, but this would complicate the unit and require replacement. Company experiments showed the largest unit would supply oxygen for 27 minutes of hard work, and management had found no reports showing that CO_2 build-up had ever caused more than a severe headache. Mr. Tucker commented, "I think this matter of CO_2 build-up raises an important question: Are you using breathing equipment to beef up the men and send them into places they normally wouldn't go or are you using breathing equipment to protect the men?"

Some equipment competing with the Self-contained unit used chemicals instead of oxygen cylinders. Mr. Tucker pointed out that any one chemical combination was not effective against all gases. The user of a chemical unit had either to predict that a certain gas in a limited quantity would be released in a fire, or, at the outbreak of a fire, to ascertain exactly what gases were released and then attach the proper canister. He felt that while such predictions were possible in industry or in mines such was not the case in ordinary fire fighting.

Because Pocketaire's all-nasal mask protected the lachrymal tear duct in the nose, management said eye protection was unnecessary unless there was a gas present which directly attacked the eyes, such as sulphur dioxide, or the skin, such as a heavy concentration of ammonia, chlorine, and some aldehydes. They recognized that the goggles were not overly satisfactory but pointed out that men can see better and feel temperature increases quicker with goggles and some men suffer from claustrophobia in a full-face mask.

Several manufacturers produced units similar to the Portable oxygen unit, but Mr. Fuller, assistant to Mr. Cole, said these were usually much heavier, less compact, and more expensive. He said that surgical supply houses sometimes reported that doctors made objections to Pocketaire, such as, "I don't want that unknown brand—I'll take the other one made by a manufacturer who makes other equipment I use. Sure it's more expensive than Wayland's, but it's a lot more substantial and complete." Mr. Fuller thought, however, that a light neat-looking unit

Exhibit 4

WAYLAND COMPANY

Examples of Products Competing with the Self-contained Unit

Mr. Cole commented on competitive equipment as follows: Wayland Self-contained units were inhalators that delivered a constant flow of oxygen. They competed mostly with Demand-type units, in which the user's breathing regulated the flow of gas. Because they were costly and complicated, the use of Rebreathing units was limited to mines. The Self-generating units were used in mines and, to some extent, in industry, but the canisters were costly and not effective against all gases. The Demand-type equipment made by the Scott Aviation Corporation and the Mine Safety Appliances Company (MSA) required larger cylinders than ours because they did not use a rebreathing bag. The Scott Air-Pak and some MSA units used air, not oxygen. Mr. Cole pointed out that many people believed it was safer to use air units in petroleum vapors and other explosive gases; however, he emphasized that atmospheric temperature, not oxygen content, was the key to spontaneous combustion.

The brief descriptions and photographs of the products shown were furnished and approved by the manufacturers.

Mr. Cole made the following comments about competitive equipment: The Oxygen Equipment Manufacturing Company (OEM) inhalator was most similar to and competitive with the Wayland Portable unit, but 25 minutes was too short a time. Portable resuscitators provided automatic breathing for a victim through alternating positive and negative oxygen pressures; such units were popular with police and rescue squads, despite their weight and cost, because

Exhibit 4—Continued

WAYLAND COMPANY

Examples of Products Competing with the Self-Contained Unit

REBREATHING TYPE

MSA ONE-HOUR OXYGEN BREATHING AP-
PARATUS: This Rebreathing unit permits the
most efficient utilization of O_2 supply. The wearer's breathing regulates the O_2 supply from the
relatively small cylinder. Chemicals in the $1
replaceable canister remove CO_2 from the ex-
haled breath, and the O_2 remaining is reused.
Unit weighs 18 pounds and costs $250.

DEMAND TYPE

SCOTT AIR-PAK (illustrated): Uses pure compressed
air, not oxygen. Nonrebreathing type, delivers fresh air
on each inhalation through a demand regulator to the
mask in any quantity and at any rate required by the
user. It has Bureau of Mines approval, minimum air
duration of 30 minutes at extreme exertion, weighs 30
pounds, and costs $229. Smaller 15-minute, 19½-pound
unit costs $184.50. Recharging equipment sells for
approximately $225. MSA makes three sizes of De-
mand-type apparatus, using either air or oxygen: the
$149.50, 11-pound SLING MASK designed for 8–10-
minute jobs or escapes; the $169.50, 18-pound CUB
MASK with a 15–20-minute supply; and the $214.50,
30-pound AIR or O_2 Mask which has Bureau of Mines
approval for its 30-minute duration at hard work.

SELF-GENERATING TYPE

CHEMOX: Instead of cylinders and valves, this
MSA unit uses a $6.60 replaceable chemical can-
ister which evolves oxygen as needed and removes
carbon dioxide. The unit has Bureau of Mines
approval, lasts a minimum of 45 minutes at hard
work, weighs 13½ pounds, and costs $165.

Exhibit 4—Continued

WAYLAND COMPANY

Examples of Products Competing with the Portable Unit

resuscitation had been found more effective than manual artificial respiration. If O_2 was not piped into the rooms, hospitals generally used units similar to the McKesson one, although nurses sometimes complained about pushing around the large cylinders.

The brief descriptions and photographs of the products were approved and furnished by the manufacturers.

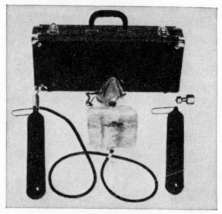

OEM PORTABLE UNIT: Two special cylinders supply 25 minutes of oxygen through a reusable mask. Packed in a case, it weighs 8 pounds, costs $54.50, including recharging adapter.

EMERSON RESUSCITATOR: Unit performs three functions: resuscitation; inhalation; and aspiration, which is the removal of fluid obstructions from the throat. Utility Model shown weighs 33 pounds, can provide nearly 1.5 hours of resuscitation, and sells for $410. A "Featherweight" $253 model weighs, with one tank, only 18 pounds. By admixing air with the O_2, it can resuscitate for 50 minutes.

McKESSON EMERGENCY OXYGEN AND RESUSCITATION UNIT: By squeezing the rebreathing bag and forcing air into the patient, unit may be used as a resuscitator. Depending whether standard E or D cylinders are used, oxygen is supplied for approximately 80 minutes, or 25 minutes; weight is 22 pounds, or 17½ pounds; height is 30 inches or 20 inches; and cost is $77.80 or $74.20. The regulator alone sells for about $35.

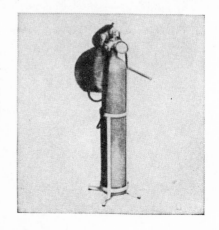

would appeal for personal use to people with breathing difficulties.

In 1955 Wayland became the distributor for municipalities and industry of the Kreiselman Bellows Resuscitator, which was made by Ohio Chemical and Surgical Equipment Company, Madison, Wisconsin, and sold for $65. The resuscitator consisted of a face mask, a valve, and a small bellows and was used to revive a trapped or otherwise immovable victim where heavy equipment could not be brought into action.

SALES

Management believed that the potential market for the Self-contained apparatus was very large but had found the information available from sources such as the National Fire Protection Association, insurance companies, and publications such as *Fire Engineering, Occupational Hazards, National Safety News* very sketchy. "The main problem in the sales area is that neither we, nor, as far as we know, the people like Linde and Ohio Chemical we work with, nor our competitors have any real market information; we all work by guess," Mr. Cole said.

The *Reader's Digest* estimated in 1953 that 6,000 firemen were injured or killed each year from smoke or gas poisoning.[1] Mr. Cole had been unable to find actual statistics but pointed out that with 20,000 fire departments and 700,000 paid or volunteer firemen in the United States, "We have a long way to go before we give protection to even the key men." One competitor claimed to have sold over 18,000 units to fire departments and industry since World War II. In industry such equipment is used for hazardous areas, plant fire protection, tank cleaning, sewage inspections, and so forth. "Ever-increasing awards and workmen compensation claims are enforcing an expanding market," Mr. Cole said. He quoted an editor of a technical journal as saying, "It is a waste of time to try and get statistics on the number of present units in use, because the market has not been touched."

Mr. Cole also foresaw a wide market for the Portable oxygen unit. He believed there were some five million persons in the United States who suffered from breathing difficulties caused by heart condition, asthma, and other allergies and that many of these people could get relief by the administration of oxygen during their periods of distress. This estimate was made by the medical department of a national company that checked the record of its employees needing oxygen equip-

---

[1] August, 1953, p. 33.

ment during the past four or five years. The proportion was then extrapolated to give some indication of the United States market. Commented Mr. Cole, "The figure is impressive, although I don't know if we've really delved into it too much. Of course, it doesn't mean that all five million people necessarily need our unit, that they could afford it, or that doctors recommend our unit. It does indicate, however, that we have a large market and perhaps can sell a thousand units a month." Mr. Cole felt that the availability of oxygen was important to such people and the more portable the unit the freer the life such a person might live. He also thought the unit might be sold to doctors, particularly to those country general practitioners who would save time if they had an emergency unit available in their cars. Units could be used by hospitals, rescue squads, beach life guards, and in police prowl cars and hospital first-aid stations.

Wayland sold its products to three types of distributors: fire equipment distributors, safety supply houses, and surgical supply houses. The first two outlets sold the Self-contained units and most of the Portable units; surgical supply houses sold only Portable units. To qualify as a distributor, a firm had to carry and demonstrate Wayland products. Discounts to all types of distributors on all products were 30% off list price on complete units and replacement parts. Terms were 1%, 10 days, net, 30 days. For a year a national manufacturer had had exclusive national distribution rights to the medical supply field of the Portable unit and received a discount of 45%; however, Wayland was disappointed with the sales volume and terminated the agreement.

The international distributor that handled Wayland's export sales received a chain discount of 30% and 20%, making the margin 44%, but it paid for all advertising and promotion.

Mr. Cole and Mr. Fuller said that distributors, especially those in the New England area, made very little effort to sell Wayland products. One surgical supply distributor commented, "Ed Cole comes in here and talks to the boys, and then they pick up the Portable unit and sell a couple more of them but then they drop it, because it isn't an everyday item that everybody wants." Another said, "Sure, I guess the doctors could use it, and a couple of the boys tried to sell it, but let's face it they make lousy money when they call on doctors so they go where the volume is, the hospitals, and the hospitals can't see using those small cylinders." Mr. Fuller then tried unsuccessfully to get the distributor to sell regulators to the hospitals. A third surgical distributor explained his refusal to sell Pocketaire: "I never heard of Wayland before, but it looks like a good product. Still, I guess I'm old fashioned but I'd just as soon some other distributor makes the fast buck introducing it. When the others are interested, you come back and see me." Mr. Fuller thought he would make a sale on his next visit.

Fire equipment distributors and safety supply houses, while generally smaller and less well established than surgical supply houses, made more effort, Mr. Cole thought, to sell Wayland products and were faster paying. According to Mr. Fuller, many fire equipment distributors occupied small inaccessible offices, offered no terms or discounts, but relied solely on long-time friendship with the fire chiefs for getting sales. Some firms became Wayland distributors by answering Wayland advertisements or direct mailings and sending in several initial orders. Under these circumstances, Mr. Cole sometimes had to decide whether or not to grant a new distributorship in the territory of an old but inactive distributor. He had found it unwise to rely only on credit ratings in selecting distributors, because small and seemingly financially shaky firms often generated the most volume. Wayland billed the ultimate consumer directly if it was worried about receiving payment. Mr. Cole said one small unpromising firm bought a demonstrator and later returned it; months afterwards the same firm ordered four units and eight months later bought ten. Mr. Fuller believed this example illustrated the time lag that often existed between demonstration and sale. "I once demonstrated a unit, heard nothing for two years, and then got an order for eight units," he said.

Wayland kept records of distributors by state, city, type of business, sales of each unit, and total sales. Exhibit 5 shows a summary of sales by state together with selected data related to the markets for both products. The following table of sales to Pennsylvania is an example of Wayland sales data, minus the city identification:

Distributor	Self-contained	Portable Unit	Total Sales
Fire equipment distributor, selling to both industry and municipalities............	$ 653.29	$ 634.46	$1,287.75
Surgical supply house....................		125.30	125.30
Fire equipment distributor................	443.00	110.60	553.60
Surgical supply house....................		125.30	125.30
Safety supply house.....................		62.65	62.65
Multistate scientific organization..........	1,836.24		1,836.24
Fire equipment distributor................	71.45	140.44	211.89
Fire equipment distributor................	1,186.92		1,186.92
Fire equipment distributor................		117.02	117.02
Total sales........................	$4,290.90	$1,315.77	$5,506.67

Exhibit 5

WAYLAND COMPANY

Market Data and Sales by States

November 1, 1954, to October 31, 1955

State	Population	All Physicians	Physicians in General Practice	Hospitals	Firehouses	Firemen*	Wayland Distributors	Wayland Sales	Average Sales per Outlet
Alabama...	3,033,000	2,321	807	118	218	1,257	1	$ 200.20	$ 200.20
California .	13,032,000	20,763	5,764	442	686	11,218	8	3,756.50	469.56
Colorado ..	1,549,000	2,385	565	103	158	968	1	210.29	210.29
Conn......	2,241,000	3,777	1,055	73	292	2,762	10	4,384.93	438.49
D.C.......	853,000	2,483	503	30	1	1,098	1	79.82	79.82
Georgia ...	3,621,000	3,391	1,048	158	204	1,918	2	2,122.75	1,061.38
Illinois....	9,361,000	12,529	4,271	365	961	6,400	6	1,494.28	249.05
Indiana....	4,330,000	4,420	1,726	142	553	3,341	1	160.82	160.82
Iowa......	2,692,000	2,829	1,068	117	928	1,149	2	2,162.14	1,081.07
Kentucky..	3,005,000	2,638	1,060	126	279	1,247	1	105.68	105.68
Mass......	5,016,000	8,715	2,445	228	364	9,739	7	3,777.31	539.62
Michigan..	7,236,000	7,900	2,082	272	781	5,126	1	117.91	117.91
Miss.......	2,111,000	1,562	732	110	147	619	1	1,118.25	1,118.25
Nebraska ..	1,381,000	1,581	630	116	486	713	1	62.65	62.65
New Jersey.	5,420,000	6,737	2,151	163	428	5,477	7	2,452.77	350.40
New York.	16,124,000	31,146	8,890	525	1,693	18,437	21	11,715.00	557.86
N.C.......	4,285,000	3,913	1,270	189	232	1,542	1	364.67	364.67
Ohio......	8,966,000	10,873	3,376	263	1,088	6,912	5	1,226.94	245.39
Oklahoma .	2,168,000	2,226	771	129	248	1,383	1	192.84	192.84
Oregon....	1,669,000	2,098	719	79	362	1,318	1	133.53	133.53
Penn.......	11,159,000	14,727	4,497	353	2,011	6,300	9	5,506.67	611.85
R.I........	845,000	1,036	303	25	104	1,186	2	540.33	270.17
Texas.....	8,563,000	8,750	2,650	567	592	5,829	1	297.37	297.37
Vermont...	378,000	563	183	28	170	189	1	126.00	126.00
Virginia...	3,579,000	3,652	1,324	129	337	1,518	1	94.33	94.33
Wash......	2,570,000	3,238	953	140	481	2,129	4	2,029.02	507.26
Wisconsin .	3,694,000	3,926	1,398	223	587	2,845	2	2,304.79	1,152.40
Canada....	14,009,429	17,076	7,754	1,120	2,223	n.a.	1	5,129.13	5,129.13
Other Exp..	....	....	....	....	....	....	1	980.31	980.31
Totals..............							101	$52,779.38	$ 522.57
Office Direct Sales....								6,256.71	
Total Sales..........								$59,036.09	

* Full-time equivalent employment of state and local governments, October, 1955; breakdown of volunteer firemen not available.

NOTE: Paid fire departments usually keep all equipment, including fire suits, on the trucks; volunteer fire departments usually have the firemen keep their own equipment in their cars and bring it to the fire.

Source: Sales from company records; Population, Bureau of the Census, *Current Population Reports;* Firehouses, from survey by the National Fire Protection Association; Physicians and Hospitals, from *American Medical Directory,* 19th Edition, published by the American Medical Association; Firemen, Bureau of the Census, *State Distribution of Public Employment.*

Mr. Cole explained that an initial order for a demonstrator made a man a distributor, a fact which helped depress the average sales per outlet.

Mr. Cole intended Wayland advertising to generate leads for distributors to follow up rather than to induce orders itself for company products, which he felt must be demonstrated. During 1955 the company advertised in *Fire Engineering, Occupational Hazards, Law and Order, National Safety News, Journal of the American Medical Association,* and *Best's Safety Directory.* Wayland had had several publicity articles published, including one which, Mr. Cole said, was in 63% of all U.S. newspapers using Associated Press service. It "not only created interest but was responsible for a large boost in actual sales." To increase sales volume, Mr. Cole said it would be necessary to have an $8,000 to $10,000 advertising program planned by a publicity agent. He pointed out that there were currently no channels to reach effectively the biggest market for the Portable unit, those people with breathing difficulties; the public rarely entered surgical supply houses, some of which required prescriptions to buy O_2 units. Therefore he wanted a publicity firm to plan articles which the medical profession would consider ethical, whether doctors or the lay public read them. Mr. Cole wished to run a series of 13 advertisements, one-sixth of a page, in *Business Week,* which would cost about $500 apiece.

Mr. Cole hoped Wayland eventually could afford to supplement its advertising with four salaried salesmen. In 1955 the company had five salesmen besides Mr. Cole and Mr. Fuller: one full-time man, who had the Metropolitan New York, Long Island, and New Jersey area and received 25% on direct sales and an 8½% override on distributor sales; and four part-time men, who got a 30% discount on all sales and passed on 20% to the distributors. As an experiment, Mr. Cole had hired three medical students to sell Portable units directly to doctors. "In short, I think we've got to do the selling, because the firms certainly aren't going to do it for us," Mr. Cole said.

The Wayland Company had found it difficult to get distributors because of the entrenched position of established manufacturers. In 1955 Wayland announced it had entered suit against a competitor for $250,-000 in triple damages, or a total of $750,000. It charged that company with spreading false, misleading statements in regard to Pocketaire equipment, unlawful contracts and combinations with some dealers and distributors to restrain trade, thereby tending to bring about a monopoly on the sale of artificial breathing devices. It further charged that company's method of doing business precluded certain dealers and distributors from selling the products of the Wayland Company.

In 1955 Wayland was engaged in internal discussion on the level of its products' prices. Originally, the company had deliberately priced one of the three models of the Self-contained unit below $100, because it believed municipalities generally required fire chiefs to get approval on all purchases over $100. Mr. Cole recognized that his company's prices were lower than his competitors' but was opposed to raising them:

I think it would be a tragedy to raise prices at the time I feel sales are beginning to grab hold. We've doubled our sales of the Self-contained units. It is the first real feeling we've had that we're getting hold of the market, and I'd hate right now to throw a monkey wrench in it anywhere along the line. I would rather see Pocketaire accepted and stronger and then raise the prices. As for the Portable unit, we've just made an arrangement with Sears, Roebuck & Company to have it placed in their catalog, and so it would be embarrassing to both of us if we raised the prices now.

Others in the company disagreed with Mr. Cole. Mr. Carson and Mr. Tucker were in favor of a price rise, while Mr. Fuller was uncertain. Mr. Carson said, "Only one unit is under $100, and with the case or goggles the price automatically goes over $100. One or two fire chiefs have to order under $100, so they merely order it without one cylinder and order extras such as goggles, recharger, or case later." Mr. Tucker added:

I don't think price is that important. You see, I'm a backwoods boy from Ohio. If we did $60,000 in sales and lost $6,000 last year, I suggest we charge 10% more. To me it is just that simple. If we sell at that price, we make a profit; if not, we're out of business. Therefore let's try it and see what happens. I don't see any other alternative, and I can't see how talking week after week about prices does any good at all.

PRODUCTION

Wayland products were assembled in a 1,200-square-foot room by Messrs. Tucker, Fuller, and Carson. All parts were bought; typical assembly operations were gluing together the parts of the face mask and bag, welding the parts of the regulator and adjusting it, and packing the finished product for shipment.

Mr. Carson, production manager, described his job as follows:

My biggest interest is to make sure things are right when they are shipped out of here. I'd rather be here than in the field selling to be sure everything is thoroughly tested. After all, I am a volunteer fireman, too, and maybe I'll have to wear this equipment some day. I do everything from floor sweeping to assembling. On Saturdays I come in here to clean the floor because no one else seems to be interested in doing it. I had a man come in to quote on that job sometime ago but he wanted $12 a week; I didn't think we could afford that. Sometimes my wife and I come in at night to get things ready for the next morning. I think my future lies with this company, but I was trained as a mortician and still pay $10 a year dues so I can always have a mortician's job in the future.

Mr. Tucker spent about one-third of his time keeping the perpetual inventory cards on parts and finished units and running the cost control system he had devised. He said he did not get bids on all of the parts: "I know about what the prices ought to be and I have a little machine shop near by which makes most of our parts so that it is a waste of time getting quotes."

In 1954 Mr. Tucker built up cost sheets for each of the different Wayland products. He added up the cost of parts, using the original prices from the perpetual inventory cards. He said this system raised a difficulty because of an initial order of $62 worth of parts; $32 might be for the original tools so additional orders would cost $30. He was uncertain what price should be transferred to the product cost sheet.

Ed Cole and I argue about this all the time. I want to keep this as though I am buying tools all the time, because I want to be able to change my source of supply and be flexible in our methods of construction. Therefore I could get a second supply of any part or change an item $\frac{1}{16}$ of an inch without showing any change in the product cost list. . . . As I have often said, I feel we are not charging enough for our products. I think we need more money for research and development, and since Ed turns everything into a percentage-of-sales basis the higher I price the goods the more he will have to sell them for. So if direct arguing fails, I can give my cost not dishonestly, but toward the high side, and help with my own argument. What do you think I should do?

Mr. Cole commented:

Dick Tucker's not fooling me; I've tried for two years without success to explain how I use percentages for budgeting. Anyway, I don't like surprises, especially on the annual statements. Dick's overpricing of raw material provides a margin of safety in my calculations—a margin that wouldn't begin to allow for the time and money we've given this business for nothing.

Exhibit 6 shows Mr. Tucker's product cost estimates for selected periods, 1954 to 1955.

Two other figures were added to the list of parts costs in compiling a product cost list. Mr. Tucker added 10% of total parts cost to cover spoilage, shrinkage, and freight-in. For a few months during 1954 he and the other two assemblers kept daily time charts from which he compiled standard times for each job. Then he divided these times by an arbitrary 70% efficiency factor and multiplied by an arbitrary rate, $3 an hour, to get a total labor cost for each product.

Actually, this is all an addition of lies. These costs can't mean much. For example, over the period of the last six months we had such sales as to justify one man for 24 hours a week. . . . I think these figures (in Exhibit 6) are interesting and useful to see if our costs are going up or down, but I think

Exhibit 6

WAYLAND COMPANY
Mr. Tucker's Product Cost Estimates

	Jan., 1954	Dec., 1954	Nov., 1955
1. Portable Unit (without cylinders):			
Total parts	$15.73	$13.51	$13.65
10% allowance	1.57	1.35	1.37
Labor	3.00	3.00	3.00
Total manufactured cost	$20.30	$17.86	$18.02
2. 4½-Pound Self-contained Unit:			
Total parts	22.54	24.41	26.12
10% allowance	2.25	2.45	2.61
Labor	6.00	6.00	6.00
Total manufactured cost	$30.79	$32.86	$34.73
3. 6½-Pound Self-contained Unit:			
Total parts	26.77	28.92	31.72
10% allowance	2.61	2.90	3.17
Labor	6.00	6.00	6.00
Total manufactured cost	$35.38	$37.82	$40.89
4. 9-Pound Self-contained Unit:			
Total parts	27.44	30.06	32.76
10% allowance	2.74	3.00	3.28
Labor	6.00	6.00	6.00
Total manufactured cost	$36.18	$39.06	$42.04
5. 4¾-Pound Industrial Self-contained Unit:			
Total parts	22.78	24.07	26.08
10% allowance	2.28	2.41	2.61
Labor	6.00	6.00	6.00
Total manufactured cost	$31.06	$32.48	$34.69

Source: Company records.

trying to extrapolate them into profit or loss statements is a waste of time, although Ed Cole likes to do it.

In the fall of 1954 Mr. Carson took over the inventory control system, but three months later Mr. Tucker relieved him. Mr. Carson afterwards was at a loss to explain this move: "Running the system came easily to me." Mr. Tucker explained, "I like to keep track of the parts myself since I'm constantly improving the products."

Mr. Cole, who noted that he had been used to complicated control systems in the large companies in which he had worked, said he had carried most of the control information in his head but now he wanted more accurate costs for budgeting purposes. At a breakeven point he figured his costs as a per cent of net sales would run as follows: purchased materials, 37%; direct costs and factory overhead, 13%; selling costs, 10%; advertising, 10%; general and administration, 12%; royalties, 4%; and profit, 14%.

Mr. Cole was not sure at what sales figure these percentages would be made but thought it might be in the neighborhood of $100,000 to $250,000 of sales.

FINANCE

"My cousin and I have invested money in the company, loaned money to the company, guaranteed loans to the company, but now the company needs more money," Mr. Cole said. "We need $5,000 to $10,000 in the immediate future and another $40,000 to $50,000 later on."

Mr. Cole had investigated four ways of obtaining new money: (*a*) He talked to the banks, the regional Small Business Administration, and a local development corporation, and he came to the conclusion that credit, as far as Wayland was concerned, was frozen. He said at times he even thought of moving the company to another state because of the local banking situation. (*b*) He asked the banks about the possibilities of a loan against a big order from a large and reputable company but was told he could only get a loan on the accounts receivable. (*c*) He checked through a Boston finance company to investigate the possibilities of a factoring arrangement and found that such an arrangement could be made when accounts receivable ran about $30,000. (*d*) He found that trying to sell blocks of stock through underwriters was financially unfeasible for his size of issue.

Mr. Cole wanted to sell stock at par, $10, to such people as would not interfere with his management. He said he did not want to sell the stock to another company because he wanted to keep management control. "We're trying to develop a business, not milk it, and we don't want anyone else to come in and milk it either. The question is, can we get this capital and at the same time keep control?" Originally, he was wary of selling small blocks of stock because he didn't want to be bothered by the small stockholders, but he had discovered that his fears were unfounded. According to Mr. Cole, selling small amounts of stock locally posed some difficulties: "I need to sell the stock but it takes a lot of time, and for the company's growth I must spend that time on sales. I've lived most of my life in Europe and I don't know many people in this area. I don't belong to the clubs, I don't go to the cocktail parties and mix, so, frankly, I am considered an outsider."

In 1955 there were outstanding 5,289 shares of Wayland common stock, of which 4,419 shares, or 83.5%, were held by company personnel. Most of the other stockholders were friends or acquaintances of Wayland management and had bought stock after hearing of the company's problems. Mr. Cole did not believe in soliciting friends. "Getting your friends to buy stock is a fast way to lose friends; however, if they come and ask to become stockholders, that's all right." The stockholders and their holdings were as follows:[2]

Name	Number of Shares	%
Mr. AB	20	0.4
Mr. BC	100	1.9
Mr. BC and company	200	3.8
Mr. CD	100	1.9
Mr. DE	200	3.8
Mr. EF	200	3.8
Mr. FG	50	0.9
Mr. Edward H. Cole	1,503	28.4
Miss Helen D. Cole	1,505	28.4
Mr. Richard M. Tucker	369	7.0
Mr. Paul A. Fuller	1,005	19.0
Mr. Herbert L. Carson	30	0.6
Mrs. Audrey Bradley	5	0.1
Lawyers	2	....
Total	5,289	100.0%

ORGANIZATION

Employees described Wayland as a close-knit organization; everyone knew everyone else's salary. They each felt they reported directly to Mr. Cole, for whom all expressed great admiration. Mr. Fuller thought that Mr. Tucker should be in charge of production with Fuller and Mr. Carson reporting to him but added that he, Fuller, would report to Mr. Cole on sales matters. Descriptions of company personnel are given in Exhibit 7.

Employees described Mr. Cole as polite, but strong when he had to be, a very patient explainer, and an executive who "works like a dog in trying to see all of the angles." Mr. Cole said of himself:

Somebody has to say yes or no around here, and that is me. . . . I want to spend most of my time on sales but, in fact, I do whatever seems to be necessary. . . . To run a company, I think, takes a good second-class mind and a singleness of purpose; if you have a first-class mind, you go mad, if no singleness of purpose you don't have the drive. I don't like driving others but I like to stimulate them into action. I think my value to the company is that I've had broad experience and a fair amount of training in marketing; I pick good salesmen. I think people like to work for me, at least they say they do. I think my most important quality—be it temperament or luck—is that I am resilient and I bounce and I am determined. If I can find a door or way out of the box we are in, I'll go through it; if not, I will just go through the darn wall.

---

[2] Five shares per employee were distributed in December, 1954, in lieu of annual vacations.

Employees agreed that Mr. Cole had no mechanical ability, or was "ham-handed," as one employee put it. One person felt the president sometimes oversold a client. Another said that Mr. Cole sometimes spent too long trying to decide between two alternative courses of action. "If it's that hard to decide, it couldn't matter *much* which alternative he picked. Still, some of the mistakes he has made within the last three

Exhibit 7

WAYLAND COMPANY

Descriptions of Company Personnel

Edward H. Cole*   Age: 54
Position: President   Salary: $75/week
Background:
    After finishing Yale Sheffield in 1924, became liaison officer in Germany, France, and England and finally managing director of the English interests of Lehn & Fink Products Corporation. In 1937 joined Jergens Woodbury Sales Corporation as eastern sales manager. After six years with the Royal Air Force, worked first for G. Frank Sweet, Inc., advertising agency, and then became vice-president of Pierce's Proprietaries in Buffalo.

Helen D. Cole*   Age: Over 40
Position: Treasurer and Secretary   Salary: $40/week
Background:
    A.B., University of Vermont, 1932. Worked for the Black Rock Bank and during World War II was in the accounting department of McGuire Industries. Joined Wayland as a part-time employee in 1952.

Richard M. Tucker*   Age: 40
Position: Design Engineer   Salary: $120/week
Background:
    B.S. in Engineering, Massachusetts Institute of Technology, 1942. After a year in industry, worked in M.I.T. Radiation Laboratory until it was dissolved in 1945. From 1945–47 ran a radio repair shop, and from 1947–50 taught high school physics. After two years with Aero Medical Research Unit of Yale Medical School, joined Burgin Machine Works from which he came to Wayland in 1953.

Paul A. Fuller*   Age: 26
Position: Assistant to Mr. Cole   Salary: $75/week
Background:
    Graduated from the Kent School in 1947, worked two years as a salesman for Bridgeport Hardware, and then attended the University of Bridgeport for a year before going into the Army. From 1951–52 was a salesman for Johnny Seesaw Ski Equipment. Joined Wayland in 1952.

---

* These people, with the lawyer, are on the board of directors.
Source: Interviews with company personnel.

Exhibit 7—Continued

WAYLAND COMPANY

Descriptions of Company Personnel

Herbert L. Carson   Age: 33
Position: Production Manager   Salary: $70/week
Background:
   Graduated from N.H. Junior College in 1942 and entered the Navy.
In 1945 attended the American Academy of Embalming and, following
a year of apprenticeship, managed a funeral home for five years. Worked
for Burgin Machine Works prior to joining Wayland early in 1953.

Audrey Bradley   Age: Over 30
Position: Secretary   Salary: $23/week
Background:
   Widow with two children receiving social security benefits which
prevent her working full time. When benefits expire in 1964, hopes to
have a full-time job with Wayland.

---

years have shaken his confidence a bit; I don't think he's gambling anymore." Commented Mr. Cole, "I think I know my own flat sides; I don't
broadcast them."

Mr. Richard M. Tucker was the design engineer and also the highest
paid person in the company (see Exhibit 7). Mr. Tucker said of himself:

Sometimes I'm worth $100 an hour because I happen to know something
that improves our product; sometimes I'm worth $5 an hour; sometimes I'm
worth 50 cents an hour; sometimes I'm worth nothing at all. I have to wear
many hats—I'm not only the engineer but I also have to work on production,
do the purchasing, and keep the cost system going. I like working in a small
company; in fact, I think I'd go crazy if I had to go back to a big one. I don't
want to be a school teacher again. I had enough of trying to teach a bunch of
auto mechanics. I'm the kind of guy who can work at triple speed for three
days and then collapse. With my engineering background and the work I have
done in physiology, both before coming here and after, I think I know about
as much about breathing equipment as anyone; however, I need someone out
here to talk to who has a technical background such as mine. As to my future
here, I don't have any particular ambition to be president, although I think I
could do the job; I want to run a research and development department.

Fellow employees expressed great admiration for Mr. Tucker's technical ability, mind, and knowledge of his field but had doubts about
his administrative ability. Mr. Carson said:

We think we have to have a top-notch engineer like Dick to make improvements and invent new products, but, unfortunately, he has to do many jobs

for which we could hire a girl. Perhaps it would be better if he just stuck to one problem at a time, although I realize they all have to be done.

Mr. Paul A. Fuller, son of a long-time friend of Mr. Cole, divided his time between sales and production work. In October, 1955, he was in charge of Wayland exhibits for the Chicago safety show. Mr. Fuller said:

I'm interested in capital appreciation; that's why I invested $10,000 in this company and took out a loan to finance it. When I was looking for a job, all the companies that I talked to told me about the pension I'd have when I was 65 if I didn't make mistakes. . . . As to my future here, I will run the company some day unless someone else comes in that is more qualified to do the job. I think I am capable of taking over the company tomorrow; you have to be tough to run a company, and, unlike some of the men here, I could fire half of the employees tomorrow if it was necessary for the company's growth. In fact, I'd do it at the drop of a hat.

Others in the company said Mr. Fuller had a good mind, a fertile imagination, and much ambition; he had suggested many ideas for new products or improvements. With his young wife, he had rebuilt an old cabin into a house, a job which included digging a cellar, adding rooms, and installing heating. Mr. Tucker considered this a pretty good example of Mr. Fuller's being "uninhibited" and willing to try anything. One person described Mr. Fuller as a strong starter and a weak finisher: "He starts off knowing all the answers but soon finds he doesn't, gets bogged down, and starts on something else. Now he's asking questions far more quickly than he ever did before." Miss Cole commented, "Paul's enthusiastic, liable to jump to conclusions, and inclined to make decisions himself when Ed's away without awaiting his return; later he realizes that he should have waited." Most employees agreed that Mr. Fuller would some day run the Wayland Company.

FUTURE PLANS

Mr. Cole talked about the future as follows:

I feel that if this company fails there's only one person that is responsible, and that is me; if we succeed, everyone has had a hand in the success. I think if we can get over the present hurdles of finance and marketing problems, which will take a couple of years, there's a real future for the people here. We need financing, we must find some new products or find new markets for our present products, and we must develop a marketing organization. I'll put whatever financing we get into working capital rather than into bricks and mortar. In other words, I'd rather work on the marketing end than expand our production facilities. I'm sure the Wayland Company has a great future.

HMH Publishing Company, Inc.

"I WOULDN'T TRADE PLACES with anyone else in the world. I have everything I've ever wanted—money, success in business, success in the arts. What I've done anybody else can do if he's willing to display a little of the initiative and derring-do that made the country great in the first place, instead of settling for job security, conformity, togetherness, anonymity, and slow death," remarked Hugh M. Hefner, 35-year-old president of HMH Publishing Company, Inc., in July, 1961.

HMH revenue had grown from $268,000 in 1954 to $8 million for the 11 months ending May, 1961.[1] Over the same period, after-tax earnings had increased from a deficit of $23,000 in 1954 to a profit of $313,000 (see Exhibits 1 and 2).

In July, 1961, Mr. Hefner was concerned with furthering the company's growth and development. He planned to achieve this by: (1) the introduction of a new magazine, *Show Business Illustrated;* and (2) an increase in the number of *owned* and *operated* Playboy Key Clubs, the first of which had been in business for 16 months. Because of the uniqueness of each of these activities, relatively little published information was available to Mr. Hefner for analysis; however, he foresaw no difficulties in adding these additional activities.

HMH Publishing was started in 1953 in Chicago by Mr. Hefner to publish *Playboy,* a monthly magazine. In 1961 he explained that *Playboy* was created as an outlet for his own creative ability which had been stifled during his career as copywriter for *Esquire* magazine, and later as a circulation manager for *Children's Activities.*

The first issue of *Playboy* was published in December, 1954. Mr. Hefner contracted with Art Paul, then a free-lance artist, to provide the necessary art and photo work for the issue. Mr. Paul was paid in common stock of HMH Publishing. Other services for that first issue were obtained in similar fashion. In 1961 Mr. Paul was art director of *Playboy.* Mr. Hefner owned 80% of the outstanding common stock in the company, while a few key employees owned the remaining 20%.

The increasing growth in revenue from *Playboy* financed several

---

[1] Exclusive of sales and earnings of International Playboy Clubs, Inc.

Exhibit 1. HMH PUBLISHING COMPANY, INC.

Comparative Balance Sheets 1954–61

(Dollars in Thousands)

Assets	11 M/E 5/31/61	6 M/E* 6/30/60	12 M/E 12/31/59	12/31/58	12/31/57	12/31/56	12/31/55	12/31/54
Current Assets:								
Cash	$ 60	$ 103	$ 112	$ 192	$ 105	$ 33	$ 70	$15
Receivables	934	717	888	709	482	401	187	20
Inventories	715	511	389	264	211	214	44	33
Other		14	1					
Total Current Assets	$1,709	$1,345	$1,390	$1,165	$ 798	$ 648	$301	$68
Investment	†							7
Fixed Assets (Net) (Primarily Real Estate)	1,096	882	837	371	385	306	40	
Other Assets:								
Deferred Subscription Promotion‡	129	100	133	148	134			
Less: Applicable Federal Taxes	67	52	69	77	52			
	$ 62	$ 48	$ 64	$ 71	$ 82			
Other Assets§	207	94	94	57	46	100	29	4
Total Other Assets	$ 269	$ 142	$ 158	$ 128	$ 128	$ 100	$ 29	$ 4
Total Assets	$3,074	$2,369	$2,385	$1,664	$1,311	$1,054	$370	$79
Liabilities								
Current Liabilities:								
Bank Notes	$ 100	$ 50		$ 66	$ 20	$ 100	$ 6	$ 3
Taxes (F.I.T., Payroll and Excise)	284	95	$ 34			36		
Other	667	720	808	450	535	428	98	45
Total Current Liabilities	$1,051	$ 865	$ 842	$ 516	$ 555	$ 564	$104	$48
Land Contract Payable	244	255	259					
Unearned Subscriptions	1,139	879	982	825	553	380	204	
Deferred Taxes	48	91	95	77	52	14		40
Preferred Stock								1
Common Stock	7	7	7	15	15	14	18	13
Surplus	585	272	200	231	136	82	44	(23)
Net Worth	$ 592	$ 279	$ 207	$ 246	$ 151	$ 96	$ 62	$(9)
Total Liabilities	$3,074	$2,369	$2,385	$1,664	$1,311	$1,054	$370	$79

* Company changed to fiscal year ending June 30.
† 25% interest in International Playboy Clubs, Inc. $400 cost; approximate book value $75,000.
‡ Under a 1957 ruling by the I.R.S., the company was allowed to write off this expense over the months in which the income was taken into consideration.
§ Composed of advances to authors and artists.
Source: Company records.

Exhibit 1a

HMH Publishing Company, Inc.

Ratio Analysis

	5/31/61	6/30/60	12/31/59	12/31/58	12/31/57	12/31/56	12/31/55	12/31/54
Current ratio (R)	1.6	1.6	1.7	2.3	1.4	1.1	2.9	1.4
Net working capital ($)	$658,016	$480,138	$547,609	$649,002	$243,427	$83,930	$196,733	$20,264
Acid test (R)	0.9	1.0	1.2	1.7	1.1	0.8	2.5	0.7
Net worth to debt (R)	0.23	0.13	0.09	0.17	0.13	0.10	0.20	(0.09)
Receivables turnover* (days)	38.7	40.5	57.6	60.3	48.4	46.4	59.8	26.9
Inventory turnover† (days)	32.7	32.0	24.8	23.5	23.7	17.0	18.2	NA
Net sales to fixed assets (R)	7.26	7.23	6.65	11.40	9.35	10.01	28.60	38.40
Gross operating profit to net worth (%)	300.3	234.6	395.5	241.6	236.9	391.4	596.9	Loss
Net profit to net worth (%)	53.0	25.9	10.0	38.5	20.1	62.5	110.5	Loss
Cash (days)	2.7	6.2	7.8	17.1	10.7	4.0	23.0	18.4
Other payables (days)	30	43	54	40	55	51	33	55

* Accounts receivable × 360/net sales.
† Average inventory × 360/cost goods sold.
Source: Prepared from Exhibits 1 and 2 by Harvard Business School staff.

Exhibit 2

HMH PUBLISHING COMPANY, INC.

Comparative Income Statements
(Dollars in Thousands)

	%	11 M/E 5/31/61	%	6 M/E* 6/30/60	%	12 M/E 12/31/59
Sales						
Magazine (net)...................	60.0	$4,779	67.8	$2,158	68.8	$3,820
Advertising space—gross.........	36.0	2,873	30.0	954	26.8	1,490
By-products.....................	1.7	133	1.3	43	1.5	82
Trump division..................		...	...	...	...	...
Calendar sales..................	2.3	182	0.9	30	2.9	160
Miscellaneous..................		...		...		...
Total....................100.0	100.0	$7,967	100.0	$3,185	100.0	$5,552
Cost of goods sold:†						
Magazine......................	73.4	$3,506	76.9	$1,659	81.2	$3,103
Advertising sales...............	84.5	2,428	86.6	827	95.8	1,428
By-products....................	90.2	120	100.0	43	97.6	80
Trump division.................		...		...		...
Calendar.......................	74.2	135	3.3	1	76.8	123
Total.......................	77.7	$6,189	79.4	$2,530	85.3	$4,734
Gross profit....................	22.3	$1,778	20.6	$ 655	14.7	$ 818
(Less) G & A	12.3	982	11.9	377	8.9	495
Net operating profit.............	10.0	$ 796	8.7	$ 278	5.8	$ 323
Other income (net)..............	0.0	2	0.1	1	(0.0)	(1)
Operating profit before taxes and unusual items...............	10.0	$ 798	8.8	$ 279	5.8	$ 322
Profit sharing..................		...		...	1.1	62
Federal taxes...................	5.1	410	4.5	143	2.4	131
Net profit normal operation.......	4.9	$ 388	4.3	$ 136	2.3	$ 129
Less: Loss on TV..............	(2.0)	(156)	(4.1)	(132)	(3.4)	(191)
Loss on Jazz Festival......		...		...	(0.6)	(32)
Tax reduction due to loss..	1.0	81	2.1	68	2.1	115
	(1.0)	$ (75)	(2.0)	$ (64)	(1.9)	$ (108)
Net profit........................	3.9	$ 313	2.3	$ 72	0.4	$ 21
Gross profit:‡						
Magazine......................	71.6	$1,273	76.2	$ 499	87.7	$ 717
Advertising....................	25.0	445	19.5	128	7.6	62
By-products....................	0.7	13	(0.1)	(1)	0.2	2
Trump division.................		...		...		...
Calendar sales.................	2.7	47	4.4	29	4.5	37
Total....................100.0	100.0	$1,778	100.0	$ 655	100.0	$ 818
Promotion expenditures..........				261		588

* Company changed from calendar to fiscal year.
† As a percentage of respective sales (magazine cost as percentage of magazine sales).
‡ As a percentage of total gross profit.
Source: Company records. Percentages prepared by Harvard Business School staff.

%	12/31/58	%	12/31/57	%	12/31/56	%	12/31/55	%	12/31/54
77.1	$3,265	79.3	$2,840	91.4	$2,842	98.3	$1,107	100.0	$ 268
17.3	732	14.1	507	4.2	131	0.9	10		NA
1.6	66	1.7	61	2.1	64				
		1.4	50	2.3	71				
4.0	168	3.5	125		. . .				
						0.8	9	0.0	0
100.0	$4,231	100.0	$3,583	100.0	$3,108	100.0	$1,126	100.0	$ 268
81.0	$2,644	82.4	$2,342	76.8	$2,183				
110.9	812	134.3	681	287.8	377				
86.4	57	91.8	56	68.8	44		NA		NA
	. . .	140.0	70	178.9	127				
73.8	124	60.8	76		. . .				
86.0	$3,637	90.0	$3,225	87.9	$2,731	66.9	$ 754	92.2	$ 247
14.0	$ 594	10.0	$ 358	12.1	$ 377	33.1	$ 372	7.8	$ 21
9.7	410	8.2	295	9.1	282	28.9	325	17.5	47
4.3	$ 184		$ 63		$ 95	4.2	$ 47	(9.7)	$ (26)
0.1	3	(0.3)	(10)	0.6	19	1.9	22	1.1	3
4.4	$ 187	1.5	$ 53	3.6	$ 114	6.1	$ 69	(8.6)	$ (23)
	. . .		. . .		. . .		. . .		. . .
2.2	93	0.7	23	1.7	54	0.0	0	0.0	0
2.2	$ 94	0.8	$ 30	1.9	$ 60	6.1	$ 69	(8.6)	$ (23)
2.2	$ 94	0.8	$ 30	1.9	$ 60	6.1	$ 69		$ (23)
104.6	$ 621	139.4	$ 499	174.5	$ 658				
(13.5)	(80)	(48.6)	(174)	(65.2)	(246)				
1.5	9	1.4	5	5.5	21		NA		NA
	. . .	(5.6)	(20)	(14.8)	(56)				
7.4	44	13.4	48		. . .				
100.0	$ 594	100.0	$ 358	100.0	$ 377				
	523		433		255		49		1

other enterprises; four were major parts of HMH operations in July, 1961: (1) *Playboy* by-products, the first of which was the *Playboy Annual*, were started in November, 1954; (2) a taped TV show, "Playboy Penthouse," was first produced in September, 1959; (3) International Playboy Clubs, Inc., was organized in October, 1959; and (4) *Show Business Illustrated* was announced in May, 1961.

Other more peripheral HMH ventures included a discontinued magazine and jazz festival, a currently operating travel agency, and a proposed movie.

In 1956 a Trump Division was organized in New York to publish *Trump,* a monthly magazine satire on radio and TV programs. The key people on the staff of *Trump* previously had been associated with Mad comics, the first magazine of this type. *Trump* was discontinued in 1957 because, as one HMH executive said, ". . . of a lack of effective control over the New York operation."

The Playboy Jazz Festival, held in Chicago in the summer of 1959, was produced by Victor Lownes III, promotion director of HMH. The company suffered a small financial loss on the project after donating the first night's proceeds of $50,000 to the Chicago Urban League.

Playboy Tours, a travel organization, was formed in 1960 to conduct guided tours through Europe, Jamaica, Hawaii, and Mexico. The purpose was to prove to the travel industry that *Playboy* was an effective advertising medium for travel ads. In 1961, the tours were running at about 25% of anticipated volume. Advertising revenue from the travel industry was $22,000 for the first five months of 1961 compared to $10,000 for the similar period in 1960.

Arrangements for "The Playboy Story," a movie on the life of Hugh Hefner, were pending in the spring of 1961 between HMH Publishing and Tony Curtis, the Hollywood actor.

The rest of the case will include both industry and company data: first a note on the publishing industry, followed by a description of *Playboy* and an analysis of competition; next in order, discussions of the Playboy by-products; the HMH television show; a note on the restaurant industry followed by a description of Playboy Key Clubs; and last, a description of *Show Business Illustrated*. The case ends with Mr. Hefner's comments on his plans for the company.

PUBLISHING INDUSTRY

Making generalizations about the magazine publishing industry is difficult. A variety of sizes, types, and classes of periodicals[2] are published, based on varying concepts of publishing. The extremes range

---

[2] The terms "periodical" and "magazine" are used interchangeably.

from mass magazines such as *Life* and *Reader's Digest,* which appeal to a broad cross section of the magazine market, to class magazines such as trade magazines, which are directed toward a small, well-defined segment of the magazine market. There are magazines circulated through newsstands, and magazines sold only by subscription. Some periodicals do not solicit advertising revenue; others rely heavily on this source of income. Finally, there are infinitely varied combinations of all the above.

In 1961 a number of recent trends were evident in the magazine industry.

1. According to the *Census of Manufactures,* gross receipts of the periodical publishing industry had risen steadily between 1947–58:

Periodical Receipts
(Dollars in Millions)

Census Year	Total	Subscriptions and Sales	Advertising	Advertising Per Cent of Total
1958	$1,545	$551	$988	64.0%
1954	1,394	530	863	62.0
1947	1,019	407	612	60.0

2. Again according to the *Census of Manufactures,* the number of periodicals declined from 4,610 in 1947 to 3,427 in 1954 and rose to 4,455 in 1958. The only available figures showed monthlies declined from 2,253 to 1,604 and semimonthlies from 233 to 148 during 1947–54.

3. According to a 1961 *Business Week* survey, television and rising costs were combining to decimate the general magazine field. (An excerpt from this survey to convey an impression of the industry in 1961 is given in Appendix A.)

4. According to a survey conducted for the Magazine Publishers Association, Inc., magazines with the same percentage of advertising revenue as *Playboy* were fortunate to break even in 1959 and 1960 (see Exhibit 3).

5. Again according to *Business Week,* the future held in store: (*a*) increased competition in the class audience field, (*b*) greater use of regional editions, (*c*) more merchandising services, and (*d*) rapid changes in magazine content and appearance.

PLAYBOY MAGAZINE

"What is a playboy?" the magazine asked rhetorically in 1956. It continued, "Is he simply a wastrel, a ne'er-do-well, a fashionable bum?

Exhibit 3. HMH Publishing Company, Inc.

Percentage Comparison of Costs of Magazine Publishing, 1957–60

	1960 Industry	1960 HMH (6 months)	1959 Industry	1959 HMH	1958 Industry	1958 HMH	1957 Industry	1957 HMH
Income:								
Advertising	3	26	32	25	2	16	3	13
Subscriptions (earned)	64	20	62	20	⎱98	17	88	16
Newsstand	5	54	6	55	⎰	67	12	71
Total	100	100	100	100	100	100	100†	100
Costs:								
Paper	19	21	19	21	29	21	18	24
Printing	17	21	17	23	40	26	24	29
Distribution	5	5	6	5	1	6	6	7
Circulation promotion	20	5	19	5	14	7	10	5
Circulation fulfillment	8	3	8	3		3	15	3
Advertising	9	5	9	5		5	2	5
Editorial	10	12	10	12	19	12	5	13
Accounting							4	
Administrative	10	13	8	10	10	11	⋮	9
Total costs	100	85	99	84	118	91	83	86
Profit	0	15	1	16	(18)	9	17*	14*
								5†

Comparison of Selected Costs

	1960 Industry	1960 HMH (6 months)	1959 Industry	1959 HMH	1958 Industry	1958 HMH	1957 Industry	1957 HMH
Circulation costs per reader ($)	$1.62	$0.24	$0.95	$0.47	$0.18	$0.45	$0.38	$0.33
Advertising department								
Income per page ($)	6,580	5,330	3,475	3,960	3,723	3,530	3,553	2,940
Cost per ad page ($)	1,072	1,050	636	880	684	1,210	595	1,040
Ad costs per ad income (%)	16.4	19.8	18.3	22.2	18.3	34.4	16.8	35.4
Revenue per copy sold:								
Advertising	$0.11	$0.13	$0.10	$0.11	$ ...	$0.06	$ ...	$0.05
Subscription	0.13	0.10	0.14	0.09	0.13	0.07	0.11	0.06
Newsstand	0.03	0.26	0.03	0.26	...	0.26	0.02	0.26
	$0.27	$0.49	$0.27	$0.46	$0.13	$0.39	$0.13	$0.37

* Profit before administrative costs. † Profit after administrative costs. ‡ Figures developed for each item individually; therefore, columns may not add to totals.

Note: Comparable magazine classes shift as from those with advertising income "up to 20% of total" in 1957–58 to those with advertising income "between 20%–40% of total" in 1959–60.

Far from it: he can be a sharp-minded young business executive, a worker in the arts, a university professor, an architect or engineer. He can be many things, provided he possesses a certain *point of view*. He must see life not as a vale of tears, but as a happy time; he must take joy in his work, without regarding it as the end and all of living; he must be an alert man, an aware man, a man of taste, a man sensitive to pleasure, a man who—without acquiring the stigma of the voluptuary or dilettante—can live life to the hilt. This is the sort of man we mean when we use the word playboy."[3]

Another explanation for the appeal of *Playboy* was offered by the Reverend Roy Larson in an article entitled, "The Lowdown on the Upbeats," published in *Motive*,[4] April, 1960:

. . . My own personal explanation for its popularity goes like this: *Playboy* has a strong, almost irresistible appeal for the self-conscious young man who is struggling to establish his own identity, to define his own personality, to work out his style of life. Caught up in a reaction against "blah," he does not want to be just another person, but wants to show, by his manners, his personal taste in music, food, drink, and apparel, that he is someone who is distinctive.

But he is unsure of himself. He doesn't know his "way around." He is deathly afraid of being ludicrous. He doesn't want to goof. He doesn't want to do anything which would indicate that he's a hick, a square, or a clod. And so he needs impersonal guidance and direction and help.

Where does he get it? From *Playboy,* of course . . .

Playboy magazine was published monthly in three regional editions —East, Midwest, and West—and had experienced continual growth in circulation sales and advertising revenue since 1954. In 1954, the magazine had a monthly circulation of 113,000. There was no revenue from advertising space sales. In 1961 monthly circulation was 1.2 million while advertising space sales accounted for 36% of total revenue (see Exhibits 2 and 4).

Advertising sales was under the direction of Mr. Eldon Sellers, executive vice-president of HMH, and Mr. Howard Lederer, advertising director. Ads were solicited by a staff of 20 salesmen located in offices in New York, Chicago, Los Angeles, and San Francisco, and by two publishers' representatives located in Miami, Florida, and Atlanta, Georgia. A schedule of advertising rates is presented in Exhibit 4. Advertising pages usually constituted about 30% of the pages in the magazine.

The content of the magazine was divided into four parts: fiction,

---

[3] The average *Playboy* reader was 29.6 years old, and had an income of $8,150. In addition 41.3% had an executive/professional business title or position.

[4] Magazine of the Methodist student movement.

Exhibit 4

HMH PUBLISHING COMPANY, INC.

Selected Circulation Figures and Advertising Rates

CIRCULATION *

	Date Established	January, 1953	January, 1954	January, 1955	January, 1956	January, 1957	January, 1958	January, 1959	January, 1960	August, 1961
Dude	1956									266,024
Gent	1956									318,364
Escapade	1953							257,612	328,908	313,924
Esquire	1933	819,679	800,920	787,295	747,274	778,190	824,215	812,531	848,034	875,053
Playboy	1953			113,565	227,605	687,593	788,350	858,656	940,767	1,144,077
Rogue	1959								200,000	260,901
Life	1936	5,339,565	5,536,418	5,615,075	5,655,473	5,714,310	5,851,168	6,041,778	6,107,885	6,764,686

ONE TIME BLACK AND WHITE PAGE RATES *

	January, 1953	January, 1954	January, 1955	January, 1956	January, 1957	January, 1958	January, 1959	January, 1960	August, 1961
Dude and Gent									$3,000
Escapade							$1,400	$1,400	1,400
Esquire	$4,850	$4,850	$4,850	$5,190	$5,600	$6,000	6,150	6,150	6,500
Playboy			650	2,100	3,850	3,850	3,850	5,100	7,100
Rogue								700	700
Life	19,200	19,200	20,350	21,775	23,080	26,275	29,375	29,875	31,150

COST PER PAGE PER 1,000 CIRCULATION †

	January, 1953	January, 1954	January, 1955	January, 1956	January, 1957	January, 1958	January, 1959	January, 1960	August, 1961
Dude and Gent									
Escapade								$4.26	$4.46
Esquire		$10.01	$6.16	$6.99	$7.20	$7.28	$7.57	7.25	7.43
Playboy			5.74	5.25	5.50	4.88	4.48	5.74	6.21
Rogue									2.68
Life		6.46	3.62	3.60	4.04	4.38	4.35	4.77	4.50

* No other data available.

† These costs have been "reduced by the common denominator of cost per thousand copy pages. . . . The number of thousand copy pages is determined by taking the average press run for a given period (usually a year) and multiplying it by the total number of pages run in the period and dividing by 1,000."

Source: *Standard Rate & Data Service*, January issues.

nonfiction, cartoons, and photography. In the June, 1961, issue, fiction occupied 10% of the pages; nonfiction 20%; cartoons and photography, 30%; and miscellaneous, 7%. Fictional material was submitted to the magazine by professional authors through their agents. This source accounted for 99% of the fiction used by the magazine. The remaining 1% came from a "slush pile" of manuscripts submitted directly by amateur writers. About 500 manuscripts per week came to the slush pile while 100 per week came from authors' agents. Each and every manuscript was read by a staff member.

Nonfiction material was classified as informative, such as a series on sports cars; or individual viewpoint articles, such as an article by J. Paul Getty[5] or other known personalities. Informative articles were contracted for with authors who agreed to write a definite number of articles per year. Individual viewpoint material originated either with an outside author who sold it to the magazine, or else with the magazine which contracted with an author to write the feature.

Playboy maintained a standard rate schedule for material used in the magazine regardless of the prominence of the author. The lead article or story in each issue was worth a minimum of $3,000. Authors of other articles and stories used in an issue were paid $1,500; $600 was the standard rate for a short short or one-page feature. Any member of the *Playboy* staff who submitted a story or article that was accepted for publication received the appropriate payment.

The great majority of all cartoons used in the magazine also originated outside the regular staff. Cartoons could be submitted by any individual or else contracted for on a yearly basis with professional cartoonists. All cartoons submitted to the magazine were screened by two associate editors. Those that passed the initial screening were reviewed by the entire editorial staff which made the final selections.

The photography and art work were under the direction of Art Paul, art director of *Playboy* magazine. He would determine what was needed in the way of supporting material for each issue. Art work and/or sketches, which usually accompanied the fictional material, were handled by Mr. Paul and his department.

The "Miss Playmate of the Month" section was a special feature included in every issue of *Playboy*. Photographers from all over the country were invited to submit film strips of prospective Playmates. These photos were reviewed by each editor. The selection of each Playmate

---

[5] Mr. Getty, reported to be the richest man in the world, was business and financial consulting editor for *Playboy* magazine.

was by majority vote of the editorial staff, with final approval coming from Mr. Hefner.

Final approval of the material on each page of the magazine rested with Mr. Hefner.

The production, or actual printing of the magazine, was done by Hall Printing Company of Chicago. This part of the process was under the supervision of Mr. John Mastro,[6] production manager, who was responsible to Mr. Hefner. After the contents of the magazine had been selected, edited, arranged by pages, and approved by Mr. Hefner, the magazine went to Mr. Mastro. He purchased the paper and other supplies, supervised the preparation of the printing plates, scheduled production, and supervised the printing of the magazine.

Mr. Hefner demanded that no expense be spared to make the magazine technically perfect. The first few copies off the press were examined by Mr. Mastro with a magnifying glass to check for printing quality, color separation, and other mechanical details of the printing process. These initial copies also had to be approved by Mr. Hefner. It was not unusual for him to delay final printing two or three days until the quality of the printing met with his approval.

Playboy magazine was distributed in two ways. The Independent News Company distributed 80% of each press run to magazine wholesalers throughout the country who, in turn, would resell to individual retailers. All copies of the magazine were sold on consignment. Independent paid 58% of retail; the wholesaler paid 64%; and the retailer, 80%.

The other channel of distribution was subscription sales. Mailing labels were produced from nameplates prepared and kept up to date by HMH's subscription department. These labels were sent to an outside firm that wrapped each copy of the magazine in a plain brown wrapper, affixed the label, and handled the mailing.

Mr. Hefner spoke of three policies he maintained in publishing *Playboy*. The first was a policy of no reduced rates for subscription sales. A one-year subscription to the magazine was $6; the same price as 12 issues at the newsstand price of 50¢. In September, 1960, when the newsstand price was increased to 60¢, the annual subscription rate remained at $6. He commented, ". . . We . . . believe that our advertisers are entitled to an interested audience, an audience that reads the magazine because it wants to, not because it was bribed into buying. . . ."

---

[6] Mr. Mastro's prior experience had been in the printing industry.

The second policy centered around the sale of advertising space in the magazine. The advertising acceptance committee (composed of Mr. Hefner; Mr. Victor Lownes, promotion director; Mr. Sellers, executive vice-president; and Mr. Spectorsky, associate publisher) screened all prospective advertisements to be sure that they were in keeping with the concept of the magazine. Mr. Hefner continued:

. . . *Playboy* has the toughest ad policy of any magazine in America with the possible exception of *The New Yorker*. It is one way we have of separating ourselves clearly from the cheap girlie magazines, without ever having to read a line of editorial comment. . . .

What makes an ad unacceptable in our eyes? Well, a wide variety of things —a viewpoint that seems in conflict with the concept of the magazine, ads of questionable taste, ads of questionable value, ads that sell too hard, or are unattractive or that do not complement the *Playboy* reader—his intelligence, education, income level, taste, etc. . . . For example, we will not accept any ads for weight reducing aids, earn money in your spare time, or the like. . . .

The third policy concerned publication of another magazine similar to *Playboy*. Mr. Lownes summed up this issue as follows:

. . . Every day we come across articles, stories, cartoons, etc. that just aren't good enough to be published in *Playboy*. Why not publish another magazine using this rejected material? We ruled out that idea for two reasons. First, by definition, the second magazine would not be as good as *Playboy*. There was no way to prevent this inferior magazine from becoming identified with us. We want the prestige of good magazines. Second, it would make decision-making too complicated. We would have to juggle stories, cartoons, etc., between the two magazines. For instance, if the circulation of one was lagging, we would have to take from the other in an attempt to increase sales. This would downgrade both magazines. . . .

COMPETITION

Executives at HMH believed their competition came from two sources. The first was *Esquire* magazine. *Esquire* was published by Esquire, Inc., which also published *Coronet*[7] and *Gentleman's Quarterly*. In addition, Esquire, Inc., operated radio station WQXI in Atlanta, Georgia, and Wide-Lite Corp., a manufacturer of floodlights. In 1961 Esquire, Inc., suffered an operating loss of $46,000 on sales of $23 million. Esquire, Inc., had a net worth of $5.6 million.

In defining the *Esquire* reader, Harold Hayes, articles editor for *Esquire*, said:

---

[7] Publication of *Coronet* was discontinued in July, 1961.

. . . He's mature. Whatever his field, he has arrived professionally—or he's on his way. He's a sophisticate in the classic sense: knowledgeable, selective, interested in *everything* in the world around him—or else he wouldn't be interested in *Esquire.*

He's a businessman . . . and a busy man. And *Esquire* is ready to meet his most challenging demands. . . .

Our circulation department tells me that so far, our editorial concept is clicking . . . we're getting the sort of man we really want . . . men such as Josh Logan . . . Mac Kreindler . . . Frank Stanton . . . Otto Preminger . . . Senators Jacob Javits and Barry Goldwater . . . John Crosby . . . Conrad Hilton . . . and J. S. Inskip . . . all of whom happen to be *Esquire* subscribers."[8]

Esquire drew its features from two sources. One was its own staff of eight professional columnists; the second was free-lance professional writers, many of whom were very well-known while others were comparative newcomers to the literary field. Publicity departments of both *Playboy* and *Esquire* could cite many of the same well-known contributors.

Mr. Hefner recalled, ". . . that for years *Esquire* had been all alone as the magazine for the young literate urban male. In the early 1950's, however, I felt that *Esquire* had abandoned this market in favor of the more affluent business and professional man. That's where *Playboy* came in. Now *Playboy* is firmly entrenched as the guide for the young urban male. We have far outstripped *Esquire* in circulation."

The second source of competition for *Playboy* came from the ". . . increasing number of cheap girlie magazines trying to imitate *Playboy.* There must be about 50 of them on the market now, all of them trying to hang on to *Playboy's* coattails. These imitators have not made it up to now, and they never will. We're just too far ahead for anyone else ever to catch up."

The content of these other magazines ranged from those composed almost entirely of girls in various stages of undress to formats similar to that used by *Playboy.* As far as could be determined, no research had been conducted by these magazines in an attempt to define their readers. Recent issues of many of these magazines contained little or no advertising. Further, articles by established writers did not appear in them as regularly as in *Playboy* and *Esquire.*

Mr. Hefner concluded his remarks on the competitive situation by adding: ". . . We have given the young city guy a real identification with the magazine by giving him what he wants. I've always edited on

---

[8] In a 1960 study of *Esquire* subscribers, the average subscriber was 40.8 years old and had an annual income of $14,196. In addition, 61.3% had an executive/professional business title or position.

the assumption that my tastes are pretty much like those of our readers. As I develop, so will the magazine. . . ."

Exhibit 4 presents a comparison of *Playboy, Esquire,* and four other magazines in the men's general interest field. *Life* is included as an example of a mass appeal magazine. These magazines are compared on circulation figures, the cost (to advertisers) per page per 1,000 circulation, and one time, one page, black and white advertising rates.

PLAYBOY BY-PRODUCTS

Playboy by-products were commercial products differentiated only by the *Playboy* rabbit trademark (see Figure 1). These by-products were manufactured by outside suppliers licensed by HMH Publishing.

The first by-product, the *Playboy Annual,* was a collection of cartoons, stories, and articles from the first 12 issues of *Playboy* magazines.

Figure 1

Since that time over 25 by-products had been licensed by HMH. These included tie pins, cuff links, jazz records, shirts, and ties.

There were two outlets for the by-products. The first was through International Playboy Clubs, Inc. HMH would sell to International at 50% off the retail price. International in turn would sell to the individual clubs at 40% off retail. The second outlet was mail orders. HMH maintained a complete mail-order department to fill individual customer requests for by-products.

For the 11 months ending May, 1961, by-products sales were $133,-000 with a gross profit of $13,000. Mr. Victor Lownes, commenting on this activity, said:

. . . do you know of anyone else, besides Walt Disney and *Playboy,* who can sell products distinguished by their commercial trademark? . . . We get almost 100 requests per week from people with ideas guaranteed to make a million if we would allow use of the *Playboy* rabbit. But we are in the magazine business, not the by-products business. Besides, we don't want to be in competition with any of our advertisers. For that reason we are pretty careful as to just what articles we put our rabbit on. . . .

TELEVISION

HMH produced its own television show "Playboy Penthouse" with Mr. Hefner as M.C. The show was sold by two independent distributors to individual TV stations at prices varying between $300–$700. In July, 1961, 20 out of 580 TV stations in the U.S. carried the show. As shown in Exhibit 2, the 37 hours of programing completed during 1959–60 had produced a net loss of $496,000. Mr. Hefner planned to continue to produce new shows and sell past ones as reruns.

THE RESTAURANT INDUSTRY

The term "restaurant" includes the full spectrum of types and classes of eating places. Types of chain restaurants vary from the corner delicatessen up through variety, drug, and department store chains with restaurants, and ending with Howard Johnson's 608 units coast to coast. Classes of restaurants range from the simple decor of the local sweet shoppe to the elaborate appointments of the finest night and supper clubs.

The 1958 *Census of Manufactures* reported that $11 billion was spent for food and beverage outside the home in 230,000 restaurants. It also added that 310 restaurants with annual sales of $1 million and over, representing 0.13% of total restaurants, accounted for 4.34% of total industry sales.

Cities in which Playboy Key Clubs were either planned or already in operation, along with the relative ranking of these cities according to 1958 restaurant sales, were as follows:

Rank	City	Number of Establishments	Total Restaurant Sales (000)	Revenue per Establishment
1............	New York City†	15,062	$1,347,000	$89,400
2............	Los Angeles†	9,246	672,000	72,700
3............	Chicago*	7,283	563,000	77,300
6............	Boston	2,943	246,000	83,600
7............	Detroit	4,140	234,000	56,500
13............	Miami*	1,396	125,000	89,500
26............	New Orleans†	1,001	67,000	67,000

* In operation.
† Under construction.
Source: 1958 *Census of Manufactures.* Company executives noted clubs in operation or under construction.

PLAYBOY KEY CLUBS

Ownership of International Playboy Clubs, Inc., was divided equally between Mr. Hefner; Mr. Victor Lownes, promotion director of HMH; Mr. Arnold Morton, Chicago restaurant owner; and HMH Publishing. International was set up to franchise and supervise the operation of Playboy Key Clubs (see Exhibit 5).

Exhibit 5

HMH PUBLISHING COMPANY, INC.

Balance Sheet of International Playboy Clubs, Inc., and Chicago Playboy Club for the 10 Months Ending June 30, 1961

(Dollars in Thousands)

	International June 30, 1961		Chicago Club June 30, 1961
Current Assets		**Current Assets**	
Cash	$ 29	Cash	$ 50
Accounts Receivable (Net)*	442	Accounts Receivable	198
Advances to New York Club	199	Inventories	15
Inventories	72	Other	19
Other	73	Total Current Assets	$282
Total Current Assets	$ 815	Fixed Assets (Net)	291
Investments		Total Assets	$573
In New York Club	100	**Current Liabilities**	
In Los Angeles Club	94	Accounts Payable	$ 57
Fixed Assets (Net)	27	Taxes	79
Other Assets	4	Other	54
Total Assets	$1,040	Total Current Liabilities	$190
Current Liabilities		**Long-term debt**	
Accounts Payable	$ 47	Taxes	$136
Loans Payable	250	Other	42
Due Local Clubs†	89	Total Long-Term Debt	$178
Other	37	**Capital**	
Total Current Liabilities	$ 423	Stock	$ 10
Long-Term Debt		Surplus	195
Taxes	291	Net Worth	$205
Commissions to HMH	30	Total Liabilities	$573
Other	6		
Total Long-Term Debt	$ 327		
Capital			
Common Stock	2		
Surplus	288		
Net Worth	$ 290		
Total Liabilities	$1,040		

* Only 2% of these receivables were 90 days past due.
† Chicago, Florida, St. Louis, New Orleans.

During its first year of operation, International made agreements in seven cities—Miami,[9] New Orleans, St. Louis, Boston, Baltimore, Detroit, and Pittsburgh—to permit franchised operation of a Playboy club. In June, 1961, executives at International decided that no additional franchises would be given, and that all clubs would henceforth be owned and operated by International (except for the seven cities al-

[9] International repurchased the Miami Franchise in September, 1961, for $600,000. The seven franchises were originally sold for $10,000 a piece.

Income Statement for International Playboy Clubs, Inc.,
for the 10 Months Ending June 30, 1961
(Dollars in Thousands)

	International June 30, 1961
Income	
Key fees*..	$622
Commissions on receivables.............................	209
Sale of franchise and franchise services..................	92
Miscellaneous..	2
Total income.................................	$925
Direct costs...	235
Operating profit.......................................	$690
General and administrative.............................	$184
HMH commissions.....................................	25
Profit before taxes....................................	$481
Net profit...	$235

* Income from key fees was deferred over a 5-year period.
Source: Company records.

ready franchised). In reviewing the reasons for this change in policy, Arnold Morton, vice-president of International, said:

> . . . We decided that the clubs were too profitable to give away under a franchise agreement. In addition, since International had to "OK" the design and construction of the club, order silverware, dishes, decorations and other supplies, in fact, have all of the headaches associated with ownership, we might just as well have the profits, too. Besides, it is extremely difficult to maintain control over a franchisee when he is in Miami or New Orleans or even London. . . .

International, as the parent, required the individual clubs—owned or franchised—to operate under set rules. Each club was to use the same forms and procedures for keeping records and ordering supplies, and maintain the same policies regarding prices, service, and standards of quality in their products. In addition, International acted as a factor for each of the clubs. It would purchase the receivables of a club for 90% in cash; the remaining 10% was the fee charged by International for services rendered. Finally, International retained the authority to decide which stage acts would appear at what clubs, and when.

The first club opened in Chicago in February, 1960. It was owned by International, although operated as a separate corporation. The Chicago club was the testing ground for many of the procedures and much of the physical layout used by the other clubs (see Exhibits 5 and 6 for financial data).

The second club, a licensee, opened in Miami in May, 1961. In July, 1961, additional clubs were under construction in New Orleans, New

Exhibit 6

HMH PUBLISHING COMPANY, INC.

Selected Data on the Restaurant Industry

A. Percentage comparison between urban restaurants and Chicago Playboy Club:

	Industry Urban Restaurants Serving Food and Beverage		Chicago Playboy Club 10 months ending June 30, 1961	
	1959 %	1958 %	%	$000
Sales				
Food	77.25	77.57	13.50	168
Beverages	22.75	22.43	86.50	1,079
Total	100.00%	100.00%	100.00%	1,247
Cost of sales				
Food	37.05	37.72	81.50	136
Beverage	30.83	31.18	18.50	199
Total	35.64%	36.25%	27.10%	335
Gross profit	64.36	63.75	72.90	912
Other income	1.03	0.82	4.60	57
Total income	65.39%	64.57%	77.50%	969
Controllable expenses				
Payroll	32.58	33.04	23.20	290
Employee benefits	4.90	4.48	1.70	21
Direct operating expense	6.01	5.84	4.05	51
Music and entertainment*	0.29	0.31	0.24	3
Advertising and promotion	2.24	2.09	2.73	34
Utilities	2.01	2.07	1.28	16
Administration and general	2.62	2.78	3.95	49
Repairs and maintenance	1.72	1 90	1.73	22
Fee to International	...		14.50	181
Total	52.37%	52.51%	53.38%	667
Profit before occupation costs	13.02	12.06	24.12	302
Occupation costs†	5.66	5.84	4.95	65
Profit before depreciation	7.36	6.22	19.17	237
Depreciation	1.88	2.00	3.45	45
Profit before taxes	5.48	4.22	15.72	192
Add net profit from sales of keys	...	...	12.5	157

* It was the practice in the industry to offset entertainment costs against cover-charge income.
† Chicago club leased the building for 10 years at an annual rate of 5% of gross receipts or a minimum of $20,000 per year.

Sources: Horwath & Horwath. Company records.

B. Selected data comparing restaurants with assets of $250,000–$1,000,000 and the Chicago Playboy Club:

	Restaurants of Assets Size $250,000–$1,000,000	Chicago Playboy Club
% Fixed assets	80.34	50.7*
% Current assets	19.66	49.3
Current ratio	0.68	1.48
Net worth/debt	0.70	0.56
Sales/receivables	45.96	6.32
% Profit/net worth	6.99	94.0
Sales/total assets	2.20	2.18

* Percentages prepared by case writer from Exhibits 5 and 6.
Sources: Robert Morris & Associates, 1961. Company records.

Exhibit 6—Continued

C. Selected operating percentages of The Chicago "Golliwog Club":

The Chicago "Golliwog Club," an 88-person capacity cocktail lounge, staffed with costumed waitresses, was opened by the Sheraton Corporation in May, 1961. Annual statements, projected on the basis of two months' operation, showed the following results:

Cost of food/food sales...................................31.0%
Cost of beverage/beverage sales...........................31.8
Total cost goods sold.....................................31.7
Beverage sales/total sales................................94.5
Payroll and benefit/sales.................................27.2

Source: Sheraton Corporation.

York,[10] and Los Angeles. The latter two were to be owned by International.

Playboy Key Clubs were night clubs with admission limited to holders of a Playboy key. Membership keys could be obtained after payment of a lifetime membership fee of $50 for a resident key (for persons residing within 75 miles of an operating club) or $25 for a nonresident key (for persons residing outside the 75-mile radius). A key admitted the holder to any Playboy club in operation and extended credit privileges. As of June, 1961, there were 51,000 members. An unannounced $10-annual-account-service fee was considered as a future possibility.

Club managers were experienced restaurant personnel. Each club was under the general supervision of a club manager and an assistant. The club managers were responsible to Tony Roma, operations manager at International.[11]

Playboy Key Clubs were built on four or five levels, depending upon available space. Each level contained a bar. In addition, the second level had a buffet table; the third level, called the library, offered only a floor show, while the fourth level, called the penthouse, had a different floor show, and facilities for a steak dinner. Club patrons were free to circulate among the four levels at will.

The pricing policy was unique for an operation of this kind. Each drink was $1.50, regardless of ingredients; a steak dinner was $1.50; the buffet was $1.50. The only additional charges were cover charges of $1.50 and $2.50 in the library and penthouse respectively. Tipping was encouraged since it provided the sole source of income for the costumed waitresses.

---

[10] The total cost of the New York club was $2.8 million. This cost was broken down as follows:

Land and building.......................................$ 700,000
Building renovation..................................... 1,500,000
Furniture and fixtures..................................   600,000

[11] Mr. Roma's prior experience had been with restaurants and country clubs.

A given operation in the restaurant industry, such as the Playboy Key Club, might be variously defined as a restaurant, night club, cocktail lounge, or private club. For example, a Playboy Key Club had a greater proportion of beverage sales than most comparable restaurants, lower entertainment costs than many night clubs, and a greater proportion of food sales than most cocktail lounges.

Executives at HMH felt that the Playboy club was unique in the industry. A typical comment was as follows:

. . . The [Playboy] club is not like a conventional restaurant. In any other restaurant you sit down in one room and you stay put for the entire evening. At the club there are four different levels. Each time a customer walks into a new room it's like walking in all over again and he starts drinking again. The whole club is designed for simplicity and convenience. There is something for all types of customers—for the guy who comes for the entire evening to the guy who just wants a quick drink or bite to eat. There is something doing at all hours of the day, not like other restaurants where they do the biggest part of their business during mealtimes. . . .

No other restaurant has the same ratio of food to beverage that we do. Our business is 25% food and 75% beverage, while the standard for the industry is 25% liquor, 75% food [see Exhibit 6]. When we get the rest of the clubs in operation, we'll be the largest wholesale purchaser of liquor in the country.

No attempt had been made to determine what relation, if any, existed between *Playboy* readers and Playboy club members.

SHOW BUSINESS ILLUSTRATED

In May, 1961, Mr. Hefner announced the introduction of a new magazine to be published semimonthly, *Show Business Illustrated*. ". . . SBI will be dedicated to a full coverage of the entertainment arts in the dual role of reporter and critic of current events in radio, TV, movies, records, etc."

To staff the new magazine, Mr. Hefner hired editors, artists, and writers from leading periodicals throughout the country. Mr. Frank Gibney, author of *The Operators* and other books, formerly with *Life, Time,* and *Newsweek,* was made editorial director of *SBI.*

SBI was to be divided into four main parts: (1) The first would be a "news and reviews" section. This would contain brief notes of recent goings-on as well as short critiques of present performances in all elements of the entertainment world. These would be written by "stringers," critics and writers on a retainer to the magazine, as well as by members of the *SBI* staff. (2) The second section would be a "listings and ratings" section. As the name implies this would contain a current listing of movies, plays, TV programs, records, and concerts, and an evaluation of each of these. (3) The third section would be composed of nonfiction stories or articles of current interest to *SBI* readers. The great majority would come from authors' agents with a very few originating with unknown writers. (4) The fourth part would be the photographic material accompanying most of the features and stories. There also would be a liberal sprinkling of comedy and humor.

The prime purpose of the *SBI* staff was to procure, edit, and rewrite manuscripts, and design the layout for each issue of the magazine. Mr. Hefner worked daily with Mr. Frank Gibney, and Mr. A. C. Spectorsky,[12] associate publisher of HMH.

The first edition of *SBI* was scheduled to go on sale August 23, 1961. The newsstand price was set at 50¢, making *SBI* the most expensive semimonthly on the newsstand.[13] A special introductory subscription offer of 12 issues for $4 was available for a limited time. The regular subscription price was 25 issues for $8.50.

In commenting on the introduction of *SBI,* Mr. Lownes, promotion director of HMH, said, ". . . I maintain that *SBI* will very soon become a weekly. One of the real purposes of *SBI* is to keep its readers up to date on current events. This is almost impossible to do in a monthly. Maybe we can do it with a semimonthly, but I really think that to do the job right it will ultimately have to become a weekly. . . ."

FINANCE

Throughout its history, HMH had relied on internally generated funds to finance its activities. Deferred items, such as taxes and subscription income, were also a source of funds (see Exhibit 7). A public offering of 15% ownership in International was planned for the winter of 1962.

FUTURE PLANS

Mr. Hefner commented,

. . . Right now we are concerned with immediate problems. Each day that goes by without a new club in operation costs us money, a lot of money. Now that we are no longer going to operate the clubs under franchise, we are looking for ways to raise the money we need to open up new clubs. The money we get from the stock will be a drop in the bucket compared to what we need. The new magazine, *SBI,* has a lot of problems that must be straightened out before it is

---

12 Author of *The Exurbanites.*
13 Mr. Hefner offered a circulation guarantee of 350,000 readers to advertisers.

Exhibit 7

HMH PUBLISHING COMPANY, INC.

Source and Application of Funds

(Dollars in Thousands)

	1954–55	1955–56	1956–57	1957–58	1958–59	(6 months) 1959–60	1960–61	Total
Source								
Working capital		113			101	68		282
Depreciation	5	14	42	51	65	65	132	374
Other assets						16		16
Profits	69	60	30	94	21	72	314	660
Unearned subscriptions	163	176	173	273	156		260	1,201
Land contract*					259			259
Federal taxes		14	38	25	18			95
Common stock	4		24					28
	241	377	307	443	620	221	706	2,915
Application								
Working capital	177		159	406			178	920
Fixed assets†	38	280	120	37	530	110	346	1,461
Other assets	25	71	28		30		128	282
Unearned subscriptions						103		103
Land contract*						4	11	15
Federal taxes						4	43	47
Preferred stock	1							1
Common stock		26			60			86
	241	377	307	443	620	221	706	2,915

* Purchase of Mr. Hefner's home.
† Primarily real estate.

Source: Prepared by case writer from Exhibits 1 and 2 and company records.

running as smoothly as *Playboy*. The new staff is not yet used to our way of doing things. The new movie that Tony Curtis is going to do will require some of my time.

Finally, there are a lot of inefficiencies and waste going on at HMH. We have been so busy growing that not much attention has been devoted to organization. I work best when I'm in the mood. Although I don't usually get to the office until 2 P.M. in the afternoon, I work well into the night. At least one night a week I'll go right through to dawn. That way I gain an extra day. The other people work just as hard. Even though they put in the time, the work still doesn't seem to get done. For instance, we had a promotional mailing of almost a million pieces planned for the key clubs. At the last minute we discovered that someone had forgotten to provide the envelopes. I see a lot of employees with nothing to do, and others overburdened with work. Our management group is overworked. One of our big problems will be hiring capable people to come in and lighten the load.

But even with all these plans, *Playboy* will always be most important. Not because it was my first success, but because *Playboy* provides the concept on which all the other activities are based. The magazine is the idea that underlies them all. . . .

APPENDIX A

EXCERPTS FROM *The Mass Media,* A SPECIAL REPORT*

For magazines, television all too quickly became an evil eye hypnotizing the mass audience as no other medium ever has done. At least partly through starvation inflicted by TV's greedy appetite for advertising dollars, Publishing Row is strewn with the bodies of dead magazines—*Woman's Home Companion, Collier's, Better Living,* and others.

Before television, it was the big, slick general magazines that were the glamorous stars on the mass media scene. The biggest era of the slick general magazines began 25 years ago when Henry Luce launched *Life,* quickly followed by Gardner Cowles with *Look.* This year's 25th anniversary hardly finds the industry in a mood for celebration. Just five years ago, general magazines reached a peak when they set advertising linage records. But today publishers are haunted by the fear that, unless they can somehow exorcise TV's hex, several mass magazines that seem like household institutions will have to fold.

Television has undercut the general magazines in much of their editorial function: excitement, entertainment, and the illustrating of news and information. More important, it has siphoned off advertising.

In fact, magazines are still trying to equal the record for total advertising pages that was set in 1956.

In a Bind. Up to now the mass magazines have chosen to fight TV with numbers—total readers against total viewers. They have pulled out all stops in efforts to fatten their circulation, but this has now trapped them in two vicious cost squeezes.

The costs of attracting and holding the marginal readers, through special

---

* Reprinted with permission from *Business Week Magazine* May 17, 1961.

prices and promotion campaigns, have ballooned out of all proportion to the prices that magazines can charge their readers.

So, too, have the costs of producing and delivering magazines for these expensive additional readers. Costs such as paper, postage, and many forms of labor go up in almost direct relation to circulation as magazines scratch for new readers to justify higher ad rates. Second-class postage rates alone have risen 88% in eight years.

Publishers' profit statements tell the story. Last year, from total revenues of $248.6 million, Curtis Publishing Co. squeezed out net income of only $1.08 million—not enough to cover dividends on preferred stock. In the six months ended December 31, earnings of Meredith Publishing Company (*Better Homes & Gardens*) dropped 72% below the comparable 1959 period.

This isn't merely a recession problem. *Time, Inc.,* in 1956 netted a peak 6% on income and has shown a consistent decline since then. Last year its net on revenues of $287 million amounted to only 3.2%.

Counterattack. General magazines are deep in a restudy of their fundamental function in an era of audience fragmentation and of challenge from TV. Some are crossing over to the other side by buying TV and radio stations as a diversification move. Others are considering deep-rooted changes in magazines.

In the next few years you will see:

A shift in emphasis from mass audience to class audience.

More regional editions that offer flexibility in both advertising and editorial content, even at the sacrifice of the national image that has been carefully built up.

More merchandising services—posters, coupons, and other gimmicks—to make sure the advertiser's dollars work hard at the local market place.

Drastic changes in the content and appearance of magazines.

PATTERN FOR SUCCESS

In seeking new formulas, publishers keep their eye on three magazines that have scored notable successes in the past few years: the biweekly *Look* and two monthlies, *McCall's* and *Reader's Digest*. These publications were impressive exceptions to the dour picture in 1960, and their first quarter of 1961 gave them still further gains in total revenue: 15% for *Look,* 22% for *Reader's Digest,* 36% for *McCall's*.

These magazines have some things in common: they stress the features that most distinguish them from standard TV fare; they pay handsomely for material from first-rate writers; they offer very personal, even intimate, advice to their readers; they use color lavishly.

Perhaps most important, none of them is a weekly; they don't have to clear away each issue in just seven days to make way for a new one, and they don't have to compete with TV, radio, and newspapers for each week's news.

James Forsythe

JAMES FORSYTHE[1] had achieved wide reputation for unusual skill in helping customers to work out difficult financial problems. Many companies sought his services as a director. In 1926 and 1927 Mr. Forsythe had attended the Middle Western alma mater of his father and then transferred to the school of commerce at the state university, where he received a B.S. degree in 1929. He then accepted a position in the credit department of the Merchants National Bank in Providence. In 1934, he was made assistant cashier and loan officer.

The whole policy of the Merchants National Bank became more aggressive when Steven Taylor was elected president in 1934. His election followed the death of William Saunders, who had been president of the Merchants National Bank for thirty years. Mr. Taylor had formerly been president of the United Machinery Company, with headquarters in Providence. As a businessman, Mr. Taylor believed that the credit policy of the commercial banks lacked imagination. He was soon impressed with the constructive attitude of Mr. Forsythe and promoted him to vice-president in charge of the loan department.

Mr. Forsythe and Mr. Taylor had long discussions about building the reputation of the Merchants National Bank among growing enterprises in the Providence area. As one step in this direction, Mr. Taylor was able to interest several leading merchants and manufacturers in becoming directors of the Merchants National Bank. He also encouraged Mr. Forsythe to accept directorships when he could be of real service.

FRANKLIN LEATHER COMPANY

In 1936 Thomas Franklin came into the bank and talked to Mr. Forsythe about the financial condition of his business and the possibility of retirement. Thomas Franklin was president and majority stockholder of the Franklin Leather Company. The company had the highest credit rating and, except for occasional seasonal needs, did not call for bank credit. The Merchants National Bank had worked with Mr. Franklin

---

[1] Vice-president, Merchants National Bank of Providence; director of Franklin Leather Company; and director of Pine Tree Rivet Company.

in the critical period of inventory deflation in 1921. Mr. Forsythe also had worked with Mr. Franklin in financing accounts receivable in 1932. Although there had been no recent need for credit, Mr. Franklin had, from time to time, confided in Mr. Forsythe his entire financial and family situation. These contacts had led Mr. Franklin to name the Merchants National Bank as coexecutor in his will.

Mr. Franklin had frequently expressed the feeling that his son, Merritt, was going to develop some real business ability, but he recognized that it would be a good many years before he could take over full management. Merritt was the Franklin's only child. In 1936, he was a senior at Dartmouth. He stood well scholastically and was generally popular as a varsity halfback. The strenuous years of the depression had brought Mr. Franklin to the conclusion that he ought to retire and make some interim provision for continuing the enterprise until his son had developed adequate experience.

As a result of the discussion with Mr. Forsythe, Mr. Franklin brought in Mr. Raymond Kelly as executive vice-president. Mr. Kelly was fifty years old and had spent his entire career in the leather business. In 1932 two banks had put Mr. Kelly in as president of a small competitor of the Franklin Leather Company. By 1936 it was generally recognized that the situation in this small company was practically hopeless, in spite of improvements shown under Mr. Kelly's leadership. This company was engaged in a line of specialties for which demand had shifted.

Mr. Franklin died suddenly in January, 1937. As executor, the Merchants National Bank, and Mr. Franklin's attorney, John Williams, of Williams, Thompson and Rogers, received a majority of the Franklin Leather Company stock in trust for Mr. Franklin's son, Merritt Franklin. The pertinent terms of Thomas Franklin's will were:

I have heretofore received through James Adams Franklin, now deceased, shares of the capital stock of the Franklin Leather Company which, along with shares otherwise acquired by me, put me in voting control of that company. Consistent with his wishes, it has been my effort to use that control to expand and perpetuate the reputation and business of that company upon the principal of ownership-management by maintaining quality of product and uniform fair dealing and by enlisting the intelligent and interested abilities and co-operation of its employees through fitting recognition and remuneration. It is my desire that these policies be continued. It is my earnest hope that my son may be fitted and may desire to succeed me in the ownership of voting control. To this end, having already given him some shares of stock, I direct that before they shall sell or dispose otherwise of any or all of the shares of common capital stock in the Franklin Leather Company at any time held by them, my Executors or

Trustees shall first afford my son, Merritt Franklin, such opportunity as to them shall seem reasonable to acquire the voting control for himself or for his nominee for his account and benefit at such price or prices as to them respectively shall seem to be fair and reasonable and to represent the then intrinsic value thereof, unaffected by the fact that voting control of said company may be involved in such sale to him or to his nominee; and upon such terms as to times and manner of payment and as to security for any part of the purchase price not paid in cash as to my said Executors or Trustees shall seem meet, without liability upon them for anything which they may do herein in good faith. If my said son shall fail to so acquire said stock it is my wish that, all other considerations affecting my estate or the trusts hereby created being fairly equal in their judgment, my Executors or Trustees give preference to the acquisition thereof by someone fitted in their untrammeled judgment to best serve the successful operations of said company and the interests of its employees. No purchaser of said stock shall at any time be required to make inquiry as to whether any or all of the things hereinabove provided to be done by my Executors or Trustees have in fact been done by them, but on the contrary the execution and delivery by them respectively of any undertakings with respect thereto or of the certificates for such shares and of appropriate instruments of transfer thereof shall be valid and binding upon all parties according to the purpose and intent thereof.

The executors called a special meeting of stockholders to elect a board of directors. The trust department asked Mr. Taylor to free Mr. Forsythe so that he might serve on the board of directors of the Franklin Leather Company to represent the bank. The executors also elected to the board John Williams, Raymond Kelly, and four other directors who held small amounts of stock and were employed by the company. The board, in turn, created an executive committee composed of Mr. Forsythe, Mr. Williams, and Mr. Kelly. Mr. Kelly was elected president.

Mr. Forsythe and Mr. Williams immediately had a long and thorough discussion with Mr. Kelly. Mr. Franklin had told of the plans for Merritt when he asked Mr. Kelly to take the position of executive vice-president. The three men agreed that Merritt could not qualify for the job of president for some years. They frankly considered the problems that might face Mr. Kelly when the time came to turn control over to Merritt. In all probability Mr. Kelly would not be able to or want to retire from active business at that time. Much depended upon how soon Merritt Franklin might prove his ability. Mr. Forsythe thought that, even after Merritt became president, it might be well to retain Mr. Kelly's experience by electing him chairman of the board, at a modest salary, or by continuing him as a consultant. The executive committee and Mr. Kelly came to an understanding that he should be free to continue to supervise his own enterprise, the Raymond Kelly Company, Incorporated.

This arrangement had been agreed to by Mr. Franklin when he first hired Mr. Kelly.

The Raymond Kelly Company, Incorporated, was engaged in buying and selling hides. Mr. Kelly had agents in India, Argentina, and other parts of South America. The Franklin Leather Company also had agents in South America. Up to 1941, there was an ample supply, and so competition in purchasing was limited to a few prime grades. The secret of Mr. Kelly's success lay in his knowledge of the buyers and all other key men in the trade, according to Mr. Forsythe.

Mr. Kelly came to the Franklin Leather Company on the basis of a salary plus a bonus based on profits before federal taxes; his compensation averaged about $30,000 a year.

Mr. Forsythe and the staff of the Franklin Leather Company all realized that Mr. Kelly's greatest contribution was his broad acquaintance with the trade rather than his direct supervision of operations. Mr. Kelly usually came into the Franklin Leather Company office in the morning. He talked with the key men about any problems that were brought to him and went over a daily statistical report of operations and financial position. He kept in touch with the agents of the Franklin Leather Company in South America, as well as with agents of Raymond Kelly Company, Incorporated. Mr. Kelly spent several weeks each year traveling at home and abroad in the interests of both companies. On occasion, for example, when it became necessary to decide on moving the plant or installing new boilers, Mr. Kelly laid everything else aside and made a thorough study of the alternatives.

When war broke out in 1939, and particularly after the United States entered the war in 1941, the business of Raymond Kelly Company, Incorporated, became almost dormant under various governmental restrictions. This gave Mr. Kelly time to spend in Washington clearing the red tape necessary for the Franklin Leather Company to stay in business.

After Mr. Franklin's death, Mr. Forsythe had several long talks with Merritt Franklin about his personal adjustments and the future of the business. Merritt felt that now, more than ever, he ought to stay on the job he had taken in the tannery after graduation. Mr. Forsythe had been urging him to take an advanced course in business administration. He understood the terms of the will. And, in his mind, it was clearly necessary to earn the respect and following of the organization "the hard way."

Before his death, Mr. Franklin had discussed with Mr. Forsythe a number of personnel problems growing out of family relationships. The business had been in the Franklin family for three generations. Several branches of the family held small stock interests, and Mr. Franklin had given positions to members of the various families. On the whole, there had been what Mr. Franklin termed a "strong sense of family loyalty."

Soon after Mr. Franklin's death, James Livingstone complained bitterly to Mr. Forsythe about not being made president. Mr. Livingstone was Mr. Franklin's brother-in-law. He held the position of vice-president although his duties were limited to management of one minor specialty department. He felt that at least he should be put in charge of production. Mr. Forsythe said right to his face: "As long as I have anything to do with the company, I will not put you in charge of the plant." He went on to tell Mr. Livingstone that it was up to him as senior member of the family to maintain the loyalty that had always characterized the company. Mr. Livingstone apparently accepted Mr. Forsythe's analysis of his position in the company, and the staff continued to work well with Mr. Kelly.

In the summer of 1937, Mr. Kelly outlined for the executive committee the policies and plans of organization which he had developed to continue Mr. Franklin's general ideas. The occasion for the memorandum was a trip abroad to clear up the import-export business of the Raymond Kelly Company, Incorporated. Mr. Kelly anticipated that during this trip he would also be able to develop outlets for Franklin Leather. The memorandum submitted to the executive committee follows:

OPERATING POLICY—JULY AND AUGUST

Due to my necessitated absence for a period of approximately from July 10 to September 10, I have determined upon the following operating policy to pertain for the company during that time:

The executive conduct of the business will be in charge of a steering committee consisting of Smith, Francis, Jones and Brown for all matters pertaining to general operating policies. The above committee, when functioning in respect to White department, will include Livingstone and Nelson as consultants on cost and raw stock respectively.

The steering committee is to meet in the main executive office daily to discuss the situation of the company generally, and individually as the respective responsibilities lie, namely:

> Smith—All merchandising of the Franklin lines
> Francis—Finance and cost
> Jones—Production and labor
> Brown—General consultant on all matters

Smith will merchandise both the "Franklin Kid" lines of Blacks and Whites, in co-operation and collaboration with the representatives and agents of the company.

Francis will conduct all financial transactions relating to credits, new borrowing and cost. (Arrangements for emergency borrowing will have been made before I leave with the banks with whom the company does business.)

Jones will have charge of the production, and, in consultation with *Smith* and *Nelson*, periodically check on the salability and quality of the production.

Brown will consult generally on all matters pertaining to the business.

Livingstone will consult with the general steering committee on all matters pertaining to raw stock operations after collaboration with *Jones*, and make specific recommendations in respect to the purchases, which will be carried out by *Francis*, since it would be more proper to have an officer of the company do the actual negotiating with our suppliers.

It has been our policy for the past six months' operations to carry an approximate forward-rawstock position of ninety days on the basis of full production. We have concluded that, due to the general slowing up in demand witnessed the past six weeks, it may be necessary by the first of August to cut production somewhat, and, consequently, from July 1 onward our forward position on raw stock will be limited day coverage basis. All raw stock is to be financed to the fullest extent against domestic Letters of Credit, on account of the relative advantage in interest rates, and we will conserve our cash for current requirements.

An analysis of our raw stock position to date reveals that the high-priced skins have been now almost entirely put into process, and booked orders against the majority of these skins will permit of their being worked with small loss, if any. Our coverage of raw stock, other than Brazils, we consider conservatively on the market. Our coverage of Brazils, which is our main coverage and which amounts to approximately 500,000 skins, averages, on the basis price, 71.05 cents per pound, which we know to be conservatively within the raw stock cost of our competitors.

We have approximately 34,000 dozen booked for future delivery and feel justified, our inventory position considered, in accumulating at least up to 3,000 dozen to the increase of the past six months, which amounts to 7,000 dozen, being a total of 10,000 dozen, which would even then leave our finished inventory in an abnormally low position, particularly considering that we are entering our best season for Black Kid.

The nine months' formula, considered in the trade as representing a normal position, indicates that in so far as our Black production is concerned, and irrespective of our orders on hand, it is in a very conservative, snug position, being 7.84 months' supply as against the normal nine months'.

The nine months' formula on our White position is somewhat out of line because of the still unsettled definite operating policy of this department plus the fact that, having concluded that Chinas were the safest and most profitable skin to work, we purchased requirements for next season's operations during this season. Such purchases are a necessity when operating in this market and, consequently, put our position considerably out of line in comparison with our Black position. The nine months' formula on Blacks, however, is not applicable to our White schedule on account of the seasonal character of the business. In respect to our position on Whites, however, raw stock on hand and under contract is conservatively in line with market and could be disposed of with little loss, if any, should we later decide to discontinue the operation of this department.

The arrangement which was extended with *Bevan* for an additional six months' trial period, to terminate on May 31, 1937, was extended one month on account of conditions, but terminated and settlement made on the basis agreed upon as of June 30, 1937. Henceforth the White Kid production will be merchandised by *Smith* in conjunction with the "Franklin Kid" line of Blacks.

The White Kid assorting department will be taken over on approximately July 1 by Mr. *Wilson,* a thoroughly experienced and qualified assorting room foreman and merchandiser, whose function it will be to regularize the uniformity of quality and standardization of grades to a competitive and profitable extent.

We will continue to soak what we consider to be the practical minimum of Whites, 100 dozen per day, on a type of skin, North Chinas, which is the safest to work in respect to profitable merchandising, until we determine upon a definite policy after the survey of the entire White Kid situation has been completed. We are in the slow months now for White Kid demand, which will give us opportunity to go into the question of suitability of raw stock, quality, cost, operating policy, etc., in order that we may be set for the next White selling period. During this slow period we are endeavoring to perfect the quality of our suede production and if this, as anticipated, proves to be entirely competitive, the policy of production and coverage will be determined upon along a conservative basis, utilizing what part of our present White coverage is suitable, plus additional coverage suitable to suede production.

We have entered into a one-year renewal with Walczak, as our European sales supervisor, along more restricted lines, however, whereby all his actions are subject to confirmation by the home office, and whereby his salary has been reduced from $200 to $100 per month, certain countries eliminated and the commission reduced from 2.2% to 2%. It is my purpose during my stay in Europe this summer to make an investigation and survey of our export situation, which will form the basis for determining the best policy in the interest of the company to pursue, following the termination of Mr. Walczak's agreement.

Our cash position as of the date of meeting is:

In bank	$232,113.87
Outstanding accounts receivable	180,075.08
A total current position of	$412,188.95

We do not contemplate the necessity for new money until possibly the month of August, when it should be for a temporary period and will be prompted by the rather protracted seasonal easing in demand which we are currently witnessing.

I have arranged with the office so that they will be enabled to contact me by cable or telephone at any time during my absence should it prove necessary to discuss any matters of policy in which it might be considered that I would be helpful.

The general plan of organization outlined by Mr. Kelly contained no major changes in personnel or in the policies followed by Mr. Franklin, and few questions came to the executive committee (Mr. Forsythe and Mr. Williams) in Mr. Kelly's absence. Mr. Forsythe had developed some "feel" for the leather business from his previous study of Mr. Franklin's problems. He had observed from earlier work with Mr. Franklin that, in order to make a success in the leather business, it was necessary to combine "right prices" with "right skins"; to make a good run in the tan; and to develop personal contacts in the trade. Although without previous knowledge of the leather business, Mr. Williams was an able corporate counsel with broad experience.

The executive committee did consider the suede department with some concern during Mr. Kelly's absence. Mr. Forsythe talked to Merrit Franklin about the losses in this department. Merritt Franklin shared the skepticism of the committee and expressed his doubt that the company had a man really competent to develop this specialty. Although Mr. Kelly was still enthusiastic about the possibilities of suede when he returned from Europe, he finally acknowledged the wisdom of concentrating effort on the well-known and profitable items in the Franklin line.

After he returned from his trip abroad in 1937, Mr. Kelly suggested that the Franklin Leather Company enter into a contract with the Raymond Kelly Company, Incorporated, for exporting leather and importing hides. Mr. Forsythe took what he considered to be a normal view of this problem of conflicting interests. In view of the necessity of keeping Mr. Kelly interested in the Franklin Leather Company and also maintaining his other contacts, Mr. Forsythe and Mr. Williams, as a majority of the executive committee, approved the contract as long as offers were at prevailing market prices. Merritt Franklin understood and approved the situation. After this plan was accepted by the executive committee, Mr. Kelly prepared a formal contract which was examined by the committee and later executed.

Both men had respect for Mr. Kelly's skill in the business, but they realized that in some issues they had to come to an independent judgment. This they considered to be the hazard of countenancing Mr. Kelly's dual position as president of Franklin Leather Company and proprietor of the Raymond Kelly Company, Incorporated. Mr. Forsythe felt that this relation called for more alertness on the part of the directors than he felt responsible for on other boards.

The executive committee meetings were held as occasion demanded, at first once or twice a week. They became less frequent as relations clarified. Board meetings were held when they were needed for declaration of dividends or authorization of contracts. The Franklin Leather

Company paid Mr. Forsythe and Mr. Williams each $1,000 a year. Mr. Forsythe turned this sum over to the bank.

In 1941, Mr. Williams and Mr. Forsythe had about concluded that Merritt Franklin was ready to take over the management and to use his trust income for the purchase of the controlling stock. His induction into the Army interrupted their plans. When Merritt had graduated from Dartmouth in 1936, he went into the tannery as a tanner's helper. This was the hottest, dirtiest, and heaviest work in the company. The old-timers had known Merritt from childhood and were proud of the way he took hold. He had shown an understanding of the business, had discharged minor supervisory responsibilities, and had used his income moderately. Mr. Forsythe believed that Merritt's wartime experience as a technical sergeant at a far Pacific base had further seasoned him.

During the years since the death of Mr. Franklin in 1937, Mr. Kelly and the other executives had discussed all major problems with Merritt Franklin. Actually, Mr. Kelly had made no changes in the key personnel. The younger men, who had been brought in by Mr. Kelly as understudies, had all been selected with the approval of Merritt Franklin. Many of these younger men had been taken on to conduct research for substitutes for tanning materials unavailable during the war. Merritt Franklin came in to see Mr. Forsythe from time to time to discuss operations in the business and general progress of management. According to Mr. Forsythe, everyone in the company knew Merritt and no one would think of doing anything without his knowledge.

The production manager, Mr. Jones, had worked up through forty years in the company. He supervised most of the 250 employees and watched the flow of work. Technical supervision of the actual tanning processes was a highly personal skill according to Mr. Forsythe. Fortunately, the Franklin Leather Company had an excellent head tanner in Mr. Milovitch. His skill in treating varying skins with the proper time and mixture in the tan was critically important in producing uniformly high quality leather. This uniformity had built Franklin Leather's reputation. Although Merritt Franklin was not a skilled tanner, Mr. Forsythe had confidence that he knew enough to pick the right man for the job should the need arise. Mr. Jones and Mr. Milovitch had discussed all major changes with Merritt Franklin since his father's death.

Mr. Smith was a "back-slapping," "poker-playing" sales manager of forty-five who knew everyone in the trade by nickname. The leather business was an "old-line" proposition in which Mr. Smith and his two

Exhibit 1

FRANKLIN LEATHER COMPANY

(Manufacturers of Glazed Kid)

| | Balance Sheet | | Net Change in Balances | |
	11/30/35	5/31/45	Dr.	Cr.
Assets				
Cash	$ 75,958.28	$ 377,026.24	$ 301,067.96	....
Accounts Receivable	270,493.82	330,495.01	60,001.19	....
Merchandise—Finished	322,725.44	107,573.94	....	$ 215,151.50
Merchandise—Unfinished	247,534.03	169,413.44	....	78,120.59
Raw Material	237,978.08	257,654.88	19,676.80	....
Material and Supplies	12,221.56	46,384.27	34,162.71	....
Government Holdings	....	318,182.13	318,182.13	....
Total Active Assets	$1,166,911.21	$1,606,729.91	....	....
Land	144,919.50	149,649.50	4,730.00	....
Buildings	450,374.82	462,178.08	11,803.26	....
Machinery and Equipment	257,267.56	330,877.48	73,609.92	....
Prepaid Expenses	7,533.56	18,660.71	11,127.15	....
Cash Value of Life Insurance	145,824.26	73,137.33	....	72,686.93
Notes Receivable—Officers and Employees	4,454.00	26,878.50	22,424.50	....
Other Assets	24,392.63	55,449.20	31,056.57	....
Total Noncurrent Assets	$1,034,766.33	$1,116,830.80	....	....
Total	$2,201,677.54	$2,723,560.71	....	....
Liabilities				
Open Accounts	$ 49,753.55	$ 50,623.41	....	869.86
Accruals	45,843.41	31,843.01	14,000.40	....
Letters of Credit, Drafts, and Other Liabilities	434,166.36	90,036.52	344,129.84	....
Total Quick Debt	$ 529,763.32	$ 172,502.94	....	....
Mortgages or Liens—Real Estate	33,000.00	....	33,000.00	....
Ground Rent	198,000.00	....	198,000.00	....
Total Debt	$ 760,763.32	$ 172,502.94	....	....
Contingent	(300,889.85)	....	....	....
Capital Stock—Preferred	330,000.00	330,000.00	....	....
Capital Stock—Common	330,000.00	330,000.00	....	....
Surplus and Profits	398,777.36	$1,355,432.68	....	956,655.32
Reserves Depreciation	382,136.86	535,625.09	....	153,488.23
Total	$2,201,677.54	$2,723,560.71	$1,476,972.43	$1,476,972.43

salesmen had grown up with their Franklin Leather Company customers and friends.

Mr. Smith and the salesmen called on representatives of the large shoe companies with whom they were individually best acquainted. Mr. Kelly also made calls from time to time when special questions of price arose. The salesmen consummated sales on the basis of price and quality subject to inspection on arrival. Since there were so many variations in skins and tanning runs, the personal reputation of the salesmen over the years had a controlling influence in relations with customers. According to Mr. Forsythe, the price had to be right, but intangible relations determined sales. (During World War II, the government, in effect, took all skins and allocated them to tanners at a fixed price. The government also set ceilings on tanned skins.) Mr. Smith and Mr. Kelly took Merritt Franklin with them on calls and introduced him to all the major customers.

Exhibit 2

FRANKLIN LEATHER COMPANY

Operating Data

	11 Months Ending 11/30/35	6 Months Ending 5/3/45
Sales	$2,257,219.13	$1,873,720.00
Annual profits (before taxes 1945)	159,117.71	329,527.64
Other income	51,230.48	....
Annual dividends	46,200.00	54,752.50
Other outgo	....	....
Net to surplus	164,148.18	274,775.14
Total active assets	1,166,911.21	1,606,729.92
Total quick liabilities	529,763.32	172,502.94
Working capital	637,147.89	1,434,226.98
Other net assets (excluding intangibles)	1,026,769.33	567,730.70
Total	$1,663,917.21	$2,001,967.68
Less fixed liabilities	231,000.00	....
Less other reserves	382,136.85	....
Net worth (tangible)	$1,050,780.36	$2,001,967.68

After Merritt Franklin's discharge from the Army late in 1945, Mr. Kelly took him on a trip to South America to meet the buying agents. Before the war, Merritt had worked in the inspection and receiving department long enough to become familiar with grades and price differentials.

Mr. Forsythe and Mr. Williams had conferred frequently to appraise Merritt Franklin's ability in terms of his father's will. They were agreed, by the time of his discharge from the Army, that Merritt had proved he was not a "ne'er-do-well." He got along well with the organization and didn't squander his money. He knew the main problems in production and sales. About the only thing they weren't sure of was his judgment of price trends and buying ahead. Mr. Forsythe felt that Mr. Kelly knew a good thing when he saw it and would be glad to stay on as a consultant on buying or as chairman of the board. Mr. Forsythe and

Mr. Williams also were both willing to remain on the board if asked by Merritt Franklin.

Financial statements for the period just prior to Mr. Franklin's death and for 1945 are shown in Exhibits 1 and 2.

PFEIFER OIL COMPANY

Mr. Forsythe had been instrumental in working out arrangements to finance the Pfeifer Oil Company expansion before and during World War II. The Merchants National Bank had been the only bank connection during the years in which the Pfeifer Oil Company had become one of the largest independent distributors of oil and gasoline in the Providence area. Sales amounted to about $8,000,000 a year, although net worth was only $750,000. Capital was practically all invested in fixed assets. At the peak of expansion, Mr. Forsythe was invited to become a director of the company.

Mr. Robert W. Perkins was president of the Pfeifer Oil Company, and its dominant stockholder. He gave independent oil-burner dealers a commission on contracts they secured for fuel oil to be delivered by the Pfeifer Oil Company. Mr. Perkins also had developed a comprehensive oil-burner service which he made available to associated independent oil-burner dealers. This service included a direct emergency telephone connection with offices of the oil-burner dealers. This telephone arrangement automatically connected the Pfeifer Oil Company's service department with the customer calling any of the subscribing oil-burner dealers. Mr. Perkins also had arranged an accounting and billing service which took care of billing the service customers for the oil-burner dealers.

The Pfeifer Oil Company had made a practice of never giving data to credit agencies because of the intense competitive situation. Mr. Forsythe believed that this policy accounted for some of the rumors about the condition of the company that arose from time to time. He had made independent studies, satisfying himself that the rumors were unfounded.

Even the Pfeifer Oil Company's own certified public accountants found it difficult to get clear, unemotional pictures of the Pfeifer Oil Company. Mr. Perkins just did not care about technicalities, and he was the "whole show." Mr. Forsythe had learned over the years that everybody else in the organization did what they were told to do; but, owing to the ability of Mr. Perkins, it was a highly efficient organization. The auditors stated in their certificate that trade acceptances, discounted by the Merchants National Bank, did not represent actual deliveries. However, Mr. Forsythe found upon personal investigation that the acceptances were properly secured by warehouse receipts of an independent warehouse company (controlled by Pfeifer Oil Company) delivered to the Pfeifer Oil Company customers for stocks held for their account in the only available storage facilities.

Mr. Forsythe was convinced that Mr. Perkins knew his way around in the oil business and was not dismayed by large competitors or any traditions and formalities. He illustrated this point by a suit that Mr. Perkins profitably prosecuted against one of the major companies for failing to fulfill contracts for delivery to the Pfeifer Oil Company.

Tension in the local fuel oil trade reached a climax during the heating season of 1942–43. Mr. Perkins had seen tankers being sunk and started early in the spring to build up stocks to take care of his industrial and domestic customers during the winter. He talked over his program with Mr. Forsythe, and the two of them worked out a credit formula. On this basis, the Merchants National Bank at one point had loaned the Pfeifer Oil Company more than $3,215,000.

It was during this critical period when the loan was at its peak and conditions in the industry were unsettled that Mr. Perkins approached Mr. Forsythe about becoming a director of the Pfeifer Oil Company. Advances on the oil represented inflated values arising from costs of wartime transportation, and no one knew what kind of government subsidies could be negotiated by representatives of the industry. Mr. Perkins said that he understood the concern that the Merchants National Bank might feel about the large credit extended to the Pfeifer Oil Company and that he would be very happy to have Mr. Forsythe on his board.

Mr. Perkins already had secured some outstanding businessmen as directors. He was acknowledged, even by his competitors, to be an unusually able and aggressive merchant, and he had an enviable reputation with hundreds of retail customers. Mr. Perkins' board included Mr. Murdock, president of a local steel company that made domestic oil tanks. Another member of the board was a large truck dealer with whom the Pfeifer Oil Company had made arrangements for fleet maintenance. Mr. Perkins also had secured as a director one of the vice-presidents of the Lone Star Petroleum Company, which assured the Pfeifer Oil Company of a major part of its oil requirements.

Mr. Forsythe discussed the invitation with Mr. Steven Taylor, president of the Merchants National Bank. Mr. Forsythe explained that he already had all of the data that he felt necessary to justify the credit extended to the Pfeifer Oil Company. Furthermore, he had always had complete access to any additional information that he wished. In fact, he had been in daily, if not almost hourly, contact during some of the periods of greatest stress.

Mr. Taylor and Mr. Forsythe also discussed the possible reaction of the Merchants National Bank board if Mr. Forsythe were to become a director of the Pfeifer Oil Company. Some of the directors were directly or indirectly interested in the oil business.

Finally, Mr. Forsythe and Mr. Taylor concluded that the bank had no security to gain by having an officer go on the board of the Pfeifer Oil Company. Furthermore, the trade position of the Pfeifer Oil Company might be jeopardized in this period of crisis if the name of a bank officer were to be listed among the directors. Mr. Forsythe felt that he would have additional difficulty in answering credit inquiries about the Pfeifer Oil Company if he had to explain why he had gone on to the board at this time.

In explaining his refusal to go on the board of the Pfeifer Oil Company, Mr. Forsythe commented to Mr. Perkins that under other circumstances it would have been of real interest. As it was, Mr. Perkins welcomed his opinion about liquidating inventories and other business problems. As a result of these discussions with Mr. Forsythe, Mr. Perkins had completely liquidated the abnormally large stock by June, 1944. Also he cut receivables down to normal proportions by June, 1945.

THE PINE TREE RIVET COMPANY

Mr. James Forsythe met Mr. John Knoll at a university alumni association banquet in New York in 1936. Mr. Knoll found Mr. Forsythe's aggressive attitude toward credit policy most congenial. He arranged to continue their discussion in Mr. Forsythe's office a few days later when he planned to be in Providence.

Mr. Knoll was graduated from West Point in 1912. He later took some advanced engineering courses and in 1917 completed a special course in business administration at Mr. Forsythe's alma mater. During World War I, he served as a colonel in the Quartermaster Corps, located in Washington. After the war he went to Boston and there became a successful insurance consultant and acquired a comfortable fortune.

Throughout his career in Boston, Mr. Knoll maintained his interest in business management. He frequently expressed to his friends his desire to own and manage a small business. In contacts with his insurance customers, he kept alert to the possibility of finding some business that he might take over.

In 1933, Mr. Knoll bought the Union Manufacturing Company in Brockton, Massachusetts, for $1,200 at auction. He found a capable local manager, and early in 1936 sold his interest for $35,000. The successful outcome of the venture convinced Mr. Knoll that he ought to go into business for himself, and he closed out his insurance practice.

When Mr. Knoll came down to Mr. Forsythe's office, he went over some of the business prospects and problems of the Pine Tree Rivet Company of Providence. The business was owned by George Lewis. Mr. Knoll's attention had been called to the Pine Tree Rivet Company by Edward Kendall, a New York investment broker. Mr. Kendall had planned to register the company with the Securities Exchange Commission and distribute the stock publicly. Mr. Knoll characterized Mr. Kendall as a pretty fast operator. He had spent $20,000 on preliminary surveys and arrangements but could not get a statement in satisfactory shape for the Securities Exchange Commission. After some months of these fruitless negotiations, Mr. Knoll had about decided to go ahead without Mr. Kendall and his associates. He thought he could buy Mr. Lewis' majority stock interest and hold it for himself.

George Lewis was an inventor. He had developed a unique automatic rivet-setting machine, as well as processes for making tubular rivets. Mr. Lewis, however, had a number of other inventions in mind which he was developing in a separate plant in Connecticut. These took the center of his attention, although he still attempted to manage the Pine Tree Rivet Company. Later Mr. Forsythe learned that Mr. Lewis had had some good people under him but that they had no real opportunity to take initiative. The sales manager, Mr. Edmunds, later showed excellent judgment in pricing and setting sales territories for the six salesmen. Most of the 150 employees were under the direct supervision of a foreman reporting to Mr. Lewis.

The company had frozen loans of $30,000 in one Providence bank and had $47,000 in commercial paper spread among fifteen smaller banks in New England.

Mr. Forsythe worked with Mr. Knoll on a plan to refinance the credit arrangements of the Pine Tree Rivet Company. During the discussions Mr. Forsythe learned more of Mr. Knoll's philosophy and methods. His respect increased and in spite of the "shoe-string" appear-

ance of the figures, Mr. Forsythe made the following recommendation
to the loan committee of the Merchants National Bank:

PINE TREE RIVET COMPANY

Recommendation

Loan $77,000 to be used to take up loans of old management held by sixteen
banks.

Reasons for Recommendation

1. Company in quite comfortable working capital position.
2. At rate at which it is going, probably will pay down regularly and expect
   to redeem obligation by June 30, 1937. Apparently no necessity for additional loans or capital.
3. Prospects for immediate future extremely bright.
4. Management strong, aggressive, and well qualified to handle company's
   operations. Active head owns majority interest. Will be resident manager
   contrasted to previous absentee management and control.
5. By handling this credit now we can secure a fair-sized and valuable account. Cash balances are substantial.
6. Logical move at this time; account now at (   ) but management
   new to Providence, friendly to this bank, is desirous of doing business
   here. Management has no personal connections at (   ) at present
   time.

Business

Two main phases of business: manufacture and sale of tubular rivets; and
manufacture and sale of rivet-setting machines. Tubular rivets are manufactured
from brass, copper, steel, and aluminum. For rivet-setting machines, sold to
heavy users, rough castings are made by other concerns, then assembled with
patented parts designed and manufactured by the Pine Tree Rivet Company.
Other products include wide variety metal stampings and "spots" for use on
furniture, suitcases, golf bags, hand bags, and trunks.

Market for Products

Market for industrial rivets is widespread. Partial list of uses follows:

knife handles	fuses	radios
ball bearings	screens	beds
spark plugs	wheels	tools
brake linings	brooms	sewing machines
trunks & locks	metal boxes	electric instruments
leather products	furniture	measuring instruments
switches	bags	brushes
		overalls

In order to round out use of present stamping equipment, machines may be
used for wide variety of stamped articles, not taken advantage of by old manage-

ment. There are a number of allied lines which may be added without any appreciable capital investment. Company not dependent upon any one outlet for its products. Currently about 30% of the output goes into the automobile industry. This is a problem, however, which the present management expects to investigate and develop for the purpose of obtaining an even more diversified distribution of its products in the industrial field.

Management

President, active manager, and owner of majority control is John Knoll. About forty-five years old, married, three children. Mr. Knoll is well qualified by education, training, and experience to handle company's affairs. Excellent record as successful businessman.

George Lewis, former president, is associated with the company under a six-year contract at $6,000 per year. He has no executive powers whatsoever, but confines his activity to experimental and development work. Will supervise changing of present method of making rivets now being used at Pine Tree Rivet Company to new improved method. Mr. Lewis has no authority to commit the company in any way regarding purchasing, financing, or selling. It was largely due to his lack of ability along these lines that put the company in difficulty.

Financial Condition

Ample working capital; good current earnings record. (Memo continued with detailed description of accounts on financial statement.)

General

New management, John Knoll, known to our bank, and a personal friend of our Mr. Forsythe. Mr. Knoll came to Mr. Forsythe for advice in formulating his plans to buy out old interest and for aid in carrying them through. Mr. Forsythe had been in somewhat intimate contact with the new setup and operations for several months. Mr. Knoll seemed to like our methods and was friendly to us.

January 11, 1937   JAMES FORSYTHE

Mr. Knoll had determined that he wanted to surround himself with a board of directors who could supplement his experience. He asked Mr. Forsythe to become a director and to help him put into effect the financial rearrangements that Mr. Forsythe had outlined.

In talking to Mr. Steven Taylor, president of the Merchants National Bank, about the invitation, Mr. Forsythe concluded that almost anyone would be flattered to serve on the Pine Tree Rivet Company board. Mr. Knoll was a sound aggressive businessman, the other directors were honest citizens, and there was an interesting problem to be worked out. Furthermore, a director could be sort of a shield to ward off the other bankers as Mr. Knoll became better known in Providence. "Accounts can be weaned away."

The small stockholders who had been interested in the company by

Mr. Lewis and by Mr. Kendall's investment house were represented on the board, in a sense, by John Sumner, Esquire, of New York. He had been attorney in the unfruitful registration episode. Mr. Forsythe considered Mr. Sumner to be a very able corporate lawyer and a satisfactory representative for the minority stock owners. Mr. Knoll was always careful to see that these minority stock owners were carefully considered. There were about 200 of them.

Another director, Mr. Robert Larsen, owned a sizable minority interest. He had been a brigadier general in World War I and subsequently settled in Boston. He had been an insurance associate of Mr. Knoll and a close personal friend. He was also a man of substantial means.

Mr. M. J. Goldman was personal attorney for Mr. Larsen and had impressed Mr. Forsythe with his counsel on corporate law.

Robert Wilson also was a close friend of Mr. Knoll and vice-president of the Boston National Bank and Trust Company. Mr. Wilson had wide business connections and a critical point of view toward expansion.

Mr. Knoll confided in Mr. Forsythe that he also felt the need for counsel on manufacturing, production, and labor relations. He did not need the kind of technical advice on plant layout that one would expect to get from an industrial engineering firm. He felt a need for someone who understood his general objectives and could raise questions of policy on a high level. The kind of question that Mr. Knoll was concerned with had to do with scrapping all of their header machines for a new, higher output style. He felt that he needed to know the facts to consider, and also the timing. In due course, Mr. Forsythe was able to put Mr. Knoll in contact with Mr. Henry Patterson, hardware manufacturer and wholesale dealer in Providence. Mr. Patterson was glad to serve on the board because of the contacts with the other directors. His judgment was valued by Mr. Knoll because of his wide experience with somewhat similar, although not competing, companies.

Procedure in working with the directors varied from question to question. Ordinarily, Mr. Knoll would call on the directors about the specific problems on which that director might have some contribution to make. Mr. Forsythe illustrated this by commenting on frequent calls from Mr. Knoll about extending credit to customers, or about financing of equipment. Mr. Forsythe also knew that in regard to the scrapping of the header machines alternatives had been thrashed out thoroughly with Mr. Patterson. After the question had been clarified, however, Mr. Knoll presented the issues at a meeting of the full board.

Board meetings were perfunctory. Mr. Forsythe emphasized that the main work of the directors was in conferring with Mr. Knoll. Meetings were held sometimes in New York. In the opinion of Mr. Forsythe, this was primarily an occasion for a "night in the big city." Directors' fees in the Pine Tree Rivet Company were $20 a meeting. However, since most of their service was in informal consultation, the annual compensation was nominal. Mr. Forsythe felt that this was one reason for favoring an annual retainer fee for directors. The minutes of meetings covered only the motions required by law or by other corporate formalities. Copies of the minutes were sent to all directors after the meeting. Mr. Forsythe had accumulated so many analyses of the Pine Tree Rivet Company that he did not keep the minutes in his credit files.

Mr. Forsythe studied reports received by the directors in the Pine Tree Rivet Company by first having his assistant summarize the facts in a standard form. This short-form credit analysis was one of Mr. Forsythe's early contributions to the loan department of the Merchants National Bank. Mr. Forsythe used the graphic portrayal of the flow of funds to keep Mr. Knoll from freezing working capital in plant expansion.

The form reproduced as Exhibit 3 (pp. 87–88) showed the situation early in 1945 when the Pine Tree Rivet Company board had decided to ask the Merchants National Bank for a $150,000 line of credit. Mr. Forsythe had a special cumulative binder for the single sheets on which the data were presented.

Mr. Forsythe also found his graphic flow of funds statement was useful in keeping the board from declaring dividends on the basis of an apparently large bank account. Mr. Larsen had urged the directors to declare a dividend in 1943. The Pine Tree Rivet Company sent a printed report to its stockholders annually. This included a letter from the president discussing sales, contract renegotiation proceedings, expansion, and other activities of the year. The financial statements certified by public accountants at the end of 1943 showed an increase of $125,000 in cash. Mr. Larsen felt that he and the other small stockholders were entitled to some of this cash.

The whole issue was thrashed out at great length among the directors. Mr. Forsythe pointed out that, although they had money in the bank, there was going to be need for cash in the period of readjustment after the war. He added that their dividend policy had always been irregular. Mr. Forsythe concluded that the only safe policy was to clear up their commitments and save their cash.

Mr. Knoll agreed to this point of view. He argued that he had never made any commitments to the small stockholders and that they had bought with their eyes wide open to the risks.

In 1944, Mr. Knoll called on Mr. Forsythe to discuss the purchase of an additional rivet company in Bridgeport. Mr. Forsythe told Mr. Knoll that he would be glad to make a credit analysis of the other company. He was emphatic, however, that as a director, he would object to the acquisition. He told Mr. Knoll: "You have only so much managerial ability. If you buy this company, you will be spreading yourself too thin." Mr. Knoll ultimately agreed with Mr. Forsythe.

Soon after this decision, Mr. Knoll was approached by a large manufacturer who offered to buy the Pine Tree Rivet Company at a substan-

Exhibit 3

PINE TREE RIVET COMPANY

Providence—Manufacturers of Rivets and Riveting Equipment For Approval Line $150,000 Unsecured

LOANS

	High	Low	Balances
1942............	$ 80,000	....	$69,200
1943............	125,000	....	41,600
1944............	80,000	....	39,100
1945............	(Off since 10/1/44)		3,500 (2 mos.)

Account opened 2/3/37. Present management, headed by majority stockholder, John Knoll, acquired control 12/6/36. Since that time the company had made steady progress through excellent earnings, and its financial picture is well balanced. In rounding out its line and improving its manufacturing, there has been a considerable investment in machinery and equipment. However, no material conversion problems are anticipated as the company is manufacturing the same products and selling to the same customers as in normal years.

Starting with $77,000 loaned in 1937, we have advanced varying amounts from time to time, reaching a peak of $125,000 in 1943. Our experience has been entirely satisfactory and Line is recommended.

R. BRADLEY, *Asst.*

JAMES FORSYTHE, *Vice-President*

CHANGES: 12/31/43—12/31/44 (1 YEAR) (00'S OMITTED)

	C.A.	C.&A.	C.L.	W.C.	C.R.	T.L.	N.W.	Sales	Profits
44............	256.0	95.4	86.7	169.3	2.95	118.9	393.8	1,266.8	25.2
43............	349.1	192.7	195.4	153.7	1.79	228.3	373.8	1,328.5	34.1
Change.......	−93.1	−97.3	−108.7	+15.6	...	−109.4	+20.0	−61.7	−8.9

	Year Ending 12/31/43	Per Cent	Year Ending 12/31/44	Per Cent
NET SALES................	1,328.5	100.00	1,266.8	100.00
Cost of Sales.............	1,047.4	78.84	1,016.4	80.23
GROSS PROFIT.............	281.1	21.16	250.4	19.77
Operating Expenses.......	177.7	13.38	207.6	16.39
OPERATING PROFIT........	103.4	7.78	42.8	3.38
Other Income............	6.4	0.48	9.6	0.76
	109.8	8.26	52.4	4.14
Other Deductions.........	10.7	0.80	7.1	0.56
PROFIT BEFORE TAXES......	99.1	7.46	45.3	3.58
Reserve for Income Taxes..	65.0	4.89	20.1	1.59
NET PROFIT..............	34.1	2.57	25.2	1.99

USE OF FUNDS		SOURCE OF FUNDS	
		Current Net Profits............	25.2
Dividends...................	13.8	Prior years refunds, etc.........	7.9
Total Decrease..............	13.8	Total Increase................	33.1

Resulted in an INCREASE in NET WORTH of.................. 19.3

DISTRIBUTED AS FOLLOWS:

DEFERRED INCOME 4.9

FIXED AND NONCURRENT ACCOUNTS

Plant and Equipment..........+	25.0	Prepaid Expenses............. —	1.5
Cash Value of Life Insurance...+	2.4	Advance Purchase of Machinery—	3.5
Mortgages Payable........... —	0.7	Machines Out of Plant on Lease —	1.3
		Patents, Formulas, etc........ —	2.5
		Reserved for Depreciation..... +	20.5
Total Increase................	28.1	Total Decrease.............	29.3
		NET DECREASE..............	1.2

WORKING CAPITAL

Finished Merchandise.........+	12.8	Cash......................... —	55.1
Work in Process..............+	2.7	Accounts Receivable.......... —	42.2
Bank Debt.................... —	70.0	Raw Material................ —	11.3
Due Smaller War Plants Corp... —	3.3	Accounts Payable............. +	12.4
Accrued Miscellaneous Taxes... —	8.2	Accrued Payables............. +	4.6
Miscellaneous Accounts Payable...................... —	2.5	Employees' Deductions........ +	5.0
Reserve: for Income Taxes..... —	46.7		
Total Increase................	146.2	Total Decrease..............	130.6
NET INCREASE................	15.6		
	20.5		20.5

Exhibit 4

PINE TREE RIVET COMPANY

Manufacturers of Rivets and Riveting Equipment

	Balance Sheet		Net Change in Balances	
Assets	12/31/35	12/31/44	Dr.	Cr.
Cash	$ 51,915.20	$ 32,118.82	....	$ 19,796.38
Accounts Receivable—Net	33,484.32	63,270.80	$ 29,786.48	....
Merchandise—Finished	85,766.18	49,385.61	....	36,380.57
Merchandise—Unfinished	....	44,067.07	44,067.07	....
Raw Material	....	67,174.02	67,174.02	....
Total Active Assets	$171,165.70	$256,016.32	....	....
Land, Buildings, Equipment, etc.	438,466.58	573,224.78	134,758.20	....
Prepaid Expenses	2,556.80	4,716.67	2,159.87	....
Other Assets	78,632.73	68,276.08	....	10,356.65
Deficit	148,259.90	....	....	148,259.90
Total Noncurrent Assets	$519,656.11	$646,217.53	....	....
Total	$839,081.71	$902,233.85	....	....
Liabilities				
Notes Payable	$ 83,573.27	....	$83,573.27	....
Open Accounts	6,593.77	$ 33,337.89	....	26,744.12
Accruals	3,630.80	18,315.04	....	14,684.24
Reserve for Taxes	3,410.50	20,147.93	....	16,737.43
Miscellaneous Taxes	....	6,838.82	....	6,838.82
Defense Bond Deductions and Taxes	....	8,066.91	....	8,066.91
Total Quick Debt	$ 97,208.34	$ 86,706.59	....	....
Mortgages or Liens—Real Estate, First	55,000.00	32,175.00	22,825.00	....
Second Mortgage	110,000.00	....	110,000.00	....
Notes Payable Stockholders, Due 2/28/41	18,839.65	....	18,839.65	....
Total Debt	$281,047.99	$118,881.59	....	....
Wage Certificates Exchanged for Preferred Stock	3,725.62	....	3,725.62	....
Capital Stock—Preferred	19,690.00	....	19,690.00	....
Capital Stock—Common	278,414.33	275,116.60	3,297.73	....
Surplus and Profits—Capital	....	24,852.76	....	24,852.76
Surplus and Profits—Earned	....	116,860.25	....	116,860.25
Reserve—Depreciation	256,203.77	366,522.65	....	110,318.88
Total	$839,081.71	$902,233.85	$539,896.91	$539,896.91

tial profit to Mr. Knoll. Again he came down to the Merchants National Bank and had a long discussion with Mr. Forsythe. Mr. Forsythe acknowledged that, so far as the bank was concerned, he would like to see Mr. Knoll continue the management, since their account was attractive. The prospective purchaser had its principal banking connections in Boston. However, Mr. Forsythe pointed out that Mr. Knoll had no one to succeed him. His son was a graduate of West Point and wanted to go into aviation. Because the original plans to sell the stock publicly had not materialized, Mr. Knoll's entire fortune was invested in the

Exhibit 5

PINE TREE RIVET COMPANY

Operating Data

	PERIODS ENDING	
	12/31/35	12/31/44
Sales...................................	$434,623.70	$1,266,823.42
Annual profits (before taxes)............		45,324.27
(after taxes).............	15,536.65	25,176.34
Other income...........................	....	7,853.31
Annual dividends.......................	....	13,755.83
Net to surplus.........................	15,536.65	19,273.82
Total active assets......................	171,165.70	256,016.32
Total quick liabilities..................	97,208.34	86,706.59
Working capital........................	73,957.36	169,309.73
Other net assets (excluding intangibles)...	186,624.78	256,680.39
Total............................	$260,582.14	$ 425,990.12
Less fixed liabilities....................	183,839.65	32,175.00
Net worth (tangible)................	$ 76,742.49	$ 393,815.12

Exhibit 6

PINE TREE RIVET COMPANY

Record of Borrowings from Merchants National Bank

(In Dollars; 000 Omitted)

	1937	1938	1939	1940	1941	1942	1943	1944	1945
January......................	..	25	50	50	50	35	..	80	..
February.....................	77	25	50	50	50	35	60	80	..
March.......................	35	25	50	50	50	80	70	80	..
April........................	35	25	50	50	50	80	70	80	..
May.........................	35	25	50	50	50	..	70	80	..
June.........................	30	25	50	50	50	30	125	80	..
July.........................	30	50	50	50	50	..	100	80	..
August.......................	30	50	50	50	50	30	100	80	..
September....................	30	50	50	50	40	..	100	..	..
October......................	30	50	50	50	40	..	100	..	30
November....................	30	50	50	50	40	..	100	..	..
December....................	25	50	50	50	35	..	80	..	..

plant. Mr. Forsythe observed that if Mr. Knoll were to die, the Pine Tree Rivet Company would go on the auction block and his estate would not get much out of it. The Pine Tree Rivet Company was a "natural" supplement to the line of the prospective purchaser and the price was quite attractive. Mr. Forsythe concluded, "John, you'd better sell the damn plant."

Financial statements for the period before Mr. Forsythe became a director and the latest period before sale of the company are shown in Exhibits 3, 4, 5, and 6. The exhibits also include a monthly record of borrowings by the Pine Tree Rivet Company from the Merchants National Bank throughout the time of Mr. Knoll's management.

Commenting to Mr. Steven Taylor, president of the Merchants National Bank, on the advice given to Mr. Knoll, Mr. Forsythe observed, "Steve, I hate to see that account go, but John Knoll is a good industrialist. Wherever he goes we'll at least have our foot in the door." To which Mr. Taylor added, "Jim, we've got to live by developing new risks—not by hanging on to old connections."

HARTFORD CASUALTY COMPANY

One evening in the summer of 1945, on the Merchants Limited from New York back to Providence, Mr. Forsythe sat down in the lounge car beside an old friend, Ted Gorham. Mr. Gorham was treasurer of the Economy Shoe Store Company. The company operated a chain of moderate-priced shoe stores along the North Atlantic seaboard with headquarters in Providence.

Just before they separated, Mr. Gorham suggested: "Say, Jim, why don't you try to get an account from the Hartford Casualty Company? I ran into Jack Stone, their president, in New York this week end, and he is mad as a wet hen at the Providence Trust Bank. He can't get over the fact that they sent us to the Fire, Marine, and Casualty Company of Boston for our blanket liability policy. Jack said that he had a big account at the Providence Trust and felt he ought to get some reciprocity."

Following up this tip, Mr. Forsythe made occasion to see John Stone, president of the Hartford Casualty Company, in Hartford, Connecticut. Mr. Stone was exceedingly cordial and explained his interest in the aggressive policies of the Merchants National Bank of Providence. Mr. Stone was convinced that there was a real community of interest in the business opportunities for banks and insurance companies.

A few days later, Mr. Stone called on Mr. Forsythe in Providence, and the two men had lunch with Steven Taylor, president of the Merchants National Bank.

During the lunch, Mr. Stone said that he had been thinking a great deal of the recent discussion with Mr. Forsythe. He had discussed his qualifications with members of the Hartford Casualty Company executive committee. Members of the committee agreed with Mr. Stone that

Mr. Forsythe would be a valuable addition to the board of the Hartford Casualty Company.

"We would be glad to give you a $100,000 reserve account," explained Mr. Stone, "but primarily what we need is an aggressive director from the Providence area. The Hartford Casualty Company is a relatively new company in the field, but we are expanding rapidly. We believe that able younger executives, like Mr. Forsythe, can perform a mutual service for us and for their other business contacts by throwing business our way. I am making this frank statement of what I expect of directors because I like to have all of the cards on the table."

In the discussion that followed, Mr. Forsythe learned the board was made up of thirty directors from almost as many different cities in the Middle Atlantic and New England states. The board met quarterly at the home office in Hartford. Mr. Stone emphasized the interest that the directors took in the concentrated program of these meetings. Executives of the company arranged a condensed review of industrial developments in the area covered by the company. One of the executives usually had an illustrated talk prepared on the service rendered by the Hartford Casualty Company to customers. Mr. Stone assured Mr. Forsythe that the executive committee took care of all "formalities"; so the board lost no time in bothering with operations of the company.

After Mr. Stone left, Mr. Forsythe and Mr. Taylor reviewed his proposal.

"It looks to me, Jim," commented Mr. Taylor, "like the executive committee really runs the Hartford Casualty Company, and I have an idea that Mr. Stone keeps even the committee pretty much under his thumb."

Mr. Forsythe agreed that it was obvious that the directors, meeting only once a quarter, could not do anything about the management of the company.

"I doubt if we can get the account without going on the board, Steve, but I don't relish being a dummy director."

"I am sure you are right," replied Mr. Taylor, "and I am afraid we would get into trouble with Mr. Stone's ideas of reciprocity. Remember, we have a lot of other insurance business on our books and some insurance men on our board. I have been on the board of the New England Mutual Fire Insurance Company for twenty years, but the whole setup is different. I would never request one of our customers to take out insurance in the New England Mutual, but I do think it is appropriate to tell the boys where a piece of business may be available."

PART II

Sizing Up Situations, Formulating Policies,
Discovering Opportunities, Assessing Risks,
and Planning Programs of Action

Mathatronics, Inc.

"Like a Good 5¢ Cigar"

MATHATRONICS, INC., a small electronics firm located in Waltham, Massachusetts, manufactured and distributed a low-cost, electronic, desk-top, digital computer called the Mathatron. Sales brochures described this machine as providing "the benefits and convenience of automatic digital computation without the high cost." The machine could be used both for fully automatic computation or could be operated like a desk calculator using ordinary mathematical notations.

Mathatronics, Inc., had been organized by Mr. Roy Reach, Mr. Dave Shapiro, and Mr. William Kahn, the designers of the Mathatron, in February of 1962 for the purpose of developing, manufacturing, and distributing the machine. They believed the machine would fill what they saw as a "gigantic void" in the data-processing market between the $1,500 rotary calculator and the $20,000 full-size computer. According to Mr. Reach, president and treasurer, the needs of this void "were too complex for calculators but were not such as to require a $20,000 computer. For a long time there has been a saying in the electronics world that what the country needed most was a 5¢ cigar and a $5,000 computer. We believe we have the computer."

By December, 1962, the first prototype had been built. Within one year orders had been received for 40 Mathatrons.

Both Mr. Kahn and Mr. Reach as well as Mr. Shapiro had had extensive technical training and experience in the computer industry prior to their formation of Mathatronics, Inc. Mr. Reach had been associate director of research and systems for Minneapolis-Honeywell's computer division, having specialized in the development and design of electronic computers throughout his career. Mr. Kahn had been a senior engineering analyst at Raytheon, specializing in electronic systems analysis before organizing Mathatronics. His cohorts described him as a "genius at program and system design." Mr. Shapiro had been a project director in charge of production planning and design for RCA's data-processing group. At one time all three men had worked at

Honeywell. It was during this period that the idea of entering business together had first arisen.

THE MATHATRON

The Mathatron had been designed for use in scientific and engineering calculations, accounting procedures, and specialized business problems where speed, accuracy, low cost, and simplicity of operation were important. The recognition of the lack of machinery available to fill these needs had been an outgrowth of "many informal after-hour bull sessions" between the three men. The product itself had resulted from what Mr. Reach described as a "concentrated, nine-month design effort to try and fill these needs."

The Initial Concept. Mr. Reach described the group's initial thinking as follows:

> We realized our primary skills were computer related. Consequently we concluded very early in our discussions that anything we did had to be connected with the data-processing industry. We also were certain that the financial requirements of pursuing the large data-processing market would leave us with little ownership or control. Working with computers, we knew that no one was exploiting the possibility of economy via reduced speed, i.e., everyone was building devices with greater capacity and speed. Therefore we decided to determine what data-processing needs we could satisfy, exploiting the cost advantages of lower speed systems, which were not being satisfied by available high-speed systems.

The conclusions of the three men were incorporated into presentations made to potential investors. Direct excerpts of these presentations follow:

The Need:............Low investment.

The Problem:.........Present-day systems are economical only in large-scale, high-speed applications.

The Solution:.........Produce low-cost data-processing equipment by taking advantage of the low-speed requirements of the small user.

Proposal:............Design and produce low-cost desk-top electronic computer and design expanded line. Sell to scientific market—expand into business market.

Expand to full data systems by producing an expanded product line and selling to a captive market (captive in the sense of the machine's unique capabilities)—capture the massive, untapped, small business data system market.

The Market:..........Potential billion dollar—ultimate market— measured in total number of small businesses.

Trends:..............Growing office machine market.

	Average cost per machine
1947	$288
1954	614
1959	833

Tendency toward quality.

Expected share of calculator market: 13,000 over 10-year cycle.

ESTIMATE OF SALES BREAKDOWN

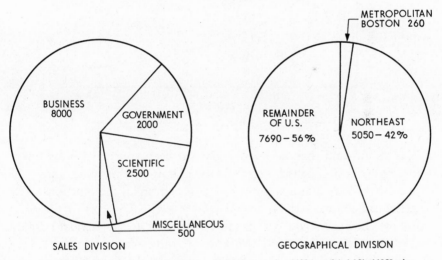

SALES DIVISION   GEOGRAPHICAL DIVISION

In 1959, 112,000 motorized calculators were sold. Mathatron sales of 100/month is 1.1% of 1959 sales.

According to Mr. Shapiro, the group concluded that to reach the customer whose data-processing needs were beyond the capacities of a calculator, yet were not large enough to efficiently utilize the $20,000–$40,000 small computer, they had to design a machine which:

1) Didn't require a large investment in programmers ("training people to fit the machine").
2) Would be "unfrightening" in appearance.

3) Could be mass-produced—one design covering the majority of applications.

4) Would require a modest investment, allowing even one individual to finance it easily.

Figure 1

PER UNIT COST OF PAPER WORK

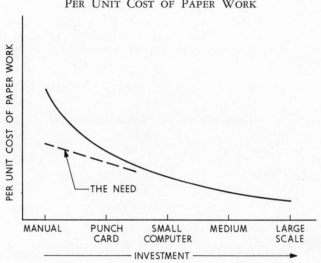

Mr. Kahn said that the Mathatron had been conceived of as essentially an extension of the electronic calculator. The basic advantage of the electronic calculator was its ability to perform all the functions of its mechanical counterpart faster and more quietly. The cost of the basic machine, however, was considerably higher than the standard rotary calculator, although the cost of expanding the electronic unit's capacity was relatively low (see Figure 2). Accordingly, the group's idea was to build an electronic calculator as cheaply as possible and then add to its features which would raise the machine's capability per cost ratio well above that of a mechanical calculator (point A).

Mr. Kahn explained:

Just the additional speed and quietness of an electronic calculator didn't seem enough to justify the higher cost of the basic machine. Consequently we added a program memory, automatic decimal point placement, and other operating efficiencies to our specifications. Now if the rotary calculator manufacturers were going to compete with us, it would have to be on an electronic basis.

By December of 1961, the three men had settled on what were to be the distinctive features of the proposed machine. These features were:

1) A very low price: $2,000–$2,700.
2) The high speed, quietness, and reliability of electronic components.
3) A printed record of all input and output data.
4) An ability to learn sequence of operations—to select a prewired sequence.
5) The ease of direct entry via "parenthication"—repeat data registers—push-button access.
6) The automatic placement of the decimal point and exponent.
7) An ability to be expanded to a full data system.

Figure 2

CAPABILITY PER INVESTMENT

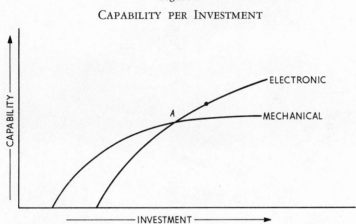

On the basis of this concept, Mathatronics was able to raise $250,000 during January of 1962. At that time no prototype or model had been built. As Mr. Kahn put it, "We were confident we could build it. Our uncertainty was how much would it cost to mass-produce it."

The Finished Machine.[1] The first prototype was completed in December, 1962. Except for changing the numbering and arrangement envisioned for the keyboard, the prototype did not vary significantly from the original technical conception. An underestimation of component costs, however, did result in an increase in price from $2,700 to $3,500.

Mr. Shapiro felt the maintenance of a disciplined design had been the

---

[1] See Exhibits 1 and 2.

Exhibit 1

MATHATRONICS, INC.

the ***MATHATRON***

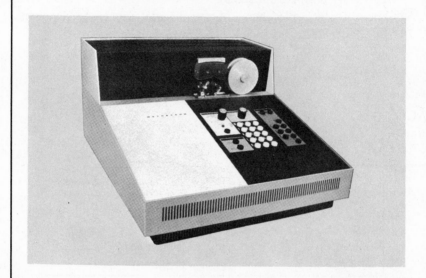

a new approach

to automatic computation

major reason behind their ability to successfully implement the idea, and he said:

The usual thing for a large corporation is to add a little something here and another transistor there until you reach the point where it is a monstrous thing. This is a characteristic of the large corporation—an inability to stick to an original, careful specification.

Exhibit 2

MATHATRONICS, INC.

KEYBOARD LAYOUT

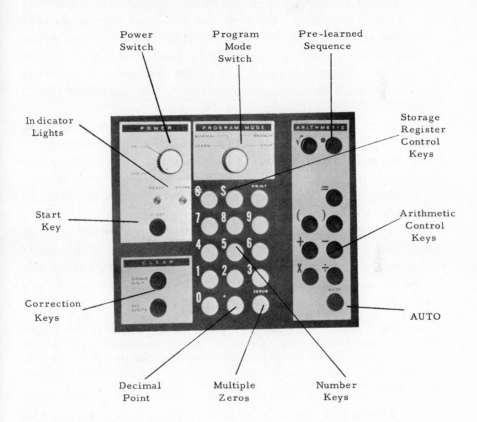

The Mathatron incorporated many of the computation abilities of large computers by adding to its desk calculating functions, storage registers, and magnetic memory units which allowed fully automative computation. The machine would accept direct entry of data using ordinary mathematical, algebraic notations (no preliminary programming was needed). Because of this feature, the three men had discovered that most individuals with a rudimentary understanding of algebra could learn to operate the Mathatron effectively within 30 to 45 minutes.

The Mathatron required no special wiring to operate. Its size (21 inches wide, 25 inches deep, 13 inches high) and weight (75–90 pounds, depending on peripheral equipment), in addition to the lack of special wiring required, made the machine relatively portable.

As each key was depressed, the corresponding number or symbol was printed out on a paper tape. Since the tape provided a continuous record of all data entered, written in conventional mathematical form, it was possible to intervene at any time during computation to display, modify, or correct formulas and numbers. The printer operated at 20 characters per second. In contrast, printer speeds in a large computer system ranged from 100 to 2,000 characters per second.

The printer had been developed along with the basic machine itself. The three men had planned to use a printer similar to those utilized by most adding machines, but due to an inability to find a printer which would meet required performance and cost specifications, they had designed their own. "This was our major technical change. It delayed us about three weeks."

Recently, the company had completed arrangements to sell 1,000 of these printers to a manufacturer planning to incorporate it into a special-purpose billing machine. Mr. Reach expected the independent sale of the printer to have a minor but a stabilizing influence on the company's growth. He stated:

Our major growth will come from the Mathatron, as the printer market requires extensive engineering coordination with the customer's design personnel—a service we are just not able to provide at the present time. In contrast, the Mathatron is ordered as an end-use item, thereby reducing to a minimum technical interface problems with the customer.

The Mathatron's unique ability was its capacity to solve the wide variety of problems that could not be worked on a mechanical calculator without the repeated reentry of intermediate steps, yet did not require the sophistication or capacity of the large computer. Some examples of these problems were:

Calculation of mortgage payment tables
Determination of bond prices
Tax calculations
Great circle calculations
Surveying calculations
Generation of random numbers
Solution of cubic, quadratic, and fifth degree equations

    Simultaneous equations (up to 3)
    Correlations and distribution
    Radic conversions

Exhibit 3 contains examples of applications.

Exhibit 3

MATHATRONICS, INC.

Representative Applications of the Mathatron

June, 1964

The MITRE Corp., Bedford, Mass., a technical consultant for the U.S. Air Force Electronic Systems Command at Hanscom Field, has two Mathatrons. One is being used for general research and development calculations. The other system is being operated by temporary office help from "Aid Employment" on a special project. (AID is a firm which specializes in providing temporary secretarial help to all types of organizations.) The engineer enters the formula with its several variables and then the AID girls spend the day working the formula by simply touching the AUTO key and entering the variable data.

Woods Hole Oceanographic Institution, Woods Hole, Mass., has been using two Mathatrons for the past eight months on the world-circling research vessel *Atlantis II.* These two Mathatrons have been operating satisfactorily under extremely difficult environmental conditions.

The MIT Instrumentation Laboratory, Cambridge, Mass., is using two Mathatrons for general engineering and design calculations. The Mathatrons, which are located in the same building as the Honeywell 1800 large-scale electronic data-processing system, are currently saving MIT time and money by providing a convenient, easy method for their engineers to do their own computations without waiting for data to be keypunched and scheduled on the large system.

Arthur D. Little, Inc., Cambridge, Mass., an industrial consulting firm, has been using the Mathatron as part of a service bureau to its outside consultants. Statistical clerks are doing the routine calculations which the consultants use for client reports. With desk calculators, a Mathatron, and an IBM computer at their disposal, these girls can now select the right machine for the size of job to be performed.

The Bell Telephone Co. of Canada, Montreal, Canada, has a Mathatron in its staff engineering headquarters. They have reported that a $3\frac{1}{2}$-day series of "great circle" type computations was completed in a single afternoon.

Boston University School of Medicine, Boston, Mass., has just established a medical statistical laboratory. Two Mathatrons equipped with nine prewired sequences were installed in this laboratory. With this prelearned sequence package, the researcher no longer has to be a machine operator to work his problems.

The MIT Lincoln Laboratory, Lexington, Mass., is doing contract research work for the government. Two Mathatrons have just been installed. One is being used by a group of R&D engineers and the other by a group of mathematicians.

Scientific Engineering, Waltham, Mass., a nonprofit research organization, is using the Mathatron to generate test data necessary to check out programs for its large computer in addition to performing their scientific computations.

United States Army Corps of Engineers, New England Division, Waltham, Mass., is using a Mathatron for civil engineering and river control calculations.

The Foxboro Co., Foxboro, Mass., a large manufacturer of industrial processing controls, is using a Mathatron in its circuit analysis group.

Polytechnic Institute of Brooklyn, Brooklyn, N.Y., is planning to use their Mathatron as a teaching tool to instruct engineering students in how to use a computer. Brooklyn Polytechnic has also completed installation of a large IBM computer which will be used for research; however, the IBM computer is much too large, sophisticated, and expensive to be used by the average engineering student. The Mathatron, on the other hand, can be used to teach the student the basic concepts of the computer, and just as important, the Mathatron can be used as an educational tool in teaching computer concepts from high school to Ph.D. level. (We have been in touch with the Department of Health, Education, and Welfare in Washington, D.C., and the Department of Education in Massachusetts. We find that 50% of the price of any educational tool will be paid for by the federal government, if it is to be used in secondary education. In many states the term secondary education extends through the sophomore year of college.)

Polaroid Corp., Cambridge, Mass., is using Mathatron to perform complex financial and production projections. Their Mathatron, which is located in the controller's department, is proving that the Mathatron can be used for business as well as a statistical and scientific application.

Emmons and Flemming, a small civil engineering organization located in Billerica, Mass., is using a Mathatron equipped with a special set of civil engineering prelearned sequences to compute automatically their closure, inverse, traverse, and all the other computations associated with surveying without the use of tables. This organization of approximately 10 employees expects the Mathatron to pay for itself, through timesaving alone, in less than two years.

Source: Company sales literature.

MARKETING

In March of 1963, a marketing manager was hired. According to Mr. Reach, the primary motivation in hiring such an individual was that "none of us knew anything about selling computers." The new manager, Mr. Charles French, was a graduate of the Harvard Business School. Mr. French had sold office machines for several years and before coming to Mathatronics had been the assistant manager of sales administration of Minneapolis-Honeywell's computer division. Mr. French was not a major stockholder, as were the three officers of the company.

In June of 1964, Mr. French described the Mathatron's markets as follows:

We have felt that the machine's greatest potential would be in the general business market, particularly over the long run, and that scientific and research applications would be significant only early in the game. But the response of the scientific market has proven to be much larger than we anticipated and to date we have concentrated on satisfying this demand. We still believe, however, that the small business, which can never afford the standard computer, is our largest potential market. But right now, the Mathatron does not do enough more, relative to the mechanical calculator, to justify its price to the small businessman. At the present time, it is primarily a scientific-engineering machine with only limited use in the business field. When we add the page printer and punched paper tape this fall, we will begin to get into more business applications.

Mr. Reach said that due to the uniqueness of the Mathatron, the potential business customer was usually unaware such a machine existed, and was therefore skeptical of its technical ability or its usefulness to him. In addition, he pointed out that the vast majority of small businessmen did not have any programming ability. As he stated it:

Selling to the engineer and the scientist greatly reduces these problems. Typically they are familiar with data-processing concepts and machinery, and they quickly recognize the innovation the machine represents. Also, because they are trained in mathematics they have no difficulty in operating the Mathatron. Consequently, the technically trained customer can make up his own mind as to how he will use the machine, greatly reducing our selling job. Such is not the case with the small businessman. It is difficult to get over to him why it is a better device than the calculator.

In response to a request by the case writer to characterize the Mathatron's distinctive abilities in layman's terms, Mr. Reach commented as follows:

The Mathatron is essentially a device which numerically evaluates mathematical functions automatically. You don't have to set the problem up for the machine, you just type in as you would write it down on a piece of paper. From this it gets answers easily and automatically, making the Mathatron different from the calculator. Certainly calculators get answers too, but not without a lot of intermediate help and mental figuring.

Mr. French explained that to overcome the difficulties in selling to the small businessman, "you have to show him the machine and how he can solve his own particular problems on it. You can't explain it to him in terms of generalized problems as you can with the engineer or scientist. The usual businessman's response to our sales literature is very small. In contrast, we have typically received from scientific-engineering firms a great deal of interest solely on the basis of promotional material."

Exhibit 4 illustrates the change in the company's market conception from 1962 to 1964.

Exhibit 4

MATHATRONICS, INC.

Predicted Composition of Sales 1962, 1964

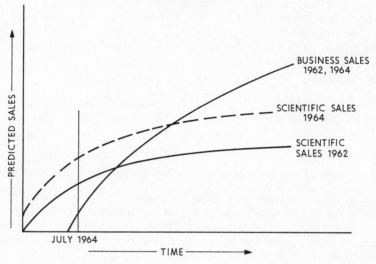

Shortly after Mathatronics incorporated in February, 1962, Mr. Reach had obtained a booth for the Northeast Electronics Research and Engineering Meeting (NEREM), held annually in Boston in November. The NEREM show was to be the company's first major promotional effort. In October of 1963, Mr. French obtained the services of a friend, for years a specialist in electronics publicity and advertising, to help prepare for the show. Company officers described the response to the Mathatron at the show as very enthusiastic. Reflecting the success of the show, front-page articles appeared in *Electronic News, Purchasing News,* and the *Electronic Design* magazines, describing the Mathatron's development and technical capabilities.

To capitalize on the interest of scientific and research firms three special-purpose models of the Mathatron were added to the product line: one for mathematical, one for statistical, and one for civil engineering computations. In essence, each model was the basic machine to which an expanded memory unit, containing several special-purpose prewired programs, had been added. Any of these internally stored programs could be used by simply dialing a program switch. The programs were selected on the basis of computations frequently utilized in each area. For example, the mathematical Mathatron contained prewired programs facilitating the automatic calculation of trigonometric ratios, the solution of simultaneous equations, the calculation of logs and antilogs, and so forth. The statistical model incorporated programs simplifying the handling of arithmetic operations such as summarization, determination of inverses, distributions, correlations, variances, etc.

According to Mr. Shapiro the decision to make the special-purpose Mathatron a standard product item had reduced manufacturing costs, and he said:

> We found that most customers were requesting prewired sequences and that 80%–90% of these requests fell into one of three categories. . . . By packaging it in this way we have also cut our spare parts problems in addition to making the marketing of the machine easier.

The price of the special-purpose machines ranged from $6,000 for the statistical model to $7,500 for the mathematical model. Mathatronics would install the special memory unit in a customer's standard machine for the difference in the original price and that of a special-purpose machine plus a $75 service fee.

DISTRIBUTION

During the spring and summer of 1963, electronics distributors who were interested in obtaining territorial franchises were told the company had not yet decided on how best to distribute the machine. However, just prior to the NEREM show, the company decided to use independent agents to sell and distribute the machine. Up to this time the principal sales effort had been confined to the direct contacts of Mr. French. The decision to use independent agencies was a result of a conclusion pushed by Mr. French that the size of the investment both in time and money which was needed to develop an effective sales and service force was too large. Described as not an insignificant factor was the immediate market created by requiring agents to purchase at least one demonstrator, if not two—depending on the type of contract agreed on.

The company offered two basic contracts. One, a distributor contract, required that the agent do the billing, assuming the credit risk. The distributor was required to buy two Mathatrons immediately. A discount was provided to him on all machines and parts. Another, a representative contract, provided a fixed commission and required the purchase of only one machine. The representative performed no billing or clerical functions. The distributor was required to carry a minimum stock of spare parts, the amount being determined by the number of machines operating within his assigned region. The representative was supplied spare parts by Mathatronics. Both contracts required the maintenance of service facilities and personnel. The initial agreements, for six months, were renewable on a year-to-year basis if all parties were satisfied. Initially agents had complained that the discount given on equipment was "tight." However, Mr. French said the company's participation in the NEREM show and a large electronics show held in New York in March of 1964 had generated a "tremendous enthusiasm" among the office equipment and machine distributors and scientific instrument dealers. His statement was:

We now realize that the demonstrator discount rates were tight for the distributor and the commission representative. However, the product was selling fast enough to provide us with a strong bargaining position. In addition, when an agent invests $5,000 to $10,000 in machinery, not counting the one-week service training we require of his personnel, he is likely to move quite quickly to recover his money. We are now planning to adjust our discount policy so it will conform more closely with standard practice.[2]

Mr. French sought agents who had the capacity to serve large regional areas as he planned to cover the United States with 10 to 11 large dealer organizations.[3] With a minor exception every agent was familiar with the scientific market. Often they were already calling on potential scientific and research oriented organizations with other lines. He added:

In each region we have tried to select the top distributors on the basis of sales volume, reputation, and service capacity. In some areas, notably New York and Washington, D.C., we have gone with new groups who will be concentrating exclusively on our products. Of course, we are limited in our search by lack of time, as we want to get the country as quickly covered as possible, as much of our early growth will come in this manner. Coverage is also important to our becoming solidly established before competition appears, for in the computer business the man with an advantage is the one who is there first. For the customer there is no economic justification for going to another computer system if he can expand his existing line.

COMPETITION

In discussing competition, Mr. French admitted that while the company had gone into "a complete vacuum" between the nonprinting $1,500 rotary calculator and the $20,000 computer, competitors were

---

[2] Standard practice in the industry was to provide discounts at 30% to distributors and representatives.

[3] See Exhibit 5 for a description of the sales agents as of July, 1964.

Exhibit 5

MATHATRONICS, INC.

List of Distributors

July, 1964

(Listed Chronologically since September, 1963)

Distributor	Office Location(s)	Territory	Number of Sales (Service) Personnel	Other Types of Products Sold	Number of Mathatronics Sold
Company	Waltham, Mass.	. . . .	. . .	Office equipment	28 (2)
A*	Framingham, Mass.	Eastern Mass.	3	Rents student dormitories	3 (1)
B*	Boston, Mass.	Eastern Mass.	2	None	1 (3)
C†	New Jersey, East New York, Pennsylvania	New Jersey, East New York and Pennsylvania	3 (½)	. . . .	6 (3)
D†	Washington, D.C.	Maryland, Delaware and Washington, D.C.	2 (2)	None	6 (2)
E	Orlando, Fla., Huntsville, Ala., Greensboro, N.C.	Florida, Georgia, Alabama, Kentucky, Tennessee, Virginia, North and South Carolina	7 (2)	Electronic components and measuring devices	4 (3)
F	Dallas, Texas	Texas, Arkansas, Oklahoma, Louisiana	6 (2)	Computer service bureau	1 (3)
G	Toronto, Ont., Vancouver, B.C., Ottawa, Ont., Montreal, Que.	Canada	7 (2)	Electronic components and measuring devices	1 (2)
H	Albuquerque, N.M.	Rocky Mt. states	3 (1)	Electronic components	(1)
I†	San Francisco, Calif.	California	2 (1)	None	(1)

* Discontinued.
† Indicates distributors.
Source: Company records.

Exhibit 6

MATHATRONICS, INC.

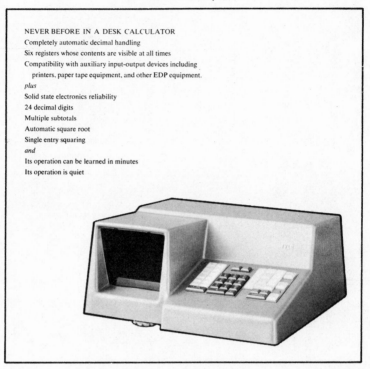

NEVER BEFORE IN A DESK CALCULATOR
Completely automatic decimal handling
Six registers whose contents are visible at all times
Compatibility with auxiliary input-output devices including
    printers, paper tape equipment, and other EDP equipment.
plus
Solid state electronics reliability
24 decimal digits
Multiple subtotals
Automatic square root
Single entry squaring
and
Its operation can be learned in minutes
Its operation is quiet

beginning "to adopt our concept of what a machine should be," and he pointed out:

Wyle Laboratories, for example, has just introduced a $4,000 electronic calculator which does have three storage registers (see Exhibit 6). However, it has no printer. Instead it utilizes a cathode ray tube display (like a TV tube) which doesn't allow you to maintain a record. But its biggest drawback, as far as we are concerned, is its lack of a program memory unit.

Mr. French expected the Wyle unit to have a program memory within 12 months, and a printer within 6.

Mr. French and Mr. Reach believed their closest competitors were companies making electronic calculators. Since mid-1962 several office and billing machine manufacturers, e.g., Sony, Friden, and Monroe, had introduced or announced development of electronic calculators (see Exhibits 7 and 8). Some of these machines featured automatic calculation of square root and decimal point placement. These machines ranged in price from $1,500–$2,500.

Exhibit 7

MATHATRONICS, INC.

SONY ALL-SOLID-STATE FULLY AUTOMATIC
ELECTRONIC CALCULATOR MODEL MD-V

SONY Electronic Calculator Model MD-V is a compact, handy, and light weight portable machine for general calculating purposes.

The MD-V can perform addition, subtraction, multiplication and division, and their serial calculation simply, instantaneously and silently.

The digits and directives for the calculation may be put into the calculator by pushing the keys according to the sequence of the mathematical expression to be calculated.

For example, to perform the following calculation:

$$[(123 \times 456) + 789 - 123] \div 456 = \quad ?$$

Simply push the keys in the following sequence:

1, 2, 3, x, 4, 5, 6, +, 7, 8, 9, —, 1, 2, 3, ÷, 4, 5, 6, =.

The answer is clearly visualized on the digital display tubes in a moment. ■ Calculation speed is almost instantaneous—within 0.5 sec. for every calculation. ■ Complete silence of operation is one of the most desirable features. ■ All solid state module construction provides compactness, light weight, reliability and long service life.

In March of 1964, Pacific Data Systems, Inc., announced a new computer priced at $21,500, designed for engineering computations (see Exhibit 9). In addition to its greater capacity, the machine provided (1) a typewriter printer, (2) a punch tape record of any pro-

Exhibit 8

MATHATRONICS, INC.

The new Friden 6010 is a low-cost electronic computer designed especially for business applications which require high-speed computation as well as descriptive alphabetic information. ■ In spite of its low cost, the Friden 6010 Electronic Computer has many characteristics of more expensive computer systems: it is fully transistorized; it has random access core storage; it performs logical functions; and it is capable of unattended operation. ■ The electronic processor of the Friden 6010 operates faster than many larger computers. For example, *in one second it can make over 750 additions—over 45,000 in one minute.* Yet, the machine takes up no more floor space than a secretary's desk and can be operated or monitored by any reasonably alert typist after a short period of instruction. ■ You can plug the Friden 6010 Electronic Computer into any standard wall outlet. Air conditioning is not necessary. ■ Friden computer specialists have devised a simple linear programming method which requires only sequential wiring on a removable program panel. You may have a separate program panel for each application, or you may wire a single panel for several applications, depending on the complexity of the programs involved. ■ The Friden 6010 Electronic Computer is versatile. It accepts input from punched tape, edge-punched cards, tabulating cards, auxiliary input units, or the familiar electric typewriter keyboard of the Friden Flexowriter* (the basic input-output unit). It produces output in the form of a printed document and punched paper tape or edge-punched cards. When required, it also controls auxiliary output units, such as tape- or card-punch machines. ■ Here is true automation, available now, at a practical cost within the range of even small companies. Let your local Friden Systems man show you how the Friden 6010 Electronic Computer can bring the benefits of automation to your company. Call him soon.

solid-state computer for business applications

Changing jobs on the Friden 6010 Electronic Computer is a simple matter. The operator removes one program panel and inserts another. It takes only a few seconds.

gram entered, (3) typewriter or punched tape input, (4) interface connections allowing expansion and/or incorporation into larger systems, and (5) ease of programming due to the use of common arithmetic language. Mr. French expected this machine, as well as similar ones being developed by Monroe, Olivetti, and Friden, to become a

Exhibit 9
MATHATRONICS, INC.

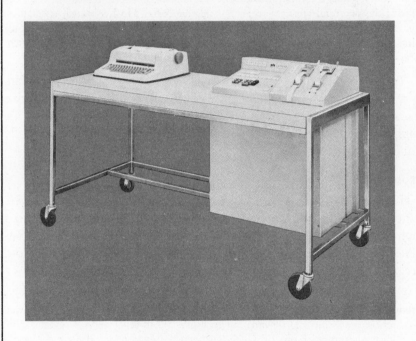

- *Low cost, versatile computer designed to be used directly by engineers*
- *Keyboard operation for rapid problem solving*
- *Internal program storage for solving more complex problems*

more significant competitive factor as the basic Mathatron system was expanded. He said:

Within six months we will have, in addition to a typewriter printer and an expanded memory to be added this fall (1964), compatible interface connections and punched taped input and output. This will raise the upper end of our price range to $11,000.

In regard to the large computer manufacturers, Mr. French believed that the team concept of selling utilized by the large computer companies would delay their entry into the market. He explained as follows:

> I think that if a large computer company tried to develop a similar machine, it would become apparent that they would have no market force available to sell it. The machine is too sophisticated for their typewriter salesmen and too inexpensive to support the team-selling approach used with their computer products. The large computer salesman is a coordinator. He makes the contacts, defines the potential application areas, and then brings in his branch specialists. Since $10,000 won't support group selling, you need one salesman who combines the technical, programming, and application skills you find in the branch. The typical typewriter or calculator salesman does not have these skills.

To the best of the company's knowledge, none of the large data system companies were within three years of introducing a competitive machine. It was the conclusion of all four men, however, that the company would face direct competition within 18 months from Wyle Laboratories and Friden.[4]

PRODUCTION

The first Mathatrons had sold for $3,500. However, because buyers continually requested an expanded number of storage registers, an eight-register machine at a price of $4,990 had become the basic unit. The ability to produce and sell the machine at that price was a function, according to Mr. Shapiro, of an "integrated design," and he added:

> Rather than wait for basic design to be solidified before worrying about production and packaging problems (the usual thing), we designed lower production costs into the system. For instance, the Mathatron has several hundred logic circuits, each one of which has been designed to use the same kind of transistor; that way we can safely order them in batches of 100,000. It is difficult to integrate design functions in a big company as by its very nature you have to break up and separate various design functions, and efforts at reintegrating these activities never seem to overcome the difficulties.

Mr. Shapiro also pointed out that a preconception as to how the machine would be serviced had also influenced the basic design from the beginning. As he stated:

> We want the maximum amount of maintenance to be performed in the field by relatively low-skilled personnel. Therefore, we made malfunctioning compo-

---

[4] See Exhibit 10 for a comparison of the Mathatron with the Friden, Sony, and Wyle machines.

nents easy to isolate and replace by the use of five large, interchangeable, plug-in subassemblies. Thus, the maintenance man need diagnose only one out of five malfunctioning subunits rather than one out of 100 or 1,000 subunits.

Because several production techniques were unique to the industry, Mr. Reach believed there was as much innovation in the packaging and production of the machine as there was in its concept of application. He noted:

Low cost has not typically been a consideration in this industry. As a result, production costs have skyrocketed due to (1) the necessity of integrating on the production line the "pet" design concepts of several small research groups, and (2) the production engineer's ability to get involved in the overall design until it is already solidified.

Because of specialized design and production procedures, the cost of the Mathatron was substantially lower than it would have been using

Exhibit 10

MATHATRONICS, INC.

Comparative Summary

	Mathatron	Friden 130	Sony	Wyle Scientific
Selling price.............	$3,490	$1,900	Approx. $1,000	$3,950
Keyboard type............	10 key	10 key	10 key	10 key
Number of digits of entry (listing columns)	9 plus exponent	13	10	24
Number of digits of total (totaling column)	9 plus exponent	13	...	24
Output.................	Printer (serial)	Cathode ray tube	Neon character tube—1 tube per digit	Cathode ray tube (like TV tube)
Individual subtotals and grand totals..........	Yes	Yes	Yes	Yes
Multiplication...........	Automatic	Automatic	Automatic	Automatic
Division.................	Automatic	Automatic	Automatic	Automatic
Cumulative multiply.......	Yes	Yes	Yes	Yes
Square root..............	Yes	No	No	Yes
Storage registers..........	4	1 plus 2 ltd. access	1	3
Program memory..........	24–48 steps	None	None	None
Electronic interface........	Yes	No data	No data	Yes
Transfer between registers...	Complete	Limited	Limited	Complete
Delivery.................	Immediate	Limited distribution	No data	July, 1964
Decimal point............	Automatic/floating point	Adjustable fixed point	No data	Adjustable
Size (inches).............	25 × 21½ × 13	c.20 × 22 × 9	20 × 20 × 8	20 × 22 × 1
Weight (pounds)..........	75	40	No data	50

Source: Mathatronics, Inc.

conventional design and procedures. Mr. Shapiro estimated that the machine would cost two to three times more if it had been designed and produced by conventional methods.

Mathatronics was located in a portion of the old Waltham Watch plant. The production area covered about 4,000 square feet, a large portion of which was used for inventory and test facilities. Except for the foreman and one mechanic, all production personnel were women. Conventional production procedure was for the computer to be wired almost entirely by hand. However, the Mathatron was wired almost entirely by semiautomatic methods which Mr. Shapiro felt to be several times more efficient than the best hand methods. Although a computer could be wired completely by machine, such wiring required several structural changes to be made in its physical design. A wiring machine cost approximately $45,000 and was considered to be about three times faster than the best hand methods, and better than the methods presently being used by Mathatronics. Mr. Shapiro estimated that the use of machine wiring would not be feasible for Mathatronics until their volume approached 200 machines per month. "Then it would be sensible to invest, say, $90,000 in machine wiring."

Partly in an effort to keep overhead as low as possible, but primarily as a result of "novel" production procedures, less than $5,000 had been invested in production tooling by July of 1964. At that time one girl required six working days to wire a machine. Mr. Shapiro indicated he would be able to reduce this to three to four working days by the use of better layout and fixtures, work flow procedures, etc. He said:

At first I didn't have the time to take advantage of these efficiencies, as our priority was just to get the machines out the door. Now we are concentrating on steadying our production by building up our inventory of subassemblies, presently the cheapest way to level our production rate. As we have steadied our work flow and gotten the paper work squared away, I have begun to tighten up our methods and procedures. But, of course, you are always faced with the difficult question of "How do you do this without increasing overhead?"

In July of 1964, the production backlog stood at 90 days. The current rate of output was 20 machines per month. By September the production was expected to reach 40 machines per month and by the middle of 1965, 80 to 100 machines per month. To speed this buildup, Mr. Shapiro thought he might subcontract certain subassemblies. "However, I anticipate that by September our efficiency will be such that the cost of farming out our work will become unattractive to me. But I plan to do some of this in order to find a capable contractor who can help us in case of sudden peaks in our growth."

In June of 1964, Mathatronics exercised an option to lease a second-floor section of the building directly above their present facilities. The added space, 10,000 square feet, it was believed, would facilitate methods improvement which would eventually double efficiency, raising the existing production capacity to 140 machines per month. The new floor area was to be in use by September, but Mr. Shapiro didn't expect actual capacity to approach 140 machines per month until February, 1966.

PRODUCT DEVELOPMENT

Mr. Kahn, whose primary responsibility was system and application development, described the company's product development efforts as follows:

So far our development effort has been to design attachments, special pre-wired sequences, etc., thereby increasing our capacity and moving toward the provision of a total data-processing system.

Beyond the development of attachments, we have done some general thinking about what a new model of the Mathatron might look like. Our approach again has been to start from scratch and ask: "What would be the best and most needed machine we could build?" We still come up with something which is essentially a superimposure on the Mathatron. It would follow the same concept of ultimate simplicity by expanding on the language breakthrough of the Mathatron I.

Because the most serious competition was believed to be coming in from the "low end, not from the top," of the low-capacity data-processing market, Mathatronics planned to add as accessory units, a page printer, punch tape input-output, and expanded memory unit to its product line by January of 1965. The increased memory capacity would significantly extend the processing power of the Mathatron by allowing it to store longer problems and a large volume of data. This new capacity was expected to cut deeply into the abilities of the $20,000 computer. Mr. Kahn pointed out:

With these attachments the Mathatron will still not do everything the $20,000 machine will, but it will perform the less complicated things more easily, e.g., surveying calculations. The expanded system will again allow us to pursue another vacant segment of the computer market—that of the $5,000 to $10,000 range which in turn will reduce the impact of the increasing competition at the lower end of the market.

As for the development of new applications, the company had begun to rely increasingly on the distributors for this service, and he added:

There is a bit of limit on what you want to work out here at the factory. However, we do provide a basic backup to the distributor, but we encourage him to define the needs. For example, we just finished a complete statistical program which one of them asked for. We have also made it available to all our distributors.

FINANCE

By midsummer 1964, the sales of Mathatronics were running at an annual rate of 240 machines per year. While financial figures were not available publicly, the company had been profitable since the last quarter of 1963 and the company was experiencing a substantial inflow of cash from its operations as of July, 1964 (see Exhibits 11 and 12).

The three founders held an estimated 60% of the common stock.

Exhibit 11

MATHATRONICS, INC.

Sales—Expense Statement

(Total Sales = 100%)

	Jan. 31, 1963	Jan. 31, 1964	April 30, 1964	June 30, 1964
Income:				
Sales	35.40%	97.35%	94.87%	95.94%
Rental	64.60	2.65	5.13	4.06
Total	100.00%	100.00%	100.00%	100.00%
Cost of sales	...	83.85	51.23	56.48
Gross profit	...	16.15%	48.77%	43.52%
Selling expense	305.88*	26.60	15.16	16.27
General and administration	...	48.40	13.85	14.78
Operating profit or (loss)	...	(58.85)%	19.76%	12.47%
Interest income	...	1.44	0.02	0.68
Net profit or (loss)	(205.88)%†	(57.41)%	19.78%	13.15%

* Total expenses since incorporation.
† Capitalized as net development cost to be written off over five years on the basis of electronic computers sold.

Exhibit 12

MATHATRONICS, INC.

Index of Total Sales & Total Assets

(January 31, 1963 = 100)

	Jan. 31, 1963	Jan. 31, 1964	April 30, 1964*	Aug. 31, 1964
Total sales	100.0	493.83	453.00	1293.57
Total assets	100.0	241.14	258.49	432.17

* 1964 fiscal year started on January 1.

The initial stock offering of $250,000 had been supported by a small group of private investors who, for each share of $100 preferred stock purchased, could purchase an additional 20 shares of common at $1. The 2% preferred stock, nonvoting and noncumulative, was callable at any time at its par value. Mr. Reach explained that the use of preferred stock had grown, to a large extent, out of "our [the founders] concern for maintaining control." In June an additional $150,000 had been raised when the original investors exercised options they held on 6,000 shares of common stock at a price of $25 a share. The majority of these proceeds were to be used to finance the expansion of production facilities.

JULY, 1964

By midsummer 1964, Mathatronics employed 60 people. In June an assistant sales manager had been hired to allow Mr. French to concentrate on the development and strengthening of the distributor organization. Also the services of the public relations consultant had been retained on a nearly full-time basis. In addition to these two gentlemen, two engineers were employed to write new program applications. However, the major growth in employment had come from the addition of testers and production personnel.

During July, a California distributorship was established and the company did not renew its contract with its first distributor. Assigned the New England territory, the distributor, an office equipment representative, had sold only three machines in a year's time. As Mr. French put it:

He was reluctant to call on the scientific-engineering types because of his nontechnical background. His difficulty in selling business firms reaffirms my belief that the primary market for the basic model of the Mathatron is the scientific-engineering firm. Fortunately, this weakness has shown up in our own backyard, where we are best equipped to handle it.

THE FUTURE

As to the future, Mr. French commented as follows:

I don't see any broad, integrated, general business applications where the Mathatron system takes care of the firm's entire data-processing needs.

We will, however, grow into segmented, specialist applications, such as estimating, bond calculations, certain billing work, etc. This will be in the foreseeable future as we add the full page printer and punch tape input. Because payroll and inventory control requires large storage capacity and the ability to sort and update data, these applications are a little further off. In the meantime we have found a potential market in process controls. The machine capabilities are as unique in this area as they were in the calculating market.

A real problem, I anticipate, is to expand at a rate which will allow our distributors to grow in their capacities as our product line grows. The complexion of our distributors will be increasingly system oriented. . . . Of course, my biggest worry is an automobile accident involving Roy, Bill, or Dave.

Discussing the future, Mr. Reach said:

Our biggest problem to date has been a matter of customer education and a difficulty in getting on people's budgets. Far too many people think a $5,000 computer just can't exist. In this respect competition will be an assistance as it will help to develop the market.

Our strength has been that we are thoroughly experienced in the digital field and we have the imagination to develop practical innovations and market them. Our ability to combine these skills with no interdepartmental squabbling is a big advantage. In this regard we try to hire bright people who are relatively inexperienced, not having been conditioned to the tight departmental boundaries found in larger organizations. . . .

As to our long-range growth we plan to get into other sorts of computers. We will try to keep ahead of the state-of-the-art, be the innovators—at least at the smaller, low-cost system level.

APPENDIX: GLOSSARY OF TERMS

Automatic Decimal Point Placement—Indicates the machine's capacity to carry the decimal point throughout its calculations, placing it correctly in the printed solution. In contrast, the standard rotary calculator prints only the digital composition of the solution, the operator being required to determine manually the proper placement of the decimal point.

Interface Connection—An outlet built into the machine which allows a "plug-in" connection with another electronic system, e.g., an electronic measuring device or a large computer system, etc.

Learning Ability—The ability to store a formula or sequence of mathematical operation in the machine's memory unit so that the operator is not required to re-enter the formula each time he wants to use it.

Memory Capacity—A general term used to describe the ability to retain either formulas or numerical data.

Program—A term used to describe the sequence of machine operations required to solve a problem.

Prewired Program—Indicates a program wired permanently into the machine's memory unit so that a specific formula and group of constants can be brought into use by the operator simply turning a switch. An example of a commonly used prewired program would be a program for the calculation of square roots.

Storage Registers—The ability to store a group of digits, each register storing only one digit at a time. A constant in an equation would be stored in such a register to be used as needed.

Typewriter or Punched Tape Input—Automatic methods of entering programs or numbers into a computer. Typewriter or punched tape input performs the same function as punched cards. Because the operator is not required to enter data manually via the machine's keyboard, the speed with which programs and numerical data can be entered into the computer is greatly increased.

Biddle Printing Company

IN 1955 Joseph Stevenson acquired the Biddle Printing Company of Drexel, Pennsylvania, and brought Arthur Johnson into the management of the 73-year-old firm. Under Mr. Johnson's direction, first as general manager and later as president, the company initiated changes designed to return it to a profitable basis and improve its market position. Between 1956 and 1961 the company moved its printing and binding operations from the original multistory plant to a more efficient one-story facility, opened a branch plant in Illinois, and added an offset printing process to its letterpress operations. Sales during this period increased 38%.

Exhibit 1

BIDDLE PRINTING COMPANY

Earnings History, 1945–55

(Thousands of Dollars)

Year	Net Sales	Gross Profit	Profit before Tax	Profit after Tax
1945	$3,078	$ 760	$370	$133
1946	4,059	1,082	590	345
1947	5,031	1,212	589	339
1948	4,579	998	467	267
1949	4,636	839	299	166
1950	4,735	867	179	154
1951	4,995	944	305	134
1952	5,316	847	126	49
1953	6,411	1,032	221	115
1954	7,366	770	(113)	(59)
1955	7,749	733	(261)	(251)

In September, 1962, Mr. Johnson believed that it was time for the company to consolidate its gains and concentrate on some internal problems. Although profits had steadily increased since the change in ownership, the president was not satisfied with the company's profitability. "Our costs are too high. The percentage of after-tax profits to sales is

Exhibit 2

BIDDLE PRINTING COMPANY

Income Statement, 1956–61

(Thousands of Dollars)

	1961	1960	1959	1958	1957	1956
Composition sales	$ 1,460	$ 1,063	$ 963	$ 979	$ 995	$ 859
Printing sales	2,281	2,215	1,998	1,864	1,650	1,828
Binding sales	8,616	7,206	6,521	6,328	5,891	5,968
Miscellaneous (paper sales)	203	145	189	169	141	152
Total sales	$12,560	$10,629	$9,671	$9,340	$8,677	$8,807
Less sales discounts	114	94	86	86	79	81
Net sales	$12,446	$10,535	$9,585	$9,254	$8,598	$8,726
Cost of goods sold	10,066	8,464	7,974	7,829	7,438	7,069
Gross profit on sales	$ 2,380	$ 2,071	$1,611	$1,425	$1,160	$1,657
Less operating expenses:						
Shipping expense	243	258	232	204	226	238
Storage expense	197	168	174	147	136	180
Transportation expense	18	16	11	14	20	28
Selling expense	253	179	162	173	166	154
Administrative expense	568	524	464	376	396	295
Total expenses	$ 1,279	$ 1,145	$1,043	$ 914	$ 944	$ 895
Net income from operations	$ 1,101	$ 926	$ 568	$ 511	$ 216	$ 762
Less other expenses:						
Interest	135	85	81	99	103	69
Miscellaneous (net)	70	76	27	42	21	62
Income before federal tax	$ 896	$ 765	$ 460	$ 370	$ 92	$ 631
Provision for federal tax	469	404	230	189	36	335
Net income	$ 427	$ 361	$ 230	$ 181	$ 56	$ 296

the best test of management, and last year our rate was only 3.4%; it should be closer to 5% or 6%." He had given considerable thought to the company's operating problems, particularly to the problem of communications, which he believed to be a major source of the company's difficulties, and had asked a firm of management consultants to review the operations of the company and suggest improvements.

THE BOOK PRINTING AND PUBLISHING INDUSTRY

The U.S. Department of Commerce estimated the total 1961 consumer expenditure for books and maps at $1.7 billion, up 46% from 1958. It explained this increase as follows: "While purchases of almost every type of consumer product or service have some effect on the printing and publishing industries, expenditures for education are of special importance. Private expenditures for higher education rose 55% from 1958 to 1961; for elementary and secondary schooling, 43%.

Exhibit 3

BIDDLE PRINTING COMPANY

Balance Sheet, 1955–61

(Thousands of Dollars)

	1961	1960	1959	1958	1957	1956	1955
Assets							
Current assets:							
Cash	$ 604	$ 281	$ 336	$ 671	$ 361	$ 589	$ 365
Treasury bills	328	...	...	...	...	...	...
Accounts receivable	1,089	829	761	583	581	538	680
Income tax refund due	...	...	...	4	4	3	77
Inventory:							
Bound books	188	113	164	151	414	651	537
Work in process	1,156	1,516	969	803	921	979	895
Raw materials	333	362	266	253	278	333	294
Fuel	2	1	...	...	...	...	...
Total current assets	$3,700	$3,102	$2,496	$2,465	$2,559	$3,093	$2,848
Plant and equipment:							
Land	128	23	23	23	23	23	23
Buildings	1,970	1,423	1,397	1,396	1,394	841	839
Machinery and equipment	3,827	3,310	3,055	2,920	2,910	2,305	2,095
Leasehold improvements	83	3	...	...	...	...	...
Total	$6,008	$4,759	$4,475	$4,339	$4,327	$3,169	$2,957
Less accumulated depreciation	(2,480)	(2,209)	(1,972)	(1,842)	(1,567)	(1,402)	(1,243)
Net	$3,528	$2,550	$2,503	$2,497	$2,760	$1,767	$1,714
Construction in progress	282	268	...	...	...	290	...
Prepaid and deferred	182	122	124	124	98	70	83
Cash sur. value, life ins.	...	...	...	...	...	...	6
Total assets	$7,692	$6,042	$5,123	$5,086	$5,417	$5,220	$4,651
Liabilities							
Current liabilities:							
Notes payable, current	$ 702	$1,155	$ 852	$ 605	$ 852	$ 907	$1,139
Mortgage payable, current	114	...	...	...	...	...	...
Accounts payable	409	487	165	151	155	331	197
Accrued liabilities	426	383	290	247	255	280	278
Federal income tax payable	289	268	117	165	20	301	...
Total current liabilities	$1,940	$2,293	$1,424	$1,168	$1,282	$1,819	$1,614
Long-term debt:							
Mortgage payable	2,027	435	435	435	435	435	414
Notes payable	...	...	275	550	825	...	...
Reserve for plant replacement	...	667	667	667	667	667	669
Capital stock:							
6% preferred	220	220	220	220	220	220	220
Common	522	522	522	522	522	522	522
Retained earnings, 1/1	1,905	1,580	1,524	1,466	1,557	1,212	1,486
Profit for the year	427	361	230	181	56	296	(261)
Transfer of reserve	667	...	...	...	...	...	...
Dividends	(13)	(13)	(167)	(116)	(148)	(46)	(13)
Adjustments	(3)	(23)	(7)	(7)	1	95	...
Retained earnings, 12/31	$2,983	$1,905	$1,580	$1,524	$1,466	$1,557	$1,212
Total liabilities	$7,692	$6,042	$5,123	$5,086	$5,417	$5,220	$4,651

Total expenditures by federal, state, and local governments for education increased 28% during the same period."[1]

The book printers shared in this market. Although the publishers arranged for the writing, the marketing, and usually the purchase of paper for a book and some also did their own printing, most publishers engaged an independent printing company for the actual printing operations. The printers' share in the increased sale of books is indicated in the following Department of Commerce estimates of the value of shipments by printers for the years 1958 to 1961:

Value of Shipments[2]
(Thousands of Dollars)

Year	Book Printing	Bookbinding and Related Work
1958............	$422,907	$190,956
1959............	472,458	290,345
1960............	531,708	223,958
1961............	551,053	223,564

According to an industry source, in 1962 the bulk of book-printing work was done in 60 major plants and in 300 to 400 medium-size plants. The same source indicated that some significant changes were taking place within the industry:

For years, primarily a sheet-fed flat-bed letterpress, single-color printing field, book work in the past 15 years has seen a decided increase in color work, greater volume in offset, and more use of webs [and] rotary letterpress. . . . Together with this greater sophistication of the printing process has come an increased mechanization of the binding process so that manufacture, in some areas, is almost on a complete in-line basis. Most significant is the steady growth of the book market, spurred by general population growth, and increase in school enrollments, higher educational standards and requirements, increased leisure time and higher incomes.[3]

To appreciate these changes it is necessary to have some knowledge of the printing process. A flat-bed letterpress consisted of a reciprocating "bed" which held a plate of inked type. As the bed reached one end of the press, a single sheet of paper was fed onto the bed. As the bed moved under a large roller, the impression of the type was transferred to the paper. This process produced a high-quality product with vivid

---

[1] U.S. Department of Commerce, Business and Defense Services Administration, *Printing and Publishing Industry Report* (October, 1962), p. 1.

[2] *Ibid.*

[3] "Offset Spurs Expansion in Book Printing," *Printing Magazine* (July, 1962), p. 80.

colors but required extensive preparation of the bed ("make-ready time") and a relatively low printing speed. The rotary letterpress increased the printing speed by placing the plate of type on a revolving cylinder and drawing the paper under the cylinder. The offset printing process achieved the speed of the rotary press with less make-ready time by transferring the ink impression from the plate to a rubber-coated roller and then to the paper. The offset process also replaced the heavy relief plate of the letterpress with a lightweight plate produced by a photographic process. Offset plates were made by burning the image to be reproduced into a thin zinc and aluminum plate with an arc lamp; the plate held ink only on that portion that had been burned. Another innovation designed to increase the speed of printing was the introduction of web-fed presses whereby rolls of paper instead of precut sheets were fed into the presses. Up to 1,200 feet of paper per minute could be printed by this process. Web printing was possible for book work with both offset and letterpress equipment but was used mostly with offset because of the reduced make-ready time of offset press plates.

Department of Commerce statistics[4] for the period 1947 to 1958 indicated that a significant change had taken place in the purchase of presses for the printing industry. In 1947, 66% of all press purchases were letterpress and 19% were offset. In 1958, however, only 45% of purchases were letterpress while 36% were offset. Proponents of the letterpress pointed out, however, that letterpress printing was the standard of quality in the industry and in 1962 was used in the manufacture of 75% of all book work. When properly used it offered:

economy, control, quality, fidelity, and flexibility. The future of letterpress has never looked brighter. Contrary to general belief, progress in lithography (offset process) has actually slowed down in the face of the new frontiers of the letterpress industry, which include improvements of letterpress equipment, new methods in typesetting, improvements in inks and paper, better and faster engravings, lighter plates, better electrotypes (typesetting machines), new kinds of relief printing plates, greater speeds in original and duplicate plate making, better make-ready procedures (preparation of the press for printing), new sheet-fed rotary presses, web-fed letterpresses, and other improvements in every department of today's letterpress plant.[5]

BIDDLE AND THE TEXTBOOK MARKET

The Biddle Printing Company was one of the oldest and largest printers of high-quality bound books in the United States. Eighty-five

---

[4] U.S. Department of Commerce, Business and Defense Services Administration, op. cit.

[5] A. R. Tommasini, "Letterpress Is in a Climate of Change," *Inland Printer/American Lithographer* (December, 1962), p. 56.

per cent of its sales were in the elementary and high school textbook market, with Bibles, hymnals, and "trade work" (bound books for sale through book stores) comprising the remainder of its sales. Biddle executives found it difficult to compare their operations with those of the company's competitors because the competition's sales mix included a smaller proportion of work in the textbook field.

The book printing industry was divided into three segments: composition, press work, and binding. Biddle performed all three operations: it set type and made printing plates from the publishers' manuscripts, printed the pages on its letterpress or offset presses, and bound the pages into book form. Ten other integrated printers provided most of the competition for the textbook business. Biddle was larger than most of these companies but only half the size of its major competitor.

Each segment of the printing industry presented a different competitive situation. The integrated printers competed actively for composition work because an order to compose a book was usually followed by orders for printing and binding. The composition portion of the market was the most competitive and the least profitable.

Specialty printers and commercial printers competed with the integrated printers for pressroom work. Although the specialty printers offered competitive prices, the quality of printing was an important competitive factor to the textbook publishers, and the book printers generally excelled in this area. The equipment capabilities of the printers also affected pressroom competition. Although Biddle was the largest printer of high school texts, its lack of offset printing capabilities prior to 1961 hampered its efforts in the elementary textbook field.

As with other integrated printers, over 70% of Biddle's press work involved reprints. The average textbook series was expected to have a seven-year life, with peak sales in the fifth year. The actual number of books printed depended, of course, upon the demand; most textbooks were printed once a year, with delivery scheduled for the opening of the school year in September, but a few books underwent two printings a year. Although orders for reprinting and rebinding were not automatic and in some cases were based upon competitive bid, the company that had done the original printing and had stored the printing plates generally received reorders. Biddle stored plates for 1,200 books at no charge to the publisher in order to obtain this reprint business.

Binding was the largest and most profitable of Biddle's operations. Before the company acquired offset equipment, 30% of the binding work had come from outside printers, but in 1962 Biddle supplied the bindery with 80% of its work. Traditionally composition, press work, and binding orders had been obtained by separate bids on each book, but in the late 1950's binderies began entering into long-term commitments; Biddle had two long-term binding agreements, including a 10-year contract with a major educational publisher.

The book printing companies solicited the business of over 700 publishers ranging in size from small marginal firms to companies with over $1 million in sales. Some publishers were known as "price houses" and based their orders predominantly on competitive bids, while other publishers considered quality and service paramount. The type of book greatly influenced the selection of the printer. The publication of a textbook series covering six or eight school grades and including teaching guides represented an investment of $400,000 to $1 million prior to printing. Textbook publishers therefore placed great emphasis upon quality and service in order to protect their investment. Similarly, difficult composition work (e.g., mathematics) was likely to be given to Biddle or other printers with proven ability in this field.

It was not unusual for publishers desiring quality work to develop strong loyalties to certain printers. Biddle sought loyal business rather than business based upon price alone, for the executives felt that "price business" could be lost as easily as it could be gained. Three of Biddle's accounts indicated the nature of the loyalty within the industry. One had been a customer since the founding of the company in 1882. Another had been helped through a period of financial difficulties in the 1920's by Biddle and, although managements had changed, remained a loyal customer. Biddle salesmen had called on a newer customer for three years before being allowed to bid on a job and for another two years before a bid was accepted. A publisher who had developed a satisfactory working relationship with a group of printers over a period of years was not inclined to try others. Although Biddle executives were concerned by the decline of orders from one publisher, the company had never lost a major account.

Mr. Johnson viewed the company as a "service organization" and believed that service was the most important factor in securing and maintaining sales. The quality of service depended to a large extent upon the degree of coordination of information between the publisher and the printer on the details of printing and scheduling deliveries. One Biddle account required 10 to 12 telephone calls a day to achieve this coordination. As an industry tradition the printers offered other services to the publishers, such as free storage of plates and bound books. In many cases the printer also acted as shipping agent for the publisher. In cases where Biddle obtained business on a competitive price basis, however, it did not provide free book storage or shipping.

HISTORY

Mr. Douglas N. Biddle had founded the Biddle Printing Company in 1882 as a book bindery. In 1897 he moved the company from Philadelphia to its present location in Drexel, Pennsylvania, where its operations were expanded to include press work and composition as well as binding. During the 1890's Mr. Biddle added a textile department to manufacture cloth for his book bindings.

In 1913 the company was incorporated under the laws of Pennsylvania, with Douglas Biddle owning the preferred stock and one fifth of the common stock. Three other executives of the company and one outsider held the remainder of the voting stock equally. As each of the original owners died, the stock was offered to executives of the company. By 1950 all the original owners had died and 12 Biddle executives owned most of the stock.

Upon Mr. Biddle's death in 1948 the presidency passed to Mr. Shore. Between 1948 and 1956 Mr. Shore dominated every aspect of the company's operations. His policy of binding books in long runs and billing as books were shipped resulted in large printing inventories. Under his iron hand both morale and profits decreased and cash was unavailable for necessary improvements.

By 1955 the need for cash became urgent. At that time nine of the 12 owners were over 60 and wanted to transfer their holdings into more marketable securities. An agreement was reached whereby Mr. Joseph Stevenson purchased all the common stock and provided the company with security for up to $2 million in loans. Mr. Stevenson had been a close friend of Mr. Biddle and had originally managed the company's textile department adjacent to the Biddle plant. In 1918 he had purchased that department from the company and built it into a profitable textile operation. After the purchase Mr. Stevenson maintained a close interest in Biddle operations but did not actively participate in its management. Upon his death in 1958 his stock was placed in trust for his widow, with Mrs. Stevenson, the Biddle Printing counsel, and Sam Warren, a vice president of his mill, as trustees.

Through the security provided by Mr. Stevenson, the company was able to extend its short-term borrowings. It also took other steps to improve its cash position. It billed large portions of its inventory and instituted a policy of producing in advance of orders only if the publisher was willing to finance the inventory. Because of the policy change the company recorded a large profit in 1956. In January, 1957, it negotiated an agreement with three Philadelphia banks for a loan of $1 million and postponement of the principal payment on the 1954 mortgage until the bank notes had been paid.

The $1 million loan was used to build and equip a printing plant in Peoria, Illinois. The executives felt that the company would obtain several competitive advantages from extending its operations into the Midwest: it would be in a better position to compete for business in the Chicago area and would save shipping charges. Furthermore, the Peoria area had suffered from unemployment and its labor force was younger and more energetic than the highly unionized local labor force.

Upon acquisition of the Biddle stock by the Stevenson interests, the president of the company resigned and the purchasing agent held the presidency until his retirement in 1958, when Mr. Johnson became president. Mr. Johnson continued the modernization effort which he had instituted with his predecessor. In 1961 the company refinanced its mortgage and negotiated an additional $2 million, 15-year mortgage which restricted dividend payments. Some of this money was used to build a warehouse for the Peoria plant and to purchase an additional 120 acres of land at the warehouse site. Most of the money, however, was spent on improving the Drexel production facilities. The adjacent Stevenson mill building was taken over for the Biddle operations, the printing and binding facilities were spread out over the one-floor plant, and some new equipment was purchased.

In 1960, Mr. Johnson learned through a customer that the New Haven Printing Company was contemplating a merger or sale of its assets. The New Haven Printing Company specialized in the "cheap printing" field, such as catalogues and telephone directories. It had been one of the first printers to enter the less costly offset printing market, an area in which Biddle had not competed. Although its early entry into the market had been impressive, union difficulties and increasing competition had subsequently made its offset operations less attractive.

Through Mr. Johnson's efforts the owners of the two companies reached an agreement to establish a holding company and issue shares in exchange for the voting stock of both companies. Since the two companies had been approximately equal in size and profitability, ownership and management of the holding company were shared equally between the owners of the former companies. Mr. Johnson became chairman of the board, and the president of the New Haven company was elected president. The other four seats on the board were allotted to the ownership interests, with Arnold Stevenson and John Smith (Biddle's lawyer and a trustee of the Stevenson estate) representing the Biddle owners. As part of the original negotiations Biddle had purchased New Haven's offset printing and photoengraving equipment and transferred this operation to the Drexel plant. This was the only operating change brought about by the merger.

Mr. Johnson described the activities of the holding company directors as an amicable "thinking together" on problems. The operations of the two companies were completely autonomous and were left to the discretion of the individual managements. In the summer of 1962 the directors were investigating means of securing additional equity capital. One of the New Haven representatives with investment experience believed that a company should have $40 million in sales before seeking equity financing, so urged another merger. One possibility was a commercial printing company with approximately $18 million in sales. Although there would be no operating advantages to such a merger, the New Haven representative believed the combined companies might prove more attractive to potential investors and allow Biddle to replace its debt with equity.

TOP MANAGEMENT

In managing the operations of the company Mr. Johnson sought "total agreement," if possible. He commented:

> There's no sense running a business as a one-man show when it's this size; it should be run with unanimity. Of course there are times when a decision must be made, but I try to talk it over with the others and reach an understanding first. For instance, recently I disagreed with the way that Sam Norman (manager of the Peoria plant) intended to handle a labor problem. Jim Pettibone (general manager) was on the fence about the matter. I talked to Jim for several hours and finally got him to agree with me before telling Sam to handle it differently. There has been only one direct conflict since I've been here when I was forced to tell a man that he had to do things my way.

Mr. Johnson sought to obtain "unanimity" through personal contact with the other Biddle executives. He worked closely with Jim Pettibone (general manager), Lee Herron (sales manager), and Jim Campbell (assistant to the president), both individually and as a group. He made frequent unannounced visits to their offices to discuss current problems. All four were familiar with the overall problems of the company and had some experience in both the manufacturing and sales areas.

These four also comprised an informal management committee which met as necessary to discuss major problems and plans. Although these meetings were held irregularly and had no formal agenda, the individuals were aware of the issues to be discussed and usually were in basic agreement. The meetings therefore usually served to work out the details of a decision. In addition to the four top executives, Mr. Johnson also sought the agreement of others in the organization. The meetings often included two of the salesmen with particular interests in the company's affairs; one was in charge of the company's largest account and the other was a son of the owner.

President Johnson. Mr. Johnson, an articulate and energetic man in his late forties, had joined the Biddle Printing Company as general manager in 1955 and had advanced to the presidency three years later upon the retirement of the interim president. In discussing his decision to join Biddle he said that he was intrigued by the challenge.

I'm the type that always wants to buy the broken-down house and fix it up. Before I came here top management had not been truthful with its customers. Prices had been secretly broken by one man and the company had made promises which it could not fulfill. The company had been run by one man who made all the decisions. We had to tell one customer that we were sorry but we would not be able to print his series; that's difficult, because in this business it takes a long time to mend your fences.

Now when we have a problem such as our recent price increase we all work together. We had a meeting of the top executives with Roy Meyers (the salesman handling the company's largest account) and worked out the details of the price changes. Perhaps when the company was smaller it could be run as a one-man show, but I think that we can get as much done by working together and persuading rather than telling somebody to do something. I know that Jim Pettibone doesn't feel as strongly about this as I do.

I feel that there is a continuous challenge here in getting the people together to resolve problems, dealing with personality differences, and spreading "the word" throughout the organization. Communications is still our biggest problem. Also we still aren't as profitable as we should be; we have a large debt to retire, and we would like to revive one of the major accounts that has slipped in the last several years.

It was Mr. Johnson's practice to spend much of his time out of his office. He toured the plant daily to "let the men know that I am on the job." Although he reviewed the machine loading schedule prepared by the planning department, he believed that he could get as good a picture of the status of operations by seeing the amount of in-process inventory awaiting binding and the amount of activity in the pressroom. He conferred with the other executives frequently and listened to the middle management people, but refrained from interfering with Jim Petti-bone's handling of manufacturing problems. In these contacts he made an effort to "show that what is being done well is appreciated."

Prior to January, 1962, much of Mr. Johnson's time had been spent in handling the company's largest account, but following a manage-ment consultants' report this account was turned over to a salesman. As the president said: "I knew I should give it up but I liked the detail of handling the account. The only selling that I do now is indirect selling." After giving up the account he still devoted over half of his time to problems in the sales area with the remainder devoted to manufacturing problems. The consultants had recommended that he withdraw from the details of the business and devote more time to planning and making policy. Mr. Johnson said:

I seldom make policy—policies are made by circumstances. In labor relations you don't sit back and make policy; you solve a problem and that becomes your policy. The other day a customer called me about a sales problem. I turned it over to our salesman for a reply to his counterpart. You could say I made a policy of having salesmen handle customer problems down the line rather than handling them myself, but I acted only to solve a particular problem.

Mr. Johnson believed, however, that the management consultants had been useful. "In general the consultants' report is good because it is not too extreme. We knew about the problems and have done many of the things that they suggested." The major problems mentioned in the November, 1961, report were low profitability in the composition and printing departments at Drexel, excessive shortages in finished orders, a sharp seasonal sales decline during the fourth quarter of every year, and inadequate methods study and cost information. The company imple-mented most of the organizational suggestions: it reorganized the general manager's duties, hired an industrial engineer, created the posi-tion of sales service manager, and started a management training pro-gram to improve middle management abilities. Two men had com-pleted this training program by August, 1962, and were working in the sales department. The officers also started releasing cost and profit information to the superintendents in order to help them develop their management skills.

Weaknesses in middle management were a concern to both the consultants and Mr. Johnson. Since 1955, 10 of the 12 executives who had owned stock had retired and other personnel changes had occurred.

Part of our problem is a lack of experience. The people in central planning don't fully realize what it's like to deal with customers. They all need one to three more years of experience. We have an annual review of salaried people where competent work is rewarded. When the middle management people were owners, the salaries were low, but we have been adjusting that since 1956, and now junior officers get reasonable salaries.

General Manager—Mr. Pettibone. Jim Pettibone, vice president, general manager, and treasurer, had joined Biddle in 1924 as a cost accountant. In 1955 a management consultants' report suggested that a central planning department be created to schedule manufacturing operations and coordinate them with the sales department. Mr. Pettibone organized the department and ran it as production manager until 1958, when he succeeded Mr. Johnson as general manager.

Prior to January, 1962, Mr. Pettibone had directly supervised the production department superintendents as well as the controller, chief purchasing agent, and production manager (scheduler). Upon the recommendation of the management consultants the position of manufacturing manager was created in January, 1962, to relieve Mr. Pettibone of direct supervision of manufacturing operations. Later the new industrial engineer was added to Mr. Pettibone's staff. Eventually it was hoped that the new manufacturing manager would take over supervision of the industrial engineer and the superintendent of shipping.

Mr. Pettibone explained:

The job of treasurer is rather nominal. I do review the contracts and cash statements and discuss investments with Mr. Warren (trustee and director) at Stevenson mills before we go ahead.

Most of my job consists of handling a fire a day. Scheduling is a problem because of the seasonal nature of the business. Out of 430 people in the binding department we will have to lay off 80 to 90 in November and hire them back in January. Most of the women will come back, but the 30 to 40 man are hard to replace. We cannot keep the people we want, and the ones we get are erratic and have a high rate of absenteeism. The absenteeism is so high that we have hired 60 girls to operate 56 jobs on the binding machines.

Now I also have an account. Dick Corpus (controller) worked with another fellow who went to work for a publisher. He asked if we intended to bid on a small encyclopedia to be sold through supermarkets. Dick and I went to see them and I found myself as a salesman. Now I'm so far into it that I can't get out. Our goal of operation is to get enough diversification to eliminate the slump in the fall quarter. Then I can settle back to manufacturing books.

Mr. Pettibone had also directed the introduction of offset printing. He believed that the company had to go into offset work because it was cheaper than letterpress. Jobs requiring up to 42 hours of preparation on a letterpress could be set up in four to six hours on an offset press. He believed that the more vivid reproductions of letterpress no longer outweighed the cost difference for most publishers.

Storage also presented a problem. Although the company had expanded its floor space from 430,000 to 560,000 square feet during the previous five years, 60% to 70% of the additional space was needed for storage, and operations were still overcrowded. Mr. Pettibone and Mr. Johnson had worked together to try to find additional warehousing space.

Since both Tod Ciro (production manager) and Bud Holman (manufacturing manager) were new in their jobs, Mr. Pettibone spent much of his time working with them informally. He stated:

> The work with Tod consists of reviewing his schedules and going over his problems more than anything else. He reports any cases of serious overtime or of presses sold out and we try to work out the problem. He is new and needs a lot of guidance.
>
> Bud used to be production manager and is now manufacturing manager. The sales and manufacturing people still come to me with problems because I am more conversant with most areas than Bud. Being an eager beaver I often give answers that I probably should refer to him. Bud still lacks aggressiveness; he still sends notes when he should come in here and press me for a decision. His present project is to get together the details for our 1963 machine program. I know he will ask for three times what we can afford.
>
> I'm also working on a plan with Dick Corpus to get our standards and estimating on IBM. Now I spend a great deal of time with sales, reviewing the prices and estimates of special situations and customers. We proposed the plan several years ago, but sales didn't think they could work with it. Dick has been doing the arithmetic for us on it for the last six months. It's very complicated and we seem to get halfway through when some fire takes place.
>
> Communications are also a problem. Perhaps we have been too informal. Last year our presses were sold out and we gave a book to a neighboring printer. He did a poor job and the customer objected. Yet this year we sent the same job to the same man and got back work that was as bad as the previous work. I asked Bud to investigate, and Bud said that the salesman claims he checked with manufacturing and that they approved the printing plans. Sometimes when these things are done informally it leads to problems.
>
> We have also had a problem since the new position of sales service manager was created. The sales service manager interposes one more person between manufacturing and the customer. The problem lies in the habits of the salesmen and to some extent in the individual selected for the position. He has not been around long enought to know all the quick ways of getting something done around here. I wanted to get "dummies" out to my account. Going through channels I would never get my books.

Assistant to the President—Mr. Campbell. Mr. Campbell, secretary of the company, had joined Biddle Printing in 1925 and by 1955 had progressed to the position of works manager. Following the change in ownership he was transferred to the sales department in order to provide a continuity in Biddle's relations with several major accounts. In addition to his duties as a salesman he handled union negotiations for the printing industry in the region and through the informal "management committee" advised on problems throughout the company.

DEPARTMENTAL ORGANIZATION

Sales. In 1959 Mr. Johnson had created the position of sales manager to expand sales activities and achieve better coordination between the sales and production departments. He hired Mr. Lee Herron, an enthusiastic salesman in his late forties with previous experience in both publishing and printing companies, to fill the position. In addition to supervising a sales serviceman charged with resolving conflicts between customers' requirements and production capabilities, Mr. Herron directed the overall efforts of the salesmen, handled a major account, and solicited new business.

Biddle had about 90 accounts, of which 20 were small and unprofitable. Ten accounts represented most of the business, three of these providing 50% of the orders and one 30%. These accounts were serviced by nine salesmen (including Mr. Herron): six worked out of the home office, two worked from a branch office in New York, and one from a branch office in Chicago. The manager of the Peoria plant also acted as a salesman, but his efforts were confined mainly to one large account.

Both the New York and Chicago offices had been established in 1961 in an effort to increase sales. The Chicago office had developed one good account which had made it a profitable venture; the New York office had been less successful. It was staffed by one new salesman and a salesman from the New Haven Printing Company who specialized in offset printing. The new salesman had received orders from seven or eight small accounts but had not yet secured any really encouraging business. Mr. Johnson was less than enthusiastic about the New York branch but conceded that "one good account would make it pay." Mr. Herron was also displeased but believed that the branch must be maintained:

If we want to grow, we shouldn't discontinue the branch just because operations here don't show the profit that we want. The other big printers recognize the importance of New York; our major competitor even moved its office to New York, although its plant is in the South. If we give up because things are not going well, we will never grow.

The acquisition of New Haven's offset business offered the company an excellent opportunity to increase its sales. New Haven had been one of the first companies to enter the textbook market with offset equipment. Offset printing had been accepted by publishers as a desirable method of printing elementary school texts because it allowed for a gradual fading of the pictures into the page, a technique believed to be appealing to the young audience and not possible on letterpress equipment. When this belief first gained acceptance, New Haven had been in the pleasant position of being able to go to the publishers and tell them how much time they could allow for printing on their presses during the coming year. As offset printing became more readily available to the publishers, this advantage disappeared, but New Haven was able to keep 15 good accounts. As Mr. Herron explained:

We must prove our ability to print with offset equipment in order to retain this business. So far we have held 13 of the 15 accounts. These accounts don't come to us automatically. When I went to see one publisher, he said: "I suppose you think that you have our account now." Of course I told him that I didn't think anything of the kind but that I hoped he would consider us for his business. We had hoped to keep more of New Haven's technical people; we only have two of their salesmen and another man acting as a consultant. One of the salesmen is working in copy preparation and the other is in New York working with the New Haven accounts. Of the 10 best accounts, four are new to Biddle and have good possibilities of becoming very important to us. We also have an opportunity to strengthen our relations with the six publishers for whom we were doing letterpress work. These regular accounts have caused some conflict. The customers are a little irritated because both our regular salesmen and Mr. Duncan (the New Haven salesman) are calling on them and their efforts are overlapping. It would be better to leave the accounts with the regular salesmen and use Mr. Duncan as an expert on offset matters. I know the decision that I should make but it would hurt offset.

The offset work is important to us for another reason. We will have to learn to handle the offset problems before we can think about going into web-fed presses. Presently companies with web presses are able to undersell us on long runs, but right now web printing doesn't look like the competitive threat that it appeared to be a year ago. Web printing allows feeding, printing, and folding at high speeds of up to 1,200 feet of paper per minute. At that rate of speed large amounts of paper can be spoiled very quickly. So far the manufacturers have absorbed the paper spoilage, but actual operations have not given the anticipated savings. There are other problems with web printing; the sizes are not flexible, so each web press can produce book pages of only one size. We can go into web printing if we want for about $1 million, but what size should we buy? At that price we can't set up two web presses and we might not have the business for one without stealing business from our other presses. Besides this, the publishers are losing their enthusiasm. They find it difficult to move their plates from one printer to another because of the size problems.

In servicing an account each customer was the responsibility of one salesman. For major accounts the salesman visited the customer two or three days every other week. At that time everything in process was reviewed with the publisher's production manager and the other interested employees. This included the printing schedules, complaints, and shipping problems. Although the salesmen solicited orders for new books and reviewed the specifications with the publisher, actual estimates were developed by the departmental estimators in the office.

A sales secretary was also assigned to each customer to help service the account. The amount and type of work performed by the sales secretaries varied considerably. In the absence of a salesman the secretary acted as the representative of the publisher at the Biddle Printing Company and obtained information the publisher required relative to his work in process. These duties could include processing and checking quotations made by the estimators; recording orders from publishers and preparing the orders for composition, press work, and binding; maintaining records of plate locations, publishers' materials, and in-process inventories; reconciling inventory differences with publishers; checking and forwarding bills; and expediting the manufacture or shipment of orders.

In performing these duties the sales secretaries occasionally duplicated work done elsewhere in the organization. The central planning department was responsible for preparing orders and controlling inventory records of paper. The secretaries felt that their occasional order-writing, expediting, and record-keeping activities were necessary to insure the proper customer service for their particular clients and to eliminate errors which had sometimes occurred through poor record keeping in the central planning department.

Since 1957 retirements and terminations had eliminated all the salesmen who had worked for the company prior to 1955. The sales secretaries had provided a continuity with the accounts and had looked out for the best interests of their particular publishers. Of the 12 sales secretaries, half had been with the company for 10 to 35 years. Although it was conceded that they were sometimes difficult to work with, the more experienced secretaries were recognized experts in expediting and handling manufacturing details and in achieving coordination with the publishers.

Mr. Herron was concerned because one of the girls was leaving:

She has been at Biddle for 20 years, and I hate to see her go, but I can understand why she is leaving. There is a lot of conflict around here and it's worse now than ever. Several weeks ago I took several of the older girls out for dinner, and after dinner we had a gripe session and brought a lot out into the open. A lot of the time "the secretaries" are blamed for the mistakes of a few of the younger girls, but most of the trouble comes from central planning. A lot of the difficulty over there is that they are undermanned, and information is very slow and often inaccurate when it reaches us. At one time they were 200 orders behind—that would take a week to process. On numerous books they have established a binding date which we would submit to the publisher. When the date arrives, they will say that the cloth isn't in. When we check it out, we find that the order sat in central planning for a week before it ever got to purchasing. This can be dangerous because occasionally a publisher will go to the textile mill in order to expedite the cloth, and if the publisher finds out that Biddle's sales department is using the lack of cloth as an excuse for being late while the Biddle purchasing department is a week late in ordering the cloth, we have jeopardized the account. Furthermore, they are inexperienced. Seven years is a short time to get the operation running smoothly, and the turnover they have had has made it worse. The bindery scheduler has only been there a year and the press scheduler is the former bindery scheduler. The plant is still able to give them answers that they shouldn't buy.

Mr. Herron hoped to have further meetings with the secretaries at some time when Bud Holman (manufacturing manager) could attend. In the meantime, until the problem could be solved in central planning, he was considering some changes in the sales department. One contemplated change was the establishment of a ranking system for sales secretaries, rating them as senior, account secretary, or trainee, which would allow for more rapid training and uniformity of operation.

Central Planning. The central planning department had been set up in 1955 to coordinate the flow of information between the sales department and the manufacturing facility. Prior to its formation, data on job specifications and inventory were not centrally located, and many jobs were scheduled by direct contact between the individual salesman and the foremen of the various manufacturing departments. The resulting conflicts and confusion led to the establishment of the department.

The department had been headed since January, 1962, by Tod Ciro, production manager. Mr. Ciro had joined the company in 1950 and had worked up through the foreman and general foreman ranks to central planning, where he served as bindery and then pressroom scheduler before becoming production manager. Under Mr. Ciro were the schedulers of the three production departments (composition, press, and bindery) and secretaries to handle the files and specifications analysis.

The major function of central planning was the scheduling of production. Mr. Ciro and the schedulers prepared a weekly master schedule for each of the departments which listed, by publisher, each order in the house. Utilizing the current information on machine breakdowns, inventory, and manpower, they set a delivery date for each order. The dates were contingent upon prompt return of proofs from the publisher and prompt delivery of paper stock from the publisher as well as timely performance within the production departments.

The department schedulers used the master schedule in preparing the detailed departmental schedules. Each department used Gantt charts to machine load the sequential operations over a period of several weeks. None of the schedulers used formal time standards because the company work was difficult to estimate and experience had proved more satisfactory and less costly than standards. The schedulers sent daily schedules to the foreman of each production area, indicating the individual machine jobs and loads for the next three days. The foremen returned daily "production status reports" to central planning. Manpower information was developed weekly from the planning schedules.

The central planning department also maintained perpetual inventory records and reviewed orders to determine purchase requirements. Paper was usually supplied by the publisher, and other materials were purchased as needed.

Within the organization the communication between the sales department and central planning was a constant source of problems. The central planning department claimed it was undermanned and found it difficult to keep up with the paper work beyond the scheduling function and impossible to follow up on schedule changes in manufacturing. The sales department complained that requests for printing and binding schedule changes were often ignored. Sales personnel also complained that they were not notified when dates were not met or schedules were changed. The sales secretaries were particularly concerned because publishers might not pay for changes unless they were notified when they occurred. Typing errors or incomplete orders originating in central planning also caused concern and delays. The resulting change orders initiated by the sales secretaries caused additional paper work throughout the organization.

The central planning personnel blamed manufacturing personnel for some of the confusion. The manufacturing department did not always report manufacturing changes or shortages. Often the shortages arose from inaccurate counts of the number of pages printed and were not recognized until the book was being bound.

Production. Bud Holman, manufacturing manager, was directly responsible for all production activities. The position of manufacturing manager was created in January, 1962, upon the recommendation of the management consultants to relieve the general manager of some of the operating details. Mr. Holman, an engineer in his late thirties, had been with the company for eight years and in charge of scheduling for four years prior to undertaking this new assignment.

In creating the position, Mr. Pettibone assigned to Mr. Holman the supervision of the superintendents of composing, press work, and binding but retained the supervision of shipping, accounting, engineering, and purchasing. Some of these activities might later be assigned to Mr. Holman after the manufacturing operations had been brought under control.

The two men occupied adjoining offices and worked closely together on manufacturing problems. Mr. Holman made a point of informing the general manager in the course of their day-to-day contacts of important problems and manufacturing changes. In addition he consulted Mr. Pettibone about important decisions such as equipment purchases. Some of his suggestions were presented to Mr. Pettibone in writing.

Bud Holman considered shortages the major manufacturing problem. During the printing process some printed pages were spoiled; the shortage of one signature (section of a book), of course, created a shortage for the entire order. These shortages were expensive; not only did they represent spoilage over and above standard allowances but they also required rework on a rush basis with the accompanying extra setup expense and disruption of the regular schedule. Furthermore, a shortage in one signature represented overages in other signatures and created additional storage and spoilage problems.

A consultants' study of 1961 orders by one major customer indicated the extent of the problem at Biddle. Of 306 orders processed, 179 were short, 99 were short by more than 50 books, and 14 were short by over 1,000 books. Although the shortage was only 2% of total books ordered, the shortages in many orders could strain customer relations and produce considerable rework. A 1% shortage was considered permissible, but in this sample 40% of the orders exceeded 1%, and 20% exceeded 3%.

Mr. Holman had devoted much of his time to trying to control shortages and believed that the problem had decreased substantially in recent months. He felt that it was the "perpetual problem of counts" which caused most of the problems. To alleviate this situation the company purchased a high-speed mechanical counter and assigned the industrial engineer to study the situation. Most of Mr. Holman's activity on this problem took the form of getting the bindery superintendent to report shortages more promptly. Previously the superintendent had held open the orders for three to six months after binding to look for lost signatures. By September, 1962, most orders were closed within two weeks of binding. Mr. Holman hoped that as the superintendents gained more experience the situation would continue to improve.

He believed that the company was not doing enough in other problem areas:

> In addition to the problem of count we should do more industrial engineering. We make an analysis of the machinery and overhaul or buy equipment as necessary, so the machines are in good condition, but we need a kitty for research. Presently nothing is budgeted for us to experiment with the equipment. There are 60 girls in the sewing department; perhaps the sewing can be mechanized. There is a machine on the market that we could buy for $2,000 to $3,000 and we might be able to tie it into the other equipment. We should be willing to try things like that. We also should think about putting the scheduling on IBM.
>
> We are also having a problem with the lines of organization, but that will work out with time. The superintendents are used to talking over their problems with Jim Pettibone and occasionally he will think of something and call a superintendent without telling me.

In addition to the daily telephone contact with the superintendents, Mr. Holman held weekly meetings with the production manager, plant engineer, and superintendents. Each meeting centered upon a specific preannounced topic, such as safety, cost control, etc., but other problems and company policies were also discussed.

Bud Holman said that he supervised each man differently according to his personality. He explained that the composition department foreman was a soft-spoken thinker and able administrator with 20 years' experience. The pressroom foreman was "rough talking and bull-headed" with but two years' experience as superintendent. The bindery superintendent had the most potential; he was highly analytical. Although he had had but one year's experience, he ran a tight department. Each of the superintendents had an assistant. All, he thought, were competent, with the composition assistant the best of the group. He added, however:

> Beyond that we are very weak. Most of the workers don't seem to want to advance. A working foreman gets an additional 25 cents an hour, and most think that the extra pay isn't worth the extra effort. We have tried to make the supervisory jobs more attractive by giving the bindery foreman membership in a

local trade association and providing foreman training by a college professor, but the results have not been good.

Composition. The composition department accounted for less than 12% of Biddle's sales and none of its profit, as shown in Exhibit 4. As the first step in the production process, composing attracted business for the sometimes profitable printing operation and the more profitable binding operation. The "foundry" or platemaking section of the composing department was responsible for this loss. The 20% to 25% loss on foundry sales offset the small gross profit realized in the rest of the department.

Exhibit 4

BIDDLE PRINTING COMPANY

Gross Profit as a Percentage of Sales

	1959	1960	1961	Average of 28 Firms (1960)
Drexel				
Composing	6.2%	5.4%	2.4%	14.8%
Platemaking	(19.8)	(21.6)	(26.4)	4.7
Pressroom	11.1	12.7	4.0	19.0
Bindery	20.2	22.7	21.3	18.2
Peoria				
Pressroom	24.8	37.6	36.0	. . .
Bindery	19.6	27.4	31.4	. . .

Source: Consultants' report.

Bud Holman did not think that composing had to be unprofitable. "People say that they expect it to be unprofitable, so it makes a loss." He believed that the reasons for the unprofitable operations were both an industry problem and a company problem. Most companies used their composing facilities to bring in business, thereby keeping the price of composing work low. He did not believe, however, that a price rise would lose much business. He also thought that Biddle could employ better methods if it had more space available and had consequently suggested some changes which would provide this additional space. He hoped that the details could be worked out with the other departments by October, 1962.

The composition section operated on the lower two floors of the company's original four-story wooden-frame building, with the heavy equipment and galley storage on the lower floor. All orders followed the same production flow. Upon receipt, each order was routed according to the publisher's instruction to the monotype or linotype machines for setting lines of lead type. The type was then assembled into galleys (trays of type in proper sequence), proofread, corrected for errors, and reprinted as "galley proofs," which were sent to the publisher for approval. Biddle had no control over the two-month to 12-month delay awaiting publisher approval.

After return of the proofs, the company corrected the galleys, divided them into pages, added plates for pictures, and sent another set of proofs to the publisher for approval.

Because of the unpredictable delays and the variety of matter produced, estimating and scheduling composition work was difficult. The composition estimator was responsible to the sales manager. Although scheduling was initiated by central planning, the salesmen and sales secretaries maintained contact with the composition foreman to see that their particular orders were being given proper consideration.

Plate Making.   Plates for letterpress printing were made in the foundry adjacent to the composing area. When long runs were expected, an electroplating process was used to make metal electroplates, but a cheaper vinylplastic plate could be used for short runs. Simply stated, the manufacturing process consisted of making a matrix impression from the galley type and using this matrix as a form to mold the plastic or produce a metal plate through electrolysis. The matrix used for a plastic impression was stored for possible reuse. After electroplating, highly skilled craftsmen prepared the plates for use on the presses.

Press Work.   In 1961 the company leased the adjacent mill and moved its presses from the original four-story frame building occupied by Biddle in 1889 to the more spacious one-story layout. In addition to the original six rotary and 10 flat-bed presses the company now had the four rotary offset presses of the New Haven Printing Company.

The men working in the pressroom were predominantly older, skilled employees. When rotary presses were introduced, the union members with the highest seniority generally refused to accept the higher paying jobs on these presses, so the younger men now handled them. The pressmen's union was reluctant to change methods, so some featherbedding existed, but by changing job assignments the company believed it had reduced featherbedding to minor amounts.

Bindery.   The company's most profitable operation was the bindery. This was a highly mechanized operation except for the feeding of the machines and the sewing operation. Here the company was dependent upon semiskilled girls instead of the skilled labor of the other departments. During August, 1962, the bindery employed 518 people as contrasted with 144 in composition and 181 in the pressroom. Prompt layoff of unnecessary workers was considered the key to profitable bindery operation. Because of an unusual order for 100,000 copies of a trade book and another order for a small encyclopedia, however, management believed that layoffs in October, 1962, would not be so severe as in past years.

In 1961 the bindery was also moved to the new area. Because the mill retained its new office building in the center of its mill buildings, there was some inconvenience in moving materials from the presses to the binding area.

The bindery operations included gathering the individual signatures into book form, sewing the books, and adding the covers. Because the sewing operation required a large amount of labor, absenteeism often caused delays. The company tried to maintain a backlog of 400,000 to 500,000 printed sheets awaiting binding in order to facilitate scheduling in the bindery.

The Peoria Plant. The pressroom and the bindery operations at Peoria were about one fourth the size of the comparable operations in Drexel but produced higher gross profits (see Exhibit 4). Company officials attributed the higher profitability to the longer press and bindery runs in the Peoria plant. They believed that the quality of printing at Peoria had improved to a point where it was comparable to that at Drexel. Biddle executives stated that the company needed a gross profit of 12% to 13% to break even on each order and that this was difficult in bindery runs of less than 2,000 books.

Labor Relations. The company dealt with seven craft unions. Five of these bargained with the company directly, while two bargained on an industrywide basis. Mr. Campbell handled both the local negotiations and, as industry representative for the region, the industry negotiations. He felt that the company had a "very good union relationship —better than most." The relations had changed considerably since the 1920's when the company was in a power position and gave some thought to breaking the union. During the 1930's the company's considerate labor relations policy and the need to have the union label to sell textbooks in many states broke down the animosity between the management and the unions. Although management believed that it faced "tough unions with strong seniority and tried to be tough with them," most problems were worked out together. No grievances had gone to arbitration in recent years.

Although Mr. Johnson and Mr. Pettibone were generally satisfied with the union relationship, they believed that union regulations impeded technological changes. Mr. Johnson had suggested a pay plan for bindery workers based upon productivity. Although the plan was rejected, he believed that it made the union leaders think about productivity.

Accounting. Dick Corpus graduated from college in 1950 and joined Biddle in 1953 as cost accountant. In 1957 he was promoted to controller and charged with the supervision of the estimating and billing departments as well as cost and general accounting.

Mr. Corpus considered the estimating area the least satisfactory of the operations under his control. The accounting department was responsible for estimating in the bindery and pressroom. Estimating for composition work was under the direction of the sales department, while Mr. Pettibone personally supervised the estimating of offset printing work. The bindery and press-work estimating was based upon long-established scales. The scales in fact were so long established that no one could remember when they had been established or what basis had been used in developing them. It was evident, however, that they bore little relationship to the current actual production costs of the company. Price changes were made yearly by adding a percentage to the scale. Mr. Corpus had been working on an improved system for several years but did not yet have a system which satisfied him. One of the problems still confronting him was the handling of material costs under a uniform markup system since the publisher supplied the paper in some cases, while Biddle supplied the paper in other cases. In the few cases that Biddle tried to present the lowest competitive bid, the standard costs were used for estimating purposes. Low-price bidding was only used when the company had serious idle capacity; it accounted for less than 5% of sales.

The bindery and the pressroom were on a standard cost system. Daily and weekly cost variances were accumulated by job order. Reports of production variance, overtime, and job profitability were received weekly by the top executives and the superintendents. The breakdown of profitability by job and by customer was studied by all the executives. Because of the continued unprofitability of one account the company was attempting to drop a customer. This was being done gradually so as not to let the industry think "that we are kicking him out." Mr. Corpus felt that the reports were not well understood by the superintendents. For this reason the quantity and price variances were not separated. Mr.

Corpus discussed weekly with the supervisors the figures that were out of line.

Mr. Corpus also developed an annual budget, and the top management had developed detailed long-range budgets for presentation to banks to obtain loans. These budgets had proved fairly realistic.

FUTURE PLANS

Mr. Johnson was optimistic about the growth of the textbook market and expected the Biddle Printing Company to retain its share of the growing business. In addition he hoped that the company's limited success in the encyclopedia area would lead to more stable production with reduced costs.

Both Mr. Johnson and Mr. Pettibone were willing to enter the web-printing field as soon as the company could afford the million dollar investment. Mr. Pettibone believed that the combination of web-fed and letterpresses held great promise if a satisfactory low-relief plate could be developed. Although the company had no formal research project, Mr. Stevenson's son-in-law had been assigned to keep abreast of the latest developments and to coordinate the company's experiments in new printing techniques.

Although the owners might agree on a merger or on equity financing, Mr. Johnson did not believe that the changes would have any effect on the operations unless the company merged with a firm that had an established web process.

Colony Trucking Company

In 1957 Colony Trucking Company operated the largest transportation system of all motor "common" carriers domiciled in the New England states. In terms of revenues, it ranked second in the area in 1956 with an income close to $8 million (Exhibit 1). As of November, 1957, the company had 970 full-time employees, and assets just under $2 million (Exhibit 2).

Colony offered regular transportation services between the metropolitan areas of Boston, Springfield, Pawtucket, Newark, New York City, and New Haven; and between most of the cities and towns in Vermont, New Hampshire, and southern Maine. To service this area the company operated 23 terminals of which 13 were in Vermont and Maine, 6 in Massachusetts and New Hampshire, and one each in New York, Connecticut, Rhode Island, and New Jersey (Exhibit 3).

COMMON, CONTRACT, AND PRIVATE CARRIERS

As a common carrier, Colony offered its services to all shippers on an equal basis. In this respect it differed from "contract" carriers which were hired on an individual contract basis and which usually served only a few shippers. Both these types of "for hire" carriers in turn could be distinguished from "private" carriers which hauled only for the company to which the carrier belonged.

Of these three categories of trucking firms, private carriers operated by far the largest number of trucks, approximately 83% of the U.S. total in 1956. Since these carriers did not operate their trucks for revenue, the freight they hauled did not add to the industry's dollar volume, though it did add to the industry's ton-miles. Common carriers accounted for 93% of total 1953 industry revenue from intercity shipments, while contract carriers accounted for the remainder. All contract and common carriers together accounted for 33% of the total intercity ton-miles hauled by trucks in 1955.

For-hire carriers were further classified by commodities hauled. A "general commodity" carrier hauled all commodities except those it

186

Exhibit 1. COLONY TRUCKING COMPANY

Comparative Income Statements

Periods Ending December 31, 1948–56 and September 30, 1957

(Dollars in Thousands)

	1948	1949	1950	1951	1952	1953	1954	1955	1956	1957 January 1 to September 30
Net freight revenue	$2,197	$2,712	$3,387	$3,678	$4,886	$5,959	$6,607	$6,905	$8,143	$6,936
Operating expenses:										
Equipment maintenance and garage	367	509	621	573	829	1,042	910	1,000	959	736
Transportation	951	1,152	1,295	1,443	2,023	2,300	2,608	2,711*	3,730*	3,410*
Terminal	249	339	533	618	796	1,049	1,276	1,365	1,632	1,282
Traffic (sales, rating, and advertising)	48	59	86	100	136	167	212	204	238	169
Insurance and safety	139	163	182	207	268	359	360	431	490	331
Administrative and general	215	244	333	372	472	570	687	736	796	621
Total operating expenses	$1,970	$2,466	$3,050	$3,313	$4,524	$5,487	$6,053	$6,447	$7,845	$6,549
Profit before provision for depreciation	227	246	337	365	362	472	554	458	298	387
Less: Provision for depreciation	142	143	168	239	277	349	370	333	261	144
Operating profit	$ 85	$ 103	$ 169	$ 126	$ 85	$ 123	$ 184	$ 125	$ 37	$ 243
Add:										
Miscellaneous and extraordinary income credits	7	17	10	5	3	3	1	30	24	1
Gain on disposition of equipment			5	6	67	83	17	14	175	41
Total other income	$ 7	$ 17	$ 15	$ 11	$ 70	$ 86	$ 18	$ 44	$ 199	$ 42
Total operating profit and other income	92	120	184	137	155	209	202	169	236	285
Less: Other charges:										
Interest paid	17	12	14	22	25	25	36	32	21	8
Provision for bad debts	5	6	2	7	6	4	10	4	6	4
Donations	3	5	8	5	6	9	5	6	3	1
Officers' life insurance premiums	2	8	8	7	7	11	6	6	6	4
Miscellaneous charges		5†				5		2	9	9
Total other charges	$ 27	$ 36	$ 32	$ 41	$ 44	$ 54	$ 57	$ 50	$ 45	$ 26
Reserve for estimated expenses							68‡			
Profit before federal income taxes	65	84	152	96	111	155	77	119	191	259
Provision for income taxes	24	35	74	45	37	58	34	47	50	120
Net profit	$ 41	$ 49	$ 78	$ 51	$ 74	$ 97	$ 43	$ 72	$ 141	$ 139

* In 1955 equipment rental fees and purchased transportation costs amounted to $207 thousand; in 1956, to $907 thousand; in the first nine months of 1957, to $844 thousand.

† Loss on sale of equipment.

‡ Reserve for estimated expenses attributable to the year's operations but not properly chargeable to expense accounts. This procedure was allowable under provisions of the 1954 Internal Revenue Code which were subsequently changed.

Source: Company records.

Exhibit 1a. COLONY TRUCKING COMPANY

Comparative Income Statements

Periods Ending December 31, 1948–56 and September 30, 1957

(As % of Net Freight Revenue)

	1948	1949	1950	1951	1952	1953	1954	1955	1956	1957 January 1 to September 30
Net freight revenue	100.0	100.0	100.0	100.0	100.0	100.0	100.0	100.0	100.0	100.0
Operating expenses:										
Equipment maintenance and garage	16.7	18.7	18.4	15.6	16.9	17.5	13.8	14.5	11.8	10.6
Transportation	43.3	42.5	38.2	39.3	41.4	38.6	39.5	39.3*	45.8*	49.2*
Terminal	11.4	12.5	15.7	16.8	16.3	17.6	19.3	19.8	20.0	18.5
Traffic (sales, rating, and advertising)	2.2	2.2	2.5	2.7	2.8	2.8	3.2	3.0	2.9	2.4
Insurance and safety	6.3	6.0	5.4	5.6	5.5	6.0	5.4	6.2	6.0	4.8
Administrative and general	9.8	9.0	9.8	10.1	9.7	9.6	10.4	10.6	9.8	8.9
Total operating expenses	89.7	90.9	90.0	90.1	92.6	92.1	91.6	93.4	96.3	94.4
Profit before provision for depreciation	10.3	9.1	10.0	9.9	7.4	7.9	8.4	6.6	3.7	5.6
Less: Provision for depreciation	6.4	5.3	5.0	6.5	5.7	5.9	5.6	4.8	3.2	2.1
Operating profit	3.9	3.8	5.0	3.4	1.7	2.0	2.8	1.8	0.5	3.5
Add:										
Miscellaneous and extraordinary income credit		0.6	0.3	0.1	0.1	0.1	0.0	0.4	0.3	0.0
Gain on disposition of equipment	0.3		0.1	0.2	1.4	1.4	0.3	0.2	2.1	0.6
Total other income	0.3	0.6	0.4	0.3	1.5	1.5	0.3	0.6	2.4	0.6
Total operating profit and other income	4.2	4.4	5.4	3.7	3.2	3.5	3.1	2.4	2.9	4.1
Less: Other charges:										
Interest paid	0.8	0.4	0.4	0.6	0.5	0.4	0.5	0.5	0.3	0.1
Provision for bad debts	0.2	0.2	0.1	0.2	0.1	0.1	0.2	0.0	0.1	0.1
Donations	0.1	0.2	0.2	0.1	0.1	0.1	0.1	0.1	0.0	0.0
Officers' life insurance premiums	0.1	0.3	0.2	0.2	0.2	0.2	0.1	0.1	0.1	0.1
Miscellaneous charges		0.2†				0.1	···	0.0	0.1	0.1
Total other charges	1.2	1.3	0.9	1.1	0.9	0.9	0.9	0.7	0.6	0.4
Reserve for estimated expenses							1.0‡			
Profit before federal income taxes	3.0	3.1	4.5	2.6	2.3	2.6	1.2	1.7	2.3	3.7
Provision for income taxes	1.1	1.3	2.2	1.2	0.8	1.0	0.5	0.7	0.6	1.7
Net profit	1.9	1.8	2.3	1.4	1.5	1.6	0.7	1.0	1.7	2.0

* In 1955 equipment rental fees and purchased transportation costs amounted to $207 thousand; in 1956, to $907 thousand; in the first nine months of 1957, to $844 thousand.

† Loss on sale of equipment.

‡ Reserve for estimated expenses attributable to the year's operations but not properly chargeable to expense accounts. This procedure was allowable under provisions of the 1954 Internal Revenue Code which were subsequently changed.

Source: Prepared from Exhibit 2 by the Harvard Business School staff.

Exhibit 2

COLONY TRUCKING COMPANY

Comparative Balance Sheets as of December 31, 1948–56 and September 30, 1957, and Selected Ratios

(Dollars in Thousands)

Assets	1948	1949	1950	1951	1952	1953	1954	1955	1956	September 30, 1957
Current:										
Cash in Bank and on Hand	$ 45	$ 44	$ 98	$ 70	$ 15	$ 131	$ 347	$ 207	$ 143	$ 428
Receivables (Net)	197	210	284	382	322	571	595	465	451	677
Materials and Supplies	23	18	24	37	48	104	89	70	117	108
Guarantee Deposits	15	13	18	18	28	18	18	18	49	48
Cash Surrender Value of Officers' Life Insurance	6	10	16	24	33	44	55	66	76	86
Prepaid Items (Taxes, Insurance, Insurance Premiums, etc.)	18	39	50	88	148	136	108	64	84	83
Total Current Assets	$ 304	$ 334	$ 490	$ 520	$ 594	$1,004	$1,212	$ 890	$ 920	$1,430
Fixed Assets:										
Cost	1,001	1,086	1,421	1,810	2,202	2,489	2,599	2,645	2,193	1,906
Reserve for Depreciation	556	578	695	888	1,058	1,253	1,583	1,875	1,594	1,406
Net	$ 445	$ 508	$ 726	$ 922	$1,144	$1,236	$1,016	$ 770	$ 599	$ 500
Other Assets	....	....	....	....	....	21	27	2	28	29
Total Assets	749	842	1,216	1,442	1,738	2,261	2,255	1,662	1,547	1,959

Liabilities and Net Worth

Liabilities:	1948	1949	1950	1951	1952	1953	1954	1955	1956	September 30, 1957
Current:										
Notes Payable on Revenue Equipment	$ 182	$ 103	$ 151	$ 256	$ 320	$ 292	$ 322	$ 264	$ 14	$ 9
Notes Payable—Unsecured	12	2	....	....	8	14	40*	75*	....	136*
Accounts Payable	124	168	213	239	278	630	551	394	498	467
City, State, and Federal Taxes Accrued	71	79	133	122	160	219	220	133	151	276
Accrued Items:										
Payroll	24	24	50	36	50	48	106	68	91	102
Claims and Other	33	35	33	7	31	99	127	56	33	78
Total Current Liabilities	$ 446	$ 411	$ 580	$ 660	$ 847	$1,302	$1,366	$ 990	$ 787	$1,068

Exhibit 2—Continued

Liabilities and Net Worth	1948	1949	1950	1951	1952	1953	1954	1955	1956	September 30, 1957
Total Current Liabilities (from p. 189)	$ 446	$ 411	$ 580	$ 660	$ 847	$1,302	$1,366	$ 990	$ 787	$1,068
Long Term:										
Notes Payable on Revenue Equipment	100	187	314	409	441	418	310	71	18	10
Total Liabilities	$ 546	$ 598	$ 894	$1,069	$1,288	$1,720	$1,676	$1,061	$ 805	$1,078
Net Worth:										
Common Stock—1,500 Shares, $100 Par Value	150	150	150	150	150	150	150	150	150	150
Retained Earnings	53	94	172	223	300	391	429	451	592	731
Total Net Worth	$ 203	$ 244	$ 322	$ 373	$ 450	$ 541	$ 579	$ 601	$ 742	$ 881
Total Liabilities and Net Worth	$ 749	$ 842	$1,216	$1,442	$1,738	$2,261	$2,255	$1,662	$1,547	$1,959
Working capital	$ (142)	$ (77)	$ (90)	$ (140)	$ (253)	$ (298)	$ (154)	$ (100)	$ 133	$ 362
Current ratio	0.7:1	0.8:1	0.8:1	0.8:1	0.7:1	0.8:1	0.9:1	0.9:1	1.2:1	1.3:1
Fixed assets to total assets	59.4	60.3	59.7	63.9	65.8	54.7	45.1	46.3	38.7	25.5
% earned on net worth after taxes	20.2	20.1	24.2	13.7	16.4	17.9	7.4	12.0	19.0	15.8

* Borrowed from Colony Trucking Company Pension Trust Fund. Under existing income tax laws, pension trust payments were considered expenses even though fund reserves were borrowed by the company on an interest-free basis.

Source: Company records.

Exhibit 3

COLONY TRUCKING COMPANY

Territory Serviced and Approximate Locations of Terminals

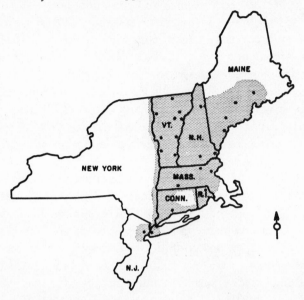

Dots represent locations of Colony terminals.
Shaded area roughly approximates the territories serviced by the company.
Source: Company records (outline sketched from American Automobile Association Highway Map).

specifically designated as excluded from its service. "Special commodity" carriers limited their services to enumerated commodities.

STATE AND FEDERAL REGULATION

Colony, in common with other truckers, operated in an industry that
was extensively regulated by both the states and the federal government. State regulation aimed primarily at achieving orderly traffic flow,
and was significant mainly in the areas of speed limits, driving practices, and size and weight limits for equipment. Variations among the
states' requirements have long posed a problem for interstate shippers,
whose equipment must conform to the most stringent regulations of
any state through which it is to pass. For example, even though a carrier hauled a load mostly through states which had legal weight limits
of 40,000 pounds or more, he could carry only 20,000 pounds if he
had to enter a state with that legal limit, unless, of course, he wished
to reload before reaching the state boundary.

Federal regulation affected all carriers engaged in interstate transportation and was administered by the Interstate Commerce Commission (ICC). It covered (1) rates, (2) rights to operate over traffic routes, (3) mergers, acquisitions, and consolidations, (4) stock issues in excess of $1 million, (5) insurance coverage, and (6) safety aspects including qualifications and maximum hours of service of employees, equipment safety, parts and accessories, and maintenance of equipment for all interstate motor carriers. Safety reports on each carrier were kept by the commission and were used to help determine the carrier's "fitness" to be granted the operating rights for which it might apply. Private carriers not competing commercially for freight movements were excluded from federal economic regulation but were still subject to the safety regulations.

Rate Regulation. Local rate bureaus, organized and operated under ICC supervision, provided the machinery through which rates were set or changed. Rates charged by common carriers might be of two types: (1) "class" rates to which commodities were assigned on the basis of such factors as density, susceptibility to damage, ease of loading, and ability of shippers to pay; and (2) "commodity" rates, which applied to the movement of a specific commodity between two designated points and were usually lower than the class rate that would otherwise apply. Requests for commodity rates most often came from carriers who wanted particular freight movements but could not take them away from competing forms of transportation without offering rates lower than the class rates. On a per-ton and/or per-mile basis, both class and commodity rates tended to vary inversely with size of load and length of haul.

Proposals for rate establishment or change were made by carriers to the local rate bureau, where they were subject to hearings at which shippers and other freight carriers often appeared to argue for or against them. A carrier proposing to lower his rates usually met opposition from other carriers who, if they did not follow suit, would stand to lose some of their traffic. Proposals for rate increases were often opposed by shippers whose transportation costs would be increased by the change. After the public hearings, the bureau decided whether or not it would approve a carrier's proposal or recommend a counterproposal. Although it had not been authoritatively adopted as a general policy, rate bureaus attempted to maintain class rate schedules which would allow the local carriers an operating profit close to 7% of operating revenues. (Since these rates were determined largely on the basis of average costs of all carriers in an area, however, there was considerable variability in profit performance.)

If the carrier was not satisfied with the bureau's decision, it could elect to give notice of independent action, after which the proposed rate was published for that individual carrier. This rate was then subject to further contest before the ICC, which had the regulatory power to approve or deny the rate or to set a different one.

Some of the tests used by the commission and its bureaus to judge the reasonableness of rate proposals were: the rates must be reasonably compensatory to the carrier so they will not "burden" other forms of transportation; they must be no lower than necessary to meet competition; and they must not be so high as to allow an unreasonable amount of profit. In order to quote a commodity rate, carriers usually had to prove before the regulatory agency that such factors as ease of loading and the frequency and stability of shipment that were associated with each movement made it economically justifiable to assign a commodity rate.

Rate regulation by the ICC varied between contract and common carriers. For the former it was limited to setting minimum rates, while for the latter the full and exact schedule of rates was regulated. In 1955 the ICC's power to set specific rates for common carriers (both truck and rail) was called in question by a special committee appointed by the President to examine existing federal transportation policy. In essence this committee charged that existing regulation was preventing adequate competition between the various means of transportation and that regulated carriers were losing out to unregulated carriers. One of the committee's major suggestions was to limit the ICC to setting maximum and minimum rates for common carriers rather than specific rates.

In supporting this change the railroads argued that existing ICC policy, which called for testing the effect of all rate proposals on the ability of other forms of transportation to compete, in effect allocated a portion of the total freight business to each type of carrier, and thus prevented real competition. In opposing the change, truckers argued that it would result in a return to the destructive competition which caused federal regulation in the first place. No legislation was passed.

Operating Rights. Under provisions of the Motor Carrier Act of 1935, which was aimed at curbing the extensive and sometimes violent competition existing in the early years of motor transport, common and contract carriers were required to obtain rights to operate over specific routes. Carriers in business before passage of the act were automatically granted rights to operate over their previously established routes under a so-called "grandfather clause." When applying for additional routes, contract carriers had to prove before the ICC that the addition of their services was "in the public interest," but common carriers had to prove such addition was "required by public convenience and necessity." Applications were frequently contested by competing truckers and other carriers serving the area.

While contract carriers generally were successful in proving a case for their applications, as the industry expanded it became increasingly difficult for common carriers to prove that their service over an applied-for route was required. As a result, by 1957 it was difficult for new firms to enter the common carrier business and for existing firms to extend their operations without purchasing or merging with companies already possessing the necessary rights.

COMPANY HISTORY

Robert Danson, president, age 59, founded Colony in 1921 by hauling milk from farms around Barton, Vermont. In the following year, George Danson, executive vice-president, age 51, joined his brother and immediately began to solicit new accounts. His efforts were successful, and by the end of 1927 the company had enough business to warrant operating a fleet of eight trucks. Headquarters had been removed from Barton to Barre, Vermont, where a large meat-packing customer was located.

In 1928 the brothers began delivering Barre products to a large retailer in Boston. They were unable, however, to obtain enough freight to fill their trucks for the return trips, and the major portion of their revenue resulted from freight hauled southward. In the early 1930's, the company was nearly bankrupted when a competing fleet owner operating primarily from Boston to Vermont began soliciting return business at rates reflecting only out-of-pocket costs.

In 1934 George Danson moved to Boston and aggressively solicited new accounts. He immediately rented terminal space in Cambridge, Massachusetts, and within a year freed Colony from overdue debts and increased its fleet from 12 to 18 trucks. The company's major operational base was moved to Cambridge, along with some of the management offices. By 1935, the major portion of Colony's revenue came from trips starting northward.

In an effort to use equipment more efficiently, George Danson began to concentrate on obtaining freight moving from northern New England to Boston. Before World War II, 11 new terminals were added. Through the acquisition in 1937 of a small company with operating rights in southern Maine and a terminal in Portland, the company acquired a triangular transportation network, which significantly increased its flexibility in equipment scheduling.

In 1946 George Danson began what he described as "our ten years of significant expansion." During the first four of these years the expansion was accomplished by extending operations to all previously unserviced points within the system. In 1950 Colony purchased the operating rights of a defunct company to routes connecting Boston and Springfield, Massachusetts, with New York City. This purchase was not approved by the ICC until 1955. According to George Danson, motor carriers operating in the New York area contested it extensively, charging that Colony was "too aggressive" a competitor. "The rights were purchased for $75,000," stated George, "and it cost us just about that much to go through the legal process." The company was allowed, however, to service the routes during the litigation and, by the time final approval was obtained, had increased the number of truckloads carried by approximately 1,000% over the level achieved by the former owner.

After 1955 the company made several acquisitions of rights allowing it to extent its service to Newark, New Jersey; Pawtucket, Rhode Island; and New Haven, Connecticut. The 10-year period of "significant expansion" ended when Colony opened a terminal in New Haven in June, 1956.

TERMINAL OPERATIONS

All the company's 23 terminals performed pickup and delivery service. At each terminal, local freight was loaded on or unloaded from trucks making line-hauls, that is, trips between terminals. The company attempted to have freight picked up and delivered within a two-day period when the distance from the origin and destination terminals could be driven in one night. Since the company served a large number and variety of shippers, realization of this objective required extensive control over terminal operations and equipment scheduling.

Scheduling and Control. Line-haul equipment was scheduled by a central dispatch department located in the Cambridge terminal. Local pickup and delivery operations were scheduled by persons at each terminal. In Cambridge, local dispatch operations were performed from an office with the aid of radio broadcast equipment used to communicate instructions to drivers while away from the terminal. At the smaller terminals this function was usually performed by the terminal manager along with such other functions as rating bills of lading, supervising freight handlers and drivers, and maintaining the terminal's office.

Formal equipment scheduling and control procedures had been devised for the central dispatch department and the larger terminals. Executives found, however, that in spite of these procedures a need still existed for making a large number of on-the-spot scheduling decisions based purely on judgment. Although some of the company's experienced dispatchers were described as "worth their weight in gold," company executives thought that better procedures should be devised though they were not certain how to do so.

Terminal Facilities. Most of the company's terminals amounted to little more than a loading dock and a minimum of office equipment. The most extensively equipped of the terminals occupied exclusively by Colony, the one in Cambridge, had been built in 1947. Freight was moved about the terminal by means of an overhead "drag-line" which could be operated continuously in conjunction with easily connected and disconnected pallets mounted on wheels.

A relatively large volume of freight was necessary to justify investment in specialized dispatching and materials handling equipment. The huge New York and New Haven terminals, which were shared by Colony with other carriers, had been built by the municipal port authorities with the most modern equipment available. Most other terminals in the company's system, however, were not considered large enough to warrant the investment.

Colony executives estimated that the size and facilities of all terminals other than the one located in Cambridge were adequate to handle volumes up to 25% greater than those handled in 1956. Terminal capacity, of course, depended not only on size but also on the efficiency of equipment scheduling. Executives believed that the Cambridge terminal, however, had reached its capacity and occasionally was so overloaded with backlogs of freight that efficient loading and unloading could not take place.

Terminal Balance. Colony terminals located in the northern part of its system were typically smaller than those located in the southern part. This fact reflected the relative concentration of industry in the area served by the company. Since there was a natural tendency for the flow of freight northward to exceed that southward, the company faced a continual problem in achieving a reasonable balance of shipments to and from its individual terminals. (See Exhibit 4 for terminal statistics.)

Exhibit 4

COLONY TRUCKING COMPANY

In and Out Tonnage by Terminal, 1955 and 1956

(In Thousands)

TERMINAL LOCATION	1955 TONNAGE		1956 TONNAGE	
	In	Out	In	Out
Bennington, Vt.	4.8	4.1	4.1	4.5
Bellows Falls, Vt.	10.8	15.8	13.6	14.6
Barre, Vt.	8.7	6.8	9.1	8.7
Bangor, Maine	15.7	13.0	17.9	14.1
Burlington, Vt.	17.8	13.7	19.8	13.8
Berlin, N.H.	1.5	2.7	2.1	2.2
Cambridge, Mass.	97.6	100.5	91.4	111.3
Gardner, Mass.	10.5	6.8	13.1	21.9
Lewiston, Maine	12.1	18.2	12.4	20.1
Manchester, N.H.	10.0	4.9	11.9	6.5
Newport, Vt.	3.6	5.1	4.0	3.2
New York, N.Y.	57.6	70.6	60.5	55.1
Newark, N.J.*	...	...	14.4	32.4
New Haven, Conn.†	...	...	2.5	1.1
Pawtucket, R.I.	7.8	5.5	11.1	6.8
Portsmouth, N.H.	10.7	3.7	12.3	4.7
Portland, Maine	27.6	17.7	36.1	20.9
Rutland, Vt.	9.8	6.0	11.9	8.4
Springfield, Mass.	22.9	16.1	29.1	24.8
St. Johnsbury, Vt.	11.9	22.8	12.7	19.8
Waterville, Maine	8.0	10.0	8.7	10.4
Wells River, Vt.	9.0	15.0	10.8	13.7
White River, Vt.	7.8	6.8	8.9	4.3

* Opened in February, 1956.
† Opened in June, 1956.
Source: Company records.

At the beginning of 1957 a management consulting firm hired by Colony recommended the establishment of monthly terminal profit and loss statements which were designed to indicate the extent of unbalanced terminal conditions. The company immediately began preparing them and found that several of the small terminals consistently showed losses. Colony executives were not satisfied, however, with the methods adopted for allocating costs and revenues to each terminal, believing that they understated the value of the unprofitable terminals to the total system. Colony's controller was attempting to devise more equitable methods but had not made any recommendations by the end of the year.

SALES

Sales Force and Advertising. The company's sales force consisted of 24 regular salesmen and four "national account" salesmen who concentrated their efforts on the larger shippers located in the company's area. These salesmen called on companies within their territories in an attempt to secure promises from responsible executives to use Colony's service. The salesmen distributed promotional brochures. The only additional advertising consisted of quarter-page spreads in the yellow pages of local telephone directories.

Regular salesmen were paid salaries averaging about $5,000 per year; national account men were paid salaries ranging from $6,500 to $7,500. Colony executives were in the process of devising an incentive system for salesmen's compensation but were not able to agree as to the basis on which it was to be computed. Statistics reflecting the change in terminal in-and-out tonnage had been recommended as a basis, but this method was not adopted. Executives explained that since the company could not determine which shipments were related to salesmen's activities and which were not, the over-all statistics would not truly reflect a salesman's worth. Salesmen did not take signed orders, and the company did not prepare analyses of its markets.

Company executives considered prompt settlement of shortage and damage claims to be of prime importance in holding customers and creating a favorable reputation among shippers. The company promptly paid the claims submitted by large customers but usually investigated those of smaller customers before settling them.

Interline Shipments. About 44% of the company's 1956 revenue resulted from interline shipments, that is, shipments originated and/or terminated by other carriers. The relative importance of interline business had grown steadily in the years since 1950 when it amounted to 35% of the company's total. Although most rates charged to shippers under interline agreements were equal to regular class rates, Colony executives thought that the company was at a disadvantage in competing on an interline basis for freight movements which other carriers could handle singly from origin to destination. Transferring freight from one carrier to another increased the possibility of damage and/or delivery delay.

Rate Participation. Colony normally participated in the class rate schedules that were developed by the New England Motor Rate Bureau. In making applications for commodity rates, the company usually would not recommend a rate below 85% of the otherwise applicable class rate. Executives thought this was the lowest the company could go without "getting into trouble with other carriers." Also, the company did not request commodity rates in an effort to "take" business from other truckers since this might lead, they thought, to destructive retaliation. "We will cut rates down to the level of rail rates to get certain types of shipments, though," indicated the company's rate officer.

Colony executives said that they always opposed applications by competing firms for rights to operate over routes serviced by Colony and for reductions in service rates. Approval of either type of application was bound to decrease the company's revenue, they thought.

EQUIPMENT

In October, 1957, the company operated 158 straight trucks, 207 tractors, and 356 trailers. About 50% of the tractors and trailers were used in line-haul operations. The remainder, always the oldest units, were used in conjunction with the company's straight trucks for local pickup and delivery operations. Company executives indicated that part of the Cambridge terminal's overload problem resulted from not having a sufficient number of line-haul units available at the "proper time."

Within the state-imposed weight and size limits, Colony, like other truckers, attempted to obtain equipment with maximum load capacity, since "running cost," for example, fuel and drivers' wages, varied little on a per-mile basis. Manufacturers' improvement in equipment design since 1944 had been significant. In 1944 trailers 35 feet long and weighing 13,700 pounds had a capacity of 1,870 cubic feet. Some 40-foot aluminum trailers produced in 1956 weighing only 7,900 pounds had a capacity of 2,900 cubic feet. Price increases accompanied the improvements in trailer design. In 1944 the average trailer was priced at about $2,000; in 1956, at about $10,000.

Since 1952 legal weight limits in most of the New England states had been increased from 40,000 to 60,000 pounds, making much of Colony's old equipment virtually obsolete. Largely as a result, the company began a major equipment rehabilitation program in early 1956. About 200 old trailers and 35 old tractors were sold, and about 300 new trailers and 75 new tractors were added.

Company executives believed that it would be a wise policy for a company with a stable-sized fleet to replace its equipment every five years. "Since we have continually expanded our operations," stated George Danson, "it has been necessary in the past for us to continue to use our old equipment longer than we perhaps would have otherwise." Prior to 1956 the company had kept its trucks and tractors for close to 10 years and its trailers for about five years.

Repair. Major repair and service work was performed at large garages located in the Barre and Cambridge terminals. Colony also maintained several light-service shops in strategic locations throughout its system. Executives recognized that there was considerable duplication of supervision and inventory costs because of the separate locations of its two major garages but thought that facilities at either location were not adequate to handle all the work.

According to company executives, many competing carriers spent relatively less than Colony on the maintenance of their equipment. Company executives indicated that they rarely questioned sums spent on maintaining equipment condition and looks.

Safety. Since 1945 the company had maintained formal driver-training programs, safety incentive systems, and periodic equipment inspections directed toward decreasing accidents. These measures had succeeded in steadily reducing the company's accident rate per driver from 1.98 in 1946 to about 0.81 in 1957. As a result of this record, the company had been recognized by the various regulatory agencies as a responsible carrier and had been granted lower insurance rates than many competing carriers.

COSTS AND PROFIT

In the period 1948–56, Colony's percentage operating profit (Exhibit 3) compared with that of all Class I carriers[1] as follows:

Year	1948	1949	1950	1951	1952	1953	1954	1955	1956
Colony	3.9	3.8	5.0	3.4	1.7	2.0	2.8	1.8	0.5
Class I Carriers	6.5	5.1	6.6	4.6	4.4	3.9	3.2	4.2	3.5

In 1955 and 1956, company and Class I carrier revenues were divided percentagewise between expenses and operating profit as follows:

---

[1] From 1950 through 1956, Class I carriers were defined as those having annual gross revenues of $200,000 or more. Before 1950 the lower limit was $100,000; in 1957 it became $1 million.

	1955		1956	
	Colony	Class I Carriers	Colony	Class I Carriers
Net freight revenue.............	100.0%	100.0%	100.0%	100.0%
Operating expense:				
Equipment, maintenance,				
garage..................	14.5	10.1	11.8	10.5
Transportation..............	39.3	55.0	45.8	55.8
Terminal...................	19.8	12.9	20.0	11.9
Traffic......................	3.0	3.0	2.9	2.9
Insurance and safety..........	6.2	4.5	6.0	4.4
Administration and general...	10.6	6.6	9.8	7.7
Depreciation.................	4.8	3.7	3.2	4.3
Total..................	98.2	95.8	99.5	97.5
Operating profit...............	1.8	4.2	0.5	3.5

Labor Costs. A major factor tending to lower the operating profits (or conversely to increase the operating ratio) of many carriers was the rising cost of labor. Wages represented, according to George Danson, "the largest single element" in Colony's cost. For all Class I intercity carriers handling general commodities, according to the ICC, wages in 1956 accounted for 53.8% of total revenues. Wage increases in the trucking industry were higher than for industry as a whole: between 1944 and 1956 the average yearly pay of employees engaged in trucking and warehouse operations increased from $2,374 to $5,065, or 113%, as compared with a general increase from $2,196 to $4,042, or 84%.

Colony's wage rates for both union and nonunion employees varied according to location. Drivers working out of New York were paid $2.52 per hour, for example, while drivers out of Boston were paid $2.17 per hour. Vermont was the area with the lowest wage and salary structure. Wage rates for members of the Teamsters' Union were negotiated yearly by statewide carriers' associations and associations of the union locals. George Danson himself was involved in most of these negotiations either directly or as a behind-the-scenes "consultant" for the mangement groups. He was regarded as a leader in the industry and knew many of the labor leaders personally.

Like other truckers, Colony was plagued by the fact that wage increases could not be promptly reflected in rate increases. Before raising their rates, carriers had to go through the formal regulatory procedure, usually including hearings, which often took several months. By the time rate relief was granted, the carriers sometimes found themselves facing another wage increase. This problem had been particularly acute for Colony in early 1957, since negotiations in Massachusetts had resulted in a relatively large rise in labor costs. Since it was difficult if not impossible to anticipate the extent of cost increases, Colony usually did not submit applications for rate increases in advance.

Cost per Ton-Mile. In the trucking industry, costs per ton-mile tend to vary inversely with (1) length of haul and (2) weight of load. Costs per ton-mile varied inversely with length of haul principally because the longer hauls provided more mileage over which to spread terminal loading and unloading and other overhead costs, and because truckers tended to carry heavier loads on the longer hauls. Between 1948 and 1956 industry average terminal costs increased from $1.89 to $3.58 per ton.

In 1954 Colony's cost per ton-mile was approximately $0.112 which compared with an average of $0.095 for other Class I companies domiciled in New England. Ton-miles hauled by Colony in 1954 amounted to 57.3 million.

As compared with other New England and U.S. Class I carriers, Colony's record on average length of haul, average load in tons, and average revenue per intercity ton was as follows:

	1950	1951	1952	1953	1954	1955	1956
LENGTH OF HAUL IN MILES							
Colony	116	168	185	186	195	193	207
N.E. average	133	131	NA	135	132	132	135
U.S. average	235	237	240	242	233	235	230
AVERAGE LOAD IN TONS							
Colony	4.76	6.96	7.46	8.26	7.36	7.78	9.48
N.E. average	7.5	7.5	NA	7.61	7.61	7.82	8.00
U.S. average	9.0	9.12	8.94	9.01	9.11	9.26	9.58
AVERAGE REVENUE PER INTERCITY TON IN DOLLARS							
Colony	14.58	14.68	16.47	17.22	19.81	18.86	19.18
N.E. average	NA	10.00	9.36	NA	11.43	11.25	11.96
U.S. average	10.91	11.24	12.26	12.61	12.33	12.49	12.62

NA = not available.

FINANCE

For financing terminal buildings and equipment, the Danson brothers employed different methods. All but six of the terminal buildings were owned by the Dansons through legally independent real estate investment firms, and all the owned buildings were mortgaged. According to company executives, the rents charged to Colony by the Dansons' firms were determined largely on the basis of estimated market value. The six terminals not owned by the Dansons were leased from other investors.

About 75% of the cost of equipment was paid for with funds borrowed either from banks or equipment manufacturers. In recent years the latter had been relied on most heavily.

Prior to 1956 Colony had purchased all its own equipment. Early in 1956, however, the Dansons organized a separate firm to finance about 75% of the equipment added during the year. This was leased to Colony at rates based on depreciation charges plus a small fee for administrative handling of the transaction. The rates were generally 5% to 10% lower than those of other equipment-leasing firms which included substantial financing charges.

While discussing Colony's financial position, George Danson stated, "At present, I don't have as much money as I need to do everything I want, but our financial structure is adequate for our present level of operations."

For the industry as a whole the financing of motor-carrier equipment and terminals presented two major problems: lack of credit sources and unfavorable terms in the purchase of equipment. Banks frequently would lend only under terms that many motor carriers felt were too stringent. While commenting on this problem in early 1957, an industry spokesman pointed out that small firms have had to finance by "piecemeal methods, on a one-truck or one-terminal basis." Equipment was often purchased under vendor-credit arrangements. Recently, several firms had begun to lease their equipment from manufacturers or separately organized leasing companies. Various means of financing terminal facilities had been developed, including renting of space by a motor carrier to other motor carriers, co-operative association of motor carriers, with each sharing the investment, and privately owned terminal companies which operate on the basis of leases with carrier tenants.

Public Financing. By 1957 the number of highway carriers publicly financed had increased to 26 from a prewar total of one. In commenting on this trend, *Barrons* noted that Wall Street's interest was not confined to carriers that were already large as of the date of issue. For example, when their stock was first offered, several firms had gross revenues under $20 million and at least one had less than $10 million. According to *Barrons:*

These moves, and others like them, point up one of the latest and most interesting twists in transportation—the rough and tumble trucking business is coming of age financially. . . . In short, a spree of empire building, reminiscent of the railroads in their heyday, may well be in the making for the truckers.

OWNERSHIP AND MANAGEMENT

Stock ownership in the company was split 40% each to Robert and to George Danson and 20% to Charles, the youngest of the three brothers. The company relied heavily on profits as a source of funds to finance its expansion, and no dividends on its stock had been declared since the date of incorporation (Exhibit 5). Both Robert and George

Exhibit 5

COLONY TRUCKING COMPANY

Source and Application of Funds, 1948–56

(Dollars in Thousands)

	Application	Source
Increase in current assets............	$1,126	
Purchases of equipment.............	905	
Increase in other assets..............	29	
Reduction of short-term notes payable on revenue equipment......	173	
Increase in unsecured notes payable...		$ 124
Increase in other current liabilities...		671
Retirement of long-term notes payable on revenue equipment.......	90	
Increase in retained earnings.........		678
Depreciation charged..............		850
	$2,323	$2,323

Source: Prepared from Exhibit 2 by the Harvard Business School staff.

Danson drew yearly salaries of $52,000. Charles, who had been active in the management of the company since 1938, was paid $32,000.

George Danson was regarded by most company executives as the "real president" of Colony, although Robert held the title. George's office was located in the Cambridge terminal where executives in charge of operations and personnel also had offices. Robert's office was located in Barre, Vermont, where the company's accounting operations were performed. Communication between offices was conducted by telephone and truck-mail. No regularly scheduled meetings of the executive group were held.

Charles, age 36, was formally assigned responsibility for co-ordinating line-haul operations, equipment maintenance, major equipment purchases, and general purchasing. In describing his activities, Charles stated, "Most of my decisions are made in conjunction with my brother, George. Nothing goes on that he doesn't get into somehow. Actually, most of my activity consists of fact-finding and fault-finding. I spend a lot of time raising hell about something going on out in the terminal such as improper loading of freight."

Almost all Colony executives had been exclusively in the trucking business since starting their business careers. Many started as truck drivers and worked their way up through the ranks to their present positions. None had earned college degrees. Most of them were in their forties or fifties.

According to George Danson, a major organizational problem existed in home office-terminal relationships. One home office executive described his experience in dealing with terminal managers as follows:

There is a general feeling around here that the terminal managers cannot be replaced, and it's true we don't have the people to replace them. This presents some real problems in getting the managers to follow instructions sent out from the home office. Mistakes resulting from failure to follow instructions got so bad that I finally decided to put a coupon on the bottom of my instructions which the managers are to clip off and send back to me. Then I file them so that I will have them when a manager uses the excuse that he never received the instruction.

Colony's board of directors consisted of the three Danson brothers, the company's vice-president and general manager, and its controller.

COMPETITION

In 1954 there were 1,176 general commodity carriers and 3,805 other than general commodity carriers holding certificates or permits to operate in New England. The federally regulated highway carriers domiciled in New England numbered 2,202, of which less than 10% were Class I carriers. In addition, 65 firms domiciled elsewhere operated in New England, including the largest firm in the industry.

In competing with the railroads, New England truckers, both private and for-hire, in 1954 accounted for an estimated 50% of total rail-highway ton-miles for intercity transport, as compared with a national average of 28%. Indexes of intercity truck tonnage for Class I carriers, however, indicated that the New England trucking business was expanding less than the national average:

Indexes of Intercity Class 1 Tonnage (1957-1949 = 100)

	1949	1951	1954	1956
New England	99	126	134	153
United States	107	148	154	183

For-hire truckers, such as Colony, competed not only with nontruck transport but also with private truckers. Indexes of intercity ton-miles for the various classes of motor carriers indicated that, on a nationwide basis, the latter was the fastest growing group:

Indexes of Intercity Ton-Miles, Trucks (1947-57 = 100)

	1949	1951	1954	1956
Regulated Common and contract carriers	109	164	164	188
Private and nonregulated carriers	111	163	201	241
Total—all trucks	110	164	187	221

The largest common carrier domiciled in New England had 1954 revenues from intercity operations of $9.5 million. The largest carrier operating in New England—and also the largest in the United States—was Associated Transport, Inc., with 1956 revenues of $99.1 million. For this company, operating costs as a percentage of operating revenue were 97.1% in 1954, 100.4% in 1955, and 99.1% in 1956 in spite of a $3.1 million increase in gross revenue during the latter year. In his 1956 annual report, Associated's president attributed low profits to rising costs and stated that emphasis would shift in 1957 from increasing sales to cutting costs.

On the other hand, some large carriers had lower than average operating ratios. For example, 1956 statistics for five large publicly held firms were as follows:

COMPANY	1956	
	Gross Revenues (In Millions)	Operating Ratio
U.S. Truck Lines	40.7	93.6
Pacific Intermountain Express	52.3	95.6
McLean Trucking	21.4	92.1
Interstate Motor Freight	30.2	96.0
Denver-Chicago Trucking	26.2	92.0

A comparison of 102 carriers domiciled in New England with 65 carriers domiciled elsewhere but operating in the New England region showed that the latter typically carried heavier loads and had much longer hauls: In spite of the fact that freight capacity of the trucks most commonly used in New England in 1954 ranged from 12 to 15 tons, 50% of the 102 New England carriers in 1954 had an average load of less than 8 tons, while only 13% had an average load of 12 tons and over. In contrast, only 25% of the 65 outside firms averaged under 8 tons per load, while 40% averaged at least 12 tons. Similarly on length of haul, 75% of the 102 New England firms averaged no more than 200 miles, while only 17% of the outside carriers had so short an average. And only 6% of the New England carriers averaged over 300 miles as compared with 54% of the outside carriers.

In referring to competitors from outside the region, George Danson indicated that the company had "felt the effects" when in 1955 several large carriers formerly operating only in the South and Southwest extended their regular service into the New England area.

INDUSTRY TRENDS AND OUTLOOK

In the years from 1946–56, according to *Business Week,* an estimated 8,000 mergers and acquisitions had taken place in the U.S. trucking industry. Reportedly, many of these transactions involved the aging founders of small, privately owned firms seeking protection from inheritance taxes. Also, many small carriers were reportedly finding their financial problems too difficult to face alone and were looking to merger or sale as the best possible solution. Moreover, according to one executive, "The merger climate is favorable down in Washington . . . The resistance is less. More of the expanding truck lines have decided that it is an unnecessary waste of time and money to oppose a competitor's merger application."

Outlook. As to whether the trucking industry will continue to expand at the expense of the railroads, there was some difference of opinion. A spokesman for one of the large motor carriers predicted that truckers would obtain increasingly large shares of the transportation market on the assumption that the nation's output would tend to be composed of more and more highly fabricated products. Being more valuable per pound and per cubic foot, such products would be better able to afford the generally more costly but more rapid and flexible service of motor carriers. Another source, on the other hand, predicted that the industry's future rate of growth will be slower than that of the general economy and of industrial production. This prediction was based on the fact that ton-mile carriage by regulated truckers had remained approximately level in the years from 1951 to 1955.

In the future, it was expected by several sources that there would be increased co-ordination between the various means of transportation. "Piggy-backing," the movement of loaded motor carrier trailers on railroad flatcars, had already achieved significance by 1957. Within the previous year or so, several airline companies had signed agreements with truckers which resulted in regular air-surface transportation systems. Similar agreements had been made between truckers and waterway carriers. The movement toward co-ordination was being sponsored by several of the Interstate Commerce Commissioners who hoped it would result in a more efficient national transportation system.

BIBLIOGRAPHY OF SOURCES FOR INDUSTRY DATA

AMERICAN TRUCKING ASSOCIATIONS. *American Trucking Trends*, 1950–53, 1955–59 editions.

Barrons, April 2, 1956, pp. 3 ff.

Business Week, June 22, 1957, pp. 168 ff.

Commercial and Financial Chronicle, October 18, 1956, pp. 184 ff.

MOODY'S *Transportation Manual*, 1957–58 editions.

NEW ENGLAND GOVERNORS' COMMITTEE ON PUBLIC TRANSPORTATION. *Motor Freight Transport for New England*, Report No. 5, October, 1956.

Railway Age, April 2, 1956, pp. 40 ff.; April 22, 1957, pp. 43 ff.

TAFF, CHARLES A. *Commercial Motor Transportation*. Homewood, Ill.: Richard D. Irwin, Inc., 1955.

Superb Biscuits, Inc.

CRACKERS AND COOKIES bearing the Superb name appeared on the shelves of about 80% of all retail food stores in the four-state area of Illinois, Michigan, Indiana, and Ohio. Superb Biscuits, Inc., of Chicago produced and distributed a wide line ranging from simple, square salt crackers to filled chocolate-coated cookies sold in foil-wrapped assortments. More than 80 different items and package sizes were available, and company sales reached $7.6 million in 1956. (For financial statements, see Exhibits 1 and 2.)

COMPETITIVE SITUATION

Superb encountered competition of two types. Most important were the "Big Three"—National Biscuit Company, Sunshine Biscuits, Inc., and United Biscuit Company—with combined sales of almost $700 million in 1956 (see Exhibits 3 and 4). According to Superb's estimates, National Biscuit reached 90% of all outlets and had about 40% of the market, while Sunshine sold to about 70% of the outlets and held about 25% of the market. Superb was believed to run a good third in its own territory, with about 22% of total sales.

Competition also came from about six medium-sized or small companies, either local or regional in character, operating in part or all of Superb's territory. Several dozen such firms were scattered throughout the United States.

Product lines of the big companies were essentially the same as Superb's, although they put more emphasis on crackers and on offering a wider variety of items. The smaller companies generally specialized in high-priced fancy cookies, custom recipes, or accessories like ice cream cones.

In contrast to Superb and most other smaller companies, the three large firms were to some extent both horizontally and vertically integrated. Together they had acquired almost 50 small baking or supply companies during the last 30 years, which were either operated as divisions or supplied large portions of the parent companies' flour and packaging requirements. Furthermore, two of the large firms had divi-

Exhibit 1

SUPERB BISCUITS, INC.

Income Statement, Years Ending December 31
(Thousands of Dollars)

	1956	1955	1954	1953	1952	1951	1950	1949	1948	1947	1946	1945
Net sales	$7,555	$7,001	$7,156	$7,508	$6,829	$6,374	$5,311	$4,841	$4,676	$4,933	$3,825	$3,704
Cost of goods sold	5,182	4,800	5,002	5,229	4,763	4,516	3,647	3,321	3,398	3,471	2,519	2,434
Gross profit	$2,373	$2,201	$2,154	$2,279	$2,066	$1,858	$1,664	$1,520	$1,278	$1,462	$1,306	$1,270
Selling, delivery, and administration	2,199	2,029	1,990	2,036	1,814	1,672	1,469	1,389	1,289	1,148	946	899
Operating profit	$ 174	$ 172	$ 164	$ 243	$ 252	$ 186	$ 195	$ 131	$ [11]	$ 314	$ 360	$ 371
Other income	23	29	10	10	4	17	14	15	13	4	9	[11]
Total income	$ 197	$ 201	$ 174	$ 253	$ 256	$ 203	$ 209	$ 146	$ 2	$ 318	$ 369	$ 360
Interest expense	11	5	10	20	22	13	16	22	21	7	8	19
Income before income tax	$ 186	$ 196	$ 164	$ 233	$ 234	$ 190	$ 193	$ 124	$ [19]	$ 311	$ 361	$ 341
Federal income tax	91	95	82	119	121	95	73	47	[5]	119	140	246
Net profit	$ 95	$ 101	$ 82	$ 114	$ 113	$ 95	$ 120	$ 77	$ [14]	$ 192	$ 221	$ 95
Preferred dividends	$ 40	$ 41	$ 42	$ 42	$ 43					$ 43	$ 21	......
Percentage Analysis												
Net sales	100.0%	100.0%	100.0%	100.0%	100.0%	100.0%	100.0%	100.0%	100.0%	100.0%	100.0%	100.0%
Cost of goods sold	68.6	68.5	69.9	69.6	69.7	70.9	68.7	68.6	72.7	70.4	65.9	65.7
Gross profit	31.4%	31.5%	30.1%	30.4%	30.3%	29.1%	31.3%	31.4%	27.3%	29.6%	34.1%	34.3%
Selling, delivery, and administration	29.1	29.0	27.8	27.1	26.6	26.2	27.6	28.7	27.5	23.3	24.7	24.3
Operating profit	2.3%	2.5%	2.3%	3.3%	3.7%	2.9%	3.7%	2.7%	[0.2]%	6.3%	9.4%	10.0%
Other income	0.3	0.4	0.1	0.1	0.0	0.3	0.2	0.3	0.3	0.1	0.2	0.3
Total income	2.6%	2.9%	2.4%	3.4%	3.7%	3.2%	3.9%	3.0%	0.1%	6.4%	9.6%	9.7%
Interest expense	0.1	0.1	0.1	0.3	0.3	0.2	0.3	0.4	0.5	0.1	0.2	0.5
Income before income tax	2.5%	2.8%	2.3%	3.1%	3.4%	3.0%	3.6%	2.6%	[0.4]%	6.3%	9.4%	9.2%
Federal income tax	1.2	1.4	1.1	1.6	1.8	1.5	1.4	1.0	0.1	2.4	3.6	6.6
Net profit	1.3%	1.4%	1.2%	1.5%	1.6%	1.5%	2.2%	1.6%	[0.3]%	3.9%	5.8%	2.6%
Preferred dividends	0.5%	0.6%	0.6%	0.6%	0.6%					0.9%	0.6%	......

Bracketed figures are negative.

Source: Company records.

sions making bread, fresh cakes, cake mixes, dried fruits, potato chips, or similar foods.

Most crackers and a few sweet cookies were standardized high-volume products that carried a low margin and required large-scale automatic production to return a profit to the producer. Most sweet cookies, on the other hand, were specialized products or assortments commanding better prices at lower volumes. Their manufacture called for special machinery or hand operations, while shorter runs necessitated frequent changeovers, especially in single-plant companies. An industry spokesman indicated that the large companies favored the high-volume items that were better suited to their automatic production lines.

There was little differentiation among the high-volume products offered by various makers, except for package design. Significant price differences appeared only during special promotions. Specialties, on the other hand, were claimed to be new and different. Superb officials said new products had to be introduced periodically in order to "show new faces in the market." The large companies were active in this respect, and one of them was reported to have introduced about ten new items over a six-month period. If a new product proved highly successful, however, competitors would probably develop similar items, and it would eventually become standard for the industry. Round cocktail crackers and fig bars, for example, had started out as specialties of two companies. On the other hand, according to Superb officials, many specialties showed a tendency to be "fads" that "went flat" after 90 days or so.

It was customary among the large- and medium-size companies, including Superb, to employ a sales force charged with order-taking in the food stores, and with arranging fresh stock on the shelves or in special displays featuring price reductions or new products. In most stores the salesmen checked stocks and replenished merchandise entirely on their own responsibility. In these cases they had developed a relationship with the store managers, who trusted them to keep the right amounts of salable products on hand. The men also exchanged stale, unsalable packages and rotated the stocks according to age dates on the cartons.

These services were considered important to keep the goodwill of the store and its customers. Industry spokesmen indicated that volume in a given store depended a great deal on the personality and aggressiveness of the biscuit salesman, and they considered it unlikely that independent

Exhibit 2

SUPERB BISCUITS, INC.
Balance Sheets, December 31
(Thousands of Dollars)

	1945	1946	1947	1948	1949	1950	1951	1952	1953	1954	1955	1956
Assets												
Cash	$ 268	$ 180	$ 149	$ 98	$ 93	$ 123	$ 120	$ 199	$ 134	$ 188	$ 160	$ 189
Receivables—Net	105	175	155	156	182	192	256	273	281	234	241	274
Inventories	205	306	332	317	326	375	518	449	572	608	753	983
Investments—Restricted	52	56	64	74	82	92	100	109	119	.....	.....	.....
Total Current Assets	$ 630	$ 717	$ 700	$ 645	$ 683	$ 782	$ 994	$1,030	$1,106	$1,030	$1,154	$1,446
Land, Building, and Machinery	$ 454	$ 473	$ 892	$ 926	$ 947	$ 995	$1,085	$1,141	$1,229	$1,327	$1,432	$1,487
Reserve for Depreciation	254	236	259	302	351	379	410	463	495	574	636	710
Net Property	$ 200	$ 237	$ 633	$ 624	$ 596	$ 616	$ 675	$ 678	$ 734	$ 753	$ 796	$ 777
Prepayments	25	53	28	42	26	42	76	34	41	53	75	80
Goodwill	450	450	450	450	450	*						
Organization Expense	88	88	.....	.....	.....							
Total Assets	$1,393	$1,545	$1,811	$1,761	$1,755	$1,440	$1,745	$1,742	$1,881	$1,836	$2,025	$2,303
Liabilities												
Notes Payable	$ 30	$ 30	$ 75	$ 11	$ 22	$ 22	$ 19	$ 38	$ 113	$ 75	$ 150	$ 570†
Accounts Payable	89	104	158	232	124	139	238	173	175	205	235	206
Accruals	68	98	73	82	82	119	146	156	188	229	217	209
Federal Income Taxes	351	288	268	241	278	264	238	245	241	178	223	64
Total Current Liabilities	$ 538	$ 520	$ 574	$ 566	$ 506	$ 544	$ 641	$ 612	$ 717	$ 687	$ 825	$1,049
Notes Payable—Long Term	$ 180	$ 150	$ 300	$ 289	$ 266	$ 244	$ 356	$ 319	$ 281	.....	.....	.....

Cumulative Preferred Stock ($0.50 Dividend Rate)	$ 419	$ 419	$ 419	$ 428	$ 428	$ 428	$ 427	$ 428	$ 428	$ 428	$ 428	$ 428
Common Stock	122	122	122	122	122	122	122	122	122	122	122	122
Earned Surplus	723	669	610	340	269	198	103	433	356	387	325	125
Total Stock and Surplus	$1,264	$1,210	$1,151	$ 890	$ 819	$ 748	$ 652	$ 983	$ 906	$ 937	$ 875	$ 675
Less: Reacquired Preferred Stock	10	10	2	7	8							
Net Stock and Surplus	$1,254	$1,200	$1,149	$ 883	$ 811	$ 748	$ 652	$ 983	$ 906	$ 937	$ 875	$ 675
Total Liabilities	$2,303	$2,025	$1,836	$1,881	$1,742	$1,745	$1,440	$1,755	$1,761	$1,811	$1,545	$1,393
Net Current Assets (Thousands of Dollars)	$ 397	$ 329	$ 343	$ 389	$ 418	$ 353	$ 238	$ 177	$ 79	$ 126	$ 197	$ 92
Current Ratio	138:1	140:1	150:1	154:1	168:1	155:1	144:1	135:1	114:1	122:1	138:1	117:1
Number of Shares—Preferred (1,000)	41	41	42	42	42	43	43	43	43	43	43	43
Earned per Share—Preferred	$ 2.26	$ 2.47	$ 1.98	$ 2.72	$ 2.70	$ 2.23	$ 2.81	$ 1.79	$	$ 4.49	$ 5.18	$ 2.24
Dividends per Share—Preferred	$ 1.00	$ 1.00	$ 1.00	$ 1.00	$ 1.00	$	$	$	$	$ 1.00	$ 0.50	$ ....
Arrearages per Share—Preferred	$ 1.75	$ 2.25	$ 2.75	$ 3.25	$ 3.75	$ 4.25	$ 3.75	$ 3.25	$ 2.75	$ 2.25	$ 2.75	$ 2.75
Total Arrearages (Thousands of Dollars)	$ 71	$ 92	$ 115	$ 136	$ 158	$ 182	$ 160	$ 139	$ 118	$ 96	$ 118	$ 118
Number of Shares—Common (1,000)	122	122	122	122	122	122	122	122	122	122	122	122
Earned per Share—Common	$ 0.44	$ 0.66	$ 0.51	$ 0.76	$ 0.75	$ 0.60	$ 0.81	$ 0.45	$[0.29]	$ 1.39	$ 1.63	$ 0.61
Net Tangible Assets per Share—Common	$ 6.31	$ 5.70	$ 5.02	$ 2.67	$ 1.89	$ 1.13	$ 0.53					
Per Cent Return on Net Worth (after Tax)	7.5%	8.4%	7.2%	12.9%	13.9%	12.5%	18.4%	7.8%	[1.6%]	20.3%	25.3%	14.1%

*Goodwill was written off against earned surplus—now carried at $1.
†Short-term funds of $500,000 for seasonal inventory needs included.
Bracketed figures are negative.
Source: Company records.

Exhibit 3

SUPERB BISCUITS, INC.

Per Cent Changes in Sales and Profits
Three Large Biscuit Companies* and Superb Biscuits, Inc.

	THREE LARGE COMPANIES*				SUPERB BISCUITS, INC.			
Year	Sales (Millions)	% Change from Past Year	Net Profit (Millions)	% Change from Past Year	Sales (Millions)	% Change from Past Year	Net Profit (Millions)	% Change from Past Year
1956..	$698.1	+9.8%	$31.1	+11.9%	$7.6	+8.6%	$0.095	−6.0%
1955..	635.9	+3.8	27.7	....	7.0	−2.8	0.101	+21.9
1954..	612.8	+2.6	27.7	−2.1	7.2	−4.0	0.082	−28.1
1953..	597.4	+4.8	28.3	+1.4	7.5	+10.3	0.114	+0.9
1952..	570.2	+2.5	27.9	+3.7	6.8	+6.2	0.113	+18.9
1951..	556.1	+13.5	26.9	−19.7	6.4	+20.8	0.095	−20.8
1950..	489.9	+2.0	33.5	−3.7	5.3	+10.4	0.120	+57.9
1949..	480.1	−1.3	34.8	+32.3	4.8	+2.1	0.077	−⎫ (negative basis)
1948..	486.5	+10.9	26.3	+4.4	4.7	−4.1	[0.014]	−⎬
1947..	438.5	+22.6	25.2	−5.3	4.9	+28.9	0.192	−13.1
1946..	357.4	+8.4	26.6	+26.0	3.8	+2.7	0.221	+132.6
1945..	329.6	....	21.1	....	3.7	....	0.095	....

* National Biscuit Company, United Biscuit Company, Sunshine Biscuit Company, Inc.
Bracketed figures are negative.
Source: Compiled by Harvard Business School Research staff from Moody's company records.

brokers or jobbers would give similar attention to service. Supermarkets and larger stores generally assigned fixed shelf space to each of the important firms in the area and rotated special promotion privileges among them. Nevertheless, the relationship of the salesman to the store personnel influenced any preferential treatment the company might receive.

Two of the Big Three carried on national advertising programs, using magazines, radio, and television. Smaller companies had to rely more heavily on advertising allowances to retailers, store promotions, and limited local radio, television, and billboard displays. Expenditures proportional to those of the large competitors were considered by Superb officials to be less than proportionately effective.

HISTORY AND ORGANIZATION

Superb Biscuits, Inc., was founded at the turn of the century; it thrived for 25 years, expanding its product line through new items. The depression, however, hit the company hard, and after experiencing severe losses, Superb changed hands in 1936. The new majority stockholder was Earl T. Kingsbury, father of the current president, Richard F. Kingsbury. Although the plant was equipped with modern machinery, the previous management had allowed the quality of the product to slide

Exhibit 4

SUPERB BISCUITS, INC.

Per Cent Return on Net Worth over Twelve Years
Typical Industry Performances and Superb Biscuits, Inc.

COMPANY	PER CENT RETURN											
	1956	1955	1954	1953	1952	1951	1950	1949	1948	1947	1946	1945
National Biscuit Company	11.5%	10.7%	11.9%	11.5%	11.6%	10.8%	14.2%	15.3%	10.7%	12.4%	10.2%	15.9%
United Biscuit Company	8.2	8.1	4.2	9.8	11.2	12.3	14.7	17.2	26.7	32.4	37.4	15.7
Sunshine Biscuits, Inc.	12.5	12.0	12.2	12.8	12.8	14.3	17.9	20.6	20.4	15.4	24.0	11.2
Average of six large and medium companies (weighted average)	10.7	10.1	10.3	11.0	11.3	11.1	14.3	15.4	12.8	13.6	14.2	14.9
Superb Biscuits, Inc.	7.5	8.4	7.2	12.9	13.9	12.5	18.4	7.8	[1.6]	20.3	25.3	14.1

Relative Volume of Three Largest Biscuit Companies
(Selected Years; Millions of Dollars)

COMPANY	1956		1954		1951		1948		1945	
	Sales	%	Sales	%	Sales	%	Sales	%	Sales	%
National Biscuit Company	$410.4	59.0%	$376.4	61.5%	$329.9	59.5%	$296.2	61.0%	$205.0	62.2%
United Biscuit Company	137.1	19.7	117.2	19.4	107.2	19.1	87.7	17.9	50.6	15.4
Sunshine Biscuits, Inc.	150.6	21.3	119.2	19.1	119.0	21.4	102.6	21.1	74.0	22.4
Total	$698.1	100.0%	$612.8	100.0%	$556.1	100.0%	$486.5	100.0%	$329.6	100.0%

NOTE: Comparability is limited by the fact that the large companies have diversified or integrated their operations to some extent. For instance, NBC produces 80% of its own flour requirements and 50% of packaging supplies. NBC also produces bread and cake in the East. Similarly, Sunshine Biscuit and United Biscuit are engaged in comparable fields.

Bracketed figures are negative.
Source: Prepared by Harvard Business School Research staff.

when reverses set in, and Earl Kingsbury was faced with the task of up-grading standards and recovering the acceptance of Superb biscuits in the trade. He believed that poor sales service and lack of freshness control had created considerable ill will.

Bringing with him a number of new executives, Earl Kingsbury attempted to reorient the company to his philosophy of giving high quality for the lowest possible price. Working against heavy financial odds, he effected changes in the production and sales departments, and sales and profits increased. Mr. Kingsbury was characterized by company officials as a shrewd financial operator whose frugality and determination were the main driving forces behind Superb's recovery. They said he had assumed close personal direction of the business and continually made decisions on both details and policy. His door was always open to subordinates, with whom his contacts were many and varied. Many who had worked under Mr. Kingsbury spoke of him as "wonderful" and "smart." When his health deteriorated seriously in 1954, Mr. Kingsbury was forced to resign all duties, and his son Richard, then 26, was elected president. Richard Kingsbury had served under his father for two years in production and traffic.

The company was organized into four departments—sales, production, finance, and legal and personnel. Each was headed by a vice-president (see Exhibit 5). The president met monthly with this group of officers. The board of directors consisted of the president and four members representing some 300 stockholders; the Kingsbury family held a majority of the shares. These board members were the company's banker, an investment broker, and vice-presidents of two suppliers. Meetings were held regularly every month, usually after the officers' meeting, and the board maintained a close interest in operating results and major capital expenditures.

SALES AND PROMOTION

The company's sales organization, under James V. Cannon, vice-president, aimed at three different markets. The first was composed of food stores in the company's four-state home territory. These were called on by 110 salesmen supervised by 10 district managers. Deliveries were made by company trucks, either from the plant or from eight scattered warehouses. William R. Stewart, territorial sales manager, personally administered the large chain store accounts where formal authorization by central buying offices was required for sale of products in the stores. This market accounted for about 60% of sales.

Exhibit 5

SUPERB BISCUITS, INC.

Organization Chart

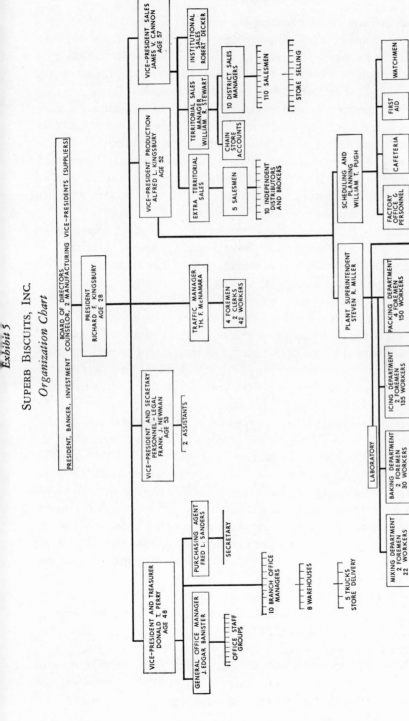

Source: Company officials.

The second market, accounting for about 15% to 20% of Superb's volume, was outside the home territory in scattered centers of population like Milwaukee, Kansas City, and even Washington, D.C. Five company salesmen, working directly under Mr. Cannon, called on the ten independent distributors who served these areas.

The third market consisted of various private and governmental institutions to which special types of biscuits were supplied on a contract basis. Competition was keen in this field, and bids were negotiated individually. While the first two markets showed only moderate seasonal fluctuations, the third required its heaviest volume during the first four months of the year. Institutional sales were managed by Robert Decker, who had 21 years of service with Superb.

Mr. Cannon had joined the company in 1936 after spending 14 years in the sales department of Scott Paper Company. A relative of Earl Kingsbury, he started as a Superb route salesman and rose to his present position after serving as district manager and territorial sales manager for a number of years.

Mr. Cannon commented that he believed one of the company's bigger problems was the high cost of distribution for the home territory. "Bill Stewart and I wonder about the merits of the present system, which is the most expensive form of selling," he said. He indicated that costs in the home territory totaled about 35% of sales in 1956. This figure included sales salaries and commissions, trade discounts, advertising, delivery, and sales administration expenses, all allocated on the basis of dollar volume. In the large cities outside the territory, where limited advertising was carried on, total costs averaged about 31.5% of sales, while sales costs on institutional business averaged about 20% of net sales. Mr. Cannon said that while institutional accounts were the most desirable in terms of selling costs, their seasonal character and competitive nature prevented the company from taking on a higher volume. In general, Mr. Cannon foresaw even higher selling costs for all types of accounts. He mentioned, for example, that drivers' wages were bounding upward along with rail rates.

In the home territory, company salesmen averaged about 175 accounts each, on which they called weekly. It was estimated that one-fourth of these stores purchased as little as $5 to $10 per month. On an average, it required at least one hour per month to service even the smallest account. Salesmen received a base salary of about $300 per month, plus graduated percentage bonuses for sales in excess of the quotas set with their co-operation by Mr. Stewart. Salesmen generally exceeded their base quotas, and yearly contests were held for the best salesman. The men kept detailed records of calls made, new accounts opened, and sales volume by accounts. From this information, weekly summaries were prepared for the district managers and the home office. All salesmen worked from route books and timetables prepared by the district managers. Turnover among salesmen was low, according to Mr. Stewart.

The president commented that he felt the need for increased volume on present routes. He believed that his big competitors had an advantage in terms of selling costs. He estimated that their volume per salesman was from one and one-half to two times that of Superb, owing to larger territories or wider product lines. Furthermore, he estimated that Superb's delivery costs per sales dollar ran about 20% higher than competitors' costs, and sales administration about 10% higher. Advertising and promotional costs he considered about equal percentage-wise (see Exhibit 6).

Mr. Cannon was weighing the pros and cons of changing from direct selling in the home territory to independent distributors, as used in the extraterritorial market. These middlemen, located in the large cities, generally received a flat 25% discount off list price. Mr. Cannon stated that they had been very successful in selling Superb products and he was considering adding several more to the present ten to enlarge the field. He stated that selling through these channels was "hard selling" but "good selling," explaining that distributors generally asked for "special deals" in terms of price concessions or free goods (e.g., one carton free for every dozen), but at the same time they assumed all risks and the company was not forced to stand behind them with a guarantee to take back unsalable stock. "Selling direct through salesmen is almost like selling on consignment," he said, "while distributors have no recourse. But then, distributors take on only 'good sellers'—which in a way is an advantage. Why clutter a store with slow-selling items?" Mr. Cannon stated that the company's rate of returned goods was not quite 2% of net sales. He added that selling through distributors required strong men "able to say no" to the many demands for special favors. Furthermore, he said, the company would be subjected to greater price pressures, since distributors generally carried more than one brand of biscuits and would tend to push the brand most profitable to them.

Another change weighed by Mr. Cannon was modification of salesmen's compensation. He said, "We are considering the possibility of putting our men on straight commission, which would also cover their expenses. At the moment we have two or three of our district managers

Exhibit 6

SUPERB BISCUITS, INC.

Comparative Breakdown of Sales Dollar
Superb versus Large Companies (Estimates)

	Superb	Estimate for Biscuit Operations of Large Competitors
Gross sales	110.0%	110.0%
Trade commissions	8.0%	8.0%
Returned merchandise	2.0	2.0
	10.0%	10.0%
Net sales	100.0%	100.0%
Raw materials and supplies	52.8%	50.0%*
Direct labor	9.3	9.5
Manufacturing overhead	6.5	7.5
	68.6%	67.0%
Gross margin	31.4%	33.0%
Selling expenses:		
Advertising and promotion	2.8%	3.0%
Sales salaries and commissions	5.8	4.6
Other	1.1	0.8
	9.7%	8.4%
Delivery, warehousing	3.3%	2.3%
Freight	5.1	4.5
General and administrative	10.7	11.2
Interest	0.1	0.1
	19.2%	18.1%
Total expenses	28.9%	26.5%
Net income (before taxes)	2.5%	6.5%
Federal income taxes	1.2	3.2
Net income	1.3%	3.3%

* Lower, according to Superb officers, because of vertical integration.
Source: Company records and estimates of company officers.

stewing over the problem. If they think it is a good idea, we shall tell the other managers, and in turn have them sell it to the salesmen."

Mr. Kingsbury thought the company might well be forced to change its distribution system in the long run. He stated that National Biscuit and some small firms had experimented with a split arrangement, putting salaried men in charge of large chain accounts, while paying the salesmen who covered independent stores on straight commission. "Under such a system," he said, "we would be better set for the eventual transition in food marketing to complete predominance of the large supermarket."

Mr. Kingsbury visualized, as a long-term possibility, the institution of direct delivery of biscuits to chain warehouses, eliminating the individual store deliveries made at present. The few remaining small independent stores would be served by driver-salesmen carrying the necessary stocks in their trucks. This would reduce the number of men required to one-third or less, he said.

Mr. Cannon indicated that the company's resources were insufficient for the extensive market research carried on by its large competitors. The company used an outside firm to supply monthly reports on relative market shares. "Everyone is in research," he said, "but when you are small you must sell hard instead, get more outlets, and keep them well stocked." He said that Superb had to rely on its sales force to bring back information about competitive developments. The district managers held regular monthly meetings with their men, and occasionally all salesmen and sales personnel were brought together to discuss advertising or promotional problems. During 1956 there had been four such meetings, a considerable increase over previous years.

New product and promotional ideas at times greatly stimulated sales according to Mr. Cannon. For example, during 1955 Superb had introduced three products aimed at different nationality groups, using authentic recipes; sales had jumped as much as 35% to 50% in outlying centers of population where these groups were heavily represented. Mr. Cannon believed that such specialties helped to promote regular sales by making the Superb name better known. Promotional ideas of the present year included handing out sample cookies, with an advertising message attached, in the elementary schools of Kansas City. The expense of the samples was borne by the distributor. "We must make little things pay," commented Mr. Cannon, and stated that he was glad the company had begun moving toward such new product ideas and promotions.

Advertising had undergone changes and was still being modified. Before 1936 the company had spent up to 10% of net sales on advertising, especially when sales began to slip. Earl Kingsbury had drastically cut expenditures to an average of $100,000 to $115,000 per year, including co-operative advertising for the home territory which amounted to about 40% of the total. In the recent past, most of the budget was spent on billboards (35%) and on some radio spots (25%). Magazine advertising was negligible. In 1956 the company initiated spots on local television and signed up for another billboard campaign (30% of budget) during the summer. Furthermore, the advertising agency was asked to come up with a suitable slogan tying the product line to reasons for consumer preference for Superb biscuits. The 1957 advertising budget was set at almost $250,000, an increase of about 24% over past years.

Richard Kingsbury believed that during his father's management the lines of authority in the sales department had become blurred because district managers were allowed to carry their problems directly to the president. "This custom resulted in nobody knowing who was to tell what to whom," he said, adding that it was not until five years ago that the sales vice-president had begun to spend most of his time in the central office. Prior to that time he had been mainly occupied with extraterritorial sales. Mr. Kingsbury commented that, except for approving the size of the advertising budget, he made it a point not to interfere in the sales department. He wanted to foster the rebuilding of authority for the department head. He believed that morale and turnover among sales personnel had improved greatly in the last five years, especially because there were no longer numerous hirings and firings.

PRODUCTION

Increased efficiency and better mechanization were the main problems that concerned the vice-president of production, Alfred Kingsbury, an uncle of Richard Kingsbury. He believed that it was vital for the company to increase production without increasing labor costs. "We have not been able to pass on increased costs to the consumer—competitors have not been able to do this either. Automation is the ultimate answer, and we are compelled to go into it, but in the intermediate period we must buy better and produce better. If I could schedule longer runs, for instance, I could double our tonnage output, but our sales force needs variety," he said.

Alfred Kingsbury was made a vice-president when Earl Kingsbury took over the company. He had been a sales representative with another biscuit company and had run food stores before that. Reporting to him were Steven R. Miller, plant superintendent, and William T. Pugh, head of scheduling. Mr. Miller, a chemist and former head of the laboratory, was placed in his present position early in 1956 by Richard Kingsbury, who explained that he had fired two men formerly serving as joint superintendents because they were unwilling to delegate authority and accept new ideas. Mr. Miller, aged 30, was in charge of production, efficiency control, the laboratory, and maintenance. Mr. Pugh, a man of 18 years' experience in the biscuit industry, was in charge of scheduling, hiring of production workers, and related personnel services.

The plant, together with the offices, was located in a four-story building in a suburban area and was served by a spur track of the Rock Island Railroad. The ground floor was used for warehousing and shipping, while the second and third floors contained offices and manufacturing area. The fourth floor was rented to another firm. Major items of equipment were four 200-foot continuous band ovens, a battery of dough mixers that handled about 400,000 pounds of flour and shortening per week, several kneading machines, packaging lines serving the ovens, and three icing, sandwiching, and coating lines. Most of the equipment had been of very advanced design at the time of installation and had been kept in good condition, according to Mr. Kingsbury. Several conveyor arrangements allowed continuous product flow.

Production operations were divided into four sections, mixing, baking, icing, and packing. The plant worked in two shifts, and the work force totaled close to 400 men and women. Labor relations were peaceful, and all workers were unionized. Both Mr. Kingsbury and Mr. Miller indicated that they made sure to consult with union representatives before making any change in operations that affected the workers, and they thought this policy was one of the foundations of labor peace. "We have to build the strength of the union for our own good," said Mr. Miller, who indicated that union stewards attended the monthly meetings of foremen and production management.

Mr. Miller was considered by Alfred Kingsbury to be aggressive, smart, and progressing well in his new job. Mr. Miller said he made it a point to rebuild the authority of his foremen who had been undermined by his predecessors. He indicated that he allowed them more freedom to make operating decisions and required workers to see their foremen first before bringing complaints to him. At the same time he was concerned with quality and efficiency. "Every Friday I get together with my foremen and discuss what we mean by quality—I prefer to call it constancy —and analyze systematically how to do better in it. I also look for savings; just recently we cut expenses $400 per month by using paper towels instead of cloth to clean machinery." To avoid costly stoppages of the continuous production lines, Mr. Miller insisted on extensive preventive maintenance.

Mr. Miller shared the president's concern about introducing better machinery, and kept a file of new developments. He had joined Richard Kingsbury on an extended trip to machinery suppliers in the United States and Europe, and had assisted in selecting several new packaging machines.

Scheduling was described as complicated owing to the large variety of products offered. Both Alfred Kingsbury and Mr. Pugh spent most of their time working out the daily and weekly programs for the four sections. A minimum run of two hours was required for any one product, and the problem was to dovetail inventories and current requirements of the eight warehouses and the extraterritorial markets.

New product development had historically been concentrated in the production area, where one specialist was spending his full time on trying out new recipes. Several years ago a committee had been formed which consisted of Messrs. Alfred Kingsbury, Cannon, Perry (vice-president and treasurer), Stewart, as well as the new products specialist, and the company's part-time art director. According to the president, the committee produced little and met very infrequently until about a year ago when it was realized that more new products were needed. Since that time six new items had been developed and approved, and the committee now met three times per month. Of the six items which had been introduced through in-store promotions, only two showed continued success, two were "slowly dying," after a three-month life, while two never "went off the ground," he said. One of the successful items was a medium-priced assortment, while the other was a new form of cookie. Mr. Kingsbury believed that there were "too many thumbs" in the new product field and said that he was still looking for the best possible method of "hatching ideas" and accelerating their utilization. He said the majority of new ideas actually came from jobbers and distributors, while a few original ideas had emerged from production personnel. "There are not too many ideas that are completely new in this field," he said, and told of an instance where a new cookie had been developed by mistake when a worker used the "wrong" spices.

Alfred Kingsbury stated that new products had to meet high turnover requirements in addition to being different. "In the recent past all biscuit companies have lost five to ten items each due to stores wanting products with faster turnover. More and more items are competing for the available shelf space in a market." He believed that the industry would have to stimulate the basic demand for biscuits if it wanted to grow further.

FINANCE AND CONTROL

Donald T. Perry, vice-president and treasurer, had spent his entire career in varying positions in the biscuit industry. Previously plant manager for a medium-size biscuit manufacturer, he had joined Superb as assistant to the president in 1936, and was appointed vice-president soon thereafter.

Mr. Perry was in charge of finance and purchasing. The general office manager, Mr. Banister, supervised the office and accounting staffs. The company employed a product-cost system that traced labor and materials costs for each product, based on the daily runs through the four production departments. At least four times per year the average costs for each product were compiled and compared to current sales prices, and the gross margin was determined to see whether the product was profitable. Costs, except labor costs, were not recorded by department, but were allocated on the basis of weight of the finished product. Other data collected included average weight of output, barrels produced per hour, percentage yield from raw materials, and cost of finishes. Small variations in coatings, for instance, could prove very costly, according to Mr. Perry. Richard Kingsbury indicated that he favored several changes in the accounting area, particularly an attempt to establish basic standards of output on which to base a "more realistic" allocation of burden. He also wanted a more detailed breakdown of departmental expenses and reorganization of the company's monthly financial reports.

Inventories were taken weekly in each warehouse, and the central office maintained close control over the ordering procedures which were based on four-week moving averages. Owing to the semiperishable nature of the products, no more than one week's inventory of finished goods was kept on hand. Similarly, raw materials were kept down to four weeks' supply at the most. The company's spoilage experience was less than one-fourth of 1% of sales, according to Mr. Perry.

The treasurer considered his most serious problem to be "how to balance the budget." He worried over increased costs due to a rise from wage negotiations which were to start in the spring of 1957. Costs of raw materials and freight showed an upward trend. "There is no end to increases," he said, "and the Middle East troubles have sent commodities way up." He said that the biscuit industry had made general price advances in early 1957, but that this had been just enough to offset some of the cost increases of 1956, leaving no room for the expected 1957 rise. "Price advances are generally made uniformly by the whole industry with the large companies taking the lead," he said, "and only occasional reductions on single products are made individually."

Mr. Perry believed that the company was too small to do any hedging in the commodity markets, which he considered a special field in itself, not even tackled by the large companies. Superb generally bought flour requirements for about 120 days ahead, under standard millers' contracts, and once in a while ventured to buy six months' supply. The latter action involved a risk of paying storage charges to millers should the company be unable to take delivery within the stated period; thus the advantage of lower prices might be eliminated. The purchasing agent, Mr. Sanders, who had 35 years' experience in procurement, believed that Superb paid essentially the same prices for its raw materials as the large competitors, owing to the fact that the large companies generally bought on the plant level rather than centrally.

Quarterly budgets were tentatively prepared, focused mainly on the cash flow required to meet seasonal swings. The president commented that since about one year formal budgeting procedures had "all but gone out of the window," because of the difficulties of forecasting demand and costs.

Every year, to meet seasonal needs, Mr. Perry borrowed several hundred thousand dollars in short-term funds on a line of credit. Superb was still saddled with arrears of $71,000 on its preferred stock, but the president hoped to be able to pay this off within the next year and then start paying dividends on the common.

Proposals made by the production department or the president for expenditures on new machinery were analyzed by Mr. Perry. On the basis of his calculations, Mr. Richard Kingsbury decided on the merits of the purchase and defended it before the board, which passed on every expenditure over $2,000. The board gave its approval on almost all projects presented by him, he said. Richard Kingsbury spent most of his time on finding new ways to mechanize the processes of manufacture.

In the past, many special machines had been developed and built by Superb, but this had become increasingly difficult in recent years, said Mr. Perry. In the early years, Earl Kingsbury had economized greatly and held back on capital expenditures where possible. Up to 1956 Superb had relied solely on internally generated funds for capital outlays and had not considered outside money. The president now felt it was high time the company started looking for long-term loans to finance more machinery.

Mr. Perry also assisted in setting product prices based on cost data, but he said the company had little leeway in pricing standard products where prices tended to be industry-wide. "We must find more specialties on which we can put a price tag of our own," said Mr. Perry, "but still most of the volume is done with a limited number of standard varieties that you must have in order to be competitive. If we withdrew these low-margin products, the customer in the store might not pick up the specialty items either, and our display space would be cut. Moreover, our factory would have greatly reduced volume which would shift burden costs onto other products."

PERSONNEL AND LEGAL

Frank J. Newman, vice-president and secretary, was in charge of the legal affairs of the company and also directed personnel policies. He hired all personnel except production workers. A lawyer by training, Mr. Newman left private practice in 1936 to join Earl Kingsbury first as counsel, later as secretary and clerk; he was made vice-president in 1954. Mr. Newman obtained leases for district warehouses, appraised distributors' contracts, and gave advice on provisions of the Pure Food and Drug Act. Furthermore, he negotiated union contracts with the teamsters' and bakery workers' locals.

Mr. Newman also prepared the agenda for officers', directors', and stockholders' meetings. He said that about a year ago the officers' meetings had "petered out," and Richard Kingsbury had temporarily stopped them altogether. About six months later they were resumed and had been kept up regularly to date. Mr. Newman said that in these meetings the officers considered "matters of over-all policy," which included items like group insurance coverage, the problems of uniform package design, and the volume of institutional sales desirable.

TRAFFIC

Superb maintained a shipping and receiving department under Mr. Thomas McNamara, who had spent 20 years with the Great Northern Railroad before joining the company in 1936. Mr. McNamara supervised the compilation of truck and rail loads of finished products and determined the best possible routing. He worked closely with the sales department.

ORGANIZATIONAL DEVELOPMENTS

Before becoming president, Richard Kingsbury had worked in two functional departments looking for improvements. His interest in efficiency had led to substantial labor savings in shipping. He said it had been easier to convince the teamsters' union of the need for changes than some of the foremen, and he believed that resistance to new ideas had been fostered by the centralized control of his father. Mr. Kingsbury described the two plant superintendents he had fired as unco-operative, hardheaded, antilabor, and as standing in the way of improvements. He said he had eliminated three additional foremen showing similar attitudes. Mr. Kingsbury felt he now had the right man in the superintendent's position, one who could lead the foremen and look for better manufacturing methods.

Soon after becoming president, Richard Kingsbury had issued a directive that prohibited on-the-spot firing by foremen. He said his father had never agreed to this change while he was in control, but Richard Kingsbury believed the exercise of firing authority was inconsistent with good supervision. The directive stated that written requests for the release of a worker should be sent by the foreman to Mr. Newman and be approved by Alfred Kingsbury and Mr. Miller.

Mr. Kingsbury stated that his own youthful age had been a "small powderkeg" at the time of his father's resignation. "There was not much doubt in the minds of the directors about the succession," he said, "but the other executives did not share that certainty as they had little contact with the board. It became a question of whether I was taking over in name or in fact, and at least two of the officers had aspirations. Many lingering animosities came into the open at that time, and I finally had to stop the officers' meetings in early 1956 because nothing could be accomplished in them."

"Co-ordination was lacking between the departments," he continued, "and I stuck my neck out to cut bottlenecks. But the people involved had to cool down first, and I did not resume the meetings for about half a year."

Richard Kingsbury commented on the current meetings as follows: "We are now operating with the vice-presidents as heads of functional line departments. Actually we never act as a management group. The only real co-operative efforts occur if two department heads have an overlapping problem like priority schedules of production. But other matters are treated separately and will likely continue to be treated as such. For instance, advertising policy is handled solely as a sales problem. Actually, the vice-presidents have been used to operating this way since my father's time. There was even terrific interdepartmental animosity; each department tried to push the other around," he said. Mr. Kingsbury explained that there had been so-called "policy meetings" under Earl Kingsbury, but although ideas were debated collectively, Earl Kingsbury personally set policies.

"It is my prerogative to set policies which are self-governing, as contrasted with day-to-day affairs. I mainly concern myself with interdepartmental matters, or with weaknesses in any one department. For instance, I felt I had to take action in the production area—but I take action only if initial suggestions do not bring results," he explained.

In speaking of interdepartmental co-operation, Mr. Cannon said that until recently co-ordination between his department and the factory had not always been the best. During 1956, however, William Stewart had the idea of forming a production planning group to consist of Mr. Cannon, Alfred Kingsbury, the heads of scheduling and sales service, and himself. The group began by working on the problem of slack periods caused by seasonal demand for certain high-volume products, especially institutional biscuits. An attempt was made to forecast such fluctuations and schedule appropriate substitute products to keep the factory operating at capacity. Similarly, the group helped to schedule production on products for which demand was especially heavy. Mr. Cannon stated he felt this group had helped both his department and the production area.

Richard Kingsbury also thought the group was a good idea, as it taught certain sales personnel "the physical facts of life about the factory." He said that salesmen tended to push certain items too hard, thinking they could have more supplies immediately. This resulted in temporary but embarrassing shortages, during which the home territory was generally neglected in favor of outside areas. "This was quite contrary to the natural emphasis required—I still believe that our home territory is our mainstay," he said. "On the other hand," he added, "the factory was tempted to produce items that best fitted its production schedules."

The older executives commented that Richard Kingsbury showed great insight and capabilities, especially for his age. They said his interest in new machinery foreshadowed promising developments. Mr. Perry remarked: "Richard can do a lot of things with people who of themselves would not think of changing their old ways. By being in a position of authority he can spark new thought and urge its acceptance." Alfred Kingsbury said that no major steps were taken either by the president or by the officers without mutual consultation. "Dick is naturally more dependent on the department heads because his experience is shorter. He would not think of doing something without bringing it up with one or all of us. Likewise, we talk to him about our problems and listen to his views."

THE FUTURE

Mr. Kingsbury visualized a need for stricter cost controls and a more unified sales promotion. "I consider our present product line a hodgepodge in terms of appearance," he said, and indicated that, as one step toward improving package design and uniformity, Superb had asked its paper and cardboard suppliers to analyze current packages and suggest changes. This practice was common among small biscuit companies that were unable to afford large sums for professional designers.

The question of product diversification had arisen several times during the past three years. The idea of going into cereals and cake mixes had been discarded owing to the difficulties envisioned in competing with nationally advertised brands. Mr. Kingsbury stated that he and some of his officers felt the company should expand its line "if and when the right opportunity comes." New products might be added either through subcontracting of production or through utilizing the present plant. Mr. Kingsbury felt that the potential of the present sales force might be more fully realized with additional compatible products.

Instruments Incorporated

DURING ITS FIRST YEAR and a half of operations, ending September 30, 1949, Instruments Incorporated of Bridgeport, Connecticut, showed steady growth (see Exhibit 1) and on October 1, the company's back-

Exhibit 1

INSTRUMENTS INCORPORATED

Sales, Employees, and Backlog of Orders by Quarters

Year	Quarter	Approximate Sales	Employees	Approximate Backlog of Orders: at End of Period
1948				
3/15–6/30	1st 3 months	(No Operations)		
7/1–9/30	2nd 3 months	$ 40,000	26	$ 50,000
10/1–12/31	3rd 3 months	45,000	32	75,000
1949				
1/1–3/31	4th 3 months	57,000	45	90,000
4/1–6/30	5th 3 months	87,000	50	185,000
7/1–9/30	6th 3 months	115,000	65	310,000

Source: Company letter to prospective investors.

log of orders aggregated over $300,000 (see Exhibit 2). Mr. Arthur Johnson, the company's president, stated that the most pressing and critical problem at that time was a shortage of funds which was inhibiting the company's growth, and that his efforts to solve it were consuming a large portion of his time.

At the time of incorporation the cofounders of the company, Mr. Johnson and Mr. Henry Brown, the vice-president, expressed the intention to specialize primarily in ". . . engineering development, design, and fabrication of electromechanical precision instruments such as . . . gyroscopes, automatic pilots, special indicators and mechanical instruments, and hydraulic and electric control systems." Mr. Johnson and Mr. Brown believed they could apply these instruments and controls to industrial processes. They were especially interested in hydraulic and electric control systems and thought these could include, in addition to

231

Exhibit 2

INSTRUMENTS INCORPORATED

Backlog of Orders as of September 30, 1949

Customer	Type Contract	Product	Operations	Contract Price	Extent in Process				Number of Units
					Manufacturing Expense			Total	
					Material	Labor	Administration		
Armed Forces	Prime	Electronic equipment	Machining and assembly	$ 33,000	5,711	6,907	7,918	20,536	100 + spares
Armed Forces	Prime	Mechanical controls	Machining and assembly	24,000	0	1,502	1,371	2,873	766
Armed Forces	Prime	Development	Study contract	22,600	5,446	2,352	3,023	10,821	2
Armed Forces	Prime	Mechanical measuring equipment	Machining and assembly	4,750	2,068	2,306	2,875	7,249	109
Development, Inc.	Subcontract	Aircraft instrument	Development	16,300					model
Development, Inc.	Subcontract	Electronic control system	Development	22,000	3	99	134	236	model
Bendix	Purchase order	Mechanical assemblies	Machining and assembly	25,185	4,018	2,903	3,742	10,663	60
Westinghouse	Purchase order	Electromechanical equipment	Machining and assembly	135,000	821	934	1,333	3,088	94
Electronics, Inc.	Purchase order	Precision parts	Machining fabrication	5,750	169	607	778	1,554	102
Rensselaer Polytechnic Institute	Purchase order	Miscellaneous laboratory equipment	Machining and assembly	6,000	1,084	1,587	2,112	4,784	50
Electronics, Inc.	Purchase order	Signal generator	Machining and assembly	10,000					1
Miscellaneous	Purchase order	....	....	6,000	0	93	88	181	
Total				$310,585	19,321	19,291	23,375	61,987	

Source: Compiled from company records.

adaptations of the special indicators and instruments noted above, ". . . new elements which will apply to the control of machine tools and to the chemical process industry." Both men had resigned from promising positions with a large manufacturer of mechanical and electronic equipment and had formed their own company in order to be unfettered in putting into effect their own ideas.

As of the end of September, 1949, practically all the company's income had been from government contracts or contracts with other companies engaged in government work. The rapid growth of this business, however, had produced a continuous strain on working capital. This shortage, besides actually restricting the company's rate of expansion, had limited funds for the research and development of the company's own products (referred to by the executives as "commercial development") to somewhat less than the amount of company earnings.

In July, 1949, Mr. Johnson said he had "learned enough politics" while he was negotiating unsuccessfully for a loan with the Reconstruction Finance Corporation the previous year to justify a second attempt, and planned again to negotiate for a loan of $150,000 which he contemplated using as follows: working capital, $25,000; research and development of company's own new products, $25,000; refinancing of outstanding indebtedness, $40,800; purchase of equipment previously leased from War Assets Administration, $45,500; and new equipment, $13,700.

The following analysis was prepared by Mr. Johnson for submission to the RFC:

Instruments Incorporated is in a rapidly expanding field with multitudinous opportunities. The company, without additional financial aid, is in an awkward position. It has expanded its personnel and organization to the point that short-term orders and contracts may not be sufficient to provide a stable continuity of employment and scale of operations (fortunately, not a major problem to date). Yet, on the other hand, large, extended-term contracts cannot be bid, or subsequently financed, without an improved working capital position. Although the company can and will expand, and increasingly profit without such new funds over a longer period of time, temporary slack periods and the resulting difficulties therefrom can probably be expected in the period of general adjustment ahead.

This company has expended a great deal of time and effort in attempts to obtain financial assistance from other sources. The risk-capital tree in general, and in New England decidedly, is markedly barren of fruit these days—a discouraging handicap to new enterprises. The banking situation in New England is similarly described. Numerous contacts have been made with New York banks as well, without satisfactory solution.

Cost-of-sales figures show that approximately 50%–60% of Instruments Incorporated's gross sales dollar is spent on payroll. Our present working capital position ($30,000) is producing (based on just-ended, last-quarter results) a yearly gross sales volume of about ten times that amount ($360,000). Of this amount, payroll amounts to over half ($200,000 on a 12-month extension of current payroll figures).

The physical facilities, including building and tools presently at hand, are capable of supporting a severalfold increase in productive output, without major increases in the amount of tooling or in present fixed charges, such as depreciation, real estate tax, etc. For this and other reasons, it is estimated that doubling the present working capital position will much more than double gross sales. With the earmarking of $25,000 of the additional funds for working

Exhibit 3

INSTRUMENTS INCORPORATED

Comparative Statement of Profit and Loss and Earned Surplus for Selected Periods

	9 Months Ending March 31, 1949	April 1949	May 1949	June 1949	12 Months Ending June 30, 1949	15 Months Ending Sept. 30, 1949
Net sales	$141,368	$18,189	$38,766	$30,586	$228,909	$345,521
Less: Cost of goods sold:						
Raw materials	$ 18,621	$ 4,289	$ 7,688	$ 4,063	$ 34,661	$ 61,060
Direct labor	62,852	10,086	9,336	9,758	92,032	126,391
Manufacturing expenses	52,318	7,214	7,326	7,530	74,387	104,463
Total	$133,791	$21,589	$24,350	$21,351	$201,080	$291,914
Add: Inventories at beginning:						
Work in process	.....	$17,396	$24,014	$17,652	.....	
Commercial products in process	.....	2,822	6,022	7,381	.....	
Commercial products development	.....	6,708	6,708	6,708	.....	
Total	.....	$26,926	$36,744	$31,741	.....	
Less: Inventories at end:						
Work in process	$ 17,396	$24,014	$17,652	$22,748	$ 22,748	$ 61,987
Commercial products in process	2,822	6,022	7,381	9,097	9,097	11,543
Commercial products development	6,708	6,708	6,708	6,708	6,708*	6,708*
Total	$ 26,926	$36,744	$31,741	$38,553	$ 38,553	$ 80,238
Cost of goods sold	$106,865	$11,771	$29,353	$14,539	$162,527	$211,676
Gross profit on sales	$ 34,503	$ 6,418	$ 9,413	$16,047	$ 66,382	$133,845
General and administrative expenses	25,424	2,886	3,006	4,540	35,856	48,740
Net income from operations	$ 9,079	$ 3,532	$ 6,407	$11,507	$ 30,526	$ 85,105
Less: Discounts on sales	.....	107	139	302	548	1,692
Net income before federal and state taxes	$ 9,079	$ 3,425	$ 6,268	$11,205	$ 29,978	$ 83,413
Less: Federal and state taxes	900	....	....	8,300	9,200	30,206
Net profit to earned surplus	$ 8,179	$ 3,425	$ 6,268	$ 2,905	$ 20,778	$ 53,207
Less: Organization expenses	650	....			650	3,457
Earned surplus before adjustments	$ 7,529	$ 3,425			$ 20,128	$ 49,750
Add: Income tax adjustment					450	
Earned surplus after adjustments					$ 20,578	

* From the company's records it could not be readily determined exactly how this item was carried on the company's balance sheets.

Source: Company records.

capital, the new working capital position would allow bidding-in and financing, with available progress payment assistance, of new longer term government contracts up to $750,000 face value. This would be expected to at least double present employment and payroll.

The results to be expected from the use of $25,000 earmarked for new commercial products are not as readily predictable, but it is deemed to be in the best interest of the general economy actively to develop and enlarge nongovernment sponsored business activity. Because of the barely scratched applications to industrial processes of new control and instrumentation techniques, the potentialities of our planned developments are considered excellent. This has been confirmed by considerable and continuing contact with and inquiries from the potential market. An important aspect is the fact that application of the devices and equipment planned for development and sale will result in higher manufacturing productivity at a lower cost. Such equipment is salable in our country even during depressions; and contrary to disproved theories, new technological developments always result in an increased general economy and employment. (See Exhibits 3 and 4 for comparative income statements and balance sheets.)

Exhibit 3a

INSTRUMENTS INCORPORATED

Profit and Loss Analysis—Percentage

	9 Months Ending March 31, 1949	April 1949	May 1949	June 1949	12 Months Ending June 30, 1949	15 Months Ending Sept. 30, 1949
Net sales	100.0%	100.0%	100.0%	100.0%	100.0%	100.0%
Less: Cost of goods sold:						
Raw materials	13.2	23.6	19.8	13.3	15.2	17.6
Direct labor	44.4	55.4	24.1	31.9	40.1	36.6
Manufacturing expenses	37.0	39.7	18.9	24.6	32.5	30.2
Total	94.6%	118.7%	62.8%	69.8%	87.8%	84.4%
Add: Inventories at beginning:						
Work in process	...	95.6%	62.0%	57.8%	...	...
Commercial products in process	...	15.5	15.5	24.2	...	...
Commercial products development	...	36.9	17.3	21.9	...	...
Total	...	148.0%	94.8%	103.8%	...	...
Less: Inventories at end:						
Work in process	12.3%	132.0%	45.5%	74.4%	9.9%	17.9%
Commercial products in process	2.0	33.1	19.1	29.8	4.0	3.3
Commercial products development	4.7	36.9	17.3	21.9	2.9	1.9
Total	19.0%	202.0%	81.9%	126.0%	16.8%	23.1%
Cost of goods sold	75.6%	64.7%	75.7%	47.6%	71.0%	61.3%
Gross profit on sales	24.4%	35.3%	24.3%	52.4%	29.0%	38.7%
General and administrative expenses	18.0	15.9	7.8	14.9	15.7	14.1
Net income from operations	6.4%	19.4%	16.5%	37.5%	13.3%	24.6%
Less: Discounts on sales	...	0.6	0.3	0.8	0.3	0.5
Net profit before federal and state taxes	6.4%	18.8%	16.2%	36.7%	13.0%	24.1%
Less: Federal and state taxes	0.6	...	...	27.2	4.0	8.7
Net profit to earned surplus	5.8%	18.8%	16.2%	9.5%	9.0%	15.4%

Source: Compiled by case writer.

Exhibit 4

INSTRUMENTS INCORPORATED

Comparative Balance Sheet for Selected Dates, May 15, 1948, to September 30, 1949

Assets	May 15, 1948	December 31, 1948	June 30, 1949	September 30, 1949
Current Assets:				
Cash on Hand and in Banks	$14,734	$ 2,465	$ 5,211	$ 21,906
Accounts Receivable	3,500	20,611	22,309	11,898
Work in Process	....	7,519	22,748	61,987
Commercial Products in Process	....	....	9,097	11,543
Finished Goods	....	1,463	....	....
Prepaid Expenses	4,330	7,465	7,790	9,144
Total Current Assets	$22,564	$ 39,523	$ 67,155	$116,478
Fixed Assets:				
Land	$ 1,000	$ 1,013	$ 1,013	$ 1,013
Building and Structures	$54,300	$ 62,980	$ 64,448	$ 64,448
Less Reserve for Depreciation	....	1,262	2,263	....
	$54,300	$ 61,718	$ 62,185	
Machines and Tools	$15,258*	$ 24,204*	$ 32,704*	$ 35,660*
Less Reserve for Depreciation	....	2,499	4,890	....
	$15,258	$ 21,705	$ 27,814	
Laboratory Equipment	$ 2,075	$ 2,345	$ 3,175	$ 5,613
Less Reserve for Depreciation	....	507	959	....
	$ 2,075	$ 1,838	$ 2,216	
Furniture and Equipment	....	$ 2,736	$ 3,145	$ 4,197
Less Reserve for Depreciation	....	99	252	....
	....	$ 2,637	$ 2,893	....
Total Land, Plant, and Equipment at Cost	....	....	....	$110,931
Less Reserve for Depreciation	....	....	....	10,855
Total Fixed Assets	$72,633	$ 88,911	$ 96,121	$100,076
Other Assets:				
Commercial Products Development	....	....	$ 9,474	$ 13,903
Organization Expenses	$ 539	$ 650	....	....
Total Other Assets	$ 539	$ 650	$ 9,474	$ 13,903
Total Assets	$95,736	$129,084	$172,750	$230,457
Liabilities and Net Worth				
Current Liabilities:				
Accounts Payable	$ 5,971	$ 7,716	$ 9,767	$ 17,524
Accounts Payable, Long Term	2,705	6,130	5,995	4,733
Other Accrued Payables	560	6,125	21,455	41,944†
Total Current Liabilities	$ 9,236	$ 19,971	$ 37,217	$ 64,201
Mortgage Payable on Real Estate	27,000	35,200	34,400	34,000
Net Worth:				
Class A Common Stock	$31,100	$ 45,000	$ 48,000	$ 50,100
Class B Common Stock	25,400	27,400	29,200	29,200
Stock Subscribed	3,000	3,954	3,355	2,805
	$59,500	$ 76,354	$ 80,555	$ 82,105
Surplus (Deficit)	....	(2,441)	20,578	50,151‡
Total Net Worth	$59,500	$ 73,913	$101,133	$132,256
Total Liabilities and Net Worth	$95,736	$129,084	$172,750	$230,457

* Does not include approximately $50,000 of machine tools leased from WAA for purchase of which the company was negotiating.
† Provision for state and federal taxes, $30,206.
‡ Includes $400 paid-in surplus.
Source: Company records.

ORGANIZATION

In October, 1949, the company employed over 60 people and was organized as indicated in Exhibit 5.

Each of the company's executives or supervisors was an engineer by training or experience except Mr. Robbins, who had graduated from the Harvard Law School in 1943. Mr. Johnson, after receiving his Master's degree in physics from the University of Chicago in 1936, had worked with the Philco Radio and Television Corporation on vacuum tube application and radio receiver design and from there had gone to Westinghouse to do commercial engineering on receivers and then to General

Exhibit 5

INSTRUMENTS INCORPORATED

Organization Chart

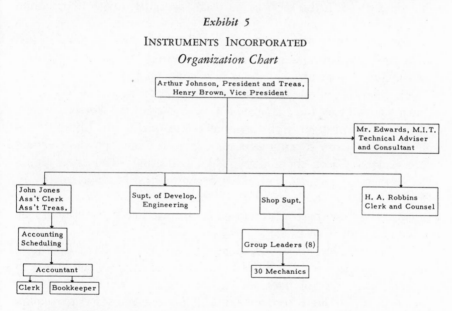

Electric as manager of a research, development, and production group of 160 people working on special radar equipment. Mr. Johnson and his associates believed this latter experience to be the equivalent of engineering and management responsibilities of a business firm of about the same size.

Mr. Brown had received an A.B. degree in chemistry from Purdue in 1936 and had subsequently worked in the research laboratory of the Allied Chemical Company as chief instrument designer and machine-shop superintendent. During the war he was in charge of test work on ammunition and various mechanical and electronic equipment, including radar and antiaircraft gun control. Mr. Brown had gone to General

Electric after the war as senior engineer, designing servo mechanisms.

Mr. Jones, after receiving his degree in engineering from Harvard, served in the Navy as an engineering officer and later in a liaison group responsible for engineering compliance with contract requirements.

The shop superintendent had held positions as plant superintendent of a small machinery company, and, consecutively, as assistant shop superintendent, head tool designer, and shop superintendent with three small manufacturing companies in the Bridgeport area.

The company's consultant, Mr. Edwards, associate professor at Massachusetts Institute of Technology in the instrumentation section of the Aeronautical Engineering Department, had had experience in his field in industry and in the service and was a specialist in gyroscopics and vector kinematics.

Several other men whom Mr. Johnson and Mr. Brown contemplated adding to this management group as the company grew possessed similar backgrounds, or at least comparable experience.

Mr. Johnson and Mr. Brown, through stock ownership, held voting control as well as the management of the company between them. Their purpose in organizing Instruments Incorporated had been to create a company run by engineers for engineers. Their previous experience had convinced them that good engineering supervision would enable them to compete with other organizations, large or small. Mr. Brown considered the market which the company intended to invade so large and new that "a half-dozen companies like it could exist side by side and all prosper."

Within three months of incorporation, the company had a $150,000 plant in operation, consisting of a modern, well-lighted building with 14,000 square feet of floor space, more than adequate for the company's 1949 volume of production, and machine tools and test equipment necessary for precision production. Mr. Brown stated that this relatively large investment in fixed assets was designed to "keep the company's feet on the ground." Both he and Mr. Johnson agreed they did not want to have their company's existence dependent upon someone "having a new idea a minute." They intended to develop manufacturing skills and a reputation for quality and precision which would bring production orders to the company, and foresaw their commercial development as contributing new machines and control devices to be manufactured by means of these skills. They stated that they were not interested in products for a mass market. Mr. Johnson believed his employees possessed a high degree of skill and intelligence so that, as a result, operations were efficient and there would be no "administrative communication" problem. He believed "administrative headaches" would develop if the company became involved in production line operations employing unskilled labor.

Mr. Johnson expressed no interest in becoming a "financial tycoon." He stated that he and Mr. Brown wanted to enjoy running the business and could do this only if it were small enough to be supervised personally. It was his opinion that large companies operated on the wrong side of the "efficiency curve" and that Instruments Incorporated's peak efficiency would be reached at about 400 to 450 employees. He said he had no desire to operate above this point, where he believed output per machine and per man would tend to go down.

During June, July, and August, while sales continued to increase and backlog to grow, commercial development on the company's own products was stopped as all available funds were channeled into working capital. Negotiations with the War Assets Administration for transfer of the $45,900 worth of surplus machinery to Instruments Incorporated were completed, although title was not transferred, and one foreman and twelve workers were added as a night shift.

A large part of Mr. Johnson's time during this period was devoted to raising additional funds or helping Mr. Brown, whose time was spent scheduling orders and directing production so as to take advantage of progress payments[1] on partial shipments in order to meet current obligations. Mr. Brown maintained a close watch over production to insure against last minute errors that would jeopardize the shipping schedule. Both men felt these exigencies were dictating their activities to an undue extent. Mr. Johnson believed additional funds were justified if for no other reason than on the grounds that they would free both men from worry and unnecessary unproductive activities, and allow them time to study and take care of the company's operating problems and commercial research. Both men were anxious to get into the laboratory themselves to work on their own ideas for new products. From the beginning they had each worked seven days a week and evenings. They received the same salaries paid them in their previous positions, but to help financially had taken, to the limit of their means, stock in lieu of a portion of these salaries.

---

[1] The government would provide advances called "progress payments" of up to 90% of actual direct labor and material, payable upon receipt of portions of a contract completed and shipped. In case of fixed-price contracts these costs as well as all others were subject to renegotiation.

PRODUCTION

Next in importance to the critical shortage of working capital, according to Mr. Brown, was a shortage of the "best engineering supervision." The company had a nucleus of three men, considered to have good engineering and production abilities, who acted as project engineers. Each was assigned a specific project, such as a government contract or a commercial product, and given responsibility for its development or production engineering from raw materials through processing and manufacture to shipment. A fourth man, the shop superintendent, also acted as project engineer on some jobs. His main duty was to supervise the actual work of the groups which were of various sizes depending on the magnitude of individual projects. Mr. Brown considered the night-shift foreman capable of supervising the workmen, but not capable enough to develop schedules and appraise an entire project. Mr. Brown was proud of both supervisors and workers. The average age of the entire group was 31 years. Most of them had come from the community in which the company was located or from nearby towns and had been upgraded considerably since coming to the firm. Mr. Brown stated that many of the men were approaching a highly skilled level and possessed enough intelligence to co-operate in scheduling work on various machines used jointly. An exception to this general efficiency occurred on the night shift where, according to Mr. Brown, the right type of worker had not been secured. Although a 10% premium over day wages was paid, the best workers could work days elsewhere for approximately the same wage. This shift did not measure up to day-shift standards of productivity or quality. The plant was not unionized and Messrs. Johnson and Brown believed it would not be. They both contended that this nonunionized working force constituted one of Instruments Incorporated's most important competitive advantages.

ACCOUNTING

Mr. Brown estimated that raw material cost was perhaps 8% of total selling price, whereas total payroll expense approached 55%. (The work-in-process figures show higher material costs than this, because of carrying vendor subcontract work, such as heat-treating, plating, and gear cutting, as a material charge.) He therefore believed the latter deserved the closest watching and control. Mr. Jones was in charge of the company's accounting, records, and office personnel and until August, 1949, had also been acting as purchasing agent. In August a man was brought in to perform this latter function under Mr. Jones's direction. Purchasing generally was on a project-requirement basis, since the variety of materials used was too great to permit stocking raw materials. Invoices were paid net 30 days in order to conserve working capital. According to Mr. Brown, the large diversity of materials purchased in small quantities constituted a continuing problem which often determined the production rate on rush jobs.

Direct material, labor, and manufacturing overhead costs were collected in considerable detail by Mr. Jones, who had devised an actual job-order cost system to provide the information necessary for government contract work. Because of the production organization, it was relatively easy to provide such costs by product or by contract. Labor costs and hours worked were collected by months and cumulatively, and by type (such as shop mechanics, junior draftsmen, senior engineers, etc.) From these was developed a current cost per hour for each type of labor, to be used for contract negotiation (see Exhibit 6). Manufacturing expense, comprising indirect expenses, factory overhead, and all depreciation, also included any employee's time not assignable to projects. These expenses were collected monthly and cumulatively and were related percentagewise to both total direct-labor dollars and hours. General administrative expense (executive salaries, office salaries and financial expenses) were treated similarly. Manufacturing expense and general and administrative expense were then divided by total direct labor hours charged to projects to give a per hour figure which, when added to the actual cost for any type of labor, could be compared to the government allowance for that type and thus furnish a rough check on company efficiency. This system also provided Messrs. Johnson and Brown and stockholders with monthly income statements and balance sheets and the former two men with material, labor, and overhead figures by month and by completed contract. In addition Mr. Jones also furnished Mr. Johnson with daily data on cash on hand, accounts payable, and accounts receivable.

Mr. Brown believed that the diversified nature of the products precluded the use of any standard costing system but that good estimates were essential for bidding. Mr. Johnson estimated hours for various types of labor on each new contract and, using the current total cost per hour, computed an over-all estimate for the contract. This estimate for the contract as a whole was broken down into shippable units, and the actual cost on completion of each such unit was checked against the

Exhibit 6

INSTRUMENTS INCORPORATED

Selected Data from Cost Accounting Record for Government Contract Negotiations

	I	II	III	IV	V	VI	VII
	Productive Labor Costs			Manufacturing Expense per Direct Labor Hour[d]	General and Administrative Expense per Direct Labor Hour[e]	(III + IV + V) Total Expense per Hour	Government Approved Allowance per Hour[g]
	Dollars	Actual Hours	Average Dollars per Hour				
Shop Mechanics:							
1949—first six months	$41,661	26,292	$1.585	$1.317	$0.598	$3.50	$3.62
Total since inclusive through 6/49	71,037	44,810	1.59	1.362	0.657	3.61	
Junior Engineers:							
1949—first six months	5,357	3,488	1.54	1.317	0.598	3.46	3.75
Total since inclusive through 6/49	8,169	5,372	1.52	1.362	0.657	3.54	
Senior Engineers:							
1949—first six months	5,716	1,548	3.69	1.317	0.598	5.61	6.92
Total since inclusive through 6/49	10,416	2,590	4.02	1.362	0.657	6.04	
Laboratory Technicians:							
1949—first six months	2,228	1,604	1.39	1.317	0.598	3.31	3.61
Total since inclusive through 6/49	2,793	2,045	1.365	1.362	0.657	3.38	
Total Productive Labor[a]							
1949—first six months	$55,688	33,240	$1.675				
Total since inclusive through 6/49	93,142	55,247	1.685				

	Manufacturing Expense			General and Administrative Expense		
	Total Dollars	Per Cent of Productive Labor Dollars[c]	Dollars per Direct Labor Hour[d]	Total Dollars	Per Cent of Productive Labor Dollars[f]	Dollars per Direct Labor Hour[g]
1949—first six months	$43,802	78.7%	$1.317	$19,886	35.7%	$0.598
Total since inclusive through 6/49	75,286[b]	80.8%	1.362	36,292[b]	38.9%	0.657

a Total of dollars and hours shown above but reflecting also cost of one senior and one junior draftsman after May.
b This item shows a relatively small variation from the amount as given in the operating statement (Exhibit 3).
c Manufacturing expense as percentage of total productive labor costs.
d Manufacturing expense divided by the total productive labor hours for corresponding period.
e General and administrative expense divided by the total productive labor hours for corresponding period.
f General and administrative expense as a percentage of total productive labor costs.
g This rate was set from experience to cover all costs plus profit allowance and was open to renegotiation after and re-examination prior to each contract

Source: Company records.

estimate. In September the company began including these estimates on the job cost sheet, thus making the estimate part of a permanent record to be used subsequently in estimating similar contracts. On no large contract had the company failed to make a profit, although on several smaller fixed-price contracts the bid price had been slightly lower than the company's actual costs.

Until March, 1949, company officers estimated that from 70% to 80% of prime and subcontract work had been on a cost-plus-fixed-fee basis, but after that date the percentage of fixed-price contracts had increased until in September fixed-price contracts accounted for an estimated 90% of sales. The company was still very much interested in "cost-plus" contracts, especially development contracts which called for a large amount of the time of senior engineers and draftsmen. Cost-plus was also preferred because such contracts, according to company officers, involved lower estimating risks. Company bids had usually been in the lower 5% to 10% of those submitted, but Mr. Johnson stated that by August the range of bidding was beginning to narrow. Bids were being decided on the basis of a few dollars, and he believed some companies were bidding on the basis of direct costs alone.

The executives indicated that they were not interested in taking a job on which they could not make a profit. Mr. Johnson stated that up to September there had been no trouble, principally because ". . . We've got an engineering management that can do some cute tricks in the plant and get the stuff out."

PRODUCTS

The company's backlog of unfilled orders at the end of September was representative of orders to that time. Most of these were the result of personal visits and the reputations of Mr. Johnson and Mr. Brown. Both of the men had friends in the armed services and in various companies with whom they had worked during the war. In addition, a part-time representative who worked in behalf of the company in securing contracts was stationed at Wright Field. Another representative sold Instruments Incorporated abilities and products along with other noncompeting products to some industrial concerns in the Middle Atlantic area. A third representative was located in Washington, D.C. Sales by these men had not been large; indeed, up to September, sales expense had not been deemed large enough to justify its segregation from the general expense category.

In addition to production and development contract work for others,

Instruments Incorporated had in the early months begun development of its own commercial products, limiting itself to those requiring a small amount of funds to develop. A strain-gauge pressure transducer for measuring rapidly changing pressures had been invented and pat- ented by a faculty member of the Rensselaer Polytechnic Institute. Instruments Incorporated had developed the invention to the point where it could be placed on the market, and by March, 1949, began to promote its sale. Work on a complete line of pressure transducers,[2] a fluid flowmeter, and several small items, such as instrument relays and hydraulic valves, had been halted by the shortage of funds while they were still in the developmental stage. Mr. Johnson and Mr. Brown had personally observed the need for, or application of, these products over the period of their employment prior to coming to Instruments In- corporated, and Mr. Johnson believed each had a market in labora- tories, industries, and the military services.

The company's pressure transducer was reported by management to have technical qualities for precision measurement which surpassed competitive products. It consisted of: (1) a sensitive metal gauge, precision-machined, capable of translating engine pressures into an electrical signal; and (2) a compact and sensitive electronic amplifier capable of enlarging the signal for presentation on a Du Mont oscillo- scope. The company's price of $500 per unit did not include the oscillo- scope. Without the amplifier the unit price was $325.

The pressure transducer had been purchased in pilot quantities of one or two by such firms as Ethyl Corporation and General Motors (see Exhibit 7), both for laboratory work in analyzing the properties of fuels and engines and as an aid in engine production and tuning. A small advertising program was launched in July, 1949. In September, the instrument still presented production difficulties, and three or four had been returned. If the hardness of the steel in some of the parts varied, the established tolerances were not sufficient for proper opera- tion. One gauge had for unknown reasons cracked in operation. A problem of corrosion of some parts had been overcome by the com- pany, and work was being done to correct the other difficulties. Of- ficers stated that they believed it would be some time before sales of the instrument resulted in an over-all profit to the company and that, although it was sold on customer demand, sales should not be pushed until technical difficulties had been overcome. The instrument was first

---

[2] A device to give accurate pressure reading at a location other than where the pressure itself existed.

Exhibit 7

APPROXIMATE CHRONOLOGICAL SALES
RECORD OF PRESSURE TRANSDUCER
April 25 to September 30, 1949

Quantity	Customer	Accessories
1	General Electric Co.	(With amplifier)
1	General Electric Co.	
4	Pratt-Whitney Aircraft	(With amplifier)
1	Univ. of Michigan	(With amplifier)
1	Univ. of Michigan	
1	Nash Kelvinator	(With amplifier)
2	Ethyl Corporation*	(With amplifier)
2	E. I. Du Pont de Nemours	
1	U.S. Dept. of Interior† (Bureau of Mines)	
1	General Motors Corp.	(With amplifier)
1	General Motors Corp. (Electro Motors Division)	
1	U.S. Navy	
1	Mack Manufacturing Co.	(With amplifier)
3	Demonstrators	

* One of these was a replacement.
† Later replaced.

Source: Company records.

used in Rensselaer laboratories where it was observed by some of its subsequent purchasers. From the latter others learned of its characteristics. In August, 1949, Mr. Brown estimated total market for the pressure transducer at between 500 and 1,000, and believed several hundred could be sold annually. He believed the market was known and easily reached. He anticipated using direct-mail promotional material but believed the best and primary source of sales would be through "word of mouth." Mr. Brown stated that, lacking expensive market-research facilities, only very general estimates of market potential for company products could be determined. These estimates, however, he believed sufficiently accurate, and he explained further that a capable man who knew the product could generally tell whether it had an extensive, medium-size, or small market, and that from the company's standpoint, in view of its scale of operations, this was probably all that was necessary.

Mr. Johnson stated that, although none of the foregoing developments was likely to "mushroom into a mass market," collectively they could provide a sizable commercial business and a steady and profitable sales volume.

These items, however, were considered by the executives to be "specialty" products and of minor importance as compared with the possibilities of the company's plans in the field of automatic machine-tool controls. In the latter part of August, 1949, Mr. Johnson wrote: ". . . The economies of mass production under current high labor costs are such that automatic equipment which will produce a better product at a lower cost is extremely salable, leasable, or profitable to operate in a competitive market. The whole machine tool industry is aware of the potentialities in this direction. We have discussed some of our ideas and the control devices which we have in hand, with major tool manufacturers. These discussions have definitely outlined specific areas in which need for such developments is real and current. At the expense of losing our potential patent position, we could undoubtedly close a deal with some of these firms to finance our development costs. To date, we have not thought this desirable for obvious reasons. . . ."

In the latter part of 1948, Instruments Incorporated had bid on and received an order for the machining of a quantity of precision-instrument gears. This order offered an opportunity to study production techniques for this part and resulted in several new ideas for a basically different automatic precision gear cutter and new ideas for employing servo controls and precision positioning devices. Since Mr. Brown's and Mr. Johnson's ideas were more specific with regard to this machine, the company's entrance into the machine-tool field was planned by way of the development of such a gear cutter. Mr. Johnson stated that millions of dollars worth of such gears were produced yearly at high unit labor cost and that Instruments Incorporated contemplated building and operating the gear cutter since he believed the company had the subsidiary equipment and know-how to "make a dent in the gear market."

He anticipated that by the end of 1950 the company's own commercial specialty products, such as the pressure transducers, microrelays and flowmeters, would comprise 30% of total sales, the remainder coming from government contracts. He hoped that by the end of 1951 this percentage would have increased to 50% of total sales and that Instruments Incorporated would be well on its way into the production of new machine tools also.

FINANCE

Mr. Johnson stated that this projected rate of growth was dependent upon the funds available. For instance, if $30,000 were secured, only a modest development program could be undertaken, while if $500,000 became available, the company could immediately begin work in the machine-tool field.

Originally the company's financing had been solely through equity capital. To retain voting control in the hands of the two founders and to secure the funds necessary for operations, two classes of stock were authorized: (1) 10,000 shares of Class A nonvoting common at $20 par value and having preference on liquidation with regard to assets; (2) 5,000 shares of Class B voting common no par, issued at $20 per share. The first issue for 5,000 shares of Class A and 2,470 shares of Class B was not subscribed in full. Mr. Johnson and Mr. Brown each received 500 shares of Class B for services rendered in incorporating and were to receive 60 shares a year for a period of five years. In addition Mr. Johnson purchased 500 shares of Class B at $20 per share and Mr. Brown bought 100 shares of Class B at $20 per share with an option to purchase at the same price another 400 shares within a five-year period. Mr. Jones purchased 250 shares of Class B and was to receive 30 shares per year for a period of five years for services rendered in incorporating. By July, 1948, 2,430 shares of Class B stock had been issued to seven individuals, all either active in company management or intending to take an active part sometime in the future. By this time, 2,080 shares of Class A stock had been sold to 23 individuals, including all the holders of Common B with the exception of Mr. Johnson and Mr. Brown. Although no single individual held more than 250 shares of Class A, the family of one member of the board held the largest block. By April, 1949, this family held 650 shares.

Despite the efforts of the company executives between July, 1948, and April, 1949, only 320 more shares of Class A and no additional Class B stock had been sold. In addition to specific factors, such as changes in stock market quotations affecting potential investors, Mr. Johnson attributed this lag in equity financing to the fact that he was not a salesman. "I told investors the truth—that it was a long-term pull and they could not expect dividends for three or four years, but that we were in a field with unlimited opportunities." Mr. Johnson was further restricted in that both he and Mr. Brown wanted to know their stockholders. Several individuals expressed interest in investing sums large enough to dwarf contributions by other individual stockholders, but Mr. Johnson stated, "I do not want anyone who might try to finagle control when times get better."

When it became evident that sufficient funds would not be forthcoming through sale of stock, Mr. Johnson investigated the possibilities of debt financing. Actually, as sales and profits grew, he had become less inclined to sell stock at all. Banks and commercial credit institutions were willing to lend up to 80% of accounts receivable, but both requested, along with other requirements such as purchase by the company of accounts overdue by 30 days, the personal signatures of Mr. Johnson, Mr. Brown, and Mr. Jones. On this basis, however, the company refused to borrow and Mr. Johnson stated, "Of what benefit is the limited liability of a corporation under such circumstances?"

Preparations for a second attempt at negotiation with the RFC were abandoned in August, 1949, when a group of New York businessmen who had organized to invest in small businesses on a speculative basis sent a representative to the plant in response to an approach made by the company early in the year. The visit resulted in considerable interest on the part of this group in Instruments Incorporated, and in September Mr. Johnson was preparing a letter to them outlining the company's plans and a basis for financing. He was inclined to favor the typical method of financing employed by the group, which generally invested a relatively small amount, perhaps 5% to 20% of total funds furnished, in common stock and the rest in preferred stock, debentures, or notes. On this basis Mr. Johnson believed $100,000 should be considered, one-third to be used for working capital, one-third for fixed assets, and one-third for commercial development. Mr. Johnson was favorably impressed with this group of businessmen. He stated that advice and contacts provided by them might be well worth the price of the loan and that he would welcome one or two of the men as additions to his board of directors. This group had successfully backed several small companies, helping them to grow into sizable and profitable concerns.

STOCKHOLDERS AND DIRECTORS

Mr. Johnson believed that any sizable investment, whether through equity or debt, should be represented by a membership on the company's board of directors. The board was composed of Messrs. Johnson, Brown, and Robbins from the company and the following outside directors: Mr. Steven L. Leslie, president of a small textile-finishing company, trustee of the Committee for Economic Development, and president of the American Business Congress (formerly the Smaller Business Association for New York, New Jersey, and Connecticut, an association of several hundred small businesses in the area); Mr. Ralph Newman, associate counsel and auditor for the firm of Arthur Andersen & Co.; and Mr. Joseph McLennen, vice-president of the Fairfield County Trust Company of Stratford, Conn. This board had several times expressed confidence in the management by helping to furnish information and contacts necessary in carrying out policies decided upon by the company officers. In fact the board had left the direction of the company almost exclusively in the hands of its management, giving help only in the direction which the officers indicated they desired to take.

COMPETITION

Depending upon the product considered, Instruments Incorporated competed with a wide range of companies in several industries possessing diverse characteristics.

Electronic control devices for industry had their inception in the early thirties and prior to the war accounted for about $15,000,000 at factory prices, or about 5% of the total output of the electronics industry. During the postwar period the annual total industry average was about $1,000,000,000; 15% or $150,000,000 of this was accounted for by industrial control systems and allied devices. By 1944,[3] approximately 17,000 devices were reported in use by 796 industrial manufacturers, and about 8,500 of these were in use in the metalworking industry. Most important other users were metal-producing, chemical-processing, and electric-utility industries. Control devices and measuring and analysis instruments were by far the most important applications, accounting for about 6,000 instruments each. Companies competing for this business ranged from such firms as General Electric, Radio Corporation of America, Westinghouse and Raytheon, to smaller specialists such as Woodward Governor, or to smaller one- or two-man companies fostered by the war. Altogether there were about 500 companies capable of producing major electronic equipment and about 2,000 to 2,500 manufacturers of component parts. Not all of these were engaged in industrial work; in fact, most such companies manufactured communications equipment, but very few produced only one type of equipment. The war, however, had fostered a rapid trend toward vertical integration within the industry.

The metalworking industry was also marked by a large number of competing companies varying widely with regard to size. Major machine-tool companies such as Ex-Cell-O Corporation of Detroit, Heald of Worcester, Massachusetts, or Jones and Lamson of Springfield, Vermont, known for the design and manufacture of high-quality machine tools, in both standard and special-purpose types, obtained a large per-

---

[3] "Present and Potential Applications of Electronic Devices in Industry," Research Department, McGraw-Hill Publishing Company, Inc., 1944. Gordon K. Bell, Jr., "Electronics from War to Peace," *Industrial Record* (National Industrial Conference Board), Vol. V, No. 3 (April 30, 1946).

centage of their income from the machining and heat-treating of precision parts. These large companies (and others such as the Cincinnati Milling Machine Company, Gisholt Machine Company, Brown & Sharpe Manufacturing Company) maintained mechanical, metallurgical, and electronic engineering staffs sometimes numbering in the hundreds. In addition, in the Bridgeport area alone there were over 200 machine shops of varying capabilities. About 20% of the latter claimed to qualify as experimental shops. Products such as gears for which extensive markets existed were manufactured not only by many of the foregoing companies and many machinery and instrument manufacturers but by a sizable number of nationally advertised companies specializing in this product. Thus, there were approximately 10 manufacturers specializing in gear-cutting machinery about equally divided geographically between the Midwest, Middle Atlantic, and New England areas and over 25 specialists in gear production. Approximately 50% of these companies were located in the Detroit-Chicago area, 30% in the New York and Pennsylvania area, and 20% in New England.[4]

---

[4] *Thomas' Register of American Manufacturers* and *American Machinist.*

Heublein, Inc. (A)

WITH GROWTH in sales and profits since 1959 far outstripping the liquor industry's "Big Four," Heublein, Inc., producer of Smirnoff vodka and other liquor and food items, had moved up to become the

TABLE 1*

Industry Rank in 1965	Company	1964 Liquor Sales (Millions)	1965 Total Sales (Millions)	Total Sales Gain 1959–65 (Per Cent)	Profit Gain 1959–65 (Per Cent)
1....	Distillers Corporation	$718	$1,005	37%	52%
2....	Hiram Walker	498	530	28	46
3....	National Distillers	430	829	44	24
4....	Schenley Industries (est.)	390	461	0	33
5....	Heublein, Inc.	123	166	89	259

* Derived from various company annual reports.

fifth largest liquor company in the United States by 1965. (See Exhibits 1 and 2 for Heublein financial statistics.)

Mr. Hart, Heublein's president since 1960 and a former executive vice president of international marketing for the Colgate-Palmolive Company, commented on the company's business as follows:

Although liquor products account for most of our sales at the present time, we consider ourselves in the consumer goods business, not the liquor business. Liquor is a consumer good just like toothpaste and is sold the same way.

To be successful in this business, you need three things: a good product, distribution, and advertising. You must have a good product. If you don't, the consumer will find you out and you will not get any repeat purchases. You also need good distribution, so the consumer will be able to get your product easily and conveniently. Finally, you must have a good convincing story to tell the consumer about why he should buy your product and you tell it through advertising.

In 1965, Heublein's management had three long-range goals: (1) to make Smirnoff the number one liquor brand in the world; (2) to continue a sales growth of 10% a year through internal growth, acqui-

Exhibit 1

HEUBLEIN, INC. (A)

Consolidated Balance Sheets as of June 30

(Dollars in Thousands)

Assets

Current assets:	1955	1960	1963	1964	1965
Cash	$ 2,298	$ 3,925	$ 2,744	$ 3,357	$ 3,338
Time deposits	...	...	6,000	1,750	...
Marketable securities	9	4,883	1,000	...	4,048
Investment in whiskey certificates	...	593	1,069	150	...
Accounts and notes receivable	5,157	12,426	17,835	18,668	19,010
Inventories	5,825	8,269	9,127	13,347	16.323
Prepaid expenses	297	382	356	325	548
Total current assets	$13,586	$30,479	$38,130	$37,597	$43,267
Long-term assets:					
Property, plant and equipment— net	$ 3,254	$ 5,793	$ 6,363	$ 7,339	$ 7,502
Deferred charges, other assets and goodwill	223	416	1,068	3,659	5,383
Total long-term assets	$ 3,477	$ 6,209	$ 7,431	$10,998	$12,885
Total assets	$17,063	$36,688	$45,561	$48,595	$56,152

Liabilities and Stockholders' Equity

Current liabilities:	1955	1960	1963	1964	1965
Notes payable to banks	$ 2,000	...	...	...	...
Accounts payable	687	$ 1,933	$ 2,078	$ 2,417	$ 3,584
Federal income tax	531	2,857	3,607	4,129	4,701
Accrued liabilities	513	2,688	4,044	5,175	5,774
Cash dividends payable	98	299	733	721	986
Long-term debt due within one year	301	631	777	850	1,013
Total current liabilities	$ 4,129	$ 8,408	$11,239	$13,292	$16,059
Long-term liabilities:					
Long-term debt due after one year	$ 4,699	$ 5,388	$ 3,239	$ 2,416	$ 1,403
Deferred federal income tax	...	...	154	248	316
Minority interest	...	...	...	272	...
Total long-term liabilities	$ 4,699	$ 5,388	$ 3,393	$ 2,936	$ 1,719
Stockholders' equity	8,235	22,892	30,929	32,368	38,374
Total liabilities and stockholders' equity	$17,063	$36,688	$45,561	$48,595	$56,152

Source: Heublein records.

sitions, or both; and (3) to maintain Heublein's return on equity above 15%.

Some industry observers, however, predicted a more normal growth rate for Heublein over the coming years because of the increasing competition from the four largest distillers in the vodka and other nonwhiskey markets from which Heublein derived the majority of its sales.

Exhibit 2

HEUBLEIN, INC. (A)

Consolidated Statement of Income for Year Ending June 30

(Dollars in Thousands)

	1955	1956	1957	1958	1959	1960	1961	1962	1963	1964	1965
Net sales	$37,222	$68,543	$82,064	$87,839	$87,647	$103,169	$108,281	$116,142	$121,995	$135,848	$165,595
Cost of sales*	29,503	53,219	63,234	67,231	67,276	78,028	80,419	85,793	89,500	99,575	121,503
Gross profit	$ 7,719	$15,325	$18,830	$20,608	$20,372	$ 25,140	$ 27,862	$ 30,349	$ 32,495	$ 36,273	$ 44,092
Expenses:											
Selling and advertising	$ 4,650	$ 8,013	$10,617	$12,613	$12,710	$ 14,276	$ 16,089	$ 16,444	$ 18,271	$ 20,477	$ 24,551
Administrative and general	1,479	2,288	2,699	2,822	2,561	2,783	3,205	4,111	3,710	3,485	4,257
	$ 6,130	$10,301	$13,315	$15,434	$15,271	$ 17,060	$ 19,293	$ 20,555	$ 21,981	$ 23,962	$ 28,808
	$ 1,590	$ 5,024	$ 5,515	$ 5,176	$ 5,100	$ 8,080	$ 8,569	$ 9,794	$ 10,514	$ 12,312	$ 15,284
Other†	$ 189	$ 316	$ 407	$ 519	$ 638	$ 293	$ 168	$ 199	$ (339)	$ (18)	$ (112)
	1,401	4,708	5,109	4,654	4,462	7,788	8,401	9,595	10,852	12,330	15,397
State and federal income taxes	733	2,531	2,697	2,524	2,399	4,232	4,587	5,188	5,830	6,516	8,021
Net income	$ 667	$ 2,177	$ 2,411	$ 2,130	$ 2,063	$ 3,556	$ 3,814	$ 4,407	$ 5,022	$ 5,814	$ 7,376

* Cost of sales includes federal excise taxes on the withdrawal of distilled spirits from bond. For the fiscal year 1965, these totalled $90 million.
† Interest income, interest expense, and miscellaneous.
Source: Heublein records.

THE LIQUOR INDUSTRY[1]

Product. Ten categories of liquor (distilled spirits, excluding beer and wine) were listed by the U.S. Department of Commerce in 1964. Of these, five were whiskeys and five were nonwhiskeys.

Whiskeys	*Nonwhiskeys*
Straight	Gin
Blended	Vodka
Bonded	Rum
Scotch (100% imported)	Brandy
Canadian (100% imported)	Other (cordials, aperitifs, bottled cocktails, etc.)

The labeling of liquor products within these categories was subject to federal standards, as follows:

TABLE 2

Product	*Requirements*
Straight whiskey	Aged not less than 24 months in new charred-oak barrels; distilled from not less than 51% of the designated grain (corn,* rye, or wheat).
Bonded whiskeys	Straight whiskeys; aged at least four years; bottled at 100 proof; the product of a single distiller, a single distillery, and a single season and year.
Blended whiskey	A mixture of two or more straight whiskeys.
Scotch and Canadian	Aged not less than 24 months,† straight or blended; if blended, then designated as such.
Gin	No aging requirement;‡ at least 80 proof; containing the juniper berry flavor; made by direct distillation of mash or redistillation of distilled spirits.
Vodka	No aging requirement;‡ no distinctive character, flavor, or taste; approved by the federal government;§ usually made by filtering grain neutral spirits through activated charcoal.
Rum	Produced from sugar cane; no federal requirements regarding method of production.
Brandy	Obtained solely from the fermented juice, mash, or wine of fruit; distilled at less than 190 proof.‖
Other	Requirements depend on the product type.

* Of the straight whiskeys, 98% were bourbons distilled from corn.
† Usually aged four or more years.
‡ Gin and vodka were unique among the distilled spirits since they required no aging. The principal distinction between gin and vodka was that the juniper berry flavor was added to grain neutral spirits to produce the former, while as many flavor-producing ingredients as possible were filtered out from grain neutral spirits to produce the latter.
§ Federal requirements complex, but essentially as stated above.
‖ Usually produced from white grapes and bottled at 80 proof or higher.

---

[1] Several terms in common use in the industry require definition:
   Proof is a term used to specify the proportion of alcohol in a product. The proof

Exhibit 3

HEUBLEIN, INC. (A)

Liquor Consumption vs. Population

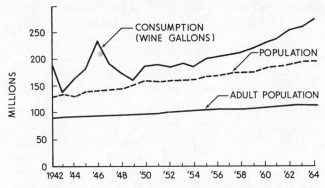

Source: Garvin Jobson Associates, Inc., *The Liquor Handbook, 1965;* cited by
Glore Forgan, Wm. R. Staats Inc., in *Heublein, Inc.* (December, 1965).

Market. Between 1955 and 1964, U.S. consumption of distilled
spirits increased from 199 million to 277 million wine gallons, or 39%
(see Exhibit 3). By the latter year, some 60 million Americans—about
53% of the adult population—drank some sort of alcoholic beverage.
These Americans spent about $6.5 billion for liquor, about one third of
the amount spent for public elementary and secondary school education.
Excise taxes[2] on these sales provided the federal government with about
$2.5 billion in 1964, more than any other single source of revenue,
except for personal and corporate income taxes. According to *Barron's*,[3]
illegal distilling was increasing as a consequence of these taxes. In 1964,
an estimated 50 million wine gallons of liquor was "bootlegged," representing about 18% of the 277 million wine gallons of legally produced
liquor.

Rising sales of liquor could be attributed to various causes, including
a rising population; increased personal discretionary income contributing to higher per capita consumption; changing social mores; the declining proportion of people in "dry" states; and changes in the population
makeup by age groups.

---

number is equal to twice the per cent of alcohol (by volume) in the product.
A *proof gallon* is any volume which contains the same amount of alcohol as a
gallon of 100-proof spirits.

A *wine gallon* is a gallon by volume (regardless of proof). Thus, a gallon (five
fifths) of 80-proof vodka would be one wine gallon but only 8/10 proof gallons.

[2] The federal excise tax on distilled spirits was $10.50 per proof gallon in 1965.

[3] Dana L. Thomas, "Flush of Success: New Competitive Spirit Has Given a Healthier
Glow to the Distillers," *Barron's* (July 20, 1964), p. 3.

Exhibits 4, 5, 6, and 7 contain the best publicly available information on some of these trends. Mr. Edward Kelley, Heublein's executive vice president, cautioned that statistics about liquor consumption by demographic groups were not as dependable as for some other consumer

Exhibit 4

HEUBLEIN, INC. (A)

The Origins of Demand by Age Group

(Urban Family Expenditures for Alcoholic Beverages,* 1960–61)

SHARE OF MARKET PERCENT DISTRIBUTION

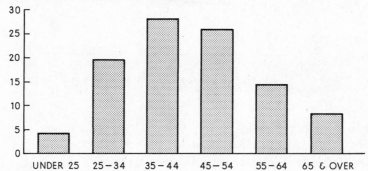

AVERAGE ANNUAL EXPENDITURES: DOLLARS

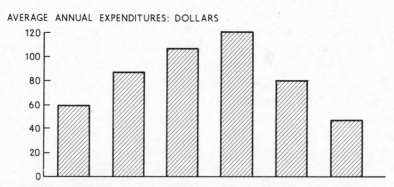

* Includes beer and wine.
   Source: Department of Labor; The Conference Board; cited by Glore Forgan, Wm. R. Staats Inc., in *Heublein, Inc.* (December, 1965).

goods. Mr. Kelley felt the growth in liquor consumption between 1955 and 1964 was primarily the result of the increase in per capita consumption, which appeared to be related to the growth in personal discretionary income, and the spread of drinking to more segments of the population and on more occasions, resulting from the trends of social living habits.

Predicting the future in relation to income and demographic changes, industry sources looked forward to an even faster growth in consumption from 1965 to 1970 than from 1955 to 1964: 4.5% or more a year, compared with 3.6%. Since the Bureau of the Census forecast that the 25 to 54 age groups would increase an average of nearly 17% between 1970 and 1980, many industry observers felt the picture beyond 1970 looked better than that between 1965 and 1970.

Market Changes. Demand for the various categories of liquor was changing as well as growing between 1955 and 1964 (see Exhibits 8, 9, 10, and 11). Thus there was a dramatic shift in consumer preference to straight whiskeys, imported whiskeys, and the nonwhiskeys, and away from the blended and bonded whiskeys. While some observers felt this represented a return to the pre-World War II relationship, which provided straight whiskeys with a slight edge over blended whiskeys, most industry sources felt the shift in consumption reflected a trend toward lightness in liquor taste. According to Roger Bensen:

The most probable reason [for the trend toward lightness] is that people drink mainly to satisfy social and status needs and for effect and not inherently for taste. The taste of many liquors is something which new drinkers find difficult to assimilate. Hence, they turn to various cocktails or mixed drinks to disguise the original flavor of the liquor product. And to complete the pattern, people achieve further fulfillment of social and status needs by using the newer, more current, more exotic liquors and cocktail formulations as a vehicle for their drinking.[4]

Exhibit 5

HEUBLEIN, INC. (A)

Total Population by Age

(Millions)

Year	Total	Under 15	15–19	20–24	25–34	35–44	45–54	55–64	65 and Over
1950	151.7	40.6	10.8	11.7	24.0	21.6	17.4	13.3	12.3
1960	180.7	56.1	13.4	11.1	22.9	24.2	20.6	15.6	16.7
1965	195.1	60.6	17.0	13.6	22.4	24.5	22.1	17.0	18.1
1970	211.4	65.7	18.9	17.1	25.2	23.0	23.4	18.5	19.6
1980	252.1	81.9	21.4	20.6	36.1	25.3	22.2	21.5	23.1

Per Cent Increase (Decrease)

1950–60	19.1	38.2	24.1	(5.1)	(4.6)	12.0	18.4	17.3	35.8
1960–65	8.0	8.0	26.9	22.5	(2.2)	1.2	7.3	9.0	8.4
1965–70	8.4	8.4	11.2	25.7	12.5	(6.1)	5.9	8.8	8.3
1970–80	19.3	24.7	13.2	20.5	44.8	10.0	(5.1)	16.2	17.9

Source: Department of Commerce, Bureau of the Census, figures updated as of July 9, 1964; cited by Glore Forgan, Wm. R. Staats Inc., in *Heublein, Inc.* (December, 1965).

[4] Roger Bensen, *Heublein, Inc.,* Investment Research Dept., Glore Forgan, Wm. R. Staats Inc. (December, 1965), p. 21.

Some of the most important of these changes are reflected in the following figures for distilled spirits entering trade channels:

TABLE 3*

PRODUCT TYPE	VOLUME (Millions of Wine Gallons)		MARKET SHARE (Per Cent)		CHANGE IN VOLUME (Per Cent)
	1955	1964	1955	1964	1955 to 1964
Whiskeys:					
Bonded	12.9	7.9	6.3%	2.8%	(39)%
Straight	46.1	69.6	22.7	24.3	51
Blend	81.5	74.7	40.0	26.1	(8)
Scotch	12.3	28.3	6.0	9.9	130
Canadian	9.2	17.2	4.5	6.0	87
Total all whiskey	161.5	197.9	79.5%	69.1%	22%
Nonwhiskeys:					
Gin	20.7	31.1	10.2	10.9	50
Vodka	7.0	28.1	3.4	9.8	302
Rum	2.7	5.9	1.3	2.1	119
Brandy	4.6	8.7	2.3	3.0	89
Other (cordials, etc.)	6.6	14.6	3.3	5.1	121
Total nonwhiskeys	41.8	88.4	20.5%	30.9%	111%
Total distilled spirits	203.3	286.3	100.0%	100.0%	41%

* For greater detail, see Exhibit 8.

According to many industry observers, one of the more important developments in the liquor industry between 1960 and 1965 was the growth of bottled cocktails. Although bottled cocktails had been on the market for over 50 years, they had shown little growth until 1960. In that year, Heublein, which had almost 100% of the market at that time, developed a new product formulation, package, and promotional campaign for its line of bottled cocktails. By 1965, volume had increased 100% to an estimated 1.9 million wine gallons, as Distillers Corporation, Hiram Walker, Schenley, and others entered the market. Nevertheless, Heublein, whose volume increased 60% during the period, still had 55% of the market in 1965. The convenience, low consumer price (only a few pennies more than comparable drinks mixed at home), and trend toward lightness caused one liquor authority to predict that bottled cocktails might represent close to 10% of the industry's volume by 1975.

Bulk imports were also expected to be an area of potential future growth. Bulk imports consisted of Scotch or Canadian whiskeys that were imported in barrels rather than bottles. They were then reduced to

Exhibit 6

HEUBLEIN, INC. (A)

The Origins of Demand by Income Class

(Urban Family Expenditures for Alcoholic Beverages,* 1960–61)

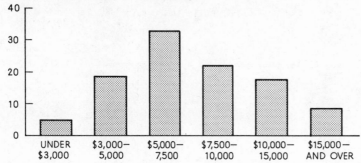

SHARE OF MARKET PERCENT DISTRIBUTION

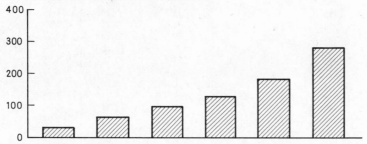

AVERAGE ANNUAL EXPENDITURES: DOLLARS

* Includes beer and wine.
Source: Department of Labor; The Conference Board; cited by Glore Forgan, Wm. R. Staats Inc., in *Heublein, Inc.* (December, 1965).

the desired proof by the addition of water and bottled in the United States. Since Scotch and Canadian whiskeys imported in bottles were taxed at a rate of $10.50 a proof gallon while the same whiskeys imported in barrels were taxed at a rate of $10.50 a wine gallon, bulk importing resulted in a tax saving of from $0.30 to $0.42 a fifth. This tax savings, coupled with lower transportation costs and reduced mark-ups by the wholesaler and retailer, resulted in a price savings of as much as $1 per fifth to the consumer. Although the demand for bulk whiskeys increased during the early sixties, some bulk importers felt their gains were made primarily at the expense of American straight and blended whiskeys rather than the higher priced, bottled imported whiskeys.

Trends in Competition. Between 1955 and 1965, the majority of

the companies in the liquor industry followed one of two broad strategies. Most of the medium-sized companies aggressively marketed their
products in traditional ways. They did not increase, decrease, or change

Exhibit 7

HEUBLEIN, INC. (A)

Liquor Consumption

Wine Gallons

YEAR	TOTAL (Millions)	PER CAPITA	
		Total Pop.	Adults
1964	276.0	1.44	2.44
1963	259.0	1.38	2.32
1962	253.7	1.37	2.30
1961	241.5	1.33	2.21
1960	234.7	1.31	2.17
1959	225.5	1.28	2.12
1958	215.5	1.24	2.05
1957	212.1	1.25	2.03
1956	215.2	1.29	2.08
1955	199.6	1.22	1.95
1954	189.5	1.18	1.87
1953	194.7	1.23	1.94
1952	183.7	1.18	1.85
1951	193.8	1.26	1.97
1950	190.0	1.26	1.95
1949	169.6	1.14	1.76
1948	171.0	1.17	1.80
1947	181.7	1.27	1.94
1946	231.0	1.65	2.51
1945	190.1	1.44	2.23
1944	166.7	1.26	1.95
1943	145.5	1.09	1.68
1942	190.3	1.42	2.20
1941	158.2	1.19	1.85
1940	145.0	1.10	1.72
1939	134.7	1.03	1.62
1938	126.9	0.98	1.55
1937	135.4	1.05	1.67
1936	122.1	0.95	1.53
1935	89.7	0.70	1.14
1934	58.0	0.46	0.75

Source: Distilled Spirits Institute and U.S. Department of Commerce; cited by Gavin
Jobson Associates, Inc., in *The Liquor Handbook, 1965.*

their product line, nor did they attempt to diversify out of the liquor
business. None of these companies had a complete line of liquor products, and some had only one or two products. Several of these companies, however, experienced extremely rapid growth during this period.
Their success could generally be attributed to having a leading product

Exhibit 8

HEUBLEIN, INC. (A)

Estimated Distilled Spirits Entering Trade Channels

Class and Type	1955 Gallons (Millions)	1955 Market Share (Per Cent)	1960 Gallons (Millions)	1960 Market Share (Per Cent)	1964 Gallons (Millions)	1964 Market Share (Per Cent)	Growth, 1964 from 1955 (Per Cent)
Domestic whiskey							
Bonded........................	12,869	6.3%	9,394	3.9%	7,911	2.8%	(38.5)%
Straight........................	44,838	22.1	58,939	24.6	68,802	24.0	53.5
Blend of straights.............	1,249	0.6	793	0.3	758	0.3	(39.2)
Blend of neutral spirits........	81,494	40.0	74,074	31.0	74,731	26.1	(8.0)
Other..........................	(449)	(0.2)	(119)				
Total......................	140,001	68.9%	143,082	59.8%	152,203	53.2%	8.9%
Imported whiskey							
Scotch.........................	12,284	6.0	20,585	8.6	28,249	9.9	130.5
Canadian......................	9,158	4.5	12,552	5.3	17,170	6.0	87.5
Other*.........................	13	...	79	...	251	...	1,822.0
Total......................	21,455	10.6%	33,215	13.9%	45,670	16.0%	113.0
Total whiskey.............	161,457	79.5%	176,297	73.7%	197,873	69.2%	22.5%
Gin							
Domestic.......................	20,447	10.1	22,001	9.2	28,963	10.1	41.5
Imported.......................	291	0.2	1,149	0.5	2,167	0.8	645.0
Total......................	20,738	10.2%	23,150	9.7%	31,130	10.9%	50.0%
Vodka..........................	6,968	3.4	19,406	8.1	28,130	9.8	304.0
Rum							
Puerto Rican, Virgin Islands....	1,873	0.9	2,724	1.2	4,189	1.4	124.0
Other domestic.................	663	0.3	804	0.3	1,543	0.5	133.0
Total domestic............	2,537	1.3%	3,528	1.5%	5,731	1.9%	126.0%
Imported domestic..............	181	...	219	0.1	186	...	3.0
Brandies							
Domestic.......................	3,726	1.8	5,300	2.2	7,575	2.6	103.0
Imported.......................	893	0.4	1,163	0.5	1,113	0.4	24.5
Total......................	4,619	2.3%	6,463	2.7%	8,688	3.0%	88.0
Cordials and specialties							
Domestic.......................	6,173	3.0	9,156	3.8	12,761	4.5	106.0
Imported.......................	455	0.2	812	0.4	1,052	0.4	131.5
Total......................	6,629	3.3%	9,968	4.2%	13,813	4.9%	109.0%
Not elsewhere specified........	178	...	342	...	750	0.3	320.0
Grand total....................	203,306	100.0%	239,373	100.0%	286,301	100.0%	41.0%
Total domestic.................	179,916	88.5%	202,594	84.6%	235,743	82.2%	41.0%
Total imported.................	23,390	11.5	36,779	15.4	50,559	17.7	121.0
Grand total....................	203,306	100.0%	239,373	100.0%	286,301	100.0%	41.0%

* Mainly Irish and Belgian.
Source: Distilled Spirits Institute: cited by Glore Forgan, Wm. R. Staats Inc., in *Heublein, Inc.* (December, 1965).

Exhibit 9

HEUBLEIN, INC. (A)

Whiskey Consumption Trend, 1955–64

(Expressed as a Three-Year Moving Average)

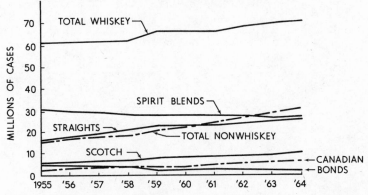

Source: Gavin Jobson Associates, *The Liquor Handbook, 1965;* cited by Glore Forgan, Wm. R. Staats Inc., in *Heublein, Inc.* (December, 1965).

in one or two of the more rapidly growing segments of the liquor market.

The four major distillers also marketed their products in traditional ways. However, with the exception of Hiram Walker, each of these

Exhibit 10

HEUBLEIN, INC. (A)

Nonwhiskey Consumption Trend, 1955–64

(Expressed as a Three-Year Moving Average)

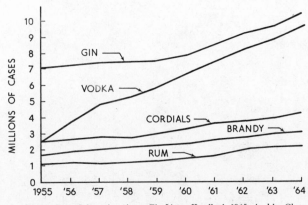

Source: Gavin Jobson Associates, *The Liquor Handbook, 1965;* cited by Glore Forgan, Wm. R. Staats In *Heublein, Inc.* (December, 1965).

Exhibit 11

HEUBLEIN, INC. (A)

Projected 1968 Sales of Liquor

(Millions of Cases)

(Based on Extension of 1960–64 Sales)

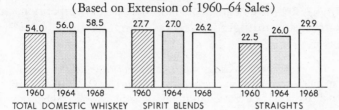

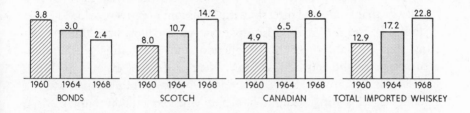

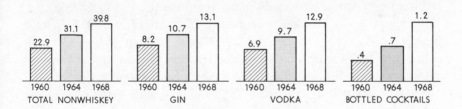

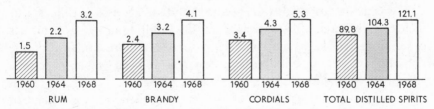

Source: Gavin Jobson Associates, *The Liquor Handbook, 1965;* cited by Glore Forgan, Wm. R. Staats Inc., in *Heublein, Inc.* (December, 1965).

companies attempted to diversify out of the liquor industry through acquisitions between 1955 and 1965. Even with this diversification, however, liquor accounted for the major portion of the sales of each of these companies in 1965. Moreover, with the possible exception of

National Distillers, the major distillers no longer seemed to be interested in further diversification outside of the liquor business in the middle 1960's. Rather they began to compete more vigorously in all segments of the liquor market during 1964 and 1965, particularly the more rapidly growing segments. This increased competition, coupled with the trend toward lightness, caused John Shaw of Equity Research Associates to predict that:

> Marketing efforts will become more consumer-oriented, stressing "appetite appeal" in much the same way as the food industry. Over all, advertising and promotional costs can be expected to trend higher, as brand competition remains intense.[5]

Thumbnail sketches of a few of the companies that have grown rapidly or that competed directly with Heublein are given below.

James B. Beam Distilling Company was a medium-sized liquor company that specialized in the production and marketing of premium Kentucky straight bourbon whiskey. Nearly 80% of Beam's $92 million sales in 1965 were derived from its Jim Beam brand, which was the second largest selling straight bourbon whiskey in the country. As a result of the expansion of the straight whiskey market, Beam was able to increase its profits by over 20% per year between 1953 and 1965.

Paddington Corporation[6] was the exclusive importer of J & B Rare Scotch whiskey, the number two brand of Scotch in 1964. Although J & B was Paddington's only product, the company sales and earnings growth were the highest in the industry between 1960 and 1964. In the latter year, Paddington earned 37.5% on its stockholders' equity, and gross sales reached over $125 million.

Distillers Corporation–Seagram's, Ltd., a Canadian-based corporation, was the largest worldwide producer and marketer of distilled spirits in 1965. Although 80% of Seagram's $897 million in 1964 gross sales came from whiskeys, the company also had a complete line of the nonwhiskeys. The breadth of its product line allowed Seagram's to take advantage of changing consumer preferences. Seagram's VO, for example, was the major recipient of the growing demand for Canadian

---

[5] John Shaw, "Trends in the Liquor Industry," *Equity Research Associates* (August 30, 1965), p. 6.

[6] Paddington Corporation was acquired by Liggett & Myers Tobacco Company in April, 1966. L & M also acquired Star Industries, a wholesale liquor distributor, liquor importer, and owner of 40% of Paddington's voting securities, at the same time. In 1964, Star's net sales (sales less federal and state excise taxes) were $82 million. During the same year, L & M had net sales of $293 million and total assets of $401 million.

whiskey. However, the company also changed old products or introduced new products in response to changing consumer preferences.
When sales of Calvert Reserve had declined for over seven consecutive
years, Seagram's replaced it with a restyled "soft whiskey," Calvert
Extra, in the spring of 1963, and experienced an immediate sales gain of
over 17%. In 1964, Seagram's withdrew Lord Calvert, a premium
blended whiskey, and replaced it with Canadian Lord Calvert, a moderately priced Canadian whiskey bottled in the U.S., to take advantage of
the trend toward bulk imports. In addition, Seagram's introduced nine
new liquor products between 1961 and 1964 to capitalize on the trend
toward lightness. Among these were two Scotches (100 Pipers and
Passport) and four liqueurs as well as a gin, a vodka, the first Hawaiian
rum, and a line of Calvert bottled cocktails.

Schenley, the fourth largest liquor company in 1964 with gross sales
of $406 million, had one of the lowest growth rates in the liquor
industry between 1955 and 1964. The company's gross sales decreased
about 3% during that period, even though Schenley had three of the
top 10 straight whiskey brands and had made several nonliquor acquisitions. However, in 1964, Schenley acquired Buckingham, the importer
of Cutty Sark, the number one brand of Scotch, and introduced a line of
bottled cocktails. As a result of these actions, several industry observers
were predicting a turn around at Schenley by 1967.

Methods of Distribution. Distribution of liquor took two basic
forms at the beginning of 1966. In 18 "control states," a state-regulated
agency was responsible for the distribution and sale of distilled spirits.
In these states, the marketer usually sold the product to the state agency
at the national wholesaler price and allowed the state to distribute the
products as it saw fit. These states often had laws which restricted the
type of point of promotion advertising that a company could undertake.
In the other 32 states, called "open states," distribution was accomplished through wholesalers who redistributed the product to the retailers who sold the product to the ultimate consumer. From 1958 to 1964,
the number of these independent wholesalers declined almost 43%, so
there were only 2,305 wholesalers left in 1964 who were licensed by
the Federal Alcohol Administration to deal in distilled spirits. This
trend, which was similar to that in other consumer product industries,
was primarily caused, according to industry observers, by a serious profit
squeeze on the wholesaler as his costs of operation increased while the
retail prices of inexpensive liquors declined because of intense competi-

tion—a situation which was aggravated by the spread of private labels. While distillers had not felt the effects of this squeeze by 1964, there was a feeling among some industry observers that distillers might have to lower their prices to wholesalers or lose lower volume lines if the trend continued.

Cost Structure. The cost of producing liquor products, excluding federal and state taxes on the raw materials, was relatively low compared to the retail selling prices. For example, high-quality vodka reportedly cost about 61 cents a fifth to produce, and retailed at $5.75. Federal taxes on raw materials (assuming an 80-proof product) were $1.68 per fifth. In addition, the costs of production, excluding federal and state taxes on raw materials, were often not much different for high-priced and low-priced liquors, even though they were often made by different processes. The different methods of production resulted in differences in taste and quality between the high-priced and low-priced liquors, however.

HEUBLEIN'S HISTORY

The House of Heublein was founded in 1859 in Hartford, Connecticut, by Andrew Heublein, a painter and weaver by trade. At that time, the House of Heublein was a combination restaurant, cafe, and small hotel. By 1875, Andrew's two sons, Gilbert and Lewis, were running the business. They branched out by conducting a wholesale wine business in addition to expanding the original operations. In 1892, through a combination of fortuitous circumstances, Heublein invented the bottled cocktail. From this time until the start of national prohibition, Heublein's principal business was the production and sale of distilled spirits.

In 1907, Heublein began importing Brand's A-1 steak sauce and later, when World War I disrupted the importation, acquired the manufacturing rights to the product in the United States. When prohibition forced Heublein to close down its liquor plant in 1920, the company transferred key personnel to food operations. Until the repeal of prohibition in 1933, A-1 steak sauce was Heublein's principal product.

In 1939, John Martin, Heublein's president and one of the company's principal stockholders, acquired the rights to Smirnoff vodka from Mr. Rudolph Kunett. Although Heublein sold only 6,000 cases of Smirnoff that year, a carefully planned promotional campaign, which was put into operation immediately after World War II, aided in boosting the sales of Smirnoff to over one million cases per year by 1954. As the vodka market expanded, Heublein introduced Relska vodka in 1953 and Popov in 1961 to have entries in the middle-price and low-price segments of the market.

Although Smirnoff's remained Heublein's principal product from 1959, when it accounted for over 67% of sales, to 1965, when it accounted for 51% of sales, Heublein began to diversify its product line and to expand its international operations in the former year.

Heublein used both internal growth and acquisitions to broaden its product line. In 1960, Heublein began a campaign to increase the sales of its bottled cocktails by introducing new kinds of cocktails and promoting the entire line more heavily. As Heublein's sales began to increase, other distillers, principally Distillers Corporation, began to market their own cocktails. By 1965, bottled cocktails sales exceeded 850,000 cases a year, more than double the 1960 sales. At that time, Heublein still claimed 55% of the market.

In 1961, Heublein made two acquisitions which strengthened its specialty food line. Timely Brands, which manufactured and marketed a complete line of ready-to-use, home dessert decorating products, including Cake-Mate icing and gels, was acquired in June. In July, Heublein acquired Escoffier, Ltd., of London, England, makers of 23 famed gourmet sauces and specialties.

Heublein made two more acquisitions during this period, both of which were designed to broaden and strengthen Heublein's liquor line. In April, 1964, Heublein acquired Arrow Liquors Corporation for an estimated cost of $5.7 million. Arrow's principal products were its line of cordials, including Arrow Peppermint Schnapps, Arrow Blackberry Brandy, and its domestically bottled, bulk-imported Scotch, McMaster's. According to Mr. Edward Kelley, the three principal reasons for the Arrow acquisition were that Heublein expected the cordial and Scotch markets to grow in the future, that Arrow had products that were among the leaders in these markets in the control states, and that Arrow had a small but extremely competent management.

In January, 1965, Heublein acquired Vintage Wines for approximately $2.2 million. Vintage, whose sales were about $4 million at the time of the acquisition, was integrated with the Heublein Liquor Division. Vintage's principal product was Lancers Vin Rose, an imported Portuguese wine that accounted for about 50% of the company's sales.

The expansion which occurred in Heublein's international operations consisted primarily of the establishment of franchise operations in 21 additional foreign countries. This raised the number of such operations from 11 in 1959 to 32 in 1965.

HEUBLEIN'S PRESENT OPERATIONS

Financial Situation. During the 1965 fiscal year, Heublein earned $7.4 million on sales of $166 million, which represented about a 19% return on stockholders' equity. Between 1959 and 1965, Heublein's sales growth, profit growth, and return on equity far exceeded the average of the four major distillers (see Table 1). In addition, even though Heublein was spending nearly twice as much (as a percentage

Exhibit 12

HEUBLEIN, INC. (A)

Heublein Sales Mix for Selected Years

Year	Smirnoff Vodka	Other Vodka	Total Vodka	Other Alcoholic Beverages	Food	Total
1965..........	51%	11%	62%	30%	8%	100%
1964..........	58	12	70	21	9	100
1963..........	62	12	74	16	10	100
1962..........	63	11	74	16	10	100
1961..........	64	11	75	19	6	100
1960..........	67	9	76	18	6	100
1955..........	61	2	63	32	5	100
1950..........	27	...	27	63	10	100

Source: Heublein records.

of sales) on advertising as the average of the four major distillers, and had increased the company's dividend payout ratio to 50% of earnings, the company had a cash flow of $8.6 million in 1965, about 22% on equity, which compared favorably to the 9% average of the four major distillers.

Product Line. At the end of 1965, Heublein was marketing well over 50 products through its four divisions. While vodka was the company's principal product, accounting for 62% of 1965 sales, the company's product base had been broadened considerably since 1960 by acquisitions, internal growth, and new marketing agreements (see Exhibit 12 for sales-mix trends). Heublein's product-line strategy was to market high-quality consumer products which provided the high margins necessary to support intensive advertising. Heublein aimed its promotions of these products at the growing, prosperous, young adult market. The company was also interested in phasing out some of its less profitable lines whenever possible.

The liquor products division accounted for over 80% of Heublein's 1965 sales. Its principal product was Smirnoff vodka, the fourth largest selling liquor brand in the United States in 1965, with estimated annual sales of 2.3 million cases. Company officials expected that Smirnoff, with its faster rate of growth, would move ahead of the third place brand (Canadian Club: 2.4 million cases) and second place brand (Seagram's VO: 2.5 million cases) within three years.

In 1965, Smirnoff had 23% of the total vodka market and outsold the second place vodka brand by over four to one. In addition, Smirnoff was the only premium-priced vodka on the market in 1965, since Wolfschmidt, formerly another premium-priced vodka, had lowered its wholesale price in 1964 in an effort to stimulate sales. After considering this action, Mr. Hart decided the appropriate response was to raise Smirnoff's wholesale price $1 per case and to put the additional revenue into advertising. Although Wolfschmidt's sales more than doubled, this increase appeared to come from the middle-priced segment of the vodka market, since Smirnoff's sales also increased 4% over the previous year and was running over 10% ahead in 1966. Smirnoff also appeared to be immune to the spread of the hundreds of private label vodkas, since company officials felt that these products obtained their sales from the 15% to 30% of the vodka market that was price conscious.

As a result, many industry observers expected Smirnoff to dominate the vodka market well into the future, particularly since Smirnoff could, on the basis of its sales volume, afford to spend $7 million to $8 million on advertising, while its closest rival could afford to spend only $2 million before putting the brand into the red.[7,8]

Relska, a medium-priced vodka, and Popov, a low-priced vodka, were produced and sold primarily to give Heublein's distributors a full line of vodka products. They accounted for 11% of company sales in 1965. They were cheaper to produce than Smirnoff but were not as smooth to the taste, according to company officials.

Heublein bottled cocktails sold an estimated 500,000 cases in 1965,

---

[7] Roger D. Bensen, *Heublein, Inc.,* Glore Forgan, Wm. R. Staats Inc. (December, 1965), p. 25.

[8] In 1963, according to the *Liquor Handbook,* Heublein spent $1.4 million to advertise Smirnoff, while total advertising for all other vodka brands during the same year was $1.2 million.

about 55% of the bottled cocktail market. Nevertheless, Heublein was beginning to receive competition from the national distilling companies, particularly Distillers Corporation, whose United States subsidiary, Seagram's, was marketing a similar line. Mr. Hart, however, welcomed this competition. He commented to the Los Angeles Society of Security Analysts in 1965:

> We believe the idea of bottled cocktails has not been completely sold to the American public. We were therefore delighted when we learned that one of the major companies in the liquor industry was introducing a new line of cocktails and that there would be heavy expenditures in advertising and merchandising to promote their usage to the public.[9]
>
> We are of the opinion that, as the cocktail market expands, our share will decrease, but Heublein cocktails will continue to be the leader, and that our sales will show remarkable increases.

Mr. Hart explained to the case writer that distribution was one of the principal reasons Heublein would keep its number one position:

> We secured distribution in 1960 when the other companies weren't too interested in cocktails. Since a distributor will usually carry only two or three lines, this means that he will have Heublein and Calvert or Heublein and Schenley: in other words, Heublein and somebody else. . . . In addition to being first, Heublein's wide line will also help us get and maintain distribution.

In 1965, Heublein's bottled cocktail line included Manhattans, Vodka Sours, Extra Dry Martinis, Gin Sours, Whiskey Sours, Side Cars, Vodka Martinis, Daiquiris, Old Fashioneds, and Stingers.

During 1964, the liquor products division reintroduced Milshire gin. For years, Milshire had been a regional gin selling about 100,000 cases a year. However, in 1963 the promotional budget was deemed sufficient to devote some real attention to Milshire. To prepare for this, the old inventory was sold off, the product was reformulated, and the package was redesigned. The principal difference in the product was that its botanical and aromatic content was lowered since it was filtered through activated charcoal in a process similar to that used to make Smirnoff. The net effect of this was to make the gin "lighter." Sales for 1964 increased to 150,000 cases, a significant jump, but still very far behind the 2.1 million cases of Gordon's, the leading brand.

In 1966, Heublein reached an agreement with Tequila Cuervo S. A. to be the exclusive U.S. marketer of Jose Cuervo and Matador tequilas and a cordial based on the same spirit. Heublein planned to market

---

[9] Heublein spent $2 million advertising its line of bottled cocktails in 1965. Seagram's spent $1.5 million advertising its Calvert line the same year.

these products on a nationwide basis through the liquor products division.

The liquor products division also marketed Harvey's sherries, ports, and table wines; Bell's Scotches; Gilbey's Canadian whiskeys; Byrrh aperitif wine; and the products of Vintage Wines, Inc.

The Arrow division accounted for about 10% of Heublein's sales in 1965. The division's principal products were Arrow cordials, liqueurs, and brandies, and McMaster's Scotch. Arrow's distribution system was particularly strong in the control states. In addition, Arrow's distribution in the open states was strengthened in 1965, when Heublein

Exhibit 13

HEUBLEIN, INC. (A)

Advertising Expenditures of Major Liquor Companies for 1965

Company	Advertising (Millions)	Sales (Millions)	Advertising as a Percent of Sales
Distillers Corp. Seagram's Ltd.	$43,750	$762,520	5.7%
Schenley Industries	23,100	380,200	6.1
National Distillers & Chemical Corp.	19,668	810,900	2.4
Hiram Walker	17,750	498,174	3.6
Heublein, Inc.	17,495	165,522	10.6

Source: *Advertising Age* (January 3, 1966), p. 46.

discontinued the production of its line of Heublein cordials and substituted the Arrow line.

Although the sales of the food division more than doubled between 1961 and 1965, it accounted for only 8% of the company's 1965 sales. Nevertheless, A-1 steak sauce was the company's number two profit producer in 1965, second only to Smirnoff vodka. Other food products included Cake-Mate icings and gels, Escoffier sauces, Grey-Poupon Mustard, and Maltex and Maypo cereals. In 1965, Heublein reached an agreement with the Costal Valley Canning Company of California to distribute and market Snap-E-Tom Tomato Cocktail. Snap-E-Tom was a tomato juice flavored with onion and chili pepper juices. It was designed for the pre-meal juice and the cocktail mixer markets, both of which had high profit margins.

Marketing. The case writer felt that Heublein's unique advertising and promotion policies and campaigns set Heublein apart from the other liquor companies (see Exhibit 13 for the advertising expenditures of various liquor companies). Heublein considered liquor to be a branded consumer product, and viewed itself as a marketer of high-quality consumer products rather than as a liquor company. As a result, Heublein developed intensive advertising campaigns to sell its products for the growing, affluent young adult market, since it believed it was easier to get a new customer in this market than to get a 40-year-old Scotch drinker to switch to vodka. Because of the importance attached to advertising, Heublein spent 10.6% of sales for advertising in 1965, nearly double the 5.7% of Distillers Corporation.

In addition, Heublein was an aggressive innovator among liquor industry advertisers. In the 1950's, industry self-regulation prohibited depicting a woman in an advertisement for a liquor product. In 1958, Heublein advised the Distilled Spirits Institute that it believed this ban on the portrayal of women was "obsolete, hopelessly prudish, and downright bad business." Finally the DSI agreed and Heublein became the first liquor company to portray women in its ads under the new DSI self-regulation, an advertising practice later followed by nearly every major distiller. Heublein also pioneered a change in DSI regulations to permit liquor advertising in Sunday supplements. At the end of 1965, Heublein was pushing for the use of liquor advertisements on radio and TV similar to beer and wine advertisements.

Another unique feature of Heublein's marketing was the promotions it used. These were designed to appeal to the young adult group and used celebrities and offbeat approaches to gain attention (see Exhibit 14). An example of this approach was the Smirnoff Mule promotion launched in May, 1965. The promotion, Heublein's largest for a single drink, was designed to catch the discotheque popularity on the upswing. The total investment was about $2 million for advertising, merchandising, and sales promotion. *The New York Times* commented that:

> Included in the Smirnoff advertising mix are a drink, called the Smirnoff Mule; a song and dance, called simply The Mule; a recording called Skitch Plays "The Mule"; a copper-colored metal mug in which to drink the Smirnoff Mule; and a recent phenomenon called the discotheque . . . the Gumbinner-North Company [Heublein's advertising agency] has recruited such vodka salesmen as Skitch Henderson, Carmen McRae, and Killer Joe Piro to put it over. . . . In addition to Smirnoff ads, The Mule will be featured in local advertising by the 7-Up people.[10]

Distribution. Heublein sold its products directly to state liquor control boards in the 18 control states and to approximately 235 whole-

---

[10] Walter Carlson, "Advertising: Smirnoff Harnesses the Mule," *The New York Times* (June 27, 1965).

Exhibit 14
HEUBLEIN, INC. (A)
Smirnoff Mule Ad

THE SMIRNOFF MULE—SKITCH HENDERSON MADE IT A SONG. "KILLER JOE" PIRO MADE IT A DANCE.

NEW DRINK...SMIRNOFF® MULE
It swings!

Taste the new party favorite that's sweeping the country, the swingingest drink since Smirnoff invented vodka. It's the Smirnoff Mule, made with Smirnoff and 7-Up®. Just pour a jigger of Smirnoff over ice. Add juice of ¼ lime. Fill Mule mug or glass with 7-Up to your taste. *Delicious!* Only smooth, flawless Smirnoff, filtered through 14,000 pounds of activated charcoal, blends so perfectly with 7-Up. That's why the fuel for your Mule must be Smirnoff! *It leaves you breathless®*

SMIRNOFF VODKA 80 AND 100 PROOF. DISTILLED FROM GRAIN. STE. PIERRE SMIRNOFF FLS. (DIVISION OF HEUBLEIN). HARTFORD, CONN.

sale distributors in the 32 open states and the District of Columbia. Food products were sold through food brokers and wholesalers. It was Heublein's policy to strive to create mutually profitable relationships with its distributors. For example, one of the reasons for the creation of

Popov vodka was to give Heublein's distributors a low-priced vodka brand to sell.

International Operations. At the end of 1965, Heublein was involved in three types of overseas activities. The largest and most important was its licensing operation. Distillers in 32 foreign countries were licensed to manufacture and market Smirnoff vodka. Among the countries in which Heublein had such franchises were Austria, Denmark, Greece, Ireland, New Zealand, South Africa, and Spain. When selecting a franchise holder, Heublein looked for a local distiller who had good production facilities and who was a good marketer in his country. Heublein felt this policy allowed it to get established faster than if Heublein tried to set up its own plant. Heublein also felt it improved relations with the local government.

Under these franchise agreements, the distiller produced the neutral spirits in the best way possible in his country. To maintain quality control, however, Heublein installed and owned the copper filtration units and shipped the charcoal to these locations from Hartford. This was done at cost. The contracts called for a license fee (about 10% of sales) and also stipulated that certain amounts be spent by the franchisee for advertising. Usually, during the first three or four years, Heublein would add its 10% license fee to these advertising funds in order to help build up the business. Plans were under way at the end of 1965 to begin operations in six more countries, including Ecuador, India, and Nigeria.

Heublein also exported Smirnoff, primarily to military bases overseas. In addition, Heublein opened an operation in Freeport, Jamaica, in 1965, to produce Smirnoff and other Heublein liquor products, and to market these products to customers such as ships' chandlers and diplomatic agencies who could purchase tax-free liquor.

Between 1961 and 1965, Heublein's export sales increased 99%, royalties from licenses 145%, and profits from international operations 458%. In 1965, net export sales stood at $1.2 million, and profits before taxes from international operations, including license fees, were $880,000.

Production. At the end of 1965, Heublein owned and operated three plants throughout the United States, with an annual capacity of 20 million wine gallons for all product lines, and was building a plant in Detroit to replace the old Arrow plant. This plant was to cost $4.5 million and to have an annual capacity of 5.5 million wine gallons. When completed, this plant would give Heublein a total annual capacity of 25.5 million wine gallons. All these plants were highly auto-mated.

Heublein had about 975 employees in 1965, of whom slightly less than half were hourly employees. In 1965, labor costs were only 3% of the total cost of sales.

Heublein did not produce the grain neutral spirits for its gin and vodka production, but rather purchased these requirements on contract and the open market from four distillers. Heublein maintained facilities in the Midwest for the storage of 8 million proof gallons, however, in case none of these suppliers could meet Heublein's stringent quality requirements. At 1965 consumption rates, this represented about a one-year supply.

According to Heublein, even the high-quality grain neutral spirits it received from its suppliers contained too many impurities for direct use in Smirnoff. The first step in Smirnoff production was, therefore, to redistill these grain neutral spirits. At the end of the redistillation, the alcohol was 192 proof. It was then blended with distilled water to reduce the mixture to 80 proof. This mixture was then filtered slowly through 10 copper tanks which contained over 14,000 pounds of acti-vated charcoal. The filtering process required eight hours. According to company officials, it was during this process that the vodka became smooth and mellow and acquired its mild but distinctive taste. The only remaining step was to bottle the finished product, since vodka required no aging.

Heublein also redistilled the grain neutral spirits used in the produc-tion of its charcoal-filtered Milshire gin. However, the company did not redistill the liquors (purchased on the open market) used in the produc-tion of Heublein cocktails.

Most of the food products were manufactured at Hartford or at the plant in Burlington, Vermont. Heublein insisted on the same high-quality standards in the purchase of raw materials and production of its food products that it required in its liquor production.

Heublein, Inc. (B)

HAVING ACQUIRED four companies during the past six years (both Timely Brands and Escoffier, Ltd., in 1960—manufacturers and marketers of specialty food products; Arrow Liquors Corporation in 1964; and Vintage Wines in 1965),[1] Heublein's management at the end of 1965 expressed continued interest in further acquisitions.

The kinds of companies being sought were not just profitable financial deals, but rather firms in which Heublein's management believed it could improve operations. Heublein's acquisition policies were explained more fully by Mr. Ralph Hart, Heublein's president, in a 1965 presentation before the Los Angeles Society of Security Analysts:

> Frankly, we take a long hard look at any potential acquisition. We ask ourselves: "Will the new product or company we acquire have a potential at least equal to existing Heublein products, in order not to dilute present equity? Will new products lend themselves to our channels of distribution and marketing techniques? Will these products have sufficient gross margin to allow for our type of distribution, advertising, and merchandising?"

THE PROPOSED HAMM ACQUISITION

Early in the fall of 1965, Heublein's top management was seriously considering the possible acquisition of the Theo. Hamm Brewing Company. They were particularly interested because they felt Hamm's could profit immensely from what they felt was Heublein's major strength—the ability to market a consumer product extremely well. If the acquisition were consummated, Heublein would become the first company to engage in the production and sale of both beer and liquor.

Under the proposed agreement Heublein would acquire all of the outstanding shares of Hamm's common in exchange for 420,032 shares of Heublein's 5% preferred, and 200,031 shares of Heublein's 5% convertible preferred. Both preferreds had a par value of $100; the latter was convertible into three shares of Heublein common, subject to certain provisions against dilution of earnings. Although Hamm's stock was held by a family group and did not have a market price, Heublein's board estimated that the aggregate fair value was in excess of $62

---

[1] For further particulars, see Heublein, Inc. (A).

million, or book value (see Exhibit 1). The proposed agreement stipulated that each class of preferred would have the right to elect one
member to Heublein's board. In addition, it was provided that the $25
million of securities indicated on the Theo. Hamm Brewing Company
consolidated balance sheet as of 9/30/65 would be liquidated and used
to buy out dissident Hamm's stockholders prior to the acquisition by
Heublein. This would have the effect of reducing Hamm's working
capital and stockholder equity before the purchase by about $25 million.

Exhibit 1

HEUBLEIN, INC. (B)

Theo. Hamm Brewing Company Consolidated Balance Sheets
(Dollars in Thousands)

	Nov. 30, 1964	Sept. 30, 1965
Current assets:		
Cash	$ 3,475	$ 3,153
Certificates of deposit	2,000	500
Commercial paper and marketable securities (at cost)*...	26,560	24,044
Accounts receivable (net)	5,452	7,959
Inventories	5,352	6,479
Prepaid expenses	898	891
Total current assets	$43,737	$43,027
Investments and other assets	6,467	6,536
Property, plant, and equipment (net)	26,381	26,930
	$76,585	$76,493
Current liabilities:		
Trade accounts payable	$ 2,639	$ 2,926
Salaries and wages	1,207	1,304
Customers' deposits	932	1,151
Miscellaneous accounts payable and accrued expenses....	470	1,301
Taxes other than taxes on income	2,038	2,299
Federal and state taxes on income	2,657	2,559
Dividends payable	1,538	660
Sinking fund deposits due in one year	100	100
Total current liabilities	$11,580	$12,302
Eight per cent debenture bonds	1,400	1,400
Stockholders' equity		
Capital stock	55,083	26,432
Capital surplus	...	26,273
Earned surplus	8,521	10,086
	$76,585	$76,493

* The market value of these securities was $28.1 million in 1964 and $25.7 million in 1965.
Source: Heublein acquisition study.

Hamm's History and Competitive Position.   Hamm's was a family-
owned brewing company. During the five years preceding the proposed
acquisition, sales and profits had remained relatively stable (see Exhibits 2 and 3). However, since industry sales had increased slightly more

Exhibit 2

HEUBLEIN, INC. (B)

Theo. Hamm Brewing Company Consolidated Statement of Income

(Dollars in Thousands)

	Years Ended November 30					Ten Months Ended September 30 (Unaudited)	
	1960	1961	1962	1963	1964	1964	1965§
Revenues:							
Sales less allowances	$119,881	$115,874	$114,885	$119,584	$124,233	$106,109	$109,449
Interest	161	240	270	575	958	748	941
Dividends	81	62	50	51	61	58	42
Other	283	95	175	196	351	301	359
	$120,407	$116,272	$115,380	$120,405	$125,602	$107,217	$110,791
Costs and expenses:							
Cost of goods sold*	89,843	86,314	86,595	90,878	95,388	81,004	84,597
Selling, delivery, advertising, general and administrative expenses	16,263	17,065	16,200	18,534	21,423	18,196	19,026
Interest:							
Long-term debt	235	164	120	120	120	100	100
Other	8	159	2	16	13	12	...
	$106,349	$103,702	$102,918	$109,548	$116,945	$99,312	$103,723
Earnings before taxes on income	$14,057	$12,570	$12,462	$10,857	$8,657	$7,905	$7,068
Taxes on income:							
Federal	6,750	6,150	6,100	5,100	3,900	3,550	3,000
State	450	400	400	275	300	275	225
	$7,200	$6,550	$6,500	$5,375	$4,200	$3,825	$3,225
Net earnings (excluding the operations of the Eastern division and related distributing subsidiaries)	$6,857	$6,020	$5,962	$5,482	$4,457	$4,080	$3,843
Loss on operations of Eastern division and related distributing subsidiaries less applicable income tax benefits†	1,092	1,717	2,124	1,408			
Net earnings	$5,765	$4,303	$3,838	$4,074	$4,457	$4,080	$3,843
Preferred stock dividend requirements	210	210	210	210	210	175	142
Earnings applicable to common stock	$5,555	$4,093	$3,628	$3,864	$4,247	$3,905	$3,701
Per common share (dollars) earnings applicable to:							
Common stock‡	$2.14	$1.57	$1.40	$1.49	$1.63	$1.50	$1.40
Cash dividends declared	...	...	0.40	0.95	1.25	0.50	0.75

* Cost of goods sold includes federal and state excise taxes of between $32 and $38 million for each of the above periods.
† In 1960, the company acquired brewing facilities in Baltimore, Maryland, which were sold in 1963 for $6 million, the approximate net carrying amount of the facilities. Applicable income tax benefits ranging between $1.2 and $2.1 million have been netted against loss on operations of Eastern division and related distributing subsidiaries for the years 1960–63 inclusive.
‡ Earnings applicable to common stock are based on the number of shares outstanding at the end of each period as adjusted for the recapitalization during the year ended November 30, 1961.
§ Earnings for the 10 months ended September 30, 1965, were adversely affected by nonrecurring legal and centennial expenses aggregating approximately $400,000.
Source: Heublein acquisition study.

Exhibit 3

HEUBLEIN, INC. (B)

Heublein, Inc., and Theo. Hamm Brewing Company

Pro Forma Combined Statement of Income

(Dollars in Thousands)

	June 30, 1960 / Nov. 30, 1960	June 30, 1961 / Nov. 30, 1961	June 30, 1962 / Nov. 30, 1962	June 30, 1963 / Nov. 30, 1963	June 30, 1964 / Nov. 30, 1964	Ten months to Sept. 30, 1965
Heublein / Hamm						
Net sales	$223,050	$224,156	$231,027	$241,579	$260,082	$249,056
Cost of sales	$167,872	$166,732	$172,389	$180,378	$194,963	$187,059
Selling, general and administrative expenses	33,323	36,359	36,755	40,515	45,385	43,164
Other income (deductions):						
Interest and dividend income	352	417	444	865	1,287	1,217
Interest expense	(560)	(595)	(363)	(344)	(342)	(215)
Miscellaneous—net	198	85	93	503	308	320
	$ (10)	$ (93)	$ 174	$ 1,024	$ 1,253	$ 1,322
Income before income taxes	$ 21,845	$ 20,972	$ 22,057	$ 21,710	$ 20,987	$ 20,155
Provision for income taxes	11,432	11,137	11,688	11,205	10,716	9,966
Net income before loss on discontinued operations of Hamm	$ 10,413	$ 9,835	$ 10,369	$ 10,505	$ 10,271	$ 10,189
Loss on discontinued operations of Hamm, less applicable income tax benefits	1,092	1,717	2,124	1,408		
Net income	$ 9,321	$ 8,118	$ 8,245	$ 9,097	$ 10,271	$ 10,189
Deduct pro forma adjustments:						
Interest and dividend income	219	275	290	591	981	950
Interest expense	1,209	983	975	501	122	85
Income taxes	(738)	(638)	(652)	(549)	(496)	(418)
	$ 690	$ 620	$ 613	$ 543	$ 607	$ 617
Pro forma net income	$ 8,631	$ 7,498	$ 7,632	$ 8,554	$ 9,664	$ 9,572
Preferred dividend requirements:						
Heublein:						
5% preferred stock	$ 2,100	$ 2,100	$ 2,100	$ 2,100	$ 2,100	$ 1,750
5% convertible preferred stock	1,000	1,000	1,000	1,000	1,000	833
	$ 3,100	$ 3,100	$ 3,100	$ 3,100	$ 3,100	$ 2,583
Pro forma earnings applicable to common stock	$ 5,531	$ 4,398	$ 4,532	$ 5,454	$ 6,564	$ 6,989
Pro forma earnings per share (dollars):						
Assuming no conversion of convertible preferred stock	$ 1.15	$ .91	$ .93	$ 1.12	$ 1.37	$ 1.43
Assuming full conversion of convertible preferred stock	1.21	1.00	1.01	1.18	1.40	1.43
Actual Heublein earnings per share*	0.74	0.79	0.91	1.03	1.21	1.30

* Heublein shares outstanding in June of 1965, 4.9 million; approximate market price/share in 1965 (to September) $26–$27.
Source: Heublein acquisition study.

than 11% during this period, Hamm's market share had declined from 4.5% to 3.7%. In addition, Hamm's return on sales had lagged behind the industry leaders (see Exhibits 4, 5, and 6).

Exhibit 4

HEUBLEIN, INC. (B)

Beer: Larger Markets, Tougher Competition*

The bigger it gets, the rougher it gets. That sums up the brewing industry, which has just had its best year ever. But no one brewer had an easy time of it, and the competition will get even stiffer in the years ahead.

by Kenneth Ford, Managing Editor

No one in the brewing industry had anything but kind words last week for the nation's growing number of young adults.

Not only were they quaffing their share of brew and more besides, but even more significant, they appeared willing to cast aside some old-fashioned concepts about beer being a "blue-collar" drink.

For the nation's 190 brewers (four fewer than the year before) the moral was that patience pays off. All during the long, dry decade of the Fifties the industry watched total consumption lag behind population growth and per capita consumption remain static at a low level. Brewers pinned their hopes on the vast crop of war babies of the Forties, hoping that when they reached drinking age they would set off a beer boom, but also fearing they might move from the innocence of Coke to the decadence of Martinis in one easy step.

They didn't. When the 1963 figures were totaled up at this time last year, there were clear signs that the brewing industry was on the move at last. No one outside the industry realized how fast it was moving until the 1964 totals came in last month.

The results: total sales (consumption) climbed to 98.5-million barrels, up five per cent from 1963's 93.8-million barrels. Per capita consumption, the more meaningful measure of marketing effectiveness, jumped to 15.7 gallons, up 2.6 per cent from 1963's 15.3 gallons. Both gains were the best year-to-year increase posted by the industry since 1947.

It is a certainty that the industry will cross the 100-million barrel barrier in 1965. The only question is whether it will reach 101-million or 102-million barrels. No one will be unhappy if it doesn't go that high—the industry's most optimistic forecasters hadn't expected it to reach the 100-million barrel level until 1967.

But though the overall industry outlook is sudsy, neither leaders nor laggards are finding it easy selling.

Competition has never been fiercer. The nation's top ten brewers have staked out 57.7 per cent share of the total market, selling 56.6-million barrels of that 98.5 million total. The next 14 ranking brewers take 25.4 per cent of the total, or 25-million barrels. All together, the top 24 brewers, each doing better than one-million barrels apiece, account for 82.9 per cent of total sales, some 81.6-million barrels.

---

* *Printers' Ink* (Feb. 12, 1965). Reproduced by permission.

Exhibit 4—Continued

But even what would be a normally respectable gain was not enough to hold the previous year's position, much less advance, in the top 24 standings.

LOSSES AND GAINS

Carling dropped in 1964 from fourth to fifth; Hamm from seventh to eighth; Rheingold from tenth to 11th; Lucky Lager from 13th to 16th; Pearl from 17th to 18th; Narragansett from 19th to 21st and Jackson from 23rd to 24th. Yet five had made sales gains—Carling's posted a 1.7 per cent increase; Rheingold a 3.1 per cent increase; Pearl a 5.4 per cent increase; Narragansett a 2.8 per cent increase; and Jackson a 2.2 per cent increase.

The leading brewers had set such a blistering pace that merely running to keep up just wasn't fast enough.

First-place Anheuser-Busch (Budweiser–Busch Bavarian–Michelob) achieved a 10.1 per cent gain that carried it across the ten-million-barrel level, an industry record, and gave it a 10.5 per cent share of the total market. A–B phenomenal performance was the culmination of marketing programs set in motion as long as a decade ago. Basically, these concentrated on development of marketing executives, achieving the best possible communication with its 900 wholesalers throughout the country and expanding plants into growing markets. (Its new Houston brewery will be ready next year.)

Though A–B is one of the heaviest advertisers in the industry, it makes only evolutionary changes in its advertising program from year to year. "Where There's Life There's Bud" (1963) became "That Bud, that's beer" (1964) and now becomes "It's Worth It, It's Budweiser" (1965).

Expansion-minded Schlitz, eyeing the heavier-beer-drinking Canadian market (per capita consumption 16.4 gallons) tried to migrate north by buying control of Canada's Labatt Brewing, but found itself ensnarled in antitrust actions and other legal complications. The time and attention it had to devote to these were reflected in only a 5.3 per cent gain, in contrast to 1963's 13 per cent gain.

Another 11.6 per cent gain like the one Pabst made last year might well knock Schlitz out of second-place. And fast-rising Falstaff is a factor that Schlitz and Pabst marketing executives both must reckon with in the year ahead.

Falstaff surprised everyone by clipping Carling out of fourth place in the brewing industry. Carling had made sixteen consecutive sales gains that brought it up from 19th in the industry and was generally conceded to be the brewer to watch. Controlled by Canadian entrepreneur E. P. Taylor, its marketing strategy is based on two rules: build plants where the markets are growing (it now has nine in the U.S.) and advertise heavily.

But it was Falstaff's ambition and innovation that carried it ahead. It markets only one brand of beer, Falstaff, in 32 states westward from Indiana. These states have 45 per cent of the nation's population but consume less than 45 per cent of total beer production.

A COMPETITOR TO RESPECT

"If we were in the other 18 states, we'd be selling 10.5-million barrels instead of 5.8-million," says George Holtman, vice president, advertising. Holtman's

Exhibit 4—Continued

boast is not idle. That Falstaff is a competitor to respect is attested to by Hamm's decline of 2.5 per cent. Both collided competitively in the Midwest generally and the Chicago market in particular. Falstaff began moving into Chicago three years ago and the 1964 figures reflect its arrival. Similarly, it began moving into the West Coast in recent years where traditional beer sales patterns are changing, too. Lucky Lager, long the leading West Coast brand, slumped 15.1 per cent, dropping below the two-million barrel level under the impact of competition from Falstaff and other interloping brewers. Among them: the Schlitz–Burgemeister brand team, Falstaff, Budweiser, and Carling. The latter is going to build its own brewery in the San Francisco area, which should make conditions in the important California market (it accounts for about 7.5 per cent of total consumption alone) even more competitive.

But the moral is not that the big bad national brands come in and knock off the poor little locals. Washington-based Olympia, strong in the Northwest, and Denver-based Coors both are making significant progress on the West Coast. Olympia scored a 22.1 per cent increase, and Coors, long the strong man of the Rocky Mountain empire, boosted advertising budgets by 11 per cent and barged into California. Result: a 12 per cent sales increase.

In the big New York market it was a locally-based brewer that led the pack—Brooklyn's F&M Schaefer Brewing. Schaefer soared to 4,250,000 barrels up 10.1 per cent, while Newark-based Ballantine dropped 3.9 per cent and Rheingold, up 3.1 per cent, slipped out of the top ten and found its claim to being top brand in the New York metropolitan area under severe pressure.

Ballantine, long handled by the Wm. Esty Co., is now looking for a new advertising agency. Rheingold, sold by the Liebmann family to Pepsi-Cola United Bottlers, switched agencies again. In recent years it has gone from Foote Cone & Belding to J. Walter Thompson, back to FCB, and is now at Doyle Dane Bernbach. Rheingold, under the aegis of its new management, reportedly was moving ahead at year's end behind a barrage of television and radio spots.

COMPETITION KEEN IN EAST, TOO

Throughout the East, competition was similarly strong. Philadelphia-based Schmidt (Schmidt–Prior–Valley Forge) gained 13.3 per cent, Baltimore-based National climbed 21.5 per cent, and Manhattan-based Ruppert, strong in New England, moved ahead 22.5 per cent. Rochester-based Genessee (up 20.2 per cent) cemented its already strong position in upstate New York.

One result of this fierce competition was increased ad budgets. With most brewers offering what economists call "poorly differentiated products"—i.e., sameness—images were the most important function in marketing. Most brewers in *Printers' Ink's* annual marketing survey, of course, declined to give data on ad expenditures, though a few admitted increases ranging from four to six per cent. However, the industry operates on a so-much-per-barrel basis in its ad budgeting. *Printers' Ink's* study of beer advertising expenditures (October 2, 1964, page 25) found the industry average was 96-cents a barrel for the four measured media. This would put total spending in a 98.5-million barrel year at $94.4-million in those media. This, however, is only about one-third of total expenditures. Big chunks of money go for "rights" to broadcast sports events, a

Exhibit 4—Continued

staple of beer marketing. For instance, Schlitz, now building a new brewery in Texas, paid out $5.3-million for rights to the Houston Colts games.

"It's all part of becoming a new resident of the area," a Schlitz spokesman explained. "We want to get known fast and this is how you do it."

So important are sports sponsorships that they significantly influence marketing strategy. For example, Schmidt's bought the old Standard Beverage plant in Cleveland from Schaefer (which then bought the old Gunther plant in Baltimore from Hamm). Schmidt originally intended to use the Cleveland brewery to supply its markets in Western Pennsylvania and Western New York state and had no immediate intention of entering the northeastern Ohio market. But the opportunity arose to buy a participation in radio-sponsorship of the Cleveland Browns' games. Schmidt's bought it and entered the market immediately.

CAN U.S. COMPETE ABROAD?

For the past few years, American brewers have enviously watched the success of imported European beers in the U.S. The European imports sell less than one per cent of the total sold in the U.S. but their profit margins are far better than the domestic brewers achieve on a unit basis. Would the same not hold true for U.S. and Canadian beers overseas? It is also a way to rise above the cannibalistic competition in the U.S. The other way is to increase the beer consumption of the American drinker. Though 1964's 3.3 per cent increase in per capita consumption was the best in recent years, the industry lags far behind the high of 18.7 gallons set in 1945 or even the postwar 18.4 gallons quaffed in 1947.

New products may help. Schlitz, Pabst and National are now strongly promoting malt liquor brands. A–B's Michelob and Hamm's Waldech in the super-premium class are upgrading beer's image and adding a new group of customers.

But it is a packaging development that may be of the most far-reaching significance. This is the home keg or draft beer that fits neatly into the family refrigerator. In the consumption battle, beer's increase in share must come from soft drinks, coffee, tea, and such—not merely from population growth or competitors' customers.

In the decade ending in 1963, beer consumption increased only 12 per cent while the population grew 19 per cent. Soft drinks shot up 48 per cent, soluble coffee 158, and tea 20 per cent.

The confirmed beer drinker guzzles about six quarts a week on a yearly averaged-out basis. That's about two and a half 12-ounce cans at a time.

What the industry must attract is the glass-at-a-time sipper. That's not much at a time, but there are an awful lot of them and enough sips by enough people can boost beer back near the 20 gallons per capita consumption level of pre-World War I days.

It will take a revolution in American beer-drinking patterns to do it, but it could happen.

BEER: A REVOLUTION IN DRINKING?

Beer's flat consumption curve may get the upward kick it needs from the new refrigerator keg that the man in the picture is "pulling."

Exhibit 4—Continued

Some brewers privately hail it as the most significant development in beer marketing in the postwar era. They think a keg of draft beer in the family refrigerator can't help but cause a gusty increase in per capita consumption.

Units like the one above have been in test markets for more than two years now, and indications are that a rush into this type of packaging is about to begin. Nine brewers now offer draft beer in one of three such packaging variations; more than a dozen others are negotiating with a leading supplier.

There are two basic types of kegs being used, the more elaborate, made by Reynolds Metals and Alcoa, utilize carbon dioxide to shoot the beer out; the other, made by National Can, utilizes squeeze-bulb-generated air pressure.

Falstaff, Hamm and National are using the Reynolds unit, called the "Tapper." Schlitz is now testing the Alcoa unit in eight markets. It's called the Home Keg.

Atlantic Lederbrau, Sterling Brew, Koch Brewing, Gettelman (owned by Miller's), Standard Rochester and National (using both) are marketing in National Can's Home Tap.

There are important differences in the units. Reynolds' Tapper holds $2\frac{1}{4}$ gallons, measures nine inches by $11\frac{1}{2}$ inches so that it will fit in 98 per cent of existing refrigerators, weighs seven pounds empty and 26 pounds full, contains the equivalent of 24 12-ounce cans, and will keep draft beer flavor-fresh for three weeks under refrigeration.

The Alcoa unit, being tested by Schlitz, differs from the Reynolds unit in two ways—the carbon dioxide mechanism, and size. The Alcoa unit holds only 144 ounces but Schlitz is packing two to a carton so the consumer buys the same amount of beer as in the Reynolds unit. Because of quirks in state liquor laws, the Reynolds size is illegal in a few states. Falstaff is now testing a $3\frac{1}{8}$-gallon size in Louisville that will meet such objections.

National Can's Home Tap, which holds one gallon, also fits snugly on the refrigerator shelf.

Because the Tapper carries a four-dollar deposit, Falstaff pioneered in extensive testing the Reynolds unit in Springfield, Ill.; Fort Wayne, Ind.; Tulsa, Okla.; Detroit; and Chicago. The beer itself is comparable in price to a case of 24 cans, making the initial outlay between eight and nine dollars, but the second-time cost is between four and five dollars.

Falstaff found that the average Tapper buyer was male and relatively prosperous. "These results tie in exactly with our predictions of what the beer drinker of coming years will be like," says Alvin Griesedieck, Jr., vice president, marketing. "Our projections show that although he will continue to be married, he will have a higher level of education, be a professional man or in the service industries, live in suburbia, and enjoy a higher income."

Griesedieck is enthusiastic about its potential. It should, he says, create "a revolution in beer-drinking habits." Others agree. Schlitz president Robert Uihlein, Jr., views the potential of draft beer in the home as "outstanding."

And that's what beer needs most.

Exhibit 5

HEUBLEIN, INC. (B)

Hamm and Industry Sales

(In Millions of Barrels)

	Brewing Industry, Tax-Paid Only*	Hamm's Beer Sales, Tax-Paid Only	Tax-Paid Hamm's Sales as % of Tax-Paid Industry Sales
1955.	85.0	3.1	3.6
1956.	85.0	3.3	3.9
1957.	84.4	3.4	4.0
1958.	84.4	3.4	4.0
1959.	87.6	3.5	4.0
1960.	87.9	4.0	4.5
1961.	89.0	3.7	4.1
1962.	91.2	3.7	4.0
1963.	93.8	3.8	4.1
1964.	98.6	3.7	3.7

* The data given with respect to the brewing industry represent tax-paid withdrawals of malt beverages as reported by the Internal Revenue Service.
Source: U.S. Treasury Department data.

Hamm's sold three brands of beer at the end of 1965: Waldech (premium price), Hamm's (premium and popular price), and Buckhorn (lower price). The 1964 sales breakdown among these brands had been 17,800 barrels[2] for Waldech, 3,624,700 barrels for Hamm's, and 57,800 barrels for Buckhorn, for a total of 3,700,300 barrels. In addition, Hamm's had produced some beer for sale to the F.&M. Schaefer Brewing Company under the Gunther brand in 1964.

In 1965, Hamm's beer was sold in 31 states and the District of

Exhibit 6

HEUBLEIN, INC. (B)

Returns on 1964 Sales of Leading Brewers

	Total Revenues (000)	Pretax Net (000)	Profit Margin (Per Cent)	Barrels Sold (000)	Pretax Returns/ Barrel
Anheuser-Busch.	$491,384	$39,312	8.00%	10,235	$3.84
Schlitz.	311,394	28,277	9.08	8,266	3.42
Pabst.	227,610	20,421	8.97	7,444	2.74
Falstaff.	211,943	13,604	6.42	5,815	2.33
Hamm.	125,602	8,657	6.89	3,719	2.33

Source: Company annual reports.

[2] A barrel was equivalent to 31 U.S. gallons.

Columbia. Most sales, however, were made in the midwestern, western, and southwestern parts of the United States. Hamm's relied exclusively on 479 independent wholesalers for its distribution, most of whom carried other brands of beer. Although any of these wholesalers could terminate his relationship with Hamm's at will, none of them accounted for more than 2.5% of Hamm's 1964 sales.

According to some industry observers, Hamm's four breweries were one of its principal assets. Three of these were owned outright, while the fourth was leased. The location and annual productive capacity of each of these plants was as follows:

Location	Annual Productive Capacity (barrels)
St. Paul, Minnesota	2,550,000
San Francisco, California	1,000,000
Los Angeles, California	500,000
Houston, Texas (leased)	450,000
	4,500,000

According to industry estimates, the cost of replacing Hamm's 1965 capacity would be about $135 million, or more than double the proposed purchase price. This estimate was based on the industry rule of thumb which set the costs of new plant construction at $30 to $35 per barrel at the end of 1965.

Like Heublein, Hamm's purchased most of the raw materials needed for its production—malt, barley, hops, and corn grits—from various independent suppliers. About one fourth of the malt and hops requirements were met by wholly owned subsidiaries, however.

The Brewing Industry. At the end of 1964, the beer market was approximately the same size as the distilled spirits market, or about $6.4

Exhibit 7

HEUBLEIN, INC. (B)

Alcoholic Beverages—Consumer Expenditures, 1942–64

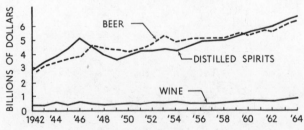

Source: *The Liquor Handbook, 1965;* cited by Glore Forgan, Wm. R. Staats Inc., in *Heublein, Inc.* (December, 1965).

Exhibit 8

HEUBLEIN, INC. (B)

Indexes of Per Capita Beer Consumption, 1940–64

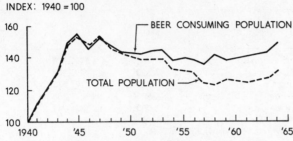

Source: United States Brewers Association; cited by Glore Forgan, Wm.
R. Staats Inc., in *Heublein, Inc.* (December, 1965).

billion a year (see Exhibit 7). In addition, from 1960 to 1964, the beer
market had grown at approximately the same annual rate as the liquor
market, i.e., at about 2.5%. Per capita beer consumption had increased
moderately during the period (see Exhibit 8).

Since people began consuming beer at a younger age than liquor,
industry observers expected beer consumption to increase as much as, if
not more than, liquor consumption through 1970. Most of this increase
was expected to be in the sale of packaged beer, since the sale of draught
beer had decreased from 22% of total beer sales in 1955 to 19% in
1964.

The same observers felt that brand loyalty was not as strong for beer
as for liquor. Nevertheless, the economies of high-volume production
and the use of high dollar advertising seemed to be causing a gradual
concentration of the beer industry, for the number of breweries operated
in the United States decreased from 329 to 211 between 1953 and
1963. Moreover, the percentage of sales accounted for by the largest
brewing companies had recently been increasing (see Exhibits 4, 9, and
10).

Exhibit 9

HEUBLEIN, INC. (B)

Market Share of Major Brewers

(Per Cent)

	1964	1963	1962	1961	1960	1959	1958	1957	1956	1955	1954	1953	1952	1951
Top 25	83.7%	82.2%	79.9%	77.4%	75.1%	73.8%	70.5%	69.2%	67.5%	64.3%	62.1%	61.3%	60.2%	57.5%
Top 10	57.7	56.8	55.0	52.8	51.4	50.0	45.9	45.2	44.4	42.7	40.8	40.1	40.8	39.2

Source: Research Company of America.

Exhibit 10

HEUBLEIN, INC. (B)

Advertising Expenditures of Major Brewers in 1965

Company	Advertising (000)	Sales (000)	Advertising Per Cent of Sales
Jos. Schlitz Brewing Co..........	$34,200	$311,375	11.0%
Anheuser-Busch, Inc.............	32,500	491,384	6.6
Pabst Brewing Co...............	15,900	227,610	7.0
Carling Brewing Co.............	15,500	412,306	3.8
Falstaff Brewing Corp...........	15,000	211,943	7.0

Source: *Advertising Age* (January 3, 1966), p. 46.

THE PROPOSED WIDE LINE ACQUISITION[3]

At the same time as the purchase of Hamm was being evaluated, several other possible acquisitions were being considered. One of these was the Wide Line Soft Drink Company, which in 1963 had total assets of $15.5 million (see Exhibit 11). Although Heublein's management felt that Wide Line could benefit from Heublein's ability to market

Exhibit 11

HEUBLEIN, INC. (B)

Wide Line Soft Drink Company

1963 Balance Sheet for Year Ending December 31

(Dollars in Millions)

Current assets:
Cash.............................$ 0.7
Accounts receivable (net)............ 3.6
Inventories........................ 3.3
Short-term bonds................... 0.6
Other............................ 0.2

Total current assets..............$ 8.4
Property, plant, and equipment (net).... 6.6
Other assets...................... 0.5

Total assets...................$15.5

Current liabilites:
Bank notes........................$ 1.3
Notes payable..................... 0.5
Current portion long-term debt....... 0.2
Accounts payable.................. 2.6
Federal and state income taxes........ 0.5
Other taxes........................ 0.1

Total current liabilities..........$ 5.2
Long-term debt..................... 2.4
Customer deposit liability............. 1.2
Deferred federal and state income taxes.. 0.4
Stockholders' equity
Common stock.................... 1.3
Capital surplus.................... 2.7
Retained earnings.................. 2.3

Total liabilities and equity.......$15.5

Source: 1963 Wide Line Soft Drink Company annual report.

---

[3] For purposes of security, the name, geographic location, and certain income statement figures of the company have been changed. The description of the industry and other aspects of the company's operations (e.g., market share, product line, etc.) are accurate.

consumer products, management nonetheless entertained some reserva-
tions. The most significant of these related to Wide Line's relatively
weak competitive position. While Wide Line—with sales of $26 mil-
lion in 1964—was among the top eight soft drink manufacturers in the
country, its 2% to 3% market share was far below Coca-Cola's 31%
and Pepsi-Cola's 23%. Also significant was the fact that Coca-Cola,
Pepsi-Cola, and Seven-Up were three of the most experienced marketers
of consumer goods in the country. In addition, while Wide Line's sales

Exhibit 12

HEUBLEIN, INC. (B)

Wide Line Soft Drink Company

Income Statements for Year Ended December 31

(Dollars in Millions)

	1959	1960	1961	1962	1963
Net sales	$18.6	$21.7	$21.9	$24.4	$26.0
Cost of goods sold	13.5	15.3	15.2	17.0	18.9
Gross profit on sales	$ 5.1	$ 6.4	$ 6.7	$ 7.4	$ 7.1
Selling, general and administrative expenses	3.1	3.7	4.0	4.7	4.2
Advertising	1.4	1.6	1.6	1.7	2.0
	$ 4.5	$ 5.3	$ 5.7	$ 6.4	$ 6.2
Income from operations	0.6	1.2	1.0	1.0	0.9
Other income (charges)	0.0	0.1	0.0	0.0	0.0
Federal taxes	0.3	0.5	0.5	0.5	0.4
Net income	$ 0.3	$ 0.6	$ 0.5	$ 0.5	$ 0.5

Source: Various Wide Line Soft Drink Company annual reports.

had increased 40% between 1959 and 1963, profits had remained
relatively steady (see Exhibit 12). Moreover, profits represented only a
2% return on sales, even though Wide Line was spending only half of
the industry average (as a percentage of sales) for advertising and
promotion.

The Wide Line Company. Wide Line manufactured carbonated
beverage concentrates which it sold to franchised bottlers in the United
States and foreign countries under its own brand names. During 1964,
sales of Wide Line soft drinks by these franchise holders exceeded 45
million cases. Under these franchise agreements, Wide Line's franchise
holders had to maintain certain quality conditions in their bottling
operations, and were required to spend certain minimum amounts for
advertising.[4] They were, however, allowed to produce carbonated beverages in addition to those sold under Wide Line's trademarks.

[4] Usually 30% of the cost of the concentrate. Half of the amount spent by the
franchise holder, up to 50% of the concentrate cost, would be refunded by Wide Line

In addition to its sales to franchised bottlers, Wide Line also sold concentrates to private-label bottlers, to the dairy and ice cream industries, and to the fountain trade as syrups.

Wide Line also bottled and sold carbonated beverages under its own brand name in the south central region of the country. Wide Line entered the bottling business in 1962 when it acquired its largest franchise holder. This operation, now the bottling division, used about 20% of the Wide Line's concentrate production. The bottling division not only produced carbonated beverages under Wide Line's trademarks, which it sold to independent distributors who redistributed these beverages to various retail outlets such as chain stores, drug stores, and hotels, but also produced a lower cost beverage, which it sold directly to chain stores, independent supermarkets, and cooperative food stores. In addition, the bottling division produced beverages under private-label brands to meet the demand for a low-priced product.

Wide Line's product line was one of the most complete in the industry. The company produced 24 different flavors, including the basic four: cola, lemon-lime, orange, and root beer. Ten of these flavors were also produced in low-calorie form. Although no figures were available, it was the case writer's judgment that low-calorie flavors accounted for about 20% of Wide Line's total concentrate sales.

Wide Line maintained its executive offices and concentrate manufacturing facility in El Paso, Texas. It also maintained sales offices and cold storage facilities in California, New York, and Toronto, Canada. The bottling division owned or leased plants with a total of 20 bottling lines in seven cities spread throughout the south central region.

The Soft Drink Industry. Soft drink sales increased 27% between 1955 and 1964, from 1.5 billion cases in the former year to over 1.9 billion in the latter (see Exhibit 13). Over one third of this increase resulted from the increase in per capita consumption from 218 bottles a person in 1955 to 240 bottles in 1964. The most important industry trend during this period was the increasing importance of low-calorie soft drinks. These beverages increased their market share from less than 2% in 1955 to 10% in 1964, and estimates of future growth ranged from a plateau of 10% (predicted by Coca-Cola) to a forecast of 35% by 1970 (predicted by Pepsi-Cola and Canada Dry). While the market positions of the four major soft drink manufacturers—Coca-Cola, Pepsi-Cola, Royal Crown, and Seven-Up—had not changed much between 1955 and 1964, Royal Crown had advanced slightly as its Diet-Rite Cola captured 40% of the low-calorie market (see Exhibit 14). There

Exhibit 13

HEUBLEIN, INC. (B)

Soft-Drink Market

COMPANY	CASES (Millions)		MARKET SHARE (Per Cent)	
	1963	1964	1963	1964
Coca-Cola...............	560	600	31%	31%
Pepsi-Cola...............	420	440	23½	23
Royal Crown.............	185	200	10	10
Seven-Up................	160	165	9	9
Canada Dry..............	145	155	8	8
Beverages Int'l...........	55	60	3	3
Dr. Pepper..............	55	55	3	2½
Cott....................	35	35	2	2
Squirt..................	18	20	1	1
Shasta..................	15	20	1	1
No-Cal..................	10	10	½	½
No Grape...............	10	10	½	½
All others...............	133	160	7½	8½
Grand total........	1,801	1,930	100%	100%

Source: *Printers' Ink* (April 9, 1965), p. 22.

was some concern among the industry leaders that the private-label brands, which were sold primarily on a price basis, might try to use low-calorie drinks to increase their market share still further, since low-calorie drinks provided a greater opportunity for price cutting than regular soft drinks because of their lower cost. The increased volume of low-calorie soft drinks was also partially responsible for the growing

Exhibit 14

HEUBLEIN, INC. (B)

Soft-Drink Market by Company and Flavors (1964)

COMPANY	COLA MARKET		LEMON-LIME		DIET SOFT DRINKS	
	Per Cent	Cases (Millions)	Per Cent	Cases (Millions)	Per Cent	Cases (Millions)
Coca-Cola.............	44%	530	21%	65	20%	38
Pepsi-Cola.............	33	400	11	35	20	38
Royal Crown.........	15	180	2	6	41	77
Seven-Up.............	...	...	50	155	included in all others	
All Others...........	8	100	16	50	19	37
Total..........	100%	1,210	100%	311	100%	190

Source: *Printers' Ink* (April 9, 1965), p. 23.

Exhibit 15

HEUBLEIN, INC. (B)

Soft-Drink Market by Flavors

Flavor	1964	1963	1958
Cola	62%	60%	53%
Lemon-lime	16	15	10
Orange	8	9	5
Root beer	4	5	3
Other	10	11	29
Grand Total	100%	100%	100%

Source: *Printers' Ink* (April 9, 1965), p. 23.

importance of the two basic flavors: cola and lemon-lime (see Exhibit 15).

Although adequate distribution was a crucial factor in soft drink sales, the primary selling tool used by most national carbonated beverage companies and their franchised bottlers was advertising. During 1964 these companies and their bottlers spent about $200 million on promotion. According to an industry rule of thumb, companies should spend about 10 cents per case on advertising. A comparison of actual and estimated advertising expenses for 1964 is contained in Table 1:

TABLE 1

Company	Rule-of-Thumb Estimate (Millions)	Actual Expenditure (Millions)
Coca-Cola	$60.0	$59.0
Pepsi-Cola	44.0	35.0
Royal Crown	20.0	24.0
Seven-Up	16.5	12.0

In this advertising, most of the companies developed themes which they repeated for several years. For example, Coca-Cola developed, "Things Go Better with Coke." Soft drink companies also used special advertising and promotional campaigns to attract additional sales during the summer sales peak.

In 1964, industry sales were divided into four categories: the take-home business, 66%; the vending of soft drinks in cups, bottles, and cans, 15%; fountain sales, 10%; and bottles in nonvending coolers, which accounted for the remaining 9% of sales.

According to *Printers' Ink,* "Bold advertising strategies, new or revi-

talized products, new packages, and fast action characterize the carbon-
ated-beverage industry. This decade and the next will see a continuation
of changing consumer tastes and consequent changes in the soft-drink
industry itself."[5]

---

[5] "Battle of the Brands: Soft Drinks," *Printers' Ink* (April 9, 1965), p. 26.

PART III

Organizing Administrative Personnel and
Putting Plans into Action

Flawless Foundry
and Equipment Company

IN MARCH, 1950, an incident occurred which caused Henry D. Williams, chief executive of Flawless Foundry and Equipment Company of Cleveland, Ohio, to wonder about the effectiveness of his management organization. The sales manager, personnel manager, and plant superintendent had become sufficiently concerned over the increasing frequency of late delivery to customers of Flawless' products to insist that the general manager, Joseph D. Stocker, hold an executive meeting at which they would endeavor to get at the roots of the trouble.

Henry Williams had known about the increase in late deliveries during the past year, and that two large customers had been lost consequently. He had not worried previously about the company's operation, however, because Flawless had been operating at a profit. Too, he realized that Joseph D. Stocker, a former castings salesman and general manager since 1948, needed time in which to learn how to handle his new job.

The demands on Stocker made by the subordinate executive group in March did disturb Williams, however, and caused him to wonder about the effectiveness of his management organization.

For a year prior to the March meeting, the foremen of Flawless' six production departments reported directly to general manager Stocker. Mr. Stocker still devoted a great deal of his time to casting sales work. He expected each foreman and department head to run his own department and to work directly with other departments with only occasional checks on his part. Stocker's assistant in production management, plant superintendent William D. Miller, was responsible for interdepartmental scheduling and for product deliveries, but held no authority over the production foremen (see Exhibit 1).

The numerous late shipments of orders in the past year had been due primarily to material shortages and to late deliveries of work-in-process between departments. The material shortages had resulted not so much

Exhibit 1

FLAWLESS FOUNDRY AND EQUIPMENT COMPANY

Organization Chart, July, 1949

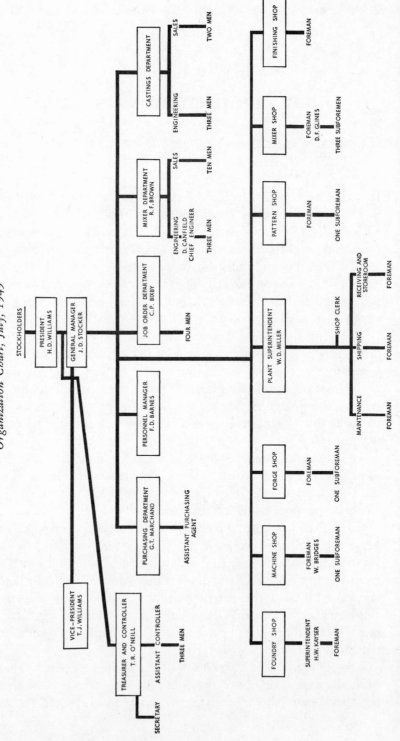

from lack of these items in the open market, according to Miller, but rather from the inadequacy of material inventory controls and from the difficulty of procuring the special parts which many orders required. Operated on a functional basis, the departments were interdependent; a holdup at one place could cause delays in several departments. Such occurrences had increased substantially in 1949 and early 1950.

At the request of the subordinate executive group, John Stocker had held an executive meeting in March to discuss the increase in late deliveries of orders. At this meeting he announced that Miller was responsible for the delays. The latter stated that this surprised the whole group; he then requested authority over the foremen and was granted it by Stocker (see Exhibit 2).

Henry Williams, chief executive of Flawless since 1946, had prior experience only in the accounting department and did not feel that he knew enough about the operation of the company to judge the effectiveness of his management organization. Therefore, in April, 1950, he hired a management consultant to study the problems of the company for him.

In July, 1950, Flawless Foundry and Equipment Company was engaged in the custom manufacture of (1) gray iron castings, (2) industrial mixing machines, and (3) industrial machinery parts of many varieties. Since 1939, the company had tripled its sales volume with sales of $2,984,000 and profits of $99,000 in 1949 (see Exhibits 3 and 4). During the same period the organization had expanded from 173 to 276 employees with the addition of employees, equipment, and buildings in random fashion as the needs increased.

During 1950, four of the company's six production departments were running below full capacity because of the dwindling of the gray iron castings business. Industrial mixer orders were at a higher level than in 1949, compensating somewhat for the low volume of gray castings orders and keeping the machine shop busy. Stocker estimated that, regardless of high volume in the mixer line, about 25% of the company's equipment was not being utilized.

Stocker felt that gray iron castings would never again be the most important factor in the company's business. He stated that his thinking and planning were shifting away from this part of the business on which the company had been built to mixer and industrial parts production, and that he had given considerable thought to the acquisition of a new product which would be suitable for production with the idle facilities.

Exhibit 2

FLAWLESS FOUNDRY AND EQUIPMENT COMPANY

Organization Chart, July, 1950

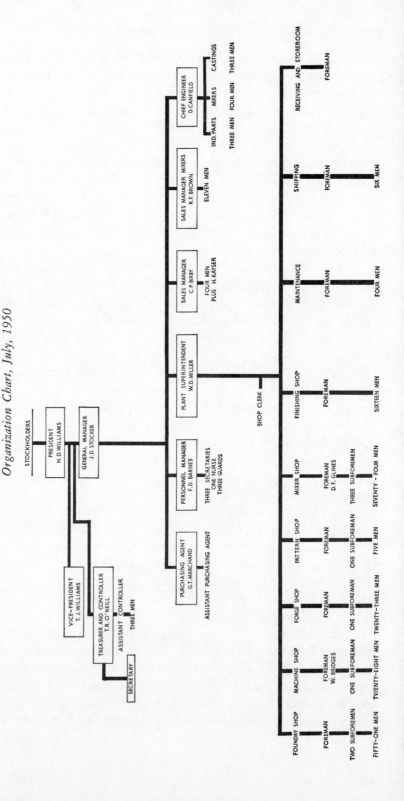

Exhibit 3

FLAWLESS FOUNDRY AND EQUIPMENT COMPANY

Comparative Balance Sheets for Selected Years Ending December 31
(In Thousands)

Assets	1949	1948	1947	1946	1944	1941	1937	1933	1927	1924
Cash	$ 116	$ 33	$ 8	$ 46	$ 153	$ 5	$ 31	$ 15	$ 51	$ 11
Accounts Receivable (Less Reserve)	320	244	189	188	114	215	125	55	179	123
Notes Receivable	...	...	...	...	82	3	6	19	...	8
Accounts—Officers and Employees	19	14	...	24	14	...	...	23	...	...
Stock Investments	23	22	22	114	188	49	61	61	29	37
Inventories	711	1,076	937	627	574	505	137	120	157	114
Total Current Assets	$1,189	$1,389	$1,156	$ 999	$1,125	$777	$360	$293	$416	$293
Other Assets	15	31	39	21	14	17	33	57	6	...
Fixed Assets	827	823	768	684	632	613	564	486	439	394
Less: Reserve for Depreciation	603	584	574	539	423	465	359	277	129	47
Net Fixed Assets	$ 224	$ 239	$ 194	$ 145	$ 209	$148	$205	$209	$310	$347
Total Assets	$1,428	$1,659	$1,389	$1,165	$1,348	$942	$598	$559	$732	$640
Liabilities										
Accounts Payable	$ 25	$ 67	$ 105	$ 53	$ 59	$ 78	$ 9	$ 3	$ 28	$ 3
Notes Payable	...	123	258	240	70	57	1	26	...	31
Accrued Liabilities	138	120	154	139	7	62	49	20	16	5
Accounts Payable—Officers and Employees	112	214	71	6	199	163	24	15	55	36
Taxes Payable	79	159	62	35	184	25	12	...	...	...
Total Current Liabilities	$ 354	$ 683	$ 650	$ 473	$ 519	$385	$ 95	$ 64	$ 99	$ 75
Capital	123	123	123	123	123	123	123	122	122	123
Surplus	951	853	616	569	706	434	380	373	512	443
Total Liabilities	$1,428	$1,659	$1,389	$1,165	$1,348	$919	$598	$559	$732	$640
C.A./C.L.	3.36	2.03	1.78	2.11	2.17	2.02	3.77	4.58	4.20	3.91
N.C.A./C.L.	1.35	0.46	0.34	0.79	1.06	0.71	2.35	2.70	2.62	2.39

HISTORY

E. A. Williams founded Flawless in 1900 and soon began the custom manufacture of cast iron vessels and parts for plumbing, stove, and furnace manufacturers. In 1910 he was joined by his brother, D. R. Williams, forming a brother team which ran the company until 1942. E. A. Williams controlled finances and always held final authority. D. R. Williams, as general manager, made all decisions concerning operations. The latter was described by Henry Williams, his nephew, as a man of "dynamic personality" who inspired personal loyalty from the

Exhibit 4

FLAWLESS FOUNDRY AND EQUIPMENT COMPANY

Comparative Operating Statements for Selected Years Ending December 31
(In Thousands)

	1949	1948	1947	1946	1944	1941	1937	1933	1927	1924
Sales	$2,984	$3,933	$2,716	$2,441	$3,427	$1,554	$1,041	$398	$767	$459
Cost of sales	2,340	3,035	2,422	2,450	2,999	1,379	905	312	677	415
Gross profit	$644	$898	$294	($9)	$428	$175	$136	$86	$90	$44
Selling and administrative expense	412	414	161	151	168	85	81	80	86	43
Net profit from operations	$232	$484	$133	($160)	$260	$90	$55	$6	$4	$1
Other income	9	14	25	14	16	15	3	3	11	14
Gross income	$241	$498	$158	($146)	$276	$105	$58	$9	$15	$15
Other deductions	76	158	91	24	115	59	35	6	9	3
Net income before taxes	$165	$340	$67	($170)	$161	$46	$23	$3	$6	$12
Income taxes	66	139	20	......	109	16	5	......	......	......
Net profit	$99	$201	$47	($170)	$52	$30	$18	$3	$6	$12

	%	%	%	%	%	%	%	%	%	%
Sales	100.00	100.00	100.00	100.00	100.00	100.00	100.00	100.00	100.00	100.00
Cost of sales	78.42	77.16	89.18	100.37	87.51	88.74	86.94	78.39	88.27	90.41
Gross profit	21.58	22.84	10.82	(0.37)	12.49	11.26	13.06	21.61	11.73	9.59
Selling and administrative expense	13.80	10.53	5.93	6.18	4.90	5.47	7.78	20.10	11.21	9.37
Net profit from operations	7.78	12.31	4.89	(6.55)	7.59	5.79	5.28	1.51	0.52	0.22
Other income	0.30	0.35	.92	0.57	0.46	0.97	0.29	0.75	1.43	3.05
Gross income	8.08	12.66	5.81	(5.98)	8.05	6.76	5.57	2.26	1.95	3.27
Other deductions	2.55	4.02	3.35	0.98	3.35	3.80	3.36	1.51	1.17	0.65
Net income before taxes	5.53	8.64	2.46	(6.96)	4.70	2.96	2.21	0.75	0.78	2.62
Income taxes	2.21	3.53	0.73	......	3.18	1.03	0.48	......	......	......
Net profit	3.32	5.11	1.73	(6.96)	1.52	1.93	1.73	0.75	0.78	2.62

Exhibit 5

FLAWLESS FOUNDRY AND EQUIPMENT COMPANY

Sales by Products

(In Thousands)

	6 Mos. 1950	1949	1948	1947	1946	1945	1944	1943	1942	1941	1940	1939	1938	1937	1936	1935	1934
Castings	$ 294	$ 979	$1,255	$ 828	$ 708	$ 762	$ 458	$ 536	$ 638	$ 767	$ 642	$ 469	$ 370	$ 699	$ 683	$ 588	$ 597
Mixers	649	1,172	1,583	1,180	1,374	1,419	1,355	776	441	460	209	218	89	88	99	19	8
Industrial machinery parts	155	776	1,043	637	307	330	286	100	109	207	283	204	217	254	138	91	11
Miscellaneous	25	57	52	71	52	31	24	38	18	9	6						
War products						73	1,304	3,696	2,680	110							
Total sales	$1,123	$2,984	$3,933	$2,716	$2,441	$2,615	$3,427	$5,146	$3,886	$1,553	$1,140	$ 891	$ 676	$1,041	$ 920	$ 698	$ 616
	%	%	%	%	%	%	%	%	%	%	%	%	%	%	%	%	%
Castings	26.2	32.8	31.9	30.5	29.0	29.1	13.4	10.4	16.4	49.4	56.3	52.6	54.7	67.1	74.2	84.2	96.9
Mixers	57.8	39.3	40.2	43.4	56.3	54.3	39.5	15.1	11.3	29.6	18.4	24.5	13.2	8.5	10.8	2.7	1.3
Industrial machinery parts	13.8	26.0	26.6	23.5	12.6	12.6	8.3	1.9	2.8	13.3	24.8	22.9	32.1	24.4	15.0	13.1	1.8
Miscellaneous	2.2	1.9	1.3	2.6	2.1	1.2	0.7	0.8	0.5	0.6	0.5						
War products						2.8	38.1	71.8	69.0	7.1							
Total sales	100.0	100.0	100.0	100.0	100.0	100.0	100.0	100.0	100.0	100.0	100.0	100.0	100.0	100.0	100.0	100.0	100.0

Backlog of orders August 1, 1950:

Castings	$ 164
Mixers	520
Industrial parts	239
Total	$ 923

Estimated* total sales for 1950, $2,243

*By plant superintendent Miller.

men, and whose philosophy was to encourage competition between individuals and between departments. As one of the older foremen recalled, "In the old days under D. R., Flawless was a hard-driving outfit from top to bottom."

The depression of the early thirties hit the gray iron business hard. Flawless sales dropped from a peak in 1927 of $767,000 to $398,-000 in 1933. New products were sought to maintain employment and to hold the company together. In 1933, Flawless began custom production of industrial mixing machines. In 1936, Flawless began production of machinery parts on a job order basis for nearby industrial customers. By 1939, Flawless had doubled its 1933 size, employing 173 men.

In 1941, Flawless received its first war contracts. A wartime sales peak of $5,146,000 was reached in 1943. During the wartime period the company received several citations for its service in the building of ordnance parts.

In 1943, a national independent labor union, after two unsuccessful attempts, organized the workers of the company though this was done against the opposition of D. R. Williams and his production manager, Paul S. Hofstetter, who felt that such action was an encroachment on their management prerogatives. The following year production was halted for 35 days by a strike in protest of department transfer of a worker by Hofstetter. During the strike, workmen demonstrated their protest by overturning Hofstetter's car.

In 1942, the bachelor president, E. A. Williams, died, leaving half of his stock to Henry D. Williams, son of a deceased third brother, and dividing his remaining stock equally between D. R. Williams and a sister. Henry D. Williams thus became the largest stockholder in the company.

D. R. became president upon his brother's death. Later in the same year, however, his health failed, and on doctors' orders he relinquished active management of the company to his production manager, Paul Hofstetter. Henry Williams later described Hofstetter as a good production man, hard driving and very decisive. "Paul's doing the job was the most important thing to him."

"During these years under Hofstetter," said Henry Williams, "discord increased between management and employees; the former had little respect for the union and the union grew in favor with the men so that although production continued high, trust between management and the workers had largely disappeared by 1946."

Henry D. Williams returned from three years' Navy service in 1946 to become vice-president and executive head of Flawless with his uncle, D. R., acting in an advisory capacity. Educated in liberal arts and interested in business chiefly as a "human community," Henry Williams stated that he disliked the conflict which he saw in the company and was determined to bring it to an end.

In 1946, he allowed Hofstetter to resign because of a "basic disagreement" in their management philosophies. Henry Williams then promoted the head of the castings department, Joseph O'Brien, to the post of general manager. Intending to exert no pressure on the organization, Mr. Williams gave O'Brien full charge of the company's operations while he concerned himself with the problems of management-union relations. Mr. Williams later described O'Brien, who remained in office until 1948, as having been a good salesman but inadequate as a general manager, getting bogged down in details.

In the spring of 1948, D. R. Williams died; Henry Williams became president and O'Brien resigned to take the post of sales manager for a large foundry company. A few months later Henry Williams chose Joseph D. Stocker, a castings salesman for the company, as the man best qualified to become general manager. Stocker was given the same broad powers of full, free control which had been granted to his predecessor.

"Since Henry took over in 1946," said general manager Stocker, "things have been a lot different. When Paul Hofstetter was here, it was his word or else. Henry went to the other extreme to correct this situation, allowing others to have a hand in running the company with as much leeway as possible. In the last two years the workers have taken advantage of Henry's leniency and the company has suffered. Now we must tighten up."

PRODUCTS—GRAY IRON CASTINGS

Flawless' original products, cast iron vessels and plumbing, stove, and furnace parts, as well as other gray iron machinery parts, were manufactured in many different shapes and sizes. These gray iron products were used by other manufacturers as parts for a large variety of applications.

Flawless made gray castings largely on a custom basis, although certain shapes were of standard design. Gray cast iron parts, as opposed to malleable shapes (not made by Flawless), were relatively brittle and less apt to stand up under strong impact. Malleable shapes and alloys adapted to individual needs and conditions had made inroads into fields formerly served by gray iron products.

INDUSTRIAL MIXERS

Flawless built on a custom basis a line of industrial mixing machines, mainly for the mixing and blending of liquids in the chemical, plastics, and related industries. Certain basic designs of the mixers were standard, and although a variety of sizes and types was offered, the same general production routines were followed for most of the mixers produced. Flawless would build almost any mixer that a customer desired—lined with stainless steel, alloy metals, plastic, rubber, or something else.

The most common type of mixer built consisted of a large cylindrical tank with agitator mechanisms built on the sides or on the top. Other types included conical or horizontal cylinder machines. Most mixers had a capacity of 500 gallons and over. The assembly of the machines involved plate and sheet metal work, a certain amount of precision machining of moving parts, and construction of suitable bracketing. At times special orders called for unusual designs or materials with specified characteristics to fulfill unique and difficult needs of the customer.

INDUSTRIAL MACHINERY PARTS

Located in a heavily industrialized region, Flawless did a large volume of job order casting, machine work, and welding fabrication to produce machinery parts for industrial customers of all kinds. "Anything we think we can build, we quote on," said chief engineer Donald Canfield.

OWNERSHIP

Flawless was owned jointly by the D. R. Williams estate, a Williams sister, and Henry D. Williams. Henry Williams stated that the sister placed full reliance upon him and that he held unquestioned authority of ownership in the company.

Thomas J. Williams, son of D. R., was vice-president representing his father's estate, a trust for Mrs. D. R. Williams and three children. "No major disagreement with Tom is possible," said Henry Williams. "We always agree, working well together, and discussing freely all matters."

All major stockholders were represented on the payroll of the company. Consequently, it had been the policy of the company not to pay dividends as none had been paid since 1938.

ORGANIZATION

Henry D. Williams, president of Flawless, was a tall, slender man of 38, immaculate in dress and mild in manner. His conversation indicated a wide command of the English language and a close acquaintanceship with the literature and arts of Western culture.

Aware of his lack of technical training and his stated lack of aptitude or desire for it, he approached his job as one of general administrative supervision, leaving the operational management to his subordinates. Mr. Williams considered his primary function as a human one, to serve as a catalyst that would blend the human elements into a smooth organization to work toward his own and the company's end. He did not keep in touch with the daily operations of the company except for matters where subordinates judged that company policy was involved, thereby requiring his attention. He had no scheduled report from anyone, although in July, 1950, at the suggestion of the management consultant, he was considering the installation of some control reports to keep himself more closely informed on the company's operation. He talked with the chief officers along very general lines every day and kept closely informed on personnel and labor matters, frequently talking with the personnel manager and listening to the men's personal problems.

"It is hard to say how good a job we are doing now," said Henry D. Williams. "I don't know whether Joseph Stocker is doing a good job, or whether anyone is. Perhaps none of us is doing as good a job as if driven—though I doubt it. If each man is allowed to find his own level, to express himself as he sees fit, I think that in the long run we can accomplish more and have a better time doing it than if we were working under pressure.

"I personally abhor conflict and competition. Sometimes I wish that I had some of it in my nature. Nevertheless, I do not believe in it as an end in itself—as such it is evil.

"This love of 'drive' pervades our whole life—a nation of gladiators; if we win, O.K.; if not, thumbs down. It's vicious. It presupposes an ability by all of us to fit into that system, and all of us don't. Those who do not fit are made to feel inadequate, whereas actually they may be entirely adequate. I don't like this game spirit, this get-in-there-and-fight, but I may abhor it for a wrong reason.

"I think the life that one builds for himself must be judged on its own merits and not in juxtaposition to that of Henry Ford!

"The drive itself is not evil, but the system that deifies that drive I'm inclined to be skeptical of. The only excuse for material development is to make it possible for men to think about something else. Shaw expressed it well—first acquire an independent income, then practice virtue . . . he may have them backwards, however, overlooking the material rewards of ethical living. It is necessary that men have enough, but what they do with the residue appalls me."

Thomas J. Williams, vice-president and son of the late D. R. Williams, took little active part in the management of Flawless. He was in close touch with his cousin, Henry, on matters of policy, acted occasionally as a representative for Henry, and did favors for the men such as making personal loans in times of individual distress. He concerned himself primarily with the matters of his father's estate and with the general supervision of a real estate business of his own.

Joseph D. Stocker, general manager since 1948, was a quiet, calm man in his late 40's who had been a casting salesman for the company since 1942. A graduate mechanical engineer, he had worked for a similar company since 1927 as salesman and later as sales manager.

"My job here," said Mr. Stocker, "is chiefly a checking job. Unless there's friction, the departments work directly together, and when they get into trouble I step in to smooth things out. I'm not tied down to anything. Of course, there are some things that I must handle myself. I make some big selling trips. I will still have to fool with castings sales from now on; Charles Bixby [sales manager and former manager of job order department] doesn't know how to handle them, and it's no trouble to me."

Mr. Stocker received a monthly report of sales by products; he did not receive any other regular written reports. Each day he checked all castings orders and did the necessary sales managerial work on these orders. Typically, Mr. Stocker did not visit the department heads but would discuss their problems when they brought them to him.

In 1949 he had created a "policy committee" composed of the five major department heads. With the exception of the meeting called in March when they discussed the late delivery problem, no meetings of this committee had been held in 1950.

"I tried to run the company without bothering Henry with details— that's what he wants, I believe, isn't it? This is a one-man job; if he's going to take a more active part, then I don't see what there is for me to do here."

During the past year general manager Stocker had made several changes in the organizational setup of Flawless. Formerly, (see Exhibit 1) Stocker had had 16 direct subordinates, including all production foremen and the castings department personnel—an arrangement inherited from his predecessor. The changes reducing his direct subordinates to six in number, consolidated all sales, except mixers, under one man, Charles P. Bixby; placed all engineering under the chief design engineer, Donald Canfield; and transferred authority over the production foremen to plant superintendent Miller (see Exhibit 2).

BOARD OF DIRECTORS

The owners of Flawless (H. D., T. J. and his two brothers, T. J.'s mother and aunt) plus the treasurer, Thomas R. O'Neill, comprised the board of directors. Regularly scheduled meetings of the entire board were very infrequent.

COMPETITION

Foundry Industry. In 1950, there were 5,300 foundries in the United States engaged in the manufacture of castings ranging from gray iron castings (which tonnagewise accounted for the highest share of the output), malleable iron and alloys, to casting in nonferrous metals like nickel and aluminum. In recent years there had been a noticeable trend towards alloys and nonferrous castings inasmuch as the number of companies specializing in these fields had increased at the expense of the gray iron foundries. Flawless to some extent had followed suit when part of its foundry was devoted to the making of alloy and nonferrous castings for its job order division.

About half of the foundries in 1950 were strictly jobbing shops of the type Flawless had represented in its past, while one-sixth were "captive shops" being departments of larger corporations making castings used for their own products. The remaining one-third were establishments producing for both their own needs and for sale on the outside. The size of the 5,300 foundries ranged from the tiny owner-run "neighborhood operation" with a limited product line to the large, multimillion dollar establishments, offering any conceivable cast shape made efficiently on mechanized equipment.

Mr. Stocker stated that in recent years it had become increasingly difficult for the smaller foundries to get the business of large customers because of the powers of reciprocal buying possessed by the larger integrated companies. Flawless had to compete by giving personalized service and quality but could not match the reciprocity arrangements.

Furthermore, the larger companies had been continually successful in developing new and more efficient casting techniques.

Industrial Mixing Machines. Machines for the mixing and blending of liquids, powders, and viscous substances were used in large numbers by the growing chemical, drug, plastic and food industries, as well as by the various building trades. In 1950, there were over 200 companies engaged in the manufacture of a variety of devices to serve mixing and blending needs.

The smallest of these machines were so-called laboratory "stirrers," a "beater" on a long rod, turned by air or electricity, which could be immersed in barrels or pails of liquid and held by hand. The largest of the mixing machines were huge tanks, with capacities of hundreds or thousands of gallons, fitted with agitator mechanisms or consisted of power-driven vibrating or rolling containers. Other examples were the familiar stationary or truck-mounted concrete mixers used in the building trade.

Some of the larger companies in the field, like Eastern Industries or Patterson Foundry & Equipment Company, manufactured mixers for the whole range of conceivable applications. Other smaller companies, including Flawless, specialized in a more limited field, making machines for solids or liquids only, or specializing in concrete mixers, hand mixers, or dough kneading machines, and the like. Sales of industrial mixers had expanded along with the industries served, and new developments like plastic-lined vessels or new heating methods had been pioneered.

Most of the companies, including many firms which offered a standardized line of mixers, made "tailored-to-order" machines upon request by the customer. Meeting the special needs of many customers required engineering skill and quality production, and Flawless was able to compete along these lines. This offset the fact that it did not offer a standard line of products. Flawless thus was typical of the smaller producer in the industry and sold directly to users on a custom basis.

PRODUCTION

Flawless had six production departments: foundry shop, machine shop, forge shop, pattern shop, mixer shop, and finishing shop (see Exhibit 2).

William D. Miller, plant superintendent, explained in July, 1950, that two production departments were in excellent shape with regard to orders: there were 254 mixers on order, enough to last the mixer department until the first of the year; and the machine shop had industrial parts ordered sufficient to carry it through November. Among the other departments the situation was not so good; the forge shop and the finishing shop which finished plumbing, stove, furnace, and some other cast iron parts each had only five weeks' work. The foundry and pattern shops had two weeks' work in standard parts but were better situated for the nonferrous work and job order iron casting, with a two-month backlog of orders.

FOUNDRY

Oldest of Flawless departments, the foundry for most of its history had made cast iron vessels and plumbing, stove, and furnace parts. Flawless, however, was not equipped to produce the steel parts which had gained in favor with many customers in recent years. With the decline of these products, foundry operations had been diversified to include production of soft-iron machine and parts casting and nonferrous castings. Most recently, permanent mold casting of nonferrous metals on a job order basis appeared to be a promising field, according to Miller and Stocker.

About half of the foundry floor was devoted to rows of standard parts molds; the rest was used for smaller soft-iron and nonferrous castings. Two 40-foot-high cupolas were used to melt iron, and two small electrical furnaces melted the nonferrous metals. Pouring of large castings was done by snap molders[1] who used ladles suspended from overhead monorails. Other workers poured smaller castings with 100-pound-capacity hand ladles. Molds were prepared in the morning and pouring was done in the afternoon. In July, with a shortage of orders, snap molders were working only two days a week.

The foundry was supervised by one foreman and two subforemen. About half of the men in the foundry were laborers who were shifted from one phase of the operations to another as the labor needs changed during the day. The management consultant felt that although there were three supervisors, the foundry was only about 60% efficient. President Williams believed the foundry was only moderately profitable at best, though there were no separate department records to substantiate this feeling.

Part-time technical adviser to the foundry was Herbert W. Kayser who had been with Flawless for 27 years and who had been foundry superintendent for several years prior to 1950. In January, 1950, Stocker relieved Kayser of authority over the foundry and placed him

---

[1] Snap molding is a process which employs molding flasks consisting of two halves which are closed with a snap fastener.

in the sales department "to cut down on the number of foundry super-visors and to gain a solicitor for foundry orders."

Kayser had a knowledge of metallurgy which no one else in the company possessed; thus, when difficult foundry problems arose, it was necessary that he be called back to the foundry as a technical adviser. Kayser maintained a primary interest in the foundry, dropping his sales work when foundry troubles materialized. Neither sales manager Bixby nor plant superintendent Miller considered himself to have authority over Kayser while the latter held this dual capacity. Both men wanted general manager Stocker to clarify Kayser's position.

The most recent job in the foundry involving "permanent" molds had been the production of 500 intricate, thin-walled aluminum castings. Two engineers had tried to design the mold without success, and Kayser was called in to aid. After conducting experiments for five weeks, he remedied the flaws in the mold design so that volume production could be begun in late July.

FINISHING SHOP

Vessels, standard plumbing, and stove and furnace parts made in the foundry were taken to the finishing shop where, under the supervision of one foreman, these parts, as well as some of the gray iron machine parts, were machined, cleaned, and made ready for delivery to outside customers.

MACHINE SHOP

The nonferrous castings from the foundry generally were taken to the machine shop for finishing operations. Equipped with all conventional machine tools, the machine shop handled most industrial machinery parts orders.

With the aid of one subforeman, this department was run by foreman Walter Bridges, a thin, energetic New Englander who was continually worried about the lack of ambition of the men: "They just don't seem to want to improve themselves." Bridges planned all of his department's operations, did most of the cost and time estimating for bids on machine work, and designed the department's tools and jigs. The latter work, he said, was taking too much of his time. He had formerly kept job times by machining operations which aided greatly in estimating. Upon a complaint by the labor union that this was unfair, general manager Stocker, without consulting Bridges, had ordered the discontinuance of this recording of incremental operation times. "They won't tell me why they do things and they don't give a damn whether you like it or not," said Bridges in reference to this incident. "They won't allow me enough control, but they sure raise hell when something goes wrong."

FORGE SHOP

The forge shop was the starting place for most of the parts used in mixing machine manufacture. It was equipped with plate and bar shears, metal punches and saws, heavy drill presses, bending machines, hot working forges, and a blacksmith shop. Most of the equipment was old, and the area was crowded, with the result that the aisles were usually blocked with wagonloads of work-in-process materials. A shop foreman with the aid of one subforeman controlled the flow of materials visually. Materials were moved from machine to machine on small steel wagons which were pushed by hand and which sometimes required six men or more to move. Aisles were considered too narrow for lift trucks, and the ceiling too low to install a bridge crane. With inadequate space and a great variety of heavy materials to be moved, the material-handling problem contributed to frequent temporary bottlenecks which in turn caused delays in production in the mixer shop.

MIXER DEPARTMENT

Located on the other side of, and adjacent to the forge shop, was the mixer department, biggest of Flawless' production departments. This department was under the supervision of Daniel F. Glines, Jr., and three subforemen. Glines was a son of the forge shop foreman. The department consisted of a single production line with six stations, several subassembly areas, a mixer repair area, and a paint shop. Mixers of every type were built on the one production line. Subassemblies such as frames, bracketing, and agitator assemblies were built in side areas and fed into the main production line.

The work of the mixer department was an assembling operation done chiefly by welding and riveting. The work at the first two stations was nearly standard, with the custom variation in the mixing machines being handled at the later stations. More than half of the mixers produced were tank type mixing machines. Even with these semistandard jobs, however, the necessary variations in production time hampered uniform flow of work from station to station. Also, there might be six different types of mixing machines on the line at one time, with the slowest job setting the pace for the whole group. Mixer production averaged slightly more than two per day.

In addition to handling the mixing machine work, Glines with one of his subforemen supervised welding operations on industrial orders. In June, at the suggestion of the management consultant, part of this work had been shifted into a separate area.

The plant superintendent in charge of all production departments was William D. "Bill" Miller, 35-year-old mechanical engineer. After several years with the company as an engineer before the war, he became production control manager in 1946; in 1947, he was named plant superintendent, but with no substantial change in his duties of production control and with no authority over the foremen, this authority being vested in the general manager.

Shortly after becoming plant superintendent in 1947, Miller installed a "Productrol" system for control of production scheduling. The Productrol boards with the accompanying records and one clerk served as a message center through which all orders and information came into the shop. Records were kept of all orders moving between departments. Miller asserted that the system, coupled with frequent checks with the foremen, had afforded good control on long orders but had been less effective on short-run orders.

In April, 1949, Miller requested another clerk to help in operating the Productrol system. Stocker felt that the system was inadequate and too expansive; rather than grant Miller's request, he discontinued the Productrol system completely. As a substitute each foreman was to control his own department completely and was to be responsible to general manager Stocker. All orders were handled directly between foremen and the engineering department without any central control point such as had existed under the Productrol system.

Miller continued to be responsible for interdepartmental scheduling of work and for the prompt delivery of orders to customers. He conferred with each foreman daily to keep informed on the progress of work and to try to smooth the flow of work-in-process between departments.

After the discontinuance of the Productrol system, the number of late deliveries to customers of products increased. "By March, 1950, the situation had become intolerable and very confusing to all. There was no co-ordination between departments," said Miller. "I was bypassed by the foremen and by those in the engineering office so that I had no real control of production scheduling, and Joseph Stocker was still acting like a castings salesman.

"We had an executive meeting last March when the late orders' problem became acute," continued Miller. "Much to everyone's surprise, Joseph Stocker told us that I had the full responsibility for the plant. Then I demanded, and got, authority over the foremen. We still have a lot of educating to do, but the foremen are getting to know now that I am their boss. No one gives them orders except me, and no one is going around me anymore—either up or down. The consultant has helped me a lot in organizing my work. Now that I know what my job is, and just what my bounds of authority are, this change of command is going to work or else."

In May, 1950, Miller had installed biweekly foremen's meetings at which mutual problems were discussed and at which the foremen were informed of developments and company policies which affected them. "A good foreman will stand on his own hind legs; we haven't got but three who do so now. The rest usually try to shift responsibilities wherever possible; for example, if a worker tells a foreman to 'go to hell,' he just takes it to Floyd (personnel manager). That's no way for a foreman to act. There has been a lot of apathy among foremen and workers. Since the 'renaissance,' however, I believe that they will come around."

After the March meeting Miller decided to confer with the sales and purchasing departments twice weekly. The status of all orders was reviewed, and the information of all three was pooled regarding material needs, sales prospects, production facilities available, and the expected delivery time on orders. Miller carried a clip board with him on which the status of work in every department was noted. He conferred daily with each production foreman, checking on the progress of new and late orders and helping them with their problems.

Delivery time estimates were asked by most industrial parts and mixing machine customers, with less frequent requests for such promises from castings customers. These estimates were given to the sales manager by Miller. With the aid of the production foreman he would make such estimates after consideration of production requirements of an order and the current availability of production facilities.

Because of the custom nature of the shop and the consequent great variety of jobs, no production standards had been employed. Labor times by whole jobs[2] were collected through a job-card time-clock system and recorded by a shop clerk. No record of elemental work times had been kept except in the instance of Mr. Bridges' efforts in the machine shop. Delivery time estimates, as well as cost estimates, were made on the

---

[2] Whole jobs might include several products.

basis of previous work for whole jobs, with the limited aid of the job-card information. Such estimating was considered satisfactory for jobs closely similar to previous work, according to treasurer O'Neill who was responsible for the collection of time and cost information. The lack of elemental work standards, however, greatly limited the accuracy of estimates on new types of work. "Our products are so varied that we can't establish standard costs," said Mr. O'Neill. "I wish someone could devise a system for us which wouldn't require a whole flock of men to operate it."

ENGINEERING

Donald Canfield, chief engineer, age 38, came to Flawless in 1935 as a draftsman-engineer with a degree in mechanical engineering. He was named chief design engineer in 1941. Subsequently he had been concerned primarily with mixer design and engineering until all engineering was consolidated in the fall of 1949 and placed under his direction.

This department, containing ten engineer-draftsmen, was responsible for most of the price estimating work for product design, for plant engineering, and for inspection of finished mixers. In addition, Canfield made infrequent selling trips.

When customer inquiries were received, the engineering department made price estimates for the sales manager with the aid of the accounting and purchasing departments. The accounting department supplied labor cost information on past work completed, which was used as an aid in estimating the labor cost of new work. Material cost estimates were obtained from the purchasing department. On items concerning which the purchasing agent had to make outside inquiries, Canfield complained that action had usually been slow. Overhead rates were fixed by the accounting department, expressed as a fixed percentage of direct labor for most departments. Canfield stated that overhead rates had been changed only three times in the past 15 years and that he doubted the accuracy of these rates.

All customer orders came to Canfield. There, shop orders were written up, materials were requisitioned from the purchasing department, the necessary engineering work was done, and the order was sent to the shop for production. The engineering department had no control over the production department except indirectly in an advisory capacity and in an inspecting capacity.

The required engineering work usually consisted of adapting a standard design to meet the specific requirements of the customer. Engineering work usually was necessary on every mixing machine order. Most of the industrial machinery parts required no engineering work as designs were supplied by the customer. In cases where original design work had to be done, this work was performed sometimes at the time of customer inquiry but more usually after the receipt of a firm order. In the past year they had developed two new agitator assemblies for mixing machines, a new stainless steel mixer, and had improved the present mixing machine designs. "We seem to be just one jump ahead of the sheriff all the time around here," said Canfield. "There is no time to plan for the future."

ACCOUNTING

Thomas R. O'Neill, controller and treasurer, was a slight man of about 60 years who said that he had been trained by the first president, E. A. Williams, to "keep the figures close to himself." An executive with the company since 1925, O'Neill was the financial adviser to Henry Williams, supervisor of all accounting and financial work, and personal handler of the private ledger (profits, officers' salaries, etc.).

An assistant controller and four other men completed the department. Conventional company accounting was practiced. The department kept all Flawless records and handled most financial transactions.

There was no interdepartmental accounting, and no records were made of departmental profitability. Total costs by product were not kept. "We just throw it all together and see how it comes out at the end of the year," said the assistant controller.

PURCHASING

George T. Marchand, purchasing agent, stated that he was responsible for all purchases. With an assistant to handle local purchases and routine work, Marchand concerned himself with major items of supply, inventory control, and the making of purchase inquiries.

On receiving a material requisition from engineering, he would determine whether the material could be taken from stock or must be ordered. In the latter case he would make outside inquiries, getting price and delivery date from material suppliers. "Getting special stuff is a headache, and we seem to need a lot of it—odd-sized bolts for some mixers, special material for an industrial part, and so on. The engineering department always wants it in a hurry, and I have to keep pushing the suppliers to get the stuff here on time."

Inventory control was decentralized and nearly all visual. Marchand kept records of plate, shape, and bar stock (steel), checking frequently with the foremen to insure adequate supply of the right sizes, and taking quarterly actual inventories. Foremen kept inventories on less critical items such as sand or limestone for the foundry. The plant superintendent kept castings inventories, and the sales manager for mixers, R. F. Brown, kept inventories of mixing machines and accessories. "Inventory control is sort of a joint responsibility among the foremen, Stocker, Brown, and myself," said Marchand. "If it had been my full responsibility, we wouldn't have run out of stainless steel sheet here last month like we did; they just didn't tell me that the supplies were low. Then the market tightened up, and we couldn't get nearly enough."

SALES

When responsibility for all the sales (except mixers) had been consolidated in late 1949, the job of sales manager was given to 33-year-old Charles Bixby, who had previously been head of the job order sales department. Henry Williams considered him to have been an excellent man in handling these industrial orders and in handling government war contract negotiations during World War II.

There were four engineer salesmen under Bixby. Formerly, three of these had been castings salesmen exclusively and one had been a parts salesman. After consolidation all four were authorized to sell both lines of products, but actually there had been little change in their work, the three still being "99% castings salesmen." Bixby also sold industrial parts about 25% of his time.

The salesmen were paid on a commission basis with a small drawing account. Bixby in his new capacity did not believe that he should continue to draw sales commissions since it put him in an embarrassing position with his salesmen at the time. He wanted his salary tied to the sales of the whole department and had made such a proposal to Stocker in late 1949, but as yet no action had been taken.

Prior to the new sales setup general manager Stocker had been castings sales manager in addition to his job as general manager. When the sales switch had been made, Bixby had understood that Stocker was to transfer the castings business gradually to him. In July, 1950, Stocker was still handling all castings sales work. The two castings salesmen had been told of the new setup but were confused because Stocker still handled their accounts. "I haven't pushed this castings control," said Bixby. "It will work out eventually. As long as the castings orders are being handled, it's O.K. by me."

At the time of the consolidation of sales, the handling of all mixer sales was transferred to Robert S. Brown, a former mixer salesman. Henry Williams described Brown as a "wonderful salesman—the alpha and omega of the mixer division." The mixing machines made by Flawless had been successful in gaining a good reputation in the market, according to Brown, and were well received by old and new customers alike.

Brown operated with three office men and eight salesmen who called on customers directly. "During the past few years we could have sold all of our mixing machines over the telephone but we need the contacts so we have maintained the sales force. We sell mixing machines for a few hundred dollars more than our big competitors at times, but we give quality custom service and the customers know it. We haven't had a serious failure of our machines in 14 years," said Mr. Brown.

Mr. Brown added that their chief customers had been the large chemical and food manufacturers who bought both on price and quality. "We can't keep mixers in stock because of the custom nature of our work and because of the expense, but we can deliver within about five weeks after an order is placed."

Bixby stated that the production co-ordination meetings with Miller and Marchand were working reasonably well. "We get expediting and delivery promises pretty accurately from Miller now. This has been a sore subject in the past, but we are rocking along all right now. We still fall down on a few promises, but it isn't as bad as it was last year.

"These production meetings are the only ones of any sort that we have in this company," continued Bixby. "We need more meetings. They would prevent lots of our problems. No one ever asked my advice on company problems. I don't like to keep running and complaining, but I would like my thoughts heard nevertheless. Also, we shouldn't have to ask what's going on; we ought to be informed automatically. I don't see how a company runs without the executives getting together once in a while."

The Flawless sales program was almost entirely direct selling by engineer salesmen. Occasional advertisements were run in trade journals, and some direct-mail advertising was used, including calendars and product brochures.

LABOR RELATIONS

Floyd D. Barnes, age 32, had been personnel manager since the spring of 1949. An engineer, previously he had been assistant to Charles Bixby in the industrial job order department. He was familiar with every phase of the company's operations, acting as plant superintendent for two weeks in July when Miller was on vacation. Common interests in the human problems of the business and in philosophical matters had drawn him close to Henry Williams. The latter felt that Floyd was one of the few men in the company with whom he had much in common and was one of the few whom he knew well.

In July, 1950, Barnes had just completed a wage negotiation with the union granting a 5-cent-per-hour general wage increase plus six paid holidays.

Year-end profit bonuses had been paid to the men for the past two years, 11 cents per hour and 5¼ cents per hour, respectively. The men stated that they did not want such bonuses but would rather have the money in their regular pay envelopes. With the negotiated raise the company did not intend to grant any further such bonuses.

Bonuses were to continue, however, for office and supervisory personnel. These bonuses had been on an arbitrary basis "according to a man's value to the company," as decided by president Williams.

"There was a complete lack of trust in the early days of the union," said Barnes. "Things are much better now, but some of that distrust still exists among the workers. In trying to overcome this, we have been actually too lenient. No one has been fired for inefficiency or insubordination in over a year. Petty grievances have multiplied. I now believe that we must handle the men with a firm but fair hand.

"The men don't have any enthusiasm for the work as they did before the war," Barnes added. "The snap molders are only putting out 60 molds a day each, where we know they can do 100 easily. In the mixer shop the men did put on a little drive in June to increase production while the consultants were here, but now they have slipped into their old complacent ways; furthermore, the supervisors have done little to get more work out of the men. I don't know—perhaps the basic trouble is that no one knows exactly what he is supposed to do."

OPERATIONS AND PLANS

In the spring of 1950, Flawless designed a special casting for a prospective customer who intended to buy 1,200 units. The design was approved by the customer's engineering department; this design was given to a large competitor for bidding. Flawless quoted a lower price than the other firm, and the Flawless bid was accepted tentatively. When sent to main company headquarters for final action, however, the order was changed, going to the large competitor presumably for reasons of reciprocity, according to Stocker.

With the memory of this incident freshly in mind and the knowledge of developments in the foundry industry, general manager Stocker was searching for new ways and ideas to make use of the idle casting facilities and men.

By July, 1950, the management consultant firm, which had been hired by Mr. Williams to analyze the operations of the company, had studied the mixer shop and the foundry and expected to complete the study of the management organization and of the whole company by early fall.

In the mixer department the consultants believed that production could be doubled on the single assembly line without any basic changes. Because of the great variations in work they stated that close supervision was needed for efficiency and that foreman Glines previously had not been spending enough time in direct work supervision. During June, the consultants put three extra supervisors on the mixer line for methods study; the workmen made a sustained effort to increase production, turning out 67 units, an increase of 18% over the months of 1950. Foreman Glines did not receive the help of the consultants willingly. Miller asked that he congratulate the men on the June performance, but Glines refrained from doing so. In early July the consultants had made several minor suggestions about improvements in production methods, but none had been acted on. In July, mixer production dropped to 38.

In June, 25 of the mixers produced had to be taken off the line incomplete for lack of certain rubber parts; in July, the production line was held up three days for lack of rivets of a special size. An improvement on the visual control of mixer parts inventory was being devised by the consultants with written records and one man to act as a full-time stock chaser. It was hoped that this new system of inventory control would eliminate holdups from material shortages and would allow Glines more time in the future for direct work supervision.

The consulting firm was also devising a standard cost system and production control system for the mixer department. The methods would be to set standards for the basic fundamental operations performed in the shop and then to synthesize a set of job standards from these elements for each variety of mixer that was produced. Use of the system would require the services of one timekeeper; it was hoped to extend this system later to all departments.

After studying the foundry, the consultants made recommendations in July to rearrange the layout, reducing the floor area assigned to standard molds and increasing the nonferrous area. It was recommended that two bridge cranes be installed to replace the present single-rail system and that a separate building be constructed for the permanent mold work. It was further recommended that the pattern shop be combined with the foundry and that the combined supervision be reduced from five to two foremen. Mr. Stocker said that at least the physical changes would be made in the near future.

With an old plant, overcrowding had become a serious problem, particularly in the forge and mixer shops. Several plant layout revisions had been made by the consulting firm. On the one hand, a new mixer building was considered. "Stainless steel mixers are going extremely well," said Stocker, "and to get volume production on them it would be best to have a new building." On the other hand, Stocker was considering moving the forge shop out under the adjacent craneway and expanding the mixer shop with two parallel production lines into the present forge shop area. This revision would give these departments much needed additional space and would allow the establishment of a second mixer line, mitigating the problems of building so many different types of mixers on one production line. Mr. Stocker stated that he wanted to get a full plant revision worked out before taking any action on an individual department layout.

Old equipment was another problem, much of it being over 20 years old. It was realized that this contributed to high cost production, though no figures had been accumulated to substantiate this feeling. "When the money is available out of earnings, we will buy new equipment as we can," said Mr. Stocker; "we don't want to borrow to buy equipment." In recent months new mixer shop tools and an automatic turret lathe had been purchased. Most critical needs were considered to be a new plate punch, a plate shear, and a milling machine. The new plate punch would effect labor savings which would pay off its cost in three years. At present, however, there was not an adequate space in the forge shop in which to put it.

Returning from a week's selling trip on July 26, 1950, general manager Stocker beamingly presented Henry Williams with the first big order for standard castings which the company had received in over a year; "I sewed it up just before the big boys arrived!"

Appleton Machine Company (A)

INTRODUCTION

THE APPLETON MACHINE COMPANY was a small, family-owned producer of capital goods located in Durham, New Hampshire, a city about 60 miles north of Boston with a population of 4,000. The company employed about 300 people in 1961. Its product line included four quite separate items of equipment: (1) textile machinery, (2) heat exchangers, (3) water control equipment, and (4) industrial rolls.

DESCRIPTION OF PRODUCTS AND MARKETS

Textile Machinery. The textile machinery produced by the company was primarily for the washing and dyeing operations in the processing of cloth. These machines consisted primarily of a stainless steel tank, which contained the liquid, and a drive mechanism for pulling the cloth through the tank at carefully controlled tension.

The stainless steel tank was made by Appleton. The drive parts were designed and patented by Appleton, but included mostly purchased parts.

The company had an excellent reputation in this field, and its U.S. customers included American Viscose Corporation, Burlington Mills, and Cluett Peabody Company. Plans were being made to establish a joint venture in Italy for the manufacture and distribution of these machines to the Common Market countries. The company's machines were also sold through agents in South America and the Far East, especially in India and Vietnam.

The Appleton Heat Exchanger. The Appleton heat exchanger was a patented device which permitted efficient heat transfer to and from viscous materials. The heart of the exchanger was a device which maintained a thin, even film of the material along the tank wall, permitting the material to be heated and cooled evenly and quickly. This process was particularly important in the processing of chemicals, foods, and pharmaceuticals, and the company had sold much of its output to these industries. It was frequently necessary to make the exchanger of stainless steel to avoid contamination.

The company had attempted to increase its sales of process equipment by working with chemical companies and developing new equipment for existing processes. As an illustration of its success in this area it cited the fact that of 12 urea plants recently designed by a leading chemical engineering firm, 11 had included Appleton equipment.

Water Control Equipment. The major product of this division was sluice gates, which the company sold primarily to contractors engaged in a variety of projects. Frequently these involved municipal water supply or sewerage projects, but power companies and state and federal agencies were also important customers.

Sluice gates were ordinarily made of bronze. They were cast, and then machined to dimension.

Industrial Rolls. The company produced rolls of metal, rubber, wood, and plastic for a variety of industries. Most were sold to the textile industry, but many other applications were common. Rolls had been sold by direct mail, but in 1961 the company was considering whether this should continue to be the case.

MARKETING

Marketing. Each of the products in the product line was marketed by a group of people reporting to a "division manager." (See Exhibit 1, Organization Chart.)

With the exception of rolls, the company's products were sold both by its own salesmen and by manufacturers' agents.

All of the company's products were custom products, in the sense that a basic design had to be modified to fit each customer's particular requirements. Consequently, the company placed considerable emphasis on its own salesmen having a great deal of technical knowledge concerning the company's products.

In early 1962, the company was looking for new products to add to its product line. Executives of the company felt that the choice of any new product should conform with the policy enunciated by the president of the company in 1959:

We are now serving a market which is no longer limited to New England. It is a national market and, to an increasing extent, international. We can't compete with the rest of the country in hauling tons of metal. We have to be interested in patented, proprietary products where we are adding engineering brains and manufacturing skill. Any product we add must fit into this philosophy, as well as our existing plant facilities.

Exhibit 1

APPLETON MACHINE COMPANY (A)

Organization Chart—January, 1962

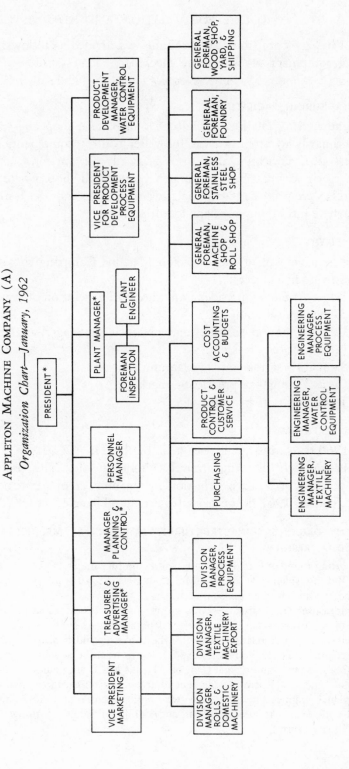

* Member of management group.

Source: Case writer impression, based on interviews with company officers.

In 1962 the company's sales volume was divided as follows: water control equipment, 45%; textile machinery, domestic, 15%; textile machinery, export, 15%; process equipment, 15%; and rolls, 10%.

MANUFACTURING FACILITIES

Manufacturing facilities included (1) a pattern shop and foundry, used primarily to produce parts for water control equipment; (2) a stainless steel fabricating shop, used primarily for the construction of textile machinery and heat exchangers; (3) a roll shop, where industrial rolls were produced—especially wooden rolls; and (4) a machine shop, where machining was done for all products.

MANAGEMENT

The management of the Appleton Machine Company consisted of the following five officers:

1. Roger Appleton, president, and the third generation of Appletons to manage the company.
2. David Appleton, treasurer and advertising manager, and younger brother of the president.
3. Samuel Dyer, manager of planning and control.
4. Cyrus Young, vice president—marketing.
5. James Johnson, plant manager.

PROFIT PERFORMANCE

In 1960 the company incurred a sizable loss. In 1961 it had a profit on approximately the same overall volume of sales. This profit was made possible by a sharp reduction in the number of personnel employed. During 1961 the office staff was reduced from 120 to 80.

COMPANY ORGANIZATION STRUCTURE: STATEMENT BY MR. ROGER APPLETON, PRESIDENT

Reporting to me as President are the following four major officers:

1) Vice President–Marketing—Mr. Young is in charge of both domestic sales and exports for those divisions.

2) Treasurer and Secretary—This is my younger brother, David. He is in charge of the cash payroll, receivables and payables, and our external financial arrangements, such as relationships with the banks. In addition, he is in charge of advertising, although he reports to Mr. Young when he acts in this capacity.

3) Manager of Planning and Control—This is Mr. Dyer; he has under him a variety of functions. These include general accounting, cost control, purchasing, and product engineering. Mr. Dyer was until recently our chief industrial engineer, reporting to the president and doing all kinds of things except industrial engineering.

4) Plant Manager—Mr. Johnson is in charge of all of our manufacturing facilities.

In addition, the following people also report to the president: The Manager of Product Development—Water Control Equipment; the Vice President for Product Development (Mr. Gates), who is responsible for product development primarily in the chemical field; and the Personnel Manager. If we were twice our present size, I suppose we would have a single Vice President—Product Development who would handle product development for everything. But right now that function is split among two people.

I am not sure that the function of product development—chemical products should still be awarded a vice president's title. Our Vice President of Product Development (chemical) is a vice president because he is a long-term and highly respected employee. He is a highly innovative individual, but he is not by nature a manager. One reason he was given the title was in order to endow him with authority—to give him stature within the company. It was hoped that it would give him the "spark" to manage people, but it didn't have that effect.

Mr. Young, our Vice President—Marketing, became a vice president about seven years ago—naturally because the scope of his responsibility is so broad. Also, at that time he handled almost all of our large orders personally, and he considered that his ability to speak for the management was most significant.

Mr. Dyer, our Manager of Planning and Control, is not a vice president. I don't know how many officers a company our size needs. I also don't know if we would work differently if he were a vice president—maybe we would.

Our board of directors has only one outside member on it—a lawyer. He retains that position not so much because of his profession, but because I respect his judgment on many of the problems that we face. The other members of the board of directors are myself, our Vice President—Marketing, the Treasurer (my brother), and the Vice President—Product Development. I should add that the board of directors in this company fulfills a largely perfunctory purpose. It meets only once a year and then just to pass a previously proposed set of minutes.

ORGANIZATION: FORMAL GROUPS

The three major groups at the company were the management group, the executive group, and the better relations group.

The management group was the company's top operating group. It consisted of the president, vice president—marketing, the treasurer, the manager of planning and control, and the plant manager. This group met almost weekly from 1:30 to 8 P.M. All the members of the group were enthusiastic about it. A typical comment was made by Mr. David Appleton:

With the management group, we are now requiring more of the organization, and it has responded. Also, there is less departmentalization. If I have to get 100 letters out, I know I can get it done all over the company, and no one will refuse to help because they aren't in my department.

The company is much more of a team, primarily because the management is much more of a team. Each function knows what the other group is doing, and why.

The executive group was a group which existed for communications purposes only, rather than as a problem-solving body. Membership in the executive group was as follows:

Roger Appleton	President
Cyrus Young	Vice President—Marketing
David Appleton	Treasurer—Advertising Manager
Edward Gates	Vice President—Product Development
Samuel Dyer	Manager, Planning & Control
James Johnson	Plant Manager
Robert Bash	Purchasing Agent
Philip Freed	Manager, Product Development— Water Control Equipment
Edward Holmes	Manager, Water Control Equipment, Sales Division
Carl Schultz	Manager, Textile Machinery & Industrial Roll Division
Peter Fuller	Manager, Process Equipment Division
Herbert Colino	Manager, Export Division

As typical illustrations of the kind of occasions on which this group would be convened, Mr. Dyer cited the following:

It is our policy to always distribute information to our supervisors first. We recently put out several new policy directives on matters of importance. On such an occasion, I call the executive group together and discuss it with them first.

As another example, our Vice President—Marketing recently got back from a trip around the world, and we had him speak to the executive group. I would say that training and communications are the principal purposes of these meetings.

The better relations group was different from the other two in that it consisted of both workers and executives. Its operation is described in the following statement by Mr. James Johnson, plant manager:

We felt responsible for the poor communications last year. Roger and I felt that we didn't spend enough time in the plant. The fellows out there are hungry for information about the company. And they don't want it from just their supervisors. They want to hear it right from the president.

Roger and I went right out into the shop, department by department, and we had a bull session. Roger did most of the talking, and I answered a few questions. We are planning to do more of this. It is a very effective way of getting to the people.

Incidentally, we had quite a revelation when we went through the list of fringe benefits we have, in order to be able to explain it to our people. When we got all the data together, you could see that it was quite an impressive package of benefits. I don't think the man on the machine realized how much of a contribution the company was making to such things as Blue Cross and life insurance, vacations, paid holidays, etc.

The machinists' union knocked at the door but did not succeed in gaining certification. After it was all over we asked ourselves, "Where have we failed?" We decided that we should spend more time in the shop. Also, we decided that the fellows want a channel to the president. They want to know: "Does Roger Appleton know about this problem in my department?" The result was the establishment of a group to improve relations—the better relations group.

We have 12 members in the group who are hourly rated people from the plant; and three members from management. We meet every Wednesday from 7 to 9; and the president of the company is the chairman.

The members from the plant are selected as follows. I nominate them, after talking to the personnel manager and supervisors. We pick fellows who will represent their group and who will speak up. We would rather have the problem of controlling it than of jacking it up, so we don't care whether or not a fellow was campaigning for the union when we select nominees.

We post the nominations in the shop, together with a petition. The fellows can sign the petition if they don't want him. If a majority of the men he's to represent sign, he's rejected. If he is not challenged, he is appointed by Roger and he serves for a year.

If a fellow in the shop has a problem, he goes to his supervisor. If he isn't satisfied with the answer he gets, he takes it to the better relations group. At first we had some problems with this, because people would bring things to the better relations group before taking it up with their supervisor. But we now insist that it go to the supervisor first.

Each week we have two guests at the meeting: one from the supervisory group and one from the hourly rated workers. We are trying to use this guest approach to speed up the amount of firsthand acquaintance with the group. We don't want to wait for the rotation of members to give others a chance to see how it operates.

The group sometimes raises issues on its own. For example, they asked if we could have a hot food dispensing machine in the production room. We put one in, and it is doing a booming business.

THE PRESIDENT'S JOB

Statement by Mr. Roger Appleton, January 23, 1962.

I have the responsibility for developing—causing to be developed—objectives to give the company direction.

I have the responsibility for developing policy, within which we will operate to achieve those objectives.

I have the responsibility for developing an efficient organization, and to have plans for a future organization. Also, to fill the positions reported to me with the right people.

To cause the people throughout the organization to know their responsibilities, to be compensated, and to be trained appropriately.

I must cause to be developed plans and programs such as status reports. I maintain controls to measure our progress.

I have a written position description. We are close to formalization of this process. I have a description of my own job.

We lost a lot of money in 1960. This soul-searching that we went through, plus the fact that I have been puzzling about how to accelerate our rate of achievement, and what my role in fact should be, has resulted in many changes in our operating methods. I set up a group, and asked them to advise me. These fellows said: "The president ought to act like a president." I think that this meant that the president should give the company more direction, should establish objectives.

A year ago I had trouble caused by crowding in my schedule. This job was running me, instead of me running the job. So I took a couple of weekends off, and did a lot of thinking about it.

I have had this interesting experience. When I got back, I had found all the answers, and I began to tell them to my management group, individually. However, I thought I sensed a little antipathy to this. So, in our management meetings, we started with the following questions: What factors caused our performance to improve in 1961, and what could be learned from them?

What we found from this was the recurrence of such things as: policy clarification in personnel, policy clarification in pricing, etc. Finally, we came up with five words: (1) objectives, (2) policies, (3) organization, (4) plans, (5) controls.

Now, you see, this is very interesting. I had come up with the same conclusions myself over the weekend thinking about my job.

And here at the mangement meeting we came up with the same conclusion. The right people were in the right jobs. Plans—we learned how to come out of a meeting with plans. Controls—for the first time, we had an accounting system that everyone had confidence in. We concluded this: during the past year, one of the basic improvements was a greater unanimity among the members of the management group. It was also observed that we did not have to cancel as many decisions as before—or to leave them to die. This must mean that the decisions are "righter." That five heads are better than one. That when the president makes decisions now, he has better advice.

The big companies have committees, such as finance. Well, the finance committee is really the office of the treasurer. What this means is that the president's job can't be one man—we have to have more than that. We have really five presidents now instead of one. We said that the president's position description was, in effect, a description of the functions of the management group. That's why, when you ask "what is the function of the president," I am able to rattle it right off.

I don't think I have the final answer, by any means, but I think I am closer than I ever have been. I am also aware that any criteria for the evaluation of my performance is very difficult. In addition, I am trying to decide what I should be doing myself, and what I should be delegating to others—especially in terms of the contribution that I myself ought to be making to various company activities.

There is also the problem of dealing with top management problems—as against the lures of operating problems.

Mr. Appleton then picked up a folder, took out a memorandum from it, and proceeded to read:

Notes of Meeting: Dyer, Schultz, and myself.

Issue: Do we have enough initiative?

We also discussed: Should we have an assistant for Roger Appleton? Also, how can we get Roger Appleton to think and act like a president?

1) Evaluate the next 24-hour schedule.

2) Evaluate his desk drawer.

3) Evaluate omissions—the things that do not get done now.

Advise the management group that from now on Roger Appleton will think and act like a president; tired of bellyaches and excuses, from now on anything can happen: firing, transfers, etc. Available for counsel.

They were very critical of me for being so tolerant of poor performance.

Mr. Appleton replaced the memo, and picked up another sheet of paper, on which was a list of duties:

This sheet [*points to sheet*] I have exploded into about 22 pages of detail. This sheet is my position description. We call it the "function of the management group."

Q: Would you say something about the reports you get, about the way you act in your control capacity?

It's a puzzle to me. I have about two and a half pages of notes about this.

In terms of what we have at present, we keep progressing and making improvements in such mechanical-financial controls as we have. We have a "forecast review" folder, and Sam Dyer is the one responsible for getting one into the hands of each member of the management group. It contains forecasts for the coming month for shipping, new orders, and the P.&L. statement.

Q: Is there anything which goes to you, as an individual, that does not go to the other members of the management group?

Yes. I get a monthly financial review including all cost center summaries, statistics, as well as a balance sheet and P.&L. statement. However, cost center reports also go to each of the cost center managers.

In this control area, I am impressed by this. When I was in the Army, I thought my commanding officer knew everything that was going on all over an extended area. I have always admired that, but I am not sure that I could match that performance.

For example, we have a better relations group, and I use that as a control group. From the complaints that come out of that group, I am able to tell what is happening in the plant. In the marketing area, I have a lot less control. I don't get out into the field at all.

One of the things that we need to develop our skills in is this area of control.

It's the things that numbers don't report, that are the hard things to control, and yet they may be the most important ones—like how do you measure morale? We are going to put in a compensation system to compensate people fairly. We can install it, but how do you find out what the effect has been?

THE JOB OF THE VICE PRESIDENT—MARKETING

Statement by Mr. Cyrus Young.

We have a problem in process equipment—not enough agents. For example, we had no agents in Illinois and in Ohio, where a lot of our customers are. We have a new division manager in process equipment, so I helped him by getting two new agents that we are happy with.

I get into export quite a bit lately. For example, in India we aren't getting the business that we used to. On my last trip out there I found out that our agents there were more interested in manufacturing than in selling for us. So I fired them and got a new agent, a very reputable firm, to represent us.

We are now having some legal problems with the termination, but when I get through with that I want to spend more time on process equipment. I recommended transferring the process equipment engineer into the division as administrative manager.

We also work with chemical companies and develop new equipment for other people's processes. The contact with chemical companies on this is part of the responsibility of the marketing division.

I get a list of all quotes. I go to the division manager with this list. At first, he was surprised to see that we knew all the jobs that had been quoted. I ask him for the status of each job; whether it has been ordered, lost to a competitor, or still pending. If it was lost, I also want to know which of our competitors got it.

We then break the lost orders down by territories. This gives us good control of our agents. An agent who loses a lot of orders after quotes are submitted should be replaced.

Q: Do you meet with your division managers as a group?

My meetings are more with each individual manager, but that's not right—the team should be together.

I've started those meetings with the division managers several times, but I've had to give them up because of the management group meetings that we are having.

With the planning group that we have now, there are more directives going down than we used to have with our sales management meetings.

Our marketing divisions have quite different problems, but they are related. For example, there is only one man who can set the pricing policy, and that's the president. We have been having about two management meetings a month on this problem.

We asked each division manager to submit to us what he thought was the best price he could get for each of his machines. We discussed it, but in general accepted it. We told him to start bidding at that level. Previously, they were leaving a margin for negotiation; but very often you don't even get a chance to negotiate if your first price is too high. The result has been that in the textile machinery business, we have lost a lot less quotes.

Every month the division managers submit an estimate for the next month, the following two quarters, and the final half-year to give us a forecast for a year ahead. This is reviewed by me and forwarded to the management group.

We found when we started that we had several sets of control figures in the company. The division managers and the control group were using different figures. Now we are all using the same set.

Once a week I call the division manager on the phone and follow up on his estimates. I'll ask him about the status of some of the jobs he's quoted on.

Every lost order must be reported immediately now on a special form. The textile machinery division always used that procedure, but we had never formalized it in all divisions.

We also now require prior reporting of company visitors. We bring a lot of people up here with our company plane, and we never used to know who was coming or how long he would be here. Now we get a report in advance, and we try to have some of the company officers around to meet them.

Monthly operating reports show actuals for total selling costs; and we are going to have the budgeted figures shown on the report, too, for easy comparison. Sam Dyer is doing this sort of thing, and doing it very well.

We found that if a machine failed, the salesman was inclined to fix it at our expense, and to just put the charge in the custom goodwill account. We now want to know why the machine failed, so we can take action to see that it doesn't happen again. Also, often it's not our fault at all, and we can call this to the attention of those responsible.

Q: How does product development work with marketing?

Product development works with Roger. They report to him, and he has the position descriptions.

The job descriptions of the division managers were written with the consultant sitting with me. Then he discussed it with the division manager, and then all three of us sat down and talked about it.

We used to brag that everyone that works for Appleton Machinery wears six hats. That's all right to brag about, but sooner or later you have to write down what a fellow is supposed to be doing.

On several occasions I asked Roger for my job description. Finally he bought the idea, and the consultants have just finished. He has yet to go over mine with me (see Exhibit 2). These position descriptions have only been done in the last three months.

As a result of these position descriptions, I can sit down with my division managers and tell them where I think they're doing a good job and where they're not.

Advertising is delegated to David Appleton, since he's had a lot of background in advertising work. This was made possible by Sam Dyer's taking part of his work. He works directly with the division managers.

We establish the number of catalogs to be sent, the number of direct mail pieces, and the number of "Apple Seeds" (company information sheets); and he works with the division managers on content.

We are not set up to do market research. We've had customer attitude surveys done in the textile industry by an advertising agency.

In water control equipment, we had a consulting engineering firm do a survey of the sluice gate market. They said that what we had to do was get a greater share of the market. Particularly in small gates, we were not competitive, but we have some fine ideas about what we can do to bring our costs down.

In process equipment, we also had a study done on the projected market for the Appleton heat exchanger.

These things are all part of my job. I work out the arrangement with the consultant, and then the division manager comes in. You might say that Roger Appleton and I pick the consultant, and then the consultant works with the division manager.

Roger and I work very closely together, and have done so through the years. I've been here for 15 years—not many people here any more that have been here longer.

Exhibit 2

APPLETON MACHINE COMPANY (A)

Position Description

The Basic Function of This Position Is to plan and manage all aspects of the marketing program; to maintain and equip a well-trained organization to carry out the program; and to direct all marketing operations so as to attain stated objectives within company policy and budgets.

Major Responsibilities:

1. Sales planning and policy
2. Sales organization, training, and compensation
3. Sales forecasts, budgets, and controls
4. Selling operations
5. Industry and customer relations
6. Pricing
7. Advertising, sales promotion, publicity, and customer relations
8. Product and market research and development
9. Sales operation research
10. Employee relations

Major Responsibility No. 1: Sales Planning & Policy

The Standard of Performance for This Responsibility is Met When marketing objectives and policies are clearly stated in writing and are understood and accepted by all marketing division people; sound plans are formulated for their attainment and appropriate action assigned; and the president is provided with recommendations enabling him to develop practical companywide objectives, policies, and plans.

Exhibit 2—Continued

Key Duties:

1. Submits to the president recommendations on the company's share of industry volume, long-range marketing objectives, and policies.

2. Participates in top management discussion and planning of overall company activity, methods, and facilities.

3. Informs the president and other appropriate officers on especially adverse or favorable competitive conditions and on needs and opportunities for changes and improvements in company objectives, policies, plans, and methods.

4. Develops long-range marketing programs to meet objectives and to balance sales, advertising, and promotion efforts between current and projected products and markets.

5. Plans and coordinates specific short-term programs and action to obtain business currently needed to operate manufacturing facilities advantageously and to meet company objectives.

6. Informs subordinates on plans and programs; reduces policy and decisions under policy to writing and promulgates to marketing executives concerned; assigns specific action and follows through to insure satisfactory completion.

7. Participates in top-level marketing and field sales meetings to develop full understanding and acceptance of policies and programs.

Major Responsibility No. 2: Sales Organization, Training & Compensation

The Standard of Performance for This Responsibility is Met When an organization suited to attainment of company objectives is maintained and continually improved; all position functions and responsibilities are understood and carried out effectively; and compensation is commensurate with performance and company objectives.

Key Duties:

1. Determines the organization pattern and personnel needed to attain company objectives; directs immediate subordinates in developing and maintaining it.

2. Appraises his immediate subordinates and helps them to improve; directs them in appraising and improving their subordinates.

3. Reviews and approves (or rejects) all recommended appointments to key positions within his division; appraises candidates for continuing growth and potential and directs corrective action where needed.

4. Determines field salary and incentive schedules and sales credit methods, to encourage aggressive and balanced activity in line with company objectives and policies.

5. Consults with the personnel department on transfers, promotions, additions, and changes in compensation of marketing people, to insure adequate compensation in line with performance and company policies.

6. Directs his subordinates in administering compensation plans; assists them in handling unusual problems.

7. Investigates personally organization structures, employment, training and

Exhibit 2—Continued

development methods, and compensation plans of comparable outside concerns, to insure that the company's plans and programs enable it to obtain and hold desirable marketing people.

Major Responsibility No. 3: Sales Forecasts, Budgets, & Controls

The Standard of Performance for This Responsibility is Met When the president and other appropriate officers are supplied with realistic sales forecasts; marketing division people are supplied with expense budgets, reports, procedures, and controls, and are using them effectively; and marketing operations are fully coordinated with manufacturing requirements.

Key Duties:

1. Directs his immediate subordinates in gathering information for annual and periodic sales forecasts; reviews and submits, with recommendations, to the president and other appropriate officers.
2. Reviews departmental expense budgets submitted by his immediate subordinates; submits, with recommendations, to the president for approval; recommends to the president desirable expenditures not included in the budget.
3. Counsels with the controller's division in developing and establishing effective, economical controls, forms, and frequency of reports on sales and expenses; maintains and analyzes records supplied by the controller's division; reviews them regularly with his immediate subordinates and directs corrective action as required.
4. Advises the manufacturing division on changes and trends in sales and in marketing plans which affect production scheduling, inventory policies, and decisions.

Major Responsibility No. 4: Selling Operations

The Standard of Performance for This Responsibility is Met When selling operations consistently result in the attainment of company and marketing division objectives, and are carried out within company policies and budgeted expenses.

Key Duties:

1. Develops among his subordinates complete understanding and acceptance of all company and marketing division objectives, policies, and programs.
2. Directs all selling operations in the conduct of all domestic and export selling and sales service operations; reviews operations regularly and directs corrective action as required.
3. Directs his immediate subordinates in coordinating all line and staff marketing operations and in developing concerted team effort.

Major Responsibility No. 5: Industry and Customer Relations

The Standard of Performance for This Responsibility is Met When the company is contributing materially to the progress and stability of the industry; good

Exhibit 2—Continued

trade and customer relations are maintained; and practical suggestions are made for improvement in the performance of customer service functions whenever they are required.

Key Duties:

1. Directs his immediate subordinates in the maintenance of good customer relations and the determination of needs and opportunities for improving performance of service functions; directs corrective action as required.
2. Directs his immediate subordinates in the handling of emergency aspects of product quality complaints; supervises them in analyzing complaints and in notifying the manufacturing and other appropriate divisions on action already taken and other action required.
3. Directs his immediate subordinates in effective participation in trade association activities and conventions of major importance; designates specific individuals among his subordinates for membership in such trade associations and attendance at their conventions.

Major Responsibility No. 6: Pricing

The Standard of Performance for This Responsibility is Met When prices, terms, and discounts are provided to the marketing organization people, enabling them to gain the company's desired share of industry sales volume and profit; and operations are carried out in conformity with them.

Key Duties:

1. Recommends to the president for approval effective pricing policies; establishes prices, terms, and discounts in line with approved company sales and profit objectives; reviews proposed new products and establishes prices for them in line with approved policies.
2. Studies competitors' products, prices, terms, and discounts to insure that company policies, prices, terms, and discounts are realistic in all fields.
3. Directs his immediate subordinates in maintaining conformity with approved prices, terms, and discounts in all operations of his selling departments.
4. Determines desirability of special prices, terms, and discounts to move unusually slow inventories or to support special sales efforts.
5. Consults with the company's legal advisers to insure that contract forms are in accordance with applicable laws and regulations, and consistent with company policy, and are fair and equitable to customers and the company.

Major Responsibility No. 7: Advertising, Sales Promotion, Publicity, and Public Relations

The Standard of Performance for This Responsibility is Met When advertising, sales promotion, publicity, and public relations programs are developed and

Exhibit 2—Continued

carried out so that they contribute effectively to the attainment of company objectives and are in line with company policies and budgeted expenses.

Key Duties:

1. Reviews advertising, sales promotion, publicity appropriations requested by the advertising manager, and their ratios in relation to company objectives; approves or rejects, with appropriate explanation and instructions.

2. Directs the advertising manager in formulating specific plans and programs for attainment of objectives within company policy and budgets.

3. Directs his immediate subordinates in coordinating advertising, promotion, publicity, and programs with selling activities; directs immediate subordinates in developing full understanding and effective and efficient utilization of programs by the selling departments.

4. Directs the advertising manager in the preparation for publication of all catalogs, bulletins, manuals, and point-of-sale materials, and in transmitting them promptly and efficiently to the marketing organization.

5. Participates in activities of professional and other groups to the extent necessary and economical to maintain the company's name and recognition in industry and with the public.

Major Responsibility No. 8: Product and Market Research and Development

The Standard of Performance for This Responsibility is Met When product and market needs and opportunities are continually recognized, investigated, and analyzed; appropriate action is taken to induce new product development; and ideas are developed resulting in improved advertising, promotion, and selling techniques.

Key Duties:

1. Initiates and directs, through his immediate subordinates, programs and specific projects for obtaining information on product and market needs and opportunities.

2. Reviews and discusses information obtained with his immediate subordinates; directs appropriate action within the division; and submits to the president requests for action outside the division.

3. Directs his immediate subordinates in maintaining close cooperation between their people and those of the product and market research and development department, in developing and maintaining a smooth and effective two-way flow of information between the marketing departments and prompt and effective action on ideas and information exchanged.

Major Responsibility No. 9: Sales Operation Research

The Standard of Performance for This Responsibility is Met When information is provided upon which to base changes and improvements in organization pattern, in the distribution of manpower and effort, and in methods and channels of distribution for marketing company products.

Exhibit 2—Continued

Key Duties:

1. Initiates and directs the planning and conducting of research on marketing operations, in analyzing the information obtained, and in suggesting specific improvements.

2. Reviews the information and the suggestions submitted; determines corrective action needed and directs his immediate subordinates in carrying it out; follows through to insure that his immediate subordinates and their people carry out the assigned action effectively and efficiently.

3. Recommendations to the president for approval of needed changes and improvements affecting company divisions.

Major Responsibility No. 10: Employee Relations

The Standard of Performance for This Responsibility is Met When company employee relations policies are fully understood and applied throughout the division, and result in harmonious employee relations.

Key Duties:

1. Applies basic company employee relations policies in all dealings with his subordinates.

2. Collaborates with the personnel manager in developing complete understanding and acceptance of company employee relations policies throughout the division.

3. Directs his immediate subordinates in applying company employee relations policies; assists them in handling unusual problems.

4. Develops a spirit of harmony, cooperation, and interest in company welfare.

THE JOB OF THE TREASURER AND ADVERTISING MANAGER

Statement by Mr. David Appleton.

I am now responsible for cash flow, meaning receivables and payables, payroll, advertising, and such other aspects of the treasurer's job as taxes, insurance, and relationships with the banks. I am also clerk, with infrequent corporate matters to handle.

We may build a new foundry. There are some financial implications to this. Sam Dyer has done most of the work on the economic justification of it. I expect we'll handle it through loans, and check it out on a cash flow basis.

We have to do some work on improving our cash forecasting, and on credit and collections.

Q: Is credit and collections part of your responsibility?

We continue to hold our division managers responsible for the orders that are entered, so it is still a split responsibility. The division manager will come to me and say: "Look, we're quoting this company for this amount—what should I do?" More and more I find that what they want is a red light or a green light. They don't want to be involved in detailed credit analysis. It's still a split function right now, although soon I intend to set limits (dollar limits by class of credit rating) and they will just bring me the exceptions. Our biggest credit and collection problem is the water control equipment division, where we deal with contractors, and the construction industry, with higher credit risks.

Q: Would you say something about your job as advertising manager?

I picked up the responsibility for advertising in March of last year. At that time, because of a variety of advertising agency changes, our work was being done by several agencies. The first thing I did was to consolidate all the work with a single agency.

In the last few years our advertising expenditures have been dwindling. Our advertising activities suffered. Along with the rest of the cost reduction steps, our advertising budget was cut severely. This was done despite the fact that Roger is a very promotion- and advertising-minded guy.

At midyear, I decided that the agency wasn't capable of doing what I thought should be done. I therefore recently made an arrangement with a direct mail agency in Boston. Our markets are specialized, and we feel that direct mail should be a large part of our effort. We now work with two agencies: one in Boston for direct mail; and the one in New York for the rest of our advertising program.

During 1962 we expect to produce a lot of literature, and will have a general stepup of our advertising effort in all areas. Our incoming inquiries have been going steadily down for the last three years, and this trend will have to be reversed.

Roger has put out a directive that division managers will be in the field 10 days each month; that all basic promotional literature will be prepared by the end of the first quarter; that all inquiries will be replied to, in some way, within 48 hours; and that our field agents will be reviewed for effectiveness.

We have also been cleaning up price policies—getting agreement on what margins are expected on each of our products, and pricing accordingly.

The division problem has always been with us. The scope of responsibility, or sphere of influence, of division managers has been a problem with us. They are becoming more and more sales managers. We have relieved them of engineering, order-entering, and other responsibilities. We are focussing more and more on getting them to be sales people.

The advertising expenditures are in their budget. I expect to be working very closely with them. I have been working on a budget for 1962. When it is ready, I'll take it to Roger and Cyrus and they'll say whether they think it's too high or too low. Then we'll adjust it and get it into operation.

I require the division managers to meet with me and the agency when I feel it must be done.

The only reason that as a treasurer I'm the advertising manager is that I did this thing before; and I did it during a period when we had our major growth. And, of course, I have staff people in finance, but I have no staff people in advertising.

We always felt that we have to overcome the disadvantages of our position here in New England by spending more for advertising than do similar companies located elsewhere. If the average advertising expenditure in our industry is 1 or 1½% of sales, we spend 1½% to 2½% of sales.

As treasurer, I can direct the division managers to get me what I need more than an advertising manager would normally be able to.

For about the next six months, advertising will be the major part of my job—because of the need to repair the damage done by the reduction of previous advertising budgets.

Perhaps I'm spending too much time on this part of the job. I feel I have to meet with the agency people and sales people when the agency people come here. Later on, I suppose they can work out a lot of details without me.

I can see where the policy implications lie in the advertising field. I'm in a position to bring the management group the marketing and sales weaknesses that I've become aware of through my work in advertising.

THE PLANT MANAGER'S JOB

Statement by Mr. James Johnson.

Q: Would you say something about what your job is?

My title is Plant Manager. My responsibility used to start when work came out of engineering. We made a recent consolidation—which I thought was an excellent move—in setting up a customer service department. They no longer report to me, although we still work very closely together. This new arrangement is primarily a matter of reporting.

My responsibility now starts when the work is scheduled, and ends when the product is manufactured and in operation. I emphasize that "in operation," because I also have the responsibility for supplying personnel for putting the machine into operation whenever modification after installation is required.

We kick titles around quite a bit here. To give you an idea of mine, the title I have could be all the way from Vice President in Charge of Manufacturing to Plant Superintendent. I think the title of Plant Manager is as good as any, although probably Manufacturing Superintendent could also be used.

The organization chart for my part of the operation looks as follows: [*draws chart on easel, which he has on table behind the desk—see Exhibit 3*].

The department head group gets together every Monday morning, and we kick around either problems that I want their help on, or information that I have. In these Monday meetings, I sometimes talk about sales data. For example, such items as the low volume in water control equipment in a given period and the influence this would have on foundry manpower needs.

When we have a general company information meeting, we take that group, and a similar group from the office. These are all cost center managers.

Roger frequently follows that up with a first-line supervisors' meeting.

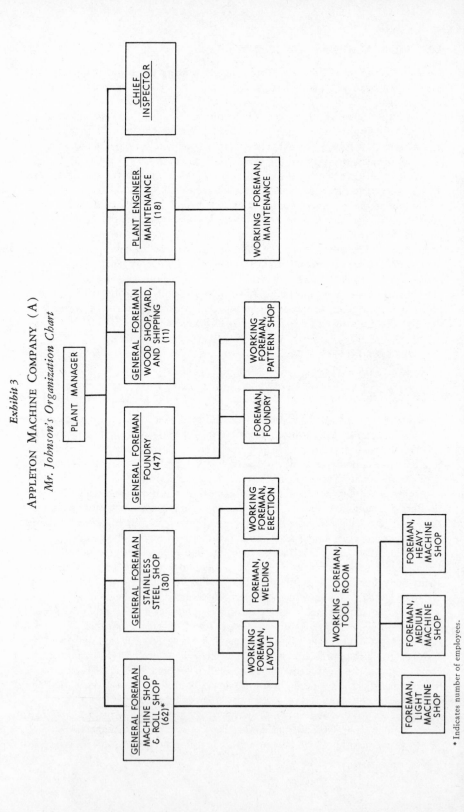

Exhibit 3

APPLETON MACHINE COMPANY (A)

Mr. Johnson's Organization Chart

* Indicates number of employees.

Q: What would you say is the most important part of your job?

Thinking over the past five years on this job, I would say that the main part of my job is coordination of these departments. Not only between the jobs in my area, but also between these jobs and the rest of the firm. I don't mean by this that I do all the contact—there are hundreds of contacts between the various departments going on all day that I don't get into.

My department heads also look to me for help on personnel policy. However, these problems are rapidly diminishing in number because of our policy manual.

THE JOB OF THE MANAGER FOR PLANNING AND CONTROL

Statement by Mr. Samuel Dyer.

Reporting to me are the following:

1) The purchasing agent.
2) The production manager. He is also head of the customer service department. He handles production control and scheduling, repair orders, and customer contact in relation to nontechnical matters, such as delivery dates.
3) Three engineering managers for three production divisions: textile machinery, process equipment, and water control equipment. The roll division handles their own sales and engineering.
4) The manager of the accounting department.

All together, there are about 45 people in the units reporting to me. This is about half of the total office force. The distribution of personnel in the various categories is as follows: in the units reporting to me, 45 people; in marketing, 24 people in all divisions; in administration and product development, 15 people—including the president of the company; in the plant, 253 people.

I spend a goodly part of my time on general management, and a small part of my time on the operational activities of the division. I feel very strongly that the communication that my people have with each other and with others in the firm should not be interfered with by myself. I stick strictly to policy.

Appleton Machine Company (B)

APPLETON (A) described the products and markets of the company, and the way in which it is now organized. Appleton (B) adds the dimension of time, by presenting a brief summary of the recent history of the organization, and statements concerning how its future is seen by two executives.

RECENT HISTORY OF THE ORGANIZATION

During the past 10 years many changes had taken place in the nature of Appleton's business as well as in the way it had organized itself to carry on that business.

From 1946 to 1956 the total annual sales volume of Appleton increased from $600,000 to $5,600,000. Thereafter, it remained relatively constant, subject to fluctuations in the economy as a whole. During recent years, considerable emphasis was placed on cost reduction. The difference this made can be seen in the following data:

Year	Annual Sales Volume	No. of Employees
1956	$5,600,000	375
1957	5,200,000	...
1958	4 700,000	...
1959	5,700,000	325

Product Mix. In addition to changes in sales volume, there had also been a major change in the relative volume of various products, as can be seen from the following data:

PRODUCT	% OF TOTAL SALES	
	1948	1961
Textile machinery (domestic & export)...	80%	30%
Industrial rolls.	10	10
Water control equipment.	10	45
Process equipment.	..	15

Profit Performance. Up until 1960, the company had made money in every year since World War II. In 1960 it had a loss. Vigorous action was taken, including the establishment of the management group, the dismissal of 40 people from the office staff, and some departmental consolidation. The result was to restore profitable performance in 1961.

Executive Turnover. During the last 15 years, the company had experienced a high rate of executive turnover. In the textile machinery division, there had been seven managers in eight years. In process equipment, there had been four managers in eight years. In water control equipment, there was one manager until 1960. When he became ill, he was put in charge of product development for this field, and a new manager for water control equipment was appointed. In industrial rolls, there had been one manager who recently retired, and there was now a new one.

In the plant, James Johnson was made acting plant manager when the previous plant manager left. A man was then hired as plant manager. When he left, Johnson became acting plant manager again, and was then made plant manager.

In 1956 a man was hired in the dual capacity of controller and vice president of manufacturing. He was discharged after one year. Mr. David Appleton explained that "he just didn't fit in well with the people here."

Organizational Changes. During the past 10 years, major changes had been made in each of the following aspects of the organization: (1) marketing, (2) engineering, (3) the job of the treasurer and advertising manager.

Marketing. The recent history of the marketing activity is summarized in the following statement by Mr. Sam Dyer, manager of planning and control:

> In 1948 Mr. Bell, who was head of the textile machinery division, was perhaps the most influential man in the company. He had been here a long time. When Roger Appleton became president, Mr. Bell became sales manager for all products, and we had an active program of putting salesmen into the field. At that time, all of our salesmen sold all of our products, and engineering was part of the divisions.
>
> About 1952 engineering was taken out of the divisions and put into a central group. It was felt that a centralized group would increase our engineering capability.
>
> In 1953 Mr. Bell left the company and Mr. Young became sales manager. In 1954 engineering was put back into the divisions. In 1960 it was again centralized with the idea of having the salesmen concentrate only on selling. In all of these moves, personalities were naturally very important.
>
> In 1950 a process equipment division was established.
>
> More recently two additional changes have been made in the marketing

organization. First, the textile machinery division was split into two divisions: a domestic division and an export division. And second, the manager of the industrial roll division had been put in charge of both industrial rolls and domestic textile machinery. Officers of the company were very enthusiastic about this last move. They said that sales of textile machinery had subsequently soared.

Engineering. The evolution of the engineering department to 1959 is summarized in the following statement by Mr. David Appleton:

Prior to 1950 engineering was done in each of the product divisions. At that time, a division manager was in charge of both marketing and engineering. Mr. Gates was with us then, as an all-around technical man and inventor. And Mr. Dyer, our industrial engineer, was reporting to the plant manager.

In 1950 we were doing five times the annual volume that we had done in 1946, and we weren't sure that our engineering organization was right for this expanded scale of operations. We therefore called in a firm of consulting engineers from down in Boston and asked them to review our engineering organization. They suggested we take the engineering function out of the divisions and centralize it under a chief engineer. We thought that was a good idea. Consequently, we made our industrial engineer the chief engineer, made him report directly to the president, and put all of the engineers under him. Mr. Gates, who developed our textile washer, was made technical director.

In 1953 our technical director asked us to relieve him of his title because he felt he was spending too much time on engineering administration. We therefore worked out an arrangement whereby he separated himself from the company and became a consultant working exclusively for us. In this way he could spend all of his time on technical work.

In 1954 we began to realize that the centralization of the engineering department just wasn't working, so we decentralized again to the divisions. Finally, we have just decided that the centralization of the engineering function is best after all. We have therefore set up the job of vice president in charge of engineering and brought Mr. Gates in for the job.

By 1961 several additional changes had been made. Mr. Gates was made vice president—product development, and assigned the task of developing new products for the process equipment division. The reasons for this move were summarized by Mr. Appleton as follows:

This division had to have some product development because it only has one product now. In addition, we felt we had to design our own product and do it quickly. So Gates was relieved of all other responsibilities and asked to do product development. At that time engineering was under Sam Dyer, who had previously been chief engineer.

The Job of Treasurer and Advertising Manager. Mr. David Appleton reviewed the changes that had taken place in his job over the past few years as follows:

In 1956 we decided that our old treasurer, who had been with us for 37 years, should retire. We therefore worked out an arrangement with him and he left. In his place we hired a fellow as treasurer and vice president in charge of manufacturing combined. He was also made a director of the firm. However, he just didn't fit in well with the people here. He was dismissed after two years, but in the meantime the controller had left as well as the chief accountant. Since I was then assistant treasurer, I became treasurer by default. Soon after that the new chief accountant left.

I am not an accountant myself although I have had some training in business administration. I was advertising manager for five years after I got back from Korea. I took the job of treasurer as a nonaccountant, but with a strong backup man as controller. Our controller left us in July of 1960. He was disappointed with his opportunity to contribute and I was disappointed with his sense of values as compared with mine and Appleton Machine's. Prior to that the company had never had a controller as such. Either he was not a capable controller or the organization was not ready to accept one. When he left I had to decide whether to replace him or to build from within. I decided to try to handle it from within—not to hire a new man because of the usual risks involved in such a move.

Our new control system was working pretty well. It had some bugs in it, but these were responsibility bugs—policy bugs—rather than system bugs. So we entered the fall of 1960 in that way. Looking back on it, I didn't have either the time or bent for that kind of job. And, as the policy clarification needs became more involved, we began to look at the whole thing more clearly.

We decided that my background in accounting was not strong enough to make progress in this area. At this time we decided that Sam Dyer should take on the cost and reporting job, since he had abilities in that field, even though he lacked up-to-date training. I remained with the responsibility for finance.

I am pleased with the decision. He has been able to make progress and to force policy decisions on the part of management where these have been necessary. The reporting system is now being refined and acted upon more than ever before.

During the same period I had charge of purchasing and a similar thing took place. I was spread too thin and could not manage these functions with the people I then had. As I recall, it was about a month after he took over costing that we decided that Dyer should also take over purchasing.

In November, 1960, Sam Dyer was made manager of planning and control.

Looking Ahead—Statement by Mr. David Appleton, President, January 23, 1962.

Q: Would you say something about the future objectives of the Appleton Machine Company?

In this area of objectives we are pretty weak. For the time being, practicality forces us into short-range objectives. We know we should have long-range objectives too; at least we read that in books. But I am convinced that if we have at least two- or three-year objectives, it would add great meaning to our short-run program.

We have objectives in the following areas: new orders, shipping, gross profits, selling and administrative expenses, general and administrative expenses, and operating profits. That's our measure of division performance. However, we recognize that we have to create conditions for these to be achieved. We are the bottleneck here.

We have some other objectives that are not stated in terms of timetable. About five years ago we developed a list of things like: "We shall maintain a fair return to stockholders in order to ensure the long-run survival of the company," and platitudes like that.

Of course we had objectives as we went along. We got out of water wheels into chemical equipment. We mean to maintain a diversified company through products which have a high degree of value added. But what is our objective concerning rate of growth? We haven't got this blueprinted.

As I look at the future, I see three big problems: our depth of management, financial problems we will encounter if we grow as we might, and the high cost of research. Regarding depth of management, we are in between being a small company where the five members of our management group could really run the whole show and being large enough to afford an extended management team in depth, like Food Machinery Corporation. In the field of finance, we are a family company and it is clear that our present rate of growth will soon raise some serious financial issues. We will need additional funds, not only for capital equipment, but also for working capital. In the area of research, if we allocated an economic amount to research, such as 2% of sales, it isn't enough to do anything serious.

Q: What are the future opportunities for the Appleton Machine Company?

The chemical industry and export. When we went into chemical equipment, we looked at it carefully. We saw the chemical industry as one having a high rate of growth and having a high rate of equipment obsolescence. We did not think we should go into the industry, however, as a job shop because of our policy of having a high value added. So we found the thin film processor and decided to produce it. We think we could do a volume of $5 million annually in chemical equipment alone instead of our total sales of $5 million annually for the whole company. We have put a lot of resources into product development in this field and we have done it consciously.

In the field of water control equipment we have done the same thing.

In textile machinery, it is so cyclical that we don't plan to do much more in product innovation.

We believe that export has great promise for us. Right now we are only doing this in textile machinery and chemical equipment. We have a plan to reinvigorate our organization in exports. Now that we are free of licensing restrictions in the chemical field, we have a great opportunity in that area.

We intend to start manufacturing for the Common Market. We intend to start manufacturing in India, and we intend to have new agents in South America.

Right now we are having meetings about the roll division with our key people to develop a market for rolls. We have just invented a new roll—a curved roll—which is used in the paper and textile industry. Right now there is only one company supplying this type of roll and it could be a good thing.

You know, at one of our meetings, the assistant manager of our roll division asked us: "Is the company going to stay in the roll business?" To me, this means that the man who asked it has been so little communicated with that he is operating in the dark. Of course we are going to stay in the roll business, and the assistant manager of the roll division is now quite enthusiastic about its prospects.

Incidentally, one of the organization problems that we now have is that the former manager of the roll division now runs both the roll and the textile machinery division. His assistant manager is now in charge of the roll division and we are not quite sure what his status should be.

Looking Ahead—Statement by Mr. Cyrus Young, January 8, 1962.

Export is something that can only continue as long as the United States is pouring money into foreign countries with the tag on it that the machinery has to be bought in the U.S. We can't compete with the Germans in the Far East.

We think the future is to manufacture a product in Italy for the Common Market. Also our intention is to manufacture in India on a phased five-year program.

In South America we are better able to compete with European manufacturers.

In process equipment we think the chemical industry is the industry of the future. However, it is still a one-product division and we need to buttress it with one or two new products. But the chemical field is a good field. It is so highly competitive for processors that even if they have a machine that is only one year old, they'll throw it out if you bring in a better one.

In textile machinery we have a good product. Our prices tend to be high but we have a good reputation and we give good service. Textile machinery is a staple item with us.

In water control equipment water is becoming more and more important all the time. The projected growth of this field over the next 10 years is considerable.

The Rose Company

MR. JAMES PIERCE had recently received word of his appointment as plant manager of Plant X, one of the older established units of the Rose Company. As such, Mr. Pierce was to be responsible for the management and administration at Plant X of all functions and personnel except sales.

Both top management and Mr. Pierce realized that there were several unique features about his new assignment. Mr. Pierce decided to assess his new situation and relationships before undertaking his assignment. He was personally acquainted with the home office executives, but had met few of the plant personnel. This case contains some of his reflections regarding the new assignment.

The Rose Company conducted marketing activities throughout the United States and in certain foreign countries. These activities were directed from the home office by a vice-president in charge of sales.

Exhibit 1

THE ROSE COMPANY

Old Organization

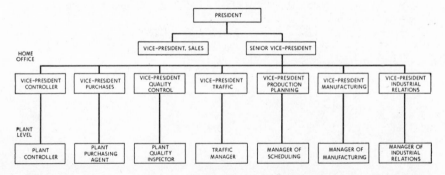

Manufacturing operations and certain other departments were under the supervision and control of a senior vice-president. These are shown in Exhibit 1. For many years the company had operated a highly centralized functional type of manufacturing organization. There was no general manager at any plant; each of the departments in a plant reported on a line basis to its functional counterpart at the home office. For instance, the industrial-relations manager of a particular plant reported to the vice-president in charge of industrial relations at the home office, the plant controller to the vice-president and controller, and so on.

Mr. Pierce stated that in the opinion of the top management the record of Plant X had not been satisfactory for several years. The board had recently approved the erection of a new plant in a different part of the city and the use of new methods of production. Lower costs of processing and a reduced manpower requirement at the new plant were expected. Reduction of costs and improved quality of products were needed to maintain competitive leadership and gain some slight product advantage. The proposed combination of methods of manufacturing and mixing materials had not been tried elsewhere in the company. Some features would be entirely new to employees.

According to Mr. Pierce the top management of the Rose Company was beginning to question the advisability of the central control of manufacturing operations. The officers decided to test the value of a decentralized operation in connection with Plant X. They apparently believed that a general management representative in Plant X was needed if the new experiment in manufacturing methods and the required rebuilding of the organization were to succeed.

Prior to the new assignment Mr. Pierce had been an accounting executive in the controller's department of the company. From independent sources the case writer learned that Mr. Pierce had demonstrated analytical ability and general administrative capacity. He was generally liked by people. From top management's point of view he had an essential toughness described as an ability to see anything important through. By some he was regarded as the company's efficiency expert. Others thought he was a perfectionist and aggressive in reaching the goals that had been set. Mr. Pierce was aware of these opinions about his personal behavior.

Mr. Pierce summarized his problem in part as follows: "I am going into a situation involving a large number of changes. I will have a new plant—new methods and processes—but most of all I will be dealing with a set of changed relationships. Heretofore all the heads of departments in the plant reported to their functional counterparts in the home office. Now they will report to me. I am a complete stranger and in addition this is my first assignment in a major 'line' job. The men will know this.

"When I was called into the senior vice-president's office to be informed of my new assignment he asked me to talk with each of the functional members of his staff. The vice-presidents in charge of production planning, manufacturing, and industrial relations said they were going to issue all headquarters instructions to me as plant manager and they were going to cut off their connections with their counterparts in my plant. The other home office executives admitted their functional counterparts would report to me in line capacity. They should obey my orders and I would be responsible for their pay and promotion. But these executives proposed to follow the common practice of many companies of maintaining a dotted line or functional relationship with these men. I realize that these two different patterns of home office–plant relationships will create real administrative problems for me."

Exhibit 2 shows the organization relationships as defined in these conferences.

Exhibit 2

THE ROSE COMPANY

New Organization

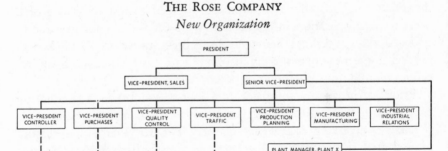

The Larger Company (A)

THE PHONE RANG, and highly indignant words blared: "Masters, what do you mean by submitting a report to all the executives without first talking it over with the division manager!"

Masters replied, "My men made every effort to see him. They never got past his secretary. He instructed her to have them talk to the works manager."

"I don't believe a word of it. Vining is up in arms. He says the report is vindictive. What are you trying to do—embarrass the division manager? I don't believe your men ever tried to see Vining and I question the veracity of their statements!" The phone on the other end was hung up with a bang.

Masters said to himself, "Gunn must be hot under the collar or he wouldn't have called me when I was away from my own office, visiting another plant."

The next day Masters' office received Gunn's letter confirming this telephone conversation and demanding an explanation. A week later Masters received a letter from Gunn's superior, a Mr. Jordan, stating, "I have read the aforementioned report and discussed it with Mr. Gunn. He has advised me that the report is essentially untrue, inaccurate, and overstated. I am not satisfied to have such wide differences of opinion and have scheduled a meeting to be held in my office on ———. I would appreciate it if you would be present."

In light of the phone call and the two letters, Mr. Masters decided to reassess all events leading to this climax.

. . . .

The cast of characters is as shown in Exhibit 1. The Larger Company had an elaborate organizational structure as a result of its scale of operation. At the headquarters office of the corporation the president had a group of staff vice-presidents in charge of functions. Mr. Masters was a staff department head reporting to the vice-president, manufacturing. The headquarters staff departments assisted in policy formulation and made staff studies for the operating organization when requested. Members of such departments were encouraged to offer ideas for the good

Exhibit 1

THE LARGER COMPANY (A)

Organization Chart

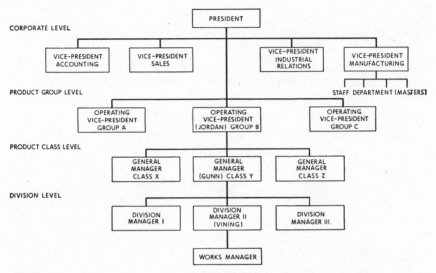

of the company. Their proposals were considered by a management committee consisting of the vice-presidents at the headquarters level and the operating vice-presidents in charge of product groups. Mr. Jordan of this case was the operating vice-president, Product Group "B."

Under the product groups there were general managers of product classes. They supervised the division managers, who were in charge of the sales and manufacturing operations of one or more plants. Mr. Gunn was general manager of Product Class "Y." One of the four division managers under him was Mr. Vining of Division II.

. . . .

Two years before this incident occurred, Mr. Masters' staff department proposed to the management committee, with the approval of the vice-president, manufacturing, that representatives of Mr. Masters' office join with representatives of the vice-president, accounting to make studies in each plant of the procedures for and actual practices regarding expense control. The suggestion was approved, and enthusiastically endorsed by the general managers. They sent a letter through channels to each division manager advising that periodically a team of two men would visit each plant to make a comprehensive analysis of expense-control practices and systems.

After a visit these field representatives of headquarters were to prepare a report giving findings and recommendations. They were to discuss it with the appropriate division manager and his staff. Thus they would be able to incorporate any specific plans of action set in motion by division managers. Next, a report was to be submitted to Mr. Masters. Both his department and the accounting office were to make comments. The final document was then to be submitted to the vice-president, accounting; the vice-president, manufacturing; the operating vice-president, product group; the general manager, product class; and the division manager concerned.

This general procedure had worked smoothly within the company until general manager Gunn of Product Class "Y" exploded. In the first plant studied, the two team members spent approximately four weeks examining documents, interviewing line management, interrogating industrial engineers, observing operations, etc. The employees of this plant were very co-operative. Some of the facts revealed by them could have been embarrassing to the division manager. The team was enabled to make specific recommendations for improvement to the division manager. His reception of the report was good. According to him, the study had given an opportunity to review his situation and get his house in order. He intended to implement the recommendations unless they were changed in the review process at the higher level. Sixteen other plants were visited with reasonably good acceptance of the work of the team.

. . . .

In his review of the Division II situation, Mr. Masters found that the team had observed all the required organization routines. Mr. Sawyer, representing Mr. Masters, had a master's degree in industrial engineering and had twelve years with the company. Mr. Peters, from the accounting office, had served that department for thirty years. Both men had shown ability to gain confidences and to use them discreetly. They were considered straightforward, conscientious, and unobtrusive in their work. In Division II the team obtained from plant personnel considerable information which pointed up a number of practices and procedures requiring improvement. In the opinion of the team members, the operating organization at the lower levels sincerely wanted to make these changes. The team thought that there was some resistance at some level within the division to these suggestions and, in fact, to any from headquarters.

While the study was in process, Mr. Sawyer advised Mr. Masters about the possible impact of the information which was being collected.

Mr. Masters emphasized the necessity to report to the division manager, and Mr. Sawyer promised that he and Mr. Peters would do so.

The team made several efforts to see the division manager, but his secretary informed them that he was busy. They questioned the secretary closely to learn if the manager had knowledge of the procedural requirement that he and his staff go over the report with the team. She replied that he knew the requirements, but was too busy to discuss a headquarters program. He would ask his assistant, the works manager, and several staff members to go over it, and what they approved would be all right with him. Eventually this meeting was held.

The members of the local management staff took a very reasonable attitude; they admitted the bad situation portrayed in the analysis and offered their assurances that immediate steps would be taken towards improvement. The team members thought that the local management staff was glad to have their problem brought out in the open, and were delighted to have the suggestions of the headquarters representatives.

. . . .

When Mr. Masters reviewed the report, both team members expressed their complete dissatisfaction with the brush-off they got from the division manager. Masters took this as a cue to question them extensively concerning their findings and recommendations. In view of the sensitive character of the situation and the possible controversy that it might create, he was reluctant to distribute the report. It was the consensus of the remainder of the staff and the representatives of the accounting office that the usual transmittal letter should be prepared, and distribution made. Mr. Masters signed this letter and took no other action until the telephone call came from Mr. Gunn.

The Larger Company (B)

MR. JORDAN, operating vice-president, Product Group "B" of the Larger Company, called a meeting to review the report submitted by Mr. Masters' staff department and the accounting office. Mr. Jordan, Mr. Gunn, Mr. Masters, the vice-president, accounting and the vice-president, manufacturing attended. In a very constructive, two-hour meeting, the report was evaluated and many conclusions were confirmed.

Division manager Vining was not present. Mr. Jordan had not invited him because he wanted to keep "heat" out of the meeting. Mr. Jordan regarded Mr. Vining as an "individual operator" who on more than one occasion had shown definite disrespect for headquarters' functions and programs.

There was some heat in the meeting, nevertheless. Mr. Gunn stated that Mr. Masters should have discussed the report with him. Thus he might have had an opportunity to take executive action at his level. When a division manager failed to consider a report the superior should have a chance even though the formal procedure did not provide for it. Mr. Gunn said that Mr. Masters should have known that. Mr. Gunn also read a letter that had been prepared by Mr. Vining. It generally and categorically denied most of the statements in the report that were unsatisfactory to him. The vice-president, accounting and Mr. Masters, however, had certain information and supplementary reports which seemed to discount the effectiveness of the letter of rebuttal.

Before too much time elapsed, Mr. Jordan turned the discussion into ways of bringing about improvement in the future. "Where there was so much smoke," he observed, "there might be some fire." He suggested that men of higher rank review the work of the two team members; this would serve either to confirm or modify their findings. This step seemed advisable in order to assuage the feelings of the local division manager.

The meeting ended on a very harmonious note. Mr. Jordan asked Mr. Gunn to see Mr. Vining. "He needs to understand and appreciate

357

that he has a responsibility to find time to review and comment on the type of reports being made by team members."

Mr. Masters was pleased by the results of the meeting and the follow-up actions. Mr. Gunn must have talked with Mr. Vining. Whatever was said may have contributed to better working relationships. Plant co-operation immediately improved. The division manager cleared any obstacles interfering with the success of the program. His influence was particularly noticeable in its effect on the behavior of the line supervisory organization. According to Mr. Masters, co-operation rather than resistance was now encouraged. The home office team became the advisory team it was intended to be.

In reviewing this experience Mr. Masters said, "There was bound to be some form of blow-up because Vining had the reputation of thinking he did not have to conform to company-wide programs unless it was to his advantage. Further, he was more rugged in nature than Gunn. On many occasions Gunn was inclined to support Vining. There has been a very definite change in this respect during the latter part of this year."

Consolidated Vultee Aircraft Corporation

CONSOLIDATED VULTEE AIRCRAFT CORPORATION was in 1944 the largest single producer of aircraft in the world. Before the end of World War II, the company was manufacturing 14 different types of airplanes, ranging in size from the small Sentinel Flying Jeep to the giant XB-36 and the Dominator (B-32), companion to the Super-Fortress (B-29). Among the better-known planes designed and manufactured by Consolidated Vultee were the Liberator (B-24), Catalina (PBY), Coronado (PB2Y-3), Privateer (PB4Y-2), and Valiant (BT-13). The com-

Exhibit 1

CONSOLIDATED VULTEE AIRCRAFT CORPORATION

Location and Activities of Divisions as of January, 1945

Division	Location	Principal Activities
San Diego Division.........	San Diego, Calif.	Manufactured PBY, PB2Y, RY-3, B-32, B-24, PB4Y-2
Fort Worth Division.......	Fort Worth, Texas	Manufactured B-24, C-87, XB-36, B-32
Vultee Field Division.......	Vultee Field, Calif.	Manufactured BT-13, 15; parts for B-32, B-24, PB4Y-2, P-38
Allentown Division........	Allentown, Penn.	Manufactured TBY-2
Elizabeth Division	Elizabeth, N.J.	Modification center for Navy planes
Louisville Division.........	Louisville, Ky.	Modification center for B-24
Intercontinent Aircraft Corporation...............	Miami, Fla.	Manufactured parts for A-31, A-35, B-24, F4U, P-38
Nashville Division.........	Nashville, Tenn.	Manufactured A-31, A-35, P-38, parts for B-24
New Orleans Division......	New Orleans, La.	Manufactured PBY, modification center for PB2Y-3
Stinson Division..........	Wayne, Mich.	Manufactured AT-19 and L-5, "Flying Jeep"
Tucson Division..........	Tucson, Ariz.	Modification center for B-24
Stout Research Division....	Dearborn, Mich.	Experimental and development
Consairways..............	Fairfield, Calif.	Operation of Consairways, ATC contract airline

pany had 13 divisions located in various parts of the United States, employing over 100,000 workers. Exhibits 1 and 2 indicate the location and activities of the company's divisions and the aircraft sales volume during the period of 1940–44.

Exhibit 2

CONSOLIDATED VULTEE AIRCRAFT CORPORATION

Net Sales for the Period 1940–44

(In Millions)

Year	Consolidated	Vultee	Consolidated Vultee
1940....................	$ 9.3	$ 5.6	....
1941....................	94.8	34.0	....
1942....................	304.0	109.7	....
1943....................	....	....	$797.2*
1944....................	....	....	960.0

* The Consolidated and Vultee organizations merged in March, 1943.

Consolidated Vultee, formed in 1943 as a merger of Consolidated Aircraft Corporation and Vultee Aircraft, Inc., was an associated company of the Aviation Corporation,[1] a manufacturing and holding company owning 30% of Consolidated Vultee common stock. Through its stock ownership the Aviation Corporation had the controlling interest in the management of Consolidated Vultee. The Aviation Corporation acquired Vultee in 1934 when it was a small designer and manufacturer of light planes. By 1940 Vultee was known as one of the major producers of training planes for the armed forces.

Consolidated Aircraft Corporation, founded in 1923 by R. H. Fleet, first specialized in the design and manufacturing of Army and Navy training planes, and then expanded into the field of large, multiengine aircraft. In December, 1941, Vultee purchased Mr. Fleet's stock interest, and Consolidated became an associated company of the Aviation Corporation. Consolidated and Vultee operated independently until March, 1943, when they were merged, forming Consolidated Vultee Aircraft Corporation.

After 1940, aircraft production expanded rapidly and both Consolidated and Vultee encountered numerous management problems. The Aviation Corporation enlisted management personnel from outside the aircraft industry to assist in its expanding production program. Mr. T. M. Girdler, well-known industrialist and chairman of the board of directors of the Republic Steel Corporation, became a director of Aviation Corporation; subsequently he became chairman of the board of

---

[1] The Aviation Corporation had five manufacturing divisions and three associated companies. The manufacturing divisions produced aircraft products and some automotive parts. The associated companies were Consolidated Vultee; the New York Shipbuilding Corporation, one of the country's largest producers of naval combatant ships during the war; and the American Central Manufacturing Corporation, manufacturers of household kitchen equipment. The Aviation Corporation also held substantial investments in American Airlines, Inc., and Pan American Airways System.

directors of Vultee and Consolidated, and later of Consolidated Vultee. An associate of Mr. Girdler, Mr. Harry Woodhead, whom Mr. Girdler succeeded as chairman of Vultee's board of directors, became president of Vultee and Consolidated, and later of Consolidated Vultee. Under Mr. Woodhead's management, Vultee pioneered the use of powered assembly lines in the aircraft industry.

While Vultee's expansion during 1940 and 1941 was rapid, Consolidated's expansion as a major producer of heavy bombers was even greater. During this period, Mr. R. H. Fleet, Consolidated's chairman and president, maintained personal control over the company's operations. In January, 1942, however, Mr. Girdler became chairman of the board of directors of both Consolidated and Vultee. The following quotation from *Fortune* magazine indicates some of the circumstances incident to this change in management:

There were no brass bands or welcoming committees waiting for Tom Girdler one Saturday last January when the Board Chairman of Republic Steel arrived at San Diego to take charge of the Consolidated Aircraft Corporation, producer of long-range flying boats and four-engine bombers. He came over the Rockies in Republic's private airplane and next day walked through the plant with several men directly responsible for Consolidated production. Monday morning he called all the department heads together, two dozen or more, to lay down his plans. Among them were men who had been in aviation since their youth, and some who were with Consolidated when it had nothing but a few thousand dollars, mostly borrowed, "Rube" Fleet's colossal nerve, and "Mac" Laddon's designs.

Mr. Girdler sat at a big desk, feet up, hat slanted rakishly over owlish horn-rimmed glasses, as he set forth what he proposed to do. . . . In the hush that followed, a Vice President, one of the powers of the old Fleet regime, stepped forward. He called the steelman "an interloper," a money man who, with gross impertinence, had bought his way into an art of craftsmen and pioneers, and in accents sharp with rage he told Girdler that the best thing he could do was to go back where he came from.

If T. M. Girdler had ever before tolerated a tongue-lashing, there is no record of it. But this time he made no answer. The man whose boast is "I put together Republic" understood. After his castigator had finished, he turned to one of the Fleet men and said quietly, "You straighten this out. . . ."

. . . .

The events that persuaded this toughest of industrial operators to change careers at sixty-five, to sacrifice a sure berth in steel for the "hot seat" of a war production job, have curiously passed almost unnoticed. They begin with the difficulties in which Major Reuben H. Fleet, founder and boss of Consolidated, found himself a year ago after the President had called for a concentration of production behind the heavy-bomber program. This meant a terrific expansion for Consolidated, whose B-24 (Liberator) was one of only two four-engine

American land bombers, and whose two-engine PBY's (Catalina) and four-engine PB2Y's were the only long-range flying boats then in production. From 1939 to the summer of 1941, Consolidated went from 1,500 to over 30,000 workers, and floor space increased many times.

Rube held almost a third of the stock and absolute control. He had married a young wife, his second, and it was no secret that he wanted to sell out—partly to convert his equity into cash while tax schedules were comparatively easy, partly to spread responsibility in a war corporation where he had such a heavy stake in every dollar. Also, the Army and Navy, with hundreds of millions of dollars worth of airplanes in Consolidated's backlog, wanted to see him replaced with a first-class industrialist. While the services were grateful to Rube for having run a shoe-string hawker of trainers into a potential source of enormous striking power, he had taxed their patience with his continuous wrangling with labor and his bullheaded arguments over tactical changes. Worst of all, his inability or disinclination to shake Consolidated down into something more substantial than a one-man show was injecting grave doubts into the stability of the heavy-bomber program.

From the point of view of Mr. Robert A. Lovett, Assistant Secretary of War for Air, and Rear Admiral John H. Towers, chief of the Bureau of Aeronautics, who took a hand in the task of showing up Consolidated, the problem was not to find a purchaser with money, but rather one with the production experience and intestinal fortitude to man perhaps the most crucial single strong point on the whole production battle line. Several companies were tempted, but eventually shied away; their managements already had their hands full. Then . . . Mr. Victor Emanuel [The Aviation Corporation] secretly entered the negotiations. . . .

.   .   .   .

The deal . . . was closed last December [1941]. Vultee, now 76 percent owned by Aviation Corporation, was the purchaser. . . .

As Mr. Emanuel tells the story:

"When we finally took Consolidated over, I was deeply worried, since we knew nothing about big airplanes and the situation was almost a danger to the country. . . . I became more and more concerned, and finally told him [Tom Girdler] that he'd have to take over—and fast.

"After the facts were laid before him, Tom finally said he would. He never bothers much about details—he knew there was a stipulated production rate and that was all that mattered."

As Chairman of the Board and chief executive officer of both Consolidated and Vultee, while still retaining the chairmanship and policy direction of Republic, Mr. Girdler has moved into one of the top production assignments of the war. His interests extend from coast to coast. Already an estimated 130,000 workers are on the payrolls of the three companies that he managed directly; the companies' assets at the end of 1941 stood at nearly $600 million, and their backlog runs into the billions. . . .

.   .   .   .

Girdler, by his own definition, is an executive rather than a production man —"and there's a hell of a difference." An executive is one who lays down general policy and then delegates to other men responsibility of execution. "The trick," he once advised Victor Emanuel, "is in putting a man in a job, giving him complete responsibility, not bothering him, and not letting anyone else bother him." In theory, this leaves the executive free to ponder long-range problems, and Girdler believes that he has so nearly approached the ideal that, when testifying before the La Follette Committee about who in Republic reported to him, he said, "The President, . . . two secretaries, and one airplane pilot.". . .

.   .   .   .

A quick look [at Aviation Corporation] convinced him that aviation could be a big market for his [Republic's] light steels. And with the double purpose of forearming Republic while also helping his friends, he lent them Mr. Harry Woodhead, Vice President and General Manager of a subsidiary, Truscon Steel, to apply the "Republic touch."

Under the combined drive of the first rearmament orders and of Mr. Woodhead, a tireless, amiable, towering Yorkshireman, what is now Aviation Corporation began to right itself productionwise. . . . Except for keeping "a friendly eye" on Mr. Woodhead's progress . . . Girdler remained pretty much out of sight. He did not emerge as a power behind Aviation Corporation until . . . Victor Emanuel swung his great coup: the purchase of Consolidated.

.   .   .   .

As Mr. Girdler points out: "A lot of people think we busted in here to salvage a broken-down plant. That's bunk. We bought Consolidated because it already had the kind of strength we could use." The 3,000-foot assembly line that Rube started, though radically modified, remains the beginning and end of everything, and many of his executives, whose light had lain under a bushel, have moved up. One is thirty-four-year-old George J. Newman, a factory manager, whom Girdler put in charge of the Texas plant; another is the Major's thirty-two-year-old son, David Fleet, now Executive Vice President of Vultee. And the third and most important is I. M. (Mac) Laddon, designer of the B-24, the PBY, and the PB2Y, now Executive Vice President and General Manager. Mac Laddon learned his profession in the last war at McCook Field where he worked on some of the earliest armored and turbosupercharged warplanes, and where he eventually designed the first all-metal airplane produced in this country. "You're my kind of guy," the steelman said impulsively, after their first fishy-eyed exchange. It is a good thing, for the services rightly cherish Mac Laddon, a gentle, self-effacing soul.

On the other hand, Mr. Girdler has crowded his own brand of management around the top. To be Vice Chairman and No. 2 man of Vultee, he imported Mr. G. M. (Monte) Williams, President of Russell Manufacturing Co. (textiles), before the head of the now defunct Marmon Motor Car Co. . . . Mr. Woodhead was brought down from Vultee to be President of Consolidated. Young Mr. C. W. Perelle, Vultee's production strategist, whom Girdler calls "a tough cookie," was drafted to "help knock the man-hours out of the B-24." And Mr. Francis A. Callery, an Emanuel man, was made Vice President in charge of finance. Major Fleet, who is still around under a five-year, $60,000-a-year contract as "adviser," remarked one day, "Well, it's taken five men, including Tom Girdler, to fill my shoes."

.   .   .   .

. . . Girdler, after breaking several Army schedules, has pushed his potential well beyond the government's ability to supply him with parts and materials. This has been the result of introducing a straightline production system; of pushing more and more of the final assembly back into the subassemblies; of patient worker education; of introducing incentive bonuses; and of delegating authority. . . . By fall [1942], Consolidated will have the final assembly lines moving continuously, if slowly, under power. "The only thing that can stop production," Mr. Girdler has said, "will not be management or brain power, but the gadgets over which we have no control."[2]

. . . .

After January, 1942, there were several changes in the top management personnel in Consolidated and Vultee as indicated in the foregoing statement. Mr. Woodhead and Mr. Laddon became officers of both Consolidated and Vultee, and Mr. Perelle was made vice-president in charge of production for Consolidated. Mr. Girdler made the following statements concerning Mr. Laddon and Mr. Perelle:

Rich though [Consolidated] is in talent, and especially in engineering talent, I. M. Laddon is the genius. Laddon's is the fundamental creative force which the Consolidated organization is expressing. Laddon now is our executive vice president. Each kind of business has to have its emphasis on some special talent; in a mail order house the emphasis probably is on merchandising; it would be on showmanship in a circus; but in aircraft manufacturing the emphasis is definitely and unmistakably on engineering and design. Mac Laddon is an engineer who became a great designer.[3]

Woodhead brought [to Vultee] C. W. Perelle, a young engineer with a superb understanding of production. Perelle did a swell job. He never rested until he had Vultee making more pounds of airplane per man-hour than any other plant in the world. Before he worked for us, Perelle had worked in the Boeing plant in Seattle. He is forty-one and looks twenty-five. As if by instinct he knows that he can't get the best done unless every man under him knows only one boss—Perelle. . . . That is the way I [Girdler] have always felt.[4]

In addition to Woodhead and Perelle, several other Vultee executives were brought to Consolidated to strengthen the latter's organization. Consolidated's organization by March, 1942, is shown in Exhibit 3.

Both Consolidated and Vultee continued to expand rapidly during 1942. Consolidated's employment reached 44,300 during that year. Two new plants commenced operations producing B-24's—one in Fort Worth, Texas, and the other in San Diego. The latter plant supple-

---

[2] "Tom Girdler's Truce," *Fortune,* Sept., 1942, pp. 89 ff.

[3] Tom M. Girdler, *Boot Straps* (New York: Charles Scribner's Sons, 1943), pp. 425–26.

[4] *Ibid.,* p. 424.

mented the company's existing plant facilities in San Diego. Modification centers were established at Tucson, Arizona, and Elizabeth, New Jersey, to handle war-theater modifications of B-24's and PBY's. Vultee added a modification center at Louisville, started the Allentown Division (manufacturing), acquired Intercontinent Aircraft at Miami, and increased production at its home plant (Vultee Field), at the Nashville Division in Tennessee and at the Stinson Division (Wayne, Michigan). During this period, preliminary to the eventual merger, efforts were made to standardize company procedures and organizations.

Consolidated Vultee Aircraft Corporation was formed in March, 1943. The company's organization chart at the time of the merger is shown in Exhibit 4. There were 11 divisions of the company operating throughout the country, in addition to Consairways, an airline operated by the company, and the research activities located at Dearborn, Michigan. In order to standardize the organizations within each division, a standard division organization was established. Each division was to conform with this organization, and any deviations were subject to the approval of the executive vice-president, Mr. Laddon.

To supervise all company operations, a central staff was formed consisting of the directors of the various company functions. Frequent meetings of the central staff officers and division managers were held to discuss mutual problems, among which were matters relative to the company's form of organization. The first meeting, held in San Diego on March 29, 1943, served primarily to introduce this new form of organization. The following statements are excerpts and notes taken from the minutes of this and subsequent meetings of Consolidated Vultee's division managers:

DIVISION MANAGERS' MEETING—SAN DIEGO—MARCH 29, 1943

In opening this meeting Mr. Girdler stated that a lot of time had been spent on the setting up of the new organization chart in an effort to work things out so that they would function smoothly. The chart represented the combined thinking of Mr. Woodhead [President], Mr. Laddon [Executive Vice President], Mr. Leigh [Vice President], and some others. He emphasized that now that the merger had taken place, there was neither a Vultee outfit nor a Consolidated outfit, but rather it represented the Consolidated Vultee Aircraft Corporation.

Mr. Girdler stressed the fact that the management wanted everyone to feel that he could talk to everyone else but that he wanted him to do it logically. In [explaining] the division manager's setup, Mr. Girdler spoke as follows:

"As far as Consolidated Vultee is concerned I have one President and one secretary and no one else reports to me. Mr. Woodhead has two secretaries and two or three assistants. I have a couple of assistants but they do not report to

Exhibit 3

CONSOLIDATED AIRCRAFT CORPORATION
Organization Chart, March 26, 1942

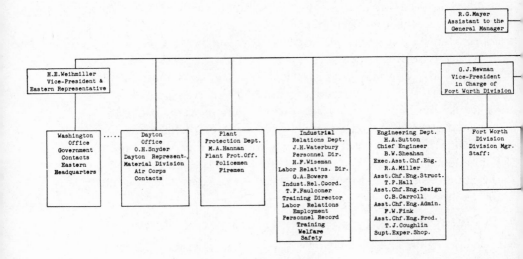

R.G.Mayer
Assistant to the
General Manager

H.E.Weihmiller
Vice-President &
Eastern Representative

G.J.Newman
Vice-President
in Charge of
Fort Worth Division

Washington
Office
Government
Contacts
Eastern
Headquarters

Dayton
Office
O.H.Snyder
Dayton Represent.
Material Division
Air Corps
Contacts

Plant
Protection Dept.
M.A.Hannan
Plant Prot.Off.
Policemen
Firemen

Industrial
Relations Dept.
J.H.Waterbury
Personnel Dir.
H.F.Wiseman
Labor Relat'ns. Dir.
G.A.Bowers
Indust.Rel.Coord.
T.P.Faulconer
Training Director
Labor Relations
Employment
Personnel Record
Training
Welfare
Safety

Engineering Dept.
H.A.Sutton
Chief Engineer
B.W.Sheahan
Exec.Asst.Chf.Eng.
R.A.Miller
Asst.Chf.Eng.Struct.
T.P.Hall
Asst.Chf.Eng.Design
C.B.Carroll
Asst.Chf.Eng.Admin.
F.W.Fink
Asst.Chf.Eng.Prod.
T.J.Coughlin
Supt.Exper.Shop.

Fort Worth
Division
Division Mgr.
Staff:

Exhibit 3—Continued

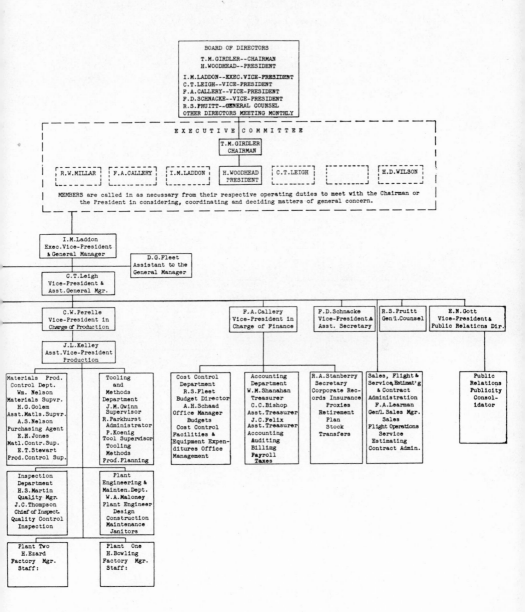

Exhibit 4

CONSOLIDATED VULTEE AIRCRAFT CORPORATION

Organization Chart, March 30, 1943

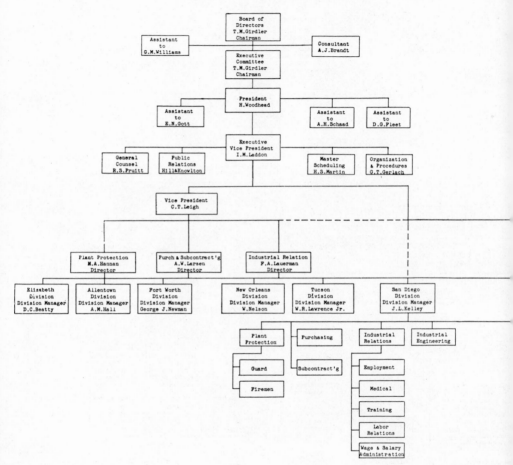

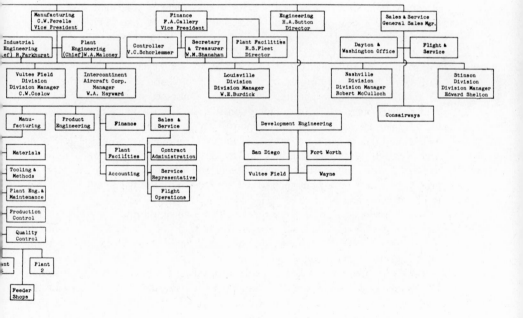

me; they spend most of their time reporting to Mr. Woodhead and Mr. Laddon. Everybody else in the company, other than the few I mentioned, report to Mr. Laddon as Executive Vice President. Now I want to give you this organizational setup as I see it—this is what I call a straight line organization. If a Division Manager talks to Mr. Woodhead about something, that is perfectly all right, but if he forgets to talk to the people he is supposed to report to on the subjects they have in hand, and forgets to tell his boss in that line about it, that is something for his boss to handle in his own good way. In other words, if Mr. Coslow [Division Manager, Vultee Field] or Mr. Newman [Division Manager, Fort Worth] or Mr. Burdick [Division Manager, Louisville] takes something up with Mr. Woodhead or Mr. Laddon and forgets to take it up with Mr. Perelle, if it is in Perelle's line, then Mr. Perelle has a perfect right to raise Cain about it. Mr. Perelle has no right to object to them talking to Mr. Woodhead and Mr. Laddon about it but he does have a perfect right to insist that he be kept informed. On some matter of purchases or some matter of credit or some matter of finance, he should, of course, take it up with Mr. Schorlemmer [Controller] or Shanahan [Secretary-Treasurer] or Callery [Vice President—Finance] or whoever he should take it up with. He is subject to censor if he does not do it. In other words, there is a straight line way of doing it and a straight line should be followed. I hope that when you gentlemen leave here and go back to your respective locations that you will have everything perfectly clear in your mind as to how this organization is to function. I think they say in law that ignorance of the law is no excuse. I think everybody will have time before he goes back to go to people and ask for interpretations on certain subjects so that there will be no ignorance of the law. I am very glad to have men talk to me. Don't consider that you have talked to anybody but me because I don feel any responsibility to passing it on to anyone else. You should talk to Mr. Perelle, Mr. Laddon or Mr. Callery or even to Mr. Woodhead through the proper channels, and then if I don't hear what I am supposed to hear, I will raise the dickens with them and not with you. To get down to brass tacks, there is only one man to tell me everything I ought to know, and that is Mr. Woodhead."

Mr. Woodhead next stressed the fact that one of the main reasons for the merger was to give authority to the Division Manager. The central staff affords men who can furnish guidance in the handling of specific problems. Again loyalty to the Corporation was emphasized.

Mr. Laddon was then asked to explain the basic idea of the new organization. He pointed out that the various divisions of the company were bolstered by the addition of a central staff. The people on this central staff were the people regarded as the best brains in the organization for the specific function to which they were assigned. In answer to the question "For whom do I work" it was stated that the Division Managers would work for everybody on the staff. In other words if there were a division that had nothing but manufacturing in it, it would be working 100 percent for Perelle. If there were a division having only engineering work, it would be working for Sutton [Engineering Director]. The plan did not mean that the staff man was going to come down to the division to specify every move that was to be made—it meant that the Division Manager was to act to the best of his ability and, when he needed help, a staff man would be available to look over the situation and to make suggestions as to what should be done to improve the function. It was emphasized that these suggestions were to be complied with. The Division Managers were to have responsibility and reasonable authority. This method of organization was felt to be the basis for operating a big corporation, and it was stated that other large companies had operated very successfully along this line. The central staff plan makes it possible to make better brains available to the entire corporation than would otherwise be the case.

It was announced that the purpose of the meeting was to go over the general form of organization taking it point by point and answering any questions that the Division Managers might have. It was felt that specific details growing out of this meeting would aid in the preparation of a more detailed functional write-up. The meeting was then thrown open to questions.

[The] question was raised concerning the organization chart which showed a line running from Laddon to Kelley [Division Manager, San Diego], bypassing all the staff. The question was whether the Division Managers reported through central staff representatives only. The answer was that on most things the Division Manager should report to the staff representative concerned, but that on a small percentage of general policy matters they should report directly to Mr. Laddon.

The following . . . statement was made [Mr. Girdler] in amplification of the above discussion:

"If you [Laddon] issued an executive order to each Division Manager and it affected production, you would send it also to Perelle [Vice President—Manufacturing] or, in the matter of finance, to Callery [Vice President—Finance], but over your signature as Executive Vice President."

The Division Managers were requested to make up an organization chart of their divisions, not paying particular attention to titles at this stage of the game, as it was intended to standardize titles throughout the Corporation.

By way of illustration of the way plant departments would work in relation to division managers and central staff heads, the title of "Chief of Plant Protection" was discussed. Each plant has its own Chief of Plant Protection; he was required to report everything with reference to plant protection to the Division Manager and it was also stated to be the duty of that Chief of Plant Protection Officer to report to the Director of Plant Protection at San Diego in order to keep the central office thoroughly in touch with everything that was going on.

Mr. Woodhead stressed the fact that the Plant Protection Officer had to be sure that he reported everything to the Division Manager, but nevertheless paralleled this to report to the Plant Protection Chief of the whole Corporation.

With regard to Engineering, the Division Engineer was responsible to the Division Manager for producing the drawings in time to meet the schedule as set. The Division Manager was not in any sense responsible for design. The design of the airplane was something that was controlled by the Director of Engineering. The fact that the Division Engineer does parallel his report to the Division Manager and the central office does not take away any of the responsibility or authority of the Division Manager. He was responsible for the discipline and for the fact that the engineering department functioned as a part of his organization.

One Division Manager raised the following question: "Suppose I have a man in my organization who gets an answer from a staff representative of which I have also received a copy. He doesn't put that into effect until he checks with me,—is that right?" The answer given this Division Manager was that he was still the Division Manager and the man in his organization was still working for the Division Manager but receiving guidance and suggestions from the central office. It was again emphasized that the central staff group was responsible for the successful conduct of their line of activity at the divisions. The question was answered negatively in that it was stated that the directions from the central staff officer constituted a direct order on both the department head and the Division Manager and that the department head didn't have to wait to talk to the Division Manager about it but rather could put the instruction into effect. The question was then posed as to whether such action relieved the Division Manager of responsibility for the specific matter. . . . It was said that if the Division Manager disagreed with instructions issued by the central office he could bring it to the Executive Vice President's attention or go directly himself to the central staff officer involved and try to work out a better course of action.

Mr. Laddon said that he believed there were many things that the Division Managers would have to contact him on directly—matters of general policy which affected the whole division. He felt that that was all right but that they should not contact him on anything that had to do with a specific function for which there was a staff man. On those things the Division Manager should work through the staff representative. He further pointed out that only one report per week was wanted from each Division Manager, that report to be a discussion of weekly progress with decisions arrived at, etc. If definite and special reports were requested by a central staff man those reports should be sent to the person in charge of that particular function by the division department head concerned but simultaneously a copy of the report should go to the Division Manager.

The question was raised as to whether the Division Engineer was responsible for scheduling engineering to meet production and whether the engineering schedule would have to be approved by the Director of Engineering. The answer was that the Division Engineer should submit the schedule of what he promises he can do. After all he was the man on the job who knew local conditions and it was then up to him to live up to it. It was not felt that the Director of Engineering could be responsible for that schedule because he couldn't keep in close enough touch with it. If things did not work out satisfactorily then probably the Division Engineer was not the man for the job. There was no reason under this arrangement why a Division Engineer should accept a larger work assignment from the Director of Engineering than he felt he could handle.

Another example of relationship was that the Division Flight man supervised the Flight Operations but that there was one man on the central staff particularly concerned with flight operations. It was stated that he did not have the right to order the Division men around without going through the Division Manager. The Division Flight Operations Department reported "directly, concurrently, simultaneously, instantaneously" to the Division Manager. It was then said that the central staff man had a right to ask the Division Flight Operations people questions about a particular problem and that the Division Manager would get a copy of the response. . . . It was said that 99 times out of 100 the central staff man would not give the Division Flight Operations Department a direct order. . . .

Delivery schedules were to be set up by Master Scheduling with Perelle, Martin [Scheduling Director] and the Division Manager taking part in their formulation. The Division Manager should look over what the Army or Navy calls for and advise the central office as to what they think they can do.

Mr. Woodhead injected the thought that the Division Managers didn't want to get the idea that the central office was going to run the Division Manager's plant. He said that the Division Manager should bother the central office the smallest amount possible but use them when necessary. Otherwise the company might as well separate into subsidiary companies and there wouldn't be a reason for the Consolidated Vultee Aircraft Corporation. He suggested that they not worry too much about authority. He said he had gone into Division Managers' offices where the desk was littered with papers and everything was beautifully bottlenecked because the Division Manager didn't want anybody to do anything until he had told them to do it. This simply illustrated the need for greater delegation.

The staff people were, to the best of their ability, to work through the Division Managers and there was to be no intent to work without them. However, in order to speed up action and to prevent bottlenecking, it was felt that it might help for the central staff men to go direct to their corresponding department heads with coordination through the Division Manager; for if all negotiations went through the Division Manager only, it might easily be held up for several days.

Another point that was raised was in regard to schedules. Take, for instance, a modification center where the Air Force representative asks if a division can turn out some additional airplanes. The situation was to be handled by the Division Manager saying that he would investigate it. He was then to report to San Diego what he felt he could do and San Diego would, in 99 cases out of 100, okay the proposed action and the Division Manager could then report the proposed schedule to the A.A.F. The Division Managers were not to say "we can't tell you what the schedule is until we get in touch with San Diego." The idea of the San Diego check was so that the central office could coordinate the whole program. It wasn't a matter of asking permission of San Diego but merely reporting what it was felt could be done.

With regard to procedures or standard practices, any one of the staff heads could issue a procedure. If it affected plant protection or purchasing or subcontracting, it would come out over Mr. Leigh's signature and, in the case of manufacturing, would come out over Mr. Perelle's signature.

On the matter of the Division having no responsibility for engineering schedules discussed earlier, Mr. Laddon said that he thought Sutton should have a staff assistant assigned particularly to that problem. He felt that engineering schedules were difficult to establish and that there should be a certain amount of staff supervision and responsibility over them. Mr. Girdler did not see how Sutton could take full responsibility or how the Division Manager and the Division Engineer could take full responsibility for such schedules. He felt that it had to be a cooperative thing and if Sutton could have an assistant who spent his whole time checking on such schedules it would be a substantial help.

Labor matters were considered definitely a matter of Corporation policy and in that connection it was stated that Mr. Lauerman [Industrial Relations Director] would sit in on all negotiations of contracts with labor. He was to cover all divisions in person.

DIVISION MANAGERS' MEETING—SAN DIEGO—MAY 3, 1943

. . . .

It was proposed that all company general policies should be issued in the form of Corporation Standard Practice Instructions. . . . By way of explanation it was stated that a Corporation Standard Practice Instruction was to be issued only when it affected more than one function. If Mr. Perelle wished to issue a directive with regard to the Production Department it was to be issued as a directive covering the functioning of the Production Department. If, however, it affected production and also contract administration, in other words, more than one department, it should be issued as a C.S.P.I. over Mr. Laddon's signature or Mr. Leigh's. On the subject of organization charts it was stated that they were not to be taken too seriously. The functioning of the organization as a whole was said to be dependent upon the people in the organization wanting to do the job.

Mr. Woodhead said that no matter how perfect you make an organization chart, if the disposition to make the organization work isn't there, it won't work. The original chart was a tentative outl:ne of how the organization was supposed to function for the following few months, and there would probably be a considerable number of changes as things were found not to be exactly as they should be.

Mr. Laddon again emphasized that he did not want the Division Managers coming to him on things that should be handled through the staff. If the matter had to do with production it should go through Perelle; if it had to do with engineering the Division Manager should go through Sutton. If it concerned Industrial Relations they should go through Lauerman. There were, however, certain things as relations with the customer and matters of general policy that should continue to come to Mr. Laddon.

Mr. Woodhead stated that they were going to discourage any deliberate effort to go around and not through the channels they were supposed to go through.

. . . .

Many questions were directed by the Division Managers concerning accounting, cost matters and contractual matters. It was stated that no satisfactory clarification of the accounting structure could be accomplished until the functional organization had been set up on a uniform basis throughout all divisions.

It was stated that a typical organization chart for any division was being developed and that it should be ready for the next Division Managers' meeting.

DIVISION MANAGERS' MEETING—DOWNEY, CALIFORNIA —JUNE 30, 1943

Mr. Laddon announced that the decision had been made that the Division Managers should not appoint key personnel such as assistant managers, general superintendents, etc., without first clearing with the general office at San Diego. One reason why this was requested was that smaller divisions would not require as many top personnel as larger divisions. It was emphasized that this was not so much a matter of receiving permission to appoint new personnel but was rather a matter of organization. Everyone should remember that he was part of a large organization; that a man might be placed in a particular position and for reasons known to the general office it might be advisable to move him. This would have to be done, of course, from the standpoint of over-all good for the organization. It would not be a case of taking away the Division Manager's authority but rather of having Division Managers recognize the fact that they are part of a large organization. There seemed at this time to be a tendency on the part of some of the smaller divisions to adopt the organization which existed at San Diego and Fort Worth. There was no justification for this as many functions could be combined and thus simplify the smaller divisions' operations. This meant that the Division Managers should follow the general outline of the chart but would not necessarily have identical positions. The necessity for approval of changes on the part of San Diego would go down only to the point where the functions corresponded to the major functions on the central staff. Below those positions it was not necessary for the Division Managers to refer to San Diego.

Mr. Girdler pointed out in this connection that it wasn't a question of the Division Managers getting permission but rather giving the central staff heads a chance to make suggestions. In most cases the Division Manager would probably get the man he wanted anyhow.

.   .   .   .

DIVISION MANAGERS' MEETING—SAN DIEGO— JANUARY 18–19, 1944

Relation Between Corporation Staff and Corresponding Personnel in Divisions

MR. COSLOW [Division Manager]: In directing department heads in a Division just how far down the line should the staff man go in selecting the personnel of the department? It was your statement at one Division Managers' Meeting that control should go as far as the top man. Since that time there has been some change in thinking on that—at least I have indications that the staff man is interested further down in the organization.

MR. LADDON: When the merger took place we eliminated the job of General Manager. The staff as it exists fulfills the function of a General Manager. They are my representatives with regard to their particular functions and function as a General Manager functions in their particular field. For instance, the staff man on industrial relations has the responsibility in that field that the General Manager would have. Say you want to appoint the head of a department. It is a good idea for you to consider the staff man's opinion in picking a candidate for that office. If the staff man is not satisfied that the job is properly handled in your Division and comes to you and suggests a change in personnel, you should listen to him. He is the one to whom I have assigned the responsibility. If he desires he can go down a man or two below the department head. He can step in to the degree he deems necessary to make the function work at your Division. If you want to appoint a new man to any function call the staff man concerned and get his suggestion. Take his advice. If you get the basic idea that the staff man is part of the General Manager you will be all right. This Corporation is too big to have any one man as General Manager. I found that out on numerous occasions. We have got to have people consider the accomplishment of the individual job more and forget their personal situations and prerogatives. Stop worrying about whether someone is stepping on your toes. Your personal advancement will be based on accomplishment and not on anything else. The corporate organization is well charted. I can answer any question about it. What we need is better team work. Worry about getting a thing done in the best and fastest way. There has been considerable improvement in the past six months but there is room for a lot more.

MR. WOODHEAD: Personal prestige in this Corporation means less than nothing. The thing that counts is the Corporation's success. A team success. There will be very little sympathy for the Division Manager who creates a situation and it is found the only thing that suffers is his own prestige and feelings. There is enough glory and reward for everyone to get his share. Personal prestige means nothing.

MR. McMAHON [Division Manager]: Agreed that you can and must have harmony. Just suppose the staff man says something can go and the Division Manager says it can not?

MR. WOODHEAD: You may have a difference of opinion with the staff man. You have a perfect right to straighten it out. You don't have to take everything the staff man says. Be sure it is an honest difference of opinion and for the good of the Corporation and not a difference because you feel your own prestige is affected.

MR. LADDON: Every employee has the right of appeal. Go up through channels and state the case. I don't anticipate we should get many of these. There have been only two or three in the last four months. They usually get resolved by common sense meeting of minds. No one can take an unreasonable stand and get away with it, whether Division Manager or staff man.

Utilizing Staff and Division Experience

MR. MARTIN: The matter that brought this to my attention was a recent trip to Fort Worth in connection with inspection. They were having the same troubles San Diego had a year or so ago. It seemed to me that instead of trying to find their own solution they might have wondered if other Divisions had run into those troubles and how they had solved them. For example, Fort Worth was trying to write an inspection manual. San Diego had written several thousand pages of inspection procedure and it seems to me it would have been a big start on an inspection manual if Fort Worth had asked what had been done here along that line.

MR. LADDON: There is a very natural tendency on the part of everybody to endeavor to work out their own problems in their own way. We should bear in mind that there is a great deal of experience available in the Corporation and before we start experimenting on a particular problem it would speed things up immeasurably if we talked it over with those Divisions where experimentation on that item has already taken place. This is one of the major advantages of a large Corporation and it is the specific responsibility of staff function concerned to see that all Divisions utilize to the fullest degree the entire corporate knowledge and experience.

DIVISION MANAGERS' MEETING—STINSON DIVISION (WAYNE, MICHIGAN)—AUGUST 14-16, 1944

Issuance of Directives by Staff Members to Department Heads at Divisions

MR. LADDON: At our very first staff meeting we defined what we considered to be the staff responsibility and we said at that time that it would not be necessary for every staff man to do all of his work through the Division Manager. We said at the time that he would work directly with his counterpart at the Division but that he should be very careful that the Division Manager was kept informed. We have had a number of instances where directives are issued or phone calls made to the department head or the staff counterpart involved without informing the Division Manager and that practice must be discontinued. The staff has a definite responsibility but nevertheless in fulfilling that responsibility they must do it in such a fashion that they do not belittle the authority of the Division Manager. He still is to function as the boss. We have in our Corporation a couple of people who have had considerable experience with a staff setup, F. A. Lauerman and M. A. Hannan. We have had little or no trouble with them. They decide on the proper course of action and tell their counterpart to talk it over with the Division Manager and, if he has no objections, put it into effect, or, if he has any, to call them. On the other hand, we have people who call up and give orders and the Division Manager does not know about it. In the final analysis the Division Manager is responsible for the functioning of the entire Division. The staff man involved may want a particular person hired to take care of a particular function in the best possible way, but getting that man may upset the over-all wage scale in the Division. Before any final action is taken it should be taken up with the Division Manager. That is particularly true in matters of organization. We have had situations where directives have been issued or changes of organization made by the staff man involved and the information sent directly to his counterpart in the Division. In the case mentioned it was issued in its final form and a copy was sent to the Division Manager. This is not the way to do it. In a number of cases conflicting directives have been issued. When a directive is issued by a staff man it should be okayed by the head of that function. Industrial relations or purchasing or materials or plant protection matters should all go through one place and follow the same procedure. . . . I am sure these are not issued with the idea that they will conflict with any other directive, but, in many cases, they do not know what directives have been issued.

MR. WOODHEAD: I would like to raise a point. When a staff man goes to a Division, the first thing he should do, for no other reason than common courtesy, is to check in with the Division Manager. After he talks with the man who is handling his particular phase of activity it would seem to me the right thing for the staff man to check out with the Division Manager so that he is familiar at all times with what is going on. One of the reasons for having a big Corporation rather than having a lot of small companies is to have the benefit of the added strength and talent by combination staff activities,—that is the primary purpose of having a Corporation. There are certain rules and regulations laid down because of the Corporation's setup. There is nothing to stop the Division Manager from working through the particular staff man. When there is something which you think is wrong or you object to, the party you must object to is the party that is responsible for it. If the matter is something to do with the Contract Department, go to Frank Watson and not through other sources. The thing which we do not like is that there is too much criticism and too much conversation in the wrong direction. There is absolutely no reason why the Division Manager should continue with something which he thinks is wrong and just keep his mouth shut, nor do we like people who open them too wide. That is the policy which we have set up and that is what we are going to follow.

MR. LADDON: The staff man is always thinking of his particular function; the Division Manager has to think of the whole Division. If the staff man insists that his directive be followed and the Division Manager does not agree, call Mr. Woodhead or me and get a decision on it. I get few such calls. I have had about two in a year and a half. The right of free speech still exists. Go to the top. Mr. Girdler's door is always open. So are Mr. Woodhead's and mine. We definitely do not want the staff to become consultants, to give advice but have no responsibility. That is not the way we want them to operate. If you cannot get together with the staff man and settle your difference of opinion, come to us. There has been a lot of behind-the-scenes complaining, and I want to see an end to it. Bring your complaints out in the open. All of the fault is not with the staff. We have had several instances where the Division Managers made changes in personnel without consultation with a staff man. That has to be stopped.

MR. WOODHEAD: With reference to this business of working together with the staff, I served as Division Manager for approximately seven years for Republic Steel under the same setup that we are working under here. In all that time I never once found a situation embarrassing to me or belittling to my position or which took away my authority. If two reasonable people, the staff man and the Division Manager, want to make the situation work, they can make it work perfectly without subordinating themselves or abdicating any of their authority. The Industrial Relations Manager for Republic Steel would come first to my office at Truscon Steel and say whom he came to work with. He would spend two or three days working with the man and then come back to my office and say how the man was working and then leave. We had the same thing with the Purchasing Department and with the Accounting Department. We had a good Chief Accountant who worked for me, who took my orders. When the Central Office

Auditor would come out, he would come into my office and say he was going to work with Jack Stanton. He would work with him three days and, if they had changes to make, he would present them to me when he was leaving but wouldn't go into detail. I never felt for one moment that I didn't have any control over that department. If I found out that anything had happened, how long do you think it would have been before I would have been on the phone finding out what was going on? I had the combined power of the whole Republic Steel Corporation to back me up. That was how I felt about it. I had all this strength behind me to use. The success of Consolidated Vultee isn't Louisville, or Nashville, but it is Consolidated Vultee. The success of a Division Manager is going to be the success of Consolidated Vultee. The thing we have to put over is the Corporate setup. Any time any little thing comes up like a conflict in orders or if a staff man comes into your Division and says something he shouldn't have said, we don't want to hear it from five different people. It is to be settled right on the spot between the Division Manager and the staff man. There has been altogether too much of this business of telling somebody else of the difficulties which you have had with a staff man. There is too much trying to play the individual game. This conversation is not meant for any particular individual. We do not want to know these things through a number of individuals. We want to hear them direct. We don't want to hear about it from anyone whose job has nothing to do with it. When we had trouble in the Police Department at Republic, we called up James Williams. We didn't call up the Police Department who would call up the Accounting Department. We called up James Williams and got it settled right then. Ninety-nine percent of our difficulties, irritations, complaints and criticisms will clear up if you fellows will work direct. I am going to go one step further and say this. If you do not do this, we are going to begin to question your motives and think you are trying to cross things up. If you persist in doing it, we are definitely going to question you as to whether you are really honestly trying to do the job and play the game as it should be played. We are going to be less charitable. When we get to the reconversion period and we have to begin to shrink operations, we are going to shrink it back corporation-wise. The organization that will be with this Corporation postwar is the organization which has earned its right to be with the Corporation. No one has an inside track. We are going to determine the permanent organization based on the record, ability and the personality of the individual.

MR. LADDON: Is there any discussion on that subject? I believe Mr. Coslow has some definite ideas on it.

MR. COSLOW: My thoughts on the matter were expressed in the memo which I wrote in answer to Mr. Martin's request. I used the word "consultant" which was wrong. My only thought was that when a staff man comes in to see you once in three or four months, he can't be too familiar with every little detail and can't watch things too closely. I work with every staff man that comes in, in nearly every case. The staff man is willing to work with and through the Division Manager. The only trouble is that they give their counterpart information which I don't learn about.

MR. LADDON: We said at our very first meeting that we didn't want to have everything flow through the Division Manager. We didn't want to get in the position where one man was a bottleneck. When important changes are to be made, they should be decided tentatively between the staff man and his counterpart and then confirmed with the Division Manager. When the staff man calls the counterpart he should not give him instructions on important changes which have not first been talked over with the Division Manager.

MR. GIRDLER: I have been functioning under this system for a good many years. It is pretty hard to lay down any rule which does not have a few exceptions and you can't wear people out by trying to set it up so every minute detail has to go through a straight channel. If Mr. Hannan [Plant Protection Director] calls up the Plant Protection Department at Nashville and says he just got some information on one of the men and wants him fired right away, in my opinion it isn't necessary to find Joe Hennen [Division Manager] to fire that particular guard. Say Hennen has a foreman in the plant who fires a man, he does not tell Hennen,—that is a relatively commonplace case. But on the other hand if Hannan has a Plant Protection man in Nashville and wants to transfer him from Nashville to Allentown, he cannot talk to the man about it until he has talked to Hennen about it. The spirit of cooperation is the most important part of this setup.

MR. WOODHEAD: Mr. Coslow mentioned the fact that a staff man may only go into a Division once every three or four months and therefore he is not too familiar with what is going on. How often do the Division Managers call up the staff men—not wait for the staff man to call them? Ask the staff man for assistance and help. The staff man is responsible for his particular function in the Corporation. How often do you ask for that assistance? Again, if a Division Manager is having trouble with his Engineering setup, does that Division Manager try to work with his Division Engineer or does that Manager call up Mr. Sutton? Do they go right to the staff man who would help them at that time?

MR. LADDON: It is all part of the idea that we do not want the staff to work just as consultants. When the Division Manager is in trouble, we want him to call the staff for help and when he isn't getting help, we want to know about it. We want the staff people to have responsibility, not be just advisors and consultants. They may know someone who can be spared at some other Division to help out. The staff man can demand that help be given. I want to get away from this idea of a consultant.

.   .   .   .

In discussing the corporation's organization, Mr. Laddon stated that one of top management's difficulties concerned the selection of division managers. It was desirable for a division manager to possess both outstanding administrative ability and wide manufacturing and engineering experience. Such men were difficult to find, and frequent compromises were made as between desired abilities and available men with somewhat lesser qualifications. An example concerned a manager of a major manufacturing division assigned to that position because of his ability as a strong administrator. Although associated with the aviation industry for several years, this man had had no previous experience with large-scale manufacturing operations. He effectively brought together an organization which functioned well for a time. After a change in production to a new and more complicated type of plane, however, some serious production shortcomings developed, notably in the control of quality. Mr. Perelle, central staff officer in charge of manufacturing, first tried to solve the division's manufacturing problems by advising and making suggestions to the manager and his organization. Progress was slow, however, and Mr. Perelle became dissatisfied with his lack of direct authority over manufacturing operations which he believed required immediate attention. He later received temporary authority from Mr. Laddon and Mr. Woodhead to assume direct control of production at this division in order to deal effectively with this immediate problem. Significant improvements in manufacturing efficiency followed, although major changes in operating personnel and manufacturing methods were required. During the period of Mr. Perelle's direct management of manufacturing operations the division manager resigned.

Mr. Perelle resigned on September 1, 1944, to become vice-president and general manager of the Hughes Tool Company at Houston, Texas, and manager of the Hughes Aircraft Company at Los Angeles. In these positions, Mr. Perelle was to have sole responsibility for manufacturing at the two companies.

In April, 1945, Mr. Girdler resigned as chairman of the board of Consolidated Vultee. The following statement was published in the *American Aviation Daily* at the time:

Consolidated Vultee Aircraft Corporation announces the resignation of Tom M. Girdler as chairman of the board and a director after almost three and a half years of service. Consolidated directors accepted Girdler's resignation "with profound regret."

In his letter of resignation, Girdler said that when he accepted the position with Consolidated he did so with the understanding that he would relinquish it "when I felt my portion of the job was finished. I believe that the time has now come. The defeat of Germany is assured."

Girdler said that "the urgent need for large production of aircraft will remain until Japan falls, but the industry is now geared to meet every production requirement. All that is necessary is for production lines to keep moving."

Girdler continues as chairman of the board of Republic Steel Corporation. He became chairman of the Consolidated and Vultee aircraft corporations in December, 1941, to help accelerate military aircraft production.[5]

---

[5] *American Aviation Daily,* April 24, 1945, p. 270.

Exhibit 5

CONSOLIDATED VULTEE AIRCRAFT CORPORATION

Organization Chart, July 25, 1945

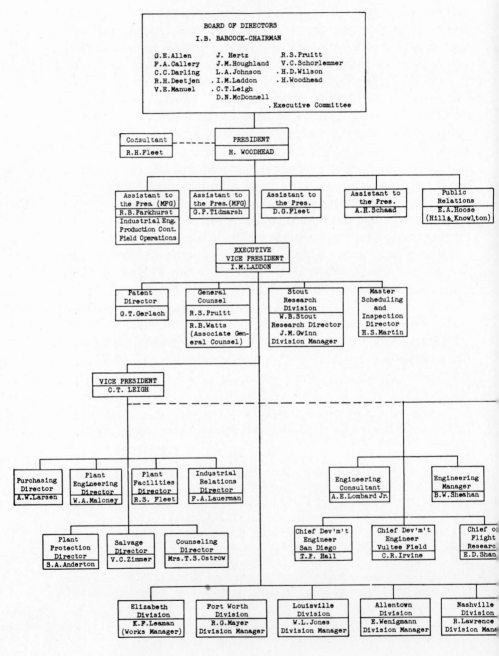

Exhibit 5—Continued

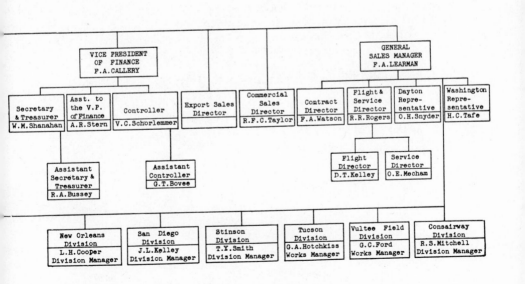

In comparing the organizations of Consolidated Vultee and Republic Steel, Mr. Girdler said:

> The splendid performance of Republic Steel Corporation during the war is to be explained by one simple fact. For thirteen years Republic has been "boiling out." We got rid of all those who could not or did not fit. Up and down the line the men in Republic have learned where their authority ends, where that of another begins. Lines of demarcation are respected. Since there is no friction, the whole enterprise runs as a well-oiled machine. Every man in it seems to delight in doing his best.
>
> Of course, there has not been time for such a "boiling out" in the big aircraft companies. For one thing, they have expanded so greatly, as much as fortyfold and more within a couple of years. Yet at Consolidated I found an organization far better than I had expected, one that was extraordinarily rich in talented men.[6]

Mr. Girdler was succeeded at Consolidated Vultee by Mr. Irving B. Babcock. Mr. Babcock, formerly a vice-president of General Motors and president of Yellow Truck and Coach Manufacturing Company, had joined the Aviation Corporation as president in February, 1945. The Aviation Corporation's annual report for 1944 included the following statement concerning Mr. Babcock:

> The addition of Mr. Babcock to the organization greatly strengthens it because of his wide general manufacturing and commercial experience. He not only has first-hand knowledge of production, but is familiar with the problems of finance, sales, engineering and development. It is evidence of Mr. Babcock's belief in the future of The Aviation Corporation that he should sever his long association with the automotive industry to apply his executive abilities in a new field. His background of experience will be of value not only during the war, but also in the postwar program on which The Aviation Corporation will embark when the end of the war permits the resumption of normal activities.[7]

Consolidated Vultee's organization by July, 1945, is shown in Exhibit 5.

Exhibit 6 is an analysis of changes in division manager personnel during the period March, 1943—July, 1945.

---

[6] Girdler, *op. cit.*, p. 425.

[7] The Aviation Corporation and Associated Companies, *Annual Report for the Fiscal Year Ended November 30, 1944*, p. 10.

Exhibit 6

CONSOLIDATED VULTEE AIRCRAFT CORPORATION
Analysis of Changes in
Maunfacturing Division Manager Personnel
March, 1943—July, 1945

Divisions	March, 1943	July, 1943	December, 1943	May, 1944	July, 1945
San Diego............	J. L. Kelley			R. G. Mayer	
Fort Worth..........	G. J. Newman				G. C. Ford
Vultee Field..........	C. W. Coslow				E. Wenigmann
Allentown............	A. M. Hall	R. J. McMahon			K. F. Leaman
Elizabeth............	D. C. Beatty		L. H. Cooper		
Louisville............	W. E. Burdick	W. L. Jones			
Intercontinent Aircraft Corporation........	W. A. Hayward		N. C. Sather		
Nashville............	R. McCulloch	J. W. Hennen			R. Lawrence
New Orleans.	W. Nelson				L. H. Cooper
Stinson..............	E. Shelton				T. Y. Smith
Tucson..............	W. R. Lawrence				G. A. Hotchkiss

Westinghouse Electric Corporation (A)

THE WESTINGHOUSE ELECTRIC CORPORATION, with headquarters in Pittsburgh, Pennsylvania, had long been one of the largest and most diversified corporations in the United States. In terms of the annual *Fortune* survey of the 500 largest United States industrial corporations, Westinghouse ranked 17th in sales ($2.3 billion) and 24th in total assets employed ($1.6 billion) for 1964. The company had about 64 plant locations in the United States, sales offices throughout the country, and employed about 115,000 people in 1964. In addition to its domestic operations, Westinghouse also had investments in about 35 foreign countries and had over 150 foreign licensees.

Westinghouse was generally classified as an electrical equipment manufacturer, and produced a wide range of industrial and consumer equipment for the generation, transmission, distribution, control, and utilization of electric power. Some measure of the diversity of its operations can be inferred from the following comments in a *Time* article:

> Any company that makes both reactors for nuclear submarines and $1.25 magnets for extracting wire and nails from cows' stomachs has some claim to diversity—and Westinghouse Electric claims to be the world's most diversified company. The oldest electronics firm and the second biggest producer of electrical equipment (after General Electric) in the U.S., Westinghouse makes 8,000 different products in 300,000 variations. The company's 59 divisions with their 64 plants spread through 20 states, daily confront almost every American with some Westinghouse product, from 6,000 types of light bulbs to the output of five TV and seven radio stations.[1]

A more complete listing of Westinghouse products and facilities as of 1964 is shown in Exhibit 1. Of the product groups shown, the Electric Utility group had been the largest in terms of sales, followed by the Industrial and the Atomic, Defense & Space groups.

Single divisions ranged in size from about $5 million to well over $100 million in sales, and had from 500 to 5,000 employees. If listed as independent companies, all of the product groups listed as well as

---

[1] *Time* (October 30, 1964), p. 97.

many of the divisions would have been included in the *Fortune* list of the 500 largest U.S. industrial companies.

The great diversity of the products and services offered by Westinghouse is shown in somewhat more detail in Exhibit 2, which is a reproduction of several pages selected from a booklet entitled "The World of Westinghouse." It was stated in the booklet that the list of over 1,300 products was constantly growing and changing, and it was emphasized that multiplying the products listed by "ratings, sizes, styles, enclosures, colors, combinations, and all the other variables which fit them to specific needs" would explode the list into one of thousands and thousands of items.

Exhibit 1

WESTINGHOUSE ELECTRIC CORPORATION (A)
Westinghouse Divisions and Products

ATOMIC, DEFENSE AND SPACE

AEROSPACE ELECTRICAL DIVISION, Lima, Ohio
Electric power systems, generators, motors, control apparatus, thermoelectric devices, power conditioning and conversion equipment, and support equipment for military and commercial aircraft, missiles and spacecraft.

ASTRONUCLEAR LABORATORY, Large, Pa.
Nuclear power for space and other advanced applications; specialized equipment for space applications.

ATOMIC EQUIPMENT DIVISION, Cheswick, Pa.
Main coolant pumps, valves, control rod drive mechanisms, and other specialized apparatus for nuclear reactors; pumps for controlled circulation boilers; thermoelectric cooling devices for military applications.

ATOMIC FUEL DIVISION, Cheswick, Pa.
Nuclear reactor cores and core components for Naval applications.

BETTIS ATOMIC POWER LABORATORY, Pittsburgh, Pa.
Government-owned facility operated by Westinghouse for the Atomic Energy Commission. Development of nuclear reactors for Naval propulsion and electric power generation under contracts with U.S. Government.

DEFENSE AND SPACE CENTER:
Aerospace Division, Baltimore, Md.
Aerospace systems, equipment and associated support items: reconnaissance; detection; surveillance and weapon control; navigation; data handling and display; missile launch, guidance and control; space vehicle guidance and control; communications; com-

ATOMIC, DEFENSE AND SPACE (CONTINUED)

mand and control; instrumentation; scientific satellites and space vehicles; advanced weapons and electronic warfare.

Surface Division, Baltimore, Md.
Ground, ship and mobile surface systems, equipment and associated support items: surveillance; detection and weapon control; navigation; data handling and display; command and control; communication; instrumentation; satellite control; tracking and discrimination; anti-missile protection; advanced weapons and electronic warfare.

Underseas Division, Baltimore, Md.
Underwater systems, equipment and associated support items: torpedoes, mines and advanced weapons; mine, weapon and CW countermeasures; surveillance; sonar detection; data handling and display; instrumentation; oceanographic systems and equipment; manned submersibles.

Systems Operations, Baltimore, Md.
Management, design and integration of major defense and space systems and systems involving resources and capabilities of several Westinghouse divisions.

PLANT APPARATUS DIVISION, Pittsburgh, Pa.
Procurement of reactor plant equipment for Naval applications.

SUNNYVALE DIVISIONS:
General Products Division, Sunnyvale, Calif.
Electrical, mechanical and shock mitigation components for missile and rocket programs; missile launching and handling equipment; wind tunnel equipment, including axial-flow compressors; special apparatus such as tele-

Exhibit 1—Continued

ATOMIC, DEFENSE AND SPACE (CONTINUED)

scope drives and mountings, centrifugal machines, shock machines and large hydraulic valves.

Marine Products Division, Sunnyvale, Calif.
Equipment for marine applications, including propulsion, providing ship service electrical power, ship handling equipment such as anchor and cargo winch controls, automatic ship and engine room controls, marine condensers, air ejectors, and marine wet winding submersible motors.

CONSTRUCTION

AIR CONDITIONING DIVISION, Staunton, Va.
Packaged air conditioning and heating equipment for residential, commercial and industrial applications; engineered air conditioning systems; heat pumps and electric heat systems for residential and commercial installations.

BRYANT ELECTRIC DIVISION, Bridgeport, Conn.
Wiring devices; lampholders; fluorescent devices; outdoor fixtures for reflector backed lamps; circuit breaker load centers.

ELEVATOR DIVISION, Jersey City, N.J.
Passenger, freight, and shipboard elevators; electric stairways; electric walks; security systems.

ENVIRONMENTAL SYSTEMS DIVISION, Grand Rapids, Mich.
Micarta-clad doors; movable partitions and walls; controlled atmosphere work areas; clean rooms.

LAMP DIVISION, Bloomfield, N.J.
Lamps of all types for all applications: incandescent; fluorescent; mercury; sealed-beam; reflector; miniature; medical; photographic; Christmas tree; flashlight; sun; heat.

LIGHTING DIVISION, Cleveland, Ohio
Commercial, industrial, fluorescent and incandescent fixtures; fluorescent and mercury ballasts; flood, roadway, and marine lighting; lighting accessories; Sterilamp equipment.

STURTEVANT DIVISION, Hyde Park, Mass.
Air distributing units; fans, blowers—general purpose and heavy duty; heaters; heating and cooling coils, steam and hot water; Precipitron air cleaners; dehumidifiers.

PRINTING DIVISION, Trafford, Pa.
Nameplates, printed circuits, all forms of printing.

CONSUMER

AUTOMATIC MERCHANDISING DIVISION, East Springfield, Mass.

CONSUMER (CONTINUED)

Automatic beverage coolers for bottlers of Coca-Cola.

COLUMBUS APPLIANCE DIVISIONS:
Dishwasher & Specialty Products Division, Columbus, Ohio
Dishwashers; waste disposers; water coolers; water heaters.
Refrigerator Division, Columbus, Ohio
Refrigerators and freezers.
Room Air Conditioning Division, Columbus, Ohio
Air conditioners.

MANSFIELD APPLIANCE DIVISIONS:
Laundry Equipment Division, Mansfield, Ohio
Laundromat® automatic washers; dryers; dry cleaners.
Portable Appliance Division, Mansfield, Ohio
Electric housewares; bed coverings; fans; floor polishers; vacuum cleaners.
Range Division, Mansfield, Ohio
Ranges and ovens; kitchen cabinets.

THE C. A. OLSEN MANUFACTURING COMPANY, Elyria, Ohio
Residential heating and air conditioning; incinerators; unit heaters.

TELEVISION-RADIO DIVISION, Metuchen, N.J.
Television receivers; radios, portable and consoles; high fidelity and stereo phonographs; tape recorders.

ELECTRIC UTILITY

ATOMIC POWER DIVISION, Pittsburgh, Pa. (Forest Hills)
Advanced concept development programs, atomic fuel, nuclear steam supply systems, turn-key nuclear power plants—for commercial atomic power installations.

EAST PITTSBURGH DIVISIONS:
Distribution Apparatus Division, Bloomington, Ind.
Capacitors; lightning arresters; fuse cutouts; surge protective devices; reclosers; sectionalizers; load pick-up switches.
Large Rotating Apparatus Division, East Pittsburgh, Pa.
Large generators, motors, motor-generator sets; electric couplings; frequency changer sets; synchronous condensers.
Power Circuit Breaker Division, Trafford, Pa.
High voltage power circuit breakers; condenser bushings, insulators; arc heaters.
Power Control Division, Research and Development Center, Pittsburgh, Pa. (Churchill)
Dispatching control; digital datalogers;

Exhibit 1—Continued

ELECTRIC UTILITY (CONTINUED)

load-frequency control; printed circuit modules; steam plant automation; steam plant computer systems; turbine control systems.
Switchgear Division, East Pittsburgh, Pa.
Assembled switchgear; high voltage fuses; network protectors; nuclear plant control; regulators; substations; generator synchronizers.

MEASUREMENTS DIVISIONS:

Meter Division, Raleigh, N.C.
Watthour, demand, recording meters and accessories; sockets and mountings.
Relay-Instrument Division, Newark, N.J.
Electrical measuring instruments of all types; protective relays and relaying systems.

STEAM DIVISIONS:

Heat Transfer Division, Lester, Pa.
Surface condensers, air ejectors, circulating and condensate pumps, priming ejectors, flash evaporators, water conversion plants— for installation on land; nuclear steam generators.
Large Turbine Division, Lester, Pa.
Large steam turbine generators—for installation on land.
Small Steam and Gas Turbine Division, Lester, Pa.
Gas turbines, small steam turbine generators, steam turbines for mechanical drive— for installation on land.

TRANSFORMER DIVISIONS:

Distribution Transformer Division, Sharon, Pa.
Dry and liquid immersed distribution transformers; current and potential instrument transformers; metering units.
Power Transformer Division, Sharon, Pa.
Power transformers; power regulators; reactors; self-contained unit substations.

ELECTRONIC COMPONENTS AND SPECIALTY PRODUCTS

ELECTRONIC TUBE DIVISION, Elmira, N.Y.
Electronic tubes of all kinds; power amplifiers, oscillators, pulse, rectifier, cathode ray tubes; television camera and picture tubes; miscellaneous special tubes—industrial and military.

INDUSTRIAL CERAMICS DIVISION, Derry, Pa.
Porcelain insulators; industrial ceramics.

MATERIALS MANUFACTURING DIVISION, Blairsville, Pa.
High temperature, permanent and soft magnetic alloys; nonfuel nuclear and refractory metals.

MICARTA DIVISIONS:

Decorative Micarta Division, Hampton, S.C.

ELECTRONIC COMPONENTS AND SPECIALTY PRODUCTS (CONTINUED)

Decorative Micarta sheets.
Industrial Micarta Division, Hampton, S.C.
Laminated fabricated plastics, Micarta shapes, sheets; insulating enamels and materials (Trafford, Pa.).

MOLECULAR ELECTRONICS DIVISION, Baltimore, Md., Newbury Park, Calif.
Epitaxial material; functional electronic blocks; integrated circuits.

NEW PRODUCTS TASK FORCE, Research and Development Center, Pittsburgh, Pa. (Churchill)
Cryogenic systems; scientific equipment (Edgewood Site); electronic capacitors (Irwin, Pa.)

SEMICONDUCTOR DIVISION, Youngwood, Pa.
Transistors; power rectifiers; diodes; solid state relays; thermoelectric devices; specialty devices.

SPECIALTY TRANSFORMER DIVISION, Greenville, Pa.
Cores; charging reactors; transducers; specialty transformers.

X-RAY DIVISION, Baltimore, Md.
Medical and industrial X-Ray apparatus, supplies and accessories; electro-medical products.

INDUSTRIAL

MOTOR DIVISIONS:

Motor and Gearing Division, Buffalo, N.Y.
Integral hp. motors for general industry and specific purpose applications; brakes; couplings; motocylinders; drives; gearing and gear motors; speed reducers.
Small Motor Division, Lima, Ohio
Small motors, general and special purpose for all types of domestic, appliance and industrial purposes.
Copper Wire Division, Buffalo, N.Y.
Copper and aluminum conductors.

CONTROL DIVISIONS:

General Control Division, Buffalo, N.Y.
Motor starters and controllers; special purpose control; control components; static control; pilot devices; power supplies.
Hagan Controls Corporation, Pittsburgh, Pa.
Control components; control devices; control systems for combustion, flow and level, pressure and differential pressure, temperature, and chemical systems.
Low Voltage Distribution Equipment Division, Pittsburgh, Pa.
Control centers; panelboards; switchboards; custom control assemblies; special switchgear; custom power centers; high voltage bus.

Exhibit 1—Continued

INDUSTRIAL (CONTINUED)

Standard Control Division, Beaver, Pa.
Controls for motors; starters, contactors, relays, pushbuttons; bus duct; circuit breakers; safety switches.

INDUSTRIAL EQUIPMENT AND SERVICE DIVISIONS:
Electric Service Division, Pittsburgh, Pa.
Field engineering; technical direction; installation and startup service; inspection and maintenance.

Homewood Division, Homewood, Pa.
Non-current apparatus and parts.

Industrial Electronics Division, Baltimore, Md.
Induction heating equipment; ultrasonic devices for cleaning and process equipment.

Repair Division, Pittsburgh, Pa.
Repair, rewind, rebuild, update, modernize electrical and mechanical apparatus, in the field or in one of 42 repair plants.

Transportation Equipment Division, East Pittsburgh, Pa.
Motors, generators, gearing and control for transit vehicles; transit expressway vehicles.

Westing-Arc Division, Buffalo, N.Y.
Electric arc welders, electrodes, accessories; brazing alloys.

INDUSTRIAL (CONTINUED)

INDUSTRIAL SYSTEMS DIVISIONS:
Computer Systems Division, Research and Development Center, Pittsburgh, Pa. (Churchill)
Digital computers.

Industry Systems Division, Research and Development Center, Pittsburgh, Pa. (Churchill)
Design and management for large scale systems; includes the Metals Industry Systems Department, the General Industries Systems Department and the Public Works Systems Department.

Systems Control Division, Buffalo, N.Y.
Mill and marine materials handling control systems; numerical control; packaged drives; power rectifiers; Semitron® rectifier equipment (East Pittsburgh).

THERMO KING CORPORATION, Minneapolis, Minn.
Air conditioning for automobiles, trucks, buses and other personnel vehicles. Refrigeration-heating for semi-trailers, trucks, van bodies and other produce carriers.

Source: "The World of Westinghouse," a company publication.

Exhibit 2

WESTINGHOUSE ELECTRIC CORPORATION (A)

Sample Listing of Westinghouse Products

Coolers, Portable, *Portable Appliance Division, Mansfield, Ohio*
Evaporative

Cores, *Specialty Transformer Division, Greenville, Pa.*
Cubex®
Hipersil®
Wescor®

Corona Detectors, *Distribution Apparatus Division, Bloomington, Ind.*

Couplings, Electric, *Large Rotating Apparatus Division, East Pittsburgh, Pa.*

Couplings, Flexible, *Motor and Gearing Division, Buffalo, N.Y.*

Cryogenic Systems, *Cryogenic Systems Department, Research and Development Center, Pittsburgh, Pa. (Churchill)*

Cryptographic Equipment, *Aerospace Division, Surface Division, Defense and Space Center, Baltimore, Md.*

Cutouts, Fuse, *Distribution Apparatus Division, Bloomington, Ind.*
Enclosed
Open

Data Processing and Display Equipment, Ground and Shipboard, *Surface Division, Defense and Space Center, Baltimore, Md.*

Data Processing Equipment, Airborne and Spaceborne, *Aerospace Division, Defense and Space Center, Baltimore, Md.*

Data Processing Systems, *Systems Operations, Defense and Space Center, Baltimore, Md.*

Data Transmission and Reception Equipment, Ground and Shipboard, *Surface Division, Defense and Space Center, Baltimore, Md.*

Decorative Micarta®, *Decorative Micarta Division, Hampton, S.C.*

Degaussing Equipment, Marine, *Marine Products Division, Sunnyvale, Calif.*

Dehumidifiers, *Dishwasher and Specialty Products Division, Columbus, Ohio*

Dehumidifiers, *Sturtevant Division, Hyde Park, Mass.*
Sprayed coil type

Digital Datalogers, *Power Control Division, Research and Development Center, Pittsburgh, Pa. (Churchill)*

Exhibit 2—Continued

Dishwashers, *Dishwasher and Specialty Products Division, Columbus, Ohio*
  Built-in
  Portable
Doors, Micarta-Clad, *Architectural System, Grand, Rapids, Mich.*
Drives, *Motor and Gearing Division, Buffalo, N.Y.*
  Mechanical adjustable speed (Adjusti-Flow®)
  Planer
Drives, Packaged, Electrical, Adjustable Speed, *Systems Control Division, Buffalo, N.Y.*
Dry Cleaners, Commercial, *Laundry Equipment Division, Mansfield, Ohio*
Dryers, *Laundry Equipment Division, Mansfield, Ohio*
  Commercial
  Domestic

Pushbuttons, *Standard Control Division, Beaver, Pa.*
  Heavy duty
  Oil tite
  Standard duty
Radars, Airborne and Spaceborne, *Aerospace Division, Defense and Space Center, Baltimore, Md.*
Radars, Ground and Shipboard, *Surface Division, Defense and Space Center, Baltimore, Md.*
Radios, *Television-Radio Division, Metuchen, N.J.*
  Clock
    AM, AM/FM, pushbutton
  Portable
    AM, AM/FM, transistor, shortwave
  Table
    AM, AM/FM, FM stereo
  Transceivers
Ranges, Electric, *Range Division, Mansfield, Ohio*
  Built-in
    Cooking platforms
    Electronic
    Ovens
  Free standing
    Conventional
    Eye-level ovens
Reactors, *Power Transformer Division, Sharon, Pa.*
  Current limiting
    CL, oil-immersed and dry type
    MSP, dry type
  Shunt, oil-immersed and dry type
Reactors, Charging, *Specialty Transformer Division, Greenville, Pa.*

Reactors, Saturable Core, *Distribution Transformer Division, Sharon, Pa.*
Reclosers, *Distribution Apparatus Division, Bloomington, Ind.*
Reconnaissance Equipment, Airborne and Spaceborne, *Aerospace Division, Defense and Space Center, Baltimore, Md.*
Reconnaissance Systems, *Systems Operations, Defense and Space Center, Baltimore, Md.*
Rectifier Assemblies, *Semiconductor Division, Youngwood, Pa.*
  High voltage
  Standard
Rectifier Diodes, Silicon, *Semiconductor Division, Youngwood, Pa.*
  Controlled avalanche
  Fast recovery
  "O.E.M." line
  Standard
Rectifier Equipment, Semitron®, *Rectifier Product Group (Systems Control), East Pittsburgh, Pa.*

Self-Lubricating Bearing Materials, *Materials Manufacturing Division, Blairsville, Pa.*
Service, Electric, *Electric Service Division, Pittsburgh, Pa.*
  (Available at all Westinghouse sales locations)
  Field engineering services
  Inspection, maintenance and repair service
  Starting service on apparatus and systems
  Technical direction and advice
Service, Steam, *Steam Divisions Service Department, Lester, Pa.*
  Complete installation service, maintenance service, repair service and modernization programs for all products marketed by the Steam Divisions, including generators, exciters and regulators sold with turbines and waterwheel generators marketed by Large Rotating Apparatus Division.
Silicon Rectifier, *Rectifier Product Group (Systems Control), East Pittsburgh, Pa.*
  Subassemblies for replacing Ignitron tubes
Sockets and Mountings, Meter, *Meter Division, Raleigh, N.C.*
Sonar, *Underseas Division, Defense and Space Center, Baltimore, Md.*
Space Propulsion Concepts, *Astronuclear Laboratory, Large, Pa.*
Space Systems, *Systems Operations, Defense and Space Center, Baltimore, Md.*
  Electrical
  Mechanical
Specialty Devices, *Semiconductor Division, Youngwood, Pa.*

Exhibit 2—Continued

Speed Reducers, *Motor and Gearing Division, Buffalo, N.Y.*
Helical
Moduline®
Shaft
Worm gear

Spot Film Devices, X-Ray, *X-Ray Division, Baltimore, Md.*

Starters, Electric Motor, *Standard Control Division, Beaver, Pa.*
Magnetic
Manual

Steam Generators, Marine, *Marine Products Division, Sunnyvale Calif.*

Steam Generators, Nuclear, *Heat Transfer Division, Lester, Pa.*

Steam Plant Automation Systems, *Power Control Division, Research and Development Center, Pittsburgh, Pa. (Churchill)*

Steam Plant Performance Computer Systems, *Power Control Division, Research and Development Center, Pittsburgh, Pa. (Churchill)*

Steam Turbine Generators, Land, *Large Turbine Division, Lester, Pa.*
20,000 to 1,000,000 kw

Steam Turbine Generators, Land, *Small Steam and Gas Turbine Division, Lester, Pa.*
20 to 15,625 kw

Source: "The World of Westinghouse," a company publication.

Westinghouse Electric Corporation (B₁)

ASSUME that you are the general manager of a product group with total sales of about $400 million in 1964. (See Exhibit 1, Westinghouse (A), for brief descriptions of typical product groups and divisions.)

Assume that each division manager reports directly to you. Profit objectives are established each year by corporate officers for your group as a whole, and by you and your division managers for the divisions in your group. A full set of financial statements is prepared by each division in your group. Your performance, and the performance of the division manager, is evaluated to a considerable extent each year on performance with respect to the objectives established.

While attending a management seminar made up of division managers and group managers from a number of large, diversified companies, you have been asked to indicate the degree of delegation you feel is appropriate in your organization for a number of problem situations. The "Delegation Questionnaire"[1] is reproduced as Exhibit 1. In order to facilitate comparisons among companies, you also have been asked to assume, for your company, that:

1. Business conditions have been fairly good, and are expected to continue to be favorable;
2. All of your divisions have been profitable, although generally not as profitable as desired by corporate management;
3. Each division has had at least one major product line that has shown losses, but you stand a fairly good chance of meeting your profit goals for the group this year; and
4. You have held your job for some time, and each of the division managers in your group has been in his job at least three years.

---

[1] Source of delegation questionnaire and problem situation: Mr. William Nesbitt, Director, Organization Planning, Westinghouse Electric Corporation.

Exhibit 1 —Westinghouse Electric Corporation (B₁)
Delegation Questionnaire

As a group general manager you would expect your division managers to:	See legend below for detailed explanation of headings:					
	Take action		Advise you		Provide information	
Problem requiring action	A	B	C	D	E	F

1. Hire a replacement for the division manager's secretary who is leaving.
2. Authorize a temporary $50,000 increase in division raw material inventory in anticipation of a possible steel strike.
3. Establish next month's manufacturing schedule for the division, at an increased level which will require the hiring of two additional people in the factory.
4. Establish next month's manufacturing schedule, at a substantially higher level which will require the addition of 50 people in the factory.
5. Pass final approval on the design of a new product, and authorize work to start on production tooling.
6. Postpone the scheduled introduction of a new model by 45 days, and authorize a crash program estimated to cost $100,000 which will modify the design and permit incorporation of a recently developed design feature.
7. Establish the list price of a major product line, which in the aggregate amounts to 30% of division volume.
8. Increase the price of an existing product line by 4%, to attempt to recover cost increases that have taken place in material and labor; this will place the price above the competitive level.
9. One product line has an extremely seasonal pattern, with all sales occurring in the summer. Authorize the production schedule for the year, which will create a $6 million shipping stock of this product at the time of its peak selling season.
10. Make a change in the division inventory standards, which will reduce field shipping stocks but increase factory work-in-process inventory, maintaining the same total investment.
11. Increase the investment in inventory on a different product by approximately $1 million, because the sales department feels that they can get more sales if they have greater product availability.
12. Initiate a computer activity, estimated to cost $1 million for feasibility study and programming, and which will require a commitment for a computer that will ultimately cost $200,000 per year.
13. Introduce a new system into the factory that is recognized to have a 20% chance of precipitating strong opposition, possibly leading to a strike on the part of the union.
14. Change advertising program for the division, reducing magazine advertising, increasing direct mail and trade show promotional activities.
15. Authorize the manager of manufacturing to increase the methods and industrial engineering activity and reduce the size of the quality control department, maintaining the same total manufacturing expense.
16. Authorize the marketing manager to increase the number of salesmen in the field, reduce the number of manufacturing engineers by a corresponding amount to maintain the same total cost.
17. Select the replacement for the manufacturing superintendent who will retire soon.
18. Take the superintendent off the job for poor performance; replace him with another man now serving as a general foreman.
19. Select the replacement for the general foreman position now open.
20. Increase the number of general foremen positions in the division from four to six. Select the individuals to fill the new positions.
21. Authorize an 8% salary increase for the manufacturing superintendent, allowed for in the budget and within the rate range for the job.
22. Authorize an 8% salary increase for the division sales manager, allowed for in the budget and within the rate range.
23. Authorize the factory to work overtime two Saturdays next month to reduce the backlog of overdue orders.
24. Increase the job classification and rate range for the engineering manager, to reflect the growth of his department and the increased responsibility of his position.
25. Authorize a change in job classification for the six general foremen positions, as a result of changes in their responsibility.
26. Cancel two engineering development projects included in this year's program, and concentrate the $250,000 effort on a new development believed to have real commercial potential, identified as a result of research performed in the corporate research center.

Explanation of Headings:
A. Take action without any contact with you.
B. Take action; mention the action taken later if he happens to see you.
C. Advise you in advance of the action he intends to take; act unless you tell him not to.
D. Advise you in advance of the action he would like to take; delay action until you give him approval.
E. Give you an analysis of the alternative actions possible, with their merits and disadvantages, supporting his choice of the one he recommends for your approval.
F. Give you as many facts about the case as possible so you can identify alternatives and select the action you want to be taken.

Westinghouse Electric Corporation (B₂)

ASSUME that you are the manager of a division with total sales of about $60 million in 1964. Your division is a part of a product group which accounted for about $400 million in sales in 1964. (See Exhibit 1, p. 387 for brief descriptions of typical product groups and divisions.)

Assume that you and all of the other division managers in your group report directly to the group general manager. Profit objectives are established each year by corporate officers for your group as a whole, and by you and your group general manager for your division. A full set of financial statements is prepared by each division in the group. Your performance, and the performance of your group general manager, is evaluated to a considerable extent each year on performance with respect to the objectives established.

While attending a management seminar made up of division managers and group general managers from a number of large, diversified companies, you have been asked to indicate the degree of delegation you feel is appropriate in your organization for a number of problem situations. The "Delegation Questionnaire"[1] is reproduced as Exhibit 1. In order to facilitate comparisons among companies, you also have been asked to assume, for your company, that:

1. Business conditions have been fairly good, and are expected to continue to be favorable;
2. All of the divisions in your group have been profitable, although generally not as profitable as desired by corporate management;
3. Each division, including yours, has had at least one major product line that has shown losses;
4. You feel that you have a reasonable chance of meeting your division profit goals for the year;
5. Your group general manager has said that the group will probably meet its profit goals for the year "if everyone comes through";
6. You have held your job for some time, and the group general manager as well as the other division managers have all been in their jobs for at least three years.

---

[1] Source of delegation questionnaire and problem situation: Mr. William Nesbitt, Director, Organization Planning, Westinghouse Electric Corporation.

Exhibit 1 —WESTINGHOUSE ELECTRIC CORPORATION (B₂)

Delegation Questionnaire

As a division manager, you would:

SEE LEGEND BELOW FOR DETAILED EXPLANATION OF HEADINGS:

Problem requiring action	Take action		Advise group manager		Inform group manager	
	A	B	C	D	E	F

1. Hire a replacement for the division manager's secretary who is leaving.
2. Authorize a temporary $50,000 increase in division raw material inventory in anticipation of a possible steel strike.
3. Establish next month's manufacturing schedule for the division, at an increased level which will require the hiring of two additional people in the factory.
4. Establish next month's manufacturing schedule, at a substantially higher level which will require the addition of 50 people in the factory.
5. Pass final approval on the design of a new product, and authorize work to start on production tooling.
6. Postpone the scheduled introduction of a new model by 45 days, and authorize a crash program estimated to cost $100,000 which will modify the design and permit incorporation of a recently developed design feature.
7. Establish the list price of a major product line, which in the aggregate amounts to 30% of division volume.
8. Increase the price of an existing product line by 4%, to attempt to recover cost increases that have taken place in material and labor; this will place the price above the competitive level.
9. One product line has an extremely seasonal pattern, with all sales occurring in the summer. Authorize the production schedule for the year, which will create a $6 million shipping stock of this product at the time of its peak selling season.
10. Make a change in the division inventory standards, which will reduce field shipping stocks but increase factory work-in-process inventory, maintaining the same total investment.
11. Increase the investment in inventory on a different product by approximately $1 million, because the sales department feels that they can get more sales if they have greater product availability.
12. Initiate a computer activity, estimated to cost $1 million for feasibility study and programming, and which will require a commitment for a computer that will ultimately cost $200,000 per year.
13. Introduce a new system into the factory that is recognized to have a 20% chance of precipitating strong opposition, possibly leading to a strike on the part of the union.
14. Change advertising program for the division, reducing magazine advertising, increasing direct mail and trade show promotional activities.
15. Authorize the manager of manufacturing to increase the methods and industrial engineering activity and reduce the size of the quality control department, maintaining the same total manufacturing expense.
16. Authorize the marketing manager to increase the number of salesmen in the field, reduce the number of manufacturing engineers by a corresponding amount to maintain the same total cost.
17. Select the replacement for the manufacturing superintendent who will retire soon.
18. Take the superintendent off the job for poor performance; replace him with another man now serving as a general foreman.
19. Select the replacement for the general foreman position now open.
20. Increase the number of general foremen positions in the division from four to six. Select the individuals to fill the new positions.
21. Authorize an 8% salary increase for the manufacturing superintendent, allowed for in the budget and within the rate range for the job.
22. Authorize an 8% salary increase for the division sales manager, allowed for in the budget and within the rate range.
23. Authorize the factory to work overtime two Saturdays next month to reduce the backlog of overdue orders.
24. Increase the job classification and rate range for the engineering manager, to reflect the growth of his department and the increased responsibility of his position.
25. Authorize a change in job classification for the six general foremen positions, as a result of changes in their responsibility.
26. Cancel two engineering development projects included in this year's program, and concentrate the $250,000 effort on a new development believed to have real commercial potential, identified as a result of research performed in the corporate research center.

Explanation of Headings:
    A. Take action without contacting group general manager.
    B. Take action; mention action later if you happen to see the group general manager.
    C. Advise group general manager in advance of action you intend to take; act unless he tells you not to.
    D. Advise group general manager in advance of action you would like to take; delay action until he gives you approval.
    E. Give the group general manager an analysis of the alternative actions possible, with their merits and disadvantages, supporting your choice of the one you recommend for his approval.
    F. Give the group general manager as many facts about the case as possible so that he can identify alternatives and select the action he wants taken.

PART IV

Measuring, Controlling, and Motivating
Administrative Personnel

Breitman & Company (A)

I. INTRODUCTION

"YOU OUGHT TO GET a case from my uncle, Judson Fischer, vice-president of Breitman & Company," a second-year student at the Harvard Business School suggested in early 1952 to Mr. John Williams, a case writer at the School. "The company is in New York and makes women's belts and handbags. It's a highly successful business, and its executives are wonderful people. Neither of the two partners who own the business, however, is much interested in management. Felix Breitman, the president, is primarily a designer, and there's no question that his skill there has a lot to do with the company's success. Jud, my uncle, has the title of vice-president, but he really is the one who runs most of the actual operations. He's primarily a salesman, though, not an administrator; and I suspect that if you look into the matter, you may well find that as the company has grown, there has been inadequate attention to production and to the use of control and cost information on the part of the two partners.

"I think you'd find them very receptive to giving you a case. For several years my uncle's lawyer, Irving Lasser, has been telling Jud that the company badly needs 'more and better administration,' and I suspect Jud would welcome an outsider's look at the situation, even if you don't give him any advice."

As an outgrowth of this conversation, the nephew made arrangements for Mr. Williams to see Mr. Fischer on Monday morning, March 15, 1952, about the possibility of a case on Breitman.

II. MR. WILLIAMS' FIRST DAY WITH THE COMPANY

Mr. Williams arrived at 10:35 A.M. on the appointed day for his first interview with Mr. Fischer in the company showroom and headquarters, on the sixth floor of a "loft"-type building, 31 East 32d Street, New York, New York. Mr. Fischer's "office" consisted of a desk and a couch in one corner of the colorfully decorated L-shaped showroom. After some discussion about how Mr. Fischer's nephew was doing at the Business School, Mr. Fischer turned to the question of the case.

We're very glad to have you study our operation. Irving Lasser—you know who he is?—thinks we don't know how to run this business, but we've been pretty successful. If this isn't going to take too much of my time, we'll be delighted to tell you anything you want to know. What is it you'd like to know about us?

WILLIAMS: Well, Mr. Fischer, before we start, I should explain that in letting us go ahead, you are in effect making a contribution to the Harvard Business School, without getting anything directly in return. Naturally, you will see whatever we write up, but I won't attempt to offer any direct advice.

FISCHER: Yes, I understand that, but we still think this will be of great value to us.

WILLIAMS: Well, at least to get started, I'd like to learn a little bit about your products, whatever figures you have to show how you've done sales- and profitwise, who the members of your executive staff are, and something generally about how you operate.

FISCHER: Well, to begin with, this is a young business—about 13 to 15 years old. I came in 10 or 11 years ago, and since then sales have jumped from $300,000 to over $5,000,000. Would you like some more figures? (*He pulls out some 5″ × 8″ catalogue cards.*) In 1948 we did $2,500,000; 1949, $3,200,-000; 1950, $4,000,000; 1951, $5,000,000. That last figure isn't quite accurate— let me get Miss Voss, the office manager, in here. (*He calls Miss Voss on the phone, asking her to come in.*) During the time I've been here, my interest in the business has increased from $25,000 to over $300,000, but we still don't really have enough capital.

Good morning, Miss Voss. This is Mr. Williams, who's going to make a study of Breitman & Company. (*The two exchange greetings.*) Miss Voss, the latest figure on 1951 is off by $100,000. Is that right?

MISS VOSS: Yes, Mr. Fischer.

FISCHER: How do I correct the monthly figures?

MISS VOSS: Well, I think the simplest way, since these are rough, would be to add $10,000 to each of 10 months. (*She corrects the card and remains seated in the office during the remainder of the interview.*)

FISCHER: To continue, let's start with the bag department, headed by Sidney Teplow. Would you like to know what he makes? He's our highest-priced executive, making $35,000, and does $2,000,000 worth of business in fabric bags. You'll want to visit our 14th Street factory, which he runs. He also controls five contractors, who make bags for us. Shall I give you the rest of the people who work for him?

WILLIAMS: Yes, please.

FISCHER: We've recently hired a designer who's making $10,000. There's also an assistant in buying—he's paid $10,000; the production manager, $10,000; and the man who ships handbags and handles raw materials, $7,000.

We also buy straw bags from Rostyn Brothers, one of our large contractors, run by three partners whom, incidentally, we were put in touch with by the millinery union. They operate on about $100,000 to $150,000 of capital.

Another part of our business is the Highline Corporation in Dandridge, Tennessee. Mr. Breitman and I own the stock of that, and I think now we were very foolish in opening it. We make there washable bags of scrap nylon and acetate. Our general manager there is paid $7,800 a year. Last year we sold $600,000 worth of handbags from Dandridge.

Now as to the belt business. Have you met Byron Steinmetz, our belt sales manager? (*Mr. Steinmetz is called on the telephone, comes in, is introduced to Mr. Williams, and leaves to return to a buyer with whom he has been working.*) We sold $2,750,000 worth of belts last year, which is a lot for this business. Our second competitor did only about a million dollars volume.

The secret of our success is Mr. Breitman, just an ordinary guy who happens to have a genius in this design field. Some people will tell you you can buy talent. I say "nuts!" The scarcest commodity in this business is talent.

You want to know something about our problems—I can very quickly tell you about our biggest problem—the one that has given my partner ulcers and makes me so nervous I have to take sleeping pills at night. This is a style business—we live on the special designs Mr. Breitman creates, and because our customers would like us to ship their orders yesterday, we have to maintain large inventories. The trouble is, that inventory could become worthless tomorrow—we couldn't even get 10 cents on the dollar on it—and we could be forced out of business tomorrow. As I told you, we're undercapitalized, and if we wake up tomorrow with a half-million dollars of worthless inventory, we'd be out of business. If you want something to worry about, tell us what to do about that.

Going back to Mr. Breitman and the belt business, one of our most successful lines—and one on which we have no competition—is the Breitweave line, a novelty fabric belt which Mr. Breitman designed. As a matter of fact, he worked with the yarn manufacturers to design a new yarn and worked out a new way of making braid. This originally started out as something primarily for the Southern market, but it's now a big thing in our summer line.

You might be interested in this "throwaway" which describes these belts. This, incidentally, is the only kind of advertising we do—to prepare these leaflets to be mailed out as enclosures by our customers. Last year we spent $50,000 on this kind of advertising. Regular fashion advertising is no good in this business—it just doesn't work in the belt business.

Is this the kind of thing that interests you?

WILLIAMS: Yes, certainly.

FISCHER: Well, to get back to the belt business. As I said, Byron Steinmetz is the sales manager of the belt department. We hired him from a competitive organization four years ago. Fred Apfel is our production man—you'll want to talk with him. He's paid $10,000. Our Breitweave belts are made in our factory on 25th Street, run by Mrs. Long, who is our oldest employee in point of service. You'll probably want to visit that factory. We sell roughly $600,000 a year in the Breitweave belt line. We also sell a line of metal belts, doing about

$250,000 a year, and leather belts—about the same. In addition to our own factory, we also have seven contractors who make belts for us. All our belts, though, are shipped from our stockrooms on this floor. You'll want to talk with Mr. Harry Block, who is responsible for shipping all our belts. Our bags, incidentally, all go out from the 14th Street factory.

You've met Miss Voss, our office manager. You'll probably also want to talk with our accountant, Mr. Morris Firth, and Mr. Irving Lasser, our attorney.

I should also mention that we have ten salesmen, all over the country, all on a commission basis. If you want to help us, you might tell us why our New York salesman hasn't been able to get our belts into ———— and ———— [New York City department stores].

Miss Voss, is there anything else you think Mr. Williams should know about?

MISS VOSS: Well, Mr. Fischer, I think Mr. Williams might be interested in knowing how important your own abilities are to Breitman & Company.

FISCHER (*laughing*): Oh, come now, Miss Voss!

MISS VOSS: I mean that sincerely, Mr. Fischer. (*To Mr. Williams*) Mr. Fischer is a marvelous person for this business. He knows the line, he has a sense of fashion, a sense of timing, and he knows the merchandise of the stores—all of which are very vital.

FISCHER (*laughing*): Well, that's all very flattering, Miss Voss, but I'm sure Mr. Williams knows an exaggeration when he sees it.

MISS VOSS: No, really, Mr. Fischer, I mean it.

FISCHER: Well, Mr. Williams, do you at this point have any questions?

Mr. Williams asked if he might restate what he had written down to be sure he had it correct. In the process he also learned that the company had another activity—French Lines, a one-man organization that made high-priced belts in very limited quantities; that Breitman's general line of merchandise was considered medium-priced; that the company in 1952 sold to over 5,000 accounts all over the United States, including department stores, specialty stores, and a variety of specialized retail outlets. He also learned that in addition to the people mentioned by Mr. Fischer originally, the executive group included Mr. Frank Rich, sales manager of the handbag department, who had been hired within the last six months; two girls who worked in the showroom; and Mickey, Simon, and Joe, three men in their twenties who performed "a variety of jobs." (See Exhibit 1.)

Mr. Fischer also indicated his belief that selling was the most important part of the business:

Anyone can manufacture belts and bags, and I don't even claim that our merchandise is necessarily any better quality than our competitors'. It's the job of selling that's most important. I'm no big-shot executive, and I don't know all there is to know about business or management, but I do know something about how to sell, which is one of the reasons we've been so successful.

On his first visit, Mr. Williams had a short interview with Mr. Breitman, who indicated he was quite busy getting ready for a trip to Japan:

We're delighted to have you work with us, and I think you'll enjoy your visits because we think we have a nice bunch of people working here. It may be that you'll come up with something in our methods to indicate that they aren't all they should be, and you may be very helpful by taking a look at them. Another question that we'd like the answer to is whether or not it's smart for us to keep on growing, or whether we have any choice in the matter.

I imagine you'll want to spend more time with Judson and with the rest of our people than you will with me, but don't hesitate to see me at any time you have any questions. I've learned, though, that the less I have to do with the business end of things, the better they work out.

On his first day Mr. Williams was served lunch at Mr. Fischer's desk, together with Miss Voss and Mr. Fischer, with whom he discussed the possibility of looking over the company records. Miss Voss indicated that her office was primarily a record-keeping operation—that the company accountants compiled all the regular statements. She gave Mr. Williams a copy of the latest balance sheet but told him that any other financial records would have to be obtained from the accountants:

We don't have enough space to store any records here that we don't have to keep.

Mr. Fischer added that space was one of Breitman's major problems:

You'll see a lot of confusion here which results from the fact that we're too crowded. The difficulty is that this building is *the* location to have a showroom, and we can't get any more space here. We could move our belt stock room elsewhere, but I like to be able to have the merchandise right here to show customers. I think it really helps our business to have it here. You can take a buyer out back, and if she sees the merchandise there, she's more likely to place an order.

Mr. Williams learned from a brief visit with Mr. Apfel that, although the latter felt the company had no major problems facing it, he thought that Mr. Williams might be interested in taking a look at the way the company was organized:

I've been taking a course in organization and management at N.Y.U., and I know you ought to have better definitions of responsibilities than we have here. One of these days I'm going to have to have a showdown with the boss on this matter. I'm particularly referring to the way Mr. Fischer works with Harry Block and me. As a matter of fact, things are now a lot better than they were

Exhibit 1

BREITMAN & COMPANY

Company Personnel

32D STREET

Location	No. of People	Name	Title or Duties	Approx. Age
President's office....	1	*Felix Breitman*	*President, Treasurer*	50
Showroom.........	1	*Judson Fischer*	*Vice-President*	50
	1	*Byron Steinmetz*	*Belt Sales Manager*	45
	1	*Frank Rich*	*Bag Sales Manager*	45
	1	*	Assistant to Mr. Steinmetz-Advertising	35
				..
	1	*	Saleswoman	35
	12†	*	Salesmen	25–50
	1	*	Telephone Operator	..
Bookkeeping Department........	1	*Muriel Voss*	*Office Manager*	30
	2	*	Stenographers	..
	20	*	Clerks, Bookkeepers	..
Order Department..	1	*Fred Apfel*	*Belt Production Manager*	35
	1	*Harry Block*	*Belt Shipping Manager*	45
	1	*Mickey*	*Order Processing*	25
	1	*	Account-Card Supervisor	..
	4	*	Account-Card Clerks	..
	2	*	Billers	..
Belt Storage Area...	1	*Joe*	*Assistant to Mr. Breitman*	25
	1	*Simon*	*Outside Calls, Misc. Duties*	25
	5	*	Order Pickers	..
	3	*	Lay-away Clerks	..
	1	*	Supervisor, Receiving Department	..
	25	*	Receiving Department Employees	..
	6	*	Shipping Clerks	..
	5	*	Miscellaneous Employees	..
Total at 32d Street..	99			

* Names given only for people mentioned by name in the case.
† Most salesmen usually traveling away from office.

when Harry first came in here. Mr. Fischer has a habit, though, of wanting something done right away—right now, for example, I'm preparing a report on our stocks of aluminum belts—and he's likely to ask the first person he can get ahold of to take care of it for him.

Mr. Williams spent much of his first day sitting in Mr. Fischer's office or waiting in the showroom while Mr. Fischer talked on the telephone, discussed problems with his people, or talked with customers. It seemed to Mr. Williams that many of the impressions he gained that day were relevant to his interest in the company, particularly if, in fact, Monday was a relatively slow day, as Mr. Fischer had indicated. Breitman & Company appeared a "beehive" of activity. After ten o'clock in

Exhibit 1—Continued

BREITMAN & COMPANY

Company Personnel

14TH STREET

Location	No. of People	Name	Title or Duties	Approx. Age
Office............	1	*Sidney Teplow*	*Bag Department Manager*	55
	1	*	Bag Production Manager	35
	1	*	Bag Designer	40
	3	*	Clerks	..
Factory..........	1	*	Factory Superintendent	30
	3	*	Cutters	..
	21	*	Pasters	..
	24	*	Sewing-Machine Operators	..
	13	*	Assemblers	..
	4	*	Inspectors	..
	1	*	Shipping and Receiving Superintendent	55
	2	*	Billers	..
	2	*	Receiving Clerks	..
	6	*	Shipping Clerks	..
Total at 14th Street.	83			

25TH STREET

Location	No. of People	Name	Title or Duties	Approx. Age
Factory..........	1	*Mrs. Long*	*Factory Superintendent*	30
	1	*	Cutter	..
	2	*	Crocheters	..
	16	*	Sewing-Machine Operators	..
	2	*	Tackers	..
	4	*	Trimmers	..
	9	*	Miscellaneous Factory Workers	..
	1	*	Clerk	..
Total at 25th Street.	36			

OTHERS MENTIONED IN CASE

Name	Position
Irving Lasser............................*Lawyer*
Morris Firth..........................*Accountant*
Larry Goodman.........................*Former Partner*
Jake Levy.............................*Former Partner*

the morning the showroom nearly always contained at least half-a-dozen buyers, looking at sample bags and belts, and being waited on by someone from the Breitman organization. The call bell, controlled by the telephone operator, seemed to be in continual operation, necessitated by the fact that the people being called appeared to be away from their desks as much of the time as they were there. Mr. Williams observed that Mr. Fischer especially seemed to be engaged in a continuing stream of activity—talking to buyers, taking orders over the phone, reviewing orders as they came in, talking to his people about their particular problems, and checking up on orders.

At the end of his first day, Mr. Williams concluded that a study of Breitman & Company might well make an interesting case and that at least it would be worth his while to follow up the lead. At Mr. Fischer's suggestion, Mr. Williams also made arrangements to see the company's accountant, Mr. Morris Firth, before visiting the company again. Mr. Fischer also expressed interest in having Mr. Williams meet Mr. Lasser at an early date and promised to schedule such an interview whenever Mr. Williams was ready.

Following a visit with Mr. Firth during the last week in March, Mr. Williams made the definite decision to go ahead with a case. Over the next several months, therefore, he spent an aggregate of approximately 20 working days with various people in the Breitman organization. During much of this time he was unable to get the undivided attention of the people he wished to see, but this fact gave him the opportunity to watch what was going on. At the end of his stay with the company he felt he had become sufficiently "part of the scenery" so that he had a rough "feel for" how the Breitman organization worked.

III. INFORMATION OBTAINED FROM THE ACCOUNTANT

Mr. Williams' initial interview with Mr. Firth in the latter's office lasted a full day, and at Mr. Firth's suggestion, Mr. Williams returned again several weeks later to follow up the topics discussed during the first visit. Mr. Firth gave Mr. Williams the balance sheets, income statements, and ratio information shown in Exhibits 2–5. He also provided most of the data on the company history, summarized below, as well as a statement about the relationship between his accounting firm and the company. Mr. Firth also volunteered a number of comments about Breitman & Company's problems, which are summarized below.

Company History. Breitman & Company was established in 1937 by Mr. Felix Breitman and Mr. Jake Levy, both of whom made an initial investment of $4,000. When the firm started, it made only women's novelty fabric belts, which it sold to local department and retail stores, and the two partners constituted the entire management group. They personally designed the merchandise, sold it, supervised production and purchasing, and with the aid of a bookkeeper kept the records. As sales grew from $69,000 the first year to over $200,000 a year in 1940–41, Mr. Levy invited Mr. Fischer, then selling in the

Exhibit 2

BREITMAN & COMPANY

Comparative Balance Sheets, 1938–51

(Thousands of Dollars)

Assets	1938*	1939*	1940*	1941*	1942*	1943*	1944*	1945*	1946*	1947*	1948†	1949†	1950†	1951†
Cash	$0.6	$2.6	$7.4	$7.6	$10.2	$7.6	$24.7	$33.1	$47.7	$91.9	$22.1	$53.4	$141.6	$63.0
Notes and Accounts Receivable	8.7	16.4	30.4	43.1	122.9	91.4	96.1	174.3	226.1	236.0	224.2	287.4	336.8	595.5
Inventories	2.3	2.7	3.8	4.1	73.1	96.8	96.0	135.2	233.8	246.0	250.2	103.5	126.2	265.7
Merchandise at Contractors													168.4	231.1
Current Assets	$11.6	$21.7	$41.6	$54.8	$206.2	$195.8	$216.8	$342.6	$507.6	$573.9	$496.5	$444.3	$773.0	$1,155.3
Treasury Stock	$2.2	$2.6	$3.5	$6.6	$17.0	$17.9	$28.2	$52.0	$61.1	$64.1	$70.6	$65.0	$65.0	$65.0
Machinery and Equipment	0.1	0.1	0.3	0.7	1.0	2.7	1.6	12.7	7.5	7.1	13.0	70.8	75.2	80.6
Other Assets												33.3	31.4	39.5
Fixed Assets	$2.3	$2.7	$3.8	$7.3	$18.0	$20.6	$29.8	$64.7	$68.6	$71.2	$83.6	$169.1	$171.6	$185.1
Total Assets	$13.9	$24.4	$45.4	$62.1	$224.2	$216.4	$246.6	$407.3	$576.2	$645.1	$580.1	$613.4	$944.6	$1,340.4
Accounts Payable	$2.7	$5.5	$15.3	$20.7	$78.5	$75.6	$54.0	$71.7	$191.2	$121.3	$144.0	$130.8	$114.2	$209.2
Notes Payable			5.0	7.0	45.0		50.0	100.0	125.0	200.0	100.0	75.0	350.0	450.0
Accrued Expenses	1.2	0.9	3.0	3.9	12.3	25.8	6.0	29.6	26.4	60.7	57.6	65.9	85.5	171.6
Other Liabilities	5.6	5.0			13.5	3.2	4.6	5.6	18.1	30.4	56.9	45.8	39.9	104.5
Officers' Loans to Business	0.1		0.6	1.7		5.5								
Corporate Income Tax Liability		1.0						100.0	100.0	100.0				
Current Liabilities	$9.6	$12.4	$23.9	$33.3	$149.3	$110.1	$114.6	$306.9	$460.7	$512.4	$358.5	$317.5	$589.6	$935.3
Capital Stock—Common	$4.0	$7.4	$12.6	$12.6	$45.0	$66.1	$132.0	$100.4	$115.5	$115.2	$115.2	$115.2	$115.2	$115.2
Earned Surplus	0.3	4.6	8.9	16.2	29.9	40.2				17.5	106.4	180.7	239.8	289.9
Total Capital	$4.3	$12.0	$21.5	$28.8	$74.9	$106.3	$132.0	$100.4	$115.5	$132.7	$221.6	$295.9	$355.0	$405.1
Total Liabilities and Capital	$13.9	$24.4	$45.4	$62.1	$224.2	$216.4	$246.6	$407.3	$576.2	$645.1	$580.1	$613.4	$944.6	$1,340.4

* 1938–47, year ending April 30.
† 1948–51, year ending February 28 or 29.
Source: Records furnished by accountant.

Exhibit 3

BREITMAN & COMPANY*

Comparative Profit and Loss Statements, 1938–52

(Thousands of Dollars)

	1938†	1939†	1940†	1941†	1942†	1943†
Net Sales	$69.1	$100.6	$169.5	$239.3	$803.4	$870.2
Less Cost of Goods Sold	49.1	60.6	120.2	189.6	649.4	725.9
Gross Profit from Sales	$24.9	$ 40.2	$ 49.3	$ 49.7	$154.0	$144.3
Commissions—Handbag					29.1	29.9
Total Income	$24.9	$ 40.2	$ 49.3	$ 49.7	$183.1	$174.2

Deductions

	1938†	1939†	1940†	1941†	1942†	1943†
Compensation of Officers	$ 6.7	$ 16.2	$ 16.8	$ 23.0	$ 39.7	$ 31.8
Salaries and Wages	10.3	11.5	14.2	15.1	22.6	20.6
Rent	1.5	1.6	2.4	2.6	5.7	6.6
Repairs						
Bad Debts	0.1		0.3	0.2	0.2	0.2
Interest	1.2	0.1	0.1	§	0.9	0.1
Taxes (Other than Federal Income)	0.7	1.4	3.2	2.5	6.9	7.0
Contributions					0.4	1.3
Depreciation	0.2	0.3	0.4	0.5	2.1	2.7
Commissions					53.1	52.7
Traveling and Selling	0.6		2.4	2.5	8.9	7.7
Advertising and Promotion					2.2	2.8
Packing and Shipping—Freight and Cartage					3.1	2.4
Stationery and Postage	1.2				4.2	3.0
Legal and Professional	0.4	0.4	0.7	0.9	2.4	2.1
Insurance—Life					1.0	1.0
Other	0.2	0.7	0.5	0.5	1.1	1.9
Light and Power					1.2	1.0
Telephone and Telegraph	0.4	0.4	0.6	0.8	1.1	0.8
Credit and Association						0.7
Designing Expense and Sample Making						
Factory Expense					0.8	
California Office Expense						
Chicago Office Expense						
Sundry Expense	1.1	2.2	2.8	2.2	6.4	2.6
Health and Vacation Fund						
Belt and Bag Corrugated Boxes						
Auto Expense						
Hospitalization						
Total Deductions	$24.6	$ 34.8	$ 44.4	$ 40.8	$164.0	$149.0
Net Income	$ 0.3	$ 5.4	$ 4.9	$ 8.9	$ 19.1	$ 25.2
Federal Income and Excess Profits Tax	§	1.1	0.6	1.6	5.4	4.9
Net Income after Taxes	$ 0.3	$ 4.3	$ 4.3	$ 7.3	$ 13.7	$ 10.3
Surplus—Beginning of Year		$ 0.3	$ 4.6	$ 8.9	$ 16.2	$ 29.9
Surplus—End of Year	$ 0.3	$ 4.6	$ 8.9	$ 16.2	$ 29.9	$ 40.2

* Operated as corporation, April 30, 1937—November 30, 1942; as partnership, November 30, 1942—February 14, 1946; as corporation after February 14, 1946.
† Year ending April 30.
‡ Year ending February 28 or 29.
§ Less than $50.
‖ Includes partners' personal taxes on income.
Source: Records furnished by accountant.

BREITMAN & COMPANY (A)

Exhibit 3—Continued

BREITMAN & COMPANY

Comparative Profit and Loss Statements, 1938–52

(Thousands of Dollars)

1944†	1945†	1946†	1947†	1948‡	1949‡	1950‡	1951‡
$1,428.9	$1,440.1	$1,810.5	$2,394.9	$2,218.6	$2,508.9	$3,146.8	$4,194.5
1,020.7	1,075.6	1,291.8	1,733.2	1,404.5	1,627.2	2,195.2	2,989.0
$ 408.2	$ 364.5	$ 518.7	$ 661.7	$ 814.1	$ 881.7	$ 951.6	$1,205.5
$ 408.2	$ 364.5	$ 518.7	$ 661.7	$ 814.1	$ 881.7	$ 951.6	$1,205.5
$ 45.0	$ 45.0	$ 45.0	$ 61.6	$ 68.6	$ 81.6	$ 91.9	$ 106.1
56.4	94.9	100.4	159.7	164.2	201.9	216.6	282.3
12.1	18.8	17.5	20.3	20.7	20.8	29.7	29.6
			1.9	3.7	6.9	9.6	10.9
			2.2				
1.2	3.6	4.4	4.8	2.2	2.0	5.6	9.7
16.7	17.9	16.8	20.7	26.1	23.1	22.7	32.4
4.8	4.2	3.8	8.2	5.5	3.3	7.1	5.8
6.1	10.2	12.8	14.9	12.2	12.0	14.3	19.3
48.7	65.1	96.1	144.6	121.1	145.3	207.7	288.4
30.8	30.9	40.1	42.6	57.8	46.5	60.3	83.4
26.2	4.8	25.4	23.4	35.5	66.5	32.9	24.3
8.1	15.2	10.1	15.8	19.2	17.5	21.8	53.3
5.8	7.9	10.2	22.7	29.2	25.6	13.8	6.9
8.3	10.3	17.9	18.9	20.2	19.9	18.8	14.0
7.5	3.2		8.2	3.9	3.6	6.3	8.2
		8.2	13.5	9.5	12.3	9.2	13.3
2.1	4.8	6.4	5.3	5.4	5.3	4.8	4.7
1.5	2.4	3.0	4.1	5.3	5.4	5.9	7.8
2.5	1.9	2.2	2.2	2.9	4.6	3.5	4.0
	3.6	21.6	3.1	4.3	1.2	3.0	35.9
8.1	12.1	15.4	7.2	8.7	6.7	7.3	8.8
					1.4	1.9	2.9
			2.1				
5.5	9.1	9.5	16.4	12.5	9.8	9.5	9.3
		1.8		4.8	3.8	3.0	3.6
				24.8	32.5	43.6	43.9
					3.1	1.9	2.2
					2.1	1.9	2.2
$ 297.5	$ 366.1	$ 468.6	$ 624.4	$ 668.3	$ 764.7	$ 854.6	$1,113.1
$ 110.7	$ (1.6)	$ 50.1	$ 37.3	$ 145.8	$ 117.0	$ 97.0	$ 92.4
85.0‖	30.0‖	35.0‖	20.4	56.9	42.8	37.9	42.3
$ 25.7	$ (31.6)	$ 15.1	$ 16.9	$ 88.9	$ 74.3	$ 59.1	$ 50.1
$ 40.2	$ 132.0	$ 100.4	$ 0.6	$ 17.5	$ 106.4	$ 180.7	$ 239.8
$ 65.9	$ 100.4	$ 115.5	$ 17.5	$ 106.4	$ 180.7	$ 239.3	$ 289.9

Exhibit 4

BREITMAN & COMPANY

*Accountant's Analysis of Income Statements
and Balance Sheets, 1938–51*

	1938	1939	1940	1941	1942
Ratio of Current Assets to Current Liabilities........	1.2 to 1	1.7 to 1	1.7 to 1	1.6 to 1	1.4 to 1
Average Capital Turnover in Relation to Sales:					
Capital Beginning of Year (in thousands of dollars)..		$ 4.2	$ 12.0	$ 21.5	$ 28.8
Capital at End of Year (in thousands of dollars).....	$ 4.2	$ 12.0	$ 21.5	$ 28.8	$ 74.9
Average Capital (in thousands of dollars)..........	$ 4.2	$ 8.1	$ 16.7	$ 25.2	$ 51.9
Average Capital Turnover in Relation to Sales....	16	12½	10	9½	15½
Percentage of Net Profit (before Federal Taxes) to Average Capital............................	6.8%	66.0%	29.5%	35.7%	36.9%
Sales (in thousands of dollars).....................	$69.0	$100.6	$169.5	$239.4	$803.4
Percentage of Gross Profit to Sales.............	36.1%	39.9%	29.1%	20.8%	22.9%
Percentage of Net Income (before Federal Taxes) to Sales....................................	0.4%	5.3%	2.9%	3.8%	2.5%
Inventory Turnover in Relation to Sales............	30	40¼	52	60½	20⅝
Inventory Turnover in Relation to Cost of Merchandise Sold..................................	19¼	24¼	37	48	16⅝
Percentage of Officers' Salaries to Sales............	9.8%	16.1%	9.9%	9.6%	4.9%
Percentage of Other Salaries to Sales...............	14.9%	11.4%	8.4%	2.2%	2.8%
Percentage of Commission Selling and Advertising Expenses to Sales............................	0.8%		1.4%	1.0%	8.0%
Percentage of Shipping, Packaging, Fitting Bags and Boxes to Sales................................					0.4%
Percentage of All Other Expenses to Sales..........	10.2%	7.1%	6.5%	4.2%	4.3%
Percentage of Total Expenses to Sales..............	35.7%	34.6%	26.2%	17.0%	20.4%

Source: Records furnished by accountant.

South for a nationally known men's clothing firm, to join Breitman & Company as partner and sales manager.

In 1941 the then three partners formed a separate corporation to sell women's handbags, but a year later merged it with Breitman & Company. They also started to distribute their belts and handbags through salesmen throughout the United States, most of whom also represented manufacturers of other noncompeting items (e.g., children's underwear, sweaters, luggage). Sales jumped from $293,000 in 1940–41 to $1,428,000 in 1944–45, and in 1945 the firm bought out the leather and fabric handbag business of Mr. Larry Goodman, making him a fourth partner. According to Mr. Firth, Mr. Goodman did not add to the firm the bag "know-how" that his other partners had expected of him, so he withdrew in 1946, selling his interest to the other three partners. A year later, in February, 1947, Mr. Levy suddenly withdrew from the firm after a dispute with Mr. Fischer. According to Mr. Firth, this dispute was almost entirely the result of Mr. Levy's desire to be "the complete boss." Mr. Levy received $65,000 from the corporation for his interest, and in 1952 he was the head of his own high-priced handbag business.

Exhibit 6, prepared by Mr. Williams from the balance sheets, shows the growth of the firm's financial position.

Exhibit 4—Continued

BREITMAN & COMPANY

Accountant's Analysis of Income Statements and Balance Sheets, 1938–51

1943	1944	1945	1946	1947	1948	1949	1950	1951
1.8 to 1	1.9 to 1	1.1 to 1	1.1 to 1	1.1 to 1	1.4 to 1	1.4 to 1	1.3 to 1	1.2 to 1
$ 74.9	$ 106.3	$ 132.0	$ 100.4	$ 115.5	$ 132.7	$ 221.7	$ 295.9	$ 355.0
$106.3	$ 132.0	$ 100.4	$ 115.5	$ 132.7	$ 221.7	$ 295.9	$ 355.0	$ 405.2
$ 90.6	$ 119.1	$ 116.2	$ 107.9	$ 124.1	$ 177.2	$ 258.8	$ 325.4	$ 380.1
9½	12	12½	17	19½	12½	9½	9½	11
27.8%	93.0%	(1.4%)	46.4%	30.0%	82.3%	45.2%	29.8%	24.3%
$870.1	$1,428.8	$1,440.1	$1,810.5	$2,394.9	$2,218.6	$2,508.9	$3,146.8	$4,194.6
20.0%	28.6%	25.3%	28.6%	27.6%	36.7%	35.1%	30.2%	28.7%
3.0%	7.8%	(0.1%)	2.7%	1.5%	6.7%	4.6%	3.1%	2.2%
10¼	14⅜	12½	9⅝	10	9	14⅜	15⅝	10½
8½	10½	9¼	7	7½	5¾	9½	11	7½
3.6%	3.1%	3.1%	2.5%	2.6%	3.1%	3.3%	2.9%	2.5%
2.4%	3.9%	6.6%	5.5%	6.6%	7.4%	8.0%	6.9%	6.8%
7.2%	7.4%	7.0%	8.9%	8.8%	9.5%	10.3%	9.6%	9.4%
0.3%	0.6%	1.1%	.6%	0.7%	2.0%	2.0%	2.1%	2.3%
3.5%	5.8%	7.6%	8.4%	7.4%	8.0%	6.9%	5.6%	5.5%
17.0%	20.8%	25.4%	25.9%	26.1%	30.0%	30.5%	27.1%	26.5%

The addition of executive personnel had more or less followed the growth of the firm's sales. Miss Voss had been taken on from Mr. Firth's accounting firm in 1945 to act "temporarily" as office manager and head bookkeeper. In 1952 she was still acting in that capacity. Mr. Fred Apfel was added at about the same time as belt production manager. Mr. Sidney Teplow was brought in to manage the bag department when Mr. Goodman left. The two sales managers, Mr. Byron Steinmetz (belts) and Mr. Frank Rich (bags), had been hired from competitive firms in 1949 and 1952 respectively. Besides the two officers, the executive group in 1952 included 16 people. Of this group 10 worked in the 32d Street office, 5, including Mr. Teplow, worked in the bag factory at 14th Street, and 1 was superintendent at the 25th Street belt factory.

Accounting Firm's Relations with Company. Mr. Firth's accounting firm, of which he was one of four partners, was retained by Breitman & Company in 1941. According to Mr. Firth, his firm performed the same services for Breitman & Company as it did for its other clients, which were mainly manufacturing concerns of about the same size as Breitman. Four times a year two junior accountants audited the Breitman books and also prepared quarterly and annual balance sheets and income statements as well as the company's tax returns. After each statement, Mr. Firth sat down with Mr. Fischer and Mr. Breitman, and occasionally some of the other Breitman people, to appraise the op-

Exhibit 5

BREITMAN & COMPANY

Sample Five-Month Income Statement in Form Used by Accountants
for Company Review
July 1—November 30, 1950

(Figures Rounded to Thousands by Case Writer)

	Total	Per Cent	Bag Department	Per Cent	Belt Department	Per Cent
Sales: Regular	$ 700.3		$669.5		$ 30.8	
Straw	17.2		17.2			
Job	555.9				555.9	
Metal	447.8				447.8	
Total Sales	$1,721.2		$686.7		$1,034.5	
Gross Profit: Regular	$ 206.4	29.5%	$187.9	28.1%	$ 18.5	60.2%
Straw	Loss					
Job	153.0	27.5%			153.0	27.5%
Metal	151.9	33.9%			151.9	33.9%
	$ 511.3	29.7%	$187.9	27.4%	$ 324.4	31.3%
Mark Downs	21.6	1.3%	8.2	1.2%	13.4	1.3%
	$ 489.7	28.4%	$179.7	26.2%	$ 310.0	30.0%
Commissions	124.4	7.2%	41.9	6.1%	82.5	8.0%
Profit after Mark Downs and Commissions	$ 365.3	21.2%	$137.8	20.1%	$ 227.5	22.0%
Expenses						
Direct: Manufacturing	$ 108.5	6.3%	$ 56.0	8.2%	$ 52.5	5.1%
Selling	20.8	1.2%	2.5	0.4%	18.3	1.8%
Shipping	37.2	2.2%	18.4	2.7%	18.8	1.8%
Total Direct Expenses	$ 166.5	9.7%	$ 76.9	11.3%	$ 89.6	8.7%‡
†Allocable: Manufacturing	$ 34.6					
Selling	65.3		$ 62.9		$ 95.3	
General Administration	58.3					
Total Allocable Expenses	$ 158.2	9.2%	$ 62.9	9.1%	$ 95.3	9.2%‡
‡Total Expenses	$ 324.7	18.9%	$139.8	20.4%	$ 184.9	17.9%
Net Profit	40.6	2.3%	($ 2.0)	(0.3%)	$ 42.6	4.1%

( ) Loss.
† Allocable Expenses distributed to various departments on basis of sales.
‡ Supporting schedules normally furnished to officers not included here. See Exhibit 3.
Source: Furnished case writer by Mr. Firth.

erating results and discuss items of cost which appeared out of line.
Mr. Firth, together with Irving Lasser, the lawyer, also met once a year
with vice-presidents of each of the two banks with which Breitman did
business to establish lines of credit for the coming year. Bank practice
required that loans not exceed the company's working capital, that the
company maintain a deposit balance of at least 20% of loans outstanding, and that the composition and size of the inventories on hand
play a major part in determining the size of loans. The company was
also required to "stay out of the banks" for at least 30 days each year.

Exhibit 6

BREITMAN & COMPANY

*Case Writer's Analysis of Source and Application
of Invested Capital, 1938–51*

(Thousands of Dollars)

| FISCAL PERIOD | SALES | INCREASES IN INVESTED CAPITAL FROM | | | TOTAL CAPITAL INCREASE | INVESTED CAPITAL INCREASES APPLIED TO INCREASES IN | | |
		Profits	Deprecia-tion	Money Put in by Partners		Machinery and Equip-ment*	Other Assets	Net Working Capital
1938–39......	$ 100.6	$ 4.3	$ 0.3	$ 3.4	$ 8.0	$ 0.7	$ ...	$ 7.3
1939–40.......	169.5	4.3	0.4	5.2	9.9	1.3	$ 0.2	8.4
1940–41......	239.3	7.3	0.5	...	7.8	3.6	0.4	3.8
1941–42......	803.4	13.7	2.1	32.4	48.2	12.5	0.3	35.4
1942–43......	870.2	10.3	2.7	21.1	34.1	3.6	1.7	28.8
1943–44......	1,428.9	25.7	6.1	...	31.8	16.4	(1.1)	16.5
1944–45......	1,440.1	(31.6)	10.2	...	(21.4)	34.0	11.1	(66.5)
1945–46......	1,810.5	15.1	12.8	...	27.9	21.9	(5.2)	11.2
1946–47......	2,394.9	16.9	14.9	0.3	32.1	17.9	(0.4)	14.6
1947–48......	2,218.6	88.9	12.2	...	101.1	18.7	5.9	76.5
1948–49......	2,508.9	74.3	12.0	(65.0)	21.3	12.2	20.3	(11.2)
1949–50......	3,146.8	59.1	14.3	...	73.4	18.7	(1.9)	56.6
1950–51......	4,194.5	50.1	19.3	...	69.4	24.7	8.1	36.6
Cumulative Total, 1938–51...		$338.4	$107.8	$ (2.6)	$ 443.6	$186.2	$ 39.4	$218.0

( ) Negative figure.
* Net increase based on book value of machinery and equipment.
Source: Compiled by Mr. Williams from company balance sheets.

The seasonal nature of the company's business was such that loans were usually repaid at the end of June. At various times in recent company history, Mr. Breitman and Mr. Fischer had lent as much as $100,000 of their own funds to the business, in addition to the money provided by the bank. According to Mr. Firth, the company's bank credit had always been unusually good. At the same time, Mr. Firth regarded it as his responsibility to see that Breitman & Company did not ask for too much credit. In 1951 he had persuaded Mr. Fischer to ask for $100,000 less than the latter had contemplated.

Mr. Firth said that it was Miss Voss's responsibility to see that sufficient funds were on hand to meet expenses (sometimes as high as $500,000 a month) and that she had done "an exceptional job" in "keeping on her toes" and handling her operation of the business efficiently. The accounting firm handled all credit inquiries about Breitman & Company.

Mr. Firth's Appraisal of the Company. In talking about Breitman & Company, its history, and its way of doing business, Mr. Firth made frequent references to the company's unusual record of success and, by way of contrast, spoke of a number of other companies of the size of Breitman with less fortunate records:

Judson Fischer and Felix Breitman are wonderful people. They've been successful because they've been willing to work like dogs—because they have been able to work together in harmony and build up a wonderful spirit of co-operation in their organization. What, of course, is just as important is the fact that between them they've had the vision to stay ahead of the market in style trends.

In response to questions from Mr. Williams, Mr. Firth expressed skepticism as to the desirability for any more elaborate record-keeping, information, budgeting, or cost-control operations at Breitman & Company. He also indicated some concern about the continued operation of the business after the retirement of either of the partners, but doubted whether anything could at present be done about this problem. He also expressed doubt as to whether much could be done to improve Breitman's financial position, particularly since neither of the partners was a wealthy man. The company's financial strength, he felt, would put an automatic brake on future expansion:

You must remember that this is a highly risky business and a fast-moving business, and that it takes a lot of personal supervision to keep such a business alive. One bad season and Breitman & Company could be in serious trouble; two, and they'd be out of business. The kinds of things you teach your boys at the Harvard Business School about management are all very well, but they don't exactly fit this business.

IV. THE LAWYER'S VIEW OF THE COMPANY

Mr. Williams obtained another view of company operations from Mr. Lasser, whom he saw early in May. Mr. Williams had considerable difficulty in arranging an appointment with Mr. Lasser because of illness in the latter's family. Mr. Williams' one interview with Mr. Lasser took place at the home of Judson Fischer, where he and Mrs. Fischer entertained Mr. Lasser and Mr. Williams for dinner. From notes he took at the dinner table, Mr. Williams reconstructed the following transcript of what took place that evening.

LASSER: I'm delighted to have this opportunity to talk with you about Breitman & Company, particularly since it gives me another chance to preach to my good friend Judson, here, some things I've been trying to hammer into him for over two years now.

It won't take me very long to say what I have to say because my theme is pretty simple, and I don't pretend to be able to work out all the details. Besides, if you're from the Harvard Business School, you'll know what I'm talking about.

Perhaps I should begin by qualifying myself to talk about this. I, too, incidentally, am a graduate of Fair Harvard—the Law School. Our firm specializes in combining business and legal advice to manufacturing corporations; I myself am a director of several corporations, including the ———— Company, of which Mr. ————, a graduate of your Business School, is president. Our firm is retained by Breitman & Company to do all its legal work; and, in addition, this son-of-a-gun and I are very good friends. We think we've given pretty good advice so far.

There are four things I think this firm needs, and it needs help to get them: first, a critical look at its market acceptance and the reasons for its success; second, a modern, up-to-date control system with somebody to run it; third, some acceptance of the rudimentary concepts of good administration in its day-to-day operation; and fourth, a more diversified product line to protect it against a dip in the market and against being run by its salesmen, as is now the case.

Let me talk about each of these in turn. Market acceptance—you've been watching the company long enough to know something about how it operates. Have you seen anyone there who ever has had time to sit back and take a look at where this company ought to be getting its business from, find out where Breitman stands in relation to competition, and plan its marketing activities accordingly? You know what I mean.

My second point ought to be equally obvious, even after a quick look at the company. This firm badly needs some element of financial and cost control.

FISCHER: Are you saying that Miss Voss doesn't do a good job?

LASSER: She does a good job of seeing to it that she's all things to all people, and she probably does an efficient job as head bookkeeper; but in terms of providing management information, she doesn't do a thing. Why, do you realize that this company has no analyses of sales by products, profitability by product lines, or costs by operations?

FISCHER: We get all that from Mr. Firth.

LASSER: Well, if you do, you've never shown it to me. And as far as that goes, Mr. Firth is a good accountant, but he's highly conservative, and I'm not sure that he sees what I'm talking about.

And now for a point that I'm glad I can make with Judson here. I'm as fond of him and Felix as I can be of anybody, and in each of their lines they're both geniuses. Felix can come up with belt designs that are literally works of art, and Jud can smell what the market will buy in a way that's uncanny. But the point is, they're both lousy administrators. What they know about running an organization would fit on the head of a pin. Have you noticed the number of things Jud gets involved in? Have you ever seen him really delegate responsibility? Can you tell me who's responsible for what in that firm? Does either of these two know anything about training their people? Do you know who's responsible for production or purchasing?

FISCHER (*smiling*): He really thinks I'm a lousy boss, doesn't he?

LASSER: I know you are.

And now for the final point. Maybe, Mr. Williams, you can help me sell this to Jud here. As you know, this is a highly risky kind of business. You may not know that sales costs—salesmen's commissions—are a highly expensive item. And it's my contention that when Breitman & Company bargains with its salesmen, the salesmen have the upper hand. Clearest proof of that is the fact that in spite of what you pay them, they still aren't working full time for you. They're also selling other lines. And your name doesn't mean anything in the trade, so you need them more than they need you.

FISCHER: You're out of date on one point. We now only have two salesmen carrying other lines.

LASSER: Well, that doesn't invalidate my basic point. What I am proposing then is very simple. That in addition to belts and handbags, Breitman & Company carry what for want of a better name I call a "gift line"—scarves, handkerchiefs, umbrellas, leather goods—I'm not enough of an expert on these matters to say just what. My point is that by broadening the base of their products, the company will do several things: they will protect themselves against style trends in just one line; they can expand their volume without expanding their sales cost proportionately; and what is more important, they can afford to start advertising the Breitman name, to strengthen their position in the market.

Now notice one thing—I'm not suggesting they start to manufacture these items. I like to think that I've already done these guys some good by hammering at them hard enough to get them to take care of their present increased sales volume without expanding their production. And what I'm proposing doesn't contemplate their producing any of these things either.

Which, incidentally, is another point. The talent these guys possess is a design talent, a selling talent, not a manufacturing talent. Besides, you don't make money manufacturing in this business. I'm not even sure they need to do any manufacturing at all, although Judson here thinks differently.

FISCHER: You know what I think about that, Irving. If buyers get the idea you're just a jobber, they'll want to go directly to the manufacturer because they think they get a better buy that way.

LASSER: And you know what I think about the mentality of most buyers. With the appeal you have now, it doesn't make one bit of difference whether you make your merchandise or whether someone else does.

Well, Mr. Williams, I'm terribly sorry, but as I told you earlier, I have to leave now—but those are my essential ideas, and if you—or anyone else—can ever make Judson see them, you'll be doing him a favor.

FISCHER: Are you quite through, Irving?

LASSER: For the moment, yes.

FISCHER: Just so Mr. Williams doesn't get the wrong idea—you and I are old friends—but as I've said many times, you're really full of hot air, and on that idea of a gift line you're just plain nuts.

LASSER: Tell me why.

FISCHER: It just won't work. Besides, we've got enough problems on our hands without asking for more.[1]

V. BREITMAN, COMPETITORS, AND THE MARKET

Although in preparing his case Mr. Williams concentrated on the day-to-day activities of Breitman & Company, he thought that a picture of how business generally was done in the belt and bag industries emerged gradually from his study. Breitman, it appeared, was "typical" of belt and bag firms generally in a number of respects. Such companies usually had a rapid turnover of styles. They operated on a two-season-a-year basis with marked seasonal fluctuations in volume (see Exhibit 7). They themselves did little or no advertising and virtually no brand promotion. They sold directly to retail buyers from their own

Exhibit 7

BREITMAN & COMPANY

*Case Writer's Analysis of Seasonality
in Breitman and Department-Store Sales by Months, 1951*

| | MONTHLY SALES AS PER CENT OF YEAR'S TOTAL | | |
| | Breitman | | U.S. Department Stores |
	Handbags	Belts	Handbags and Small Leather Goods
January....................	10.9%	7.3%	5.0%
February..................	11.4	7.8	5.3
March.....................	14.4	5.4	9.5
April......................	13.1	6.8	6.6
May.......................	7.8	4.8	8.3
June......................	5.6	8.0	7.2
July.......................	5.1	6.7	4.7
August....................	7.1	11.2	5.9
September.................	5.5	14.0	8.7
October...................	5.7	12.6	8.7
November.................	6.0	11.4	10.3
December.................	7.4	4.0	19.8
	100.0%	100.0%	100.0%

Source: Breitman figures computed from monthly figures furnished by accountant. Department store figures computed from Federal Reserve Board Index.

---

[1] At this point Mr. Lasser left for the evening, and Mr. Williams spent several hours with Mr. Fischer discussing the administration of Breitman & Company.

showrooms or through commission salesmen. They usually designed particular style items to fit an established price[2] rather than the reverse; that is, a typical price decision would be to decide whether a particular belt could be sold for $7.50 or $10.50 a dozen. Cash discounts to customers of 8% on belts and 3% on bags were allowed on payments within 10 days after the end of the month.

Most of the companies in the belt and handbag industries were located in or around New York City. They were, for the most part, closely held companies with relatively limited financial resources. Mr. Williams had learned of no publicly owned belt or handbag manufacturing companies. Executives with training and experience outside the garment or soft-goods industries were the exception, while the staffing of key jobs with the relatives of the owners was a common practice.

At the same time Breitman was unique, so far as Mr. Williams could determine, in being a relatively large company that sold both belts and nonleather handbags. A number of bag houses sold both leather and nonleather merchandise, although this was not a universal practice. ("We tried making leather bags when we had Larry Goodman in here and nearly lost our shirts," Mr. Fischer reported.) A number of lower priced belt houses sold directly to dress manufacturers, which Breitman & Company did not do.

Mr. Firth had reported that the belt and bag industry (like most fashion industries) was stratified into at least three layers: 1) those companies with well-known name designers, very high-priced "original" merchandise, and exclusive distribution; 2) those companies which employed their own designers, created some of their own styles, but also copied "originals" and sold medium-priced merchandise with wider distribution than the first group; and 3) those companies whose design activity consisted exclusively of copying higher priced designs and of competing on a low-price volume basis. Breitman & Company, Mr. Firth said, fitted in the second group.

Some of the questions that Mr. Williams believed were of importance in understanding Breitman's position in the market he had been unable to answer with any degree of completeness, since his study of the industry had been limited and had been confined to conversation with Breitman people and buyers in the showroom, and to a search of ma-

---

[2] Breitman sold its belts in 30 prices, ranging from $7.50 a dozen to $120 a dozen. These were typically sold at retail from $1 to $16 apiece, with the retailer's markup percentage varying according to the particular price. Breitman's bags sold at $35.65 or $57 a dozen, with the corresponding retail price usually $5.98 and $7.98.

terial in Baker Library of the Harvard Business School. How successful had the company, volumewise and profitwise, been in relation to competitors? The information shown in Exhibits 3 and 8–11 was his only

Exhibit 8

BREITMAN & COMPANY

Quarterly Sales by Products, 1949–52

(Thousands of Dollars)

Year	Handbags	Belts	Total
1949			
1st Quarter...............	$650.6	$283.4	$ 934.0
2nd Quarter...............	617.3	293.2	910.5
3rd Quarter...............	349.6	351.6	701.2
4th Quarter...............	366.3	330.8	697.1
Year..................	$1,983.8	$1,259.0	$3,242.8
1950			
1st Quarter...............	$614.8	$392.9	$1,007.7
2nd Quarter...............	706.8	358.5	1,065.3
3rd Quarter...............	382.3	600.8	983.1
4th Quarter...............	424.8	489.0	913.8
Year	$2,128.7	$1,841.2	$3,969.9
1951			
1st Quarter...............	$997.0	$563.0	$1,560.0
2nd Quarter...............	719.9	534.5	1,254.4
3rd Quarter...............	481.3	871.1	2,352.4
4th Quarter...............	520.0	765.0	1,285.0
Year..................	$2,718.2	$2,733.6	$5,451.8
1952			
1st Quarter...............	$728.6	$894.3	$1,622.9
April–May...............	561.8	817.9	1,379.7
Five Months............	$1,290.4	$1,712.2	$3,002.6

Source: 1949–51, Company accounts.

clue to that question. Exhibit 5 shows a loss in the handbag department for one period of operation. Mr. Fischer explained that while over the years the handbag operation had been profitable, it was never as profitable as the belt department. "One of the principal reasons for this," he explained, "is the highly competitive nature of the handbag industry in contrast to the belt industry. We just can't get as good a gross margin." How did the company's coverage of various segments of the market compare with that of competitors? Since neither Breitman & Company nor Mr. Williams had made any recent statistical analysis of Breitman account cards, the best clues Mr. Williams felt he had to answering that

Exhibit 9

BREITMAN & COMPANY

Comparative Rates of Growth—Company and U.S. Department-Store Sales, 1937–51

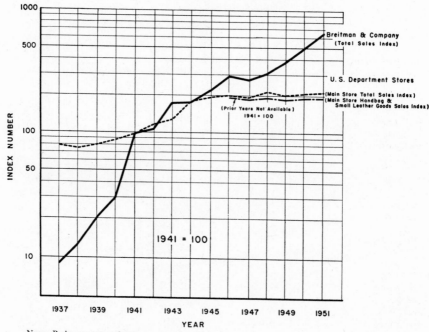

NOTE: Breitman year = fiscal year.

Sources: Breitman—Profit and Loss Statements; Department Stores—Federal Reserve Board Bulletins·

question lay in putting together an executive's statement that the company had 5,000 accounts, and that 75% of its business was with department stores with the information shown in Exhibit 12. Was it customary in the industry to subcontract production to the extent that Breitman & Company did? So far as Mr. Williams could learn, it was highly unusual. One buyer had reported that since buyers generally thought they could get better prices and better service by dealing directly with manufacturers, Breitman could subcontract to the extent that it did only because it was known as a manufacturer. How did Breitman's line compare with competitors' in number of items, style, quality, price? (See Exhibit 13.) Mr. Williams could only draw inferences from the rest of his data. He visited several department stores to see belts and bags displayed, but considered that he was incapable of making any qualitative judgments about Breitman merchandise in relation to competitors. One out-of-town department-store buyer with

Exhibit 10

BREITMAN & COMPANY

Industry Data on Handbags and Belts—1947

	Total	Establishments with an Average of							
		1-4 Employees	5-9 Employees	10-19 Employees	20-49 Employees	50-99 Employees	100-249 Employees	250-499 Employees	Over 500 Employees
Handbags and Purses:									
Number of establishments, 1947	734	176	139	140	163	70	43	3	
Number of proprietors and firm members	601								
Number of employees, average for year	20,301	431	963	1,925	5,120	4,809	6,056	997	
Units produced, in thousands:									
Leather	16,854								
Nonleather	37,488								
Value added by manufacture	$ 76,586	$2,025	$3,726	$8,165	$21,356	$16,794	$21,173	$3,347	
Net sales value, f.o.b. plant	$159,693*								
Leather	$ 74,306								
Nonleather	$ 75,991								
Belts:									
Number of establishments, 1947	396	91	94	99	75	26	8	2	1
Number of proprietors and firm members	361								
Number of employees, average for year	9,162	227	640	1,381	2,300	1,766	1,056	1,792	Withheld
Units produced, in thousands of dozens:									
Leather	6,464								
Nonleather	5,702								
Other, not specified									
Value added by manufacture	$ 38,037	$1,104	$2,824	$6,009	$ 9,009	$ 6,730	$ 4,625	$7,736	Withheld
Net sales value, f.o.b. plant	$ 60,117†								
Leather	$ 39,981								
Nonleather	$ 17,864								
Other, not specified	$ 2,272								

* Includes $4,396 value of other products manufactured by members of the handbag industry.
† Total value of all belts shipped by manufacturers classified in the belt industry and in other industries was $68,982.
Source: *U.S. Census of Manufactures*, 1947.

Exhibit 11

BREITMAN & COMPANY

Excerpts from WOMEN'S Wear Daily *on Handbag Industry*[3]

Manufacturers Operating at Profit Held Rarities in Industry

Because of the discriminatory features of the 20% excise tax and the reduction of duty rates, handbag manufacturing firms that operate at a profit have become rarities. Testimony to this effect will be delivered by Max Berkowitz, codirector of the National Authority for the Ladies' Handbag Industry, when he appears before the Senate Finance Committee. . . .

Mr. Berkowitz will point out that the handbag industry has shrunk from 800 firms doing a wholesale volume of 200 million dollars in 1946 to 500 firms doing 135 million in 1951.

—April 25, 1952, p. 32.

Tendency to Overproduce Is Held Bane of the Industry

What's wrong with the handbag industry? . . .

Critics point out that foremost among the industry's shortcomings is its tendency toward overproduction . . . hungry manufacturers quickly copy a successful item and the market is almost immediately glutted. . . .

It is too easy for a would-be manufacturer to go into the handbag business. . . . The industry attracts an excessive number of marginal producers [who are] prone to undersell in order to attract business. . . . When conditions are unfavorable . . . salesmen, production workers [and others] who may suddenly find themselves unemployed frequently form partnerships and go into the manufacturing business for themselves.

Another industry defect is an apparent indifference to the scientific production approach . . . not enough attention is paid to the accurate compilation of costs. . . .

Still another defect, which is less the fault of producers, but perhaps more basic, [is] the tendency to dress informally.

—May 2, 1952, p. 29.

whom Mr. Williams talked indicated that there were about four or five belt manufacturers and a half-dozen bag manufacturers whose lines most buyers tried, or at least examined, each season and that Breitman was included in both groups. Mr. Williams was of the opinion that there was much more he could have done to widen his understanding of the industry and Breitman's position in it.

VI. THE ORGANIZATION AT WORK

As Mr. Williams began to gain a mental picture of the internal workings of the company, he determined to concentrate on trying to see

---

[3] Reproduced by permission of the publisher.

Exhibit 12

BREITMAN & COMPANY
Selected Data on Retail Outlets Selling Handbags—1948

	ALL RETAIL STORES THIS TYPE		STORES THIS TYPE SELLING HANDBAGS†				
TYPE OF STORE	1948 Number (Thousands)	1948 Volume (Millions of Dollars)	1948 Number (Thousands)	1948 Handbag Volume (Millions of Dollars)	1948 Total Volume (As Per cent total Volume All Stores)	1948 Average Handbag Volume per Store (Thousands of Dollars)	1948 Average Total Volume per Store (Thousands of Dollars)
Women's ready-to-wear	30.7	$ 3,305	10.6	$101.0	63.0%	$ 9.6	$ 198
Department stores	2.6	10,645	2.3	98.0‡	96.5	42.1‡	4,380
Family clothing	12.5	1,791	5.1	40.9	64.3	8.0	227
Women's shoes	3.2*	377	1.5*	25.1	74.5	17.1	192
Apparel, accessory, specialty	7.7	328	1.5	21.3	30.8	13.7	66
Family shoes	13.2*	859	3.3*	16.3	45.4	5.0	119
Millinery	5.7	109	1.9	7.8	41.4	4.2	24
Corsets and lingerie	2.7*	92	0.3*	1.2	17.4	3.8	49
Men's shoes	2.3*	198	0.1*	0.6	8.1	5.9	152
Dry goods, general merchandise	29.7	2,824	18.3	NA	81.4	NA	126
Variety stores	20.2	2,507	14.7	NA	93.5	NA	159
General stores	21.6	1,233	10.9	NA	63.4	NA	71

NA Not available.
* Figures not exactly comparable with others in series.
† All figures except those for "Apparel, accessory, and specialty" and "Corsets and lingerie" based on reports from more than 90% of stores in each category. Forty per cent "Apparel, accessory, and specialty" reported breakdowns. Per cent of "Corset and lingerie" reporting not available.
‡ Includes small leather goods.

Source: *U.S. Census of Business*, 1948.

Exhibit 13

BREITMAN & COMPANY

Statistics on Product Line—Fall, 1952

Basic Type	Number of Styles	Number Carried Over from Spring Line	Approximate Number of Style-Color Combinations	Approximate Number of Style-Color-Size Combinations	Range of Manufacturers Price per Dozen
			BELTS		
Leather..........	109	76	400	2,000	$ 7.50–$ 60.00
Metal............	90	47	171	600	7.50– 96.00
French line.......	33	13	110	400	21.00– 120.00
Velvet...........	32	12	110	400	7.50– 66.00
Elastic..........	29	5	112	300	7.50– 72.00
Metallic leather...	21	17	47	107	7.20– 66.00
Suede...........	18	11	40	120	7.50– 60.00
Patent...........	14	10	25	100	7.25– 22.50
Reptile..........	13	4	35	120	7.50– 96.00
Satin............	5	0	5	20	10.50– 66.00
Calf staples.......	4	4	20	110	7.50– 16.50
Plastic alligator...	2	2	2	11	7.50– 10.50
Faille...........	2	1	9	54	7.50– 30.00
Total........	372	202	1,086	4,342	
			BAGS		
Faille...........	25	NA	75	*	$35.65
	15		45		57.00
Velvet..........	20	NA	60	*	35.65
	14		42		57.00
Novelty.........	14	NA	112	*	35.65
	15		120		57.00
Patent..........	11	NA	11	*	35.65
Evening.........	8	NA	80	*	35.65
Broadcloth.......	7	NA	21	*	57.00
Quilted..........	3	NA	3		35.65
Total........	132		569		

NA Not available.
* Not applicable.
Source: Tabulated by case writer from company listing of fall line.

whether he could understand what he believed to be five essential processes that were going on continually: (1) merchandising the line; (2) selling that line; (3) producing the merchandise; (4) keeping production and purchasing abreast of sales; and (5) processing orders. If he could fit the activities of people into these processes, he believed he would have a pretty good idea of how Breitman & Company worked on a day-to-day basis.

1. *Merchandising the Line.* For the most part, the belt and bag activities were carried out separately, although some of the same people were involved in each. The activities referred to as "merchandising the line" culminated in the decisions as to what styles (at what prices) would constitute Breitman's offering to the trade in both its fall and spring lines. The bulk of the activity involved in preparing a fall line was completed by late May, and the spring line by late November, although once a line had been established, particularly in the case of belts, additions or withdrawals were by no means uncommon.[4]

Within the belt line a limited number of styles, mostly leather, were known as "staples," or basic belts. These had been in the line for several years, and salesmen had been informed that the company would continue to carry enough inventory on these numbers at all times to permit shipments within 24 hours of receipt of orders.

SELECTING THE BELT LINE. Final selection of a season's full belt line took place in eight or ten 4–6-hour after-dinner meetings, usually attended by Mr. Breitman, Mr. Fischer, Byron Steinmetz, Fred Apfel, Harry Block, and any of the salesmen who happened to be available. Such selection appeared to Mr. Williams to be very much a group activity, involving the exchange of a great many opinions before a consensus was reached on which of the many samples examined by the group should constitute the line.

The following interchange from one such meeting, recorded by Mr. Williams in his notes, illustrates the type of discussion that took place in these meetings:

STEINMETZ: How do you like this number, Judson? It's very popular in Paris.

FISCHER: Haven't we already got enough wide contour belts? How much would we get for that?

APFEL: Mr. Fischer, I could give you that for $15. We'd get Leatherco to make it.

BLOCK: You'd never get $15 for that belt.

APFEL: Harry, we couldn't make a nickel on it if we sold it for less.

---

[4] Mr. Williams did not obtain any conclusive evidence as to the extent to which the line changed from season to season or within any particular season. According to Mr. Steinmetz, the belt sales manager, the company did not save records which would make such an analysis from season to season readily possible, although an analysis of changes in the spring, 1952, line could perhaps have been made from bulletins to salesmen. Mr. Steinmetz estimated that less than 25% of the belt line was ever carried for more than one season, with perhaps a higher carry-over in handbags. According to Mr. Williams' analysis of changes from the spring to fall line in 1952, 202 of the 372 numbers in the spring line remained in the fall line.

STEINMETZ: How about eliminating the pendant? That ought to save something.

BREITMAN: If you don't use the pendant here, maybe we could put it on the last number we looked at.

FISCHER (*smiling*): You don't like it when we throw away all your hard work, do you, Felix? (*To a salesman.*) What do you think, Abe?

ABE: For $15 I like it better than some we've already picked out.

BLOCK: How many sizes would we need in this one?

APFEL: This would be easy to make in 24 through 32, Harry. I could easily get it for $10.50 if we cut out the pendant, and show a nice profit.

STEINMETZ: Why don't we leave it in for now and come back to it?

FISCHER: All right, but I'm not sure I like it.

The samples from which selections were made were produced by the company's own belt factory or one of the contractors. Ideas for styles arose from a variety of sources; Mr. Breitman spent most of his time sketching belts or ornaments for them, and these provided the major source; salesmen, Mr. Fischer, or others of the executives brought in competitive merchandise they had seen in stores; and contractors and occasionally buyers made suggestions. In 1952 an important source of ideas developed from the several trips abroad made by various members of the organization: Byron Steinmetz made a trip to Europe looking for new belt styles in March, and Mr. Teplow planned a similar trip for the bag department during the summer. Mr. Breitman also made a six weeks' trip to Japan, during which he made arrangements with a number of Japanese manufacturers to produce novelty designs (both belt and bag) for the company, and in addition he brought back ideas for Breitman's own production.

As a season progressed, lines which did not "go" were dropped, and others added. Sometimes such decisions were made on a group basis, and sometimes they were arrived at as a result of suggestions initiated by Fred Apfel, Byron Steinmetz, a salesman, or one of the partners and approved by one of the partners.

"Merchandising" the handbag line was accomplished in much the same way, except that a number of decisions on the bag line were made by Mr. Teplow and his designer, sometimes, but not always, after discussing them with Mr. Breitman, Mr. Fischer, and Mr. Rich.

2. *The Selling Process.* Selling the Breitman line involved three essential relationships or activities, as Mr. Williams saw it: (1) The work done away from the showroom by salesmen in soliciting business from buyers; (2) the selling done in the 32d Street showroom, plus entertaining visiting buyers in New York; (3) the calls made by 32d

Street people on department-store resident buyers in New York City. In addition, the company prepared advertising material each season for the use of its customers.

THE SALES FORCE AND ITS FIELD ACTIVITIES.   Although Mr. Williams had met each of the salesmen at least once, his knowledge of their activities was limited to what Mr. Fischer and the two sales managers told him and to what the salesmen themselves reported about the jobs. Mr. Williams learned thus that salesmen received, with very few exceptions, 10% commissions on all sales made to their accounts, regardless of whether or not they personally made the sale. Most of them lived in their territories, except the men covering the New York, Philadelphia, and New England areas. Some of them had gross earnings larger than the salaries of the partners (see Exhibit 14). Mr. Williams understood that this was not at all uncommon in the soft-goods and style-merchandise industry. The group ranged in age from about twenty-five to forty-five, he judged, with three or four of the salesmen apparently under thirty.

Mr. Fischer said that salesmen usually tried to call on large department-store buyers at their offices but in many instances, in accordance with trade practice, set up their samples in a hotel room, where buyers came to inspect the merchandise. On one occasion Mr. Fischer remarked:

Maybe you can tell me how you get the lead out of some of these salesmen, when making a good living these days is not too difficult. Actually most of our salesmen are first rate, but I don't know what you do about the few lazy ones.

Sales territories were assigned by Mr. Fischer, who said that the reason the territories were not divided on a strictly geographical basis was to take account of particular salesman-buyer relationships that had grown up. Mr. Fischer believed that having a salesman call on a store where he knew a particular buyer was more important than having a strict geographic division of territories.

Mr. Fischer indicated to Mr. Williams that Byron Steinmetz and Frank Rich were sales managers more in title than in fact:

I guess at Harvard you'd say that was poor organizational practice, but I don't think you can just bring in two men and suddenly turn over to them something you've been doing for years. The salesmen know me, and I know them intimately. Besides, I sometimes wonder if either Byron or Frank knows what it takes to be a sales manager.

So far as Mr. Williams could tell, Byron's and Frank's principal sales-management functions consisted of preparing sales bulletins to the field,

Exhibit 14

BREITMAN & COMPANY
Product Sales by Salesmen and Salesmen's Commissions
July, 1950—June, 1952

	July, 1950—June, 1951				July, 1951—June, 1952				Territory
	Belts	Bags	Total	Commission	Belts	Bags	Total	Commission	
House Sales	$145,340	$151,532	$296,872	$22,985	$198,193	$158,934	$357,127	$30,764	New York City area: 45 stores, 4 belts only
Salesman #2	145,666	110,389	256,055	3,322	258,518	101,027	359,545	5,387	New England, New York, and Pennsylvania: 8 states, 138 cities
Salesman #3	139,143	215,876	355,019	28,266	214,734	225,928	440,662	35,962	
Salesman #4	207,427	352,848	560,275	42,335	336,342	433,965	770,307	59,388	South Central: 3 states, 53 cities
Salesman #5	376,399	253,847	630,246	48,618	482,053	306,245	788,298	66,916	West and Southwest: 12 states, 3 foreign cities
Salesman #6	211,996	266,562	478,558	38,366	299,379	333,989	633,368	51,543	Central: 6 states, 241 cities
Salesman #7	99,696	219,829	319,525	25,602	197,162	284,795	481,957	38,343	South: 9 states
Salesman #8	241,618	287,222	528,840	42,983	449,571	382,807	832,373	70,355	Middle West: 10 states
Salesman #9 (1 month only: June, 1952)					2,410	1,710	4,120	360	South: 4 states, 95 cities
Salesman #10 (11 month totals: missing June, 1951, and June, 1952)	214,284	266,874	481,158	38,760	319,326	307,579	626,905	51,715	South: 4 states, Mexico
Salesman #11 (11 month totals: missing June, 1951, and June, 1952)	141,592	145,765	287,357	23,876	145,585	156,041	301,626	24,303	Six large cities, plus parts of New York City and Chicago
Salesman #12 (11 month totals: missing June, 1951, and June, 1952)	53,743	88,209	141,952	11,277	111,362	97,649	209,211	17,716	East Central: 4 states plus suburban New York City and Philadelphia
Salesman #13 (8 months: October, 1951, through May, 1952)					4,801	3,807	8,608	674	
Totals: (11 month totals: missing June, 1951, and June, 1952)	$1,790,238	$2,238,219	$4,028,557	$318,362	$2,786,938	$2,663,069	$5,450,007	$423,793	

Source: Mr. Fischer's desk records.

indicating changes in the line and numbers that were selling well, and reporting sales progress generally.

The particular individual whom a buyer saw in a customer organization varied from account to account. In the largest retail organizations the buying organization was a highly specialized activity. Many large department stores had at least one buyer who bought only handbags. A few stores with a separate bargain basement had two handbag buyers. Relatively few department stores had buyers responsible only for belts. That merchandise was often bought in large stores by individuals handling a variety of accessories—umbrellas, luggage, wallets, scarves, etc. —occasionally by the handbag buyer. In smaller stores the number of types of merchandise purchased by a buyer was greater—one buyer might, for example, be responsible for women's apparel and accessories as a group. In still smaller stores all buying might be done by the proprietor. To get some notion of the varying responsibilities of store buyers in a place like New York City, Mr. Williams put together the information in Exhibit 18.

During his visits Mr. Williams was told many times that good salesman-buyer contacts were the most important part of the business. One salesman described these contacts thus:

> Obviously, you've got to have the right merchandise, but if you can't get along with the buyers, you're through. Most of the time you're on a first-name basis with these people; you know about their private lives; you take them out to lunch or dinner; and in a lot of cases you spend a great deal of time with them, never even mentioning business. This week, for example, I took the belt buyer for ——— [a New York department store] to lunch—the third week running. We had a few drinks, I kidded her along—more like a date than a business conference—and as I dropped her off after lunch, she suggested I come in next Friday. Maybe she'll buy, maybe she won't, but it's all part of the game.

An important part of a salesman's job, Mr. Fischer reported, was seeing to it that stores did not overload with merchandise that would not sell:

> Twenty per cent of our customers are smart enough to know better than we do what will go, but the other eighty per cent don't. And it would be very poor business for us to overload a buyer with merchandise that she'd have to mark down—or try to return—at the end of the season.[5]

---

[5] Mr. Williams had never been able to get any exact information on customer returns, but had been assured by several people that this had never constituted a serious problem for Breitman & Company.

SHOWROOM SELLING ACTIVITIES. In terms of the demands on a number of people's time, waiting on customers in the showroom was the principal activity at 32d Street. This activity also contributed substantially, Mr. Williams believed, to the continued impression he had of the organization as an exceptionally busy place. Mr. Williams made only one brief visit to the showroom during "market season," the semiannual two-week period when all the salesmen came to New York, and the flow of out-of-town buyers into the showroom was occasionally so heavy that a line of buyers waited in front of the elevators in the first-floor lobby. At the same time, even during the so-called "slack season," Mr. Williams had never seen the showroom empty of buyers between ten in the morning and five at night, and it was not exceptional for a few buyers to be waiting in the lobby because the eight showroom tables were full.

During Mr. Williams' visits to the company, he observed that 11 members of the Breitman organization, in addition to whatever salesmen might be on hand, spent at least some part of their regular work week waiting on customers in the showroom. For the two girls who regularly worked there, this was apparently the only activity, except for such duties as putting samples back in their cases and, for one of them, working on preparation and distribution of advertising material. For Byron Steinmetz and Frank Rich, waiting on customers, Mr. Williams guessed, typically occupied at least one-half to two-thirds of most working days. Simon, Mickey, Fred Apfel, Harry Block, and Joe were called on as the occasion demanded, or as their immediate jobs permitted, more or less in that order. Mr. Williams estimated that each of them typically put in 10 to 15 hours a week in the showroom. Waiting on customers appeared to have "top priority." If any one of the showroom people already waiting on someone saw another customer unattended, he usually tried to locate someone else to come into the showroom.

Mr. Fischer himself also appeared to spend more than half of most working days either waiting on buyers or talking to them as someone else showed samples to the buyers. Mr. Breitman, on the other hand, usually came into the showroom briefly to greet someone he already knew or to meet a new customer if the salesperson working with that customer suggested it.

Mr. Fischer was acknowledged to be the best salesman in the house, and Mr. Williams could only sense—rather than describe—why this was so. Mr. Fischer appeared to have a very genuine warmth when he greeted people. He had an unusual capacity for remembering names and his previous conversations with customers, and he made only a limited number of references to himself. Mr. Williams had been told on a number of occasions by salesmen, the 32d Street group, and buyers that "Judson Fischer's personality is the most important asset this business has."

In addition to the showroom contacts with buyers, Mr. Fischer and the two sales managers spent most noon hours entertaining buyers at lunch, and it was not uncommon for Mr. Fischer to entertain buyers at home all the evenings in a week that he did not spend in the showroom.

CALLS ON RESIDENT BUYERS. Mr. Fischer and, starting in the spring of 1952, Simon, one of the young men in the 32d Street office, made calls about once a week on the larger "resident buyer" organizations in New York City. "Resident buyers" represented either a large department-store chain, like Federated Department Stores, or a group of independent department or other retail stores. The larger resident-buying offices had as many as from 50 to 75 buyers, specializing in various kinds of merchandise in the same way that the department-store buyers themselves did. A resident buyer had several functions: to keep the buyers of various department stores throughout the country informed on style trends; to select the source and type of merchandise to fill orders placed with them by the stores they represented; and to assist their affiliated stores in following up on merchandise deliveries. At least in the large stores, resident buyers were used as aids to the store buyers themselves; the store buyers typically maintained their own contacts with suppliers as well.

ADVERTISING. Breitman's advertising, Mr. Williams was told by Mr. Fischer, was limited to preparation of material for use by its customers because "people just won't decide they want a Breitman bag or belt and then go looking for it. It's the store name, rather than the manufacturer's name, that pulls in this business."

Breitman's principal advertising expense was for a semiannual "belt enclosure," a leaflet describing eight or ten items in a season's line and made available in quantity to the stores that bought from Breitman. These stores sent this leaflet, with monthly bills, to their customers. Breitman also provided customers with "mats" for newspaper ads, showing Breitman merchandise. In 1952 the company was having a 40-second film prepared on Breitman belts for use by department stores in local TV spot advertisements.

Mr. Steinmetz was responsible for working with artists and printers in preparing advertising material and was assisted in this work and in the mechanics of distributing the material by one of the showroom saleswomen. The final copy on enclosures was usually reviewed by the group which made decisions on belt merchandising.

3. *Production.* BELT OPERATION—THE 25TH STREET FACTORY. The 25th Street factory consisted of a 5,000-square-foot, third-floor loft, and numbered 43 production people supervised by Mrs. Long, whom Mr. Williams judged to be in her early thirties. In contrast to the 32d Street operation, and to some extent the 14th Street bag factory, the 25th Street factory appeared to have adequate room for its activities. On the day Mr. Williams visited the factory, it was making only Breitweave braided belts, but Mr. Williams understood that at other times of the year the factory also made other types of fabric belts. He observed seven different types of operations during his visit, done either by hand or by a variety of sewing or braiding machines: cutting, braiding, stitching, eyeletting, trimming, "tacking" (fastening buckles), and assembling (fastening ornaments, pasting leather strips, etc.). The supervisor appeared quite willing to explain her job:

This is really very simple, and I don't know what there is to explain. None of our operations is any different from what you'd find in any belt factory.

Mr. Apfel gives me cutting orders over the phone. I then write up cutting tickets, which stay with the belts until they are shipped. I also enter all cutting orders in a book. We ship to 32d Street once a day, and I write up shipping tickets for all shipments. On the basis of "feel," I order material over the phone from 14 different suppliers as we need it and find buyers for raw material that doesn't move. I'm not concerned with prices—that's Mr. Apfel's job. I discuss with him the places I buy from and send purchase requisitions up to 32d Street on everything I buy.

We can turn out 150 to 200 gross of belts here a week and can get most orders out in a couple of days after Mr. Apfel gives them to us. Every once in a while Mr. Breitman comes down and we figure out together how we'll make some new style.

I'm not concerned with prices or costs, except that, of course, it's up to me to see that waste is kept down and that we turn out good merchandise.

I guess you'd say we have a very happy place here, largely because my two bosses, Mr. Breitman and Mr. Fischer, are such wonderful people.

BAG OPERATION—THE 14TH STREET FACTORY. The 14th Street factory, equipped—according to the factory superintendent—to turn out 78 gross of bags in a 40- or 45-hour week, numbered approximately 65 employees who were engaged in four types of operations: cutting, pasting, sewing and assembling, and inspecting. "I don't know what there is to explain," the superintendent reported. "We get orders on what to make from the bag production manager, usually in three-gross lots; they go through the works, and it's my job to keep the factory going."

The 14th Street factory, in contrast to the belt factory, shipped its merchandise directly to customers and maintained its own shipping department, supervised by a Mr. Fox. The bag factory also sent out its own invoices, typed by a girl located in the shipping room.

THE DANDRIDGE, TENNESSEE, OPERATION. While Mr. Williams was visiting Breitman, Mr. Fischer and Mr. Breitman decided to close the Tennessee operation. Frank Rich had made a visit to the Southern plant, and as a result of this trip an audit was made of that firm's books, which were, according to Miss Voss, "in terrible shape." Mr. Fischer reported: "We think actually we may have been cheated, and we're probably going to lose $100,000 in this before we're through. We were persuaded to make this mistake by a handbag competitor of ours—he put up half the funds involved."

Because the Dandridge company was personally owned by the partners, its profits—or losses—were not reflected in Breitman income statements. Its sales were reflected in Breitman's total sales figures, since it sold all its merchandise through Breitman & Company.

THE CONTRACTORS. Mr. Williams had learned very little about the operations of the belt and bag manufacturers who did contract work for Breitman. He had at one point asked Miss Voss for a breakdown of the relative volume done by each of them. But when he was told that to furnish such data would involve running subtotals from the purchase register, he decided to withdraw his request. Exhibit 15 indicates the information on contractor and company manufacturing maintained in Mr. Fischer's desk records.

Mr. Williams had sat in on the negotiations with one belt manufacturer who began working with Breitman & Company in April and talked with another manufacturer who had made belts for Breitman for over a year. Both these men owned, and constituted the entire supervisory force of, their businesses; both had been recommended to Breitman by the garment workers' union representing Breitman workers. Both had been "in and out" of the business once before, one for reasons of health and the other because of voluntary liquidation.

4. *Keeping Production and Purchasing Abreast of Sales.* The duties of co-ordinating belt production and purchasing with sales were performed entirely by Mr. Fred Apfel, who also was responsible for determining belt prices. Mr. Apfel worked closely with Mr. Fischer and Mr. Breitman. His counterpart in the bag department, except for differ-

Exhibit 15

BREITMAN & COMPANY

Breakdown of Sales Showing Merchandise Manufactured by Company and by Contractors, 1948–51

(In Thousands)

	1948	1949	1950	1951
Belts:				
Company manufactured.	$ 748.4	$ 551.4	$ 581.7	$ 735.7
Job*.........................	373.4	354.2	761.6	1,354.6
Job—metal*..................	192.3	353.4	504.9	643.3
Total belts...............	$1,314.1	$1,259.0	$1,848.2	$2,733.6
Bags:				
Company manufactured........	$1,111.3	$1,237.9	$1,362.3	$1,954.4
Job—straw..................	80.4	741.5	729.6	736.8
Job—other..................		4.4	67.1	27.0
Total bags...............	$1,191.7	$1,983.8	$2,159.0	$2,718.2
Total sales..............	$2,505.8	$3,242.8	$4,007.2	$5,451.8

* Most of the contractors making metal belts were located in Rhode Island. Other contractors were, for the most part, in the New York City area.
Source: Mr. Fischer's desk records.

ences noted below, performed about the same duties as did Mr. Apfel.

BELT PRODUCTION SCHEDULING AND PURCHASING—MR. APFEL'S ACTIVITIES. "If you aren't an executive when you start this job, you sure are once you've been at it a while," Mr. Apfel reported. "I make more decisions a week about how to spend the bosses' money than I can count, and they've got to be right."

Mr. Williams observed that Mr. Apfel's activities, in addition to his participation in evening meetings, included deciding at what price each of the various belt items should be sold; deciding the amounts of the various styles to be produced, in what colors, and by whom; determining where various raw material items could be purchased; and in many cases placing orders, usually over the telephone, for shipments to contractors. In the process of deciding merchandise prices, Mr. Apfel also made frequent suggestions to Mr. Breitman about ways in which designs might be changed or new ones added to the line. Furthermore, Mr. Apfel in the late spring was handling all company contracts with a large mail-order house, which had ordered belts from Breitman for the first time that season. It was, moreover, not uncommon for Mr. Apfel to spend several hours in an afternoon working in the showroom.

Mr. Apfel made his price decisions[6] by using a table he had prepared, listing each of the various prices at which belts were sold and, for each price, the amount that should be spent on raw material and labor. This last amount he had calculated in each instance by deducting sales commission (10%), purchase discount (8%), a net profit figure (15%), and a "cost-of-doing-business" figure from the sales price. In making a particular price decision, he started with the price at which he believed a belt had to be sold, compared the appropriate balance for raw material and labor with his estimate of what a particular style would cost, and concluded that either the company could sell the particular belt at this starting price or that he must find ways to reduce the cost by minor modifications or review with Mr. Breitman or Mr. Fischer the basic decision to include the number in the line. His "raw material and labor" cost estimates were based on his own knowledge of what costs were, or on estimates he got over the phone from suppliers. His cost-of-business figure, he said, he reviewed approximately once a year with Mr. Fischer. His net profit figure was a target from which he frequently varied.

Mr. Apfel's activities in purchasing and production scheduling were based on a running record of (1) orders placed on suppliers, (2) merchandise receipts, (3) orders received from customers, and (4) merchandise shipments. This information was recorded by individual style numbers in a loose-leaf notebook. Mr. Apfel himself kept this record up to date and based it on information he obtained periodically from the account-card desk. In addition to placing orders, he kept in frequent telephone contact (and had an occasional personal visit) with suppliers and contractors to follow up on his orders and to issue instructions to them. He also wrote up personally all purchase invoices involved in his activities.

Mr. Apfel also kept a record of monthly shipments by belt types (metal, leather, velvet, etc.) and used it as the basis for making initial purchase decisions at the beginning of a season. He said to Mr. Williams:

I always try to get Mr. Fischer's ideas before I commit the firm for any major amounts, but sometimes I just have to go ahead on my own. It works something

---

[6] Mr. Apfel's price decisions were, of course, an integral part of the merchandising process described earlier but are included here for convenience in describing his activities as a whole.

like this: At the beginning of a season I may decide we're going to sell at least $250,000 of aluminum belts, and I get Mr. Fischer or Mr. Breitman to let me go ahead with that much at the beginning of the season. Then after sales have come in for a month or so, I'll use my own judgment in placing more orders.

Mr. Apfel and Mr. Williams on several occasions had discussed the "frantic pace" that this job necessitated, particularly since Mr. Apfel's only assistance came from the girls at the account-card desk. On one such occasion, Mr. Apfel said:

This is what it's like in this business, and, of course, there are a lot of compensations in working for people like Mr. Breitman and Mr. Fischer. At the same time I don't know if I can continue this way. You see, the difficulty with my job is that it would be very difficult to train anyone to assist me, particularly since so much of what I do is based on my feel for the business, my knowledge of the line and of customers, and my personal contacts with suppliers. They'll do things for me they won't do for anyone else because they know I'm fair.

After this season is over, I hope to be able to turn some of my clerical work over to Olga [at the account-card desk] and that should straighten things out. Of course, it would be a lot easier if people weren't interrupting me all the time —and the boss is one of the biggest offenders on that score. He's always asking for information on how we stand on a particular number or a particular part of the line. And of course, there's the time in the showroom, but that helps keep me posted on what customers are buying.

BAG PRODUCTION SCHEDULING AND PURCHASING. From his single interview with the bag production manager, Mr. Williams understood that he had approximately the same responsibilities as Mr. Apfel, with such differences in day-to-day operations as resulted from the following circumstances: he worked directly under Mr. Teplow's supervision; he occupied an office located adjacent to the bag factory and shared only by three clerks who worked for him; he had to cope with only a relatively small number of styles in the bag line; and he did not deal at all with customers. These differences apparently resulted in his being subjected to few interruptions in his "normal" work, although the bag production manager was in frequent telephone contact with Mr. Fischer or salesmen about the status of orders.

5. *The Processing of Orders.* Mr. Williams devoted particular attention to understanding the detailed mechanics of the process of getting orders through the Breitman organization in view of: Mr. Breitman's initial comment to him about methods; the number of comments made to him about the difficulties in keeping up with this operation, particularly in the belt department; his own observation that Mr. Teplow discussed the system with Fred Apfel and Harry Block with

increasing frequency as he visited the company; and on several occasions Miss Voss's indicating to him that if space could be found, a mechanized operation would be highly desirable. Mr. Williams, in the course of his study, sat in on an evening conference when a young lawyer (Mr. Fischer's nephew) discussed with most of the executives of the company his views on the company's methods and procedures. The lawyer's two recommendations, made in general terms, were that the company should standardize its record forms in the belt and bag

Exhibit 16

BREITMAN & COMPANY

Steps Involved in Processing Orders

Steps	Performed by
STEPS COMMON TO BELT AND BAG ORDERS	
1 Mail orders opened...............................	Telephone operator
Orders taken in the showroom or by telephone............	Showroom sales person
2 Orders reviewed.......................................	Mr. Fischer
3 Orders coded...	Mickey
4 Credit checked.......................................	Miss Voss or assistant
STEPS IN PROCESSING BELT ORDERS ONLY	
5 Orders entered on account cards.......................	Account-card clerk
6 Orders stapled to cardboard holders and placed in order bin..	Harry Block or order pickers
7a Orders picked.......................................	
7b Prices entered.......................................	Harry Block or order pickers
7c (Back orders sent to lay-away bin)...................	
8 Invoice typed..	Biller
9 Merchandise packed and shipped.......................	Shipper
10 Shipments entered on account cards...................	Account-card clerk
11 Orders placed in file................................	Account-card clerk
STEPS IN PROCESSING BELT BACK ORDERS	
7a Back orders entered in shortage book..................	Lay-away clerk
7b Incoming belt merchandise checked against shortage book...	Lay-away clerk
7c Back orders filled...................................	Lay-away clerk

operations and that immediate steps should be taken to mechanize some of the order processing and record-keeping operations. In Mr. Williams' opinion, the lawyer did not succeed in convincing Mr. Fischer or the group of the soundness of his recommendations, although Mr. Williams understood that the lawyer was to continue his study.

Exhibit 16 lists the steps involved in processing all belt orders, as well as the four steps common to both belt and bag orders. Each of these steps required the physical movement of orders from one part of the office to another, and orders were usually carried from point to point by the person who last handled them. That movement, according to Mr. Williams' observations, caused particular congestion in the area where Mr. Apfel, Mickey, the account-card clerks, and Harry Block had their desks. The processing of bag orders at 14th Street was essentially the same as the 32d Street belt process, except that no separate provision was made for handling back orders.[7] According to Mr. Teplow's production and purchasing assistant, such a system was unnecessary in the bag department because fewer styles were involved, back orders were less common, and it was considerably easier to follow through production such back orders as did arise.

According to Miss Voss, an average of 2,500 orders were processed each month. Some orders were taken in the showroom; some were received via the salesmen; and some directly from the customer. Although all orders were coded to show their source, no tabulation—to Mr. Williams' knowledge—was made of the relative volume of business which came in each way. Orders from outside the showroom came in by mail, telegraph, or telephone. As part of her normal routine the switchboard operator placed all telegraph and mail orders on Mr. Fischer's desk. Orders were taken over the telephone by either Mr. Fischer, the salesmen, or the showroom people.

Several salesmen and one or two others in the organization had indicated to Mr. Williams their belief that Mr. Fischer's insistence on seeing all orders was both a source and a symptom of one of Breitman & Company's chief problems—an overload on Mr. Fischer. Objections to this part of the system had also been raised directly to Mr. Fischer by members of his organization in Mr. Williams' presence. Mr. Fischer had replied to one of these objections by saying:

> This doesn't really take much of my time, and it's a very important way for me to keep posted on what's going on. I can learn more about what's selling and who's buying from a quick look at orders than I ever could from a report. This is a fast-moving business, and I can't wait for a report. Besides, whom have we got to prepare it?

Orders were normally picked up by Mickey from Mr. Fischer or taken by whoever might pass Mr. Fischer's desk to Mickey, for a routine processing to indicate source of order and salesman's credit.

Mickey, a young man in his twenties, had joined Breitman & Company in 1950. He indicated to Mr. Williams that the order-coding part

---

[7] A back order is one which cannot be filled from merchandise in stock.

of his job involved no particular difficulties. This responsibility, however, was combined with the job of following up customer inquiries, "plus a few other things," and Mickey reported:

I sometimes don't know whether I'm coming or going. Look, right now I'm three days behind in answering correspondence. I spend so much of my time walking around trying to find where the orders are that I can never catch up. Another problem is that I have to separate bag and belt orders. Our salesmen know enough to write them up separately, and so do many of our customers, but I have to copy off the bag orders if they're not separate.

Mickey, or a passer-by, carried orders to Miss Voss's office, where a credit check, in most cases routine, was made, and then the belt orders were returned to the account-card desk. After a clerk made a notation of the orders on the customer account cards, the orders were placed on Harry Block's desk.

HARRY BLOCK'S ACTIVITIES.   "You know, Doc, you're from Harvard, and you probably know a lot about management, and you probably think getting orders out is simple and unimportant," Mr. Block said to Mr. Williams toward the end of Mr. Williams' stay. "Well, if you do, you're wrong. What we do here has as much to do with whether we stay in business as what the salesmen do, even if they do make more money—particularly if we foul up. I know something about the problems of this game, since I spent almost 20 years with Sears, Roebuck in their traffic department before coming here, and I set this system up."

Mr. Block and his group were also responsible for taking periodical physical inventories, an operation that usually took place over a week end. This group customarily was augmented by five or six other people from the executive group. Partly from his initial interviews with Mr. Block, partly from subsequent visits, Mr. Williams learned that Mr. Block worked with his four to six "order pickers" in taking the orders placed on his desk and stapling them on large cardboard cards together with an order sheet, and physically taking the merchandise off the shelves. This job of filling orders, Mr. Block explained, required a detailed knowledge of the "line" and of customers because in many cases it was necessary to make substitutions for what the customers ordered or to fill so-called "open orders" in which the customer left the particular merchandise to be shipped to the discretion of the manufacturer. He also explained that the job involved some judgment as to establishing priorities on orders:

Our system has to be designed on the basis that we take care of orders as they come in, but at the same time we've got to give preference to big accounts.

The trouble is every salesman thinks his orders should be taken care of first, and I have to use my judgment. You can't please everyone, Doc.

Mr. Block also pointed out that a unique feature of the belt department, as contrasted to the bag department, was the so-called "lay-away system." If orders could not be filled, even by substitutions, they were carried to a lay-away area, where they were entered in a "back order" or "shortage" book and filed by date. When incoming merchandise was received, it was normally checked against the back-order book before being placed on the shelf, although Mr. Block explained that the need for giving priority to good customers meant that the system was not followed rigidly.

Like Mr. Apfel, Mr. Block was subject to a number of interruptions in his daily routine. He was frequently asked by salesmen, showroom people, or Mickey to assist them in locating unfilled orders. He also was asked by a variety of people when particular merchandise was expected; sometimes he referred such questions to Fred Apfel. He worked in the showroom as the occasion demanded, and took telephone calls from customers inquiring about their orders. Mr. Block indicated to Mr. Williams that a certain amount of the confusion that existed in his operation was the inevitable result of the very crowded situation in the back room and in the belt storage area:

The boss is reluctant to get our belt inventory out of this building, but we're going to have to do it.

With Mr. Fischer's approval, Mr. Block had placed an ad in the *New York Times* early in June, indicating an opening in a belt shipping department for a traffic executive. From the hundred-odd replies he received, he interviewed five and hired a man to work with him at $60 a week. "The guy left in a week," Mr. Block reported. "He seemed to have the notion that all executives sit with their feet up on the desk."

BELT RECEIVING. An additional activity, related to the processing of orders and located adjacent to the belt storage shelves, was the belt receiving department. Here approximately 25 people, under the supervision of a man known to Mr. Williams only as "Smitty," checked all incoming belt merchandise, inspected it, and packed it in half-dozen or dozen lots in the boxes in which the merchandise was placed on the shelves. It was Mr. Williams' understanding that "Smitty" was responsible to Fred Apfel and Harry Block, although he observed Mr. Fischer and Mr. Breitman talking to "Smitty" about his operations on a number of occasions.

6. *Record-Keeping and the Process of Keeping Management Informed.* Exhibit 17 summarizes the data gathered by Mr. Williams on Breitman's record-keeping process. Mr. Fischer kept a set of 5" × 8" cards in his desk, on which Miss Voss entered monthly records of orders, shipments, and salesmen's sales and commissions, and the annual tabulation of sales going back to 1948. Mr. Fischer occasionally asked Mr. Block or Mr. Apfel for special reports in more detail on the status of particular numbers or types of merchandise in the line.

Although Mr. Williams did not go into the details of the bookkeeping operation, he was invited on half-a-dozen occasions to join Miss Voss for lunch at her desk and had talked with her on a number of other occasions. The bookkeeping operation, with the exception of Miss Voss's own activities, was almost entirely self-contained, and from Mr. Williams' general impressions of its day-to-day workings, he saw no need to investigate its activities in any detail. Miss Voss had indicated her belief that less crowded quarters would enable her to run a more efficient operation. She also expressed the hope that if more room were made available, she might be able to persuade Mr. Breitman to mechanize some of her operations:

> We had an estimate from Remington Rand a year ago on a $25,000 installation which would speed up our billings considerably. Mr. Breitman wanted to know how quickly we could save that, and I had to tell him that we wouldn't realize any direct cash savings, so he turned it down.

Miss Voss indicated that one of her continuing headaches was not being able to maintain her help on the salaries she was permitted to pay. "In this business the money goes to the selling end. We don't pay either our office help or our production people competitive wages." Because of this fact, and because of her own college courses in personnel, she reported that she tried to take an interest in some of the personnel problems not only of her own people but also of the production people. "Last week I conducted what you'd call an exit interview with one of the boys out back who quit."

VII. MR. WILLIAMS' CONTACTS WITH MR. BREITMAN, MR. FISCHER, AND MR. TEPLOW

In view of Mr. Williams' interest in the over-all management problems of Breitman, he had been particularly interested in learning as much as he could about the two owners of the business, as well as about Mr. Teplow, whom several people in the organization had referred to

Exhibit 17

BREITMAN & COMPANY

*Analysis of Company Records and Reports**

BASIC RECORDS OF NORMAL BUSINESS TRANSACTIONS

Records	Number of Copies	Prepared by	Sent to	Use
Customer order....	1	Customers (mail orders) Breitman sales personnel	See Exhibit 16	Processing all orders
Customer invoice..	4	Biller	Customer as bill Customer as shipping ticket Completed order files Miss Voss	Establishing shipments made and accounts receivable
Purchase invoice...	2	Mr. Apfel Miss Voss Mrs. Long Bag Production Manager	Supplier† Miss Voss	Recording merchandise or material ordered
Supplier invoice....	1	Supplier Contractor	Receiving Departments Miss Voss	Checking incoming shipments Establishing accounts payable
Time cards........	1	Production employee	Miss Voss	Establishing payroll
Shipping receipts...	1	Post Office Railway Express	Clerk	Establishing shipments made
Cutting tickets....	1	Mrs. Long Bag Production Manager	Accompanies merchandise through factory—filed in production files	Getting merchandise produced in factory

* Does not include all records at 14th Street or 25th Street factories.
† Copy not always sent to supplier on telephone orders.
Source: Case writer's interviews with people involved.

INFORMATION ACCUMULATED BY ACCOUNTING DEPARTMENT
(MISS VOSS'S DEPARTMENT)

Ledger or File	Description
Purchase registers:......................... Handbags Handbag contractors Belts Expense	Chronological record of purchases and payments
Payroll register............................	Chronological record of payroll
Cash receipts and disbursements...............	Chronological record of other cash receipts and disbursements
Accounts receivable register.................	Customer accounts receivable cards

Exhibit 17—Continued

BREITMAN & COMPANY

Analysis of Company Records and Reports*

INFORMATION ACCUMULATED TO KEEP TRACK OF ORDERS AND SHIPMENTS			
Record or File	Description	Maintained by	Use
Belt account cards...	5 × 8 cards, filed alphabetically by customer showing all belt orders and shipments made to customer	Account-card clerks—32d Street	Permanent record of customer activity. Follow-up on orders
Bag account cards...	Same for bags	Account-card clerk —14th Street	
Belt active-order file.	Orders awaiting processing, filed by date	Harry Block	Source of orders to be processed. Follow-up of orders
Belt lay-away file...	Orders awaiting belt shipments, filed by date	Lay-away clerk	Processing back orders
Belt shortage book..	Chronological record of back orders, filled and unfilled		Follow-up of orders
Belt completed-order file........	Completed orders, filed by customer	Account-card clerk	Permanent record
Bag active-order file.	Orders awaiting shipment, filed chronologically	Bag Department clerks	Order processing
Bag completed-order file........	Completed orders, filed by customer		Permanent record

* Does not include all records at 14th Street or 25th Street factories.
† Copy not always sent to supplier on telephone orders.
Source: Case writer's interviews with people involved.

INFORMATION ACCUMULATED BY MR. APFEL FOR HIS OWN USE	
Record	Description
Cost cards............................	5 × 8 cards showing cost breakdowns on each style
Individual style sheets..................	8 × 11 sheets showing shipments, receipts, and orders placed for each style, broken down by size and color
Tabulation of monthly sales and shipments.	Cumulative monthly record of belts sold and shipped, under headings: metal, leather, other

Exhibit 17—Continued

BREITMAN & COMPANY

*Analysis of Company Records and Reports**

REPORTS FOR MANAGEMENT USE

(Prepared within the Organization)

Tabulation	Prepared by	For
Daily belt shipments by basic types......... ⎱ Daily belt orders by basic types............ ⎰	Account-card clerks	⎰ Mr. Fischer ⎱ Mr. Apfel ⎰ Mr. Block
Monthly sales by salesmen...................	Miss Voss	Mr. Fischer
Monthly sales and shipments by types of bags and belts.............................	Account-card clerks Miss Voss	Mr. Fischer
Annual sales by customers listed geographically (includes bags and belts)..................	Whoever available	Mr. Fischer Salesmen
List of styles in the belt and handbag line......	Mr. Steinmetz's assistant	Salesmen Shipping departments

(Prepared by Outside Accountants)

	Frequency	Description
Balance sheet......................................	Four times a year	See Exhibit 2
Income statement.................................	" " "	See Exhibit 3
Ratio analysis.....................................	" " "	See Exhibit 4
Income tax form...................................	Once a year	

* Does not include all records at 14th Street or 25th Street factories.
† Copy not always sent to supplier on telephone orders.
Source: Case writer's interviews with people involved.

as "a kind of informal general manager." By the end of his preliminary investigation, Mr. Williams had had much less opportunity to talk in detail with either Mr. Breitman or Mr. Teplow than he had with Mr. Fischer, and his picture of the former gentlemen's respective places in the organization was much less detailed.

Mr. Breitman, as both president and treasurer, talked frequently to Mr. Fischer about such matters as hiring of personnel, decisions on spending money, questions as to whether or not to add new lines (e.g., the novelty line Mr. Breitman brought back from Japan), and the volume of business being done. Otherwise, Mr. Breitman apparently devoted most of his time to his office or design room, working on new styles. (Joe, one of the younger men in the group, spent much of his time in acting as general assistant to Mr. Breitman.) "I've learned that the business gets along better if I keep out of most of the operating details," Mr. Breitman told Mr. Williams.

Mr. Teplow, general manager of the bag department, seldom discussed many of the day-to-day details of the handbag operations with either Mr. Fischer or Mr. Breitman, so far as Mr. Williams could learn. He did, however, review with Mr. Breitman and Mr. Fischer the items he proposed to include in the line as well as the results of his operation in terms of volume. Mr. Teplow had little day-to-day contact with Frank Rich, the bag sales manager, and had almost no contacts with customers. His system of follow-up in matters he regarded as requiring attention had been pointed out to Mr. Williams by others on several occasions. Mr. Teplow carried a sheaf of tablet paper in his coat pocket, on which he made notes of matters needing attention. "This gives him an unfailing memory," one person reported, "and if you haven't done what you said you would, look out." Mr. Teplow had answered freely any specific questions put to him by Mr. Williams, but had never volunteered much information about company problems.

Mr. Williams believed that his picture of Mr. Fischer's place in the organization was much more nearly complete, and Mr. Fischer had on several occasions talked at length about his views about the organization. Twice in his study Mr. Williams had spent a full day with Mr. Fischer, observing in detail his activities and listening to his conversations with others. Each day Mr. Fischer had kept up a pace of activity that made it perfectly clear why so many references had been made to his "busyness." In a single hour, for example, he might talk to half-a-dozen people in the organization about particular orders or particular problems, look at 20 or so orders, talk to a salesman on the long-distance phone, sign some checks, and say "Hello" to three or four buyers.

From numerous conversations Mr. Williams pieced together a number of Mr. Fischer's attitudes toward his own problems. "I know I'm too busy, but can you give me an easy answer on what to do about it? A great deal of my problem arises out of the fact that it's good business for the head of the firm to talk to buyers." Mr. Fischer reported on several occasions to Mr. Williams that once after he had turned over a customer to one of his sales managers, the customer had said: "What's the matter with Judson Fischer? Does he think he's a big shot?"

Mr. Fischer had offered the job as his assistant to a belt buyer for a large department store, but the buyer had turned down the job to enter his own business. Mr. Fischer indicated to Mr. Williams that he planned to offer the same job to one of his best salesmen:

But will you tell me what I do then? I'm no big shot—I'd go crazy cooped up in an office like Felix. I really enjoy what I'm doing now.

After Mr. Williams' interview with Mr. Lasser, Mr. Fischer had discussed some of Mr. Lasser's points with Mr. Williams:

> Irving talks about delegation, but let me talk about it. Do I tell Mr. Teplow how to do his job? Do I tell Miss Voss? The answer is, of course not. But what do you do when it's your business, and people don't always do what they're supposed to? I think I've got good people around me, but they slip up—let me give you a couple of examples. Last week I told Byron Steinmetz to get a belt rack for ——— [a Philadelphia department store]. Here a week later, he hasn't done it. And the week before last Fred Apfel and I were walking with a buyer past ——— [a department store], and she saw a belt she liked. I told Fred to get her one like it, and it still isn't done. Those may be details, but this business runs on details.
>
> Let me talk about another of Irving's points. He wants me to do some things now and spend some money while excess profits taxes are still in effect. The one thing he forgets is that it's my money. I've known what it's like not to have it, and I'm going to be careful spending it now that I have it.

On this same occasion Mr. Fischer talked about his attitude toward the absence of a board of directors (he and Mr. Breitman constituted the board):

> Where am I going to get some people who understand my problems, who aren't going to try to act important? Irving Lasser is very smart and a good friend of mine, but he just doesn't understand our problems.

Mr. Fischer also expressed to Mr. Williams his "dream" that he might some day retire, but said he was uncertain as to how this could in fact be accomplished. (Mr. Fischer had no children, and Mr. Breitman's only daughter was in high school.)

.   .   .   .

One of Mr. Williams' last visits to Breitman & Company took place on Monday, July 14, a day when Mr. Fischer had returned to work after a two weeks' minor illness. A description of this visit will be given in Breitman & Company (B).

Exhibit 18

BREITMAN & COMPANY

Selected Information on Belt and Handbag Buying in 36 New York City Department Stores

Size of Buying Group	Number of Stores	Number of Buyers Buying			Number of Belt or Handbag Buyers Who Also Buy					
		Hand-bags Only	Belts Only	Hand-bags and Belts	Jewelry	Leather Goods	Um-brellas	Neck-wear	Gloves	Hand-ker-chiefs
1–10 buyers	4	0	0	2	3	3	2	1	2	1
11–25 buyers	15	2	0	6	6	4	3	4	4	2
26–50 buyers	9	5	0	3	4	3	4	3	1	1
51–75 buyers	4	1	0	1	1	2	1	1	0	1
76–100 buyers	4	1	0	1	0	0	0	0	1	1
	36	9	0	13	14	12	10	10	7	6

Source: Compiled by case writer from trade sources.

Breitman & Company (B)

THE JULY 14TH CONFERENCE

AT THE REQUEST of Mickey, Simon, and Joe, an evening meeting was held on July 14th to take up some urgent problems which these three men wished aired. At eight o'clock, after the group[1] had eaten dinner together in the showroom, Mr. Fischer asked:

Well, what is it we're going to talk about tonight?[2]

JOE (*pulling out a sheet of paper on which he has written some notes*): Well, Mr. Fischer, we've been waiting for you to come back to get the answers to a lot of questions that have been bothering us. I've got a list of things here and if it's all right, I'd just like to go down some of them.

FISCHER: Sure!

JOE: The first thing that I think we probably ought to settle is about open orders.[3] We've got a problem there because they aren't filled when they first come in, and they go into the lay-away bins and we have no system for seeing that they get followed up.

FISCHER: That's a question of merchandise deliveries. Do we need to talk about that this evening?

JOE: Well, we can't just fluff it off. I think that's quite important.

APFEL: Mr. Fischer, this is a very important problem. Right now, a lot of our salesmen are writing open orders. Maybe as many as 10% of our orders come in that way. What happens is, when the boys go out to pick them in the "back," they can't find the merchandise, so they put the orders back in the lay-away bins. These orders don't appear in the shortage books, though, and there's no way of making sure they get filled.

---

[1] Present were: Mr. Fischer, Vice-President; Mr. Breitman, President; Mr. Teplow, Manager, Bag Department; Simon, resident-buyer calls, order processing; Joe, assistant to Mr. Breitman; Fred Apfel, Belt Production Manager; Frank Rich, Bag Sales Manager; Mickey, order-processing; and Mr. Williams.

[2] The transcript of this conference was dictated by Mr. Williams from notes he took during the conference.

[3] An "open order" is one on which the customer permits the manufacturer to ship whatever merchandise is available.

448

FISCHER: Is that your problem? I can solve that very simply. Why can't we just have Harry [Block, belt shipping manager] take all those orders aside and have him pick them and keep track of them?

APFEL: Mr. Fischer, Harry is a very busy man. He's already got too much to do. That isn't any answer.

FISCHER: Too bad Harry isn't here tonight. He ought to be here to discuss this. Well, what about Smitty [an order picker]? Could he do this?

BREITMAN: Smitty is working out nicely and doing a very fine job, but I don't think he knows enough yet to handle this kind of thing, and besides, we need him where he is.

APFEL: Mr. Fischer, I don't like to say this because I know Joey isn't going to like me to say it, but I think he's just the man to handle that. I think it might be a good idea if we got him to take care of it. He may not want to, but I think it's an important job, and it's to his interest and our interest that it be done.

FISCHER (*to Joe*): Do you want to?

JOE: Well, I'd like to talk to you about that and some other things later.

FISCHER: All right.

JOE: There's another matter here that I think I might bring up, which I think is related to this—and that is that we don't have any follow-up system on our orders.

FISCHER: Isn't that a little off the subject? We were talking about open orders.

JOE: No, not at all. That's very closely related to it.

SIMON: One of the reasons these open orders don't get taken care of is that we have no follow-up system at all on our orders.

FISCHER: Mickey, isn't that your job?

MICKEY: Well, I'm supposed to answer correspondence and inquiries about orders. To that extent it is my job, but I'm not supposed to follow up all orders; and, at that, I'm so busy now I can't keep up with the correspondence.

SIMON: Part of the problem is that we've never had any system, but it's gotten now completely out of hand because instead of taking orders in turn the way the system says we should, it's getting all messed up because everybody is making promises in taking care of "specials."[4]

FISCHER: Why, that's ridiculous. Do you mean to tell me that you're suggesting we shouldn't give special attention to our good customers?

---
[4] A "special" is an order handled out of sequence.

That's the way we built this business, and you're not suggesting we should be so foolish as to take care of the little stores ahead of our very best accounts, are you?

APFEL: Mr. Fischer, that's not the point. Of course we have to give special attention—have to have specials. We're so far behind now that even the promises on the specials don't do any good. Part of our problem is that we give customers a promise and then aren't able to keep it. And you've got to admit, Mr. Fischer, that you can never say "No" to anybody; even if somebody comes in who's only a small account, you still are going to make a promise to them.

SIMON: That's one of our big problems. We have a lot of people coming in here and you make promises, Mr. Fischer; Harry makes promises, the salesmen make promises, and when it's all done, none of those promises means anything. What makes it even worse is that a lot of our promises are to people who have never done any business with us before.

FISCHER: Do we have a lot of new accounts now?

BREITMAN: We really do, Judson.

SIMON: We opened up over a thousand in the last year. At the beginning of the season our cards were up to 4,000, and now they're up to 5,200.

RICH: A lot of people are coming in here to buy from us who have never bought anything from us before because of the shortage of cinches.[5]

FISCHER: There's one thing we can do something about. Simon, could you go through the [account] cards tomorrow and pick out all the orders that have been placed by people who've never dealt with us before?

APFEL: We can't pull out the cards because the girls will be working on them continually.

FISCHER: Well, then you can make a list.

RICH: One of the things you've got to be careful about is that some of the people who will appear on those cards as new accounts will actually be old bag accounts. You don't want to turn them down, do you?

FISCHER: Well, Simon, then when you get that list, you can check it with Sidney Teplow.

RICH: If you bring the list to me, I can tell you which of them are bag accounts.

---

[5] An elastic belt, for which a demand had arisen rapidly in the late spring of 1952.

FISCHER: But that still doesn't settle the basic problem about promises, does it?

APFEL: May I make a suggestion, Mr. Fischer? Right now I'm getting in about 30 gross of belts a day. That's 150 gross a week. You want to be able to make promises to your good customers. Supposing I were to take, say, 10% of those belts, which would be 15 gross a week, and set them aside, and you can promise them any way you see fit. Do you think that would be a good idea?

FISCHER: You mean you'd give me 15 gross of belts to promise any way I see fit? Gee, that would be wonderful.

BREITMAN: Do we need to set them aside?

SIMON: I don't think we should set them aside. Remember what happened last year when we had a lot of belts set aside for ———— [a salesman] and the other salesmen came in and took them all away from us. That, incidentally, is another problem. ———— [a salesman] was out back today picking out a lot of belts for his special customers.

FISCHER: After all, ———— is a good Breitman man, and I think he's probably entitled to get a little special treatment once in a while.

SIMON: Well, it isn't just ————. He's probably no worse than the rest, but the other salesmen will all come in here and want to do the same thing, and then we'll get all mixed up.

FISCHER: Well, then we don't need to put them aside. Is there anything wrong with Mr. Apfel's suggestion?

RICH: Is Mr. Breitman going to have the same, another 15 gross set aside for him?

BREITMAN: I wouldn't want to have that.

SIMON: What about Harry and all the salesmen?

APFEL: No, this is just for Mr. Fischer. If we do that, Mr. Fischer, you've got to limit yourself to that 15 gross, and if somebody else comes in, you've got to get tough with them. You've got to admit that you're soft, and if anybody comes in here and wants a promise, you'll give it to them.

FISCHER: Well, I just can't say "No" to a customer—you know that. We built this business by being agreeable to people, and I just don't think you ever say "No" to someone. You've got to play along with them. If you get tough with them, they'll get disgruntled and leave.

BREITMAN: Well, while you were gone, Judson, I got tough with some of these people and said "No" to them and made them like it.

FISCHER: Well, I think Fred's suggestion is a good one, but before we get too many more things, what about that open-order thing? Maybe we should cut out all open orders. How about this order which I have here in my pocket, which I wrote this afternoon? How is this as a way to write orders? (*Mr. Fischer pulls out an order in which he has listed all the style numbers, roughly 40 of them, which the customer wants in varying quantities to make up an order worth several thousand dollars.*) Is this perhaps a better way to do it?

BREITMAN: Well, I think open orders are a good idea, Judson. I don't think we ought to cut them out.

FISCHER: Well, then we have to have somebody to handle them, don't we? Could we perhaps hire somebody new?

TEPLOW: Well, it would have to be somebody who knows belts. You can't just take somebody off the street to do that.

FISCHER: Well, Simon, what about you? Would you like to go out back and handle them?

SIMON: If you're asking me if I *want* to, the answer is "No." There's more to this than simply the problem of open orders. People are running around there all the time not knowing what they're doing, everybody's trying to do everything. . . .

FISCHER (*interrupting*): Are you trying to tell me that you think that Harry Block is disorganized?

SIMON: Mr. Fischer, it isn't that I don't like Harry, and I know he works hard, and I know he's done a lot, but I think the answer to your question is, "Yes."

FISCHER: You mean, you don't want to work for Harry Block?

SIMON: It isn't that I don't like him.

FISCHER: You've never told me this before.

SIMON: You never asked me, and just now you did ask me, point-blank. My job is to do what I'm supposed to, not to go around and tell you about the faults of other people.

FISCHER: Gee, I wish Harry Block was here. You did try to get him, didn't you, Fred?

APFEL: Yes, and he had already left.

JOE: Coming back to this question of a follow-up system, Mickey's supposed to check on the orders, but right now there's just so much of that, he can't keep up with it. That results in the fact that everybody is going into the files, pulling out the cards to see what's happened to orders, and we're getting all mixed up. Three of the salesmen were out there this afternoon, for instance.

FISCHER: Well, that's one thing we can put a stop to. We just don't want to have any salesmen out back.

SIMON: Well, a lot of people have been calling Harry, too, to get orders. Right now when people call in here, they only want to talk to two people, either you, Mr. Fischer, or Harry Block. We could get rid of the entire rest of our sales force because they want to get a promise out of you, they know they can get it from you, and they've been getting it from Harry. Harry has been giving a lot of people promises and a lot of people special attention. A lot of customers have written in to say, in effect, that Harry was able to give them orders when nobody else could. Now he's finding that he can't continue that either; he's beginning to make a lot of enemies out of people he made promises to.

JOE: Well, another part of the problem is that when these orders get pulled out to be checked, they don't get put back, and so you have a lot of orders sitting around and nobody knows where they are.

FISCHER: Well, couldn't we take care of that by having somebody assigned simply to see to it that all the orders got put back in the files properly?

SIMON: We'd have to hire somebody new to do that. We haven't got anybody we can spare now.

FISCHER: Well, let's hire them.

SIMON: Well, I think that would help, but that wouldn't solve the problem.

(*At this point there was a discussion, primarily between Mr. Teplow, Fred Apfel, Mr. Breitman, and Frank Rich, as to whether or not a different system for handling orders would eliminate much of this difficulty. It was not clear to Mr. Williams exactly what was being proposed. After about five minutes of this discussion, Mr. Fischer resumed.*)

FISCHER: Well, it's getting late, and we're not going to change the system this season. I don't think there's any point in carrying this discussion on any further.

JOE: Well, whatever system we have, when a guy comes in for a sale, you still have to have a good system to tell him what you can give him.

FISCHER: Well, we've been talking about a lot of things here and we still haven't answered some of the questions we've brought up. What about this question of Mickey's load? Are you really overloaded, Mickey?

MICKEY: Well, I'm getting three or four hundred letters in here a day. Sally has been helping me, but I just can't possibly keep up with it.

FISCHER: How quickly are you answering telegrams?

MICKEY: Well, I try to get a letter out on them in about 48 hours.

FISCHER: How far behind are we on our promises?

MICKEY: Well, we've got some things that were promised for June 1, which still aren't shipped yet.

APFEL: Mr. Fischer, this is a tremendously difficult problem. We all know that Mickey's been working very hard to keep up. Probably we can't solve it completely, but I don't think. . . .

FISCHER: Well, there's no need to make a speech about it, is there? What do you have in mind?

APFEL: Well, the point is, Mr. Fischer, I don't think that when these letters come in, the customers want to know what we're going to do— I think they want goods. Maybe it isn't necessary to give them all the information that we're now giving them.

FISCHER: Well, what about that, Mickey?

(At this point there was a discussion among Mickey, Fred Apfel, Mr. Fischer, and Mr. Teplow as to whether or not to give customers who had written in to check on orders complete information as to the status of those orders, and after three or four minutes of discussion it was agreed that such a procedure was, in fact, necessary and that Mickey should have an assistant. Discussion then turned to what to do to speed up shipments.)

APFEL: Well, I'm going to spend tomorrow morning getting all the new people squared away on what they're supposed to do. Ninety per cent of our troubles come from improper training, and now that we've gotten some new people, if we can get people started on the right foot I think we can lick a lot of these things.

SIMON: Well, you may have some new people, but you still have a lot of the same old faces.

JOE: Our problem is that we have no organization out back.

SIMON: Our problem is that we have no organization, period.

FISCHER: Well, now you've said that before. Let's talk a little bit about that. Just what do you mean?

SIMON: Well, we have no organization. You've never broken down the duties that each of us is supposed to do.

MICKEY: Well, now in the Army you have tables of organization. You have a chart showing what each person is supposed to do. Everybody has an assignment of a responsibility. We don't have that here.

SIMON: You have no delegation of responsibility whatsoever. A lot of people are getting blamed for things they aren't even supposed to be responsible for.

FISCHER: Well, can't we do something about that right now? Suppose we took Mickey off his job and put Sally [one of the girls in the showroom] on that job and gave her some help and put Mickey out back and gave him some definite responsibility for, say, these open orders. Simon, you know what you're supposed to do. You're responsible for the locker stock.

SIMON: Yes, and I call on the resident buyers, take stock, work in the showroom, and help Mr. Breitman.

APFEL: Let's not forget that we're in this pickle now because of an unusual buying situation.

SIMON: You haven't got this situation because there's any emergency. You have this emergency because we've been in this type of situation for a long time.

APFEL: Mr. Fischer, supposing we did this. (*He takes out a pencil and a piece of paper and starts drawing an organization chart.*) Take out back. Now, we all recognize that Harry's got to be in charge. He's done a marvelous job under the circumstances, he's worked as hard as anybody possibly could work, and I think the thing is going to straighten itself out. But supposing now we gave him some help and some people with actually assigned duties. I still think that Joey ought to go back there. Supposing we made Joey responsible for all new orders and for the lay-away. Supposing we put Smitty [an order picker] in charge of shipping and receiving, and supposing that we took somebody else and put them in charge of, say ——— and ——— [mail-order houses]. I think perhaps he ought to report to me rather than to Harry. Suppose we have somebody else to follow up our old orders. Each of these people would have definite duties, definite responsibilities, but still all reporting to Harry Block.

FISCHER: Well, I don't think we ought to settle any of this without Harry Block's being here. After all, he's in charge out back, but I think I'd better call him in here tomorrow morning, and we'll talk about this. (*Turning to the case writer.*) Maybe what we need in here is an efficiency expert. Do you think we need an efficiency expert?

SIMON: That's just what we don't need, Mr. Fischer. The people who are working on this problem know what the answers to some of these problems are, but nobody ever asks them for their opinions. You've been having a survey in here every three months, but none of them has done any good. An outsider can't come in here and give us answers, but if you listen to us, we can work this thing out.

JOE: I'd like to bring up one more thing. As a result of a lot of things we've been talking about this evening, a lot of our salesmen are following the practice—when a customer doesn't get his shipment—of simply sending us in a whole new order. The result is that sometimes we know about that duplication and cancel the original order and sometimes we don't, and we ship out double shipments. Now in times like these when people will take anything they can get, that's fine, but if the business should ever fall off, we may find ourselves with a great many returns on our hands that we'll be stuck with.

RICH: Do you have good figures on your returns?

BREITMAN: Well, we tried keeping them for a while, but they didn't tell us very much, and we didn't think they were worth bothering with.

FISCHER: Well, it's getting late, and I want to have a talk with Mr. Teplow and Mr. Breitman before Mr. Teplow goes off to Europe, so maybe we ought to go back over what we settled this evening. Simon, first thing tomorrow morning you're going to go through the cards and pick out those accounts that have ordered from us for the first time. You'll check with Frank, and we'll pull all those orders out and set them aside.

RICH: Are you going to tell the salesmen and the showroom not to accept new accounts?

FISCHER: Yes, we'll put that into effect immediately. If somebody comes in here who hasn't bought from us before, we'll explain the situation to him and try to get him interested in buying from us next year but not take any of his orders this year.

SIMON: I'd like to make one more point, people, before we break up. I think this is very serious. We've talked a lot about this before, but we've never done anything, and I think it's about time we took some action.

FISCHER: Well, I'm going to get Harry in here and talk to him about this first thing tomorrow morning. What about this open-order thing? Simon, would you be willing to take over there for a couple of weeks just to help out?

SIMON: Well, yes, if you say so, Mr. Fischer, but I'm already behind on my locker stock work. I've been doing all that work at home at night, and I'm still far behind, and that plus calling on the buying offices, I just don't have time.

FISCHER: Well, maybe we could cut out the calls on the buying office.

SIMON: Well, I don't think that's a good idea, Mr. Fischer. Right now we're having a lot of trouble keeping them friendly as it is without problems on shipment, and if we don't pay any attention to them at all, the thing will get even worse.

BREITMAN: Well, I'd be glad to go over for the time being and pull those orders—just to get caught up.

TEPLOW: That's an awfully expensive way to pull orders.

FISCHER: Well, Joe, what about you? Felix, could we take Joe off the Japanese stuff for a while?

BREITMAN: Sure, we can get along without him for a while.

JOE: Well, of course that isn't all I'm doing right now, Mr. Fischer.

BREITMAN: I'll be glad to do it for a while, Judson. I think that's the answer. Well, it's getting late, and I think we'd better quit.

FISCHER: Sidney, when do you leave for Europe?

TEPLOW: Friday.

FISCHER: Well, I can see you tomorrow then.

(*As the group broke up, Mr. Breitman turned to Mr. Williams.*)

BREITMAN: This is all very well, but after all, we've been successful, and you can't argue with success.

FISCHER: Yeah, we could be very logically organized and get this place nicely set up, and we'd probably do about a half a million dollars' worth of business a year.

SIMON: I don't think so.

A Note on the Manufacture and Distribution of Portland Cement in the United Kingdom*

CEMENT MANUFACTURE

PORTLAND CEMENT was developed from an invention of a laborer in Leeds, England, in 1824. It was called "portland" cement because the concrete made from it resembled the well-known portland building stone in color and texture. Its manufacture is today a major world industry. World consumption has risen from 81 million tons in 1938 to 315 million in 1960 and is still rising.

Cement itself is manufactured from a closely controlled mixture of calcium carbonate, alumina, and silica. Calcium carbonate is found in various forms of limestone fairly liberally throughout the world. To be suitable for the manufacture of cement, the calcium carbonate content of the limestone must be relatively free from impurity. Soft chalk, which is very high in calcium carbonate, is found uniquely on either side of the English Channel toward the southern part of the North Sea. Chalk is easier to process than hard limestone, and its availability accounts, in part, for the fact that nearly half of British production is located in southeastern England.

Alumina is found in some forms of clay or shale. A relatively small amount of sand supplies the silica requirements.

From 3,000 to 3,600 pounds of raw materials are required to make a ton of cement. These are quarried with large diesel or electric power shovels and conveyed to the works, which is normally placed nearby. There they are crushed and ground to a fine powder, and—in what is known as the "wet process"—mixed in strictly controlled proportions with water to form cement slurry. (Slurry normally contains about 40% water by weight.) The liquid state of the mixture is necessary to

---

* Much of the material included in this description was taken, with permission, from a paper "The Manufacture and Distribution of Cement" prepared by the Chairman of The Rugby Portland Cement Company Ltd., Rugby, England.

facilitate a perfectly homogeneous mixture of the raw materials and to permit rapid adjustment of the proportions by merely adding materials which quickly become uniformly dispersed throughout the liquid.

The slurry, when chemically correct, is fed to the kiln, which in a modern works is a large steel cylinder from 3 to 500 feet in length and 9 to 14 feet in diameter. It rotates at the rate of approximately once every 45 seconds, on a slightly inclined axis. The slurry is fed in at the higher end.

Near the lower end of the kiln is the burning zone, where fuel is injected into the kiln and fired to produce a temperature of about 2,500° F. Pulverized coal is the usual fuel in Britain, but oil and natural gas are used in other countries where these fuels are readily available. The water in the slurry is driven off as steam, together with the carbon dioxide content of the calcium carbonate and minor quantities of other gases. The remaining materials are fluxed in the intense heat and leave the kiln in the form of pea-sized nodules called cement clinker. The chemical part of the process, completed at this point, is closely controlled throughout by chemists who test the raw materials, the coal, and the slurry every hour, day and night.

Thereafter, the process is largely mechanical. The cement clinker is ground in large water-cooled mills to a predetermined fineness, and a small amount of calcium sulphate, or gypsum, is added in order to control the "setting time" of the resultant powder, now finished cement.

As it leaves the mills, the cement is weighed automatically and then pumped through pipes by compressed air to the large concrete silos in which it is stored. It remains in storage until it is withdrawn by mechanical means to the packing plant, where it is packed into paper sacks, which are automatically fitted, sealed, weighed and delivered by means of conveyors to the truck, the rail car, or the ship. It may be withdrawn from the silos into special bulk trucks which deliver it unpacked.

THE USES OF CEMENT

Cement is used as the binding agent in concrete and in mortar. Concrete, one of the world's primary construction materials, is composed of cement, sand, aggregate (clean gravel and stones), and water. Cement reacts chemically with the water and hardens within a few hours after mixing, binding the sand and gravel particles in a solid mass. Concrete can be used without reinforcing (as in highway pavements which contain only wire matting for temperature stresses), or it can be used with steel reinforcement, as in buildings and bridges.

STRUCTURE OF THE INDUSTRY IN THE UNITED KINGDOM—1960

The cement industry in the United Kingdom consists of nine financially independent groups, all of which have been members of the Cement Makers' Federation since its establishment in 1934.

The three largest interests held, in 1960, about 83% of the home market and have provided much of the leadership within the federation. Associated Portland Cement Manufacturers Limited is considerably the largest company, with about 62% of the United Kingdom market. The Tunnel Group has about 12.4%, and The Rugby Portland Cement Company Limited 7% of the United Kingdom market. Practically all the United Kingdom export trade is conducted by these three makers, which are also the only companies having manufacturing subsidiaries abroad.

The federation regulates the internal affairs of the industry and arranges an interchange of technical information and industry-wide statistics. By far its most important function, however, is establishing the basis of selling prices and conditions of sale, in order, it is asserted, that the costs of distribution—which average nearly 20% of delivered cost of cement—can be controlled. Membership is voluntary and voting power is proportionate, although not directly, to the previous year's home deliveries. Approval of any proposal, however, requires the concurrence of at least four of the nine members. The federation has no control over the production of any manufacturer, nor is it concerned with the export trade.

The British cement industry also maintains a large research and promotional organization, the Cement and Concrete Association, part of whose function is to increase the use and uses of concrete. Cement itself has no substitute; however, it is used only to form concrete, which is in competition with steel, brick, stone, tile, timber and many other materials.

The industry also organizes its conduct of labor relations. For more than 35 years it has operated a National Joint Industrial Council at which industry-wide wage rates and working conditions are set. The industry has never had a national strike or lock-out. Holidays with pay and profit-sharing plans were features of the industry for many years before World War II.

POSTWAR GROWTH OF THE INDUSTRY

The postwar progress made by the industry is shown in the following exhibit:

Exhibit 1

THE MANUFACTURE AND DISTRIBUTION OF
PORTLAND CEMENT IN THE UNITED KINGDOM

United Kingdom Cement Deliveries
(000 tons)

	Home	Export	Total
1961 (est.)	13,800	800	14,600
1960	12,463	1,000	13,463
1959	11,683	1,088	12,771
1958	10,675	1,145	11,820
1957	10,709	1,382	12,091
1956	11,275	1,600	12,875
1955	10,759	1,766	12,526
1954	10,079	1,769	11,848
1953	9,335	1,917	11,253
1952	9,147	2,055	11,202
1951	8,144	1,974	10,119
1946	5,479	1,095	6,574
1939	7,587	665	8,252

THE ECONOMICS OF THE INDUSTRY

Siting of the Plant. It is considered a matter of prime importance that cement plants be located as close as possible to raw material deposits. Adequate water supplies, fuel, and electricity, and access to road, rail, and water transport must also be available. Thorough technical investigation is required since both the physical and chemical properties of the raw materials will influence the design of many of the factory components.

Costs of Production. The manufacture of cement is a highly mechanized process and employs comparatively little labor. The capital investment is among the highest for any industry; it equals almost £20,-000 per man employed, which is over six times what it was before World War II. Depreciation is therefore a heavy charge, and will become progressively heavier as prewar plants are replaced.

Coal is the largest individual item in the cost of production. It takes approximately 800 pounds of coal, including the coal used to generate electricity, to make a ton of cement.

In general, industry production costs are distributed as follows:

```
Coal and power.............................45–50%
Direct labor...............................10–15%
Consumable equipment........................ 9–12%
Depreciation (installed cost)............... 9–12%

Indirect factory labor and other overheads (super-
    vision, testing, maintenance, cost accounting,
    etc.)..................................15–20%
Manufacture cost........................... 100%
Average haulage............................20–30% of Manufacture Cost
Sales expense.............................. 5– 8% "        "        "
General administrative overhead...............10–15% "        "        "
```

Profit margins are not disclosed. It has been asserted that current prices allow profits only because the manufacturers are still using, in part, equipment installed in the late 1930's. As greater proportions of new, more expensive plant installations are brought into use, prices may rise to cover increased depreciation charges.

Leaders of the British cement industry have repeatedly stated that manufacture of cement in the United Kingdom has for years been conducted with the highest efficiency and one of the lowest unit costs of any producing country in the world.

Distribution. The distribution of cement to the site where it will be used is a more technical and complicated problem than at first sight appears, for it is not the cost of production at the place where the cement is made but the cost at the site where it will be used that is important. The geographical distribution of demand, which in itself varies quite considerably from year to year (and can be materially distorted at different times by large airport programs, road works, reservoirs and similar forms of construction using large quantities of cement) is not coincident with the geographical distribution of the works.

Most companies in the industry maintain a fleet of trucks for road delivery. Little goes by rail, owing to the costs of double-handling. Delivery in bulk (in special vehicles) has rapidly increased in recent years and now accounts for nearly 50% of the home trade.

PRICING AND THE ROLE OF THE CEMENT MAKERS' FEDERATION

The manufacturers feel that a joint policy of distribution and price can avoid the severe price competition which, in the early 1930's created difficulties for both producers and users. For example, a works near to a large consuming area might be able to supply only one-third of the demand in that area, leaving the remaining two-thirds to come from a much greater distance. If there were not a co-ordinated price policy, it has been said, a builder taking his supplies from the nearer works would pay one price, while his competitor would have to pay a higher price for cement coming from a more distant works. This would assertedly lead to endless complications in bidding for construction projects.

The federation's pricing arrangements, therefore, have the following objectives:

1. To sell and distribute cement throughout the country in the most efficient and economical manner commensurate with the interests of the country as a whole, of the users of cement, and of the manufacturers—in particular by:
    a) Encouraging the delivery in any particular area from the nearest works with the object of avoiding unnecessary and wasteful haulage.
    b) Eliminating depots (except where these perform useful functions) and delivering straight from works to construction sites.
    c) Providing a stable system of prices which takes into account the high proportion of the cost of transport in the price of cement and avoids disproportionate price differentials which would otherwise arise between various parts of the U.K.
2. To provide a price system giving sufficient stability to enable manufacturers individually and collectively to plan production in advance efficiently and economically, and individually to undertake the heavy expenditure required to meet increasing demand for cement.
3. To ensure during any temporary shortage of cement that prices remain at a reasonable level.
4. To eliminate unnecessary and expensive advertising.
5. To provide for standard forms of packages, bulk delivery and the like.
6. To arrange for the convenience of both manufacturers and buyers, standard conditions of supply and forms of quotation and contract.
7. To facilitate joint research and exchange of information to improve the standard and the potential utility of cement.[1]

To achieve these aims, the federation's present system provides for the same delivered price at the same point of delivery for all brands of cement, irrespective of the works from which the cement may come.

There are 48 cement works in the United Kingdom. (Cement works very near one another usually have the same base price.) There are 37 base prices, one for each location where cement is manufactured, and one for each cement importing center on the coast. These base prices are nearly the same at every factory, although there are slight variations made for the type of raw materials used, and the delivered

---

[1] Summarized from a policy statement of the federation.

price of fuel to the works. For the former, for instance, plants using chalk as their source of calcium carbonate have base prices about 5% lower than those using limestone, since all limestone crushing and grinding expenses are eliminated. In 1961, the base factory price (delivered within five miles of plant) of ordinary portland cement ranged from 111/6d. to 127/6d. per ton.

Radiating from each works is a series of concentric circles at four- or five-mile intervals, the circles from any particular works continuing until they meet the circles radiating from another works. The delivered price within each of these circles increases by 1/6d. for each circle. (See Exhibit 2.)

These price increments do not, in fact, cover actual transportation costs; therefore, manufacturers allow 10–15% of the base price plus the zone price increments for covering haulage costs. As a result, between 20 and 30 miles from a producing unit is considered the "breakeven" haulage distance, below which haulage costs are less than the allowance in the base price plus the incremental price increases, and above which the converse is true. The more efficiently a producer can operate his truck fleet, the greater will be his breakeven haulage distance.

The pricing scheme means that every buyer at a particular point will pay exactly the same price for his cement. It also means that there is every inducement for a manufacturer to save transport costs by selling as much of his production as possible within the circles controlled by his own works. The further he delivers cement from his own works, the more likely he is to run into the circles controlled by another works, where the price he will receive will begin to decrease. The federation asserts that the effect of this arrangement is to save as much as possible of the heavy transport costs and so maintain throughout the country, on the average, a lower level of prices than would otherwise be the case.

There exist standard merchant discounts. Retail building material suppliers are entitled to a merchant's discount, but they in turn must sell cement at the same prices, in the particular zones, which apply to the manufacturers. Thus, a buyer pays the same price whether he buys from a manufacturer or a merchant. Merchants play a major role in supplying small orders, since the minimum order normally accepted by a manufacturer is 6 tons. A relatively small percentage of industry sales is made directly to merchants for their own accounts, but much more cement is delivered to the customer "on site" at a merchant's order.

Exhibit 2

THE MANUFACTURE AND DISTRIBUTION OF PORTLAND CEMENT IN THE
UNITED KINGDOM

Illustration of the Federation's Pricing Agreement

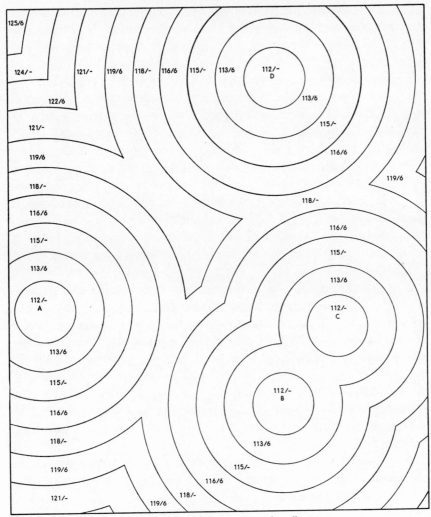

Sales price in shillings and pence per ton shown for each four- or five-mile zone.

THE RESTRICTIVE TRADE PRACTICES ACT

In 1956, England passed the Restrictive Trade Practices Act, which required that all trade agreements be registered with the Registrar of the Restrictive Practices Court. These agreements subsequently had to be justified before the Court, which would decide whether they were contrary to the public interest. On March 16, 1961, the Restrictive

Practices Court handed down its decision: it upheld the federation's price agreements with only minor modifications.

In essence, the federation argued that, because of its price-fixing agreement, U.K. cement manufacturers could operate with more certainty of profit than under free competition. Because of this greater security, they were willing to accept a lower return on investment and thus could sell cement appreciably lower than if prices had not been fixed.

Experts on both sides agreed that, in order to attract new capital into the industry, a net return on investment of at least 15% would have to be available. The federation proved that, in order to yield such a return, a new cement plant would have to price its cement at least 25 shillings per ton higher than the current average price. It also established that federation members were earning, on the average, less than 10% return on investment. The Court therefore concluded that, had the price-fixing arrangement not existed, the price of cement would have been "significantly" higher, and the public would have suffered accordingly. Thus the Court upheld the main price-fixing clause. It found that the industry was efficient and had acted with a sense of responsibility.

The presiding judge was concerned only that the price-fixing agreement should be as honorably administered in the future as had been true in the past. Thus he requested, and the federation agreed, that if at any future date the Registrar should wish to determine whether prices were still being kept at a fair level, the federation would cooperate fully by making cost and price data available for inspection.

The federation's practice of giving quantity discounts based on total annual purchases from *all* federation members was disallowed by the judge, on the grounds that it did not reflect true economies from volume sales.

The court also scrutinized, and upheld with one exception, minor agreements regarding terms of sale. In summing up his decision, Mr. Justice Diplock remarked:

In the result, therefore, the Respondents have satisfied us that the main price-fixing conditions, other than those providing for general rebates to large users and large merchants, are not contrary to the public interest, and that the ancillary restrictions, other than that relating to the prohibition upon the quotations and contracts for the supply of cement for periods exceeding twelve months, are also not contrary to the public interest. . . .[2]

---

[2] *Judgement in the Restrictive Practices Court on an Agreement between Members of the Cement Makers' Federation,* printed by the Cement and Concrete Association, 1961.

In commenting on the Court's decision, Sir Halford Reddish observed:

I am not being wise after the event if I say that the judgement accorded closely with our expectations, for we were confident throughout that a detailed examination of our arrangements would show conclusively that they were in the public interest. And the cement makers were not alone in their satisfaction with the outcome of the case. Over four thousand buyers of cement sent us replies to a questionnaire before the hearing: something like 97 per cent of them were strongly in favour of a continuation of the present system.[3]

---

[3] *Investors Chronicle,* March 24, 1961.

The Rugby Portland Cement Company Limited (A)

HISTORY, GROWTH, AND ORGANIZATION

THE RUGBY COMPANY began producing lime in the early nineteenth century at a works near Rugby, England. Cement manufacture, under the company's "Crown" Cement trade-mark began at the works in the 1820's, and thereafter became its principal product. In 1925, the company, which hitherto had been a partnership, became a private limited company with share capital of £100,000 owned by descendants of the previous partners. In 1929, Mr. (now Sir[1]) Halford Reddish, a young chartered accountant with a consulting practice, joined the board which previously had comprised only representatives of the two descendant branches of the original owners. Four years later, upon the death of the general manager, Mr. Reddish became managing director, and shortly afterward, chairman.

At that time, the cement industry was in the middle of a deep depression. Prices were at a very unprofitable level. In spite of this crisis, the chairman decided to expand and modernize the company's production facilities. Contrary to previous industry tradition, he also decided to operate the plant 52 weeks per year, thus ensuring steady employment for the workers. Despite the depression and difficulties of selling the increased output, a profit was realized at the end of the first year of the new management. A second manufacturing site was obtained when a nearby company went into receivership. Erection of a new factory at the second site plus the modernization and expansion of the Rugby works required substantial fresh capital. In 1935, the company became a public company with its shares quoted on The London Stock Exchange, and additional capital of £140,000 was introduced. Since that time, additional equity capital had been raised by occasional "rights" issues.

---

[1] In early 1958, Her Majesty Queen Elizabeth II knighted Mr. Halford Reddish for his public services.

In 1936, Rugby acquired a third site and erected its Rochester works. In 1939, another company was purchased and its facilities were combined with those at Rochester. In 1945, Rugby acquired another company, and although its production facilities were closed, Rugby used its brand name and distribution organization.

Rugby made major additions to its three plants in Great Britain after 1946.

During the immediate postwar years, export trade was very profitable, with unit margins several times those of the home market sales. The proportion of Rugby's deliveries accounted for by exports reached a maximum in 1951 and 1952 at about 43%. In 1961, however, Sir Halford Reddish said that in recent years export sales had become almost marginal because of the increased competition (much of it subsidized) from non-British manufacturers and the growth of cement industries in areas formerly importing cement. Rugby had itself established overseas subsidiaries and built manufacturing plants in Trinidad and western Australia. The former started production in 1954, and the latter in 1955. Both units were able to supply cement at substantially lower prices than existing imported cement and made useful contributions to Rugby's consolidated profits.

With a rapidly developing local market plus export trade in the eastern Caribbean, the Trinidad factory required the doubling of its capacity within less than five years of starting its operation. Management decided in 1961 to extend the Australian plant in the near future.

In highlighting Rugby's growth, Sir Halford said in 1961:

> In 1933 we had the one not very modern works at Rugby and total net assets with a book value of £109,250. Today all our works at home and abroad are modern and up-to-date and the total net assets of the company at book values amount to £13,404,369. (The real value is probably in excess of £18,500,000.) Additional capital introduced from 1st January 1933 to 31st December 1960 amounted to £13,295,119. Here's how the money has been found.

Shareholders have subscribed for shares (including premiums and loan stock)	£ 5,890,863
by leaving profits in the company	5,666,076
And others (by minority interests in, or loans to, subsidiary companies) have found	1,738,180
	£13,295,119

Net profit before taxes rose from less than £4,000 to almost £1.8 million in the same period. Postwar growth produced 11 years of successively record deliveries from 1945 to 1956 and 16 years of successively record group profits, 1946–61 (see Exhibits 1–3).

Exhibit 1

THE RUGBY PORTLAND CEMENT COMPANY LIMITED (A)

Consolidated Balance Sheet Statements 1946 and 1951–61

(1,000's of £)

Assets	1946	1951	1952	1953	1954	1955	1956	1957	1958	1959	1960	1961
Current Assets	576	1,847	1,982	2,616	3,836	4,211	4,521	4,195	4,692	6,744	7,597	*
Fixed Assets (1937 Valuation or Cost If Subsequently Acquired)	1,673	3,271	3,591	3,876	6,171	7,861	8,613	9,309	9,487	9,809	10,627	
Less Accumulated Depreciation	436	987	1,125	1,261	1,562	1,635	1,969	2,306	2,601	3,008	3,456	
Net Fixed Assets	1,237	2,285	2,466	2,616	4,609	6,226	6,644	7,003	6,886	6,801	7,171	
Investment in Subsidiary Companies (Not Consolidated)	209	33	393	793	760							
Total Assets	2,022	4,165	4,841	6,025	9,205	10,437	11,165	11,198	11,578	13,545	14,768	
Liabilities and Net Worth												
Current Liabilities	367	1,355	814	776	1,327	1,498	1,759	1,292	1,190	1,191	1,364	
Debt Capital:												
4% Debenture	420	.....	.....	.....	.....	.....	.....	.....	.....	.....	.....	
Mortgage Loans	.....	.....	.....	.....	.....	400	480	560	640	720	800	
4¾% Unsecured Loan 1957–62	.....	.....	1,000	1,500	1,500	1,500	1,500	1,500	1,500	1,500	1,500	
Total Debt	420	.....	1,000	1,500	1,500	1,900	1,980	2,060	2,140	2,220	2,300	
Share Capital:												
4% and 6% Preference Shares	325	825	825	825	825	825	825	825	825	825	825	
Ordinary Shares 5/par	325	500	500	750	1,250	1,500	1,500	1,500	1,500	1,750	2,000	
"A" Shares 1/par	.....	.....	.....	.....	50	50	50	50	50	50	50	
Capital Reserve	325	610	563	810	1,265	1,300	1,358	1,415	1,275	2,133	1,950	
Revenue Reserves:												
General Reserve	100	500	500	750	1,125	1,500	1,750	2,000	.....	.....	.....	
Reserve for Future Taxation	.....	249	408	504	352	390	320	303	350	1,000	1,217	
Reserve for Ordinary and "A" Share Dividend Payment (Net)	161	52	55	55	115	201	230	230	276	329	383	
Undistributed Profit	.....	73	175	56	120	106	275	451	2,947	3,067	3,741	
Total Capital and Reserves	1,236	2,809	3,026	3,750	5,102	5,873	6,308	6,774	7,223	9,154	10,166	
Interest of Outside Shareholders in a Subsidiary Company								1,072	1,025	980	938	
Total Liabilities and Net Worth	2,022	4,165	4,841	6,025	9,205	10,437	11,165	11,198	11,578	13,545	14,768	
Net Working Capital	210	491	1,168	1,841	2,510	2,712	2,762	2,903	3,502	5,553	6,233	
Equity/Debt Ratio	2.9/1	no debt	3.0/1	2.5/1	3.4/1	3.1/1	3.2/1	3.3/1	3.4/1	4.1/1	4.4/1	

* Balance sheet information for 1961 not available.

Exhibit 2

THE RUGBY PORTLAND CEMENT COMPANY LIMITED (A)

Consolidated Profit and Loss Account 1946 and 1951–61

(1,000's of £)

	1946 £	1946 %	1951 £	1951 %	1952 £	1952 %	1953 £	1953 %	1954 £	1954 %	1955 £	1955 %	1956 £	1956 %	1957 £	1957 %	1958 £	1958 %	1959 £	1959 %	1960 £	1960 %	1961 £	1961 %
Consolidated trading profits	213		522		656		744		904		1,256		1,369		1,397		1,500		1,877		2,183		2,569	
Other income			19		20		24		27		39		65		51		52		57		99			
Less depreciation	79		124		142		136		210		270		340		342		381		443		506		550	
Net profit before taxes	134	100	417	100	534	100	633	100	721	100	1,025	100	1,093	100	1,106	100	1,171	100	1,491	100	1,777	100	2,019	100
Taxation—profits tax‡			100		102		125		62		115		109		135		60		45		88			
Income tax‡	39		150		255		300		313		325		255		235		260		475		550			
Total taxes	39	29	250	60	357	67	425	67	375	52	440	43	364	33	370	34	320	27	520	35	638	36	776	
Net profit after taxes	95		167		177		208		346		585		729		736		851		971		1,139		1,244	
Preference dividends	12	9	21	5	21	4	22	3	22	3	23	2	23	2	23	2	23	2	24	2	24	1	24	
Ordinary dividends (net)	22	16	52	12	55	10	55	9	115	16	172	17	194	18	194	18	230	20	268	18	306	17	306	
"A" share dividends (net)											29		36	3	36	3	46	4	61	4	77	4	77	
Retained in business	61	46	94	23	101	19	131	21	209	29	361	35	477	44	484	44	553	47	618	41	732	41	837	
Ordinary dividend per share (gross)	7½d		1/-d		1/-d		1/-d		1/-d		1/-d		1/1½d		1/1½d		1/3d		1/3d		1/3d		1/3d	
Capital distribution per share (gross)	3d		3d		3d		3d		..															
"A" share dividend per share (gross)											1/-d		1/3d		1/3d		1/6d		2/-d		2/6d		2/6d	
Net profit before taxes as return on total capital and reserves	10.85%		14.87%		17.65%		19.50%*		17.65%*		17.42%		17.30%		16.30%		16.20%		16.29%		17.48%			
Gross ordinary dividend as return on capital employed, i.e., ordinary plus disclosed reserves (less reserves credited to "A" shares)	4.36%		5.04%		4.54%		4.12%*		6.20%†		6.09%		6.36%		5.84%		6.06%		5.43%		5.56%			

* Excluding the £500,000 of additional capital introduced at end of 1953.

† Excluding the £1,000,000 of additional capital introduced at end of 1954.

‡ *Profits Tax* was the estimated liability for the year ending with the statement. *Income Tax* was the estimated liability for the subsequent two-year period. This procedure gives rise to the Reserve for Future Income Tax in the balance sheet. The estimated income tax for the future period is put into this reserve; and at the end of each year, the actual tax liability for the year is withdrawn from the reserve and put into current liabilities, from which the actual remittance is made.

Exhibit 3

THE RUGBY PORTLAND CEMENT COMPANY
LIMITED (A)

Indices of Deliveries, Profit, and Net Worth 1946–61
(Base: 1946 = 100)

Year	Deliveries*	Capital†	Profits
1946	100	100	100
1947	105	184‡	140
1948	138	203	195
1949	139	208	214
1950	155	219	262
1951	168	227	311
1952	208	245	398
1953	214	303§	473
1954	238	413‖	538
1955	302	475	765
1956	307	510	816
1957	294	548	825
1958	296	584	874
1959	319	741¶	1,113
1960	357	822	1,326
1961	388		

* These are total group deliveries, in tons, used as an index basing point.
† "Capital" here equals total equity capital, including reserves.
‡ In 1947, £1,000,000 of new capital was raised: £500,000 from new preference shares sold, and £500,000 from new common shares. Without this sale of shares, the index would have remained at 100.
§ In 1953, £500,000 of new common shares were sold. Without this sale, the index at the end of 1953 would have been 265.
¶ In 1954, £1,050,000 of new capital was raised, £50,000 by the sale of "A" shares, £1,000,000 by the sale of new common shares. Without this new capital, the index would have been 330 at the end of 1954.
‖ In 1959, £1,075,000 of new capital was raised through sale of common shares. Without this sale, the index would have been 655 at the end of 1959.

Late in 1961, a new kiln, with an annual capacity of 180,000 tons, was installed at the Southam works. After this addition, the five company works and their annual capacities in tons were:

Southam (England)	500,000
Rochester "	400,000
Rugby "	320,000
Trinidad	165,000
Australia	120,000

The company also maintained a chalk quarry at Totternhoe, some 48 miles from Rugby.

At the end of 1961, The Rugby Cement Company had about 1,600 employees in its three United Kingdom factories, other U.K. subsidiaries, overseas operations, and headquarters in Rugby, England. The headquarters was organized into seven functional departments: accounting, production, engineering, transportation, domestic sales, export sales, and legal. There was also a secretarial department. Above these departments was a small control and co-ordination group called the administration department. This group, consisting mostly of assistants to top management, directed and co-ordinated the activities of the functional departments and served as the intermediate link between subsidiary companies, which addressed all inquiries and reports to Sir Halford Reddish, who was the chairman of each, and to the headquarters staff departments.

The board of directors comprised seven members, three of whom were top executives in the company. These three were: Sir Halford Reddish, chairman and managing director; Mr. R. L. Evans, deputy managing director; and Mr. M. K. Smith, head of the legal department. Sir Halford and Mr. Evans worked closely with one another attempting to attain an interchangeability of talents. Sir Halford played a leading role in all major policy decisions, but was particularly concerned with financial management and public relations. Mr. Evans' background was also in accounting; he was considered the expert on accounting and technical phases of the operations. As second in command, he in effect headed the administration department. Mr. Smith generally confined himself to the company's legal matters and did not become involved in routine company operations.

Sir Halford, who served on the boards of three other corporations and on a number of semipublic councils, spent the greater part of each week in London. His days in Rugby included the weekend, and he normally met with Mr. Evans on Sunday morning to discuss current operations and problems, and also to do financial planning up to "two or three balance sheets ahead."

REASONS FOR GROWTH

Sir Halford felt that the company's growth and profitability were attributable to several interrelated activities.

1. *Emphasis on operating efficiency* was considered one of the most important of these activities. Sir Halford said that the key to lower unit costs when producing with expensive, continuous process equipment was keeping the plant operating as close to full capacity as possible and minimizing every element of operating and overhead costs. Therefore, avoiding down time, improving efficiency of men and machines, and fuel and power economies were all important. To accomplish these ends, Rugby employed an elaborate monthly cost reporting system which facilitated pin-pointing the items of excessive costs. The factory

managers were held responsible for costs under their control, and the chief engineer and production manager were continually watching fuel and power costs and working on means of increasing machine efficiency. Excess overtime, costly repairs, stores usage and factory staff costs were other items which attracted the attention of the central cost control department. One manager said: "We continually work on the weakest point reflected by the cost analyses."

The company's research on improvement of its manufacturing process produced several cost savings. The major outcome of such research was the recent development of a "wetting" agent for the slurry. Without affecting the chemical properties of the finished product, this agent produced the same "liquidity" and thus the same mixing and handling properties in a slurry containing only 35% water contrasted with 41% previously required. The smaller amount of water to vaporize meant appreciable fuel savings.

Worker efficiency was also a matter of continuous attention. Because of the expensive equipment and need to operate without stoppages, misconduct on the job, unexcused absences, and excessive tardiness were considered grounds for release. Such strictness was necessary because, for example, a kiln burner[1] could, through 10 minutes' neglect, permit many thousands of pounds' worth of damage to the equipment. Sir Halford said that his insistence that all employees "play the game according to the rules of the organization" was not only necessary for efficiency but was also a matter of loyalty. "But," he added, "I hold firmly to the view that loyalty should be two-way traffic. If the head of a business expects a man to be loyal to him, then I say that man has every right to expect the same loyalty from the head of the business."

Finally, emphasis was placed on clerical and procedural efficiency. Sir Halford said that greater use of mechanized accounting and invoicing, and continuous analysis and improvement of office procedures had slightly reduced the head office staff in the past few years. Periodic evaluation of the forms and paper work systems was conducted to eliminate unnecessary ones. "We have even had our competitor friends," he said, "come to look over our reporting and accounting systems. They are amazed by the fact that we get our data faster than they do with a proportionately smaller clerical staff."

2. *An effective sales organization* was the second contributing factor to growth and profits. Manufacturing savings effected by maintaining

---

[1] The kiln burner was the worker in charge of operating one or more kilns.

peak production were attainable only as long as the output could be sold. Mr. Yeatman, the general sales manager, remarked, "Since the industry sells on a common price arrangement, you don't sell cement by selling cheaper than the next man. You sell on delivery service, goodwill, product quality, and on contact with the customer. We like to think that we rate very high on all these counts. Selling cement is very much of a team effort, and we have a fine organization here, which naturally makes my job much easier." Under Mr. Yeatman were two area sales managers, one for midland sales and one for southern and export sales. Each manager had eight salesmen, most of whom worked from their homes. Three of the southern salesmen were located in the London office. The salesmen were paid entirely by salary, because, Mr. Yeatman said, "It's very difficult to say who's responsible for an individual sale. Most of our orders are sent in to one of our four offices: London, Birmingham, Rochester, or Rugby, rather than through the salesman. Our salesmen sell the company in general rather than the product; they are chiefly purveyors of goodwill."

Mr. Yeatman added that many customers bought from two or more manufacturers as a matter of policy. "I might mention," he added, "that all the U.K. cement manufacturers make cement which is so much higher in quality than standard British specifications that our customers have come to expect such quality from us. Accordingly, all manufacturers are constantly checking one another's product quality. Finally, since most large users have their own expert technical information on cement, we find ourselves giving technical advice only to an occasional small user. It's not an important tool in our sales kit."

3. *Overseas manufacture and other subsidiary activities* accounted for much of the company's growth and its increased profits in the past five years. Rugby was continually conducting site investigations and negotiations in search of new overseas opportunities for expansion.

4. *Transportation* of the U.K. cement sales was another reason for RPC's growth and profitability. Rugby's fleet had grown from 52 trucks in 1946 to 196 in 1961 (77 flat-bed trucks, 17 bulk tippers, and 102 pressurized bulk wagons)[2] plus extra trucks hired in the peak construction season. Rugby was proud of the efficiency of its fleet, the operating costs of which remained below the transportation allowance in the delivered price. During 1960, the fleet averaged less than 7% delays for

---

[2] Flat-bed trucks carried cement in bags; pressurized bulk wagons carried loose cement in large tanks which were slightly pressurized to remove the cement at the delivery site; bulk tippers were fully enclosed dump trucks which carried loose cement.

repair, less than 10% nonoperating idleness, and 6% on-the-job delays. Company officials believed that their truck fleet was one of the most efficient in the industry. The major reason for this efficiency, the directors believed, was the highly centralized scheduling of truck dispatches. Each day the central transportation department, working with the sales department, prepared schedules of the following day's dispatches of all trucks from each of the three works. Scheduling attempted to maximize the number of deliveries by each truck and to make as uniform as possible the work-load at the packing and loading plants.

5. *A philosophy of teamwork:* Sir Halford and the other directors of Rugby believed that the most important reason for the company's success was the achievement of company-wide teamwork through the chairman's human relations philosophy and application of profit-sharing and employee-shareholding plans. Rugby had no "personnel" department; development of teamwork was the job of managers at all levels within the firm. The impersonal term "personnel" and the word "welfare," with its connotation of charity, were banned from the Rugby vocabulary.

During the course of his career, Sir Halford had developed a philosophy of business as a team effort. A concrete expression of this philosophy was his introduction at Rugby of employee shareholding and profit-sharing plans. Commenting on the relationship between his philosophy and these plans, he said:

I am convinced that no scheme of profit-sharing or employee shareholding can succeed unless it is built on a firm foundation of confidence within the business and of real esprit de corps, of a strong feeling on the part of all employees of pride in the company and its achievements. The goodwill of those working together in an industrial enterprise cannot be purchased for cash—of that I am sure. A scheme which is put in with the primary object of buying goodwill is almost certainly doomed to failure from the start. It may indeed not only do no good but may even do positive harm by creating suspicion, however ill-founded.[3]

Teamwork, commendable in any organization, was held to be doubly important in the cement industry where production in large units of continuous-process plant made it impossible to associate individual effort with specific product output. Mutual confidence was felt to be the basic ingredient of teamwork: the board's confidence that all employees would put forth a fair day's work, operate and maintain the plant in-

---

[3] Quotation from "This is Industrial Partnership," a pamphlet written by Sir Halford in 1955 explaining his philosophy and the profit-sharing and employee share-holding schemes of Rugby.

telligently, and follow the leadership of the company; the employees' confidence in the capability and integrity of the directors and that discipline "which is as fair as it is firm" will be maintained.

ESPRIT DE CORPS AND COMPANY POLICIES

The following paragraphs summarize the most important company policies which Sir Halford felt had established *esprit de corps* within Rugby.

1. Personal contact between top executives and operating people all over the world was relatively frequent. Sir Halford visited the Trinidad and Australian plants at least once a year, and someone from the central headquarters staff visited them, on an average, every two or three months. At home, Sir Halford not only delivered his annual "Message to My Fellow-Workers," but he always personally made presentations which were given to men with 25 years' service and again after 50 years' service. Such presentations were made in the presence of the recipients' colleagues, and Sir Halford usually gave a brief review of the recent progress of the company.

2. In his annual messages to the employees, he described recent developments within the company, emphasizing the co-operative roles played by employees and shareholders. He frequently discussed the importance of profits. The following is part of his message following the 1951 operations:

> I want now to say something about profits, because a lot of nonsense has been talked about profits in the last few years, often by politicians of all parties who have never been in industry and have no practical knowledge of industry.
>
> You and I know that profits are the reward and the measure of economy and efficiency, and are essential to the maintenance and expansion of a business. They are, in fact, the real and only bulwark behind our wages and salaries, for if this company ceases to make profits it can be only a comparatively short time before you and I are out.
>
> Let us recognize that it is up to every one of us in this team to go all out all the time, to give of our best, to maintain and increase our production with economy and efficiency, and, in turn, the profits of the company: first—and note that I put this first—because it is the job we are paid to do, and it is only common honesty to our shareholders to do it; and secondly in our own interests to safeguard our jobs for the future.

3. Another aspect of the teamwork was the "works committee" at each plant. Composed of the works manager, the works engineer, the safety officer, and five representatives elected from the factory work force, the committee met without exception each month with a senior

member of the headquarters staff in attendance. The committee discussed matters of particular interest to the works concerned, and suggestions for operational improvements. The head office staff took this opportunity to clarify and discuss newly announced changes in policy and other company developments such as the annual financial statements.

Late in 1961, an IMEDE[4] researcher had the opportunity to attend a works committee meeting at the Rochester works. Mr. R. L. Evans was the representative of top management in attendance. The committee chiefly discussed matters of plant safety and of amenities for the workers, such as a sink and hand towels for workers at a remote plant location. Mr. Halfden Lav, the Rochester works manager, said that this meeting was typical, especially insofar as it was primarily concerned with safety and working conditions. The researcher was impressed at the free and easy manner in which the workers entered into the discussions. Mr. Evans explained in great detail some minor points of company policy on tardiness and vacation time. Mr. Lav commented that the worker representatives occasionally brought up very minor points in the committee; "I think," he added, "that some men do this just to show that they are on their toes and doing a good job for their fellow-workers. We let them talk as long as they want to, and the result is that the committee functions very well, and in a very good spirit."

4. Another policy was that no one but Sir Halford had the authority to release people during slack periods. He had in fact never authorized a layoff. For instance, the rail strike in 1955 almost closed the Rochester factory as coal reserves ran low. As the shutdown date approached, Sir Halford announced that no one would be laid off, but that:

    a) Some men would have to take their vacations during the shutdown.
    b) Everyone would have to agree to do any job given him (at his usual pay rate) during the shutdown.

(Last minute settlement of the rail strike saved Rugby Cement from its contemplated shutdown.)

5. Since 1954, the company had offered its weekly paid employees the option of having their contract of employment determinable not by the usual one week's notice but by one month's notice by either side for employees having 10 years' service, two months for those having

---

[4] IMEDE is the abbreviation of l'Institut pour l'Etude des Méthodes de Direction de l'Entreprise at Lausanne, Switzerland.

15 years, and three months for those having 20 years. Of those to whom the offer applied, over 85% had accepted one of these options.

In commenting on the fact that 15% of the workers had not chosen to take one of these options, company officials said that some workmen preferred the independence of being able to leave on short notice. "Our employee turnover is, however, quite low," one executive pointed out. "If we set aside employees with less than two years of service, our average worker has been here about 13 years. We do find that some new employees, especially young men, are not prepared for the demanding work in a cement plant, and such men leave, usually within 12 months. Thus new employees should not be fairly included in our average turnover figure. Incidentally, taking total annual wages and bonuses as an indicator, the cement industry ranks in the top half-dozen British industries in terms of earnings."

6. The final key policy of the company was summarized by Sir Halford:

If there is to be a lively interest and pride in the company and its doings, then it is necessary that all employees be kept informed as far as possible about what is going on. . . .

We try as far as we can to ensure that everyone has an opportunity of reading on the company's notice boards a few hours *before* it appears in the newspapers any release issued to the Press. We do not think it right that a man should learn from the newspapers something which he could quite properly have heard at first hand within the company.[5]

Besides all of the aspects of teamwork within an organization, two other features of any profit-sharing or employee-shareholding plan were felt necessary by Sir Halford. The first was that any such scheme must be tailored to suit the circumstances of the company and the outlook, philosophy, and intention of its leader. The second feature was simplicity.

THE PROFIT-SHARING SCHEME

Sir Halford said that the Rugby profit-sharing scheme, inaugurated in 1935, was designed to emphasize two things:

a) That the efforts of the employees are the efforts of a team—that we are all working to one end.

b) The essential partnership which exists between the ordinary shareholders and the employees.[6]

---

[5] "This Is Industrial Partnership."

[6] *Ibid.*

In speeches both to shareholders and workers, Sir Halford **referred** to the partnership between capital and employees. He said that capital was nothing more than the "labour of yesterday—the production of yesterday which was surplus to the consumption of yesterday."

Fundamental to the partnership was the following bargain:

. . . the labour of today is guaranteed payment for its services and the profit is calculated only after the remuneration of that labour has been paid. Capital, therefore, takes the risk and in return takes such profit (or loss) as arises *after* the labour of today has been paid in full.

But to my mind this difference in the basis of their respective remuneration in no way destroys the conception of industrial enterprise as essentially a partnership between the labour of yesterday (capital) and the labour of today. Nor is it destroyed if the "bargain" is varied slightly by guaranteeing the greater part of labour's remuneration irrespective of profit or loss and by making an additional but smaller part of it dependent on the results of the enterprise as a whole.[7]

The employees' profit-sharing scheme provided for an annual bonus in excess of industry-negotiated wages (wage-earners) or contracted salary (staff) for all Rugby workers. Basic points of the scheme are summarized below:

1. To qualify for the profit-sharing bonus, an hourly or salaried employee must have completed, on December 31, twelve months' unbroken service to the satisfaction of the Directors.

2. For the purpose of calculating the bonus, each qualified employee is treated as if he held a certain number of ordinary shares in the company. A staff employee received two "notional shares" for each £1 of annual salary. An hourly worker received shares in proportion to his length of service. For example, a worker with one year's service had 250 "notional shares"; a worker with five years' service, 375; a worker with 20 years, 750; and a worker with 40 or more years had 1,250.

3. The bonus is calculated at the full rate per share of the gross dividend declared and paid to the ordinary shareholders for the financial year in question and is paid immediately after the Annual General Meeting. For example, in 1960 the ordinary dividend declared was 1s.3d. per share. Thus a worker with five years' service, holding 375 notional shares, would receive a bonus of (375 × 1/3d.) or £23/8/9.

4. Certified sickness or compulsory National Service are ignored in calculating the number of years of unbroken service.

5. Any employee who leaves or is under notice to leave prior to the date of payment forfeits his bonus.

6. The scheme confers no rights in respect of any capital distribution, or distributions other than those declared as dividends on the ordinary shares of the company out of profits.

---

[7] *Ibid.*

7. The scheme is subject to modification or withdrawal at any time at the discretion of the Directors.[8]

Sir Halford emphasized that the bonus was not automatic. In a very small number of cases each year, bonuses were withheld completely or in part because service was not "to the satisfaction of the directors." If a man's record for the year was questionable, including several unexplained tardinesses, for instance, it was submitted, without name, to the works committee of the factory. In all cases, the directors had abided by the committee's recommendation. Sir Halford said that withholding the bonus was not so much a penalty to the slack worker, but was necessary in fairness to those who gave 100% service during the year.

Summarizing, Sir Halford said:

I believe that this is important: the bonus must be something that is earned —not something which becomes a right. I also feel that the link with the ordinary shareholders' dividend is fundamental: if the dividend per share goes up, so does the bonus; if the dividend is reduced, the bonus falls too—which is as it should be.

THE "A" SHARE SCHEME

After the war, Sir Halford saw two factors that made the profit-sharing scheme inadequate in emphasizing the partnership between capital and labor. He felt that the twin virtues of hard work and thrift no longer assured a man of personal savings for his old age—*taxation* restricted savings and inflation *devalued* them. Unlike the ordinary shareholder's income which flowed from an asset whose market value reflected both the company's prosperity and inflationary pressures, the employee's profit-sharing bonus was not reflected in a realizable capital asset. Thus he did not have a "hedge" against inflation.

To supply this need, Sir Halford presented his "A" share plan, in late 1954, for approval by the ordinary shareholders. He said that the scheme was designed to do three things:

To give practical form to the unity of interest which I have always held to exist between the ordinary shareholders and the employees; to give a return to the ordinary shareholders on profits "ploughed back" in the past; and to give to every full-time employee the opportunity to have in his hands a capital asset readily realizable on death or retirement. It was received enthusiastically by shareholders and employees alike.[9]

---

[8] This explanation of the profit-sharing scheme contains only the major aspects. Full details are available in Sir Halford Reddish's booklet, "This Is Industrial Partnership."

[9] Explanation of "A" share plan summarized from "This Is Industrial Partnership."

One million "A" shares of 1s. each were created with the following conditions attached to them:

1. For any financial year after 31st December 1954 for which (*a*) the net profits before tax are not less than £900,000, and (*b*) the gross amount distributed as dividend to the ordinary shareholders is not less than £300,000, the holders of the "A" shares shall be entitled to an amount of £70,000 plus 20% of any excess of the said net profits over £900,000 (see Exhibit 4). However, (*i*) the amount attributable to the "A" shares shall not exceed 12½% of the net profits; and (*ii*) in the event of the issue of additional ordinary share capital by the company after 31st December 1954, otherwise than by way of a capitalization of reserves or undistributed profits, the said figure of £900,000 shall be increased by a sum equal to 6% of the proceeds or other consideration received by the company.[10]

2. Any amount atributable to the "A" shares as ascertained under (1) above may be distributed as dividend or carried forward in the books of the company to the credit of the "A" shares for subsequent distribution, as the Directors may decide.

3. The holders of "A" shares have no voting rights.

4. In a winding-up, the "A" shares may participate only insofar as the amount of their paid-in capital value and the "A" share credit carried forward on the company books, but no further participation in assets.

5. No further "A" shares shall be created without the sanction of an Extraordinary Resolution passed by the holders of the "A" shares.[11]

Half of the "A" shares were offered to the ordinary shareholers at par and half to the employees.

"*All* full-time employees of the company were included: this was not a get-rich-quick exercise for the favoured few," said Sir Halford.

Allocation to the employees was done by dividing all employees into groups according to remuneration, responsibility, and status within the company (length of service was not a factor). Those in the first group were offered 250 shares, followed by groups of 500, 750, 1,000, 1,500, 2,000, and so on. (Most factory production workers were in the first group, for example.) Over 90% of Rugby's employees had exercised their option and purchased the "A" shares.

Sir Halford was particularly concerned about two aspects of the scheme. About the first, he said:

I was anxious that there should be no element of a "gift" from one partner (the holders of the ordinary shares) to the other (the employees); and that the equity owned by the ordinary shares should be unimpaired. I was convinced that the holders of the ordinary shares could have no legitimate cause for complaint

---

[10] Because additional equity had been introduced since 1954, the "A" shares now began participating at net profits of £964,500.

[11] Explanation of "A" share plan summarized from "This Is Industrial Partnership."

if the profits were so substantially increased in the future and some comparatively small part of the increase went to the employees as a reward for their efforts.

The "A" shares should be worth no more than was paid for them when issued, so that the employees could feel that whatever increased value accrued thereafter was due to their teamwork, with, I do not forget, nor do I allow them to forget, the capital provided by their partners in the enterprise.[12]

This reason, and tax considerations (discussed later) dictated that the minimum profit level at which the "A" shares would start participating (£900,000) should be well above the profit levels when the "A" shares were issued.

The second aspect was that the main object of the scheme was to insure employees of a capital sum on death or retirement. Sir Halford foresaw that the "A" shares might have some speculative attraction to the general public and he did not want the employees to be tempted into selling and thus depriving themselves of retirement or death benefits from the plan. He also felt that anyone leaving the firm be required to sell his shares back at par and thus enable newcomers to participate. To accomplish these ends, Sir Halford designated that the shares allocated to the employees were held in their behalf by Staff Nominees Limited which was accountable to the employees for dividends declared and authorized to act in their behalf in all matters relating to the "A" shares. The following conditions applied:

1. Initially and whenever an employee moves upward to a new group, he is given the opportunity to buy his allocation of shares at par. Failing to do so, he is not given a subsequent opportunity.
2. "A" shares may be sold by the employee at any time *at par* to Staff Nominees Limited and *must* be sold any time he leaves the company.
3. An employee's share may be sold at market value (market price was established by quotation on The London Stock Exchange of the "A" shares allotted originally at par to the ordinary shareholders) *only* in the event of the employee's death while in the service of the company, or upon his reaching the age of 65 (55 for women).
4. Any dividend declared on the "A" shares is paid immediately to the employee.

Fifty thousand shares remained unallocated to the employees after the initial sale. The Directors felt that this block of shares and those shares which Staff Nominees Limited bought back, at par, from employees who left, would be sufficient to offer shares to new and promoted employees for the foreseeable future.

---

[12] *Ibid.*

In his message to his fellow-workers in the company following the 1958 operations, Sir Halford said the following about the "A" share plan:

. . . Quite often a man will say to me: "This 'A' share scheme of yours—tell me, has it increased production?" And I reply: "I haven't the slightest idea, but I shouldn't think so." So he says: "But surely that was the object. It's an incentive scheme, isn't it?" "On the contrary," I tell him, "I have always insisted that it should *not* be called an incentive scheme, because that to my mind would imply that we in Rugby Cement were not already doing our best, were not doing our duty in return for our wages and salaries. And that I will not have."

What our "A" share scheme does is to give to the employees the opportunity to build up capital available on retirement or on earlier death, and to promote the feeling that we are all one team working to the same end in partnership with our shareholders. The value of the "A" shares depends in the long run on the success of our efforts in making profits. And don't overlook the fact that half the "A" shares were issued, also at par, to the holders of our ordinary shares. They very rightly benefit too, as they have seen these 1s.0d. shares change hands on the Stock Exchange at prices up to 42s.0d.[13]

Apart from the capital aspect, the holding of "A" shares by the employees of the company, and also, of course, our "profit-sharing" schemes, give some reward for successful endeavour—which is surely right.

The Taxation Aspect. For the company, the profit-sharing bonus was considered a wage bonus and therefore a before-tax expense. The "A" share dividends, however, were similar to ordinary dividends, being paid out of after-tax profits.

For the employees, the profit-sharing bonus was taxed as ordinary wage or salary income. Taxation of the employees in connection with "A" share distribution was a most difficult problem and one for which Sir Halford spent many hours in consultation with the Board of Inland Revenue.

The law held that if at the time of issue the value of the shares was greater than the amount the employees paid for them, the difference was taxable as a "benefit" arising from employment. The Rugby "A" share sale to its employees, however, had two characteristics which affected any ruling under this law:

1. "A" shares were not quoted on the market until two months after issue; thus it was a matter of discussion whether at time of issue they were worth more than the par value paid for them.
2. Employees were not free to sell their shares at market price except on retirement or death.

---

[13] In 1961, "A" shares were quoted on the stock exchange at up to 100 shillings per share.

Final agreement with the Inland Revenue was reached which assessed the value of the "A" shares at time of issue slightly above par.

Tax assessment for shares issued subsequently to newcomers or to promoted employees required a different arrangement with the Inland

Exhibit 4

THE RUGBY PORTLAND CEMENT COMPANY LIMITED (A)

Profit Participation of the "A" Shares

Graph of Participation "Formula"

and

Schedule of Gross Profits *before* Taxes

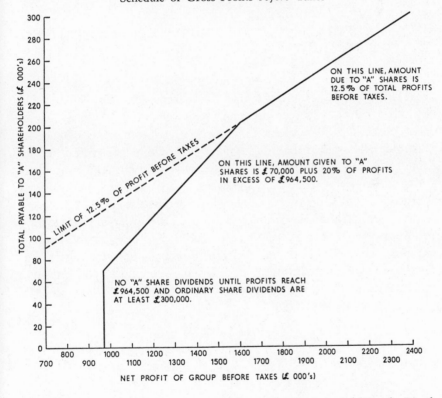

NET PROFIT OF GROUP BEFORE TAXES (£ 000's)

Revenue, since by that time a market value was established. Final agreement resulted in considering a variable fraction of the difference between current market value and par value as taxable income. The fraction varied inversely with the length of time between the recipient's age and 65 when he could realize the market price of the "A" shares. For instance, a 25-year-old newcomer receiving 500 "A" shares would have to consider as income, for income tax purposes, only 10% of the

Exhibit 4—Continued

THE RUGBY PORTLAND CEMENT COMPANY LIMITED (A)

Summary of Earnings and Gross Dividend Payments 1954–61

(1,000's of £)

Year	1954	1955	1956	1957	1958	1959	1960	1961
Profit before tax....................	721	1025	1093	1106	1171	1491	1777	2020
Gross ordinary dividend..............	200	300	338	338	375	437	500	500
Gross payable to "A" shares.........	..	95	109	111	124	179	222	252
Actual "A" share dividend...........	..	50	63	63	75	100	125	125
Difference carried forward as "A" share credit...........................	..	45	46	48	49	79	97	127
Cumulative "A" share credit*........	..	45	91	140	189	268	365	493

* The "A" share credit was contained in the Undistributed Profit account in the balance sheet. The directors considered this credit as a "dividend equalization reserve" to supply "A" dividends if they were not earned according to the formula (i.e., if pretax profits were below £964,500).

difference between market value and the price paid (one shilling per share), because he could not realize the market value for 40 years. On the other hand, a 50-year-old man receiving 500 "A" shares would have to consider 60% of the difference as taxable income, because he was much closer to realizing the gain. (The United Kingdom had no "capital gains" tax, but all dividends received by employees on their "A" shares up to retirement age were treated, for tax purposes, as "earned" income and therefore taxed at income-tax rates.)

Overseas. An employee profit-sharing plan, similar to that existing for Rugby workers in the United Kingdom, had been established for workers in the Trinidad and Australian plants. "A" shares were offered only to workers in the United Kingdom, including staff assigned temporarily to the overseas operations.

The Rugby Portland Cement Company Limited (B)

LATE IN 1961, an IMEDE[1] research team decided to attempt to expand the Rugby Portland Cement case by adding information on the ways in which various employees of the company viewed their jobs. To this purpose, an IMEDE researcher toured each of the company's three cement works in England; he also conducted interviews with a number of hourly paid workers and with a substantial number of middle- and top-management executives. This case includes excerpts from some of these interviews, as well as some of the researcher's impressions of what he saw.

VIEWS OF SOME RUGBY WORKMEN

Rugby's management was very co-operative in helping the researcher to interview some of the workmen. Although in theory it would have been useful to interview a rather large number of workers selected at random, this was not practicable for certain reasons:

1. There were limitations on the research time available for these interviews.
2. There was a chance that some men, if chosen at random, might:
    a) Not be able to articulate their views.
    b) Be less than wholly frank.
    c) Be unable to leave their work posts at the desired time.

Accordingly, Mr. R. L. Evans (deputy managing director) and Mr. Baker (works manager of the Rugby works) selected from the Rugby work force four workers who, they thought, would be articulate, honest, and as representative as possible of the general sentiments of the entire Rugby worker group. The researcher interviewed the four men separately, in an office at the Rugby plant; nobody else was present during the interviews. The names of the four men interviewed have been disguised.

---

[1] Once again, IMEDE is an abbreviation for l'Institut pour l'Etude des Méthodes de Direction de l'Entreprise at Lausanne, Switzerland.

INTERVIEW WITH MR. RYAN

Mr. Evans and Mr. Baker, in arranging the interviews, mentioned that Mr. Ryan should provide a highly entertaining and useful interview, that he was outspoken and highly articulate. Mr. Ryan, who had been working for the company since 1956, was an Irishman; he appeared to be about 40 years old. He worked in the transport department of the company as a truck driver and had been a member of the Rugby works committee for some time. The researcher asked each of the four men only one question to begin: what did the man think about working for the company, what were the bad points and the good points? Mr. Ryan began:

Well, I might tell you I'm an old union man, been a sort of union agitator all my working life. Before I came here I never held a job longer than eighteen months. I've been here almost six years now and I can tell you this, I'm going to stay here the rest of my life. And, mind you, I got a lot less to gain by staying here than most of the men. I have no A-shares, because you know you only get one chance to buy them A-shares, and when I had to buy them, I didn't have the money because my wife just had to have an operation. So now for the rest of my life I got to work here knowing that I'll never have no A-shares, and I think this is unfair, and I keep fighting to get me shares, and maybe I will and maybe I won't, but I'll stay on here no matter what.

And another thing is I'm a very bad timekeeper—sometimes it's my fault, and sometimes it was because I had to take my wife to the doctor and so I'd come in late, and so for three straight years I lost my profit-sharing bonus on account of being late so much. [Mr. Ryan had actually lost his bonus in two nonconsecutive years, management reported.] So you can see what I mean when I tell you that I got much less to gain by working here than the other men.

But even though there's lots of little things could be done, this is a wonderful place to work, and that's the Lord's own truth. I'm not saying anything to you I wouldn't say right to the Chairman's face if he asked me—I'm not a man to say what he doesn't mean.

You got to remember this: it's no good coming down to a cement works if you don't want to work hard. But they pay you good and, the main thing is, you always get treated fair. If you got a complaint, you can take it as high as you want, right up to the Chairman himself, but it's no good complaining unless you give 'em the facts. That's what they want to see: facts.

Another thing you ought to write down is this: in this company, I'm just as good as anybody, as good as the Chairman or Mr. Evans—that's what you won't get anywhere else. We all know this here, and we know you've got to work as a team. And I'll tell you this, I know the Chairman would let me buy my A-shares if he could, but you see he's got to be fair to the other workers too. But I do think that you get punished awful hard for being late. [Mr. Ryan's profit-sharing bonus would have amounted, in those years when he lost it, to about £30. His weekly wages were about £15.]

Over in Coventry, you know [about 15 miles away], in the car and airplane factories a man can make £30 a week while here he'll only make about £15, but we get the £15 for 52 weeks of the year, plus the profit-sharing, the A-shares, and lots of other benefits. The company buys up lots of clothes for us so we can get them cheaper. I once compared what I earned in a year with a friend of mine who works in Coventry for £29 a week, and you know what? I came out £48 ahead of him for the year, because those fellows are always getting laid off.

And let me tell you this: you'd never get a better firm to work for, no matter where you went; there isn't another company like this, at least none I've ever heard about.

You know, when I tell you we work hard here, you've got to remember that the Chairman doesn't ask us to to do anything he doesn't do himself. You know, he works eighteen hours a day, and when he come down sick recently and had to have that operation, his doctors told him to take it easy, and so he did—he only worked ten hours a day.

[Mr. Ryan then gave the researcher a very detailed description of what was involved in his truck-driving. He stressed that the equipment was the best obtainable, that the company paid much more attention to driver safety than to delivering a maximum daily tonnage of cement, that scrupulous care was taken at great expense, to be certain that the customer received all the cement he had been billed for.]

You see my truck out there? That truck, it's brand new, and it cost £10,000, and they expect me to take care of it like if it was my own, and I do. [The truck in fact cost slightly over £3,500.] And I know I've got 42 hours a week guaranteed, and more hours on weekends if I want to make extra money, and that's a hell of a nice thing for a truck driver. And as soon as I've driven 11 hours in a single day, even if I didn't get home with the truck by the time my 11 hours was up, the company would send out another lorry with two drivers to drive me and my truck home, that's how careful they are about the 11-hour rule. And you see them fine overalls we drivers got, and them jackets? Mr. Reddish, I believe, bought them for us out of his own pocket. That's just the kind of man he is. [In fact he didn't: they are provided by the company.]

I told you I used to be a union man, but I tell you this, if a union came in here now, it would hurt the workers—they'd get less pay, they couldn't touch anything they weren't supposed to. That's the kind of a union man I am today.

In summing up, and this is God's own truth, I think Sir Halford Reddish ought to be England's Prime Minister, and Mr. Evans ought to be the Secretary for Foreign Affairs.

INTERVIEW WITH MR. MASON

Mr. Mason was a foreman in the "raw plant," where the slurry was made. He had been working for the company about 14 years and appeared to be about 50. He began:

Well, wherever I went, I don't think I could better myself, that's what I'd say. The Chairman puts us in the picture about what's going on, he has more of a fatherly concern for us, I think. I've known the Chairman 30 years and if he says a thing he means it. He's put in some wonderful plans for the men, he has. For example, when my father died, we got about £1000 for his A-shares, and this was a big help, because I've got a sister who isn't very well, and this money pays for her. From the workman's point of view, if you want it, I find that they're very, very satisfied. I've got 30-odd men working for me, and I get all the points of view, so to speak, and I think I can say that they're all happy to be working here. Now, of course, there's some men as will always find something to complain about, you're going to have that anywhere, but in the main I think that the men like working here very much.

You're an American, so I'll put it in American: damn it all, we're on to a good thing here and we know it.

I've got a brother, a son, and two brothers-in-law working here, and my father before he died. They all came to work here after I did. Now do you think they'd have come if this wasn't a good place to work?

I do believe honestly, and I'm not handing you any bull, that we couldn't better ourselves. And you've got to remember this: Sir Halford will give any of his men a proper hearing anytime. And what's astonishing is that as the firm gets larger, the company seems to give us more attention, when you'd think it'd be the other way around.

Now you take your average Englishman, he's the biggest grumbler in the world, about anything at all. But you won't find much grumbling here. You'd have to kick them out to get the men here to leave.

INTERVIEW WITH MR. TOOT

Mr. Toot, who appeared to be about 50, had been with Rugby about seven years. The researcher received the distinct impression that Mr. Toot was temperamentally a sort of cynic who only grudgingly would admit that a workingman's life could be decent, although this impression was formed on the basis of very little evidence. Mr. Toot began:

Taken all around, I should say that this is a very good place to work. A workman here knows that he can go as high as he likes, if he has the ability. You get fair treatment here. I suppose that work here is 80% satisfactory. For the other 20%, it's hard to say what the objections might be. But one thing is, when a man first came to work here, he didn't get enough participation in the bonus system (the profit-sharing scheme), but they've changed that now.

If a man's willing to do an honest day's work, he'll generally be satisfied here. I suppose I could say this: the longer a man's been here, the more he wants to stay.

Now, you get some fellows, especially young ones, come in and they can't stick the work; it's too heavy or too hard for them. They usually leave, if they're this type, in 12–18 months. If a man sticks it a year or a year and a half, he'll probably stay here until he's through working.

This is a long-term policy job, so to say. It's good if you're thinking about your old age, because the company really takes care of you after you retire. I don't suppose you know this, but all the company's pensioners [retired workers] get a ton of coal from the company at Christmas. There's a Christmas party for the pensioners. And men like Mr. Evans and Mr. Baker visit the pensioners very regularly. The company doesn't just forget you when you've stopped working for them—they take care of you.

I suppose when I think of it, it's hard to say what kind of objections, you might say, a man could have to working here, if he's not just a casual laborer who doesn't care about doing an honest day's work, if he doesn't care about doing a good job. This is a good place to work.

INTERVIEW WITH MR. FORSTER

Mr. Forster had been working for Rugby for 48 years, and he worked in the quarry. He talked rather little, much less than the previous three men.

Well, I've been working here all my life, and that's a fact. It's hard work, and no doubt about it, but it's a wonderful company to work for. I was here, you know, when Sir Halford took over, and it was wonderful when he did. He promised us steady work, and we've had it ever since. Some of your casual lads, now, who come here looking for an easy day's work and high pay, they don't stay, but a real man, a man who doesn't mind work, he'll be happier here than anywhere else I've ever heard of.

RANDOM IMPRESSIONS OF THE RESEARCHER

In the course of his tour of the three different works, the researcher spent a great deal of time with Mr. R. L. Evans, who toured each plant with him, and with the works managers. The researcher was especially struck by two facts. First, Mr. Evans and the works managers appeared to know a great deal about the background of every company employee. The researcher was, while walking through the plant, introduced to one worker who had been a chef in Wyoming some years ago. Another worker was pointed out as having been (he was now 72) a good Rugby player in his youth. These and similar details were forthcoming quite frequently from Mr. Evans or the works managers. Second, the workers all said "hello" to Mr. Evans as he passed through the plant, and Mr. Evans would chat with them about their families and how things were going.

Another impression, although a difficult one to justify with explicit evidence, was that the various managers were more than superficially concerned with their workers and their lives. Words and phrases which often recurred in the four days of conversation included: "fair treatment," "decent work for a man," "take care of our men," "except them to work as part of a team." Workers and managers alike constantly referred to themselves as being part of a single team; they did so either implicitly or explicitly.

Precision Controls, Inc.

IN December, 1962, Steven Dietrich, chief executive officer of Precision Controls, Inc., of Los Gatos, California, believed that the biggest problem facing the company was its overhead cost structure. Since 1954 the company had added to its original product line, which consisted of relatively simple electro-mechanical controls, increasingly complex electronic control devices and aerospace components which created additional engineering and technical work. In commenting on the situation, Mr. Dietrich said:

I suspect that the overhead costs in some areas are high, but I want to prove it. Our overhead has inceased to six or seven times direct labor on many of our items. Overhead is hard to control for several reasons. One is that we have $10 million in sales, and for our company the area between $10 and $15 million is an awkward one. We are big enough to need a good accounting facility, standard practices and systems, a relatively strong management group, and other assets of a modern corporation, but these same overhead items, by and large, are capable of handling a much higher level of sales. It takes more overhead now that we are out of the little business stage, but our company needs about $15 million in sales to make the overhead pay.

Another reason is that standard cost accounting is no help in allocating costs among our product lines because it uses overall percentages for allocation. Our 28 product lines are in various stages of development, and we are sure that some of the newer products are taking more of the development and engineering time than the older products, but we just don't know what they really cost. Last July I asked our new controller, Harold Dickenson, to make a complete review of the 28 product lines and determine exact costs for each. We will have his results soon and then we will have facts instead of guesses to evaluate our operation.

The following discussion of the Precision Controls company deals with (1) the operations of the company prior to the accounting review, (2) the details of the accounting review, and (3) the management decisions made following the accounting review.

See Exhibits 1 and 2 for financial data for the years 1952–62.

OPERATIONS OF THE COMPANY PRIOR TO THE ACCOUNTING REVIEW

History. Precision Controls, Inc., had been organized in 1936 by Paul Nelson, a Stanford University professor, and three students to exploit their patented electro-mechanical control devices. The company originally was located in the Palo Alto, California, home of Mr. Nelson, but prior to 1940 it moved to leased quarters in Los Gatos, 20 miles south of Palo Alto. World War II provided a great impetus to the young company. Precision Controls' products were readily adaptable for use in military applications, and the company devoted all its efforts to war production, principally for use in military airplanes. During the war, sales increased to approximately $6 million.

In 1946 Precision Controls, like many other California firms associated with the aircraft industry, faced the problem of adjusting to the peacetime economy. Although the company had developed an engineering and manufacturing proficiency in the mass production of high-quality control devices during the war, it lacked products geared to the lower quality mass commercial market. Early in the postwar period the original owners brought in Steven Dietrich as executive vice president to manage the company during the transition period. Mr. Dietrich had previously been an executive with a major industrial company specializing in electric equipment for civilian and military uses. Under his administration the company began to develop its commercial market. The original products were adapted to a variety of commercial uses and a lower priced control device was added to the product line to give a broader product coverage. During these changes the company did not lower its quality standards but continued to concentrate on quality controls for both the commercial and military markets. It also built a strong distribution system, composed largely of manufacturers' representatives, to handle its products nationally.

With the outbreak of the Korean War the company was prepared to provide quality instruments to the government on short notice for military requirements. Although most of the government work called for aircraft applications of the original electro-mechanical product line, the company also developed several completely electronic control devices for military use. In 1954 Precision Controls hired a market research firm to investigate the company's market. The consultants forecast an eventual decline in the aircraft control applications, which then represented 90% of the company's business. Following the Korean War the company again emphasized commercial applications and concentrated on refining and adapting its electronic controls to the civilian economy. The electronic controls subsequently developed into the company's Division No. 2 products. Precision Controls also began to build a direct sales organization in order to reach the more technically oriented electronic control market.

Exhibit 1

PRECISION CONTROLS, INC.

Income Statements for the Years 1952 to 1962

(Dollars in Thousands)

	1952	1953	1954	1955	1956	1957	1958	1959	1960	1961	1962
Net sales	$6,662	$5,895	$5,680	$7,067	$8,371	$8,923	$8,333	$10,028	$9,715	$10,280	$10,348
Cost of sales	3,313	3,179	2,912	3,379	5,152	5,794	5,369	5,912	5,990	6,451	5,562
Gross profit	$3,349	$2,716	$2,768	$3,688	$3,219	$3,129	$2,964	$4,116	$3,725	$3,829	$4,786
Selling, administrative and general expenses	2,101	1,972	2,030	2,427	2,249	2,587	2,616	2,962	3,043	3,014	4,242
Operating income	$1,248	$744	$738	$1,261	$970	$542	$348	$1,154	$682	$815	$544
Other income	73	68	72	51	86	97	67	24	54	88	146
Other expense (interest)	351	221	261	353	301	218	64	46	56	52	251
Profit before taxes	$970	$591	$549	$959	$755	$421	$351	$1,132	$680	$851	$439
Taxes	539	208	60	282	299	200	198	622	367	467	237
Net income	$431	$383	$489	$677	$456	$221	$153	$510	$313	$384	$202

Exhibit 2

PRECISION CONTROLS, INC.

Balance Sheets for the Years Ending December 31, 1952 to 1962

(Dollars in Thousands)

	1952	1953	1954	1955	1956	1957	1958	1959	1960	1961	1962
Cash	$ 253	$ 218	$ 279	$ 179	$ 332	$ 272	$ 346	$ 383	$ 304	$ 316	$ 318
U.S. Treasury notes		87	38	101			248	977	977	749	
Accounts receivable	347	460	447	641	728	707	820	1,117	907	1,166	1,346
Inventory	667	617	585	836	1,072	1,072	1,230	1,527	1,273	1,326	1,588
Prepaid expenses	26	31	30	30	38	41	57	53	108	66	130
Total current assets	$1,293	$1,413	$1,379	$1,787	$2,170	$2,092	$2,701	$4,057	$3,569	$3,623	$3,382
Investment in subsidiary companies	715	794	1,204	1,708	290	330	213	168	211	245	200
Real estate not used					41						
Net fixed assets	399	422	417	520	616	717	549	596	537	666	1,108
Due from Precision Real Estate Co.										456	475
Patent rights							41	37	30	25	9
Total assets	$2,407	$2,629	$3,000	$4,015	$3,117	$3,139	$3,504	$4,858	$4,347	$5,015	$5,174
Notes payable					$ 375	$ 375					$ 250
Current installment of long-term debt								$ 85	$ 85	$ 85	85
Accounts payable	$ 102	$ 59	$ 83	$ 177	140	122	$ 210	335	233	274	220
Payroll taxes payable	40	41	35	44	61	71	135	154	105	110	85
Accrued expenses	301	226	246	282	252	197	191	275	150	250	157
Due to subsidiaries										22	
Other reserves											99
Federal and state taxes due	223	168	69	268	288	163	223	609	181	418	233
Total current liabilities	$ 666	$ 494	$ 433	$ 771	$1,116	$ 928	$ 759	$1,458	$ 754	$1,159	$1,129
Long-term debt							752	918	836	752	666
Capital stock	375	375	375	375	375	375	375	375	375	375	375
Earned surplus	1,366	1,760	2,192	2,869	1,626*	1,836	1,618	2,107	2,382	2,729	3,004
Total liabilities	$2,407	$2,629	$3,000	$4,015	$3,117	$3,139	$3,504	$4,858	$4,347	$5,015	$5,174

* Investment in subsidiary charged off to surplus.

In 1957–58 the company asked another consulting firm to review Precision Controls and recommend plans for the future direction of the company. The consultants approved of the expansion in the electronic controls field and recommended the development of a broader line of industrial products. They also recommended that the company develop precision components for aerospace applications but that it not endeavor to undertake complete aerospace control systems. The recommendations were never fully adopted, for the company continued to specialize in the measurement and control of only one environmental factor; but the company did hire a new vice president of engineering who directed the company's engineering efforts toward the government's aerospace requirements. This aerospace and systems research work continued as the company's Division No. 3 after the vice president left the company in 1960. During the late 1950's the development of the Division No. 2 and Division No. 3 products took most of Precision's engineering time. The owners believed that investment in the engineering department was an investment in the firm's future growth and at times sacrificed current profit to develop new products.

The company's expanded activities also required additional space. In 1957 Precision Controls leased a three-story building (Plant No. 2) in San Jose, five miles from its original plant. In 1962 it built a modern, climate-controlled, dust-free, two-story plant to replace the four-story frame building that it had leased since 1940 and used as a main plant. The company hoped eventually to expand the new building and consolidate the operations which were presently located in various leased buildings in the area.

Ownership. By 1962 the ownership of the company was divided fairly evenly among five officers: Lester Clark (chairman of the board), Steven Dietrich (president), Paul Nelson (treasurer), John Hurley (director of engineering), and Bill Cole (secretary). Although only Steven Dietrich was active on a full-time basis, each of the owners had an office in the company's main plant and maintained a close interest in company affairs. Mr. Clark visited the office weekly and served as a consultant to the other officers. As one of the company's founders he had a thorough knowledge of the company's technology and through several businessmen's associations he had contacts and a breadth of business experience that were of great value. Mr. Hurley also operated on a part-time basis and provided extensive experience and engineering ability. Mr. Nelson had invented the original product and maintained an active interest in the technical and financial activities of the company. Mr. Cole was on the faculty of a local university and also acted as an engineering consultant. The four semiactive owners had extensive outside interests which required much of their attention. All of the owners were in their early 50's, except Mr. Nelson, who was 65.

The five owners also comprised the board of directors, which met weekly to review the activities of the company. Although the board discussed the full range of company business, including insurance programs, major personnel decisions, and tax and financial policy, Mr. Dietrich described the main interest of the directors as technical rather than economic. "The members of the board are sympathetic to research and have had a lot of fun blazing trails." Although the members of the board reviewed the policies of the company, they left the actual operations to Mr. Dietrich.

Top-Management Organization. The five men who reported directly to Mr. Dietrich were Harold Dickenson (controller), Jim Moore (vice president of manufacturing), John Stykes (vice president of engineering), Don Hudson (vice president of sales), and Joe Morrell (director of labor relations).

Harold Dickenson had joined the company in 1950. He had previously graduated from college with an accounting degree and had worked for 10 years in the manufacturing department of another company. Until his promotion to controller in 1962 he had been sales service manager. Part of his duties as sales service manager had included preparation of sales forecasts. He had also reviewed the profit from engineering projects suggested by the sales department and had earned a reputation as an advocate of better cost control.

Jim Moore was described by Mr. Dietrich as a "very good man who followed me here. We had worked together prior to joining Precision Controls." Jim supervised, through the division managers, the manufacture of the electro-mechanical controls (Division 1) at the company's new plant and the electronic controls (Division 2) at the company's plant No. 2. Two thirds of the Division 3 products were produced in the facilities of the other divisions and also came under his manufacturing supervision.

John Stykes, vice president of engineering, worked under the supervision of Steven Dietrich in all operating matters; in formulating technical policies and appraising technical approaches to problems he also worked closely with John Hurley. Mr. Stykes had graduated from college with an engineering science degree and had taught for several years before joining Precision Controls in 1950. His department provided engineering support for Divisions 1 and 2 and also operated a separate research group which investigated new product possibilities.

Don Hudson, vice president of sales, had joined Precision Controls in 1953 after graduating from the engineering and business schools of Stanford University. His department provided a direct sales effort for the more complex control devices manufactured in Divisions 2 and 3 and supervised the manufacturers' representatives in the commercial market.

Joe Morrell, the labor relations director, was past retirement age. In addition to acting as director of labor relations he supervised the company's credit department. Mr. Dietrich explained that Joe Morrell's long experience in both fields and the staffing behind him in anticipation of retirement made it possible for him to bridge both functions with considerable effectiveness.

Mr. Dietrich described his direction of subordinates as informal and based to a high degree upon delegation. Each department head was responsible for developing a capital budget and controlling costs within his department, but capital and departmental budgets were consolidated on a companywide basis and were reviewed by the board of directors. In general, the ratio of capital expenditures to depreciation charges was used as a measure of the adequacy of the maintenance of the existing facilities with additional expenditures authorized by the board of directors for economic, technical, or growth reasons where the value of the individual piece of equipment could be proven.

Mr. Dietrich met weekly with his five subordinates and the assistant treasurer as a "Planning Committee." He described the objectives and limitations of the committee as follows:

It is the job of the operating department heads to operate within general policies as laid down by the board of directors or communicated by general management. Committees sometimes can be effective in decision making, but I feel that the real value of these meetings has been to provide a regular reporting session in which we are forced to consider problems of the company as a whole. In return, operating heads are given an opportunity to voice their opinions, to learn more intimately the problems of their associates, and also jointly to arrive at certain guidelines of mutual operation. Effective decisions, however, I believe, are most often handled directly by the line and staff organization functioning with assigned duties and responsibilities and with what I hope is reasonable guidance from the top.

Obviously, in a technical company many matters of a technical nature come to the foreground during planning committee meetings, representing problems or opportunities for the company. However, the meetings are also a vehicle for examining our monthly statements, reviewing business activity in terms of incoming orders, comparing expenditures with budgets, and reviewing personnel matters and the host of general problems which come up to any management. Many hours have also been spent over many years in trying to foresee the future and to modulate the company's policies in terms of changing times.

One officer pointed out that the name "planning committee" for this group was actually a misnomer. Prior to its formation Mr. Dietrich had held staff meetings which were attended by department heads and their subordinates. The new planning committee had been established as a means of reducing attendance at the staff meetings without hurting the feelings of the individuals who were excluded rather than to signify a different purpose. Meetings of the entire staff had been discontinued.

Divisional Organization. Although the top-management positions were divided along functional lines, the production and engineering efforts were separated into three product divisions. Mr. Dietrich explained the divisional organization as follows:

> When we divided the company into divisions, it was as an expedient for controlling the operations. We didn't really create the divisions separately; we just divided up what we already had. The divisions identify the different kinds of businesses that we are in and vary across the spectrum. The industrial products of Division 1 require the least engineering time and are the most stable. The electronic products of Division 2 require more engineering, and the exotic products of Division 3 require the highest engineering content and the fastest reaction time. In Division 1, material cost is extremely low as compared with Division 2 and often Division 3. Our first effort to get a handle on our costs was by identifying these kinds of businesses, segregating them, and treating them as separate businesses in manufacturing and operating areas, including engineering.

Exhibits 3, 4, and 5 describe the product lines of the three divisions, Exhibit 6 indicates the total 1962 company sales and costs by division, and Exhibits 7, 8, and 9 indicate the sales and cost by product line for each division as determined by the accounting review.

Division 1. The electro-mechanical control devices of Division 1 comprised the original products of the company and were based largely upon the same patented applications developed by the original inventors. They were sold to a wide range of industrial users. The customers who purchased from this division were basically of two types: the industrial user, who bought small quantities at the time of installation of equipment or for replacement, and the original equipment manufacturer, who bought large quantities on a price basis for inclusion in a variety of equipment ranging from small appliances to aircraft. Prices varied by quantity purchased to allow the company to compete for the large quantity business and still cover the cost of the more expensive small orders.

Exhibit 3

PRECISION CONTROLS, INC.

Product Lines in Division 1

	PRODUCT LINE										
	1	2	3	4	5	6	7	8	9	10	11
Date of introduction	1936	1948	1949	1946	1951	1955	1954	1954	1954	1936	Various
Approximate price	$10	$15	$15	$1.75	$13.50	$30	$3.75	$50	$11	$10	(see below)
Type of purchaser	O.E.M. Commercial	Government	Commercial	O.E.M.	Commercial	Aircraft	Military Electronics	O.E.M. Commercial	Commercial	Commercial Commercial	
Type of distribution	Mfg. Reps.	Direct	Mfg. Reps. & Direct	Mfg. Reps.	Mfg. Reps.	Direct Sales	Mfg. Reps.	Mfg. Reps.	Mfg. Reps.	Mfg. Reps.	
Company evaluation	Stable	Declining	Stable	Stable	Stable	Declining	Declining	Growing	Stable	Stable	

Comments:

Product #1—The company's original product reaches a wide market and has enjoyed stable sales for many years. The company has patent protection on this product and is presently suing one of the two small competitors that make similar products for patent infringement.

Product #2—A run-out product being used only for replacement parts.

Product #3—Limited by design features to this stable volume. The company is designing a new product which will eventually replace this one. This product has undergone almost yearly major engineering changes over the past 12 years.

Product #4—A low-price but quality instrument which differs from the regular line of more complex products. It is needed to maintain a full line.

Product #5—A special unit of very high quality with a constant limited demand. Competitors sell only low-quality units at one-fourth the price.

Product #6—A special unit designed for aircraft which are no longer manufactured. The company sells only replacement units.

Product #7—A product with wide industrial application which is expected to remain stable for one year and then decline because of changes in industrial design requirements. The company's design efforts with Product 8 and other instruments have contributed to the decline of this product.

Product #8—A widely used product with good growth potential which has just been completely redesigned by the company. The company expects sales of about $600,000 in 1963 without the excessive development, tooling and manufacturing costs of 1962.

Product #9—A special product with limited stable sales.

Product #10—A part used exclusively with Product #1.

Product #11—Includes a variety of replacement parts for other products and sales in foreign countries through licensing agreements.

Exhibit 4

PRECISION CONTROLS, INC.

Product Lines in Division 2

	PRODUCT LINE					
	1	2	3	4	5	6
Date of introduction.........	1959	1959	1960	1961	1961	Various (see below)
Approximate price.........	$45	$165	$100	$125	$2,000 & up	
Type of purchaser.........	Commercial	Commercial	Aircraft-Military	Commercial	Commercial	
Type of distributor.........	Mfg. Reps.	Mfg. Reps.	Direct	Mfg. Reps.	Mfg. Reps.	
Company evaluation.........	Growing	Growing	Dead	Growing	Declining	

Product #1—The company executives believe that a $1.5 million market exists for this product and its recent modifications and that the company can capture most of that market because of its superior distribution system even though it is competing with a number of electronic firms and enjoys no patent protection. The company expects a 30% growth in 1963.

Product #2—Although not a mass market item the company expects a growth of about 20% in 1963.

Product #3—This item was developed for an aircraft firm which had difficulty selling its planes. No more will probably be sold.

Product #4—Used with Product #1 and should enjoy the same growth potential.

Product #5—This is a system made up of components from the other products in Division 2. It is declining and will probably be replaced by Division 1 products.

Product #6—Composed of parts and miscellaneous sales.

Exhibit 5

PRECISION CONTROLS, INC.
Product Lines in Division 3

	PRODUCT LINE										
	1	2	3	4	5	6	7	8	9	10	11
Date of introduction	1961	1946	1958	1953	1960	1959	1958	1958	1954	1957	Various (see below)
Approximate price	...	$9	$105	$130	$150	$12	$1–$120	$30,000–$50,000	$220	$1–$200	
Type of purchaser	Government	Aircraft	Aircraft	Aircraft	Aircraft	Various	Various	Commercial	Aircraft	Government	
Type of distribution	Direct	Direct	Direct	Direct	Direct	...	...	Mfg. Reps. & Dir.	Direct	Direct	
Company evaluation	Stable	Declining	Uncertain Slight Growth	Static or Declining	Declining Rapidly	Growing	See Below	Growing	Static	Fluctuating	

Product #1—This account represents cost plus fixed fee contracts. About half of this is an open service contract which the company will keep in 1963 but intends eventually to drop because it has not led to the hoped for new products. The other half represents research contracts in the company's area of interest. The company has contracted for equivalent work in 1963.

Product #2—A replacement item which will be needed as long as present aircraft fly. The company has a strong patent position.
Product #3—A combination of instruments replacing Product #2 in newer planes. The company has some patent protection.
Product #4—A high-quality product for a small but competitive market.
Product #5—A product designed primarily for one aircraft manufacturer. Since planes did not sell well a 75% decline is expected in 1963.
Product #6—A component part of Product #5 and of Division #2 products. Although a competitive item, cost problems have been "solved" and the company expects a 33% increase in 1963.
Product #7—This represents sales through cross licensing agreements. The company is turning this business over to its representative and in the future will receive a commission from their efforts.

Product #8—A promising item in the "investment stage." This item represents complete control systems installed and serviced by Precision Controls in large industrial plants. The company hopes for $450,000 sales in 1963 and an eventual market of $700,000 per year with $300,000 additional service contract income. The manufacturers' representatives are finding prospective customers, with sales handled by company salesmen.

Product #9—An item designed for aircraft. Only replacement parts are sold.
Product #10—Replacement parts for aircraft control systems not developed by the company.
Product #11—Represents other small parts sold and engineering service performed.

Exhibit 6

PRECISION CONTROLS, INC.

Sales & Costs by Division—1962

(Dollars in Thousands)

	Division 1	Division 2	Division 3	Total
Sales..	$6,050	$1,200	$3,098	$10,348
Costs directly applicable to products:				
Materials................................	$ 730	$ 368	$ 820	$ 1,918
Direct labor............................	392	132	208	732
Commissions...........................	446	102	106	654
Other....................................	168	22	54	244
Indirect production expense..............	786	80	344	1,210
Division period costs....................	502	202	712	1,416
Corporate period costs:				
Building.................................	314	60	200	574
Engineering............................	198	184	234	616
General administrative................	300	58	128	486
Selling..................................	424	116	314	854
Total allocated costs...............	$4,260	$1,324	$3,120	$ 8,704
Income after allocated cost...............	$1,790	$ (124)	$ (22)	$ 1,644
Nonassignable costs.....................	884	144	356	1,384
Income after total cost...................	$ 906	$ (268)	$ (378)	$ 260
Add:				
Volume variance (to adjust direct cost-				
ing to accrual basis).................	174	41	69	284
Income per books.....................	$1,080	$ (227)	$ (309)	$ 544

Employment Breakdown 12/31/62:	*Total*	*Production Workers*
Division 1	283	173
Division 2	53	29
Division 3	51	16
Corporate building	38	
Corporate engineering & research	75	
Corporate administration	54	
Corporate selling	77	
	631	

Each of the 11 product lines mechanically measured the same environmental factor. Most of the instruments were also equipped to activate electronic controls when indicated by the mechanical measurements. The product lines ranged widely in size and complexity, depending upon the purpose of their application. Although the price and quality of the instruments generally were higher than those of similar instruments used in mass consumer applications, the Division 1 products had a wide range of industrial uses. They could be varied to serve the purpose of the individual industrial customer by changing the calibration and mountings to fit a particular application. In any single month the company might produce 1,000 different models for 8,000

Exhibit 7

PRECISION CONTROLS, INC.

Division 1 Profit & Loss Statement by Product Line—1962

(Dollars in Thousands)

	PRODUCT LINE											TOTAL
	1	2	3	4	5	6	7	8	9	10	11	
Sales	$3,296	$96	$562	$224	$342	$44	$670	$264	$314	$52	$186	$6,050
Direct product expenses:												
Material cost	$ 265	$10	$ 33	$ 37	$ 38	$ 8	$ 63	$ 76	$125	$ 4	$ 71	$ 730
Labor cost	190	6	34	22	24	2	54	22	22	4	12	392
Commissions	257	2	34	17	31	1	42	27	28	5	2	446
Other	90	4	11	8	7	1	9	3	3	1	31	168
Total direct product expense	$ 802	$22	$112	$ 84	$100	$12	$168	$128	$178	$14	$116	$1,736
Division production expense	359	16	80	40	52	8	99	58	60	8	6	786
Division period costs	176	19	62	20	34	7	52	68	48	6	10	502
Total direct and division costs	$1,337	$57	$254	$144	$186	$27	$319	$254	$286	$28	$132	$3,024
Income contribution after total direct and division costs	$1,959	$39	$308	$ 80	$156	$17	$351	$ 10	$ 28	$24	$ 54	$3,026
Corporate period costs:												
Building	$ 147	$ 6	$ 28	$ 14	$ 24	$ 3	$ 40	$ 29	$ 18	$ 3	$ 2	$ 314
Engineering	71	4	14	6	4	4	8	70	14		3	198
Selling	206	5	32	16	17	3	54	35	31	8	17	424
Administrative	158	5	22	12	15	2	30	14	19	5	18	300
Total corporate period costs	$ 582	$20	$ 96	$ 48	$ 60	$12	$132	$148	$ 82	$16	$ 40	$1,236
Income contribution after corporate costs	$1,377	$19	$212	$ 32	$ 96	$ 5	$219	($138)	($ 54)	$ 8	$ 14	$1,790
Nonproduct assignable costs ($884,000) net of volume variance to adjust direct costing to books	390	11	46	28	30	2	67	26	41	11	58	710
Operating profit by product per books	$ 987	$ 8	$166	$ 4	$ 66	$ 3	$152	($164)	($ 95)	($ 3)	($ 44)	$1,080

Exhibit 8

PRECISION CONTROLS, INC.

Division 2 Profit & Loss Statement by Product Line—1962

(Dollars in Thousands)

	PRODUCT LINE						TOTAL
	1	2	3	4	5	6	
Sales	$567	$270	$6	$136	$137	$84	$1,200
Direct product expenses:							
Materials cost	$162	$86	$2	$42	$50	$26	$368
Labor cost	80	24	..	12	14	2	132
Commissions	53	28	..	14	6	1	102
Other	12	4	..	2	3	1	22
Total direct product expense	$307	$142	$2	$70	$73	$30	$624
Division production expense	48	18	1	8	3	2	80
Division period costs	116	44	1	22	11	8	202
Total direct and division costs	$471	$204	$4	$100	$87	$40	$906
Income contribution after total direct and division cost	$96	$66	$2	$36	$50	$44	$294
Corporate period costs:							
Building	$37	$11	$0	$6	$4	$2	$60
Engineering	96	18	2	27	34	7	184
Selling	43	37	..	26	2	8	116
Administration	28	12	..	5	4	9	58
Total corporate period costs	$204	$78	$2	$64	$44	$26	$418
Income contribution after corporate costs	($108)	($12)	$0	($28)	$6	$18	($124)
Nonproduct assignable costs ($144,000) net of volume variance to adjust direct costing to books	36	22	..	11	4	30	103
Operating profit by product per books	($144)	($34)	$0	($39)	$2	($12)	($227)

Exhibit 9

PRECISION CONTROLS, INC.

Division 3 Profit & Loss Statement by Product Line—1962

(Dollars in Thousands)

					Product Line							Total
	1	2	3	4	5	6	7	8	9	10	11	
Sales	$274	$767	$777	$240	$138	$437	$88	$199	$26	$102	$50	$3,098
Direct product expenses:												
Materials cost	$ 84	$115	$179	$ 45	$46	$151	$62	$ 66	$14	$ 52	$ 6	$ 820
Labor cost	58	49	45	18	8	18	..	4	2	..	6	208
Commissions	..	23	18	3	2	40	3	15	1	1	..	106
Other	9	29	7	3	1	3	..	1	..	..	1	54
Total direct product expense	$151	$216	$249	$ 69	$ 57	$212	$65	$ 86	$17	$ 53	$13	$1,188
Division production expense	8	106	136	37	7	29	1	7	1	3	9	344
Division period costs	55	73	228	50	26	72	8	172	6	18	4	712
Total direct and division costs	$214	$395	$613	$156	$ 90	$313	$74	$265	$24	$ 74	$26	$2,244
Income contribution after total direct and division cost	$ 60	$372	$164	$ 84	$ 48	$124	$14	($ 66)	$ 2	$ 28	$24	$ 854
Corporate period costs:												
Building	$ 6	$ 45	$ 73	$ 14	$ 6	$ 14	$..	$ 37	$ 2	$ 2	$ 1	$ 200
Engineering	2	25	93	4	22	34	5	36	13	..	..	234
Selling	21	27	151	8	12	44	..	32	2	5	12	314
Administration	11	24	32	8	4	26	1	7	1	5	9	128
Total corporate period costs	$ 40	$121	$349	$ 34	$ 44	$118	$ 6	$112	$18	$ 12	$22	$ 876
Income contribution after corporate costs	$ 20	$251	($185)	$ 50	$ 4	$ 6	$ 8	($178)	($16)	$ 16	$ 2	($ 22)
Nonproduct assignable costs ($368,000) net of volume variance to adjust direct costing to books	13	46	70	13	9	72	6	17	2	11	28	287
Operating profit by product per books	$ 7	$205	($255)	$ 37	($ 5)	($ 66)	$ 2	($195)	($18)	$ 5	($26)	($ 309)

customers from its 11 product lines by varying the components and adding special parts.

All production in Division 1 took place in the company's main building. There were two major stages in the production process—manufacturing and final assembly. The first phase included receiving and storing stock metal, fabricating basic component parts, machining the parts to exact specifications, brazing parts to form subassemblies, painting, and storing the parts until required by the assembly departments on the second floor. The production control department established inventory levels for basic component parts. When a part reached the minimum inventory level it was scheduled for production and the required number cut from the raw stock and turned on the company's 12 automatic screw machines. Although the company's original product line was easily manufactured on the automatic screw machines, the more recent additions to the line and most of the Division 2 products were housed in casings that were more easily produced by die-casting techniques. The company lacked die-casting equipment and was considering investing $25,000 for this type of operation.

After the preliminary work had been completed, the parts were moved to the finishing department, where they were ground to exact specifications, drilled, and brazed together to form finished subassemblies. In the finishing department large production lots were completed on automatic equipment and small lots were finished by hand or semiautomatically. After the relocation of the equipment in the new plant, the department had an over-supply of machines, and workers could move from one machine to another rather than reset the same machine for the various operations; thus both overtime and setup time were temporarily minimized. The operations were highly automated; one punch press combined with an automatic feeder could produce a three months' supply of one small part in one shift. The company hoped to find additional uses for the feeder. At the present time, Mr. Moore stated, the department was working at about 60% of capacity; he did not anticipate a higher capacity in the machining or finishing department during 1963.

After the completion of the subassembly, the parts were placed in inventory until needed in the assembly area on the second floor. The company maintained a raw stock and semifinished inventory of about $1 million. Assembly of the finished products was scheduled by the production control department on the basis of sales orders and past sales experience. Production in the assembly area remained fairly stable;

where possible, the company produced its instruments for inventory and then calibrated them for individual customers as orders were received. Small orders could be processed quickly from finished stock inventory, but large modifications were scheduled into the regular production runs.

The assembly operation was divided into product line areas; the basic product line required about half of the available space. The company had devised numerous control devices of its own to aid in the manufacture and calibration of its products, with the result that the actual assembly process was not a highly skilled operation.

Division 2. Division 2 had been added to the company in 1955 after the company had entered the electrical control field. Products in the electrical division were designed to measure the same conditions as the products in Division 1 but electrically rather than electro-mechanically. The Division 2 products were therefore more complex and more easily adapted to use in extensive control systems.

Except for two parts produced in the main plant, all of the electrical products were manufactured in plant No. 2 which also housed the sales and accounting offices, Division 3, and the office of the executive vice president. The division's engineering department, however, was housed with the Division 1 engineering department in a small building adjacent to the main plant.

Whereas most of the Division 1 products were manufactured from stock, Division 2 was primarily an assembly operation. The division purchased the die-cast housing and the delicate sensing devices for its instruments and assembled them into the final product. While the Division 1 operation was done on an assembly-line basis, the Division 2 operation was on a job-order basis.

The company had encountered difficulty with one particularly sensitive purchased part which was a key component in most of the electronic devices. Much of the activity of the division had been spent in determining how to replace this part without having to recalibrate the instrument. The company finally succeeded in solving this engineering problem and in obtaining a small price reduction in the cost of the part.

Don Hudson, vice president of sales, worked closely with the Division 2 manager. He believed that in addition to a concern for the production and the quality of his items, the manager also understood the sales problems of the line and was of assistance in developing a coordinated marketing and manufacturing effort.

Division 3. Division 3 could be more accurately described as an engineering capability than as a production division. The only production facility of the division was a small model shop. The "products" of the division included government development contracts, the end result of some of the company's extensive research work, and combinations of the company's more standard products for installation in control systems for military and industrial purposes.

The division consisted of three engineering groups and a manufacturing section plus additional units as required to service particular development contracts. The electro-mechanical and the electronic engineering groups within Division 3 (five engineers and four technicians each) were responsible for applying the company's technology and products in these areas to military and industrial control system applications. Although these groups occasionally re-engineered the standard products for their own use, the re-engineering of the standard products and the special engineering for products in the general industrial line were the responsibility of the Division 1 and 2 engineering sections.

The division's third engineering group, consisting of five engineers and three technicians, worked only on the division's product line No. 8. The company hoped that the development of a complete plantwide control system would eventually become a large outlet for the company's standard products and would also lead to a steady income from service contracts.

Engineering. The company considered itself engineering oriented, and engineering activities were carried on throughout the organization. The sales and manufacturing staffs consisted largely of engineers. The engineering department, however, included only the activities under the direction of Mr. Stykes, the vice president of engineering. He supervised two groups of engineers. The first group concentrated on the engineering problems of Divisions 1 and 2 products, while the second concentrated on research.

While Mr. Stykes was described by his associates as a researcher and teacher, the chief engineer in charge of Divisions 1 and 2 engineering, Mr. Olson, was pictured as a strong-willed, "hard-nosed," highly competent engineer. Mr. Olson used weekly and monthly project reports to keep track of the engineering projects in his department. These included reports, by project, on the hours spent in engineering and design and reports on the costs of the model shop, the laboratory, and materials. An analysis of the project reports of the engineering department as a whole indicated that activity was evenly divided between support engineering for existing projects, engineering for major customer application, and engineering for adapting present products to new uses.

Mr. Dietrich believed that the company offered engineers several advantages that they could not get in other companies. It not only paid the going rate for engineering talent, but it also offered steady work that was not dependent on government contracts and the advantages of living in a pleasant suburban community.

Sales. Don Hudson, vice president of sales, controlled his department through four sales managers. Three of the sales managers were in charge, respectively, of aerospace programs, international sales, and market development. The fourth sales manager was responsible for the four regional sales managers, a service manager who ran the clerical staff and handled returned instruments, a warehouse manager responsible for shipping, and the four sales engineering teams at headquarters which supported the regional sales departments. Each of the sales engineering teams included a sales engineer and a customer service supervisor.

The four regional sales managers handled direct sales and maintained contacts with the manufacturers' representatives. The company also employed five salesmen; three worked under regional managers and two other salesmen operated out of the main office and covered industrial accounts in California.

The activities of the sales department varied greatly because of the wide range of products it handled. The company believed that one of its greatest assets was its manufacturers' representatives and had spent a great deal of time and effort in providing them with a variety of training courses, including a two-week course at the company plant, to indoctrinate them in the proper sales techniques for the company's products. The company arranged for the representatives to carry products complementary to Precision products so that they could present a more complete and attractive line to their customers. The company also had arrangements with special representatives to cover certain government installations and aircraft companies. The representatives, therefore, in addition to handling the bulk of the commercial sales, sold the other lines of the company, sometimes with the aid of the company salesmen.

The company set up its direct selling organization in the late 1950's because it believed that the representatives did not reach the market which it hoped to enter with its more complex electronic and aerospace equipment. The regional managers and the regional salesmen concentrated their efforts upon locating and selling large accounts in their regions. In selling the services of Division 3 the salesmen usually found the customer and then relied upon the engineers of the division to complete the sale.

Building. In 1954 the company began planning for the new building which a management consulting firm had recommended as part of the company's growth program. The plans were postponed in 1956–57 when the predicted profits failed to materialize and the company underwent some personnel cutbacks, and again delayed in 1958 by the recession. In 1961 the plans were revised and the modern, two-story, atmosphere-controlled building was built in early 1962. The move to the new plant was made during the company's two-week shutdown period in July, 1962. Little new machinery was purchased, since the company had continually modernized its equipment following the Korean War.

The new building was a source of pride to both the executives and the employees of the company. The actual plans, developed over a period of eight years, were designed to overcome the problems that had become evident during 20 years of operating in a four-story plant originally designed as a shoe factory. Although the final decisions had been made by the board of directors, many of the suggestions for the building came from Jim Moore, and he was pleased with the manufacturing engineering in the new building. The company's former plant had required substantial movement of products, which resulted in inefficient operation, particularly in processing the large government orders. As much of this inefficiency as possible had been eliminated in the new plant through the detailed planning efforts of the manufacturing engineering department.

The 106,000-square-foot building was specifically designed to allow an even work flow and to accommodate the special requirements of the firm. It was well lighted, spacious, dust free, climate controlled and contained special, closely controlled work areas for highly sensitive operations. All painting and "dirty" operations were confined to one end of the building; the air conditioning was designed to take air toward the dust rather than away from it. Additional features included automatic shoe cleaners at the entrances, hydraulically operated loading platforms that rose to the height of any truck bed, and a roof sprinkling system to increase the effectiveness of the air conditioning in the summer.

One officer described the building as "an extension of the direction in which we were going." By this he meant that the production line techniques were designed to produce efficiently a large number of high-quality precision electro-mechanical components, while some of the climatically controlled rooms were designed to do the most complicated of electronic subassembly work. The building could be expanded as the requirements of the electronics division warranted; with a small addition and two-shift operation the plant could employ 1,000 production workers. The company did not, however, plan an expansion in the next five years.

The planned capacity of the new building had been based upon the company's sales plus an additional margin based upon the forecast growth of each product line. Mr. Dietrich explained that the move to the new building had resulted in a consolidation of equipment and overcapacity in some departments.

Production in the old building was utter confusion and highly inefficient. When we laid everything out in the new plant, we had more machine tools and other equipment than we needed. We realize that some of the departments are out of balance and have more capacity than is necessary, but we would get very little for the extra equipment if we sold it. We plan to bring the plant into balance through our capital purchasing and replacement policies. We have always done a good job of replacing our equipment and keeping our operations modern so we are not planning on getting rid of anything useful but we are only buying those things that we require. With the eventual growth in sales things will come into balance.

Original estimates of the savings to be gained by producing in the new building were $260,000, but as of the end of 1962 it was doubtful that these savings would be fully realized. Material handling savings had been offset by higher power costs and a 250% rent increase paid to an affiliated company on a sale-leaseback basis. It was hoped that savings would increase to the expected level when work was completed on the office area of the building. In December, 1962, the manufacturing offices and the offices of four of the owners had been moved to the new building. Eventually the company hoped to transfer all headquarters operations to the new plant.

Adjacent to the new plant was a new engineering building housing the engineering staffs of Divisions 1 and 2. Since 1957 the company had also leased three stories of a building five miles away (plant No. 2) where were housed the operations of Division 3, the sales and accounting offices, the vice president of engineering, and the president, who "wanted to be close to the inputs of the operation." He believed that his presence influenced the sales department to hold down its demands on the engineering and production departments. As of December, 1962, the third floor of this building was unoccupied.

THE PRODUCT COST ANALYSIS

In January, 1963, Mr. Dietrich received the results of the detailed product cost analysis prepared by Mr. Dickenson. The results covered the year 1962 and broke down the cost figures into their elements by division and product line according to the company's responsibility accounting and direct costing systems (see Exhibits 6, 7, 8, and 9). In commenting upon the results Mr. Dietrich said:

The traditional accounting allocates overhead costs by using overall ratios. When you have to multiply labor and material by high rates, it's a problem to identify and get at actual overhead costs. I never believed the accounting results. I knew by feel that certain areas were making money and that we were losing our shirt in others, but we never could get beyond the accounting to identify costs.

Now we have an allocation of costs by time and effort expended that will show the true distortion of our overhead. I can go to the board with facts rather than conjectures.

Mr. Dickenson went on to explain further the importance of the accounting review as follows:

Under our regular cost accounting procedures we were generating a great deal of cost accounting information, but only about half of the cost could be directly assigned to products. We have a responsibility accounting system which charges salary and the indirect costs of each individual to his superior's account and then distributes the cost to the products, usually on the basis of direct labor dollars. Since we introduced the system, a number of changes have occurred that have tended to distort the results of the monthly product line accounting statements. When the system was initiated, all the company's products bore about the same ratio of labor costs to total costs, and the total company overhead as compared with the labor cost was a relatively low $2\frac{1}{2}$ to 1. Since then the company has started to develop products with differing proportions of direct labor cost and with a great deal more engineering and other overhead cost attached. In 1962 the allocated charges had increased to 8.2 times the direct labor and showed signs of increasing even more; therefore any distortions that we used to have are magnified many times over.

Mr. Dickenson also believed that the use of the same overhead formula in evaluating new products resulted in a distortion of the statements. New product proposals were evaluated on the basis of direct cost plus eight times labor cost compared with the probable sales at the price the market would bear. In selection, those products with low labor costs and with purchased rather than manufactured parts were more attractive regardless of actual overhead costs.

In order to achieve a more realistic picture of the actual costs by product line, Mr. Dickenson began an intensive investigation of the allocated costs. This involved examining in detail all cost records, surveying plant capabilities, and questioning those contributing to the indirect charges to determine the actual projects worked on during the year. Under this procedure many costs which had been allocated were determined exactly and others that had to be allocated were done on more justifiable grounds. In total, 86% of the company's expenses were associated with particular product lines.

EXPLANATION OF ACCOUNTING REVIEW

The results of the accounting review are presented in Exhibits 6, 7, 8, and 9. The accounts for Divisions 1 and 2 were kept on the same basis. The actual manufacturing costs associated with Division 3 were incurred largely in the other two divisions and transferred to Division 3; minor amounts of special items were incurred in the Division 3 model shop. Various company executives gave the following explanations of the accounting entries.

Sales. The sales figure represented the shipments made by the company during the accounting period as a result of orders received by both the company salesmen and the manufacturers' representatives. The representatives carried practically no inventory of company products.

Material Cost. This cost represented the standard cost of the material used during the period. Material variances were minor and were included with the other direct expenses. The quality of materials used during production affected the material cost more than did the quantities consumed. Because of the mechanical nature of the products in Division 1, a wide variety of purchased and manufactured parts with exacting specifications were needed. Decisions to make or buy a part were made by the engineering department during the design of the product.

Direct Labor Cost. Direct labor was entered at the standard costs determined by the manufacturing department. The company considered these standards realistic. The executives were very conscious of direct labor costs and sought to use labor with the greatest possible efficiency. Robert Moore, the manufacturing vice president, believed that some room for improvement still remained in obtaining the maximum productivity from the direct labor.

Commissions. Commissions included only the commissions paid to the 33 manufacturers' representatives throughout the country. Company salesmen were paid on a salary basis and the cost of direct sales and assistance to the manufacturers' representatives was included as part of selling expense. The company was completely satisfied with its representatives. They were encouraged to carry a full line of noncompetitive control devices for sale to industrial users and received the same commission on the Precision Controls products as on other control instruments. The sales department maintained that the representatives' only complaint was that the company had confined its products to one area of the control field.

Other Direct Expenses. This account contained other miscellaneous costs which could be directly assigned to a specific product line, including small amounts of material variance, employee benefits for direct labor personnel, and outside costs associated with the development and production of specific lines.

Indirect Production Expense. This account included costs incurred by the production departments as well as the cost of providing auxiliary services for the production departments. Sixty per cent of this expense was associated directly with production and included the difference between standard and actual direct labor, manufacturing supplies, perishable tools, setup time, overtime premiums, and salaries through the assistant foreman level. These charges were distributed to the product lines on the basis of direct labor costs in the various departments.

The 40% of indirect production expense not associated with the departments consisted of the supplies and salaries of those directly engaged in supporting the departments. The quality control inspectors and toolmakers accounted for most of this cost. Quality control personnel entered into every phase of the company's operations. When bar stock was received, it was checked before storage; when a machine was set up, the first piece of the run and as many more pieces as necessary were inspected. In addition, statistical samples of parts were made to insure quality. Special climate-controlled areas were available for testing, and certain delicate calibrations were made by the quality control personnel. Other charges in this account included stock clerks and shipping clerks and a customer return section. Very few of the instruments were returned, and in half of the cases the return was due to the customer's failure to properly install or read the instrument. In these cases the manufacturers' representative sent an engineer to instruct the customer in the proper use of the instrument.

Division Period Costs. One fourth of this account represented depreciation, the salaries of factory superintendents and the expense of operating the offices of the division managers. Division managers attempted to coordinate manufacturing and selling operations. Another 16% represented the cost of the methods engineers in the manufacturing engineering department. The remainder represented the salaries and clerical costs of the quality control department, the tool engineering department, factory supervision, and production control (including time study). Management hoped that Division 2 manufacturing cost would decrease with greater volume.

Corporate Period Costs.

1. BUILDING. Building expenses were allocated to departments on the basis of square feet of floor space used and then were allocated to products according to the historical record of work done. An additional $300,000 charge representing unused space and cafeteria area was designated as "nonassignable cost," of which $175,000 was a nonrecurring item representing the expense of moving into the new building and continuing rental payments on the original four-story, wooden-frame "firetrap" occupied since 1940. This lease expired at the end of 1962.

2. ENGINEERING. For purposes of product accounting the engineering account included only the engineering activities which were directly associated with the division product lines. The operations of the research department ($190,000) and $98,000 of other engineering work not related to present products were considered nonassignable costs.

Most requests for engineering projects were initiated by the sales department to meet the special requirements of a potential customer. An analysis of the engineering investment during 1958 and 1959 in Division 1 and the sales returns during the period 1958 through 1960 is set out in Table 1.

A similar analysis of engineering expense on Division 2 projects indicated that no sales were made on $130,000 of investment and that the gross profit on other investments had not always reached the estimate.

Following this analysis in early 1961 the company adopted a policy of rejecting customer projects with less than a 10 to 1 return on engineering investment and of rejecting work for Division 2 in excess of $3,000 unless other considerations warranted the investment. Because of the difficulty of estimating the prospective sales of an engineer-

TABLE 1

DIVISION 1 PROJECTS

	Projects with Less than a 10 to 1 Return on Engineering Investment	Projects with a More than 10 to 1 Return on Engineering Investment	Total
Sales (1958 through 1960)...........	$284,000	$1,003,000	$1,287,000
Cost (material + labor + 2½ times labor)........................	137,000	440,000	577,000
Gross profit.......................	$147,000	$ 563,000	$ 710,000
Engineering investment..............	127,000	16,000	143,000
Average return	1.16 to 1	35.10 to 1	4.97 to 1

TABLE 2

DIVISION 2 PROJECTS

PROJECT	DEVELOPMENT COST	GROSS PROFIT		RETURN
		Estimated	Actual	
A.................	$ 652	$ 8,140	$*	0 to 1
B.................	11,971	113,400	1,935†	0.2 to 1
C.................	13,679	160,000	86,376	6.3 to 1
D.................	227	31,000	276	1.2 to 1
E.................	331	10,000	4,870	14.7 to 1
F.................	1,744	2,700	1,807	1.1 to 1
G.................	425	6,700	3,180	7.5 to 1

* $3,000 on order.
† $144,000 on open order.

ing idea and the company's desire to develop products in the electronics area, this policy had not been strictly enforced.

3. SELLING. The sales department cost figures were developed from the individual reports of department members.

Nonassignable Cost. $1,384,000 of costs could not be assigned to individual products. This amount was composed of the items listed in Table 3.

TABLE 3

NONASSIGNABLE COST

Nonrecurring building cost.............$	175,000
Unassigned space, including cafeteria....	125,000
Research department...................	190,000
Other engineering activities...........	98,000
Space advertising......................	200,000
Other sales activities..................	49,000
Personnel department..................	96,000
Executive after partial distribution of the planning committee...........	390,000
Other...............................	61,000
Total...............................	$1,384,000

MANAGEMENT DECISIONS FOLLOWING THE ACCOUNTING REVIEW

After receiving the final results of the accounting analysis in January, 1963, Mr. Dietrich used the report as the basis for making significant changes in the operation of the company. He commented:

Once I had the facts on which to base a decision, I went through a reappraisal of the objectives of the company. My personal and corporate desire is to make this a flourishing company. I want to see us in a good solid business position with sound products. The owners have not yet reached a decision on the eventual future of the company but we realize, of course, that a good earnings and growth record will give us more flexibility no matter what we do.

When I had the figures, I went to the board with a cost reduction program and they agreed to it unanimously. The first thing that we did was to knock the hell out of the blue-sky stuff. We eliminated all research and development on items which would not be in production within a reasonable period of time. We had some research with a five- to 10-year payout and nothing for a market but hope. We also eliminated most of our central research staff.

We defined the area where we are successful and hope to concentrate on the electronics and electro-mechanical area and drop the exotic research. We also are limiting our government work. We have done too much engineering on missiles that were canceled after three firings. We have no complaints about the government, but it's a lot of cost and bother to put up with over 40 renegotiation audits. It's hard for us to drop some of the things that we have brought along. Some of our special work is unique and has a lot of people connected with defense activities excited, but it's just not close enough to our main interest.

A third thing that we are going to do is establish new criteria for projects coming in. We are going to be real tough on input. The sales department will have to make an assessment of the opportunity of each project. Then the sales, engineering, and manufacturing people will get together periodically and go over the projects. They should be able to decide on the spot the value of 80% of the projects on a go, no-go basis. The rest will have to have a detailed analysis. We want a return in two years.

We are always looking for weak spots in our operations. Now that we have started on the overhead problem we hope to continue by putting our new accounting procedures on IBM and furnishing the top management with a continuity of effective operating data. Eventually some relaxing of the cutbacks will have to be done but we hope to establish a ratio of overhead to volume and keep within that limit. That should keep our overhead in line with our growth. We also want to start thinking about probing new market areas in depth with our products.

As far as the future is concerned we want to grow to keep up with the economy and we want that growth to be at a profit and on a strong economic footing. I am hoping for a growth of 15% next year, with a gross profit on sales of 10%. Eventually we should have a gross profit of 15% to 18% and a net profit of 7% to 8%. We are looking for a heavy growth in the electronics area of Division 2. The commercial products of Division 1 will also increase, but our more exotic products will become stable or decline. One thing that will help us is the government's emphasis upon conventional weapons and new airplanes. Ten years ago a consultant forecast a decline in aviation business, so we shifted from 90% aviation to 80% commercial; but the recent emphasis on conventional weapons makes the aviation business look good. We are close to the aviation industry and can project sales five years in advance through the experimentation and production stage to the spare parts market; this market now looks promising. We also expect a rapid growth in our commercial market, but new commercial markets are hard to define and forecast. We are now aiming at certain specific markets in the commercial field.

Budgeted Cutbacks. The actual budgeted cutbacks in the 1963 operations of the company involved a two-phase reduction. In the first phase, begun in the fall of 1962, the department heads voluntarily made cuts in their operations and personnel. Following the board of directors' review of the accounting study, a second arbitrary cut of $150,000 each was made in the projected budget of the sales and engineering departments. Although the department heads were allowed to make the cuts as they pleased within their departments, they were told of the directors' general decision to eliminate the exotic ventures from the budget. The total voluntary and compulsory cuts by department follow:

TABLE 4

TOTAL DEPARTMENT CUTS

Manufacturing	$180,000
Sales	150,000
Accounting	70,000
Engineering	175,000
	$575,000

In January, 1962, the company had 725 employees. During 1962 it reduced its employment to 631, largely through the improvement in manufacturing methods in the new building and a reduction in the accounting department. Phase two of the cutback further reduced employment to 600 by eliminating higher priced positions in the engineering and sales departments. After the cuts had been made, the various department heads commented on the new policy and its effect upon the future operations of the company.

Engineering. John Stykes commented:

Understanding the significance of the cutback requires an understanding of the company itself. This is a technically oriented company in a peculiar sort of way. Mr. Nelson, the treasurer, originated the product. The other four owners are extremely creative engineers. They are so creative that their creativity cannot help but spread beyond the company's area of interest. Technically we have almost an academic climate. The owners have tried to resist the technical enthusiasm but have never been able to resist it 100%. It's a cliche in this company that our activities are spread too thin and the criticism starts with engineering. A director will talk to an engineer at lunch about a problem and sometime later the engineer will put a new gadget on the director's desk. They will be fascinated by it and have difficulty understanding why everyone won't want it, but the sales people won't know what to do with it because it doesn't fit into the product line.

The owners are all close to the company, and each has his special interest. These interests have created ambivalence. Emotionally, the owners want to try new, exotic things that cost money, but when they do they are brought up short by the P.&L. figures. That's why the cuts in the engineering budget don't hurt the department and may have made it stronger. The morale certainly has improved, for the people in the department know that at last the owners have made a decision. Even some of the people who left were happy to see the decision.

We made the biggest cut in the research and development department. Over the years this department has developed from a director's interest facility into a very sophisticated engineering operation. Most of its original work was in the glamour areas like aircraft and other big deals that the directors and the organization were interested in. When it looked as though the aircraft market was declining, the company brought in a new vice president of engineering who urged the company to "get exotic." Under his direction the research department increased its aerospace efforts and developed a strong scientific capability. In 1960 he resigned and we were left with a crippled industrial effort. We kidded ourselves along and tried to develop products out of this work, but we were going in all directions at once.

Now we are concentrating again on the industrial line. The engineering department has eliminated the exotic research, and that allows the other departments the opportunity to eliminate the personnel that had been established to handle these items. That doesn't mean that we have stopped all of our research and development, but we are concentrating on the items that are close to the production stage for commercial sale. We are quite encouraged about three items in particular.

The first of these is a new low-cost controller which is an attempt to extend the electronic products into the low-price field—low for us, that is. [Included in Product Line 1, Division 2.] It will still not be as low as some of the competitive controls, but it will be a low-price quality control that will be the Ford of our line. It should be ready for production in four months, and the sales people think that it will sell about 10,000 units per month.

Another product that we are working on is a special application for the textile industry that should be ready for production in about 10 months. We are also working on a new concept for the electro-mechanical line that will change the original concept of the product and make it more adaptable to a wider range of business applications. The preliminary work has been completed, to a large extent, and we have added one adaptation of it to the product line.

While we terminated most of the R.&D. people, we did hire a new research engineer with a lot of practical experience and some patents in our area of control instruments. Whereas many of our new controls call for die-casting which we cannot do ourselves, his interest is in the type of control that can be made on our screw machines. He is doing work now in a new area which we hope to develop.

In selecting the areas for engineering we are now much more under the guidance of the sales department. That's why my office is here with the sales people rather than in the engineering department. We and the manufacturing people make an estimate of the cost of developing an application and the sales people give us practically all of our guidance. Most of our present work is for a particular industry that the sales people have selected, such as the packaging industry, the textile industry, or the frozen food industry. We used to have a new products committee composed of the chief engineers, the division managers, the sales coordinators, and the top people from sales and engineering, but that was stopped last December when we shifted emphasis to increasing sales for our present products.

The elimination of the nonessentials in the engineering department has not solved all of our problems. Probably the biggest problem in the company is making Division 3 work. The new approach has placed the financial responsibility for developing its products in the hands of the division instead of spreading it among the total activities of the company, which is an improvement, but the division still has not shown the ability to sell its service and product. The sales department is still separate from the activities of the division, and the service must be sold by the division engineers.

Another problem is product direction, which has a psychological effect upon the engineers in the department. An engineer likes to work on something that is important and that has a chance of development. The directors have always been good about talking to the engineers and keeping them interested in the projects, but the directors have never talked about where the company was going. There is an iron curtain there that you just can't talk about. The directors give no indication about the possibility of going public or selling out. If the company stays as it is, there are great advantages to the engineers. Although the wages are a little lower than those paid by the electronics firms in the city, this is a better place to work and has a friendly atmosphere. We are the highest paying industry in a small town where all the people have roots and are a part of the community. We are not a high-pressure business like some of the government contract firms where the people have to put in seven days a week. Maybe this is not the kind of place that can keep highly skilled engineers who are extremely ambitious in terms of technical competence or business success, but we offer decent employment and a sense of being wanted.

Sales. In discussing the reductions in the sales department, Don Hudson, vice president of sales, said that the reduction in his budget had eliminated the development of future programs for the company. His statement was:

The biggest cut came in our market development section. The market development section includes the advertising, product planning, market research, and sales analysis functions. We kept our advertising man and gave him the job that was formerly handled by a technical publicity agency. We eliminated the product planning section and the sales analysis section, and for the time being we are also doing without the market research section, but I hope to fill that position as soon as I can get the money. Basically we have taken the attitude that we have five years of product direction mapped out for us and we are concentrating on selling our present products.

We had been using advance promotion for our new products; we are eliminating most of that and all aerospace advertising. We also have cut out all of the aircraft advertising, have reduced the aircraft section of the home office to one man, and have dropped the sales engineer in Los Angeles who worked with the aircraft industry. The only thing that we are going to do for the aircraft industry is shoot for the big jobs instead of trying to cover the whole field.

One of the other things that we have done to cut expenses is to eliminate the home office training program that we offered to the representatives' salesmen. We are substituting a correspondence course which will allow the salesmen to learn about the products at home. It will take a little time to get it organized, but it will be just as good and will cost a lot less when we get it established. Most of the actual sales force has been maintained. We did have three regional salesmen working with the aircraft industry, but now we have only two. We retained the four regional managers, the two manufacturers' representatives that were on a retainer, and the two local salesmen.

We are still looking for a sales increase during 1963 of about 10% in dollar sales and about 20% in orders received. We can make a fairly good prediction of the amount of the present products that will sell during the year from the number of orders on hand at the beginning of the year. Over the years our sales have been running at the rate of about four times the beginning orders, and we expect that some of the newer products will increase the amount of orders during the year. Division 1 products have doubled over the past five years and we expect them to double in the *next* five years. We have developed a new product that we are not ready to produce that differs radically from our original concept of measurement, and this should provide an increase in sales. It will replace line 3 in Division 1 but will have more growth potential. Since design and testing have not yet been completed, we will not have it field tested until 1964 and in general use until 1966.

I am predicting a 25% yearly increase in the Division 2 products, particularly because of a new product that we will soon bring onto the market. We expect to have production of 10,000 units per month at a sales price of about $15 each. This will in part replace product No. 1 in the electronics line. It will be a quality electronics instrument at a low price. It will be the Ford of our line, but the competition will still undersell us with lower quality.

In Division 3 we are also picking up some new contracts in our area of interest and will pick up sales with our present products, even though we have dropped some of the ideas that we were working on. Much of the market research work was done for the systems line (product No. 8) of Division 3, and although we have stopped our market research work, I hope to be able to start this program again soon.

A big part of the change in the procedures in the last few months is the new policy of increased justification of the engineering work that we do. After dropping the market research group, we have had a difficult time predicting the future of some of the applications that we work on, and I am doing most of it now although it is a very loose thing. I hope as soon as possible to get some help in the market research area. We in the past have been looking for particular markets and trying to develop one market, such as the food packing market. We are now using a factor of 10 times investment in two years to determine which projects to try. Each of the directors also has his own interest in certain markets, and we have tried to fit them in if we could. Mr. Clark is particularly interested in the scientific market for control equipment; Paul Nelson invented the original product and is interested in improving and applying it to more varied industries; John Hurley is interested in systems; Bill Cole is interested in the food industry; and Steve Dietrich has always been fascinated with aircraft. When we cut out the aircraft work, it cut a piece out of Steve.

Our biggest problem is deciding just what our market should be. I think that we should concentrate on our own specialized type of controls from the appliance market up to but not including complete process instrumentation. I feel that our market should include components for complete process systems but that we should not go into the completed systems. Some of the others want to go further to include the smallest appliances, the complete systems, or to expand into the full range of controls.

Manufacturing. Jim Moore, the manufacturing vice president, took his own steps to reduce the overhead in his department during the first phase of the overhead reduction program. He eliminated the division managers for Divisions 1 and 2 and took over the operations of the divisions himself. He reduced the staff personnel and expected that once the plant was running on a normal basis more efficient operations would permit still further reductions.

Mr. Moore made the following comments on the problems facing the company:

This has always been a most exciting company to work for. We have had our fingers in so many pies and they all have looked so delicious that we have had difficulty deciding which one we are going to sit down and eat. It is difficult to drop any line because almost all of them are promising.

I think that we should charge more for some of the things that we are doing. As a manufacturing man I have a horror about work stoppage, and some of our controls are vital to the operation of a plant. The sales people don't understand this or they would put the price where it belongs—sky high. If we are control experts, let's get paid for it, because we are already taking the risk of a failure. Lately, however, we have done a better job of pricing. We have set a price on small quantities which reflects the additional cost of handling the small order and have established a $20 minimum for them. We also have improved our pricing on special orders.

I think that we need on a companywide basis a sound plan for increasing profit. We should have an overall plan for the company. As far as my own problems are concerned, my immediate problem is the 1963 program. We are trying to reduce cost on a day-to-day basis. We are constantly reviewing our processes and looking for better methods, and we are making economic evaluations of tooling cost and of other manufacturing operations to determine if we should use special tooling. On the die-cast control instruments that you saw we used metal fabricated parts for many years because we didn't have the confidence in ourselves to go ahead and spend the $25,000 necessary to make the parts for less.

Of course we could use volume, but we have just about given up hoping for that rare product which would give us large volume operations. We are concentrating on doing our present work more simply. We have intoduced argon arc welding which allows us to weld without flux, thus producing a better quality instrument at reduced cost. We are also trying to eliminate the secondary operations from the lathes so that the whole operation can be performed at one time. We are standardizing our finishes to reduce the cost of the painting department. Another thing that we are working on is productivity. If the coffee break is supposed to be 10 minutes, we are trying to get it down to 10 minutes. We are trying to get the people to work right up until 3:30 and to move faster on the job. This is mostly a problem of discipline; we have never been really rough around here, so it's a matter of disciplining children. First you tell them, and then when you have to, you punish them.

Accounting. Mr. Dickenson was pleased with the results of his work in implementing the budget changes, and he explained:

I think that the directors now have confidence in the figures. We have been talking about cost for a long time around here, but mostly in generalized terms. Our recent approach of furnishing more detailed data has proven very effective. I know the company can be more profitable on a long-term as well as short-term basis and can obtain a better growth rate with proper controls. Now the question is: Can they keep it up, or when we get a little money in the bank will we go right back to where we were? We had a cutback in 1959, and you can see how effective it was, but look at what happened in the next two years when we relaxed.

The real problem was one of realism. In seeking growth, we tried to carry on too many good things. Meanwhile our government business changed to lower volume orders with higher engineering costs. For commercial work we had to engineer each product individually. About $1 million of our sales each year were re-engineered. Now that we have the necessary information we are trying to be more selective and use better evaluation before taking on projects. When we look at each thing that we are doing, we can decide to reduce cost, increase price, or get out.

As far as next year is concerned, I think that we will definitely be more profitable by the amount that we have cut the budget. Once we set a budgeted figure, we are pretty good at living up to it. But I think that the sales figures that some of the others are talking about are overly optimistic. Remember that I have been making the sales forecast for the past 10 years, and I have never been more than 5% off and usually am much closer than that. My budget, which is based upon products now in production plus the one item that we know will be added, is for $10,973,000 in 1963, with $6,075,000 in Division 1, $1,335,000 in Division 2, and $3,563,000 in Division 3.

Business Machines Corporation

In March, 1963, Stewart P. Saunders had been president of the Business Machines Corporation (BMC) of Trenton, New Jersey, for 19 months. In that time he had restored profitability to the near-bankrupt firm, revamped the executive organization, and made plans for future expansion of the company's operations.

The June 30, 1961, annual report of the BMC indicated a net loss of $986,566 for fiscal 1961 and a negative earned surplus account of $2,929,102. The company had suffered increasing losses in each of the previous four years. Its principal stockholder had tried three different chief executives during that time but still was not satisfied with the results. On September 1, 1961, he hired Stewart Saunders, president of a hospital supply firm and an executive with a reputation for "reviving sick dogs," and gave him complete freedom to revive the company. Between September 1, 1961, and July 30, 1962, the top management of BMC experienced a 100% turnover and lower management experienced extensive changes in personnel. The fiscal year ended June 30, 1962, was the first profitable year of operation since 1957. (See Exhibit 1.)

Although the rejuvenation continued during the last half of 1962 and early 1963, it did not sustain the rate of the previous fiscal year. Mr. Saunders explained that in March, 1963, the company had reached the point it should have reached in September, 1962. He attributed the setback to several unusual occurrences. First, the distributor sales had proved disappointing; second, the company had had a great deal of trouble with a government contract; and finally, in February, 1963, the company was struck by the local union. These developments had diverted much of Mr. Saunders' attention from his primary task of building an organization capable of rapid and profitable growth.

PRODUCT AND COMPETITION

BMC sold three different types of recording equipment: commercial office dictating equipment (70% of sales), long-playing tape recorders (20%), and government contracted equipment (10%). The company

Exhibit 1

BUSINESS MACHINES CORPORATION

Statement of Income and Earned Surplus for the Fiscal Years Ending June 30
(Thousands of Dollars)

	1956	1957	1958	1959	1960	1961	1962
Sales and service contracts......	n.a.	n.a.	$3,016	$4,038	$ 4,192	$ 4,037	$ 5,278
Operating costs...............	n.a.	n.a.	3,341	4,284	4,868	4,809	4,779
Depreciation..................	$ 51	$ 57	91	96	112	133	124
Operating profit (loss)........	$ (13)	$ 349	$ (416)	$ (342)	$ (788)	$ (905)	$ 375
Interest expense..............	30	31	71	99	35	82	114
Federal income taxes...........	...	2	(1)	...	...	...	...
Net profit (loss).............	$ (43)	$ 316	$ (486)	$ (441)	$ (823)	$ (987)	$ 261
Retained earnings at beginning of year....................	(88)	(136)	207	(279)	(725)	(1,548)	(2,929)
Adjustment (primarily the writeoff of patents and development expense)........	(5)	27	...	(5)	...	(394)	(92)
Retained earnings at end of year......................	$(136)	$ 207	$ (279)	$ (725)	$(1,548)	$(2,929)	$(2,760)

n.a. = Not available.
Source: Published reports.

competed with three well-established firms (Dictaphone, Gray, and McGraw-Edison) and one newcomer (IBM) for sales in the office dictation market. Dictaphone, the largest and most competitive of the established companies with 50% of the total market, was BMC's major source of competition. Financial difficulties had made the Gray Company a strong price competitor in competitive bidding, but BMC's executives felt that the BMC Model 7 had basic design advantages over both the Gray Audograph and the McGraw-Edison Ediphone. In December, 1960, IBM entered the office equipment dictating field by purchasing the Pierce Recorder Company and introducing an all-transistorized magnetic belt recording machine. This equipment was distributed by the IBM typewriter salesmen throughout the country. The Ediphone with 15% of the market was second to Dictaphone, with the other companies and foreign competitors sharing the remainder of the market about equally.

Each company offered a full line of dictating and transcribing equipment with accessories. Each company claimed that certain features of its own machine made it superior to those of its competitors. IBM claimed that its magnetic belt could be used "thousands of times" by erasing the message and recording again. The magnetic belt held 14 minutes of recording time. BMC claimed that its equipment had been designed as a total communications system and therefore had advantages over its competitors. Part of this system was the BMC Model 7, which provided a microphone and controls at the executive's desk and the machine next to his secretary's desk to relieve the executive of the bother of servicing the machine. The BMC machine could also be used to record conferences. Mr. Saunders believed that BMC made sales in about 95% of the cases where it demonstrated its equipment in competition with other manufacturers. The machines of each company were competitively priced and sold nationally through a branch or a distributor's sales-service organization.

BMC's 24-hour transverse tape recorder had been developed during the late 1950's for governmental use. Not until 1962 did the company seek to sell its equipment in the commercial market on a large scale. The tape recorder could hold 24 hours of continuous recording on a wide magnetic tape. A time index was preprinted on the tape. The widest application so far had been the use of tape recording devices to replace court recorders. This system was accepted by the Alaska courts and was also used in some courts of lower jurisdiction which previously had not been courts of record. The advantage of this system was that it gave an exact reproduction of the proceedings which did not need to be transcribed unless a case was appealed. The system also had been used successfully in police dispatching offices and was accepted by the FCC as a method of recording radio broadcasts for FCC monitoring. The tape units were also used as component parts of many airplane and communication systems products.

The company had no competitors in the transverse tape recording field who could exactly duplicate the performance of its equipment. Many other companies did have available combinations of more conventional equipment which would provide the same service. However, their equipment was more bulky and did not provide a continuous tape record. BMC intended to equip its plant with a 24-hour recorder and microphones at convenient locations throughout the plant so that workmen could record their starting and stopping times on various job orders. If this system of production control proved successful, BMC felt that it would reduce its own production control costs and would also provide a marketable service to other industrial firms.

Most of the company's government contract work had been done for the Federal Aviation Agency. This work consisted mainly of one large contract for 100 30-channel recorders. These recorders would ultimately be used by airport control towers to record the conversations between the control towers and the pilots in airplanes. Each unit could record 30 conversations at a time.

The FAA contract had been a major source of difficulty for the company. It had been negotiated prior to Mr. Saunders' arrival and called for the completion of the units in February, 1962. In the fall of 1961 it became evident that the company was behind schedule in developing the project, and new engineers were brought in to assist in the development. The technical problems of the contract were not solved until the summer of 1962. During the fall of 1962 the FAA tried to cancel the contract and found fault with the company for failure to follow its specifications. Mr. Saunders spent much of his time in Washington arguing about the specifications and working to retain the contract. He pointed out that some of the minor flaws were the fault of the FAA-approved supplier, that the circuits called for in the specifications were the wrong ones for the unit, and that the government did not need delivery until April, 1963.

Through these efforts the contract was maintained. The company had completed its first unit in March, 1963, and it was undergoing acceptance testing. The company anticipated the delivery of 12 units by April.

Although most of the company's engineering effort between September, 1961, and March, 1963, had been devoted to the FAA project, the company had also been able to improve the design of its basic commercial unit and introduce several new items to the market. One of these items was a combination recorder and slide film projector for use in sales presentations. In the fall of 1961 Mr. Saunders entered into an agreement with a Japanese manufacturer to create BMC of Japan, an affiliate company 50% owned by the American company. The affiliate company produced a small portable dictating and transcribing unit designed for sale through the regular BMC sales outlets. As of March, 1963, sales of these other items were negligible.

HISTORY

1940–1961. The Business Machines Corporation had been incorporated in New Jersey in 1940 to exploit the patents of an inventor, Mr. Rollins. The company's original office dictating machine, marketed in 1940, was a drastic innovation in the dictating equipment field. The BMC machine recorded electronically on a plastic disc while its two competitors, Dictaphone and Edison, recorded acoustically on wax cylinders. Subsequently both competitors started to make electronic equipment, although they continued to use wax cylinders.

During World War II BMC devoted extensive effort to military contracts and the dictating line was not pushed. Following the war the company continued with its original line until 1949, at which time it introduced an improved lightweight machine, "The Century," with a metal, instead of wood, frame and an improved indexing system. This redesigned machine was in response to new machines offered by the Gray Manufacturing Company in 1947 and by Dictaphone and Edison in 1948.

Although improvements had been made in the machine periodically and accessories added, no drastic changes were made between 1949 and 1960. By 1960 profits had vanished and management considered a new line of equipment necessary. The company quickly designed the "System 660" to replace its then current line and scheduled it for production in July. In July, 1960, the company stopped producing the Century and started setting up for the new line, but production problems delayed the final introduction of the line until October. During the summer of 1960 salesmen had no machines to sell and became increasingly dissatisfied. Several large distributors gave notice of canceling their distribution contracts.

By the fall of 1960 the company was producing at a maximum capacity of 2,000 units per month to refill the channels of distribution. By early 1961 it became apparent that the new machine had basic design problems, particularly in the bearing and motor board system. Rework rose sharply and sales declined. In March of 1961 sales were so low that 40% to 50% of the production force had to be laid off.

Between 1949 and 1960 BMC's competitors had improved their products but none had brought out a completely revised product line. The design failures in the 1960 BMC model were caused by a multitude of small problems throughout the system rather than a single major problem. Therefore customers made frequent calls for service and the cost of service calls and rework mounted. Before the problem was solved, the company had replaced parts on every machine produced in the fall of 1960. In July, 1961, an additional 10% of the original production force was laid off because of further declining orders.

September, 1961–June, 1962. On assuming the presidency in September, 1961, Mr. Saunders soon found that the company faced serious problems in all areas of its operations and insufficient managerial talent to cope with them. The first 10 months of his efforts were devoted to working on the most serious of these problems and finding capable men for top-management positions.

He believed that the basic problem of the company was the "attitude of the people." Prior managements had created a "rough union situation" where workers were paid for 100% of a measured day's work while producing at only 30% efficiency. Manufacturing overhead was 360% of standard direct costs. Although the company had a great deal of excess capacity because of declining sales, the company still purchased many component parts for its machines. A defeatist attitude pervaded the sales organization. Because of past design problems the servicemen were overworked and the salesmen found it difficult to sell machines. The engineering department's concern with the BMC machine had placed it behind on several important government contracts. In addition, Mr. Saunders believed that the company was incurring excessive costs through overstaffed office personnel and overvalued auditors and patent attorneys.

Mr. Saunders' first action was to take charge of all check-signing and purchase-order approval in order to control expenses. He also replaced the manufacturing manager in the hope of bringing more efficiency to that operation and personally controlled all hiring within the firm. In November, 1961, it became apparent to Mr. Saunders that neither the

Exhibit 2

BUSINESS MACHINES CORPORATION

Sales and Profit by Quarter

(Thousands of Dollars)

	Sales	Profit (Loss)
Fiscal Year Ending June 30, 1961		
First quarter	$ 840	$(128)
Second quarter	866	(216)
Third quarter	1,236	(304)
Fourth quarter	1,095	(339)
Total	$4,037	$(987)
Fiscal Year Ending June 30, 1962		
First quarter	$ 930	$(165)
Second quarter	1,262	(47)
Third quarter	1,604	118
Fourth quarter	1,482	355
Total	$5,278	$ 261
Fiscal Year Ending June 30, 1963		
First quarter	$1,064	$ 34
Second quarter	1,210	46
January, 1963	306	(33)

Source: Company quarterly reports.

Exhibit 3

BUSINESS MACHINES CORPORATION

Balance Sheets for the Fiscal Years Ending June 30, 1956, to 1962, and January 31, 1963

(Thousands of Dollars)

	1956	1957	1958	1959	1960	1961	1962	January 31 1963
Assets								
Current assets:								
Cash........	$ 167	$ 247	$ 111	$ 100	$ 188	$ 68	$ 92	$ (131)
Receivables (net)...	393	467	572	739	952	782	1,224	1,329
Inventories...	754	1,265	1,080	1,161	1,787	1,479	2,255	2,540
Prepayments...	32	44	31	30	40	33	28	21
Total current assets...	$1,346	$2,023	$1,794	$2,030	$2,967	$2,362	$3,599	$3,759
Property, plant and equipment...	$ 457	$ 652	$1,359	$1,494	$1,672	$1,586	$1,661	$1,726
Reserve for depreciation...	175	203	244	341	411	418	523	598
Net property...	$ 282	$ 449	$1,115	$1,153	$1,261	$1,168	$1,138	$1,128
Construction in progress...		556						
Patents (net)...	43	45	51	57	71	92		
Deferred charges and development expense...		107	256	380	398	2		
Tax claims...	14	25						
Total assets...	$1,685	$3,205	$3,216	$3,620	$4,697	$3,624	$4,737	$4,887
Liabilities								
Current liabilities:								
5½% demand notes payable to bank...							$ 701	$1,200
5% convertible notes payable June 1, 1963...							120	120
5½% convertible subordinated notes payable June 9, 1963...							500	500
5½% convertible subordinated notes payable November 10, 1963...								750
Current installment of mortgage and of notes prior to 1961...	$ 15	$ 746	$ 251	$ 730	$ 330	$ 30	$ 26	26
Accounts payable and accrued liabilities...	656	711	819	945	1,221	867	850	443
Customer service contracts prepaid...						242	291	316
Total current liabilities...	$ 671	$1,457	$1,070	$1,675	$1,551	$1,139	$2,488	$3,355

Long-term debt:								
6% mortgage note payable August 7, 1968			275	245	215	185	159	145
5% convertible notes payable June 1, 1963		700	700	125	125	125		
5½% convertible subordinated notes payable June 9, 1963					500	500		
5½% convertible subordinated note payable November 10, 1963						750	750	200
5½% convertible subordinated note payable September 15, 1964							200	200
Other notes payable	363	228	137	163				
Stockholders' equity:								
Common stock	715	1,204	1,204	1,515	2,022	2,022	2,053	2,053
Paid-in surplus	72	109	109	622	1,832	1,832	1,847	1,847
Earned surplus (deficit)	(136)	207	(279)	(725)	(1,548)	(2,929)	(2,760)	(2,713)
Total liabilities	$1,685	$3,205	$3,216	$3,620	$4,697	$3,624	$4,737	$4,887

Notes to the 1962 financial statements:

1. *Demand notes payable*
The 5½% demand notes payable to bank are secured by an assignment of accounts receivable. Subsequent to June 30, 1962, the company borrowed $1 million from a bank under a revolving credit agreement which provides, among other things, for loans up to $1 million for 90 days at 5½% at any time until October 1, 1963. The proceeds of this borrowing have been used to repay outstanding 5½% demand notes and for working capital purposes. (The unsecured loan limit is $1,200,000.)

2. *Patents*
Prior to July 1, 1961, the company followed the policy, for financial statement purposes, of amortizing patent costs over the life of the respective patents. Effective as of July 1, 1961, the company adopted the policy of expensing patent costs as incurred and charged to earned surplus (deficit) the unamortized patent costs at June 30, 1961, amounting to $91,905. This change in policy had no significant effect on the company's financial statements.

3. *Long-term debt*
The notes due June 1, 1963 (included under current liabilities) are convertible into 10,000 shares of common stock at the rate of one share for each $12 of principal amount. The notes due June 9, 1963 (included under current liabilities), November 10, 1963, and September 15, 1964, are subordinated to bank loans and are convertible into 131,817 shares of common stock at the rate of one share for each $11 of principal amount. A total of 141,817 shares of authorized common stock is reserved for the conversion of notes.

4. *Restricted stock option plan*
At June 30, 1962, 44,200 shares of common stock were reserved under options granted to directors, officers, and employees, and 23,800 additional shares were reserved for future grant. Option prices (not less than the fair market price of the stock at dates of grant) range from $9.25 to $19 per share. During the year ended June 30, 1962, options were granted for the purchase of 33,700 shares. Options were exercised during the year for the purchase of 7,500 shares aggregating $41,250.

5. *Federal income taxes*
The company and its subsidiary have a tax loss carryover of approximately $2,476,000 which, under present law, may be applied against future earnings for federal income tax purposes. Unless utilized, a loss carryover of $123,000 will expire on June 30, 1963, $517,000 on June 30, 1964, $915,000 on June 30, 1965, and $921,000 on June 30, 1966.

6. *Contingent liabilities*
The company is contingently liable on assigned retail time payment sales contracts of approximately $151,000.
The company is involved in certain legal proceedings in which various claims and counterclaims have been filed. In the opinion of management, claims asserted against the company, if sustained, would have no material effect on the consolidated financial position of the company.

Source: Published reports and company records.

new manufacturing manager nor the general sales manager was achieving the results that he expected. He replaced the new manufacturing manager and personally assumed control of sales. At the same time he hired Allen Parker as director of research and development and charged him with the task of improving the company's engineering capabilities. Through an industrial psychologist and other business contacts he sought other managerial personnel to improve the quality of his own staff while concerning himself primarily with sales and overall corporate problems. In late 1961 he negotiated an arrangement with a Japanese firm for the production and foreign distribution of a lightweight transistorized portable dictating machine. This machine was to be sold through the BMC distribution channels in the United States and through the company's distribution channels in 63 foreign countries.

In February, 1962, Mr. Saunders hired George Shea to accelerate his program of returning the manufacture of component parts to the BMC factory and to handle all the company's purchasing. By June of 1962, the company had purchased equipment to do its own metal stamping, cutting, and screw turning.

In the summer of 1962, Mr. Saunders completed his management reorganization by hiring a new controller (June), a new director of employee relations (July), and a new manufacturing manager (August). In recruiting management and engineering talent the company offered generous salaries. The financial data during this period showed a steady increase in sales and profit (see Exhibit 2).

July, 1962–March, 1963. During the fiscal year 1963 the company continued its development with a permanent top-management organization. Although sales and profits continued to increase, the rate established in 1962 slackened. Some of the trends in labor efficiency registered during the 1962 fiscal year reversed themselves. The company operated under the continued threat of a strike. It sustained a six-day wildcat strike in December, 1961, and a brief strike upon expiration of the contract in July, 1962; it operated without a contract until November. After a labor contract had been obtained and labor efficiency restored, the union again went out on strike in February, 1963. The distributor organization also failed to live up to its previous sales record. The company had to continue to drop established distributors and institute sales branches. Furthermore the FAA contract problems continued to plague the company's engineering staff and took time from other projects. The company had anticipated that the fiscal year 1963 would be a period of cash shortage; this forecast proved accurate. Prior to 1961 the company had made extensive use of convertible notes to finance its losses. A total of $1,320,000 in convertible notes was due for redemption or conversion in June and November, 1963 (see Exhibit 3 for details). During 1962 the company had issued $200,000 in convertible debentures and secured additional working capital by assigning the company's receivables. In January, 1963, the company used the limit of its $1,200,000 line of credit. Through inventory reduction during the strike, however, the company was able to pay back $59,000 by March, 1963. Mr. Saunders expected the convertible debentures to be converted to stock rather than redeemed in cash because the stock price in March, 1963, was $19 per share while the conversion amounts were between $11 and $12 per share. The company's immediate objective was to clean up the subordinated notes so that it could finance future operations through loans and retained earnings.

ORGANIZATION

In late October, 1962, Mr. Saunders said:

I told the board of directors at their last meeting that for the first time I'm beginning to feel enthusiastic about the future of the company. I explained that I meant I had finally found the people that I think can do the job. It will take three or four months before we have eliminated the past problems and can start thinking about current problems, but now we have the organization that can do it. We have a new man by the name of Peter Sharp as manufacturing manager. He is doing a magnificent job. Also we have a new personnel manager, and he is doing an excellent job. Basically, I am still filling the general sales manager's spot, but within the past three weeks I have hired a fellow by the name of Sam Caldwell, who was one of IBM's better regional managers, and he is now field sales manager until he becomes acquainted with the product, with our organization, and with our problems. In engineering, Allen Parker is a fine engineer and administrator but a little weak on follow-through. He doesn't like unpleasantness, no one does; so in those areas I usually have to take over instead of his carrying through as he should. Now that I know his weakness I can watch him. Mike Spadone, our controller, is also coming along nicely.

None of them is on his own as yet. That's why the other two manufacturing managers didn't last; they wanted to take on the full responsibility too soon. I look at successful management like an amoeba. I know what I want and am sure of what is going to be successful. When a new man comes, I take over most of his problems myself and then give him more of the problems as he becomes familiar with the job. I figure that I know the problems better than a new man does, so I give him in writing a list of goals that I want him to carry out when he first gets here. Then, as he gets to know the job, we can revise and change the objectives. Eventually I can pretty much forget about watching him. He will carry out his department objectives and I know he will keep me informed on major problems.

I manage the men here individually. Frankly, I don't believe in meetings. I think they are a waste of time and I think they are just another reason for people to excuse their responsibilities. I give them a goal and an objective and I expect them to meet it; if they have any problems with their counterpart in another department, I expect them to work them out jointly or come to me. I don't believe in this meeting business or this committee business. I think this is the one thing that has wrecked American companies more than anything else in the last 25 years.

Production. All production was carried on in the company's five-year-old plant at Trenton, New Jersey. The company planned, however, to transfer all production of commercial items to Florida by the spring of 1964. After the production workers showed a marked increase in productivity during the spring of 1962, plans were abandoned to close down and sell the Trenton plant and a revised expansion program was initiated which contemplated the production of government orders and of newly acquired products at Trenton.

The manufacturing operation was divided into three departments. A machining and metalworking department cut the frame for the machine and did machining operations on component parts. The assembly department assembled the commercial machines on an assembly-line basis. The third department was the military department where government equipment was assembled on a job-order basis. The assembly and military departments required no special skill. The company, however, had encountered problems in hiring skilled machinists for the metalworking department because of the announced move to Florida. The severe layoff in July of 1961 had eliminated all employees with less than eight years' seniority.

Upon taking over the manufacturing operations in September, 1961, Mr. Saunders noted two particularly costly deficiencies. First, the company was purchasing many parts which it could manufacture while at the same time it had excess capacity in its own operations. The company was also getting extremely low productivity from its production workers as compared with the measured daywork system used in the plant.[1] Productivity for the major department was at 30% of the rated stand-

---

[1] The measured daywork plan, according to the union contract, measured each employee's daily production against a 100% efficiency rate defined as "the number of production units of consistently required quality which may reasonably be expected from an experienced, first-class operator working at normal and reasonable speed." Standards were set by the employer but subject to the grievance procedure, including final arbitration by a mutually acceptable engineering firm. During the spring of 1962 the company hired an outside engineering firm to review the standards. Their report indicated that the BMC work pace was 50% to 60% of the work pace of other Trenton area plants.

ard; the company had retained its 40 overhead personnel after reducing the work force to half of the original 300 workers in July, 1961.

In the fall of 1961, Mr. Saunders reduced the overhead production personnel from 40 to 6 and brought in a new manufacturing manager to improve productivity and to bring some of the subassembly work back into the plant. When the new man failed to show satisfactory progress he was replaced. Although his replacement made some improvements in the methods and added a shear to the machining department so that the company could cut its own metal frames from stock instead of buying finished metal, he also proved unsatisfactory and in the spring of 1962 was fired. Mr. Saunders took over the production supervision until August, 1962, when he hired Peter Sharp as manufacturing manager.

Under Mr. Saunders' direction productivity in the manufacturing department increased sharply, rising by July to about 92% of the measured daywork standard. Mr. Saunders believed that much of this was done simply by enforcing the union contract. Under the contract the pay of a worker was determined by the percentage of a measured day's work performed. Workers who continually performed below their pay scale were subject to pay cuts or dismissal. When a few workers were dismissed and others cut, the productivity increased. Manufacturing overhead decreased from 360% of standard direct costs to 150% by June, 1962.

Quality control also had been a major production problem. In the fall of 1961, 75% of all units in the commercial line were rejected at final inspection. To remedy this problem the company eliminated the union inspectors and substituted quality assurance engineers to inspect parts on a sample basis during production and on a 100% basis after assembly. It also enforced the provisions of the union contract which called for payment only on the basis of acceptable units produced.

Mr. Saunders also assigned his purchasing agent to investigate several ideas for bringing operations into the plant. The improvements made during the spring included winding the coils for the company's motors, purchasing a centerless grinder and doing the grinding of shafts in the plant, changing the work methods so that the dual winding machine could wind two coils at once, and rearranging the machines so that one man could attend three machines instead of one. During this time he managed the manufacturing operations through daily production meetings with the production control supervisor and the purchasing agent. At these meetings they discussed the day's production, analyzed the results of the previous day and the efficiency reports from accounting, and determined the improvements that could be made in the operations.

In July, 1962, Mr. Saunders believed that the operations had improved to a point where the manufacturing operation could be turned over to another man. Production had increased from 400 to 1,000 units per month without an increase in personnel. Through a placement service he met Peter Sharp, an engineer with 16 years' experience in manufacturing, and hired him to run the operation. Before hiring him, however, Mr. Saunders fired all of the company's production foremen in order to give Mr. Sharp a fresh start and ease the personnel problems.

Mr. Sharp began directing the production activities in September, 1962. He earned the respect of Mr. Saunders through the improvements that he made in the housekeeping and material flow in the plant. Between October, 1962, and January, 1963, however, the efficiency of the workers declined from 90% to 60%. Mr. Saunders told Mr. Sharp of his displeasure with the results and told him to enforce the contract and improve the efficiency. This Mr. Sharp did and the efficiency improved during January (see Exhibit 4).

While the plant was on strike during February, Mr. Sharp, at the

Exhibit 4

BUSINESS MACHINES CORPORATION

*Weekly Worker Efficiency Reports for the Period
October, 1962, to February, 1963*

WEEK ENDING	PER CENT OF MEASURED DAYWORK EFFICIENCY	
	Assembly Department	Machine Department
October 12, 1962	91%	87%
October 19, 1962	89	91
October 26, 1962	81	93
November 2, 1962	78	103
November 9, 1962	74	102
November 16, 1962	73	93
November 23, 1962	73	93
November 30, 1962	71	76
December 7, 1962	74	90
December 14, 1962	75	86
December 21, 1962	75	85
December 28, 1962	Christmas shutdown	..
January 4, 1963	61	66
January 11, 1963	69	85
January 18, 1963	72	91
January 25, 1963	74	104
February 1, 1963	78	92

Source: Company records.

insistence of Mr. Saunders, rescheduled the operations of the assembly department and devised a method of reducing the assembly line workers from 10 to 5. Through this and other methods improvements he was able to eliminate about 25 production jobs.

Mr. Saunders was very pleased with Mr. Sharp's progress in the company. In March, 1963, he said: "Peter Sharp has probably come along faster than any of the others. His final lesson in how bad things really were came during the strike when he found that he could cut the production line in half."

Labor Relations. Since 1954, all production workers had been members of the International Brotherhood of Electrical Workers (IBEW). Wages and working conditions were collectively bargained biannually; the most recent contract expired on July 15, 1962. The union contract contained many provisions which were not enforced by management prior to the arrival of Mr. Saunders. The director of labor relations had modified the contract through numerous private agreements with the union officials; these agreements were never reduced to writing. Mr. Saunders' attempts to increase productivity in the fall of 1961 contradicted some of the private agreements but did not violate the contract. During the fall of 1961, the union members became increasingly resentful of management's policies and initiated a large number of grievances against management's actions. The resentment culminated in a wildcat strike in December, allegedly in protest of management's replacement of the union inspectors with quality assurance engineers. Management asserted that it had upgraded the jobs beyond the union's jurisdiction and the union agreed to return to work and settle the issue during the July negotiations. The union officials disclaimed all responsibility for the strike.

Mr. Saunders believed that labor relations had been one of the basic problems of the company before his arrival.

Management sat back on its dignity and let the union run the company. The union contract was never enforced. The contract calls for the workers to be paid on the basis of their percentage of production as compared with a measured day's work. They were not making production but they were still getting the top pay. A lot of the fault rests with the personnel manager, who was straddling the fence. He wasn't enforcing management's part of the contract and was making secret agreements with the union. I got rid of him and brought in Joe Ventrella as personnel manager. Joe's problem now is to win the respect of the union. So far he has done a pretty good job.

During the contract negotiations, management sought to eliminate from the contract a number of provisions which it felt were economically unreasonable. Mr. Saunders believed that the former management had engaged in "a giveaway program" by including in the contract such provisions as a day off with pay for the death of a relative as far removed as second cousin; a bumping plan whereby a man could not be furloughed for half a day without changing job assignments throughout the plant; and a vacation payment plan which provided payment on a sliding scale up to 8% of a year's pay for a worker with 20 years' seniority. Mr. Saunders also believed that overall wage scales were too high, particularly in light of the fact that the production workers were not meeting the efficiency rates required by the measured daywork plan.

No settlement was reached on July 15. After a brief walkout, both parties agreed to extend the contract until October 31, 1962, to allow more time for negotiations. During the negotiations Mr. Saunders announced the company's intention to move its plant to Florida. The union became more militant and, as one executive said, took the attitude that "We'll break you before you go."

Management was represented at the negotiations by Joe Ventrella Peter Sharp, Allen Parker, and Mike Spadone. Stu Saunders did not participate because he believed that the management actions should be ratified outside the negotiating room just as the union committee decisions had to be ratified by the membership before they became final. In commenting on the negotiations Joe Ventrella said: "I probably would have given in sooner, but Stu wouldn't give an inch; finally the union gave in. Whenever we sit down with the union, they get emotional and bring out a long list of grievances that should go through the grievance procedure. We are taking a strict interpretation on all grievances and Stu isn't giving an inch, so they will all go to arbitration."

An agreement was reached in October, without a strike, in which management offered an improved insurance program and no wage decreases. The union agreed to reduce vacation benefits, allow temporary furlough without regard to seniority, reduce the time off for death of a relative, accept management's jurisdiction over inspectors, and accept the new engineering standards for work performed. Several grievances still pending were compromised. Mr. Saunders was generally pleased with the outcome of the negotiations.

Just before the conclusion of the negotiations in late October, 1962, Mr. Saunders announced that because of the increased productivity in the plant during the spring and summer the company intended to continue the operation of the Trenton facility even if the commercial operations were moved to Florida. The union asked for and received a letter of intent to this effect as part of the agreement. As Mr. Saunders said: "The productivity has shown a good increase lately; that's why we decided to stay in Trenton. If the workers here will just behave themselves, we have no intention of leaving" (see Exhibit 5).

In January, 1963, labor relations deteriorated. The union threatened several times a week to strike over various issues. During the first week in February, management furloughed two girls in the machine department without regard to seniority because there was no work available for them. Management claimed that the action was covered by the contract because the only place where they could go was the assembly department, where they could be furloughed without regard to seniority under the new contract. Instead of taking the issue through the grievance procedure, the international representative went to Joe Ventrella and demanded that the two girls be reinstated with pay or the company would have a strike.

When management would not concede, the union struck, claiming that no contract was in effect since the international union had not yet approved the October agreement and had not yet returned signed copies to the company. Management had a copy of the agreement signed by the local officers and claimed that this was sufficient evidence of a contract.

During the strike and the subsequent mediation, the union centered its attacks upon Mr. Saunders personally. In a letter to the company's directors it claimed that Mr. Saunders was the cause of the strike and that the union would not return to work until the "cause was removed." During the mediation Mr. Saunders decided to let the other officers of the company handle the negotiations, but the union requested that Mr. Saunders come to the session since he had the ultimate decision in the company and because many of the grievances were directed at him personally. In a final session lasting from the early evening to 6 A.M. Mr. Saunders had an opportunity to answer the union charges.

Each time the international representative made a charge that was untrue, I pointed out that he was a liar. When the industry representative asked me to let them finish, I did, but I took notes and refuted each statement. They said that they wouldn't come back to work while I was here. Well, I told them that I didn't want them back. Look at the efficiency figures and you can see that they have been on a slowdown between October and January (see Exhibit 4). They were smart about it; it was a gradual slowdown, the kind that is hard to detect. The police caught two of them stealing machines, and we had them arrested. I then had a security check on the employees and found that 30% of them had

Exhibit 5
BUSINESS MACHINES CORPORATION
Newspaper Article, October 25, 1962

BMC MAY REMAIN, EXPAND HERE

President Says Decision Hinges on Production, Tax Adjustment

Trenton—There is a strong possibility today that the Business Machines Córp., instead of closing its Hollins Street plant as announced some months ago, may remain here and expand its operations.

Stewart P. Saunders, president and chief executive officer of BMC, made this disclosure Wedenesday night in a talk before the Society for the Advancement of Management at Anthony's Restaurant.

Continuation of Trenton operations, he said, depends on the present quality of work and an adjustment of taxes, described by Saunders as "high."

BMC is now building a plant near Winter Gardens, Fla. Removal there will cut $400,000 in labor costs, eliminate union problems, eliminate sales and property taxes, and place production nearer the center of sales, saving on transportation, Saunders said. The Florida plant will be used when ready. The question is how much can be salvaged at Trenton.

"BMC found its people in New Jersey were not energetic," Saunders said. "A one hundred per cent (workday) turned out to be no more than three and a half to four hours of work a day," according to consultants.

The president said quality in Trenton was so poor that the firm had to spend $300,000 to $400,000 annually in field branches rebuilding units before they could be delivered to customers.

"We employed a consultant and found that 56% of BMC's market was located in the Midwest, Southwest and West," he continued. "The freight on a unit to the West cost $2.93."

Then came wildcat strikes, grievances and a second strike, Saunders said, and earlier this year the firm made its decision to move to Florida.

"We planned to close and sell our Trenton plant," he continued, "but since we started planning the move to Florida, quality and production have gone up here. . . . If this improvement trend continues and we can get reduction in present high taxes, we may even expand in Trenton."

Saunders said Florida, like many southern states, would build a plant for an incoming firm, and move it free. Combined with this is a work force that is paid $1 to $1.50 an hour less than in New Jersey. "They make it very difficult for you to walk away," he added.

In answer to a question, however, Saunders said he didn't expect this "honeymoon" to last more than 10 years, to the time when workers would be demanding wages equal to the North. "But in 10 years you save $5 million," he remarked.

BMC, which manufactures and sells communications systems, monitors, and office dictating equipment, is moving to Winter Gardens, Fla. It also has a Japanese branch.

Exhibit 5—Continued

Blames Management

Saunders joined the firm in September, 1961, and feels some of the present problems were caused by former management. "I feel management gave in to demands to the point of bankruptcy," he said. "I blame management as much as I do the people."

"In Florida," Saunders continued, "people are unspoiled. They are not used to getting as much as they can for as little as they are able to do."

He said freight costs would be $75,000 higher because of the move, but that $400,000 would be saved in labor costs.

In answer to a question on whether his firm would be unionized in Florida, Saunders said, "Not if I can help it."

One member of the audience who said he lived in Trenton took issue with Saunders' statement that taxes in the town were too high.

"Taxes for BMC are too high," Saunders replied. He had noted earlier that they totalled $38,000 annually, and added that, combined with state taxes, it was too much.

Saunders said he hoped to get a tax reduction from the town, but had received no commitment from town officials.

police records. I did some more checking and found that a lot of them came from another local company after they had driven it into bankruptcy. We finally reached an agreement on callback; we would have carte blanche to call back the people that we needed for the first 30 days after the strike was over, and for 60 days after that we could call back on a job-seniority basis rather than on a plantwide seniority basis. With three weeks of strike and a slow callback we should be able to get rid of the troublemakers. We also won the right to keep the people that we hired during the strike. With the 15 or so that we hired and the total jobs in the plant cut to about 100, there won't be any room for all of the 128 who went out on strike. I'm not trying to break the union—I just don't want them to run the manufacturing department.

Purchasing and Material Control. One of the areas which Mr. Saunders found particularly perplexing was purchasing. Upon joining BMC he learned that the company contracted extensively for the manufacture of parts while its own manufacturing facilities were operating at only a portion of normal capacity. He immediately started pulling back as many as possible of these manufacturing operations. He questioned the ability and motives of the purchasing agent and felt that he should approve all further purchase orders himself.

In January, 1962, he fired the purchasing agent and replaced him with George Shea. Mr. Shea, a 1945 graduate of Tufts, had taken the

General Electric value analysis course for purchasing agents. He had worked for several large companies and had joined BMC after meeting Mr. Saunders through a mutual friend.

During the spring and summer of 1962, Mr. Shea and one girl handled all purchasing for the company, a drastic reduction from the four-man department. He at first thought that another purchasing agent would have to be hired but finally accustomed himself to the new situation. Mr. Shea was given the authority to release purchase orders without Mr. Saunders' approval.

The basic purchasing guide was the weekly inventory report. This was a tab listing of inventory along with the company's estimated requirements in the next two-month period and the amount of inventory over or under requirements. The basis for the requirements was the company's authorized manufacturing schedule developed from sales estimates and approved by Mr. Saunders. The inventory over or under figure was only a purchasing estimate; Mr. Shea also considered lead time, economic order size, etc., before placing orders. Although inventory had been reduced during early 1962 through closer supervision, he felt that further reduction could be obtained through a "maximum-minimum" inventory system for small parts; he was developing the figures necessary to control such a system.

Mr. Shea felt that the company "has had a lot of bad suppliers," and he had devoted much of his time to developing more dependable and less costly sources. In general this change resulted in manufacturing many of the parts which had previously been purchased and in reducing the number of suppliers for other items to the two or three best sources.

In addition to his regular duties Mr. Shea also investigated capital purchases suggested by Mr. Saunders. The purchase of the 10-foot shear in the fall of 1961 had cost $8,000 but had allowed the company to buy sheet steel at $300 a month instead of cut metal at $1,400 per month. Both Mr. Saunders and Mr. Shea believed that similar savings could be made through additional capital purchases. With this in mind Mr. Shea had visited several suppliers to look over their heat-treating equipment. He also believed that the coil-winding, metal-finishing, and thread-grinding operations could be brought into the plant as well as the manufacture of some other electrical components. These suggestions were eventually adopted.

The company not only absorbed a great deal of overhead by making rather than buying its parts, but also achieved better control over inventory and scheduling. By consolidating its remaining sources it had achieved a closer relationship with the suppliers and reduced problems of poor heat treating, plating, and grinding. This had proved particularly troublesome on government work which had stricter specifications.

In the fall of 1962, Mr. Saunders expanded Mr. Shea's duties to cover all material control within the company. In November Mr. Saunders explained his duties as "purchasing, materials control, receiving, shipping, stores—the whole gamut of materials. We were going through a shifting period here and it was a question of developing him to the point where he could take over. This was the plan all along, although I don't think he knew it—in fact, I know he didn't."

During the winter Mr. Shea had a chance to put his ideas into operation and did so to the satisfaction of Mr. Saunders. In March, 1963, Mr. Saunders reported that "George has developed more than anyone else. He has done wonders. Nothing is too hard for him to tackle. He handled inventory control while we were in a tight cash position, in addition to purchasing. He could develop into a good operations manager. He has the internal drive and is quick to get things done."

Engineering. Allen Parker, an electrical engineer in his early 40's, joined BMC in October, 1961, after 14 years with a major competitor. He was promoted from director of research and development to vice president in charge of engineering in February, 1962, because of his initiative in introducing improvements into the development engineering section; these improvements included project accounts, time scheduling for research projects, and periodic progress reports. As vice president and No. 2 man in the organization, his expanded duties involved the supervision of five departments: research and development, quality assurance, production control, manufacturing-engineering, and technical publications. Upon assuming these responsibilities it was understood that he would be relieved of some of them as soon as other competent executives could be developed within the company. Consequently, the responsibility for production control was transferred to Mr. Shea and the responsibility for manufacturing-engineering to Mr. Sharp in September, 1962.

In October, 1962, Mr. Parker believed that the engineering department had survived its most critical period.

When I arrived last fall we were behind on the FAA contract; it wasn't until February that I realized how far behind we were. It wasn't until this summer that we finally worked out all of the problems on the job. It took almost all of our engineering staff to get the job done. Now we can start thinking about other projects for the engineers. Our engineering staff is still developing. We had about 20 development engineers when I first came here; we have replaced most of them and built up our engineering staff to about 32. Our budget calls for 50, so we are still looking for good engineers.

Most of my time is spent hiring new engineers and looking for development contracts to fill this plant when our commercial work is moved to Florida. Now I am gone about 40% of the time and as we get closer to the move I expect to be away practically all the time.

Mr. Saunders, although not an engineer, maintained an interest in engineering, suggested topics to be worked on, and even took home machines and tore them apart in an effort to find easier methods.

I've started something new here; each month the project manager and the director of engineering meet with me to report on progress on the projects during the month. I'm doing this for three reasons: first, to be sure that they are getting the right direction in the engineering area, because, by and large, the engineers are not very good managers; second, to acquaint myself with the progress that is being made; and third, to serve as a morale builder for the project group to get a hearing with me and tell me what they have accomplished. This is the third month we have done it.

Bob Carter, director of research and development, attended these meetings in the fall of 1962. He had joined the company in November, 1961, and had succeeded Mr. Parker as director. Mr. Carter said that he was having a problem getting the right people to fill out his engineering department.

It's hard to pick up the right people at the salary offered. We feel that the salaries are high but we're not willing to pay for experience outside of our interests. Also the Florida move is not helping. It hasn't cost us any men because these men want to stay around for the experience, but besides wanting the challenge and money, engineers want to stay put. I don't know what will happen when we move to Florida, or who will go. I have a lot of ties here and a new home.

During the winter of 1962 Bob Carter left the company and was not replaced. Mr. Saunders took over the direction of the research and development engineering department himself because he had become increasingly displeased with the progress that Allen Parker was making with the company. Mr. Parker's failure to follow through on the problems of the FAA contract disappointed Mr. Saunders.

I don't know what happened to Allen, but after I made him a vice president he seemed to sit back and relax. I don't know if it's the weight of the problems or the lack of cash or what, but he doesn't seem to be challenge-motivated.

Yesterday morning I asked him to see about $4,000 that the FAA owes us and he said that he would. When I asked him about it today, he hadn't done anything. Allen just does not follow through. The thing that he seems to like to do is sell to government agencies. I am going to give him a chance to do that; if he doesn't make the grade, I will have to get rid of him. Right now he is not producing for the dollars being spent.

Accounting. Mike Spadone, controller and treasurer, joined BMC in May, 1962. After graduating from college in 1950, he worked with a CPA firm and an electronics company before answering an ad in *The Wall Street Journal* and learning about BMC.

Mr. Spadone was high in his praise for Mr. Saunders.

He is a really dynamic person who knows where he wants to go and is going to get there. In the accounting area he knows what he wants. He was an internal auditor for Continental Can for many years and knows as much about accounting as anything else. When I arrived, I received a letter telling me all the things that he wanted done in this department. The goals included reporting balance sheet figures and P.&L. figures by the 15th of the month, installing budgets and new inventory procedures, reducing manpower, and projecting levels for receivables and payables. Before I came here the accounting was not very sophisticated. All we really had were the standard P.&L. accounts and a very loose cost accounting system. We have introduced better sales analysis and responsibility accounting in sales and have revised the reports. We also have made the cost accounting reports more specific. Stu Saunders is very interested in the labor efficiency report and the internal statements. He receives these daily and uses them to control operations.

We have made a lot of progress in the accounting department but we have been hampered by the turnover in personnel. Almost all of the people in accounting are new; five of the six tab people are new since May. One girl in cost accounting has been here 20 years, but the rest are new. Only a few of the other girls have been here more than three years. Our future plans will have to wait until some of these people come along.

There are a lot of things that we want to do in the future. We hope to get an organizational chart set up soon. We also want to get the complete statements out in eight days, whereas now we take 30 to 35 days to get them out. There are a lot of other things that should be done, too, such as putting accounts payable on tab, devising better inventory control and production control programs, developing economic order quantities, and improving the standards.

As of March, 1963, Mr. Saunders was generally pleased with Mike Spadone's progress but conceded that he too was weak on follow through. "During the strike the timekeeper refused to work on the production line, so we fired him. I told Mike Spadone and Peter Sharp that this was a good time to put in our new production control system which will replace the timekeeper with a 24-hour tape recorder. When the strike was over, they wanted to hire a new timekeeper but I wouldn't let them. They have to learn to use their problems as opportunities."

Mr. Spadone also made cash projections and kept Mr. Saunders advised of the company's cash position. In financial matters Mr. Saunders relied upon the treasurer's figures but made all decisions himself.

In reviewing the cash position of the company in March, 1963, Mr. Saunders said the past year had been very tight. "The worst came in January. We have a $1,200,000 line of credit with a New York bank and in January we had to use all of it. The strike actually helped the cash position. Because of the labor problems, we have had to keep a four-month inventory of finished machines, but when the strike came it freed a lot of money that was in inventory. Since then we have been able to repay $59,000 of the loan. We should be able to get $300,000 to $400,000 from the FAA for April deliveries. The total due on the contract is $600,000, which will ease the cash situation considerably. With that and better purchasing and inventory control we should be past the worst of our cash problems."

In the past the company had used convertible debentures and factored receivables to finance its operations. The company expected that the increasing profitability of the company would reduce the convertible debt. In September, 1962, it negotiated a $1,200,000 unsecured line of credit and ceased its receivables financing.

Sales. As general sales manager, Mr. Saunders spent 60% of his time on sales problems. A major source of concern was the ineffectiveness of the distributors.

The distributor organization has not developed well; in fact, we are closing out our distributors because they just aren't doing the job for us. I don't think this is a good distributor product; unless you give away too much of the profit to the distributor, he isn't interested. We have closed out our distributors in Des Moines, Flint, Rochester, and Syracuse. We have bought out one in New York and are closing Akron. We are putting our own branches in all of these areas; we have opened new branches in Philadelphia, Washington, and Sacramento and will open branches in Florida soon. As far as I'm concerned, if the distributor does the job we won't throw him out. But many of them just aren't doing the job. We set quotas for each sales area based upon the area's sales potential as established by the Office Machine Equipment Institute. In many areas the distributors not only aren't meeting their quotas but aren't making any sales at all.

We have had some problems with the product, but our big problem is convincing the sales organization that the company is behind them. I find that by and large the BMC sales organization has always had a crutch as to why they couldn't sell. First, they couldn't sell because of design difficulties. That's now behind us. Then, they couldn't sell because we weren't giving them enough machines. Well, that's behind us, too. I don't know what the latest excuse is, but we are not accepting excuses any more.

Once we have developed a strong sales organization, we will look for new products that can be sold by the same people. Primarily, we are interested in office equipment but are also considering other items in the electronics field. We have offers all the time from people who want to come in with us. What we are looking for is something like a dry photocopy process which would increase our sales without much increase in overhead. It will take two years to really build the sales force, but I hope that in three or four months the sales organization will be in shape so that we can start thinking about diversification.

Branch Sales Operations. Mr. Saunders believed that successful sales branches were vital to the overall success of the firm and spent a majority of his time visiting sales offices and recruiting new branch managers. In December, 1962, he reorganized the Boston office of the company and installed Dick Frankel as branch manager. By February the Boston office led all branches in sales. Dick had left the company in September, 1961, and had returned as a salesman in the Trenton office when he heard of Mr. Saunders' accomplishments. The following para-phrased comments by Dick Frankel indicate some of the changes that Mr. Saunders had accomplished in the branch offices:

Mr. Saunders has made some real changes in the sales organization. I think his biggest change has been giving the sales department strong leadership and confidence in the company. He also gives the sales offices more direction through his review of the results and his letters. Before, the branch managers used to get only a profit and loss statement. Since my background is in marketing, I couldn't tell if the results were good or bad. Now we not only have the P.&L. but he also gives us specific goals and objectives for each of the accounts. We have a budget and a forecast of sales to strive for and each month we get a P.&L. which shows not only the amount of each account but the percentage that each account should be of total sales. I get a monthly letter from him reviewing my accounts and questioning me on items that may be out of line. Of course he evaluates by results; when the results are not good, he can really put the pressure on you.

We now have production backing us up, which we didn't before. I used to phone in a rush order and get promised a machine only to have it arrive late because of production problems or some shipping clerk who would refuse to work five minutes overtime to get it out. Saunders is a production man and has made some real changes there.

Another improvement is simplified reporting. We used to have to report our transactions daily. Now we report weekly and get back a tab run that we can use to make up our monthly reports. This lets me spend more time out of the office. I'm afraid, though, that Sam Caldwell has just come up with another report comparing forecast and actual sales that will take us about four hours a month to fill out. I could give this to my girl to fill out, but she is new and I don't feel that this should be general office information.

Another thing that I like is that I have complete freedom in running the office. I do the hiring, firing, training, and the management of expenses. I can do what I want as long as I produce results. I think that most of the people now selling are out to prove something. Stu has gotten rid of the ones who sat back waiting for the business to come to them, even though many of them were good salesmen. The men we have now are more eager. It's not just a matter of energy; it's a matter of desire to do a job right. I sometimes come in early and work until 11 o'clock, and so do the others.

I think it's necessary to have that desire to sell BMC products. Our salesmen have to be creative sellers who are able to meet the arguments of our competitors. One of the arguments that competitors use is that we are a small company with P.&L. problems while the others are long-established firms. Now we are better on that count. Another is that they give better service. They can't say that in Boston anymore because we have a very good service department, but a company like Dictaphone or IBM is bound to have more facilities in some parts of the country because of its size. Finally they talk about their design features. I'm sure that we have the best all-around design on the market, but its features have to be sold. The big feature of our equipment is that it is the easiest operating system on the market and has been designed to save the time of the high-priced executive rather than that of the office girls. Our system is easy to load, has accurate backspacing and identification of corrections, and returns quickly and simply to the place where it stopped recording. The equipment is so simple that the executive can operate it with one hand without looking. The actual recording is serviced by the secretary at her desk, so the executive never has to take discs to her; she can change discs and start typing at her convenience.

The new salesmen are always concerned about the price of the equipment. All the companies are within $5 of each other at around $400, except IBM which I think is about 5% higher. But the big feature in selling dictating equipment is not the initial investment but the savings in time for the executive. The salesmen have to be creative to put this across. Of course, if it's a big account that we want to get into, we will go low with a competitive bid and hope to get back to list price with future business.

Another reason that we have to be creative is that we can't sit back and wait for sales to come to us, like Dictaphone. Dictaphone has been established so long that the name has become generic in the business. When a Dictaphone salesman goes out, he has over $70 of advertising helping him. We are lucky to have $2 per salesman. We have to fight uphill for sales and we make sales in most of the competitive situations. The sales that we lose are the sales that we never hear about. We don't have the salesmen to cover the market like Dictaphone or IBM. Actually IBM helped us when they came in with their machine. The IBM salesmen get businessmen to think about dictating equipment, but most companies want to see several machines before they buy. The typewriter salesmen are not familiar enough with dictating equipment to sell it. About 60% of our business comes through leads from people who call us and ask for a demonstration. The other 40% we have to find ourselves.

The most important part of our selling effort is done before we see the customer. Right now we are making a telephone survey and a survey of some office buildings to find prospects. Even when a customer calls us we have to give some thought to his particular problems before we make a presentation.

In this office the new equipment has not been as much of a help in increasing sales as the changes in the management operations have been. Our sales increase has been mainly in the standard dictating line. We have sold few of the memoscribers (Japanese imported machine at half the price) because the quality is not so good as the regular equipment, it does not form a complete office system, and it takes as much of a salesman's effort to sell a $200 memoscriber as a $400 regular machine—and to a salesman working on commission that makes a big difference. The memoscriber is the type of thing that should be sold through Western Auto or a camera store to individuals; we look for most of our business in offices where we have a chance to sell more machines at a higher price. We haven't been selling the audio-visual system because we can't get production on it. When we do get it, I will have to go out and determine the best prospects and the best presentation for it. Right now with three men and a quota set for six we have all that we can do to keep up with the office dictating business.

I think that the company has taken care of the biggest problems that faced the sales force, but the things that remain to be done as far as I am concerned are in the area of training and motivating salesmen. The branch managers do all the training now. Even with only a skeleton force here I spend a lot of time in the field with the salesmen and I have put together three books full of information for training. As we add salesmen, training will become a problem.

Motivating the salesmen is another problem. We pay well at BMC, but salesmen work for more than money. Motivating salesmen is a matter of attention to every detail. You have to see that they have a pat on the back at the right time and that they keep up the pressure on sales. You have to see to it that they never lose faith in the product or the company and that they never work through fear. A salesman who has too many problems of his own can't concentrate on the customer's problems. In production a man can come to work after a fight with his wife and he will only produce 20 units instead of 30, but he is all right as long as he keeps his finger out of the machine; a salesman in the same circumstances, however, will produce nothing. That's why I didn't tell the salesmen about our strike until it was over and that's why I get irritated when things from the home office come in the mail or by telegram and the people in the office see them before I do.

PROPOSED MOVE TO FLORIDA

In December, 1961, one of the BMC stockholders tried to interest Mr. Saunders in moving his plant to Florida. The stockholder was building a completely new city in Florida and hoped to bring in light industry and attract workers to his homes. The stockholder had taken an interest in BMC because of its handling of the union problem and the turnaround in the profit picture and became determined to get BMC for his new city. The overcapacity at BMC and the value of the four-year-old plant combined with the problems of the workers' attitude at Trenton made the offer appealing. The stockholder offered to build a new plant and lease it to BMC on reasonable terms. Florida offered savings in labor costs of about $1.50 per hour. Mr. Saunders estimated that the total cost of the move would be $350,000 to $400,000. In addition, the company expected to incur about $75,000 per year of additional transportation costs but believed that the savings in labor costs would more than offset this.

Mr. Saunders announced his decision to retain the Trenton plant in October, 1962 (see Exhibit 5). "We planned to close and sell our Trenton plant, but since we started planning the move to Florida, quality and production here have gone up. If this improvement trend continues and we can get reduction in present high taxes, we may even expand in Trenton."

Only the commercial segment of the operations would move to Florida. The Trenton plant was to be used for expanded government work and to house other operations which the company hoped to acquire.

Groundbreaking for the Florida plant was expected in the summer of 1963 with the building to be completed in the spring of 1964.

What we plan to do is produce about a four months' supply of machines which we will store. Then we will produce probably five to six months' supply of parts needed to assemble machines here, ship the parts to Florida, and gradually start an assembly process there. In selecting people in Florida, we plan to do what RCA did. As I understand it, they actually set up the units to be assembled or the job to be performed and gave the prospective employee three or four hours to play with the material and watched him to see how he made out. If they thought he had an aptitude for the work, they would say fine, in three months you have a job; if not, they would just forget it. We will probably do something along this line, too. We will probably take all of the good supervisors with us or ask them to go with us. If there are any dogs in the group, no, we won't even invite them. We haven't specifically asked them yet, but most of them have come and said that they hope they are invited to go. Mr. Sharp will probably go down as overall manager of production. We haven't really decided about the other people. Some of the engineers will have to go and probably the personnel man.

THE FUTURE

Mr. Saunders believed that the company was still working on problems created by the past management and would continue to do so for the next several months. After that he believed that the only problems remaining would be

. . . the standard, everyday problems that occur in any other business. You will always have personnel problems, finding the right people for the right task. I don't mean at the top level; I mean at the foreman level and under. You will always find people who will function perfectly in the next three months as a foreman and then all of a sudden will fall apart. I don't foresee anything other than normal everyday problems facing us—mostly people.

I have no intention of leaving the company after our present problems are overcome. I took a cut in pay to come here but was given a sizable stock option, so I intend to stick around and see that the company grows.

So far we aren't looking for companies to acquire—they are coming to us. I wouldn't acquire anything that we couldn't move into our facilities and eliminate the duplicate administrative and overhead costs. Every one of these companies is in serious trouble because they have too much overhead; unless we could consolidate and eliminate overhead, I wouldn't even touch them at the moment. We aren't going to pick up anything that is going to upset our profit position. We've been on the loss side so long that this is detrimental to our selling efforts, so we're not going to slip back.

Mr. Saunders believed that the company's growth could be accomplished through retained earnings and, if necessary, cash supplied by the major stockholders. There were no limits to the size of company acquired so long as BMC would remain the "ultimate company." Acquisition plans were confined, however, to the electronics and office equipment fields.

With our present machine and modifications to it, we expect to expand our present business to about $12 to $15 million in annual sales in the next two years. My long-range plan is that in five years we will be worth at least $50 million through acquisitions as well as expansion of our present products, and in eight to 10 years I want to be well over $100 million.

Linton Company, Inc.

"I THINK lack of capital is our biggest problem," Mr. Frank Corbett, president of the Linton Company, a wholesale grocery firm, told a case writer from the Harvard Business School in April, 1954. "We need additional sales volume, but our present capital is not large enough to finance additional receivables and inventory. We could make a substantial increase in profits by increasing sales, because most of our expenses are fixed or would rise very little with higher volume. I have prepared some figures that show you how this looks (see Exhibit 1). At present gross margin and other income just cover our operating expenses. For five years now, we've been trying to get volume over this 'break-even' point to where we will be making sizable profits. At first I thought our break-even point was about $2,500,000. Then it increased to $3,000,000, and now it seems as though we need about $4,000,000 sales before we'll show real profits!

"Each time our bank loan comes up for renewal, the loaning officer, Mr. Eaton, asks us when we are going to make some money. I've been giving him this same explanation since 1947. Last time Mr. Eaton saw Bob, who is my brother and partner; he said, 'Your brother Frank sounds like an old broken record being played over and over. When is he going to have something new to tell me?'

"One reason we haven't made larger profits is that we took the calculated risk of lowering margin and prices to increase volume. If I had an additional $100,000 capital I could risk cutting margins even further. This, I am positive, would enable us to secure additional large customers and increase sales to a point where we would really be making money. What I couldn't do with this business if I only had some capital to use!" (See Exhibits 2, 3, 4, 5 and 6 for financial data.)

The Linton office and main warehouse were in Elgin, Illinois, a city of 44,000 population, approximately 30 miles northwest of Chicago. The company rented a smaller frozen-food warehouse in another suburb about 15 miles nearer Chicago. The grocery line, which included over 2,000 grocery products, was sold to 405 retail accounts within a

Exhibit 1

LINTON COMPANY, INC.

Estimates of Projected Weekly Income and Expense Figures

YEAR	Mr. Frank Corbett's Assumptions of Sales Volume		Grocery Income*	Frozen-Food* Income	Total Income	Expense†	Profit or (Loss)	Annual Profit or (Loss)
	WEEKLY							
	1	2	3	4	5	6	7	8
	Groceries	Frozen Foods						
	$32,000	$16,000	$2,410	$1,690	$4,100	$4,400	$(300)	$(15,600)
	32,000	18,000	2,410	1,740	4,150	4,400	(250)	(13,000)
	32,000	20,000	2,410	1,950	4,360	4,400	(40)	(2,080)
	32,000	22,000	2,410	2,180	4,590	4,400	190	9,880
	35,000	16,000	2,635	1,690	4,325	4,400	(75)	(3,900)
	37,000	16,000	2,795	1,690	4,485	4,400	85	4,420
	40,000	16,000	3,010	1,690	4,700	4,400	300	15,600
	40,000	18,000	3,010	1,740	4,750	4,400	350	18,200

VERY LIKELY VOLUME IN 1954

37,000	18,000	2,795	1,740	4,535	4,400	135	7,020

POSSIBILITY IN 1954

37,000	20,000	2,795	1,950	4,745	4,400	345	17,940

GOAL

40,000	22,000	3,010	2,180	5,190	4,400	790	41,080

ACTUAL RESULTS 1950–53

1950....	25,500	3,500	2,702	357	3,059	2,950	109	5,668
1951....	22,800	8,600	2,572	809	3,381	3,268	113	5,876
1952....	22,900	13,100	2,054	1,465	3,519	3,428	91	4,732
1953....	29,000	16,600	2,186	1,927	4,113	3,921	192	9,984

* Total income includes gross margin, advertising allowances, and purchase discounts as estimated by Mr. Frank Corbett.
† This was Mr. Frank Corbett's estimate of "highest conceivable operating cost" at these volumes.
Source: Mr. Frank Corbett.

50-mile radius of Elgin, in Illinois and Indiana. Linton was also the distributor for Apex Frozen Foods in the same territory.

HISTORY UNDER PREVIOUS MANAGEMENT, 1903–45

Linton was founded in 1903 by Messrs. S. F. Linton and J. C. McIvor, wholesale flour, grain, and feed dealers. After their original warehouse burned down in 1914, the company built a new warehouse and added

Exhibit 2

LINTON COMPANY, INC.
Balance Sheets, 1945–53

Assets	Dec. 31 1953	Dec. 31 1952	Dec. 31 1951	Dec. 31 1950	Dec. 31 1949	Dec. 31 1948	Dec. 31 1947	Dec. 31 1946	June, 1945
Cash on Hand and on Deposit	$ 54,659	$ 27,923	$ 18,240	$ 26,906	$ 11,818	$ 6,030	$ 5,873	$ 12,841	$ 14,380
Accounts Receivable—Trade	86,875	73,436	53,550	62,813	37,506	50,028	40,485	35,989	28,077
Accounts and Claims Receivable—Nontrade	174	4,095	395	388	1,402	1,105	2,441	1,121	.....
Inventories: Groceries	201,954*	176,180*	179,599*	200,251*	116,021*	128,777	159,364	201,142	.....
Frozen Foods	20,027	13,777	6,679	10,751	14,485	29,381	0	.....	58,805
Total	221,981	189,957	186,278	211,002	130,506	158,158	159,364	201,142	58,805
Total Current Assets	$363,689	$295,411	$258,463	$301,109	$181,232	$215,321	$208,163	$251,093	$101,262
Cash Surrender Value—Life Insurance	2,180	1,563	1,020	276	20	.....	.....	.....	.....
Land	1,500	1,500	1,500	1,500	1,500	1,500	1,500	1,500	1,500
Buildings	15,437	16,150	16,863	17,575	18,288	19,000	19,713	20,425	21,494
Improvements	5,105	4,525	3,201	3,783	4,365	4,948	.....	.....	.....
Total Real Estate	22,042	22,175	21,564	22,858	24,153	25,448	21,213	21,925	22,994
Furniture and Equipment	2,643	3,291	2,901	2,763	3,217	7,833	9,232	3,560	98
Delivery Truck	100	320	699	1,937	2,970	3,734⎱	7,820⎱	3,632⎱	
Automobiles	2,886	3,174	4,242	1,521	1,117	1,866			3,739
Total Fixed Assets	$ 27,671	$ 28,960	$ 29,406	$ 29,079	$ 31,457	$ 38,881	$ 38,265	$ 29,117	$ 26,831
Miscellaneous Receivables			310	612					
Deposit Premiums and Unexpired Insurance	2,734	1,743	2,080	2,393	1,261	1,648	1,913	542	610
Other Deferred Charges	199	199	341	106	104	240	186	.....	636
Officers and Employees' Accounts	2,064	1,696	.....	.....	978	.....	.....	.....	77,339
Total Other Assets	$ 4,997	$ 3,638	$ 2,731	$ 3,111	$ 2,343	$ 1,888	$ 2,099	$ 542	$ 78,585
Total Assets	$398,537	$329,572	$291,620	$333,575	$215,052	$256,090	$248,527	$280,752	$206,678

Exhibit 2 (Continued)

LINTON COMPANY, INC.

Balance Sheets, 1945–53

Liabilities	Dec. 31, 1953	Dec. 31, 1952	Dec. 31, 1951	Dec. 31, 1950	Dec. 31, 1949	Dec. 31, 1948	Dec. 31, 1947	Dec. 31, 1946	June, 1945
Notes Payable—Unsecured	....	....	....	....	$ 4,000	$ 13,000	$ 20,000	....	....
Notes Payable—Autos	....	....	$ 1,215	....	....	....	....	....	....
Due Officers	....	....	715	$ 461	....	....	682	....	....
Accounts Payable—Trade	$150,871	$113,880	77,684	113,810	37,970	55,897	39,992	$ 82,814	$ 26,784
Notes Payable—Bank (Secured by Inventory)	120,000*	90,000*	90,000*	100,000*	73,500*	106,479	102,844	124,606	33,000
Notes Payable—Secured by Equipment	310	400	....	....	256	....	....	....	....
Provision for Taxes	6,342	6,621	4,261	7,150	6,739	7,830	11,279	8,645	6,484
Accrued Expenses and Other Liabilities	4,032	1,953	3,340	3,353	980	1,590	2,261	2,187	1,254
Amortization of Mortgage Payable	1,500	1,500	1,500	1,350	1,500	1,500	1,500	1,500	....
Total Current Liabilities	$283,055	$214,354	$178,715	$226,124	$124,945	$186,296	$178,558	$219,752	$ 67,522
Mortgage Payable—Real Estate	24,000	25,500	27,000	28,650	23,625	25,125	28,500	28,500	20,000
Capital Stock	75,300	74,200	70,000	63,800	53,000	32,500	32,500	....	24,000
Earned Surplus	16,182	15,518	15,905	15,001	13,482	12,169	8,969	....	95,156
Total Capital	$ 91,482	$ 89,718	$ 85,905	$ 78,801	$ 66,482	$ 44,669	$ 41,469	$ 32,500†	$119,156
Total Liabilities and Capital	$398,537	$329,572	$291,620	$333,575	$215,052	$256,090	$248,527	$280,752	$206,678

*Inventory of $116,021 pledged to secure note of $ 73,500 on 12/31/49.
  " " $194,834 " " " " $100,000 " 12/31/50.
  " " $173,388 " " " " $ 90,000 " 12/31/51.
  " " $169,829 " " " " $ 90,000 " 12/31/52.
  " " $195,971 " " " " $120,000 " 12/31/53.

† Partner's capital.
Source: Company records.

Exhibit 3

LINTON COMPANY, INC.

Breakdown of Capital Stock

Capital Stock:

First Preferred, 7% Cumulative, Par..........$	100		
Authorized: 800 shares			
Issued: 426 shares.....................	42,600		
Subscribed: 2 shares.....................	200	$42,800	
Second Preferred, 4½% Cumulative, Par........$	100		
Authorized: 300 shares			
Issued: 300 shares.....................		30,000	
Common, No Par Value			
Authorized: 1,000 shares			
Issued: 100........................		2,500	
Total Capital Stock......................		$75,300	

Source: Auditors' report.

groceries to the line. Regarding the previous management, Mr. Corbett stated:

"The company as managed by Linton and McIvor was a slow-moving, low-volume, high-markup operation. Neither management nor the salesmen were merchandising-conscious: they thought a sale was complete when the goods were delivered and did little to help move products off the retailer's shelf. They bought at the best prices available and added a high enough margin to ensure a net profit of 4% or 5%. This high-price policy, coupled with a sales emphasis on the company's own private brands, resulted in a profitable record until the early 1940's when the company began to have difficulties. Mr. Linton nevertheless continued to run the business on these policies until the day he retired."

In the early 1930's two trends emerged in the grocery business, stated Mr. Corbett. First, margins dropped as increasing chain-store competition caused many independent retailers to turn to higher-volume, lower-markup co-operative and voluntary chain wholesalers. Secondly, advertising by large manufacturers promoted consumer acceptance of national brand names, often at the expense of local wholesalers' private brands.

Continuing, Mr. Frank Corbett said, "Linton's policies, which resulted in high prices, private-label emphasis, and inadequate service to retailers, made the fast-growing, merchandising-conscious, independent supermarket operator stay away from them."

.After losses in 1943 and 1944, Mr. Linton sold out to Mr. Frank Corbett in June, 1945. Net sales and net profits had declined slowly

LINTON COMPANY, INC.

Graphs of Cost of Goods Sold, Gross Profit, Total Operating Expenses, and Net Profit

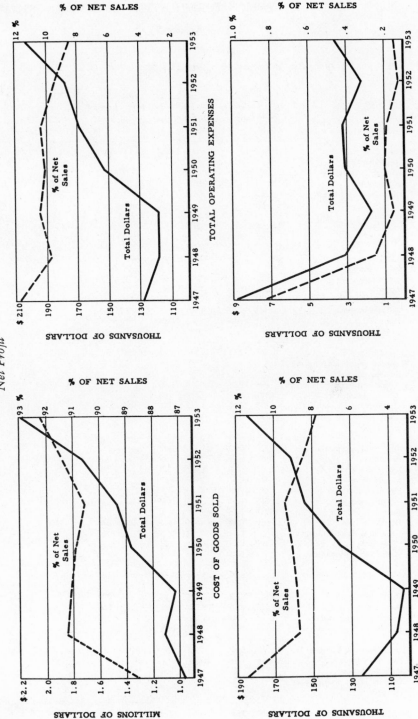

Source: Prepared by case writer from Exhibit 4.

Exhibit 5

LINTON COMPANY, INC.

Operating Statements—Years Ending December 31, 1950–53

	1953						1952			
	Combined		Groceries		Frozen Foods		Combined		Groceries	
	Dollars	Per Cent	Dollars	Per Cent	Dollars	Per Cent	Dollars	Per Cent	Dollars	Per Ce
Sales........................	2,403,389	101.44	1,526,533	101.43	876,856	101.45	1,899,760	101.34	1,209,359	101.4
Returns and allowances..........	34,126	1.44	21,577	1.43	12,549	1.45	25,182	1.34	17,809	1.4
Net sales......................	2,369,263	100.00	1,504,956	100.00	864,307	100.00	1,874,578	100.00	1,191,550	100.0
Cost of goods sold										
Beginning inventory...........	189,957		176,180		13,777		186,279		179,599	
Net purchases.................	2,210,991		1,440,655		770,336		1,712,742		1,098,814	
Freight and other expense.......	5,535		5,535				4,723		4,723	
	2,406,483		1,622,370		784,113		1,903,744		1,283,136	
Closing inventory.............	221,981		201,955		20,026		189,957		176,180	
	2,184,502	92.20	1,420,415	94.38	764,087	88.40	1,713,787	91.42	1,106,956	92.5
Gross profit....................	184,761	7.80	84,541	5.62	100,220	11.60	160,791	8.58	84,594	7.1
Operating expenses:										
Selling expense:										
Advertising.................	1,813	0.07	1,813	0.12			*		*	
Payroll—sales	41,482	1.75	17,270	1.15	24,212	2.80				
Sales promotion.............	5,412	0.23	1,603	0.11	3,809	0.44				
Payroll burden..............	1,591	0.07	661	0.04	930	0.11				
Incentive commissions.......	.....	....								
Total selling expenses..........	50,298	2.12	21,347	1.42	28,951	3.35	45,114	2.41	23,489	1.9
Warehouse and handling expense:										
Building expenses:										
Taxes—real estate.........	898	0.04	898	0.06			*		*	
Mortgage interest.........	1,188	0.05	1,188	0.08						
Repairs..................	1,612	0.07	1,612	0.11						
Depreciation.............	1,545	0.06	1,545	0.10						
Insurance................	283	0.01	283	0.02						
Total building expenses.......	5,526	0.23	5,526	0.37						
Rent......................	2,889	0.12			2,889	0.34				
Light and heat..............	1,993	0.08	1,993	0.13						
Burglar alarm...............	449	0.02	449	0.03						
Fire and extended coverage on inventory..............	585	0.03	456	0.03	129	0.01				
Payroll—warehouse........	17,631	0.75	9,074	0.60	8,557	0.99				
Payroll—burden...........	959	0.04	494	0.03	465	0.05				
Cornwall Warehouse Company payroll.................	3,491	0.15	3,491	0.23						
Maintenance and miscellaneous	229	0.01	229	0.02						
Total warehouse and handling...	33,752	1.43	21,712	1.44	12,040	1.39	26,774	1.43	16,418	1.3
Delivery expenses:										
Gas, oil, repairs, dry ice.......	3,141	0.13	2,159	0.14	982	0.11	*		*	
Truck rentals...............	13,316	0.56	5,238	0.35	8,078	0.93				
Insurance—autos, trucks.....	1,179	0.05	1,138	0.08	41	0.01				
Depreciation—autos, trucks...	1,308	0.06	1,308	0.09						
Total rolling stock expense......	18,944	0.80	9,843	0.66	9,101	1.05				
Payroll—delivery...........	20,951	0.88	12,169	0.81	8,782	1.02				
Payroll—burden............	1,124	0.05	654	0.04	470	0.06				
Cornwall Warehouse Company payroll.................										
Total delivery expenses.........	41,019	1.73	22,666	1.51	18,353	2.13	41,573	2.22	24,012	2.

* Subtotals not available for 1952.

		1951 Combined		1951 Groceries		1951 Frozen Foods		1950 Combined		1950 Groceries		1950 Frozen Foods	
Frozen Foods		*Combined*		*Groceries*		*Frozen Foods*		*Combined*		*Groceries*		*Frozen Foods*	
Dollars	Per Cent	Dollars	Per Cent	Dollars	Per Cent	Dollars	Per Cent	Dollars	Per Cent	Dollars	Per Cent	Dollars	Per Cent
0,401	101.08	1,655,196	101.31	1,206,445	101.51	448,751	100.77	1,531,189	101.35	1,348,946	101.46	182,243	100.55
7,373	1.08	21,348	1.31	17,898	1.51	3,450	0.77	20,392	1.35	19,400	1.46	992	0.55
3,028	100.00	1,633,848	100.00	1,188,547	100.00	445,301	100.00	1,510,797	100.00	1,329,546	100.00	181,251	100.00
6,680		211,002		200,251		10,751		130,506		130,506			
3,928		1,449,650		1,050,903		398,747		1,446,945		1,273,787		173,158	
		4,539		4,137		402		7,548		7,265		283	
0,608		1,665,191		1,255,291		409,900		1,584,999		1,411,558		173,441	
3,777		186,279		179,599		6,680		211,002		200,251		10,751	
6,831	88.85	1,478,912	90.52	1,075,692	90.51	403,220	90.55	1,373,997	90.95	1,211,307	91.11	162,690	89.76
6,197	11.15	154,936	9.48	112,855	9.49	42,081	9.45	136,800	9.05	118,239	8.89	18,561	10.24
*	*	5,195	0.32	5,149	0.43	46	0.01	5,408	0.36	5,253	0.39	155	0.08
		26,405	1.61	23,736	2.00	2,669	0.60	36,165	2.39	30,545	2.30	5,620	3.10
		1,060	0.06	698	0.06	362	0.08	1,160	0.08	1,017	0.07	143	0.08
		1,247	0.08	1,122	0.09	125	0.03	1,170	0.08	920	0.07	250	0.14
		305	0.02	305	0.03			88	0.00	88	0.01		
1,625	3.16	34,212	2.09	31,010	2.61	3,202	0.72	43,991	2.91	37,823	2.84	6,168	3.40
*	*	1,019	0.06	1,019	0.09			1,047	0.07	1,047	0.08		
		1,324	0.08	1,324	0.11			1,145	0.08	1,145	0.08		
		1,330	0.08	1,330	0.11			945	0.06	945	0.07		
		1,294	0.08	1,294	0.11			1,295	0.08	1,295	0.10		
		134	0.01	134	0.01			140	0.01	140	0.01		
		5,101	0.31	5,101	0.43			4,572	0.30	4,572	0.34		
		225	0.01			225	0.05	2,019	0.13	2,018	0.15	1	0.00
		1,254	0.08	1,254	0.10			1,638	0.11	1,638	0.12		
		449	0.03	449	0.04			412	0.03	412	0.03		
		297	0.02	211	0.02	86	0.02	414	0.03	378	0.03	36	0.02
		15,294	0.94	6,512	0.55	8,782	1.97	17,750	1.17	14,848	1.12	2,902	1.60
		959	0.06	428	0.04	531	0.12	1,022	0.07	856	0.06	166	0.09
		2,270	0.14	2,270	0.19			1,656	0.11	1,656	0.13		
		197	0.01	158	0.01	39	0.01	158	0.01	141	0.01	17	0.01
0,356	1.52	26,046	1.60	16,383	1.38	9,663	2.17	29,641	1.96	26,519	1.99	3,122	1.72
*	*	3,789	0.23	3,075	0.26	714	0.16	6,630	0.44	3,767	0.28	2,863	1.58
		10,139	0.62	4,284	0.36	5,855	1.32						
		1,127	0.07	1,119	0.10	8	0.00	1,073	0.07	1,073	0.08		
		1,927	0.12	1,927	0.16			1,670	0.11	1,670	0.13		
		16,982	1.04	10,405	0.88	6,577	1.48	9,373	0.62	6,510	0.49	2,863	1.58
		17,008	1.04	10,757	0.90	6,251	1.40	12,025	0.80	9,326	0.70	2,699	1.49
		985	0.06	623	0.05	362	0.08	658	0.04	510	0.04	148	0.08
								318	0.02	318	0.02		
7,561	2.57	34,975	2.14	21,785	1.83	13,190	2.96	22,374	1.48	16,664	1.25	5,710	3.15

Exhibit 5—Continued

LINTON COMPANY, INC.

Operating Statements—Years Ending December 31, 1950–53

	1953 Combined		Groceries		Frozen Foods		1952 Combined		Groceries	
	Dollars	Per Cent	Dollars	Per Cent	Dollars	Per Cent	Dollars	Per Cent	Dollars	Per Ce
Administrative expenses:										
Office and clerical expenses:							●	●	●	●
Payroll—clerical and IBM..	15,293	0.64								
Payroll—burden..........	444	0.02								
IBM rentals..............	5,852	0.25								
IBM supplies.............	1,632	0.07								
Other office and clerical supplies..................	5,377	0.23								
Total office and clerical expenses.................	28,598	1.21								
Payroll—executive..........	22,790	0.96								
Payroll—burden............	693	0.03								
Miscellaneous insurance......	716	0.03								
Legal and audit.............	2,226	0.10								
Telephone..................	3,994	0.17								
Travel.....................	2,045	0.09								
Dues and subscriptions.......	543	0.02								
Depreciation—furniture and fixtures..................	617	0.03								
Miscellaneous administrative expenses...............	433	0.02								
Cornwall Warehouse Company payroll.................	3,491	0.15								
Miscellaneous taxes and licenses................	491	0.02								
Intracompany charges (red)...										
Total administrative expenses...	66,637	2.81	42,328	2.81	24,309	2.81	55,975	2.98	35,694	3.
Financial expenses:							●	●	●	●
Bank service charges........	729	0.03								
Cornwall Warehouse Company expenses...............	2,200	0.09								
Interest expense (except mortgage interest)...........	6,706	0.29								
Estimated loss on accounts receivable................	2,369	0.10								
Donations and contributions..	190	0.01								
Total financial expenses........	12,194	0.52	12,194	0.81			8,820	0.47	8,820	0.
Total operating expenses.........	203,900	8.61	120,247	7.99	83,653	9.68	178,256	9.51	108,433	9.
Gross operating profit or (loss).....	(19,139)	(0.81)	(35,706)	(2.37)	16,567	1.92	(17,465)	(0.93)	(23,839)	(2.
Other operating income:										
Promotional advertising........	5,876	0.25	5,876	0.39			4,284	0.23	4,284	0.
Purchase discounts............	22,892	0.97	22,892	1.52			17,911	0.95	17,911	1.
Miscellaneous................	342	0.01	342	0.02			17	0.00	17	0.
Total other operating income......	29,110	1.23	29,110	1.93			22,212	1.18	22,212	1.
Net income or (loss) before taxes and other expenses.......	9,971	0.42	(6,596)	(0.44)	16,567	1.92	4,747	0.25	(1,627)	(0.
Federal and state taxes.........	3,945	0.17					2,331	0.12		
Net cost of life insurance........	2,406	0.10					177	0.01		
	6,351	0.27					2,508	0.13		
Net profit for year..............	3,620	0.15					2,239	0.12		

● Subtotals not available for 1952.

Frozen Foods Dollars	Per Cent	Combined Dollars	Per Cent	1951 Groceries Dollars	Per Cent	Frozen Foods Dollars	Per Cent	Combined Dollars	Per Cent	1950 Groceries Dollars	Per Cent	Frozen Foods Dollars	Per Cent
*	*	12,444	0.76	12,444	1.05			12,510	0.83	11,326	0.85	1,184	0.65
		370	0.02	370	0.03			530	0.03	480	0.04	50	0.03
		4,685	0.29	4,685	0.39			4,254	0.28	4,254	0.32		
		3,048	0.18	3,048	0.26			1,215	0.08	1,215	0.09		
		2,084	0.13	1,935	0.16	149	0.03	2,659	0.18	2,516	0.19	143	0.08
		22,631	1.38	22,482	1.89	149	0.04	21,168	1.40	19,791	1.49	1,377	0.76
		28,860	1.77	28,860	2.43			20,280	1.34	20,280	1.53		
		436	0.03	436	0.04			270	0.02	270	0.02		
		415	0.02	371	0.03	44	0.01	376	0.03	347	0.03	29	0.02
		2,007	0.12	2,007	0.17			1,046	0.07	1,046	0.08		
		2,974	0.18	2,790	0.23	184	0.04	2,751	0.18	2,672	0.20	79	0.04
		1,467	0.09	1,467	0.12			272	0.02	272	0.02		
		484	0.03	484	0.04			499	0.03	495	0.03	4	0.00
		490	0.03	490	0.04			453	0.03	453	0.03		
		606	0.04	506	0.04	100	0.02	483	0.03	461	0.03	22	0.01
		3,405	0.21	3,405	0.29			1,529	0.10	1,529	0.12		
				(15,000)	(1.26)	15,000	3.37			(1,040)	(0.08)	1,040	0.58
20,281	2.97	63,775	3.90	48,298	4.06	15,477	3.48	49,127	3.25	46,576	3.50	2,551	1.41
*	*	499	0.03	499	0.04			444	0.03	444	0.03		
		2,051	0.13	2,051	0.17			1,416	0.09	1,416	0.11		
		6,356	0.39	6,356	0.54			4,937	0.33	4,937	0.37		
		1,655	0.10	1,206	0.10	449	0.10	1,353	0.09	1,171	0.09	182	0.10
		350	0.02	350	0.03			129	0.01	129	0.01		
		10,911	0.67	10,462	0.88	449	0.10	8,279	0.55	8,097	0.61	182	0.10
69,823	10.22	169,919	10.40	127,938	10.76	41,981	9.43	153,412	10.15	135,679	10.20	17,733	9.78
6,374	0.93	(14,983)	(0.92)	(15,083)	(1.27)	100	0.02	(16,612)	(1.10)	(17,440)	(1.31)	828	0.46
		4,187	0.26	4,187	0.35			3,268	0.22	3,268	0.24		
		16,331	1.00	16,331	1.38			18,758	1.24	18,758	1.41		
		384	0.02	384	0.03			227	0.01	227	0.02		
		20,902	1.28	20,902	1.76			22,253	1.47	22,253	1.67		
6,374	0.93	5,919	0.36	5,819	0.49	100	0.02	5,641	0.37	4,813	0.36	828	0.46
		2,788	0.17					2,132	0.14				
		(23)	(0.00)					464	0.03				
		2,765	0.17					2,596	0.17				
		3,154	0.19					3,045	0.20				

Exhibit 6

LINTON COMPANY, INC.

Condensed Statements—Years Ending December 31, 1947–53*

	1953		1952		1951	
Net Sales	$2,369,263	100.00%	$1,874,578	100.00%	$1,633,848	100.00%
Cost of Goods Sold	2,184,502	92.20	1,713,787	91.42	1,478,912	90.52
Gross Profit (Before Purchase Discounts)	184,761	7.80	160,791	8.58	154,936	9.48
Total Operating Expenses..$	203,900	8.61%	$ 178,256	9.51%	$ 169,919	10.40%
Gross Operating Profit or (loss).	(19,139)	(0.81)	(17,465)	(0.93)	(14,983)	(0.92)
Other Operating Income Including Purchase Discount	29,110	1.23	22,212	1.18	20,902	1.28
Net Income before Taxes and Other Expenses	9,971	0.42	4,747	0.25	5,919	0.36
Net Profit for Year.......$	3,620	0.15%	$ 2,239	0.12%	$ 3,154	0.19%

* See Exhibit 7 for industry averages.
Source: Company records.

from their peak in 1928 until 1944, when sales of $475,000 brought a loss of $4,870. Sales in the first six months of 1945 were $220,000.

Speaking of the business when he took it over, Mr. Corbett said, "Because Linton was a tightfisted old man who saved everything he made, he spent little on the upkeep of the buildings. The warehouse was dark and dingy. Warehousemen who had been employed by the company as long as 10 years were being paid $30 per week, and there were office girls making $25 per week. I sometimes think Linton was forced to sell out because his employees were disgruntled and the organization was going stale."

PURCHASE OF THE BUSINESS

The purchase of the business by Mr. Frank Corbett in June, 1945, was negotiated through Mr. Thomas Kahn, a broker and personal friend of both the Corbett brothers. At that time, Mr. Frank Corbett was general manager of the National Wholesale Company, a large Chicago co-operative grocery wholesaler.

After preliminary negotiation a price of $108,200 was set for the building (subject to a mortgage of $20,000), inventories, and other assets. Since Mr. Corbett had only $800, he obtained a 30-day option for which he paid $500, and then set out to borrow the rest of the purchase price. His first step was to approach the bank he dealt with on behalf of the National company. This bank agreed to lend him $50,000 secured on the Linton inventory. Mr. Corbett described his further money-raising efforts as follows:

1950		1949		1948		1947	
$1,510,797	100.00%	$1,140,752	100.00%	$1,216,110	100.00%	$1,089,120	100.00%
1,373,997	90.95	1,038,473	91.03	1,109,612	91.24	964,536	88.56
136,800	9.05	102,279	8.97	106,498	8.76	124,584	11.44
$ 153,412	10.15%	$ 119,481	10.47%	$ 119,663	9.84%	$ 128,099	11.76%
(16,612)	(1.10)	(17,202)	(1.50)	(13,165)	(1.08)	(3,515)	(0.32)
22,253	1.47	18,282	1.60	19,366	1.59	15,163	1.39
5,641	0.37	1,080	0.10	6,201	0.51	11,648	1.07
$ 3,045	0.20%	$ 1,801	0.16%	$ 3,199	0.26%	$ 8,969	0.82%

"My brother Bob was overseas in the navy, but I knew he would come in with me as a partner. We both were reared in our father's wholesale grocery business, and after we got out of college, Bob took a job as sales manager for a large Detroit grocery wholesaler, and I went to work for National. We often talked about how much we would like to be in business together. After I was sure of the bank loan on Linton, I cabled him in Italy and soon had his answer that he would put $6,000, nearly all his savings, in the venture. I then approached friends and relatives, and several of them lent me amounts varying from $500 to $10,000. A final loan of $14,800 from Tom Kahn enabled me to complete the purchase of the business."

OPERATION UNDER NEW MANAGEMENT

"When I took control," Mr. Corbett stated, "I retrained employees in new sales, merchandising, order handling, and billing routines. I attempted to increase efficiency and lower costs in every department. We also exerted every possible effort to increase sales volume. In the 24-month period beginning June, 1945, when certain types of merchandise were still in short supply, stock turnover was more rapid, and markups were higher than in 1953. We earned a net profit of $40,000 on sales of $1,600,000."

Mr. Corbett believed these results were mainly owing to his good friends who stood by him with generous credit lines and extra supplies of hard-to-get merchandise. Because of his contacts and record of increasing sales volume at National, he received preferential treatment from many manufacturers and salesmen.

Exhibit 7

LINTON COMPANY, INC.

Financial Data for Linton Company and Wholesale Grocery Trade

(In Per Cent)

Grocery Wholesalers with Asset Size $250,000 to $1,000,000

	Linton Co.	Industry		
Year..........................	Dec., 1953	1952	1951	1950
Number of statements analyzed...	.....	93	80	79
Assets:				
Cash.............................	13.72	5.25	5.45	4.22
Marketable securities.............	....	0.42	0.56	1.48
Receivables (net)................	21.84	21.13	20.05	21.16
Merchandise (net)...............	55.70	51.92	53.32	52.02
All other........................	....	1.33	1.18	0.90
Total current.................	91.26	80.05	80.56	79.78
Plant and equipment.............	6.94	14.23	13.05	13.45
All other........................	1.80	5.72	6.39	6.77
Total noncurrent...............	8.74	19.95	19.44	20.22
Total.....................	100.00	100.00	100.00	100.00
Liabilities:				
Due to banks....................	30.11	12.45	12.34	13.68
Due to trade....................	37.86	17.10	13.96	15.44
Federal income taxes.............	1.59	1.80	2.33	1.80
All other........................	1.46	7.05	7.93	5.42
Total current.................	71.02	38.40	36.56	36.34
Due to banks (long term).........	6.02	1.39	1.81	1.10
Other long-term debt.............	....	3.71	3.98	4.54
Total debt...................	77.04	43.50	42.35	41.98
Reserves........................	....	0.48	0.52	0.78
Net worth......................	22.96	56.02	57.13	57.24
Total.....................	100.00	100.00	100.00	100.00
Income data:				
Net sales........................	100.00	100.00	100.00	100.00
Cost of sales....................	92.20	92.24	91.51	91.42
Gross profit..................	7.80	7.76	8.49	8.58
All other expense (net)...........	7.48	7.02	7.24	7.42
Profit before taxes...........	0.32	0.74	1.25	1.16
Federal income taxes.............	0.17	0.34	0.54	0.39
Net profit or loss.............	0.15	0.40	0.71	0.77
Ratios:				
Current.........................	1.28	2.09	2.20	2.20
Net worth/total noncurrent assets.	2.80	2.81	2.94	2.83
Net worth/total debt.............	0.30	1.29	1.35	1.36
Sales/receivables................	27.22	26.13	24.93	21.88
Receivables turnover (days).......	13.00	14.00	14.00	16.00
Sales/merchandise................	10.67	10.64	9.38	8.90
Merchandise turnover (days)......	34.00	34.00	38.00	40.00
Sales/total noncurrent assets......	72.53	27.69	25.72	22.89
Sales/net worth.................	25.90	9.86	8.75	8.09
Profits/net worth...............	3.96	4.00	6.24	6.21
Sales/total assets................	5.94	5.52	5.00	4.63
Profits/total assets..............	0.91	2.24	3.57	3.55

Source: Adjusted data from Robert Morris Associates Statement Studies (1948 to 1952, inclusive).

In January, 1946, Mr. Robert Corbett received his discharge from the Navy and joined the company. He immediately assumed responsibility for sales and merchandising efforts.

During 1947 the merchandise heretofore hard to get became more plentiful. Pricing became more competitive, and the company cut margins to maintain volume. Selling effort and service were also increased with resultant extra costs. Profits as a percentage of sales declined over the next six years until in 1953 they were 0.15%.

During 1950 Mr. Frank Corbett succeeded, after considerable effort, in obtaining an exclusive distributorship for Apex Frozen Foods, a popular nationally advertised brand. Apex was a subsidiary of the Oshawa Foods Corporation, a large integrated manufacturer with a varied product line. Apex sold all its products through exclusive wholesale distributors until 1952, when it started selling direct to all grocery chains. Former exclusive distributors, however, continued to sell Apex products to all food retailers except chains, and they voluntarily continued to maintain territorial boundaries previously in effect.

"One of our biggest problems is whether we can hold out long enough financially to get the increased volume we need to cover costs and show a better profit," said Mr. Frank Corbett in August, 1953. "We have placed our emphasis on securing large new customers who run modern supermarket-type stores and this policy has kept us in an ever-widening vicious circle of getting more and more volume and at the same time, of needing to cut costs in order to sell these customers on a low-margin basis."

For 1953, Linton Company showed a net profit of $3,620 on sales of $2,369,262 (see Exhibit 5). "The low net profit of 0.15% for 1953 re-emphasizes the fact that our most pressing task is to get the business showing a better net profit," said Mr. Frank Corbett. (See Exhibits 7 and 8 for related industry statistics and information.)

CAPITAL SOURCES

Earnings from June, 1945, to June, 1947, enabled Mr. Frank Corbett to repay all the individuals from whom he had borrowed except those who agreed to transfer their loans to a preferred stock equity. In June, 1947, the capital structure of the business was changed to provide for three different classes of stock (see Exhibit 3). Common stock was owned 90% by Frank Corbett and 10% by Robert Corbett. Voting power was vested in the common unless the first and second preferred dividends were unpaid for two and three years respectively. The Cor-

Exhibit 8

LINTON COMPANY, INC.

Excerpts from Robert Morris Associates
1952 Issue of "Highlights of the Wholesale Grocery Trade"

SUMMARY

The year 1951 marked the sharpest decline in profitability for wholesale grocers in postwar years. Gross profit on sales decreased. Net profit on sales fell from .70% to .45%. Net profit on worth was reduced from 6.1% to 4.3%.

Inventory and receivables turnover rates increased with the increase in sales volume. Turnover of working capital improved without much detrimental change in the working capital position. This again emphasizes the importance of the increased sales volume. Again firms with extremely high turnovers in inventory and receivables earned a higher return on worth. Purchase discounts surpassed the profits before taxes. Percentage of purchase discounts to total purchases declined with an increase in size.

The industry is still characterized by long-established firms with seasoned management. Lower current ratios and a higher proportion of debt characterized the larger firms. Smaller firms showed higher equity. Percentage of wholesale grocers with outstanding bank loans at some time during the year fell from 95% to 93%. Peak borrowing was in the winter and early spring months. Effects of competitive conditions, higher cost of sales, and continued taxation were evidenced in the extremely low profits of the wholesale grocery trade during 1952.

INTRODUCTION

The wholesale grocery business unit is apt to be a one-man operation. The low margin on each product magnifies the importance of small savings in cost and slight improvements in turnover rates. This emphasis on detail may have a tendency to dim perspective on major policy decisions. Good organization and controlled delegation of authority are at a premium.

This study includes 229 companies most of whom are located in the North Central region of the United States. Of these, four are affiliated with a holding company engaged in food distribution; 54, 24%, are in a voluntary group; five are operated as a retailer-owned cooperative; 72, 31% of the sample, sell at cost plus a fixed markup or service charge fee. The information was so incomplete concerning the type of operation that it did not support special tabulation of financial patterns by these types.

Wholesale grocers are generally the most active group of bank borrowers.

The gross profit ratio is highly significant in this business. Oddly enough, a decrease in the ratio can be a signal of greater efficiency. An increase could result from speculation. Sometimes a company with sales that are declining (or at least increasing less rapidly than others) may show an increase in gross due to taking on lines that, while having a better gross, are harder to sell, develop slower turnover of inventory and carry credit problems. Outstanding companies in this business have had an almost steady decrease in gross profit, but the in-

Exhibit 8—Continued

crease in turnover of inventory and receivables has given as much or greater return on invested capital.

The ability of the wholesaler to survive depends upon his capacity to adjust to changing conditions in the performance of his basic economic function of distribution. The credit man should be on the alert for changes in individual companies and judge them in relation to competition. Credit guideposts of the wholesale grocery trade include: the age of the company and the tenure of the present management, the trend of the gross profit ratio, turnover of inventory, purchase discounts earned, receivable turnover, size of average receivable and area sold, aging of accounts and bad debt experience, turnover of working capital seasonal borrowing pattern, and comparative financial progress. In addition, it has been suggested that the credit man should be aware of transportation and selling costs, investments in or loans to retail outlets, changes in proportion of private brand sales and sales to public institutions.

MANAGEMENT

One clue to the quality of management is the age of the business. Another clue may be provided by the length of tenure of present management.

While not statistically provable, there is the belief in informed quarters that the going concern value of a wholesale grocery business is deteriorating. This follows from the rather unique characteristic of more modest but rather constant profits on capital. Under today's tax laws rarely will there be found a case of glamour from a capital gains standpoint. Hence, the capital value suffers from this limited market for transfer of ownership. As a creditor, however, the banker can be reassured on the liquidation value of inventory if it is well balanced and does not contain an important amount of own brand or other stock less advertised and marketable.

betts owned all the stock except $6,000 of the first preferred and $10,000 of the second preferred. Stock owned by outsiders was distributed among eight of their friends and relatives in amounts ranging from $300 to $6,000. For some of these people this investment was a substantial portion of their savings.

Increasing sales had substantially multiplied the need for working capital to enlarge inventories, carry receivables, and provide cash to enable the firm to take discounts. The main sources of funds were increased bank loans and trade credit.

BANKING RELATIONSHIP

In 1946, the original line of credit was increased from $50,000 to $75,000. In 1947, the bank that granted this line merged with another bank, which subsequently withdrew from the Linton arrangement and referred Mr. Corbett to a third bank. Upon reviewing the situation this bank's officers stated that they did not wish to take over the Linton line. They referred Mr. Corbett to Mr. Eaton, vice-president and loaning officer of the North West Bank. After investigating Mr. Corbett's case, Mr. Eaton agreed to have the $75,000 line of credit transferred to the North West Bank. The line of credit, which had gone as high as $160,-000, stood at $120,000 as of April, 1954.

FIELD WAREHOUSING ARRANGEMENT

The bank loan was secured by a field warehousing arrangement involving the entire grocery inventory. Ordinarily warehouse receipts were accepted as collateral by the North West Bank only when they were issued by a bonded warehouse in which the merchandise was clearly marked, segregated, and inventoried. Merchandise was withdrawable from the warehouse only on repayment of the warehouse receipts[1] which had been assigned to the bank as security. Because of the increased labor and paper work entailed in handling merchandise under an ordinary field warehousing arrangement, Mr. Frank Corbett and Mr. Eaton worked out what Mr. Corbett said was a unique system they called "bulk field warehousing." Under this arrangement, which had been in effect since 1947, the Cornwall Warehousing Corporation, a warehouse service organization, was engaged by the bank to be responsible for the segregation, storage, and inspection of the pledged goods,[2] which were all kept in the Linton warehouse. Two Linton employees were placed in the employ of the Cornwall company. One was a warehouse worker, who padlocked all the doors every night; the other worked in the office and checked the IBM inventory system report on the total merchandise. The Linton Company reimbursed the Cornwall company for the salaries of these two men.

Under the warehousing agreement Linton was allowed a shipping leeway of 10,000 case units amounting to a $45,000 weekly volume. The office manager examined the IBM records of the units shipped each

---

[1] For example, if 10,000 cases of salmon valued at $5 per case were put in a field warehouse and the bank specified a margin of 25% on the loan, the company would be able to borrow $37,000 on the $50,000 worth of salmon kept as security by the bank. The warehouse manager would then, in effect, sell the salmon back to the wholesaler or grocer for $3.75 per case. In this manner the bank lent the grocer funds to pay for inventory and the grocer repaid the bank in proportion as he drew on the inventory.

[2] Large signs in the warehouse stated, "The merchandise in this warehouse is the property of the Cornwall Warehousing Corporation." Stickers on the merchandise also identified it as belonging to the Cornwall Warehousing Corporation. The company padlocked all the doors of the warehouse every night as required by law. In accordance with the bank's insurance requirements, a sprinkler system had been installed throughout the office and warehouse.

day to make sure that the company was not shipping more than the quota allowed. Every Friday a special report of the total units shipped and received daily for the past week was sent to the bank and the warehousing company.

"Mr. Eaton understands our problem and is a real help in managing our financial situation," stated Mr. Corbett. "However, he is anxious about the loan and has to justify the amount to the bank's board, which seems to be putting pressure on him to get out of the loan so that the money can be lent to a more profitable business under a simpler and more secure collateral arrangement. I don't know what I would do if the loan were called."

"Our long-term objective," said Mr. Corbett, "is to pay the bank loan off and own the business free of debt."

SUPPLIER CREDIT RELATIONS

In Mr. Corbett's opinion Linton received more generous credit accommodations than the average grocery wholesaler. The Oshawa Food Company, for example, extended $45,000 and $25,000 lines of credit on Apex frozen foods and grocery items respectively.

Supplier's credit departments ordinarily checked closely on wholesalers' financial conditions and required certified copies of all financial reports. Grocery manufacturers generally maintained strict terms of 2% discount 10 days from invoice date, net 30 days, except in unusual situations. The nondiscounting of an invoice by a wholesaler was a serious indication of financial weakness. When an invoice was not paid within 30 days, grocery manufacturers had been known to cancel all credit and place the wholesaler on a cash-payment basis. Terms on frozen foods were typically net 10 days. Mr. Corbett stated that the average wholesaler was considered to have made par on discounts if he averaged 1.5% of grocery purchases.

Since cash discounts were one of the most important sources of "income" or cost savings to a grocery wholesaler, it was vital that the company take discounts. "We've been in a few jams in the past when our cash was so low we weren't able to take discounts," said Mr. Corbett.

POSSIBLE SOURCES OF CAPITAL

To obtain more permanent capital Mr. Frank Corbett was investigating the possibility of a sale and lease-back arrangement on the warehouse and office building. Although this building was mortgaged for $26,000, he thought it could be sold for $70,000 to $80,000, which would give the company additional capital amounting to approximately $50,000. It had been appraised at $165,000 by an engineering consultant in February, 1953, and was insured for $130,000.

The Corbetts thought they might be able to sell more stock to some of their friends and relatives but had not yet approached anyone in this matter. "We both have too much pride to ask any of our friends or relatives for money. Possibly some of them could help us, but this is about the fastest way I know to lose their friendship," said Mr. Frank Corbett.

SALES

Mr. Corbett stated that grocery wholesaling was extremely competitive. Brand merchandise was the same no matter which wholesaler sold it, and a price difference of only a few cents on a $100 purchase would cause a retailer to change suppliers unless he received some important service for the additional cost. "There are about 25 dry grocery wholesalers, 3 frozen-foods wholesalers, and 3 wholesalers carrying both lines that compete with us in some area of our territory," said Mr. Corbett.

"In order to keep our product line up to date with the retailer's needs," said Mr. Corbett, "we usually take on about 20 new items each month and drop 10 to 15 old ones. Most of these changes are in package sizes, but we do add some new products every month. In 1954, new products seem to have been mostly baking mixes and drug items. All new products are taken on an experimental basis and continued permanently only if results warrant."

"Private labels," stated Mr. Corbett, "are 'a thing of the past' because advertising has made the consumer want national brand names. Fifteen years ago Linton made a good profit on private brands because the firm was able to sell at a price differential of $2 or $3 a case. Now, because of increased costs for small manufacturers and cost savings by large-volume producers, we are able to undercut name brands by only 25 to 30 cents per case of 24 cans. When figured on a per can basis, the private-brand price differential has fallen so much it can't overcome name-brand appeal."

Because of limited working capital Linton concentrated its sales efforts on customers who were able to pay on short terms, rather than on the type of retailer who required extended credit. The latter usually purchased in small quantities and could be charged higher prices, stated Mr. Corbett.

In addition to Mr. Robert Corbett, who covered 25 of the best accounts, the company had 2 other grocery salesmen. Number and size of accounts covered by each are shown in Exhibit 9. There were also 4 frozen-food salesmen who were order takers only and were paid on a salary-plus-bonus basis.

A policy of reduction on the number of retail accounts and salesmen began in 1952 as the result of a survey which showed that 80% of sales volume came from less than 20% of the customers. Since this survey also showed that most customers split their purchases between two or three different wholesalers, the Corbetts concluded that they could increase volume and cut cost by dropping their smaller accounts and trying to obtain a larger percentage of their large customers' business. The total number of customers had been reduced from about 700 to 405 between September, 1952, and July, 1953. The company had also reduced the number of grocery salesmen from 6 to 2 in the same period. The objective was to cut back further to 60 customers who without a salesman's call would make purchases amounting to at least $500 weekly by mail or phone.

The 1952 customer survey was made as a preliminary study before Linton initiated a "cost plus 3, plus 9" plan under contract with the Nation-Wide voluntary chain of wholesale and retail grocery outlets. Under the Nation-Wide plan prices to selected retail customers were cost plus freight in before discounts, plus a 3% markup and a flat $9 weekly service charge, f.o.b. Linton's warehouse. There was in addition a transportation fee of 4 cents a case. For example, if a retailer bought $1,000 worth of merchandise weekly, he would pay $30 for markup plus the $9 service fee, or a total of $39 plus transportation and the basic cost of merchandise. For accounts of $300 and $1,000 weekly volume, this plan gave a markup of approximately 6% and 3.9%, respectively. The objectives of the plan were to effect an increase in the size of accounts and attract larger ones on which the company could operate profitably with a much smaller margin. Sales and delivery expenses on "cost plus 3, plus 9" business were reduced because the customer ordered weekly on an order sheet without a salesman calling. Also, the number of deliveries was set at one per week plus a limited number of emergency deliveries. A policy of a $100 minimum order for each delivery was strictly enforced under the plan. "Cost plus 3, plus 9" customers paid for merchandise by sending signed "blank" checks with each order.

The Nation-Wide organization was one of the oldest voluntary

Exhibit 9

LINTON COMPANY, INC.

Grocery* Customer Analysis—September, 1953

VOLUME OF PURCHASE

Class	Purchases per Week
A+	$300 or over
A	$100 to $300
B	$ 50 to $100
C	$ 25 to $ 50
D	$ 15 to $ 25
E	Under $15

SALESMAN	NUMBER OF CUSTOMERS ON BOOKS	TOTAL SALES	CLASS A+			CLASS A			CLASS B			CLASS C			CLASS D			CLASS E		
			Number	Per Cent	Approximate Weekly Volume	Number	Per Cent	Approximate Weekly Volume	Number	Per Cent	Approximate Weekly Volume	Number	Per Cent	Approximate Weekly Volume	Number	Per Cent	Approximate Weekly Volume	Number	Per Cent	Approximate Weekly Volume
Office.................	178	$ 5,009	2	1%	$ 700	6	3%	$1,200	11	6%	$ 825	13	7%	$ 494	33	18%	$660	113	65%	$1,130
Cost + 3 + 9†.........	25	8,000	20	80	7,000	5	20	1,000	...	...	...	...	...	...	...	...	...	...	...	...
W. F. Keeler.........	92	7,736	3	3	1,050	16	17	3,200	28	30	2,100	32	35	1,216	5	5	80	9	10	90
D. C. Manio.........	110	9,768	4	4	1,400	22	20	4,400	32	29	2,400	36	32	1,368	4	4	80	12	11	120
	405	$30,513	29	7%	$10,150	49	12	$9,800	71	18%	$5,325	81	20%	$3,078	41	10%	$820	134	33%	$1,340

* Frozen-food customer analysis not available.

† Sold on the basis of a weekly order sheet mailed or phoned to the office.

Source: Company records.

wholesaler-retailer co-operative groups. Under the Nation-Wide plan selected wholesalers were granted a franchise for an exclusive territory. Each wholesaler paid the Nation-Wide organization a fee based on annual sales volume. The wholesaler granted local grocery stores a retail franchise in the Nation-Wide Food Store Service Fee Plan.

Under the Nation-Wide contract with the retailer Linton agreed: to allow the retailer the use of Nation-Wide store signs and insignia; to service the retailer's merchandise needs satisfactorily; to supervise retailer merchandising efforts; to supply advertising material; to assist in planning store layout; to educate and train retail store personnel by means of letters, bulletins, and meetings; and to furnish store signs on a rental basis. In return the retailer agreed: to pay for merchandise on Linton's terms; to pay for other services and material on a nominal fee basis; to order merchandise on a weekly basis; and to co-operate in advertising and merchandising plans, including local newspaper advertising.

Since joining the organization Linton had succeeded in getting 25 large independent supermarket accounts on this plan. "Naturally," said Mr. Corbett, "we signed up our best and most co-operative customers first, and from now on it undoubtedly will be much harder to get additional customers on the "cost plus 3, plus 9" plan. Mr. Robert Corbett stated that he was planning to retrain the two remaining grocery salesmen as sales supervisors under the Nation-Wide sales plan. Their main job then would be to check displays, floor planning, and other merchandising aspects of the stores on the "cost plus 3, plus 9" plan.

Exhibit 9 shows an analysis of retail customers by volume of purchases according to the company's IBM records as of September 20, 1953.

Exhibit 10 shows a customer breakdown by frequency of purchase as of September 20, 1953. From this exhibit it can be seen that customers who, according to Mr. Corbett, were practically valueless made up 50% of the customer list. Mr. Corbett stated that extra profits could be made if invoicing, delivery, selling, and other services, which were of a "roughly fixed-cost nature" for each customer, could be eliminated for this 50% of Linton outlets. Nevertheless, there were important practical difficulties in dropping the smaller customers, stated Mr. Corbett. A "D" or "E" customer was often in the same vicinity as an "A" or "A plus" customer, and under these circumstances a salesman could call and delivery could be made to handle the business at practically no additional cost.

Exhibit 10

LINTON COMPANY, INC.

Grocery Customer Analysis by Frequency of Purchase—1953

Mr. Frank Corbett's Classifications	Number of Customers	Percentage of Customers
Customers who all buy once a week ("Cost + 3 + 9").	25	6%
Regular customers who buy every week.	89	22
Buy regularly at least twice a month.	76	19
Buy regularly once a month.	27	7
Buy irregularly less than once a month— practically no value.	72	18
Buy irregularly and very seldom—hardly worthy of the name "customer".	116	28
Totals.	405	100%

Source: Company IBM records.

Mr. Frank Corbett went over an IBM sales analysis summary sheet with each of the salesmen every Friday afternoon. This sheet listed customers by name, address, amount of sales for the week, and amounts owed to the company. Except for "cost plus 3, plus 9" customers, the company sold to retail outlets on a net 7-day basis. Institutions were allowed net 30-day terms. The average collection period of accounts receivable had been kept down to approximately 15 days through enforcement of a strict credit policy, stated Mr. Corbett.

Because of the small net profit, Mr. Frank Corbett had been searching for some plan to increase sales volume over what he called the "break-even point" which he believed was $3,500,000 in October, 1953. He thought that exceeding this volume would make the difference between a substantial net profit and the marginal profits the company was earning.

Mr. Robert Corbett had made the suggestion of trying to increase profits by raising markup on all products 1%. This action was not feasible, Mr. Frank Corbett said, because such an increase would price many products out of competition. He stated, however, that they were always trying to raise total markup by increasing the margin on some items as much as 3% and edging it up possibly ½ of 1% even on competitive staple items. Mr. Frank Corbett stated that he and his brother studied all markup and turnover ratios regularly to eliminate slow-moving or low-profit products.

The 1953 net profit proved, said Mr. Frank Corbett, the need for a sales increase in the more profitable large-volume customers. He estimated that, if the company could sell an extra $2,000 weekly in frozen foods at only 5% gross margin, instead of the regular 10%, gross income would increase $100 per week. If $5,000 extra grocery volume could be sold at 2% instead of the regular 6%, there would be an additional $100 gross margin, or a total of $200 per week. Mr. Corbett said that the cost of the total additional volume could not possibly exceed $100 per week. This meant that the $7,000 extra weekly volume would give an additional net profit before taxes of $5,200.

The foregoing line of reasoning caused Mr. Corbett to consider whether the company should enter into a *sub rosa* agreement with one or two large independent supermarkets. Under such an agreement the supermarket would buy in large volume at a lower price than regular customers. Because this type of supermarket did a heavy volume, Mr. Frank Corbett thought his company might possibly sell as much as $15,000 a week to any one of them. He thought that within 10 miles of the warehouse there were seven or eight stores of this type that might be agreeable to such an arrangement. Many wholesalers, he said, were turning to this expedient of offering a price advantage to a few large independent supermarkets to induce them to buy in large volume that could be handled at a low cost, while at the same time they tried to maintain, and break even on, sales to their regular customers to whom they sold on their usual terms. Thus these wholesalers were able to increase sales over the break-even point and realize an added profit.

Because a wholesaler was ultimately dependent on retailers, Mr. Frank Corbett was thinking of eventually entering the retail business by owning or leasing a chain of supermarkets. In order to do this, the company would have to enlarge its facilities to handle perishables, dairy products, health and beauty aids, and other items formerly carried mainly by drugstores. A meat department would also be necessary. Mr. Corbett stated that he and his brother did not know the meat business, and that in five to ten years they might be in a position to hire a man who knew this business.

WAREHOUSE AND OFFICE FACILITIES

Grocery warehouse and office space in Elgin totaled 21,000 square feet on three floors (see Exhibit 11). Because the Elgin warehouse had no cold storage, Linton rented a frozen-food warehouse, 7,000 square feet in area. In March, 1954, every available inch of warehouse and office space was being used for storage. Even in the garage cases of merchandise were stacked to the ceiling. "To attain sales of $4,000,000,

Exhibit 11

LINTON COMPANY, INC.

Plan of Elgin Warehouse and Offices

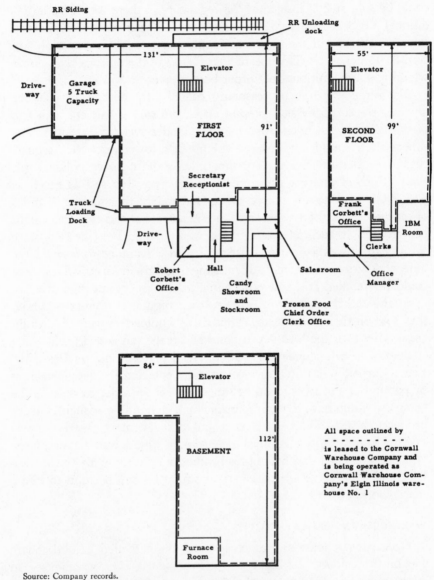

Source: Company records.

which is our immediate goal, we definitely need extra space," Mr. Corbett said. "In addition, we are severely hampered by the multiple-story building, which prevents the use of a modern conveyor system, lift trucks, or other new techniques of merchandise-handling. At present we are handling merchandise five or six times before it reaches a customer, whereas competitors handle their merchandise only two or three times on the average." Mr. Corbett estimated that warehouse salaries could be cut by $7,500 annually if space were available to use more modern methods. "This extra salary cost is a direct drain on profits," he said.

Mr. Corbett had recently asked a carpenter to estimate the cost of building an additional 3,000 square feet of warehouse space adjoining the present building. In his opinion, however, what the company actually needed was a one-floor warehouse of at least 35,000 square feet in area. Mr. Corbett had seen estimates of $5 per square foot to build an ordinary cement-block building without offices. "Eventually," he said, "we wish to sell the building and move."

"The present location," Mr. Corbett stated, "is not the best possible in 1954 because the center of the company's market area has shifted toward the South. On goods sold south or west of Chicago there is a double haul because we have to transfer nearly all merchandise from Chicago, which is the lake port and shipping terminal, to Elgin and then back again." Mr. Frank Corbett thought the best location would be in Chicago or possibly Springdale, where the frozen-food warehouse was located.

Because of the company's restricted financial position and the risk of losing volume if the business were moved, Mr. Frank Corbett thought the bank would not allow a move until the walls were actually "bulging." He considered the move at least five years away and was not looking for another building at present. He was reluctant to talk to Mr. Eaton on this subject.

Lack of space and capital made it impossible for the company to add to its line the meats, perishables, or beauty items[3] which were becoming increasingly a necessity to a wholesaler serving the large supermarket-type store. Candy products and various sundries, however, had been added to fill out the line during the previous year.

OFFICE OPERATION

The office staff handled all the paper work necessary in processing accounts payable, invoicing, collections, and general accounting.

In 1947 the company began to change its accounting operation to IBM machines. Inventory accounting was the first to be put on IBM

---

[3] Items such as deodorants, lipsticks, cold creams, lotions, etc.

and it required one and one-half years to get the new system functioning smoothly. Sales and invoicing were put on IBM in 1950, and in the
spring of 1953 the accounts receivable tabulation for frozen foods was
added. The frozen-food receivables tabulation had worked out so well
that in July, 1953, the company changed grocery receivables accounting to IBM. When the transition from the old manual system of bookkeeping to IBM had been completed, five people would be able to do
the work that six were previously doing. Moreover, because all accounting personnel would be trained on all IBM operations, jobs would be
interchangeable and the company would not have to keep an extra
worker to allow for absences. When the switch to IBM was complete,
over one-third more work could be handled in the office without addition to the present staff, stated Mr. Frank Corbett, since the company
was "practically on a minimum-charge basis" with respect to expenses
for IBM operation. Commenting further on the company operations in
general, Mr. Corbett stated, in August, 1953, "We have just reached
the break-even point. Right now our volume just gets rid of cost. With
a higher volume and the same expense we'll be making a better profit."

Weekly office payroll included Mr. Davis, office manager, at $75, a
billing clerk working for the Cornwall warehouse company at $52, two
IBM girls at $47 each, and two clerks at $40 each.

CONTROL

In an effort to find where he could save on cost to increase profits,
Mr. Corbett had studied the cost breakdowns on the operating statements carefully. He thought that costs could not be lowered appreciably
and that an increase in volume was necessary. "I am no longer interested in percentages," he said, "because the trend in the grocery business
is to take a lower profit percentage on a higher volume. If we strive for
lower margins and higher volume, competitors in the territory would
be squeezed out," he stated. As volume increased, Mr. Corbett said,
overhead expenses became less in proportion, and the company could
cut costs still more and therefore get a higher volume, which ultimately
meant more profit.

ORGANIZATION

As shown in Exhibit 12, Mr. Frank Corbett, the president and Mr.
Robert Corbett, vice-president and sales manager, shared the management function of the business. Each could handle the other's job without difficulty; but, Mr. Frank Corbett stated, his brother took more of

Exhibit 12

LINTON COMPANY, INC.

Organization Chart

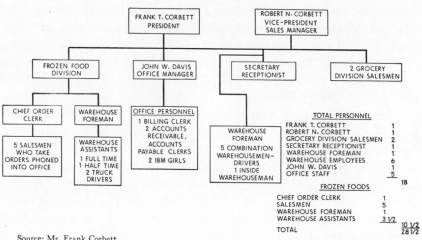

Source: Mr. Frank Corbett.

the responsibility for the grocery division. Mr. Robert Corbett did most of the grocery purchasing and spent a good deal of his time on grocery sales, warehousing, and delivery operations. Mr. Frank Corbett spent a large amount of his time supervising the office staff that handled payments and billing. Mr. Frank Corbett also took the major responsibility for the frozen-foods division. Under him were the chief frozen-food order clerk, the frozen-food warehouse foreman, two warehouse assistants and two truck drivers who also worked in this division. Although each brother spent most of his time on these respective duties, each usually knew what the other was doing and they talked over problems many times a day.

The office manager, Mr. John W. Davis, age forty-two, was with the company when Mr. Frank Corbett bought it. Under Mr. Corbett's almost constant supervision he was responsible for seeing that the routine payment and invoicing work was done by the office staff.

"If he or his brother were taken from the business suddenly," Mr. Frank Corbett stated, "one of the older warehouse hands could come in and perform most of the jobs except buying." This he thought could be done only by himself or Robert. He said that there were "three or four warehouse men who knew the business well." They had been trained under Mr. Linton. "The organization would be capable of carrying on adequately if either Bob or I had to leave for some time," said Mr. Corbett.

In 1953 the board of directors was composed of Frank and Robert Corbett and Mr. Davis. It functioned, said Mr. Corbett, in name only. He wanted to ask both Mr. Eaton and Mr. Kahn to serve on the board but hesitated because he thought it might take too much of their time. "There is also the question of whether they would consider it an honor to be asked to serve on our board and whether they could do anything for us at present," he stated.

DUTIES OF MR. FRANK CORBETT

"The first thing I do every morning, usually between 8:00 A.M. and 8:15 A.M., is to talk with Mr. Davis to see what his schedule is for the day," said Mr. Frank Corbett. "I check back several times each day to see what the office staff is doing and whether payments and billing are being kept up to date. I also check the IBM operators once or twice a day to make sure they are not falling behind. Every morning I go over credit accounts with Mr. Davis to see that payments are up to date. I often phone overdue accounts myself to put pressure on them to pay bills. Another major aspect of my work is scheduling the payment of all bills. Mr. Davis might be able to do this, but I don't let him because it requires my judgment to decide which bills should be paid quickly and which can go for two or three days longer. I keep a running summary of all receipts and disbursements so that I know what the bank balance is at any time during the day. This helps avoid overdrawing our account." In handling this task Mr. Corbett examined with Mr. Davis all incoming invoices, checks from customers, and adding-machine tapes of cash receipts two or three times each day. Mr. Corbett was also in charge of payroll, an activity which took four or five hours of his time each week. He stated that about 30% of his time was spent on careful control of the credit and financial aspects of the business. This control was necessary, he said, because of the company's lack of working capital. In conference with his brother he made daily checks on turnover, markup, and pricing statistics, and they discussed markup and turnover ratios and any complaints received on pricing, delivery, or quality of the merchandise.

He also checked with the frozen-foods chief order clerk to keep posted on total sales and sales by each salesman. In the frozen-foods division, Mr. Frank Corbett set prices and handled all the purchasing except for basic staple items, on which the chief order clerk could purchase up to seven days' supply in advance. He received two calls a day from each of the salesmen regarding complaints, questions, and prices. He often talked to salesmen in the office regarding complaints or other matters. He also supervised the frozen-food warehouse man and with him checked the drivers' routes and mileage, since the frozen-food drivers were paid by mileage. He received visits from customers and suppliers, averaging about five a day.

Mr. Frank Corbett very seldom had time to work on even a 10-minute job straight through until it was finished and was nearly always working on two or three problems at the same time. His secretary counted 72 telephone calls that he handled in one day from 8:30 A.M. to 5:00 P.M.

Mr. Frank Corbett handled the company's bank relationship and worked with the auditors. He left the office at about 6:00 P.M. daily except for one or two nights a week when he worked until 11:30 P.M. or 12:00 midnight. Since the regular help left at 5:00 P.M., he used the time from 5:00 to 6:00 to finish odd jobs and talk over the events of the day with his brother. He and Robert both came in every Saturday morning to discuss general policy questions and finish up work they had not been able to do during the week.

DUTIES OF MR. ROBERT N. CORBETT

Mr. Robert Corbett came to work every morning at 6:00 A.M. His first job was to pick up merchandise invoices that had come in the previous day and plan the early morning Chicago pickup trips by the company's trucks.[4] About 7:00 A.M. the shipper came to work and together they planned the truck routes for the day and attended to the paper work of filling orders. After the truck routing was started, Mr. Robert Corbett looked over the mail and checked the previous day's cash-and-carry sales. As grocery sales manager he dealt with problems of the grocery salesmen and customer complaints, except those that were referred to his brother. He also was responsible for the Nation-Wide "cost plus 3, plus 9" program. He passed on customers brought into the program and handled all details and problems arising from it. On Mondays and Tuesdays, which were the heaviest days of the week for telephone orders, he helped take telephone orders. Two days a week he spent on the road handling directly 25 of the company's biggest-volume customers. He set all grocery-division prices and markups and kept customers and salesmen posted on changes. He worked closely with the grocery-warehouse foremen to make sure that orders were being shipped promptly and that stock was being moved out quickly.

---

[4] By doing its own trucking from Chicago to Elgin, the company saved approximately $40 per week on the haulage of goods from Chicago warehouses to Elgin.

On Wednesdays from 9:00 to 11:00 A.M. and from 1:00 to 3:00 P.M., he interviewed suppliers' salesmen and did the buying. Most afternoons were spent working on promotion plans and making up advertisements for retailers. He also planned the company's bulletin, a small newspaper that under the Nation-Wide heading was sent to the Nation-Wide Plan retailers.

"I like working the long hours and often stay at the office until 11:00 P.M.," said Mr. Robert Corbett. "I have done it all my life and find it thoroughly enjoyable. This is the usual thing in the wholesale grocery business and many of our competitors do the same. It is nothing to stay late and finish up the work that hasn't been done when there aren't enough hours in the day." Mr. Frank Corbett stated that "Bob was into everything" in some way, that he was generally the first one in the office every morning and the last out every night. He handled a minimum of 50 incoming phone calls each day and made about 25 himself to handle the business he was responsible for.

. . . .

Following are two incidents which the case writer recorded in his notes on the Linton Company:

A

After receiving his mail one morning in March, 1954, Mr. Frank Corbett hurriedly called his brother Robert into his office. The following conversation then took place:

FRANK CORBETT: Bob, here's a check for $7,000 from Tom Kahn. It just came through the mail. He wants this much of our first preferred stock.

ROBERT CORBETT: Well, that's good news! But what are we going to do with it? (*Points to the check.*)

FRANK CORBETT: Well. . . .

ROBERT CORBETT: How about buying some of that frozen broccoli? We could make an extra two cents a package on it because the price is going up again next week. We could take 90 cases,[5] and that would be . . . let's see (*figures on a piece of paper*) . . . an inventory profit of $43.20. On second thought, Frank, don't you think we should just slap this in the bank?

FRANK CORBETT: Well . . . yes, I guess we should, but I was talking to the

---

[5] A case of frozen broccoli contained 24 packages and cost Linton $2.91. The company's policy was to pass cost increases on to customers one week after the manufacturer changed his price regardless of what the company paid for the merchandise it already had in inventory when the price increase was announced. Since inventories purchased at the old price were seldom sold out during the week the company made an "inventory profit" on the remaining stock purchased at the lower price.

Federal Foods salesman on the phone this morning, and three of their canned baby foods are going up 10 cents a case tomorrow. If we ordered today, we could take 50 cases of each.

ROBERT CORBETT: Wait just a minute till I check the IBM clerk to see what we have on hand. (*Phones clerk regarding stock on hand.*) We've already got plenty of broccoli and baby foods in stock so this would all be extra.

FRANK CORBETT: Well, we don't have much space to put it in, but I hate to pass this up. It's the easiest way there is to make money in this business!

ROBERT CORBETT: Say, that's my phone, and I've got to get right over to Silver's. Why don't we talk this over at lunch?

FRANK CORBETT: Okay, see you then!

The sale of $7,000 of the Linton Company's first preferred stock to Mr. Kahn had been accomplished as a result of a long talk about the business that Mr. Frank Corbett had with Mr. Kahn during a game of golf in Florida earlier in the winter.

"I explained the difficulties we were having because of our lack of capital, and Tom offered to help us out to this extent. He has been a good friend to Bob and me for many years now, and this probably was an important factor in his risking $7,000 in our business," said Mr. Corbett. Mr. Kahn had interests in several businesses and owned a large office building in Chicago. He was considered by both the Corbetts to be a very astute businessman.

. . . .

B

In April, 1954, Mr. Robert Corbett received the following letter at his home:

PATTERSON FOODS, INC.[6]

Office of the President

April 5, 1954

PERSONAL - CONFIDENTIAL

Mr. Robert N. Corbett
732 Irving Drive
Elgin, Illinois

DEAR MR. CORBETT:

In our program of investigating possible candidates for the newly created executive position of merchandising manager in the Ready-Mix division of

---

[6] The Patterson Foods Company was one of the nation's largest grocery product manufacturers with sales over $100,000,000 annually.

our company your name has been recommended to me from several sources in the grocery trade. In this regard I am wondering if you would be interested in meeting with me and several other members of our management sometime before Friday, April 23, to discuss the possibility of your joining our company in this capacity.

The position of merchandising manager of the Ready-Mix division has been created as a result of a definite need for someone to assume responsibility for the combination of sales promotion and advertising efforts at the wholesaler and retailer levels of our business.

From inquiries made in our own organization and other trade sources we feel that your background and experience in the grocery business are ideally suited to the requirements of this position.

We expect that this position would lead, in a short time, to a top-management position in the marketing department of our business.

We are prepared to offer you a salary in the five-figure bracket with a substantial increase over your present earnings.

May we hear from you on this?

> Sincerely,
> /s/ JEFFREY C. ROBBINS
> *President*

When he came to work the next morning, Mr. Robert Corbett showed the letter to his brother Frank. After Frank had read and studied the letter for several minutes, the following conversation took place:

FRANK CORBETT: That's some letter, Bob! What do you think of it?

ROBERT CORBETT: Well, my first reaction was "no"! We've put so much time, effort, and money into this business that now it seems like part of us . . . (*pause*).

FRANK CORBETT: Sure.

ROBERT CORBETT: I would never pull out if I didn't think that would be the best move in the long run for you and me and the business. But you know, Frank, I got to thinking about the possibilities here for you if I took this job. You could take over sales, let Davis take over responsibilities for the office and bank balances, break in Bill or Tony on purchasing, and run the business by yourself. Without my salary and expenses, profit would take a real jump.

FRANK CORBETT: You're saying this is really a one-boss business? And that I could make more. . . .

ROBERT CORBETT: I don't know. I'm really just thinking out loud—but what do you say? I should reply to this letter sometime in the next day or two at the most. I could get enthusiastic about this job (*points to letter*), but if we could make out better in the long run together here I'd sooner stay put. What do you think?

Robbins, Inc.

IN DECEMBER, 1966, Mr. Robert Kurtz became the new general manager of Robbins, Inc., a firm operating in the electrical equipment field. In 1966, it was estimated, Robbins' sales were $100 million and the enterprise employed over 2,500 people.

Robbins, Inc., had recently been purchased by a group of wealthy investors. In view of their other varied business interests, the investing group planned to operate Robbins as a separate, independent company. Mr. Kurtz was given complete responsibility for the direction of Robbins' affairs. He had achieved an excellent reputation among industrialists as a manager capable of dealing with difficult business problems, and the investors had agreed that he was to have a free hand to make whatever changes he thought necessary to improve the company's "obviously unsatisfactory" profit performance.

Robbins manufactured and sold electrical equipment for industrial and consumer use. Its industrial products included a wide variety of standard and specialty motors. The company had achieved an excellent reputation for engineering design work. Over the years its legal staff had built up an imposing number of patents protecting improvements created by company engineers. In the consumer products line, the firm manufactured and sold a line of small "traffic" household appliances for the American and export markets.

In recent years company sales had increased substantially but profits had gradually declined to a point where only a very small profit was anticipated for 1966. While industrial products had been extremely profitable in early postwar years, the competitive situation had changed substantially in the early 1960's. Consumer appliance operations varied from early losses to small profit contributions in 1964 through 1966. Robbins was encountering increasing competition for its appliances from full-line companies, e.g., Sunbeam. Despite this, Mr. Kurtz believed that in the long run the consumer appliance area would become the most important and profitable part of the firm's business. He hoped to add new appliance items as rapidly as production and marketing facilities permitted.

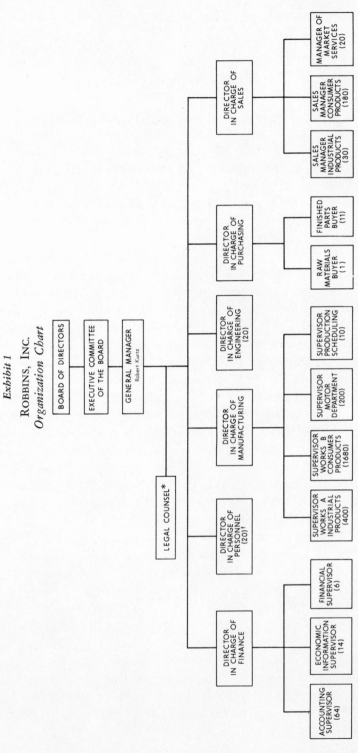

Exhibit 1

ROBBINS, INC.

Organization Chart

BOARD OF DIRECTORS

EXECUTIVE COMMITTEE OF THE BOARD

GENERAL MANAGER
Robert Kurtz

LEGAL COUNSEL*

DIRECTOR IN CHARGE OF FINANCE

DIRECTOR IN CHARGE OF PERSONNEL (20)†

DIRECTOR IN CHARGE OF MANUFACTURING

DIRECTOR IN CHARGE OF ENGINEERING (20)

DIRECTOR IN CHARGE OF PURCHASING

DIRECTOR IN CHARGE OF SALES

ACCOUNTING SUPERVISOR (64)

ECONOMIC INFORMATION SUPERVISOR (14)

FINANCIAL SUPERVISOR (6)

SUPERVISOR WORKS A INDUSTRIAL PRODUCTS (400)

SUPERVISOR WORKS B CONSUMER PRODUCTS (1680)

SUPERVISOR MOTOR DEPARTMENT (200)

SUPERVISOR PRODUCTION SCHEDULING (10)

RAW MATERIALS BUYER (1)

FINISHED PARTS BUYER (11)

SALES MANAGER INDUSTRIAL PRODUCTS (30)

SALES MANAGER CONSUMER PRODUCTS (180)

MANAGER OF MARKET SERVICES (20)

* Full-time legal counsel.
Figures in parentheses indicate number of staff and/or employees.

In the manufacture of these products, Robbins purchased substantial quantities of two raw materials ($16 million in 1966). These raw materials were subject to substantial price fluctuations and it was important for Robbins to buy at "the right time and price."

The new owners of Robbins requested that Mr. Kurtz prepare salary recommendations, for board consideration, in December, 1966. His recommendations were to cover the top 20 executives in the company including himself. Knowing the backgrounds of the new owners, Mr. Kurtz knew he would have to be able to defend his assignments of salary to specific jobs. He also knew that the new owners had been critical of the "haphazard way" in which salary payments had been made by the former general manager.

To carry out this assignment, Mr. Kurtz asked the member of the personnel department in charge of the executive payroll for the amount paid in salaries to the top 20 managers of the firm in the year 1966. This sum amounted to $860,000. He excluded individual bonus payments and incidental privileges such as company-furnished cars. Bonus payments for the Robbins management group had declined steadily during the past four years, and salary payments were now the important element in the firm's compensation program.

He then prepared to assign funds from this "common pool" to individual jobs in the organization. Mr. Kurtz realized that, after he had determined an ideal salary structure, he would have to modify his assignments on the basis of historical precedent as well as other factors. But he believed that the process of allocating the total salary fund to individual jobs, without prejudice of past history, would help him in thinking through the factors that should influence salary payments.

Exhibit 1 charts the organization of Robbins, Inc.

Research, Inc.

IN EARLY 1958 Research, Inc., commonly referred to as Searchco, with home offices in Waltham, Massachusetts, and three branch offices in the Northeast, was primarily engaged in research and development, largely under government contract. Commercial business—mainly a limited line of gamma radiography equipment[1] together with some research and development for commercial concerns—accounted for about 8.2% of the approximately $2.2 million gross income for 1957. Another 7.1% of gross income came from partly owned subsidiaries working on company-developed electrical power supply and photographic products. (See Exhibits 1 and 2 for selected financial data.)

In 1958 the company, founded in 1951, employed about 190 people, 70 of whom were administrative, the rest technical. The latter, about one-fourth of whom held Ph.D.'s, were trained and experienced in such fields as operations research, physics, chemistry, nucleonics, electronics, and applied mechanics. In its six-year history, however, the company had specialized in operations research. A layman's definition of this term was provided by one company scientist as follows:

> Operations research is an analytical process in which several people representing several different scientific disciplines get together to solve a problem They may spend some time defining the problem in a way they can handle it, determining the kinds of data they will need, and selecting the best way or ways of analyzing these data. The big advantage of operations research lies in the interdisciplinary talents it brings to the problem. A physicist, for example, can see the limitations of the way an electronics engineer would usually approach the problem, and vice versa. Between them, they should be able to devise a better way of solving a particular problem than they could severally. This approach is particularly good for very complex technical problems requiring high-powered computing equipment.

---

[1] Gamma radiography is a nondestructive method of testing solids by using the rays of radioactive isotopes to produce radiographs which reveal internal flaws in the material being tested. It resembles radiography by X rays, except that the equipment is typically smaller, requires no reliance on electrical power, and is hence more flexible. In 1958 Research, Inc., was one of very few producers of a standard line of gamma radiography equipment. The cost of a typical installation was about $2,500.

Exhibit 1

RESEARCH, INC.

Selected Financial Data

(Dollars in Nearest Thousands)

OPERATING RESULTS	PERIOD ENDING SEPTEMBER 30	
	1952	1957
Gross income:		
R & D contracts (government)..........	$160	$1,902
Commercial..........................		185
Subsidiaries*		
Watts, Inc.........................		149
Developers Company.................		10
Total...........................	$160	$2,246
Operating profit on R & D contracts.......	$ 4	$ 122
Operating profit on commercial sales.......		$ 32
Total net operating profit before federal income tax†..............	$ 1	$ 131

* These amounts were paid to the company for technical services performed, at cost.
† Total operating profit less "other expenses."

Net Income after Taxes for the Five Years, October 1, 1952 to September 30, 1957

	PERIOD ENDING SEPTEMBER 30				
	1953	1954	1955	1956	1957
Net income....................	$9	$10	$17	$40	$66
As % of gross income..........	3.0%	2.1%	2.8%	3.2%	2.9%
Shares of common stock outstanding................	114,541	106,266	107,282	230,595	230,595
Net income per share of common (in actual dollars)....	$0.08	$0.09	$0.16	$0.17	$0.28

Source: Company records.

According to company officers, Searchco was highly regarded, especially among the various government contracting officers, for its competence in this field.

FACILITIES

Company-owned facilities in Waltham, Massachusetts, included approximately 70,000 square feet of laboratory, shop, and office space in a building of modern design constructed in 1956. The laboratories were equipped with the latest standard devices for experiments in electronics,

Exhibit 2

RESEARCH, INC.

Balance Sheets, as of September 30, 1952, and 1955–57

(Dollars in Nearest Thousands)

Assets	1952	1955	1956	1957
Current Assets:				
Cash	$ 46	$ 31	$ 106	$ 41
U.S. Government Securities, at Cost	...	10	72	...
Accounts Receivable:				
U.S. Government	24	37	117	437
Other	24	9	19	75
Unbilled Expenditures on Research and Development Contracts and Estimated Profits Thereon	50	100	156	101
Inventories, at Lower of Cost or Market	10	42	41	45
Prepaid Expenses	6	7	22	12
Total Current Assets	$160	$236	$ 533	$ 711
U.S. Government Securities, at Cost	...	...	$ 400	...
Investments in and Advances to Affiliates	...	...	5	$ 151
	...	...	$ 405	$ 151
Property, Plant and Equipment, at Cost	$ 21	$ 75	$ 206	$ 681
Less: Reserves for Depreciation and Amortization	2	30	49	84
	$ 19	$ 45	$ 157	$ 597
Total Assets	$179	$281	$1,095	$1,459
Liabilities				
Notes Payable	...	...	...	$ 275
Other Current Liabilities	$ 9	$ 80	$ 199	208
	$ 9	$ 80	$ 199	$ 483
Reserve for Deferred Federal Income Taxes	...	...	...	$ 14
Stockholders Equity:				
Common Stock Outstanding, Par Value $0.10 per Share	$ 12	$ 12	$ 23	$ 23
Capital Surplus	163	166	799	799
Earnings Retained in the Business	(5)*	34	74	140
	$170	$212	$ 896	$ 962
Less: Treasury Stock, at Cost	...	11	...	...
	$170	$201	$ 896	$ 962
Total Liabilities	$179	$281	$1,095	$1,459

* The figure for earnings retained in the business in 1952 was subsequently adjusted to approximately $1,000.

Source: Company records.

physics, nucleonics, and chemistry, as well as with special apparatus designed by the company staff.

The company's machine shop, designed for research and versatility rather than volume production, included only very flexible general-purpose equipment. It was capable of handling work ranging from heavy radiation shields to precision electronic-optical instrumentation. Part of the shop facilities was devoted to producing the gamma radiography equipment.

The building also housed a large number of individual offices, equipped with desks and blackboards, and a library containing standard reference works and texts as well as a representative collection of specialized volumes on nucleonics, photography, atomic medicine, and current issues of a number of research periodicals. Included in the company's equipment were an analog and a digital computer.

OWNERSHIP

Until 1956 Research, Inc., was largely owned by its three founders, Drs. Henry R. Garrard, William S. Scott, and Willis M. Wharfedale. Due to the company's rapid growth, however, the founders began in 1956 to feel restricted by limited capital, and started to search for additional funds. Their efforts resulted in a major recapitalization in 1956. Two large institutional investors together contributed, for slightly less than one-half of the stock, funds amounting to about 320% of the approximately $201,000 owner's equity as of September 30, 1955.

BOARD AND OFFICERS

After the recapitalization, the company's board, which had previously comprised only the three founders and two lawyers and two industrialists without significant ownership interest, was expanded to include three representatives of each of the two institutional investors. In 1958 board meetings were being held monthly, and according to Dr. Scott, the new directors demonstrated a very active interest in company affairs.

In mid-1957 a vice-president for administration, Mr. Robert Marcello, was added to the ranks of company officers, which previously included only the three founders. According to the latter, Mr. Marcello was hired to assume some of the administrative burdens that had resulted from the company's rapid expansion, and that were becoming too heavy for the founders' time, experience, and interest.

Immediately prior to forming Searchco, all three founders had held responsible technical positions (for example, project director, physics and electronics division) in a large New England research and development organization, Trajectories, Incorporated. Each had become at least moderately dissatisfied with what one termed "the bureaucracy of a large organization," and had decided that he could find greater fulfillment in a company where he would have more control over his own and the organization's activities.

Before joining Trajectories, each of the founders had spent several years on the staffs of highly regarded research and academic institutions.

Each had earned his Ph.D. before 1940. All three became special technical consultants to the U.S. Air Force in 1951. Dr. Scott differed from the others in that he had also had two years of experience as assistant to the president of a small development company, a job which encompassed a wider range of responsibilities than those typically involved in technical (project) administration. The ages of the founders ranged from 35 to 41.

Mr. Marcello, age 41, came to Searchco with a broad background in government contract administration. After receiving his license as a certified public accountant, he spent several years in public accounting. For about five years he worked for the government, first negotiating contracts for the purchase of Army transport vehicles, later handling the procurement and supply of truck and automotive spare parts as a deputy branch chief in the Ordnance department. In 1948 he joined the research office of a large university as chief accountant, and six years later became business manager. The research office was principally engaged in research and development for the Navy. Mr. Marcello left it to join Searchco.

ORGANIZATION

A visualization of the company's organization is presented in Exhibit 3. The management did not maintain a formal organization chart or manual.

Dr. Garrard, president, and Dr. Scott, executive vice-president and treasurer, regarded themselves as sharing "top executive responsibilities." In addition, Dr. Scott was responsible for the administrative departments headed by Mr. Marcello, for the group of scientists specializing in electronics, and for the radiography equipment department. Both of the latter were headed by managers. Dr. Garrard was technical director for operations research projects performed in the home offices in Waltham ("on site"), and was responsible for the mechanical engineering and chemical groups. Both these groups were headed by program chairmen, who co-ordinated, controlled, and supervised the individual projects. Dr. Wharfedale, vice-president, worked as technical adviser or project leader on projects, usually in the field of physics, of interest to himself.

Prior to 1957, the technical personnel located in Waltham—approximately 80% of the total of 120—worked as individual scientists with no departmental or group affiliation. As the company grew, however, the difficulty of fixing responsibility in this type of setup was beginning to present some real problems, according to Dr. Scott. Consequently in 1957 almost all technical personnel were organized into research "groups," each of which was to specialize on problems in one of the scientific disciplines. With the aim of fixing financial responsibility on the group managers and program chairmen, the company's accounting system was modified to yield dollars and cents performance data by group.

Dr. Garrard stated that, prior to the establishment of the research "groups," company personnel had taken an interdisciplinary approach

Exhibit 3

RESEARCH, INC.

Organization Chart, Early 1958

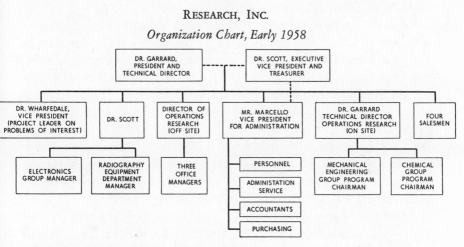

Source: Prepared by case writer from interviews with company executives.

to a large portion of the research problems. This practice continued, according to Dr. Garrard, in that individuals frequently shifted from group to group, "usually without troublesome formality."

Besides the headquarters in Waltham, in 1958 the company included three "off-site" offices, located in leased facilities at or near government units with which the company had long-term contracts. Established for work on specific contracts, these offices would not be maintained when the contracts were terminated. The managers of these off-site locations reported directly to a director of operations research, a post established in early 1958. All three offices worked exclusively in the field of operations research.

Also included in the organization were four technically trained part-time salesmen who reported directly to Drs. Garrard and Scott. These salesmen, who worked about one-half of the time as scientists, called on government and commercial offices in an effort to secure requests for bids on planned projects or in an effort to stimulate the formulation of new projects on which the company might later bid. They did not sell the company's radiography equipment, which was distributed through a separate organization.

SALES

According to Dr. Garrard, about "one-half to two-thirds" of the company's business resulted from contract renewals. The rest resulted from successful bids on new projects. Contracts ranged in amount from $10,000 to $650,000.

Requests for bids on projects came from commercial and government offices either through a "sale" by the salesmen or founders, or simply as a result of the company's reputation for competence in a certain field. Contracts were generally awarded to the lowest bidders. Under government cost-plus-fixed-fee arrangements, the bid and accepted price supposedly amounted to a maximum reimbursable cost-plus-fee figure. This price might, however, be adjusted upward with the approval of the government contracting officer, once work under the contract had begun. Because of the prevalent practice of underestimating overhead costs in order to turn in a low bid, many government offices had bids audited before deciding which one to accept.

At the end of February, 1958, the company had a backlog of government work amounting to slightly less than $1 million. Dr. Garrard regarded this backlog as unsatisfactorily low, and thought that the company's estimated overhead rate was too high to meet the competition on bids. This condition was largely the result, according to Dr. Garrard, of having recently expanded the company's facilities and personnel at a rate faster than business had expanded. In early 1958 two new part-time salesmen were added to the previously existing two-man sales force, and Drs. Scott and Garrard resolved to focus more of their attention on obtaining new business.

COSTING

On the basis of a project description accompanying a request for a bid, an estimate was made of direct labor costs—that is, salaries of technical personnel who would work on the project—to which overhead costs were added. Overhead accounted for about 60% of the total cost of work performed by Searchco in 1957. Two classes of expense were included: indirect costs such as heat, light, depreciation, and fringe benefits; and general and administrative costs such as financial expenses, officer salaries, and nonproductive labor time.

Overhead cost estimates were made for the period in which work under the contract would be performed. Mr. Marcello stated that in making these estimates he projected the company's past cost performance into the future, making adjustments for all foreseeable changes in salaries, average amount of nonproductive labor hours, facilities, and so forth.

RESEARCH "PRODUCTS"

According to company officers, research, particularly operations research, was Searchco's major "product." Several members of the organization suggested that, although they could define operations research in scientific terms, not much effort had been made in the company to define it in terms of what it could do for various potential users. As one of the company's salesmen put it, "The government has come to us to ask us to do some operations research work for it, and our approach has been to conclude that the government is our market for operations research."

In early 1958 an operations research group, specially formed for this project, was working on a study of the best tactics for the civilian populace to employ in minimizing the effects of radioactive fall-out. This study was being performed for the Federal Civil and Defense Agency. Dr. Garrard stated that he was very interested in the problems of minimizing the devastation from an atomic attack, and was hoping that the company's performance on the Federal Civil and Defense Agency project would result in additional work in this area.

Projects in the field of operations research at Searchco ranged from the formulation of analytic models of motor vehicle convoys, to the evaluation of insect eradication problems, to the development of safety programs for nuclear power plants. Some of the techniques used by company personnel in operations research projects were: operational simulation (tactical gaming); cost-effectiveness analysis; queueing theory; and the design and analysis of experiments for studying behavior in terms of Monte Carlo models.

In the fields of physics, chemistry, nucleonics, and applied mechanics, company personnel had been involved in a variety of projects. For example, one project of the chemical group involved determining the sources of photographic "fog" and the mechanisms of superadditive photographic development. According to members of the group, the data being collected were expected to aid in the formulation of new and more active chemical developers, leading to increased photographic sensitivity. Projects of the electronics group, which had turned out more "physical" products than any other, involved the development of radiation detection devices, electro-optical instruments, and weapon simulators. Projects of the mechanical engineering group involved working on the theoretical analysis of the use of high energy fuels to power armored vehicles, and on the determination of the causes of wear and galling in submarine gear couplings. In the past, projects handled by the physics group had ranged from the theoretical calculation of the "transport" of radiation through finite scattering media, to the analysis of the physics underlying the operation of technical instruments. The theoretical study of radiation "transport" resulted in a new theory which, according to members of the physics group, proved to be more accurate than the widely adopted radiation-diffusion theory, especially when studying highly absorbent media and regions close to radiation sources.

COMPETITION

The company faced competition from a number of research and development organizations, most of which had come into existence in the early 1950's, from government research offices, from educational institutions, and from the research departments of industrial concerns. Mr. Marcello, in citing a National Science Foundation study, stated that in 1953 approximately 20,000 companies contributed $3.7 billion to the country's research and development effort. About 3,700 of these supported projects performed by outside organizations; the remainder conducted research and development in their own facilities. Total expenditures for research and development amounted to more than $5 billion in 1953, $1.4 billion of which was spent by the federal government.[2] Mr. Marcello estimated that expenditures of private companies for research and development had increased from about $3 billion in 1951 to over $9 billion in 1957.

Mr. Marcello stated that these figures were not very useful to him in getting a clear idea of the market for the company's products, or of the company's performance in relation to its competitors. "About all we know, and we are not too sure of that," said Mr. Marcello, "is that

---

[2] *Science and Engineering in American Industry, Final Report on a 1953–1954 Survey,* National Science Foundation, NSF 56–16, October 10, 1956, p. 3.

Searchco is the largest publicly owned research and development organization in the field of operations research."

COMMERCIAL PRODUCTS AND PRODUCT DEVELOPMENT

"In addition to the fact that product development work is almost frowned on around here," stated one member of the administrative staff, "a product that the technical people want to develop is usually not the kind of product that might turn out well from a marketing standpoint." Since its founding the company had produced three products which the founders believed had enough commercial potential to warrant exploitation.

The first of these products was the gamma radiography equipment, which derived from an idea conceived during a research project for the government very early in the company's history. It was developed by the founders on company time, and the first piece of such equipment was sold in 1953. Sales of the line accounted for most of the company's commercial business in 1957.

The next product derived from some new concepts developed by the company in transistorized electrical power circuitry. These concepts found their practical application in a small volume of special-purpose equipment designed for several industrial firms.

To produce and sell its transistorized power supplies, Searchco in 1956 joined with Electronic Tubes, Inc., a nearby company which had become a leader in the field of microwave tubes, to form a subsidiary, Watts, Inc., in which each parent had a half interest. Searchco allocated technical personnel to the new company, and Electronic Tubes allocated production personnel and facilities. As of September 30, 1957, Searchco had made investments in and advances to Watts, Inc., amounting to $107,000, and Searchco's share of the accumulated losses to date was approximately $51,800. Company officers, however, believed that Watts would show a moderate profit in fiscal 1958. Sales, which had expanded rapidly, were expected to reach a level of $600,000.

Since transistorized electrical power supplies were not yet competitive on a cost basis with the conventional vacuum tube, rotary, and vibrator power supplies, their use had been mostly in applications where extreme operating conditions had forced the user to reject conventional circuitry for the more reliable transistorized type. The concept of transistorized circuitry, according to Dr. Garrard, was "revolutionary," and the possibilities of its application to commercial products were "unlimited."

The last of the products developed and exploited by Searchco was a new machine for processing Kodachrome film. Previously, all Kodachrome had been processed by Eastman Kodak Company by a complex method which required accurate and continual control of temperature and flow rates, and continuous chemical analysis of developing solutions. The machine developed by Searchco meant lower labor and equipment costs, and greater quality reliability. The idea for this machine was developed by company personnel who had previously worked on a number of government projects in the field of photographic chemistry.

To exploit this new film processing technique, the company in 1957 joined with an investment group to found Developers Company, 60% owned by Searchco. Personnel experienced in the field of film processing were hired by the investment group to operate the plant in Cranston, Rhode Island, while technical assistance was provided by Searchco personnel. Losses, attributed by Searchco's management to "start-up" costs, were sustained in the first year. Searchco's share of these losses was $15,900. The company's investment in and advances to Developers amounted to $44,000 as of September 30, 1957. Developers' sales were expected to reach $200,000 in fiscal 1958.

Prior to creating Developers, according to Dr. Scott, the founders of Searchco spent considerable time discussing organizational means of exploiting the new film processing machine. The alternatives discussed were licensing the new machine to an existing firm; processing film with it in Searcho's existing facilities and organization; and creating a subsidiary such as Developers. The founders chose the last alternative after long debate, principally between Dr. Scott and Dr. Garrard. The first alternative of licensing was quickly dismissed, according to Dr. Scott, because of the limited royalty payments which could be expected. Since both Drs. Garrard and Scott believed that keeping the new development in the existing organization would provide additional management opportunities for company personnel and greater control over operations, the issue turned, according to Dr. Scott, on whether it "could be done." Dr. Scott summarized his point of view as follows:

> We are scientists. We have had no training or experience in production methods and techniques. We don't have the basic production skills. It would have been foolish for us to try to produce anything other than the limited amount of radiography equipment we turn out.

Dr. Garrard thought, however, that "there is nothing so difficult about production, especially film processing, if you make up your mind to do it." He indicated that he did not continue to press the issue because Dr. Scott felt so strongly opposed to processing the film in the present organization, and because, financially, he did not think it would make much difference either way.

In commenting on the founders' decision to form Developers, one of the company's technical personnel said:

It seems very wise to me to keep production out of the operation here as much as possible. We just don't have a production atmosphere around here. Most of us would go nuts in a controlled, orderly, efficient, and sterile production atmosphere.

In fiscal 1957 the company spent approximately $16,000 on its own research and development projects. Dr. Garrard thought that some of these projects would result in additional contracts for the company's direct research and development activity. In addition, Dr. Garrard thought there was some "slight" possibility that an idea with commercial potential would arise from work on these projects. Expenditures by the company for its own research and development projects were allowable costs under most government contracts.

OBJECTIVES

When asked about their objectives for the company, the three founders and Mr. Marcello replied as follows:

DR. GARRARD: Our objective is to reach a volume of $10 million within the next three years. In achieving this objective, we want to stay out of commercial business. You know, you can't get into too much trouble with C.P.F.F. [cost-plus-fixed-fee] work, while you could really get into a mess in doing work for commercial concerns. If the government procurement agents have the money, they will want to spend it and they have no vested interests which would prevent us from doing what we think is best on each project. Commercial concerns, on the other hand, do have vested interests and would always be running in here to tell us what to do, and to prevent us from spending too much money.

Before the Sputnik, I didn't think we had a chance of reaching $10 million just doing government work. But now I am certain that government funds will free up and we will be able to get more work than we can handle for a long time to come.

DR. SCOTT: In my opinion, the company doesn't have a well-defined set of objectives. Oh! We talk about objectives such as a volume of $10 million. But to me, the way we talk about them is very general and very subjective. The three founders of the company have three different personalities, three different sets of motivations in life. Fortunately, though, the divergencies in our motivations are not so great that we can't come to some kind of decision on the questions we have to consider.

I believe that we would all rather do the technical work than run the business. But at the level of $10 million, for example, I don't believe we will be able to get into the technical end at all. If we get that big, we will just have to be satisfied with being surrounded by the stimulation of scientific atmosphere.

DR. WHARFEDALE: We talk about a volume of $10 million, but I'm not too sure I would want the company to get that much bigger. Already the volume of business is getting almost too big for us to handle. The job I have carved out for myself is to get some of the projects that come in here outlined for others to work on. And this job is not one that you can delegate any more than a judge can delegate his job.

MR. MARCELLO: My objectives for Searchco are for it to grow into a bigger and more profitable company and to keep growing. As far as I'm concerned, the profit motive is the greatest factor influencing my decisions. Of course, I also want the company to turn out very high quality work, but primarily because it is necessary to turn out good work to get more and more business.

I don't think the founders get together very often to decide how the company is going to grow in the future. They have come up with an objective of $10 million, but it doesn't seem to me that they have really worked out how they are going to get it. As I see it, there are several ways this volume could be achieved. It certainly won't happen by continuing to engage exclusively in government research, which is dangerous as well. One of these ways would be to take on commercial jobs as well as government jobs in the same place. This would be hard to do because those companies big enough to have the money to put into R & D usually already have their own research units. Another—and I think the more probable—way of being able to do it would be to take on new products, either producing them ourselves or setting up subsidiaries to produce them. This would mean that we would probably have to concentrate more on research which would be likely to result in developable products.

Drs. Garrard, Scott, and Wharfedale, and Mr. Marcello were characterized by several members of the organization as follows:

Dr. Garrard: He is the most competent, nonanalytical, and confident administrative scientist I have ever seen.

Dr. Scott: He actually is the only one of the founders of the company who *worries* about the business aspects of the operation.

Dr. Wharfedale: He refuses to be concerned about the business side of the company. He is a top notch scientist and obviously wants to remain just that.

Mr. Marcello: He has experience in working with us eggheads, so some of the things we do don't really upset him. He can be trusted to see our viewpoint.

PART V

Follow-up and Reappraisal

Aerosol Techniques, Inc.

IN JANUARY, 1966, Mr. Robert Meyer, a 1965 Harvard MBA, joined Aerosol Techniques, Inc., in Bridgeport, Connecticut, as director of corporate development. While his immediate concern was the evaluation of numerous acquisition proposals that ATI had received, Mr. Meyer was also responsible for appraising overall corporate strategy. Shortly after assuming his position, Mr. Meyer concluded that environmental trends might require a strategy change.

Founded in December, 1955, by Mr. H. R. Shepherd, a chemist and biologist with aerosol R.&D. experience dating back to the end of World War II, ATI was a "contract filler," or producer and packager of items marketed to consumers by others. With 1965 sales of $47 million, or about 22% of the total contract filling market, ATI was the largest contract filler of aerosol products in the United States. Yearly growth since 1960 had averaged 46% for sales and 65% for profits. (For financial statements, see Exhibits 1 and 2.)

From the start, ATI's policy had been to emphasize service and development research for new products. As a result, about 95% of 1965 dollar volume was made up of products that ATI had developed in its laboratories either alone or jointly with customers. Mr. Shepherd indicated that ATI did not want to have to compete on a price basis, or to compete with customers by marketing products under its own name. Thus ATI's name was not on any products packed for other firms.

In 1965 ATI was the only contract filler with plants in each major section of the country. These provided an economic advantage over other contract fillers because of the relatively high cost of transporting filled aerosol containers. Nevertheless, Mr. Meyer was worried about ATI's strategy of developing and manufacturing aerosol products for national marketers because of several trends that had developed between 1960 and 1965. Of these, he felt the most important were a general decline in prices and profit margins for filling operations and a tendency on the part of some national marketers to install their own aerosol filling lines as sales volume increased.

Exhibit 1

AEROSOL TECHNIQUES, INC.

Balance Sheets for Years Ended September 30, 1960, through 1965
(Dollars in Thousands)

	1960	1961	1962	1963	1964	1965
Current assets:						
Cash	$ 60	$ 449	$ 290	$ 359	$ 1,067	$ 1,433
Accounts receivable—net	461	832	1,279	3,373	4,924	6,566
Inventories—lower cost or market	465	238	468	2,136	2,329	3,098
Prepaid expenses	15	15	16	103	185	185
Miscellaneous	3	23	22	90	40	65
Total current assets	$1,005	$1,557	$2,076	$6,061	$ 8,544	$11,348
Fixed assets:						
Land	0	0	0	13	13	179
Buildings	0	0	0	362	365	880
Machinery and equipment	479	496	541	2,024	2,497	3,226
Other	134	144	154	308	384	1,429*
	$ 613	$ 640	$ 695	$2,707	$ 3,260	$ 5,715
Less: acc. dep. and amort.	175	240	307	1,377	1,556	1,805
Total fixed assets	$ 438	$ 401	$ 388	$1,330	$ 1,704	$ 3,909
Other assets	19	18	24	155	75	125
	$1,462	$1,976	$2,488	$7,546	$10,322	$15,383
Current liabilities:						
Notes payable	$ 0	$ 0	$ 0	$1,298	$ 1,500	$ 0
Accounts payable	596	527	758	2,480	2,842	4,151
Federal and state taxes payable	89	164	238	564	695	886
Other	179	209	200	388	396	1,318†
Total current liabilities	$ 864	$ 901	$1,196	$4,730	$ 5,434	$ 6,356
Long-term debt	217	98	34	241	200	3,152
Deferred federal taxes	36	43	47	53	55	60
Contingent deferred credit	0	0	0	355	257	184
Stockholders' equity:						
4% voting, cumulative, preferred	0	0	0	715	715	715
Common stock: 10¢ par value	30	43	44	61	76	78
Capital in excess of par value	20	20	20	20	20	20
Paid in surplus	0	421	456	131	2,083	2,179
Retained earnings	295	450	691	1,240	1,480	2,639
Total stockholders' equity	$ 345	$ 934	$1,211	$2,167	$ 4,375	$ 5,631
	$1,462	$1,976	$2,488	$7,546	$10,322	$15,383

* Incudes $934,000 for construction in progress.
† Includes $672,000 of current portion of long-term debt.

Source: ATI annual reports.

THE AEROSOL INDUSTRY

Aerosol Products. The term "aerosol product" was used to describe any product packed in an aerosol container. The total item consisted of a pressurized container, a propellant to supply the desired pressure, the usable product fill, and a cap-and-valve combination that controlled the release of the product and propellant. While almost any product

Exhibit 2

AEROSOL TECHNIQUES, INC.

Income Statements: 1960–65

(Dollars in Thousands)

	1960	1961	1962	1963	1964	1965
Net sales.	$7,052	$7,734	$10,776	$21,327	$34,632	$46,975
Cost of goods sold, selling, administrative, and general expense.	6,835	7,415	10,302	20,159	33,079	44,705
	$ 218	$ 319	$ 475	$ 1,169	$ 1,553	$ 2,270
Other income.	10	12	24	66	222	36
	$ 228	$ 331	$ 498	$ 1,235	$ 1,775	$ 2,306
Other deductions.	27	16	11	85	104	124
	$ 200	$ 315	$ 487	$ 1,150	$ 1,671	$ 2,182
Provision for federal income taxes.	99	159	247	567	751	980
Net earnings.	$ 101	$ 156	$ 240	$ 583	$ 920	$ 1,202

Source: ATI annual reports.

that was liquid or gaseous at ordinary temperatures could theoretically be packaged in an aerosol container, in actual practice it was often difficult to "marry" the product, the propellant, and the cap and valve into a workable combination. Nevertheless, by 1965 such diverse products as shaving cream, perfume, starch, furniture polish, hair sprays, and room deodorants were sold in aerosol containers.

Industry History and Growth. The first aerosol product was the "bugbomb," of which some 40 million units were produced for issue to servicemen during the last two years of World War II. When the war ended, the bomb was modified for civilian use.

While these first aerosols were high-pressure, refillable types which retailed for $3.98, myriad technical developments soon reduced both pressure and price. As a result, aerosol packaging spread to dozens of other products, as seen in Table 1.

According to industry sources, aerosol packaging would continue to spread to other fields in the future.

TABLE 1

	Year First Marketed in Aerosol Packages
Room deodorants, lacquers, mothproofers.	1948
Hair sprays, paints, automobile waxes.	1949
Shave lather.	1950
Whipped cream.	1951
Perfumes.	1954
Starches.	1955
Glass cleaners.	1956
Furniture waxes and polishes.	1959
All purpose cleaners, antiperspirants.	1962

Also important to the rapid growth (about 17% a year between 1955 and 1964) of the aerosol market was the increasing penetration of aerosols as a packaging form in each of the above product areas. The percentage of room deodorants, shave lathers, and colognes packaged in aerosol containers increased from 0% in 1947 to 91%, 82%, and 64%, respectively, in 1964 (see Exhibit 3). Moreover, some products, such as hair sprays, were made possible by aerosol packaging.

Exhibit 3

AEROSOL TECHNIQUES, INC.

Percentage Penetration of Aerosols as a Packaging Form in Various Market Segments: 1951–64

(Per Cent of Dollar Volume)

	1951	1952	1953	1954	1955	1956	1957	1958	1959	1960	1961	1962	1963	1964
Insecticides	30%	32%	37%	37%	39%	38%	39%	42%	47%	47%	47%	47%	48%	44%
Room deodorants	0	0	40	44	58	56	67	73	82	79	85	89	91	91
Shave lathers	0	12	29	38	47	51	59	60	65	69	71	79	81	82
Colognes	0	0	0	13	33	45	48	51	57	58	62	64	66	64

Source: Eighth Annual Aerosol Market Report, 1964, prepared by Freon Products Division of Du Pont. Data supplied to Du Pont by *Drug Trade News* (New York).

In 1964, total sales of all aerosol-packaged products reached over 1.3 billion units. All but 6% of this total was made up of nonfood items, of which 46% were personal products, 30% household products, and 24% miscellaneous products (see Exhibit 4). Table 2 gives examples of the types of products included in each category:

TABLE 2

Personal Products	*Household Products*	*Miscellaneous Products*
Shave lathers	Room deodorants and disin-	Paints and coatings
Hair sprays and dressings	fectants	Insecticides
Medicinals	Cleaners (all types)	Automotive waxes
Colognes and perfumes	Household waxes and	Veterinarian and pet prod-
Personal deodorants	polishes	ucts
Other (shampoos, suntan	Starches	Industrial products
preparations, hand	Shoe and leather dressings	
lotions, etc.)		

Industry observers expected each of these major categories to grow at least 8% a year during the coming decade. Du Pont, for example, in a 1965 market report, forecast that between 1965 and 1967 sales of personal products would increase 14% a year, household products 12%, and all other nonfood products 10%.

Estimates of aerosol growth for foods were more uncertain.. While sales of nonfood aerosols had increased more than 19% a year between

Exhibit 4

AEROSOL TECHNIQUES, INC.

Du Pont Company Estimate of Aerosol Production (Nonfood Products Only)

(Millions of Units)

	1953	1954	1955	1956	1957	1958	1959	1960	1961	1962	1963	1964	1965
Personal products													
Shave lather	27.3	47.0	53.1	51.0	59.3	65.0	75.0	79.1	84.7	94.8	97.6	102.6	108.1
Hair sprays and dressings	16.1	34.5	55.8	83.4	95.6	112.1	88.7	120.9	152.5	245.6	294.0	314.0	337.0
Dental creams						23.0	11.8	5.8	3.1	3.1	3.0	3.0	3.2
Medicinals and pharmaceuticals	0.8	1.1	1.5	2.4	6.2	8.1	10.5	12.3	19.5	36.9	39.8	45.6	49.4
Colognes and perfumes	0.1	3.0	7.0	8.8	18.6	30.0	37.9	43.1	54.7	55.1	60.4	66.2	69.2
Other*	3.8	4.4	7.2	7.7	7.1	9.6	12.9	18.7	18.5	36.9	38.5	47.1	52.8
Total	48.1	90.0	124.6	153.3	186.8	247.8	236.8	279.9	333.0	472.4	533.3	578.5	619.7
Insecticides†	47.0	47.0	57.0	61.4	50.7	71.3	78.9	92.5	87.3	89.2	73.2	75.1	76.4
Household products													
Room deodorants	17.3	21.3	33.1	38.4	44.6	62.8	62.9	78.1	86.3	99.0	118.5	126.4	131.6
Snow	8.9	7.1	6.8	8.9	9.0	9.8	9.5	10.5	8.6	9.5	10.5	12.5	13.5
Glass cleaners				8.0	11.2	6.6	24.2	22.2	26.0	31.0	47.3	52.3	54.3
Shoe or leather dressings				1.5	4.3	7.7	14.1	16.6	7.3	4.7	8.9	11.1	13.0
Waxes and polishes (all types)							12.1	40.6	42.1	52.9	50.9	57.8	61.0
Starches								20.6	50.5	65.4	86.9	99.0	107.3
Other	2.3	3.1	8.2	16.4	8.3	11.6	25.4	10.5	15.7	18.6	11.8	13.2	14.8
Total	28.5	31.5	48.1	73.2	77.4	98.5	148.2	199.1	236.5	281.1	334.8	372.3	395.5
Coatings	13.0	13.1	14.7	22.5	43.0	50.0	63.2	77.1	95.6	110.3	137.9	158.4	174.5
Miscellaneous products													
Veterinarian and pet products	0.3	0.5	1.0	1.5	2.3	3.3	4.3	6.3	8.3	7.1	7.6	8.7	9.4
Automotive products‡											33.2	36.9	39.6
Other§	3.1	5.9	10.3	13.3	15.0	14.3	30.2	42.2	52.8	44.7	23.6	21.4	19.7
Total	3.4	6.4	11.3	14.8	17.3	17.6	34.5	48.5	61.1	51.8	64.4	67.2	71.0
Grand total	140.0	188.0	255.7	325.2	375.2	485.2	561.6	697.1	813.5	1004.8	1140.1	1251.3	1334.8

* OTHER PERSONAL PRODUCTS include shampoos, suntan preparations, personal deodorants, hand lotions, powders, depilatories, etc.
† INSECTICIDES include high-pressure and low-pressure products (including space, residual, and mothproofers).
‡ AUTOMOTIVE PRODUCTS included in other miscellaneous products prior to 1963.
§ OTHER MISCELLANEOUS PRODUCTS include antistatic sprays, industrial applications, fire extinguishers, etc.

Source: Eighth Annual Aerosol Market Report, 1964, prepared by the Freon Products Division of Du Pont, p. 24.

1955 and 1964, the sales of aerosol-packaged foods had increased less than 2% a year (see Exhibit 5). However, in 1963 and 1964, Du Pont gained approval from the Food and Drug Administration for two new tasteless propellants. According to some industry sources, these promised to overcome previous technical problems and to open the way to aerosol packaging of a wide variety of foods—from staples, such as peanut butter and cheese spread, to additives, such as vermouth. As a consequence, some industry sources were predicting in 1965 that the growth curve for food products would soon begin to resemble that of nonfood aerosols.

Exhibit 5

AEROSOL TECHNIQUES, INC.

Growth of the Food Aerosol Market
(Millions of Units)

Year	Sales	Year	Sales	Year	Sales
1951	43	1956	69	1961	58
1952	50	1957	75	1962	63
1953	56	1958	80	1963	67
1954	60	1959	79	1964	75
1955	64	1960	59	1965	100 (est.)

Source: Eighth Annual Aerosol Market Report, 1964, prepared by the Freon Products Division of Du Pont, p. 18.

Reasons for Aerosol Usage. According to a study by the Freon Products Division of Du Pont, there were three primary reasons for the use of aerosol packaging: (1) increased product effectiveness, (2) greater user convenience, and (3) time savings. The study noted that not all successful applications exhibited all three advantages; even where effectiveness was not improved, convenience alone was often enough to stimulate sales.

Nevertheless, aerosol packaging was relatively expensive (see Exhibits 6 and 7). Some observers felt that cost would restrict the use of aerosol packaging for products with low profit margins.

Industry Structure. During World War II, the Bridgeport Brass Company produced most of the bugbombs used by the armed services. After the war, this company continued to make bugbombs, which it sold through its regular sales force. Soon, however, Bridgeport, which had no product development activities, was forced out of the aerosol market by contract fillers, which carried on intensive product development programs. These contract fillers were small, regional companies which would purchase the cans from national firms such as American

Exhibit 6

AEROSOL TECHNIQUES, INC.

Cost Estimates for Various Aerosol Products

Product Type	Starch*	Hair Spray†	Shave Cream‡
Product fill........................	1.0¢	4.0¢	1.5¢
Propellant........................	0.3	12.0§	0.1
Can‖.............................	7.0	6.3	5.0
Valve............................	3.0	2.6	3.0
Cap..............................	0.5	1.0#	0.5
Carton**.........................	0.6	0.5	0.5
Direct labor......................	1.0	1.0	1.0
Overhead.........................	1.5	1.5	1.5
Profit (max.).....................	1.0	1.0	1.0
Factory price.....................	15.9¢	29.9¢	14.1¢
Approx. retail price..............	39¢	$1–$1.20	$.79 to $1
Approx. retail price of comparable product (nonaerosol)...........	19¢ for 12 oz.	none available	$1 for 10 oz.

* 16 oz. size, for laundry use.
† 12 oz. size, alcohol-base, most "name brands."
‡ 6 oz. size, most "name brands."
§ Much more expensive than others shown because the product requires Freon as a propellant, which amounts to 70% of the weight of the contents. The propellants used in the other products shown are hydrocarbons and are only 4% of the weight of the contents. Water-based hair sprays, with somewhat different characteristics, are available; these entail a lower propellant cost.
‖ Printed cans; no separate labels.
More expensive only because usually fancier.
** Carton for a dozen cans.
Source: Estimates furnished by an industry source other than ATI. Estimates are for an established product with a volume per production run of about 25,000 units or more.

Exhibit 7

AEROSOL TECHNIQUES, INC.

Cost of a Typical Aerosol Food Product

(Food Product: Pancake Mix)

Cost	*Per Unit*
Direct labor..	$.04
Can (16 oz.)...	.09
Gas (nitrous oxide)..................................	.005
Valve and release....................................	.05
Product (pancake mix)...............................	.04
Overhead (interest and depreciation)*................	.01
Profit margin..	.015
Cost to marketer before distribution charges..............	$.250

* Assumes an investment of $300,000 for a line that produces 9.6 million units a year for eight years with indirect labor and storage costs of $50,000 a year.
Source: Harvard Business School student reports conducted for ATI.

Can Company, the propellants from firms such as Du Pont, and the caps and valves from small companies like themselves. They would then assemble these components, including the product fill, which they usually manufactured, into the final aerosol product. The contract fillers would then sell the finished product to marketing firms, which resold to retailers under their own brands. By 1950, at least 50 firms met the contract filler definition.

As the demand for aerosols grew, two changes occurred in industry structure. First, the contract fillers became larger through both internal growth and acquisition of other contract fillers. Second, some national marketers began to erect their own filling facilities since they felt their volume now warranted such a move. Such a marketer was called a "captive filler."

By 1964, output of nonfood aerosols was about evenly divided between captive and contract fillers (see Exhibit 8). Most industry observers felt a definite trend toward captive filling had not yet emerged among national marketers, however. While firms such as Colgate, S. C. Johnson, Alberto-Culver, Johnson & Johnson, Mennen, and Gillette had established their own filling lines, firms such as Procter & Gamble and Breck still relied on contract fillers. Moreover, most of the firms that had established their own filling lines still relied on contract fillers to supplement their own production during peak sales periods.

The difficulty of deciding between captive vs. contract filling was partly responsible for the lack of a definite trend. The economics of the decision required the marketing company to consider not only the cost of filling equipment and personnel, but also distribution costs, inventory costs (since the contract filler usually kept part of the inventory), and research and development costs (since many contract fillers developed new product formulations for the marketers). In addition, the marketing company had to consider noneconomic factors, such as the need for security in protecting the product formulation and the need for tight quality control.

One industry observer (not ATI) agreed that the issue of captive vs. contract filling was complex. He estimated, however, that a yearly volume of five million units in a standard product might be an "average break-even point" as far as the economics of the filling operation were involved. Although some companies used captive operations for as few as one million units a year, and others used contract fillers for annual volumes as high as 10 million, he felt that these companies were clear exceptions and were probably influenced by other-than-economic factors. He also thought that it was becoming easier for companies to set up their own filling operations since the necessary equipment could readily be purchased, and an increasing number of people with experience in aerosol filling operations were becoming available.

Other industry observers felt that many marketers would not go

Exhibit 8

AEROSOL TECHNIQUES, INC.

ATI's Share of the Contract Filled and Total
Aerosol Filling Markets: 1963–64 (Nonfood Products Only)

	PER CENT OF MARKET CONTRACT FILLED		ATI SHARE OF CONTRACT MARKET		ATI SHARE OF TOTAL MARKET	
	1963	1964	1963	1964	1963	1964
Household products:						
Room deodorants........	36.9%	22.1%	7.1%	17.0%	2.6%	3.7%
Cleaners...............	64.1	62.0	34.8	31.0	22.3	18.9
Waxes and polishes......	18.9	22.1	28.9	23.5	5.5	5.2
Starch.................	82.9	84.0	26.7	25.0	22.2	21.0
Shoe and leather dress-						
ings.................	86.9	96.1	1.3	3.9	1.1	3.8
Other.................	69.4	82.0	21.5	5.7	14.9	4.7
Personal products:						
Shave lather...........	23.0	37.0	7.1	1.6	1.6	.6
Hair spray.............	60.0	61.0	30.9	35.1	18.6	21.4
Medicinals and pharma-						
ceuticals.............	63.0	68.8	13.9	21.4	8.8	15.0
Colognes and perfumes...	51.0	38.1	15.9	31.0	8.1	12.0
Other.................	36.1	38.9	29.3	3.2	10.5	1.3
Miscellaneous products:						
Insecticides...........	34.0	31.0	54.4	30.5	18.5	9.5
Coatings..............	52.0	41.0	4.5	4.3	2.4	2.0
Veterinarian and pet.....	96.3	77.5	3.9	1.4	3.8	1.1
Automotive and in-						
dustrial..............	59.0	70.3	14.6	8.8	8.6	6.4
Other.................	...	36.7	...	10.3	...	3.8
Total..............	51.1%	50.4%	22.0%	21.9%	11.2%	11.1%

Source: ATI marketing statistics.

captive because of the low profit margins on filling. They reasoned that such marketers would be far more interested in new marketing opportunities which promised high margins than in a production activity with a rapid rate of technological change. (For further discussion of the advantages of using a contract filler, see Exhibit 9).

Contract Fillers and Their Strategies. Although the aerosol filling industry had grown tremendously, it had nevertheless become increasingly competitive during the mid-60's as the 98 independent contract fillers fought for a large but limited supply of contracts. The intensity of competition was suggested by the fact that three contract fillers had been forced into bankruptcy in 1963, and Old Empire, Inc., of Clifton, New Jersey, one of the oldest and most respected names in aerosols, had also filed a bankruptcy petition.

On the other hand, several large companies entered the aerosol

Exhibit 9

AEROSOL TECHNIQUES, INC.

Advantages of Using a Contract Packager

by

A. S. Pero

1. *Research & Development Advantages*
   a. Can draw from lab personnel already experienced in aerosols.
   b. Developments by fillers, either directly or in cooperation with other suppliers, are available promptly to marketers.
   c. Prevents added load being placed on marketers' lab facilities.
   d. Reduces marketers' outlay for research and development.
2. *Production Advantages*
   a. Can select latest and best equipment available for particular job required.
   b. Two or more products can be run simultaneously.
   c. Contract packagers offer facilities to cope with seasonal demands, or unexpected market fluctuations either of higher or lower volume than anticipated.
   d. Personnel of long, varied, and impartial experience available for quality control.
   e. Marketer can ask, and often gets, tighter specifications on his product.
   f. Supplier problems are handled by the filler.
   g. Can eliminate or minimize labor-management problems.
3. *Service Advantages*
   a. Marketer can warehouse both raw and finished materials, often at no charge, on filler's premises.
   b. Filler's trucking facilities can be used for drop shipments, emergency services, etc.
   c. Marketer can draw on know-how and information sometimes not available within his own organization.
4. *Economic Advantages*
   a. No money outlay for equipment and maintenance, plant building or expansion, or personnel and training of same.
   b. A contract packager is actually a co-op manufacturer who divides his labor, overhead, etc., among a wide group of customers and products.
   c. Working capital is conserved on material purchased by filler until product is completed.
   d. Material purchases are often less, due to filler's volume buying.
   e. Lowest costs on final product can be obtained through competitive bidding.
   f. Use of strategically located fillers can offer substantially lower shipping costs when products are to be nationally distributed.

How high a volume of product must an aerosol marketer be turning out before it pays him to consider doing his own filling?

Actually product volume is relatively unimportant in itself. More important is to seriously study the overall advantages a good filler has to offer vs. the overall advantages of the marketer doing his own work. Once this is determined, a

Exhibit 9—Continued

further evaluation is needed on the aerosol product or products to be manufactured.

Is the product to be a low-profit, highly competitive one? In this case a larger volume will be needed to justify the total expenditure involved. Or is the product a high-profit one, in a noncompetitive line? In the latter, a lesser volume might justify doing one's own filling.

In general, a careful analysis of all factors involved by the marketer, in the light of his own capacities and business interests, should provide him with a satisfactory answer. A survey of the aerosol field today clearly indicates that most marketers have already decided it is to their advantage to have their aerosol lines produced by contract packages. The aerosol filling industry is today so competitive that the margin above direct labor is small enough to discourage not only the marketer's equipment plan, but also new competitive contract packagers as well.

Source: Article by A. S. Pero of the Fluid Chemical Co., Newark, N.J., *Aerosol Age* (June, 1975), p. 28.

business through acquisitions. Borden's, for example, in 1963 and 1964 acquired Krylon, an aerosol paint manufacturer, and Aerosol Brands, a general contract filler. During the same period, Corn Products Company bought Peterson Filling in order to package its products in aerosol containers.

In an article in *Aerosol Age,* the industry trade journal, Mr. H. R. Shepherd, president of ATI, discussed the future role of the independent contract filler as follows:

It is clear that in the future there will be only two types of contract fillers—first, the filler with national distribution and plants strategically distributed throughout the nation (or in several countries) which can adequately service a national or international marketing concern. The other type of successful contract filler will be the small filler, who can handle low volume runs of specialty products or products that are only beginning to be felt in the marketplace.[1]

Vim Laboratories exemplified the latter type of company. One of the few publicly owned fillers, Vim had annual sales only slightly above $1 million. Custom filling represented part of its business, but the company's own specialty line, which included insecticides, paints, room deodorants, shaving cream, Christmas snow, insect repellent, suntan lotion, and charcoal lighter, represented a significant portion of aerosol capacity.

George Barr & Company, which had been purchased by Pittsburgh

[1] H. R. Shepherd, "The Contract Filler's Role in Aerosol Product Development," *Aerosol Age* (December, 1963), p. 48.

Railways Company in 1962, was the second largest contract filler in the United States in 1965. Barr's 1962 sales had exceeded $15 million, but had not been reported separately since 1962. In May, 1965, the company unveiled a new filling plant in Piles, Illinois, which was described as "the largest aerosol filling plant in the world." Barr's apparent strategy was to become a "packaging consultant." With this objective in mind, Pittsburgh Railways in 1963 and 1964 had acquired Advance Packaging Company, a filler of nonaerosol packages and Aero Valve Corporation, a manufacturer of caps and valves for aerosol containers.

Power-Pak, Inc., of Bridgeport, Connecticut, was a medium-sized contract filler. In 1962, Power-Pak formed agreements with three other contract fillers—one English, one Canadian, and one midwestern domestic—under which Power-Pak licensed these companies to use some of Power-Pak's product formulations. Power-Pak also performed R.&D. activities for these firms for a fee. While Power-Pak did not see any direct increase in the sales of its own products, Mr. Edward Helfer, Power-Pak's president in 1962, felt that this arrangement might lead to a penetration in continental Europe, which was just beginning to experience an aerosol boom similar to that in the United States between 1955 and 1960.

Industry Suppliers. The four principal components of an aerosol product—containers, propellants, caps and valves, and product fill—were supplied by diverse groups of companies.

The market for propellants was dominated by five large chemical companies: Du Pont, Allied Chemical Corporation, Union Carbide, Pennsalt Chemicals Corporation, and Kaiser Aluminum & Chemical Corporation.

The market for aerosol containers was also dominated by large firms. Among the most important were Continental Can Company, Inc., American Can Company, Crown Cork & Seal Company, Inc., and National Can Corporation. Glass container manufacturers included Owens-Illinois Glass Company, Foster-Forbes Glass Company, and T.C. Wheaton Company.

Small companies, similar to many of the contract fillers, played an important part in the supply of caps and valves. The major supplier was Precision Valve Corporation, which had an estimated 50% of the market. The other half of the market was split among many suppliers.

The aerosol filler, contract or captive, usually produced the product fill. In the case of certain products, such as perfumes, however, the contract filler secured the product fill from the marketing company.

ATI HISTORY

Immediately after World War II, Mr. H. R. Shepherd joined the Bridgeport Brass Company as administrative assistant to the director of research. About a year later, he and three friends founded Connecticut Chemical Research Corporation. After eight years, Mr. Shepherd resigned to form his own company, Aerosol Techniques, Inc.

ATI was launched in 1955 with $20,000 capital invested by Mr. Shepherd, a $125,000 bank loan, and $600,000 in trade credit. Although contracts were obtained almost immediately to load hair sprays and colognes, ATI was $75,000 in the red after six months. At year's end, however, the company emerged with a modest profit of $5,000 on sales of $1.5 million. *Aerosol Age* reported as follows:

> During this stage of growth, Mr. Shepherd emphasized that the theme will be "give service—expand research—put profits into new equipment and technical development". . . . The company has started a research program with an eastern university on basic problems with aerosols. . . . A complete aerosol service center is a must for proper handling of customers in aerosol packaging, according to Mr. Shepherd.[2]

By 1960, sales had risen to $7.1 million and net profit to $101,000. Although hair sprays remained ATI's most important single product, the line had been expanded to include shaving creams, toothpaste, furniture polishes, and other items. In addition, R.&D. laboratories had been established. A continuing effort was being made to improve formulae for customers and to develop or adapt aerosol packaging to new products. Though product diversification and research had reduced ATI's dependence on a few major clients, three customers still accounted for almost 60% of sales in 1960.

Although ATI lost an account which contributed 13% of 1960 sales because the customer went captive, the addition of new products and growth of established lines pushed 1961 sales to a new high of $7.7 million. Early in 1961, ATI issued 130,000 shares to the public, representing a 30% interest in the company, at $4 per share. This financing helped to alleviate the financial pressures caused by the company's tremendous growth. Even though ATI had decided to retain all earnings and to conserve funds for working capital by leasing rather than purchasing facilities, creditors were supplying over three fourths of the firm's invested funds in 1960. In October, 1961, the stock was listed on the American Stock Exchange.

---

[2] *Aerosol Age* (July, 1956), p. 21.

In 1962, ATI's spectacular growth trend was resumed as sales reached $10.8 million and net income climbed to $240,000. In addition, ATI established a subsidiary, Aeroceuticals, Inc., to produce and market an assortment of ethical drugs which company R.&D. had developed for aerosol containers. Major reasons for this move were the high growth rate (over 40% per year between 1957 and 1962) of pharmaceuticals and the relatively high gross margin on these products.

In 1963, ATI moved into first place in the contract filling business with sales of $21.3 million and profits of $583,000, partly as a result of the acquisition of two contract fillers: Western Filling Corporation in Los Angeles, California, and Continental Filling Corporation in Danville, Illinois.

When acquired, Western had shown a rapid growth similar to ATI's. Sales had doubled between 1960 and 1962 from $2.3 million to $4.7 million, while earnings had increased from $19,000 to $278,000. The Western acquisition was basically an exchange of stock.

Continental's sales had fluctuated in the four years prior to the acquisition, dropping from $9.6 million in 1960 to $6.9 million in 1962, but recovering somewhat in 1963. Profits had declined continuously during the period, however, from $118,000 in 1960 to $5,000 in 1962 and then to a $27,000 loss in 1963. Because of this weaker record, the Continental acquisition was a cash and deferred payment agreement, even though Continental's capacity was somewhat greater than Western's: 40 million vs. 35 million units annually.

To finance these acquisitions, ATI negotiated a $1 million loan with its New York bank, and in November, 1964, offered 80,000 shares to the public at $18 per share.

In 1964, ATI acquired Armstrong Laboratories, Inc., of West Roxbury, Massachusetts, through an exchange of stock. Armstrong's sales had been $1.1 million in 1963, with profits of $52,000. Armstrong had already achieved a strong reputation as an aerosol producer specializing in pharmaceuticals and other close-tolerance filling operations. Armstrong had also opened a new building with advanced production and research facilities just prior to acquisition.

With this addition, ATI's sales increased to $34.6 million in 1964, with a net income of $920,000. This growth continued in 1965, with sales increasing to $47 million and profits to $1.2 million.

In December, 1962, and again in December, 1963, ATI declared 5% stock dividends.

ATI'S CURRENT OPERATIONS

Product Line. ATI's 1965 product line consisted of over 200 products manufactured for nearly 150 customers. The largest customer, however, accounted for over 45 million units, or nearly 17% of 1965 production. In addition, the top five customers accounted for about 50% of ATI's production, and the top 10 for slightly more than 75%.

By product class, ATI was concentrated in personal products, which represented nearly 65% of 1965 volume—hair sprays alone accounted for over 45%. Household products were next in importance, representing about 28%. Most of this was starches, which accounted for 15%.

John Thomson, corporate director of sales, indicated that ATI's product line strategy was to reduce the company's dependence on personal products by placing more emphasis on household products and pharmaceuticals. Nevertheless, Mr. Thomson indicated that ATI planned to continue its outstanding record in hair sprays and personal deodorants.

According to Mr. Thomson, coatings, paints, and food products represented special cases for ATI. While he felt that the market for coatings and paints would not grow as fast as other product categories, he indicated that they might become more important for ATI. However, he also indicated that if ATI decided to enter the coating and paint field at all, it would probably market as well as manufacture these products. This move would represent a major change in ATI's present strategy of not marketing products to end-use consumers.

In Mr. Thomson's opinion, food products represented a far more promising field for ATI. Up to 1965, ATI had not devoted much effort to this area because of the technical problems encountered in propellants and caps and valves. However, Mr. Thomson indicated that ATI would increase its effort in this direction as the food aerosol market developed—perhaps within three to seven years, he believed. ATI was also studying the possibilities of aerosols for the industrial cleaning and sanitation markets, Mr. Thomson said.

Marketing. ATI's sales objective was a volume of $100 million in contract manufacturing by 1969. To reach this goal, the company planned to broaden its line, particularly in the household products area, and to concentrate its selling efforts on national marketers in the continental United States. In this sales push, ATI planned to rely heavily on what it considered its two distinctive competences: low distribution costs resulting from having plants in the East and Midwest and on the

West Coast; and a continuing flow of new and improved products resulting from its R.&D.

Mr. Thomson felt that ATI would have to price more competitively if it expected to hold its large national accounts. However, he felt that a new plant which was being erected at Milford, Connecticut, would allow production economies which would keep ATI competitive for at least the next five years. In addition, Mr. Thomson felt that ATI might acquire or build a southern production facility which would permit lower prices because of reduced distribution costs.

In 1963, ATI started to develop a corporate marketing staff to coordinate sales activity and develop marketing plans. One of the staff's first jobs was to develop a yearly sales forecast. This was accomplished through account-by-account analyses by each ATI salesman, which were later combined at headquarters into a national sales forecast.

Throughout 1965, the corporate marketing staff was assisting ATI's salesmen with major presentations to national marketing companies. These presentations represented a relatively new development for the industry. They were made to old customers whom ATI hoped to retain by developing new products for them, and to prospective customers who were either existing or potential aerosol marketers. As a result of one of these presentations, ATI developed a complete program—product, package design, and advertising theme—for marketing an aerosol hair spray for the American Home Products Company. Even though American Home had never marketed a hair spray before, this new brand, Sudden Beauty, became one of the top four hair sprays in 1965.

At the end of 1965, ATI had two men on its corporate marketing staff, four divisional sales managers, and six field salesmen. In addition to helping make the major presentations, the salesmen served as a liaison between the customer's purchasing, research, and marketing groups and the ATI organization.

Research and Development. In late 1965, ATI formed a new corporation called the Aerosol Techniques Research Center, Inc. This division was building a new research center in Milford, Connecticut, which would eventually be staffed by 15 to 25 people, headed by Mr. Clarence Clapp, an ATI vice president formerly with Western Filling. At the same time, a new technical services department was formed under ATI vice president Fred Presant, who had worked in the aerosol industry for 18 years. Technical services encompassed all the operating division's customer service, quality control, and product development laboratories. In Mr. Clapp's opinion, the new research center, combined with the technical services department, would give ATI the best research and product development activity among all contract fillers.

While the technical services department worked hand in hand with ATI's customers to improve product formulations, the research center was to be devoted solely to the development of new or improved products and new or improved technology in the aerosol field. According to Mr. Clapp:

> The direction of the research and development effort at the research center will be determined to a large degree by the market research department. Market research will be involved at both the initial and final stages of most projects. This is necessary because the ultimate dependence of our success rests with the consumer.

This policy implied that most projects chosen were expected to become commercially feasible within one to three years. Nevertheless, Mr. Clapp said that ATI would still have some commitment to "blue sky" projects, provided the financial commitments were not too heavy. He also indicated that ATI would seek technical assistance from its suppliers as much as possible but, when necessary, would perform research in the areas of new containers, valves, and propellants. To help protect accomplishments, ATI planned to seek far more patents than in the past. Mr. Clapp indicated that, when patents were not obtainable, ATI would seek contractual agreements with its customers or utilize secrecy.

The importance of R.&D. to ATI's success up to 1965 is indicated by the company's record for new products and technical developments generated. These included the first personal deodorant, Right Guard; a patented water-based hair spray, which allowed cost savings of 10% to 30%; the first aerosol mouth freshener; the first dimethyl ether propellant system, which reduced costs because it was water soluble; and the first aerosol barbecue sauce. In conjunction with a leading can company, ATI developed the first three-piece high-pressure container, which reduced costs since less propellant was required. ATI also developed new formulations which became leading products in their respective markets, e.g., Sudden Beauty hair spray, Dust and Wax furniture polish, Perform aerosol starch, and Fuller's oven cleaner. In addition, ATI had a complete cross section of all types of aerosol products on the market in 1965, even though the company might not have been the original developer of some of these products.

Another indication of ATI's commitment to R.&D. was contained in Mr. Shepherd's exposition on "The Contract Filler's Role in Aerosol

Product Development," which appeared in the December, 1963, issue of *Aerosol Age:*

In order to know of the future and to predict, within reasonable bounds, what we [the contract fillers] should be doing, we must understand the past and recognize the trends that are already discernible . . . we must understand what are the distinctive competences of the filler today and what these will be in the future. How should they be shaped and guided in order to continue the development of the aerosol industry? In the application of the resources at the disposal of the contract filler, how and when should these resources be allocated? How should they be developed? When I write of "resources," I mean things such as men, money and materials. I also mean the fund of knowledge and experience of the contract filler and new technological changes which shall come from the contract filler. . . . I think we can expect to see a continual increase in the concentration of power in the hands of the marketing companies. We can expect to endure severe conditions of excess capacity and price competition among fillers. Because of these increasing economic pressures on marketers and contract fillers, there will be an even greater need for creative, new product and marketing concepts. In order to continue to play a role in the development of this industry, the contract filler must now begin to use effectively those distinctive competences and resources which he has developed over the years. These distinctive competences are first *creativity* and the *ability to innovate technologically.* The second distinctive competence . . . is that of the many years of experience in the organizations of the members of this industry. The next resource is that of having capacity to manufacture a wide spectrum of aerosol products. Next, those contract fillers who have moved toward putting facilities up in strategic locations, in this country and on the continent, have moved toward offering more complete servicing of both national and international markets in terms of distribution. Finally, one distinctive competence which is not universally held by contract fillers organizations is that of capably using new management techniques and tools.

Production.   Aerosol products were manufactured in two basic ways in 1965. The slower but more accurate method was called cold filling. In this method, the propellant and product fill were liquefied by refrigeration and "poured" into the containers in carefully measured amounts. The cap and valve were then inserted by hand and sealed by machine, after which the filled containers were passed through a hot water bath to test for pressure leaks. Finally, labels were applied and the product was packaged for storage or shipment. The more rapid method was called pressure filling. In this method, the cap and valve were inserted in the container and then sealed at the same time a vacuum was created in the container. Next the product fill and propellant were injected through the valve into the empty container by the application of extremely high pressure. The filled container was then labeled and packaged for storage or shipment. In 1965, filling speeds of 200 cans per minute were considered high for aerosol production. However, speeds of 100 cans per minute had been considered high in 1960. Mr. Donald Schoonmaker, ATI's eastern division production manager, indicated that filling speeds might double again by 1970.

At the end of 1965, ATI had four plants with 21 filling lines located across the United States so as to insure national distribution at minimal cost. About 50% of ATI's equipment was new and 50% was relatively old. However, Mr. Schoonmaker said ATI's production efficiency was equal to or better than that of other contract fillers. Mr. Schoonmaker also felt that ATI had extremely good quality control, which he thought most contract fillers would be hard pressed to match. At this time, ATI's annual production capacity was about 390 million units.

Table 3 indicates the location and number of filling lines for each of ATI's four plants.

TABLE 3

Location	Number of Filling Lines	Approximate Annual Production Capacity (Millions of Units)	Warehouse Space (Thousand of Square Feet)
Bridgeport, Conn. (leased)	6	150	150
Los Angeles, Calif. (leased)	4	95	130
Danville, Ill. (owned)	6	100	100
West Roxbury, Mass. (leased)	5	45	30
Total	21	390	410

The Bridgeport facility, a converted piano factory, also contained the company's executive offices and research laboratories.

In June, 1965, ATI began an expansion program designed to raise capacity to 430 million units by the end of 1966. This $4.2 million program included (1) a new building in Milford, Connecticut, to house the company's main offices and eastern division plant, replacing the overcrowded Bridgeport factory and offices; (2) a new research center, also located at Milford; (3) acquisition of a new building and property in Danville, Illinois, to double the facilities of the company's Continental Filling division; (4) addition of a production line and new warehouse area in Los Angeles to increase the capacity of the Western Filling division; and (5) completion of a new aerosol pharmaceutical development and filling installation at Armstrong Laboratories in West Roxbury.

All facilities were designed to permit the installation of additional lines in the future. Expenditures required to bring capacity into line with future sales targets were estimated as shown in Table 4.

TABLE 4

Fiscal Year	Target Sales (Millions of Units)	Production Capacity* (Millions of Units)	Capital Expenditures to Obtain Additional Capacity (Thousands of Dollars)
1967...............	330	467	$480
1968...............	400	497	490
1969...............	460	532	520

* Reserve capacity in excess of sales targets was required to handle emergency orders and seasonal fluctuations.

According to Mr. Schoonmaker, expansion would be aimed at meeting the needs of national marketers who had medium-volume, high-quality, high-margin products. He felt this policy would enable ATI to make better use of its distinctive competences in R.&D. instead of having to sell on a price basis, as was necessary on mass-produced standardized products.

Organization and Control. In late 1965, ATI had four operating divisions in addition to the corporate staff and the research and technical services divisions. The name, location, and general managers of these divisions are listed in Table 5.

TABLE 5

Division	Location	General Manager	Previous Position of General Manager
Eastern division.....	Bridgeport, Conn.	John Kossak	Plant manager, General Foods, and operated own company
Western division....	Los Angeles, Calif.	John Manara	President, Western Filling Company
Continental division.	Danville, Ill.	Chris Canaday	President, Continental Filling Company
Armstrong Laboratories division.....	West Roxbury, Mass.	Robert Armstrong, Jr.	President, Armstrong Laboratories

Each of these general managers was an ATI vice president. According to Mr. Rossetti, corporate treasurer, these general managers operated their divisions somewhat like independent entrepreneurs. For example, while the divisions sent monthly and quarterly profit reports to corporate headquarters, these reports were not standardized, and Mr.

Rossetti said the divisional general managers were not evaluated on the basis of these reports. Nevertheless, Mr. Rossetti felt that the divisional general managers tried to maximize profits. The primary purpose of the reports was to enable the corporate staff to assist the divisional general managers by uncovering unfavorable performance trends.

In 1965, ATI did not employ a standard cost system or accumulate actual costs in such a way that it could estimate the relative efficiency of its different pieces of equipment or the relative profitability of its different products. While Mr. Rossetti indicated that such estimates might be desirable in the future, he felt it more important for ATI to keep up with rapidly expanding new product areas than to allocate its resources on the basis of estimated profitability.

In addition, since materials accounted for 85% of the total cost of finished products, Mr. Rossetti felt that costs could be effectively controlled by having efficient, modern equipment, by having careful quality control to minimize rejects and insure proper filling operations, and by purchasing high-quality materials at competitive prices. In order to help control materials usage, ATI was installing an IBM 1401A computer at the end of 1965.

Financial Situation. To finance new fixed assets and increase working capital, ATI sold 80,000 shares of common stock to the public in October, 1965, at $22 a share. An additional $3 million was raised by the sale of 5½% 25-year secured notes of subsidiaries to an insurance company.

PROBLEMS AND ALTERNATIVES AT THE END OF 1965

An internal policy memorandum issued in December, 1965, stated:

. . . ATI's position of leadership in the aerosol industry may not be sufficient to sustain ATI's objectives of $100 million in sales and 7% after taxes by 1969. This gap between our abilities and our goals has been brought about by factors underlying both the company's environment and the company's resources.

Environmental trends noted in this memorandum included the maturation of industry structure and aerosol technology, the increasingly heavy competition among contract fillers, the attendant threat to high-level profits, and the increasing power of the marketing companies. Mr. Shepherd commented as follows on these and other problems:

Most of the problems ATI faces now—customers going captive and pressured profit margins—we faced 10 years ago, and in a sense, they're no more serious now than then. However, because of the trend toward competition on the basis of price, we are increasingly aware of the fact that ATI will have to become more formalistic and number-oriented—a prospect I would dislike *if* it saps creativity. Thus, if the only thing I can do is beat a competitor's price, I don't feel that I'm contributing much—and more to the point—I don't feel that ATI is contributing. Our historical excellence is in creating profits for our customers through the kind of innovation which helped us to develop Right Guard for Gillette and, more recently, miniatures, a development which was written up in *The Wall Street Journal.*[3]

Again, this trend toward a more formalistic organization will have to be balanced with what I believe are my responsibilities to the people who make up our organization and its social and business interrelationships. Up until now our creativity has given us an opportunity to allow the people within our organization to find their own particular niche—even though this process takes time and in the short run uses up profits. However, in a really price competitive market there would be no time for slack, no time for learning, and no opportunity for personal change. I believe that, in the long run, such an atmosphere would be damaging to our organization and to the interests of the company. So it is for this reason, in addition to our natural desire to achieve economic success, that we are looking at other businesses where we can use the technical and organizational creativity that we have developed over the past ten years.

This doesn't mean that we plan to de-emphasize the aerosol business altogether. However, we are considering other businesses which we might enter to hedge against the threats we see in the aerosol business. Ten years from now I expect that the aerosol business might be like the can business today: efficient production, tight control, low margins, and no fun—except when creating new opportunities for new products through technical and marketing research.

In looking at other businesses, there are three things I consider important. First, we should get closer to the consumer, where price isn't the only reason for survival. This is where the real opportunity for product innovation lies. Second, the acquired company should have good management so that we can build on it, rather than being forced to decimate the company and start from scratch. Finally, I would like to have a "feel" for the business.

As a result of environmental trends and Mr. Shepherd's concern about the future nature of the aerosol business, considerable attention was being focused on the question of what economic opportunities were available to ATI.

Although the European aerosol market was expanding rapidly, ATI

---

[3] "Marketing Miniatures: Now Products Come in One-Use Packages," *The Wall Street Journal* (April 13, 1966):

Make way for the teeny-weeny economy size.

It contains one serving or application, and it's one of the hottest packaging concepts since the super-duper economy size. What's more, despite the increased cost per ounce the one-shot helping can prove to be a consumer's most economical buy.

.   .   .   .

Many of the goods are sold in pressurized aerosol containers. Aerosol Techniques, Inc., for example, is about to start commercial production of a breath freshener in a small aerosol container—not one shot but much smaller than any previous models—and is testing small containers of an antiperspirant, a man's hair spray, and a nasal spray.

paid little attention to expanding its operations overseas. However, it was considering strategies that would allow continued success in the domestic aerosol business. At the end of 1965, it had three groups of Harvard Business School students working on projects related to forward or backward integration. One group was considering possible acquisitions of plastic cap-and-valve manufacturers, even though this industry appeared at first glance to suffer from strong price competition and from profit margins lower than for contract filling. Another student group was concerned about the future of the food aerosol business. The third was studying markets for other types of packaging services that ATI might provide.

Possible Forward Integration. Some members of management felt that ATI should begin marketing products to the end-use consumer in order to get the higher profit margins associated with this business. There was, however, considerable concern lest such action cause ATI to lose some of its present customers, who would not want their supplier as a competitor. On the other hand, there had been little reaction from these same customers when ATI took Sudden Beauty hair spray to American Home Products, Inc., a company that had never been in the hair spray business, and essentially established AHP as one of the country's leading hair spray marketers. ATI's management also wondered whether ATI had the financial and managerial resources to market a consumer product nationally.

Diversification Guidelines. The major focus of ATI's attention, however, was directed toward diversification out of the aerosol business. According to the December policy memorandum,

The need for an unconventional miracle is prompted by our objectives, by an assessment of the present economic progress of our aerosol business and by the question of whether ATI's strategy is viable for the next decade. . . . It is the contention of this paper that at least the following criteria must be met if a profitable diversification is to be achieved:

1. The company should promise a growth rate compatible with ATI's own rate of growth.
2. The company should promise a return on investment compatible with ATI's own R.O.I. performance.
3. The company's management should not retard the growth of our own management structure.
4. The company should be a company to which ATI should be able to contribute synergetically so that there will exist the best possible opportunity for reaching the above listed financial criteria. In this context ATI's distinctive competences have been suggested as:
   a. Nationwide manufacturing and management facilities;

   b. A capacity to direct technological innovation toward supplying consumer and/or industrial needs;
   c. A strong series of relationships with the chemical industry; and
   d. A strong series of relationships with the financial community.
5. The company should be a company which has the capacity to contribute an additional distinctive competence to ATI. Examples of the kind of contribution we have in mind are:
   a. A sales force for the sale of (say) industrial specialty chemicals;
   b. A technological niche in a nonaerosol packaging service so that ATI can be in a position to develop an integrated system of packaging services backed by nationwide manufacturing facilities, a nationwide sales force, unique packaging machinery of our own design, and a research facility specializing in formulation chemistry related to personal, household, pharmaceutical, and food products;
   c. The ability to manufacture nonaerosol personal products—e.g., specialty soap, eye makeup, lipsticks, etc.
6. The size of the company should be such as to make possible a noticeable contribution to ATI's earnings per share after taking into account the potential effect of a synergetic relationship. In this regard the generation of an incremental 10¢ per share in earnings would be considered by ATI to be a noticeable financial contribution.

Such opportunities could lie in industries as diverse as microencapsulation and radiation as well as in consumer and/or industrial packaging and/or product services, but what is most important for us to develop is a sense for the future and a technological and marketing ability to meet this challenge within the framework of the financial criteria listed above and our own resources.

The Quality Products Company. At the beginning of 1966, Mr. Meyer was engaged in the evaluation of over 20 possible acquisitions in light of the above guidelines for diversification. He indicated that the guidelines did not adequately emphasize the desire of ATI's management for developing an end-consumer marketing activity. According to Mr. Meyer:

ATI's management would like to reduce both the risks associated with being a one-product company and the risks associated with being solely a supplier to those companies which market a product to the end consumer. While Mr. Shepherd would prefer to serve industrial end customers, the real emphasis is to get closer to an end-use market where ATI can best exploit its distinctive creative and innovative talents and yet not prejudice its relations with its existing customers. In this connection, it will be an interesting task to identify the "legitimate" path between customer loyalty and new opportunities in those end-use markets suited to our strengths.

Presently we're not sure whether we should acquire several small companies or one large one. Having a family of small companies is certainly a situation which we have learned to live with in a constructive and profitable way. It is also true that having several associated companies might help us to solve some management problems if it becomes necessary to move toward more centralized management of our aerosol operations, since these associated companies might then provide a constructive way to utilize the talents of those of our present divisional managers who are experienced and gifted entrepreneurs. On the other hand, a large acquisition might be the essential step necessary to help us build a reputation of excellence in a new field and this strategy might have substantial appeal to the entrepreneur who looks forward to corporate size as a means of at long last achieving the institution of a stable enterprise.

Basically then, no acquisition is too big or too small. Rather different, and at first sight perhaps conflicting, criteria must be used to judge each individual case. Meanwhile, we are trying to use the time we have to test the assumption that we have the brains and feelings necessary for growth into a different and changing environment with a different and changing organization.

The Quality Products Company[4] was one of the more promising acquisition prospects that Mr. Meyer was considering. Quality Products was a small company in the women's hand lotion business. During the fiscal year ended December 30, 1965, Quality earned about $92,000 on sales of $2.3 million, which represented an increase of $28,000 in profits and $300,000 in sales from the 1964 fiscal year (see Exhibits 10 and 11).

Exhibit 10

AEROSOL TECHNIQUES, INC.

QUALITY PRODUCTS COMPANY

Income Statements

(Dollars in Thousands)

	1961	1962	1963	1964	9 months 1965
Income from sales	$1,258	$2,024	$1,890	$2,002	$1,744
Cost of sales	1,036	1,596	1,579	1,575	1,380
Gross profit	$ 222	$ 428	$ 311	$ 427	$ 364
Selling expenses	60	74	102	107	88
General and administrative	60	72	91	109	81
Other expenses	3	2	9	7	7
Total deductions	$ 123	$ 148	$ 202	$ 222	$ 176
Income before officers' salaries, profit sharing, and taxes	$ 100	$ 280	$ 109	$ 205	$ 188
Officers' salaries	58	58	58	61	60
Profit sharing	16	24	23	30	..
Federal and state income taxes	8	103	10	50	59
Net income	$ 17	$ 95	$ 19	$ 64	$ 69

Source: Quality Products annual reports.

---

[4] For reasons of security, ATI desired that the name of the company and the name of the industry be disguised. The basic characteristics of the company and of the industry (e.g., size, nature of competition, product-market characteristics, etc.) are not disguised, however.

Exhibit 11

AEROSOL TECHNIQUES, INC.

QUALITY PRODUCTS COMPANY

Balance Sheet for Year Ending December 31, 1965

Current assets:

Cash	$135
Treasury bonds	2
Accounts receivable	193
Inventory	357
Other	38
Total current assets	$275

Fixed assets (net):

Machinery and equipment	$122
Laboratory equipment	1
Furniture and fixtures	22
Leasehold improvements	34
Total fixed assets	$179
Other assets	46
Total assets	$950

Current liabilities:

Accounts payable and accrued expenses	$105
Notes payable to bank	225
Other	3
Taxes payable	72
Total current liabilities	$406
Deferred tax credit	11

Stockholders' equity:

Capital stock $25 par value	$ 94
Capital surplus	83
Retained earnings	356
Total stockholders' equity	$533
Total liabilities and stockholders' equity	$950

Source: Quality Products 1965 annual report.

Quality specialized in the manufacture of high-grade women's hand lotions, which it then sold to various prestige marketing companies which marketed the products under their own brands. Quality also manufactured hand lotion of normal quality, which it sold to various supermarkets on a private-brand basis. At the end of 1965, Quality was constructing a new plant in Philadelphia which would increase capacity from $2.5 million to $4 million and would make possible more efficient operations than the present three-building plant.

Quality's management felt that, as soon as the new plant had "shaken down," a minimum sales increase of $1.3 million could be expected on the basis of preliminary contacts it had made with potential customers. Quality's management also expected that demand for high-grade hand lotions would increase because of several trends: the increased wealth and general desire for luxury, the rapid growth of the fragrance market and the impact thereof on sales of higher priced hand lotions, and the public's increasing receptiveness to greater luxury in hand creams as a result of mass advertising by the larger manufacturers who were improving their lower priced, mass-marketed hand creams.

Mr. Meyer indicated that the proposed acquisition was not without risk, however. His primary concern was that almost 50% of Quality's 1965 sales came from one customer, and that this percentage was expected to increase to 75% after the new factory was in operation. Mr. Meyer felt that with Quality producing nearly 30% of this customer's requirements, representing $3 million in sales, there was some risk the customer might decide to manufacture for himself. Nevertheless, given the willingness of ATI's management to live with this kind of risk, which was common in the packaging industry, Mr. Meyer felt that the decision to acquire Quality would rest on the cost of the deal and the degree to which ATI's resources could help Quality to grow and to minimize its vulnerability to the decisions of its major customer.

Mr. Meyer also indicated that if ATI acquired Quality, it would probably try to purchase the high-grade hand cream division of one of the large national manufacturers that was located in the Midwest, giving ATI national coverage of this grade of hand cream business. He felt the chances of negotiating this purchase would be better than fifty-fifty, since the national manufacturer had not exhibited a deep interest in this division for over 15 years.

Patterson & Swift, Inc.

PATTERSON & SWIFT, INC., of Philadelphia, produced two lines of electrical relays[1] that it sold to manufacturers of communications equipment and industrial, aircraft, and missile controls. One line, with 15 basic types and many hundreds of variations, was considered "specialized" and was engineered to work under conditions of shock, vibration, and extreme temperatures. These relays reacted to electric impulses of fractions of a watt, or to small amounts of light in photoelectric applications. According to a government survey, the company produced almost 30% of United States output of these relay types.

The other line consisted of about 20 standardized relay types designed to work under less extreme conditions. In addition, the company manufactured some industrial control systems on a custom order basis and produced an electronic household timer in limited numbers.

Specialized relays generally required modification to fit particular customer requirements. Company executives believed that design, quality, reliability, and service were of greater importance than price in competing with six larger manufacturers having diversified lines, and with about 100 smaller companies specializing in certain relay types. Executives further believed the company had a technical lead of a year or more in several specialized relay types.

The standard relays competed through price as well as through rigid adherence to standards, service, and innovations in design. There were numerous large competitors in this field. Household timers were made by a limited number of manufacturers. The company's product was a high-priced quality item sold through better mail-order and department stores.

In the fall of 1956, company sales reached an $8 million level, of which 62% went to military uses. Relays accounted for about 86% of total sales. (For financial statements and an analysis of sales, see Exhibits 1, 2, and 3.)

---

[1] Circuit breakers or switches activated by electric current.

Exhibit 1

PATTERSON & SWIFT, INC.
Sales Analysis
(Thousands of Dollars)

	9 Months Ended 9/30/56	1955	1954	1953	1952	1951	1950	1949	1948	1947	1946	1945
Relay sales	$5,318	$5,544	$5,547	$8,342	$5,820	$2,348	$1,001	$ 870	$533	$390	$228	$613
Other products	866	879	731	571	433	442	463	301	176	86	71	27
Total sales	$6,184	$6,423	$6,278	$8,913	$6,253	$2,790	$1,464	$1,171	$659	$476	$298	$640
Relay sales	86%	86%	88%	94%	93%	84%	68%	74%	81%	82%	77%	96%
Other products	14	14	12	6	7	16	32	26	19	18	23	4
Total sales	100%	100%	100%	100%	100%	100%	100%	100%	100%	100%	100%	100%
Sales to military	$3,836	$4,065	$3,961	$6,914	$4,979	$1,852	$ 877	.....	.....	.....	.....	$416
Civilian sales	2,348	2,358	2,317	1,999	1,274	938	587	$1,171	$659	$476	$298	224
Total sales	$6,184	$6,423	$6,278	$8,913	$6,253	$2,790	$1,464	$1,171	$659	$476	$298	$640
Sales to military	62%	63%	63%	78%	80%	66%	60%	NA	NA	NA	NA	65%
Civilian sales	38	37	37	22	20	34	40	(Military Sales Dropped)				35
Total sales	100%	100%	100%	100%	100%	100%	100%	100%	100%	100%	100%	100%
Backlog—relays	$1,613	$1,915	$1,824	$3,574	$8,105	NA	NA	NA	NA	NA	NA	NA
Backlog—other products	137	75	43	61	19							
Total backlog	$1,750	$1,990	$1,857	$3,635	$8,124							
Inventory—relays	$1,118	$ 867	$ 508	$1,009	$ 715	$ 517	$ 167	$ 93	$ 36	$ 28	$ 22	$ 21
Inventory—other products	275	269	233	144	65	84	52	38	16	8	5	4
Total inventory	$1,393	$1,136	$ 741	$1,153	$ 780	$ 601	$ 219	$ 131	$ 52	$ 36	$ 27	$ 25

NA Not available.
Source: Company records.

Exhibit 2

PATTERSON & SWIFT, INC.

Balance Sheets as of December 31, 1945–55, and September 30, 1956

(Thousands of Dollars)

	Sept. 30, 1956	Dec. 31, 1955	Dec. 31, 1954	Dec. 31, 1953	Dec. 31, 1952	Dec. 31, 1951	Dec. 31, 1950	Dec. 31, 1949	Dec. 31, 1948	Dec. 31, 1947	Dec. 31, 1946	Dec. 31, 1945
Assets												
Cash	$ 385	$ 423	$ 268	$ 220	$ 178	$ 100	$ 73	$ 66	$ 21	$ 31	$ 13	$ 17
Accounts Receivable—Trade	1,004	834	682	854	310	250	193	112	77	28	57	86
Accounts Receivable—Assigned	…	…	…	190	681	352	…	…	…	…	…	…
Loans to Employees	50	24	11	21	4	5	…	…	…	…	…	…
Notes Receivable	6	11	3	3	…	…	…	…	…	…	…	…
Notes Receivable—Employees	60	62	62	69	…	…	…	…	…	…	…	…
Inventory	1,393	1,136	741	1,153	780	601	219	131	52	36	27	25
Total Current Assets	$2,898	$2,490	$1,767	$2,510	$1,953	$1,308	$ 485	$309	$150	$ 95	$ 97	$128
Land and Buildings—Net	160	215	265	303	357	447	36	38	21	23	20	21
Machinery and Equipment—Net	127	120	158	171	164	152	48	36	24	20	11	13
Goodwill	…	…	…	…	…	…	…	…	7	7	7	7
Other Assets	12	20	16	13	16	5	12	9	5	4	2	4
Total Assets	$3,197	$2,845	$2,206	$2,997	$2,490	$1,912	$ 581	$392	$207	$149	$137	$173
Liabilities												
Accounts Payable—Trade	$ 291	$ 343	$ 253	$ 475	$ 161	$ 206	$ 97	$ 87	$ 58	$ 14	$ 24	$ 24
Notes Payable—Bank	…	…	…	176	157	608	…	…	…	11	12	…
Accrued Payroll and Taxes	178	336	243	194	164	138	34	28	13	9	8	7
Accrued Profit Sharing	84	23	115	231	78	30	18	1	…	…	…	…
Reserve for Year End Adjustment	133	…	…	…	…	…	…	…	…	…	…	…
Reserve for Federal and State Taxes	542	475	214	726	856	166	89	57	6	11	4	43
Total Current Liabilities	$1,228	$1,177	$ 825	$1,802	$1,416	$1,148	$ 238	$173	$ 77	$ 45	$ 48	$ 74
Reserve for Past Emergency Costs	50	90	90	90	90	…	…	…	…	…	…	…
Mortgage Payable—Real Estate	…	27	84	84	259	316	62	45	…	…	…	…
Notes Payable—Employees	183	122	89	61	78	54	…	…	…	…	…	…

Capital Stock—Common	7	7	7	7	7	7	19	19	19	19	19	19
Capital Stock—Class A	16	16	1	1	....	....	....	....	....	....	....	....
Paid in Surplus	33	9	16	16	12	12	....	....	....	....	....	....
Earned Surplus	1,830	1,397	1,094	936	628	376	262	155	87	85	70	80
Total	$1,886	$1,429	$1,118	$ 960	$ 647	$ 395	$281	$174	$106	$104	$ 89	$ 99
Less: Treasury Stock	150	....	....	....	....	1	....	....	....	....	....	....
Total Capital Stock and Surplus	$1,736	$1,429	$ 960	$ 960	$ 647	$ 394	$281	$174	$106	$104	$ 89	$ 99
Total Liabilities	$3,197	$2,845	$2,206	$2,997	$2,490	$1,912	$581	$392	$207	$149	$137	$173
Working Capital	$1,670	$1,313	$ 942	$ 708	$ 537	$ 160	$247	$136	$ 73	$ 50	$ 49	$ 54
Current Ratio	2.4:1	2.1:1	2.1:1	1.4:1	1.4:1	1.1:1	2.0:1	1.8:1	1.9:1	2.1:1	2.0:1	1.7:1
Acid Test	1.2:1	1.2:1	1.2:1	0.8:1	0.8:1	0.6:1	1.1:1	1.0:1	1.3:1	1.3:1	1.4:1	1.4:1
% Earned on Net Worth after Taxes	25.0%	22.2%	14.1%	32.1%	52.9%	29.2%	37.4%	43.6%	1.9%	14.4%	....	26.3%

Source: Company records.

Exhibit 3

PATTERSON & SWIFT, INC.

Statements of Income and Expense

(Thousands of Dollars)

	1945	1946	1947	1948	1949	1950	1951	1952	1953*	1954	1955	9 Months Ended 9/30/56
Net sales	$640	$298	$476	$659	$1,171	$1,464	$2,790	$6,253	$8,913	$6,278	$6,423	$6,184
Cost of goods sold:												
Direct labor	$ 85	$ 59	$ 65	$101	$ 152	$ 186	$ 363	$ 710	$ 900	$ 712	$ 823	$ 692
Materials	196	87	122	226	397	438	1,072	2,091	4,086	1,622	2,058	1,891
Factory burden	156	95	145	184	308	419	854	1,581	2,092	1,821	1,782	1,554
Total	$437	$241	$332	$511	$ 857	$1,043	$2,289	$4,382	$7,078	$4,155	$4,663	$4,137
Inventory adjustment	2	3	8	16	79	88	382	180	373	(413)	394	257
Cost of goods sold	$435	$238	$324	$495	$ 778	$ 955	$1,907	$4,202	$6,705	$4,568	$4,269	$3,880
Gross profit	$205	$ 60	$152	$164	$ 393	$ 509	$ 883	$2,051	$2,208	$1,710	$2,154	$2,304
Operating expenses:												
Selling and administration	$101	$ 90	$101	$110	$ 185	$ 198	$ 364	$ 551	$ 706	$ 732	$ 844	$ 708
Commissions	35	21	31	51	86	134	239	390	548	452	463	441
Total	$136	$111	$132	$161	$ 271	$ 332	$ 603	$ 941	$1,254	$1,184	$1,307	$1,149
Net operating profit	$ 69	($ 51)	$ 20	$ 3	$ 122	$ 177	$ 280	$1,110	$ 954	$ 526	$ 847	$1,155
Profit sharing										217	228	280
Net income before federal taxes	$ 69	($ 51)	$ 20	$ 3	$ 122	$ 177	$ 280	$1,110	$ 954	$ 309	$ 619	$ 875
Provision for federal income taxes	43		5	1	46	72	165	768	646	151	301	442
Net income after taxes	$ 26	($ 51)	$ 15	$ 2	$ 76	$ 105	$ 115	$ 342	$ 308	$ 158	$ 318	$ 433

Net sales	100.0%	100.0%	100.0%	100.0%	100.0%	100.0%	100.0%	100.0%	100.0%	100.0%	100.0%	100.0%
Cost of goods sold:												
Direct labor	11.2	12.8	11.3	10.1	11.4	13.0	12.7	13.0	15.3	13.7	19.8	13.3
Materials	30.6	32.0	25.9	45.8	33.4	38.4	29.9	33.9	34.3	25.6	29.2	30.6
Factory burden	25.2	27.8	29.0	23.5	25.3	30.7	28.6	26.3	27.9	30.5	31.9	24.4
Total	67.0%	72.6%	66.2%	79.4%	70.1%	82.1%	71.2%	73.2%	77.5%	69.8%	80.9%	68.3%
Inventory adjustment	4.2	6.1	(6.6)	4.2	2.9	13.7	6.0	6.8	2.4	1.7	1.0	0.3
Cost of goods sold	62.8%	66.5%	72.8%	75.2%	67.2%	68.4%	65.2%	66.4%	75.1%	68.1%	79.9%	68.0%
Gross profit	37.2%	33.5%	27.2%	24.8%	32.8%	31.6%	34.8%	33.6%	24.9%	31.9%	20.1%	32.0%
Operating expenses:												
Selling and administration	11.4%	13.1%	11.6%	7.9%	8.8%	13.0%	13.5%	15.8%	16.7%	21.2%	30.2%	15.8%
Commissions	7.2	7.2	7.2	6.2	6.2	8.6	9.2	7.3	7.7	6.5	7.0	5.4
Total	18.6%	20.3%	18.8%	14.1%	15.0%	21.6%	22.7%	23.1%	24.4%	27.7%	37.2%	21.2%
Net operating profit	18.6%	13.2%	8.4%	10.7%	17.8%	10.0%	12.1%	10.5%	0.5%	4.2%	(17.1)%	10.8%
Profit sharing	4.5	3.6	3.5	....	....	....	....	....	....	....	....	....
Net income before taxes	14.1%	9.6%	4.9%	10.7%	17.8%	10.0%	12.1%	10.5%	0.5%	4.2%	(17.1)%	10.8%
Provision for federal income taxes	7.1	4.7	2.4	7.2	12.3	5.9	4.9	4.0	0.2	1.0	....	6.7
Net income after taxes	7.0%	4.9%	2.5%	3.5%	5.5%	4.1%	7.2%	6.5%	0.3%	3.2%	(17.1)%	4.1%

* Subcontracts of about $1.0 million let to other companies are included.
Note: Figures in parentheses indicate loss.
Source: Company records.

HISTORY

The company was founded by its president, Chester F. Patterson, and the engineering manager, Henry T. Swift. Friends since the early thirties, the cofounders started business before the war, first producing a jointly developed navigational instrument, and thereafter experimenting with job-order manufacturing. During the war they acquired control of a small company making specialized relays which was put on a paying basis after considerable experiment. It reached a peak in 1945, with 150 employees and sales of well over $500,000.

After the war, loss of Navy contracts and the two-year lead time generally required to develop products for a low-margin commercial market proved to be difficult, but by 1949 the company had been successfully converted. The Korean conflict brought back military contracts, and by 1953 the company employed 700 people and reached a sales volume of almost $9 million. This expansion was accomplished with the help of a $725,000 V-Loan that was paid off in 18 months. However, financial stress during these years was so great that "reasonable salaries were not paid to management until after 1953," according to Mr. Patterson. "But today the banks are looking for business with us," he said.

During expansion additional difficulties arose from moving to the present building and from the use of subcontractors, some of whom could not master the technical intricacies of the product. "In short, we were the third bottleneck in the United States electronics industry, and the government was furious," said Mr. Patterson.

ORGANIZATION AND OWNERSHIP

"We don't like titles around here," said Mr. Patterson. He stated that Mr. Fritz ("Red") Gruber was in charge of sales, Henry Swift of all engineering, James Clark of accounting, and Joseph Adams of "everything else." (See Exhibit 4.)

Mr. Patterson was the major stockholder, owning just over 50% of the company's stock, while his brother Thomas and Henry Swift together owned just under 50%. A recent proxy arrangement gave voting supremacy to any two of the three major stockholders. These three men composed the board of directors, together with James Cooper, company clerk, who was a partner in a local law firm.

Mr. Patterson characterized the board, which met infrequently as a "very minor vehicle for gripe sessions and a means to tease the president." He said it rarely made decisions of any consequence. In his opinion,

Exhibit 4

PATTERSON & SWIFT, INC.
Organization Chart

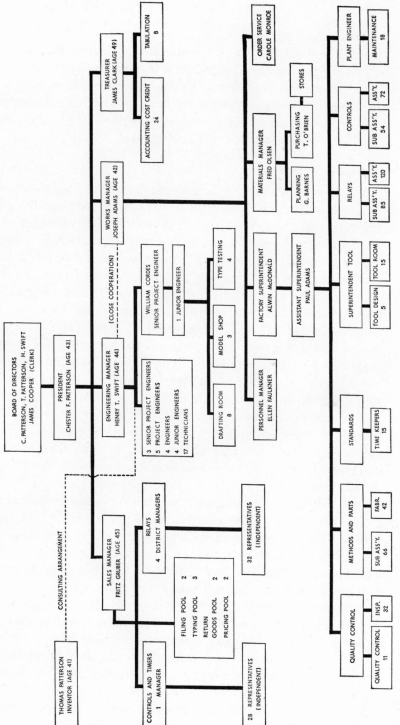

Source: Company executives.

there was no need for any outside members. For example, he said had the board deliberated on the expansion of civilian business back in 1946, the main questions would have been technical, so outsiders could have contributed little. Similarly, the issue of profit sharing was not handled as a "vast policy decision," but was talked about informally in two or three meetings. "We consider ourselves able to reason carefully about the problems that come up," he said.

PRESIDENT PATTERSON

Mr. Patterson, a philosophy major in college and a self-educated engineer, was described by his associates as a gifted designer with a searching mind that could get at the core of the most difficult technical or administrative problems by isolating key issues through sharp questioning. Although he was admired for this ability, some executives believed there was reluctance, especially in the middle-management group, to seek his advice for fear of being shown up. He had a reputation for keeping somewhat aloof from his subordinates. Mr. Patterson himself commented that he loved to talk, and that "some people get scared because I tend to talk too loud, too fast, and too insistent. I like to discuss a problem 'coequally,' and I get along with people who manage to rise to this relationship. I prefer to discuss things in the way roommates in college would do it, and I don't like to pull rank. But some people here believe that my influence counts more than my attempt to avoid authoritative behavior and that there are some who do things not because they are convinced, but because they wish to please Chet Patterson. I don't think this is true; I try to act as if I had only one vote along with the rest."

In building his organization, the president was attempting to "get away from having all the answers," as he put it. "Some time ago," he said, "I began to feel the effect of knowing more than other people. I then realized that this condition could develop yes-men around me, and luckily managed to avoid that. In the past, I used to know every person and job in the place, but this was a long time ago."

Mr. Patterson stated that at one time he had found an effective means of control in taking direct charge of the disposition and handling of returned goods. By investigating customer complaints, he was able to spot weaknesses, especially in engineering and production. As new technical developments grew in number, however, he was forced to assign this responsibility to the engineers.

Mr. Patterson currently received three monthly reports at which he looked if he was "concerned about something." Two one-page summaries showed orders on hand, shipments, backlogs, and materials on order. The third statement, which he called "blueprint," contained detailed balance sheets and operating statements that compared actual with budgeted performance by months and gave cumulative totals to date.

Most of Mr. Patterson's activities, he said, reflected his particular interests. "I look over the shoulders of the engineers who are working on new products or new processes, and I pinch-hit there once in a while."

Another interest was advertising for the sensitive relay line; he personally supervised this activity, suggesting ideas or writing copy, often of a conversational, witty character for the advertisements that appeared from time to time in magazines like *Scientific American* and *Electronics* (see Exhibit 5). Over a period of two years he had delegated most of the detail work here to his secretary, and he had recently appointed her advertising manager, but the job still took about 10% of his time. Occasionally, to test customer response, he advertised new products still in the development or prototype stage. This at times resulted in a frantic effort by engineering and production to overcome "bugs" in the new item in time to fill the orders pouring in.

A private hobby, which Mr. Patterson believed was shaping up as a commercial possibility, took almost one-half of his productive time. He had developed a new method of using plastic foam for making large, high-strength, light-weight panels and molded shapes, and he believed this method might eventually find application in production of aircraft and automotive parts. About $30,000 had been spent on this development, largely for experiments.

Occasionally Mr. Patterson concerned himself with tax or financial matters. For example, he participated in a particularly involved contract renegotiation; he also originated the idea of the profit-sharing plan which the company was currently using.

A large part of his time was, he said, "wasted" on walking around talking to people, or on business reading. "In this, like everything else, I follow my tastes and interests, and I tend to spend a disproportionate amount of time with persons working on something that fascinates me. My contacts are thus not balanced, and I know that this is not what the textbooks on management recommend a president should do, but one has to live with shortcomings."

Mr. Patterson believed the best way to direct a company was to select competent people to head the various subdivisions. He said he had succeeded in doing this in general, although the executives varied in com-

Exhibit 5

BENJAMIN DELANO ELECTRON
1791-1942
FOUNDER*

We take our share of pompous pride, shyly calling attention
to our own contribution, in fatuously welcoming the Billenium. General Motors
has built 50,000,000 self-propelled hydrocarbon energy converters, General-
Whats-his-name has gotten his family of scientists to develop the prestige-pump.
The BEV is dashing the modesty of the nucleus, and the lowly potato,
long the friend of the TV-less, deepfreezeless proletariat, now coyly
minces garbed in snobba-peel.

Our own bosom-swelling pride stems from our tradition of back-slapping familiarly with the greats of electricity and magnetism, whose august names are memorialized by the lower-case initial — joe volt, sam ampere, ed gauss, john henry, fred faraday — to us, each of these is a saint of science, their spirits blazoned on our banners boldly.

And now, in our humble way, we place on the altar of science at the epicenter of the Billenium our intellectual contribution for posterity. We are memorializing one of our staunchest researchers, who has reduced to hitherto unknown limits of accuracy, the measurement and observation of energy loss (or FRICTION), both magnetic and mechanical.

The New Unit is equal, for obvious reasons of national pride, to the friction overcome when the Battleship Missouri was pulled off the mud. As with the farad, in ordinary use, it is prefixed micro, or micro-micro, and for export to Europe, pica. It is the mccarthy (micromccarthy, micromicromccarthy, picamccarthy). M. K. S. and C. G. S. adherents may obtain metric conversions from Navy Bu-Ships data on the big Mo. Absolute units are of course the abmccarthy and the statmccarthy.

Sensitive relays with good repeatability of operating characteristics never have more than 130 centimeter-micromicromccarthys (50 inch-micromicromccarthys) of pivot friction at all extremes of temperature. Our relays don't even have that much.

*THIS ISN'T OUR FOUNDER, BUT WE THINK HE SETS THE RIGHT TONE, AND IS MORE PICTURESQUE THAN OURS, WHO ISN'T EVEN DEAD YET!

Source: Company records.

petence. "Things get done here like in a company with committee management, where the committee never meets," he said. "People with sufficient influence, and not necessarily by sheer authority, get things accomplished in their respective area. For instance, if I left here for six months, the company would encounter no operational difficulties. Hank Swift, who is highly respected, understands how to handle engineers and is skilled in analyzing problems and finding solutions. He and Joseph Adams, who is a very able man, would have no trouble directing the company in my absence.

"I run this company by the 'exception principle,' which means that I get into the act when something is out of line," he continued. "For instance, when expected sales increases did not materialize last summer, and the 'blueprints' showed a deviation from expected performance, I instigated a budget revision. But I made sure by talking to people that I had concurrence of opinion. Usually I find, however, that the people responsible for a job have taken corrective action by the time I get around to them."

When Mr. Patterson disagreed with current policies or arrangements, he often made this known by dropping subtle hints in casual conversations. He believed this method usually worked, since he thought the "grapevine" was a very effective method of communication, one on which he relied himself as a good indication of people's feelings. "I have never known the grapevine to get excited without reason," he said.

Occasionally, however, Mr. Patterson's hints were not understood. For example, in 1953, he had discussed his plan for a reorganization of engineering with the chief engineer and believed that the grapevine had carried the news to the rest of the department. However, many engineers were shocked when the new setup was announced. In speaking of this episode, Mr. Patterson commented, "There I was the closest to a solo decision that I ever came to."

Some of Mr. Patterson's subordinates believed he acted by "creating crises," either when he felt his hints had not been understood or when he wanted to jar members of the organization out of what he thought were unproductive or complacent ways of thinking. The engineering reorganization was dubbed such a crisis. Similarly, some engineers believed Mr. Patterson's premature advertising created small crises, and they were careful to hide developments from him until workability was assured. "It's Chet's way of putting on the heat," they said; Mr. Patterson, however, denied the intention of upsetting anyone.

DEVELOPMENT AND ENGINEERING

The general comment was that a majority of the company's successful products had been created by Mr. Thomas Patterson, brother of the president, and one-time head of the former development engineering section. He was unanimously described as a mechanical genius with a flair for conceiving of brilliant and simple solutions to "any technical problem." Somewhat eccentric, Thomas Patterson shunned "red tapey" engineering organizations and preferred to have his way in group efforts. Currently he had arranged to be retained by the company on a part-time consulting basis where he set his own pace, working in spontaneous spurts and alternating between the invention of relays and his major interest, the construction of harpsichords.

"My brother and I share a funny disease," commented Chester Patterson; "we don't mind explaining things, but we quickly get annoyed at superficiality. Neither of us can stand a 'stuffed shirt' or people who don't know what they are talking about. Tom is much worse in this respect than I am." He went on to tell how Thomas had caused friction by showing his annoyance at several electrical engineers who displayed only a superficial knowledge of mechanical aspects of the product. "Tom is a mechanic of whose quality there are not five in this whole country, but he must be left alone," he added. He explained that in past years he had quarreled with his brother about the latter's "government work," or private hobbies carried on during working hours, but he had found that his brother's mind worked best when allowed to pursue ideas of his own. "It took me longer than most people around him to realize that," he said.

The engineering department was currently headed by Henry Swift, self-educated engineer and cofounder of the company. He assumed this position in the spring of 1956 when the former chief engineer, William Cordes, relinquished most of his administrative functions after prolonged illness and overstrain. Mr. Cordes remained in charge of the drafting room, model shop, and testing facilities only.

During 1953, the organization of the engineering department had been substantially changed by the president. Prior to that time, the engineers had worked as groups or teams: A development group did research on relay applications and new product ideas; a product group took over at this point, transforming prototypes into models with specifications acceptable to production as well as customers; an applications group worked closely with the sales department in analyzing customers' problems and adapting standard products to their use. Each engineering group had electrical, mechanical, and other specialists who worked cooperatively together.

While this system was in effect, a number of difficulties arose. Increasingly, special problems or ideas forwarded by the sales organization were shelved and lost. At times products were designed which could not be manufactured profitably; poor service, delays, errors, and embarrassing situations resulted. Furthermore, no sales manual had been drawn up, although the increasing numbers of basic relays and common variations called for a comprehensive survey and presentation.

In the summer of 1953, the president unexpectedly announced a number of changes. He dissolved the application engineering group and abolished the existing group system. From that point on, he said, each of the five senior engineers was to be responsible for one or more relay types. Theoretically, one engineer now decided on all aspects of design, specifications, and materials used; he assisted customers and field representatives, as well as foremen in the plant. Under this "King Theory," responsibility for success of the product was his alone.

By this move, Mr. Patterson intended to force the engineers to take a broader view, in fact to make them "businessmen" interested in serving the customers.

However, upset and confusion attended the change, since, as one engineer pointed out, it forced former specialists to cope with problems outside their experience.

One of the senior engineers later said he had been against the idea, since he believed that groups could accomplish more than individuals. Thomas Patterson opposed the change because it caused unrest. Another engineer thought making one person responsible for a product was a risk because he might become ill or quit. Mr. Cordes stated that the "King Theory" prevented a co-ordinated program. A member of the sales department thought it facilitated pursuit of fruitless projects.

On the other hand, it was conceded that some good emerged quickly from the shake-up. "Before the change, we never knew the whole product in all its aspects, but afterward we had to see it," commented one senior engineer. Also, customer service was improved, and the sales manual, which Mr. Patterson had ordered completed in six months, was made ready within the year.

After 1953, further development took place. Gradually the engineers began to consult informally among themselves, with specialists helping each other on problems. After Mr. Swift took over the department, he started a series of monthly meetings and newsletters in order to improve co-ordination and to familiarize the project engineers with each other's activities. In speaking of the "King Theory," Mr. Swift stated that he thought it worked well, but required modification by introducing group effort. Consequently he tried to put at least two people of different skills on any one project.

In 1956 there were 11 project engineers, including Mr. Swift and Thomas Patterson, assisted by 28 other engineers and technicians.

Mr. Swift described his duties as two-thirds supervision and one-third working on engineering projects of his own. Advising on technical questions and handling "political" problems took about equal amounts of time, he said. The latter included problems arising from the reorganization, questions of procedure, and the relationships between the engineers and the factory. "The political problems are the hardest," said Mr. Swift; "for instance, I find that some engineers want to do projects all by themselves, while spreading the task among at least two people makes things easier and better. The problem is how to do it without hurting individual pride."

Members of the engineering staff indicated that they welcomed Mr. Swift's efforts to achieve co-ordination through newsletters and meetings. They also felt that working in a small department allowed them to achieve unusually close contact with all aspects of the product, and that this gave the company a competitive advantage over larger manufacturers.

Mr. Patterson stressed that engineers were encouraged to travel in order to keep up customer contact. He said that new product ideas came from "exposure" to present and potential customers, and that he "raised hell" if the engineers did not travel enough. Expense accounts were not questioned. "I myself and many others just pick up enough money and bring back the change, and no questions asked," he said. Similarly, Mr. Patterson strongly urged the use of long-distance calls instead of letters, since he believed the engineers could learn more and faster by talking to a customer directly.

Mr. Cordes said the company had to take exceptional care in selecting engineers, as they became its symbol. "Every company has its strong group around which it is built, and with us it is engineering." He regretted that steps had not been taken earlier to hire more young engineers, since men with the qualifications desired had become scarce. Mr. Cordes believed recruiting activity had been slowed up by Mr. Patterson's requirement that he personally interview every incoming engineer. On this the president commented that it was a general and necessary policy to screen applicants through a committee consisting of Messrs. Patterson, Gruber, Swift, and others.

Mr. Cordes also thought the company's competitive advantage of making specialized products was slowly decreasing, as the growing market attracted more competitors, and that the company thus had to rely on self-generating engineers with business sense to help it move ahead.

Mr. Patterson said that new product development utilized a "shotgun approach," but he believed the money frequently spent on projects that turned out to be useless or obsolete was a necessary cost, especially since the experience gained could be usefully applied in different projects.

PRODUCTION

All products of the company were manufactured in a two-story building of 100,000 square feet in northern Philadelphia, adjacent to a railroad and a highway. The first floor contained office space and laboratories as well as the relay manufacturing area, while the second floor contained part of the accounting department, a cafeteria, additional assembly space, and rooms for the experiments with plastics. Materials and finished goods were stored in side rooms on the ground floor. An 18,000-square-foot addition for office space was currently under construction.

Joseph Adams, works manager since 1945, had joined the company in 1942 as an expediter in the purchasing department. He had previously managed restaurants and food stores for the Food Products Co., during which period he acquired a degree in industrial management by attending night school.

Mr. Adams described his job as including all contacts and procedures involved in manufacturing; in addition, he supervised budgeting and capital expenditures. Reports going to him on a monthly basis included operating statements, inventory status by parts, subassemblies and finished products, and variance analyses. Weekly reports showed backlog on hand, orders past due, orders held, and materials on order. Daily shipments were also reported. In addition, the personnel manager presented a monthly report on absenteeism and labor turnover, and she reported frequently on exit interviews. Every three weeks or oftener the planning section furnished a forecast of allocation of plant capacity to the various relay types, based on statistical analysis plus "seat of the pants estimates."

As the company expanded, Mr. Adams had delegated certain duties; for example, a former employee interviewer, Mrs. Ellen Faulkner, was made personnel manager, while a former project engineer, Alwin Mc-Donald, was made factory superintendent. As the latter described it, Mr. Adams told him "to find out for himself what it entails to run the factory," and to come back to him should he encounter problems. Mr. McDonald commented that he later used the same approach successfully in building his own factory "staff group." Mr. Adams said that he believed in a firm chain of command, but was careful to give his subordinates full responsibility for the execution of their jobs once he had defined them.

Mr. Adams said he generally spent about two hours daily with the factory superintendent, one hour each with the materials manager and the treasurer, and one-half hour each with the order service manager and the personnel manager. Other executives sought him out for consultation, and he worked especially closely with Henry Swift, the engineering manager. "Hank and I consult on major steps I take, or we talk over operating statements. We discuss also what we can do to improve the company in general," he said.

Mr. Adams considered it one of his main problems at present to help the new engineering manager take over the leadership in his department after the past reorganization. Of this event he said, "No matter what one hears about the whole thing, no real change took place except that the responsibility of the engineers was focused. It also fostered better understanding between the formerly separate engineering sections. But now Hank is trying to put back the teamwork which had gotten lost when the engineers began to pursue individual projects." Mr. Adams went on to tell of instances where duplication of engineering effort had formerly resulted in spending several thousand dollars on excess tooling. "McDonald put in an 'Iron Curtain' to avoid similar occurrences, and there has been a lot of improvement in the last six months," he said.

Mr. Adams, together with Henry Swift, served as a mediator of conflicts between project engineers and the factory superintendent: If an engineer should be dissatisfied with the method of production used for a particular relay, the foreman in charge brought the matter first to Mr. McDonald; if he could not settle it, then Mr. Adams and Mr. Swift settled it jointly. Mr. Adams explained, "Although the engineers were decreed to have full authority over their relays, the important factors are whether you can build it and whether you can sell it. Under the theory as developed by Chet, the engineer could stop production if he was not satisfied. However, as far as I know, that has not happened. To the contrary, there were instances in which I personally ordered production halted to force the project engineer to redesign or modify his relay because 90 out of 100 relays made did not work. Similarly, customer acceptance starts or stops production of a relay."

Looking to the future, Mr. Adams spoke of the main problem confronting the company as that of getting more "idea men" to develop new products, inasmuch as most of the successful products of the past had been invented by the two owner-brothers. Visualizing a potential sales volume of $12 million within the next five years, Mr. Adams felt that "the thing to do is to keep our sales volume of the present products and to get the engineers to develop more products the world can use."

Mr. Adams stated that another job of vital importance was the planning, scheduling, and control of production; upon it hinged the size of inventories, materials purchases, labor requirements, and delivery schedules. At any one time, about 700 orders were in process, or 18,000–24,000 relays per week. In the course of a month, 1,000 orders were handled, averaging 28 basic types and thousands of variations.

Orders were expedited on the manufacturing floor by special order clerks, but there was confusion in many cases. According to the planning manager, Glen Barnes, the company's rapid growth was responsible for many control practices not best suited to the purpose. For example, he felt that production schedules were at times unduly influenced by the order service department's efforts to placate or help particular customers. This department had been set up especially to handle customer inquiries and complaints. It had been determined that each customer on an average checked two and a half times on his order, and frequently confusion resulted before the status of a particular order, or the reason for delays, could be traced through the various departments. As a special project for the future, Mr. Adams was planning an examination of the paper flow used in keeping customers informed of the progress of their orders.

Both Mr. Barnes and Mr. Adams believed that excessive duplication and red tape were present in production control. Mr. Barnes ascribed this to a "reaction" from having almost no formal procedures in the period five years earlier. A project to improve paper work, or "red tape flow," as it was called, had recently been set on foot by Mr. Adams, who delegated this responsibility to his brother, Paul Adams, and to Mr. Barnes. As Mr. Adams put it, "For all I know, we may have too little in the way of papers, but we are going to find out and eliminate wasted effort, which arose when, during the last four years, the nature of our business changed from a few high-volume items to a great variety of products." Mr. Adams stated that timekeepers on the production floor were maintaining essentially the same records which the cost department kept independently. "I believe," he injected, "that once the staff people are doing a good enough job, the factory people will cease to make their own efforts."

Mr. Barnes was planning the introduction of a formal production control system. In conjunction with this he hoped to consolidate the forms used by each department. "It is just like one department not trusting the other, and therefore each makes up its own forms," he said. To illustrate this problem, he pointed to the difficulty of making sure that alterations in blueprints reached the production floor, since engineering and production records were essentially separate.

Until recently, most relays had been manufactured on an order basis. In order to alleviate scheduling problems and because the company could now finance it, an increasing percentage of the more common relays and subassemblies was kept in stock. By the fall of 1956, about 60% of orders, accounting for 15% of dollar volume, were shipped from inventory.

Inventory control, under Mr. Olsen, had to cope with 6,000 to 7,000 parts and subassemblies, about double the number of five years before. It had formerly been the policy to write off as obsolete any parts or subassemblies not sold after three months, but recently policy here had grown more flexible. Mr. Adams said the growing number of products forced a steady increase in inventories, but he had found that competing companies were carrying even higher inventories relative to sales volume. He estimated that finished goods accounted for about 17% of inventory, work in process for 35%, the rest being raw materials and parts either procured outside or made by the company.

Delivery schedules generally called for a seven- to eight-week manufacturing period, which was about average for the industry. This time allowance, greater than actual manufacturing time, enabled the foremen to schedule the work force to best advantage. Many customers desired delivery spaced over a period of time which conformed with their own manufacturing operations. The company found that a backlog of orders of about three months was necessary to keep scheduling efficient.

In managing the production department, Mr. Adams frequently initiated special projects, carried on under his direct supervision, such as those planned to "improve red tape flow" and the paper work for checking on customer orders.

Partially completed was a project for establishing standard operation times for many different products and processes—though Mr. Adams saw the possibility of conflict between an emphasis on time standards and the company's traditional emphasis on quality.

Another special project, already accomplished, was a survey of job requirements for all operating and clerical personnel, through which job definitions and wage ranges were established. A similar survey of supervisory and executive positions was planned.

For use in determining employment policies, a survey of opinions on personnel practices had recently been carried out among all ranks. Mr. Adams' interest in employee and wage problems had resulted in the practice of clearing everyone's wages through his office.

LABOR RELATIONS

The company employed about 600 persons, 60% of whom were women whose skill and dexterity were required in assembling the many intricate metal, glass, and plastic parts. Each relay required a number of adjustments and tests during and after assembly. "Our products work only because the girls on the benches *want* them to work," said an engineer.

Labor relations in the company were characterized by all as friendly and peaceful. The plant was not unionized, a fact which Mr. Adams considered a great advantage because he or any other executive or supervisor was under no restriction about visiting the manufacturing area, talking to the workers, and examining products at various stages of completion. He believed these circumstances made it much easier to keep close liaison between production and other departments interested in quality and progressive innovation.

According to Mr. Adams, the company's employment policy helped to promote the friendly spirit among the workers. Stable employment was emphasized, and to avoid layoffs, production schedules were frequently stretched, and workers were shifted between jobs. The company relied on "natural turnover" among its employees to cut back in slow periods, and new workers were hired only if an increase in orders indicated a long-term rise in sales. Many employees brought relatives or friends to work for the company. Mrs. Faulkner interviewed each new employee and administered a vocational interest test to assure correct placement.

Wages averaged at or slightly above the going rate in the community, and, in addition, the company had instituted a profit-sharing plan several years ago, under which one-third of profits before taxes were distributed among all employees of two years' uninterrupted service. About five-sixths of the employees were eligible under the plan. Bonuses generally amounted to 20% or more of annual wages. The company had established a trust, administered by Messrs. Adams, Swift, and a senior engineer, into which all bonuses up to 15% of wages were paid for investment in general market securities. The balance of the bonus was paid in cash.

BUDGETING AND CAPITAL EXPENDITURES

In addition to his production duties, Mr. Adams was in charge of financial planning. Drawing up the budget involved co-ordination of forecasts made by the sales department with departmental spending estimates obtained from foremen and supervisors, and past performance as shown on Mr. Clark's cost records. Mr. Adams commented that he set the budget as he saw fit and was not forced to seek Mr. Patterson's approval. "Chet often displays the attitude, 'Don't bother me unless I ask you,'" he said.

Mr. Patterson received a copy of the budget at the same time the other executives did. He said he thought the problems of budgeting in the past few years had consisted mainly of determining the capacity of the plant and filling in the orders from the large backlog on a first-come, first-served basis. Then it was a matter of estimating the expenses. Mr. Adams concurred, adding that the company was still riding the boom in the electronics business. "We have had no worries yet—but the real test for this place will come should we experience a recession in our industry."

Mr. Adams also handled most requests for capital expenditures. No formal system of project appraisal was used for the yearly capital outlays of $60,000–$75,000, and Mr. Adams served as a clearing center. For instance, when Mr. Gruber, Mr. McDonald, and the purchasing agent complained about the lack of office space, Mr. Adams arranged the preparation of a master plan for a $180,000 addition to the building. After discussing this plan thoroughly with Mr. Swift and Thomas Patterson, he submitted it to the board. It was on this level that Chester Patterson first reviewed and voted on the plan.

SALES

The sales department had been developed by Mr. Fritz Gruber, who had joined the company in 1946 as the only sales engineer, after spending over eight years with the Factory Insurance Corporation. Reporting directly to him were five district sales managers who supervised a total of about 35 sales representatives working as independent agents on a commission basis.

Selling the company's products required considerable understanding of the customer's technical problems and requirements. Since the salesmen worked for independent agents, the district managers spent much time visiting the representatives and accompanying salesmen on their calls. District managers enjoyed a high degree of independence in the pursuit of their duties, having authority to "hire and fire" representatives. "It looks like I have successfully worked myself out of a job," was Mr. Gruber's comment on the amount of delegation practiced in his department.

Mr. Gruber, an "applications engineer at heart," disliked purely administrative duties. He said about one-third of his time was spent on personnel matters, since he considered it highly important to get people who fitted into the company's spirit of independent thinking. Another third of his time went to administrative duties that consisted mainly of approving new sales representatives, "pinch-hitting" for his district managers, and preparing sales forecasts. The remainder of Mr. Gruber's time was spent on the problem of new product development, which he considered, along with selling, one of the two chief responsibilities of his department.

In making sales, salesmen looked first to see if customer specifications could be met by one of the semistandard relays listed in the company's sales manual. This volume listed all basic relays and over a thousand variations that had a relatively wide or steady market. If, however, the sale required a special application, the salesman referred the problem to the company's district manager, who in turn sought advice from whichever company engineer he considered expert in the field involved.

After the product had been selected or designed, the sales department wrote up the orders and the specifications obtained from the engineer. The order was then handed to the planning and scheduling group, which arranged for materials and production.

In pricing the company's products, Mr. Gruber relied on cost data supplied by Mr. Adams and Mr. Clark to set a "floor" below which business was considered unattractive. Actual selling prices varied with the size of the order, and depended on market conditions.

The company did not always try, however, to meet competitors' prices. For example, in a conversation with Mr. Patterson, Mr. Gruber referred to a sizable order lost because of price cutting by a smaller competitor. After rapid questioning, Mr. Patterson agreed with Mr. Gruber's decision not to meet the lower price, but he urged the sales manager to protect the company from getting the reputation of a high-price concern impervious to market pressure. Mr. Gruber replied he felt strongly that it was time to re-examine the pricing policy for relay types on which the company no longer held a technical advantage. Mr. Patterson agreed, and he asked to be informed if steps were taken to adjust pricing policy to the basic changes in the growing relay field, which attracted more and more competitors.

So far, no prices were listed in the company's sales manual, but Mr. Gruber hoped in the long run to change this situation.

NEW PRODUCTS COMMITTEE

Mr. Gruber believed that seeking out new product ideas was as important a part of his job as selling. As chairman of a "new products committee," which consisted of himself and the five district managers, Mr. Gruber every two or three weeks reviewed a number of the 200–300 new ideas in his files.

This committee, composed exclusively of sales personnel, had developed about a year ago out of a larger committee which had consisted of Messrs. Patterson, Gruber, Adams, Cordes, and Thomas Patterson. Mr. Gruber said the old committee fell into disuse because its members were too far removed from detailed knowledge about customer problems, and because the five men were difficult to assemble at one time. He characterized the new group as an "idea screening committee" whose members, all engineers by training, were intimately familiar with the capacity of the plant and its people as well as with the demands of the market. He believed that more efficient selection of product ideas could result in reduced effort and man-hours wasted.

In speaking of new products selection, Mr. Patterson commented that "every once in a while someone in the company wants a new products committee." He said that he was not aware of the need for such a group at present, since facilities of the engineering department were now adequate to permit the engineers to pursue all new ideas that sufficiently fascinated them. "Should we not be able to do this any more, then I can see a need for a screening committee, although I always think of the saying: 'Had Moses been a committee, the Israelites would still be in Egypt today.'"

The former chief engineer, Mr. Cordes, stated that in his experience, committees of this nature were doomed to failure because the interest of all participants could not be sufficiently aroused, because there was lack of authority, and because no really new information could be given.

Mr. Adams said the sales department was the right place for a new products committee should there be a need for one. He could not recall seeing any information on the activities of the present group. He commented that the first committee described by Mr. Gruber had functioned for about a year in the early 1950's when Mr. Thomas Patterson had "dreamed up" so many new product ideas that a committee was needed to classify them in order of importance. But the need dwindled when no new products were forthcoming for a longer period. "I think it is necessary to distinguish between real innovations or just improvements, and a committee should really deal only with the former," he said.

ACCOUNTING AND FINANCES

James Clark, treasurer and controller, joined the company in 1945 as assistant treasurer, and became treasurer shortly thereafter. His department consisted of 32 people who prepared the company's general accounting records and maintained a job-cost system which analyzed actual production costs, departmental overhead, and inventories.

Mr. Clark was greatly interested in the application of mechanical tabulation and had introduced it to the company when he joined it. Progressively he rented IBM equipment until he completed the system with a high-speed tabulator. Rental charges amounted to about $2,000 per month. The IBM equipment required the services of six full-time employees, but Mr. Clark said mechanization had brought more than proportionate reductions in the office force.

In the fall of 1956, conversion to card tabulation was not yet complete. Major projects still to be tackled included inventory controls and accounts receivable records. Mr. Clark indicated that the equipment made possible speedy completion of monthly operating statements and detailed analyses of sales, orders, commission statements, territorial backlogs, etc.

Mr. Clark was concerned with the problem of selling the use of mechanized equipment down through the ranks. He expected to hold an "open house" for everyone in the company once he had completed the accounting system. "I think when people see what can be done, there will be questions," he said.

The peak load on the machines occurred around the first of each month, when monthly reports and statements were run. This was a stumbling block to using the equipment in areas like production scheduling or analyses of orders in process. Mr. Barnes commented that successful use of IBM methods for production purposes would require some control over the equipment, since tabulations would have to be made as needed, at any time during the month. However, he had begun studies on the application of the equipment for production purposes.

Furnishing data for renegotiation purposes was another duty of the treasurer, especially important for the company because of the high percentage of military contracts. Mr. Clark had spent considerable time in past years on preparing cost analyses to support the company's profits on military orders. The allocation of overhead costs had proved difficult because the regular accounting records did not contain such allocations, but the company had finally been cleared every year.

Mr. Clark had received full authority to run his department as he saw best fit, and this authority continued to be maintained. "I can run my machines with pink cardboard if I want to, and no one would bother me," he said. In running his operation, he had little contact with most other phases of the company. "I am rather isolated here," he commented, "and I see no outsiders at all; sometimes I wish I were in purchasing to see more people."

THE FUTURE

In discussing the future, Mr. Patterson commented on planning:

We—or maybe I better say "I"—generally prefer to work and plan ahead in small steps. We think of the immediate situation, spending as much time and money as we can afford at the moment on the problem, and then take a look again. We may not like a particular situation, such as a decline in orders for a particular product, but there is nothing drastic to do—we kick ideas around until we find the best thing in our reach. For instance, when Clark wanted some IBM equipment, we did not decide on the over-all installation right then and there, but each part was justified at the time by him. It is just like building a wall—the basic decision to put the wall up was made when I decided to go into business; now it is a matter of putting the stones in squarely, one at a time. Or take the plastic foam: Every one of us sees each dollar that is being put in the experiments, and we all see the results as they come. Now and then we take a look to see what opportunities are coming up.

We try to justify our decisions as they arise. At times we must establish basic policy, like going into the manufacture of industrial controls. But we avoid going into a new area or a competitive field with full steam. We would rather drive a small car of our own than ride the tail gate of a fast moving truck driven by some of the big firms in the business. This is how we would feel by committing ourselves heavily into the future.

Mr. Patterson considered the most important problem of the company to be the high percentage of government work. He felt that he should actively seek more civilian business. "We exist all right on government contracts," he said, "but I hate to trust it. It is not so much a question of the additional red tape; rather, there is no sense of achievement in producing for outside inspectors. For instance, I am sure I could turn my ideas on plastic foam processing into military applications, but frankly, I don't want to do it. It is just not a pleasant way of doing business."

Another problem cited by the president was that of finding the right people for his company as it grew. "We are generally aware of the need for bringing people along," he said, "and there are prospects for young people with us." He referred to his policy of putting no pay ceilings on jobs, but he was conscious of the fact that promotions in rank could not be given as fast as desirable, since the company was still small. "We have consistently promoted from within whenever possible, and have had a number of conspicuous successes. But we have some people in positions who are not able to go further, which may become even more of a problem, since their jobs grow bigger as we grow."

A DAY WITH MR. PATTERSON

On this particular day Mr. Patterson spent considerable time with four individuals. First, he conferred with a senior project engineer for about an hour on a new product. In Mr. Patterson's own words, he "pretty strongly urged him to use a different approach to the technical problem involved."

The rest of the morning Mr. Patterson spent with the engineer in charge of the plastic process, actively participating in experiments. Both men solicited reactions to new ideas from each other; in several instances the case writer thought Mr. Patterson helped to clarify the engineer's suggestions by thorough questioning.

Shortly before lunch, Mr. Patterson was asked by the sales manager, Mr. Gruber, about a trip he had made some time ago. The conversation developed into a discussion of the loss of a contract due to price cutting by a competitor, moving from there to pricing policy in general.

About half the afternoon was spent on a series of product tests which Mr. Patterson conducted, together with the project engineer in charge, for the benefit of Mr. Gruber, who had inquired about the characteristics of this product some time ago. Thereafter, Mr. Patterson returned to the plastics experiments. The last half hour of the day was spent on reading mail and reworking a sales pamphlet.

"This day was more typical than yesterday would have been, if there is such a thing as a typical day," commented Mr. Patterson. He had spent more than half of the previous day with two visitors who presented him with "some hare-brained product idea" for diversification. Mr. Patterson had finally declined to invest in the new product. "While you might consider that a typical problem with which I concern myself every day, it certainly is not," he said.

A DAY WITH MR. SWIFT

The case writer observed that the major part of Mr. Swift's time was spent walking about the department talking to his engineers. Several times he chatted with a particular engineer engaged in modifying a prototype relay, asking technical questions and making suggestions. Another time he was called by a laboratory technician to attend a test of three samples of a new product. Mr. Swift participated in testing, suggested changes, and inquired into the possibility of compiling statistics on the variations encountered. After the senior project engineer in charge had mentioned ways of implementing such research, Mr. Swift walked away.

Later he met another project engineer who was weighing the merits of several suppliers of plastic parts for his product. Mr. Swift sat down with him to analyze the pros and cons. Finally the engineer decided to call personally on one supplier to insure correct production of the intricate part. At no time did Mr. Swift overrule an opinion by authority, or ask for a follow-up report.

In the afternoon one of the senior engineers asked Mr. Swift about a request by Mr. Patterson to list specifications in the manual on a new series of relays. After discussing the technical merits of the product, they jointly decided that such a listing was not yet feasible. This same engineer then raised the issue of getting an assistant, and Mr. Swift said he would see the personnel manager about it.

While in his office, Mr. Swift was visited by one of the district sales managers who presented a customer's request for a guarantee of rather tight specifications on a relay. Mr. Swift went to see the plant superintendent and the chief inspector, who agreed to his suggestion that the product be inspected for the purpose. Later in the day Mr. Swift attended tests of the relay and told the district manager that he could give the guarantee.

A district sales manager came in to ask about procedures for notarizing a bid for the City of Chicago. Mr. Swift, a notary public, proceeded to supply the information through a series of phone calls.

Intermittently, Mr. Swift read pamphlets on the shortage of engineers and dictated letters in connection with the last directors' meeting. Then he discussed one of his own projects with the chief tool designer who asked for a change in specifications. Mr. Swift decided to request a sample product with the new specifications to test personally the effects of the change.

Later, Mr. Swift discussed with the senior engineer sharing his office two memos received from the plant superintendent. The memos inquired about the status of a parts cleaning procedure suggested by production "a long time ago," and further asked for a listing of each engineer using a certain expensive raw material. Mr. Swift was tempted to let the memos "die," but after some consideration he decided to pass along the first one to the project engineer in charge of the product, "to see what he thought of it." Technical discussions accounted for the remainder of his time.

A DAY WITH MR. ADAMS

The case writer observed in the works manager's office that Mr. Adams mainly made himself available for counsel and advice. "Your presence scares off quite a number of people who would ordinarily come here to talk to me about their jobs, as well as their own personal problems," Mr. Adams said. Nevertheless, he had several visitors: Mr. Gruber came in to talk about the change in pricing policy which he had been discussing with Mr. Patterson the previous day. A lengthy conversation developed during which both men commented that the company was undergoing a basic change as its products met increasing competition. Mr. Adams listened to the arguments of the sales manager, who supported his views by drawing price-cost curves, and stated that he would turn the matter over in his mind for a few days.

Thereafter Mr. Adams spent two hours with a company accountant to review the profit-sharing arrangement in the light of a new tax ruling. Mrs. Faulkner, the personnel manager, dropped in to ask Mr. Adams' views on a want-ad for a testing engineer. After hearing his criticisms, she suggested a more unusual approach. Mr. Adams gave suggestions as to where help for the ad could be obtained.

The engineering manager came to Mr. Adams' office to ask whether the time-payment policy for the office force was also applicable to engineering personnel. Mr. Adams said it was, but that so far it had not been possible to reduce a general policy to writing.

A spontaneous meeting of the planning and order service heads in the superintendent's office next door drew Mr. Adams' attention. It involved the fact that "short orders" (rush orders) were increasing in number and that a change in scheduling these special requests might be warranted. Mr. Adams suggested that no changes be initiated until completion of the current study of the paper flow.

Later the treasurer stopped by to announce that the next monthly statement would be available shortly. Finally, Mr. Adams authorized a request for a $6,000 machine tool after the factory superintendent explained briefly the need for the machine and his search for the best possible supplier.

Blakeston & Wilson

BLAKESTON & WILSON, of Chicago, Illinois, was a manufacturer of medium-price, high-quality chocolate candy. Its chocolates, sold under the brand name "Perfection," were distributed through company-controlled stores and by candy wholesalers (usually called "jobbers" in the candy trade).

The company was organized in 1938 when it purchased the assets of the bankrupt Sidwell Wilson Company. Mr. Wilson, who had been president of the defunct company, was instrumental in securing necessary capital and in organizing the new firm, of which he also became president. Whereas the original company had had an unsuccessful profit record, Blakeston & Wilson achieved immediate financial success. Profits were earned each year from 1938 through 1946. Mr. Wilson believed that the failure of his first company resulted from excessive sales costs; in turn, he believed that the success of the new company resulted from the fact that lower sales costs had been achieved. Profits for the first quarter of 1947 were the highest in the firm's history.

During 1947, Blakeston & Wilson planned to double the number of Perfection Chocolate Shops which marketed its candy. This expansion in retail store operations was the outgrowth of a policy adopted in 1943. Prior to that time, the company had sold its chocolates solely to wholesalers and large chain buyers. Mr. Wilson stated that his company had entered the retail sales field in 1943 to assure a stable, profitable postwar market for a part of his factory's manufacturing capacity. The opening of these Perfection Chocolate Shops was a real innovation in the company's distribution procedures; Blakeston & Wilson executive personnel had not had previous experience in retail store operation. Operating results from 1943 through April of 1947, however, had convinced Mr. Wilson of the success of the policy, as well as of the wisdom of further retail sales expansion.

PREDECESSOR COMPANY

The Sidwell Wilson Company, incorporated in 1923, had sold packaged and bulk chocolates under several brand names. Sales volume had averaged $700,000 annually, with selling expenses of approximately $100,000 (see Exhibit 1). The company had employed eight salesmen, who, under the direction of Mr. Wilson, served wholesalers and buying syndicates in the Middle West and the East.

Stock ownership had been originally divided between Mr. Wilson (25%) and the majority stockholders (75%). By borrowing money from a company supplier, Mr. Wilson had purchased complete ownership of the company in 1926. Serious losses during the early thirties made repayment of the loan impossible, and in 1937 company assets were sold to satisfy creditor claims.

Exhibit 1

PREDECESSOR COMPANY—SIDWELL WILSON COMPANY

Profit and Loss Statement for the Year Ending December 31, 1935

	Amount	Percentage of Net Sales
Net sales	$623,069.97	....
Less: Cost of sales	520,616.71	83.56%
Gross profit	$102,453.26	16.44
Less: Selling, general, and administrative expenses:		
Freight and cartage outward	$ 22,618.72	3.63
Shipping wages and supplies	10,505.42	1.69
Advertising	4,373.97	0.70
Selling expenses	40,536.91	6.50
Administrative expenses	19,740.40	3.17
Miscellaneous expenses	9,015.74	1.45
Total expenses	$106,791.16	17.14
Net loss for period	$ 4,337.90	0.70

Source: Company records.

"The company failed," Mr. Wilson stated, "primarily because our selling expenses were too high. Moreover, we were selling to wholesalers who played one manufacturer against another to force prices down. We worked and sweated to make a few dollars manufacturing candy while the wholesalers and retailers took large margins for distributing and selling our products. Consequently, the consumer paid a high price for candy on which we did not make profits." The company had also been troubled by shortages in working capital. "We had just $3,000 plus equipment when we started in 1923, and, when we did occasionally make money, the stockholders took it all out in dividends."

FORMATION OF BLAKESTON & WILSON

After analyzing the difficulties which he had encountered in his first business, Mr. Wilson concluded that by reducing sales expense he could successfully compete in the candy business. To secure capital for his new enterprise, Mr. Wilson approached Mr. Blakeston, a director and operating executive of a large Midwestern variety chain. Mr. Blakeston and three of his associates furnished the minimum amount required, $30,000. They received 500 shares of preferred stock; in addition, when all preferred stock had been retired from earnings, they were to be issued 48% of the company's authorized common stock. For services rendered, Mr. Wilson was then to receive 52% of the common stock.

By March of 1938, necessary machinery had been installed and production was initiated. Company offices, located in the factory building, were furnished simply; all administrative and overhead expense was kept to a minimum. The executive organization of the new company consisted of two men: Mr. Wilson, president and general manager, who was in charge of sales and promotion work, financial administration, and supervision of administrative personnel; and Mr. Herman Smith, production manager, who directed manufacturing, purchasing, and cost accounting work, in addition to performing some other miscellaneous duties.

PRODUCT

Blakeston & Wilson, in 1947, manufactured quality boxed and bulk chocolates. The company's boxed chocolates were packed in attractive, but inexpensively designed, paper boxes. All Blakeston & Wilson candy was hand-dipped, a process normally used only for expensive packaged chocolates; medium-price and some expensive chocolates were usually dipped by machine. Hand-dipping was reputed to create thicker, creamier chocolate coatings over the candy centers—qualities which the company believed were recognized and appreciated by consumers. Mr. Wilson stated that his chocolates (75 cents per pound) were equal in quality to those sold in the high-price range ($1.00–$2.50) and superior in quality to other medium-price chocolates ($0.75–$1.00). "The difference in price between medium- and high-price chocolates lies primarily in expensive boxes and decorations and in large promotional expenditures, not in the quality of the candy," he stated.

Prior to World War II, the company had manufactured some standard hand-dipped chocolates for variety chains and grocery chains. Shortages of raw materials had forced the company to reduce sharply production for these outlets during the war years.

ORIGINAL SALES PLAN OF BLAKESTON & WILSON

Blakeston & Wilson, until 1943, sold chocolate candy under a variety of brand names only to wholesalers and to two large chains. The company sold to 121 wholesalers in an area bounded by Madison, Wisconsin, Rock Island, Illinois, Louisville, Kentucky, and New York City. Wholesalers were given usual trade discounts (wholesale, 20%; retail, 33⅓%) and exclusive sales rights for a specified area. A typical wholesaler's sales varied in volume from $4,000 to $25,000, with an average of $8,000. He, in turn, sold to outlets such as drug and department stores, clubs, and grocery stores. Wholesalers did not carry other brands of chocolates in a competitive price range. They did, however, carry both lower-price and higher-price chocolates.

"My theory was that there were more people who would buy our product because of its quality value than there were people who would have to be coaxed into buying it by expensive sales efforts," said Mr. Wilson. In carrying out his policy to cut sales expenses, Mr. Wilson personally handled all sales work; he had no salesmen or sales representatives. Mr. Wilson periodically visited wholesalers and syndicate buyers, determined credit policies, supervised sales accounting work, selected candy items, and designed candy packages. "My selling costs for the wholesale and syndicate trade vary between 1.5% to 2% of gross sales," Mr. Wilson stated, "whereas usually costs in the industry for selling to that trade amount to 6%." He attributed the industry's high selling costs to its use of numerous salesmen, expensive missionary sales work, and high promotional expense. "We do very little promotional work for our wholesalers, and the wholesalers do not do any promotional work on our candy. They have recognized our effort to shave expenses and therefore place the best box of candy in the consumer's hands at the lowest price." Company sales promotional material initially consisted of circulars describing candy manufacturing processes and counter display cards. "The quality of our candy will sell these chocolates without sales promotion," Mr. Wilson emphasized.

Mr. Wilson had personally selected his wholesalers when the new company was first organized. Thereafter, he visited each distributor approximately three times a year. These visits were informal and frequently amounted to a game of golf with the executives of the concern. Mr. Wilson knew each executive personally, and all business relations were on a first-name basis. During World War II, his visits to company wholesalers became more infrequent, since selling at that time consisted of allocating scarce supplies of candy among these firms.

In 1947, commenting on the excellence of his original wholesaler selection, Mr. Wilson noted: "We haven't gained or lost a new account in over nine years." Shortages of candy, as well as a heavy personal work load, had prevented Mr. Wilson from returning to his prewar schedule of visits to wholesalers.

ENTRANCE INTO RETAIL SALES OPERATIONS

During the depression years of the early thirties, the candy industry had been described as "sick"; its chief symptom was overcapacity with its attendant pains of price cutting, secret rebates, and overextension of credit. Since the incorporation of Blakeston & Wilson in 1938, however, candy production, as well as the price per pound received by the manufacturer, had increased substantially (see Exhibit 2). Company sales, following the general industry pattern, increased from $286,000 in 1938 to $909,000 in 1942. Although wartime sugar rationing had hampered production, this difficulty had been partially eliminated through the increased use of nonrationed substitute materials. Moreover, manufacturers of medium- and high-price packaged chocolates had benefited greatly from the sharply increased national income. Consumers were willing to buy these more expensive candies, on which the manufacturer realized excellent margins, instead of cheaper bulk candy formerly purchased in variety stores.

Mr. Wilson, despite his firm's prosperity, was apprehensive over future prospects for sales to the wholesaler trade. On the basis of the experience with his former company, he believed that competition would first appear and be most severe on sales made to wholesaler organizations. Manufacturers selling through wholesalers, Mr. Wilson stated, could never be certain how much they could sell, and they had little control over prices received for their products. Mr. Wilson believed that a market for at least a part of his productive output could be secured at a controlled price by opening company-operated candy stores. He was not sure of making profits in these stores. "If we could just break even on store operations, our profits would come from manufacturing the candy."

Mr. Wilson, although he had worked in the candy industry since 1909, had not had any experience in retail sales work or in retail store management. He therefore discussed his idea for retail candy stores with his board, company bankers, and associates in the industry; they were unanimous in their disapproval of his plan. Despite these objections, Mr. Wilson announced that he planned to open a retail store, if necessary by supplying funds from his personal resources. The board of directors, after this statement, reluctantly approved the new policy.

Perfection Candy Stores, Inc., was organized to finance operations of the new retail store; the necessary capital was subscribed by

Exhibit 2

AVERAGE WHOLESALE VALUE PER POUND OF CONFECTIONERY SOLD BY
MANUFACTURER-WHOLESALERS AND MANUFACTURER-RETAILERS, 1925–45

YEAR	MANUFACTURER-WHOLESALERS*		MANUFACTURER-RETAILERS	
	Number of Firms	Average Value per Pound	Number of Firms	Average Value per Pound
1925	386	$0.229	96	$0.392
1926	386	0.226	96	0.396
1927	369	0.222	113	0.348
1928	381	0.224	118	0.319
1929	394	0.210	123	0.335
1930	405	0.196	113	0.386
1931	404	0.174	114	0.366
1932	337	0.136	81	0.340
1933	301	0.131	44	0.376
1934	354	0.137	44	0.387
1935	308	0.142	48	0.385
1936	308	0.143	40	0.420
1937	265	0.153	33	0.451
1938	265	0.144	33	0.453
1939	244	0.143	29	0.449
1940	244	0.144	29	0.436
1941	224	0.153	24	0.468
1942	235	0.188	29	0.489
1943	258	0.218	26	0.414
1944	258	0.232	40	0.490
1945	353	0.244	51	**

* Includes cocoa-bean processors specializing in solid chocolate items.
** Applicable information not available.
Source: U.S. Department of Commerce, *19th Annual Report on Confectionery Sales and Distribution* (1946), p. 23.

Mr. Blakeston and his associates. They received the preferred stock of the new corporation plus 48% of its common stock. Mr. Wilson received the remaining 52% of the common stock for "services rendered." The 6% cumulative preferred stock did not have voting power unless three consecutive annual dividend payments were passed. The new corporation had the same management and board of directors as did

Blakeston & Wilson; it was a separate corporate entity only for tax purposes and as a method of limiting the financial liability of Blakeston & Wilson.

The first Perfection Chocolate Shop was opened in Chicago in the fall of 1943. At that time all former brand names of the company, with the exception of those used for the syndicate trade, were abandoned, and the name "Perfection" was adopted for chocolates sold to the company store and to the wholesale trade.

OPERATION OF RETAIL STORES

Success in the operation of the first Perfection shop led to further expansion during 1946. Between January and August of that year, five

Exhibit 3

BLAKESTON & WILSON

Intercorporation Relationships

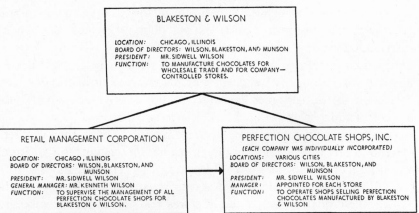

NOTE: Stock ownership of all companies was held by Mr. Wilson, Mr. Blakeston, and Mr. Blakeston's associates. Over-all management of all companies was handled by Mr. Sidwell Wilson.

additional Perfection shops were opened in the business section of Chicago. Each new shop was organized, financed, and individually incorporated, as was done in the case of the original store. (See Exhibit 3.)

Perfection Chocolate Shops were located in sections of Chicago where pedestrian traffic passing each store was heavy, as well as where the possibilities that passers-by would purchase candy were high, i.e., near hotels, department store shopping areas, and financial districts. Shops featured Perfection packaged chocolates in ½ pound, 1 pound, and 2 pound boxes, in addition to Perfection bulk chocolates; they sold only Blakeston & Wilson products and did not handle accessory lines, such as nuts and novelties. Most chocolates were 75 cents a pound or $1.45 for a 2 pound box. A few specially packed boxes of chocolates retailed at higher prices—$1.25–$1.50 a pound.

Each shop had a manager and, usually, four clerks. These were all girls and they were selected with regard to their appearance, character, and education. Starting weekly wages were $30, which were advanced to $35 after three months' service; competing firms started their sales girls at $22 a week. Managers were paid between $40 and $50 a week. In addition, both clerks and managers were paid a bonus if each girl sold over $480 of candy per week; clerks averaged between $2 and $14 per week in bonuses. Managers were eligible for an additional supervisors' bonus.

Mr. Wilson believed that any Perfection Chocolate Shop was in a strong competitive position because (1) it sold high-quality, reasonably priced candy; (2) all stores were efficiently operated; and (3) each store had a large sales volume.

Perfection chocolates were superior in quality to other medium-price chocolates. They were five cents less per pound, however, than chocolates sold by the leading competitor of Perfection Candy Shops—a seminational chain of retail candy stores. Savings resulting from reduced retail selling costs and efficient manufacturing operations were passed on to the customer through the use of highest-quality candy ingredients, Mr. Wilson stated.

Perfection Candy Shops were operated more efficiently than competitive shops, Mr. Wilson said, because of several unique operating features which he had developed. He had designed all Perfection shops with a small display window, in which several boxes of candy were highlighted. Traditionally, retail candy stores had large display windows which, he believed, took several hundred dollars of display stock, as well as many hours of time for decoration. Furthermore, Perfection bulk chocolates were packed in specially designed 5 pound boxes at the factory; these boxes fit into display cases in the retail stores without rehandling. Competitive stores, said Mr. Wilson, packed their candies in stock boxes at the factory, and the candy had to be repacked for store display. Moreover, he continued, through the operation of the bonus-payment plan for store clerks, there was an incentive upon their part to keep store personnel at a minimum—the fewer clerks in a store, the higher the individual bonus payments to each girl.

He believed that Perfection sales volume per store (1947) was substantially higher than the sales volume of competitive candy outlets.

Originally Mr. Wilson (1943 through August of 1946) personally directed all retail store operations. He visited each store daily to check on operations and to assure himself that everything was being handled satisfactorily. He hired all store personnel, supervised advertising and promotion campaigns, and determined details of operating procedures. Daily reports of cash and sales, as well as a weekly report of inventory, constituted his formal check on store operations. "It worked out beautifully," said Mr. Wilson. The primary management difficulty during this period was to find sufficient supplies of candy to meet the accelerated wartime demand for quality products.

To secure critically short materials, such as butter, sugar, and chocolate, which were necessary for the manufacture of Perfection chocolates for his retail trade, Mr. Wilson reduced production of all low-margin chocolates sold to chain buyers; this sharply diminished sales to those two customers. Sales to wholesalers were maintained at varying percentages of their 1941 purchases. These material sources were not sufficient, however, to fill the retail store demand for Perfection chocolates, and a wartime customer ration of one pound per day was instituted. In April, 1947, the improved materials situation permitted the removal of this wartime customer ration in all shops.

RETAIL MANAGEMENT CORPORATION

To relieve a heavy personal work load, as well as to prepare for intensive postwar competition, Mr. Wilson organized the Retail Management Corporation; that company was to supervise the operations of all Perfection Chocolate Shops. "My usual business day was fifteen hours long," he stated. "With conditions in the industry returning to normal I knew that more intensive management efforts were going to be required. I did not have the time to supervise retail store operations, in addition to my regular work." Retail Management Corporation was incorporated on August 1, 1946; it was organized and financed in the same manner employed in the incorporation of Perfection shops. Mr. Wilson, as president of Retail Management Corporation, made all major decisions for the new concern.

Mr. Wilson appointed his son, Kenneth, as manager of the new company. Kenneth, upon graduation from college in 1937, had been employed by the Sidwell Wilson Company as a salesman. He was assigned to develop wholesale business in the Michigan area. After a six months' trial period, this attempt had been abandoned as unprofitable. Kenneth later worked in the leather industry until his induction into the army. He returned to work for his father in November of 1945. At that time Mr. Wilson planned to have his son handle sales to wholesalers in the Middle Atlantic states. "Sugar rationing continued during 1946, however, and selling to wholesalers was still primarily a matter of ordertaking," said Mr. Wilson, "so we placed Kenneth in charge of the Retail Management Corporation." Kenneth's experience with retail sales and with the candy industry was limited to his earlier work with his father. "I wanted to give my son a chance at the business. He doesn't know much about it, but the way I look at it, I would have to teach either a stranger or my son. I might as well gamble on my son."

The staff of Retail Management Corporation consisted of four persons, in addition to Kenneth Wilson. A supervisor of stores inspected (weekly) the appearance of store property, displays, and personnel and filled out an inspection report which noted the results of his investigation; this report was given to the store manager with a duplicate copy forwarded to Kenneth Wilson. To correct any inadequacies noted on the inspection report, each manager checked her *Perfection Operating Manual*. This manual, written by Sidwell Wilson, outlined in detail approved operating procedures to be used in his retail stores. He believed that, through the use of this manual, store operations and activities were so systematized that necessary supervision was limited to an occasional check by the supervisor of stores, Kenneth Wilson, or himself. Sidwell Wilson's daughter, Thelma, was director of merchandising and purchasing. She determined inventory requirements for the shops and purchased supplies of chocolates from Blakeston & Wilson. A commercial artist developed display and counter card promotional material; radio and newspaper advertisements were prepared by a Chicago advertising agency. A bookkeeper kept necessary accounting records. Neither of the Wilson children had had previous experience in retail sales work.

Retail Management Corporation, in supervising the management of all Perfection Chocolate Shops, hired personnel, inspected the appearance of stores and store personnel, kept necessary accounting records, purchased candy and supplies, and furnished necessary financial service and advice. It received 10% of the gross sales of all Perfection shops as a management fee. Retail Management agreed to spend at least one-half of this sum for advertising purposes, the exact amount to be determined by Blakeston & Wilson.

The number of Perfection Chocolate Shops supervised by Retail Management increased from six to seventeen between August, 1946, and April, 1947. Store sales averaged $90,000 per unit. Store rentals ranged from $5,000 to $20,000 a year, with an average payment of $8,000. Overhead costs were approximately 3% of gross store sales. Invested capital, per store, varied from $10,000 to $15,000. All shops were successful financially.

Eight of the eleven new shops had been established in cities within a 200-mile radius of Chicago—i.e., Gary, Indiana, and Peoria, Illinois. Perfection shops in all eight non-Chicago cities came into competition with retail outlets, such as drug and department stores which also sold Perfection packaged chocolates distributed by company wholesalers. This created a great deal of resentment on the part of the wholesalers, who felt their market was being usurped.

PRICE

Perfection chocolates had originally retailed at 65 cents a pound; by 1946, as has been previously stated, the retail price had been increased to 75 cents a pound or $1.45 for the 2 pound box. Retail prices were the same at both Perfection Chocolate Shops and retail stores supplied by company wholesalers. In 1947, Blakeston & Wilson sold Perfection chocolates to its wholesalers at 40 cents a pound and to Perfection shops at 42 cents a pound.

Manufacturing costs had increased 17 cents per pound between 1943 and 1946. Furthermore, prices of chocolate and other raw materials had continued to increase during the first quarter of 1947, and the possible removal of sugar rationing in October of 1947 was expected to raise the price of that important commodity.

Despite rising material costs, retail-price reductions were already appearing among some brands of packaged chocolates. One leading chain competitor of Perfection had reduced the price of its 2 pound box of candy from $1.55 to $1.50 in March of 1947. Mr. Sidwell Wilson did not plan to reduce the retail price of his candy to meet this competitive development. Any price reduction, he believed, would first have to be made to the wholesaler trade, since he was well acquainted with the extremely competitive aspects of wholesaling.

When material prices returned to normal, Blakeston & Wilson planned to use any savings resulting from lowered costs to improve the quality of Perfection chocolates. "Our chocolates, which we sold for 65 cents a pound in 1943, were of better quality than chocolates which we now sell for 75 cents a pound," Mr. Wilson stated. The company had been forced to reduce product quality, as had its competitors, to take care of increased raw-material prices.

ADVERTISING

"We spent over $100,000 in 1946 advertising Perfection chocolates," said Mr. Wilson. Two-thirds of this money was expended for radio advertisements, the remaining one-third for newspaper advertisements. Blakeston & Wilson financed but a small part of the Perfection advertising fund; most of the money had been supplied by the Retail Manageagement Corporation with assistance from individual Perfection stores. Radio and newspaper advertisements were concentrated in the Chicago area and in cities where Perfection shops were located. These advertisements stressed the quality of Perfection chocolates but did not mention that Perfection candies were hand dipped; this was in conformity with industry advertising practices. By mutual agreement, candy manufacturers did not advertise whether their chocolates were hand dipped or machine dipped.

Advertising expenditures for Perfection chocolates, among packaged and bulk chocolate manufacturers, were second only to those of the Stephen F. Whitman & Son Company in Philadelphia. That company manufactured nationally advertised and distributed Sampler chocolates which retailed at $1.75 for a 20 ounce package. Mr. Sidwell Wilson said that expenditures for advertising in 1947 would be substantially higher than 1946 totals.

MANUFACTURING

The Blakeston & Wilson factory originally occupied the first three floors of a warehouse; the company had recently expanded into two floors of an adjoining building. Manufacturing operations and storage facilities were located on each floor so that raw materials would be in close proximity to the production activities in which they were used. All manufacturing departments were air-conditioned, and the plant was equipped with cold-storage facilities capable of holding 300,000 pounds of finished candy. Candy-making machinery was old but in good repair. In 1947 the plant was producing approximately 22,000 pounds of candy per day, five days a week. Capacity plant production was 30,000 pounds per day.

Mr. Sidwell Wilson believed that company manufacturing operations were efficient because (1) he personally owned and operated his business, which gave him a close check on all operations; (2) he had invented a continuous process production line which enabled him to hand-dip chocolates at a lower cost than other competitive hand-dip chocolate manufacturers; and (3) his labor force was more efficient and effective than employee groups in other companies.

Mr. Wilson did not believe that any company could secure a significant advantage over its competitors, as far as raw-materials purchasing was concerned. Sugar and chocolate prices, he said, were normally set by the New York City and foreign exchanges, and the price for a specified type of product was identical to all large-scale purchasers. Sugar, the primary ingredient of candy, was purchased by most companies on a day-to-day basis. "The only way normally to secure bargain sugar prices would be to gamble on futures—we tried that once and lost." Manufacturers of medium-price candies, however, could and did make some savings on minor items by using substitute or average-quality fruit centers, cream, and butter. Perfection chocolates, contrary to this practice, were always made from the highest-grade ingredients obtainable.

Mr. Smith, production manager, was assisted in factory supervision by four foremen and two floor ladies. He believed this number was the minimum staff required. In fact, when one of these assistants was ill, Mr. Smith had to take over temporarily his or her duties. He received two weekly production reports, which were also available for Mr. Wilson's use. They listed production by department, the number of manufacturing employees, total hours worked, and indirect factory expenses. He believed, however, that his most effective control technique was close personal supervision over factory operations. Mr. Smith was completely responsible for all manufacturing activities; Mr. Wilson did not concern himself with production problems, unless some major change in policy was contemplated.

Hand-dipped chocolates were more expensive to produce than machine-dipped candies primarily because of substantially increased labor costs. Mr. Smith estimated that machine-dipping resulted in savings of from 4 to 5 cents a pound in labor and material costs over Blakeston & Wilson's hand-dipping process. "We can afford to hand-dip our chocolates only because of the savings effected by our low sales cost."

Mr. Sidwell Wilson, in 1937, had developed and patented his continuous production-line process for dipping, cooling, and packing varied selections of chocolates. This process, he believed, enabled Blakeston & Wilson to hand-dip chocolates for 3 cents less per pound than competing hand-dip chocolate manufacturers. He had installed four of these units in his factory in 1938 at a cost of $4,000 per unit. In 1947 two units were operating at capacity (7,500 pounds per unit a day); the other two units, because of material shortages, were operating at partial capacity. Mr. Wilson had attempted to sell the process to other manufacturers for $100,000 per unit, but only one sale had been made to a small Evanston, Illinois, chocolate manufacturer.

The company's labor force was composed of 200 employees, most of whom were women engaged in dipping and packing chocolates. Labor and management relations were excellent; the company had never been organized. Wages equaled those of competing firms in the Chicago area; in addition to their base pay, all employees who had been with the company more than five years (96) participated in a profit-sharing plan which company officials believed stimulated employee interest and productive efficiency.

Wages of employees had risen steadily since 1938. At that time dippers were paid 30 cents an hour; in 1947 they started at 87 cents an hour. In addition to base pay, dippers were eligible for a bonus of from 1 to 9 cents an hour if they approached or reached the maximum production rate (24 pieces a minute); in 1947 most dippers were earning the maximum bonus. Mr. Smith awarded the bonus to dippers by occasionally checking production operations. "The bonus is based on my judgment as to how well they are doing," he said, "not on time or motion studies." The bonus system, which had been in effect for a period of four years, had not been extended to other employees of the company.

Mr. Smith personally handled the limited amount of cost accounting work done on all manufacturing operations. He had established standard costs on materials and direct labor for producing 100 pound lots of each type of candy included in the Perfection selection. Standards for burden had not been established, he said, since these charges were fairly constant from year to year. Standard costs were occasionally checked against actual costs when Mr. Smith believed this necessary. Although many of the company's standard cost sheets were obsolete because of changes in materials prices, Mr. Smith did not believe revisions were necessary so long as the company secured a 28% gross manufacturing operating profit (exclusive of burden charges). Exhibit 5 lists standard cost information on a typical chocolate item manufactured both for bulk and package sale.

Exhibit 4

BLAKESTON & WILSON

Balance Sheets, 1938–46
(In Thousands)

	1938	1939	1940	1941	1942	1943	1944	1945	1946
Assets									
Current Assets:									
Cash in Bank and on Hand	$ 11	$ 10	$ 13	$ 8	$ 32	$161	$202	$134	$227
Accounts Receivable	21	24	33	26	54	73	60	61	26
Inventories at Cost or Market, Whichever Is Lower	9	21	24	90	44	36	56	62	118
Total Current Assets	$ 41	$ 55	$ 70	$124	$130	$270	$318	$257	$371
Cash Surrender Value of Life Insurance Policy	1	2	8	9	9	10	11	16	17
Total	$ 42	$ 57	$ 78	$133	$139	$280	$329	$273	$388
Postwar Refundable Portion of Estimated Excess Profits Tax	..	..	..	..	..	12	26	..	..
Fixed Assets	13	39	45	45	38	34	38	33	39
Deferred Charges	8	13	19	11	10	9	17	17	14
Total Assets	$ 63	$109	$142	$189	$187	$335	$410	$323	$441
Liabilities and Capital									
Current Liabilities:									
Note Payable at Bank	..	..	$ 7	$ 37	$ 7	$ 7	$ 6	..	..
Accounts Payable and Accrued Expenses	$ 15	$ 19	31	25	20	29	67	$ 41	$ 58
Reserve for Federal and State Taxes	3	5	5	10	21	139	200	133	160
Total Current Liabilities	$ 18	$ 24	$ 43	$ 72	$ 48	$175	$273	$174	$218
Postwar Refund of Estimated Federal Excess Profits Tax	..	..	..	..	..	$ 12	$ 26	..	..
Capital Stock:									
Preferred Stock:									
Authorized and Issued—500 Shares of $6 Cumulative without Par Value	$ 30*	$ 50	$ 50	$ 50	$ 50	$ 50	$ 50	$ 50	$ 50
Less: Held in Treasury	..	..	..	..	..	..	18	50	50
Common Stock:									
Authorized, Issued, and Outstanding 1,040 Shares without Par Value	..	..	..	..	..	..	104†	104	104
Total Capital Stock	$ 30	$ 50	$ 50	$ 50	$ 50	$ 32	$104	$104	$104
Earned Surplus:									
Balance, January 1	..	$ 15	$ 35	$ 49	$ 67	$ 89	$116	$ 7	$ 45
Add: Net Profit	$ 15	21	17	21	25	32	34	28	74
Postwar Refund of Excess Profits Taxes	..	..	..	..	..	..	..	26‡	..
Less: Dividends Paid	..	1	2	3	3	3	39	16	..
Amount Transferred to Capital Stock Account	..	..	..	..	..	..	104‡	..	..
Under Accrual of Prior Years' Taxes, etc.	..	..	1	..	..	..	..	..	..
Balance, December 31	$ 15	$ 35	$ 49	$ 67	$ 89	$116	$ 7	$ 45	$119
Total Liabilities and Capital	$ 63	$109	$142	$189	$187	$335	$410	$323	$441

* 300 shares of preferred issued and outstanding December 31, 1938.
† Stated value of $100 per share of common voted by board of directors.
‡ Treated as deferred income in prior years, transferred to earned surplus December 31, 1945.

Source: Company records.

CHAIN STORE CUSTOMERS

By April, 1947, increased sales of bulk and packaged chocolates were again being made to the variety chain with which Mr. Blakeston was associated. Mr. Wilson had not re-established sales relations with the retail grocery chain to which he had sold chocolates prior to World War II. That company was building its own large candy factory and was installing candy departments in all its retail outlets. "We don't want to sell to any customer who is in competition with us in the manufacture of candy," Mr. Wilson declared. He had not yet attempted to secure another large grocery chain outlet, since a shortage of raw

Exhibit 5

BLAKESTON & WILSON

*Standard Costs for 100-Pound Mix
of Chocolate-Covered Cream Candy*

Materials $26.97
Direct labor 7.65
   Total $34.62

Source: Company records.

Exhibit 6

BLAKESTON & WILSON

Income Statements, 1938–46 (In Thousands)

| | 1938 | | 1939 | | 1940 | |
	Amt.	% of Sales	Amt.	% of Sales	Amt.	% of Sales
Net sales	$286	100.0%	$562	100.0%	$668	100.0
Cost of sales	231	80.8	470	83.6	561	84.0
Gross profit on sales	$ 55	19.2%	$ 92	16.4%	$107	16.0
Selling, general, and administrative expenses:						
Freight and cartage outward	$ 10	3.6%	$ 22	3.9%	$ 29	4.5
Shipping wages and supplies	3	1.0	11	2.0	15	2.2
Advertising, travel, entertainment, commissions, and other selling expenses	6	2.1	11	2.0	13	1.9
Executive and office salaries	12	4.2	18	3.2	19	2.8
Contributions to profit-sharing plan	..	..	..	..	..	..
Provision for state excise and federal capital stock tax	1	0.3	2	0.4	2	0.3
Miscellaneous	5	1.7	3	0.5	9	1.3
Total expenses	$ 37	12.9%	$ 67	12.0%	$ 87	13.0
Net profit before federal taxes on income	$ 18	6.3%	$ 25	4.4%	$ 20	3.0
Provision for estimated federal taxes on income and excess profits	3	1.0	4	0.7	3	0.4
Net profit carried to surplus	$ 15	5.3%	$ 21	3.7%	$ 17	2.6

NOTE: Totals from 1943 through 1946 include sales made by Blakeston & Wilson to company-controlled Perfection shops.

materials still hampered production. Such an outlet would be necessary during normal times, he felt, to insure his plant of capacity operations during the entire year.

CONTROL

In conformity with Mr. Wilson's desire to keep administrative expenses to a minimum, only a few reports were prepared for his use. He received a monthly balance sheet and profit and loss statement from all corporations, as well as daily reports on Blakeston & Wilson production and sales made by individual Perfection Chocolate Shops.

Mr. Sidwell Wilson, in addition to the investigations made by Retail Management Corporation, inspected several Perfection shops on one day each week. "As far as store operations are concerned, our best indicator of trouble is when customers begin to complain—then we start action," he said.

Mr. Sidwell Wilson personally checked wholesaler relations on his visits to those concerns. "That gives me all the control I need over those operations. I believe this system will be effective as long as I am personally running the business; it may not prove effective under other operating conditions." He further believed that the widespread adver-

| | 1941 | | 1942 | | 1943 | | 1944 | | 1945 | | 1946 |
mt.	% of Sales	Amt.	% of Sales	Amt.	% of Sales	Amt.	% of Sales	Amt.	% of Sales	Amt.	% of Sales
'99	100.0%	$909	100.0%	$1,160	100.0%	$1,239	100.0%	$1,110	100.0%	$1,349	100.0%
563	83.0	762	83.8	877	75.6	906	73.1	867	78.1	1,041	77.2
136	17.0%	$147	16.2%	$283	24.4%	$333	26.9%	$243	21.9%	$308	22.8%
23	2.8%	$16	1.8%	$18	1.6%	$20	1.6%	$15	1.4%	$17	1.3%
22	2.8	21	2.3	22	1.9	24	1.9	25	2.3	27	2.0
20	2.5	11	1.2	17	1.5	21	1.7	34	3.0	23	1.7
26	3.2	40	4.5	40	3.3	40	3.3	45	4.0	50	3.7
..	..	..	..	..	..	19	1.5	21	1.9	27	2.0
2	0.3	3	0.3	8	0.7	11	0.9	5	0.5	8	0.6
14	1.8	13	1.4	15	1.3	14	1.1	20	1.8	22	1.6
107	13.4%	$104	11.5%	$120	10.3%	$149	12.0%	$165	14.9%	$174	12.9%
29	3.6%	$43	4.7%	$163	14.1%	$184	14.9%	$78	7.0%	$134	9.9%
8	1.0	18	2.0	131	11.3	150	12.1	50	4.5	60	4.4
21	2.6%	$25	2.7%	$32	2.8%	$34	2.8%	$28	2.5%	$74	5.5%

Source: Company records.

tising campaign for Perfection chocolates would provide an incentive, both for his wholesalers to continue to carry the line and for the retailers supplied by these firms to hold to the advertised price.

EXECUTIVE ORGANIZATION

The executive organization of Blakeston & Wilson in April, 1947, was substantially the same as in 1938. An assistant treasurer had been engaged in 1946 to take charge of all detailed accounting work, with the exception of cost accounting records. Mr. Sidwell Wilson, fifty-six years of age, was still actively engaged in all company operations. "I can do anything from firing a boiler to selling packaged chocolates," he stated. He personally approved all major policy and operating decisions made for Blakeston & Wilson, Retail Management Corporation, or any of the seventeen Perfection Chocolate Shops.

At quarterly meetings of the board of directors, Mr. Wilson discussed general company problems with the board. All Perfection Chocolate Shops were operating at a profit, and Mr. Blakeston and his associates were convinced that the decision to enter the retail-sales field had been a wise one. All Blakeston & Wilson preferred stock had been retired by this time, and Mr. Wilson owned 52% of the outstanding common stock.

Mr. Smith, forty-five years of age, had been an accounting instructor before becoming associated with the company. The office staff of the company, excluding secretarial help, consisted of three women who handled all sales and production records, as well as payroll accounts. "Other companies of comparable size have large administrative organizations—up to twenty-five persons. By keeping a small stable customer list and using a minimum of expensive records, our administrative section can be kept to a minimum size," said Mr. Smith.

EXPANSION

Mr. Wilson was planning to expand his chain of retail shops. Four additional store leases had been signed, and before the end of 1947 the company planned to operate between twenty-five and thirty shops. "If I were a younger man, we would open 500." He believed that Perfection shops should expand immediately: (1) to get as many consumers as possible familiar with Perfection chocolates and (2) to become established in the retail candy business during 1947, a time when raw-material shortages prevented other companies from entering

Exhibit 7

BLAKESTON & WILSON

Perfection Chocolate Shops (Combined),
Balance Sheet as of December 31, 1946
(In Thousands)

Assets

Current Assets:		
Cash		$130
Inventories (at Cost)		18
Total Current Assets		$148
Fixed Assets		41
Deferred Charges:		
Improvement to Leased Premises	$ 56	
Unexpired Insurance Premiums	7	
Total Deferred Charges		63
Total Assets		$252

Liabilities and Capital

Current Liabilities:		
Accounts Payable		$ 32
Reserve for State and Federal Taxes		52
Total Current Liabilities		$ 84
Capital Stock and Surplus:		
Capital Stock:		
Preferred	$ 47	
Common	19	66
Earned Surplus:		
Balance, December 31, 1945	$ 20	
Net Profit, 1946	113	
	$133	
Less: Dividends Paid	31	
Balance, December 31, 1946		102
Total Liabilities and Capital		$252

Source: Company records.

this field. In 1947 about one-third of Blakeston & Wilson production was being sold through company-controlled stores, and Mr. Wilson wanted to increase substantially that amount.

Among the potential sites for new Perfection shops were Cleveland and Detroit. Retail candy shops, both locally owned and chain stores, were already in operation in these cities. Previous expansion had placed Perfection shops in direct competition with a seminational chain of retail candy stores. That company, incorporated in 1919, operated several hundred stores in the Middle West and along the East Coast which sold medium-price hand-dipped chocolates and salted nuts. Mr. Wilson believed that that company's sales volume averaged only $50,000 per store. "We know how to sell in volume at low costs."

Competition for Perfection chocolates sold by company wholesalers came from hundreds of locally and regionally promoted packaged chocolates, as well as from several brands of nationally distributed candies.

Mr. Wilson estimated that the productive capacity of the candy industry had expanded by 30% since 1939. In addition to the expansion of established companies, other firms were building entirely new candy plants. "Competition is going to be severe," he concluded. (See Exhibits 4, 6, and 7.)

NOTES ON THE CONFECTIONERY INDUSTRY

TYPES OF PRODUCERS

The confectionery industry may be divided into three types of producers: (1) manufacturer-wholesalers; (2) chocolate manufacturers; and (3) manufacturer-retailers.

Manufacturer-wholesalers (manufacturers who distribute their candies through wholesalers) are the predominant type of producer in the industry from the viewpoint of number of firms, volume, and value of output. These concerns, although they make the largest proportion of inexpensive candies, sell in every price class from penny goods to expensive boxed chocolates. While most manufacturer-wholesalers make a variety of goods with wide price differentials, some concentrate on one price line; in some cases the entire plant is designed to produce just one type of candy bar.

Manufacturer-wholesalers are divided into six basic types of producers: (1) general-line houses, which supply national or regional markets with a wide range of candies, such as penny goods, five- and ten-cent packages or pieces, and bulk goods; (2) bar-goods houses, which supply the national market with chocolate-covered candy bars; (3) specialty houses, which distribute either nationally or regionally one item or several types of variety candy (such as toy boats filled with candy); (4) package-goods houses, which distribute boxed and some bulk chocolates to a regional market; (5) bulk-goods houses; and (6) penny-goods houses.

Chocolate manufacturers (for example, Hershey, Baker, and Nestle), in addition to supplying the candy industry with chocolate items, such as coatings, syrups, and cocoa products, also manufacture molded chocolate bars. These products are sold both directly and through wholesale concerns.

Manufacturer-retailers (manufacturers who market the bulk of their output directly through their own stores) have the smallest volume among the three types of candy manufacturers. These manufacturers frequently build up reputations as specialists in making certain types of candy. Smaller manufacturer-retailers customarily make candy on the premises of their own store and sell it directly; larger companies have a factory and supply company-owned stores in a local or regional area.

PRODUCT

The candy market in the United States is dominated by the 5-cent candy bar. Shortly after the end of World War I, the first nationally advertised candy bar was introduced. Currently, there is a large number of nationally advertised bars on the market. In fact, more than one-half of all the candy sold in 1945 consisted of candy bars, 90% of which retailed for 5 cents. Packaged confectionery (primarily boxed chocolates) was the second largest selling item in 1945, the total making up about 20% of dollar sales. Bulk candy (approximately 15% of 1945 sales) and specialty candies (approximately 10% of 1945 sales) were the next largest selling items.[1]

INDUSTRY LOCATION AND SIZE

Candy manufacturing operations are geographically concentrated in the states of Illinois, New York, Pennsylvania, and Massachusetts, with Chicago the candy manufacturing center. In 1944 these four states produced, as measured by value, about 65% of the confectionery manufactured in this country.[2]

Sales by manufacturing concerns are likewise concentrated. In 1944, 87% of confectionery sales were made by 80 firms, each with more than a million dollar per year business.[3] Total industry manufacturing activities were carried on in 1,473 plants.

CHANNELS OF DISTRIBUTION

In the pre-war years the confectionery industry was making important changes in its methods of distribution. The chain store as a distributor of candy doubled in importance from 1927 to 1944. In 1927, 10 per cent of the candy distributed was marketed through chain stores, but by 1941 the proportion had risen to 21.4 per cent. Apparently this gain was at the expense of the independent retailer. The independent retailer's share of candy sales decreased from 27.5 per

---

[1] U.S. Department of Commerce, *19th Annual Report on Confectionery Sales and Distribution* (1945), p. 23.

[2] Edward T. Bullock, "Candy Takes Its Place at the Dinner Table," *Dun's Review,* July, 1946, p. 16.

[3] Fred Smith, "Sweetness and Light," *Advertising and Selling,* Vol. XXXIX, No. 2 (February, 1946).

cent in 1927 to 11.7 per cent in 1941. . . . Distribution through factory-owned stores has remained in the neighborhood of 9 per cent. . . .[4]

The candy wholesaler has been, and remains, the most important factor in the distribution of confectionery. The percentage of industry output which those wholesalers handled dropped from 61% (1937) to 40% (1942) and then rose to 48% (1945), following a marked reduction in military purchases of candy.[5]

SEASONALITY

Despite wartime scarcities of raw materials and the leveling influence of military demand, the candy industry never lost its characteristic seasonality.

The characteristic seasonal pattern of sales by the candy industry, shows that the highest activity is reached just before the Christmas holidays, with the market falling off in January. As the year progresses, there is a minor but well-defined rise in sales for Easter. In addition, the manufacturer-retailers experienced a pickup in sales for the February holidays, especially in the box trade for St. Valentine's Day. The bottom for all candy sales is reached in mid-summer, almost universally in July, with an upswing geared first to Thanksgiving and culminating in the Christmas trade.[6]

FLUCTUATIONS IN COSTS AND SALES VALUE

Confectionery material costs are subject to wide fluctuations. From 1927 to 1932 the average price of materials declined 50 per cent. By contrast, wholesale confectionery prices fell 40 per cent. In the recovery period to 1937, material costs rose 47 per cent and confectionery prices only 15 per cent. During the recession of 1937–1938, material costs again declined considerably more than the sales value of confectionery. The declines were 16 per cent and 7 per cent for materials and confectionery respectively. From 1938 to 1944 material costs and sales value have each risen 54 per cent.

If price history repeats itself, the next recession of any consequence will find material prices weaker than confectionery prices.

The demand for candy is but moderately affected by changes in general business conditions. In the severe depression of the early 1930's the quantity of candy consumed decreased only about 8 per cent.

Individual items, however, are subject to wide fluctuations. In 1933, for example, fancy package goods were down 70 per cent from the 1930 average. Bars other than chocolate declined 53 per cent. In the mild recession of 1937–1938, the only decline of magnitude was one of 20 per cent in plain package goods.[7]

---

[4] Bullock, *op. cit.*, p. 15.
[5] *Ibid.*
[6] Selina Caldor, "Seasonal Trends in the Candy Business," *Domestic Commerce,* Vol. XXXIV, No. 3 (March, 1946).
[7] Bullock, *op. cit.*, p. 16.

COMPETITION

The candy industry has always been characterized by intense competition. The situation in the industry during the 1920's was summarized, in 1927, by the Secretary of the National Confectioners Association as follows:

> The candy industry, representing a capital investment of approximately $300,-000,000 and annual sales aggregating $400,000,000, is beset with fears and doubts as to its future. . . . During the prewar period (1912–1917) . . . there was the keenest kind of competition and profits were things hoped for but seldom realized. . . . During the war period conditions were changed almost overnight from a buyers' to a sellers' market. . . . Manufacturers were able to dictate terms and conditions of sale. . . . What was the result? Plants were over-expanded. . . . I estimate that the potential capacity of the entire industry is anywhere from 25% to 35% more than is required to supply the demand . . . conditions tempted manufacturers to resort to practices which have developed situations that are decidedly detrimental to the industry. Free goods are given; secret rebates and special discounts are given to favored customers; over-extension of credits as to terms and quantity; special deals and concessions; rewards to customers' salesmen; and many others.[8]

During the depression years of the 1930's, competition in the industry continued to be severe; the average price per pound received by the manufacturer dropped from 23.2 cents per pound in 1927 to 13.9 cents in 1933. In addition to intense competition within the industry, external factors were limiting the confectionery market. Ice cream and soft-drink consumption had increased tremendously during this period, as did the consumption of cigarettes. The latter was aided to no small degree by increased sales to women smokers. Production (physical volume) increased 8% from 1929 to 1939, despite the fact that there were then 38% fewer plants and 22% less workers in the industry.[9]

A further factor currently affecting the competitive situation has been the rapid rise of chain grocery store candy sales.

> Grocery stores, food chains such as the A & P, and supermarkets are assuming increasing importance as distributors of confectionery. Grocery stores now sell a larger volume of candy than of coffee or butter.[10]

WORLD WAR II

The effect of World War II on the industry was reflected in three major developments: (1) rationing of basic raw materials used in candy manufacture; (2) a tremendous increase in industry sales, both

---

[8] *Confectioners Review*, August, 1927, p. 73.
[9] Bullock, *op. cit.*, p. 16.
[10] *Ibid.*, p. 18.

in terms of value and in pounds of candy manufactured; and (3) a distinct change in the types of candy manufactured.

Sugar rations for candy manufacturers were first set at 70% of the 1941 base use period; this quota was increased to 80% in July, 1942. The highest level of ration was reached from August, 1943, to December, 1944, when the sugar ration was 80% of the 1941 base, plus a 10% bonus. The lowest ration level was 50% for the last six months of 1945. In 1947 the ration was 75%.

Industry dollar sales rose from $308,000,000 in 1939 to peaks of $658,000,000 in 1944 and $620,000,000 in 1945. The gain resulted from both a higher output of candy and an increase in the price per pound. In 1939 the wholesale price of candy averaged 15 cents a pound; in 1946 it averaged 26.9 cents a pound. This price increase received by the manufacturer was primarily achieved by the producer diverting material from inexpensive lines to higher-priced boxed candies. From 1939 to 1944, production of plain and fancy packaged goods (primarily boxed chocolates) rose 30% and 310%, respectively.

EXPANSION

Sugar shortages during World War II had handicapped the expansion of established confectionery companies, as well as the development of new enterprises. In 1947, however, numerous companies were planning or were already in the process of plant expansion; for example, the Kraft Cheese Company, which had entered the caramel business before the war, planned erection of a $750,000 candy plant in Kendallville, Indiana. In addition to this new plant expansion, the manufacturing capacity of the industry had already been greatly increased by improved war-developed manufacturing processes.

Superior Separator Company

INTRODUCTION

IN JULY, 1950, the board of directors of the Superior Separator Company, Hopkins, Minnesota, decided not to take advantage of an opportunity to purchase for $300,000 the name and fixed assets of a firm which manufactured construction equipment, a line of products not related to those produced by the company. The decision was motivated by a fear that the economic consequences of the outbreak of war in Korea might greatly increase the difficulties facing a management group attempting to operate two businesses concurrently. This action caused Charles F. Pierson, president, to consider fully the problems created by an over-all management policy designed to promote the maximum growth and development of the company. Mr. Pierson was concerned both with the direction and the rate of future expansion.

Superior manufactured seed- and grain-cleaning and grading machinery for country and terminal elevators and farm lifting, loading, and moving equipment (see Exhibit 1).

Net sales for the fiscal year ending October 31, 1949, were reported as $4,539,774 and net profit after taxes as $352,154. This marked the thirteenth consecutive year of profitable operation. In the 20 years of the company's existence, net worth had grown from an initial capitalization of $30,000 to $1,655,791, almost entirely through the reinvestment of earnings. (Balance sheets for selected years are shown in Exhibit 2; income statements for selected years, in Exhibit 3.)

COMPANY HISTORY, 1929–45

The Superior Separator Company was incorporated in November, 1929, to engage in the manufacture of grain-separators for country elevators. Carl C. Gray and Harry Johnson had developed an improved process for separating impurities from grain while employed by a Minneapolis manufacturer of grain-cleaning machinery. With the aim of securing financial backing for a new enterprise, the pair approached Harry C. Piper, partner in the Minneapolis investment banking house of Lane, Piper, and Jaffray. Mr. Piper and a few associates agreed to supply $15,000 in return for 5,000 shares of common stock, one-half of the amount issued. Mr. Gray and Mr. Johnson each received 2,500 shares as compensation for their inventive skills.

From 1929 until 1936 manufacturing operations were carried out in rented space in an old building in St. Paul. Mr. Johnson would design and build a machine, and Mr. Gray, the president, would go out to a grain elevator and sell it. In spite of a basic conflict in personalities and the prevailing adverse economic conditions, sales grew from $27,000 in 1930 to $126,000 in 1936; profits were earned in three of the first seven years.

The company purchased an old plant in southeast Minneapolis in 1936 and began to expand its line. Sales rose to a prewar peak of $306,000 in 1939 but declined to $232,000 in 1940. Afraid that maximum growth had been attained, Mr. Johnson sold his stock to the other stockholders but remained with the company as chief engineer.

Until 1939 all earnings were reinvested. In that year the first dividend, $10,000, was paid. (In the period 1940–49, $45,300, in total, was returned to stockholders.)

Late in 1939 a North Dakota farmer who was an acquaintance of Mr. Johnson came into the main office with an invention which he had previously offered to several large manufacturers of farm equipment without acceptance. The product was a high-lift hydraulic loader, designed to be affixed to any standard-size tractor to utilize its power to lift and stack hay.

Although the hydraulic loader bore little relation to grain-cleaning machinery, management believed that a large potential market existed for the farm implement and took an option to purchase the patent. Following a successful patent search, rights were purchased and ten experimental units were built and sold in 1940.

The Hydraulic Farmhand, as the new machine was called, met with an enthusiastic response from farmers, but Mr. Gray proceeded cautiously, and Superior built only 336 units in 1941. When war broke out in December, 1941, the War Production Board instituted controls restricting the annual production of a manufacturer of farm equipment to 125% of the company's 1940 output, and Superior was unable to produce the Farmhand in any quantity until 1944. In that year Farmhand sales exceeded grain-cleaner sales for the first time. (See Exhibit 4 for a comparison of the sales of the Farmhand Division and the Grain-Cleaner Division, 1940–49.)

With grain-cleaner production also limited by wartime controls,

Exhibit 1

SUPERIOR SEPARATOR COMPANY

Company Sales Brochure

"At last ... a farm implement maker that specializes in farm lifting, loading, and moving equipment"

Now farming's toughest chores are completely mechanized!

You've seen it coming for years . . . "Power Farming" . . . the mechanization of all the expensive, time-taking, back-breaking work involved in operating a farm. . . .

You've seen machines take over the labor and drudgery of seeding, cultivation, harvesting and other difficult jobs. . . .

NOW . . . thanks to the research and inventiveness of a specialized farm implement company . . . you're seeing a revolution in the last stronghold of old-fashioned farming methods . . . the laborious tasks involved in lifting, loading, hauling and moving of materials.

NOW . . . for the first time . . . one company makes efficient and thoroughly proved machines to perform almost *every* job of materials handling on your farm!

These FARMHAND machines, produced in a completely modern implement plant, are designed and built by *specialists* in materials handling tools. FARMHAND makes no other type of farm imple-

ment. All the skill and experience of FARM-HAND'S master machinists and engineers is devoted solely to the problems of handling materials on the farm . . . lifting and loading materials for storage and transport . . . hauling materials in every kind of loose or bulky form . . . unloading materials in the easiest way . . . in the least possible time . . . with the utmost savings in money and manpower . . . with the greatest output of work of any implements per dollar invested.

The FARMHAND line includes well designed machines "tailored" to fit the requirements of nearly every type of farm in the country, large or small, engaged in the production of practically any kind of crop.

Look them over. See how these specialized lifting, loading, hauling and moving tools can save time and money for you. Then write for free literature on the machines that interest you . . . or see your nearest FARMHAND Dealer for a demonstration and all the facts about "Power Farming" the FARMHAND way.

Farmhand Specialized machines for every farm lifting, loading, moving job

made by Superior Separator Company, Hopkins, Minnesota

Exhibit 1—Continued

SUPERIOR SEPARATOR COMPANY

FARMHAND HIGH-REACH HYDRAULIC LOADER ... America's No. 1 farm loader choice (according to impartial survey). 3,000 lb. lift ... 21-foot reach ... gentle "wrist-action" control for accurate, easy handling and placement of big loads.

A COMPLETE LINE OF ATTACHMENTS for performing r of the year with the FARMHAND Hydraulic Loader. 1. Gra from stacks, prevents them from blowing. 2. High-capacity feed corn, etc. 4. High-capacity Hay Basket. 5. Push-Off fo

FARMHAND LOADER FOR SMALLER TRACTORS ... a rem smaller tractors. Compactly built for low clearance. Easy to Power take-off shaft brought through pump for operating leveling ... 16-foot reach ... full 2,000 lb. lift. Four attachm Basket; 3. Push-Off for Hay Basket; 4. Sand and Gravel Plate

FARMHAND "POWER-BOX" ... revolutionary 4-ton capacity wagon box with tractor-powered unloading mechanism across full width of bed. Handles almost any kind of load—silage, corn, manure, etc. Precision engineered. Ball and roller bearings throughout.

MANURE SPREADER AND MIXER-FEEDER ATTACHMENTS ... fit on the "Power-Box" ... add new ease and speed to two of farming's toughest chores.

FARMHAND "90 permits full 90° tu tensible Tongue fo front bolster ... ex

The FARMHAND Hydraulic Loader fits more than 76 well-known tractor models and may be mounted or unmounted easily in a few minutes

than 50 farm jobs in every season Fork, ideal for taking hay or straw ure Fork. 3. Scoop for snow, silage, ay Basket builds high stacks to 27 feet, folds flat against rear of Hay Basket when not in use. 6. Manure Fork Scoop attaches to fork for lifting sand, gravel, etc. 7. Heavy-duty Forage Fork for breaking frozen stacks and handling biggest, bulkiest loads, such as machinery, out buildings, feed bunks, etc. 8. Bulldozer Blade for earth moving, ground leveling, etc. 9. Rugged 8-foot V-Plow.

ble performer especially designed for use on on and off. No cables or braces in your way. implements while loader is on tractor. Self-available: 1. Full Width Manure Fork; 2. Hay

FARMHAND DUMP-RAKE · · · doubles speed of ordinary dump rakes. Simple rope trip mechanism and steel clutch roll the rake a half-turn at a time without leaving unraked hay. Low-cost single-purpose machine.

FARMHAND POST HOLE DIGGER · · · a rugged, power-driven digger that fits easily on Farmhand Loader. Pull posts, carry new wire and new posts, with loader. A complete fencing outfit in one unit.

WAGON . . . the famous 5-ton capacity wagon that without backing, slipping or tilting. Quick-Hitch Ex-st coupling . . . extensible reach . . . fixed or rocking wide 72" construction . . . other great features.

FARMHAND 2½ TON WAGON . . . a lighter version of the FARMHAND "90" Wagon with all the special features, including 90° turns with full support under load.

FARMHAND SINGLE-AXLE TRAILER · · · ruggedly built for heavy loads. Takes any box. Adjustable height hitch and front support stand.

One of America's finest specialized farm equipment plant

PRECISION ENGINEERING and sound design make FARMHAND machines tops for efficiency, low-cost operation.

CAREFUL INSPECTION all along the line assures top quality, most dependable performance for you.

FINEST QUALITY MACHINING to e ceptionally close tolerances goes into precision parts and controls.

EXPERIENCED WELDERS are responsible for the sound, solid construction and exceptional strength of machines.

TYPICAL EXAMPLE of our complex manufacturing work is this CC16 Cylinder machine, product of our grain cleaner division.

IN THIS SHEET METAL SHOP are craft many of the FARMHAND machines ar accessories that save work, time for yo

THE FARMHAND MAIN PLANT where 300 people work with precision equipment to make long lasting machines for handling materials on American farms. This large plant in Hopkins, Minnesota, contains more than 100,000 sq. ft. of factory, office and warehouse space. It is fitted with the most modern metal working tools, the finest of manufacturing facilities.

Exhibit 2

SUPERIOR SEPARATOR COMPANY

Comparative Balance Sheets for Selected Fiscal Years Ending December 31,
1930–48, and October 31, 1948–49, with Condition at June 30, 1950

(In Thousands)

Assets	Dec. 31, 1930†	Dec. 31, 1939†	Dec. 31, 1942	Dec. 31, 1944	Dec. 31, 1946	Dec. 31, 1947	Oct. 31, 1948	Oct. 31, 1949	Jun. 30, 1950
Current Assets:									
Cash	$ 1	$ 20	$ 78	$119	$ 96	$ 239	$ 85	$ 352	$ 5
Accounts Receivable	4	46	22	38	345	276	286	147	649
Inventory	2	29	47	103	492	658	1,224	1,042	1,440‡
Total Current Assets	$ 8	$ 95	$147	$260	$ 933	$1,173	$1,595	$1,541	$2,094
Fixed Assets:									
Patents and Patent License	...	$ 8	$ 5	$ 4	$ 2	$ 2	$ 5	$ 5	
Miscellaneous Receivable	...	...	...	19	...	6	6	...	
Prepaid Insurance and Deferred Charges	...	1	1	1	7	4	5	27	
Investment in Subsidiaries	...	...	...	...	53	114	112	137§	
Due from Subsidiaries	...	...	...	...	...	49	76	194‖	
Plant and Equipment—Net	...	29	60	125	153	231	291	299	
Total Fixed Assets	...	$ 38	$ 66	$ 149	$ 215	$ 406	$ 495	$ 662	
Total Assets	$124	$185	$326	$1,082	$1,388	$2,001	$2,036	$2,756	

Liabilities and Net Worth	Dec. 31, 1930†	Dec. 31, 1939†	Dec. 31, 1942	Dec. 31, 1944	Dec. 31, 1946	Dec. 31, 1947	Oct. 31, 1948	Oct. 31, 1949	Jun. 30, 1950
Current Liabilities:									
Accounts Payable	...	$ 6	$ 16	$ 174	$ 134	$ 216	$ 82	$ 162	
Notes Payable	...	...	...	104	...	...	...	450	
Accruals and Reserves	...	7	13	117	99	161	68	127	
Advance on Orders	...	...	6	3	...	19	10	...	
Reserves for Income Taxes	...	29	87	182	267	302	22.	226	
Total Current Liabilities	...	$ 37	$ 42	$122	$ 580	$ 500	$ 698	$ 381	$ 965
Common Stock	$30	$ 30	$ 30	$ 30	$ 30	$ 31	$ 31	$ 31	$ 31
Paid in Surplus	...	...	...	...	2	6	6	6	6
Earned Surplus	3*	57	113	174	470	851	1,266	1,618	1,754
Total Net Worth	$27	$ 87	$143	$204	$ 502	$ 888	$1,303	$1,655	$1,791
Total Liabilities and Net Worth		$124	$185	$326	$1,082	$1,388	$2,001	$2,036	$2,756

* Deficit.
† Complete statement not available.
‡ Raw material, $891,000; work in process and finished goods, $598,000; inventory reserve, $57,000*; variance, $8,000.
§ Includes investment of $105,000 in and loan of $25,000 to the First Street Realty Company and $7,000 in the Superior Separator Company of Canada, Ltd.
‖ Accounts Receivable, the Superior Separator Company of Canada, Ltd.
Source: Company records.

Mr. Gray solicited subcontracts from several large manufacturers of war equipment. This production reached its peak in 1943 when war orders accounted for 41% of net sales, but total war production in the period 1940–45 amounted to only $221,000.

As raw materials again became available, the company placed primary emphasis on Farmhand sales. In anticipation of a period of rapid expansion, the board of directors attempted to strengthen the executive organization by bringing into the company in 1944 a group of men headed by Charles F. Pierson, son-in-law of Mr. Piper, the largest stockholder. Following a year as acting general manager, Mr. Pierson was named president to succeed Mr. Gray.

Exhibit 3

SUPERIOR SEPARATOR COMPANY

Comparative Profit or Loss Statements for Selected Fiscal Years
Ending December 31, 1930–47 and October 31, 1948–49

(In Thousands)

	1930	1939	1942	1944	1946	1947†	1948† (10 Mos.)	1949†	1950† (8 Mos.)
Net sales..............	$27	$306	$415	$681	$3,048	$5,068	$5,955	$4,539	$2,721
Cost of goods sold........	16	166	279	481	2,296	3,962	4,716	3,374	1,989
Gross profit.............	$11	$140	$136	$200	$ 752	$1,106	$1,239	$1,165	$ 732
Administrative, general, and selling expenses.............	14	93	74	80	336	461	523	617	432
Operation profit..........	$ 3*	$ 47	$ 62	$120	$ 416	$ 645	$ 716	$ 548	$ 300
Additions-deductions and taxes......	...	13	26	80	168	262	292	196	138
Net profit............	$ 3*	$ 34	$ 36	$ 40	$ 248	$ 383	$ 424	$ 352	$ 162
Net sales..............	100.0%	100.0%	100.0%	100.0%	100.0%	100.0%	100.0%	100.0%	100.0%
Cost of goods sold........	61.4	54.3	67.3	70.5	75.4	78.1	79.2	74.3	73.1
Gross profit.............	38.6	45.7	32.7	29.5	24.6	21.9	20.8	25.7	26.9
Administrative, general, and selling expenses.............	51.2	30.2	17.8	11.8	11.0	9.1	8.8	13.4	15.9
Operation profit..........	12.6*	15.5	14.9	17.7	13.6	12.8	12.0	12.3	11.0
Additions-deductions and taxes......	...	4.2	6.4	11.8	5.5	5.2	4.9	4.3	5.1
Net profit............	12.6%	11.3%	8.5%	5.9%	8.1%	7.6%	7.1%	8.0%	5.9%

* Loss.
† Subsidiaries excluded.
Source: Company records.

Exhibit 4

SUPERIOR SEPARATOR COMPANY

Sales by Divisions, 1940–49

(In Thousands)

	1940	1941	1942	1943	1944	1945	1946	1947	1948 (10 Mos.)	1949	1950 (8 Mos.)
Grain-Cleaner Division...........	$229	$241	$251	$144	$247	$ 412	$ 457	$ 822	$ 577	$ 612	$ 294
Farmhand Division.	3	95	111	61	410	620	2,591	4,247	5,379	3,928	2,427
War Production....	...	...	54	144	24	...	...	...	...	...	...
Total.........	$232	$336	$416	$349	$681	$1,032	$3,048	$5,069	$5,956	$4,540	$2,721
Grain-Cleaner Division...........	98.7%	71.8%	60.3%	41.2%	36.2%	40.0%	15.0%	16.2%	9.7%	13.5%	10.8%
Farmhand Division.	1.3	28.2	26.7	17.5	60.3	60.0	85.0	83.8	90.3	86.5	89.2
War Production....	...	...	13.0	41.3	3.5	...	...	...	...	...	...
Total.........	100.0%	100.0%	100.0%	100.0%	100.0%	100.0%	100.0%	100.0%	100.0%	100.0%	100.0%

Source: Company records.

COMPANY HISTORY, 1946–50

To provide more extensive production facilities, the company purchased an 11-acre industrial site in Hopkins, a suburb of Minneapolis, for $4,000, and constructed a modern one-story plant with nearly 40,000 square feet of floor space. Later additions increased this area to over 100,000 square feet. The total cost of the building and additions exceeded $600,000. The old building was sold, and the company moved to Hopkins in December, 1945.

When the new plant was constructed, a direct subsidiary, the First Street Realty Company, was incorporated to own the properties and lease them to the parent company. By such action mortgage indebtedness was removed from the balance sheet of the parent company and a line of credit of $150,000 was obtained from a Minneapolis bank. (By June, 1950, this line had been extended to $750,000.) The Superior Separator Company purchased 84% of the stock of the First Street Realty Company. Stockholders of Superior owned the remaining shares directly.

A second subsidiary, the Superior Separator Company of Canada, Ltd., wholly owned by the parent company, was established in 1947 with main offices in Winnipeg, Manitoba, to serve as sales agent for the company's products in Canada.

From 1945 through the first ten months of 1948 total net sales of the Superior Separator Company increased almost 600%. While sales of grain cleaners increased moderately, the Farmhand was principally responsible for the extent of growth. During this period the demand for farm equipment far exceeded the available supply, and all manufacturers were sorely pressed to fill dealers' orders. Because the farmer preferred to purchase haying machinery in the spring before the period of use, the productive capacity of the plant was particularly strained during the late winter months.

In an attempt to even out seasonal variation in shipments, the sales manager of the Farmhand Division had devised in 1947 a scheme to grant an additional 5% seasonal discount on all orders placed between November 1 and March 1. Shipments in November and December of 1948 and January and February of 1949 remained at a high level as dealers ordered in anticipation of a normal spring demand.

"However, for several reasons retail sales did not materialize in the spring of 1949 as expected," Mr. Pierson said. An unusually severe winter had delayed the haying season. The deferred demand for farm equipment resulting from nonavailability during the war had been largely satisfied. Net farm income, off slightly in 1948 from a 1947 peak, began to fall sharply. Increasing competition for the farmer's dollar was developing rapidly from all consumer goods.

When Farmhands did not move from dealers' floors, factory orders fell off considerably. Shipments in March, 1949, were down 35% from February, and April showed a further decline. Plant production planned on a normal seasonal sales curve began to build up finished-goods inventory in Hopkins. In the middle of March overtime was eliminated. On April 8, the second shift was dropped, all schedules were drastically reduced, and 108 plant and office employees were laid off. Forty-nine other employees accepted a wage cut and downgrading in preference to a layoff. Changes were not made soon enough, however, and the company found itself on April 30 in an overextended position with: (1) a heavy inventory of raw material and work in process, (2) practically no cash, (3) a $100,000 bank loan, and (4) 1,500 Farmhands in finished-goods inventory.

"We faced a major policy decision. We could cut back production still further and attempt to hold on until dealer inventories had worked down to a level where they would reorder, or we could attack the situation aggressively by revamping our entire organization, slashing costs to the bone, and modernizing and expanding our product line. We decided to gamble on a bold attack," said Mr. Pierson.

The sales manager of the Farmhand Division, who had not informed the president of the failure of retail sales to develop as anticipated because "he didn't want to worry him," was dismissed and Mr. Pierson assumed the added responsibility. Several sales territories were combined and the field salesforce was reduced one-third. The office staff was decreased further and the engineering staff cut in half.

The remaining members of the engineering department were charged with the responsibility of redesigning all machines then in production and adding several new ones to the line. With the department working around the clock, blueprints were drawn, experimental models were tested briefly and the first machines were delivered to dealers in late summer. Although dealer reaction was favorable, the season of heavy demand had passed and farmer acceptance could not be tested adequately in 1949.

Net sales for 1949 were 24% below the record figure of $5,955,891, achieved in the first ten months of 1948, but net profit after taxes was off only 17%. To Mr. Pierson the annual report indicated that the bold measures taken in the spring had been successful. By October "expenses had been cut, inventories reduced, the bank loan paid off, and an adequate cash balance accumulated."

Shipments through June, 1950, were almost $1 million below the comparable period in 1949. Reasons stated by the sales manager of the Farmhand Division were: (1) heavy floods in the Red River Valley and a late spring throughout the Midwest, (2) droughts in Kansas, and

(3) dealer reluctance to carry any machines in inventory. Sales in the month of June, 1950, were 54% greater than in the corresponding month in 1949. Mr. Pierson thought that this increase indicated that the season was merely late and that total 1950 sales would compare favorably with those of 1949 (see Exhibit 5). Net profit after taxes for the first eight months of 1950 was 5.9% of net sales, 2.1% lower than the figure for the year 1949.

Exhibit 5

SUPERIOR SEPARATOR COMPANY

Comparative Monthly Sales and Profit Figures for Fiscal Years Ending October 31

(In Thousands)

	1949†				1950			
	SALES		PROFIT AFTER TAXES		SALES		PROFIT AFTER TAXES	
	Month	Total	Month	Total	Month	Total	Month	Total
November	$488	$ 488	$27	$ 27	$177	$ 177	$ 9*	$ 9*
December	526	1,014	41	68	210	387	5	4*
January	487	1,501	32	100	251	638	14	10
February	570	2,071	42	142	260	897	13	23
March	377	2,448	4*	138	352	1,249	17	40
April	341	2,789	5	143	362	1,611	15	55
May	393	3,182	10	153	390	2,001	27	82
June	468	3,650	45	198	720	2,721	74	156
July	283	3,933	6	204				
August	285	4,218	10	214				
September	170	4,388	5*	209				
October	152	4,540	..‡	352				

* Loss.
† In 1949 a 5% seasonal discount was granted during the first four months.
‡ October profit figure unreliable because of year-end adjustment.
Source: Company records.

COMPANY PRODUCTS

The products manufactured by the company fell into two categories: grain-cleaning machinery and farm equipment. The Grain-Cleaner Division made a full line of cleaning, grading, scalping, and aspirating equipment for the processing of grains and seeds.

The Farmhand Division produced a selected line of materials-handling equipment for the farm. The principal product of the division was the Hydraulic Farmhand. The loader was built in two sizes, one for standard-size tractors and one for small-size ones. To increase the versatility of the loader, the company had designed a number of attachments for it. Among them were a hay basket, manure fork, grapple fork, forage fork, bulldozer blade, and snowplow.

Other farm implements manufactured were the Prairie Mulcher, a tractor-drawn rotary rake which spread straw into freshly plowed land to prevent erosion; the Power Box, a four-ton capacity wagon box with tractor-powered unloading mechanism for manure-spreading and automatic feeding of livestock; a two and one-half ton capacity wagon with a tongue permitting full 90 degree turns; a five-ton capacity wagon; a single-axle trailer; a tractor-drawn high-speed dump rake; a three-level forage unit; and a portable power pack to motivate the forage unit.

When the design for a new corn picker was shown to the engineering department in 1947, there was an executive difference of opinion as to whether or not rights should be purchased. Although the corn picker was considered to be a better machine than those then on the market, the board of directors decided that the cost of development work was too great for the company to bear and decided not to add the picker to the product line.

EXECUTIVE ORGANIZATION

After graduating from Yale University in 1934, Mr. Pierson was employed for four years by the Minneapolis-Honeywell Regulator Company, Minneapolis. He spent six months as a punch-press operator, one year in the dispatching crib, six months in the production-control department, one year as a correspondent in the sales department, and one year as a salesman assigned to the Detroit territory. "It was a four-year postgraduate course in manufacturing," said Mr. Pierson.

Desiring to return to Minneapolis following the death of his father in 1938, he accepted a position with Superior as assistant to the president, Mr. Gray. After handling various jobs in the production and sales departments, he became sales manager in 1940. In this capacity he soon encountered the same difficulty working with Mr. Johnson that Mr. Gray had experienced. Mr. Pierson remained with the company until he enlisted in the Navy in April, 1942. When he received a medical discharge in the spring of 1943, he went back to Minneapolis-Honeywell as an assistant production manager. On the condition that Mr. Johnson be dismissed, he returned to Superior in 1944 and brought a group of new men in with him to fill key positions.

None of these executives remained in 1950. Mr. Pierson said, "We faced a problem basic to many rapidly expanding companies. Executive growth did not keep pace with the growth of the company. When we hired a controller in 1945, we couldn't afford to pay more than $300 a month so we hired the best man we could get at that salary. As the company grew, the job got too big for him, and his health broke under the pressure. His retirement in 1948 saved us the unpleasantness of firing him." Several executives were dismissed.

"We have a team now," said Mr. Pierson, describing the executive organization in 1950. "Sure, we have our disagreements, but we get along pretty well." The following men were key executives in the organization:

John Randall, vice-president in charge of manufacturing, joined Minneapolis-Honeywell following graduation from Tuck Business School, Dartmouth College, in 1935. He was employed in the accounting and production departments and rose to the position of plant manager of the Minneapolis assembly plant. Before coming to Superior in December, 1947, he was sales manager of the Moduflow Division (residential home heating). In June, 1950, Mr. Randall was named general manager of the Grain-Cleaner Division. He remained responsible for all company production as well.

Bernard Carlson, chief engineer, was assistant chief engineer of the Moline plant of Deere & Company before coming to Superior in January, 1947. Following graduation from the University of Montana he spent seven years with the Allis-Chalmers Manufacturing Company and several with the army engineers. In 1950 he was thirty-eight years old.

D. L. Wahl, secretary and controller, graduated from the University of North Dakota and entered the accounting firm of Touche, Niven, Bailey, and Smart. After nine years he joined Minneapolis-Honeywell, where as head of the cost department he handled renegotiation and forward-pricing of government contracts. He came to Superior in June, 1948, as controller, and was named secretary two years later. He was forty-one years old in 1950.

Arthur W. Ostrander, sales manager of the Farmhand Division, worked for Superior for several summers during the late 1930's to help pay his expenses while attending Dartmouth College. In the summer of 1940 he traveled through Minnesota, North Dakota, and South Dakota enlisting dealers to handle the hydraulic loader. With this work as a background, he presented his master's thesis entitled "A Farm Market Analysis for the Hydraulic Farmhand" for graduation from Tuck Business School in 1941. He returned to Superior after graduation and remained until Farmhand production was restricted. From 1942 until 1945 he worked in the production-control department of the P. F.

Exhibit 6

SUPERIOR SEPARATOR COMPANY

Organization Chart—July, 1950

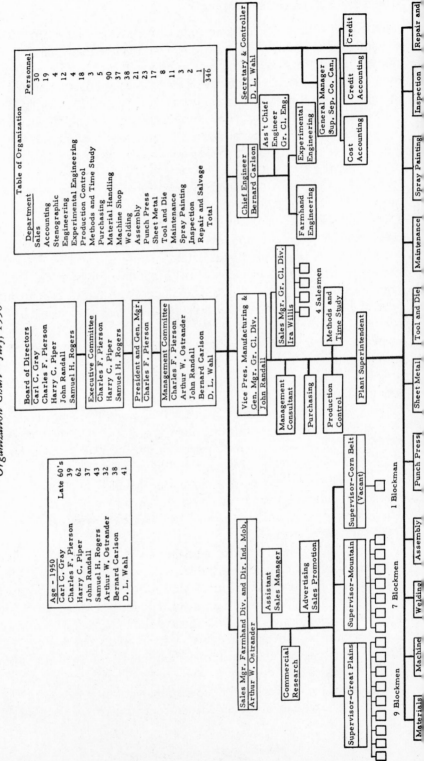

Table of Organization

Department	Personnel
Sales	30
Accounting	19
Stenographic	4
Engineering	12
Experimental Engineering	4
Production Control	18
Methods and Time Study	3
Purchasing	5
Material Handling	90
Machine Shop	37
Welding	38
Assembly	21
Punch Press	23
Sheet Metal	17
Tool and Die	8
Maintenance	11
Spray Painting	3
Inspection	2
Repair and Salvage	1
Total	346

Board of Directors
Carl C. Gray
Charles F. Pierson
Harry C. Piper
John Randall
Samuel H. Rogers

Executive Committee
Charles F. Pierson
Harry C. Piper
Samuel H. Rogers

President and Gen. Mgr.
Charles F. Pierson

Management Committee
Charles F. Pierson
Arthur W. Ostrander
John Randall
Bernard Carlson
D. L. Wahl

Age – 1950	
Carl C. Gray	Late 60's
Charles F. Pierson	39
Harry C. Piper	62
John Randall	37
Samuel H. Rogers	43
Arthur W. Ostrander	32
Bernard Carlson	38
D. L. Wahl	41

Secretary & Controller
D. L. Wahl

Chief Engineer
Bernard Carlson

Ass't Chief Engineer
Gr. Cl. Eng.

Farmhand Engineering

Experimental Engineering

General Manager
Sup. Sep. Co. Can.

Cost Accounting

Credit Accounting

Credit

Vice Pres. Manufacturing & Gen. Mgr. Gr. Cl. Div.
John Randall

Sales Mgr. Gr. Cl. Div.
Ira Willis

4 Salesmen

Methods and Time Study

Management Consultant

Purchasing

Production Control

Plant Superintendent

Sales Mgr. Farmhand Div. and Dir. Ind. Mob.
Arthur W. Ostrander

Assistant Sales Manager

Advertising Sales Promotion

Commercial Research

Supervisor-Great Plains

Supervisor-Mountain

Supervisor-Corn Belt (Vacant)

9 Blockmen

7 Blockmen

1 Blockman

Materials | Machine | Welding | Assembly | Punch Press | Sheet Metal | Tool and Die | Maintenance | Spray Painting | Inspection | Repair and

Corbin Division of The American Hardware Corporation, New Britain, Connecticut. He then spent three years with Robert Heller and Associates, management consultants, and a year in the commercial research department of General Mills, Inc., before joining Superior in November, 1949. After submitting a report based on a two-month market analysis of the company's products, he was named sales manager of the Farmhand Division in January, 1950. In July, 1950, he was also named director of industrial mobilization.

These four executives, with Mr. Pierson, constituted a management committee which met formally at irregular intervals. Mr. Pierson usually ate lunch with these men, however, and saw them several times a day to discuss current developments.

GRAIN-CLEANER DIVISION

In the first eight months of the fiscal year 1950, grain-cleaner sales amounted to only 10.8% of total sales. Operations showed a net loss of $25,606, 8.9% of net sales (see Exhibit 7). What for ten years had been the only group of products manufactured was in 1950 a minor factor in the total operations of the company.

The rapid expansion of Farmhand sales in the postwar era had required an increasing amount of executive time. As a result the Grain-Cleaner Division was allowed to shift for itself. When he joined Superior to becomes sales manager of the Grain-Cleaner Division in 1947, Ira Willis became in effect acting general manager of the division as well. In February, 1949, he surveyed the market for grain-cleaners and reported that service was the basic factor in building sales. He discerned a definite feeling of animosity toward Superior because of poor service rendered during war years and up to and including 1948. To remedy the situation, he planned an aggressive program to contact all potential customers and convince them that Superior wanted their business.

These customers were scattered throughout the United States and Canada. In addition to the original customers—country and terminal elevators—the company sold machines to flour mills, feed plants, hybrid-corn houses, cereal plants, rice mills, seed houses, and malting plants. The four salesmen were stationed in Minnesota and North Dakota and sold direct to the user. To cover the remaining territories the company employed distributors located in principal cities throughout the country. There were few large companies in the grain-separator industry. Superior's greatest competition came from the Hart-Carter Company. Both had the reputation of producing quality machines using

Exhibit 7

SUPERIOR SEPARATOR COMPANY

Profit or Loss Statement for 8-Month Period Ending June 30, 1950, by Division

(In Thousands)

	Company		Farmhand Division		Grain-Cleaner Division	
Sales, less cash discount available	$2,776		$2,469		$307	
Deduct: returns and allowances	49		37		12	
	$2,727		$2,432		$295	
Cash discount available to customers	$ 121		$ 117		$ 4	
Cash discount allowed to customers	119*		115*		4*	
Out freight	...		2		1	
Truck rental	9*		9*		..	
Net sales	$2,721	100.0%	$2,428	100.0%	$294	100.0%
Cost of goods sold:						
At standard cost	$1,660	61.0%	$1,423	58.6%	$237	80.6%
Adjustment to standard cost	38*	...	....	...	38*	...
Variances:						
Labor	39	...	23	...	16	...
Burden	111	...	113	...	1	...
Material	165	...	163	...	1	...
Provision for inventory shrinkage	52	...	49	...	4	...
Total cost of sales	$1,989	73.1%	$1,771	72.9%	$219	74.5%
Gross profit	$ 732	26.9%	$ 657	27.1%	$ 75	25.5%
Selling expenses:						
Field expenses	$ 219	...	$ 158	...	$ 62	...
Home office	69	...	54	...	15	...
Total selling expenses	$ 288	10.6%	$ 212	8.7%	$ 77	26.2%
General and administrative expenses	86	3.2	75	3.1	10	3.4
Engineering	58	2.5	45	1.9	13	4.4
Total selling, general, and administrative expenses	$ 432	16.3%	$ 332	13.7%	$100	34.0%
Profit or loss from operations	$ 300	10.6%	$ 325	13.4%	$ 25*	8.5%*
Other charges	$ 9	...				
Net income before adjusted compensation and tax provision	$ 291	...				
Provision for adjusted compensation	17	...				
Net income before income taxes	$ 274	...				
Provision for income taxes	112	...				
Net profit for the period	$ 162	5.9%				

* Loss.

Source: Company records.

the separation-through-weight principle, although the operation of the competing machines was slightly different.

For some time Mr. Pierson had been concerned about the unprofitability of the Grain-Cleaner Division. He believed that the major reason why the division had not been making money lay in its pricing policy.

The line had been priced to produce a profit after granting salesmen 5% commissions. Distributors demanded 15%, however, and an increasing percentage of sales was being made through this channel.

To remedy the situation, the division raised its list prices 10–20% in August, 1950. Henceforth, the price range would be $310–$3,885. Mr. Pierson did not believe that the price increase would affect sales adversely. "Most purchasers probably won't even notice the change."

Another reason why the division had not been operating profitably, Mr. Pierson thought, was partly psychological. The division had long believed that it was necessary to separate physically the manufacture of grain-cleaners from the manufacture of farm implements. After the inventory crisis of 1949, in order to conserve cash management shelved a plan to build a separate building for the division. Mr. Pierson felt that, as a result of this decision, the personnel of the division were not exerting enough effort to make maximum use of present quarters.

Mr. Wahl believed that one reason for the unprofitable operation lay in the lack of information on costing. The company was not sure it knew its costs in the production of grain-cleaners, and this project was, therefore, a current assignment of the accounting department in June, 1950.

In that month Mr. Randall was appointed general manager of the Grain-Cleaner Division to pin responsibility. "Since 1940 we have been on the verge of 'getting grain cleaners straightened out' . . . ridiculous to continue this business unless it can be done at a profit," said Mr. Pierson.

FARMHAND DIVISION

Competitive Situation. The Department of Commerce estimated in March, 1949, that there were about 1,600 firms engaged in the manufacture of farm equipment. Of this number, 7 companies, led by the International Harvester Company and Deere & Company, produced approximately 65% of the total output of the industry. These large companies manufactured a long line of farm machinery. "However, since these firms concentrate on the manufacture of equipment used in the production and harvesting of the major field crops, they are not major producers of all types of agricultural equipment."[1] Many of the short-line concerns specialized in one item or in a certain type of equipment. The area in which Superior desired to compete was the specialized field of materials-handling.

---

[1] Department of Commerce, *Progress and Prospects in the Farm Equipment Industry,* March 31, 1949.

Direct competition for the Hydraulic Farmhand came not so much from other high-lift loaders as from other machines designed to put up hay. Indeed, salesmen ordered to report the appearance of competitive equipment in the field had revealed that only a few high-lift loaders produced by obscure small companies had been encountered. Usually a

Exhibit 8

SUPERIOR SEPARATOR COMPANY

Comparison of Performance of Superior with Performance of Six Long-Line Manufacturers, 1939–49

	Superior	Allis-Chalmers	J. I. Case	Deere	International Harvester	Minne-apolis-Moline	Oliver
NET SALES (1939 = 100)							
1949	1,481	472	819	515	428	547	530
1948	1,942*	442	741	441	445	544	541
1947	1,653	285	390	302	349	381	386
1946	972	126	184	207	227	237	266
1945	337	391	383	196	293	314	306
1944	222	511	366	244	301	319	227
1943	114	385	342	268	216	278	161
1942	136	264	242	190	172	222	149
1941	109	164	189	178	172	175	121
1940	76	117	111	120	129	122	100
1939	100	100	100	100	100	100	100
NET INCOME AS A PERCENTAGE OF NET SALES							
1949	8.0	5.3	10.3†	10.9†	6.7	8.6	6.1
1948	7.1	4.7	6.7	8.9	5.9	8.8	7.7
1947	7.6	2.6	6.1	6.5	6.5	9.2	5.5
1946	8.1	0.1	4.2	6.6	4.6	5.3	3.9
1945	4.7	2.4	3.9	6.3	3.9	2.5	2.9
1944	5.9	2.4	2.8	6.3	4.0	3.0	4.0
1943	12.0	2.8	3.4	6.2	5.6	4.1	5.7
1942	8.5	3.0	4.9	9.5	7.3	5.1	5.8
1941	6.5	4.7	8.3	11.4	8.4	8.8	7.2
1940	5.3	5.8	6.0	14.5	8.4	7.1	4.6
1939	11.3	3.3	1.7	10.9	3.8	0.4	2.3

* Ten months.
† Before reserve for inventories.
Source: Standard & Poor's *Industry Surveys*, "Machinery—Agricultural," February 23, 1950; company records.

machine would make a brief appearance and then would disappear as the company went into bankruptcy. Although rumors were constantly cropping up that several long-line companies were prepared to introduce a high-lift loader, not one had done so by mid-1950. Instead, the big companies concentrated on a low-lift manure loader, apparently in the belief that there was a much larger potential market for this machine, particularly in the Corn Belt. The low-lift manure loader which would lift material a height of about 9 feet sold for about $325, while a high-lift hay loader which would lift material as high as 27 feet retailed with the major attachments for almost $600. Thus the two machines tended to reach a different market.

The two wagons were directly competitive with a great many other farm wagons on the market after the war. According to Mr. Pierson, the market was overcrowded when the products were introduced, but the wagons were added to the line to complement the Power Box. There was little direct competition for the fully equipped Power Box in its range of about $900; again, the size of the market was the restricting factor. The mixer-feeder attachment, for instance, was well received by the large stockman, but the farmer with a small herd of cattle could not see the economy of automatic feeding. If he needed a manure spreader, he could buy a conventional one for about one-third the price of the Power Box.

Competition for the dump rake came from two sources. The horse-drawn dump rake was still being used widely in areas where it was the custom to rake cut hay into small piles in the field to be picked up later by a stacker, such as the Farmhand. Where a tractor-drawn hay loader was used to elevate the hay into a wagon, the farmer preferred to use a side-delivery rake which would produce a continuous windrow.[2]

The demands of World War II and international food shortages following the war stimulated a major increase in U.S. food production and farm prices in the period 1940–48. Gross farm income rose from $11.0 billion to $35.1 billion, and net farm income (gross receipts less costs of production) from $4.8 billion to $16.5 billion. Prices received by the farmer increased 185% and prices paid by the farmer rose 159%. While farm wages rose 242%, the average price of farm machinery increased only 46%. Two factors, therefore, spurred mechanization of the American farm: (1) necessity for the maximum production, and (2) economy of substituting machines for men. In 1948 shipments of all manufacturers of farm machinery were 250% greater than 1940 shipments, and 1948 shipments of manufacturers of haying machinery were 665% larger than the 1940 figure (see Exhibit 9).

Net farm income began to decline in 1948 from its 1947 peak, and the trend continued in 1949 and the first half of 1950. Nevertheless,

---

[2] "Windrow"—a row of hay raked up to dry.

Exhibit 9

SUPERIOR SEPARATOR COMPANY

Industry Statistics, 1940–50

(In Millions)

Year	Total Gross Farm Income	Total Net Farm Income	All Farm Equipment Manufacturers' Shipments	Manufacturers' Shipments Haying Machinery
1950	E $31,500	E $13,000	$	$...
1949	32,167	14,129	1,815	152
1948	35,071	16,526	1,734	153
1947	34,643	17,794	1,295	95
1946	29,255	15,017	850	60
1945	25,419	12,790	700	49
1944	24,159	12,126	617	45
1943	23,008	9,086	344	26
1942	18,551	6,412	659	34
1941	13,881	4,525	671	35
1940	11,009	4,783	498	20

E: Estimated.
Source: U.S. Department of Agriculture, Bureau of Agricultural Economics.
U.S. Department of Commerce, Bureau of the Census.

most observers predicted that net farm income in 1950 would be almost three times net farm income in 1940 and that the federal government would continue to support prices to prevent a substantial drop in farm income in the immediate future.

Sales. The company sold its line of farm equipment to approximately 900 retail dealers in 20 states in the Midwest and Far West, and about 100 dealers in western Canada. The company had tried to obtain the strongest established dealer in a community. Usually the dealer selected represented one of the major long-line manufacturers of farm machinery. Mr. Pierson estimated that in the 1945–50 expansion of from 300 to 1,000 dealers the company had been successful in securing the best or the next-to-best farm equipment dealer in nearly every locality. Approximately 40% were International Harvester Company dealers, 40% were Deere & Company dealers, and the remaining 20% represented miscellaneous manufacturers. Although a report of sales by dealers in 1949 was not available to Mr. Ostrander, he estimated that 50% of the dealers would do 80% of the business in 1950. Dealers were given a 20% margin.

Mr. Pierson hoped to work toward a system of independent Farmhand dealers handling the line exclusively. In July, 1948, the company opened a retail store at Moorhead, Minnesota, to determine whether a store handling only Farmhand equipment could be operated profitably.

After ten months operations showed a net loss of $1,305 with no allocation of general and administrative expenses of the home office, and the store was closed. The president felt that the number of items in the line would have to be increased materially to warrant a system of independent Farmhand dealers.

When the supply of farm equipment once again became plentiful in 1949 and the farmer reverted to his prewar habit of buying at the moment of greatest need, speed of delivery became of prime importance. Since the factory was located over 1,000 miles from many dealers, Mr. Pierson in May, 1949, took two steps to ease the situation:

1. Seven trucks were leased to supplement rail delivery with the dealer billed at the carload rate for shipment by rail. (The trucking operation was realizing a small profit in 1950.)

2. Eleven large dealers in the Mountain and Pacific states were secured to serve as warehouse distributors. In return for storing machines and parts on consignment, the distributor was paid by the dealer a handling charge of 60 cents per 100 pounds on machines and $2.00 each on mountings used to secure the Farmhand loader to various makes of tractors. The dealer in turn passed this charge on to the farmer. The distributor agreed to make the merchandise available to any dealer in his area.

As sales manager of the Farmhand Division, Mr. Ostrander supervised 3 territorial sales managers in the United States and the sales manager of the Canadian subsidiary. These men, in turn, oversaw 17 blockmen in the United States and 5 in Canada. (A block was defined as an area with an annual sales potential of $200,000.) The three territories in the United States—Mountain, Plains, and Corn Belt—were established as areas in which crops and methods of farming were largely similar. In 1950 there was no territorial manager for the Corn Belt. In 1949, 217 dealers in the Mountain territory accounted for 35% of total Farmhand sales, 381 in the Plains territory for 58%, and 315 in the Corn Belt for 7%.

Mr. Ostrander explained this poor performance in the Corn Belt territory: "The farmers' methods of putting up hay determine whether there's a market for a high-lift loader. In the Plains and Mountain territories the Farmhand does the best job of stacking hay in the field. In the Corn Belt you can drive for miles without seeing a hay stack. (See Exhibit 10.) Farmers put their hay up in barns and don't see the need for a high-lift loader. The farmer doesn't think about the 50 other materials-handling jobs the Farmhand will do until he buys the ma-

Exhibit 10

SUPERIOR SEPARATOR COMPANY

Hay: Percentage Stored in Stacks or Ricks at Haying Time, 1944

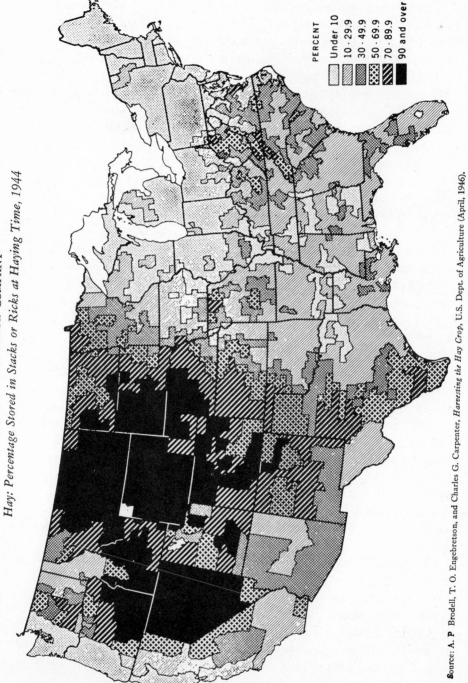

PERCENT

Under 10
10 - 29.9
30 - 49.9
50 - 69.9
70 - 89.9
90 and over

SOURCE: A. P. Brodell, T. O. Engebretson, and Charles G. Carpenter, *Harvesting the Hay Crop*, U.S. Dept. of Agriculture (April, 1946).

chine for its primary purpose. One of our biggest problems in marketing the Farmhand is to sell the Corn Belt farmer on the many uses of the machine. So far we haven't done it."

The company hoped that the addition of the Power Box, the five-ton wagon, the two and one-half ton wagon, the single-axle trailer, and the three-level forage unit would increase Farmhand sales in the Corn Belt by giving the dealer a longer line to demonstrate.

A blockman received a guaranteed monthly draw which varied from $250 to $350 depending upon his ability to meet monthly quotas and his over-all record. In addition each blockman was given a fixed amount, $50 a week, to cover expenses.

The volume required to cover the expense and draw for a blockman, based on 3½% of net collections, determined the quota for each block. Once his quota was attained, the blockman received a 3½% commission on all subsequent volume. Annual compensation varied from $5,500 for the salesman who did not make his quota to about $10,000 for the top salesman in the field. A weekly report on the status of sales-quota accomplishment was compiled and distributed to all blockmen and territorial managers. The July, 1950, report revealed that in the United States six blockmen had already attained their annual quota, six were ahead of where they should be at the 8½-month mark, and five were below this point. No Canadian blockman had reached 40% of his 1950 quota.

Two Farmhand products presented particular marketing problems. The Prairie Mulcher was "either 20 years ahead of its time or 20 years behind," according to Mr. Ostrander. When the machine was introduced in 1947, farmers showed marked interest and dealers stocked heavily. But retail sales soon declined to almost nothing. Dealers were caught with unsalable machines and became wary of other new products introduced to the line. Consequently, little effort was being made by the sales department to push the mulcher.

Mechanical defects in the dump rake, introduced in 1949, were uncovered in the field, and the company in July, 1950, was in the process of recalling all machines to the factory for engineering changes.

Advertising and Sales Promotion. The company expended $167,000 for advertising in 1949, about 3.7% of net sales. By far the greatest proportion of this amount was spent by the Farmhand Division around the basic theme "Designed by farmers . . . engineered for farmers. For every big lifting and loading job on your farm!" As a contribution to advertising expense the dealers were charged a fee of 1% of total bill-ings. For this charge they were supplied with newspaper mats and pro-motional material for mailing to prospects on a regular basis. There was some dealer criticism of this 1% charge since other manufacturers pro-vided direct-mail literature without charge and paid half of the cost of local newspaper advertising. The company believed, however, that the dealer would make better use of the mats and direct-mail folders if he were aware that he was paying a share of the cost.

The company backed up local advertising with page advertisements in regional farm papers. In the summer of 1950 this advertising em-phasized a contest offering $3,000 in prizes to 107 contestants who listed the largest number of farm jobs illustrated in a drawing as being done by hand which could be done better by a Hydraulic Farmhand. By July, 1950, over 80,000 entries had been received. At this rate it was estimated that the total response would reach 150,000 by the closing, September 30, 1950. The company employed the advertising agency of Batten, Barton, Durstine, and Osborn.

Sales-promotion efforts varied according to the season. In the summer exhibits were set up at state and county fairs. All Farmhand equipment was displayed, and the dealers and blockmen solicited inquiries from interested farmers. In the winter three films were made available to dealers to show to large gatherings with the central idea: "While tractor power has been the greatest single factor in mechanizing the American farm, it has not taken the back-break out of materials handling. The Farmhand line completes the mechanization of the farm." The block-men also held demonstrations in dealer towns.

Pricing. Although cost studies were made on a product before it was added to the Farmhand line, the price arrived at was generally the most accurate guess as to what the market would bear. Company officers often decided to price a basic machine low to stimulate the initial sale and to make high margins on attachments for it. Management had encountered difficulty with such a pricing policy because market information on a new machine was sketchy at best. The fear of overpricing a machine had led to underpricing several new products introduced in 1949. Once the price had been established, the sales manager was reluctant to raise it even though the higher price would have proven acceptable initially. Exhibit 11 reveals a cost and margin appraisal of selected items in the Farmhand line. Unit shipments for the eight-month period through June, 1950, are also included.

Exhibit 11

SUPERIOR SEPARATOR COMPANY

Summary of Profit Margin in Selected Farmhand Products February 15, 1950, and Shipments October 31, 1949—June 30, 1950

Description	Total Cost	Profit Margin	Net Price	Dealer Discount	List Price	Per Cent Margin	Shipments (Units) 8 Months through June 30, 1950
Basic machine—large loader	$194.11	$26.29	$220.40	$69.60	$290.00	12%	3,828
Main support standard angles	14.86	9.46	34.32	7.68	32.00	39	2,849
Torque tubes 178″ long	21.21	12.99	34.20	10.80	45.00	38	3,265
International W-9 mounting	22.49	13.23	35.72	11.28	47.00	37	.....
Hay basket	57.07	18.32	75.39	23.81	99.20	24	3,436
Manure fork	28.20	21.39	49.59	15.66	65.25	43	2,796
Gravel plate	4.62	3.17	7.79	2.46	10.25	41	2,659
Forage fork	34.49	19.47	53.96	17.04	71.00	36	851
Snow Scoop	43.35	48.61	91.96	29.04	121.00	53	490
Bulldozer blade	29.72	21.58	51.30	16.20	67.50	42	114
Basic machine—small loader	168.88	44.98	207.86	65.64	273.50	22	402
Hydraulic system	40.26	11.42	51.68	16.32	68.00	22	1,105
Basic Power Box	196.58	16.22	212.80	67.20	280.00	8	7†
Mixer-feeder attachment	262.03	22.97	285.00	90.00	375.00	8	44
Front and rear truck assembly:							
5-ton wagon	104.27	1.75	106.02	33.48	139.50	2	157
2½-ton wagon	92.43	3.89*	88.54	27.96	116.50	4*	141
Basic single-axle trailer	92.67	7.51*	85.16	26.89	112.05	9*	47
Dump rake	148.74	1.74	150.48	47.52	198.00	1	420

* Loss.
† 119 "complete" Power Boxes shipped.
Source: Company records.

RESEARCH AND DEVELOPMENT

Research and development were a combined responsibility of engineering and sales. The engineering department was constantly experimenting with new machines and new adaptations to present ones. The sales department tried to keep aware of equipment performance in the field and to measure the market for a machine before it was added to the line, but executives said they had often felt forced to introduce an implement before it was thoroughly tested or the market for it fully determined. The effect of such a policy was to require the farmer to do part of the testing job. Mr. Pierson believed that the higher rate of returns would be detrimental only if the reputation of the Farmhand name suffered.

Following the loss of an appeal to the Circuit Court of Appeals from a decision of the District Court against Superior in a suit brought against a small company for infringement of the patent on the Hydraulic Farmhand, Mr. Pierson had come to feel that the established brand name, "Farmhand," was more valuable than any patent in meeting competition.

In an attempt to gain closer co-ordination between sales and engineering in the summer of 1950, an engineer from the methods department was sent out into Wisconsin with the forage box to analyze farmer reaction and to suggest improvements, and a former commercial researcher for General Mills was brought into the sales department by Mr. Ostrander to perform permanent market analysis of the Farmhand line in the field.

PRODUCTION

The production of farm machinery was basically a fabricating and welding job which did not require close tolerances. Manufacture of certain parts, however, required close precision work. While many manufacturers of loaders purchased their hydraulic pumps, for instance, Superior manufactured its own. The only finished parts purchased were such items as ball bearings, chains, and tires.

The manufacture of grain-cleaners was a more complicated process, but still the operation principally involved the assembly of parts crafted in the sheet-metal shop.

The sharp seasonal nature of Farmhand sales presented a major problem to production control. The company had neither the space nor the financial resources to build up a large inventory of finished goods in the off season. As a result, the rate of production varied widely from season to season, depending on current demand. Grain-cleaner sales did not show the same seasonal variation, but the high cost per specialized machine and the limited market required almost a job-order operation. No more than 20 machines would be run through at a time, and very low finished stocks were maintained. There was some transfer of workers to grain-cleaner production when farm-equipment volume was at a low level, but the company had not yet been successful in developing a product which would level out yearly output. An increasing parts business was expected to help level off the cyclical variation in farm implement sales, but the seasonal variation was still a problem.

PURCHASING

The shortage of raw materials following the war made purchasing a serious problem area for most manufacturers. Steel, in particular, was in short supply, and most steel companies adopted a voluntary allocation system whereby a customer was entitled to purchase in proportion to his 1940 orders. For Superior, a company which had expanded 20 times over in the space of 10 years, such an allotment did not begin to satisfy its needs. The purchasing agent was forced to buy steel wherever he could obtain it. Even in early 1950 when the general situation had eased considerably he had been forced to pay a broker 11 cents a pound for sheet steel when the mill price on sheet steel was a little over 4 cents a pound.

LABOR RELATIONS

The company employed 160 to 240 factory workers, depending on the season. The contract between Superior and District 77 of the International Association of Machinists provided for a union shop and a check-off system for the deduction of union dues by the company. The wage scale was generally in line with surrounding manufacturing concerns. The 1950 contract provided for a minimum wage of $1.20 for a janitor to $1.88 for a tool and die maker. Joint wage review was to be held twice a year, in January and July.

In an attempt to promote a spirit of labor-management teamwork, Mr. Pierson in 1948 offered the union a profit-sharing plan and revealed production and financial records to the employees. The adjusted compensation proposal, offered to all employees whether union or non-union, set a base rate profit of 7.5% after taxes for the investors. Above that, for each $\frac{1}{10}$ of 1% increase in profits, each worker was to receive

an extra 1% of his gross earnings. Above 8%, the workers would receive 1% for every 1% increase in profits. The members of the union
twice rejected the proposal before final acceptance. One year later both
the union and the company praised the plan:

> As the company and the International Association of Machinists renewed the
> agreement last week, they announced that the plan had:
> 1. Eliminated layoffs in spite of seasonal nature of the firm's farm equipment
>   and grain cleaner business.
> 2. Increased employees' pay by 5% of their annual gross earnings.
> 3. Established a basis for mutual understanding between employee and em-
>   ployer which removes many of the usual frictions in labor-management
>   relations.[3]

Three months later the company was forced to lay off 108 men in
the face of an inventory crisis, and labor-management relations deteriorated. When a review of wages was held in the summer of 1949 the
union discarded the profit-sharing plan in favor of a flat 6 cents an hour
increase in wages by a 74 to 61 vote. Office employees retained the plan,
but because the highly profitable months of November and December,
1948, had been included in determining the 1948 bonus, no adjusted
compensation was declared on 1949 profits.

In March, 1950, the union struck for a 25 cents an hour wage increase. The strike was settled within 48 hours on a 7 cents an hour raise
across the board, but ill feelings lingered on both sides.

"You must expect that you're going to have occasional trouble with
your labor force in any manufacturing operation," said Mr. Pierson. He
credited the strike not so much to a desire for higher wages but to a dissatisfaction with management neglect of human relations problems
created in the shop by the product redesign and expansion program of
1949. Another executive spoke of the strike and the high office turnover as due to the nature of the company. "We're an aggressive, hard-
driving concern. Some people can't stand the pressure."

Superior did not have a personnel manager in June, 1950. "A personnel manager is no good unless he's top grade. Right now we can't
afford such a man," said Mr. Pierson.

A labor-management committee of 40, under the leadership of
Mr. Randall, met monthly to consider problems and to review the progress of the company. "It looks as if the office employees will get a bonus
this year," said Mr. Pierson in July, 1950. "The reaction of the shop
workers should be very interesting."

---

[3] *The Minneapolis Tribune,* January 3, 1949.

INTERNAL CONTROLS

The company used two standard cost systems. In one the standard was maintained unchanged throughout the year, in the other it was changed monthly. On each job, therefore, two variances were recorded for material, labor, and burden. In addition to detailed monthly financial statements, Mr. Pierson received from Mr. Wahl a daily management report which presented a rough balance sheet as of the day before and a profit and loss statement for the previous day and the month to date. Mr. Pierson also received weekly and monthly shipping reports and the weekly sales report by salesmen and territories.

FINANCE

In the spring of 1950 the company investigated the possibility of stimulating lagging sales by assisting Farmhand dealers financially. Mr. Pierson was aware that most long-line companies aided their dealers by several devices. The International Harvester Company and the Dearborn Motor Company had established credit companies for the purpose of financing dealer receivables. Other firms had worked out similar arrangements with sales-finance companies. Some companies offered floor-planning (extension of credit on inventory) to their dealers. Others shipped equipment on consignment. Almost all were returning to the prewar practice of seasonal dating whereby the dealer would be allowed as much as 130 days to 140 days to render payment.

The company felt that it did not have the financial resources to compete with the long-line companies, but it did take two steps to help its dealers:

1. On June 1, 1950, payment terms for all dealers entitled to receive shipments on open accounts were changed from 5%/10 days to 5% the tenth of the month following date of shipment. A month later management appraised the effect of this move and decided that the change in terms had not increased shipments significantly but that it had improved dealer relations.

2. Negotiations were conducted with a sales-finance company to offer all qualified dealers a factory-sponsored time payment plan covering the major items in the Farmhand line. Such a plan would have involved a 25% down payment, a 6% finance charge on the unpaid balance for 12 months' maturity, and assignment of the paper with recourse[4] on the

---

[4] "With recourse"—term used when endorser of negotiable instrument remains contingently liable to subsequent holders.

dealer. A questionnaire was sent to the dealer organization soliciting their opinion. While there was some feeling that such a plan might boost retail sales, most dealers stated that local banks were meeting their credit needs and the credit needs of the farmer in a satisfactory manner. There was an almost unanimous reaction against any plan with a recourse clause. As a result, negotiations were discontinued.

SUPERIOR SEPARATOR COMPANY OF CANADA, LTD.

Management had established the Canadian subsidiary in 1947 to serve as sales agent for the company's products in Canada. It had planned to begin manufacturing and assembling Farmhand machines there in 1949. About $50,000 was borrowed by the subsidiary from a Canadian bank with the parent company's guarantee, and subcontract negotiations were initiated with several Canadian firms. Difficulties arose, according to Mr. Pierson, largely as a result of the incompetence of the general manager, and plans for manufacturing were temporarily abandoned. In 1950 a new general manager was appointed, and the subsidiary commenced manufacturing operations in St. Boniface, Manitoba.

Sales of the Farmhand line in Canada were hampered by an 8% sales tax, and, until a change of tariff regulations occurred in February, 1950, by a 10% duty on all farm equipment suitable for nonfarm use. Since the Canadian subsidiary did not increase its prices, the devaluation of the Canadian dollar further restricted profitable operations. In 1949 on sales of $631,423 the subsidiary showed a net loss of $5,153.

BOARD OF DIRECTORS

The board of directors was composed of five men, two representatives from management and three outsiders. Management men were Mr. Pierson and Mr. Randall. The outside members of the board were Mr. Gray, the retired president; Mr. Piper, the principal stockholder; and Samuel H. Rogers, vice-president of the trust department of the Northwestern National Bank, Minneapolis.

Mr. Gray, in his late sixties in 1950, had moved from Minneapolis and did not take an active part in company affairs.

As senior partner in the investment banking house of Piper, Jaffray, and Hopwood, Mr. Piper had been asked to serve as a director of several prominent companies. In 1950, at the age of sixty-two, he was chairman of the board of Munsingwear, Inc., and a director of Pillsbury Mills, Inc., the Truax-Traer Coal Company, the Cream of Wheat Corporation, the Minneapolis-Moline Power Implement Company, the Diamond

Iron Works, Inc., the Vassar Company, and the Superior Separator Company.

Mr. Rogers represented the estate of James Vaughan, which owned the second largest block of stock. In addition to serving as a director of Superior, he was on the board of the Archer-Daniels-Midland Company, the Northwestern Terminal Company, the Home Gas Company, the Atlas Lumber Company, and three Canadian firms. Mr. Rogers was forty-three years old in 1950.

Together, Mr. Piper and Mr. Rogers held a controlling interest in the company. Officers of the company owned relatively few shares of stock. "One of our biggest problems," said Mr. Piper, "is to find a way for the young men who are running this company to share in its earnings. The present tax policy of the federal government makes it almost impossible for them to buy in."

"Management depends quite heavily on the board in the Superior Separator Company," said Mr. Rogers. Any expenditure over $10,000 had to be approved by the executive committee, consisting of Mr. Pierson, Mr. Piper, and Mr. Rogers. "I spend considerably more time in the capacity of a director of this company than I do for several other firms of which I am a director," said Mr. Rogers. Mr. Rogers had been largely responsible for the establishment of good bank relations in 1945. For several years he had been listed as a vice-president so that he could sign papers as an officer of the company. He had no other duties in this capacity.

Mr. Piper and Mr. Rogers conferred with senior executives frequently between monthly board meetings on a variety of executive problems. Mr. Rogers occasionally drove out to the plant and spent several hours with department heads. Mr. Piper often talked in his office with Mr. Pierson about company affairs over a morning cup of coffee.

Both Mr. Piper and Mr. Rogers believed that the future of the company lay in building a strong reputation as a manufacturer of materials-handling equipment for the farm. By producing a specialized line of products with limited demand, Superior, they felt, could avoid direct competition with the big concerns in the farm-machinery industry.

"There has never been a major clash between management and the board," said Mr. Piper.

FUTURE PLANS

In the summer of 1950 the company had been considering two major policy issues. A $200,000 program designed to improve existing plant facilities was rejected because, in the opinion of the board of directors, the anticipated savings in more efficient materials-handling were not adequate to warrant the investment. The purchase of the plant and equipment of a manufacturer of construction machinery was rejected because the board feared that there was an insufficient number of trained executives to control both operations and to meet the problems resulting from such a move.

"A little company gets to be a big one only by moving rapidly and aggressively," said Mr. Pierson. But the president was not sure just how fast it was safe to expand without unduly straining finances, facilities, and personnel, or in what direction this expansion would best take place. Should Superior try to increase sales of its present line of products by extending the Farmhand dealer organization geographically? Should it try to increase sales in present territories by adding new products to the line? If new products were to be added, should they be strictly materials-handling devices for the farm, or should management consider any product which appeared to offer a ready market? Should the company attempt to grow by purchasing other businesses? If so, should there be any product limitations in an absorption? These were questions executives were pondering. These were questions which Mr. Pierson felt were very important to the long-run future of the company.

One long-range goal of product development work was a self-propelled loader. Such a machine would combine the wagon, Power Box, and Hydraulic Farmhand with an integrated power unit. Mr. Pierson envisioned it as the answer to the materials-handling problem on the farm.

Provided the international situation did not necessitate production controls, Mr. Pierson still hoped to find a product which would level off the sharp seasonal variations in sales and make it possible to stabilize the volume of production throughout the year.

Should production controls be instituted, Mr. Pierson hoped to obtain a priority for the Farmhand line of equipment solely on the basis of their laborsaving features. The plant was surveyed by a representative of the War Department in the summer of 1949 to determine its ability to produce war material, and Mr. Pierson, Mr. Randall, and Mr. Ostrander were currently investigating in several quarters the possibility of securing government contracts. The engineering department was studying the possibility of the military application of the loader and Power Box as a self-propelled machine. Such a machine was perhaps five years away. A division of production with 65% of output destined for civilian use and 35% for military use was regarded by Mr. Pierson as a desirable ratio in the event of the establishment of economic controls.

Consolidated Drugs, Inc.

MR. RICHARD TRUCKS had been transferred to the Syracuse (New York) Division of Consolidated Drugs, Inc., in the first week of May, 1952. At this time he was appointed sales manager of the Syracuse wholesale drug division. Formerly he had been an assistant to the vice-president in charge of sales at the company's headquarters in New York.

At the month-end sales meeting on the last Friday of June, 1952, Mr. Asa Bush, a salesman in one of the division's rural territories, informed Mr. Trucks that he wished to retire at the end of July when he reached his sixty-fifth birthday. Mr. Trucks was surprised by Mr. Bush's announcement because he had been informed by the division manager, Mr. B. D. Burton, that Mr. Bush had requested and received a deferment of retirement until he reached his sixty-sixth birthday in July, 1953. The only explanation offered by Mr. Bush was that he had "changed his mind."

The retirement of Mr. Bush posed a problem for Mr. Trucks, in that he had to decide what to do about a successor to Mr. Bush's territory.

BACKGROUND OF THE SYRACUSE DIVISION

When Mr. Trucks became the divisional sales manager he was twenty-nine years old. He had joined Consolidated (as the firm was known in trade circles) as a sales trainee after his graduation from Stanford University in 1946. During the next two years he worked as a salesman. In the fall of 1948 the sales manager of the company made Mr. Trucks one of his assistants. In this capacity Mr. Trucks helped the sales manager to arrange special sales promotions for the lines of different manufacturers.

Mr. Trucks's predecessor, Mr. John K. Martin, had served as divisional sales manager for 15 years before his death in April. "J. K.," as Mr. Martin had been known, had worked as a salesman for the drug wholesale house that had been merged with Consolidated to become its Syracuse Division. Although Mr. Trucks had made Mr. Martin's acquaintance in the course of business, he had not known Mr. Martin well. The salesmen often expressed their admiration and affection for

Mr. Martin to the new sales manager. Several salesmen, in fact, made a point of telling Mr. Trucks that "Old J. K." knew every druggist in twelve counties by his first name. Mr. Martin had died of a heart attack while trout-fishing with the president of the Syracuse Pharmacists' Association. The Syracuse Division manager said that most of the druggists in town attended Mr. Martin's funeral.

The Syracuse Division of Consolidated was one of 25 wholesale drug houses in the United States owned by the firm. Each division acted as a functionally autonomous unit having its own warehouse, sales department, buying department, and accounting department. The divisional manager was responsible for the performance of the unit he managed. There were, however, line functions performed by the regional and national offices that pertained directly to the individual departments. A district sales manager, for instance, was associated with a regional office in Albany for the purpose of implementing marketing policies established by the central office in New York.

As a service wholesaler, the Syracuse Division sold to the retail drug trade a broad line of approximately 18,000 items. The line might well be described as consisting of everything sold through drugstores except fresh food, tobacco products, newspapers, and magazines. In the trading area of Syracuse, Consolidated competed with two other wholesalers; one of these carried substantially the same line of products; the other, a limited line of drug products.

The history of the Syracuse Division had been that of a profitable family-owned wholesale drug house before its merger with Consolidated in 1928. The division had operated profitably since that date with the exception of three years during the 1930's, although it had not shown a profit on sales equal to the average for the other wholesale drug divisions of Consolidated. Since 1945, the annual net sales of the division had risen each year. But since its competitors did not announce their sales figures, it was impossible to ascertain whether this increase in sales represented a change in the competitive situation or merely a general trend of business volume in the Syracuse trading area. Mr. Martin had been of the opinion that the increase had been at the expense of competitors. The district drug sales manager, however, maintained that, since the trend of increase was less than that of other divisions in the northern New York region, the Syracuse Division may have actually lost ground competitively. A new measuring technique for calculating the potential wholesale purchasing power of retail drugstores, which had been adopted shortly before Mr. Trucks's transfer, indicated that the share of the wholesale drug market controlled by the Syracuse Division was below the median and below the mean for Consolidated divisions.

Only a few of the employees working in 1952 for the Syracuse Division had also been employed by the predecessor company. Mr. Martin had been the only person in the executive echelon whose employment in the Syracuse Division antedated the merger. Most of the executives and salesmen currently active in the organization had come into the organization either between 1933 and 1941 or after the end of World War II. Two salesmen, however, Mr. Bush and Mr. John Jameson, had worked for the predecessor company before the merger.

Of those who were employed as executives or salesmen before World War II, only Mr. B. D. Burton, the division manager, had a college degree, which he had earned at a local Y.M.C.A. night school. All the young men employed since 1946 were university or pharmacy-college graduates. None of the younger men had been promoted when vacancies had occurred in the job of operations manager (who was in charge of the warehouse) and of merchandise manager (who supervised buying) in the Syracuse Division; however, two of the younger men had been promoted to similar positions in other divisions when vacancies had occurred.

THE SYRACUSE DIVISION SALES FORCE

From the time that Mr. Trucks took over Mr. Martin's duties he had devoted four days a week to the task of traveling through each sales territory with the salesmen who covered it. He had, however, made no changes in the practices or procedures of the sales force. The first occasion on which Mr. Trucks was required to make a decision of other than routine nature was when Mr. Bush asked to be retired.

When Mr. Trucks took charge of the Syracuse Division sales force, it consisted of nine salesmen and four trainees. Four of the salesmen, James Pepper, Michael Waller, Daniel Carmack, and Paul Smith, had joined the company under the sales training program for college graduates initiated in 1946. Concerning the other five salesmen, who had been with the company many years, Mr. Trucks was given the following information: Asa Bush and John Jameson were senior in terms of service to the others. John Dangler joined the company as a warehouse employee in 1928 when he was nineteen and became a salesman in 1933. Homer Babbidge came to Consolidated as a salesman in 1933 when the wholesale drug firm for which he had previously worked went out of business. In 1952 Mr. Babbidge, who was then forty-eight years old, had been a wholesale drug salesman for 28 years. Russell Means at the age of twenty-six came to Consolidated in 1938 after working as a missionary salesman for a manufacturer. Mr. Means served as an officer in the Army Medical Corps during the war and was discharged as a captain in hospital administration in 1945. He returned to Consolidated immediately after his discharge.

The four trainees had graduated from colleges the preceding June. When Mr. Trucks arrived in Syracuse, these men were in the last phase of their twelve months' training program. The trainees were spending much of their time traveling with the salesmen. Mr. Trucks, who now had the full responsibility for training these men, believed that Mr. Martin had hired four trainees to cover an anticipated turnover both among the salesmen and among the trainees themselves, as well as to implement the New York head office's policy of getting more intensive coverage of each market area. The trainees, he understood, expected to receive territory assignments either in the Syracuse Division or elsewhere on the completion of their training period.

Mr. Trucks had not seen very much of the salesmen. His acquaintance with them had been formed at the sales meetings and in traveling with them through their territories.

Mr. Trucks judged that Homer Babbidge was an easygoing, even-tempered person. He seemed to be very popular with the other salesmen and with his customers. Mr. Babbidge was proud of his two sons, one of whom was in high school and the other married, with a son named after Mr. Babbidge. Mr. Trucks thought that the salesman liked him, because Babbidge had commented to him several times that his suggestions had been very helpful.

Asa Bush had not, in Mr. Trucks's opinion, been particularly friendly. Mr. Trucks had observed that Bush was well liked because of his good humor and friendly manner with everyone; however, Mr. Trucks had noticed that on a number of occasions Bush had intimated that his age and experience should cause the sales manager to defer to his judgment. Mr. Bush and his wife lived in the town of Oswego.

On June 4, 1952, Mr. Trucks had traveled with Mr. Bush, and they visited five of Mr. Bush's accounts. On a routine form for sales managers' reports on field work with salesmen, copies of which were filed with the district sales manager and the New York sales manager, Mr. Trucks made the following comments about Mr. Bush:

Points Requiring Attention: Not using merchandising equipment; not following weekly sales plan. Pharmaceutical business going to competitors because of lack of interest. Too much time spent on idle chatter. Only shows druggist what "he thinks they will buy." Tends to sell easy items instead of profitable ones.

Steps Taken for Correction: Explained shortcomings and demonstrated how larger, more profitable orders could be obtained by following sales plan—did just that by getting the biggest order ever written for Carthage account.

Remarks: Old-time "personality." Should do terrific volume if trained on new merchandising techniques.

On a similar form made out by J. K. Martin on the basis of working with Mr. Bush on March 3, 1952, the following comments were made:

Points Requiring Attention: Not getting pharmaceutical business. Not following promotion plans.

Steps Taken for Correction: Told him about these things.

Remarks: Bush made this territory—can sell anything he sets his mind to—a real drummer—very popular with his customers.

Daniel Carmack, twenty-nine years old, was the oldest of the group of salesmen who had passed through the formal sales training program. Mr. Trucks considered him earnest and conscientious. He had increased his sales each year. Although Mr. Trucks did not regard Carmack as being the "salesman type," he noted that Carmack had been fairly successful in the use of the merchandising techniques that Mr. Trucks was seeking to implement.

John Dangler handled a number of the big accounts in downtown Syracuse. Mr. Trucks believed that Dangler was an excellent salesman who considered himself "very smooth." Mr. Trucks had been surprised at the affront Dangler had taken when he had offered a few suggestions about the improvement of Dangler's selling technique. Mr. and Mrs. Dangler were good friends of the Burtons. The Danglers were social friends of merchandise and operations managers and their wives. Mr. Trucks suspected that Dangler had expected to be Mr. Martin's successor.

John Jameson seemed to Mr. Trucks to be an earnest and conscientious salesman. He had been amiable, though not cordial, toward Mr. Trucks. Mr. Trucks's report on calls on ten accounts on June 5, 1952, with Mr. Jameson contained the following statements.

Points Requiring Attention: Rushing calls. Gets want book and tries to sell case lots on wanted items. Carries all merchandising equipment but doesn't use it.

Steps Taken for Correction: Suggested change in routing; longer, better-planned calls; conducted presentation demonstration.

Remarks: Hardworking, conscientious, good salesman, but needs to be brought up to date on merchandising methods.

Mr. Martin's comments on observations of Mr. Jameson on March 4, 1952, reported on the same form, were as follows:

Points Requiring Attention: Uses the want book on the basis of most sales. Not pushing promotions.

Steps Taken for Correction: Discussed shortcomings.

Remarks: Jameson really knows how to sell—visits every customer each week. Hard worker—very loyal—even pushes goods with very low commission.

On the day Mr. Trucks had traveled with Jameson, the latter suggested that Mr. Trucks have dinner at the Jamesons' home. Mr. Trucks accepted the invitation, but at the end of the day Jameson took him to a restaurant in Watertown, explaining that he did not want to inconvenience his wife because his two daughters were home from college on vacation.

Russell Means had caused Mr. Trucks considerable concern. Means complained about sales management procedures, commission rates, the "lousy service of the warehouse people," and other such matters at sales meetings. Mr. Trucks believed that most of the complaints were founded in fact, but concluded that the matters were usually trivial, since the other salesmen did not complain about them. Mr. Trucks mentioned his difficulties with Means to Mr. Burton. Mr. Burton's comment was that Means had been very friendly with Mr. Martin. Means seemed to be quite popular with his customers.

James Pepper was, in Mr. Trucks's opinion, the most ambitious, aggressive, and argumentative salesman in the Syracuse Division. He had been employed by the company since his graduation from the University of Rochester in 1948, first as a trainee and then as a salesman. Pepper had substantially increased the sales volume of the territory assigned to him. He had persuaded Mr. Martin to assign him six inactive hospital accounts in July, 1950. Within six months Pepper made sales to these accounts in excess of $36,000. The other salesmen considered him "cocky" and a "big spender." Mr. Trucks thought his attitude was one of independence. If Pepper agreed with a sales plan, he worked hard to achieve its objectives, but if he did not agree, he did not cooperate at all. Mr. Trucks thought that he had been very successful in working with Pepper.

Paul Smith, who was twenty-four years old, impressed Mr. Trucks as being unsure of himself. Smith seemed to be confused and overworked. Mr. Trucks attributed this difficulty to Smith's trying to serve too many accounts in too large an area. Smith was very interested in Mr. Trucks's suggestions on improvement in his work. Mr. Trucks believed that he would improve in time with proper help. Smith had raised his sales to the point where he was on commission instead of salary in March, 1952.

Michael Waller, twenty-five years of age, was the only salesman who worked on a salary. His sales volume was not sufficient to sustain an income of $325 a month, which was the company minimum for salesmen with more than one year's experience Waller was very apologetic about being on a salary. Mr. Trucks believed that Waller's determination to "make good" would be realized because of the latter's conscientiousness. When he had been assigned the territory two years before, it had consisted largely of uncontacted accounts. The volume of sales had tripled in the meantime. Mr. Trucks felt that Waller appreciated all the help he was given and that in time Waller would be an excellent salesman.

Both Bush and Jameson earned about 2⅛% of sales in commissions. The other salesmen all earned about 2¼% of sales as commissions, except Pepper and Carmack who earned about 2⅜%. Mr. Trucks said that expense accounts amounted to about ¾% of sales for both city and country salesmen. The differences in percentage rates of commissions were explained by Mr. Trucks in terms of the differential commissions set by the company. Higher commission rates were given on items the company wished to "push," such as pharmaceuticals and calendar promotion items.

The trainees were something of an unknown quantity to Mr. Trucks. He had training conferences with them in which he had thought they had performed rather poorly. He believed that Mr. Martin had neglected the training of the new men. All four of them seemed to be good prospects and were eager to be assigned territories, as they informed Mr. Trucks as often as possible.

The turnover of the Syracuse Division sales force had been very low among the prewar salesmen. Six of the sales-training program men had left the division since 1947. Two of these men had been promoted to department heads in other divisions, whereas four had left to work for manufacturers. Because manufacturers valued salesmen with wholesaling experience and competing wholesalers did not have training programs for young men, there were many opportunities for a salesman who desired to leave.

SALES MANAGEMENT

Since Mr. Trucks had become sales manager, he had devoted considerable thought to the problem of improving the sales performance of the Syracuse Division. He had accepted a transfer to the new job at the urging of Mr. Cameron Crow, the vice-president in charge of sales. Mr. Trucks was one of a dozen young men whom Mr. Crow had brought into the New York office since the end of World War II to work as assistants to the top sales executives. None of the young assistants had remained in the New York office for more than three years, for Mr. Crow made a policy of offering the young men field assignments so that they could "show their stuff." Mr. Trucks believed that the sales performance of the Syracuse Division could be bettered by an improved plan of sales management. He knew that the share of the Syracuse market for wholesale purchases of retail drugstores[1] held by Consolidated was only 19.5% as against a 48% share for some of the other divisions in their respective markets.

Mr. Crow, for whom Mr. Trucks worked immediately before his transfer, had focused his staff's attention upon the qualitative aspects of sales policy. Mr. Trucks had assisted Mr. Crow in implementing merchandising plans intended to utilize the salesmen's selling efforts in such a way as to minimize the handling cost of sales and maximize the gross margin.

The company encouraged the salesmen to use a threefold plan for increasing profitability:

1) Sales of larger average value per line of the order were encouraged because the cost of processing and filling each line of an order was practically constant;

2) Sales of larger total value were encouraged because the delivery cost for orders having a total weight between 20 and 100 pounds was practically constant;

3) Because some manufacturers offered margins considerably larger than others, sales of products carrying higher margins were encouraged. Salesmen's commissions varied with the margins available to Consolidated on the products they sold.

The executives of the company also sought to increase the effectiveness of Consolidated promotions by setting up a sales calendar. The sales calendar co-ordinated the activities of all Consolidated divisions so that during a given calendar period every account would be solicited for the sale of particular items yielding satisfactory profits. The type of activity represented by the sales calendar required that the salesmen in

---

[1] The potential wholesale sales for retail drugstores were calculated by the New York office market-analysis section. This market estimate, called the P.W.P.P. (potential wholesale purchasing power) was calculated for each county by adjusting retail drugstore sales to an estimate of the purchases of goods from wholesalers.

each division follow a pattern in selling to every individual account. The sales manager was responsible for co-ordinating the activities of his own salesmen.

The matter of selling patterns was largely the responsibility of the division sales manager. Mr. Trucks believed that his predecessor had never really accepted the changes that had taken place in the merchandising policy of the New York office.

Mr. Trucks had inherited from his predecessor a system of sales-department records which had been carefully maintained. The national offices required each division to keep uniform sales and market-analysis records. During the period of Mr. Trucks's work in the New York office, he had developed a familiarity with the various uses for these records.

The basis of the sales and market-analysis record was the division trading area. The limits of the trading area were determined by the economics of selling costs, and the factors on which the costs were based were transportation costs of delivery and salesmen's traveling expenses. Mr. Trucks knew from his own experience that delineation of trading areas was influenced by tradition, geographic conditions, the number of salesmen, the number of calls a salesman could make, the estimated market potential, competition, and agreements with adjacent Consolidated divisions. The Syracuse Division was bordered by the trading areas of Consolidated divisions located in Rochester and Albany on the east, south, and west; to the north was the Canadian border. A map of this division is included here in Exhibit 1.

Within the divisional trading area the market was broken into sales territories. Exhibit 2 includes data on salesmen's territory assignments; Exhibit 3 shows the salesmen's territories by counties; Exhibit 4 indicates estimated potential sales and sales by counties for various classification of customers. During the time since his arrival, Mr. Trucks had formed the opinion that the present salesmen's territories had been established without careful regard for the number of stores in the area, the sales potential, or the amount of traveling involved. Although Mr. Trucks had not yet studied any one territory carefully, he suspected all his salesmen of skimming the cream from many of their accounts because they did not have adequate time to do a thorough selling job in each store.

Mr. Trucks had been able to observe the performance records of other divisional sales managers while he worked in New York. He knew that some sales managers had achieved substantial improvements over the past performances of their divisions.

Exhibit 1

CONSOLIDATED DRUGS, INC.

Syracuse Division Trading Area

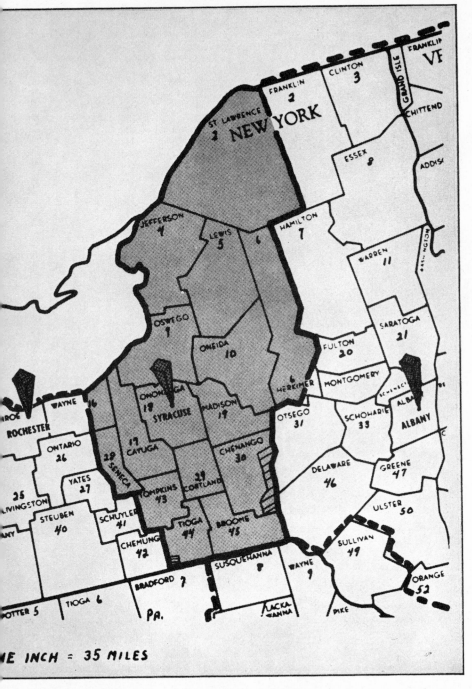

ONE INCH = 35 MILES

Exhibit 2

CONSOLIDATED DRUGS, INC.

Selected Data on Salesmen's Territory Assignments and Performance

Salesman	County	Sales, 1951*	Active Accounts	Estimated Potential†	Assigned Accounts‡
				(000)	
Babbidge	Chenango.....................	$ 20,634	4	$ 189	15
	Tompkins.....................	63,226	9	388	19
	Tioga........................	39,839	4	161	11
	Broome.......................	122,968	22	1,807	45
	Total......................	246,667	39	2,545	90
Bush	Jefferson.....................	81,162	16	371	20
	Lewis........................	28,798	8	87	11
	Oswego.......................	148,073	25	517	37
	Total......................	258,033	49	965	68
Carmack	Onondaga.....................	76,339	14	297	14
	Madison......................	86,950	12	417	19
	Cortland.....................	46,005	6	146	11
	Total......................	209,294	32	860	44
Dangler	Onondaga.....................	252,051	33	743	44
	Total......................	252,051	33	743	44
Jameson	St. Lawrence.................	136,058	25	364	32
	Jefferson....................	123,681	19	353	19
	Oswego.......................	1,091	1	200	1
	Total......................	260,830	45	737	52
Means	Onondaga.....................	244,642	29	1,009	48
	Total......................	244,642	29	1,009	48
Pepper	Onondaga.....................	212,691	28	500	29
	Total......................	212,691	28	500	29
Smith.....	Herkimer.....................	48,530	10	312	19
	Oneida.......................	113,607	46	1,053	85
	Total......................	162,137	56	1,365	104
Waller	Wayne........................	22,675	4	103	5
	Cayuga.......................	70,598	14	312	18
	Seneca.......................	36,260	8	186	13
	Total......................	129,533	26	601	36
	Hospitals, Syracuse (Pepper).......	$ 36,079			
	All others......................	$ 8,595			
	House accounts..................	$ 76,622			
	Total division sales...........	$2,197,174			

* This figure includes sales to chain and independent drugstores, and to miscellaneous accounts but does not include sales to hospitals.
† No potential is calculated for hospitals or miscellaneous sales. Where a county is divided among several salesmen, the individual-sales figure for each salesman is obtained by allocating the county potential in proportion to the *number* of drugstore accounts in that county assigned to that salesman.
‡ Includes hospitals and other recognized drug outlets in the territory.
Source: Company records.

SALES TERRITORIES OF BUSH AND JAMESON

The territory that Mr. Bush covered included accounts scattered through small towns in four counties of the rural area northeast of Syracuse (see Exhibit 5). Mr. Bush had originally developed the accounts in the four-county area for the predecessor company. At the time

Exhibit 3

CONSOLIDATED DRUGS. INC.

Syracuse Division Salesmen's Territory Assignments,
by Counties

Code Number	County	Salesmen
1	St. Lawrence	Jameson
4	Jefferson	Bush, Jameson
5	Lewis	Bush
6	Herkimer	Smith
9	Oswego	Bush, Jameson
10	Oneida	Smith
16	Wayne	Waller
17	Cayuga	Waller
18	Onondaga	Means, Dangler, Pepper, Carmack
19	Madison	Carmack
28	Seneca	Waller
29	Cortland	Carmack
30	Chenango	Babbidge
43	Tompkins	Babbidge
44	Tioga	Babbidge
45	Broome	Babbidge

he undertook this task the competing service wholesaler already had established a mail-order business with the rural druggists in this area. Mr. Bush had taken to the road in a Model-T Ford in 1922 to build up the sales in all four counties. He had been hired specifically for this job because he was a native of the area and an experienced "drummer."

Five years later Mr. John Jameson, a friend of Mr. Bush, became a division salesman, and, at the suggestion of Mr. Bush, covered other accounts in the same four-county area. Mr. Jameson had been a salesman for a proprietary medicine firm before he joined the wholesale drug house. He was seven years younger than Mr. Bush. Since that time Mr. Jameson had serviced a number of accounts in the four-county area. The list of accounts that each of these men handled appears in Exhibits 6 and 7. Mr. Trucks noticed that the incomes which Messrs. Bush and Jameson had received from commissions were very stable over the years.

A VISIT FROM MR. JAMESON

On the Wednesday morning following the June sales meeting, Mr. Trucks saw Mr. Jameson come in the front door of the Syracuse Division offices. Although the salesman passed within 30 feet of Mr. Trucks' desk he did not appear to notice the sales manager. Mr. Jameson walked through the office area to the partitioned space where Mr. Burton's

Exhibit 4

CONSOLIDATED DRUGS, INC.

Selected Data on Sales and Sales Potentials, by Counties

County	Code	Population	Per Cent	CHAIN AND INDEPENDENT STORES								HOSPITALS			MISCELLANEOUS
				Sold	Inactive Accounts	Accounts Not Sold	Total	P.W.P.P. (in Thousands)	Per Cent Area P.W.P.P.	Sales (in Thousands)	Per Cent P.W.P.P.	Sold	Not Sold	Sales (in Thousands)	Sales (in Thousands)
St. Lawrence	1	99,400	7.0	19	2	5	26	$ 364	3.9	$ 107	29.4	2	4	$ 3	
Jefferson	4	86,700	6.1	26	8	.	34	724	7.8	201	27.8	2	2	2	
Lewis	5	22,800	1.6	8	.	.	8	87	0.0	29	33.1	.	1	.	
Herkimer	6	46,800	3.3	10	6	1	17	312	3.3	49	15.6	.	2	.	
Oswego	9	78,300	5.5	22	4	.	26	537	5.7	124	23.1	1	2	.	
Oneida	10	226,000	15.9	46	14	12	72	1,053	11.3	111	10.5	.	13	.	
Wayne	16	14,400	1.0	4	.	1	5	103	1.1	23	22.0	.	.	.	
Cayuga	17	71,100	5.0	12	4	.	16	312	3.3	56	17.9	2	.	2	
Onondaga	18	346,600	24.3	104	7	9	120	2,549	27.3	722	28.3	6	9	36	
Madison	19	47,000	3.3	12	2	3	17	417	4.5	87	20.9	.	2	.	
Seneca	28	29,700	2.1	6	1	3	10	186	2.0	28	15.1	2	1	2	
Cortland	29	37,700	2.6	6	2	1	9	146	1.6	46	31.5	.	2	.	
Chenango	30	39,900	2.8	4	2	6	12	189	2.0	21	10.9	.	3	.	
Tompkins	43	60,200	4.2	9	1	4	14	388	4.2	63	16.3	.	5	.	
Tioga	44	30,600	2.1	4	.	7	11	161	1.7	40	24.7	.	.	.	
Broome	45	187,800	13.2	22	2	13	37	1,807	19.4	115	6.3	.	8	.	
Total		1,425,000	100.0	314	55	65	434	$9,335	100.0	$1,819	19.5	15	54	$45	$334
Totals, 1951															
Totals, 1950											$1,659	18.6			$27	$ 256

Source: Company records.

Exhibit 5

CONSOLIDATED DRUGS, INC.

Counties Sold by Messrs. Bush and Jameson

Exhibit 6

CONSOLIDATED DRUGS, INC.

Accounts Sold by Asa Bush, by Counties, with 1951 Purchases

Jefferson County:		Oswego County:	
Adams Center, D*	$ 1,986	Caloose, D*	$ 684
(Alexandria Bay, D	10,192)	Central Square, D	743
(Alexandria Bay, D	8,764)	Constantia, M	29
Bellville, D	1,165	Cleveland, M	156
(Carthage, D	33,903)	(Fulton, D	6,051)
Chaumont, D	336	(Fulton, D	9,817)
(Clayton, D	5,901)	(Fulton, D	11,116)
(Clayton, D	9,113)	(Fulton, D	15,396)
Deferiet, D	205	Hannibal, D	1,558
Dexter, D	6,481	Hastings, M	1,539
Ellisburg, D	131	Lacona, M	185
LaFargeville, D	290	Mexico, D	6,371
Plessis, D	490	Oswego, D	4,827
Redwood, M	60	(Oswego, D	8,307)
Rodman, D	1,787	(Oswego, D	9,641)
Sackets Harbor, D	358	(Oswego, D	16,415)
		(Oswego, D	17,593)
County total	$81,162	(Oswego, D	8,982)
		Oswego, H	6
Lewis County:		Parish, M	2,065
Beaver Falls, D*	$ 1,270	Phoenix, D	3,895
Croghan, D	8,199	(Pulaski, D	3,501)
Harrisville, D	6,172	(Pulaski, D	11,636)
Lowville, D	7,896	Sandy Creek, D	5,655
Lowville, D	1,438	West Monroe, D	1,911
Lyons Falls, D	2,008		
Port Leyden, D	775		
Turin, M	1,040	County total	$148,079
County total	$28,798		

Territory total $258,039

Increase over 1950 . . . . 0.9%

*D: Independent Drugstore; C: Chain Drugstore; M: Miscellaneous Account; H: Hospital.
NOTE: Accounts in parentheses are those indicated by Mr. Jameson as the ones he wanted.
Source: Company records.

private office was located. Twenty minutes later Mr. Jameson emerged from the division manager's office and made his way to Mr. Trucks' desk. "Hi there, young fellah!" he shouted as he approached.

"Howdy, Jack. Sit down and chat awhile," Mr. Trucks replied. "What got you out of bed so early?" he asked, knowing that the salesman must have risen at 6 o'clock to make the drive to Syracuse from his home in Watertown.

Mr. Jameson squeezed his bulky frame into the armchair next to the desk. "It's a shame Asa is retiring," he said. "I never thought he could stand to give it up. I never knew anyone who enjoyed selling as much

Exhibit 7

CONSOLIDATED DRUGS, INC.

Accounts Sold by John Jameson, by Counties, with 1951 Purchases

St. Lawrence County:

Canton, D*	$ 13,080
Edwards, D	672
Edwards, M	1,885
Gouverneur, D	226
Gouverneur, D	9,383
Gouverneur, C	16,519
Heuvelton, D	108
Massena, D	11,259
Massena, D	3,397
Massena, C	2,448
Massena, C	2,225
Massena, H	38
Madrid, D	1,432
Morristown, D	2,731
Norfolk, D	2,995
Norwood, D	3,139
Ogdensburg, D	8,090
Ogdensburg, D	22,555
Ogdensburg, D	7,203
Ogdensburg, D	3,380
Ogdensburg, M	149
Ogdensburg, H	2,653
Potsdam, D	15,444
Potsdam, C	7,371
Rensselaer Falls, D	367
Total county	$138,749

Jefferson County:

Adams, C*	$ 1,049
Carthage, C	1,176
Evans Mills, D	1,229
Philadelphia, D	2,101
Watertown, D	16,782
Watertown, D	2,632
Watertown, D	4,889
Watertown, D	17,041
Watertown, D	10,262
Watertown, D	14,622
Watertown, D	21,249
Watertown, D	12,791
Watertown, D	5,388
Watertown, D	475
Watertown, D	6,282
Watertown, C	2,019
Watertown, C	3,318
Watertown, M	378
Watertown, H	70
Watertown, H	2,009
Total county	$125,760

Oswego County:

Pulaski, C	$ 1,091

Territory total $265,600
Increase over 1950 .... 11.6%

*D: Independent Drugstore; C: Chain Drugstore; M: Miscellaneous Account; H: Hospital.
Source: Company records.

as Asa—'cept, maybe me." Mr. Jameson continued praising Mr. Bush and telling anecdotes which illustrated his point until Mr. Trucks began to wonder whether Mr. Jameson thought that the sales manager was biased in some way against the retiring salesman. Mr. Trucks recalled that he had made some critical remarks about Mr. Bush to Mr. Burton, but he could not recall any discussion of Mr. Bush's shortcomings with Mr. Bush himself or any of the other salesmen. Mr. Jameson ended his remarks by saying, "Old J. K., God rest his soul, always said that Asa was the best damn' wholesale drug salesman he had ever known."

There was a brief silence as Mr. Trucks did not realize that Mr. Jameson was finished. Finally Mr. Trucks said, "You know, Jack, I think we ought to have a testimonial dinner for Asa at the July sales meeting."

Mr. Jameson made no comment on Mr. Trucks's suggestion; instead, he went on to say, "None of these green trainees will ever be able to take Asa's place. Those druggists up there are old-timers. They would resent being high-pressured by some kid blown up to twice his size with college degrees. No sir! You've got to sell 'em right in those country stores."

Mr. Trucks did not believe that Mr. Jameson's opinion about the adaptability of the younger, college-educated salesman was justified by the evidence available. He recalled that several of these men in country territories had done better on their May sales quotas than either Mr. Bush or Mr. Jameson. He was proud of his self-restraint when he commented, "Selling in a country territory is certainly different."

"That's right, Dick. I wanted to make sure you understood these things before I told you." Mr. Jameson was nervously massaging his double chin between his thumb and forefinger.

Mr. Trucks looked at him with a quizzical expression. "Told me what?"

"I have just been talking to Mr. Burton. Well, I was talking to him about an understanding between Asa and me. We always agreed that if anything should happen to the other, or he should retire, or something —well, we agreed that the one who remained should get to take over his choice of the other's accounts. We told J. K. about this and he said, 'Boys, what's O.K. by you is O.K. by me. You two developed that territory and you deserve to be rewarded for it.' Well, yes sir, that's the way it was."

Without pausing, Mr. Jameson went on, "I just told Mr. Burton about it. He said that he remembered talking about the whole thing with J. K. 'Yes,' he said, 'Tell Trucks about it,' he said, 'Tell Trucks about it.' Asa and I went over his accounts on Sunday. I went over his list of accounts with him and checked the ones that I want. Here is the list with the accounts all checked off.[2] I already know nearly all the proprietors. You'll see that—"

"Wait a minute, Jack! Wait a minute!" Mr. Trucks interrupted. "You've lost me completely. In the first place, if there is any assignment of accounts to be made I'll do it. It will be done on a basis that is fair to the salesmen concerned and profitable to the company. You know that."

"Dick, I'm only asking for what is fair." Mr. Jameson's face was flushed. Mr. Trucks noticed that the man he had always believed to be

---

[2] Mr. Jameson's selected accounts are the accounts in parentheses in Exhibit 6.

deliberately confident and self-possessed was now so agitated that it was difficult for him to speak. "I don't want my territory chopped up and handed to some green kid!"

Mr. Trucks noticed that everybody in the office was now watching Mr. Jameson. "Calm down, Jack," he whispered to the salesman, indicating with a nod of his head that others were watching.

"Don't talk to me that way, you young squirt!" replied Mr. Jameson. "I don't care. A man with 25 years' service deserves some consideration!"

"You're absolutely right, Jack. You're absolutely right." As Mr. Trucks repeated his words Mr. Jameson settled back in his chair. The typewriters started clattering again.

"Now, first of all, Jack," queried Mr. Trucks, as he tried to return the conversation to a friendly basis, "where did you get the idea that your territory was going to be 'chopped up'?"

"You said so yourself. You said it at the very first sales meeting when you made that speech about how you were going to boost sales in Syracuse." Mr. Jameson emphasized his words by pounding on the side of the desk with his masonic ring.

Mr. Trucks reflected for a moment. He recalled giving a talk at his first sales meeting at the end of May entitled, "How We Can Do A Better Job for Consolidated." The speech was a restatement of the merchandising policy of the New York office. He had mentioned that getting more profitable business would require that a larger percentage of the total purchases of each account would have to come to Consolidated; that attaining a larger share of the business from each store would require more selling time in each store; and that greater concentration on each account would necessitate reorganization of the sales territories. He realized that his future plans did entail reorganization of the territories; he had not anticipated, however, any such reaction as Mr. Jameson's.

Finally, Mr. Trucks said, "I do plan to make some territorial changes —not right away—at least not until I have looked things over pretty darn carefully. Of course, you understand that our first duty is to make greater profits for the company. Some of our territories would be a great deal more profitable if they were organized and handled in a different manner."

"What are you going to do about Asa's territory?" asked Mr. Jameson.

"Well, I just haven't had a chance to study the situation yet," he replied. "If I could make the territory more profitable by reorganizing it,

I guess that is what they would expect me to do." Since Mr. Trucks had not yet looked over the information about the territory, he was anxious not to commit himself to any course of action relating to it.

"What about the promises the company made to me about letting me choose the accounts I want?" the salesman asked.

"You don't mean the company's promise; you mean Mr. Martin's promise," Mr. Trucks corrected him.

"Well, if Mr. Martin wasn't 'the company' I don't see how you figure that you are!" Mr. Jameson's face resumed its flush.

"O.K., Jack. How about giving me a chance to look over the situation. You know that I want to do the right thing. Let me go over your list of the accounts you want. In a few days I can talk intelligently about the matter." Mr. Trucks felt that there was no point in carrying on the discussion.

"All right, Dick," said Mr. Jameson, rising. The two men walked toward the front entrance of the office. As they reached the top of the steps leading to the front door, Mr. Jameson turned to the sales manager and offered his hand, "Look, Dick. I'm sorry I got so mad. You just can't imagine what this means to me. I know you'll see it my way when you know the whole story." Mr. Jameson's voice sounded strained.

Mr. Trucks watched the older man leave. He felt embarrassed at the realization that Mr. Jameson's parting words had been overheard by several manufacturers' representatives standing nearby.

A CONVERSATION WITH THE DIVISION MANAGER

Mr. Trucks decided to talk at once to Mr. Burton about his conversation with Mr. Jameson. He walked over to Mr. Burton's office. He hesitated in the doorway; Mr. Burton looked up and then indicated with a gesture that Mr. Trucks was to take a seat.

The sales manager sat down. He waited for Mr. Burton to speak. Mr. Burton was occupied for the moment with the problem of unwrapping a cigar. Mr. Trucks opened the conversation by saying, "Jack Jameson just stopped by to speak to me."

"Yeah?" said Mr. Burton, removing bitten flakes of tobacco from the end of his tongue.

"He said something about getting some of Asa Bush's accounts when Asa retires," Mr. Trucks said in a deliberately questioning manner.

"Yeah."

The sales manager continued, "Well, this idea of his was based on a promise that he said J. K. had made."

"Yeah. He told me that, too."

"Did Martin make such a promise?" Mr. Trucks inquired.

"Hell, I don't know. It sounds like him." He tilted back in his swivel chair.

"What shall I do about it?"

"Don't ask me; you're the sales manager." Mr. Burton paused, holding his cigar away from his lips as if he were about to speak. Just as Mr. Trucks was about to say something Mr. Burton lurched forward to flick the ashes from his cigar into his ash tray. "Look here, Dick. I don't want any morale problems around here. You're the first of the 'wonder boys' to be put in charge of a department in this division. I don't want you to do anything to mess up the morale. We never had any morale problems when Martin was alive. We don't want anything like that in this division."

Mr. Trucks was momentarily bewildered. He knew by the way that Mr. Burton used the phrase "wonder boys" that he was referring to the college men who had been brought into the Syracuse Division since the war.

Mr. Burton went on, "Why the devil did you tell the men that you were going to reassign the sales territories without even telling me?"

"But you were there when I said it."

"Said what?"

"Well, at my first sales meeting, that one of the ways we were going to get more business was to reorganize the sales territory," Mr. Trucks replied.

"I certainly don't remember anything like that. Dick, you gave a good inspirational talk, but I sure can't remember anything about reassigning territories."

"Actually, I just mentioned the reorganization of territories in passing," the sales manager smiled.

"I'll be damned. That sort of thing is always happening. Here everybody is frothing at the mouth about something that they think we are going to do and we haven't the slightest idea why they think we're going to do it. You know, the real reason Asa Bush asked to be retired instead of staying on as he planned was probably this fear of having his territory reorganized. Both he and Jameson know that their pension on retirement is based on their earnings in the last five years of active employment. Now that I think of it, three or four of the other salesmen have stopped in during the last couple of weeks to tell me what a fine job they were doing. They probably had this territory reassignment bogey on their minds."

Mr. Burton's cigar was no longer burning. He began groping under the papers on his desk for a match.

Mr. Trucks took advantage of this pause in the conversation. "Mr. Burton, I think there are some real advantages to be won by an adjustment of the sales territories. I think—"

"You still think that after today?" the division manager asked in a sarcastic tone.

"Why, yes! The profit we make on sales to an individual account is related closely to delivery expense. The larger the total proportion of the account's business we get, the more profit we make because the delivery expense remains more or less constant."

"Look, Dick. You college men always have everything all figured out with slide rules, but sometimes that doesn't count. Morale is the important thing. The salesmen won't stand for having their territories changed. I know that you have four trainees that you'd like to put out on territories. You put them out on parts of the territories belonging to some of the more experienced men—bam! God knows how many of our good salesmen would be left. Now, I've never had any trouble with sales force morale since I've been manager of this division. Old Martin, bless his soul, never let me down. He wasn't any damn' Ph.D., but, by golly, he could handle men. Don't get off on the wrong foot with the boys, Dick. With the labor situation in the warehouse being what it is, I've just got too much on my mind. I don't want you to be creating more problems than I can handle. How 'bout it, boy!"

Mr. Burton ground out his half-smoked cigar, looking steadily at Mr. Trucks.

Mr. Trucks was upset because the division manager had imputed to him a lack of concern for morale problems. He had always thought of himself as being very considerate of the thoughts and feelings of others. He realized that at the moment his foremost desire was to get away from Mr. Burton.

Mr. Trucks rose from his chair saying, "Mr. Burton, you can count on me. I know you are right about this morale business."

"Atta boy," said the division manager. "It does us a lot of good to talk like this once in awhile. Now, you see if you can make peace with the salesmen. I want you to handle everything yourself."

"Well, thanks a lot," said the sales manager, as he backed out of the office door.

As he walked through the office after talking with Mr. Burton, he saw two manufacturers' representatives with whom he had appointments already seated near the receptionist's desk. His schedule of appointments that day did not permit him to do more than gather the material pertaining to the Jameson and Bush territories.

MR. TRUCKS GOES HOME

Mr. Trucks left the office shortly after five o'clock to drive to his home in a suburb of Syracuse. It was a particularly hot and humid day. Pre–Fourth-of-July traffic lengthened the drive by nearly twenty minutes. When he finally turned into his own driveway, he felt as though his skin were caked with grime and perspiration. He got out of the car and walked around the house to the terrace in the rear. Nancy, his wife, was sewing in a deck chair under the awning.

"Hello, Dick. You're late," she said, looking up with a smile.

"I know it. Even the traffic was bad today." He dropped his coat on a glass-topped table and sprawled out full length on the glider. "Honestly, I'm so exhausted and dirty that I am disgusted with myself."

"Bad day?"

"Awful. You just can't imagine how discouraging it is trying to get this job organized. You would think that it would be obvious to everybody that what ails the Syracuse Division is the organization of the sales force," said Mr. Trucks, arranging a pillow under his head.

"I didn't realize that you thought anything was wrong with the Syracuse Division."

"Well, what I mean is that we get only 20% of the potential wholesale business. If I could organize the salesforce my way—well, God knows, maybe we could get 40% of the business. That is what the New York office watches for. The sales manager who increases his division's share of the market gets the promotions when they come along. I knew Mr. Crow transferred me to this division because he knew these possibilities existed."

"I don't understand. Is Mr. Crow still your boss, or is Mr. Burton?" asked his wife.

"Nancy, it's terribly discouraging. Mr. Burton is my boss, but I'll never get anywhere with Consolidated unless Mr. Crow and the other people in New York promote me."

"Don't you like Mr. Burton?"

"I had a run-in with him today."

"You didn't!" she said crossly as she laid her sewing aside.

Mr. Trucks had not anticipated this reaction. He gazed up at the awning as if he had not noticed his wife's intent expression. "We didn't argue particularly. He just—well, he doesn't know too much about sales management. He put his foot down on my plans to reorganize the territories."

"I can't understand why you would go and get yourself into a fight with your boss when you haven't been here even two months. We should never have bought this house!"

"Honestly, honey, I didn't have any fight. Everything is O.K. He just —well, do you want me to be a divisional sales manager all my life?"

She smiled and said nothing.

He continued, "I'm sorry you married such a grouch, but I just get plain mad when somebody calls me a 'wonder boy.'"

"You're tired," she said sympathetically. "Why don't you go up and take a shower while I feed the children. We can have a drink and then eat our dinner whenever we feel like it. It's only meat loaf anyway."

"That sounds wonderful," he said, raising himself from his prone position.

AN UNEXPECTED CALLER

Mr. Trucks had just stepped out of the shower when he heard his wife calling to him. "Dick, Jim Pepper is here to see you."

"Tell him I'll be down in just a minute. Give him a drink, Nancy."

As he dressed, Mr. Trucks wondered why the salesman had chosen the dinner hour to call. During the month since he had moved into his new home no salesman had ever dropped in uninvited.

When Mr. Trucks came downstairs, he found Mr. Pepper sitting on the living-room couch with a Tom Collins in his hand.

"Hello, Jim," said Mr. Trucks crossing the room with his right hand extended. "You look as if you had had a hot day. Why don't you take off your coat? If we go out to the terrace, you may get a chance to cool off."

"Thanks, Dick," the visitor said as he moved out to the terrace. "I'm sorry to come barging in this way, but I thought it was important."

"Well, what's on your mind?" said Mr. Trucks as he sat down.

Mr. Pepper started to speak but hesitated as Mrs. Trucks came out of the door with two glasses in her hand. She handed one glass to Mr. Trucks, then excused herself, saying, "I think I better see if the children are all right."

After she had disappeared into the house, Mr. Pepper said, "I heard about what happened at the office today, so I thought I'd come over to tell you that we stand 100% behind you."

Mr. Trucks was perplexed by Mr. Pepper's words. He realized that the incident to which the salesman referred was probably his meeting with Mr. Jameson. Mr. Trucks said, "I'm not sure what you mean, Jim."

"I heard that you and Jameson had it out this morning about changing the sales territories," Mr. Pepper replied.

Mr. Trucks smiled. Two thoughts entered his mind. He was amused at the proportions that the brief conversation of that morning had assumed in the minds of so many people; but, at the same time, he was curious as to how Mr. Pepper, who had presumably been in the field selling, had heard about the incident so soon. Without hesitation he asked, "Where did you hear about this, Jim?"

"Jack Dangler told me! He was down at the warehouse with Homer Babbidge when I stopped off to pick up a special narcotics order for a customer. They are all excited about this territory business. Dangler said Jameson came out to his house at lunch time and told him about it. Everybody figured that you were going to change the territories when you started traveling around with each of the boys, especially after what you said at your first sales meeting."

"Well, the reason I went on the road with each of the men, Jim," said Mr. Trucks, "was so that I could learn more about their selling problems and, at the same time, meet the customers."

Mr. Pepper smiled, "Sure, but when you started filling out a rating sheet on each account, I couldn't help thinking you had some reason for it."

Mr. Trucks realized that the salesman had spoken with irony in his voice, but he thought it was better to let the matter pass as if he had not noticed it. Since he was planning to use the information he had gathered for reorganization of the sales territories, he decided that he would be frank with Mr. Pepper in order to find out what the young salesman's reaction might be on the question of territorial changes. He said, "Jim, I've thought a lot about making some changes in the territories—"

Mr. Pepper interrupted him, "That's terrific. I'm sure glad to hear that. I don't like to speak ill of the dead, but old Martin really gave the trainees the short end of the stick when he put us on territories. He either gave a man a territory of uncontacted accounts so he beat his head against a stone wall until he finally quit, and that is just what happened to two guys who trained with me, or else he gave him a territory where somebody had to be replaced and where some of the best accounts had been handed over to one of the older salesmen. Well, I know for a fact that when I took over my territory from Rick Hunt, Jack Dangler and

Rusty Means got twelve of Hunt's best accounts. And, damn it, I got more sales out of what was left than Hunt ever did, but Dangler and Means' total sales didn't go up at all. It took me awhile, but, by golly, I had the laugh at every sales meeting when our monthly sales figures were announced."

"Is that right?" said Mr. Trucks.

"Damn' right! And I wasn't the only one. That's why those old duffers are so down on the four of us that have come with the division since the war. We've beaten them at their own game."

"Do you think that Waller and Carmack and Smith feel the same way?" asked Mr. Trucks.

"Think, hell! I know it! That's all we ever talk about. If you reorganize those territories and give us back the accounts that Martin took away, you'll see some real sales records. Take, for example, the Medical Arts Pharmacy out by Mercy Hospital. Jack Dangler got that one away from my territory and he calls there only once a week. If I could get that one back, I'd get in there three times a week and get five times as much business."

Mr. Trucks had to raise his hands in a gesture of protest. "Don't you have enough accounts already, Jim, to keep you busy?"

"Dick, I spend fifty hours a week on the road and I love it; but I know damn' well that if I put some of the time I spend in 'two-by-four' stores into some of those big juicy accounts like Medical Arts Pharmacy, I'd do even more business."

Mr. Trucks commented, "I'm not particularly anxious to argue the point now, but if you start putting your time into Medical Arts Pharmacy, what's going to happen to your sales to the 'two-by-four' stores?"

The salesman replied, "Those druggists all know me. They'd go right on buying."

Mr. Trucks did not agree with Mr. Pepper, and he thought that the salesman realized this.

After a moment of silence Mr. Pepper rose from his chair saying, "I'd better scoot home. My wife will be waiting for me with a rolling pin for being late so I'd better get out before your wife gets at me with a skillet." Mr. Pepper laughed heartily at his own joke.

The two men walked around the house to Mr. Pepper's car. As the salesman climbed into the car, he said, "Dick, don't forget what I said— Waller, Carmack, Smith, and I stand 100% behind you. You won't ever hear us talk about going over to a competitor!"

"Who's talking about that?" asked Mr. Trucks.

"Well," said Mr. Pepper as he started the motor and shifted into gear, "I don't want to tell tales out of school."

"Sure," Mr. Trucks said quickly. "I'm sorry I asked. So long, Jim. I'll see you soon."

Mr. Trucks watched the salesman back out of the driveway and drive away.

PART VI

Management of Foreign Operations

Devonian Electronic Components Ltd. (A)*

"I tell you, I will just not put up with any more of it—and you can tell them so from me. I'm sick and tired of being subjected to a day-to-day administration from 3,000 miles away and I've just about had enough. . . ."

The speaker was Henry Masterman, managing director of Devonian Electronic Components Ltd. (DECL), which was an English subsidiary of Newark Electronic Parts Corporation (NEPCO). His listener was Antony Ross, a young consultant who had been hired by the parent organization to study and report on the situation in the English subsidiary.

ROSS'S BACKGROUND

Ross was, in fact, an Englishman who had recently completed a two-year course of study at a school of business administration in the western part of the United States. He had gone to America with the intention of staying only the necessary two years, and towards the end of the second year he had begun to wonder how he could earn funds to pay his return passage. He had conceived the idea of offering his services as a consultant to a few small and medium-sized American firms in the electronics field who had newly started subsidiaries in England. He had a strong electronics background and he believed that some of these firms would be glad of the chance to have an impartial observer with a dual American-English background look at their English operations for a comparatively small fee.

Ross's efforts had met with mixed success. Some firms were anxious to employ him full-time in England, but not as a consultant. Others said they already had more information about their subsidiaries than they knew what to do with. However, there were a few who definitely were interested in his proposal. NEPCO was one of these.

THE VISIT TO NEPCO

Ross had stopped in at NEPCO for a day on his way back across the States to obtain background information about the parent company. He felt it important to understand as thoroughly as possible the problems of the parent company and its attitude towards its subsidiary, so that his report could be tailored to those who would receive and perhaps act on it.

He found that NEPCO's product line consisted of a wide range of small, high-quality component parts for the electronics industry. Though most of these products were simple in themselves, they usually became extremely essential parts in large and very complex pieces of electronic apparatus. The number of different parts manufactured by NEPCO was large—perhaps three to four thousand—but they could be classified into four general groups: relays, switches, sockets, and connectors.

After walking through the plant and the stockroom, Ross had the impression that the majority of the parts required precise stamping and machining by fairly complex machines and skilled workers. In the stockroom, he saw hundreds of neatly labelled wooden boxes ranged on steel shelves, most of which contained parts of millimeter dimensions, varying one from another only in minute details. It was obvious that great attention was paid to quality. Ross learnt that NEPCO's customers rejected an average of between 1 percent and 2 percent of parts sent to them. This reject rate compared very favourably indeed with that obtained by any other manufacturer of similar parts. This quality, in fact, allowed NEPCO to remain very competitive even though its prices were, in general, somewhat above the industry average.

Ross inquired about NEPCO's selling organization and was told that the company sold either through manufacturers' representatives (who were allowed a commission of 8 percent) or through stocking distributors (who typically received a margin of 27 percent).[1] NEPCO's commissions and margins were above the industry norm and its delivery promises could definitely be relied upon. These two factors, plus the quality of NEPCO products, had caused sales over recent years to keep pace with the growth of the electronics industry as a whole. See Exhibit 1. NEPCO financial data for recent years are presented in Exhibit 2.

---

[1] A "stocking distributor" may be defined as a manufacturer's agent who carries inventory and holds title to the goods in his possession, in addition to performing the sales function.

Ross gained from the plant and the stockroom an impression of a well-organized and successful company, and this impression was confirmed by a tour around the offices. Since the company was situated in a part of suburban Newark that had experienced rapid growth, it had not been able to acquire surrounding land at a rate that allowed the physical expansion to match the growth in sales. As a result, there was a severe shortage of office space. Only the president had a private office. The remaining executives worked in groups in rooms that were noisy and overcrowded. However, despite these handicaps, there was a definite air of efficiency. The executives all seemed to have an ability to concentrate firmly on their own tasks while ignoring the lack of material comfort and quiet in their immediate environment. Exhibit 3 shows the NEPCO organization at the time of Ross's visit.

CONVERSATION WITH NEPCO EXECUTIVES

As his day at NEPCO drew to a close, Ross felt that, although he had not acquired as much information about the company as he would have liked, he had learnt the maximum possible in the seven or eight hours that had been available. It had been arranged for him to have dinner with the three leading NEPCO executives so that he could become acquainted with developments in the English subsidiary and be better aware of his mission in England. The three executives were the president, James Whidden; the executive vice-president, Al Nelson; and the sales manager, Sam Morey.

Ross had arranged to meet the executives in Mr. Whidden's office at about 6:30. When he arrived, he found them all still at their desks. No one suggested a drink before dinner, so the four of them went around the corner to the most convenient restaurant and took a corner table.

They had scarcely finished ordering before Al Nelson said, "Well, I guess I'd better give you a little background information on our English company. It is at present only a small operation with 16 employees, not including the three English directors. They have at the moment five machines and have attained a very reasonable rate of production. The company is situated in the county of Devonshire at a town called Okehampton, which is midway between Exeter and Plymouth—perhaps you know the place?"

Ross shook his head, "No, but I have a rough idea of the area."

"Well, no matter," Al Nelson continued, "the situation isn't important. The 16 employees of whom I spoke include one salesman, a couple of office staff, a quality control inspector, and 12 production workers."

"Who's in charge of all operations there?" Ross asked.

Al glanced at Sam Morey and Mr. Whidden before answering. "That's just the problem. We are at the moment looking for a man to fill the role of general manager, and this has caused us one hell of a lot of trouble so far."

"What about the directors?" asked Ross. "Isn't one of them a managing director?"

Mr. Whidden, who had been making some calculations on his paper napkin, now tore off the relevant part, put it in his pocket, and looked up. "I think you'd better explain the setup with the directors, Al, before we go any further."

Al nodded. "I should perhaps have begun at the beginning and told you how the company was started. About a year ago—in May, 1960, in fact—we decided to form an English subsidiary. After an exchange of correspondence with a cousin of Mr. Whidden who lives in England and with whom he has kept in touch over the years, it was decided that this man, by name Henry Masterman, should assist us in starting an English subsidiary. He therefore came over here and we discussed what should be done. When he went back to England, Henry looked around and purchased the buildings and property of a local slate-quarrying firm which had gone bankrupt. One of the conditions attached to his promise to help us was that our subsidiary had to be situated within easy distance of his home in Devonshire."

"Can I interrupt a moment," said Ross, "and get some further background on Mr. Masterman? What is his age and how much business experience has he had?"

Mr. Whidden answered the questions. "He will be 56 this winter. He's a mechanical engineer by training who served his apprenticeship with one of the largest engineering companies in Britain. For a long while now he has been engaged in business of his own which involves selling for various heavy engineering firms in the Exeter, Plymouth, and Bristol areas. But I think that he has pretty much retired from this, particularly in view of our requirements."

"He's an Englishman, I take it," said Ross.

"Yes, certainly."

"And you know him well, or only through meeting him on a few family occasions?" asked Ross.

"I knew him very well in the 1930's when he used to come to

America to stay with my family. Since the war we have kept in touch with one another fairly regularly, and I was delighted to have such a close contact, with excellent business experience, who could help me start a company in England."

Ross nodded. "I see. Go ahead, Al, I'm sorry to have interrupted you."

"Well," Al resumed, "English law requires that a company registered in England have a majority of English directors. Since Mr. Whidden and I wanted to be directors of this subsidiary, it was up to Henry to obtain another two and he chose two friends of his—Colonel Sykes, a retired army officer, and Anthony Paton-Jones, a lawyer who had handled a good deal of business for Henry in the past. Henry himself is, of course, managing director, and that is how things have stood since last year. We are now trying hard to find a general manager who can be a full-time employee and who has our fullest confidence, but we are having some real problems which we want you to help us solve."

Ross looked puzzled. "Isn't it just a simple matter of interviewing candidates? There must be many people who would jump at a job like that, and if you had real doubts about picking the right man, it would surely be worth your while in the long run for one of you to fly over to England to do the selection."

All three NEPCO executives laughed, somewhat mirthlessly. "That's what we thought," Al said, "but it just hasn't been that easy. We seem to be up against three fellow directors who are intent on keeping the company in their own pockets."

Ross looked surprised. "You mean that Mr. Masterman has turned out to be thoroughly untrustworthy as managing director?"

Al hesitated and glanced at Mr. Whidden, clearly not knowing what to say. The latter came to his help. "I certainly don't think one could call Henry untrustworthy in any dishonest sense. The real trouble seems to be that he has become too interested in the English company and seems to be in danger of throttling its growth by trying to control every detail of its operations himself."

"And the net result," Sam Morey put in, "is that we are finding it impossible to keep in that company anyone whose authority and control will rival, if not supersede, Masterman's own."

Ross frowned. "I'm afraid I still don't quite understand."

"Well," said Al, "two months ago, for instance, we thought that we had a very promising candidate for general manager, and the English directors seemed to agree. However, when they held a formal directors' meeting to decide the question, they suddenly turned round and went against him for no very good reasons that we could ascertain."

"Were any of you present at that meeting?" Ross asked.

Sam Morey nodded. "The meeting was planned to coincide with a trip I made to England to try and boost their sales. I was able to talk with Jones—that was the man's name—a good deal. In fact, I talked with him intensively over a period of two days, testing his ideas and his technical knowledge. I concluded that as a manager he might need a steadying influence from his superior from time to time, but that his grasp of the business from a technical standpoint was very good. I was amazed and upset at the meeting when all the directors voted against him."

"Have you no idea why they voted against Jones?" Ross queried.

Sam shook his head emphatically. "Very little. It seemed to me to be personal prejudice of some kind, or some other equally intangible reason."

"And then there was the Harvey incident," put in Mr. Whidden. "I myself went to England five months ago after a visit to Switzerland to buy some screw machines. Henry had had an assistant called Harvey doing the office work, but he had dismissed this assistant shortly before my arrival. When I looked over a lot of the work the man had done, it seemed to me to be very competent, and I judged him exactly the sort of assistant that Henry needed. In fact, I was so certain of Harvey's value that I tried to get him back in the company."

"Well, I must say, I find their behaviour very odd," said Ross, who was becoming more and more curious about the situation. "I take it, then, that you still have no general manager there and that Mr. Masterman is still exercising general control over all the company's operations."

"Exactly," said Al, "and since the company has been going nearly a year, you can understand why we are concerned. We would like you to try and find out why the directors are behaving as they are and to recommend what we might do about it."

"No easy assignment," laughed Ross, "particularly if two of you were unable to obtain satisfactory answers to your problems. Are you sure that I will be able to contribute enough at this point to make it worthwhile hiring me?"

"Quite frankly," said Mr. Whidden, "the whole situation is now so difficult that we are prepared to try anything, and we all feel that an outsider, even if he has not got our experience, might be able to see something which we ourselves have missed."

"Do you mind if I ask a few more questions?" said Ross. "I know that we haven't got the time to talk as thoroughly as I would wish, but I think that already I have a pretty good background, and a few more pieces of information will complete the picture."

"Sure, go right ahead," said Al. "We'll tell you anything you want to know."

"Well, let's see." Ross paused and consulted his notebook. "Do you receive any information regularly from Okehampton?"

"Certainly," answered Al. "We have a weekly report sent to us which gives full details of day-to-day production, details of all expenses, and information about sales. This report is compiled almost entirely by Norris, Harvey's successor, and I must admit that it is done well."

"What are you producing in England?"

"Mostly stampings, but also a few connectors. So far, we are limited by the number of machines and the knowledge of the men operating them."

"Are all the production workers English?"

"Yes, all the workers are, and this has caused something of a training problem. When we despatched the first machines, we sent over Bill Ryles, our production superintendent, for six weeks and he got production started. Since his return we have been very pleased with the results that have been obtained, both as to quality and quantity of production."

Ross was making notes. "How much has been sold so far?"

"Much less than we expected. You will be able to get the exact figures in England."

"Who is doing the selling?"

"Basically, only one man, Jack Turpin, whom we hired on Henry's recommendation and trained over here for six weeks. But Henry himself has also done some selling, and we have recently—perhaps two months ago—engaged the services of a stocking distributor in the London area."

Ross again consulted his notes. "Am I right in saying that the only NEPCO personnel who have visited England to date are Mr. Whidden, Sam, and Bill Ryles? You have not been yet, Al?"

Al shook his head. "And remember that Henry and Jack Turpin have each been over here—Henry for a few days and Jack for six weeks."

"Which of you is responsible at this end for attending to English matters?"

"It depends on the American situation. I guess all of us spend a moment or two with English stuff that needs attention. Who actually does it at any one time depends on who can manage to take time off his American work. We're pretty thin on the ground here, you know, and all of us are probably overworked."

"What were some of the reasons for starting an English company?"

"The usual things—we wanted a foothold in the Common Market area, and it seemed pretty likely that England would join. Also, we felt that we had quite enough know-how to make the English market and the European market in general sit up and take notice. We don't regret our decision."

At this point the conversation became more general and little was added to the information Ross had already gained. It was apparent that the Americans were very perplexed and Ross sympathised with them. During his two years in America, and particularly during the second year, Ross had come to understand very well the American belief that the average European businessman was intensely conservative, rather inflexible, disinclined to take risks, and, in general, rather a pale shadow of his vigorous, flexible, dynamic American counterpart. There was one point in the conversation when Al had said, half sarcastically and half apologetically, "I'm afraid we take the somewhat naïve view that we are in business to make a profit," and the other two NEPCO executives had smiled rather sadly, shaking their heads over the mysterious and unbusinesslike behaviour of the English directors. As Ross drove back to his hotel, he reflected that he would probably have to attempt to introduce as tactfully as possible some superior American methods into the thinking of the English directors.

．　．　．　．　．　．　．　．　．　．　．　．　．　．

ROSS GOES TO OKEHAMPTON

Some six weeks later, after the necessary exchange of correspondence with NEPCO and the subsidiary, Ross set out from London to pay a four-day visit to Devonian Electronic Components Ltd. The main road from London passed through Exeter and Ross noticed that Exeter was certainly not an industrial city, and indeed, was little more than a large market town. From naval service, Ross knew Plymouth, the other large city in the neighbourhood of DECL, to be an important naval dockyard with a number of shipbuilding firms but not much other industry. Okehampton itself was situated some 20 miles from Exeter and was the largest of a number of small towns and villages that were strung out along a valley. This valley, which was heavily wooded, formed the western border of Dartmoor, an extensive tract of wild and almost

uninhabited moorland. Both Dartmoor and the Valleys which sur-
rounded it had been made into a National Park, which meant that all
further building and development within the area was subject to a strict
examination (and perhaps prohibition) by a body of local town and
county officials known as the National Park Planning Council.

As Ross slowly threaded his way through a herd of cows being driven
along the road just outside Okehampton by a straw-sucking farmhand,
he reflected that the surroundings in which NEPCO had placed their
English subsidiary could hardly be more unlike their Newark environment. He wondered what the three NEPCO executives who had come
to Okehampton had thought about it, and he remembered a remark by
Sam Morey—"You mustn't expect miracles from the plant; it's not one
of those gleaming white, well-ventilated, one-storey establishments that
electronic firms build for themselves in California."

THE FIRST MEETING WITH MASTERMAN AND NORRIS

The following morning, Ross asked in one of the shops in the main
street where he might find the DECL plant. He was directed down a
narrow and muddy lane leading to three stone buildings which looked
like farm buildings. On nearing them, Ross heard the sound of machinery and saw that two of them were apparently used to house machinery
and inventory while the third had been made into an office with fluorescent lighting. As Ross approached the door of the office building, a tall
man with untidy hair and thick-rimmed glasses flung open the door and
strode out, shouting over his shoulder, "And you can tell Turpin from
me that he's darn well going to work Saturday mornings in future."

He nearly bumped into Ross but stopped in time. There was a pause.
"My name's Masterman and you're Ross, I suppose," he said, offering a
hand perfunctorily. "You'd better come in here."

They returned through the door from which Masterman had just
emerged and Ross saw that what he had assumed to be a single office
had been partitioned into two rooms with a connecting door. They
passed into the inner office and Ross noted that the outer office was
occupied only by a secretary and several filing cabinets. In the inner
office there were two desks: one of them was occupied by Norris whom
Masterman introduced briefly; the other was an old roll-top desk, littered with piles of papers. Masterman gestured Ross to an upright
wooden chair standing against the wall and sank into a swivel chair
behind the roll-top desk.

"So you're studying NEPCO's subsidiary in Europe," he said. "Well,
you can tell them from me that I'm fed up with them. I've no doubt that

when you've finished you're going to write some sort of a report, and I think it damn well ought to tell the people in Newark that they haven't the first idea how to run a company. They query my judgement of people, they do nothing but complain about our expenses while pouring out money themselves, they refuse to do anything that we recommend because they think they know better, and now, to crown everything, they insist on telling me from 3,000 miles away who can and who cannot be fired."

Ross's surprise must have showed in his face, for Masterman continued, "I don't suppose you know anything about the latest development. It's typical of them, absolutely typical. A week ago I received a telephone call from Bill Ryles telling me that I was to dispose of six of the production workers, whom he named. As you can imagine, I was thunderstruck both because this action had been taken without my being consulted first in any way, and, even more, because they had presumed to know better than I who should be laid off if six people had to go. Two days later I received a letter from Ryles confirming the telephone call and adding that no new people were to be hired without NEPCO consent and that voluntary terminations should not be replaced. The letter ended"—and here Masterman picked up a piece of paper from his desk and began to read—" 'Of course, Henry, as you must realize, these actions are a must if DECL is ever going to become a self-sufficient and profitable venture. We sincerely hope that sales will soon become a reality and that the people you have let go will be back with us again.' "

Masterman snorted disgustedly and spread out his hands in a gesture of helplessness. "What could I do? I conferred with the production foreman and we both agreed that if anyone was to go it should be two troublemakers whom we wanted to get rid of anyway and who had not been named by NEPCO. I cabled NEPCO to advise them of this but received an answering cable this morning telling me to do exactly what I had been told to do originally. They must be mad!"

"Do the other two English directors know about this?" asked Ross.

"Well, as it happened, I was having a cocktail party up at my house last Saturday evening and Anthony Paton-Jones and Colonel Sykes, both of whom live about 100 miles away from here, were present. We had a directors' meeting on Sunday morning so that our formal protests could be registered in some Minutes."

Masterman again consulted the papers on his desk and thrust some typewritten pages in Ross's direction. Ross glanced at them and saw that they were the Minutes Masterman had referred to. Meanwhile, Masterman had looked at his watch, risen hurriedly to his feet and seized his briefcase. "I can't stop to talk to you all day," he said as he strode to the door. "I've got too much work to do in Plymouth. My time is precious—and that's something else that the Americans don't seem to realize. Norris will show you anything at all you want to see,"—he waved a hand round the office—"we have nothing to hide. See you tomorrow morning."

He slammed the door behind him and a few moments later the din of the machinery in the adjacent buildings was drowned by the roar of Masterman's red sports car, which had been parked in the yard. Ross, still trying to adjust himself to the events of the last few minutes, looked up in time to catch a look of amusement on Norris' face.

"I wouldn't have liked to have met Mr. Masterman for the first time this morning," he said, "—at least, not with these dismissals on his mind. He can be explosive at the best of times, but—" he broke off and looked at his watch—"I'll bet he makes Plymouth in even time this morning, and I wouldn't care to be driving the other way."

"Does he often go to Plymouth?" asked Ross.

Norris looked surprised. "Of course; that's where his office is. He has his own firm, you know, which is called Masterman Engineering Ltd. He does a lot of big selling, I believe. He's certainly got a lot of important contacts—he knows everyone in the county and an enormous range of important people in the rest of England. He's the sort of person I wouldn't be surprised to find in the Royal Box at Ascot. He had a very important job handling tank production in the war, I think."

Ross was beginning to feel that the NEPCO executives had painted a somewhat misleading picture of Masterman. "How often does he work here, then?" he asked Norris.

"Oh, an hour or two every morning and sometimes even more than that. I know he writes a lot of letters to NEPCO from his Plymouth office using his other secretary. Very often he comes back here in the evenings as well."

"Are you in charge at DECL whenever Mr. Masterman isn't here?"

"Yes, provided that Jack Turpin isn't here either. I've had no experience in this line of business at all, so I'm just not competent to deal with things that come up. If a decision is needed straight away on anything, I have a talk with Dowdell, the foreman, and we work something out. But if Jack Turpin is here we refer decisions to him because he's the only man in DECL who really knows what he's talking about as far as the DECL product line is concerned."

"Does he know more than Mr. Masterman?"

"Oh, yes, I think so. You see, Mr. Masterman's background is in heavy engineering and the stuff he sells in his business is worth thousands of pounds at a time. Jack's background is also heavy engineering, but at least he's had six weeks at NEPCO and a year or two selling to build up his knowledge."

Ross thought for a moment. "Do you mind if I have a look at one of your weekly reports?"

"Not at all. Here's the one that I sent off yesterday. I make them up every Monday."

A quick look at the report showed Ross that it was just as Al Nelson had described it, except that it was even more detailed than he had expected. Even the very smallest expenses had been listed. "Does NEPCO keep a very close check of all DECL expenses?"

Norris grinned. "Well, you heard what Mr. Masterman said. They certainly do a great deal of complaining about expenses one way or another. We have to get all expenses above the very smallest sums approved. For instance, we recently asked if we could hire a woman for four hours a week at 2/6 an hour to clean the offices. They refused our request. On the other hand, when Sam Morey came over, he had to spend three days in London talking to Thames Electronic Distributors Ltd. (TEDL), our distributor there. During this time, he stayed at the Savoy and we were later sent a bill for £101/3/6, which we paid and put on the weekly report. NEPCO was horrified, and not only was it insinuated that the expense was our fault, but we even had a letter from Sam Morey saying that he had added up his bill before he left and had purposely noted that it came to £99/12/6. The silly thing is that if they really wanted to save money, everyone around here could give them 101 good ways in which to do it."

Ross stood up. "I'd now like to take Mr. Masterman at his word and have a look through some of the office files, particularly the correspondence between DECL and NEPCO."

"Of course," answered Norris. "I'll move over to this table in the corner here and you can use my desk. And I'll try and answer any questions you may have."

.   .   .   .

ROSS OBTAINS FURTHER INFORMATION FROM THE DECL FILES

For the rest of the day, Ross concentrated on bringing to light factual information about the NEPCO-DECL situation. This was not easy. The only income statement and balance sheet to date had been prepared at the end of 1960 and were therefore seven months old. See Exhibit 4. Ross also guessed that there were substantial gaps in the correspondence file—probably because Masterman kept the most important letters in a personal file in his Plymouth office. Ross decided that someone of Masterman's apparent volatility probably wrote quite a few letters that he would not wish to leave lying around the DECL office.

Ross first of all looked through the Minutes, which Masterman had just given him. They were, as might be expected, strongly worded and concentrated on presenting the arguments against sacking any employees. It was argued that the dismissal of six employees was bound to give the firm a bad name in the community and that the action would have a serious long-run effect on the ability of DECL to attract skilled labour. It had been difficult enough to get the required labour in the first place; now that such labour had been trained for some months, it seemed ridiculous to run the great risk of losing those employees for good. It was also pointed out that the morale of those employees who remained would be badly upset at a time when a very willing and cheerful spirit had begun to establish itself in the plant. And the Minutes also noted that a layoff of half the work force would cause the entire valley to think that the firm was going bankrupt, no matter what denials were issued.

Ross spent some time thinking over these Minutes and the action that had caused them. He asked Norris for a list of the production workers and the dates of their employment by DECL. He found that the six who had been laid off were the six most recently employed.

Ross then turned his attention to establishing some sort of chronology of events since the foundation of DECL. It was then early July, 1961. DECL had been incorporated on September 14, 1960. September and October seemed to have been taken up with getting the buildings ready. During the previous fourteen months, Turpin, who had returned from his six weeks in Newark in July, 1959, had been making sales calls all round England trying to sell products which NEPCO had agreed, for the time being, to export from America. Bill Ryles had arrived with the first stamping machine in the first week of November, 1960, and had supervised its installation and the training of the first few workers. He had gone home in the third week in December in order to spend Christmas with his family, leaving behind him some enthusiastic workers and a second stamping machine which had arrived from America in the second week of December. On January 11, 1961, Ryles had written to Harvey from America saying, "We have lined up an ambitious program for DECL in 1961 and should have a minimum of eight stamping machines and molding presses to you by July 30." Ross gathered that this number had been confirmed by Sam Morey who, on his recent visit, had given the scheduled dates of dispatching from the States. However, since Morey's departure no machine had arrived, so that DECL had only five by the beginning of July.

Harvey had been dismissed in the first week of March, 1961, and Mr. Whidden had spent his few days in England in the second week of that month. The services of TEDL, the London distributor, were engaged at the end of March. The months of April and May were taken up with two problems: sales and the finding of a general manager. In the matter of sales, Ross found an Outline Marketing Plan that had been prepared by Al Nelson before Sam Morey's English visit during the first two weeks of May. See Exhibit 5. He also found a letter to Masterman from Al Nelson which showed NEPCO's feelings about sales at that time. The letter was dated April 3:

As you are fully aware, the major problem confronting DECL is the need for sales. The production capacity at Okehampton, even though limited, in fact exceeds the sales bookings which are being produced. In addition, you have a stock of products on the way to you from our United States plant for which we obviously need to get a turnover. Moreover, we have considerable capacity here at Newark which can support sales in your marketing territory. . . . We would appreciate at this time any comments which you, Turpin or TEDL would like to make on the Outline Marketing Plan and additional sales matters. . . .

With regard to the finding of a general manager, Ross gathered that Jones had been introduced to Mr. Masterman as a possible candidate and that the latter had been enthusiastic, at any rate at first, for there was a letter from him to Al Nelson, dated April 13, which said:

I want to make quite clear here and now that, whilst I have every confidence in Jones, the decision to hire him must be made by the Newark management rather than by the English directors.

It had obviously been agreed that the interests of all would be best served if the final decision regarding Jones were not made until Sam Morey's visit. In the month that had elapsed between the writing of this letter and the directors' meeting at which Jones had been turned down, it was clear that something had happened which had changed the minds of the English directors. The Minutes of the meeting afforded no clue.

The correspondence that had passed between NEPCO and DECL subsequent to Sam Morey's visit in the first and second weeks of May dealt with a number of issues. Sales were again a subject of much concern and a long letter had passed from Sam to Jack Turpin offering advice and instructions based on three days spent by Sam in making sales calls in England along with Jack. It appeared that there were several occasions when Jack's technical knowledge was badly needed in Okehampton, but NEPCO had steadfastly refused to allow him to spend one day a week in the DECL plant.

In the matter of finding a general manager, it was clear that the English directors wanted to advertise for one. At the same directors' meeting at which Jones had been turned down, it had, in fact, been agreed that the next step was to advertise for a general manager through the media normally employed in England for such purposes. However, a letter from Al Nelson dated June 11 firmly disallowed the expense of advertising on the grounds that advertising would simply attract malcontents and unsuitable people. Al suggested instead that DECL should work through a technical employment agency, as was the normal American practice. His suggestion had not been carried out because such agencies were rare in England, if not nonexistent. A stalemate therefore existed which, Ross felt, would only be broken by Turpin or Mr. Masterman coming across another possible candidate in the course of their everyday tasks.

In May and June, there was also a certain amount of correspondence on the subject of DECL's expenses. Ross found letters about the two or three matters Norris had referred to and in addition he saw that the NEPCO managers had complained about the £100 director's fee that Masterman had proposed should be offered to both Colonel Sykes and Paton-Jones. They had also queried the £20 spent on business entertainment by Mr. Masterman between January and May.

It was apparent to Ross, even after a very quick reading of the NEPCO-DECL correspondence, that by the middle of June, 1961, several important disagreements between the English and American managements had occurred. Since Ross himself had left America at the end of May, he read the letters sent from Newark during June with particular interest, for they afforded his only guide to the most recent thinking of the American management. He was particularly interested in the fact that Al Nelson had seized the opportunity, following a particularly indignant letter from Mr. Masterman, to set forth the American managers' thinking on most of the essential issues. This letter is reproduced in Exhibit 6, together with the substance of Mr. Masterman's reply. Ross noted that Al's letter had apparently done very little to calm the English directors even before they had been further upset by the NEPCO decision to lay off six of the production force.

A TOUR ROUND THE DECL PLANT AND A FURTHER TALK WITH MASTERMAN

On the morning of his second day at Okehampton, Ross had an opportunity to talk at some length with Mr. Masterman. The latter obviously felt he had been somewhat abrupt on the previous day, and seemed determined to atone. He showed Ross round the two production buildings and introduced him to Dowdell, the foreman, and Inman, the quality control inspector. From Inman, Ross was amazed to learn that DECL had not yet sold anything actually produced at Okehampton because NEPCO had not yet been satisfied with the quality of the parts produced.

"I just can't understand it," Inman said. "Each week we send them off a sample of what we have made during the week and always it comes back with a few minor criticisms but nothing else. They just don't realize that we are all working for the same cause. They don't give us any advice. They will never tell us which dimensions of a part are the critical ones, and, above all, they won't send us duplicates of the gauges they use to measure the various parts. As a result we are quite unable to check accurately almost all the features which they criticise and therefore we can do nothing except continue to send samples which raise the same criticisms." Inman added that DECL had received, three months earlier, the official approval of the Standards Department of the Ministry of Aviation. This approval was highly coveted, even by large electronics companies, because it influenced greatly, often decisively, a company's ability to obtain Government work. The fact that DECL's limited production staff had been able to obtain this approval had apparently not been appreciated fully by the NEPCO management.

Dowdell also had his problems. "Since Mr. Ryles left last December," he said, "we have been running these machines entirely on our own after only six weeks' training. Mind you, I'm not saying that this hasn't been a good thing in many ways because we have just had to become thoroughly familiar with the machines and the production process. Yet we still aren't using the right oil, for instance, just because we can't get an analysis of the oil NEPCO are using. All they tell us is the make and type of oil they use and that's not much use because the oil company concerned doesn't make the stuff over here."

"What's the most serious production problem right now?" asked Ross.

Dowdell plunged his hand into the bin underneath the stamping tools. He brought up a handful of something that looked like metal chippings. "See these?" he said. "Mixed in with these chippings are the finished parts. In order to get any of these parts, we have to sort out each one of them by hand—and you can imagine what that means."

"But doesn't NEPCO do the same?" Ross asked.

"The hell they do. They'd have a six-year backlog if they did," answered Dowdell. "All we know is that they use some sort of centrifugal processes, but so far we haven't even gathered what these are, let alone had permission to use them."

"How many different types of parts have you been making?" said Ross.

"Not very many, so far, simply because we can't get the go-ahead to sell even the few we are making. Until we get these right, there's no point in trying any others, though, goodness knows, there's enough left to try. In some ways it's even a good thing that some of the men were laid off, though the layoff has ruined morale in the plant. But if we still had twelve men here, we'd have stampings coming out of the chimney next month."

Outside in the yard again, Masterman turned to Ross. "You see how it is? I'm not alone in my complaints. The interesting thing is that it seems to be impossible to make NEPCO understand that we're having these problems." Ross frowned. "Couldn't you even get the point across to Mr. Whidden or Sam Morey when they were actually here?"

Masterman snorted. "Well, Sam Morey was almost useless in the plant. All he did here was to go on a few sales calls with Jack Turpin and I gather that he hadn't got much idea of how to sell to an English customer. It's true that he promised to get Inman some gauges, but we've never heard any more about them. As for Jim Whidden,"—and here Masterman looked almost puzzled—"I always thought that I'd been pretty close to him and that we got on well together. But he only spent about half an hour in the plant and he didn't seem able to answer any of the technical questions the men wanted answered. He didn't even seem very interested in things."

While they were talking, they had been walking up the yard and away from the buildings. Ross noticed that there was a fair-sized rectangular field separating the DECL buildings from the nearest Okehampton houses. Masterman now waved a hand in the direction of this field.

"See that field?" he said. "Jim Whidden decided he wanted to buy that, just in case DECL had to expand. It belongs to a Mr. Simpson who lives in one of those houses over there. Simpson himself wants to build on this land, but since it's within the boundaries of the National Park, he can't do this without the permission of the National Park Planning Council. I used my influence to make sure he didn't get this permission and now we're negotiating to buy this land from a disgruntled Simpson for £1,500. I think that if we wanted to build on it we could get permission on the grounds that the addition to local industry would be good for the valley. I need hardly tell you that all this rather unpleasant manoeuvering on my part was unappreciated by NEPCO."

Ross felt at a loss for an appropriate comment and said the first thing that came into his head. "Maybe they'll add a bonus to your salary."

Masterman stopped dead. "What do you mean—'add a bonus'? They don't pay me a damn thing. I took on this because I was Jim's cousin and that's why I'm doing it now. Family loyalty may seem a lousy reason to you for putting up with all this, but it's the only one. Besides, I liked Jim and still do. Although he's done one thing which upset me a good deal, I reckon that a lot of their stupidity is not his fault."

Having said this, Masterman turned away and Ross sensed that there would not be much point in talking further that morning. Masterman's abruptness in speech and frank way of talking was extremely disconcerting to Ross after his two years of human relations courses at the business school. He wondered whether the Americans weren't a little scared of Masterman.

They walked back along the yard in silence and Masterman got into his sports car. He reached behind the seat and brought up a thick envelope. "I brought you the correspondence file for NEPCO that I keep at my office. For goodness sake, don't let it out of your sight. I'll be away tomorrow, so you can give it back to me on Thursday when I suggest you come and have dinner at my house up on the hill. I'm not married, but my housekeeper cooks a pretty good meal. See you then."

He thrust the package at Ross, let in the clutch, and roared away, spattering mud in all directions. Ross just stood there, nursing the envelope and trying to collect his thoughts.

A MEETING WITH TURPIN

In the end, Ross walked back to his hotel, ate lunch and then spent the afternoon looking through Masterman's file. It added very little to what he already knew except that it confirmed his impression of Masterman's volatility and abruptness. Most of his letters went straight to the

point with considerable vigour and fluency and Ross felt that he would
not have liked to have been on the receiving end of many of them. He
guessed that the reason Masterman did not want them lying around at
DECL was that there was clear evidence in the letters of the last two
months of a growing feud between him and Turpin on the subject of
the latter's working hours and general approach to his job. Ross found
himself very curious to meet Turpin. On the previous day, Ross had
taken advantage of Turpin's daily telephone call to DECL to arrange to
see him. It happened that Turpin was selling in the West of England
during the period of Ross's visit, so that it was convenient for him to
call in at Okehampton. The two had arranged to meet on the evening of
the following day and have a drink together.

Turpin arrived just as Ross was finishing his coffee after dinner and
immediately suggested a tour of the various pubs in the valley. Three
hours and a good few pints later, Ross sat down before he went to bed
to make a few notes on the evening. He had found Turpin, who was
about his own age, to be extremely easy-going and friendly. He also was
a fine athlete. His wanderings with various athletic teams had led him all
over England, so that even before he began selling on a national scale,
he had a good knowledge of England and a very wide range of acquaintances. He knew someone in almost every large city in England with
whom he could be sure of spending an interesting evening.

Turpin had few strong feelings about his job. His main complaint
was that the Americans were inefficient in getting their products to
England, no matter how much their letters implied the opposite. Even
at that time, TEDL had not been provided with adequate promotional
literature, let alone stocks, and, according to Turpin, were about to write
a pretty strong letter of complaint to Newark. However, Turpin also
stressed that much delay was involved in getting products through the
British Customs and Ross gathered that Masterman was in the middle
of a bitter feud with the chief Customs officer at Plymouth as a result. In
general, the evening left Ross with the impression that Turpin would
have been an excellent salesman for a company with an established
product and reputation but that he was not imbued with the missionary
zeal necessary to gain NEPCO products a firm foothold in the English
market. He also noted that Turpin himself frankly admitted that his
knowledge of the products and their uses was still fairly patchy because
of his lack of background in the electronics field prior to his six weeks'
indoctrination at Newark.

A VISIT TO THE DECL AUDITOR

On the Wednesday morning, his third day at Okehampton, Ross went to Plymouth to call on Mr. Williamson, DECL's auditor. Al Nelson had arranged for Ross to make this call and had assured Williamson that he was free to talk to Ross exactly as he would talk to Whidden himself. Ross found Williamson, who was a partner in the Plymouth office of one of the largest accounting firms in England, to be a deliberate, elderly, conservative man with a strong inclination to talk about his early days as an accountant with the British Army in India. He was, however, a man with many years' experience as an accountant and these years had given him a shrewdness and an insight into human nature that made his comments on the DECL-NEPCO situation invaluable to Ross. They talked for nearly three hours, for, although DECL was only a small client, Williamson had become more and more interested in their affairs. He was delighted to have a chance to vent his ideas freely without betraying any professional confidence.

In the course of the conversation Ross asked Williamson if he could tell him about Harvey's dismissal. Williamson nodded and smiled. "I think it's better you should ask me rather than Mr. Masterman about that." Then he slowly refilled his pipe and drew on it with satisfaction.

"Harvey's dismissal was just one of those things. There was no major cause—only a series of little ones. Harvey is one of those people who don't know their own limitations. He rather fancied himself as a production man and there were at least two or three occasions when he actually offered customers who called on the 'phone some parts which the plant has just not got the equipment to make. And he offered them at ridiculous prices, as well. Another thing was that he had a very peculiar way of keeping the books—not dishonest, you understand, but very difficult to follow, so that I had a lot of trouble in carrying out the audit. A third thing was that Harvey had many relatives in the valley and he kept trying to get them employment in the company. This annoyed Mr. Masterman very much and I always felt it was only a matter of time before Harvey would have to leave. In the end, he left just before Mr. Whidden came over. I understand that Mr. Whidden was surprised at Harvey's dismissal because NEPCO had always been satisfied with the presentation of any information they had requested from him. In fact, I also know that Mr. Whidden went to see Harvey behind Mr. Masterman's back to try and persuade him to come back. When Mr. Masterman found this out he was, understandably, terribly offended and very angry. I myself am surprised that Mr. Whidden could have done such a thing and even more surprised that the NEPCO management could have made exactly the same mistake later on in the Jones affair."

This opening was too good to miss and Ross had then asked Williamson to tell him what he knew about the whole Jones affair.

"Well," said Williamson, frowning a little in an effort to remember, "I think it was Turpin who first introduced Jones to Mr. Masterman. And—" he added, with a quick glance at Ross, "I don't think that was the best beginning possible. Jack has some pretty wild drinking companions and I am inclined to think Jones was one of them. Nevertheless, he got on well with Mr. Masterman and soon everyone, including Mr. Masterman, seemed to take his future employment at DECL very much for granted. Norris tells me that Jones was very often down at DECL looking around and suggesting changes and even on occasion giving orders. Pretty odd behaviour for a man who hadn't even been hired, if you ask me. Anyway, nothing happened for a long time until Sam Morey came over. He spent almost two whole days with Jones, during which time I suppose he satisfied himself as to Jones's technical abilities. When the directors' meeting came along, we all sat round the table to make an official decision about Jones, now that a representative of the NEPCO management was on the spot."

"Can I just interrupt a moment and ask why you yourself were there?" said Ross.

"Oh, yes. I forgot that. I always attend the DECL directors' meetings because Mr. Masterman likes official Minutes to be taken by a disinterested party. I've attended every one including the last one which was called in protest against the NEPCO decision to lay off men. I suppose you know all about that, by the way?"

Ross nodded and smiled. "I've heard almost too much."

Williamson shook his head sadly. "That was an unfortunate business." He paused. "Well, now where was I? Oh, yes, the directors' meeting. Well, we were all sitting there and Jones came in. He at once sat down and for nearly half an hour, without any prompting, told us how he would run DECL. The other two English directors had never met Jones before and I could see they were astonished by his attitude. The door had hardly closed behind him before they shook their heads and said they couldn't possibly agree to hiring a man who had so little idea of how to behave in an interview. Morey, who had seemed to expect Jones to behave like that, protested that his electronics knowledge was pretty sound and that was what mattered. I expected Mr. Masterman to put in a word for Jones, but instead he strongly agreed with Colonel Sykes and Mr. Paton-Jones. The meeting therefore turned Jones down and Morey immediately went out, shaking his head. We all saw him get into Jones's car and go off with him."

"Have you any idea why Mr. Masterman changed his mind?" asked Ross.

"Yes, indeed—because he then told the three of us who were left a rather surprising story. It turned out that he had asked Jones up to his house to have a drink one Saturday before lunch, just about the end of April. Jones had drunk so much that Masterman suggested that they should go in separate cars down to the hotel at Okehampton, where they had decided to have lunch. Mr. Masterman says that Jones had some narrow shaves with two brick walls and a bus on the way down but that he somehow arrived intact. However, they had no sooner finished their soup than Jones stood up and was violently ill all over the table. He left at once and Mr. Masterman did not see him from that time until the directors' meeting."

"I'm surprised that none of you knew at the meeting," said Ross. "I would have thought that the story would have been all round the valley by the middle of the afternoon."

"That's what I thought," said Williamson, "but I gather that the hotel keeper is a good friend of Mr. Masterman and that there was no one else in the dining-room at the time, so the incident could be hushed up to save Mr. Masterman embarrassment. I was also surprised that he hadn't told us before the meeting; his reason for not doing so was that he didn't want to bias our opinions."

"What did you yourself think of Jones?" asked Ross.

"I agreed with the directors. Jones's electronics knowledge may be all right but his character is clearly pretty wild," Williamson said.

"What happened to Morey after that?" Ross said.

Williamson shrugged his shoulders. "He was due to catch a train back to London that evening in order to make his plane. Mr. Masterman had arranged to drive him into Exeter, but when the time came to leave Okehampton, Morey had still not appeared. Mr. Masterman drove into Exeter all the same, thinking that Jones might have driven Morey to Exeter. This is, in fact, exactly what happened—Jones and Morey had spent the whole afternoon together and they only just got to the station in time to catch the train. Morey barely had time to say a hurried farewell to Mr. Masterman, who was so angry by this time that it was probably just as well. He knew perfectly well that Morey had probably promised Jones the job despite the directors' meeting and I think he was right. The funny thing is, though, that the NEPCO people did finally turn Jones down in a letter which they did not write until June 5, three or four weeks after the meeting."

Ross, who had seen the letter, nodded. "I take it that Mr. Masterman would add little to what you have already told me about the Harvey and Jones affairs?"

"I don't think he would. Anyhow, I would advise you not to talk to him about either subject because they are very sore points with him. Not that he wouldn't be perfectly frank with you, but I doubt if you would learn anything more and you would run the risk of annoying him personally."

The conversation had then passed onto the subject of Mr. Masterman, and Williamson confirmed that he had always found him to be a slightly frightening personality because of his propensity for saying exactly what he thought in a very blunt way. He added that he understood that Masterman was a fine salesman who had built up a very profitable business of his own. He gave Ross an introduction to the managing director of a large Plymouth engineering firm for which he knew Masterman had done a lot of selling.

After lunch, Ross had called on this man and learnt that for some years Masterman had sold over a million pounds' worth of equipment annually almost single-handed. He also learnt that this volume had dropped off very seriously in the past year, largely because of the time and emotional effort Masterman was devoting to Okehampton. The managing director had, in fact, said outright, "If you ask me, this work he's doing at Okehampton is ruining his business and his health. He doesn't say much to me about it, but I knew enough from various sources to write him a personal letter about four months ago to beg him to concentrate his efforts on his own business once again. After all, he's 55 and not a young man and he should think about providing for his retirement as best he can."

Finally, Williamson commented very favourably on Norris, whom he regarded as a man who knew his own limitations and kept within them. He said that Norris had formerly been a police officer in one of the villages in the Okehampton valley and that, after an early retirement, he had decided to undertake part-time work at DECL. Williamson's comment had been—"I reckon he got more work than he bargained for."

ROSS CALLS ON HARVEY

As Ross was driving back from Plymouth on the Wednesday afternoon, he tried to make up his mind whether to call on Harvey, who was still living and working in the Okehampton valley. He had in his pocket a copy of a letter Bill Ryles had written to Harvey to ask him if he would see Ross and talk to him about the DECL situation. In addition, he was well aware that one of the few specific instructions the NEPCO management had given him was to find out more about the Harvey incident. Ross doubted that he would be able to find out more than Mr. Whidden had done in his visit to Harvey, but at last he decided to make the call. He knew, however, that gossip in the valley travelled so thoroughly and so fast that there was a strong possibility that Mr. Masterman would hear about his visit and would regard it as a repetition of American subterfuge tactics. Ross therefore determined to tell Masterman frankly, when he saw him on Thursday evening, that he had called on Harvey simply to gather some more information about the administrative details of DECL's early days.

It turned out that the visit to Harvey was hardly worth the trouble. It seemed that Harvey was still on reasonable terms with Mr. Masterman; certainly he was not at all bitter about his dismissal and recognized that it had been largely because of an extended series of disagreements with his superior. He added nothing to what Ross already knew about the first few months of DECL's existence, and his only opinion about DECL was that the company would not succeed and this was why he had not considered going back there.

AN EVENING WITH MASTERMAN

On the Thursday, Ross's final day at Okehampton, he spent most of the time in going over the correspondence files once more, taking notes of critical passages in various letters so that he would be able to substantiate some of the opinions and judgements expressed in his report. In the evening, he drove up to Masterman's large stone country house, which was set in spacious grounds half way up a hill overlooking the entire valley. As he reached the end of the drive, he saw Masterman sitting in the evening sun on one of two garden chairs set on the flagged terrace in front of the house. Masterman suggested that Ross should join him in having a martini, and the two sat making small talk for a while. Ross decided that this was an appropriate moment to tell of his visit to Harvey. He tried to sound as casual as possible in telling Masterman both about the visit and his reasons for making it. As soon as he had uttered a couple of sentences, however, Ross realized he had made a bad mistake. Masterman hardly waited for him to finish before he sat bolt upright in his chair and said with an incredulous look—

"Do you mean you actually went to see Harvey without having the courtesy to tell me first? What kind of behaviour is that? I've come to expect that kind of thing from the Americans, but you—you've had an English education, and I think you've been a disgrace to it."

He paused, and Ross watched him without saying anything. It was obvious that Masterman was with difficulty controlling his mounting anger. Ross felt like a spectator listening to a nuclear test countdown.

"It's disgraceful, absolutely disgraceful. First Jim Whidden goes behind my back. Then Morey makes an ass of himself with Jones and now, to crown everything, they even pick out an Englishman to do their dirty work. You ought to be ashamed of yourself being a pawn in such a game. As for them, they're not even fit to manage a business. Perhaps this is the sort of sly, underhand way in which all business is carried on in the States; but, for goodness sake, people just don't behave like that here. They're a pack of ill-bred people." —Suddenly he broke off and looked at his watch; then he picked up his glass and slammed it down on the table, breaking the stem. "I know what I'll do," he roared, "I've a damn good mind to call them up here and now and tell them what I think of them. It'll be the middle of the afternoon there and it'll wake up Al Nelson. Damn good thing too. And I know what else I'll do. I'll play them at their own game. I'm perfectly sure that they always tape-record their transatlantic telephone conversations so I'll start doing it too. I'll put you on one 'phone, a tape-recorder on the second one, and I'll give them hell on the third. It'll be darn well worth the expense."

Ross felt a strong desire to walk out then and there, but he thought there was a possibility that the evening still could be salvaged if he encouraged Masterman's anger to take its course. "If you feel like that," he said, "why don't you telephone Newark?"

Masterman got up without another word and strode into the house. Ross heard him giving his housekeeper firm instructions about the tape-recorder. Then Masterman motioned him to the telephone in the hall and stomped off himself to the third 'phone upstairs. There was a pause while the transatlantic operator tried to get through to Newark. Then she told Masterman to go ahead. Ross winced and held the telephone away from his ear, hearing Masterman's voice booming all over the house. "Hello, HELLO. Is that you, Al? Well, I'm just calling you up to say that I think you people are a bunch of unethical, under-hand, dishonest businessmen, and I've got Antony Ross on one of my 'phones and a tape-recorder on the other to hear me say that. First of all you go behind my back to try and get Harvey back again, then Morey tries to play his own clever little game with Jones, then you do nothing but complain about our expenses, then you keep trying to tell me how to run a business that's under my nose, then you go ahead and sack six men without telling me and don't pay a hoot of attention to anything that I've got to say on the subject, and now, as if all that wasn't enough, Ross tells me that he's just been to see Harvey and I know damn well it was on your instructions. That's absolutely the final straw—for two pins I'd resign and let the company stew in its own juice."

There was a pause while Masterman drew breath. Al Nelson's slow drawl came over the wire—"Well, I'm certainly sorry you feel like that, Henry, and I'm sure you'll feel differently when you have time to think more about it."

"Think more, be damned!" snorted Masterman. "I know damn well that I think that kind of behaviour stinks and I'm surprised at you for condoning it. You've been a senior officer in the United States Army and you should know better. Well, you can take it from me that I'm just not going to stand any more of it. You people won't do anything I say. You persist in thinking you know better, and as a result you've done nothing that's been any help whatever. The sooner you all learn how to behave, the better."

Ross found it incredible that Al Nelson's voice could still keep its slow, imperturbable, southern drawl in the teeth of such an onslaught. "Well, Henry, I agree there have been mistakes, but I'm sure we can sort them out in a letter or two. You know that we'll do anything we can to help you and I'm sure you'll see it that way tomorrow morning."

"Well, all right," shouted Masterman upstairs, "I'll put the whole damn lot in a letter and see how you like it that way. I've already spent too much time and money talking to you now. Goodbye."

Ross heard the receiver being slammed down and he replaced his own with a sigh. Five seconds later the telephone rang.

"Hello, Okehampton. Your call cost five pounds, ten shillings," said the operator.

Ross heard Masterman reply, "That's all right, operator. It was worth it."

When Masterman came downstairs again he was a changed man. All his anger seemed to have evaporated and he even made a half-apology to Ross for his rudeness. By the end of the evening, he was actually expressing admiration for the way Al Nelson had withstood the blast.

The following morning, Ross called in at DECL just before leaving. Masterman again apologised to him for the previous evening and did his utmost to be pleasant. Nevertheless, Ross grimly reflected as he drove back to London that he was going to have a very difficult time writing his report. "The position I have to assume in no-man's-land," he muttered to himself, "is not an easy one from which to try to explain to both parties that war is hell."

Exhibit 1

NEPCO Sales and Other Relevant Data*

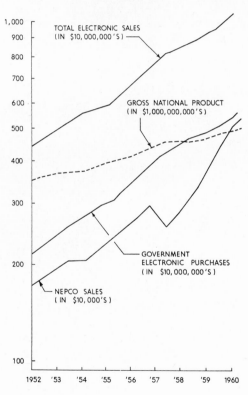

* Sales are plotted exponentially.
Source: *Fortune*, August, 1960; U.S. Government Statistics; NEPCO company records.

Exhibit 2

NEPCO Financial Information

(Figures in $000s)

I. Balance Sheets as of December 31*

	1954	1955	1956	1958	1959	1960	1961
Cash	97	39	43	262	434	589	727
Accounts Receivable	251	402	474	399	578	615	742
Notes Receivable		18	5	6			
Inventory	119	141	201	309	327	405	488
Securities				3	22	22	22
Fixed Assets	259	355	450	588	648	738	873
Depreciation†	139	163	205	328	378	451	538
Net	120	192	245	260	270	287	335
Investments	2	6	6	7	7	8	7
Prepayments				8	9	9	9
Total Assets	589	798	974	1254	1647	1935	2330
Accounts Payable	76	106	141	150	205	224	270
Notes Payable	26		134				
Accruals	30	42	41	80	132	150	180
Taxes Payable		96	45	123	193	219	268
Stock	19	19	19	19	19	19	19
Capital Surplus					6	6	6
Retained Earnings	438	535	594	882	1092	1317	1587
Total Liabilities	589	798	974	1254	1647	1935	2330

II. Sales

	1954	1955	1956	1958	1959	1960	1961
	2070	2445	3000	3195	4490	4875	5850

III. Sources and Applications of Funds

Sources of Funds:§

	1954	1955	1956	1958	1959	1960	1961
Earnings		99	59	288	210	225	270
Depreciation		36	45	123	64	73	87
Sale of Stock					6		

Applications of Funds:

	1954	1955	1956	1958	1959	1960	1961
Fixed Assets		114	98	138	75	90	135
Working Capital		17	6	264	204	208	222
Investments, etc.		4		9	1		

* No balance sheet figures were available for 1957. The sources and applications of funds for 1958 are based on the two-year period.
† It was assumed that depreciation taken during any year would be approximately 10% of the total depreciable assets outstanding at the end of that year. This is believed to have been the case in recent years.
§ In establishing sources and applications of funds, it was assumed that all earnings are retained in the business. This is justified by the fact that taxes accrued in any given year bear a relationship to the amount of earnings transferred to the retained earnings account such as to indicate that these retained earnings were the sole offsetting f [...]

Exhibit 3

NEPCO Organization Chart

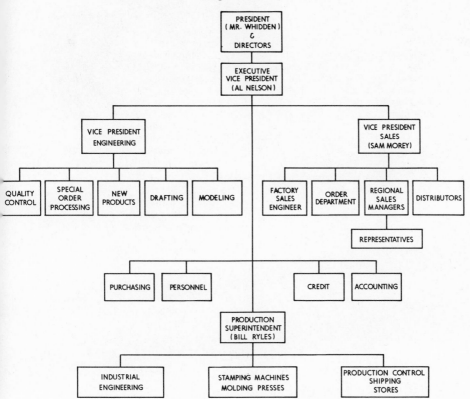

Exhibit 4

DECL Accounts for Period from 24th July 1960 to 31st December 1960
(Figures in Pounds)

I. Profit and Loss Account

Sales		1,416
Stores & Materials consumed	260	
Wages	995	
Salaries	1,061	
Travelling Expenses	589	
Directors' Expenses	94	
Other Expenses	979	
Depreciation	729	
Total Expenses		4,707
Net Loss on Trading		3,291
Add: Charges on		
Formation of Company		534
Total Loss transferred		
to Balance Sheet		3,825

II. Balance Sheet, December 31

Current Assets:		
Cash in hand	1,329	
Accounts Receivable & Pre-		
payments	3,746	
Stock	1,050	6,125
Fixed Assets (less Dep'n.):		
Land & Buildings	9,913	
Plant & Machinery	7,146	
Loose Tools & Eqp't.	601	
Office Equipment	239	
Motor Vehicles	1,205	19,104
Total Assets		25,229
Current Liabilities:		
Bank Overdraft	56	
Accounts Payable &		
Accrued Charges	7,430	7,486
Long-term Loans:		
From NEPCO	5,028	
From NEPCO of		
Canada Ltd.	13,940	18,968
Net Worth:		
Ordinary Shares (2/–)	2,600	
Less: Loss to date	3,825	(1,225)
Total Liabilities		25,229

Exhibit 5

Outline Marketing Plan for DECL Ltd.
(Prepared by Al Nelson, April 1961)

I. PURPOSE

The purpose of this Outline Marketing Plan for DECL is to serve as a basis for the development of *profitable* sales and marketing activity for the DECL organization.

II. BACKGROUND

Prior to June, 1959, NEPCO served the British and European markets by direct export to customers on the Continent. In June of 1959, arrangements were made with Masterman Engineering Ltd., of Plymouth, England, to act as NEPCO representatives in Great Britain. Mr. Jack Turpin was employed by Masterman Engineering Ltd. to act as a full time sales engineer on NEPCO's behalf. Mr. Turpin came to the United States for a period of approximately six weeks to receive training at the Newark factory. During the period July, 1959, through June, 1960, Masterman Engineering did missionary selling by calling on prospects throughout England. The results of these calls produced relatively few sales. The lack of success in this effort can be attributed to several factors. One of these factors was the relatively high price of imported NEPCO products as compared with products produced in Great Britain. Another significant factor was the nationalism expressed on the part of potential British customers. Simply stated the customer said, "We would like to buy from you if you manufacture in this country." Another important factor was insufficient management and administrative supervision on the part of Masterman Engineering and NEPCO. Still another was the narrow outlet for a broad line of products, with a limited number of distribution outlets for the line.

Exhibit 5—Continued

During the summer of 1960 the decision was made to manufacture in England. As a result of this decision, a manufacturing works was purchased at Okehampton. During the latter half of 1960, Mr. Bill Ryles, Manufacturing Engineer from NEPCO, spent a period of approximately six weeks during November and December in setting up the manufacturing facilities at Okehampton and effecting the transformation to electronic production. In March of 1961, there were four punch presses in place and actually turning out stampings of the same kind as manufactured in Newark. During March, 1961, Mr. James Whidden, President of NEPCO, went to Okehampton and further established the manufacturing facility at the British location. A revised price list for the British market was distributed in February, 1961.

III. MARKET

The market for electronic components in Europe as a whole is considerably smaller than that of the United States, due primarily to the smaller sums being expended for electronics by the various governments. However, the rate of future growth of the electronics industry in Europe appears to be greater than that in the United States. In 1961 it is estimated that the total market in countries outside the Communist bloc will be approximately the equivalent of two to three billion dollars. The population of the pro-Western countries is approximately 200 million, which exceeds the population of the United States. Past market research studies have indicated that there is a broad correlation between population and electronic potential in industrialized countries. On this basis the future growth of the electronics industry in Europe would appear to be well substantiated.

The electronics market in England is estimated to be between 5 percent and 10 percent of the U.S. market, that is, between 500 million and a billion U.S. dollars for all types of electronics. This market is strengthened by Commonwealth ties. If England is successful in becoming a member of the Common Market—and there are indications that she is thinking of joining—the future market potential for NEPCO products appears large enough to permit an economic manufacturing unit.

IV. MARKET STRATEGY

The market strategy for NEPCO products in a European environment should be based fundamentally on an engineering approach. Due to the technical nature of the product lines, the marketing focus should be directed primarily to the design engineering influences. Emphasis should be placed on the engineering characteristics and capabilities of NEPCO products in a wide variety of electronic applications.

The marketing strategy should include stress on the fact that products are "made in Britain and manufactured from a European source." The strategy should also include the concept of local availability through distributors.

The marketing image should be one that the products are competitive but the lines should be distinguished by their engineering advantages and quality rather than by price competition with existing national sources.

V. CHANNELS OF DISTRIBUTION

Initially it is conceived that NEPCO products should be made available directly from the DECL works in Okehampton and, as mentioned above, through modern electronic distributors in England and on the Continent.

The possibility of using manufacturers' agents should be considered. However, in such a consideration the problems of multi-layer channels, the availability of technically qualified manufacturers' agents, and adequate margins must be taken into account.

The channels used must also take cognisance of the physical size of territories, transportation, selling customs and techniques of the country concerned.

VI. SALES ORGANIZATION

The sales organization of DECL is conceived initially to consist of a Managing Director of DECL who has an appreciation of the essential sales function and one who is

Exhibit 5—Continued

capable of providing adequate sales engineering support to the sales force. There should be a minimum of one direct factory technical salesman capable of producing adequate sales to cover his own expenses and to produce total sales commensurate with the overall cost of maintaining this salesman on the DECL payroll.

Initially it is believed that a distributor in the London area should be utilized since the bulk of the electronics market in England is centered in the London area and since the works is located some way away from this area. One such distributor, Thames Electronic Distributors Ltd., has already been engaged as an authorized NEPCO distributor in England. It is desirable to add distributors at locations later to be determined, in order to provide better coverage through wider local availability and to avoid dependence on one or two distributors. The factory sales representative should be employed so as to provide support for the distributors, and inherent conflicts between the factory sales engineer and the distributor are to be avoided.

Manufacturers' agents, if used, should be integrated into the total marketing effort so as to support and not conflict with the factory sales organization or the distributor.

Several distributors are considered necessary in any one country or marketing territory.

VII. SALES TRAINING

Sales training has consisted of the orientation which was given to Mr. Jack Turpin when first employed in 1959, his subsequent field experience, and sales literature which has been provided to DECL. In addition, the personnel of DECL have provided training to members of TEDL.

Additional sales training is undoubtedly required to improve the sales ability of personnel already provided with earlier training. Moreover these sales people need further training in depth on established products, and training to make them effective in selling new products which are available. If additional salesmen are added by either the factory or distributors, initial training will, of course, be required for them.

Formal training sessions are needed as well as coaching on field calls.

VIII. ADVERTISING AND SALES PROMOTION

Due to the nature of NEPCO products, it is essential that sales promotion and advertising be carried out on a broad basis. The products are utilized in a wide variety of applications by almost every original equipment manufacturer in the electronics industry. Therefore it is necessary to provide for wide advertising coverage and extensive use of catalogues and product promotions. At the same time, it is essential that this advertising and sales promotion be backed up by competent sales engineering.

The advertising itself could well be directed initially towards getting catalogues into the hands of potential users. Concurrently it appears appropriate to conduct advertising campaigns to secure specific inquires on individual products.

In order to keep the cost of advertising within bounds it will probably be necessary to limit the amount of general exposure and corporate image type advertising. Different types of technical journals might well be used, and advertising should be directed towards the key buying influence, who appears to be the design engineer. The tabloid and general news-type advertising may have a certain usefulness in the earlier stages for announcement-type messages, but the overall advertising programme must be directed to the real buyer or buying influence.

In addition to trade journal advertising, direct mail advertising should be employed as a supplement. A definite and specific programme covering a definitive period should be prepared and executed. Emphasis necessarily should be placed initially on the most important types as outlined above. More detailed and extensive promotions, such as point of sale promotion, can be developed for the most part later.

IX. SALES STATISTICS

Continuing market research and sales data are needed to permit an intelligent and orderly marketing plan to materialize potential into sales.

Exhibit 5—Continued

In order to provide for standards and to measure performance, sales statistics by salesmen, by type of unit, by product, and by customer, must be developed and maintained current.

X. SPECIFIC MARKETING PLAN

Based on this marketing outline and further specific analysis of the DECL market, action is required to develop a specific marketing plan for the remainder of 1961 and for 1962 thereafter. This marketing plan is to be used to provide a clearly defined and orderly approach to securing the maximum possible sales at the earliest date in order to permit the DECL organization to operate on a profitable basis. The marketing plan so developed must also serve as a basis of measuring management and sales performance of those responsible for the profitability of DECL.

.   .   .   .

Exhibit 6

Correspondence between Nelson and Masterman

June 22, 1961

DEAR HENRY:

After receiving your letter of June 14, Mr. Whidden, Bill Ryles, Sam Morey, and I each independently devoted careful thought and consideration to this particular letter. The reason is that we all feel that in one way or another the matters contained in this letter involve the very basic objectives and policies of DECL. There are certain fundamental factors on which there must be full agreement. It is essential that these fundamentals be clearly agreed upon by all of us, and, most importantly, carried out by all of us regardless of where we may be located physically. Therefore the purpose of this letter is to redefine and clarify the basic policies concerning the operation of DECL.

Authority and Responsibility

The ultimate authority for the control of DECL, like any company, rests with its owners. In turn the principal directors of the company have the responsibility for the prudent and profitable operation of the company and the Managing Director of the company has full responsibility to the Board of Directors for his performance. The matter of prerogatives is one which is fully appreciated, and there is no question that appropriate authority must be in the hands of the Managing Director. At the same time, the Managing Director is obligated to carry out the directives of the principal directors and to demonstrate sound judgement in the execution of the duties of Managing Director.

Financial Limitations

Certain financial limits necessarily have been placed on the authority of the Managing Director. The limitations to be complied with are:
  a) Any expenditure involving capitalization requires prior written approval from the parent company;
  b) Operating expense for labour and materials is to be restricted to that directly applicable to salable products.
It should be noted particularly that these financial limitations apply *before* the commitment of funds.

It is the intent of NEPCO that the DECL subsidiary must stand on its own two feet financially. It is our further intent to limit the subsidizing of DECL in the future to the export of a certain number of manufacturing machines and associated capital equipment and to the export of manufactured products from NEPCO stocks. Otherwise DECL is expected to be self-sufficient.

Exhibit 6—Continued

Management

The most important and most urgent need for DECL is a full-time general manager. This need has often been reiterated by all concerned, yet the fact remains that the position is not now filled, nor has it been for some months.

Distribution

The relationship between TEDL and DECL has apparently been subjected to varying interpretations. It is desired that TEDL act as a stocking distributor with its territory throughout the U.K. DECL has the responsibility for sales to other manufacturers, control of factory-distributor operations, and engineering services to all customers including the distributor. The factory salesman shall have the right and the responsibility to sell to anyone, but is expected also to coordinate (but not subordinate) his efforts with those of TEDL.

The matter of how Jack Turpin has been utilized has been a source of disagreement in the past. It is the desire of the parent company that a full-time salesman be utilized in actual direct sales and sales engineering support to customers. Jack Turpin was engaged for this purpose under the agreement made two years ago with Masterman Engineering Ltd. Since there have been virtually no sales, Jack Turpin must be maintained in a full-time selling capacity. It has been the observation of our personnel that Turpin will improve in his job. Unless there are some significant sales, DECL will never be able to stand on its own feet. Although it is fully expected that TEDL can do a good job of selling and that its promotions will be of assistance, the engineering level selling required in the electronics industry can only be done by Turpin to any real degree of success. Inquiries which are directed to the factory can be handled by other personnel in the office, particularly as these individuals gain experience. For detailed technical inquiries, information must be relayed by phone to Turpin who can then contact the customer concerned. By careful planning of his time and by at least occasional work on Saturdays during these early stages of the DECL enterprise, the several demands on Turpin can be handled simultaneously and do not appear excessive.

Absentee Control

It is desired that at the earliest practical time control from the parent be minimised. However, frankly, the controls which have been exercised from Newark have been instituted because of the severe financial demands created by the enterprise. Very honestly, the amount of money put into this venture has exceeded the amount originally conceived by a considerable sum. Furthermore, certain controls have been instituted because of the technical nature of the business and the experience required for operations in such a technical field. Moreover the Managing Director has had a tremendous problem in developing a business of this kind and magnitude in a relatively short period without the help of a general manager. This has placed a great burden on the Managing Director, and the controls instituted have been for the purpose of genuine help rather than for restrictions. What we must insist upon is that we maintain complete control until sufficient profits have been realised to warrant the change in the extent of controls.

Henry, in the somewhat formalised paragraphs above, we have provided you in a forthright manner those major factors in the operation of the business on which we feel there must be absolutely no basic disagreement. The agreement on these fundamentals must be complete, and, most importantly, they must be reflected in the day-to-day actions of all of us and in the results which are forthcoming from these actions. We know that you have done a tremendous amount of work in setting up this company, and you must appreciate that we have contributed a great deal of time and effort as well as really sizeable amounts of money. We simply are not in a position to continue the financial support of the operation at its current level. Accordingly, there must be increased sales on the one hand and reduced expenses, including reduction in payroll, on the other hand.

(*Signed*)
AL NELSON

.   .   .   .

Exhibit 6—Continued

Masterman's Reply

In his reply of June 27, Masterman made four main points:

1. That there were occasions when it was desirable for NEPCO management to seek his advice before they took action;
2. That he was doing exactly what NEPCO required both financially and as regards Turpin;
3. That he now did not think that Turpin would be able to generate the sales required by NEPCO, and that TEDL were very dissatisfied with the state of affairs presently existing because they had neither stocks nor selling material in adequate quantities;
4. That there was an urgent need to advertise for a general manager and that this was the only suitable approach.

Devonian Electronic Components Ltd. (B)*

* Copyright 1963 by l'Institut pour l'Étude des Méthodes de Direction de l'Enterprise, (IMEDE), Lausanne, Switzerland. Reprinted by permission.

ON HIS RETURN to London, Antony Ross spent some time thinking about the situation that had confronted him at Devonian Electronic Components Ltd. on his recent visit there as a consultant to the American parent organization, Newark Electronic Products Corporation. When he was satisfied that he had thought through the problems he wrote the report that follows.

CONFIDENTIAL REPORT TO MR. JAMES WHIDDEN

Subject: Visit to Okehampton plant, July 1 to July 6, 1961

1. *The Present Situation*

Before I begin the body of this report, I feel that I must emphasise that I have endeavoured to be as impartial as possible during my consulting assignment. The instructions which you gave me originally were broad enough to allow me to assume to some extent the responsibility of making the first steps towards improving your present difficulties. Unfortunately these first steps involve criticism of the actions of both sides over the last few months. If you at NEPCO are to accept these criticisms, it is essential that you should be convinced that I have made every possible effort to be unprejudiced.

I'm afraid that a situation has now developed where each side is strongly suspicious of the actions of the other and much resentment and misunderstanding are being generated. It might be useful to summarise briefly what I believe to be the main feelings of the English and American participants.

The feelings held by NEPCO at this point are ones of disappointment and frustration. Although a European subsidiary would only be able to tap a market far smaller than the American one, it was judged originally that a foothold in the European electronics market might be a useful and profitable thing to have. Since you had an apparently valuable contact in England in the form of Mr. Masterman, he was approached initially, I think, with the idea of his engaging a salesman who would ascertain the degree of enthusiasm in England for NEPCO products. This seemed a suitably cautious way in which to begin the project and although few sales were effected, it was felt (see the Outline Marketing Plan) that certain plainly discernible factors were responsible for this lack of sales, and that the most important of these factors could be obviated by manufacturing in

784

Britain. Therefore, DECL was formed under the managing directorship of an enthusiastic Mr. Masterman.

From that point on, it has seemed to the NEPCO management that they have done everything possible to make things easier for DECL and to ensure the success of the English operation. It is true that misunderstandings have occurred with regard to paperwork—in pricing, perhaps, or in the various order and inventory control forms—but these were only to be expected since sheer geographical separation made the starting of an English subsidiary a difficult and complicated business. In the matter of finances, NEPCO have poured a good deal more money into DECL than was originally expected; furthermore, the top people in NEPCO have devoted valuable time—devoted at the expense of the far larger American market—to DECL's problems and no fewer than three Atlantic trips have been made so far by the Americans alone, quite apart from the two made on the English side.

To all these efforts, the English response appears to be disappointing. In fact, there seems in England to be a very serious lack of response to NEPCO's point of view. It is even doubtful if the very urgent need for sales is appreciated fully enough, and the administration at Okehampton seems often to be lethargic or unpredictable in its actions, as well as to betray insufficient realisation of the rate at which money is disappearing into DECL. Furthermore, on top of the rather surprising dismissal of Harvey—who seemed to be a knowledgeable and efficient assistant to Mr. Masterman, there was the difficult Jones incident in which Mr. Masterman's enthusiasm changed almost overnight to inexplicable disapproval and his opinion along with those of the other two Masterman-appointed directors, became ranged against that of Sam Morey who had deliberately spent a good deal of time satisfying himself about the most important facet of any future general manager at DECL, namely, his technical ability.

By the end of June, therefore, the situation, if not yet desperate, was at any rate serious enough to take the drastic action of dismissing the six most recently hired employees in such a way as to impress upon the DECL administration NEPCO's determination to cut expenses firmly until such time as money should materialise from much needed sales.

.   .   .   .

The feelings of those at DECL, on the other hand, are also, rather surprisingly, ones of frustration and a certain amount of righteous indignation. Caring little about the demands of the American market and with eyes only for the success of the English operation, they feel themselves thwarted time and again by the unwillingness of the Americans to look at the problems in the same light as that in which they are seen by those on the spot.

Up to the end of 1960, there was a considerable spirit of cooperation which made light of many of the problems which arose. But in the course of 1961, difficulties began to creep in which have slowly assumed more and more irritating proportions. As far as the actual production was concerned, the first problem was to get the initial machines installed and running; once this had been done, those in the plant began to learn more and more about the machines and their capabilities and there was a definite spirit of enthusiasm. Nevertheless problems have arisen which cannot be solved by enthusiasm alone: the finished pieces have still to be picked by hand from the chippings and this is an extremely slow and tedious business; then, no means other than straightforward drainage has been devised to separate the oil from the chippings and the finished pieces, and there is a good deal of wastage of oil at present because those at DECL feel that they still have not got the right oil for the machines; most important of all, it has so far proved impossible to perform with speed and accuracy all the measurements which are apparently necessary to maintain the quality of the smallest parts, simply because NEPCO cannot or will not get across exactly how and to what extent quality control is maintained in Newark on the parts concerned.

Nevertheless, these problems should not be overestimated, serious as they are, because there seems little doubt that in the plant itself there was, until recently, little dissatisfaction and much good morale. Such ill feeling as now exists among the DECL production workers towards NEPCO is caused by the recent dismissals, which have created a good deal of alarm and despondency.

Far more serious from the standpoint of the NEPCO–DECL relationship are the feelings of Mr. Masterman and the other two English directors and, to a lesser extent, the feelings of Norris. From their point of view, it seems the Americans are doing everything possible to make life difficult and a series of incidents, perhaps of small importance in themselves but very significant when looked at in retrospect, together with the recent dismissals as the final straw, has produced this feeling which is in so much contrast to what the NEPCO management itself thinks. The efforts to persuade Harvey to return to DECL after being dismissed; the dealings of Sam Morey with Jones after a directors' meeting had clearly turned Jones down; the constant letters about DECL expenses which often imply not only recklessness on the part of DECL but perhaps even dishonesty; the refusal to advertise for a General Manager despite the directors' advice; and, most important of all, the recent dismissals which were undertaken summarily and without the advice of the directors in England—all these things led to Mr. Masterman's outburst on the telephone the other day. By now, in fact, it seems almost incredible to the DECL management that the Americans, traditionally supposed to be very fine managers of business operations, can behave in such a way.

These two seriously conflicting points of view have caused a situation in which neither side really believes that the other knows what's best for the company, and the result has been some rather shaky administration of a comparatively simple operation. At the present time, morale at DECL is low and, far worse, sales are low as well. The machines have by now turned out hundreds of thousands of parts, not one of which has been sold because nobody seems to be sure whether these parts are of the required quality. TEDL, as you know, are contemplating sending a strongly worded letter of complaints which, as far as I can see, are justified. Finally, Mr. Masterman himself is rapidly beginning to feel that it is impossible to conduct the administration of the company in the teeth of the American insistence on management from 3,000 miles away; and meanwhile you at NEPCO appear to be getting steadily more concerned at the inability of your English counterparts to appreciate the true nature and urgency of the situation and you are unlikely to be satisfied with anything but sharply increased sales in the near future. In short, DECL looks at the moment to be anything but a promising venture.

2. Analysis of the Problem Areas

A. *Sales.* Naturally, I am not qualified to make many detailed remarks about your sales policy with DECL, but there are some observations which can and should be made on a general level. The lack of sales is clearly at the root of most of DECL's present problems and it is natural that a critical observer should review (as you at NEPCO must have done so often) the developments on the sales side to date, to try and see whether any serious mistakes were made which might yet be remedied.

One's first impression is that there has been inadequate American control and training in the very area where it is needed most. I wish I had some feel for the degree to which technical knowledge is required in order to sell NEPCO products. For it seems to me that it was a mistake to take Jack Turpin, who was not an electrical engineer by training, and expect him, after only a few weeks' indoctrination at NEPCO, to do selling work in England which was up to U.S. standards. For it meant that up to the engagement of TEDL, you were placing a good deal of responsibility for the success or failure of DECL on the shoulders of a single salesman in whom you could hardly have had the required confidence. Furthermore, you were handicapping this one salesman severely by requiring him to sell products manufactured 3,000 miles away and therefore subject to inevitable delays in passage across the Atlantic and through Customs. It may be unfounded, but I have an uneasy feeling that because the potential English market is only a small fraction of the American one, NEPCO, albeit subconsciously, regard it as an easy market to sell to by comparison with the American one and have therefore not devoted adequate time and thought to cracking it open. The tone of the letter from Al Nelson to Mr. Masterman (dated April 3, 1961) which deals with Sam Morey's forthcoming visit is definitely one of optimistic hope that Sam Morey's visit will prove to be something of a panacea to the sales problem.

In contrast to this optimism, I believe that the English market is not an easy one to enter. Not only do gentlemen's agreements and established contacts count for a great deal, but there is also widespread anti-American feeling which has to be countered. I think that only a salesman of high selling ability, considerable experience, and detailed knowledge of his sales line and its uses could be expected to generate enough volume to provide the necessary impetus for DECL.

This last comment brings me back to the subject of Jack Turpin: to judge from the variety of correspondence both to him and concerning him, I gather that NEPCO can hardly have the fullest confidence in his performance. There are constant reminders in the last half of 1960 that results are required urgently, there are even more reminders to this effect in the correspondence files for this year and, of course, there is Sam Morey's visit itself which was again followed by a long list of instructions and exhortations to Turpin. All this would seem to betray a high degree of worry about Turpin which was undoubtedly very justified. Yet on the other side of the question, the fact remains that Turpin is still employed, perhaps because you feel that you have too much invested in him already. It is entirely understandable that you should be keenly aware of the training and experience which Turpin has had selling NEPCO products; yet it must also be remembered that "sunk costs," so to speak, should not be taken into account if you think you can get a better salesman and if you need to do so.

There remains the subject of TEDL who, I understand both from Turpin and Mr. Masterman, are dissatisfied with the service they are getting from NEPCO. In fairness to Turpin, it must be said that if TEDL are feeling this kind of handicap even at this point, one wonders what kind of backing-up Jack Turpin has received over the last eighteen months.

In summary, I feel as strongly as I am able to feel without further information that NEPCO has devoted inadequate planning and effort to DECL's sales programme, at any rate until recently. I fully understand the reasons for this since I am well aware that the demands of the huge American market are incomparably more important to NEPCO. Nevertheless, I assume that at the time you decided to form DECL, you realised that a commitment would have to be made not only in terms of money but also in terms of the skill, knowledge and effort which have gone into building up NEPCO. In other words, a ten-day fire-fighting visit to England is not enough to solve DECL's sales problems, unless they are very superficial ones (which I don't believe they are). What was required—and what probably still is required despite TEDL's presence—is someone on the English side who is a skilful and knowledgeable electronics salesman and who has the trust and confidence of you at NEPCO. Such a person could have sat down at the beginning or the middle of last year and planned a strategy in detail, based on a first-hand and intelligent appraisal of the marketing problems. It is true that the problem of efficient supply would still have required drastic alteration. But at least it would have been flexible, in that it could have been controlled and altered by the man on the spot.

By contrast, as I have already stressed, NEPCO have a salesman in England in whom the officers do not seem to place much confidence and a stocking distributor who, despite the high commission he is being offered, does not seem to have accomplished very much to date. The whole sales effort has been rather patchily planned and controlled from America—and the Outline Marketing Plan is a good example of this patchiness, for it only vaguely states the problems involved in DECL's selling effort and it makes no attempt to give detailed recommendations on how to surmount these problems.

These are unpleasant comments to be faced at this stage of the operation and I would be only too glad if you could soundly refute them with evidence of a sales programme which, right from the start, was soundly conceived and executed. I suspect, however, that their substance cannot be refuted except on the grounds of NEPCO's overwhelming preoccupation with the American market. This is a preoccupation with which I completely sympathise, of course, but it is one which may yet prove disastrous for DECL.

B. Production. In this area also, I shall concentrate only on raising the major questions that my business school training prompts me to ask; for I certainly do not have the knowledge (or the experience) to make any detailed criticisms involving the machines themselves or the way they are being handled.

In the first place, I can't help wondering what would have happened if Jack Turpin had suddenly started acquiring floods of orders back in October or November of last year, and it had become necessary for NEPCO to get DECL producing as many different parts as possible to the required standards within a very short space of time. For under the present circumstances, it has been possible to run the production aspects of DECL on a comparatively leisurely timetable, and the lack of sales has covered up potentially serious shortcomings on the production side.

Here, again, the greatest lack at DECL is that of a man who is familiar with all the aspects of NEPCO's production. I say this for the following reasons:

1. When I was shown around the NEPCO plant, it was stressed that NEPCO manufactured thousands of different parts and that a great many of these parts were in frequent demand. As you know, DECL are at present manufacturing only a few different parts, and Sam Morey's letter to Jack Turpin of May 23 ordered him to concentrate first and foremost on selling the parts currently being produced by DECL. Now it may be that you decided to manufacture first at DECL those parts which you felt you had most chance of selling after you had made a study of the potential English market. I would guess, however, that the parts which are at present being made at DECL are those which are technologically the simplest to make and that this was the main determinant in choosing the parts to make.

   At any rate, it doesn't really make sense that DECL, nine months after starting production, should still be making only a very small number of the full parent company line. I am sure that even with DECL's present limited equipment, it would be possible to make a much wider range of parts and I suspect that the main reason why this has not been done is that no one at NEPCO now knows what the people at DECL are capable of or whether they can attain NEPCO standards in more than a few respects. Therefore, the easiest course is to let the DECL plant continue to pour forth stampings, etc., until the sales situation positively demands that it produce a much wider range of parts. This may well be a sensible decision, but I think it should be made by someone on the spot who knows a great deal more about the production setup both at NEPCO and at DECL than anyone on either side of the Atlantic appears to know at present.

2. Quality control is an aspect of the production process which is very important, of course, to NEPCO. It would therefore seem to be correspondingly important to have a high degree of coordination in this area between NEPCO and DECL. Yet at this point, no one seems sure whether the parts already made by DECL are fit to sell or not—and this is eight months after production has started. The problem is certainly not attributable to lack of competence at DECL as far as measuring is concerned, or even as far as the actual machining is concerned. Rather, the problem lies in the lack of adequate measuring tools and the lack of knowledge of the way NEPCO do it. Furthermore, there is no one, with the possible exception of Jack Turpin, at DECL who can say with authority which tolerances on a particular part are the vital ones to maintain. Here, again,

what is required is someone who knows *in detail* the situation on both sides of the Atlantic.

3. A number of technical problems crop up from day to day, I gather, which no one can answer satisfactorily. The separation of the oil from the chippings has been a problem for a long time, for instance, as you probably well know; as has also the matter of sorting the finished pieces. Many of the problems which come up can be solved over a period of time by the workers at DECL and they say that it is often excellent experience for them to have to do this; but there are problems also which no one at DECL can answer satisfactorily, even at this relatively uncomplicated stage in the Okehampton operation.

4. Finally, not only the production side but also the whole Okehampton operation would benefit from having someone on the spot who knew what was going to happen next and who could make sure that everyone understood what was happening and why it was happening. I refer not only to the dismissals (of which more later) but also to such letters as the one written by Bill Ryles to Harvey on January 11 of this year. In this letter, Ryles said: "We have lined up an ambitious programme for DECL in 1961 and should have a minimum of eight punch presses and molding machines to you by July 30th." Sam Morey on his visit confirmed this number and also the dates on which the machines would be despatched from the States. Yet the last machine was sent on April 15 and since then, not only have no more been despatched, but men have been laid off. You have, of course, a complete right to change your minds and make these latter decisions, but it would cause less doubt and consternation at DECL if someone were on hand to explain the reasons behind the decisions.

C. *General Administration.* Here we come to most of the problems which I think were bothering you when I was in Newark and also those aspects of the Okehampton situation which you felt required an outsider's point of view. For the most part, such comments as I have will concern Mr. Masterman directly or indirectly. Despite his relationship to you, I have decided that to be less than completely frank with regard to my own opinions would do you a disservice. Moreover, I believe that is in keeping with the spirit of my assignment from you.

It was unfortunate that the relationship between yourself and Mr. Masterman was such that he was the natural and obvious man to start up DECL. For Mr. Masterman—as he would now probably admit—is quite unsuited both by training and by temperament to doing the jobs that have been required of him over the last year. I know nothing at all about the decision to form DECL or what was said at the time. It may well be that at that time Mr. Masterman was both enthusiastic and confident of his ability to steer DECL along the right path and that you all saw no reason to doubt this, particularly as it was so convenient for you to have someone whom you knew so well as managing director of DECL.

On the other hand, a cold appraisal of Mr. Masterman's qualifications would not have borne out any optimism on your part, unless at the time you felt that he would be called upon to do very little for DECL. In the first place, his background is heavy engineering, as you well know, and it is in this field that most of his best contacts lie. Secondly, he is a salesman by experience and by temperament, and by all accounts he has been an extremely good one, who has regularly sold each year for the past several years hundreds of thousands of pounds' worth of heavy equipment. He therefore had to transfer part of his attention from a profitable business in which he was selling very heavy equipment of high value to the day-to-day managerial responsibilities entailed in the running of an operation which was turning out parts one thousandth to one millionth the size of those to which he was accustomed, and which at best would have a turnover many times smaller than that of Masterman Engineering Ltd.—at any rate in the first three or four years of its life. Furthermore, Mr. Masterman, 55 at the time, was unlikely to be extremely flexible in breaking new ground.

This is perhaps a somewhat brutal commentary on a decision which must have had far more personal and subtle undertones than I could appreciate. But I am concerned to emphasise that the initial, and almost inevitable, liaison with Mr. Masterman was for this purpose very unfortunate. It led not only to the appointment of Jack Turpin but also to the appointment of Mr. Masterman himself as managing director. These appointments, in their turn, have done much to cause the misunderstandings which have generated so much frustration and lack of confidence on either side of the Atlantic. For over the last few months, you people at NEPCO have clearly felt an ever-decreasing confidence in Mr. Masterman and have consequently taken more and more of the DECL management decisions into your own hands. Meanwhile, Mr. Masterman himself has come to see more clearly than he did originally that he is not exactly the ideal man to run DECL on the spot, despite his considerable selling abilities. Furthermore, to this injury to his confidence is added the insult of having the decisions that he still regards himself as well qualified to make either ignored or taken out of his hands completely.

Before dealing in detail with various incidents in DECL's history over the past year, I am concerned to emphasise one other thing. I spent some time at Okehampton trying to make Mr. Masterman see how you at NEPCO probably visualised the DECL operation. I did my best to point out, in the course of a longish conversation which we had one morning, that NEPCO management was very busy indeed coping with a lucrative market, which was very much larger than a European market could ever hope to be and that as a result you were very often not able to give to DECL all the time and thought which a small subsidiary in a foreign country needs if it is going to survive. In turn, I feel obliged to point out to you some things about Mr. Masterman's present position since I think from some of the remarks that were made to me in Newark, you may be over-emphasising one or two aspects and not giving enough weight to others.

When I was in Newark, remarks were made to the effect that Mr. Masterman was throttling the growth of DECL by maintaining a tight control over everything that went on and by refusing to sanction the appointment of anyone designed to take some of this control out of his hands. I think this is a little unfair. First—and this is rather important—Mr. Masterman is undoubtedly, to use Shakespeare's comment on Brutus, "an honourable man." By this I mean that in his capacity as managing director of DECL he would not think of doing anything which was not in the best interests of the company; the same, I imagine, could be said of Colonel Sykes and Mr. Paton-Jones, and no matter what the relationship of the latter two to Mr. Masterman, I am quite satisfied that each of them would have no hesitation in speaking out against a particular course of action, even if Mr. Masterman had adopted it. Thus I feel that a conspiracy, as it were, between the three of them to keep the company in their pockets is a ludicrous concept. This leaves open the question as to whether their judgement is at fault and in this respect there is definitely a danger that you have underestimated and will continue to underestimate their shrewdness and experience as far as the English scene is concerned. It is true that they all know little about the world of electronics but their ignorance in this area should not necessarily be taken as an excuse for brushing aside their opinions in other areas.

Secondly—and this again is very important—Mr. Masterman definitely has better things to do than spending time at DECL from a strictly remunerative point of view. When I was in Plymouth seeing Williamson, I also called on the managing director of a firm for which Mr. Masterman does a good deal—by no means all—of his sales work. It was told that Mr. Masterman was spending too much time with DECL and that his sales work, and probably his health also, were suffering considerably. I understand also that because Mr. Masterman was not able to devote sufficient attention to his selling activities, Masterman Engineering lost a major client in the early part of this year.

Now all this raises the question—Why does Mr. Masterman persevere with DECL? I confess I find this the most difficult question of all to answer. Undoubtedly the main driving force is a strong sense of loyalty to you personally. Ironically enough (in the light of your feelings about Mr. Masterman and DECL), I think he feels that if he were to resign, it would make things very difficult for you. There may also be some future financial rewards in remaining with DECL and this you would know far better than I. However, I can find no trace of any payment to Mr. Masterman for his services. Incidentally, I would judge that he spends anything from two to six hours a day on DECL business, which is a great deal for a man who is supposed to be running his own business. And when he is treated, as he was in the matter of the dismissals, as a man whose opinion was of virtually no consequence whatsoever, small wonder that he feels the kind of anger and resentment that must have been obvious to Al Nelson on the telephone the other day.

At this point, I must again stress that the above comments are not made from any partial feeling on behalf of Mr. Masterman—(I, too, caught the rough edge of his tongue the other day). I have tried my utmost to be impartial throughout this report and produce some facts as evidence for every opinion in it. The only reason for my making the above comments is that I think they are things that you ought to know as they appear to a disinterested observer.

It remains now to go briefly through one or two incidents and matters which have caused some disagreement between NEPCO and DECL management. These are as follows: the dismissal of Harvey; the disagreement about Jones; the recent dismissals of six people; and the control over expenses.

1. The dismissal of Harvey. I must admit that I am still not entirely certain why Harvey was dismissed. The cause seems to have been a series of incidents rather than one particular one, with the main problem being that Harvey was far too often making decisions on the spot that he simply had not got enough knowledge to make. It is significant that all those to whom I talked who were in a position to know anything about Harvey at DECL tended to approve of Mr Masterman's action. Williamson, for instance, though critical of Mr. Masterman in some respects, seemed to think that he was right in getting rid of Harvey. One must remember that whoever runs the office at Okehampton is in control of the operation for a good part of the day and it is therefore essential that the person concerned should be reliable. After Harvey had quoted, for the third time within a short period, a ridiculous figure for the making of some part or other, it was understandable that Mr. Masterman should have felt a lack of confidence in him. It is true that Harvey was probably not guilty of anything that a competent general manager could not have cured in a short time, but this comment ignores the fact that there was no such knowledgeable general manager *permanently* on the spot. I tend to think that from the standpoint of reliability, you are far better off with Norris, who knows his own limitations full well, and who has complete honesty and much common sense.

The story behind Mr. Masterman's telephone call to Al Nelson the other day is as follows. I had many misgivings about going to see Harvey primarily because I knew it would be almost impossible for me to see him without Mr. Masterman knowing sooner or later that I had done so. It is difficult to exaggerate the speed and thoroughness with which news travels in a valley like the Okehampton one. I knew that if Mr. Masterman found out this way, he would be greatly offended and this would sabotage all good relations if you were to require me to make another trip to Okehampton. Nevertheless, I decided to see Harvey and then inform Mr. Masterman that I had done so, being as casual as possible about the whole business. I told him when I went to dinner with him on the Thursday evening and said that I had gone to see Harvey, not for the purpose of raking over the details of the dismissal, but to acquire more background information about the start-up of DECL of a kind which Harvey would be the best man to provide since he had been constantly on the spot for the first four months of DECL's life.

As I should have anticipated, Mr. Masterman was very angry, despite my full explanation. After a few minutes of strong talk, he decided to call Newark and I encouraged him to do so, feeling that it might be better if his anger were allowed to take its course. So, as you know, he called Al and used the Harvey matter as a peg on which to hang a lot of strong feelings. I should add that by the end of the evening he was again in a good mood and even expressed his admiration for the way in which Al had stood the blast.

After all that, I gained very little information from Harvey, and I doubt very much if I could add anything to what you have already learnt from that quarter. We didn't talk much about DECL but we talked enough for it to be clear that Harvey certainly does not bear Mr. Masterman any great ill will—and this is perhaps a sign that he recognises that there was some justice in his dismissal.

2. **The disagreement about Jones.** The whole Jones business showed clearly many of the weaknesses in the present DECL setup. It showed, above all, that there was no one on this side of the Atlantic in whose opinion the NEPCO management could have permanent confidence. One could say that the basic issue of disagreement between Sam Morey and the three English directors concerned the importance which should have been given to Jones's technical ability. Because the three English directors were quite unable to judge his technical qualifications for the position they naturally judged him on his general behaviour and tried to see what his character was like. In these respects, Jones was found sadly wanting, not only because of his conduct in the directors' meeting itself (conduct of which Williamson disapproved strongly as well as the three directors), but also because on a recent occasion he had drunk altogether too much in Mr. Masterman's presence and had actually been ill over the lunch table in a public place when sitting opposite him. When one considers the fairly narrow criteria by which the English directors judged Jones, it is not in the slightest surprising that they should have turned him down. Sam Morey, on the other hand, being satisfied completely as to Jones's technical ability and knowing that DECL very badly needed someone in everyday charge who knew something about electronics, was naturally disposed to take an optimistic view of Jones's character and to feel that all he needed was a strong guiding hand.

The Jones situation was aggravated by the lack of other possible candidates for the general manager's position. You on your side were far too busy to do anything but hope that the right man would somehow turn up on the English side, and because you were forced to pin so much hope on Jones being suitable, you were naturally very disappointed when he turned out not to be as far as the English directors were concerned. The English directors, on the other hand, regarded the finding of a general manager as being primarily an American responsibility, if I read correctly between the lines of a letter written by Mr. Masterman to Al Nelson on April 19th of this year.

The result was that no one set about finding a general manager in the kind of way that would, I think, have been obvious to you all had you not had so many other demands on your time and thought. Surely once you had decided that a general manager was needed at DECL and you had determined how much you were prepared to pay him, the next step should have been to find out how these things are done in England (and as far as I know, Mr. Masterman is right in thinking that advertising is the best way since I don't think we have any technical employment agencies). Then you could have collected five to ten candidates and would surely have been able to agree on both the character and the competence of one of them, particularly if you personally had coincided your visit with the selection process. I realise that you were reluctant to commit yourselves to the expense of advertising if it could be avoided, but the alternative has been five months of failure to find a general manager, during which time you have not had the flow of experienced information from any aspect of the DECL operation on which alone important decisions could have and should have been based.

I have tried with the above remarks to put the Jones business in its proper perspective, and in particular to show that it has received unnecessary emphasis in your minds because too many hopes were needlessly pinned on Jones. Let me now pass on to make one or two other comments on the matter. I sympathise a good deal with your feelings of bewilderment, because you were definitely led to expect at the beginning that Jones would be very satisfactory to all concerned (see Mr. Masterman's letter to Al Nelson of April 19, 1961: ". . . whilst I have every confidence in Jones. . ."). Jones rather tactlessly took his employment for granted long before he should have done and this is largely what upset the English directors, who strongly objected to someone saying that he would do this and that before he had any authority to give orders. Sam Morey made matters somewhat worse, probably because he felt that you in America would back his opinion against that of the English directors and would appoint Jones regardless. At any rate, I feel that Mr. Masterman is probably correct in thinking that Sam Morey promised Jones the job, even after the directors' meeting on May 12, and, as you can imagine, the English directors were very offended indeed. I wish I could have met Jones if only to satisfy my own curiosity; however, I didn't think it was worth making the attempt to do so. My tentative opinion is that an unreliable general manager, no matter how good he may be technically, is the last thing that DECL should have at the present time, and that most of the evidence points to Jones being unreliable.

3. **The recent dismissals.** Perhaps the less said about these, the better. As you probably well realise by now, your failure to pay enough attention to the opinion of the English directors or to acquaint them thoroughly in writing with the reasons for the dismissals was regarded almost as an insult, and I am a little surprised that all three did not resign there and then after it had been so clearly shown that you had very little respect for their judgement. I arrived at Okehampton to find Mr. Masterman almost beside himself with indignation and I had to agree that you could have been more tactful in carrying out your decision. Yet here again, I sympathise strongly with the American point of view. I realise that you were very concerned over the amount of money being spent at DECL and that you also felt strongly that the English management did not appreciate this. I realise also that you probably felt you had given way to Mr. Masterman—at great cost to yourselves—when you decided not to appoint Jones; and that, as a result, you were in a mood to be thoroughly firm about carrying out your intentions. I think you probably foresaw that if Mr. Masterman and the

other two English directors were consulted about the dismissals, then a long exchange of views would have resulted which would have taken time and money and perhaps got you nowhere. Therefore, in a gesture of semi-desperate frustration, you asserted your authority bluntly, and the fact that you had to do so surely shows that the situation at DECL cannot continue much longer as it is.

I have not, of course, read Al Nelson's reply to the Minutes of the directors' meeting which dealt with the dismissals, so I don't know how much attention was paid to Mr. Masterman's lugubrious comments about the labour situation in the valley. There is a danger that you may not now fully appreciate the kind of community feeling that can exist in a small English valley such as the one of which Okehampton is a part. It is something that should definitely be taken into account, if only because it is advisable to behave in Rome as the Romans do. The problem lies not so much in attracting labour to Okehampton (there seem to be a number of machinists within reach who could be attracted to Okehampton by good wages), as in the tarnish which the company's image will have acquired locally as a result of the dismissals. The locals naturally feel that the company is in danger of being closed down; this, in turn, upsets the present work force and will perhaps prevent you from acquiring good men when you need them. It may also affect the willingness of the National Park Planning Council to allow you to build further if you want to. In short, your action forfeited a lot of good will in the valley. I only hope this doesn't matter in the long run.

4. **The control over expenses.** Under this heading I would like to group one or two small things. It is always sad in a situation where serious misunderstandings have occurred to see how the smallest things thereafter combine to increase the righteous indignation felt on either side. I wonder if you at NEPCO realise the resentment which is generated at DECL by very small matters: e.g., the refusal to allow a cleaning woman at 2/6 an hour, coupled with a willingness to pay £1,500 for a piece of land that may never be needed; Sam Morey's querying of his Savoy bill and Al Nelson's comment that the bill was of surprising proportions; the complaints at the proposed directors' fees (complaints which were justified, I think); the querying of expense statements, which is interpreted almost as an accusation of dishonesty; the fact that Sam Morey on his sales visit promised gauges that were never sent; etc., etc. All these things have caused irritation and my mention of them is not intended as criticism of NEPCO but merely as examples of how far each side's appreciation of the other's point of view is lacking.

D. *Summary.* You have got yourselves into a difficult situation with DECL and to get out of it I think you must be prepared to supply a lot more money and time before the company is operating on a profitable basis. The root of the trouble lies in the preoccupation of the NEPCO management with the American market to a degree which has not allowed DECL to get the planning and foresight which the parent company should have exercised in starting a subsidiary in a foreign country—and England is sufficiently different from the U.S., despite the common language, to be called "foreign." The whole point of starting a subsidiary operation in a foreign country is that it enables the parent to transplant some of its skill and manufacturing experience to an environment in which these qualities will be sufficiently unique to earn profits. Therefore two major problems present themselves: the first is that of transferring the parent's skill and experience to the subsidiary, and the second is that of adapting them to meet the demands of a different environment. Many parent companies solve the first by making a sacrifice that you have not been prepared to make and sending a member of their top management to start up operations in person; and they solve the second temporarily by keeping him there for a year or two. By that time it is hoped that the subsidiary will be beginning to earn profits and that someone will have been trained sufficiently well in the ways of the parent company to be able to manage the subsidiary from that point on with the full confidence of the parent company.

By contrast, you at NEPCO have tried to mold DECL around two people whose qualifications for the task in hand were tenuous when judged from a coldly practical point of view. And you have tried to communicate NEPCO's skill and experience to the necessary degree by having Jack Turpin in Newark for a few weeks, by a few conversations with Mr. Masterman, by sending Bill Ryles over at the outset for six weeks, by a couple of fire-fighting visits from yourself and Sam Morey, and by a stream of correspondence—all this being effected over a long period of time. Thus in DECL's life to date there has at no stage been anyone who possessed simultaneously: (a) complete authority to direct DECL; (b) complete knowledge of the skill and experience which NEPCO hoped to bring to the English market to obtain a share of it; and (c) a day-to-day knowledge of the English environment as it related to DECL.

The first of these has been divided and this has not been very satisfactory. The second is possessed by NEPCO management who, however, do not possess the third and are therefore unable to foresee problems and take steps to meet them constructively, or to find the root of troubles that arise. No one in England has the third, with the possible exception of Jack Turpin, who hasn't got any authority to speak of. Mr. Masterman does not have the time to acquire the third properly.

This analysis is, of course, somewhat oversimplified, but I trust that it gets the point across that you are at present not giving yourselves a fair chance to succeed with DECL. It remains to consider briefly some possible courses of action now open to you. I feel myself unable to make any positive recommendations since I do not possess (b) and (c) above to the necessary degree; however, you have clearly a number of alternatives before you at this point and some of these are worth comment.

1. Obviously you can continue as at present in the hope that the lack of sales is due more to a slump in the English economy than to any fault of DECL's. But I don't think you can afford to drift indefinitely in this way and, as I said above, if sales do improve I have my doubts that the production side of DECL will be able to cope smoothly without a good

deal more help from NEPCO. Finally, the present situation is thoroughly unsatisfactory as far as Mr. Masterman is concerned, both from your point of view and his. Even if nothing else changes, Mr. Masterman's workload and responsibility at DECL must be cut down. Therefore:

2. You can stick to your original course of action and get a general manager as soon as possible, while leaving everything else as it is. This would certainly cut down Mr. Masterman's workload and, provided you pick a man of good experience, it should take care of any production problems that arise. However, you will still not have a man who possesses (a), (b) and (c) above. Even if you make the man you select as general manager a director to give him authority over Jack Turpin and the same status as Mr. Masterman, you will have to know him very well or else have great confidence in him to give him (a). Frankly, I doubt if an English appointee will know enough about NEPCO to avoid his spending two or three months in the United States. You may well think that a general manager need not be given as much power as I have suggested, but I am inclined to think that the more knowledge and authority you can concentrate in the hands of one person only, the better chance you will have of managing DECL efficiently and well, at any rate initially.

3. A third alternative is to send either Al Nelson or Sam Morey or some other member of NEPCO management over for an extended period of time. This will almost certainly not be easy to do, even if someone were ready to go. It is probably the best course of action, but, even so, it would not guarantee DECL's future profitability and anyhow I doubt if you care about DECL's success to the point where you would jeopardize the management of the American concern in this way.

4. You can also, of course, cut your losses (taking a pessimistic point of view) and close down, or

5. You might be able to come to some arrangement with an English or an American competitor who would be glad to spare the time and help to run DECL. Needless to say, I am instinctively against these last two courses of action.

I think you must now decide how much you care about the success of DECL and how much financial risk you are prepared to run on its behalf. You must also take some action in the near future with regard to Mr. Masterman since we have at present the ridiculous situation that he is spending a large amount of time with DECL which he can ill afford, doing work which is far from being fully appreciated, in America anyway. I think he would be happy to see some qualified person take his place as managing director. If the change were tactfully done, and if he were retained as just a director, he would certainly be earning his keep in a way more satisfactory to all concerned. Incidentally, his influence and knowledge of the local situation in the valley should not be underestimated. He has done very well with the National Park Planning Council and he is a powerful ally to have when fighting the English Customs authorities.

I hope you will not resent those passages in this report where I have been somewhat critical of NEPCO management of DECL. I have deliberately not pulled any punches, since I think I was the only person in a position to deliver some of them at all. I sympathise very much with your problems—running a successful company like NEPCO with a small management is very much a full-time job, and I realise that by now DECL has assumed the status of a rather irritating nuisance which no one seems to have the time to deal with properly. Nevertheless, if you are to avoid further severe financial drain and get a hope of earning a return on your investment, matters cannot continue to drift.

.　　.　　.　　.　　.　　.　　.　　.　　.　　.　　.　　.　　.

Having finished his report, Ross despatched it to Newark with some trepidation.

~~~~~~

Godfrey L. Cabot, Inc.

~~~~~~

BETWEEN JANUARY, 1957, and August, 1958, Thomas D. Cabot as president of Godfrey L. Cabot, Inc., was obliged to make several major decisions. Each decision required weighing and harmonizing so far as possible various interests with a claim on Mr. Cabot's loyalty: (1) the short-run profitability of the company itself, (2) its long-run welfare, (3) national security and the foreign policy objectives of the State Department, the Commerce Department, and the Treasury, (4) the well-being of the foreign countries in which the company had plants and also that of other friendly countries, and (5) what might be called the serenity of Mr. Cabot's own conscience.

Godfrey L. Cabot, Inc., through subsidiaries in the United States and foreign countries, was the world's largest producer of carbon black, supplying 25 percent of free world demand. Cabot, together with its two largest competitors, Columbian Carbon Company and the United Carbon Company, were estimated by *Petroleum Week* (issue of May 9, 1958) to account for two thirds of total world production of all types of carbon black. Among other producers were: Phillips Chemical Company (a subsidiary of Phillips Petroleum); Continental Carbon Company (controlled by Continental Oil Company); J. M. Huber Company; Sid Richardson Carbon Company; and Thermatomic Carbon Company (a subsidiary of Commercial Solvents Corporation). Carbon black was a material of strategic importance as an essential ingredient in the production of rubber for tires.

The major specific decisions which Mr. Cabot, together with his colleagues, had to make, and the general circumstances surrounding them, were the following:

1. January, 1957. Whether to build a carbon black plant in India. The Indian government wanted it. There were reasons to believe that Russia or one of its satellites might build one if Cabot did not. The Indian government had actually had negotiations with Romanian technicians to this end.

2. February, 1957. Whether to permit the Cabot Canadian subsidi-

800

ary to sell carbon black to the Soviet Trade Commission. At that time it was legal for Canadian firms, including U.S. subsidiaries, to sell this product to Russia but not for U.S. firms to do so. The Soviets were anxious to buy.

3. May, 1958. Whether to license the Russians to produce carbon black by the Cabot processes.

4. July, 1958. Hitherto, the sale to Russia of U.S. manufactured carbon black had been prohibited, but by the summer of 1958 the Department of Commerce was considering a change in policy to permit U.S. firms to make such sales. This proposed change was under consideration by the government, at least in part, as a result of pressure from U.S. carbon black companies which had no foreign subsidiaries. Several U.S. companies, including Cabot, were asked by the Department of Commerce to express their views on the matter. What position should Cabot take?

It should be pointed out that in 1957–58 some carbon black was being made in Russia. Mr. Cabot said the amount, however, was inadequate and the quality inferior to that made in the United States or by Cabot overseas subsidiaries.

Mr. Cabot had many public interests, and had worked for the government in several capacities. He had served, for example, as director of the Office of International Security Affairs, Department of State, in 1951 and as consultant, Special Mission to Egypt, in 1953. He also had served as director of the Committee for National Trade Policy and with the Committee for Economic Development.

Mr. Cabot's attitude toward world affairs was expressed in a statement to the owners and officers of the company in early 1958 when, among other things, he said: "I cannot fail to recognize the present danger to the free world in which our society may be directly threatened. Our system of individual choice is being challenged by a system of state compulsion. The one responsibility which must transcend in importance all other objectives of all of us is to maintain the strength and leadership of the free world. In this we must be resolute, being fully prepared to sacrifice whatever it takes, and following only that leadership which clearly distinguishes the important from the less important, and puts first things first."

Some information about the company itself, about others in the industry, and about the industry's products and processes follows. Then the specific issues which the Cabot management had to resolve are amplified.

BACKGOUND INFORMATION, GODFREY L. CABOT, INC.

Godfrey L. Cabot, Inc., produced products other than carbon black and engaged in other activities, but carbon black was much the largest item in total domestic sales, which were currently in the range of $60 million. Total assets employed by the parent company and its foreign and domestic subsidiaries were about $70 million. The company had a history of profitable operations and was in good financial condition.

The domestic activities, other than carbon black manufacture, included: (a) oil and gas activities—exploration, production, and distribution; (b) the fabrication and sale of oil well equipment; (c) the processing, manufacture, and sale of minerals and chemicals; and (d) the manufacture and sale of industrial carbon products. Moreover, the company was part owner of the Texas Butadiene and Chemical Corporation.

The company had four carbon black plants in Texas and three in Louisiana, all operated through its subsidiary the Cabot Carbon Company. Through other subsidiaries the company operated a carbon black plant in Canada, one in England, and one in France.

Members of the Cabot family had begun carbon black production in 1882 when Dr. Godfrey Lowell Cabot and his older brother, Samuel, built a small carbon black plant at Buffalo Mills, Pennsylvania. Five years later Dr. Cabot bought out his brother's interest. He operated the company as a proprietorship until 1922, when it was incorporated under the name Godfrey L. Cabot, Inc. The company had continued to be closely held and family dominated.

Almost from the beginning the company had engaged in export trade. After World War II, company officials decided that the great demand for carbon black in foreign markets could best be served by foreign plants. Consequently, Cabot Carbon Ltd. was formed and started production in 1950 at Stanlow, Ellesmere Port, England. In 1951, Cabot Carbon of Canada, Ltd., was formed, and a carbon black plant was built at Sarnia, Ontario. Cabot France, S. A., was incorporated in 1955 and began production in the summer of 1957.

In 1957–58 Cabot was more active in foreign production of carbon blacks than were its competitors. One competitor, Columbian Carbon Company, owned a part interest in a plant in Brazil. Two other competitors, Phillips Petroleum Company and United Carbon Company, licensed foreign producers to use their production processes and know-how. In addition, United owned jointly with Cabot a company that was building a carbon black plant in Australia.

THE CARBON BLACK INDUSTRY

Carbon black (normally referred to as "black" in the industry) was an essential component of automobile tires because of its unique ability to increase rubber's resistance to abrasion and ultraviolet light. Each tire produced in the free world in 1957 contained beteween four and five pounds of carbon black. Natural rubber required 35 pounds and synthetic rubber 50 pounds of black for each 100 pounds of rubber. In fact, 90 percent of the more than 2 billion pounds of black produced in the free world was used to toughen rubber; the other 10 percent was used in a variety of products including printing inks, paints, stains, lacquers, tints, and dyes.

Carbon black, really a form of soot, was produced by burning a flame with a limited supply of oxygen. The exact theoretical nature of the combustion process was not known, but American firms had learned to control the combustion process so that the size of the soot particles could be varied within a range of a fine particle of 50 Å. in diameter to a very coarse particle 5,000 Å. in diameter. (An Å. is one abbreviation for an Angstrom unit, which is 1×10^{-8} cm or about 4/billionths of an inch.) Only carbon black of the quality produced in such a carefully controlled process could be used satisfactorily in compounding rubber for automobile tires.

Originally, black suitable for use with rubber could be made only by burning natural gas. At first the oxygen supply was limited by impinging the flame against long channels of metal, hence the name then used, "channel black." Later the oxygen supply was limited within a furnace, and the end product was called "furnace black." In 1945 a petroleum company developed a satisfactory process for creating carbon black by burning oil in a furnace with limited oxygen. Other companies including Cabot later developed and patented their own processes for producing oil blacks. In 1958 the oil furnace blacks were of better quality and had a larger share of the markets than the gas furnace blacks. From two to four pounds of black could be produced from one gallon of oil. The oil raw material used was an aromatic residual cut of crude oil which had to conform to rigid specifications in order to produce carbon black of the desired quality.

Carbon black had to be produced in a round-the-clock process. Production quantity could be controlled only by limiting the number of economic units which were in operation at any one time. One unit would produce 25 to 30 million pounds of carbon black annually. All United States companies in the industry were believed to have a great deal of excess capacity.

In the carbon black industry, competition on the basis of quality and service was intense. The major companies allocated substantial proportions of earnings to research programs designed to improve constantly the quality of their blacks and to develop new blacks and new applications for the product. Price changes were infrequent. Competition and technical improvements tended to keep prices down in the face of rising costs.

Exhibit 1

Estimated Carbon Black Shipments from Free World Countries, 1957

Country	Pounds (In Millions)
United States	1,800
Great Britain	215
Germany	88
Canada	50
Japan	30
Belgium	4
France	3
Italy	1
Total	2,191

Source: Godfrey L. Cabot, Inc.

Exhibit 1 shows estimated shipments in 1957 of carbon black from free world countries.

In 1957–58 the price of carbon black exports was based on the free alongside ship (f. a. s.) Gulf port price plus the cost of freight, insurance, and other export expenses. Foreign competitors also sold carbon black at a price very close to the Gulf port price plus the cost of shipping from a U.S. Gulf port. The Gulf port price for black ranged from 5.25 cents per pound for very low quality blacks to $1.77 per pound for extremely high quality blacks for special paint applications.

CANADIAN OPERATIONS

Cabot Carbon of Canada, Ltd., was the only company in Canada producing carbon black suitable for rubber reinforcement, and it supplied nearly all the oil furnace black consumed in Canada. The company's plant had been constructed originally with a capacity in excess of the current expected needs of Canadian industry. In 1956, however, Canadian needs had approached the capacity of the plant and Cabot had added another economic unit. This brought annual Canadian capacity to 60 million pounds of oil furnace black. Canadian industry in 1957 was consuming carbon black at a rate of slightly more than 40 million pounds a year, but the company estimated that by the early 1960's Canadian industry would require 60 million pounds annually.

The addition of the extra unit increased the original $3,380,000 investment in fixed assets to an undepreciated value of $4,700,000. The total investment in Sarnia operations had been increased from $4,300,000 in 1953 to approximately $6,300,000 in 1957, and Cabot was in a position to supply the entire Canadian demand for oil furnace blacks.

Cabot officials believed that, on the whole, the Canadian government was pleased to have this foreign investment in Canadian industry. They had been disturbed, however, by a speech made early in 1957 by Mr. C. D. Howe, Canadian Minister of Trade. Mr. Howe had spoken before both the Canadian Parliament and a United States commercial group in Chicago. In his speech Mr. Howe stated that Canada had three objections to the way in which United States firms then were operating in Canada: (1) Canadian nationals did not have enough opportunity for advancement in such firms, (2) Canadians were not given an opportunity to invest in them, and (3) the United States companies exerted too much control over the import-export operations of their Canadian subsidiaries.

RUSSIAN ATTEMPTS TO PURCHASE CARBON BLACK

Representatives of the Russian Trade Commission first approached the Cabot Canadian subsidiary with reference to the purchase of carbon black in February, 1957. At about the same time they also got in touch with the Cabot British subsidiary, another British producer of carbon black, and many United States and European traders who could act as intermediaries in Russian carbon black purchases. These traders began at this time to call both the foreign subsidiary companies and foreign competitors for price quotations on carbon black to be sold to Russia. About 5 million pounds of a common grade of carbon black used in rubber compounding, with Gulf port price of 8.85 cents a pound, appeared to be involved.

When Mr. P. H. Delacour, a Canadian and vice president and director of the Canadian subsidiary, first learned of the inquiries by the Russian Trade Commission, he at once informed Canadian trade authorities. They advised him that they would like Cabot Carbon of Canada, Ltd., to make the sale but that Mr. Delacour should first inform his parent company about the matter. Mr. Delacour immediately telephoned his superior in the parent company, Mr. David D. Cochrane, vice president for foreign operations, who then discussed the Soviet inquiry with the president and other senior executives of the company.

In discussing the Russian inquiries, the head of the Cabot legal department said it was his opinion that the Canadian firm legally could sell to Russia. He reported that the Commerce Department of the United States maintained a positive list of items which United States firms could not sell to Iron Curtain countries. The list was composed of two sections: Items on the A list could not be shipped to the Soviet Union by United States companies or their foreign subsidiaries; items on the B list could not be shipped to the Soviet Union by United States companies, but they could be sold and shipped by foreign subsidiaries controlled by United States firms. In February, 1957, carbon black was on the B list. An administrative decision, however, could shift an item very quickly from one list to another. Treasury regulations prohibited sales of any item to Red China or North Korea but did not affect other Iron Curtain countries.

Mr. Allen, executive vice president of Godfrey L. Cabot, Inc., telephoned an old classmate of his who was then in the Commerce Department and responsible for export licensing of United States firms. Mr. Allen informed him of the situation and inquired as to his views. This official said: "You probably could legally sell to Russia." Mr. Allen received the impression, however, that his friend did not approve of such a course.

Mr. Thomas D. Cabot, the president, gave thought to several additional factors. He wondered whether by selling to the Russians he would embarrass his brother, John Cabot, who was in the United States diplomatic corps. He thought that the big U.S. rubber producers might object to the idea of selling carbon black to the Russians. He also felt that certain people in his own company might not like the idea of trading with the Soviet Union. And he thought it possible that Canadian stevedores might strike rather than handle products sold to the Russians.

On February 27, 1957, Mr. Cabot instructed Mr. Delacour to refuse to sell carbon black to the Russians.

REAPPRAISAL

Mr. Cabot, however, was not completely satisfied with this decision. Personally, he began to think that it might be a good idea to sell carbon black to the Russians. Refusal to sell perhaps would encourage them to develop their own process for manufacturing a satisfactory grade of carbon black. He also had estimated that trade with Russia could easily increase the Canadian company's net profits by 10 to 20 percent a year.

Mr. Cabot called several of his friends and acquaintances in various government posts to find out what United States policy actually was on trade relations with Russia and their own opinions as to his responsibilities as a citizen. No definite policy statement was made by any of the officials called by Mr. Cabot, but only one, a retired admiral, expressed direct opposition to the contemplated trade. When asked if Cabot should sell carbon black to the Russians, the admiral said: "It's apparently legal for your Canadian subsidiary to sell to the Russians, so you'll have to let your conscience be your guide. But I don't see how anyone with any conscience could do it!"

Although rather vexed at not being able to get a definite policy statement on trading with Russia, Mr. Cabot was sympathetic with the situation in Washington. Because of his previous experience in government appointments, he felt he understood many of the political and administrative problems faced by individuals in government posts. Mr. Cabot believed that clear policies on certain controversial political issues were impossible to formulate without splitting a political party in two. Nor could career civil service employees be expected to denounce what they believed to be the official policy or to formulate a policy themselves. In Mr. Cabot's opinion: "The voice of a democratic government speaks with many tongues."

On March 28, 1957, Mr. Cabot held a meeting in Boston that was attended by certain other executives of Godfrey L. Cabot, Inc., as well as by the head of each foreign subsidiary. The Russian proposal was one of the primary topics of this meeting. By this time Cabot executives realized that Russia was receiving shipments of carbon black from British competitors and a West German firm licensed by Cabot to produce certain carbon blacks.

During the course of the discussion, Mr. Cabot called Mr. Sinclair Weeks, Secretary of Commerce, and asked for his views as to what Cabot's responsibility as a citizen actually was in the matter. Mr. Weeks, formerly a Boston businessman, was a personal friend to Mr. Cabot.

During the conversation Mr. Weeks pointed out the difference in the A and B classifications on the Commerce Department's positive list. But Mr. Cabot insisted that his interest went beyond the legalities involved. His company of course would observe the laws and regulations. What he wanted to know was what course of action would be in consonance with national policy and the public interest. Finally, Mr. Weeks said that if it were his company he probably would sell to the Russians. Mr. Cabot asked Mr. Weeks to repeat his views in a letter. Mr. Weeks in reply sent the following letter.

Mr. Thomas D. Cabot
Godfrey L. Cabot, Inc.
77 Franklin Street
Boston, Massachusetts

DEAR TOM:

After your telephone call of March 28, I checked with my people with regard to the questions you raised concerning regulations covering the export of carbon black to Eastern Europe.

The following statements summarize the points at issue:

1. The Bureau of Foreign Commerce is not issuing export licenses for the shipment, directly or indirectly, to these destinations. As you are no doubt aware, the Department of State is conducting discussions with Poland at the present time, and if there is any change with regard to this country such change would be announced to the public.

2. Exports of carbon black, indigenously produced, from other countries to Eastern Europe are not prohibited by any agency of the United States Government, whether or not the foreign exporter is a United States firm.

I trust that the above answers the questions which you had in mind. If there are any further points on which you need assistance, please do not hesitate to call upon me.

Sincerely yours,
(*Signed*) SINCLAIR WEEKS
Secretary of Commerce

Mr. Cabot then asked Mr. Delacour to find out whether the Russian Trade Commission was still interested in purchasing carbon black. The Trade Commission reiterated its interest, and Mr. Delacour then began price negotiations. The Russians indicated their willingness to purchase approximately 5 million pounds of carbon black at a price based on the Canadian domestic price plus charges for transportation and insurance. (The Canadian domestic price was higher than the U.S. price.)

While Mr. Delacour was negotiating with the Russians, Mr. Cabot had his vice president in charge of domestic sales sound out the attitude of the big U.S. rubber makers. The vice president reported that in his judgment these producers would not react unfavorably to trade with Russia, and that, in fact, some of them already were selling synthetic rubber to Russia.

While these various inquiries and negotiations were in process, relations between the United States and Canada were jolted by the suicide of E. Herbert Norman, the Canadian ambassador to Egypt, following his accusal as a Communist spy by the counsel for the Internal Security Subcommittee of the U.S. Senate. The Canadian authorities, although admitting that Mr. Norman had associated with Communists during his student days, denied he was a spy. The U.S. government tried to make clear that the views expressed by the subcommittee's counsel had no official standing. Nevertheless, on April 4, 1957, Norman committed suicide. Canadian officials reportedly blamed the suicide on overwork and depression arising from a feeling of persecution by the United States. Cabot executives were disturbed by the entire incident.

On May 31, 1957, Cabot Carbon of Canada, Ltd., with the approval of the parent company agreed to sell carbon black to the Soviet Union. During the remainder of 1957 substantial shipments of carbon black were made to Russia under the May 31 contract and under a second contract executed in July, 1957. Total shipments to Russia accounted for over 10 percent of the company's 1957 business. Sales to the Russians increased and in 1958 amounted to over 15 percent of the company's total shipments.

In May, 1958, the Soviet Trade Commission again approached Mr. Delacour and asked that Cabot license the Russians to produce carbon black by the Cabot processes. Such licensing would reveal U.S. production secrets to the Russians, and Mr. Cabot did not believe this should be allowed. However, he was certain the Russians must be seeking a license agreement with Cabot's competitors.

As stated earlier, during the summer of 1958 the Department of Commerce was considering a change in policy so as to permit sale of U.S. manufactured black to Russia, and the department had asked Cabot and other producers to express their views in the matter.

On August 15, 1958, Godfrey L. Cabot, Inc., complied with the request of the Commerce Department. The company did this through a letter prepared by Mr. Francis W. Peabody of its foreign operations department and addressed to Mr. Leigh Brite of the Department of Commerce, with whom Mr. Peabody previously had discussed the question. This letter expressed the considered views of Mr. Cabot and other company executives. Excerpts from the letter follow:

Mr. Leigh Brite, Assistant Director
Producers Equipment Division
Bureau of Foreign Commerce
U.S. Department of Commerce
Washington 25, D.C.

DEAR MR. BRITE:

Last Friday I had an opportunity to discuss with you the difficult position in which my company finds itself due to inquiries being made by delegations from Iron Curtain countries which are interested in obtaining licenses, patents, and know-how with respect to our oil furnace carbon black processes.

You will recall our position is that while it is in the best interests of the United States for American carbon black producers to ship oil furnace carbon blacks to Russia and the Satellites, it does not appear wise to conclude agreements which will make it possible for these Communist countries to produce the types of black in question. In brief, we can always stop shipments of carbon black but once the know-how has been exported it is gone forever. Nevertheless, if it is to be the policy of the Government of the United States that this sort of technical information may be made available to Communist countries, we want to know about it for competitive reasons.

. . . .

Although, of course, I am not familiar with the terms of the license arrangements made by our competitors, I think we can assume that none of the foreign licensees can assign their processes to third parties. If this is the case, we can conclude that unilateral control on the part of the United States Department of Commerce would be effective and go on to consider the value of the processes and know-how to Communist countries.

We, of course, have no idea how much carbon black is made behind the Iron Curtain but we do know that a significant quantity of a rather inferior quality has been made in Rumania for some time. Made from natural gas, it sometimes is offered in the world market where it finds some favor because of exchange difficulties but in no case is it considered equivalent in quality to either the gas or oil carbon blacks made in accordance with American techniques.

This low opinion of the product is apparently concurred in by Communist technicians because in 1957, 13,500,000 pounds of oil furnace blacks were shipped to the U.S.S.R. Furthermore, a recent Soviet technical article, after discussing various Russian methods of making carbon black, says:

"The principal task in the future development of the carbon black industry will be the organization of the production from oil of furnace blacks of the type of the foreign blacks, Vulcan 3 and Philblack B, which are likewise produced by combustion of oil in furnaces."

The paper then goes on to discuss the importance of and the need for automation in the Soviet carbon black industry, a step which, of course, was taken years ago in America. Finally, as an indication that our techniques are of real value, I can tell you that within the last several months delegations from Rumania, Poland, and Russia have all been actively seeking the licenses and know-how which represent years of research and development in this country.

To sum up, the most advanced techniques and processes have been developed in this country and are the property of United States corporations. Since this would seem to give your Department effective unilateral control, we urge that this be exercised, believing as we do that while it is in the interest of this country to export the carbon black produced, it is not, at the present time, wise to permit the licensing of patents and know-how to Communist countries.

Very sincerely,
GODFREY L. CABOT, INC.
(*Signed*) FRANCIS W. PEABODY
Assistant to Vice-President
Foreign Operations

INVESTMENT IN INDIA

Meanwhile, Mr. Cabot had been trying to work out a solution to the problem of carbon black production for India. The Indian government wanted a carbon black plant in India. Mr. Cabot had gone to India in January, 1957, to investigate. His initial opinion was that since the carbon black requirements of India were small (U.S. firms exported 7.5 million pounds of black to India in 1955), it would not be sound economically to build a plant there. After a few preliminary talks with Indian officials, he became even more convinced of this, and negotiations soon drifted to a standstill.

However, during his visit to India and during stops in other countries on the same around-the-world trip, Mr. Cabot had discussions with executives of rubber companies with operating subsidiaries in India, and these executives pressed him to build a black plant in India. They thought the Indian government either would build a plant itself or invite the Romanians to build one if Cabot did not agree. They pointed out that neither the Indians nor the Romanians ever had produced a high-quality black, but that they were certain the Indian government would prevent further imports of black as soon as a black plant was built in India.

At a U.S. embassy social reception during his visit in India, furthermore, certain embassy officials told Mr. Cabot they wished his company would construct a black plant in India. These official representatives of the United States asked Mr. Cabot to get in touch with the Indian officials again.

Mr. Cabot again called on the Indian officials. The Indian Minister of Trade suggested that if Mr. Cabot did not want to organize a subsidiary and build a plant himself, then he should grant a license to manufacture black with Cabot processes to an Indian manufacturer. Mr. Cabot rejected this proposal because of the special, prohibitively high taxes which the Indian government placed on profits from license agreements. The Minister of Trade then suggested a joint venture with an Indian industrialist, Mr. Lalbhai.

Mr. Lalbhai happened to be in town at this time, and Mr. Cabot agreed to meet him. After talking with Mr. Lalbhai and reviewing his record, Mr. Cabot was satisfied that he was a competent industrialist and probably would be a good partner.

The two men eventually worked out a potential arrangement with the following terms: Godfrey L. Cabot, Inc., would receive a license fee, determined by the volume of black produced by the Indian subsidiary, for the technical and engineering services with which Cabot agreed to provide the new company in the future. As compensation for its contribution of patents and know-how developed as a result of its previous experience in the business, Cabot would receive a part of the equity without cash cost. The remainder of Cabot's equity would be purchased on the same cash basis as the investment by Mr. Lalbhai.

After this tentative agreement had been reached, Mr. Cabot asked the Indian government for a promise not to nationalize the company if it were formed. The government representatives would not give this guarantee. Then Mr. Cabot asked for assurances that in the event of nationalization his company would be allowed to withdraw in dollars the value of its Indian investment. Again the Indian government would not give assurance. Mr. Cabot, however, tended to minimize nationalization risks.

Mr. Cabot also tried to get a promise that the Indian government would not raise tariffs on raw materials imported to make carbon black nor require the company to use local raw materials if it believed such materials would produce a product of inferior quality. The Indian officials again did not promise. They did agree, however, that were such tariffs increased, comparable price increases would be allowed on carbon black production.

Mr. Cabot was of the opinion that no further concessions would be made by the Indian government and that he would have to reach a decision as quickly as possible on the basis of agreements and arrangements as they then stood. No decision had been reached by the summer of 1958.

Liebig's Extract of Meat Co. Ltd.

"LOOKING BACK on the last 10 years," said Mr. K. R. M. Carlisle, chairman of Liebig's, "I am sure of one thing—that the company as a whole has made progress. Of course, I am aware that the present state of things is nowhere near perfect and that many faults could be found with the way we have tried to change things; nevertheless, we have learnt a great deal and I feel that we are a stronger company as a result of introducing new methods throughout the company and a new organization here at headquarters."

SUMMARY OF HISTORY AND PRESENT POSITION

Liebig's Extract of Meat Company (LEMCo) was a large company with worldwide operations which produced a range of food products, the most important of which were based on meat extract. The company had an interesting history. In 1847, the great German organic chemist Justus von Liebig published his famous treatise on the extract of meat which he was currently making in Munich. He offered to lend his name and assistance to any entrepreneur who was able to make extract of meat to Liebig's own high standards from the carcasses of the thousands of semiwild cattle which were slaughtered every year in South America to obtain hides and fat. Hitherto, there had been no feasible way of using these carcasses and so they were left to rot, while millions of people, both in Europe and in the rest of the world, remained undernourished.

It was not until 1863 that Liebig's offer was successfully accepted. In that year, a Belgian engineer named Giebert established a manufacturing plant at Fray Bentos in South America and started to send meat extract to a firm of merchants in Antwerp. After the extract had been tested by Liebig's representative, it was put in jars which bore a distinctive label bearing Liebig's own signature and was distributed widely throughout Europe. The meat extract at this time and, indeed, for the next 50 years was sold through a London selling agency called Corneille

David & Company. This firm was controlled by the Gunther family, of which the present LEMCo vice chairman, Mr. W. J. Gunther, is a member.

The success of the new company was immediate and it was not long before fresh capital was urgently required. In 1865, Liebig's Extract of Meat Co. Ltd. was formed in London with a capital of half a million pounds and a bigger factory was built in South America. From that point, the business expanded rapidly and the Liebig extract was sold all over the world.

During the next 75 years, the company continued to expand steadily, though it encountered a number of crises. The basic product had to be changed when competitors found ways to increase the nutritive value of meat extract by adding other materials, and it also had to be made far cheaper when refrigeration processes enabled meat to be transported to all parts of the world. There were also difficulties with the use of the Liebig name in England, and LEMCo, after trying out a variety of names, settled finally on the trade name OXO.

The expansion of the firm took place on four continents. In South America, LEMCo had taken pains in the first 30 years of this century to increase both its cattle raising and its manufacturing facilities, so that by the end of the 1920's the company was operating two large factories and was tending enormous herds of cattle in Uruguay, Paraguay, and Argentina. In North America, a small Canadian subsidiary was set up in 1932. In Africa, LEMCo had acquired, before the 1914–1918 war, large tracts of land in Southwest Africa and Southern Rhodesia and had stocked these with cattle, intending to build up its herds to the point where manufacturing facilities in Africa would be desirable. Manufacturing plants were, in fact, erected in Southwest Africa in 1930 and in Southern Rhodesia in 1932. The former had to be closed after six years of operation owing to the effect of recurrent droughts on the cattle population in that territory, and the land was also sold. The plant in Southern Rhodesia, however, continued to prosper and develop. Meanwhile, the 1920's had seen the beginning of LEMCo's marketing business in Africa when OXO Ltd. (South Africa) was formed. Finally, LEMCo had greatly expanded its marketing business in the fourth continent, Europe, between 1900 and 1930. In 1914, its English selling agency, Corneille David & Company, was voluntarily liquidated, and OXO Ltd., the largest of the present LEMCo branches and subsidiaries, was formed in its place. Between the wars, LEMCo formed a number of companies throughout Europe to deal with both sales and manufacturing in particular countries.

By the end of the 1950's, therefore, Liebig plants and selling organizations were spread widely over four continents. Exhibit 1 shows the various LEMCo companies together with the date of their founding, their location, their function(s), and the number of employees in each. Furthermore, although LEMCo's primary emphasis remained on meat products, the product line broadened considerably to include soups, both canned and dehydrated; canned meals of various kinds; flavourings; and even canned fruit and vegetables. Potato crisps, carrying the brand name "Chipmunk" and marketed by OXO Ltd. in England, were the latest addition to the company's product line. Exhibit 2 shows the proprietary products sold by LEMCo companies in the various countries which formed their major markets, together with the brand names under which those products were sold. LEMCo's main competition came from food companies which were far larger in size but which had not the same flexibility. This competition was felt most keenly in all the companies on the mainland of Europe. Competition was a less severe problem for the English company insofar as its two main products were extremely well placed in their respective markets. The OXO cube held almost a monopoly position in the bouillon cube field, while sales of Fray Bentos corned beef had expanded to the point where the company had undisputed brand leadership.

Although the ownership of LEMCo had been fairly concentrated when the company was first formed, it had become very widespread over the years, so that at the beginning of the 1960's, no stockholder held more than a very small percentage of the stock and no group could be said to have control of the company. Despite this fact, LEMCo had retained many of the marks of a family company. Two families, the Carlisles and the Gunthers, had supplied the top executives of LEMCo over the whole of the company's life. The first two top executives had been the grandfather and father of the present managing director, Mr. W. J. Gunther. A connection between the Gunthers and the family of the current chairman, Mr. K. R. M. Carlisle, had been established by a marriage at the end of the last century between a Carlisle and a Gunther relative. As a result of this marriage, Mr. K. M. Carlisle, father of Mr. K. R. M. Carlisle, had entered Liebig's and had become chairman in 1925. His son succeeded him in 1958.

Exhibits 3 and 4 give financial information for recent years. Exhibit 3 shows balance sheets and profits for the years 1955 to 1962. In speaking of the profit figures, the chairman observed that it was difficult to draw from them any firm conclusions about the performance of the Liebig management because the nature and movements of the exchange

Exhibit 1

LIEBIG'S EXTRACT OF MEAT CO. LTD.

Data on LEMCo Companies

Name and Location	Number of Employees	Function(s)	Date of Founding
U.K. and Eire			
LEMCo Ltd.	110	Headquarters	1865
OXO Ltd.	1600	Selling & secondary manufacture†	1914
Liebig's (Ireland) Ltd.*	45	Secondary manufacture	1960
OXO (Ireland) Ltd.	10	Selling	1924
North America			
OXO (Canada) Ltd.	55	Selling & secondary manufacture	1932
South America			
Paraguay:			
LEMCo Ltd. (Zeballos Cue Factory)	2400	Primary manufacture	1920
LEMCo Ltd. Estancias	560	Livestock breeding, etc.	1910
Argentina:			
LEMCo Ltd. (Colon Factory)	2635	Primary manufacture	1905
LEMCo Ltd. Estancias	60	Livestock breeding, etc.	1925
Cia. Argentina Yerbatera Liebig S.A.*	330	Livestock breeding, etc.	1925
S.A. Pastoril Correntina*	175	Livestock breeding, etc.	1935
S.A. Ganadera Entrerriana*	142	Livestock breeding, etc.	1933
S.A. Estancias y Colonias Correntinas*	32	Livestock breeding, etc.	1933
Establecimiento Pastoril el Refugio S.A.*	31	Livestock breeding, etc.	1938
Uruguay:			
Cia. Estancias y Colonias Uruguayas S.A.*	90	Livestock breeding, etc.	1928
Africa			
Tanganyika Packers Ltd.*	1900	Primary manufacture	1947
Liebig's (Rhodesia) Ltd.*	1200	Primary & secondary manufacture	1933
LEMCo Ltd. Ranch*	1000	Livestock breeding etc.	1933

Exhibit 1—Continued

Name and Location	Number of Employees	Function(s)	Date of Founding
Sunrho Ltd.*	200	Secondary manufacture	1950
Nigerian Canning Co. Ltd.*	100	Primary manufacture	1955
Central African Food Corporation Ltd.*	50	Selling	1954
OXO (South Africa) Ltd.	16	Selling	1918
OXO (East Africa) Ltd.*	10	Selling	1952
European continent			
Cie. Française des Produits Liebig S.A.*	600	Selling & secondary manufacture	1919
Compagnie Liebig S.A. (Belgium)*	420	Selling & secondary manufacture	1913
Compagnia Italiana Liebig S.p.A.*	285	Selling & secondary manufacture	1932
Nederlandse OXO Maatschappij N.V.*	35	Selling	1926
Produits Liebig S.A. (Switzerland)*	20	Selling & secondary manufacture	1936
Liebig G.m.b.H.*	10	Selling	1912
Euroliebig S.A.*	6	Coordination of continental European companies, especially in the areas of marketing and budgetary control	1962

* Companies marked with an asterisk are nonresident in the U.K. for tax purposes (see p. 835).
† The distinction between primary and secondary manufacture was clear-cut and an important one to recognize. Primary manufacture covered the slaughter of cattle, the separation of the carcasses into individual components, and the treatment required to make these components easily transportable to factories engaged in secondary manufacture, whether on the same continent or a different one. Secondary manufacture included all the supplementary processes which were required to produce the Liebig line of products in finished form.

Exhibit 2

LIEBIG'S EXTRACT OF MEAT CO. LTD.

Products Sold by Country and Brand Name

	Argentina	South Africa	Rhodesia	United Kingdom	Belgium	Denmark	France	Germany	Holland	Italy	Norway	Spain	Switzerland	Canada
Meat extract	L	—	—	L	L	L	L	L	L	L	L	—	L	—
Meat & veg. extract	—	—	—	—	—	—	—	—	—	Sapis	—	—	—	—
Veg. extract	—	—	—	—	—	—	—	—	—	Vegedor	—	—	Vegedor	—
Meat spread	—	F.B.	F.B.	F.B.	F.B.	—	—	F.B.	F.B.	—	—	—	—	—
Corned beef	L	F.B.	F.B.	F.B.	—	—	—	—	—	—	—	—	F.B.	F.B.
Canned meats	F.B.	F.B.	F.B.	—	—	—	—	—	—	—	—	—	—	—
Bouillon cubes	—	OXO	OXO	OXO	OXO&L	OXO	VX&L	L	OXO&L	L	OXO	L	L	OXO
Beef tablets	L	—	—	—	L	L	L	L	L	L	L	—	L	—
Chicken tablets	—	—	—	—	—	—	L	—	L	L	—	L	—	—
Liquid bouillon	—	OXO	OXO	OXO	OXO	OXO	VX	L	OXO	L	OXO	—	L	OXO
Arome	L	—	—	—	—	—	L	L	—	—	—	—	—	—
Tinned sauces	—	—	—	—	—	—	—	—	—	—	—	—	—	—
Granulated broth	—	—	—	—	L	—	L	L	L	—	—	—	—	—
Dehydrated soups	—	L&F.B.	L&F.B.	—	L	—	L	L	L	L	OXO	L	—	—
Tinned soups	—	—	—	—	L	—	L	L	L	—	—	—	—	—
Prepared dishes	—	—	—	—	Bentos	—	—	—	Bentos	—	—	—	—	—
Canned veg.	—	L.C.V.	L.C.V.	—	L	—	—	—	L	L	—	—	—	—
Dehydrated veg.	—	Sunrho	Sunrho	—	—	—	—	—	—	—	—	—	—	—
Potato crisps	—	—	—	Ch'munk	—	—	—	—	—	—	—	—	—	—
Jam	—	Sunrho	Sunrho	—	—	—	—	—	—	—	—	—	—	—
Tinned fruit	—	Sunrho&L.C.V.	Sunrho&L.C.V.	—	—	—	—	—	—	—	—	—	—	—

Notes: (a) L = Liebig; F.B. = Fray Bentos; VX = Viandox; L.C.V. = Liebig Cashel Valley; Ch'munk = Chipmunk.
(b) Some products, particularly bouillon cubes, beef tablets, and chicken tablets, which are manufactured in different countries, vary somewhat in weight and composition from country to country.

Exhibit 3

LIEBIG'S EXTRACT OF MEAT CO. LTD.

Balance Sheets and Group Profit for Years Ended August 31, 1955–62

(In Thousands of Pounds)

	1955	1956	1957	1958	1959	1960	1961	1962
Assets								
Bank balances and cash in hand	£ 1,610	£ 1,568	£ 1,027	£ 476	£ 648	£ 1,117	£ 605	£ 714
Accounts receivable	2,510	2,544	2,775	2,943	2,988	3,565	4,223	5,101
Livestock, produce, stores, materials	9,548	8,078	8,707	10,646	12,179	13,211	16,174	15,382
Total current assets	£13,668	£12,190	£12,509	£14,065	£15,815	£17,893	£21,002	£21,197
Ranches and agricultural lands	£ 1,269	£ 1,222	£ 1,220	£ 1,220	£ 1,220	£ 1,280	£ 1,838	£ 1,837
Leasehold properties (net)	890	872	866	734	709	712	755	846
Factories, plant, equipment, etc. (net)	3,619	3,952	4,162	4,715	4,906	5,750	6,658	7,083
Trade investments	70	48	33	33	38	17	14	24
Other investments	9	7	112	9	8	24	45	46
Total assets	£19,525	£18,291	£18,902	£20,776	£22,696	£25,676	£30,312	£31,033
Liabilities								
Short-term bank loans and acceptances	£ 2,055	£ 827	£ 1,847	£ 2,546	£ 3,104	£ 1,694	£ 3,003	£ 2,191
Accounts payable	2,330	2,258	2,116	2,293	2,313	2,361	2,330	2,584
Interest payable	—	—	—	—	—	59	49	49
Income tax payable	1,022	1,005	935	826	1,053	1,376	1,087	1,805
Dividends payable	198	158	158	158	268	323	323	392
Contingency reserves	570	510	421	439	421	934	955	1,019
Total current liabilities	£ 6,175	£ 4,758	£ 5,477	£ 6,262	£ 7,159	£ 6,747	£ 7,747	£ 8,040
Provisions against nonsterling assets	£ 2,234	£ 2,104	£ 2,021	£ 2,031	£ 2,001	£ 500	£ 500	£ 500
Amounts in suspense	Dr. 28	Dr. 71	Dr. 165	12	22	Dr. 37	395	329
Debentures and long-term bank loans	718	699	667	731	687	3,899	4,200	4,239
Deferred income tax	693	649	614	845	825	798	1,163	1,384
Minority interest in subsidiaries	910	860	810	705	728	682	681	721
Issued preference capital of parent co.	2,000	2,000	2,000	2,000	2,000	2,000	2,000	2,000
Issued ordinary capital of parent co.	2,000	2,000	2,000	2,000	4,500	4,500	4,500	4,500
Capital reserves	1,490	1,560	1,506	1,552	286	1,728	3,906	3,572
Revenue reserves and undistributed profits	3,333	3,732	3,972	4,638	4,488	4,860	5,220	5,748
Total liabilities	£19,525	£18,291	£18,902	£20,776	£22,696	£25,677	£30,312	£31,033
Group profit after interest and taxation	£ 967	£ 580	£ 335	£ 994	£ 1,164	£ 1,103	£ 911	£ 1,182
Group profit *before* interest and taxation as a % of funds employed in the group at year end	17.7%	13.4%	10.5%	17.1%	16.5%	12.5%	10.5%	14.6%

rates of the three South American countries in which LEMCo operated were such as to exert a considerable, but uncontrollable influence on the year's profits. For example, in his statement in the 1962 annual report, the chairman noted that the Paraguayan guarani had become greatly overvalued, particularly in relation to the Argentine peso, which had steadily depreciated during 1962, owing to the turn of political events in Argentina. This overvaluation made it impossible for the products of the Paraguayan meat packing industry to compete profitably in world markets.

Exhibit 4

LIEBIG'S EXTRACT OF MEAT CO. LTD.

Pattern of Group Sales by Territory and in Total, 1955–62

(Sales for 1956–62 Are Expressed as a Percentage of 1955 Sales)

	1955	1956	1957	1958	1959	1960	1961	1962
Europe								
Country A	100	109	110	138	147	170	199	239
Country B	100	105	114	108	113	121	144	117
Country C	100	129	103	113	100	115	111	124
Country D	100	101	101	125	141	116	144	148
Country E	100	111	111	121	117	136	142	156
Country F	100	94	106	125	118	120	131	124
Europe total	100	112	109	128	132	150	170	196
South America	100	47	62	75	100	118	120	103
North America	100	54	54	73	89	82	76	63
Africa	100	102	87	93	110	98	98	95
Total	100	103	101	118	125	139	155	172

Notes: (1) Percentages have been calculated with reference to sterling turnover. In cases where foreign currencies are involved, the sterling equivalents have been arrived at by converting at exchange rates at the close of the financial year. (2) Analysis is by areas in which companies mainly operate, and the percentages for some areas include some sales in other areas. This has resulted in some degree of distortion where outlets have changed.

Exhibit 4 gives an indication of LEMCo's sales between 1955 and 1962. Sales are presented in total and by continent. Sales for Europe, in which most of LEMCo's sales were effected, are broken down by manufacturing country, though these countries remain anonymous since the company was reluctant for competitive reasons to disclose their true identity. It was, however, disclosed that the sales of OXO Ltd. were greater by far than the sales of any of the continental European companies.

OUTLINE OF RECENT CHANGES

Prior to the last seven years, LEMCo headquarters were organized on a very simple basis. Offices in London were maintained only for the three inside directors and a small administrative staff which controlled such matters as transfer pricing between the various LEMCo companies and the disposal of those materials (excluding, of course, meat) which were gained from the slaughtered LEMCo cattle each year. The three inside directors were responsible for the entire top management of the company, and the top-line management supervising the various LEMCo

Exhibit 5

LIEBIG'S EXTRACT OF MEAT CO. LTD.

Directors' Responsibilities Prior to Headquarters Reorganization

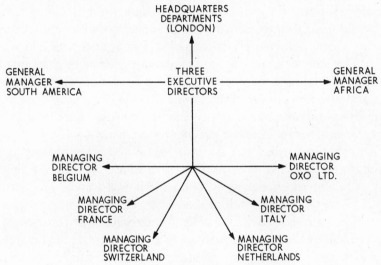

activities throughout the world reported directly to them. Although it would be inaccurate to say that the company used an overall organization chart during this period, Exhibit 5 does portray the relationships between LEMCo headquarters and the various companies. The number of people, including secretaries, at London headquarters never rose above 40–50 and sank as low as 23 during the depression.

The three directors had all served a period of apprenticeship which had enabled them to see most, if not all, of the LEMCo operations in some detail. In addition, they were constantly traveling all over America, Africa, and Europe in order to investigate local problems and sit in on the board meetings of individual LEMCo companies. Information also flowed back from the LEMCo companies to London, though the information required was not standardized and therefore varied somewhat from company to company. The three directors tried to hold to a scheme which divided responsibility between them according to three main geographical areas, Europe, South America, and Africa. Even so, they were worked very hard when particular crises occurred and they recognized that they were extremely dependent on the managerial capabilities of perhaps 10 or a dozen men scattered around the LEMCo empire.

In the early 1950's, changes began to be introduced in the areas of budgeting, work study, and marketing methods. These changes were first of all introduced locally in OXO Ltd. and then began to be introduced slowly throughout the entire range of LEMCo companies. Largely as a result of the demands on headquarters which these changes created, a new headquarters organization was born between 1956 and 1962. The number of people engaged in top management activity and based in London was considerably increased. In addition to the chairman and managing director, there were a further five people appointed to make up the composition of an "executive team." Experts were also engaged, either from inside or outside the company, who were to act as advisers in the various functional areas to top management. These advisers were expected to be ready to give advice or assistance in their own particular functional areas whenever it was wanted anywhere in the LEMCo group. As a result of these changes, there were, in 1962, no fewer than 14 people to fill the place formerly filled by three directors. The headquarters departments themselves continued approximately as before, the only changes being greater departmentalization between the various functions and the introduction of an export department.

The changes which have been dealt with in summary above are outlined in more detail below under three main headings. The above summaries which outlined the history, recent evolution, and present position of the firm were intended as a background so that the material which is presented below can be seen in better perspective.

THE INTRODUCTION OF NEW METHODS

During the Second World War and the years immediately afterwards, rationing was prevalent in many European countries. In the United Kingdom, in particular, which was easily LEMCo's largest market, both the distribution and the price of corned beef were controlled by the Ministry of Food. This control, together with the general disruption of normal patterns of consumer demand imposed by the war and the rationing, made it difficult to foresee how LEMCo would fare when conditions returned to normal. It was obvious, however, to some of the top executives of LEMCo that the company would have to introduce more up-to-date techniques in several areas if it was to remain healthy and efficient in the years of increasing competition that were foreseen ahead.

Mr. J. V. Cooper, the member of the executive team currently responsible for budgetary control, spoke as follows about the evolution of budgeting in the LEMCo group:

I myself have only been in LEMCo since 1946 when I came here to be chief accountant. Before that I was with our auditors, Binder, Hamlyn & Co. It was about that time that there was a growing demand for companies to make public their consolidated accounts—a demand which became law under the 1948 Companies Act. The effect that this had on the accounting department here at headquarters was that we began to look at the company as a *group* and no longer as a collection of separate entities.

From the time that I entered the company, I had felt the need to standardize and simplify our accounting communications in the group. In the old days, plenty of information came in to headquarters, but it was sometimes pretty difficult to understand and we seldom knew the assumptions and problems underlying the figures. We would get, for instance, a mass of cost accounting data from South America, but I don't think anyone felt confident that they understood the relationship between the figures and the facts. I personally felt that a standard system of budgetary control was urgently needed throughout the company, because I didn't see how headquarters could manage effectively if it didn't know what was happening, and no matter how much the directors traveled, accounting was still a vital means of communication.

Our first step, undertaken at the beginning of the 1950's, was to engage the services of the management advisory services department which our auditors had just formed. We then set to work to introduce budgets into one company only—OXO Ltd.—since the chairman felt strongly that we should not attempt to introduce new methods throughout the group until they had been tried and proved to be successful in a particular company.

When we set to work, we didn't encounter any real resistance to our ideas, but it was clear that many of the older managers and accountants just didn't believe in it and couldn't put their hearts into the project. There was a need for a younger point of view and the budget system did not get into its stride until some of the old employees had voluntarily retired early. For the first two or three years, the budgets were badly out. But then they began to settle down and they have been working well in OXO for some years now. Our consultants, incidentally, were very helpful and we had an excellent working relationship with them.

The chairman of LEMCo, Mr. K. R. M. Carlisle, summarized the introduction of work study and new marketing techniques as follows:

Work study was introduced concurrently with budgeting and in this area also we used OXO Ltd. as an experimental ground. I should first explain some of the managerial background, since it is very relevant to some of the difficulties we encountered. The managing director of OXO Ltd. from 1940 to 1953 was a production man by upbringing, having been manager of factories for many years before he took over as managing director. He was succeeded temporarily by the company's secretary for a period of two years while the directors looked for a new managing director from outside since there was no one left in the company who could suitably fill the position.

This was perhaps an unfortunate moment to introduce work study, because there was no strong hand to control and guide the innovations through the factory manager and the chief engineer, who resisted the changes strongly. The factory manager was a remarkable man in his way but definitely old-fashioned. He regarded himself as being responsible for a single thing called production, which embraced everything indiscriminately from quality control to maintenance, and because he kept control of all these functions firmly within his own hands, we felt that the company might be missing opportunities for improvement in various directions, simply because there is a limit to what one man can do. We had already created a separate budget department at OXO and we also wanted to change their organization in the production area so that the factory manager would have under his control three clearly defined departments—work study, quality control, and engineering. However, we were not able to do this until the factory manager retired. Thereafter we made substantial headway, having engaged from outside the group a new factory manager who had had plenty of experience with work study.

Our efforts to introduce new techniques in the area of marketing came a little later—perhaps a year or two after we had begun to introduce work study and budgeting. We brought in from outside a new marketing manager for OXO who attracted a small staff along with him. He set to work to brush up OXO's merchandising techniques and introduce widespread use of market research data. Here again, initial resistance was encountered from those who had been with the company a long time and had done things differently. But gradually things began to work well and show results, and people began to look forward to the bimonthly market research data which our market research firm sends us.

EVOLUTION OF A NEW HEADQUARTERS ORGANIZATION

By 1956–57 the process of change was making itself felt in OXO and was producing excellent results. The problem then became one of spreading new methods throughout the group with the maximum speed and efficiency. This problem drew attention to some serious inadequacies in the headquarters organization which had persisted at LEMCo up to that point.

Meanwhile, Mr. K. M. Carlisle, who had been chairman of LEMCo since 1931, had been transferring the main burden of top management to his son in anticipation of his own retirement at the beginning of 1958. Mr. K. R. M. Carlisle, though strongly sympathetic to a method of top management which he himself had followed for a good many years, nevertheless recognized that the operations of the LEMCo group had grown too large and too diverse in nature to be effectively supervised by three men. He was thus aware of and receptive to the pressures exerted from various quarters in favour of a different management structure at headquarters.

The climate at headquarters was therefore favourable to change and there were many who were pressing for it. On the one hand, the consultants were quick to point out that it was the responsibility of top management not only to control but also to assist actively the spreading of the new methods throughout the group. On the other, it was known that some of the subsidiaries themselves were anxious for more help and direction from headquarters. This point was made with particular force by Mr. J. R. Stourton, a cousin of both Mr. Carlisle and Mr. Gunther, who had joined the company three years before and had been on an extended tour of all LEMCo's operations. There was yet a third pressure at headquarters itself in the person of Mr. Cooper, who had become the secretary of the company in 1953. In a memorandum which he wrote to top management in 1956–57, he pointed out that the old system placed an enormous burden on the three directors, so that inefficiency and a lack of forward planning resulted. He also noted that there was a need for much more technical knowledge at headquarters, particularly in the production area in which the company had had some costly failures in recent years. He summarized his position thus:

It would seem that the time has come to make a fresh appraisal of our role as a parent company. The policy in the past has been one of decentralisation and there is no suggestion that this policy should be reversed; but the growth in size, scope, and number of our many interests surely demands a new and more positive attitude in London. It is more than ever necessary to have the right people "on the spot," but London should be in a position not only to receive, but also, with knowledge and purpose, to distribute the fruits of experience, technical and otherwise, of our overseas interests, and to intervene actively when things go wrong. Furthermore, London, from its relatively detached position and with its wider view of the whole sphere of our operations, should be able to produce its own constructive ideas for development in each territory and should be the mainspring of progressive policy and outlook for the group as a whole.

After much discussion between all parties concerned, during which many alternatives were considered, the organization shown in Exhibit 6 was finally decided upon. This organization reflected the two distinct needs which had been felt: the need to have both forward planning and control of the company's operations carried out without the one being detrimental to the other; and the need to have detailed knowledge of the various functional areas available to headquarters.

The exhibit shows that the number of top executives in London was increased from three to five, and responsibility both for the London departments and for the various geographical areas in which LEMCo operated was firmly apportioned among them. It was laid down that the principal concern of this executive team should be "to coordinate and stimulate the efforts of individual companies so that: (*a*) maximum profitabilty be secured, (*b*) all group companies develop themselves as fully as possible."[1]

The principal means of coordination was to be the system of budgets and management reports which it was hoped to introduce throughout the group as soon as possible. Each company in the group would therefore submit its information to a particular member of the executive team, who would discuss it both with the members of the team and with the local managing director concerned, once he had studied it carefully. It was hoped that top management in London would thereby be kept in touch with the operations of the whole group.

There were seven advisers appointed and their functions were defined as set forth in Exhibit 7. The responsibility for coordinating their activities was assigned to Mr. Stourton. Their duties were to advise on problems brought to light by the management reports and also on other matters as they arose. For instance, it was clear that their help would be very much needed during the process of spreading new and unfamiliar methods to the whole LEMCo group. The recruitment of appropriate people for the headquarters advisory services posed a difficult problem. It was clearly necessary to have, in the functional areas concerned, men who were fully abreast of the new techniques and methods which had been introduced into OXO Ltd. over the past few years. On the other hand, it was clearly not in the interests of good group relations or efficiency to despoil OXO of many of their best men. Initially, therefore, a number of the advisers were recruited from outside, in particular the sales and marketing advisers.

It was also decided that there was a need to train at headquarters men who could help in the detailed implementation of budgetary control and work study throughout the group. Accordingly, the new organization provided for the budget department in London to recruit and train,

---

[1] The quotation is from a book entitled *The Management of the Group,* which is referred to below.

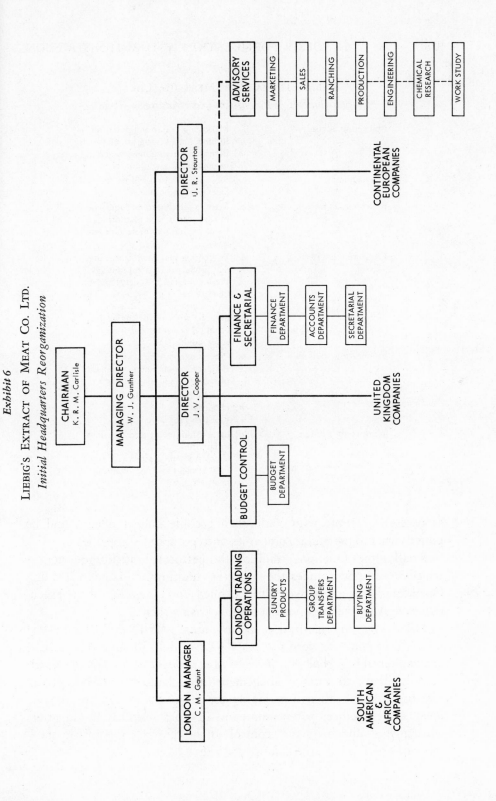

Exhibit 6

LIEBIG'S EXTRACT OF MEAT CO. LTD.

Initial Headquarters Reorganization

CHAIRMAN
K. R. M. Carlisle

MANAGING DIRECTOR
W. J. Gunther

DIRECTOR
J. V. Cooper

DIRECTOR
J. R. Stourton

LONDON MANAGER
C. M. Gaunt

BUDGET CONTROL

FINANCE &
SECRETARIAL

LONDON TRADING
OPERATIONS

ADVISORY
SERVICES

MARKETING

SALES

RANCHING

PRODUCTION

ENGINEERING

CHEMICAL
RESEARCH

WORK STUDY

BUDGET
DEPARTMENT

FINANCE
DEPARTMENT

ACCOUNTS
DEPARTMENT

SECRETARIAL
DEPARTMENT

SUNDRY
PRODUCTS

GROUP
TRANSFERS
DEPARTMENT

BUYING
DEPARTMENT

SOUTH
AMERICAN &
AFRICAN
COMPANIES

UNITED
KINGDOM
COMPANIES

CONTINENTAL
EUROPEAN
COMPANIES

Exhibit 7

LIEBIG'S EXTRACT OF MEAT CO. LTD.

Responsibilities of Parent Company Advisers—1958

Marketing adviser:	*a*) Marketing policy and potential for new and existing products
	b) Plans for entering new markets or launching new products
Sales adviser:	*a*) Sales organization and techniques
	b) Sales promotion plans
Ranching adviser:	*a*) Matters relating to management of land, cattle, and plantations
	b) Purchase and importation of livestock
Production adviser:	*a*) Production planning, processing and production control systems
	b) Production methods development
	c) Quality control systems (The production adviser will coordinate the work of the engineering, chemical research, and work study advisers.)
Engineering adviser:	*a*) Process engineering
	b) Purchase, repair, and maintenance of factory plant and equipment
Chemical research adviser:	*a*) Quality control standards
	b) Hygiene
	c) Research programmes
Work study adviser:	*a*) Establishing work study sections in factories
	b) Work study programmes for work measurement and improvement of methods

as necessary, people who could then become budget officers and be posted either to particular companies or to groups of companies.

Finally, the functions traditionally performed at headquarters—which were known under the collective heading of "London Trading Operations"—were more carefully defined, and a member of the executive team was made responsible for supervising them.

The changes in organization and procedure which were accomplished at the head office between the years 1956 and 1958 were summarized and explained in a book entitled *The Management of the Group,* which was distributed to senior management throughout the LEMCo group. The book dealt with five major topics: group policy; group management at head office; parent company advisory services; headquarters departments; and budgetary control. In his introduction to the statement of group policy, the chairman wrote:

You have already been informed, in general terms, of some of the changes being made at the head office. The board of the parent company has now approved a group plan which has been developed in the head office over the past few months. The introduction of this plan is a further step towards the strengthening of the organization and management of the group and of its individual members.

Before you read more about the plan, I would like to stress that its introduction is a natural development of existing policy rather than a change in policy. The board has always felt that each unit in the group should play a big part in its own destiny. *The group plan should make it possible for all companies and branches within the group to become strong and self-managing while cooperating for the benefit of the group as a whole.*

The chairman went on to enumerate four major policies of LEMCo:

a) to give the public good value for money,
b) to develop and expand the business as opportunity offered,
c) to offer employees attractive conditions of service and remuneration, and
d) to make the shareholders' investment a profitable one.

It was pointed out that fulfillment of the overall policies would entail each unit of the group:

a) making an effective contribution to group profitability,
b) having a sound management structure,
c) continually developing executives of sufficient calibre to maintain or, in some cases, to achieve self-management, and
d) being capable of setting up and effectively using budgets to secure optimum profitability from available resources.

In the remaining four sections of the book, the chairman concentrated on explaining in reasonable detail how the LEMCo companies would be affected by the changes that had been made. He was careful, for instance, to say that if any company required the help of an adviser in a particular area, the adviser should be requested through the medium of the executive team member concerned. In this way it was hoped that the executive team would always be in close touch with the activities of the advisers in their areas. The section of the book which dealt with the new system of budgetary control was particularly thorough and was somewhat longer than the other sections, with illustrative management report and budget forms being added as exhibits. It was stressed that budgets had worked well in OXO. Also, the functions of the prospective budget officers were explained.

DEVELOPMENTS BETWEEN 1958 AND 1962

Almost from the start of the new organization, it became a custom for those members of the executive team who were in London and not traveling to meet together every morning for a while. It was found that these meetings cut down considerably on time which had to be spent in reading documents to keep abreast of overall group affairs, and it also greatly facilitated the coordination between advisers and the executive team. With effect from January, 1963, it was also planned to have regular meetings once a month to discuss budgets and management reports.

The meetings referred to above were held in addition to the fortnightly directors' meetings which dealt with such matters as group policy and major capital expenditures. Mr. Cooper and Mr. Stourton had been appointed directors of LEMCo in September, 1957. In 1962, therefore, there were four executive directors; namely, Mr. Carlisle, Mr. Gunther, Mr. Cooper, and Mr. Stourton. In addition, there were three outside directors.

As the executive team became used to their functions, it was realized that five men were not able to meet the demands imposed by the revised conception of top management's job. Accordingly, two further men, who had each had substantial experience in LEMCo companies overseas, were added to the team. Mr. Lynn, an accountant by training, came from LEMCo management in South America and was made responsible for the subsidiary companies in Canada and Ireland. He was also given responsibility for a new headquarters department, the export department, which not only took over the functions of the old sundry products department, but also managed the sale of LEMCo products in export territories formerly attributed to OXO Ltd. and the sale, in the United Kingdom, of group products which OXO Ltd. could not conveniently handle. Mr. Wells, who had had very considerable experience with LEMCo in the production area, both in South America and Africa, came to London to become the executive team member responsible for the LEMCo African companies. Although these moves lessened somewhat the burdens formerly carried by Mr. Gaunt and Mr. Cooper, the latter still felt that his important tasks on the financial and budgetary control side were being hampered by his responsibility for coordination between headquarters and OXO Ltd. Mr. Gunther therefore assumed the duties of liaison executive with OXO and Mr. Cooper was left free to devote his whole attention to his duties as financial director. The revised organization chart is shown as Exhibit 8.

As the advisers also settled in to their duties, it became clear that further changes, albeit slight ones, were necessary. In the interests of coordination between the advisers and the executive team, a number of

Exhibit 8

LIEBIG'S EXTRACT OF MEAT CO. LTD.

Headquarters Organization, 1962, with Ages of Executive Team Members
as of December 31, 1962

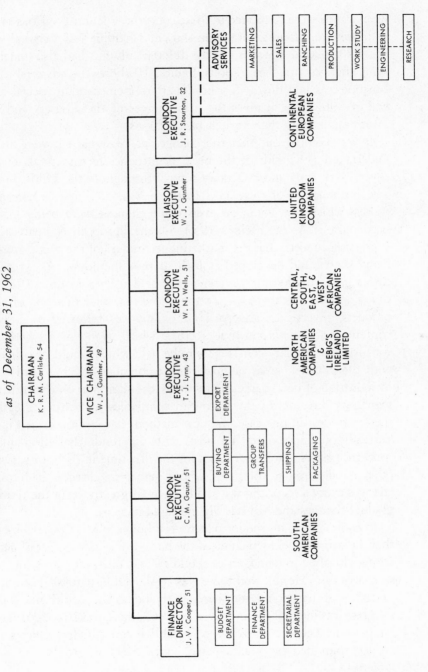

memoranda were circulated to those concerned, defining various matters of procedure. The memorandum shown as Exhibit 9 is a typical example. By 1962, the functions of the different advisers had also undergone some changes and clarifications. Exhibit 10 shows the advisers' current functions, as laid down in a headquarters memorandum issued at the end of 1962. It also gives the present ages of the advisers and some information about their various backgrounds.

It was pointed out that the changes at headquarters were in part undertaken as a result of the need to introduce new methods in work study, marketing, and budgetary control throughout the LEMCo group. The introduction of these new methods was, of course, a continuous process which was going on even while changes were being made at headquarters. As far back as 1953–54, the European companies were expressing concern that the marketing techniques of the group were not being shared and developed as fully as they should be. As a result of this, a group marketing conference was held at Paris in June, 1955, and it was decided that there was a strong need for standardisation of group products, advertising, and packaging. This was followed by a second conference at Antwerp in June, 1958, at which arrangements were made for further subsidiary conferences to be held which would be concerned with the different areas of marketing techniques. With regard to the introduction of new marketing methods, the chairman observed that the managing directors of the European companies had varied greatly in their attitudes. In one case, the new methods had been accepted enthusiastically and introduced too fast, with the result that the company concerned had suffered bad losses for the first time in its history. On the other hand, another company, whose managing director had resisted changes every step of the way, had benefited greatly from the resultant gradual changes and had steadily increased its sales.

In commenting on the introduction of budgets, Mr. Cooper observed that the real problem which faced the budget officers was that of getting along with the top managers of the LEMCo companies with which they were working. He felt that there was considerable natural resistance to budgets and that, no matter how high the hopes with which one started, progress was inevitably slow. Even by 1962, there was still a shortage of budget officers, since it had been found that more budget officers were needed than had been anticipated, particularly in Africa and South America.

A final development between 1958 and 1962 concerned the research and development activity of the LEMCo group. In 1958, a group

There is, apparently, uncertainty in some quarters as regards particular aspects of the advisers' work and relations with management. The object of this note is to answer those specific queries which have been raised as well as to amend in certain respects what has been previously laid down.

Reports on Advisers' Activities

1. Reports in draft form should be discussed with the appropriate member of the executive team before circulation in final form.
2. Items not intended for circulation outside head office should be the subject of a separate appendix.
3. Conclusions and recommendations should be so cast as to:
   a) cover all major points and especially those requiring action,
   b) act as a basis for considerations and discussion by the executive concerned.
4. If it is thought advisable to restrict circulation within a branch/subsidiary, this should be brought to the attention of local management.
5. Action on reports is the responsibility of the appropriate head office executive and/or local management, depending on the origin of the request for advice. Advisers continue to be available to amplify, elaborate, or advise on execution, and in certain cases—if invited to do so by local management—to undertake specific tasks in an executive capacity.

Correspondence

1. Advisers have their own channels of correspondence to answer questions and proffer advice. They must keep the appropriate team member in the picture and this can normally be done by the submission of copies of incoming and outgoing correspondence, or as otherwise required by the executive concerned.
2. All advisers must ensure, by the passing of copies of letters or by other means, that other advisers and executives are kept currently informed on matters which affect them.
3. In respect of individual companies or situations it may be the wish of the responsible executive to conduct correspondence himself through executive channels, in which case it is his responsibility to make the necessary arrangements with the advisers concerned.

Travel

Visits to branches/subsidiaries or elsewhere will not be made without the prior agreement of the executive concerned and/or Mr. Stourton as director responsible for the administration of the advisory team.

Coordination

Responsibility for ensuring coordination in respect of any particular project rests with the appropriate member of the executive team who, in practice, will normally instruct the adviser principally concerned to coordinate progress. This applies to all advisers, including technical ones.

Exhibit 10

LIEBIG'S EXTRACT OF MEAT CO. LTD.

Responsibilities and Background of Parent Company Advisers—1962

Adviser, Name, and Age as of Dec. 31, 1962	Background	Duties
Marketing adviser F. A. Judd (49).............	Joined LEMCo 1958 after managerial experience in economics and market research with large international competitor.	a) Market research to include: 1) research into new and existing markets 2) consumer and trade research 3) market research aspects of product research and development b) Economic intelligence c) Package design
Sales adviser P. D. Silvester (36)........	Joined LEMCo 1961. Previously director of advertising agency and with international commercial firms.	a) Marketing policy and plans and their implementation b) Selling, sales promotion, and advertising and sales administration
Ranching adviser H. E. McKie (65).........	Promoted in 1958 after 30 years on LEMCo ranches in South America as Estancia manager.	a) Matters relating to management of land, cattle, and plantations b) Purchase and importation of livestock
Production adviser J. C. R. Gornall (55)......	Promoted in 1958 after many years of service with the group's primary factories in Argentina and Africa. Posts included factory superintendent and general manager.	a) Production planning and its processing b) Production control systems c) Production aspects of process development d) Production aspects of quality control findings
Engineering adviser R. G. Condick (42).........	Joined group 1956. Promoted in 1959 from OXO Ltd., where he had been chief engineer.	a) Production engineering services b) Coordination of the engineering aspects of research and development programmes c) Specifications for the purchase of capital plant d) Repair, replacement, and maintenance of factory plant and equipment e) Costing of engineering aspects of maintenance and development budgets
Research adviser C. D. Essex (40)............	Joined group 1957. Promoted in 1958 from OXO Ltd., where he had been chief chemist.	a) Coordination of the scientific aspects of research and development programmes b) Chemical, microbiological, and physical control and investigation c) Quality standards and methods of inspection for compliance with the standards d) Scientific aspects of product and process development
Work Study adviser K. W. Cotton (42)..........	Joined group 1957. Promoted in 1959 from OXO Ltd., where he had been head of work study.	a) Work study aspects of process development b) Work study techniques for improvement of methods and cost reduction c) Work measurement and establishing suitable incentives

research programme had been established which called for a very wide range of research activity and divided this range into priorities. The work involved was split between the group research centre in London and the laboratories which were operated by subsidiaries. The programme came up for revision every six months before a committee which met regularly at headquarters and consisted of Mr. Gunther, who acted as chairman, and the advisers for market research, production, engineering, research and work study. Mr. Carlisle stressed that he felt research and development to be a very important part of LEMCo's activities.

TOP MANAGEMENT OF THE LEMCO SUBSIDIARIES

With one exception, the parent company held a majority of the stock of all the subsidiary companies in the group. However, the degree of control which could be exercised over the subsidiaries was limited in some cases by U.K. tax practice, under which the overseas subsidiaries of a U.K. parent company could only be regarded as nonresident in the U.K. for tax purposes if the parent company abstained from control over the day-to-day trading and the financial transactions of the subsidiaries concerned. LEMCo had chosen to make most of its overseas subsidiaries nonresident in the U.K. for tax purposes (all those in Exhibit 1 which are marked with an asterisk). As a result, the boards of those subsidiaries had the final say in all matters of domestic policy or capital expenditure, though they were, of course, free to ask the advice of a parent company director who was on their board as well as that of the parent company. The laying down by London of the *form* of reports to be submitted by nonresident subsidiaries under the budgetary control system was permissible as being an administrative convenience and did not constitute "control" as understood for purposes of U.K. taxation.

The organization of the various LEMCo companies was for the most part a functional one, particularly in the European companies which performed both manufacturing and selling. Typically, there would be a managing director in general charge of a particular company's operations and directly under him would be the managers of the functional areas—the production manager, the marketing manager, the chief accountant, etc. This pattern varied in South America, for instance, because the extent of the LEMCo ranches was too vast for one man to carry general management responsibility for cattle raising, and so each country had a manager who reported directly to the general manager for South America in Buenos Aires. Likewise, each of the South American factories had a general manager who reported directly to Buenos Aires. There were, however, at Buenos Aires a marketing manager, a chief accountant, and a chief engineer, each of whom carried responsibility for all South American activities in their areas.

Under the old organization, both the European companies and the outposts of the LEMCo empire had been left alone almost entirely, and as a result of this autonomy in the local companies, their various managing directors had great power. It was recognized at headquarters that the changes would inevitably diminish this power, insofar as greater control would be exercised over the activities of the group. In speaking of this aspect of the headquarters reorganization, Mr. Stourton said:

This is not as great a problem as one might think, though I agree that it might be responsible for a certain initial resistance to change. One must not forget that the European managing directors, who were the ones most affected by the changes, were also the ones who did the most clamouring for a little pooling of group skills and experience, combined with some common leadership from London. I think that most of them are now satisfied with the way things are going, though their satisfaction varies according to the performance of their own particular companies. Of course, both I, as the executive team member for Europe, and the advisers who are called on by the European companies have to be tactful in our dealings with the managing directors and their second-line management. This isn't very difficult, because the managing directors of the three largest continental LEMCo companies are all extremely capable men of great experience.

This raises another point which is worth stressing. There is danger that an outsider may fail to appreciate the finer points of the headquarters-subsidiaries relationship. On paper, it looks as if the most desirable managerial positions in the whole group are the ones here at headquarters—desirable, that is, from the point of view of salary, power, and status. But it must be remembered that we at headquarters are here not to *supervise* but simply to control and coordinate. Even the advisers are, in part, simply transferring knowledge and experience from one part of the group to another. This means that the people who are most crucial to the success or failure of the group continue to be the heads of our many different companies. I think that the managing directors themselves look at it in this way, and as a result, their ambitions are not centred on becoming members of headquarters management, but rather on the growth of their own companies. Incidentally, I assure you that the salaries they are paid give full recognition to their importance to the group.

There was another problem associated with top management of the subsidiaries; namely, one of succession. Mr. Gaunt, who had worked his way up through LEMCo after starting as an office boy and who had, in consequence, a very broad and detailed knowledge of the group, observed:

In the days when we had only three directors here and we were dependent even more than now on a handful of managers scattered around the world, succession was even more of a problem, for the structure of the group exposed us to the risk of considerable difficulties if we did not have the right man in power at a particular spot. During the war, for instance, we were almost entirely cut off from South America and the general manager there was forced to run his own operation as best he could.

Even now our problem is aggravated by the fact that our companies in the several continents are engaged largely in different activities. We raise cattle and do our primary manufacturing in South America; on the other hand, we do very little secondary manufacture there and not much selling. The reverse is true with the European companies. Africa does something of all four activities, so managerial movement does occur between Africa and the other two continents. But we are still up against a language problem. Traditionally, therefore, we have always recruited and promoted within the particular continents concerned—which meant that if a local managing director neglected to train people who could fill the key positions in his company, we would suddenly find ourselves in real difficulties with no easy remedy available. Now at least we can be sure that the local managing directors are constantly aware of the problem.

THE ROLE OF THE ADVISERS

Despite the moves LEMCo had made in the direction of greater control by headquarters, top management still felt strongly that the LEMCo companies should be left to themselves as far as possible. As a result, the advisers were in a fairly delicate position. The sales adviser, Mr. P. D. Silvester, had been recruited from outside the group at the end of 1961 and was therefore in a position to deliver impartial criticism on the adviser's role which he was called on to fill:

My first act on joining the group was to make a tour round all the subsidiaries with which I expected to have dealings. I was concerned, of course, to make myself known to the managing directors and marketing managers of these subsidiaries and also to learn as much as I could about their own particular marketing environments. In this connection, I need hardly point out that the countries of Western Europe are different enough to make it impossible to standardize at present the group's marketing techniques.

On my initial visits, I was invariably well received and managements made every effort to show me what they felt I ought to know. However, I was always aware that the real test of my usefulness would be the number of times I was "invited" back to help cope with particular problems. You see, the headquarters policy of noninterference makes it very difficult for us to revisit companies unless they actually request our services or unless a serious problem arises.

However, I am glad to say that I have already revisited several companies at their request and I feel I am beginning to perform a useful function in the group. Of course, the attitude of the local managing directors is a critical variable in getting done what I'd like to be done. If they are against a particular programme, that's it. But if they are behind it, then everything goes smoothly forward. Even if it's a programme of such a size that the expenditure has to be approved by the directors here in London, there is still a 90% chance that the local managing director will have his way.

Every now and again, an adviser has to go to a particular company because of a problem that's arisen, and he finds that he doesn't agree with the local functional manager on how it should be handled. In these cases, of course, we are justified in appealing to headquarters to mediate, no matter what the local managing director thinks. But this doesn't occur very often, and when it does, we can nearly always reach a solution without causing upset.

I should also add that the advisers are certainly not all-wise. In some cases they may not even be the best people in the group. In my own area, for instance, I am faced with the fact that OXO Ltd. now has one of the best and most up-to-date marketing organizations in the English grocery business. The OXO marketing manager is very experienced and is running a high-powered operation. As a matter of fact, we get on very well together but I can recognise a potentially difficult situation when I see one, and I would be reluctant to interfere with his activities. Besides, OXO Ltd. is a large and powerful company which dominates the English market for its two main products. It was the first LEMCo company to undergo the new methods, and as such, it is some way ahead of all the others. We therefore spend most of our time with the other LEMCo companies.

A final problem which I sometimes come up against is that I can be put in the position of having to be both judge and advocate of a particular project. One of the responsibilities of the advisers is to give top management their opinions on such large projects as the LEMCo companies put forward for directors' approval. If a subsidiary has put forward a marketing programme of such scope that it has to be approved here, the chances are that they will have called me in before starting to work it out and that a large portion of the plan will be my own work. Although this is not a serious problem, I often think that it would be easier if I had an assistant here at headquarters to resolve the dilemma. Apart from anything else, he'd be very useful in helping to cope with my growing work load.

SUMMARY

"At the present time," said the chairman, "I know that we have not got an optimal organization. When we evolved this setup, we were subject to the limitations imposed both by the very nature of the LEMCo operations and also by the abilities of the men at our disposal. Hence it would be easy for an outsider who did not understand these limitations to pick holes in what we have done. But having made this qualification, I still feel that the parent company is stuck in a somewhat precarious position between being advisory and being executive. We shall undoubtedly continue to make changes over the coming years and I don't see how they can help but be in the direction of greater centralization. This worries me somewhat because I believe that a group of companies such as ours will suffer if there is too much direction from the centre. I only hope, therefore, that we can continue to give our companies as much autonomy as possible, while ensuring the maximum distribution of superior skills, experience, or knowledge possessed at any one point in the group."

PART VII

The Business Leader
and Public Responsibility

Auto-Start Manufacturing Company

THE AUTO-START MANUFACTURING COMPANY, a maker of equipment for automobiles, was concerned during the latter part of 1965 and the early months of 1966 with problems arising from proposed and actual changes in federal excise tax laws.

On May 17, 1965, President Johnson presented to Congress a detailed proposal calling for cuts in federal excise taxes representing about $4 billion in annual revenues. This was part of the administration's efforts to stimulate growth of the economy. The President urged businessmen to "translate lower excise taxes promptly into lower retail prices for consumers."

Congress acted promptly on the proposal, presenting an excise tax bill for the President's signature on June 17, 1965, that increased the reductions even beyond those asked for by Mr. Johnson, to $4.6 billion. The bill was signed into law on June 22.

A large number of items were affected at both the manufacturer's and the retailer's level. Relief for some items, automobiles for example, was staggered over a period of years and was not to be total. The excise tax on manufacturers' sales of automobile parts, on the other hand, was totally repealed as of January 1, 1966 (with the exception of items exclusively applicable to trucks and buses).

SUMMARY: FEDERAL EXCISE TAX HISTORY

The excise form of taxation had been used in the United States for many years. This form of tax so far as it affects the ultimate consumer is based on his consumption or use of goods and services instead of on his receipt of income or other revenues. The consumer does not pay the tax directly to the government; rather, manufacturers and the various business services act as tax collectors for the government.

The first excise tax in the United States was levied in 1791 on distilled liquors, which led to the so-called Whiskey Rebellion in 1794. Over the period 1792–1802 excise taxes produced 7.1 percent of total federal tax collections. They did not represent a substantial portion of total revenue until after the Civil War. From 1863 until 1919 they were a very important part of the total, reaching a high point of 55.2 percent for the period 1899 to 1902. After 1940, their importance declined, although not the sums collected from this source. For the period 1955–63 federal excise collections amounted to $102 billion and represented 13 percent of total tax collections. In 1965 the net collections were $14 billion.[1]

An excise tax was placed on automobile parts and accessories in 1919. The rate was 5 percent of manufacturers' sales. In 1932 the rate was reduced to 2 percent; later it was returned to 5 percent; from 1952 until its repeal as of January 1, 1966, the rate stood at 8 percent.[2] Total receipts from this tax were estimated at $255 million in 1965.[3]

COMPANY HISTORY

Auto-Start began operations in the early part of the twentieth century as a small manufacturer of various parts for the new and rapidly growing automobile industry. In recent years the company's annual volume had been approximately $100 million. The company had manufacturing and warehousing facilities in 10 states and more than 4,000 employees.

Product Lines.   A–S had three major product lines:

Item	Company's Brand Name	% of Sales
Spark plugs	Thunderbolt	50
Batteries	Fail-Safe	40
Ignition system parts	Geronimo	10
		100%

The company's products also were differentiated on another basis. Approximately 85 percent of sales were of items termed counterpart, that is, parts that were either original equipment on automobiles or, in the replacement market, items identical to original equipment. The remaining 15% of sales were of items called noncounterpart. These parts were manufactured as alternates for original equipment. They were primarily a "second line" of extra performance parts and were sold in the replacement market.

---

[1] Tax Foundation, Inc., *Federal Non-Income Taxes, an Examination of Selected Revenue Sources* (New York, 1965), chap. III.

[2] *Ibid.*

[3] Tax Foundation, Inc., *Facts and Figures on Government Finance* (13th ed.; Englewood Cliffs, N.J.: Prentice-Hall, 1965), p. 102.

Distribution. A–S marketed its products under its own brand names as original equipment for new cars and to over 500 domestic distributors as replacements. (A–S, like many producers of parts, sold to only one automobile maker. In the replacement market, however, it sold parts for virtually all automobiles on the roads.) It also sold to chain operators under private-label brand names. The breakdown of sales (in millions of dollars) by product lines to the various types of customers was as follows:

Item	Automobile Manufacturers	National Chains	Distributors	Total
Spark plugs	19	8	23	50%
Batteries	6	14	20	40
Ignition system parts	—	3	7	10
	25	25	50	100%

A–S was one of the leading producers of automotive parts. It estimated that its share of the original equipment automobile market was about 25 percent for spark plugs and 8 percent for batteries and, in the replacement market, 30 percent for spark plugs and 25 percent for batteries. The company had 10 competitors.

Annual sales of the automotive parts industry in the domestic replacement market were reported to be $3 billion at the manufacturer's sales price based on federal excise tax receipts.[4] There were about 800 manufacturers of automotive parts producing one or more of the following product categories: ignition parts, mufflers and pipes, spark plugs, batteries, filters and cartridges, motor and chassis parts, paint and body supplies, brake linings and shoes, fan belts and cooling system hose, shock absorbers, piston rings, fuel pumps, lamp bulbs, carburetors, etc. There were approximately 25,000 automotive equipment wholesalers and jobbers and almost 300,000 dealer or retail outlets, including service stations, automobile dealers, and automotive equipment and parts stores. The 300,000 figure does not include department or general merchandise stores.[5]

Exhibit 1 represents graphically the distribution network for A–S and is generally representative for the entire industry. (As the exhibit shows, A–S sales to distributors were made through A–S Sales, Inc. The reason this extra step was interposed in the distribution process is

[4] *Jobber Topics,* November, 1965.
[5] *Ibid.*

Exhibit 1

AUTO-START MANUFACTURING COMPANY

Distribution Plan for Automobile Parts

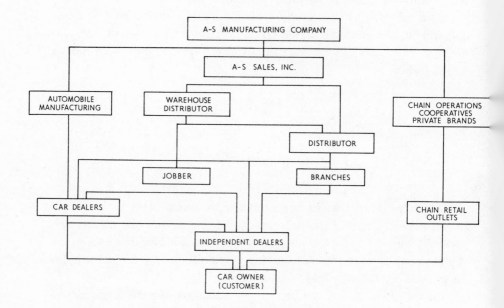

Definitions: *Primary   Customer*

Nonstocking Dealer. Service station, garage, or other
  retail outlet that does not carry an inventory of parts
  but orders as needed from a jobber or distributor.   Final consumer

Stocking Dealer. Same as above, but carries a small inventory of the most popular parts.   Final consumer

Car Dealer. Automobile agency with service facilities;
  carries inventory of popular parts.   Final consumer

Jobber. Buys from another wholesaler and carries a
  small inventory.   Independent dealer

Distributor. Medium-size wholesaler; carries fairly
  extensive inventory and buys from manufacturer or
  warehouse distributor.   Independent dealer

Warehouse Distributor. Large wholesaler, carries extensive inventory and sells only to other wholesalers.   Jobbers

Chain. Buys direct from manufacturer, usually under
  private brand, and performs the warehousing and
  wholesaling function for company's owned or fran-
  chised retail outlets.   Chain retail outlet

Automobile Manufacturer. Buys direct from parts
  manufacturer.   Car dealer

explained later.) Of A–S sales of parts to the automobile manufacturer, approximately 75 percent were used as original equipment on new cars; the remaining 25 percent were resold by the car manufacturer to franchised dealers for the replacement market. The more than 500 distributors used by A–S sold to approximately 10,000 jobbers, who, in turn, serviced about 180,000 dealers.

A–S AND INDUSTRY POSITION ON EXCISE TAX LEGISLATION

Original Position and Participation. With President Johnson's announcement on May 15, 1965, that he would ask Congress for a reduction in the 10 percent federal excise tax on automobiles, A–S and other companies in the automotive industry through a joint committee formed by various trade associations—the Industry-Wide Automotive Excise Tax Committee—undertook to guard the interests of both car and parts manufacturers. The lobbyist for the committee sought the highest possible excise tax reduction. At that time, according to A–S president, Mr. Leadtoh, no one on the committee had thought out very carefully the full implications of the program. Nothing had been said about pricing philosophy in the event of a reduction in tax. However, it soon became clear that distributors and jobbers were opposed to any price reductions, for that would reduce their dollar gross margins. Moreover, in the parts business, the market was quite inelastic. Car owners had to replace parts when they wore out. They seldom purchased ahead of that time, no matter what the price. Thus increased sales were not likely to result from a price reduction.

The auto parts dealers and distributors were also much in favor of including in the law a floor tax refund provision. (Similar provisions had been proposed for other goods also.) Stocks on hand at the time an excise tax cut became effective would decrease in value if the tax saving was passed on to consumers. Therefore, it was claimed, provision was needed for refunding by the government of the amount of tax already paid on distributor and dealer inventories.

There was some concern by the manufacturers that the burden of administering a floor tax refund would be very costly to them. For a while some manufacturers opposed the refund, but the bill as finally passed included the refunding provision.

Management's Pricing Dilemma. Under the new legislation the 8 percent tax on the manufacturer's selling price for auto parts was to be eliminated as of January 1, 1966. New price lists were usually issued at the first of each year in the industry. A–S prices had been increased in four of the last five years, the increase averaging 2.2 percent a year on spark plugs and 2.8 percent a year on batteries.

On counterpart items, which accounted for by far the larger part of A–S sales, the automobile manufacturers played a very important role in pricing. Mr. A. W. Distas, A–S marketing vice president, said, "On counterpart items, costs have little relevance to our pricing except in our negotiations with the car manufacturer over the original equipment price. But of course we sell relatively few original equipment items compared to the number of items in our aftermarket line. In our pricing of noncounterpart items, competitors' products, costs, and prices are important." On counterpart items, it was traditional for A–S and other parts manufacturers to follow car manufacturer prices. On noncounterpart items, there was no definite pattern, with A–S at times exerting price leadership and at other times following price changes of competitors.

Through bids and negotiations, A–S and the car manufacturer set the prices at which the manufacturer bought from A–S. The car manufacturer then set two prices, one at which it supplied its car dealers and the other a suggested retail price to the car owner.

When the car manufacturer announced new prices, A–S had in the past then calculated new prices for its distribution system. The basic A–S price was the distributor price, which averaged approximately 20 percent below the car manufacturer's price to dealers. Warehouse distributors usually bought at the distributor price less 20 percent, which represented a combination of functional and quantity discounts. Jobbers bought at about the distributor price plus 5 percent. Independent dealers who carried no inventory, buying parts as needed, usually bought at about one third off the consumer list price. Independent dealers who carried at least some parts in stock bought at 5 percent less than the price to the dealers with no inventory. For an example of typical price relationships throughout the distribution network before repeal of the excise tax, see Exhibit 2.

Computation of the amount of excise tax to be paid (as shown in Exhibit 2) had been as follows. An automobile part with a list price of $10 to the consumer was sold to the automobile manufacturer for $2.35 plus 8 percent federal excise tax, or $2.35 plus 19¢ for a total of $2.54. The 19¢ tax was equivalent to 7.4 percent of the total price paid by the automobile manufacturer. The price for the same part to large chain buyers was $3 plus 8 percent tax, or $3 plus 24¢ for a total of $3.24. The 24¢ was also equivalent to 7.4 percent of the total price paid by the

Exhibit 2

AUTO-START MANUFACTURING COMPANY

Typical Price Relationships and Gross Margins as of December 1965

Distribution Level	Approximate Price Relationships	Tax Paid by A–S as % of Sale Price			Gross Margin on Sales to Primary Customers
		At 23¢	At 24¢	At 19¢	
Consumer (list price)...................	$10.00	2.3%	2.4%	1.9%	
Independent dealer (no stock)..........	6.75	3.4			$3.25
Independent dealer (stock)..............	6.45	3.6	3.7		3.55
Car dealer............................	5.65	4.1		3.5	4.35
Jobber...............................	4.60	5.0			2.15
Distributor...........................	4.35	5.3			2.40
Warehouse distributor..................	3.48	6.6			1.12
Large chain...........................	3.24		7.4		
A–S Sales, Inc.........................	3.10	7.4			
Car manufacturer......................	2.54			7.4	3.11
A–S Cost.............................	2.00				
A–S Sales:					
Car manufacturer...................					.35
Large chain........................					1.00
Warehouse distributor..............					1.24
Distributor........................					2.11

chain buyers. In order to minimize the amount of tax paid on sales to warehouse distributors and regular distributors, A–S had established a separate, captive sales organization. A–S sold to this sales organization at a transfer price of $2.87 plus 8 percent tax (23¢) or $3.10. The sales organization was responsible for selling to warehouse distributors at $3.48 and to distributors at $4.35.

If the sales organization had not been incorporated into the distribution system, A–S would have been required to pay a tax of 7.4 percent of $3.48 (26¢) on sales to warehouse distributors and a tax of 7.4 percent of $4.35 (32¢) on sales to distributors. Thus, not only would the dollar amount of tax on the same part have been larger, but the dollar margin A–S received would have been less. The effect of the sales organization was to reduce the proportion that excise taxes represented of A–S total gross revenues from 7.4 percent to 5.5 percent. This was true because the 23¢ tax paid on the transfer price to the sales organization represented less than 7.4 percent of the revenues received from distributors by A–S. Also, a small portion of A–S sales were not subject to the excise tax. Use of the captive sales organization was acceptable to the Internal Revenue Service.

At the end of 1965, A–S reported revenues and sales for 1965 and projections for 1966. The percentage relationships were as shown below. Federal excise taxes A–S collected from its customers were not included as a part of gross sales.

	1965	1966 Projected
Gross revenues	100.0%	94.5%
Federal excise tax	(5.5)	—
Gross sales	94.5%	94.5%
Cost of goods sold	(77.5)	(77.5)
Gross margin	17.0%	17.0%

A–S distributors and dealers continued to oppose price reductions after repeal of the excise tax. Any price reduction that maintained the existing level of percentage mark-ups would reduce their dollar profit per item sold. These middlemen argued that it was not fair to them that they should earn fewer dollars for performing the same service and selling the same quantity just because federal excise taxes were removed.

The car manufacturer did not issue new price lists for its dealers until after January 1, 1966. A–S consequently delayed billing until it could establish its policy and prices.

A–S executives had a considerable difference of opinion as to how the excise tax cut should be reflected in new prices. Mr. Leadtoh believed quite strongly that his company should not reap any windfall gain because of the tax cut. He said:

I believe we should implement the tax cut in the manner requested by President Johnson. The consumer should receive the full benefit of the tax cut. I interpret this to mean (at least in theory) the final customer price should be reduced by the percentage of tax we have been paying, or about 5.5 percent.

But it is not that simple. We don't know what the car factories are going to do. It would do us no good to be below them—and we can't go above them. I suppose our competitors are in the same dilemma.

In addition, we must bear in mind the interests of our distributors and jobbers. They are already pressuring us not to reduce prices because they need the same dollar margins to cover their costs. If they are making a fair profit now, to reduce prices may induce other problems in the near future such as pressure for extra discounts, freight allowances, and the like. As you can imagine this could create a lot of havoc in the market as between both our customers and our competitors. If possible we would like to avoid this—it really helps no one and could potentially hurt our industry.

I'm just not sure what is right for everyone concerned or even if there is any action that we can take that will not end up hurting someone.

Another point of view was expressed by Mr. A. W. Distas, marketing vice president. Mr. Distas was in favor of retaining the prices in effect before the excise tax repeal. Mr. Distas said:

> Prices are going up, material and labor costs are going up. Why reduce our prices? And most important of all, our customers don't want prices reduced. In my job, I certainly don't want to make them mad at us. The tax we pay is only around 2 percent of the final consumer price. Since we normally raise prices about that much each year, let's just leave things as they are.

A third point of view was expressed by Mr. M. E. Mantion, financial vice president:

> I really don't see what the problem is. I think we should go along with President Johnson and pass the tax savings on to the consumer. On our sales at the distributor price, our tax amounts to 23 cents on each $10 item at the consumer level. Therefore, on a $10 item we would reduce the list price 23 cents. This is equal to 2.3 percent throughout the distribution network. This passes the tax savings on to the consumer and allows every one in the distribution network the same treatment.

Still a fourth viewpoint was expressed by Mr. Silas Eliot. Mr. Eliot, who reported to Mantion, was closely involved with the excise requirement, tax legislation, and pricing. Eliot explained his position:

> Any additional profit resulting from the excise tax cut after passing on some saving to the consumer should accrue to us. Also you must remember our competitors are earning more money than we do as a percent of sales and return on investment.
>
> I feel very strongly that we do not want to disturb the traditional percentage margins allowed in our price lists to the middlemen. Our customers understand this system. A percentage system allows great flexibility and is understandable. And it is fair and right that these people should have a given percentage margin to operate in. The margin in the past has been fair so any price reduction we make will be fair if we keep the same percentage for margins. Our customers now may want an equal reduction in dollars at each distribution level, which would change their mark-up percentages. But you can be sure that at the next price increase they will want equal percentage increases, not equal dollars.
>
> We can't afford to upset our existing pricing system. That is why I think we ought to reduce prices for the excise cut and add on our normal annual price increase. That would mean reducing prices 5.5 percent and then increasing them 2.5 percent. In effect, this would be a 3.0 percent price decrease all along the line. To make our price increase publicly acceptable, we have to net it out rather than raise prices later.
>
> Also, I don't think we ought to reduce our prices on noncounterpart items, even though they are covered by the excise repeal. We currently have a margin of about 14 percent on noncounterpart items and about 18 percent on counterpart items. If we do not reduce prices on noncounterpart items we will then have

Exhibit 3

AUTO-START MANUFACTURING COMPANY

Pricing Schedules Proposed Following Excise Tax Repeal,
January 1, 1966

Distribution Level	A–S Price Dec. 31, 1965	Car Manufacturing 1966 Prices	Base on Car Manufacturing 1966 Prices	Reduce Prices 5.5%	Reduce Prices 3.0%	Reduce Prices 23¢ (19¢ to manufacturing 24¢ to chains)	Reduce Prices 2.3%	Reduce Prices 2.3% Then Increase Prices 2.5%
Consumer (list price)	$10.00	$9.66	$9.66	$9.45	$9.70	$9.77	$9.77	$10.01
Independent dealer	6.75		6.52	6.38	6.55	6.52	6.59	6.68
Independent dealer	6.45		6.23	6.10	6.26	6.22	6.30	6.38
Car dealer	5.65	5.36	5.36	5.34	5.48	5.42	5.52	5.56
Jobber	4.60		4.44	4.35	4.46	4.37	4.49	4.48
Distributor	4.35		4.20	4.11	4.22	4.12	4.25	4.22
Warehouse distributor	3.48		3.36	3.29	3.38	3.25	3.40	3.33
Large chain	3.24		2.90	3.06	3.14	3.00	3.17	3.08*
Car manufacturer	2.54	2.35	2.35	2.40	2.46	2.35	2.48	2.41†
A–S cost	2.00	2.00	2.00	2.00	2.00	2.00	2.00	2.00

* Reduce price 24¢, increase price 2.5%.
† Reduce price 19¢, increase price 2.5%.

a margin of about 19.5 percent. If the company follows my recommendation on counterpart items we would have a margin of about 20.5 percent for those products. That would make the profitability of both types of products about the same, or at least much closer than it now is.

On Saturday, January 15, 1966, A–S received the newly published prices from the car manufacturers, which were as shown in Column 2, Exhibit 3. Mr. Leadtoh called a meeting for January 17 to discuss what pricing action A–S should take. It was essential for the company to act quickly. The president hoped to emerge from the meeting with a consensus as to appropriate action and a realistic appraisal of the effects of such action. Various pricing schedules that had been suggested are shown in Exhibit 3.

Albert Manufacturing Company

THE ALBERT MANUFACTURING COMPANY was founded in 1938 to produce various machined and fabricated components for industrial users. Shortly after the start of World War II the company began to make mechanical and hydraulic assemblies for aircraft. This part of the business grew and in April, 1947, was set up as a separate division. To house operations the company leased a newly constructed plant in Wichita, Kansas, with 1.2 million square feet of floor space. By the end of 1954 sales of the Wichita Division were running at about $120 million annually. The division had approximately 1,200 employees.

Early in January, 1955, Mr. Henderson, works manager of the Wichita Division and a vice-president of the Albert Company, called Mr. Paul Bellows to his office. Bellows was purchasing agent for the division. Henderson told Bellows he had just received a telephone call from the manager of the local office of the Federal Bureau of Investigation. The manager informed him that an investigation then in progress by the FBI had brought to light information involving certain of the division's buyers. Henderson said he had arranged for the investigators to visit the division the following morning. He asked Bellows to receive them and to keep him informed as to developments.

The next day Mr. Arnold Rand and Mr. Peter Thomas, FBI agents, called on Bellows. Mr. Ralph Nance, assistant purchasing agent, was also at the meeting. After a brief exchange of pleasantries the following discussion took place:

BELLOWS: As you can well imagine Nance and I are very curious about this matter. We have not mentioned it to anyone but we have speculated between ourselves as to the nature of the thing. What's the story?

RAND: Well, I guess I ought to go back to last fall. We were conducting an investigation on placement of government contracts at the P. B. Blake Company on the north side of town. After several weeks and rather by accident, Pete Thomas was interviewing a witness who was a buyer in Blake's purchasing department. The fellow confessed to having accepted a $4,500 bribe from a local tool supplier. Later we

854

verified that he had received the money from the company he named. The supplier involved has gone on record that the money was a personal loan from their salesman and was to have been repaid. However, the buyer involved did not support this contention. The buyer turned state witness and gave us several other instances of similar occurrences, but they were not as serious—at least there wasn't as much money involved.

NANCE: Where is the tie-in with the Albert company?

RAND: This buyer has made a sworn statement that he knows three of your buyers have also been accepting expensive gifts and perhaps being bought off as he was. . . .

THOMAS: Bellows, this thing is nebulous as hell. We don't have much to go on, but there are enough basic implications that we think these three buyers of yours may well be tarred with the same brush.

RAND: I'd like to tell you about a fishing trip that our informant was on. He stated—and we have verified this—that he was one of 12 guests at an upstate fishing lodge over a three-day week end. The whole bunch were flown up to this lodge, spent the week end in substantial style and returned. All expenses were paid by the supplier. Now get this—your three buyers were there along with the chief tool designer and two manufacturing engineers from Albert. It was at this occasion that our informant states he learned of the arrangements, shall we say, between the supplier and your buyers.

BELLOWS: What can we do to get this thing off the ground? What can we do to help clear this thing up?

RAND: We would like to examine your records to see who placed orders with the specific company mentioned in the charge and two other companies also implicated. Then we think that sworn statements will be taken. After that if there are any concrete leads we will conduct an investigation outside the company to ascertain if the individuals have increased bank balances, are living beyond their means, and stuff like that. . . .

THOMAS: There is one thing that bothers us. We don't have jurisdiction.

BELLOWS: What do you mean jurisdiction?

THOMAS: At the P. B. Blake Company we could investigate because they held prime contracts from the government. You don't, and therefore we can't come in and do the same kind of thing.

BELLOWS: Could you if we asked you to?

THOMAS: That would take care of the matter completely.

BELLOWS: Well, that settles that. We are asking you now and will give you whatever you need in the way of an official request. Now then, when and how will you start the ball rolling?

RAND: In about three days if you can be ready for us. If possible, we would like to use a private office because of the secrecy necessary until we know where we are. We will also need personnel records, purchase order files, and a lot of other things.

BELLOWS: We will be ready for you. Let me say now I am more concerned than you are and want this cleaned up one way or the other as quickly as possible but with a minimum of disruption of the purchasing department. However, even if we have got to shake this department up hard, I will give you every support. Nance, get things organized to take care of this. Don't tell anyone what is going on until we decide the time is right . . . explain the presence of strangers by, well let them be headquarters auditors or something. Gentlemen, Ralph Nance will be your contact and will personally make all the necessary arrangements. Again, I want to assure you that you have our cooperation. Tell me, who are the vendors in question?

RAND: The Supreme Engineering Company is the firm specifically mentioned in the allegation. The other two are Superior Tool and Die, Inc., and Allied Tool Company.

NANCE: Thanks, you can be assured that things will be set up for you.

Mr. Bellows was especially concerned about this investigation because he had given special emphasis to a strict code of ethical conduct with suppliers since he had assumed his current assignment. The departmental policy was that no employee was to accept any gift or courtesy that he was not in a position to reciprocate. In a variety of ways Bellows had tried to get this standard of conduct understood and accepted by all those in the department. The topic was frequently discussed at weekly meetings with purchasing supervisors. All male employees of the department had attended a company school where one of the subjects discussed was the company policy on bribery. The issue had been discussed at the monthly dinner meetings held for male employees of the purchasing department. Bellows had authorized his buyers to make a fairly liberal use of expense accounts so that they could reciprocate in buying lunches, and so on, for suppliers' representatives and not feel under any obligation to them. He knew that some of the production and engineering employees had accepted Christmas gifts and entertainment from suppliers, but he had believed that his buyers had been completely honest in dealings with suppliers.

The Wichita Division was highly specialized in that it made only a limited line of small gear trains, landing gear assemblies, hydraulic pumps and actuators, and certain fabricated assemblies. The vast bulk of the more or less common components needed were obtained from subcontractors. In 1954 the purchasing department had paid slightly over $55 million to subcontractors, or about half of the total sales of the division.

Buyers for the division were divided into groups, each headed by a senior buyer. These groups were organized along product lines, each being responsible for purchasing items that fell within a broad classification. A service group typed purchase orders, maintained the files, expedited orders that were overdue, and performed other functions of a clerical or routine nature. The entire purchasing department employed 128 people.

The flow of work into the department was in the form of requisitions that specified the items required and the date they should be available. A requisition was first processed by a member of the service group, who entered it in a master log and then routed it to the proper buying group. The assistant buyer for the group upon receipt of a requisition determined what previous suppliers had furnished the item. Any specifications that applied were pulled out together with the blueprint of the part. Then invitations to quote were sent out to approved sources or, if there was only one source, the supplier's representatives were contacted for negotiation. After a supplier had been selected, the assistant buyer filled in on the requisition the supplier's name and the price per unit. Certain other details also were added, such as the storeroom that was to receive the goods, discount terms, shipping point, and so forth. The requisition then was passed on to the appropriate buyer.

In most of the groups the effective control in selection of suppliers was in the hands of the buyers. However, in all groups every requisition had to be signed by a senior buyer. At this stage it went back to the service group. The necessary number of copies were typed, hecto masters for receiving and accounting were prepared, the facsimile signature of the purchasing agent was applied, and copies were mailed to the vendor. The requisition had been transformed from a request to purchase into a contract with a supplier.

About a week after the FBI agents started their investigation, Nance and Thomas discussed progress made during the preliminary stage.

Thomas stated that he thought matters were progressing extremely slowly but that things should speed up in the near future. He and Rand had screened all the purchase orders placed by the division with the three suppliers in question during the past six months. All the orders had been for some type of tooling, primarily for tool repair work. All had been placed by the three buyers named in the original complaint.

Thomas gave Nance the following summary of the findings of the purchase order review:

1. All 1,976 purchase orders were initialed by the senior buyer for tools, Mr. Clinton Boles. The buyers that actually handled the orders and the distribution of orders among the suppliers in question were:

	Superior	Supreme	Allied	Total
Adolph Stimmer (assistant buyer)	622	257	48	927
John Lippen (buyer)	73	159	0	232
John Ruppert (assistant buyer)	280	531	6	817

2. While only 54 purchase orders were placed with Allied, the total dollar value of these orders was $86,409. The dollar value for Superior Tool and Die was $234,765 and for Supreme Engineering it was $303,040.

3. Among the orders were three, all placed with Supreme, which radically increased in price during the period of manufacture. The original quoted prices for these orders were $257.75, $1,166, and $2,500. The final prices on the orders, as authorized by change notices to the purchase orders, were $1,186.50, $3,775, and $4,996.[1]

Nance had intimate knowledge of tool buying and of the tool buying group. He at one time had been responsible for buying tools at the home plant of the Albert Company, and Stimmer then had been an assistant buyer reporting to him. Any tool supplier usually could build a new tool. Quotations of delivery and price could be readily obtained by furnishing the supplier with blueprints and specifications. Repair of tools was an entirely different matter. It was necessary for someone from the tool firm to inspect the tool requiring repair before submitting a quotation. Time was important because the tool generally was needed for production of a scheduled part. Therefore repair jobs were often placed on an advise price basis; that is, the supplier would take the tool and after completing his inspection at his plant would submit a price. The buyer then would judge whether or not this price was fair. If he

---

[1] During the manufacture of tools, design changes often become necessary or desirable. Such changes sometimes cause revisions in the delivered prices. Change notices also may tempt the supplier, particularly one who deliberately quoted under his costs to get an order, to demand an exorbitant price increase. This practice is frowned on by reputable tool vendors but is sometimes resorted to by marginal producers.

decided it was too high, he either negotiated a new price or moved the tool to another supplier.

The tool buying group, unlike the other buying groups, dealt in general with small firms. A relatively low capital investment was required to start a tool shop and there were many local tool makers that were highly specialized and extremely small, sometimes employing no more than four or five men. Adequate credit and other information was difficult to obtain for these small firms.

About two weeks after they began their investigation, Thomas and Rand told Nance they were going to interview, under oath, Stimmer, Lippen, Ruppert, and Boles. They further stated that they wanted to discuss the progress made to date with Bellows and Nance as soon as they had had time to weigh the statements of the men. Nance suggested they meet the following afternoon. Rand and Thomas agreed.

The next afternoon Rand, Thomas, Nance, and Bellows gathered in Bellows' office. Rand opened the meeting.

RAND: Guess you will be surprised to learn that we are ending the investigation.

BELLOWS: You're all through already?

RAND: That's right. We have been unable to uncover any concrete evidence. We must have proof and, while there is no lack of suspicious circumstances, we just can't pin down anything definite.

BELLOWS: You can't come out here, tear into everything, arouse considerable doubt in our minds, and then pull out. We want these men either nailed to the cross or exonerated—is this too much to ask?

NANCE: I thought you were making satisfactory progress.

THOMAS: Paul, you must realize we work for a boss too. He gave us almost five weeks to firm the investigation up. We just can't do it. There is a lot of smoke but no fire that we can find. So we want to give you everything we have and, if you come across some new evidence later on, we promise to give you all the help we can. That's all there is to it. We're sorry it turned out this way but. . . .

NANCE: Tell us what the score is now before we discuss this aspect further.

RAND: OK. First, Lippen is clean. He was recently transferred out of the tool group and actually was in the group only three weeks during the period of time the alleged offense took place. Both Stimmer and Ruppert absolutely deny the charge. They admit close knowledge of the suppliers but were rather evasive on the question of entertainment. Stimmer stated he was at the fishing party I mentioned to you earlier.

Ruppert says he doesn't associate with salesmen outside of the office.

THOMAS: I handled the outside investigation. We went over every phase of Stimmer's and Ruppert's personal affairs—bank accounts, recent large purchases, standard of living, and so forth. Both are clean insofar as concrete evidence is concerned, but there is considerable doubt in my mind as to whether these guys are on the level. Stimmer lives well but not too far over the level he could support on his income. Ruppert took a very expensive vacation last year—two weeks in Florida at a fancy hotel. I believe a supplier paid a large part of the bills while he was there, but again I have no proof.

RAND: I think you should also know that we have checked the suppliers very carefully too. I have tried to determine the expense account entries on the salesmen's reports turned into the companies. You realize that a company is in a box with the Internal Revenue if we catch it falsifying expenses. Again nothing conclusive, but, Paul, you should know that these companies all have substantial entries listing entertaining your people. I believe your name was even listed a few times.

BELLOWS: If you could check all of the 2,200 suppliers we do business with, I bet you will find my name quite often. Needless to say, I don't even know many of the salesmen, but a purchasing agent's name on the sales report for a lunch impresses the sales manager—and who is going to check to find the salesman is doing a little padding?

RAND: That is undoubtedly true, but there were still many of Albert's personnel on the statements. I was surprised that people outside of the purchasing department were mentioned freely. However, there was nothing to implicate Stimmer or Ruppert.

THOMAS: Well, what else can we say? We have a lot of suspicion that Stimmer and Ruppert are, at best, pretty close to these suppliers. Boles, of course, could be involved in this thing too. We didn't get around to checking his personal affairs as closely as the others, but I don't think he is completely out from under, from what little we have been able to determine.

BELLOWS: What do you say, Ralph?

NANCE: Well, I don't believe we can do much more. We have the information and can be on the lookout for future indications. It is regrettable that we can't run this thing into the ground, but there isn't anything we can do about it.

BELLOWS: Then I want to thank you gentlemen for your help so far and, if we do uncover anything, we will contact you.

Exhibit 1

THE ALBERT MANUFACTURING COMPANY—WICHITA DIVISION

Organization Chart—Purchasing Department

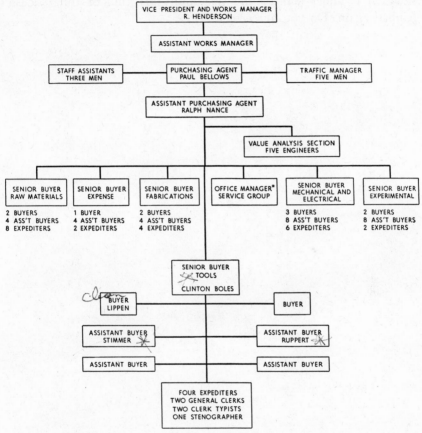

* Equal in classification to senior buyer. There were 18 women clerks, typists, and stenographers in the service group out of a total of 43 for the entire purchasing department.

THOMAS: Feel free to do that—even if we can't get out right away we can tell you what move you should make.

After Thomas and Rand had gone, Bellows and Nance talked over the situation. Nance expressed the following views.

NANCE: Paul, I'm not sure what I should do, but I'll tell you one thing: I don't want these guys in the tool group any longer. I've got to have a senior buyer that I can trust completely and buyers that are above reproach.

This whole mess is like shadow boxing. Just last November I rated Boles as ready for advancement and Stimmer and Ruppert certainly have always been considered as competent.

However, as I see it I have got to take action to make sure the situation is under control and guarantee this kind of thing doesn't happen again. Do you agree?

Skyway Electronics, Inc.

IN THE SUMMER OF 1958, Mr. Horace Jones of Jones, Evarts and Company was making an investigation of Skyway Electronics, Inc. Jones, Evarts was a small investment trust, and its officers were looking for an "up and coming" electronics firm in which to invest.

Mr. Jones met several Skyway officers, but talked chiefly with R. S. Huntley, the executive vice-president. Jones was attempting, among other things, to ascertain how the top executives of Skyway dealt with their officers and workers. It was a Jones, Evarts maxim that when one buys stock in a company one invests in its management's attitudes, traditions, and viewpoints as well as in the assets or liabilities more commonly taken into account.

Mr. Huntley and other Skyway executives answered all questions freely and frankly.

THE COMPANY AND ITS CHARACTERISTICS

Skyway Electronics had been established in 1945. It made a variety of unique electronic components developed through research and experimentation. These were protected by patents, some of which would expire between 1958 and 1962. The company also made some general-purpose components. Sales had risen from $100,000 in 1946 to about $26 million in 1957 (Exhibit 1). Production in 1958 was carried on at five locations: Ohio, Indiana, Pennsylvania, California, and Montreal. The Ohio facility was chiefly a pilot operation. The Indiana plant was a wholly owned subsidiary, the Cramden Company, acquired as a going concern in 1956.

Skyway was organized on a regional-division basis, each manufacturing unit having its own technical, sales, and manufacturing staffs. At headquarters, in Cleveland, the company maintained four supervisory groups, each under a vice-president—for marketing, technical direction, engineering services, and finance and control. A fifth vice-president was directly responsible for the performance of the five operating divisions (Exhibit 2).

The president of Skyway was Dr. Frank McLean, an electrical

engineer by training, who had risen through the technical departments of the company. His father, founder of the company, had retired from active management in 1953. Frank McLean concentrated on technical developments, while Mr. Huntley attended to organizational and managerial matters. Huntley had served Skyway since its inception.

The company enjoyed a largely unchallenged position for its specialized products, serving a variety of manufacturing customers. In

Exhibit 1

SKYWAY ELECTRONICS, INC.

Sales, Profits, and Gross Fixed Assets
Actual 1945 to 1957, Estimated 1958 to 1962
(Millions of Dollars)

Year	Sales	Pretax Profit (or Loss)	Profit as % of Sales	Annual Sales Increase	Gross Fixed Assets
1945........	$ ...	$ ...	..	...	$ ...
1946........	0.1	(0.1)	..	...	...
1947........	0.2	(0.3)	..	100%	...
1948........	0.4	(0.4)	..	100	0.2
1949........	0.9	(0.5)	..	125	1.0
1950........	2.1	(0.1)	..	135	1.3
1951........	5.4	0.5	9%	155	1.7
1952........	5.9	(0.9)	..	10	4.0
1953........	9.5	0.6	6	60	4.4
1954........	15.0	2.8	19	58	4.8
1955........	18.5	4.0	22	24	6.1
1956........	24.5	5.6	23	32	8.6
1957........	25.9	4.2	16	6	10.1
1958 (est.)...	30.0	6.4	21	16	12.0
1959 (est.)...	34.5	6.5	19	15	13.3
1960 (est.)...	40.0	6.8	17	15	15.1
1961 (est.)...	46.0	7.1	15	15	17.4
1962 (est.)...	52.0	7.4	14	15	19.4

1958, however, Mr. Huntley and Mr. McLean were concerned about the possibility of competitive developments. They considered technical obsolescence another threat from a long-range point of view. Profits had been highly satisfactory in the recent past (Exhibits 3 and 4).

The company sold its specialized components through a sales force of 145 men trained in all technical aspects and applications of the products. They sought new customers and called frequently on existing ones. Customers were exacting as to quality and delivery. Special machinery for production was required, and the work force needed a reasonable degree of skill and application to maintain satisfactory output.

Exhibit 2

S<small>KYWAY</small> E<small>LECTRONICS</small>, I<small>NC.</small>

Organization Chart
June, 1958

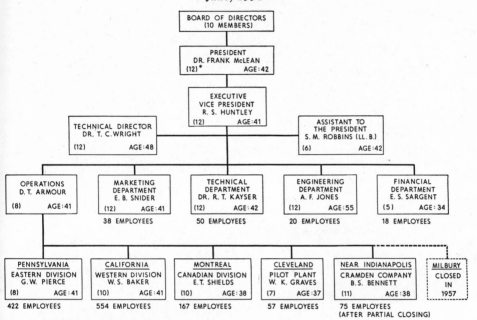

* Figures in parentheses denote years of service.

Exhibit 3

S<small>KYWAY</small> E<small>LECTRONICS</small>, I<small>NC.</small>

Operating Statements, 1956, 1957, Nine Months 1958
(Thousands of Dollars)

	1956		1957		Nine Months 1958	
Net sales	$24,500	100%	$25,920	100%	$20,500	100%
Manufacturing cost of sales	13,700	56	14,300	55	11,050	54
Gross profit	$10,800	44%	$11,620	45%	$ 9,450	46%
Expenses:						
Selling	$ 3,150	13%	$ 4,990	19%	$3,400	17%
General and administrative	800	3	650	3	550	3
Research	1,200	5	1,310	5	1,000	5
Total	$ 5,150	21%	$ 6,950	27%	$ 4,950	25%
Net operating profit	$ 5,650	23%	$ 4,670	18%	$ 4,500	22%
Other income (expense)	(20)	..	(300)	1	(100)	0.5
Net profit before tax	$ 5,630	23%	$ 4,370	17%	$ 4,400	21%
Income taxes	2,900	12	2,150	8	2,300	11
Net profit	$ 2,730	11%	$ 2,220	9%	$ 2,100	10%

Exhibit 4

SKYWAY ELECTRONICS, INC.

Balance Sheets, December 31, 1956, 1957, and March 31, 1958

(Thousands of Dollars)

Assets

	1956	1957	1958
Current Assets:			
Cash	$ 1,600	$ 500	$ 700
Receivables—Net	3,100	3,800	3,100
Inventories	5,400	7,200	8,400
Other Current Assets	100	100	100
Total Current Assets	$10,200	$11,600	$12,300
Property and Equipment	$10,100	$12,000	$12,200
Reserves for Depreciation	2,500	3,100	3,300
Net Property and Equipment	$ 7,600	$ 8,900	$ 8,900
Deferred Charges	$ 100	$ 400	$ 400
Total Assets	$17,900	$20,900	$21,600

Liabilities

	1956	1957	1958
Current Liabilities:			
Notes and Accounts Payable	$ 800	$ 1,300	$ 1,100
Accrued Liabilities	200	500	400
Federal Income Tax	2,500	1,400	900
Total Current Liabilities	$ 3,500	$ 3,200	$ 2,400
Other Liabilities	$ 400	$ 400	$ 400
Long-Term Debt	1,000	2,100	3,500
Capital Stock (Common)	$ 8,000	$ 8,000	$ 8,000
Earned Surplus	5,000	7,200	7,300
Total Net Worth	$13,000	$15,200	$15,300
Total Liabilities	$17,900	$20,900	$21,600

Mr. Jones asked Mr. Huntley what problems the company had encountered in connection with the release, transfer, retraining, and moving of personnel during its growth.

Mr. Huntley began his answer by explaining that Skyway had an unwritten rule that any officer or supervisor who had been employed for 10 or more years would be kept on even though change in scope of company operations or other factors had reduced his usefulness. "If we have not found out in 10 years whether the person is any good, it was our mistake, and we are stuck with the problem," Mr. Huntley said. The company, he added, attempted to take the best possible care of all its employees.

Speaking of future problems of personnel transfers and promotions, Mr. Huntley observed that the company's management was young, the average age being not quite 42 years for the 14 top positions. He foresaw few vacancies to absorb lower management members or men freed by changes in operations. He expected a slower rate of growth in future years as patent protection diminished and competition increased (Exhibit 1).

Huntley and other Skyway officers then described in detail the company's treatment of employees under two sets of circumstances: (1) when a plant was closed; (2) when a company was purchased and operated as a subsidiary.

CLOSING A PLANT

When Skyway Electronics was established in 1945, initial efforts had been concentrated on product development and improvement. After suitable products had been designed, the original intent was to build a new plant in Cleveland near the research facilities, the pilot operations, and headquarters. The president, however, heard of an opportunity to purchase a vacated multistory factory building, formerly used for food processing, in Milbury, a Kentucky town of 30,000 people. The purchase price was attractive in comparison with the costs of erecting a new building. Furthermore, it was thought that labor union difficulties might delay construction in Cleveland. The purchase was made and operations were begun in 1946. By 1950 the building was being used practically to capacity, and it became apparent that a major period of expansion lay ahead. Plans were then made for a plant in California, which was completed in 1951. By 1953 the need for another plant in the East was obvious, and one was built in Pennsylvania. During this period, the needs of the Canadian market had been met by exports from the United States. In 1956, however, the company began construction of a plant in Montreal, chiefly to avoid the 20% import duty.

At the end of 1956, the Skyway executives believed the period of frantic company growth was ended and it was time to review operations. The three United States plants together provided excess capacity, as much as 50% at times. Thus, the question of closing the Milbury plant arose.

A study of operating records showed the Milbury plant to be about 15% lower in efficiency than the others. Moreover, wage rates were about 10% higher. The local labor union was strong. There were in the area about 8,000 workers. Of these, 6,500 were employed by a division of General Machinery Corporation. The assistant to the president of Skyway, Mr. Robbins, characterized the situation as follows: "When our company was operating full swing in the early 1950's, it had scraped the bottom of the labor barrel. We were experimental then and needed more workers than we did when production became more routine. Because of a seniority clause in the union contract, however, most of these employees had to be kept on and this led to feather-bedding." Mr. Robbins thought the employees lacked motivation and the will to work, even though they were sufficiently skilled; workers in this plant had not been put on an incentive wage basis such as was used in the California plant. Further, Robbins said, it was common for them to live beyond their means, which led to garnishments and assignments of wages to local businesses.

The plant's location, moreover, was poor in relation to the company's major markets. Mr. Robbins pointed out that the decision to buy the plant had been made on the basis of expediency more than on considerations of location. In contrast, the new plants had been located after careul surveys of proximity to markets, local tax situations, available labor, and so on. In addition, the Milbury building was awkwardly constructed for the purposes of Skyway Electronics. The ground floor, especially, was poorly laid out and hampered manufacturing operations.

A report by the company's treasurer as of November 15, 1956, showed anticipated operating savings for 1957 from closing Milbury of $550,000 against a probable cost of shutdown of $200,000. A second estimate as of January 25, 1957, showed no net operating savings for 1957, but for 1958 and each year thereafter this estimate put net operating savings at $625,000. An estimate as of February 26, 1958 put future operating savings at $665,000 annually. Large capital savings also were expected (Exhibits 5 and 6).

The decision to shut down the Milbury plant was announced on March 8, 1957. Work stoppage was completed by June 1, with only a skeleton force remaining. The decision affected 251 workers.

According to Mr. Armour, operations vice-president, the contemplated move was kept secret until the March announcement because of the possibility of a charge by the union that the company was a "runaway employer." Mr. Huntley pointed out, however, that during the two years preceding the shutdown there had been several instances in which the inefficiencies of the operation had been called to the attention of the union and the workers. In one case, a study by a consulting firm had shown clearly that the plant's performance was substandard.

The company's relations with the union had not been cordial in the past, but neither had there been serious difficulties. In the early days of the operation a strike was called on an issue of technological unem-

Exhibit 5

SKYWAY ELECTRONICS, INC.

Memorandum on Closing Milbury
January 28, 1957

The following understanding of the situation in regard to closing the Milbury plant was reached in a meeting held January 25, 1957. This meeting was attended by Messrs. McLean, Huntley, Armour, and Sargent.

1. If we shut down Milbury in 1957, we will have to spend an additional $400,000 in the next five years (that is, through 1961) in the remaining factories in this country which would not otherwise be required.

2. Against this additional expenditure we have the following possible credits:

   a) Anything received for the sale of Milbury (book value $600,000).

   b) Reduction in working capital (estimated $100,000 for 1957, $300,000 estimated 1958–61).

   c) $135,000 ($150,000 less $15,000 duty) for miscellaneous equipment which would be shipped to Canada and which they otherwise have to buy.

   d) $50,000 production equipment which would not be needed if we close one U.S. factory.

   e) $70,000 reduction in capital needed for miscellaneous projects at Milbury.

Item (*c*) assumes that we go ahead with the Canadian plant and that the Milbury shutdown would be so timed that certain equipment could be transferred in time to take care of Canadian needs.

3. The savings which can reasonably be expected for a full year of operation with Milbury shutdown (starting in 1958) are as follows:

   a) $375,000 in lower manufacturing costs made up primarily of four items—lower labor rates, greater productivity, better flow, a greater divisor. We agree with the first three although we think there is a point beyond which the last point applies.

   b) $50,000 in reduced order and billing expenses. This is out of $125,000 contemplated for Milbury in 1957.

   c) $200,000 out of factory overhead expenses made up; $90,000 out of $500,000 of general overhead; $43,000 out of $105,000 for scheduling, production control, and so forth; $67,000 out of $107,000 for shipping and receiving. After sale of the Milbury property we can realize an additional $25,000 saving in building depreciation.

In 1957 the total operating savings are estimated at $200,000. This estimated saving will offset the estimated costs of $200,000 to be incurred in shutting down the plant and moving personnel and equipment.

We realize that a third plant gives a greater factor of safety and believe this is offset by the savings which accrue.

If sales in 1961 exceed the $46,000,000 presently estimated, a new plant will probably be needed, but we would be free to locate at the most desirable spot and build a properly laid out facility.

The mechanics of closing must be carefully planned.

Exhibit 6

SKYWAY ELECTRONICS, INC.

Memorandum on Savings from Closing Milbury Plant
Dated February 26, 1958

(Thousands of Dollars)

	For Year 1957			Annual 1958 and After
	November 15, 1956	January 25, 1957		February 26, 1958
1. *Capital Saving*	*Estimate*	*Estimate*	*Actual*	*Estimate*
a) Sale of building.............	$ 600	Undetermined	Undetermined	$503*
b) Working capital.............	100	$100	$358	358
c) Capital equipment for Canada plant............	210	135	145	...
d) Other productive equipment..	50	50	75	...
e) Reduced expenditures........	72	70	69	...
f) Miscellaneous equipment.....	...	...	50	...
	$1,032	$355	$597	$861

	For Year 1957			Annual 1958 and After	
	November 15, 1956	January 25, 1957		January 25, 1957	February 26, 1958
2. *Expense Saving*	*Estimate*	*Estimate*	*Actual*	*Estimate*	*Estimate*
a) Manufacturing costs.....$300		...	$259	$375	$400
b) Order and billing....... 50		...	13	50	20
c) Factory overhead....... 200		...	238	200	300
Total savings.....$550		$200	$510	$625	$720
d) Less carrying costs (utilities, maintenance, depreciation, taxes, etc.)......... ...		...	84†	...	55‡
e) Net savings............. 550		200	426	625	665
f) Cost of shutdown....... 200		200	303	...	...
Saving before capital loss on building........$350		...	$123	$625	$665

* Less annual depreciation.
† $52,000 maintenance, and so on; $32,000 depreciation.
‡ Only as long as we own building.

ployment. The conflict was resolved by arbitration in two hours. During contract negotiations in 1955 there had been threat of a strike, and arbitration again was successful. Much time had been spent in 1955 in negotiations on the issue of termination pay. Mr. Armour believed this indicated the union leaders thought the plant would be closed sooner or later.

During the 1955 negotiations the union had asked for a pay raise of 17 cents an hour as against the company's offer of 8 to 10 cents. The local plant manager began negotiations on the basis that the company would rather take a strike than incur the extra wage expense. Both sides were firmly entrenched in their positions when the Skyway management suddenly realized, according to Mr. Armour, that forcing the strike issue could expose the company to charges of unfair practices if it subsequently closed the plant. Consequently, the plant manager was instructed to accept the union's demands. "We rigged the figures a little so it looked like they were getting 17 cents including fringe benefits, although it actually amounted to less," Mr. Armour explained. The union dropped its termination pay clause demand at this point.

When the decision to close the plant in 1957 was announced, there was great concern at headquarters that an unfair labor charge nevertheless might result. All correspondence with the union was sent to legal counsel for approval, and all statements to be made in discussions with worker representatives were rehearsed. To the great relief of the Skyway officers, the union made no charge. Mr. Armour commented that the local union agent, though often difficult to deal with, was a realistic man who understood the facts of business. "Once he was convinced we were honest about the economics of the shutdown, he came around and did not really have much of a basis for an unfair labor charge." Moreover, the attention of the union was directed primarily at the major employer in the community; Skyway was only a small factor in the labor situation. "The agent was not dependent upon our employees for his pay; he was mainly supported by dues coming from the General Machinery plant."

Of the 251 persons idled by the shutdown, 181 were hourly employees, 150 men and 31 women. The company's controller had worked out a termination pay arrangement which in essence amounted to what the union had asked for in 1955. Each employee was to be given one week's pay for each year of service.

In its preliminary estimates the company had expected the total cost of termination payments to be about $40,000. An additional $20,000 had been set aside for the cost of transferring to other locations 15 supervisory employees the company wished to keep. The actual costs of termination and transfer, however, were estimated at $113,000. There were several factors contributing to this increase, some of the more important of which are described in the following paragraphs.

Termination payments, mainly to hourly personnel, were higher than expected by $12,000 because of a larger than anticipated number of employees at the time of shutdown.

The moving expense of the 15 supervisory personnel amounted to

$25,000 rather than the estimated $20,000. Included in this amount was $7,500 spent by the company to help with real estate transactions. The shutdown at Milbury coincided with the withdrawal of two other minor employers from the community and with the first signs of the 1958 recession affecting the General Machinery plant. Consequently, those selling their homes faced a depressed market. The company helped five persons by paying taxes, insurance, and upkeep on their homes for several months. Also, it reimbursed several employees for capital losses and made some interest-free loans until mortgage financing could be arranged. This type of assistance was voluntary; company policy on the moving of personnel, which had been established prior to this specific instance, did not call for such help (Exhibit 7). "We wanted to keep these people," said Mr. Huntley. "Good people were hard to find in 1957."

Exhibit 7

SKYWAY ELECTRONICS, INC.

Subject: Moving Expenses (Policies in effect at time of Milbury shutdown).

The company will reimburse salaried employees for all direct expenses and for reasonable indirect expenses that they incur in moving to new job assignments.

Direct expenses include the cost of packing, transporting and storing household furnishings (and of insuring them while in transit and storage), and the one-way transportation fares of the employee and his family.

Reimbursement of indirect expenses is left to the judgment of the policy book holder concerned, who will determine their reasonableness (as to object and amount) in each case in the light of the following general guides:

We will *normally* pay, if circumstances justify:

1. Travel and living expenses of one or two trips by the employee and his wife to find housing in the new area.

2. Meals and lodging for the family for a reasonable time after it moves to the new area until housing is obtained and readied for occupancy. One month is considered a maximum "reasonable time," which shall not be exceeded without the approval of the president or vice-president.

3. Occasional week-end commuting expenses of an employee who does not move his family immediately to the new area because, for example, the reassignment was made on short notice, or there is illness in his family, or there are children who should finish the school term.

4. Incidental expenses of relocation, such as reinstallation of electric stoves and other heavy appliances, and refitting of rugs and draperies. Expenses of this type must be itemized with exactness and are particularly subject to screening as to reasonableness, both individually and in the aggregate. Normally, agreement as to type of expense and the approximate magnitude should be reached with employees in advance of moving.

Exhibit 7—Continued

In a case involving hardship or other unusual circumstances, subject to the approval of the president or vice-president in advance of any commitment being made to the employee, we may:

1. Pay the broker's fee in connection with the sale of a house.
2. Help an employee carry two houses (until the old one is sold) by making an interest-free loan secured by a second mortgage.
3. Pay the "closing" costs (i.e., the costs incidental to obtaining a new mortgage) when an employee is transferred to a new location within a few months of an earlier move.

We will normally not pay:

1. Any loss on the sale of a house.
2. Expenses of a second move in the new area.

The employee, with the approval of the Division or Department Manager or his designee, will select the mover in each case. An estimate should be obtained from the mover before the move. The mover will be instructed to bill the company for his services, and the company will pay the charges only after it has received a voucher showing that the employee has declared all the goods shipped to have been delivered in satisfactory condition. Any claims for loss or damage will be handled by the employee or by the company at his request, in which latter event the employee shall release the company from any liability for loss or damage resulting from the move.

Before the mover's services are engaged, the employee should understand that the mover's liability for loss or damage is limited to 30 cents per pound and excludes certain risks unless the employee obtains proper "all risk" insurance coverage (costing about $5 per $1,000 of declared value) through the mover or through his own insurance agent.

Immediately following a move, an employee should submit to his divisional headquarters (with a copy to the assistant general sales manager) a brief report as to his satisfaction with the move. These reports, which will include records of claims for damage—their nature and settlement—will build a file of experience that will be helpful in arranging future moves.

Moving expenses should be charged to the personnel procurement expense account (150).

The company incurred additional unforeseen costs of $36,000 because not all the 15 transferred persons could be immediately employed on tasks commensurate with their salaries. Mr. Adams, for example, had been an assistant superintendent at Milbury. He had served there 10 years, and his total time with the company was 12 years. Mr. Huntley said Mr. Adams was a man of unquestioned loyalty and some members of management thought very highly of him. Mr. Huntley did not, although he considered Adams capable in some ways. When Milbury was shut down Adams was transferred to California and put on a development project. Huntley commented that he had fitted well into his new position but was being paid more than he was worth. "I don't know what we will do with him once the project is finished," he said. "He is not as good as the other assistant superintendents who are being paid $5,500 against his $7,500." Huntley thought Adams' abilities were best utilized in the position of foreman, which he had orignally held.

Unanticipated termination expenses of $35,000 were incurred because of sick leaves taken by employees. Many of the employees of the plant asked for such leaves as soon as the decision to close became known. Mr. Huntley said most of them were "no more sick than any of us"; they took advantage of the company, he said, with the help of unscrupulous doctors in the community. Employees went on sick leaves for correction of conditions, such as hernias or hemorrhoids, that had existed for years without treatment. And there were treatments for what seemed to be imaginary conditions also. The opportunity to receive something for nothing led many of the workers, particularly the women, to arrange with their doctors for certificates of illness. In some cases medical payments, made through employers' insurance, continued for several months after the plant was shut down.

Mr. Huntley added:

This hurt our insurance rating as an employer, and the only way to prevent it would have been to ask the insurance agency to investigate the local doctors. The agency representatives became suspicious anyway when this rash of illnesses occurred, but we did not wish to press the issue because it would have meant very bad feeling for our company. As things were, the community at least did not hate us.

There were other ways in which the company assisted the employees to make the transition. The personnel manager of the plant, characterized by Mr. Huntley as a very able person, remained until the shutdown was completed. He and his staff assisted hourly employees who had several years of service with the company to find employment elsewhere. Furthermore, the company paid travel expenses for nine supervisors and other salaried personnel forced to seek employment with other firms. In some instances the company paid fares up to $250. In total, about $2,000 was spent for the purpose.

When the decision to close was announced, some of the workers immediately started to look for work in other areas. Under the rules of the termination agreement they would forfeit their separation pay if they left before the company released them. The company modified this policy. It released employees who found work on their own prior to their scheduled separation and gave everyone separation pay.

The impact on the community of the plant closing, together with the departure of other employers, was severe. Mr. Snider, the marketing vice-president, described Milbury as a dying town and in general not a very desirable place in which to live. He said white-collar employees in particular had considered the location the "Siberia" of the company, and all the people who had been transferred there originally were glad to leave.

Mr. Armour said he did not know what happened to all the employees the company left behind. About 30% of them had come from the rural surroundings of the town. He did not believe the large machinery company had hired many of them. Within a radius of about 50 miles there were several other large manufacturing and processing plants, and he supposed many of the workers had found jobs there. Four valuable employees with high technical abilities chose to leave the company. One elected to stay in the area because of family ties. The other three secured good positions with large firms elsewhere. Mr. Armour regretted their loss.

The company took losses on inventories of supplies originally worth thousands of dollars. Some in-process inventories were discovered which had been spoiled and apparently hidden by the foremen in charge.

Although various closing expenses were greater than expected, the company nevertheless had direct operating savings of $123,000 in 1957 as a result of the shutdown (Exhibit 6). Gross capital savings for 1957 were placed at $597,000 with no allowance for the value of the Milbury building.

This building, with a book value in 1957 of $600,000, stood empty for six months and then was leased on a short-term basis to the General Machinery Corporation. In the spring of 1958 it had not yet been sold. An independent appraiser set its market value at little more than $100,000 in view of the depressed state of the community. The company was hoping to sell to any reasonable bidder. The capital loss on the sale would be more than made up by the savings achieved through the consolidation of operations. And loss on sale of the building would be tax deductible.

The company's capital savings, including $145,000 from transfer of equipment to the new Canadian plant, were partially offset by expenditures at other plants called for by the Milbury closing. It had been anticipated that such expenditures would amount to $400,000 over a five-year period (Exhibits 5 and 6).

PURCHASING A COMPANY

Skyway Electronics acquired the Cramden Company in April, 1956, for $500,000 in Skyway stock and payment of Cramden's long-term indebtedness of $100,000. In addition, Skyway spent $200,000 for needed equipment and added $121,000 to working capital.

The two multistory buildings that housed operations were not included in the purchase agreement. These were leased from Mr. Cramden by Skyway for a five-year period at an annual cost of $23,000.

The Cramden Company manufactured electronic components. It had been founded and managed by a family trio: father, mother, and son. The Cramden family had built the enterprise around the inventive abilities of father and son and Mrs. Cramden's management ability. The company produced two distinct lines of components. One line, accounting for 60% of sales, consisted of specialty components for a market Skyway wished to enter. The other line consisted of general-purpose components. Total sales volume in 1957 was about $1 million. There were 90 hourly employees, a plant manager, and 13 salesmen.

Labor relations in the Cramden Company had been cordial throughout its history. The plant was not unionized. Mr. Robbins characterized management's past labor relationships as somewhat paternalistic.

The major purpose of the acquisition was to obtain the technical knowledge and the facilities for manufacturing Cramden's special components. By purchasing a going concern, Skyway hoped to gain time and to avoid many of the problems and costs involved in the alternative of setting up a research and development program of its own. The sales potential for the Cramden components appeared promising, as the total market was considered to be $100 million a year. Skyway hoped to capture about 10% of this market by 1960.

When Skyway took over the company the elder Mr. Cramden was retained as president; Mrs. Cramden became the treasurer; and the son, Elton Cramden, was named chief engineer. Huntley concluded fairly soon that the plant manager, Mr. Brown, was not doing a satisfactory job. He had been with Cramden for 15 years and was being paid $11,000 a year. Huntley told him the company could not keep him on as plant manager but could make him purchasing vice-president of the subsidiary at a salary of $7,500. Huntley reported that Mr. Brown gladly accepted the post, with the cut in pay, and had done adequate work.

After about a year of operations, the Skyway officers concluded, according to Mr. Huntley, that Mr. and Mrs. Cramden were not so efficient as had been hoped in managing the company as a subsidiary. Mr. Huntley went on to say that he and Mr. McLean decided to put pressure on the couple to retire from active management. Mr. Armour described Mr. Cramden as a born promoter and inventor, but a poor business manager. Mrs. Cramden, he said, was competent but was hampered by ill health and nervous tension. Elton Cramden was a very competent electrical engineer and inventor.

Mr. and Mrs. Cramden finally agreed to retire early in 1958. Elton was retained by Skyway to continue developing the Cramden special components.

Mr. Armour pointed out some of the difficulties encountered with Mr. Cramden. Cramden had found it very hard to adjust to the fact that his company now was part of a larger enterprise and he could no longer act independently. For instance, although Skyway officials informed Mr. Cramden they had decided the subsidiary was to concentrate efforts on further development of the specialty components, he gave much more time to some of the unprofitable standard items in which he had a personal interest. He managed to stay within his budgets, but the detailed spending did not correspond with the needs of the company. Furthermore, Cramden frequently argued with Armour and Huntley about the state of development of the products and about alternative manufacturing processes. His representations had led on several occasions to embarrassment with customers. Skyway management had relied on his word that certain components were ready for the market while in fact they had not fully cleared the development stage. "We made the mistake of listening and not looking," said Mr. Armour.

In view of these difficulties, and in consideration of the uncertain health of Mrs. Cramden, the Skyway officers felt that retirement for the Cramdens was a sound solution, especially since they were financially secure. As a face-saving gesture, Skyway retained Mr. Cramden in a consulting capacity. "This makes him feel important, and he does have quite a bit of know-how," Mr. Armour explained.

Conditions at Cramden, however, did not improve materially even after the Cramdens withdrew from active management. Serious quality problems were encountered with the specialty components on the one hand, and, on the other hand, the standard components met stiff price competition and were sold at a loss sufficient to make the entire operation unprofitable (Exhibit 8). A report dated May 8, 1958, pointed out that while operations at Cramden had shown a small profit in 1956,

Exhibit 8

SKYWAY ELECTRONICS, INC.

Operating Statements by Divisions,
1957

(Thousands of Dollars)

	Western	Milbury (Closed in 1957)	Eastern	Home	Canadian	Cramden	Total*
Net sales	$13,250	$3,630	$9,890	$2,740	$2,510	$1,070	$25,920
Cost of sales	7,710	2,950	5,750	2,100	1,810	1,150	14,300
Gross profit	$ 5,540	$ 680	$4,140	$ 640	$ 700	$ (80)	$11,620
Expenses:							
Selling	$ 2,020	$ 460	$1,590	$ 160	$ 640	$ 120	$ 4,990
General and administrative	290	80	160	50	40	30	650
Research	560	120	220	280	90	40	1,310
	$ 2,870	$ 660	$1,970	$ 490	$ 770	$ 190	$ 6,950
Net operating profit (loss)	$ 2,670	$ 20	$2,170	$ 150	$ (70)	$ (270)	$ 4,670
Other income (expense)	(60)	(10)	(40)	(180)	...	(10)	(300)
Net profit (loss) before tax	$ 2,610	$ 10	$2,130	$ (30)	$ (70)	$ (280)	$ 4,370
Income tax							$ 2,150
Net profit after tax							$ 2,220

* Interdivisional sales amounting to $7,170 eliminated from total.

there was a loss in 1957 amounting to 26% of sales, and operations in the first quarter of 1958 showed an 8.6% loss. However, the report added that valuable know-how had been obtained and the desired diversification achieved.

In June, 1958, Skyway reached the decision to close down production of standard components at Cramden. The gross margin was generally much lower for standard components than for specialty items, 24% versus 43% in 1958. The specialty components showed a good potential, according to Mr. Huntley, although the quality problem was still present and competition could be expected to develop substitute products within the next five years. Huntley thought Skyway had not been sufficiently active to date in developing the market for the Cramden specialties.

The decision to discontinue production of Cramden standard components came after Skyway executives had weighed four alternatives:

Exhibit 9

SKYWAY ELECTRONICS, INC.

Cost of Alternative Ways of Dealing with Cramden Company
(Thousands of Dollars)

Type of Expense	Alternative 1 Close Down	Alternative 2 Close Down	Alternative 3 Close Partially to 1961	Alternative 4 Maintain as at Present to 1961
Immediate Expenses				
1. Cash Outlays:				
Termination—personnel	$ 25	$ 25	$ 15	$ ..
Transfer—personnel	10	10	5	..
Transfer—equipment	50	50	10	..
	$ 85	$ 85	$ 30	$ ..
2. Book write-offs:				
Equipment, building, inventory	100	180	50	..
3. Total immediate	$185	$265	$ 80	$ ..
Expenses in 1961 (Termination of lease)				
1. Cash outlays:				
Termination—personnel	$ ..	$ ..	$ 5	$ 10
Transfer—personnel	..	..	5	10
Transfer—equipment	..	..	40	50
	$ ..	$ ..	$ 50	$ 70
2. Book write-offs:				
Equipment, inventory	..	..	10	50
3. Total 1961 expense	$ ..	$ ..	$ 60	$120
Grand total	$185	$265	$140	$120

1. Close the plant completely and transfer manufacture of specialty components to other locations. The payments for the remaining two and a half years of the leasehold agreement on the buildings would be the only continuing costs for the Cramden location under this plan.
2. Close the plant completely, moving specialty components manufacture. Settle the leasehold obligation by agreeing, in return for cancellation of the remaining lease payments of $23,000 per annum, to leave intact $112,-000 in leasehold improvements, which included a sprinkler system and a freight elevator.
3. Continue production of specialty components, but not of general-purpose items, at Cramden for the remainder of the leasehold agreement. Keep overhead at a minimum.
4. Continue production of both lines at Cramden but cut administrative and sales expense to a minimum.

Exhibits 9 and 10 give a figure analysis of these alternatives. The third alternative was chosen partly because it required relatively low immediate cash outlay. Furthermore, it allowed for orderly liquidation of inventories and gradual reduction of specialty component production

Exhibit 10

SKYWAY ELECTRONICS, INC.

*Operating Data under Alternative Plans for Cramden Company
Annual Estimate, 1958 to 1961*

(Thousands of dollars)

	Alternative 1 Close Down	Alternative 2 Close Down	Alternative 3 Continue Specialties to 1961	Alternative 4 Maintain as at present to 1961
Sales:				
Special components	$550	$550	$550	$ 550
Standard components	...	...	...	600
Total	$550	$550	$550	$1,150
Cost of Sales:				
Special components	$275	$275	$275	$ 275
Standard components	...	...	...	460
	$275	$275	$275	$ 735
Gross margin	$275	$275	$275	$ 415
Leasehold expense (until 1961)	$ 65	$...	$ 68	$ 70
Factory expense:				
Special components	95	95	87	87
Standard components	..	..	..	93
Order and billing:				
Special components	15	15	15	15
Standard components	..	..	..	105
Total expense	$175	$110	$170	$ 370
Contribution	$100*	$165*	$105	$ 45

* Contribution would continue after 1961.

should expected competitive developments hurt the market outlook. Also, the effect on employees and the community would be less severe than under alternatives (1) and (2).

The company's decision meant that about half the 90 hourly employees and some of the 13 salaried salesmen would be laid off immediately. Mr. Huntley pointed out that there was a great deal of difference between the impact on the community in this case and in the case of Milbury. Although the Cramden plant, too, was in a community of only 30,000 people, it was very near Indianapolis. The Skyway officers thought the idled employees would not have extreme difficulty finding employment there.

Mr. Huntley said there was a possibility the plant would be kept open beyond the expiration of the lease, if it should appear there was use for it as a pilot operation and experimental shop. If it were closed, the company again would face the problem of personnel transfers. Huntley wished to transfer about five supervisors in case of a shutdown. He stated that Skyway also could not afford to lose all the other good employees who still were with Cramden. On the other hand, he was reluctant to resort again to organizational changes in other plants in order to accommodate more than five. "You cannot bust up the organization all the time." Huntley believed a final decision on the disposal of Cramden would come with adequate forewarning. He supposed the company would use the same termination agreements as were used at Milbury. There were, however, a few employees with 17 or 18 years of service who would be virtually unemployable anywhere else. Huntley did not know what the company would do in their cases if the plant were closed.

Belcamp Hardware Company, Inc.

IN 1950 THE GORDON family acquired virtually all the outstanding shares of stock of the Belcamp Hardware Company, Inc., of Louisville, Kentucky. This company was among the older and larger wholesale hardware distributors in Kentucky and Tennessee.

Together, Mr. Thomas Gordon and his two sons owned a little more than 94% of the stock outstanding: Thomas Gordon, aged 72 in 1950, held 164 shares, and Joseph Gordon, 45, and Charles Gordon, 40, each held 6,600 shares. Charles Gordon accepted the presidency of the company, but virtually complete responsibility for operations was given to Mr. Frank Robertson, a friend of the Gordons, who was persuaded to join the company as general manager.

Company net earnings declined sharply under Mr. Robertson's management, however, and by 1958 Charles Gordon was disillusioned as to Robertson's business judgment. The problem Gordon faced was what to do with the Belcamp Company. His own time, as well as that of his brother, was fully occupied by other family enterprises.

Company sales and earnings from 1942 through 1958 are summarized in Exhibit 1.

THE GORDON PURCHASE OF BELCAMP

Mr. Thomas Gordon had purchased 600 shares of Belcamp stock in 1934 from Mr. John Cole, then president of Belcamp. The two men were neighbors and close personal friends. Cole highly respected Gordon's business judgment and asked him to purchase the stock and serve on the Belcamp board of directors. At that time the largest single stockholder was a widow, Mrs. Fred Paine, whose husband had owned and managed the business before his death in 1912. She owned 4,800 shares. These she always voted in support of Mr. Cole's policies. Mr. Cole, after selling the 600 shares, owned 2,400. Mr. Thomas Kent, vice-president and treasurer of Belcamp, owned 1,200 shares. The remaining 5,164 shares outstanding were rather widely held by various Belcamp employees and Louisville businessmen.

When Thomas Gordon first invested in Belcamp, Mr. Cole closely

Exhibit 1

BELCAMP HARDWARE COMPANY, INC.

*Parent Company Sales and Consolidated Earnings
before Federal Income Tax*

Year	Sales Volume	Pretax Earnings or Loss
1942	$3,153,988	$115,750
1943	3,586,811	261,311
1944	3,398,858	203,340
1945	3,242,058	202,416
1946	5,509,142	409,499
1947	6,153,024	257,367
1948	5,489,823	363,614
1949	4,807,553	272,829
1950	5,092,155	256,183
1951	5,691,286	208,242
1952	6,946,265	166,213
1953	7,076,145	(36,219)
1954	5,714,067	39,794
1955	5,313,972	(61,219)
1956	5,966,467	115,637
1957	5,950,807	24,320
1958	5,780,328*	35,277*

* Preliminary figure.

supervised all company operations. Assisting him were three key individuals. Mr. Kent, who also was familiar with all phases of company operations, handled various duties assigned by Mr. Cole. Miss Carolyn Ashley, the assistant treasurer, was in charge of the company records. Mr. Harold Long served as sales manager. Cole and Kent were paid $50,000 a year. Long was paid $25,000 and Miss Ashley, $8,000. In addition, each received annual dividends through ownership of Belcamp stock. The total number of employees was approximately 170.

In February, 1950, Mr. Long suddenly died. At that time Mr. Cole was 71, Mr. Kent was 67, and Miss Ashley was 62. The purchasing agent, age 42, was made sales manager, but Cole and Kent assumed most of Long's former responsibilities.

In September, 1950, Mr. Cole, Mr. Kent, and Miss Ashley all decided to retire as soon as possible. Cole and Kent wished to sell their interest in Belcamp, and they ascertained that other stockholders with sufficient shares to make up a controlling interest also wanted to sell. As no open market existed for the stock, Cole began searching for possible buyers. One group of Louisville businessmen studied the situation but decided not to invest because no one was available to replace Cole and Kent in the company organization. A Chicago group of investors then indicated an interest and tentatively suggested, in October, 1950, a purchase price of $68 a share. This price was satisfactory to Cole, and he was confident the other stockholders would agree to any price he negotiated. The Chicago group asked to study the books in detail before making a definite offer. After this further study, these potential investors refused to pay $68. Although $50,000 "earnest money" had been deposited with Mr. Cole, the agreement stipulated that the money would be returned if the transaction failed to materialize for any reason.

The interested parties then began a series of price negotiations; prices of $63, $60, and $58 a share were suggested by Mr. Cole. Each time the Chicago group rejected the proposal, and, in November, 1950, Cole called off the negotiations.

At this point the Gordons offered to purchase 7,190 shares at $53. With the 600 shares they already held, this would give them 55% of shares outstanding. Mr. Cole accepted their offer.

The Gordons also owned and operated the Gordon Company, a building supply firm that earned after taxes $250,000 or more annually on sales exceeding $12 million and an investment of $3.2 million. Thomas Gordon was chairman of the board, Charles Gordon was president and manager of Louisville operations, and Joseph Gordon was vice-president and manager of the Nashville branch. Each of these officers received an annual salary in excess of $60,000, and each devoted at least 65 hours a week to this business. All three took great personal pleasure in their success in this highly competitive industry, in which single orders involved hundreds or thousands of dollars. In the hardware wholesale business, on the other hand, $65 was a big single transaction. The Gordons also owned majority interests in five other firms. They added Belcamp to their holdings only because they believed the company had a good chance of producing outstanding long-term capital gains. They did not intend to be active in its management.

Almost immediately after acquiring a controlling interest in Belcamp, the Gordons stopped payment of dividends to avoid increases in their personal income tax bases. Most of the minority stockholders, however, depended on the dividends as part of their livelihood. As these minority stockholders came to realize that dividend payments would not be resumed in the foreseeable future, they tried to sell their stock. Many of them asked the Gordon family to buy their holdings, since it seemed quite unlikely that any outsider would be interested in purchasing small blocks of stock in a company in which the management, with

55% of the stock, did not plan to pay dividends. Even though the Gordons did not wish to increase their holdings, they felt an obligation to purchase the stock. They tried to establish a price for each block of stock in light of such considerations as the price originally paid, contributions made by the seller to the company, and the needs of the seller. They ended by purchasing 87% of the minority holdings, or 5,574 shares, giving them ownership of 94% of all shares outstanding. Prices paid ranged between $25 and $50 a share and averaged $36. The Gordons, incidentally, were chagrined to discover that, after selling stock to them for $45 a share, the company's assistant treasurer immediately purchased the same number of shares from another party for $18 a share.

FINDING A GENERAL MANAGER

The Gordons did not anticipate any trouble in finding a good manager for Belcamp. Besides their investment in several local companies, each of the Gordons served as a director of at least one firm, and Charles and Thomas each served on the board of a local bank. Because of these varied interests, the Gordons knew or expected to meet several men seeking the type of opportunity offered at Belcamp. From among these candidates, one would be chosen for training under Cole and Kent, who had agreed to help develop a suitable replacement.

The Gordons interviewed a dozen men in December, 1950, before Charles Gordon mentioned the opportunity to Frank Robertson. Although not related, the Charles Gordons and the Robertsons had certain family ties. Charles' wife, Elizabeth, had a brother who was killed in World War II. The brother's widow, Kathleen, later married Mr. Robertson. Elizabeth and Kathleen had been close friends for many years, and the Robertsons and Charles Gordons were vacationing together in Florida at the time the opportunity with Belcamp was mentioned.

Mr. Robertson, whose father was the executive vice-president of a large oil company, was employed in Chicago as a district sales manager for another major oil firm. After graduation from college with a B minus average, Robertson worked for an oil well supply company and then for the oil firm where he was employed in 1950. Robertson, who was then 35 years of age, believed his advancement in this company had been quite satisfactory and thought his future progress seemed very promising. His salary in 1950 was $12,000 a year. After some preliminary investigation of Belcamp, however, Mr. Robertson said he definitely was interested in the job there.

Thomas and Joseph Gordon, after interviewing Robertson, agreed that he was a likeable individual who made an excellent appearance and had a good mind. Above all, the Gordons felt they could trust his integrity in handling their personal investment; consequently, they offered him the job.

Robertson deliberated about accepting the Gordon offer for approximately six months. During this time Charles Gordon was quite enthusiastic in his description of the potential opportunity offered by Belcamp. In June, 1951, Robertson accepted the offer at a salary of $9,000 a year. The Gordons also promised to sell Robertson some stock at a favorable price if things worked out, but the number of shares and price were not definitely set.

The Robertsons took up residence in Louisville. Thereafter they and the Charles Gordons were together socially at least once a week and often two or three times. Both families were boating enthusiasts, and they frequently got together for week-end boat trips, races, and regattas.

MR. ROBERTSON AT BELCAMP

A week after Robertson began working at Belcamp, Mr. Cole died suddenly, and within six months Mr. Kent was fatally stricken. Charles Gordon became president of the company, and Robertson became general manager and vice-president. As general manager, Robertson was completely responsible for the operation of the business. As a general rule, Gordon's approval was necessary only for decisions involving major policy changes or substantial investments. Gordon continued to devote most of his time to the Gordon Company.

In 1953, in an attempt to improve Belcamp's profits, Robertson undertook to modernize operations. Construction of a new building with 100,000 feet of warehouse space and 13,000 feet of office space was completed in 1954 at a cost of $700,000. The building was owned by the Corydon Company, a family investment trust company of the Gordons. Belcamp paid $73,000 annual rent plus taxes and insurance on the premises.

The new warehouse embodied the latest concepts in materials handling, and Robertson made several innovations that greatly simplified the work of the warehouse crew and cut in half the number of men needed. In addition, the new facility made it possible for the company to handle twice its current sales volume.

Robertson in 1955 supervised the installation of a modern IBM accounting system that incorporated several new ideas later reported in IBM company publications. The new system allowed further reductions in the warehouse crew, gave better control over the inventory level, speeded preparation of reports, and provided reports hitherto unobtainable. Furthermore, Robertson reduced the number of items carried in inventory from 30,000 to 18,000 without lessening the service given to retail accounts.

Nevertheless, company earnings did not improve. Exhibits 2 and 3 show the company's income statements and balance sheets, and Exhibit 4 presents a ratio analysis for selected items.

MR. ROBERTSON'S EVALUATION OF BELCAMP

Robertson believed that the moves he had made were necessary just to keep the company in business. He pointed out that during 1957 and 1958 major hardware distributors in Columbus, Kansas City, St. Louis, and Minneapolis had been forced to liquidate. Many factors were operating against the hardware wholesaler in Robertson's opinion. Average retail hardware store sales were no larger in 1957 than in 1947— $92,000 in each year, although during that period prices had increased by one third. Various types of competitors had cut into the wholesaler's unit volume: the supermarkets cut into houseware sales; the discount houses hurt electrical appliance sales; the lumber yards hit tool and building supply sales; and mail-order houses challenged the wholesaler across the board.

Furthermore, in the past few years many small operators had started distributorships operating out of their garages and car trunks. They, according to Robertson, performed all the separate jobs: purchasing, warehousing, promotion, sales, order layout, delivery, and billing. They gave personalized service to the retailers in their neighborhoods by delivering an item within an hour of receiving the order. Belcamp's quickest service in the outlying areas was four days.

In addition, manufacturers had started selling directly to some of Belcamp's large accounts, the ones most profitable to the company.

The increased number of distributors selling hardware items had cut down the time a retailer would give to a Belcamp salesman. An hour, according to Mr. Robertson, was the most that a salesmen could expect. For 55 minutes of the hour the dealer looked around his store, checking

Exhibit 2

BELCAMP HARDWARE COMPANY, INC.

Balance Sheets, December 31, 1950–57

(Thousands of Dollars) *

Assets	1950	1951	1952	1953	1954	1955	1956	1957
Cash	$ 108	$ 130	$ 15	$ 94	$ 92	$ 71	$ 149	$ 69
Accounts Receivable (Net)	482	497	827	812	716	882	1,112	1,039
Tax Refund Claim	….	….	….	20	32	….	….	….
Inventory (Lower of Cost or Market)	837	972	1,326	1,038†	939	1,149	1,098	945
Prepaid Expenses	….	1	8	13	4	14	14	9
Total Current Assets	$1,427	$1,599	$2,175	$1,977	$1,783	$2,117	$2,373	$2,062
Facilities (Net)	12	22	25	22	86	93	84	81
U.S. Securities	100	….	….	….	….	….	….	….
Life Insurance (Cash Surrender Value)	37	36	37	38	38	….	….	….
Deferred Catalogue Costs	….	20	20	33	26	16	7	….
Total Assets	$1,576	$1,678	$2,273	$2,070	$1,934	$2,227	$2,464	$2,143
Liabilities and Net Worth								
Accounts Payable	$ 258	$ 237	$ 426	$ 185	$ 167	$ 321	$ 253	$ 221
Notes Payable	….	….	325	425	300	535	725	450
Accruals:								
Wages and Commissions	25	29	40	32	30	19	24	16
General Taxes	1	23	20	11	13	10	25	23
Other	….	8	17	9	16	1	8	9
Deferred Income	….	….	….	12	….	7	….	….
Reserve for Federal Income Tax	104	97	72	27	29	15	24	10
Reserve for Loss on Purchase Commitments	….	….	….	25†	….	….	….	….
Reserve for Loss on Lease	….	….	….	….	20‡	20	….	….
Total Liabilities	$ 388	$ 394	$ 900	$ 726	$ 574	$ 928	$1,059	$ 729

Capital Stock (18,500 Shares, Including 4,336 Shares in Treasury)	$ 283	$ 370	$ 370	$ 370	$ 370	$ 370	$ 370	$ 370
Earned Surplus:								
Beginning Balance	803	905	973	1,062	1,033	1,049	987	1,093
Add Net Income (Loss)	259	110	89	(29)	16	(62)	106	15
Increase in Life Insurance Value	3	...	...	...	...	...	...	...
Less:								
Tax Deduction	...	...	...	...	...	...	...	5
Reserve for Federal Income Tax	104	...	...	...	...	...	...	...
Dividends	57	14	...	...	...	...	...	...
Adjustment to Reflect Treasury Stock at Cost	...	28	...	...	...	...	...	...
Ending Balance	905	973	1,062	1,033	1,049	987	1,093	1,103
Less Treasury Stock (4,336 Shares at Cost)	...	59	59	59	59	59	59	59
Total Net Worth	$1,188	$1,284	$1,373	$1,344	$1,360	$1,298	$1,404	$1,414
Total Net Worth and Liabilities	$1,576	$1,678	$2,273	$2,070	$1,934	$2,227	$2,464	$2,143

* Detail will not necessarily add to totals because of rounding.
† Merchandise in discontinued lines has been valued at estimated realizable values. A reserve for loss on discontinued lines has been established in the amount of $25,000.
‡ At the close of 1954 the company moved its warehouse location. The company and the lessor of the former warehouse were in dispute concerning interpretation of the former lease which expired April 1, 1955. A reserve for possible loss on the lease was provided in the amount of $20,000.
§ Includes restoration of amount provided for loss on lease less charges of $2,000 incurred in terminating dispute with former lessor.

Exhibit 3

BELCAMP HARDWARE COMPANY, INC.

Income Statements, 1950–57

(Thousands of Dollars) *

	1950	1951	1952	1953	1954	1955	1956	1957
Net sales	$5,092	$5,691	$6,946	$7,076	$5,714	$5,314	$5,966	$5,951
Less cost of sales	3,917	4,509	5,647	5,805†	4,514	4,237	4,702	4,736
Gross profit	$1,176	$1,183	$1,299	$1,271	$1,200	$1,077	$1,265	$1,215
Operating expenses:								
Sales	786	NA	NA	362	296	254	288	295
Warehouse and delivery		NA	NA	402	369	370	345	337
General and administrative	127	NA	NA	356	339	368	339	380
Other		NA	NA	163	155	171	206	181
Total operating expenses	$ 913	$ 974	$1,144	$1,283	$1,159	$1,162	$1,178	$1,193
Net income (loss) from operations	263	208	156	(13)	42	(85)	87	22
Other income	1	...	11	...	...	24	29§	2
Other expense	(5)	...	...	(24)	(2)	...	...	...
Net income (loss) before federal tax	259	208	166	(36)	40	(61)	116	24
Special charge	...	...	...	...	(47)‡	...	...	...
Provision for federal tax	...	98	77	...	23	1	10	9
Special credit for tax carry-back	...	...	...	7	...	...	...	...
Net income (loss)	...	$ 110	$ 89	$ (29)	$ 16	$ (62)	$ 106	$ 15

* Detail will not necessarily add to totals because of rounding.

† A reserve for loss on purchase commitments for discontinued appliance lines (which net sales approximated $1,113,000 in 1953) has been provided for in the amount of $25,000 and included in cost of sales.

‡ Includes $20,000 provision for possible loss on former lease incurred when company moved into a new warehouse facility. The company and former lessor are in dispute over the interpretation of the terms of the former lease.

§ The reserve for loss on lease in the amount of $20,000 which was provided for in 1954 was restored to income less charges of $2,000 incurred in 1956 in terminating dispute with former lessor.

Exhibit 4

BELCAMP HARDWARE COMPANY, INC.

Ratio Analyses

	1950	1951	1952	1953	1954	1955	1956	1957	Dun & Bradstreet 1957 Median Figures for Hardware Wholesalers
Sales	100.0%	100.0%	100.0%	100.0%	100.0%	100.0%	100.0%	100.0%	
Cost of sales	76.9	79.2	81.3	82.1	79.0	79.7	78.8	79.6	
Gross profit	23.1%	20.8%	18.7%	17.9%	21.0%	20.3%	21.2%	20.4%	
Operating expenses:									
Sales expenses	15.4%	NA	NA	5.1%	5.2%	4.8%	4.8%	4.9%	
Warehouse and delivery expenses		NA	NA	5.7	6.5	7.0	5.8	5.7	
General and administrative expenses		NA	NA	5.0	5.9	6.9	5.7	6.4	
Other operating expenses	2.5	NA	NA	2.3	2.7	3.2	3.5	3.0	
Total operating expenses	17.9%	17.1%	16.5%	18.1%	20.3%	21.9%	19.8%	20.0%	
Net income from operations	5.2%	3.7%	2.2%	(0.2)%	0.7%	(1.6)%	1.4%	0.4%	
Other income	0.0		0.2	(0.3)	(0.0)	0.5	0.5	0.0	
Other expenses	(0.1)	..						..	
Net profit (loss) before taxes	5.1%	3.7%	2.4%	(0.5)%	0.7%	(1.1)%	1.9%	0.4%	
Net profit (loss) after tax	3.0%	1.9%	1.3%	(0.4)%	0.3%	(1.2)%	1.8%	0.3%	1.5%
Net profit (loss) on tangible net worth	13.0%	8.6%	6.5%	(2.2)%	1.2%	(4.8)%	7.5%	1.1%	4.4%
Net profit (loss) on net working capital*	14.9%	9.1%	7.0%	(2.3)%	1.3%	(5.2)%	8.1%	1.1%	5.4%
Net sales to tangible net worth	4.3	4.4	5.1	5.3	4.2	4.1	4.2	4.2	3.0
Net sales to net working capital*	4.9	4.7	5.4	5.7	4.7	4.5	4.5	4.5	3.6
Net sales to inventory	6.1	5.9	5.2	6.8	6.1	4.6	5.4	6.3	4.1
Current assets to current debt*	3.7	4.1	2.4	2.7	3.1	2.3	2.2	2.8	3.9
Current debt* to inventory	46.4%	40.5%	67.9%	69.9%	61.1%	80.8%	96.4%	77.1%	40.5%
Inventory to net working capital*	80.6%	80.7%	104.0%	83.0%	77.7%	96.6%	83.6%	70.9%	83.9%
Debt to tangible net worth	32.7%	30.7%	65.5%	54.0%	42.2%	71.4%	75.4%	51.6%	54.2%
Fixed assets to tangible net worth	1.0%	1.7%	1.8%	1.6%	6.3%	7.2%	6.0%	5.7%	14.0%
Collection period (days outstanding)	34	31	43	41	45	60	67	63	33

* All outstanding debt including reserves on contingent losses is considered current debt by the Belcamp Hardware Company. Therefore, net working capital equals current assets less total liabilities.

his inventory, and saying from time to time: "Give me one of these and three of those." This left the salesman with five minutes at most to devote to presenting new items. The company had 23 salesmen. They were paid on a straight commission basis and had no personal expense accounts.

Under Mr. Robertson's management, Belcamp had been trying to help the dealers by making them more promotion conscious, but these efforts had not had much success. Robertson believed that many persons operating hardware stores had no feel for retailing. Some had inherited their stores and knew no other business. Sometimes the local plumber or carpenter just backed into the business by buying in quantities in order to gain a discount. Some individuals opened hardware stores after failing in other lines.

Robertson believed also that the wholesaler had been caught in a price squeeze. The manufacturer had raised his prices, but the wholesaler couldn't raise prices to the dealer at will. Manufacturers customarily sent notices to dealers stating the prices paid by the wholesalers and the "fair prices" the wholesalers should charge.

At the same time, Belcamp's costs had increased tremendously. Delivery costs had risen from $\frac{1}{2}\%$ to $3\frac{1}{2}\%$ of sales. Labor costs had tripled. For many years the former owners had paid sweatshop wages, Robertson said. In 1947 a warehouseman was paid $26 for a 44-hour week; in 1958 he was paid $78 for the same time. The pay scales of all other employees had risen correspondingly. In 1947 the employees had no paid holidays; in 1958 they had $11\frac{1}{2}$ paid holidays. The employees deserved many of these increases, in Robertson's opinion, and he was not surprised that the Teamsters Union had organized Belcamp drivers and warehousemen in 1948. The fact was, however, that the workers of no other distributors in the area had been organized, and the pressures from the union increased Belcamp's headaches.

Mr. Robertson had found it difficult to obtain competent employees. He had brought a chief purchasing agent with him from his old company, and a friend of Charles Gordon had become controller in 1954. Both these men had been promised better rewards than the company so far had been able to provide. The company had picked up other employees from diverse sources, but staffing had been a problem.

In the judgment of Robertson, Belcamp's only hope lay in making some radical changes. He had concluded tentatively that the soundest step would be to open a chain of retail outlets and, in late 1958, was working on details of such a plan.

MR. GORDON'S EVALUATION OF BELCAMP

Mr. Charles Gordon was convinced the company's profits were declining because of poor management. Although agreeing that the hardware wholesaling business was becoming more competitive, he pointed out that Belcamp's chief rival had continued to show through 1957 a profit in the neighborhood of $20,000 annually on a net worth of only $750,000.

Gordon believed that theoretically competition for hardware orders was based on three factors: service, terms, and "outs," or the ability to hold down the number of orders lost because the stock was unavailable. However, he thought profits also depended upon management's ability to obtain special discounts from suppliers. He thought Robertson, as general manager of one of the largest wholesale firms in the area, should "apply a little leverage on the prices charged by suppliers instead of paying the first price quoted." He believed that Robertson did not take advantage of this economic power, nor did he stock up on items offered at special prices by suppliers even though the Belcamp Company had tremendous warehouse facilities and adequate working capital.

Mr. Gordon made a five-page list of Robertson's errors. Some of what he considered the more costly mistakes were:

1. Publishing a bound catalogue at a cost of $40,000. Because of constant changes in the product line, the catalogue was out of date almost as soon as it was published. The mistake was corrected by adopting a loose-leaf catalogue, but the initial expenditure was almost completely wasted.

2. Adding several "lemons" to the Belcamp line which were very poor sellers and eventually were eliminated at losses ranging between $25,000 and $50,000.

3. Losing money during a part of his first year as general manager at the rate of $15,000 annually and not even knowing it until the end of the year because of an inadequate accounting system. Because of their intuitive familiarity with the business, Mr. Cole and Mr. Kent had not established a detailed accounting system. Robertson had not immediately recognized his need for a more formalized control system.

4. Failing to recruit a dynamic sales manager capable of stimulating the sales force to get increased business.

5. Refusing business from old established customers during the 1958 Christmas rush when the orders could have been handled by working the men overtime. When questioned by Mr. Gordon on this point, Robertson had replied that overtime premiums eliminated any profit margin, and he had thought Gordon did not approve of overtime. Gordon acknowledged that actually he had reprimanded Robertson for using overtime under conditions in which the men through laziness did not get their work done during the regular working

hours and that he had ruled that any further use of overtime must have his approval.

Gordon recognized that Robertson had made several contributions to improve the efficiency and service of the company and had worked day and night for seven days a week during the six months spent in moving to the new warehouse and installing the accounting system. However, he thought that Robertson lacked a certain quality of "sharpness." According to Gordon, this subtle quality separated a good, aggressive manager from one who was just average, and it could make a difference of thousands of dollars in profits.

Gordon was aware that Robertson was on the verge of presenting a plan for opening retail stores. Gordon's reaction to this was that a man who was unable to manage the business as it was certainly was in no position to manage a more complicated setup.

In view of the total situation, the Gordons were considering liquidating the business. They believed the inventory could be sold at no less than book value and they had been offered $900,000 for the warehouse. However, they felt some obligation to provide employment for the men and women who had worked for the company 15 to 20 years, underpaid during part of this time. As an alternative to liquidation, the Gordons also were considering selling their stock. Several individuals had indicated an interest in purchasing the firm.

By January, 1959, Robertson and Gordon held such varying opinions as to the business that they could no longer discuss the matter in front of their wives. Joseph Gordon repeatedly asked his brother: "When are you going to get enough guts to take some action?"

Exhibits 5, 6, and 7 give summary data on wholesale and retail operations in the hardware industry.

Exhibit 5

BELCAMP HARDWARE COMPANY, INC.

Operating Data—Hardware Wholesalers

Item	1948	1954
Establishments...	1,977	2,137
Sales (millions of dollars).................................	2,006	2,068*
Operating expenses (including payroll, as % of sales)........	15.6	18.3
Payroll, entire year (thousands of dollars)..................203,769		227,146
Paid employees (week ended nearest November 15)...........	59,330	54,245
Active proprietors of unincorporated (wholesale hardware) businesses, November.................................	1,016	1,110

* "Cumulative sales for hardware wholesalers for the first 11 months in 1958 were $2,005 million." *Hardware Age*, January 29, 1959.

Source: *Statistical Abstract of the United States*, 1958.

Exhibit 6

BELCAMP HARDWARE COMPANY, INC.

Wholesale Price Index—Hardware
1947–49 = 100

1947.................................... 92.9
1950....................................114.2
1954....................................139.3
1955....................................146.4
1956....................................155.9
1957 (March)............................162.2
1958 (March)............................168.9

Source: *Statistical Abstract of the United States*, 1958.

Exhibit 7

BELCAMP HARDWARE COMPANY, INC.

Retail Store Sales—Hardware*
(In Millions)

1954....................................$2,702
1955.................................... 2,788
1956.................................... 2,893
1957.................................... 2,737
1958.................................... 2,653

* Number of retail establishments was 34,009 in 1948, 34,859 in 1954, and 34,670 in 1958.

Source: *Statistical Abstract of the United States*, 1958 and 1961, and *Hardware Age*, February 26, 1959.

M. Porter
S.S.B
Personal
Finance